135-143
48-72
Garcetti
ABA Mod. R. 1.13
39 + Arb. Award

47-48
82-101
PWC
127x
174
Cir. Cites II
153+
Toyota Case
Hardison again

LABOR AND EMPLOYMENT LAW

PROBLEMS, CASES AND MATERIALS IN THE LAW OF WORK

Third Edition

By

Robert J. Rabin
Professor of Law
Syracuse University College of Law

Eileen Silverstein
Professor of Law
University of Connecticut School of Law

George Schatzki
Professor of Law
Arizona State University
College of Law

Kenneth G. Dau-Schmidt
Professor of Law
Indiana University School of Law–Bloomington

for
THE LABOR LAW GROUP

WEST
GROUP

A THOMSON COMPANY

Mat #18246090

West Group has created this publication to provide you with accurate and authoritative information concerning the subject matter covered. However, this publication was not necessarily prepared by persons licensed to practice law in a particular jurisdiction. West Group is not engaged in rendering legal or other professional advice, and this publication is not a substitute for the advice of an attorney. If you require legal or other expert advice, you should seek the services of a competent attorney or other professional.

American Casebook Series, and the West Group symbol
are registered trademarks used herein under license.

ISBN 0–314–25728–4

TEXT IS PRINTED ON 10% POST
CONSUMER RECYCLED PAPER

Preface

We cover a lot of ground in this book. You will be exposed to a number of workplace issues and a multiplicity of regulatory systems. We want to give you some organizational principle for handling them.

We have organized the casebook around four sets of workplace values, each the theme of one chapter. They are, fair treatment of the individual worker (Chapter One), worker participation in governance of the workplace (Chapter Two), health and safety (Chapter Three), and economic security (Chapter Four). Within each of these chapters we look at various models for securing these workplace values, such as the market, setting of substantive standards, protection of identified categories of workers, and the use of collective bargaining. In Chapters One and Two we set out the basic structure of each of the systems of regulation, describing its operation in some detail. When you get to Chapters Three and Four you should be familiar enough with each system to apply it to the difficult substantive issues those chapters raise.

We give considerable space in this book to the collective bargaining system. This is not meant to express a preference for that approach to resolving workplace problems. Indeed, in these changing times we are all holding our breaths as to what is the most effective means of regulation of the workplace. We explore collective bargaining in more detail because it is the approach you are probably the least familiar with at this stage of your legal education, and we want to be sure you understand how it works and what are its limits. Collective bargaining has provided some unique institutional developments that may be of value in other areas of the law. For example, it departs from ordinary contract law in providing for some regulation of the bargaining process. And it relies on a system of dispute resolution, binding arbitration, that has become a model for the movement towards alternative dispute resolution in other contexts. In Chapter Two we describe the collective bargaining process in somewhat systematic fashion as it normally unfolds.

We provide a number of problem exercises throughout each chapter. We believe that you will profit from attempting to apply the principles you have learned in the course materials to new and complex situations. In these problems we attempt to place you in roles where you must come up with creative solutions and exercise some of the lawyer's skills of drafting, negotiation and problem solving. These problems usually are not designed to convey the textual portion of the book, so that if your instructor chooses not to cover them, you will find the necessary materials in the other parts of the casebook. Where the problem includes some information or perspective that we want you to consider even if you do not actually work through the problem, we will indicate this in the text.

ROBERT J. RABIN
EILEEN SILVERSTEIN
GEORGE SCHATZKI
KEN DAU-SCHMIDT

May, 2002

Authors' Thanks

This book has diverse roots. It goes back to 1984, when Willard Wirtz and Clyde Summers spoke eloquently at the Park City conference of the Labor Law Group about rethinking labor law. With the help and encouragement of many friends, we attempted to capture those ideas in our first edition. We remain indebted to those whose contributions we acknowledged in the first edition.

Our first two editions endured for well over a decade, giving us the pleasure of a rich collaboration in which we constantly talked and argued about what materials worked and what changes should be made to improve the book. We view the many students and colleagues who have used this book as our collaborators as well, for they have not been shy about telling us what they liked and didn't like. When it finally became time to update the second edition, alas, we were not content to leave things alone. In the third edition we tinkered a bit more, and deleted and replaced some materials, all in the elusive chase of perfection. As the three senior authors prepare to pass the baton, we welcome our colleague Kenneth Dau-Schmidt as a co-author of the third edition. Ken has provided valuable insights and materials, particularly in the area of economics, which is one of his specialties. We also had considerable help for this edition from Christopher David Ruiz Cameron, who teaches at Southwestern Law School, where he is also Associate Dean. Chris joined us for our planning session for the third edition, and provided numerous helpful suggestions. We hope Chris will be able to become a co-author when the fourth edition appears.

We give special thanks to our research assistants at our respective law schools, who helped tame and perfect mountains of earlier drafts. They are Minh Nguyen, Michael Riley, Heather Varley, Marsha Lawson, Jeff White, Chris Bond, Garry Hays, Griffin Dunham, Kelly Powis, Robert Moore, and Angelina Arrington. We reserve our most extravagant praise for our hardworking and cheerful secretaries, Teia Johnson, Chris Ramsdell, Claudette Landry, Delia Roy, Deborah Eads and Sonja Quinones.

EILEEN, GEORGE, BOB AND KEN

*

Foreword

The Labor Law Group is an association of law teachers, most of whom serve on faculties in the United States; others teach in Belgium, Canada, England, and Israel.

At the December 1946 meeting of the Labor Law Roundtable of the Association of American Law Schools, Professor W. Willard Wirtz (who became Secretary of Labor in 1962) delivered a compelling paper criticizing the labor law course books then available. His remarks so impressed those present that the Roundtable Council organized a general conference on the teaching of the subject. At the conference, held in Ann Arbor in 1947, some conferees agreed to exchange proposals for sections of a hoped-for new course book. The late Professor Robert E. Mathews served as coordinator. Beginning in 1948, a preliminary mimeographed version was used in seventeen schools; each user supplied comments and suggestions for change. In 1953, a hard-cover version was published under the title *Labor Relations and the Law*. The thirty-one "cooperating editors" were so convinced of the value of multi-campus collaboration that they gave up any individual claims to royalties. Instead, those royalties were paid to a trust fund to be used to develop and "provide the best possible materials" for training students in labor law and labor relations. The Declaration of Trust memorializing this agreement was executed November 4, 1953, and remains the Group's charter.

Cooperative ventures among legal scholars are often centered around ideological orthodoxies or common experiences or identities. In contrast, the Labor Law Group has tried to expand the scope of perceptions and experiences represented within its membership. Consistent with this goal, it has attained significant diversification in the racial, gender, national, and ideological composition of its participants and, additionally, has drawn its membership and leadership from institutions that are varied in size, styles, status, and geography.

The founding committee's hope that the initial collaboration would bear fruit has been fulfilled. Under Professor Mathews' continuing chairmanship, the Group's members produced *Readings on Labor Law* in 1955 and *The Employment Relation and the Law* in 1957, edited by Robert Mathews and Benjamin Aaron. A second edition of *Labor Relations and the Law* appeared in 1960, with Benjamin Aaron and Donald H. Wollett as co-chairmen, and a third edition was published in 1965, with Jerre Williams at the helm.

In June of 1969, the Group, now chaired by William P. Murphy, sponsored a conference to reexamine the labor law curriculum. The meeting, held at the University of Colorado, was attended by practitioners and by full-time teachers including nonmembers as well as members of the Group. The conference papers and discussion summaries were distributed

to law school libraries and to participants. In meetings that followed the
conference, the Group decided to reshape its work substantially. It restructured itself into ten task forces, each assigned a unit of no more than two
hundred pages on a discrete topic such as employment discrimination or
union-member relations. An individual teacher could then choose two or
three of these units as the material around which to build a particular
course. This multi-unit approach dominated the Group's work throughout
much of the 1970s under Professor Murphy and his successor as chairman,
Herbert L. Sherman, Jr. As the decade progressed and teachers refined
their views about what topics to include and how to address them, some
units were dropped from the series while others increased in scope and
length. Under Professor Sherman's chairmanship, the Group planned a
new series of six enlarged books to cover the full range of topics taught by
labor and employment law teachers.

Professor James E. Jones, Jr., was elected chairman in 1978 and shep-
herded to completion the promised set of six full-size, independent casebooks. In addition, during this period supplements were published for
some books. The Group continued to reevaluate its work and eventually
decided that it was time to convene another conference of law teachers.

In 1984, the Group, now chaired by Robert Covington, sponsored
another general conference to discuss developments in the substance and
teaching of labor and employment law, this time at Park City, Utah. (The
conference papers were distributed to law school libraries as well as participants.) Those discussions and a subsequent working session led to the
conclusion that the Group should devote principal attention to three new
conventional length course books, one devoted to employment discrimination, one to union-management relations, and one to the individual
employment relationship. In addition, work was planned on more abbreviated course books to serve as successors to the Group's earlier works
covering public employment bargaining and labor arbitration.

In 1989, with Alvin Goldman as Chair, the Group met in Breckenridge,
Colorado, to assess its most recent effort and develop plans for the future.
In addition to outlining new course book projects, the Group discussed
ways to assist teachers of labor and employment law in their efforts to
expand conceptual horizons and perspectives. In pursuit of the latter goals
it co-sponsored, in 1992, a conference held at the University of Toronto
Faculty of Law at which legal and nonlegal specialists examined alternative models of corporate governance and their impact on workers.

When Robert J. Rabin became Chair in 1996, the Group and a number
of invited guests met in Tucson, Arizona, to celebrate the imminent fifti-
eth anniversary of the Group. The topics of discussion included the impact
of the global economy and of changing forms of representation on the
teaching of labor and employment law, and the impact of new technologies
of electronic publishing on the preparation of teaching materials. The
Group honored three of its members who had been present at the creation
of the Group, Willard Wirtz, Ben Aaron, and Clyde Summers.

The Group next met in Scottsdale, Arizona in December, 1999, to discuss the production of materials that would more effectively bring emerging issues of labor and employment law into the classroom. Among the issues discussed were integration of international and comparative materials into the labor and employment curriculum and the pedagogical uses of the world wide web.

Laura J. Cooper became Chair of the Group in July, 2001. In addition to this new edition of *Labor and Employment Law*, the Group currently has three other textbooks in print, all published by WestGroup: *ADR in the Workplace*, by Laura J. Cooper, Dennis R. Nolan and Richard A. Bales; *Employment Discrimination Law* (Sixth Edition), by Robert Belton and Dianne Avery, with Maria L. Ontiveros joining as an author beginning with the 2001 Authors' Case Update; and *Legal Protection for the Individual Employee*, by Matthew W. Finkin, Alvin L. Goldman, and Clyde W. Summers. The Group is also at work on two new projects— a book on government employment (expanding an earlier work on public sector collective bargaining) and a casebook on labor issues in the global economy.

At any one time, roughly twenty-five to thirty persons are actively engaged in the Group's work; this has proved a practical size, given problems of communication and logistics. Coordination and editorial review of the projects are the responsibility of the executive committee, whose members are the successor trustees of the Group. Governance is by consensus; votes are taken only to elect trustees and to determine whom to invite to join the Group. Since 1953, more than seventy persons have worked on Group projects; in keeping with the original agreement, none has ever received anything more than reimbursement of expenses

This book is the Third Edition of a pioneering work by the original three authors, seeking to place the more traditional focus on labor law within a broader examination of the law of work. The book is innovative in both its subject matter and pedagogy. This edition, as did its predecessors, offers provocative essays, dialogues and problems, along with cases and questions for discussion.

Professor Robert J. Rabin, formerly Chair of the Labor Law Group, is a labor arbitrator and mediator who serves as editor of *The Labor Lawyer*, the scholarly journal of the American Bar Association's Section of Labor and Employment Law. He practiced on behalf of both unions and management before joining the faculty of Syracuse University College of Law in 1971. Eileen Silverstein is the Zephaniah Swift Professor of Law at the University of Connecticut School of Law. Before becoming a law teacher in 1974, Professor Silverstein practiced labor and employment law in California on behalf of management clients. She writes and teaches in the areas of property and civil rights, along with labor law. Professor George Schatzki, now at Arizona State University College of Law, served with the National Labor Relations Board and as a union lawyer prior to commencing an academic career that had included teaching at six law schools and serving as dean at two of them. Professor Schatzki has been engaged in authoring books with the Labor Law Group for more than two decades.

    Joining as co-author for this Edition is Kenneth G. Dau-Schmidt, the
Willard and Margaret Carr Professor of Labor and Employment Law at
Indiana University, Bloomington. Professor Dau-Schmidt's economic perspective is an important addition to this new Edition. He has a doctorate
in economics and served as a state legislative labor counsel and union
attorney before becoming a law teacher. He teaches and writes in the
areas of labor and employment law and also on the economic analysis of
legal problems.

THE EXECUTIVE COMMITTEE

HARRY W. ARTHURS

DIANNE AVERY

LANCE COMPA

LAURA J. COOPER, *CHAIR*

KENNETH G. DAU-SCHMIDT

MARIA L. ONTIVEROS

ROBERT J. RABIN

Editorial Policy Committee

The Labor Law Group

*

The Labor Law Group

Currently Participating Members

Harry W. Arthurs
York University

James B. Atleson
State University of New York, Buffalo

Dianne Avery
State University of New York, Buffalo

Richard A. Bales
Northern Kentucky University, Salmon P. Chase College of Law

Robert Belton
Vanderbilt University

Roger Blanpain
Instituut voor Arbeidsrecht, Collegium Falconis

Christopher David Ruiz Cameron
Southwestern University

Ruth Colker
Ohio State University

Roberto L. Corrada
University of Denver

Lance Compa
Cornell University, School of Industrial and Labor Relations

Laura J. Cooper
University of Minnesota

Robert N. Covington
Vanderbilt University

Marion G. Crain
University of North Carolina

Kenneth G. Dau-Schmidt
Indiana University, Bloomington

Matthew W. Finkin
University of Illinois

Catherine L. Fisk
Loyola Law School, Los Angeles

Joel W. Friedman
Tulane University

Alvin L. Goldman
University of Kentucky

Joseph R. Grodin
University of California, Hastings College of the Law

James E. Jones, Jr.
University of Wisconsin (Emeritus)

Deborah C. Malamud
University of Michigan

Martin H. Malin
Chicago-Kent, Illinois Institute of Technology

Mordehai Mironi
Haifa University

Robert B. Moberly
University of Arkansas

Dennis R. Nolan
University of South Carolina

Maria L. Ontiveros
University of San Franciso

Robert J. Rabin
Syracuse University

George Schatzki
Arizona State University

Calvin W. Sharpe
Case Western Reserve University

Eileen Silverstein
University of Connecticut

Acknowledgments and Permissions

Chapter One

Abrams, Roger A., Theory for the Discharge Case, 36 Arbitration Journal 24, 25 (198 1). Reprinted by permission of the Arbitration Journal.

Brecht, Bertolt, Selected Poems, 109 (H.Hays trans. 1947).

Culp, Jerome, Water Buffalo and Diversity: Naming Names and Reclaiming the Racial Discourse, 26 Conn.L.Rev. 209, 232-233 (1993). Reprinted by permission of The Connecticut Law Review Association.

Epstein, R., In Defense of the Contract at Will, 51 U.Chi.L.Rev. 947,953-955 (1984). Reprinted by permission of The University of Chicago Law Review.

Goeghegan, Thomas, Which Side Are You On? 91-96. Copyright 1991 by Farrar, Straus & Giroux, Inc. Reprinted by permission of Farrar, Straus & Giroux, Inc.

Holmes, Privilege, Malice and Intent, 8 Harv.L.Rev. 1, 7, 9 (1894). Reprinted by permission of The Harvard Law Review Association.

Jones, Power and Prudence in the Arbitration of Labor Disputes: A Venture in Some Hypotheses," 11 UCLA L.Rev.675, 764 (1964).

Kilborn, Peter T., A Company Recasts Itself to Erase Decades of Bias, The New York Times, Nov. 4, 1990, A1. Reprinted by permission of The New York Times Company.

LaMothe, L., Snyder, J., and West, R., Women as Rainmakers, Litigation, Spring 1991, 11-15. Reprinted by permission of Section of Litigation, American Bar Association.

Summers, Clyde, The Contract of Employment and the Rights of Individual Employees, 52 Fordham L.Rev. 1082, 1106 (1984). Reprinted by permission of Fordham Law Review.

Thurow, Lester, Policy Recommendations Concerning the Second Draft of the Pastoral Letter, 5 St. Louis U. Pub.L.Rev. 281, 288-289 (1986). Reprinted by permission of The Saint Louis University Public Law Review, 1986, Saint Louis University, St. Louis, Missouri.

Wilson, August, I Want A Black Director, The New York Times, July 22, 1990, A25.

Chapter Two

Bacow, Lawrence S., Bargaining for Job Safety and Health, 12-14. Cambridge, Mass.: MIT Press, ©1980. Reprinted by permission.

Bernstein, Irving, The Lean Years, 145-146, 163-164. Excerpt from the Lean Years by Irving Bernstein. Copyright © 1960, and renewed 1988 by Irving Bernstein. Reprinted with permission of Houghton Mifflin Company. All rights reserved.

Ashford, Nicholas A. and Caldert, Charles C., Technology, Law, and the Working Environment 29-32 (Van Nostrand Reinhold, 1991). Reprinted by permission.

Chess, Caron, Winning the Right to Know: A Handbook for Toxics Activists, 13-14. Philadelphia, PA: Delaware Valley Toxics Coalition, ©1984. Reprinted by permission of author.

Feinauer, Dale M., The Relationship Between Workplace Accident Rates and Drug and Alcohol Abuse: The Unproven Hypothesis, 3 Labor Studies Journal 10-13 (1990). Reprinted by permission of author.

Friedman, Milton, and Friedman, Rose D., Free to Choose: A Personal Statement, 232-243. Excerpts from Free to Choose: A Personal Statement, copyright © 1980 by Milton Friedman and Rose D. Friedman, reprinted by permission of Harcourt, Inc.

Getman, Julius, Ruminations on Union Organizing in the Private Sector, 53 U. Chi. L. Rev. 45, 71-73 (1986). Reprinted by permission of the University of Chicago Law Review.

Gross, James A. and Greenfield, Patricia A., Arbitral Value Judgments In Health And Safety Disputes: Management Rights Over Workers' Rights, 34 Buff.L.Rev. 645-55 (1985). Reprinted by permission of the Buffalo Law Review.

Leonard, Arthur S., AIDS and Employment Law Revisited, 14 Hofstra L. Rev. 11 (1985). Reprinted with permission of the Hofstra Law Review Association.

Nelkin, Dorothy and Brown, Michael S., Workers at Risk: Voices From the Workplace, 106, 122, 164. Chicago: U. Chicago Press, 1984.

O'Reilly, James T., Driving a Soft Bargain: Unions, Toxic Materials, and Right to Know Legislation, 9 Harvard Environmental L. Rev. 307-308 © (1985) by the President and Fellows of Harvard College and the Harvard Environmental Law Review. Reprinted by permission.

Rabin, Robert J., Some Comments on Obscenities, Health and Safety, and Workplace Values, 34 Buff.L.Rev. 725, 728-30 (1985). Reprinted by permission of the Buffalo Law Review.

Rhinehart, Lynn K., Would Workers Be Better Protected If They Were Declared An Endangered Species? A Comparison of the Criminal Enforcement Under the Federal Workplace Safety and Environmental Protection Laws, 31 Am.Cr.L.Rev. 353-54 (1994). Reprinted by permission of the American Criminal Law Review © 1994.

Chapter Four

Cameron, Christopher David Ruiz, How 'Necessary Became The Mother Of Rejection: An Empirical Look at the Fate of Collective Bargaining Agreements On the Tenth Anniversary of Bankruptcy Code Section 1113(c), 34 Santa Clara Law Review 841 (1994). Reprinted by permission.

Cappelli, Peter, The New Deal At Work, 76 Chi-Kent L. Rev. 1169, 1175-78 (2000). Reprinted by permission.

Compa, Lance, The Multilateral Agreement on Investment and International Labor Rights, 31 Cornell Int'l. L. J. 683, 697-700 (1998). Reprinted by permission.

Dau-Schmidt, Kenneth G., Employment in the New Age of Trade and Technology, 76 Indiana L. J. 11, 8-12. Copyright 2000 by the Trustees of Indiana University. Reprinted by permission.

Dine, Janet, Human Rights and Company Law, in Human Rights Standards and The Responsibility of Transnational Corporations, 209-212 (ed. Michael K. Addo)(1999). Reprinted with kind permission from Kluwer Law International.

Dowling, Donald C. Jr., The Multinational's Manifesto on Sweatshops, Trade/Labor Linkage, and Codes of Conduct, 8 Tulsa J. Comp. & Int'l Law 27, 39-40, 43-46 (2000). Reprinted by permission.

Ghilarducci, Teresa, Labor's Capital: The Economics and Politics of Private Pensions, 176-78 (1992). Reprinted by permission.

Hagen, Katherine A., Fundamentals of Labor Issues and NAFTA. This work, copyright 1994 by Katherine A. Hagen, was originally published in 27 U.C. Davis L. Rev. 917 (1994), copyright 1994 by the Regents of the University of California. Reprinted with permission.

Hailstones, Thomas J., Basic Economics, 5th edition 37-39 © 1976. Reprinted with permission of South-Western College Publishing—a division of Thomson Learning.

Harrison, Bennett, Lean and Mean: The Changing Landscape of Corporate Power in the Age of Flexibility, 206-213. Copyright © 1994 by Bennett Harrison. Reprinted by permission of Basic Books, a member of Perseus Books. L.L.C.

Hepple, Bob, A Race to The Top, 20 Comparative Labor Law & Policy J. 347, 357-363 (1999). Reprinted by permission.

Keating, Dan, Good Intentions, Bad Economics: Retiree Insurance Benefits in Bankruptcy, 43 Vand. L. Rev. 161, 163 (1990). Reprinted by permission.

Langbein, John H. and Bruce F. Wolk, Pension and Employee Benefit Law 90-93 (1990). Reprinted by permission.

Olsen, Frances E., Symposium: Global Dynamics of Unfair Employment, 4 Employee Rights and Employee Policy J. 171-174. Reprinted by permission.

Ontiveros, Maria, A Vision of Global Capitalism, 3 J. of Small & Emerging Bus. Law 27, 36-37 (1999). Reprinted by permission.

Schultz, Vicki, Life's Work, 100 Colum. L. Rev. 1881, 194-27 (2000). © Vicki Schultz.

Summers, Clyde, NAFTA's Labor Side Agreement, 3 J. of Small and Emerging Bus. Law, 173, 175-187 (1999). Reprinted by permission.

Summers, Clyde, The Battle in Seattle: Free Trade, Labor Rights, and Societal Values, 22 U. Pa. J. Int'l Econ. L. 61, 66-68. (2001). Reprinted by permission.

Stone, Katherine Van Wezel, Labor and the Global Economy, 16 Michigan J. of Int'l Law 987, 998-1006. Reprinted by permission.

*

Summary of Contents

	Page
PREFACE	iii
AUTHORS' THANKS	v
FOREWORD	vii
EDITORIAL POLICY COMMITTEE	xi
THE LABOR LAW GROUP	xiii
ACKNOWLEDGEMENTS AND PERMISSIONS	xvii
TABLE OF CASES	xxxvii

CHAPTER ONE. FAIR TREATMENT OF THE WORKER 1

I. AN INTRODUCTORY PROBLEM AND SOME BACKGROUND FOR THE COURSE 2
A. Problem: The Worker Who Questions Authority 2
B. The Lawyer's Toolbox 4
C. Some Pervasive Themes in This Course 6

II. EMPLOYMENT AT WILL 11
A. The Contractarian Understanding of Work Relations 11
B. Looking Beyond the Agreement 47

III. AN OVERVIEW OF EQUAL EMPLOYMENT OPPORTUNITY LAW 72
A. Problem: The Attorney Who Does Not Make Partner 72
B. Two Models of Proof 82
C. When Differences Matter (Or Not) 101

IV. SHALL WE SWALLOW EMPLOYEES, THEIR FREEDOM, AND THEIR STATUTORY RIGHTS INTO THE WORLD OF CONTRACTS AND ARBITRATION? 165
A. Via Covenants Not to Compete, Can a Former Employer Preclude an Employee From Working? If it is the Employer Who Terminates the Contract, is the Covenant Not to Compete Still Effective? 165
B. The "Conflict" of Statute and Contract 171

V. AN INTRODUCTION TO ANOTHER EXCEPTION TO EMPLOYMENT AT WILL—UNION AND CONCERTED ACTIVITIES 190
A. The Requirement of Concertedness 191
B. The Bright, Elusive Line Between Concerted Activity That is Protected and That is Not Protected 192

Page

C. Motive (Revisited) in an Anti–Union Setting------------------------- 197

**CHAPTER TWO. PARTICIPATION IN WORKPLACE GOV-
        ERNANCE** --- **200**
A. Two Models of Workplace Participation -------------------------------- 200
B. The Boundaries, Perks and Obligations of Representation--------- 252
C. The Road to Representation -- 309
D. What Do We Talk About When We Talk About Work?—The
        Law That Regulates Collective Bargaining ----------------------- 352
E. Negotiating in the Shadow of Economic Weapons------------------ 398
F. Applying and Enforcing the Compact ---------------------------------- 466
G. Using More Global Economic Weapons -------------------------------- 487

**CHAPTER THREE. HEALTH AND SAFETY IN THE
        WORKPLACE** -- **520**
A. The Common Law Response to Employee Injuries------------------ 528
B. A Class Discussion About Workers' Compensation Laws --------- 531
C. Occupational Safety and Health Act of 1970 ------------------------ 538
D. Problem 3–1 -- 578
E. The Worker Who Takes Matters Into Her Own Hands—Prob-
        lem 3–2 --- 607
F. Problem 3–3 -- 639
G. Problem 3–4 --- 663

**CHAPTER FOUR. ECONOMIC SECURITY AND CAPITAL
        MOBILITY** -- **682**
A. Introduction --- 683
B. Legal Responses to Accelerated Capital Mobility -------------------- 698
C. International Business Transactions and the Law of Work ------- 819
D. Transnational Labor Standards and the Global Economy --------- 845

INDEX -- 881

Table of Contents

─────────

		Page
Preface		iii
Authors' Thanks		v
Foreword		vii
Editorial Policy Committee		xi
The Labor Law Group		xiii
Acknowledgements and Permissions		xvii
Table of Cases		xxxvii

CHAPTER ONE. FAIR TREATMENT OF THE WORKER 1

I. AN INTRODUCTORY PROBLEM AND SOME BACKGROUND FOR THE COURSE 2

A. Problem: The Worker Who Questions Authority 2
On Brainstorming 4
B. The Lawyer's Toolbox 4
C. Some Pervasive Themes in This Course 6
Some Statistics About Employment 7

II. EMPLOYMENT AT WILL 11

A. The Contractarian Understanding of Work Relations 11
Epstein, In Defense of the Contract at Will 12
Holmes, Privilege, Malice and Intent 14
A Note for All Cases 15
Vegelahn v. Guntner 15
Note 21
A Case Study 23
Local 1330, United Steel Workers of America v. United States Steel Corp. 23
Questions 33
Thomas Geohegan, Which Side Are You On? 34
E.B. White, The Lighthouse 36
Warn—A Statutory Approach and Other Statutory Efforts to Enhance Job Security 37
Employment–At–Will Doctrine Dominates 38
"Cause" and Arbitration 39
Sample Arbitration Award 39
Notes 46
Roger Abrams, A Theory for the Discharge Case 47
Questions 47

Page

B. Looking Beyond the Agreement --- 47
   1. Case Law --- 48
      a. Discharge That Contravenes Public Policy -------------------- 48
        Sheets v. Teddy's Frosted Foods, Inc. ----------------------- 48
        The Concern About Public Policy----------------------------- 53
      b. Implied–In–Law Good Faith and Fair Dealing -------------- 54
        Fortune v. National Cash Register ----------------------- 54
        Questions -- 57
        Kumpf v. Steinhaus -------------------------------------- 58
        Questions and Notes ------------------------------------- 61
        Clyde Summers, The Contract of Employment and the Rights of
          Individual Employees: Fair Representation and Employment
          at Will --- 61
      c. Implied–In–Fact Promises of Job Security-------------------- 62
        Pugh v. See's Candies, Inc. ----------------------------- 62
        Questions -- 68
        Damages and Attorney's Fees------------------------------- 69
        Statutory Law-- 70

III. AN OVERVIEW OF EQUAL EMPLOYMENT OPPORTU-
     NITY LAW -- **72**
A. Problem: The Attorney Who Does Not Make Partner ------------- 72
   Reasonable Cause Decision --- 72
   Issues to Think About -- 76
   Women As Rainmakers -- 77
B. Two Models of Proof --- 82
   1. Disparate Impact or Disproportionality --------------------------- 82
      Griggs v. Duke Power Co. ------------------------------------ 82
      Questions and Notes --- 88
   2. Disparate Treatment or Intentional Discrimination ------------- 89
      McDonnell Douglas v. Green --------------------------------- 89
      Notes and Questions --- 96
      Mount Healthy City School District Board of Education v. Doyle------ 97
      Notes and Questions --- 101
C. When Differences Matter (Or Not) ----------------------------------- 101
   1. The Bona Fide Occupational Qualification (BFOQ) ------------- 101
      August Wilson, I Want a Black Director------------------------- 104
   2. Affirmative Action-- 107
      Peter T. Kilborn, A Company Recasts Itself to Erase Decades of
        Bias -- 107
      Question-- 113
      The Supreme Court Speaks, Often and Variously ----------------- 113
      Johnson v. Transportation Agency, Santa Clara County, Cal. --------- 113
      Questions and Observations ---------------------------------- 123
      Lester Thurow, Policy Recommendations Concerning the Second
        Draft of the Pastoral Letter ----------------------------- 124
      Question-- 125
      Jerome Culp, Water Buffalo and Diversity: Naming Names and
        Reclaiming the Racial Discourse ------------------------- 125

Page

C. When Differences Matter (Or Not)—Continued

    3. Reasonable Accommodation 127
      Trans World Airlines, Inc. v. Hardison 127
      Notes and Questions 134
    4. Harassing Behavior 135
      Harris v. Forklift Systems, Inc. 135
      Questions and Notes 139
      Oncale v. Sundowner Offshore Services, Inc. 139
      Questions 143
    5. Pregnancy 143
      Newport News Shipbuilding And Dry Dock Co. v. E.E.O.C. .. 143
      Note 146
    6. Age 147
      Hazen Paper Co. v. Biggins 148
      Questions 152
    7. Disability 152
      Sutton v. United Air Lines, Inc. 153
      Questions 163

IV. SHALL WE SWALLOW EMPLOYEES, THEIR FREE-
    DOM, AND THEIR STATUTORY RIGHTS INTO THE
    WORLD OF CONTRACTS AND ARBITRATION? 165

A. Via Covenants Not to Compete, Can a Former Employer Pre-
    clude an Employee From Working? If it is the Employer Who
    Terminates the Contract, is the Covenant Not to Compete
    Still Effective? 165
    Robert S. Weiss and Associates, Inc. v. Wiederlight 165
    Questions 170
B. The "Conflict" of Statute and Contract 171
    Oubre v. Entergy Operations 171
    Note and Questions 174
    Gilmer v. Interstate/Johnson Lane 174
    Notes and Questions 184
    The Differences Between Arbitration and Litigation 185

V. AN INTRODUCTION TO ANOTHER EXCEPTION TO
    EMPLOYMENT AT WILL—UNION AND CONCERTED
    ACTIVITIES 190

A. The Requirement of Concertedness 191
    NLRB v. City Disposal Systems 191
    Questions 192
B. The Bright, Elusive Line Between Concerted Activity That is
    Protected and That is Not Protected 192
    NLRB v. Washington Aluminum Co. 193
    Questions and Notes 196
C. Motive (Revisited) in an Anti–Union Setting 197
    Edward G. Budd Manufacturing Co. v. NLRB 197
    Note 199

Page

CHAPTER TWO. PARTICIPATION IN WORKPLACE GOV-ERNANCE **200**

A. Two Models of Workplace Participation 200
Introductory Dialogue 200
Concord vs. Discord: Is This the Choice? 202
Irving Bernstein, The Lean Years: A History of the American Worker, 1920–1933 202
J.D. Rockefeller, Jr., Labor and Capital–Partners 203
1. Modes of Worker Participation 205
Out With the Old Ways: Reinventing the Workplace? 205
Participation With Empowerment—Collective Bargaining ... 207
R. Freeman and J. Medoff, What Do Unions Do? 207
Jack Metzgar, Striking Steel: Solidarity Remembered 210
Unions and the Market 215
Milton and Rose Friedman, Who Protects the Worker? 215
Kenneth G. Dau–Schmidt—A Bargaining Analysis of American Labor Law and the Search for Bargaining Equity and Industrial Peace 217
A Bridge Between the Union and Non–Union Models? 220
Weingarten Rights in the Non–Union Workplace 220
Epilepsy Foundation of Northeast Ohio 221
Some Observations and Questions to Guide You Through This Chapter 225
2. Does the Law Discourage Informal Worker Representation? .. 227
Irving Bernstein, The Lean Years: A History of the American Worker 227
Electromation, Inc. v. NLRB 230
Statutory Reform? 239
The "Saturn" Advice Memo and Bernhard–Altmann 240
International Ladies' Garment Workers' Union v. National Labor Relations Board 241
Summers, Employee Voice and Employer Choice 243
Weiler and Mundlak, New Directions for the Law of the Workplace 247
NLRB General Counsel Advice Memorandum: GM–UAW Saturn Project 248
Some Questions 250
Saul Rubinstein, Et Al., "The Saturn Partnership: Co–Management and the Reinvention of the Local Union," In Employee Representation, Bruce E. Kaufman and Morris M. Kleiner, Eds. 251

B. The Boundaries, Perks and Obligations of Representation 252
Introduction 252
1. Exclusivity: Does the Unity of the Majority Silence the Voices of Dissent? 254
J.I. Case v. NLRB 255
Emporium Capwell Co. v. Western Addition Community Organization 259
Note On Two Conflicting Directives in the NLRA 273
2. Exclusivity and the Duty of Fair Representation 274
Ford Motor Co. v. Huffman 274
The Duty of Fair Representation After Ford Motor Co. 278
Communications Workers of America v. Beck 280

Page

B. The Boundaries, Perks and Obligations of Representation—
　　Continued
　　3. Sharing the Costs of Exclusive Representation ------------------- 286
　　　　Note on Workers' Voice and Union Dues on Joining the Union ------ 286
　　4. The Collective Bargaining Community: Inclusive or Divisive? 289
　　　　National Labor Relations Board v. Kentucky River Community
　　　　　Care, Inc. -- 293
　　　　Future Directions in Union Representation------------------------ 300
　　　　NLRB v. Town & Country Electric, Inc. ------------------------ 300
　　　　Note on Town and Country and its Implications ----------------- 306
　　　　Medical Students and Graduate Students----------------------- 307
　　　　Katherine V.W. Stone, The New Psychological Contract: Implica-
　　　　　tions of the Changing Workplace for Labor and Employment
　　　　　Law --- 307

C. The Road to Representation --- 309
　　Paul Weiler, Promises to Keep: Securing Workers' Rights to Self–
　　　Organization Under the NLRA ------------------------------------ 311
　　NLRB v. Gissel Packing Co. --------------------------------------- 315
　　Questions and Notes About Gissel---------------------------------- 324
　　Lechmere v. NLRB--- 327
　　Note on Access -- 335
　　Getman, Ruminations on Union Organizing in the Private Sector ------- 335
　　Further Complications—Offsite and Off Duty Workers ---------------- 337
　　Note on Organizing Issues in an Electronic Workplace--------------- 337
　　Review Problem -- 339
　　Problem 2–1: The Outspoken Technician ---------------------------- 340
　　National Labor Relations Board v. Local Union No. 1229, International
　　　Brotherhood of Electrical Workers----------------------------- 342
　　Note on the Ptolemy Problem ------------------------------------ 348
　　On Concertedness--- 349
　　On Protected Remarks --- 350
　　Protection in a Non–Union Workplace----------------------------- 350
　　Weingarten Rights in the Non-Union Workplace------------------- 352

D. What Do We Talk About When We Talk About Work?—The
　　Law That Regulates Collective Bargaining ----------------------- 352
　　Introduction -- 352
　　The Power Base of Bargaining and the Law Relating to Use of
　　　Economic Weapons--- 353
　　Problem 2–2: Preparing for Bargaining--------------------------- 354
　　Surface Bargaining—A Case Study in Bargaining Strategies and Eco-
　　　nomic Weapons--- 355
　　Teamsters Local v. NLRB (Reichhold Chemicals) ----------------- 355
　　Note on Surface Bargaining ------------------------------------- 358
　　Kenneth G. Dau–Schmidt: A Bargaining Analysis of American Labor
　　　Law and the Search for Bargaining Equity and Industrial Peace 358
　　A Case Study on Bargaining Under the NLRA--------------------- 362
　　Questions --- 370
　　More Law—Mandatory Subjects of Bargaining--------------------- 372
　　First National Maintenance Corporation v. National Labor Relations
　　　Board --- 373
　　FNM and Fibreboard—Two Different Courts? --------------------- 382

xxx TABLE OF CONTENTS

Page

D. What Do We Talk About When We Talk About Work?—The
Law That Regulates Collective Bargaining—Continued
United Food and Commercial Workers v. NLRB 383
Notes on the Scope of the Duty to Bargain 386
Some Philosophical Observations About the Duty to Bargain 387
To Reiterate 388
Some Other Ways of Looking at the Carrier Case Study 389
What is an Impasse, and why is it important? 390
Ellen J. Dannin and Terry H. Wagar, Lawless Law? The Subversion of
the National Labor Relations Act 391
A Brief Exercise on Impasse 393
Some Practical Alternatives—A Dialogue on Effects Bargaining 394
The Right to Information 396
Remedies 397
E. Negotiating in the Shadow of Economic Weapons 398
Introduction 398
1. Defining the Bounds of Judicial Intervention: The Strike, Its
Limitations, and Proposals for Reform 400
NLRB v. Mackay Radio & Telegraph Co. 400
Note on the Significance of Mackay Radio 404
The Antidote to Mackay? The Striker Replacement Bill 408
The Authors And Friend Go to Congress 408
2. Do Replacement Workers Have Rights Too? 413
Belknap, Inc. v. Hale 415
Some Practical Questions About Belknap 421
3. Union Attempts to Redress the Balance 423
4. The Wisdom of Judicial and Administrative Intervention 425
NLRB v. Insurance Agents' International Union, AFL–CIO 425
American Ship Building Company v. NLRB 431
To the Cynics Among Us 439
5. Union Control Over and Persuasion of Those Who Do Not
Honor its Economic Activities 441
Clear Pine Mouldings, Inc. 441
Pattern Makers' League of North America, AFL–CIO v. NLRB 444
A Couple of Questions and Observations 448
6. What About the Economic Weapons of Non–Union Workers? 450
Section 8(b)(7) Discussion . . . at a Cast Party 451
7. Is There a Substitute for Economic Weapons? 459
State of Connecticut Interest Arbitration and Domestic Partner
Benefits 460
F. Applying and Enforcing the Compact 466
An Overview: Two Contrasting Models 466
The Typical Collective Bargaining Agreement 467
Arbitration of External Rights 469
Alexander v. Gardner–Denver Co. 470
The Gilmer Case 479
Note on Reconciling Alexander and Gilmer 479
Wright v. Universal Maritime Service Corporation Et Al. 480

Page

F. Applying and Enforcing the Compact—Continued
    Questions About Wright -- 485
    Note on a Difficult Technical Point: NLRB Deferral ------------- 486
G. Using More Global Economic Weapons ----------------------------- 487
    Introduction --- 487
    A Trip Through § 8(B)(4) --- 488
    1. The Traditional Distinction Between Primary and Secondary
       Pressure -- 489
       Local 761, Electrical Workers v. NLRB ---------------------- 490
    2. The Courts Relax the Meaning of "Coercion" ------------------- 499
       Edward J. DeBartolo Corp. v. Florida Gulf Coast Building and
          Construction Trades Council -------------------------------- 500
    3. On Neutrality --- 511
       On Finer Distinctions Regarding Neutrality ------------------- 511
    4. The Publicity Proviso and the First Amendment --------------- 512
       NLRB v. Fruit & Vegetable Packers & Warehousemen, Local 760
          (Tree Fruits) --- 513
       Some Concluding Observations -------------------------------- 519

CHAPTER THREE. HEALTH AND SAFETY IN THE WORKPLACE --- **520**

Introduction: Some Idea of the Problem and the Range of Solutions ---------- 520
Nicholas A. Ashford, Crisis in the Workplace ------------------------------- 520
Nicholas A. Ashford and Charles C. Caldert, Technology, Law, and the
    Working Environment --- 523
Some Updated Statistics About Injuries and Illnesses in the Workplace ------ 527
A. The Common Law Response to Employee Injuries --------------------- 528
    Farwell v. Boston and Worcester Rail Road Corporation --------------- 528
B. A Class Discussion About Workers' Compensation Laws ------------- 531
C. Occupational Safety and Health Act of 1970 ------------------------- 538
    1. Assessing Risks and Balancing Values -------------------------- 540
       Industrial Union Department, AFL–CIO v. American Petroleum
          Institute (Benzene Case) ----------------------------------- 540
       Several Years Later --- 550
       Cost–Benefit Analysis Under OSHA and the Value of a Life ---------- 550
       American Textile Manufacturers Institute, Inc. v. Donovan (Cotton
          Dust Case) --- 550
       Questions: -- 556
       Executive Order 12866 -- 557
       Department of Labor Occupational Safety and Health Adminis.
          Safety Standards for Steel Erection ---------------------------- 558
       Questions: -- 562
       Lawrence S. Bacow, Bargaining for Job Safety and Health ---------- 562
       Lynn K. Rhinehart, Would Workers be Better Protected if They
          Were Declared An Endangered Species? A Comparison of Crimi-
          nal Enforcement Under the Federal Workplace Safety and Envi-
          ronmental Protection Laws -------------------------------------- 564

Page

C. Occupational Safety and Health Act of 1970—Continued
  2. Learning About Risks and How to Deal With Them (Or:
     How I Learned To Stop Worrying and To Love My Job)   565
     James T. O'Reilly, Driving a Soft Bargain: Unions, Toxic Materials,
       and Right to Know Legislation 565
     Delaware Valley Toxics Coalition, Winning the Right to Know: A
       Handbook for Toxics Activists 566
     Developing Right to Know Legislation 566
     Worker Right to Know or Public–Access Legislation? 566
     Types of Toxics Information 566
       a. Under the NLRA 567
          OCAW v. NLRB 567
       b. Under "Right to Know" Statutes 571
          United Steelworkers of America, AFL–CIO v. Auchter ... 571
          Note About Employee Knowledge of Employment Dangers and
            Hazards 575
          Catherine Ruckelshaus and Fanette Pollack, Book Review,
            Women's Health in the Workplace 576
D. Problem 3–1 578
  1. Statutes 579
     a. Title VII—Johnson Controls 580
        International Union, UAW v. Johnson Controls 580
     b. OSHA—American Cyanamid Case 591
        OCAW v. American Cyanamid Co. 591
     c. The Americans with Disabilities Act 596
  2. The Collective Bargaining Contract 597
     (a) Arbitrability—Can we refuse to arbitrate? 597
         AT & T Technologies, Inc. v. Communications Workers
           of America 597
     (b) Arbitration—Is it the exclusive remedy? 600
     (c) Statutory Reference within Contract. 601
     (d) What does the collective bargaining contract
         mean? 601
  3. The NLRB and Unilateral Action 602
E. The Worker Who Takes Matters Into Her Own Hands—Prob-
   lem 3–2 607
   D. Nelkin and M. Brown, Workers at Risk 607
   Eve, Sorter, Manufacturing Plant 607
   Steve, Railroad Trackman 607
   Problem 3–2 608
   1. Arbitration and Refusals to Work 611
      James A. Gross and Patricia A. Greenfield, Arbitral Value Judg-
        ments in Health and Safety Disputes: Management Rights Over
        Workers' Rights 611
      Robert J. Rabin, Some Comments on Obscenities, Health and
        Safety, and Workplace Values 614
   2. Protected Concerted Activities, the National Labor Relations
      Board and Deferral to the Arbitral Process 616
      United Technologies Corp. and International Association of Ma-
        chinists & Aerospace Workers, AFL/CIO 616
      Taylor v. NLRB 619

Page
E. The Worker Who Takes Matters Into Her Own Hands—Continued
    3. Collective Action Without Representation 625
    4. OSHA and Refusals to Work 626
       Whirlpool Corp. v. Marshall 626
    5. The Union's Obligation to Provide a Safe Workplace 633
       United Steelworkers of America v. Rawson 633
F. Problem 3–3 639
    Vaca v. Sipes 642
    Note—The Duty of Fair Representation 649
    Warning: Damages in Fair Representation Suits 649
    Dale M. Feinauer, The Relationship Between Workplace Accident Rates and Drug and Alcohol Abuse: The Unproven Hypothesis 651
    Skinner v. Railway Labor Executives' Ass'n 653
    Note 660
    Some Questions About Braveman's Problem 661
G. Problem 3–4 663
    1. A Little Information Regarding Aids 665
       Arthur S. Leonard, Aids and Employment Law Revisited 665
    2. The Rehabilitation Act of 1973 667
       School Board of Nassau County, Florida v. Arline 667
    3. Some Questions About the Americans With Disabilities Act and the Arbitration Award 673
    4. Is the Proposed Axfel Award Enforceable in the Courts? 674
       Eastern Associated Coal Corporation v. United Mine Workers of America 674
       Note: Lessons to be learned from Eastern Associated Coal, and other questions about Problem 3–4. 679
       Another Exception to Arbitral Finality 680

CHAPTER FOUR. ECONOMIC SECURITY AND CAPITAL MOBILITY **682**
A. Introduction 683
    1. Free Enterprise Capitalism: Theory and Practice 683
       Thomas J. Hailstones, Basic Economics 683
       Charles E. Lindblom, Unions and Capitalism 686
       Peter Cappelli, The New Deal at Work 688
    2. The Changing Labor Market and its Effects 691
       Kenneth G. Dau–Schmidt, Employment in the New Age of Trade and Technology: Implications for Labor and Employment Law 691
       Vicki Schultz, Life's Work 695
       Maria L. Ontiveros A Vision of Global Capitalism That Puts Women and People of Color at the Center 697
B. Legal Responses to Accelerated Capital Mobility 698
    1. Going Out of Business 698
       a. The Law 698
       b. Does a Collective Bargaining Agreement Make a Difference? 700
         Local 461 v. Singer Co. 700
       c. Some Consequences of Going Out of Business 702
         i. Pension Plans 703
         ii. Welfare benefit plans 703
       d. Perspectives 704

Page

B. Legal Responses to Accelerated Capital Mobility—Continued
2. Reorganization Under Chapter 11 of the Bankruptcy Code --- 708
   a. Chapter 11 Reorganization and Labor Costs ------------------ 709
   b. Does a Collective Bargaining Agreement Make a Difference? -- 710
      Truck Drivers Local 807 v. Carey Transp., Inc. ---------------- 711
      Notes --- 721
         i. Section 1113 --- 721
         ii. Application of Section 1113 --------------------------------- 722
         iii. Section 1114: Retiree Insurance Benefits ----------------- 724
   c. Perspectives --- 726
3. Restructuring to Cut Costs --- 727
   Restructuring by Eliminating Jobs -------------------------------- 728
   a. Just fire people -- 728
   b. Voluntary Separations Combined With Generous Severance Benefits -- 729
      i. Voluntariness --- 729
      ii. Waivers and Releases -------------------------------------- 731
         General Release and Covenant Not to Sue ---------------- 731
      iii. What do severance benefits buy? ------------------------- 733
   c. Early retirement incentives to eligible employees ----------- 733
      i. ADEA and early retirement incentives ------------------- 734
      ii. Restrictions on future employment as age discrimination --- 735
         EEOC v. Local 350, Plumbers ----------------------------- 735
      iii. Can the employer pick and choose who is eligible for early retirement? --- 740
         McNab v. General Motors Corp. --------------------------- 740
         Eichorn v. AT & T Corp. -------------------------------- 743
   d. Cost as a Factor in Decisions to Close Operations ---------- 750
      Marley Weiss, Risky Business: Age and Race Discrimination in Capital Deployment Decisions ----------------------------- 751
      Allen v. Diebold, Inc. -- 752
   e. Does a collective bargaining agreement make a difference? -- 755
      i. Self–Help -- 755
      ii. Cooperation -- 756
      iii. The Courts --- 756
         Boys Markets, Inc. v. Retail Clerks Union, Local 770 -------- 756
         Notes -- 760
         Aluminum Workers Intern. v. Consolidated Aluminum Corp. --- 760
         Notes -- 767
4. Transfer of Ownership --- 774
   A Brief Detour Into the World of Corporate Law ---------------- 775
   Back to the World of Labor and Employment Law -------------- 776
   a. Do Promises of Fidelity Survive Transfers of Ownership? 776
      i. Covenants Not to Compete as a Limit on the Right to Work --- 776
         Freund v. E.D. & F. Man International, Inc. ------------ 777

Page

B. Legal Responses to Accelerated Capital Mobility—Continued

         Campbell v. Potash Corp. of Saskatchewan, Inc. 780

    ii. Just Cause as a Limit on the Right to Discharge 786

         Conrad v. Rofin–Sinar, Inc. 786

  b. Does a Collective Bargaining Agreement Make a Differ-
     ence? 791

    i. Must Sunshine Honor the Terms of the Frost–RCU
       Bargaining Agreement? 792

       NLRB v. Burns Intern. Security Services 792

       John Wiley & Sons, Inc. v. Livingston 796

       Howard Johnson Co. Inc. v. Detroit Joint Executive Board .. 799

       Questions 805

    ii. Must Sunshine Bargain with the RCU? 805

       Fall River Dyeing & Finishing Corp. v. NLRB 805

  c. Perspectives 816

    Join the Discussion * * * 816

C. International Business Transactions and the Law of Work 819

  1. Extraterritoriality: Domestic Jurisdiction Determined by
     Statute or Treaty 820

    Van Blaricom v. Burlington Northern R.R. Co. 821

    Notes 824

    Morelli v. Cedel 824

    The Effect of Treaties 829

    Fortino v. Quasar Company 830

    Note 832

  2. Domestic Jurisdiction Declined: Forum Non Conveniens 833

  3. Domestic Substantive Law Applied 834

    Labor Union of Pico Korea Ltd. v. Pico Products, Inc. 834

    Note 842

    Note on Doe v. Unocal 842

D. Transnational Labor Standards and the Global Economy 845

  1. Transnational Labor Rights 846

    Janet Dine, Human Rights and Company Law 846

    Lance Compa, The Multilateral Agreement on Investment and
     International Labor Rights: A Failed Connection 847

    Clyde Summers the Battle in Seattle: Free Trade, Labor Rights and
     Societal Values 850

    Questions 852

  2. International Trade and Labor Standards 852

    Bennett Harrison, Lean and Mean: The Changing Landscape of
     Corporate Power in the Age of Flexibility 853

    Donald C. Dowling, Jr. The Multinational's Manifesto on Sweat-
     shops, Trade/Labor Linkage, and Code of Conduct 855

    Frances E. Olsen, Symposium: Global Dynamics of Unfair Employ-
     ment 860

  3. Institutional Approaches 862

    Katherine Van Wezel Stone, Labor and the Global Economy: Four
     Approaches to Transnational Labor Regulation 863

    Katherine A. Hagen Fundamentals of Labor Issues and NAFTA 871

    Clyde Summers, NAFTA's Labor Side Agreement and International
     Labor Standards 872

    Bob Hepple, A Race to the Top: International Investment Guide-
     lines and Corporate Codes of Conduct 877

INDEX 881

*

Table of Cases

The principal cases are in bold type. Cases cited or discussed in the text are roman type. References are to pages. Cases cited in principal cases and within other quoted materials are not included.

Adair v. United States, 208 U.S. 161, 28 S.Ct. 277, 52 L.Ed. 436 (1908), 11

Adarand Constructors, Inc. v. Pena, 515 U.S. 200, 115 S.Ct. 2097, 132 L.Ed.2d 158 (1995), 124

Air Line Pilots Ass'n, Intern. v. O'Neill, 499 U.S. 65, 111 S.Ct. 1127, 113 L.Ed.2d 51 (1991), 278

Alexander v. Gardner–Denver Co., 415 U.S. 36, 94 S.Ct. 1011, 39 L.Ed.2d 147 (1974), 184, 185, **470,** 478, 479, 485, 487, 611

Allen v. Diebold, Inc., 33 F.3d 674 (6th Cir.1994), **752**

Aluminum Workers Intern. v. Consolidated Aluminum Corp., 696 F.2d 437 (6th Cir.1982), **760,** 768

Amalgamated Local 813, Intern. Union, Allied Indus. Workers of America v. Diebold Inc., 605 F.Supp. 32 (N.D.Ohio 1984), 768

American Hosp. Ass'n v. N.L.R.B., 499 U.S. 606, 111 S.Ct. 1539, 113 L.Ed.2d 675 (1991), 291

American News Co. (Paterson, N.J.), 55 NLRB 1302 (N.L.R.B.1944), 440

American Provision Co., In re, 44 B.R. 907 (Bkrtcy.D.Minn.1984), 722

American Ship Bldg. Co. v. N.L.R.B., 380 U.S. 300, 85 S.Ct. 955, 13 L.Ed.2d 855 (1965), 425, **431**

American Textile Mfrs. Institute, Inc. v. Donovan (Cotton Dust Case), 452 U.S. 490, 101 S.Ct. 2478, 69 L.Ed.2d 185 (1981), **550,** 557, 558, 562

Ansonia Bd. of Educ. v. Philbrook, 479 U.S. 60, 107 S.Ct. 367, 93 L.Ed.2d 305 (1986), 134

Arlington Hotel Co., Inc. v. N.L.R.B., 785 F.2d 249 (8th Cir.1986), 411

Astor v. International Business Machines Corp., 7 F.3d 533 (6th Cir. 1993), 731

AT & T Technologies, Inc. v. Communications Workers of America, 475 U.S. 643, 106 S.Ct. 1415, 89 L.Ed.2d 648 (1986), 468, 486, **597**

Automobile Workers v. Wisconsin Employers Relations Bd. (Briggs–Stratton), 336 U.S. 245, 69 S.Ct. 516, 93 L.Ed. 651 (1949), 424

Barrantes Cabalceta v. Standard Fruit Co., 667 F.Supp. 833 (S.D.Fla.1987), 834

Belknap, Inc. v. Hale, 463 U.S. 491, 103 S.Ct. 3172, 77 L.Ed.2d 798 (1983), 405, **415,** 421

Beth Israel Hosp. v. N.L.R.B., 437 U.S. 483, 98 S.Ct. 2463, 57 L.Ed.2d 370 (1978), 338

Blinne Construction, 135 NLRB 1153 (N.L.R.B.1962), 458

Boston Medical Center Corporation, 330 NLRB No. 30 (N.L.R.B.1999), 307

Bowen v. United States Postal Service, 459 U.S. 212, 103 S.Ct. 588, 74 L.Ed.2d 402 (1983), 650

Boys Markets, Inc. v. Retail Clerks Union, Local 770, 398 U.S. 235, 90 S.Ct. 1583, 26 L.Ed.2d 199 (1970), 371, 372, **756,** 760, 768

Buffalo Forge Co. v. United Steelworkers of America, AFL–CIO, 428 U.S. 397, 96 S.Ct. 3141, 49 L.Ed.2d 1022 (1976), 371

Building & Construction Trades Council (New Orleans & Vicinity) (Markwell & Hartz, Inc.), 155 NLRB 319 (N.L.R.B.1965), 499

Burlington Industries, Inc. v. Ellerth, 524 U.S. 742, 118 S.Ct. 2257, 141 L.Ed.2d 633 (1998), 139

California Federal Sav. and Loan Ass'n v. Guerra, 479 U.S. 272, 107 S.Ct. 683, 93 L.Ed.2d 613 (1987), 603, 610

California Saw and Knife Works, 320 NLRB 224 (1995), 287

Campbell v. Potash Corp. of Saskatchewan, Inc., 238 F.3d 792 (6th Cir.2001), **780**

Chamber of Commerce of United States v. Reich, 74 F.3d 1322, 316 U.S.App. D.C. 61 (D.C.Cir.1996), 408

Charter Tp. of Ypsilanti v. General Motors Corp., 201 Mich.App. 128, 506 N.W.2d 556 (Mich.App.1993), 773

Charter Tp. of Ypsilanti v. General Motors Corp., 1993 WL 132385 (Mich. Cir.Ct.1993), 772

Chateaugay Corp., In re, 17 E.B.C. 1102 (S.D.N.Y.1993), 725

Chateaugay Corp., In re, 945 F.2d 1205 (2nd Cir.1991), 725

Chevron U.S.A., Inc. v. Natural Resources Defense Council, Inc., 467 U.S. 837, 104 S.Ct. 2778, 81 L.Ed.2d 694 (1984), 335

Circuit City Stores, Inc. v. Adams, 532 U.S. 105, 121 S.Ct. 1302, 149 L.Ed.2d 234 (2001), 185, 479

Clear Pine Mouldings, 268 NLRB 1044 (N.L.R.B.1984), **441,** 448

Collyer Insulated Wire, Gulf & Western Systems Co., 192 NLRB 837 (N.L.R.B.1971), 486, 602

Commonwealth v. _____ (see opposing party)

Communications Workers of America v. Beck, 487 U.S. 735, 108 S.Ct. 2641, 101 L.Ed.2d 634 (1988), **280,** 287, 288, 289, 450

Connolly v. McCall, 254 F.3d 36 (2nd Cir.2001), 740

Conrad v. Rofin–Sinar, Inc., 762 F.Supp. 167 (E.D.Mich.1991), **786**

Coppage v. State of Kansas, 236 U.S. 1, 35 S.Ct. 240, 59 L.Ed. 441 (1915), 13

DelCostello v. International Broth. of Teamsters, 462 U.S. 151, 103 S.Ct. 2281, 76 L.Ed.2d 476 (1983), 650

Delgado v. Shell Oil Co., 890 F.Supp. 1324 (S.D.Tex.1995), 833

Detroit Edison Co. v. N.L.R.B., 440 U.S. 301, 99 S.Ct. 1123, 59 L.Ed.2d 333 (1979), 396

Diaz v. Pan Am. World Airways, Inc., 442 F.2d 385 (5th Cir.1971), 103

Doe v. Unocal Corp., 110 F.Supp.2d 1294 (C.D.Cal.2000), 842

Dormeyer v. Comerica Bank–Illinois, 223 F.3d 579 (7th Cir.2000), 146

Dothard v. Rawlinson, 433 U.S. 321, 97 S.Ct. 2720, 53 L.Ed.2d 786 (1977), 104

Dow Chemical Co. v. Castro Alfaro, 786 S.W.2d 674 (Tex.1990), 834

Dubuque Packing Co., 303 NLRB 386 (N.L.R.B.1991), 383, 386

Eastern Associated Coal Corp. v. United Mine Workers of America, Dist. 17, 531 U.S. 57, 121 S.Ct. 462, 148 L.Ed.2d 354 (2000), 485, 663, **674,** 679, 680

Edward G. Budd Mfg. Co. v. N.L.R.B., 138 F.2d 86 (3rd Cir. 1943), **197,** 199

Edward J. DeBartolo Corp. v. Florida Gulf Coast Bldg. and Const. Trades Council, 485 U.S. 568, 108 S.Ct. 1392, 99 L.Ed.2d 645 (1988), **500**

E.E.O.C. v. Local 350, Plumbers and Pipefitters, 842 F.Supp. 417 (D.Nev. 1994), 740

E.E.O.C. v. Local 350, Plumbers and Pipefitters, 998 F.2d 641 (9th Cir. 1992), **735**

Eichorn v. AT & T Corp., 248 F.3d 131 (3rd Cir.2001), **743**

E.I. du Pont de Nemours & Co., 311 NLRB 893 (N.L.R.B.1993), 238, 398

Electrical Workers v. Hechler, 481 U.S. 851, 107 S.Ct. 2161, 95 L.Ed.2d 791 (1987), 634

Electrical Workers v. N.L.R.B. (Tiidee Products), 502 F.2d 349, 163 U.S.App.D.C. 347 (D.C.Cir.1974), 397

Electromation, Inc. v. N.L.R.B., 35 F.3d 1148 (7th Cir.1994), **230,** 250

Ellis v. Brotherhood of Ry., Airline and S.S. Clerks, 466 U.S. 435, 104 S.Ct. 1883, 80 L.Ed.2d 428 (1984), 288, 289, 450

Emporium Capwell Co. v. Western Addition Community Organization, 420 U.S. 50, 95 S.Ct. 977, 43 L.Ed.2d 12 (1975), **259,** 270, 271, 272, 273, 350, 424, 451, 480, 651

Epilepsy Foundation of Northeast Ohio, In re, 331 NLRB No. 92 (N.L.R.B.2000), 220, **221,** 352

Ex–Cell–O Corp., 185 NLRB 107 (N.L.R.B.1970), 397

Excelsior Underwear, Inc., 156 NLRB 1236 (N.L.R.B.1966), 326

Fall River Dyeing & Finishing Corp. v. N.L.R.B., 482 U.S. 27, 107 S.Ct. 2225, 96 L.Ed.2d 22 (1987), **805**

Farwell v. Boston & W.R. Corp., 45 Mass. 49 (Mass.1842), **528**

Fibreboard Paper Products Corp. v. N.L.R.B., 379 U.S. 203, 85 S.Ct. 398, 13 L.Ed.2d 233 (1964), 382, 383, 386

First Nat. Maintenance Corp. v. N.L.R.B., 452 U.S. 666, 101 S.Ct. 2573, 69 L.Ed.2d 318 (1981), **373,** 382, 383, 386, 389

Ford Motor Co. v. Huffman, 345 U.S. 330, 73 S.Ct. 681, 97 L.Ed. 1048 (1953), **274,** 278, 279, 611

Forrer v. Sears, Roebuck & Co., 36 Wis.2d 388, 153 N.W.2d 587 (Wis. 1967), 38

Fort Halifax Packing Co., Inc. v. Coyne, 482 U.S. 1, 107 S.Ct. 2211, 96 L.Ed.2d 1 (1987), 704

Fortino v. Quasar Co., 950 F.2d 389 (7th Cir.1991), **830**

Fortune v. National Cash Register Co., 373 Mass. 96, 364 N.E.2d 1251 (Mass.1977), **54,** 57, 61, 70

Franks v. Bowman Transp. Co., Inc., 424 U.S. 747, 96 S.Ct. 1251, 47 L.Ed.2d 444 (1976), 270

Freund v. E.D. & F. Man Intern., Inc., 199 F.3d 382 (7th Cir.1999), **777**

Garner v. Board of Public Works of City of Los Angeles, 341 U.S. 716, 71 S.Ct. 909, 95 L.Ed. 1317 (1951), 95

General Elec. Co. v. Gilbert, 429 U.S. 125, 97 S.Ct. 401, 50 L.Ed.2d 343 (1976), 610

Gilmer v. Interstate/Johnson Lane Corp., 500 U.S. 20, 111 S.Ct. 1647, 114 L.Ed.2d 26 (1991), **174,** 184, 185, 466, 470, 479, 485, 611

Glass and Pottery Workers v. Wickes Companies, Inc., 243 N.J.Super. 44, 578 A.2d 402 (N.J.Super.L.1990), 770, 772

Globe Molded Plastics Co. Inc., 204 NLRB 1041 (N.L.R.B.1973), 411

Griggs v. Duke Power Co., 401 U.S. 424, 91 S.Ct. 849, 28 L.Ed.2d 158 (1971), 76, **82,** 88, 89, 123, 604, 610

Harris v. Forklift Systems, Inc., 510 U.S. 17, 114 S.Ct. 367, 126 L.Ed.2d 295 (1993), **135,** 139

Hazen Paper Co. v. Biggins, 507 U.S. 604, 113 S.Ct. 1701, 123 L.Ed.2d 338 (1993), **148**

Hebert v. Mohawk Rubber Co., 872 F.2d 1104 (1st Cir.1989), 730

Henn v. National Geographic Soc., 819 F.2d 824 (7th Cir.1987), 730

Hennessey v. Coastal Eagle Point Oil Co., 129 N.J. 81, 609 A.2d 11 (N.J. 1992), 662

Hines v. Anchor Motor Freight, Inc., 424 U.S. 554, 96 S.Ct. 1048, 47 L.Ed.2d 231 (1976), 680, 681

Hollywood Ceramics Co., 140 NLRB 221 (N.L.R.B.1962), 327

Hoover Co. v. NLRB, 191 F.2d 380 (6th Cir.1951), 440

Howard Johnson Co., Inc. v. Detroit Local Joint Executive Bd., 417 U.S. 249, 94 S.Ct. 2236, 41 L.Ed.2d 46 (1974), **799**

Industrial Union Dept., AFL–CIO v. American Petroleum Institute (Benzene Case), 448 U.S. 607, 100 S.Ct. 2844, 65 L.Ed.2d 1010 (1980), 538, **540,** 550

In re (see name of party)

International Broth. of Elec. Workers System Council U–4 v. Florida Power and Light Co., 784 F.Supp. 854 (S.D.Fla.1991), 768

International Broth. of Teamsters v. Almac's, Inc., 894 F.2d 464 (1st Cir. 1990), 768

International Broth. of Teamsters, Local 695, A.F.L. v. Vogt, Inc., 354 U.S. 284, 77 S.Ct. 1166, 1 L.Ed.2d 1347 (1957), 451

International Ladies' Garment Workers' Union, AFL–CIO v. N.L.R.B., 374 F.2d 295, 126 U.S.App.D.C. 81 (D.C.Cir.1967), 389

International Ladies' Garment Workers' Union (Bernhard–Altmann) v. N.L.R.B., 366 U.S. 731, 81 S.Ct. 1603, 6 L.Ed.2d 762 (1961), 240, **241,** 250

International Union, United Auto., Aerospace and Agr. Implement Workers of America, UAW v. Johnson Controls, Inc., 499 U.S. 187, 111 S.Ct. 1196, 113 L.Ed.2d 158 (1991), 288, 579, **580,** 590, 591, 596, 605, 610

Ionosphere Clubs, Inc., In re, 22 F.3d 403 (2nd Cir.1994), 710

ITT Industries, Inc. v. N.L.R.B., 251 F.3d 995, 346 U.S.App.D.C. 180 (D.C.Cir.2001), 337

Jean Country, 282 NLRB 139 (N.L.R.B. 1986), 335

J.G. Roy & Sons Co. v. National Labor Relations Bd., 251 F.2d 771 (1st Cir. 1958), 512

J.I. Case Co. v. N.L.R.B., 321 U.S. 332, 64 S.Ct. 576, 88 L.Ed. 762 (1944), **255,** 651

Johnson v. Transportation Agency, Santa Clara County, Cal., 480

U.S. 616, 107 S.Ct. 1442, 94 L.Ed.2d 615 (1987), **113,** 124

Johnson–Bateman Co., 295 NLRB No. 26 (N.L.R.B.1989), 602

John Wiley & Sons, Inc. v. Livingston, 376 U.S. 543, 84 S.Ct. 909, 11 L.Ed.2d 898 (1964), 792, **796**

Karlen v. City Colleges of Chicago, 837 F.2d 314 (7th Cir.1988), 734

Kremer v. Chemical Const. Corp., 456 U.S. 461, 102 S.Ct. 1883, 72 L.Ed.2d 262 (1982), 478

Kumpf v. Steinhaus, 779 F.2d 1323 (7th Cir.1985), **58,** 61

Labor Union of Pico Korea, Ltd. v. Pico Products, Inc., 968 F.2d 191 (2nd Cir. 1992), 842

Labor Union of Pico Korea, Ltd. v. Pico Products, Inc., 1991 WL 299121 (N.D.N.Y.1991), **834**

Laidlaw Corp., 171 NLRB 1366 (N.L.R.B.1968), 411

Lechmere, Inc. v. N.L.R.B., 502 U.S. 527, 112 S.Ct. 841, 117 L.Ed.2d 79 (1992), 311, **327,** 335, 337, 338

Lehnert v. Ferris Faculty Ass'n, 500 U.S. 507, 111 S.Ct. 1950, 114 L.Ed.2d 572 (1991), 285, 289

Local 818 of Council 4 AFSCME, AFL–CIO v. Town of East Haven, 42 Conn.Supp. 227, 614 A.2d 1260 (Conn.Super.1992), 768

Local 461 v. Singer Co., 540 F.Supp. 442 (D.N.J.1982), **700**

Local 1330, United Steel Workers of America v. United States Steel Corp., 631 F.2d 1264 (6th Cir.1980), **23,** 33, 363, 699, 772

Local 761, Electrical Workers, AFL–CIO v. N.L.R.B., 366 U.S. 667, 81 S.Ct. 1285, 6 L.Ed.2d 592 (1961), **490**

Machinists v. Street, 367 U.S. 740, 81 S.Ct. 1784, 6 L.Ed.2d 1141 (1961), 284, 288

Marafino v. St. Louis County Circuit Court, 707 F.2d 1005 (8th Cir.1983), 146

Marshall v. Barlow's, Inc., 436 U.S. 307, 98 S.Ct. 1816, 56 L.Ed.2d 305 (1978), 538

Maxwell Newspapers, Inc., In re, 981 F.2d 85 (2nd Cir.1992), 723

McDonald v. City of West Branch, Mich., 466 U.S. 284, 104 S.Ct. 1799, 80 L.Ed.2d 302 (1984), 478

McDonnell Douglas Corp. v. Green, 411 U.S. 792, 93 S.Ct. 1817, 36 L.Ed.2d 668 (1973), 76, **89,** 96, 97, 101, 196

McNab v. General Motors Corp., 162 F.3d 959 (7th Cir.1998), **740**

Meritor Sav. Bank, FSB v. Vinson, 477 U.S. 57, 106 S.Ct. 2399, 91 L.Ed.2d 49 (1986), 136

Metropolitan Life Ins. Co. v. Massachusetts, 471 U.S. 724, 105 S.Ct. 2380, 85 L.Ed.2d 728 (1985), 704

Meyers Industries, 281 NLRB 882 (N.L.R.B.1986), 350

Miami Newspaper Pressmen's Local No. 46 v. N.L.R.B., 322 F.2d 405, 116 U.S.App.D.C. 192 (D.C.Cir.1963), 512

Mike Yurosek & Son, 306 NLRB 1037 (N.L.R.B.1992), 350

Minton v. Cavaney, 56 Cal.2d 576, 15 Cal.Rptr. 641, 364 P.2d 473 (Cal. 1961), 776

Morelli v. Cedel, 141 F.3d 39 (2nd Cir.1998), **824**

Mt. Healthy City School Dist. Bd. of Educ. v. Doyle, 429 U.S. 274, 97 S.Ct. 568, 50 L.Ed.2d 471 (1977), **97,** 101, 197

National Labor Relations Bd. v. Truitt Mfg. Co., 351 U.S. 149, 76 S.Ct. 753, 100 L.Ed. 1027 (1956), 396

National Labor Rel. Bd. v. Babcock & Wilcox Co., 351 U.S. 105, 76 S.Ct. 679, 100 L.Ed. 975 (1956), 335, 337

National Lab. Rel. Bd. v. Business Mach. & Office Union, 228 F.2d 553 (2nd Cir.1955), 512

National Packing Co. v. N.L.R.B., 377 F.2d 800 (10th Cir.1967), 440

National Treasury Employees Union v. Von Raab, 489 U.S. 656, 109 S.Ct. 1384, 103 L.Ed.2d 685 (1989), 660

Newport News Shipbuilding and Dry Dock Co. v. E.E.O.C., 462 U.S. 669, 103 S.Ct. 2622, 77 L.Ed.2d 89 (1983), **143,** 146

New York University, 332 NLRB No. 111 (N.L.R.B.2000), 307

N.L.R.B. v. Bildisco and Bildisco, 465 U.S. 513, 104 S.Ct. 1188, 79 L.Ed.2d 482 (1984), 721

N.L.R.B. v. Burns Intern. Sec. Services, Inc., 406 U.S. 272, 92 S.Ct. 1571, 32 L.Ed.2d 61 (1972), **792**

N.L.R.B. v. City Disposal Systems Inc., 465 U.S. 822, 104 S.Ct. 1505, 79 L.Ed.2d 839 (1984), **191,** 196, 349, 610

N.L.R.B. v. Denver Bldg. & Const. Trades Council, 341 U.S. 675, 71 S.Ct. 943, 95 L.Ed. 1284 (1951), 499

N.L.R.B. v. Erie Resistor Corp., 373 U.S. 221, 83 S.Ct. 1139, 10 L.Ed.2d 308 (1963), 421, 422, 423, 425

N.L.R.B. v. Exchange Parts Co., 375 U.S. 405, 84 S.Ct. 457, 11 L.Ed.2d 435 (1964), 324, 325, 327

N.L.R.B. v. Fansteel Metallurgical Corp., 306 U.S. 240, 59 S.Ct. 490, 83 L.Ed. 627 (1939), 440

N.L.R.B. v. Fleetwood Trailer Co., 389 U.S. 375, 88 S.Ct. 543, 19 L.Ed.2d 614 (1967), 411

N.L.R.B. v. Fruit and Vegetable Packers and Warehousemen, Local 760 (Tree Fruits), 377 U.S. 58, 84 S.Ct. 1063, 12 L.Ed.2d 129 (1964), 513

N.L.R.B. v. General Motors Corp., 373 U.S. 734, 83 S.Ct. 1453, 10 L.Ed.2d 670 (1963), 286

N.L.R.B. v. Gissel Packing Co., 395 U.S. 575, 89 S.Ct. 1918, 23 L.Ed.2d 547 (1969), 310, 315, 324, 325, 326, 327

N.L.R.B. v. Health Care & Retirement Corp. of America, 511 U.S. 571, 114 S.Ct. 1778, 128 L.Ed.2d 586 (1994), 300

N.L.R.B. v. Insurance Agents' Intern. Union, AFL–CIO, 361 U.S. 477, 80 S.Ct. 419, 4 L.Ed.2d 454 (1960), 424, 425, 439, 440

N.L.R.B. v. J. Weingarten, Inc., 420 U.S. 251, 95 S.Ct. 959, 43 L.Ed.2d 171 (1975), 220, 221, 352

N.L.R.B. v. Katz, 369 U.S. 736, 82 S.Ct. 1107, 8 L.Ed.2d 230 (1962), 602

N.L.R.B. v. Kentucky River Community Care, Inc., 532 U.S. 706, 121 S.Ct. 1861, 149 L.Ed.2d 939 (2001), 293, 300

N.L.R.B. v. Local Union No. 1229, Intern. Broth. of Elec. Workers (Jefferson Standard), 346 U.S. 464, 74 S.Ct. 172, 98 L.Ed. 195 (1953), 342, 350, 424, 440

N.L.R.B. v. Lorben Corp., 345 F.2d 346 (2nd Cir.1965), 326

N.L.R.B. v. Mackay Radio & Telegraph Co., 304 U.S. 333, 58 S.Ct. 904, 82 L.Ed. 1381 (1938), 400, 404, 405, 408, 421, 423, 425, 440

N.L.R.B. v. Pepsi–Cola Bottling Co. of Miami, 449 F.2d 824 (5th Cir.1971), 440

N.L.R.B. v. Rapid Bindery, Inc., 293 F.2d 170 (2nd Cir.1961), 390

N.L.R.B. v. Servette, Inc., 377 U.S. 46, 84 S.Ct. 1098, 12 L.Ed.2d 121 (1964), 511

N.L.R.B. v. Town & Country Elec., Inc., 516 U.S. 85, 116 S.Ct. 450, 133 L.Ed.2d 371 (1995), 300

N.L.R.B. v. Transportation Management Corp., 462 U.S. 393, 103 S.Ct. 2469, 76 L.Ed.2d 667 (1983), 197, 349

N.L.R.B. v. Washington Aluminum Co., 370 U.S. 9, 82 S.Ct. 1099, 8 L.Ed.2d 298 (1962), 193, 196, 220, 351, 352, 424, 451, 609, 625

N.L.R.B. v. W.C. McQuaide, Inc., 552 F.2d 519 (3rd Cir.1977), 442

N.L.R.B. v. Wooster Div. of Borg–Warner Corp., 356 U.S. 342, 78 S.Ct. 718, 2 L.Ed.2d 823 (1958), 388

Oil, Chemical & Atomic Workers v. N.L.R.B., 711 F.2d 348, 229 U.S.App.D.C. 70 (D.C.Cir.1983), 396, 567

Oil, Chemical and Atomic Workers Intern. Union v. American Cyanamid Co., 741 F.2d 444, 239 U.S.App.D.C. 222 (D.C.Cir.1984), 579, 591

Oncale v. Sundowner Offshore Services, Inc., 523 U.S. 75, 118 S.Ct. 998, 140 L.Ed.2d 201 (1998), 139, 143

Oubre v. Entergy Operations, Inc., 522 U.S. 422, 118 S.Ct. 838, 139 L.Ed.2d 849 (1998), 171, 174, 184, 185, 733

Pattern Makers' League of North America, AFL–CIO v. N.L.R.B., 473 U.S. 95, 105 S.Ct. 3064, 87 L.Ed.2d 68 (1985), 444, 448, 450

Pay Less Drug Stores Northwest, Inc., 312 NLRB No. 144 (N.L.R.B.1993), 335

Payne v. Western & Atlantic R. Co., 81 Tenn. 507 (Tenn.1884), 12

Peerless Plywood Co., 107 NLRB 427 (N.L.R.B.1953), 326

Pet, Inc. v. N.L.R.B., 641 F.2d 545 (8th Cir.1981), 511

Piper Aircraft Co. v. Reyno, 454 U.S. 235, 102 S.Ct. 252, 70 L.Ed.2d 419 (1981), 833

Price Waterhouse v. Hopkins, 490 U.S. 228, 109 S.Ct. 1775, 104 L.Ed.2d 268 (1989), 101

Pugh v. See's Candies, Inc., 116 Cal. App.3d 311, 171 Cal.Rptr. 917 (Cal. App. 1 Dist.1981), 62, 68, 69, 70

Pullis, Commonwealth v. (Philadelphia Cordwainer's Case), Philadelphia Mayor's Court (1806), 190

Reeves v. Sanderson Plumbing Products, Inc., 530 U.S. 133, 120 S.Ct. 2097, 147 L.Ed.2d 105 (2000), 96

Robert S. Weiss and Associates, Inc. v. Wiederlight, 208 Conn. 525, 546 A.2d 216 (Conn.1988), 165, 170, 171

Roe III v. Unocal 170 DLR A–10 (Cal. Sup.Ct.2001), 845

Sailors Union of the Pacific (Moore Dry Dock Co.), 92 NLRB 547 (N.L.R.B. 1950), 499
School Bd. of Nassau County, Fla. v. Arline, 480 U.S. 273, 107 S.Ct. 1123, 94 L.Ed.2d 307 (1987), 663, 664, **667,** 673
Sears, Roebuck & Co., 190 NLRB 143 (N.L.R.B.1971), 512
Sewell Mfg. Co., 138 NLRB 66 (N.L.R.B. 1962), 326
Shaw v. Hunt, 517 U.S. 899, 116 S.Ct. 1894, 135 L.Ed.2d 207 (1996), 124
Sheets v. Teddy's Frosted Foods, Inc., 179 Conn. 471, 427 A.2d 385 (Conn.1980), **48,** 54, 70
Shopping Kart Food Market, 228 NLRB 1311 (N.L.R.B.1977), 327
Skinner v. Railway Labor Executives' Ass'n, 489 U.S. 602, 109 S.Ct. 1402, 103 L.Ed.2d 639 (1989), **653**
Smitley v. N.L.R.B., 327 F.2d 351 (9th Cir.1964), 453
Southern S.S. Co. v. N.L.R.B., 316 U.S. 31, 62 S.Ct. 886, 86 L.Ed. 1246 (1942), 440
Sutton v. United Air Lines, Inc., 527 U.S. 471, 119 S.Ct. 2139, 144 L.Ed.2d 450 (1999), **153**

Taylor v. N.L.R.B., 786 F.2d 1516 (11th Cir.1986), 609, **619**
Teamsters v. Lucas Flour Co., 369 U.S. 95, 82 S.Ct. 571, 7 L.Ed.2d 593 (1962), 467
Teamsters v. United States, 431 U.S. 324, 97 S.Ct. 1843, 52 L.Ed.2d 396 (1977), 603, 604
Teamsters Local v. N.L.R.B. (Reichhold Chemicals), 906 F.2d 719, 285 U.S.App.D.C. 25 (D.C.Cir.1990), **355,** 361, 362, 364, 371, 372, 386, 389, 405
Textile Workers Union of America v. Darlington Mfg. Co., 380 U.S. 263, 85 S.Ct. 994, 13 L.Ed.2d 827 (1965), 390, 699
Textile Workers Union of America v. Lincoln Mills of Ala., 353 U.S. 448, 77 S.Ct. 912, 1 L.Ed.2d 972 (1957), 467
Torres v. Southern Peru Copper Corp., 113 F.3d 540 (5th Cir.1997), 833
Trans World Airlines, Inc. v. Hardison, 432 U.S. 63, 97 S.Ct. 2264, 53 L.Ed.2d 113 (1977), **127,** 134
Truck Drivers Local 807 v. Carey Transp. Inc., 816 F.2d 82 (2nd Cir. 1987), **711,** 722, 723

United Food and Commercial Workers v. N.L.R.B., 1 F.3d 24, 303 U.S.App.D.C. 65 (D.C.Cir.1993), **383**
United Food and Commercial Workers Union, Local 1036 v. N.L.R.B., 249 F.3d 1115 (9th Cir.2001), 288
United Paperworkers Intern. Union, AFL–CIO v. Misco, Inc., 484 U.S. 29, 108 S.Ct. 364, 98 L.Ed.2d 286 (1987), 679
United Steelworkers of America v. American Mfg. Co., 363 U.S. 564, 80 S.Ct. 1343, 4 L.Ed.2d 1403 (1960), 597
United Steelworkers of America v. Enterprise Wheel & Car Corp., 363 U.S. 593, 80 S.Ct. 1358, 4 L.Ed.2d 1424 (1960), 46
United Steelworkers of America v. Warrior & Gulf Nav. Co., 363 U.S. 574, 80 S.Ct. 1347, 4 L.Ed.2d 1409 (1960), 597
United Steelworkers of America, AFL–CIO–CLC v. Auchter, 763 F.2d 728 (3rd Cir.1985), **571,** 574
United Steelworkers of America, AFL–CIO–CLC v. Rawson, 495 U.S. 362, 110 S.Ct. 1904, 109 L.Ed.2d 362 (1990), 611, **633**
United Steelworkers of America, AFL–CIO–CLC v. Weber, 443 U.S. 193, 99 S.Ct. 2721, 61 L.Ed.2d 480 (1979), 113, 117, 123, 466
United Technologies and Machinists Union, 268 NLRB 557 (N.L.R.B. 1984), 487, 609, **616**

Vaca v. Sipes, 386 U.S. 171, 87 S.Ct. 903, 17 L.Ed.2d 842 (1967), 469, 611, **642,** 643, 644, 649, 650, 681
Van Blaricom v. Burlington Northern R. Co., 17 F.3d 1224 (9th Cir. 1994), **821,** 824
Vegelahn v. Guntner, 167 Mass. 92, 44 N.E. 1077 (Mass.1896), **15,** 21, 22, 449, 450, 451, 772

Wards Cove Packing Co., Inc. v. Atonio, 490 U.S. 642, 109 S.Ct. 2115, 104 L.Ed.2d 733 (1989), 88
Waters v. Churchill, 511 U.S. 661, 114 S.Ct. 1878, 128 L.Ed.2d 686 (1994), 46, 47
Western Air Lines, Inc. v. Criswell, 472 U.S. 400, 105 S.Ct. 2743, 86 L.Ed.2d 321 (1985), 101, 102
Whirlpool Corp. v. Marshall, 445 U.S. 1, 100 S.Ct. 883, 63 L.Ed.2d 154 (1980), 610, **626**
W.R. Grace and Co. v. Local Union 759, Intern. Union of United Rubber,

Cork, Linoleum and Plastic Workers of America, 461 U.S. 757, 103 S.Ct. 2177, 76 L.Ed.2d 298 (1983), 270

Wright v. Universal Maritime Service Corp., 525 U.S. 70, 119 S.Ct. 391, 142 L.Ed.2d 361 (1998), **480, 485**

Wright Line, 251 NLRB 1083 (N.L.R.B. 1980), 197, 349, 611

Wygant v. Jackson Bd. of Educ., 476 U.S. 267, 106 S.Ct. 1842, 90 L.Ed.2d 260 (1986), 123, 124

Youngstown Sheet & Tube Co. v. Sawyer, 343 U.S. 579, 72 S.Ct. 863, 96 L.Ed. 1153 (1952), 408

*

LABOR AND EMPLOYMENT LAW

PROBLEMS, CASES AND MATERIALS IN THE LAW OF WORK

Third Edition

*

Chapter One

FAIR TREATMENT OF
THE WORKER

A Worker Reads History

Who built the seven gates of Thebes?
The books are filled with names of kings.
Was it kings who hauled the craggy blocks of stone?
And Babylon, so many times destroyed,
Who built the city up each time? In which of Lima's houses,
That city glittering with gold, lived those who built it?
In the evening when the Chinese wall was finished
Where did the masons go? Imperial Rome
Is full of arcs of triumph. Who reared them up? Over whom
Did the Caesars triumph? Byzantium lives in song,
Were all her dwellings palaces? And even in Atlantis of the legend
The night the sea rushed in,
The drowning men still bellowed for their slaves.

Young Alexander conquered India.
He alone?
Caesar beat the Gauls.
Was there not even a cook in his army?
Philip of Spain wept as his fleet
Was sunk and destroyed. Were there no other tears?
Frederick the Great triumphed in the Seven Years War. Who
Triumphed with him?

Each page a victory,
At whose expense the victory ball?
Every ten years a great man,
Who paid the piper?

So many particulars.
So many questions.

> Bertolt Brecht, Selected Poems
> 109
> (H. Hays tran. 1947).

1

I. AN INTRODUCTORY PROBLEM AND SOME BACKGROUND FOR THE COURSE

A. PROBLEM: THE WORKER WHO QUESTIONS AUTHORITY

Billie Tulip has been an employee of Enderby Communications since 1989. She started out as a telephone operator and, in 1995, as part of the company's affirmative action plan to break down sexual stereotypes in job classifications, she was trained and assigned as a line technician. Her job includes troubleshooting problems in customers' homes, maintaining telephone lines, wires and relays in the field, and identifying and repairing line problems. She normally works an 8–5 shift Monday through Friday, and is assigned a regular territory. The job is viewed as a skilled position and commands a relatively high salary within the company. Ms. Tulip's overall work record is excellent.

The Company also schedules a team of line technicians around the clock and on weekends to provide emergency coverage. While employees are assigned to emergency shifts, the Company often uses volunteers to fill vacancies on the emergency team caused by illness, vacations, special needs and the like. In addition to her usual work week, Ms. Tulip had volunteered to fill in on one such shift on a weekend last August.

About an hour into the shift, all 4 members of the emergency team were called out to replace several sets of power lines that feed one of the main co-generators in the system. The team was directed by Tony Marino, who holds the title of senior line technician. This job, while not a management position, pays a higher rate than the normal line technician in recognition of the supervisory responsibility involved. Tony had just been appointed senior line technician, and was anxious to make a good impression in his new job.

When the crew arrived at the scene, the following dialogue occurred, according to a statement later given by Marino:

> *Tulip:* Tony, this is one of those cogenerators. Nobody told me we'd be assigned here. These things are a health menace. Haven't you read those articles about the families who live under them and everyone dies from cancer? No way I'm going to work here.

> *Marino:* Come on, Billie, don't give me a hard time. This is where the company assigned us, some of us are earning overtime, and we can't string these lines unless all four of us do the work. You volunteered and now you just have to do it.

Tulip: I volunteered for a team that does emergency work. This doesn't look like emergency work to me, but a long range maintenance project that shouldn't be assigned to us. We shouldn't be doing it anyway, and certainly not when it endangers our health.

Marino: Somebody's got to do this, and we're the ones who are assigned or volunteered. The guys here want to get on with it and you are holding us up.

Tulip: Maybe the guys don't care, but I do. It is especially hazardous for a woman, because she could be pregnant and these electrical fields could do horrible things to the baby she might be carrying. I'm beyond all that, but I can't let you do something that would pose a threat to the women who work here. Let's call the union shop steward to get advice on whether this is a proper assignment under the contract.

Marino: There's no shop steward around on a Sunday and I'm not waiting for you to find somebody to call in. And I'm sick and tired of everything becoming a women's issue. This is an order. You do the work or I'm recommending disciplinary action.

Tulip: Over my dead body.

Yostremski (another worker, who has been active in the union and was once a shop steward): Billie, just do the job, and then file a grievance Monday. The union will back you. You can get in hot water for refusing to carry out an order.

Tulip: Get out of my face, Joe.

At that point Marino called the Company's weekend supervisor and reported that Tulip refused to carry out her assignment, and that without her the crew couldn't work on the co-generator. The supervisor directed Marino to take the crew back to headquarters for reassignment, and to send Tulip home. The supervisor said she'd report the matter to the personnel department. Tulip left work as instructed.

On Monday, the Director of Personnel, Mary Pickman, sent Tulip the following memo:

"Based on my investigation of the weekend incident, I conclude you were insubordinate. It is imperative that we at Enderby Communications work as a team, and your misconduct forced the team to discontinue important work. I am placing you on a two week suspension without pay. After that, you will be temporarily reassigned for six months to duty as an operator, and will receive the lower rate of pay for that job. At the end of that period, if your work performance is satisfactory, you will be restored to your former position."

You are an attorney in a small firm in the town where Ms. Tulip lives. You have no experience in labor and employment law, but you've represented Ms. Tulip in various civil matters. You agree to hear her story and to then suggest what she should do next. Ms. Tulip gives you substantially the same account as presented above. However, in her account of the tail end of the conversation she says she asked Joe Yostremski, the other worker, to get off her case for 5 minutes while she tried to call the shop steward. She's sure Joe would back her up on this statement. Ms. Tulip tells you that Ms. Pickman, the Personnel Director, never spoke with her or asked for her account of the incident.

ON BRAINSTORMING

Sometimes it helps just to let your mind range free in thinking about the issues and their possible solutions. Put aside for now any law you may know, and try to identify the various interests involved in this incident, how strong a claim they make, and how these conflicting interests could be reconciled.

Keep the Billie Tulip story in mind as we go through the course, for as you learn new areas of the law you may want to figure out how they apply to this problem.

B.   THE LAWYER'S TOOLBOX

As you begin to study this field, you will find a rich array of sources of potential relief for Ms. Tulip. Many of the approaches we now mention are the subject of statutory regulation. The relevant statutes are contained in the reference supplement for this book, and we recommend you take a first look at those materials as you work through this brief note.

- Health and Safety issues. Ms. Tulip believes that extensive exposure to electromagnetic fields may cause potential harm to a worker. The federal Occupational Safety and Health Act sets standards for workplace safety and provides procedures for abating hazards. This statute is enforced by a public agency, the Occupational Safety and Health Administration, part of the Labor Department. Ms. Tulip may want to file a complaint with that agency. However, the agency itself calls the shots on whether and how to proceed, as the statute doesn't create a private cause of action for Ms. Tulip. On the other hand, OSHA confers a rather limited right on an employee to refuse to do work that presents a clear and imminent danger. Ms. Tulip may try to invoke that section here. If there is a state agency that provides parallel protection Ms. Tulip may wish to turn there instead.

- Protections in the state courts against unjust dismissal or discipline. For over a century the dominant view of the employment relationship in this country has been that employment is at will. This means the employer is free to terminate or discipline the employee for any reason at all. In recent years, courts in many states have made inroads into this doctrine by granting relief when a discharge violates public policy. If she is in a state that embraces this approach, Ms. Tulip may be able to get redress on a theory that it violates public policy to punish her for complaining about an unsafe working condition. In addition, a few states' courts have suggested that an employment contract implies fair and reasonable treatment of employees. Ask yourself, however, what lawyer would take this case without an assured and adequate fee? Moreover, can such a claim survive the existence of a contract between the union and Enderby?

• Claims of gender discrimination. Ms. Tulip suggested in her argument with Mr. Marino that this hazard poses a special problem for women of child bearing age. She may have a claim that the company policy of forcing employees to accept such an assignment takes a heavier toll on women than on men and therefore violates Title VII of the Civil Rights Act. She may also have a claim, although it seems a long shot, that Mr. Marino reacted to her so sternly because she is a woman. This would give rise to a claim of intentional discrimination under Title VII. Finally, although it is buried in the background of the problem, the Company's affirmative action program to advance women in traditionally male dominated jobs raises issues under Title VII.

• Rights under a collective bargaining agreement. In this problem, Ms. Tulip happened to be represented by a labor union. You'll remember that she sought the intervention of her shop steward and was advised by another employee to carry out the order and grieve it later. The collective bargaining relationship provides a unique system of workplace governance. Under it, Ms. Tulip could file a grievance challenging her discipline. She could discuss the matter directly with a representative of the company. If the company's response didn't satisfy her and if the collective agreement provides for arbitration, as almost all bargaining agreements do, Ms. Tulip could, if her union agreed, take her claim to an impartial arbitrator, who would hear both sides of the story and decide whether the discipline was appropriate. The arbitrator's standard, under most collective bargaining agreements, is whether the employee was disciplined for "just cause." This amorphous sounding concept actually embraces a well established set of criteria, developed through countless arbitration decisions, of acceptable standards of workplace behavior.

The union can also represent Tulip's interests by attacking the company's apparently incomplete investigation.

There are downsides of the collective bargaining approach for Ms. Tulip. First, it is within the union's discretion to decide whether to advance her claim to arbitration. Here, because the other three workers wanted to go ahead with the job, the union may decide not to side with Ms. Tulip. Its judgment will usually block Ms. Tulip's claim based on the collective bargaining agreement, unless a court concludes that the union's decision was arbitrary or made in bad faith.

Further, as Mr. Yostremski suggested to Ms. Tulip, many arbitrators conclude that an employee must obey a workplace order and grieve it later. Ms. Tulip may have been obliged to carry out the weekend assignment and file a grievance later, challenging the company's right to make such an assignment.

Further research will tell you that as a private attorney there is little you can do for Ms. Tulip to enforce her rights under a collective bargaining agreement. Under the theory of collective bargaining, the union signs on as Ms. Tulip's exclusive representative for matters under the agreement. However, through aggressive advocacy you may be able to influence the union's direction in pursuing Ms. Tulip's claim.

• Rights under the National Labor Relations Act. Even if Ms. Tulip is not represented by a union, when she undertakes activity in collaboration with other workers or on their behalf concerning working conditions, that conduct may be protected against discharge or other discipline under the National Labor Relations Act. Ms. Tulip suggested to Mr. Marino that she wasn't acting just for herself, but had in mind the interests of other women workers at Enderby.

C. SOME PERVASIVE THEMES IN THIS COURSE

As you are introduced to the foregoing, and other, sources of workplace regulation, you should think about some pervasive themes in this course. As a policy choice, which of the various alternative models for enforcement of workplace rights makes the most sense? For example, the Billie Tulip problem involves the values of fairness to the worker, concern for workplace health and safety, and the employer's interest to run its business to maximize profits, to serve society, or both. One approach is to leave it to market forces to secure these values. If Billie Tulip is dissatisfied with the way the company treats her, she can go elsewhere. If enough workers defect, or if good workers won't take employment with Enderby, Enderby must change its employment practices to attract and retain the best workers. Under the market model, Billie also may be able to recover under tort law for any harm she can prove was caused by an unsafe condition.

The market model seems to assert its greatest hold when we deal with questions involving the employer's running of the business and investment of its capital. We are reluctant to interfere with a firm's decision to change its product mix, reduce its work force, move elsewhere. We often accept the premise that we cannot shake the forces of the market, and that it is folly to force the employer to produce or serve in a way it deems inefficient.

As you can see from the brief catalogue of responses that we found in the lawyer's toolbox, the market approach hasn't always satisfied society's interest in securing many of the values of the workplace. In the area of health and safety, for example, we have found it necessary to set and enforce substantive performance standards, even if this means that those employers that cannot meet them may go out of business, or that the cost of products or services may increase. As we will see with a number of other aspects of the employment relationship, government often intervenes.

Another regulatory approach is for the law to intervene in the market only when market forces take their toll on certain categories of employees thought to be the most vulnerable or most deserving of protection. Statutes that prohibit discrimination fall into this category: Title VII of the Civil Rights Act, the Americans with Disabilities Act, the Age Discrimination in Employment Act, and the National Labor Relations Act. We will ask how these protected categories are identified. We shall also explore whether it makes sense to single out any groups for special benefits or protection, as opposed to insisting on similar treatment of all workers.

Finally, the collective bargaining model gives employees, through their unions, a role in workplace governance. The collective bargaining model builds on the market approach, but attempts to alter the market, as recognized by the common law, by creating new employee rights, including the right to bargain collectively through a union, and by placing limitations and obligations on unions and employers.

These theoretical substantive rights are of little value if they cannot be effectively enforced. So another pervasive question in these materials is which model of enforcement of worker rights is most effective and enduring. The worker who turns to OSHA must rely on a government employee to protect her rights. Her representation is free, but she competes for the shared time and limited budget of the government agent. The worker who uses a Title VII approach generally entrusts the outcome to a private attorney who expects to be compensated adequately or will not take the case. The worker who is represented by a union enjoys day to day advocacy as partial repayment for her union dues, but she must persuade the union, which represents all the competing interests of all the employees, to exercise its considerable discretion to act aggressively and spend limited funds on her behalf.

You also should think about what a law firm would charge Ms. Tulip for the work it performs for her. She is talking about a two week suspension without pay and a reduction in salary for six months. While the principle may be enormous to her, the monetary stakes are not great. Can our legal system provide her with effective representation?

Employers too have preferences about the models for enforcement of workplace rights. Do not jump to the conclusion that an employer would always favor the market approach. A small employer, for example, might be better off with government regulation of workplace health and safety, if government regulation meant other employers would not adopt such strict standards that the smaller employer could not compete. If the employer must be regulated, the employer wants a system that is quick, fair, cheap and predictable. What about the attorney who represents the employer? Does she have the same interest in efficiency and economy as the employer?

SOME STATISTICS ABOUT EMPLOYMENT

Who are the people working in America?

In 2001, approximately 135,103,000 people were at work in the United States. Barely one-half were men over twenty years old. Women over twenty accounted for a little more than 44 percent of the working population, and the remaining 5–plus percent consisted of young men and women aged sixteen to nineteen. The number of women in the workforce has increased significantly in recent years. In 2001, 58.6 percent of the women over the age of 20 were in the workforce, compared to 40 percent in 1950. This change in the composition of the workforce has contributed to the need for new work arrangements and benefits such as flexible hours, child-care, and parental leave.

The majority (83.8%) of American workers in 2001 were categorized as white, 11.6% as black, and 4.6% as Asian, Pacific Islander, American Indian, or Alaskan Native. 4.2% of the black workers and 11.8% of the white, or a total of 10.4% of the workforce, claim an Hispanic heritage.

The unemployment rates for men and women were substantially the same; for whites, the rate was 3.8 percent, for blacks it was 8 percent, and Hispanics, 6.2 percent. Experts anticipate that the American workforce will become increasingly diverse, with Asian and Hispanic Americans experiencing the highest rates of employment growth in the early years of the twenty-first century.

The unemployment rate in 2000 of people who had not graduated from high school was 6.5 percent; for those with only a high school degree the rate was 3.9 percent; those who had some secondary education but no college degree had an unemployment rate of 3.0 percent; and, those with a college degree had a rate of 2.1 percent.

When employees set out for work where do they go?

The vast majority of American workers are employed by private enterprises. The minority (approximately fifteen percent) are employed by a variety of governmental institutions throughout the country. Of those in private non-agricultural work, 81 percent perform services while the remaining 19 percent produce goods. For the past few decades, the service industries have grown while the product industries have shrunk. All indications point to the continuation of both trends.

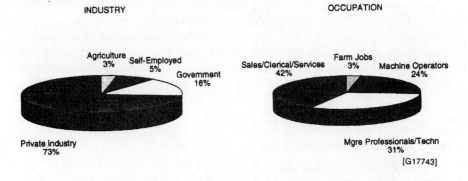

INDUSTRY   OCCUPATION

Agriculture 3%   Self-Employed 5%   Government 16%   Sales/Clerical/Services 42%   Farm Jobs 3%   Machine Operators 24%

Private Industry 73%   Mgrs Professionals/Techn 31%

[G17743]

What proportion of American workers does not hold traditional full-time jobs?

There are a significant number of so-called "contingent" workers in the United States. These workers include part-time workers, some of whom are multiple job holders, employees of temporary help agencies, and self-employed "owner-operators" or independent contractors.

In 2001, there were about 22 million part-time workers, approximately one-third of whom desired full-time work. Approximately two-thirds of the part-timers are women. Part-time workers are relatively low paid and are less likely to receive pension and health benefits from their employers.

The number of temporary workers in the United States has increased more than six-fold since 1979. In 1999, there were an estimated 12.2 million workers who did not expect their current jobs to last. Like part-time employees, temporary workers are relatively low paid and less likely to receive pension and health benefits.

In 2001, 5.5 percent of American workers held more than one job. Americans work more hours than employees in other "first-world" countries, with the possible exception of Japan.

How well are Americans compensated for their labor?

In May 2001, the average private sector employee earned $14.26 per hour, if paid on that basis, and $489.12 per week, if paid on that basis. Americans working in the goods and products industries received an average hourly rate of pay of $15.88 per hour or $645.50 per week. Service industries compensated their employees at an average of $13.77 per hour or $447.92 per week.

From 1973 to 1997, real wages for all employees declined. In fact, this was true for only the lowest paid nine-tenths of the working force. During this period, the highest paid ten percent received an increase (7.5%) in their real wages. During the same period, the productivity of our economy grew by 85%.

In 2000, women received in weekly pay approximately 75 percent of what men did. Some of this differential is due to the fact that women, on average, work less hours and have fewer years of experience than men; studies that account for these facts still show women are paid at lower rates then men. Of the over one hundred occupations identified by the Department of Labor as employing at least 50,000 men and 50,000 women, men on average were paid more than women in every such occupation. In 1998, women were the primary supporters of 18 percent of the 71 million families in the United States. 27 percent of all families primarily supported by women resided below the poverty level. Despite these numbers, which some (but not all) would argue support the conclusion that women are still the victims of irrational discrimination in the workplace, it is also indisputably clear that the gap between women's and men's wages has been narrowing consistently since the mid 1970s.

Hispanics' weekly salary in 2000, on average, was 68 percent of what the average white earned; and blacks' was 77 percent.

In 1997, approximately two-thirds of all full-time private employees received a health plan benefit of some kind from their employers. Men were somewhat more likely than women to have such a plan. Whites were slightly more likely than blacks to have such a plan, but substantially more likely than Hispanics (67 percent as compared with 50 percent).

In 1997, 50 percent of all private, full-time employees were participating in an employer supported retirement plan. Once again, men were slightly more likely than women, and whites more likely than blacks, to be in such a plan; whites were substantially more likely than Hispanics (51 percent to 28 percent) to be in such a plan.

There appears to be a direct correlation between the level of education employees have and their earnings. In 1997, as in any other year for which such statistics are available, the following pattern will be found:

Education level

Hourly pay

$8.22	Less than high school graduation
$11.02	No more than high school graduation
$12.43	Some college but no graduation
$18.38	No more than college graduation
$24.07	College education plus more

How many American workers are unionized?

Union membership has decreased since a high point in 1950, when union membership was approximately 35 percent of the private sector non-agricultural workforce. In absolute numbers, the nadir for the past twenty years (at least as of the time of the writing of this edition) was 1997, when 16.1 million people belonged to labor unions. In the year 2000, there were 16.3 million members, a number that included within it only 9 percent of the private sector non-agricultural employees in the country.

Generally, employees represented by unions receive better compensation than employees not so represented. The average weekly pay of an employee represented by a union in early 2001 was $691, while those not represented received only $542.

ated by unions were substan-
epresented to have an employ-
pared with 66 percent) and to
retirement plan (82% to 50%).

T AT WILL

UNDERSTANDING
TIONS

reference point to identify fair
, under the common law of
100 years ago, the terms of
the shop owner set their own
dition continued employment
...nday, being a vegetarian, not
joining a trade union, or not patronizing a particular retail store.
Similarly, either employer or employee could sever the working relationship for any reason, or without reason, as long as there was no explicit
undertaking to the contrary. Courts were only interested in contractual
commitments, and not in whether the conditions set out in the contract
were fair in the eyes of a judge or the product of equal bargaining power.

As interpreted by the United States Supreme Court in the early
1900s, the Constitution confirmed that the essential consideration in
employment relations is each party's right and freedom to contract;
consequently, the Court reasoned, agreements made by the parties are
the best guide for deciding what is fair. When federal and state legislatures imposed limits on the number of hours a person could work, or the
minimum age for becoming a wage earner, they relied on characteristics
or interests of the workers other than the right to contract. These
legislative judgments offended the Constitution because

> [t]he right of a person to sell his labor upon such terms as he deems
> proper is, in essence, the same as the right of the purchaser of labor
> to prescribe the conditions upon which he will accept such labor
> from the person offering to sell it. So the right of the employee to
> quit the service of the employer, for whatever reason, is the same as
> the right of the employer, for whatever reason, to dispense with the
> services of such employee. * * * In all such particulars the employer
> and the employee have equality of right, and any legislation that
> disturbs that equality is an arbitrary interference with the liberty of
> contract which no government can legally justify in a free land.

Adair v. United States, 208 U.S. 161, 174–175, 28 S.Ct. 277, 280, 52
L.Ed. 436 (1908).

Contemporary champions of market regulation continue to insist
that the relevant consideration in employment decisions is the agreement reached by the employer and the individual worker.

EPSTEIN, IN DEFENSE OF THE CONTRACT AT WILL
51 U.Chi.L.Rev. 947, 953–55 (1984).

* * * Freedom of contract is an aspect of individual liberty, every bit as much as freedom of speech, or freedom in the selection of marriage partners or in the adoption of religious beliefs or affiliations. Just as it is regarded as prima facie unjust to abridge these liberties, so too is it presumptively unjust to abridge the economic liberties of individuals. The desire to make one's own choices about employment may be as strong as it is with respect to marriage or participation in religious activities, and it is doubtless more pervasive than the desire to participate in political activity. Indeed for most people, their own health and comfort, and that of their families, depend critically upon their ability to earn a living by entering the employment market.

* * *

It is one thing to set aside the occasional transaction that reflects only the momentary aberrations of particular parties who are overwhelmed by major personal and social dislocations. It is quite another to announce that a rule to which vast numbers of individuals adhere is so fundamentally corrupt that it does not deserve the minimum respect of the law. With employment contracts, we are not dealing with the widow who has sold her inheritance for a song to a man with a thin mustache. Instead we are dealing with the routine stuff of ordinary life; people who are competent enough to marry, vote, and pray are not unable to protect themselves in their day-to-day business transactions.

* * * [I]t is hardly likely that remote public bodies have better information about individual preferences than the parties who hold them. This basic principle of autonomy, moreover, is not limited to some areas of individual conduct and wholly inapplicable to others. It covers all these activities as a piece and admits no ad hoc exceptions, but only principled limitations.

This general proposition applies to the particular contract term in question. Any attack on the contract at will in the name of individual freedom is fundamentally misguided. As the Tennessee Supreme Court rightly stressed [Payne v. Western & Atl. R.R., 81 Tenn. 507, 518–19 (1884)] the contract at will is sought by both persons. Any limitation upon the freedom to enter into such contracts limits the power of workers as well as employers and must therefore be justified before it can be accepted. In this context, the appeal is often to an image of employer coercion. To be sure, freedom of contract is not an absolute in the employment context, any more than it is elsewhere. Thus the principle must be understood against a backdrop that prohibits the use of private contracts to trench upon third-party rights, including uses that interfere with some clear mandate of public policy, as in cases of contracts to commit murder or perjury.

In addition, the principle of freedom of contract also rules out the use of force or fraud in obtaining advantages during contractual negotiations; and it limits taking advantage of the young, the feeble-minded, and the insane. * * * Fraud is not a frequent occurrence in employment contracts, especially where workers and employers engage in repeat transactions. Nor is there any reason to believe that such contracts are marred by misapprehensions, since employers and employees know the footing on which they have contracted: the phrase at-will is two words long and has the convenient virtue of meaning just what it says, no more and no less.

An employee who knows he can quit at will understands what it means to be fired at will, even though he may not like it after the fact. So long as it is accepted that the employer is the full owner of his capital and the employee is the full owner of his labor, the two are free to exchange on whatever terms and conditions they see fit, within the limited constraints just noted. If the arrangement turns out to be disastrous to one side, that is his problem; and once cautioned, he probably will not make the same mistake a second time. More to the point, employers and employees are unlikely to make the same mistake once. It is hardly plausible that contracts at will could be so pervasive in all businesses and at all levels if they did not serve the interests of employees as well as employers. The argument from fairness then is very simple, but not for that reason unpersuasive.

Even those who equate fairness with fulfillment of contractual agreements acknowledge that material inequality can affect the terms of the bargain. According to the constitutional jurisprudence of the early twentieth century and the reasoning of scholars like Epstein, however, the Constitution and the common law authoritatively establish freedom of contract as the paramount consideration in evaluating employment decisions. The argument that neither the states nor the federal government has the authority to enact legislation aimed at reducing differences in fortune or position is well articulated in the majority opinion in Coppage v. Kansas, 236 U.S. 1, 17, 35 S.Ct. 240, 244–45, 59 L.Ed. 441 (1915):

> [I]t is said by the Kansas supreme court to be a matter of common knowledge that employees, as a rule, are not financially able to be as independent in making contracts for the sale of their labor as are employers in making a contract of purchase thereof. No doubt, wherever the right of private property exists, there must and will be inequalities of fortune; and thus it naturally happens that parties negotiating about a contract are not equally unhampered by circumstances. This applies to all contracts, and not merely to that between employer and employee. Indeed, a little reflection will show that wherever the right of private property and the right of free contract exist, each party when contracting is inevitably more or less influenced by the question whether he has much property, or little, or none; for the contract is made to the very end that each may gain

something that he needs or desires more urgently than that which he proposes to give in exchange. And, since it self-evident that, unless all things are held in common, some persons must have more property than others, it is from the nature of things impossible to uphold freedom of contract and the right of private property without at the same time recognizing as legitimate those inequalities of fortune that are the necessary result of the exercise of those rights. But the 14th Amendment, in declaring that a state shall not deprive any person of life, liberty, or property without due process of law gives to each of these an equal sanction: it recognizes liberty and property as coexistent human rights, and debars the states from any unwarranted interference with either.

The Kansas statute in question condemned contractual promises not to join a union. The Court concluded that this law imposed an unwarranted intrusion into the rights of property and liberty because

there is no object or purpose, expressed or implied, that is claimed to have reference to health, safety, morals, or public welfare, beyond the supposed desirability of leveling inequalities of fortune by depriving one who has property of some part of what is characterized as his financial independence. In short, an interference with the normal exercise of personal liberty and property rights is the primary object of the statute, and not an incident to the advancement of the general welfare. But, in our opinion, the 14th Amendment debars the states from striking down personal liberty or property rights, or materially restricting their normal exercise, excepting so far as may be incidentally necessary for the accomplishment of some other and paramount object, and one that concerns the public welfare.

Accordingly, the Constitution establishes symmetrical legal rights for employee and employer, and makes liberty of contract the touchstone for defining fair employment decisions. It also authorizes questions of distributive justice to be resolved by individual negotiation and not by the popular will as captured in legislation.

Is the formula, to each according to the agreement made, truly a product of constitutional mandate? More than one hundred years ago, Justice Holmes challenged judges to acknowledge their roles in establishing the meaning of legal concepts.

HOLMES, PRIVILEGE, MALICE AND INTENT
8 Harv.L.Rev. 1, 7, 9 (1894).

Perhaps one of the reasons why judges do not like to discuss questions of policy, or to put a decision in terms upon their views as lawmakers, is that the moment you leave the patch of merely logical deduction, you lose the illusion of certainty which makes legal reasoning seem like mathematics. But the certainty is only an illusion, nevertheless. Views of policy are taught by experience of the interests of life.

Those interests are fields of battle. Whatever decisions are made must be against the wishes and opinions of one party, and the distinctions on which they go will be distinctions of degree. Even the economic postulate of the benefit of free competition * * * is denied by an important school. * * *

I make these suggestions, not as criticisms of the decisions, but to call attention to the very serious legislative considerations which have to be weighed.

A NOTE FOR ALL CASES

As you read the many cases in this book, consider whether you agree with Holmes' observation that preferences and values, not the neutral exercise of logic, determine judicial analyses. Consider, also, whether the judges in the cases weighed heavily Epstein's enshrined value, the freedom to contract, and if not, consider what values the judges did prefer. More specifically, consider these issues as you read the next two cases.

VEGELAHN v. GUNTNER

Supreme Judicial Court of Massachusetts, 1896.
167 Mass. 92, 44 N.E. 1077.

[The defendants, a group of workers, placed a patrol in front of the facility of their employer, a manufacturer of furniture, in support of their demands for higher wages. The employer moved for an injunction against the patrol. The case came up initially on a motion for an injunction *pendente lite*. An injunction *pendente lite* is often issued *ex parte* (that is, without the participation of the defendants) and on the basis of sworn statements rather than live testimony. In this case, however, the defendants were present and represented by counsel. The initial injunction was quite broad, prohibiting both the patrol and certain forms of persuasion and social pressure. The key language follows:

> It is ordered, adjudged, and decreed that an injunction issue *pendente lite* * * * restraining the respondents and each and every one of them, their agents and servants, from interfering with plaintiff's business by patrolling the sidewalk or street in front or in the vicinity of the premises occupied by him, for the purpose of preventing any person or persons who now are or may hereafter be in his employment, or desirous of entering the same, from entering it, or continuing in it; or by obstructing or interfering with such persons, or any others, in entering or leaving the plaintiff's said premises; or by intimidating, by threats or otherwise, any person or persons who now are or may hereafter be in the employment of the plaintiff, or desirous of entering the same, from entering it, or continuing in it; or by any scheme or conspiracy among themselves or with others, organized for the purpose of annoying, hindering, interfering with,

or preventing any person or persons who now are or may hereafter be in the employment of the plaintiff, or desirous of entering the same, from entering it, or from continuing therein.

Justice Holmes, then a member of the Massachusetts Supreme Judicial Court, drew the assignment of trial judge following the initial injunction, and heard the full case on the merits. In issuing a proposed final injunction he was quite explicit in the manner in which he narrowed the preliminary injunction:

"The means adopted for preventing the plaintiff from getting workmen are, (1) in the first place, persuasion and social pressure. And these means are sufficient to affect the plaintiff disadvantageously, although it does not appear, if that be material, that they are sufficient to crush him. I ruled that the employment of these means for the said purpose was lawful, and for that reason refused an injunction against the employment of them. If the ruling was wrong, I find that an injunction ought to be granted.

"(2) I find also, that, as a further means for accomplishing the desired end, threats of personal injury or unlawful harm were conveyed to persons seeking employment or employed, although no actual violence was used beyond a technical battery, and although the threats were a good deal disguised, and express words were avoided. It appeared to me that there was danger of similar acts in the future. I ruled that conduct of this kind should be enjoined."

The text of Justice Holmes' proposed final decree read "the defendants are enjoined by the final decree from intimidating by threats, express or implied, of physical harm to body or property, any person who may be desirous of entering into the employment of the plaintiff, so far as to prevent him from entering the same."

The full court then reviewed Justice Holmes' proposed final decree and restored the original preliminary injunction in its full breadth. As you read the following portion of the majority decision, consider how the court's decree differs from that proposed by Justice Holmes. Then ask yourself whether the court restrained the patrol because it was inherently coercive, or because the court disagreed with the tactics and goals of the union.

Directly following the majority opinion, we reproduce most of Justice Holmes' dissent. Now in the role of dissenter on the full court (after sitting as trial judge below), Justice Holmes asserted that he had worded his proposed final decree to prevent the use of all bodily force, so the majority's fears of coercion were unfounded. Consider his explanation of the majority's position and his view of the role of the judge when it comes to issues of policy.—Eds.]

ALLEN, J. The principal question in this case is whether the defendants should be enjoined against maintaining the patrol. The report shows that, following upon a strike of the plaintiff's workmen, the defendants conspired to prevent him from getting workmen, and thereby to prevent him from carrying on his business, unless and until he should adopt a certain schedule of prices. The means adopted were persuasion and social pressure, threats of personal injury or unlawful harm conveyed to persons employed or seeking employment, and a patrol of two men in front of the plaintiff's factory, maintained from half past 6 in the morning till half past 5 in the afternoon, on one of the busiest streets of Boston. The number of men was greater at times, and at times showed some little disposition to stop the plaintiff's door. The patrol proper at times went further than simple advice, not obtruded beyond the point where the other person was willing to listen; and it was found that the patrol would probably be continued if not enjoined. There was also some evidence of persuasion to break existing contracts. The patrol was maintained as one of the means of carrying out the defendants' plan, and it was used in combination with social pressure, threats of personal injury or unlawful harm, and persuasion to break existing contracts. It was thus one means of intimidation, indirectly to the plaintiff, and directly to persons actually employed, or seeking to be employed, by the plaintiff, and of rendering such employment unpleasant or intolerable to such persons. Such an act is an unlawful interference with the rights both of employer and of employed. An employer has a right to engage all persons who are willing to work for him, at such prices as may be mutually agreed upon, and persons employed or seeking employment have a corresponding right to enter into or remain in the employment of any person or corporation willing to employ them. These rights are secured by the constitution itself. No one can lawfully interfere by force or intimidation to prevent employers or persons employed or wishing to be employed from the exercise of these rights. It is in Massachusetts, as in some other states, even made a criminal offense for one, by intimidation or force, to prevent, or seek to prevent, a person from entering into or continuing in the employment of a person or corporation. Intimidation is not limited to threats of violence or of physical injury to person or property. It has a broader signification, and there also may be a moral intimidation which is illegal. * * * The patrol was an unlawful interference both with the plaintiff and with the workmen, within the principle of many cases; and, when instituted for the purpose of interfering with his business, it became a private nuisance.

The defendants contend that these acts were justifiable, because they were only seeking to secure better wages for themselves, by compelling the plaintiff to accept their schedule of wages. This motive or purpose does not justify maintaining a patrol in front of the plaintiff's premises, as a means of carrying out their conspiracy. A combination among persons merely to regulate their own conduct is within allowable competition, and is lawful, although others may be indirectly affected thereby. But a combination to do injurious acts expressly directed to another, by way of intimidation or constraint, either of himself or of persons employed or seeking to be employed by him, is outside of allowable competition, and is unlawful. * * *

Nor does the fact that the defendants' acts might subject them to an indictment prevent a court of equity from issuing an injunction. It is true that, ordinarily, a court of equity will decline to issue an injunction to restrain the commission of a crime of a crime; but a continuing injury to property or business may be enjoined, although it may also be punishable as a nuisance or other crime.

A question is also presented whether the court should enjoin such interference with persons in the employment of the plaintiff who are not bound by contract to remain with him, or with persons who are not under any existing contract, but who are seeking or intending to enter into his employment. A conspiracy to interfere with the plaintiff's business by means of threats and intimidation, and by maintaining a patrol in front of his premises, in order to prevent persons from entering his employment, or in order to prevent persons who are in his employment from continuing therein, is unlawful, even though such persons are not bound by contract to enter into or to continue in his employment; and the injunction should not be so limited as to relate only to persons who are bound by existing contracts. We therefore think that the injunction should be in the form as originally issued. So ordered.

HOLMES, J. (dissenting). In a case like the present, it seems to me that, whatever the true result may be, it will be of advantage to sound thinking to have the less popular view of the law stated, and therefore, although, when I have been unable to bring my brethren to share my convictions, my most invariable practice is to defer to them in silence, I depart from that practice in this case, notwithstanding by [sic] unwillingness to do so, in support of an already rendered judgment of my own. * * * I wish to insist a little that the only point of difference which involves a difference of principle between the final decree and the preliminary injunction, which it is proposed to restore, is what I have mentioned, in order that it may be seen exactly what we are to discuss. It appears to me that the opinion of the majority turns in part on the assumption that the patrol necessarily carries with it a threat of bodily harm. That assumption I think unwarranted, for the reasons which I have given. Furthermore, it cannot be said, I think, that two men, walking together up and down a sidewalk, and speaking to those who enter a certain shop, do necessarily and always thereby convey a threat of force. I do not think it possible to discriminate, and to say that two workmen, or even two representatives of an organization of workmen, do; especially when they are, and are known to be, under the injunction of this court not to do so. I may add that I think the more intelligent workingmen believe as fully as I do that they no more can be permitted to usurp the state's prerogative of force than can their opponents in their controversies. But, if I am wrong, then the decree as it stands reaches the patrol, since it applies to all threats of force. With this I pass to the real difference between the interlocutory and the final decree.

I agree, whatever may be the law in the case of a single defendant, that when a plaintiff proves that several persons have combined and conspired to injure his business, and have done acts producing that effect, he shows temporal damage and a cause of action, unless the facts disclose or the defendants prove some ground of excuse or justification; and I take it to be settled, and rightly settled, that doing that damage by combined persuasion is actionable, as well as doing it by falsehood or by force.

Nevertheless, in numberless instances the law warrants the intentional infliction of temporal damage, because it regards it as justified. It is on the question of what shall amount to a justification, and more especially on the nature of the considerations which really determine or ought to determine the answer to that question, that judicial reasoning seems to me often to be inadequate. The true grounds of decision are considerations of policy and of social advantage, and it is vain to suppose that solutions can be attained merely by logic and general propositions of law which nobody disputes. Propositions as to public policy rarely are unanimously accepted, and still more rarely, if ever, are capable of unanswerable proof. They require a special training to enable any one even to form an intelligent opinion about them.

In the early stages of law, at least, they generally are acted on rather as inarticulate instincts than as definite ideas, for which a rational defense is ready.

To illustrate what I have said in the last paragraph: It has been the law for centuries that a man may set up a business in a small country town, too small to support more than one, although thereby he expects and intends to ruin some one already there, and succeeds in his intent. In such a case he is not held to act "unlawfully and without justifiable cause," * * *. The reason, of course, is that the doctrine generally has been accepted that free competition is worth more to society than it costs, and that on this ground the infliction of the damage is privileged. Yet even this proposition nowadays is disputed by a considerable body of persons, including many whose intelligence is not to be denied, little as we may agree with them.

I have chosen this illustration partly with reference to what I have to say next. It shows without the need of further authority that the policy of allowing free competition justifies the intentional inflicting of temporal damage, including the damage of interference with a man's business by some means, when the damage is done, not for its own sake, but as an instrumentality in reaching the end of victory in the battle of trade. In such a case it cannot matter whether the plaintiff is the only rival of the defendant, and so is aimed at specially, or is one of a class all of whom are hit. The only debatable ground is the nature of the means by which such damage may be inflicted. We all agree that it cannot be done by force or threats of force. We all agree, I presume, that it may be done by persuasion to leave a rival's shop, and come to the defendant's. It may be done by the refusal or withdrawal of various pecuniary advantages, which, apart from this consequence, are within the defendant's lawful control. It may be done by the withdrawal of, or threat to withdraw, such advantages from third persons who have a right to deal or not to deal with the plaintiff, as a means of inducing them not to deal with him either as customers or servants. I have seen the suggestion made that the conflict between employers and employed was not competition. But I venture to assume that none of my brethren would rely on that suggestion. If the policy on which our law is founded is too narrowly expressed in the term "free competition," we may substitute "free struggle for life." Certainly, the policy is not limited to struggles between persons of the same class, competing for the same end. It applies to all conflicts of temporal interests.

I pause here to remark that the word "threats" often is used as if, when it appeared that threats had been made, it appeared that unlawful conduct had begun. But it depends on what you threaten. As a general rule, even if subject to some exceptions, what you may do in a certain event you may threaten to do—that is, give warning of your intention to do—in that event, and thus allow the other person the chance of avoiding the consequence. So, as to "compulsion," it depends on how you "compel." So as to "annoyance" or "intimidation." In Sherry v. Perkins, 147 Mass. 212, 17 N.E. 307, it was found as a fact that the display of banners which was enjoined was part of a scheme to prevent workmen from entering or remaining in the plaintiff's employment, "by threats and intimidation." The context showed that the words as there used meant threats of personal violence and intimidation by causing fear of it.

So far, I suppose, we are agreed. But there is a notion, which latterly has been insisted on a good deal, that a combination of persons to do what any one of them lawfully might do by himself will make the otherwise lawful conduct unlawful. It would be rash to say that some as yet unformulated truth may not be hidden under this proposition. But, in the general form in which it has been presented and accepted by many courts, I think it plainly untrue, both on authority and principle. But it is not necessary to cite cases. It is plain from the slightest consideration of practical affairs, or the most superficial reading of industrial history, that free competition means combination, and that the organization of the world, now going on so fast, means an ever-increasing might and scope of combination. It seems to me futile to set our faces against this tendency. Whether beneficial on the whole, as I think it, or detrimental, it is inevitable, unless the fundamental axioms of society, and even the fundamental conditions of life, are to be changed.

One of the eternal conflicts out of which life is made up is that between the effort of every man to get the most he can for his services, and that of society, disguised under the name of capital, to get his services for the least possible return. Combination on the one side is patent and powerful. Combination on the other is the necessary and desirable counterpart, if the battle is to be carried on in a fair and equal way. * * *

If it be true that working men may combine with a view, among other things, to getting as much as they can for their labor, just as capital may combine with a view to getting the greatest possible return, it must be true that, when combined, they have the same liberty that combined capital has, to support their interests by argument, persuasion, and the bestowal or refusal of those advantages which they otherwise lawfully control. I can remember when many people thought that, apart from violence or breach of contract, strikes were wicked, as organized refusals to work. I suppose that intelligent economists and legislators have given up that notion today. I feel pretty confident that they equally will abandon the idea that an organized refusal by workmen of social intercourse with a man who shall enter their antagonist's employ is unlawful, if it is dissociated from any threat of violence, and is made for the sole object of prevailing, if possible, in a contest with their employer about the rate of wages. The fact that the immediate object of the act by which the benefit to themselves is to be gained is to injure their antagonist does not necessarily make it unlawful, any more than when a great house lowers the price of goods for the purpose and with the effect of driving a smaller antagonist from the business. Indeed, the question seems to me to have been decided as long ago as 1842, by the good sense of Chief Justice Shaw, in Com. v. Hunt, 4 Metc. (Mass.) 111. I repeat at the end, as I said at the beginning, that this is the point of difference in principle, and the only one, between the interlocutory and final decree; * * *.

The general question of the propriety of dealing with this kind of case by injunction I say nothing about, because I understand that the defendants have no objection to the final decree if it goes no further, and that both parties wish a decision upon the matters which I have discussed.

[The dissent by FIELD, J., is omitted.]

Note

As Justice Holmes intimates in his dissent, there is a significant difference between having the law protect existing economic arrangements and using the market to allocate economic resources. A "free" market encourages the parties to pit their relative strengths against each other and tolerates the results, including a redistribution of economic power. When, however, the law disables challengers from effectively exploiting their superior market strength, legal intervention actively supports existing economic arrangements. In *Vegelahn*, for example, the injunction helped an employer who was unable to defeat striking workers by doing their jobs himself, hiring replacements or farming out the struck work. Had the Court denied the relief sought, the strikers might have prevailed or the employer might have been forced to close down.

To our present-day sensibilities, it is apparent that the injunction in *Vegelahn* undermined market regulation by giving aid to an employer with inferior market power. To Justice Allen, however, the injunction was consistent with the prevailing, unchanging common law and with the commitment to private ordering. Allen thought the injunction maintained the status quo and did not distort the operation of a "free" market, because he (along with others) considered organized labor an unnatural element in commerce. Accordingly, by turning to the law for help in labor disputes employers cleansed the community of forces with no apparently legitimate role in commercial affairs. See C. Gregory, Labor and The Law 60–76 (2nd rev. ed. 1958).

The view—organized labor has no place in commercial transactions—has a rich history. In the early 1800s, employers responded to strikes by charging the participants with violations of the criminal law. According to the public prosecutors who indicted these workers for criminal conspiracy, concerted agreements to work only at shops paying union rates and hiring union labor harmed everyone except the strikers. These agreements put employers at a competitive disadvantage by enabling workers to set the price of labor and to control the labor market. In organizing, workers harmed the community by inhibiting commercial expansion. Higher wages meant higher priced or lower quality goods; it followed that employers subject to employee price (wage) fixing were put in an inferior competitive position. The workers who did not strike suffered because they might be precluded from employment under conditions they deemed tolerable. Prosecutors implored juries to condemn the strikers as evil creatures, indifferent to the pervasive adversity caused by their selfish demands. The form of legal intervention changed during the latter part of the nineteenth century, as tort actions and injunctions replaced criminal conspiracy charges in the effort to control organized labor, but the justification underlying such intervention remained the same.

Steeped in this tradition, Justice Allen and his colleagues identified the relevant fact about business affairs as the opportunity for all employees and all employers to negotiate as individuals about employment terms. Since the nineteenth century concept of a contract did not comprehend an agreement addressing conditions of employment for many employees and involving employees (or their representatives) as a party to the agreement, attempts by workers as a group to influence rates of compensation could be restrained. Because of the group action and the collective objective, the *Vegelahn* majority did not view regulation by injunction as compromising the general proposition that private ordering, not law, controls the employment relationship. Considered from the point of view of fairness, individual identity alone was relevant to the question of just compensation for workers; benefits produced by group pressure were akin to spoils from a robbery. It is therefore easy to understand why Justice Allen rejected any thought that he was implementing policy. He believed he was enforcing a self-evident, immutable and correct principle.

Holmes personified the transitional thinker. He agreed with Allen that private ordering should regulate commerce and that the law could be used to rid the commercial world of irresponsible interlopers. But Holmes' picture of commerce included organized labor as a legitimate participant, harnessing its resource—labor power—just as business people deployed their financial power. As Holmes put it, "If the policy on which our law is founded is too narrowly expressed in the term 'free competition,' we may substitute 'free struggle for life.' Certainly the policy is not limited to struggles between persons of the same class, competing for the same end. It applies to all conflicts of temporal interests." For Holmes, then, fairness entitled trade unions to participate in commercial affairs, workers to make employment contracts as members of a group, and judges to accept the group's use of concerted action to advance its interests.

As Holmes predicted, the law has enlarged the concept of a contract to include terms negotiated by workers as a group. But the formula approved by both Holmes and Allen—to each according to the agreement made—is still considered relevant in defining fairness at the workplace.

Can We Reconcile Fairness With Efficiency?

A CASE STUDY

Decisions about fair treatment of the employee have more than one dimension. The employer may acknowledge and even embrace the principle of fair treatment of its workers, but will assert that fairness to the employee can only be measured in the context of the company's needs for productivity and efficiency. That balance was involved in the Billie Tulip problem at the start of the chapter.

The tension between fairness and efficiency is raised most acutely in situations where an employee who has done good work is terminated because the employer feels his services are no longer necessary. This is the story in the next case, a modern classic. The workers say they struck a bargain for job security, which the employer says was trumped by its need to close down an outmoded facility. As you read this decision, ask yourself whether there is any other way to resolve the tension between fairness and efficiency. How can the law respond in a constructive way?

LOCAL 1330, UNITED STEEL WORKERS OF AMERICA v. UNITED STATES STEEL CORP.

United States Court of Appeals, Sixth Circuit, 1980.
631 F.2d 1264.

[The decision by United States Steel Corporation to close two mills in Youngstown, Ohio threatened the jobs of 3,500 steelworkers and the economic stability of a community already devastated by earlier mill closings. Local unions representing affected workers joined with religious, community and political organizations to keep the mills in Youngstown operating. Their campaign included press releases, demonstrations, public hearings, a sit-in at company headquarters, and applications to the federal government for direct aid and loan guarantees to fund a feasibility study and employee buy-out. A lawsuit helped sustain these efforts by temporarily keeping the plants in operation. The lawsuit also gave voice to the claims of the steelworkers and their community-claims of unfairness and frustrated expectations that lawyers framed as violations of property and contractual rights.—Eds.]

EDWARDS, CHIEF JUDGE.

This appeal represents a cry for help from steelworkers and townspeople in the City of Youngstown, Ohio, who are distressed by the prospective impact upon their lives and their city of the closing of two large steel mills. These two mills were built and have been operated by the United States Steel Corporation since the turn of the century. The Ohio Works began producing in 1901; the McDonald Works in 1918. The District Court which heard this cause of action found that as of the notice of closing, the two plants employed 3,500 employees.

The leading plaintiffs are two labor organizations, Locals 1330 and 1307 of the United Steel Workers of America. This union has had a collective bargaining contract with the United States Steel Corporation for many years. These local unions represent production and maintenance employees at the Ohio and McDonald Works, respectively.

In the background of this litigation is the obsolescence of the two plants concerned, occasioned both by the age of the facilities and machinery involved and by the changes in technology and marketing in steelmaking in the years intervening since the early nineteen hundreds.

For all of the years United States Steel has been operating in Youngstown, it has been a dominant factor in the lives of its thousands of employees and their families, and in the life of the city itself. The contemplated abrupt departure of United States Steel from Youngstown will, of course, have direct impact on 3,500 workers and their families. It will doubtless mean a devastating blow to them, to the business community and to the City of Youngstown itself. While we cannot read the future of Youngstown from this record, what the record does indicate clearly is that we deal with an economic tragedy of major proportion to Youngstown and Ohio's Mahoning Valley. As the District Judge who heard this case put the matter:

> Everything that has happened in the Mahoning Valley has been happening for many years because of steel. Schools have been built, roads have been built. Expansion that has taken place is because of steel. And to accommodate that industry, lives and destinies of the inhabitants of that community were based and planned on the basis of that institution: Steel.

In the face of this tragedy, the steel worker local unions, the Congressman from this district, and the Attorney General of Ohio have sued United States Steel Corporation, asking the federal courts to order the United States Steel Corporation to keep the two plants at issue in operation. Alternatively, if they could not legally prevail on that issue, they have sought intervention of the courts by injunction to require the United States Steel Corporation to sell the two plants to the plaintiffs under an as yet tentative plan of purchase and operation by a community corporation [Community Steel] and to restrain the piecemeal sale or dismantling of the plants until such a proposal could be brought to fruition.

Defendant United States Steel Corporation answered plaintiffs' complaints, claiming that the plants were unprofitable and could not be made otherwise due to obsolescence and change in technology, markets, and transportation. The company also asserts an absolute right to make a business decision to discharge its former employees and abandon

Youngstown. It states that there is no law in either the State of Ohio or the United States of America which provides either legal or equitable remedy for plaintiffs.

The District Judge, after originally restraining the corporation from ceasing operations as it had announced it would, and after advancing the case for prompt hearing, entered a formal opinion holding that the plants had become unprofitable and denying all relief. We believe the dispositive paragraphs of a lengthy opinion entered by the District Judge are the following:

> This Court has spent many hours searching for a way to cut to the heart of the economic reality—that obsolescence and market forces demand the close of the Mahoning Valley plants, and yet the lives of 3,500 workers and their families and the supporting Youngstown community cannot be dismissed as inconsequential. United States Steel should not be permitted to leave the Youngstown area devastated after drawing from the lifeblood of the community for so many years.
>
> Unfortunately, the mechanism to reach this ideal settlement, to recognize this new property right, is not now in existence in the code of laws of our nation.
>
> This Court is mindful of the efforts taken by the workers to increase productivity, and has applauded these efforts in the preceding paragraphs. In view of the fact, however, that this Court has found that no contract or enforceable promise was entered into by the company and that, additionally, there is clear evidence to support the company's decision that the plants were not profitable, the various acts of forebearance taken by the plaintiffs do not give them the basis for relief against defendant.

Plaintiffs-appellants claim that certain of the District Judge's findings of fact are clearly erroneous, that he has misconstrued federal and state contract law, and that he failed to grant a hearing on their antitrust claims.

With this introduction, we turn to the legal issues presented by this appeal. * * *

The primary issue in this case is a claim on the part of the steel worker plaintiffs that United States Steel made proposals to the plaintiffs and/or the membership of the plaintiffs to the general effect that if the workers at the two steel plants concerned put forth their best efforts in terms of productivity and thereby rendered the two plants "profitable," the plants would then not be closed. It is clear that this claimed contract does not rest upon any formal written document, either authorized or signed by the parties to this lawsuit. * * *

The District Judge's rejection of any formal legal contract claims was clearly mandated by both state and federal contract law. The lack of such features as a written document, authorization by the corporate Board of Directors and the Executive Boards of the steelworkers national and local bodies, a stated contract period, specified mutual consideration, all serve to demonstrate that the minimum features of a formal legal contract are missing.

Appellants' principal argument in this appeal is, however, that the District Court should have found a contract based upon the equitable doctrine of promissory estoppel * * *.

The doctrine of promissory estoppel recognizes the possibility of the formation of a contract by action or forbearance on the part of a second party, based upon a promise made by the first party under circumstances where the actions or forbearance of the second party should reasonably have been expected to produce the detrimental results to the second party which they did produce. . . .

Thus, appellants' contract claim depends essentially upon oral statements and newspaper releases concerning the efforts of the company to secure increased productivity by enlisting the help of the workers of the plant and upon the employee responses thereto. The representations as set forth in the steelworkers' complaint include many oral statements made over the "hotline" employed by management in the plants to advise U.S. Steel employees of company policy. They began in the Fall of 1977 in the midst of much public speculation that the Ohio and McDonald works at Youngstown were to be closed. In general they follow the very first statement made by William Ashton, then superintendent of Youngstown works of U.S. Steel, on September 1, 1977, which said:

> In response to many rumors, I want to tell you that there are no immediate plans to permanently shut down either the Ohio Works or McDonald Mills.
>
> However, steps will have to be taken to improve these plants' profitability. These steps, which have been and are currently under study, will require the suspension and consolidation of some operations in the months ahead.
>
> Ohio Works and McDonald Mills are faced with very serious profit problems caused by a combination of heavy imports of foreign steel, higher energy costs, higher taxes and, of course, environmental expenditures.
>
> The continued operation of these plants is absolutely dependent upon their being profit-makers.
>
> In the months ahead, we will be calling for the full support of each and every one of you. Your cooperation and assistance is absolutely necessary if our facilities are to continue to operate.

Many similar statements were made by the company and were responded to by the employees. As 1977 and 1978 went by, there began to be statements over similar facilities and sometimes by company press releases indicating improvement in productivity at the two Youngstown facilities. Some of these included reference to "a complete turnaround" and reference to the Youngstown plants as "profitable" and once again viable.

The opposite side of the contract bargain alleged by plaintiffs consists of performance claimed by plaintiffs to have been induced by the sort of promises recited above and actions taken by them "in detrimental reliance" upon said promises.

* * *

[R]esponses and actions which steelworkers alleged were induced by these promises, and which represented detrimental reliance thereon, [included:]

"[1] Because of Defendant's promise and in detrimental reliance thereon, Defendant Youngstown employees immediately began to work harder and to increase their productivity. The results were evident as early as October 1977, when, for the first time in 1977 according to the method of accounting employed by Defendant, the Youngstown District made a monthly profit. Defendant's Manager of Accounting for the Youngstown District reported:

"In October, Youngstown made a *profit* of $34. The importance of this *profit* can only properly be comprehended if the odds against it, at this level of operations, are clearly understood. The break-even point on October's fixed expenses * * * is 74,400 tons * * *. October's shipments of 51,283 tons were 23,100 tons below the break-even point, and therefore, only extraordinary performance variance achievements from hot metal through primary rolling drove the actual variable cost (standard variable cost [plus or minus] cost variances) to $273 per ton below the Standard variable cost of $297. * * *

". . . The Ohio Works variance is the most favorable variance performance achieved since May, 1975. . . .

". . . If Youngstown is judged strictly on its own fixed expense, October's profit would have been $1,408, and the year to date loss would be reduced from the Profit Contribution reports' $19,421 to $4,947."

(Emphasis in original.)

"[2] In further illustration of the action and forbearance induced by Defendant's promise, in detrimental reliance thereon, on May 12, 1978 Mr. Kirwan stated on the 'hot line':

"Hello, this is Bill Kirwan.

Congratulations! For the second month in a row, I am happy to report that, due to your outstanding performances, Youngstown Works has again, been a profitable steel plant.

In April, the Blast Furnace Department set a new monthly record and the crews on #51 Open Hearth did the same. All of you kept on top of your individual assignments and the result is most gratifying. . . ."

"[3] Because of Defendant's promise and in detrimental reliance thereon, Plaintiff Locals agreed to combine into one seniority list the machinists at the Ohio and McDonald Works.

"[4] Plaintiff Locals permitted Defendant to combine jobs so as to reduce Defendant's costs, although the previously existing jobs were well established by past practice and Plaintiff Locals could have grieved the changes had management imposed them unilaterally.

"[5] Also in detrimental reliance on Defendant's promise, individual Plaintiffs, or some of them, gave up opportunities to take other employment and committed themselves to major, long-term expenditures such as the purchase of homes. By way of illustration:

"a. LeRoy Benson, 455 Utah Avenue, McDonald, Ohio 44437, the first-named individual Plaintiff, had been in the mill ten years as of June 1979. Since his pension became vested at that time he considered whether to seek other employment. His foreman, Thomas Augustine, advised him not to do so because he had a secure future with United States Steel. Accordingly, Mr. Benson gave up the idea of seeking work elsewhere, bought a car in July 1979, and on October 28, 1979 bought a home.

"b. Frank Georges, R.D. 2, Hillsville Road, Lowelville, Ohio 44436, another individual Plaintiff, bought a new home on November 27, 1979, and heard the news of Defendant's shutdown announcement on the car radio as he drove home from the bank.

"c. Michael Meser, 810 New York Avenue, McDonald, Ohio 44437, another individual Plaintiff, spent considerable time deciding where to send his son Mickey to college. After hearing David Roderick's statement on TV in June 1979, Mr. Meser decided on Hiram College where tuition was $2,000 a year rather than Youngstown State University where Mickey could have gone tuition free. On the strength of Mr. Roderick's assurance Mr. Meser also decided to buy a new car which he had not done since 1956. On November 21, 1979, he took out a $4,000 loan from the employee credit union."

Based on these allegations, appellant steelworkers make this fundamental assertion which is the heart of the contract claim:

"13. Defendant's promise, and the detrimental reliance thereon of Locals 1330, 1307, 3073, and 3072, and of their members gave rise to a contract between Defendant and Locals 1330, 1307, 3073, and 3072, and their members, that the Ohio and McDonald Works would be kept open if they became profitable."

They also assert that "The Ohio and McDonald works would become profitable."

As we read this lengthy record, and as the District Judge read it, it does not contain any factual dispute over the allegations as to company statements or the responsive actions of steelworkers in relation thereto. It is beyond argument that the local management of U.S. Steel's Youngstown plants engaged in a major campaign to enlist employee participation in an all-out effort to make these two plants profitable in order to prevent their being closed. It is equally obvious that the employees responded wholeheartedly.

The District Judge, however, rejected the promissory estoppel contract theory on three grounds. The first ground was that none of the statements made by officers and employees of the company constituted a definite promise to continue operation of the plants if they did become profitable. The second ground was that the statements relied upon by plaintiffs were made by employees and public relations officers of the company and not by company officers. The third ground was a finding of fact that "The condition precedent of the alleged contract and promise—profitability of the Youngstown facilities—was never fulfilled, and the actions in contract and for detrimental reliance cannot be found for plaintiffs."

The District Judge's fundamental disposition of plaintiffs-appellants' contract claims is stated in this finding of fact:

> [T]here is clear evidence to support the company's decision that the plants were not profitable, the various acts of forebearance taken by the plaintiffs do not give them the basis for relief against defendant.

Our examination of this record offers no ground for our holding that this finding of fact is "clearly erroneous." See Fed.R.Civ.P. 52(a).

The District Judge's findings on profitability bear quotation in full:

> There is a second, independent ground for denying relief under the contract and detrimental reliance theories, and that is the failure of the condition precedent to defendant's liability—the profitability of the Mahoning Valley plants.

> Plaintiffs attempted to demonstrate profitability by defining minimum profitability as the "gross profit margin", which William R. Roesch, President and Chief Operating Officer of United States Steel, described as "the revenues minus the variable costs of performing the operation to produce the product." He admitted that "technically, if you are losing money at the gross margin operation, there is no way to make that operation profitable." Plaintiffs then turned to their exhibits 32 through 37, which were summary sheets of operating profitability for the Youngstown facilities for 1977, 1978, 1979, and 1980. These exhibits revealed that the gross profit margin for 1977 was $24,899,000.00, that for 1978 was $41,770,000.00, that for 1979 was $32,571,000.00 and that the

projected gross profit margin for 1980, as of November 20, 1979, was $32,396,000.00.

These figures do indicate that at the variable-cost margin, the plant was, in a sense, profitable. It should be remembered, however, that even with the projected $32,396,000.00 gross profit margin projected for 1980, the over-all projection for the year was a loss of $9,387,000.00. This suggests that with a different definition of profit, especially one that would include fixed costs, the outcome of an accounting analysis could be made to be nonprofitability. Mr. Roesch testified that the gross profit margin "does not represent the profit of the operation," nor does it represent that the operation is necessarily profitable considered as a whole. He explained that "[t]here are other factors involved because, once you have the gross margin, you have to subtract the depreciation for the equipment which was involved and depreciate it over a period of time; you have to subtract the selling expenses which are necessary; and you have to subtract the administrative charges, the taxes, and so forth." He also explained that, because of the integrated system of the national corporation, many of the unseen costs of the Youngstown Works were absorbed by other plants and operations in the steel company. Mr. Roesch testified that it was primarily the obsolescence of the plant facilities that made the plant unprofitable.

The testimony of David Roderick, Chairman of the Board of Directors and Chief Executive Officer of United States Steel, confirmed Mr. Roesch's opinion. In answer to the question "And through the end of October, 1979, Youngstown [sic] the performance of that year was in the area of about the break even, was it not?" Mr. Roderick replied ". . . the actual number was about a $300 thousand loss, as of the end of October, cumulative for the year. And further, as I recall, they had lost money three out of the four months preceding it." Further, Mr. Roderick explained the opinion of the Board of Directors on the trend of the loss in this way:

> Well, what I really mean by an irreversible loss is based on our best judgment, or my best judgment, the loss would be incurred and there was nothing the plant could do to avoid that loss, that the market was working negatively and that it was our projection that the plant would lose money in five out of six months of the second half, that the loss for the year would be quite substantial in 1979, and with all the facts that we could see on the horizon for 1980, plus the actual performance for the second half of 1979, we felt there was no way that the loss trend could be reversed for the calendar year of 1980.

This Court is loath to exchange its own view of the parameters of profitability for that of the corporation. It is clear that there is little argument as to the production figures for the Youngstown mills—the controversy surrounds the interpretation of those figures. Plaintiffs read the figures in light of a gross profit margin analysis of minimum profitability. Defendant sees capital expenditure, fixed costs and technical obsolescence as essential ingredients of the notion of profitability. Perhaps if this Court were being asked to interpret the word "profit" in a written contract between plaintiffs and defendant, some choice would have to be made. Given the oral nature of the alleged promises in the case at bar and the obvious ambiguity of the statements made, this Court finds that there is a very reasonable basis on which it can be said that Youngstown facilities were not profitable. Further, plaintiffs have made no showing of bad faith on the part of the Board of Directors in the Board's determination of profitability, nor have they given any grounds to suggest that defendant's definition of profitability is an unrealistic or unreasonable one. The condition precedent of the alleged contract and promise—profitability of the Youngstown facilities—was never fulfilled, and the actions in contract and for detrimental reliance cannot be found for plaintiffs.

* * *

We believe that this record demonstrates without significant dispute that the profitability issue in the case depends in large part upon definition. The plaintiffs wish to employ the direct costs of operating the two plants, compared to the total selling price of their products. The difference, they contend, is "profit." This formula would eliminate such charges as corporate purchasing and sales expense allocable to the Youngstown plants, and allocable corporate management expenses including, but not limited to marketing, engineering, auditing, accounting, advertising. Obviously, any multi-plant corporation could quickly go bankrupt if such a definition of profit was employed generally and over any period of time.

Plaintiffs-appellants point out, however, that this version of Youngstown profitability was employed by the Youngstown management in setting a goal for its employees and in statements which described achieving that goal. The standard of Restatement (Second) of Contracts § 90, upon which plaintiffs-appellants rely, however, is one of reasonable expectability of the "promise" detrimentally relied upon. The District Judge did not find, nor can we, that reliance upon a promise to keep these plants open on the basis of coverage of plant fixed costs was within reasonable expectability. We cannot hold that the District Judge erred legally or was "clearly erroneous" in his fact finding when he held that the "promise" to keep the plants open had to be read in the context of normal corporate profit accounting and that profitability had not been achieved. * * *

At a pretrial hearing of this case on February 28, 1980, the District Judge made a statement at some length about the relationship between the parties to this case and the public interest involved therein. He said:

> But what has happened over the years between U.S. Steel, Youngstown and the inhabitants? Hasn't something come out of that relationship, something that out of which—not reaching for a case

on property law or a series of cases but looking at the law as a whole, the Constitution, the whole body of law, not only contract law, but tort, corporations, agency, negotiable instruments—taking a look at the whole body of American law and then sitting back and reflecting on what it seeks to do, and that is to adjust human relationships in keeping with the whole spirit and foundation of the American system of law, to preserve property rights.

* * *

It would seem to me that when we take a look at the whole body of American law and the principles we attempt to come out with—and although a legislature has not pronounced any laws with respect to such a property right, that is not to suggest that there will not be a need for such a law in the future dealing with similar situations. *It seems to me that a property right has arisen from this lengthy, long-established relationship between United States Steel, the steel industry as an institution, the community in Youngstown, the people in Mahoning County and the Mahoning Valley in having given and devoted their lives to this industry.* Perhaps not a property right to the extent that can be remedied by compelling U.S. Steel to remain in Youngstown. But *I think the law can recognize the property right to the extent that U.S. Steel cannot leave that Mahoning Valley and the Youngstown area in a state of waste, that it cannot completely abandon its obligation to that community, because certain vested rights have arisen out of this long relationship and institution.* [Emphasis in original—Eds.]

Subsequently thereto, steelworkers' complaint was amended [to add a fourth claim], as follows:

52. A property right has arisen from the long-established relation between the community of the 19th Congressional District and Plaintiffs, on the one hand, and Defendant on the other hand, which this Court can enforce.

53. This right, in the nature of an easement, requires that Defendant:

   a. Assist in the preservation of the institution of steel in that community;

   b. Figure into its cost of withdrawing and closing the Ohio and McDonald Works the cost of rehabilitating the community and the workers;

   c. Be restrained from leaving the Mahoning Valley in a state of waste and from abandoning its obligation to that community.

This court has examined these allegations with care and with great sympathy for the community interest reflected therein. Our problem in dealing with plaintiffs' fourth cause of action is one of authority. Neither in brief nor oral argument have plaintiffs pointed to any constitutional provision contained in either the Constitution of the United States or the

Constitution of the State of Ohio, nor any law enacted by the United States Congress or the Legislature of Ohio, nor any case decided by the courts of either of these jurisdictions which would convey authority to this court to require the United States Steel Corporation to continue operations in Youngstown which its officers and Board of Directors had decided to discontinue on the basis of unprofitability. * * *

* * *

We find no legal basis for judicial relief as to appellants' fourth cause of action.

Finally, appellants contend that the United States Steel Corporation has violated federal antitrust laws, 15 U.S.C. § 1 et seq. (1976). The essence of the antitrust complaint is that defendant United States Steel Corporation has refused to sell to the plaintiffs the Ohio and McDonald works which it seeks to abandon. Plaintiffs claim defendant has thus exercised monopoly power for the purpose of preventing a potential competitor from entering the steel market. * * *

Out of perhaps an excess of caution, we vacate the District Court judgment dismissing appellants' antitrust claim. * * * The antitrust issue which we perceive as arguable should be the subject of briefing, argument and trial court decision before consideration by this court. * * *

[The district court refused to reinstate its injunction restraining U.S. Steel from selling or leasing the mills. In October 1980, U.S. Steel leased the most profitable part of the McDonald Works to an investment firm for five years, with an option to buy. The plaintiffs abandoned the antitrust claim and settled the lawsuit. The settlement included a promise by U.S. Steel not to dismantle three mills for five years and an opportunity for Community Steel to participate in the deliberations of an advisory council looking into ways to expand steel operations in Youngstown.—Eds.]

Questions

Are you able to explain why the plaintiffs in *Steelworkers* did not succeed in establishing their legal claims? The district and appellate courts refused to let the legal claims rest on factors not contained in the agreement of the parties. By letting the claim of promissory estoppel turn on the narrow issue of defining profitability, did the courts duck the real issues? Were any other considerations relevant?

Are you persuaded that the parties' agreement was not violated? That profitability should have been defined as the court defined it? That the employees did not act based on reasonable reliance?

Responding with sympathy to the assertion that U.S. Steel had a legally enforceable obligation to the community in the Mahoning Valley, the court concluded that "the whole body of American law and the principles we come out with disavow a public policy that allows a company like U.S. Steel to abandon a community." The court drew a sharp distinction, however, between legislative and judicial power to take emergency action in the public interest. Can you think of any considerations grounded in public policy to which a court should respond even in the absence of legislative authorizations? Can you think of any court-made law that ignores entirely all considerations of public policy?

THOMAS GEOHEGAN, WHICH SIDE ARE YOU ON?
91–96 (1991).

Wisconsin Steel was the first of the big Chicago mills to crash, and the crash was the most dramatic, because here, unlike most mills, the workers were cheated of their shutdown benefits. Even with the payments from the PBGC[1] the workers still lost nearly $45 million. By 1988, if the interest on this money was added up, they had lost nearly $90 million. The benefits they lost, among others, include severance pay, supplemental unemployment benefits pay, extended vacation pay, "special payment," health insurance (for retirees). They even lost two weeks of wages because the paychecks bounced without warning when the mill suddenly closed in March 1980. But worst of all, 500 or so of them lost their pension benefits, often up to 60 percent, especially the "Rule of 65" pensions, which were the special shutdown benefits that went in effect only if the mill closed.

So not only did the workers lose their jobs; that would have been bad enough. But they also lost the $45 million, which was their "deindustrialization" money. The closing of Wisconsin Steel was, in many ways, like an earthquake. The first shock was that the mill closed. The second shock, like an aftershock, was that they would not get this money either. The money that would have cushioned the blow, that would have given them time to think, figure out what to do next, hold on to the car or the home a little longer: it was not much money, really, but it was enough, just enough, to make people lose their balance. Some of them could never get their balance back.

I spent all the Reagan years on this one case. It was endless. I felt like I was in prison. I used to think of that line from Richard II: "I wasted time, and now doth time waste me." I came to hate "deindustrialization." The mill had closed, but it seemed as if the litigation would never end, and I might have to clean up after this mill forever. I felt as the men must have felt: I was always living in the year 1980. I could not seem to leave 1980.

I wanted to move, go to New York, do anything else, but people told me, "You can't, you're stuck here," and they were right. I was stuck here. I was trapped in a way, just as the people in the neighborhood were trapped, trapped in homes they could not sell, like victims of an earth-

---

1. The Pension Benefit Guaranty Corporation—an entity established by ERISA—   Eds.

quake. Nobody was moving, nobody was going away. I was a labor lawyer, like it or not, until this damn case was done.

Here is how the case started:

Wisconsin Steel, in short, was unsalable. Yet Harvester did not want to close it either. If it did so, it would owe the whole $65 million in pensions, plus another $20 million in special shutdown benefits, like severance pay. It almost seemed as if Harvester was trapped into keeping the mill open. Nor was Harvester the only steel company in the 1980s to have this problem. A union lawyer once told me, "The only reason half the steel mills in this country are still going is that they can't afford to pay the pensions." It was the revenge of the weak on the strong. "Shut us down, Mr. Employer, and you die, too."

So Harvester tried to close the mill indirectly. It transferred title to a dummy corporation. Then, when this corporate shell went bankrupt, Harvester could say, "Too bad, they're not our pensions now." But Harvester had to have an accomplice. It found one in a small engineering company, Envirodyne, Inc., which knew nothing about steel. Envirodyne was not much of a company, just two yuppies in a garage. But Envirodyne did not want to have to pay the pensions either. So Envirodyne transferred title to a subsidiary it created, EDC Holding Company. Then EDC transferred title to a subsidiary it created, WSC Corporation. One corporate shell came after another. It was like a game of Chinese boxes, and when you got to the last box, nothing was in it. Nobody would be paying the pensions.

Under our law, a subsidiary can go bankrupt and normally the parent company will not be liable for its debts. So when EDC or WSC went bankrupt, Harvester and even Envirodyne could say they owed nothing. Indeed, Harvester was not even the parent. But Harvester was the biggest creditor and held on through mortgages to everything of value. That was the malign beauty of it all, which I spent seven grudging years admiring. Harvester had dumped all the pension liabilities but kept control of all the assets. It could keep running the mill as if it still owned it. Envirodyne could conduct its little engineering experiments. And the workers, who may have been there twenty or thirty years, would lose their pensions, health insurance, severance pay, etc. Dumb, stupid organized labor would take the fall.

The deal was so mean, so vile, that even the investment bankers gagged. Lehman Brothers, the investment banking firm handling the sale, went to Harvester and objected on simple moral grounds. Peter Peterson, the president of Lehman, came out to a Harvester board meeting to express his distaste. He talked about the "appearance" and the "reality" of the transaction. He was ignored, but he made a record, at least, and it does show a certain honor: sometimes, even on Wall Street, someone may write a memo to the file.

Harvester kept the mill going for a decent interval (two years). Then, on March 28, 1980, with no warning to the workers, Harvester pulled the plug. It foreclosed on the mortgages, and the mill went down the drain. In minutes, WSC was in bankruptcy.

Everybody was stunned. They thought, "How could anything be wrong?"

Right before the mill closed, production almost cruelly began to go up. People were getting more overtime than ever. They were like old ladies, on their deathbeds, rougeing up their cheeks.

But no, it was something else: they never knew they were about to die, it was a total shock. They say people who die sudden, violent deaths are most likely to become ghosts and haunt the earth. On March 28, 1980, all the workers died a sudden, violent death, no time to say goodbye.

Men were obsessed with "the last day." Even seven years later, as we prepared for trial, they could not talk about anything else. Dozens of times, I asked potential witnesses, "Now what did you lose as a result of the closing of the mill?" And they answered with non sequiturs, their little stories about "the last day."

Mr. J. said, for example, "I'm walking off the shift, and my foreman comes over and says, 'Don't come back.'

"I said, 'What?'

"He said, 'Don't come back. It's over.'

"I said, 'What? What?' "

Another man said he was asleep, and someone phoned and woke him from a dream and said, "Don't come in, it's gone."

These stories might go on for fifteen, twenty minutes, just pointless stories. As witnesses, they worried me. They did not seem to care about the loss of pensions, etc. It was that phone call saying, "Don't come back." I was afraid that, as witnesses, they would talk about nothing else, and the jury would think, "What's the big deal about the last day?"

E.B. WHITE, THE LIGHTHOUSE
Technological Progress.
7/13/35.

ON A ROCKY ISLAND in the blue sea, shining white, its tall tower naked and beautiful in the sun, a lighthouse stood, abandoned. We passed by in a boat, remembering when the place was full of life, the keeper tending his light and drawing his pay, his wife hanging out flannel drawers to the sea breeze, his children, like Captain January's daughter, roving the island, watching the ships. Now, in the channel, three or four hundred yards off the rocks, is a gas buoy, winking its mechanical warning, supplanting a whole family. To us, an idle mariner on a painted ocean, the empty lighthouse seemed a symbol of all that is going on in the world: new devices putting men and their families out of work. As we passed the forsaken island and stared at the boarded-up windows and thought about the family applying for relief and the Congress worrying about new taxes to provide the dole, we wondered whether it wouldn't just have been simpler, somehow, for the government never to have bought a gas buoy. Is it really cheaper to support a lighthouse keeper on relief than to support him in his lighthouse? Science, blessing us with gas buoys, is a hard master and perhaps an evil one, giving us steel for flesh, dole for wages, solving every problem save the essential one: what to do about the pride of a former lighthouse-keeper, who doesn't want relief, who wants bread earned by toil, seeing his light shine afar.

Of course, the defenders of scientific progress claim that for every displaced victim of technology, there is a new job opening up-if not in the service industries, or in entertainment, then in the field of invention. Maybe this is true. Certainly there are some queer new jobs that one hears about these days. There is the engineer, for instance, who carved out a niche for himself in the world by devising an apparatus which copes with the problem of the flies which hover by the thousands over the manure beds on mushroom farms. A huge fan sucks the flies across a refrigerating coil, which chills them and drops them, dormant, into large milk cans. The lids are then clamped on the milk cans and the flies are shipped to frog-growers, who chill them again and serve them, with a dash of bitters, to frogs. Maybe some ex-lighthouse-keeper can busy himself, in our brave new world, by thinking up something nifty like that.

WARN—A STATUTORY APPROACH AND OTHER STATUTORY EFFORTS TO ENHANCE JOB SECURITY

In 1988, during a Republican presidential administration, Congress enacted the Worker Adjustment, Retraining and Notification Act, known by the acronym WARN. This was widely heralded as a watershed in our approach to freedom of corporate movement, until then virtually unrestricted. Since WARN is currently one of the statutory cutting edges of job security, you should examine it now to see what protections it affords against loss of a job. If WARN had been in effect at the time of the Local 1330 litigation, would U.S. Steel have been required to give notification under the statute? If it failed to do so, what would have then been its monetary exposure in damages?

Another statutory device that may protect job security, although that is only a byproduct of its primary goal, is the Employee Retirement and Income Security Act (ERISA), a comprehensive statute that regulates pensions and other employee benefits. We will study ERISA further in Chapter IV. ERISA does not require an employer to offer pensions to its employees, but if an employer decides to undertake pension obligations, ERISA does require the employer to set aside adequate funds to cover those pension obligations. It was ERISA which, Geohegan explains, motivated Harvester to play its "shell" game.

EMPLOYMENT–AT–WILL DOCTRINE DOMINATES

Employment-at-will has often been described as follows: in the absence of express limitation on the power to terminate the employment contract and in the absence of a stated specific period of employment, either employers or their employees have the unilateral power to abrogate their relationship for good reasons, bad reasons, or no reasons at all. For virtually all common law (that is, non-statutory) cases involving employment termination, this doctrine has been adopted by the courts of the fifty states.

What is the justification for denying employees protection from bad or no-reason discharges, especially when their employer has promised permanency in order to induce the employees to commence working for the employer? The courts have not been revealingly articulate in their attempts to explain the doctrine. One of the better efforts can be found in *Forrer v. Sears, Roebuck & Co.*, 36 Wis.2d 388 153 N.W.2d 587 (1967), where the Supreme Court of Wisconsin wrote:

> The presumption [that an employment contract is at-will] is grounded on a policy that it would otherwise be unreasonable for a man to bind himself permanently to a position, thus eliminating the possibility of later improving that position. Moreover, a contract of permanent employment is by its very nature indefinite, and thus any effort to interpret the duration of the contract and assess the amount of damages becomes difficult.

While the court allows for the parties to insert explicit language into the contract to remove it from the at-will category, in the absence of such language the court is clear that the presumption of mutual terminability of an employment contract is a given. Notice that the court's justification for its presumption has nothing to do with the intentions of the parties. Rather, its primary premise is that employees in mutuality with employers are free to reject the contract and—what? Get another job, no doubt, is what the court had in mind. And, if there is no other job? One might conclude, if one was concerned about the welfare of the employees (as the court says it is), that all willing employees would be assured, by life or by the law, a job. The court's concern for the freedom of an employee to find better employment is both touching and a judicial statement in support of Professor Epstein. Is the court's concern for mutuality (that is, the court assumes that, if employees are free to quit, it follows that employers have the same freedom to sever the relationship) a reflection of the same spirit that justifies laws that forbid everyone from sleeping under bridges? Surely, whatever the Wisconsin Supreme Court and Professor Epstein mean by freedom, they do not agree with Janis Joplin that freedom means you have nothing left to lose. Or, with Ira Gershwin, who wrote that the only things that are free "are things ... like the stars in the skies"; for everything else, one needs a lock on the door.

"CAUSE" AND ARBITRATION

As the foregoing should make clear to you, the presumptive at-will doctrine is no more than a judicial imposition based on whatever values and empirical intuitions judges may have. Since the judges purport to be enforcing the will of the parties, the latter can provide for a standard other than at-will to determine whether or not discharges are proper. Typically, collective bargaining contracts between employers and unions representing employees provide that the employer must have cause, or good cause, or just cause to terminate or discipline an employee. What is more, these contracts also provide for a neutral arbitrator (really, a private judge) to decide, after a judicial-like hearing, whether the employer had cause. In such a case, the employer has the burden of justifying the discipline. While the bargaining agreements typically do not define the criteria for or the concept of just cause, there is a well-developed body of decisions written by arbitrators all over the country. Not surprisingly, cause is a highly fact specific concept which may vary with a host of factors like, for example, the nature of the workplace, the past practices of the employer, the length and quality of the employee's past service, and the quality and enormity of the alleged cause. But, regardless of the substantive meaning of cause, it is important to know that the employer must satisfy the decision-maker that the termination had a valid and justifying cause.

Similar considerations are prevalent throughout the federal and the state governments, where civil service statutes also require cause to justify discipline. Rather than private arbitrators, governments use public employees, usually referred to as either hearing officers or administrative law judges, to hear and usually decide whether the governmental employer had cause for discipline. Recently, there has been some movement in state legislatures to remove the cause protection given to employees by the civil service statutes. Whether this movement will become significant remains to be seen.

In order to have some sense of the meaning of cause, consider the following arbitration award.

SAMPLE ARBITRATION AWARD

State of New York

Arbitration between

  A   County
and
Local 815, Union
(Pauline Pear Grievance)

Decision and Award of Arbitrator

Fair N. Reasonable, Arbitrator

BACKGROUND

The County charges the grievant, Pauline Pear, with patient abuse based on an incident on the shift that began on February 24, 1992. The written charge contends that the grievant used "inappropriate, threatening and profane language toward a patient and that you also made inappropriate physical contact with this patient. This behavior constitutes patient abuse." The County deemed the incident serious enough to warrant terminating Ms. Pear. The issue before me is whether her termination was for just cause.

Three witnesses gave direct accounts of the events of that night. They differ in several important respects, so this case turns very heavily on which testimony I accept. The three accounts cover different segments of the episode, and only the grievant provides us with a complete narrative from beginning to end. Some of her testimony is uncontradicted.

THE GRIEVANT'S TESTIMONY

The grievant is an LPN who had worked for the County almost 25 years. She was assigned to an ALC (alternate level of care) unit from 11 p.m. to 7 a.m., a Sunday night. It was not her normal shift. One of her first tasks on the Sunday night shift was to enter each patient's room to take vital signs. She went into S's room (to protect his privacy, I won't use his full name) and woke him up to take this information. S. was not very happy about being awakened. She left his room while he went to the bathroom, and when she returned he was very agitated and belligerent. However, he let Ms. Pear take his vital signs.

When Ms. Pear left S's room, he started to bang things around, such as the metal door on his locker. Ms. Pear thought the noise would wake up other patients, so she came back and asked S. to stop. As Ms. Pear left the room, S. followed her and began to scream at her. Ms. Pear told him repeatedly to go back to his room. She says he cursed at her, but she did not swear back at him.

By now, S. was face to face with Ms. Pear in the hall. She told him to go back to his room, and lightly touched him on the shoulder to get him started in that direction. S. then grabbed Ms. Pear's wrist and would not let her go. She began to struggle to get free, and he said "hit me and I'll call the police." Ms. Pear said she would not hit him, and finally yanked her hand free.

At this point. Ms. Pear first saw Nurses' Aide Carla Calvino arrive on the scene. Ms. Calvino stepped between Ms. Pear and S, and led him back to his room. That was the end of the incident.

CARLA CALVINO'S TESTIMONY

Ms. Calvino was assigned to the same unit as Ms. Pear. Between them they divided up taking vital signs. While Ms. Calvino was overseeing one of her patients, she heard a commotion in the hall. She came into the hall and saw Ms. Pear and S. face to face, swearing at each other. He called her a mother fucking bitch, and she called him a mother fucking bastard. Ms. Pear began hitting S. in the shoulder, with an open palm, fairly hard. Ms. Pear repeated, in a taunting way, "S. doesn't like to be touched." Ms. Pear then said to S, as though egging him on, "go ahead and hit me, I'll have to call security." S. did not hit her. At that point Ms. Calvino got between Ms. Pear and S. and said "I'll take him." She began to lead S. back to his room.

As Ms. Calvino was leading S. back to his room, walking with him and holding his hand, Ms. Pear came up from behind and knocked S. between the shoulder blades. It is doubtful that Ms. Calvino directly saw Ms. Pear touch S., but she is certain she heard Ms. Pear hit S. from behind, and she did see S. lunge forward. After that there was at least one other time when S. saw Ms. Pear that evening, and when he did he tensed up.

OLGA KONSTANTIN'S TESTIMONY

Olga Konstantin is a RN who had just completed her prior shift and was off duty. She was waiting in the lounge to finish a conversation with Ms. Calvino, who was doing vital signs. She testified that she heard loud voices in the hall, and went out into the hall. There she saw Ms. Pear in the hall outside S's room. Ms. Pear opened S.'s door and started yelling at him. Both S. and Ms. Pear swore. At one point S. slammed his door shut. Ms. Konstantin did not see Ms. Calvino. Nor did Ms. Konstantin see any physical contact between Ms. Pear and S. Late in her testimony, Ms. Konstantin added that she heard Ms. Pear say something like "start something with me and I'll call security." At that point Ms. Konstantin left to take care of another patient.

I must assume, since Ms. Konstantin didn't see Ms. Calvino at all, that Ms. Konstantin came upon the scene before Ms. Calvino came back out into the hall and witnessed the face to face confrontation between S. and Ms. Pear. If Ms. Konstantin had seen that part of the incident she would have noticed Ms. Calvino. So Ms. Konstantin doesn't shed any light on what I consider the critical elements of the incident.

THE PATIENT S.

S. has been a patient in the various zones on which the three employees work, and all three knew him somewhat. He was a street person, an alcoholic who had suffered a recent head injury, which is probably what brought him back to the hospital. S. is an extremely aggressive patient. At the third day of the hearing I was asked to review in camera his medical records, obtained through court order. I studied these records again in preparing this award. They contain notations of potentially dangerous behavior, verbal abuse, physically threatening gestures, and occasional physical contact such as striking out, scratching and shoving. There is no doubt S. is given to belligerent outbursts, and all the witnesses testified as such. Some nurses and aides seem to have better success dealing with S. than others, as the events of this night show. While the Associate Director of Nursing Services, Ms. Edna Event, attempted to find out from S. what happened that evening, he provided her with no useful information.

THE DIFFERENCES IN THE TESTIMONY

As I said at the outset, the different witnesses saw different segments of the encounter between Ms. Pear and S. Ms. Pear dealt with S. alone in his room. There is no reason to doubt her testimony that S. became agitated when she woke him up to take his vital signs. The County makes no suggestion that it was inappropriate for Ms. Pear to wake him up. Nor does it suggest that Ms. Pear dealt inappropriately with S. when she was taking his vital signs or when she went back in his room to ask him to quiet down.

Ms. Pear testified without contradiction that S. followed her out into the hall. Voices were raised, and if I credit the other two witnesses, one of whom only heard rather than saw some of the exchange, Ms. Pear swore at S. I credit Ms. Pear's testimony that S. grabbed her firmly by the wrists and began to hurt her. Her testimony that she later soaked her wrists is consistent with this account. So is the testimony of her son, who said he saw bruises on his mother's wrists when she came home after the incident. Ms. Pear concedes she first touched S. on the shoulder, so it may be that she provoked S. into grabbing her wrists.

Ms. Pear was asked several times whether it was true, as Ms. Calvino had testified, that Ms. Pear hit S. from behind as Ms. Calvino was escorting him back to his room. Ms. Pear denied this vigorously. On the other hand, after being pressed several times on cross, Ms. Pear conceded that she might have been agitated by the events of the evening by the time she had her face to face confrontation with S. in the hall.

The discrepancies in the testimony are these: All the witnesses agree that S. was cursing, and all the witnesses except Ms. Pear say Ms. Pear cursed too. There is some disagreement as to whether it was Ms. Pear or S. who said "hit me and I'll call security." There is agreement that Ms. Pear touched S. on the shoulder. Ms. Pear minimizes the severity of it, and says she touched him only once, lightly, merely to urge S. to go back to his room. Ms. Calvino says it was a series of somewhat harder blows. Finally, there is an outright discrepancy as to whether Ms. Pear came up from behind S. and hit him in the back.

All three witnesses provided written statements shortly after the incident. I've reviewed them carefully, and they are substantially consistent with the testimony at the arbitration hearing.

The County points to the log of the shift in question, placed in evidence as part of the patient's records. It shows an entry on 2/24/92 at 0515 by Ms. Pear that the patient was extremely verbally abusive at 2400. He "made repeated threatening gestures toward nurse but did not hit nurse." The County makes much of the fact that Ms. Pear waited until after 5 a.m. to make this entry, and that she did not mention that the patient grabbed her by the wrists. The County suggests this shows Ms. Pear knew she had done something wrong, and didn't document the incident until she realized that others had witnessed it. It also argues that the omission of the wrist grabbing in the log suggests that it never happened. Ms. Pear responds that this was not her usual shift, that she was awake long beyond her normal hours, and that fatigue prevented her from making the entry earlier.

Credibility resolutions of the sort raised here can be difficult and painful. In my experience, in the brief opportunity an arbitrator has to observe witnesses in a highly artificial and strained setting, he can seldom be confident based on demeanor alone that one rather than another witness is telling the truth. I assume each of the key witnesses gave an account as she honestly recollected the events of the evening. Ms. Calvino, the key witness for the County, was straightforward, did not exaggerate, committed few discrepancies, and gave little basis to suspect error in her testimony. Ms. Pear was a little more uncertain and hesitant in her testimony. The more useful way of resolving credibility is to see how each story hangs together, and which is the more likely to have occurred in light of the facts that are undisputed.

In this case, the County stresses that the two other witnesses, especially Ms. Calvino, who provided the key testimony, were entirely disinterested. It is conceded all around that neither Ms. Calvino nor Ms. Konstantin knew Ms. Pear, and neither had any reason to fabricate a story. In contrast, I must consider the familiar truism that Ms. Pear has a strong interest in the outcome that might lead her to give testimony that would save her job.

HOW I SEE THE INCIDENT

After putting together the various pieces of testimony, and considering the various factors that bear on credibility, I conclude that the events of February 24 unfolded as follows: After a heated exchange in S.'s room, for which Ms. Pear is really not to blame, S. followed her out into the hall. Voices were raised. I conclude that Ms. Pear used some swear words, although I can't be sure of the extent, for S. swore too, and Ms. Konstantin, who heard but did not see this exchange, would have some trouble being sure who said what. Ms. Pear concedes she can speak loudly, and I conclude she did, and she concedes she was agitated. At this point she touched S. on the shoulder, although it is impossible to tell how hard the contact was. Ms. Calvino did not say it was an extremely hard or violent touching, and it probably was no more than one would expect when there is a heated, frustrating exchange. Still, as I will indicate shortly, Ms. Pear should have realized that any touching can be misunderstood, and that she as the professional should have controlled herself. S.'s rather strenuous reaction shows that he took the touching as provocative.

I am less certain about whether Ms. Pear repeating the statement to S. to go ahead and hit her is so much a taunt as a warning to him that he'd better not hit her. In any event, this exchange doesn't play a major part in my assessment of the overall incident.

At that point Ms. Calvino intervened. I credit Ms. Calvino's account that after she started walking away, Ms. Pear hit S. from behind. I see no reason why Ms. Calvino would make that up. While I believe that Ms. Pear was sincere in her denial that she struck S. from behind, I conclude that she was by then too agitated to realize what she had done. She had gone through a difficult confrontation with a patient who often causes problems, and he had just inflicted a good deal of physical pain on her. I think that in frustration she lashed out at S. I cannot tell if she did so with very much force, for Ms. Calvino didn't see it occur directly, but only heard the contact and saw S. lunge forward. I am unwilling to assume it was a very hard contact.

THE APPROPRIATE DISCIPLINE

Thus, I conclude that there was an incident of inappropriate physical contact. It involved two aspects, the touching of S. on the shoulder and later pushing him from behind. I cannot say that either physical contact was terribly forceful, and I think both were provoked. Still, a professional employee understands that physical contact is inappropriate. Ms. Event testified that nurses are trained to handle these situations. The Patients' Bill of Rights makes clear that nurses are to treat patients with respect. I am less certain of the degree of threatening and profane language that Ms. Pear actually used, but I conclude that because she continued to argue with S., rather than take steps to avoid a further confrontation, the County has sustained at least that part of its charge that alleges inappropriate language. S. presents a sad, perhaps hopeless case. Ms. Pear, the stronger person, entrusted with S.'s care, had to take every step to make sure such an incident didn't happen.

The County suggests that in a situation like this the employee is trained to call security, and that if Ms. Pear had done so the incident wouldn't have escalated. Under the circumstances, which unfolded so quickly, it may not have made sense to call, for Ms. Pear thought the incident would end. Still, it is her responsibility to do whatever is necessary to avoid a verbal and physical confrontation with a patient.

The most compelling consideration in Ms. Pear's favor is that she had almost 25 years of service with the County as an LPN. Ms. Event conceded that her record was good, and the Association introduced two recent evaluations that are very positive. For example, one (U–2) says she is very conscientious in her care and safety of patients, and very thorough and excellent in her care. There is no evidence that Ms. Pear had engaged in past behavior of this sort. The County concedes that it has consistently followed the approach of progressive discipline (which is called for in Article XXXIV, although there seems to be an exception), but contends this incident is so severe that the extreme penalty of discharge is warranted. Indeed, the County handbook for employees (Co. 3) lists threatening, intimidating or coercing any member of the public as grounds for possible immediate discharge. Still, a long and positive record of this sort entitles an employee to some consideration in mitigation, especially when the physical contact was not excessive and where the employee was under some stress and provocation. Provocation does not excuse the offense, nor does the relative mildness of the physical contact make it any less of a violation. The professional employee has to overcome these impulses. On the other hand, the circumstances show the reaction may have been an aberration, unlikely to recur. Ms. Pear's long record gives her some credit to draw upon in mitigation of the extreme penalty of discharge.

At this writing, Ms. Pear has been out of work for more than a year. Discharge is a disproportionate penalty, and so is a suspension without pay for the period of time that has elapsed. The length of a disciplinary suspension is a matter of considerable judgment. If the County had chosen to suspend rather than terminate the grievant, and had selected a period of 3 or 6 months for example, I would have deferred to its judgment. That is because the employer is in a better position than I am, and indeed has the responsibility in the first place to make such a call. But where the County has not chosen a period of suspension, I have the hard task of deciding that question. Over the years of hearing a variety of cases, appropriate patterns emerge. I conclude that a disciplinary suspension of four months without pay is appropriate under the circumstances. Ms. Pear is to be returned to her previous job, with her original seniority interrupted by a four month period in which seniority does not accrue. A notation of a disciplinary suspension may be made in her files. She is to receive back pay for the remaining period of time that she was out of work because of the termination.

Because of the potential for severe harm in cases of patient abuse, the County may as a condition of her reinstatement require Ms. Pear to undergo a reasonable program of counselling and training on dealing with difficult patients. Ms. Pear may be required to undergo this training on her own time, but at County expense.

I will retain jurisdiction on the question of remedy only, until May 1, 1993. If either party notifies me on or before that date that an issue remains as to remedy, I will continue my jurisdiction and notify the parties of the procedures that will follow. If neither party notifies me by that date, my jurisdiction will terminate.

March 22, 1993

Notes

In thinking about arbitration, consider the Billie Tulip problem, 1–1, that opened this book. Suppose that Ms. Tulip's union decided to challenge her termination through arbitration. First, there's the difficult question of which account of the facts to accept. Did Ms. Tulip refuse the job outright, as Marino says, or did she simply ask for more time to contact her shop steward. How would you as an arbitrator tell which version really happened? Maybe there is no "true" version of the incident.

In some sense, didn't each of the participants in the Billie Tulip case see the encounter differently, from his or her own peculiar perspective? Did each version, then, really happen?

But let's accept the company's version. Was the discharge justified? How you answer depends on your values, on your notions of the way a company should operate, and on how far the demands for discipline and hierarchy outweigh the tolerance of individual frailties and needs.

Just what is an arbitrator's role in these sorts of cases? Is she to substitute her judgment for management's? Or should she say: "Management was closer to the incident than I am. They have to live with this worker. I ought to uphold their decision unless I'm convinced it was dead wrong or my sense of justice is outraged."

The Supreme Court warns that in labor arbitration, the decision maker is not "to dispense his own brand of industrial justice," United Steelworkers of America v. Enterprise Wheel & Car Corp., 363 U.S. 593, 597, 80 S.Ct. 1358, 1361, 4 L.Ed.2d 1424 (1960). But Professor Edgar Jones retorts:

> [A]ny arbitrator who has looked down the long corridor of his conscience at a "just cause" disciplinary grievance is apt to feel that, at best, it is a pious sentiment, and, at worst, that it obscures and encumbers the abrasive necessity of pulling all of the elements of decision, including whatever biases he may experience, down into plain view. The parties in the "just cause" provision have conferred upon management the discretion to discipline the employees, but only for "just cause." Can it be said that the arbitrator does not sit to dispense his own brand of justice in that case? At that point, what other brand could there possibly be?

Jones, "Power and Prudence in the Arbitration of Labor Disputes: A Venture in Some Hypotheses," 11 UCLA L.Rev. 675, 764 (1964).

In a First Amendment case challenging the discharge of a public employee, a four-justice plurality of the Supreme Court held that a trial court or jury need not determine what the employee actually said that triggered her firing. Rather, the trier of fact had to ascertain whether (1) the employer made a reasonable investigation to discover what was said and (2) the employer believed the investigation's conclusion that the employee had engaged in conduct which is not protected by the First Amendment. Waters v. Churchill, 511 U.S. 661, 114 S.Ct. 1878, 128 L.Ed.2d 686 (1994). Three members of the Court believed that the only appropriate criterion was the employer's belief, regardless of an investigation. Two members were of the view that the employee's actual comments were protected by the First Amendment and, accordingly, she should have prevailed.

Are there lessons to be learned from the *Waters* case and applied to the run-of-the-mill discharge cases heard by arbitrators? If so, what might those lessons be?

ROGER ABRAMS, A THEORY FOR THE DISCHARGE CASE
36 Arbitration Journal 24, 25 (1981).

Many arbitration opinions read as if [a] retrospective and punitive focus is the appropriate approach to be taken by a neutral under a just cause provision. The opinions relate, often in great detail, what the employee did that led his employer to terminate him. The arbitrator then determines whether the employee is guilty and, if so, whether the misconduct warranted the penalty of discharge. * * * The employer is seen as punishing the employee with discharge and the arbitrator is reviewing the punishment to see whether it "fits the crime." * * *

Although commonly used, this retrospective and punitive approach is not satisfactory. Discharge should not be viewed as punishment for misconduct. Rather, an employee is discharged because his past actions are indicative of what he may do in the future, and the company considers that prospect so unappealing (in a business sense) that it no longer wishes to employ the worker. Under such an approach the events of the past are examined as prologue to the future, as predictors of future performance, and not as a contract default justifying reciprocal action on the employer's part.

* * * The inquiry might be phrased as follows: Can the arbitrator conclude with some degree of confidence that the employer reasonably has predicted that the employee cannot fulfill his employment obligations in the future? * * *

Questions

Is the proposal of Professor Abrams a useful definition of cause? Do you have a better one?

B. LOOKING BEYOND THE AGREEMENT

In the past few decades, most legislatures have rejected the absolute rule of employment-at-will and the right of management to terminate an employee for good, bad or no reason. For example, the at-will doctrine permits employers to terminate an employee because of her race, gender or disability. Statutes that we will examine later in this chapter prohibit such conduct.

Many state courts have not waited for legislative action that directly addresses the scope of the employer's discretion to discipline and discharge. These courts have adapted and applied common law doctrines to give employees "some modicum of judicial protection" at the work place. The decisions which follow raise issues being discussed in state courts throughout the country: whether a termination violates a notion of public policy (a tort claim) or whether the parties by their conduct created an implied limit on the right to discharge (a contract claim). Of course, the answers to the questions vary depending on the jurisdiction. Whatever the law of a particular jurisdiction, however, one should remember that the common law exceptions to the at-will doctrine tend to be given narrow scope and, as a result, rarely give protection to employees. This is especially true for low wage employees whose damages in a potential wrongful discharge suit are usually too small to attract an attorney's involvement on a contingency fee basis.

In reading the cases that follow, be sensitive to the following considerations:

- What is the source of the legal theory: state or federal law? common law, statute or constitution?

- What does a case look like from the plaintiffs' and defendants' perspectives? Think particularly about burdens of proof, evidentiary considerations, remedies.

- For each exception to employment-at-will, does a judge, a legislature or both have competence to formulate the exception?

- What would a comprehensive provision regulating the right to discharge provide?

- Is the goal of fair treatment best achieved through comprehensive federal or state laws, litigation, or private agreement?

- Are the costs of regulating employment decisions too high to justify second-guessing managerial decisions on discharge and discipline?

- If we assume these costs are "too high," does that assumption justify our presuming the managerial decisions were correct?

1. CASE LAW

a. *Discharge That Contravenes Public Policy*

SHEETS v. TEDDY'S FROSTED FOODS, INC.

Supreme Court of Connecticut, 1980.
179 Conn. 471, 427 A.2d 385.

Peters, Associate Justice.

. . . Since this appeal is before us pursuant to a motion to strike, we must take the facts to be those alleged in the plaintiff's complaint . . . The complaint alleges that for a four-year period, from November 1973 to November 1977, the plaintiff was employed by the defendant, a producer of frozen food products, as its quality control director and subsequently also as operations manager. In the course of his employment, the plaintiff received periodic raises and bonuses. In his capacity as quality control director and operations manager, the plaintiff began to notice deviations from the specifications contained in the defendant's standards and labels, in that some vegetables were substandard and some meat components underweight. These deviations meant that the defendant's products violated the express representations contained in the defendant's labeling; false or misleading labels in turn violate the provisions of General Statutes § 19–222, the Connecticut Uniform Food, Drug and Cosmetic Act. In May of 1977, the plaintiff communicated in writing to the defendant concerning the use of substandard raw materials and underweight components in the defendant's finished products. His recommendations for more selective purchasing and conforming components were ignored. On November 3, 1977, his employment with the defendant was terminated. Although the stated reason for his discharge was unsatisfactory performance of his duties, he was actually dismissed in retaliation for his efforts to ensure that the defendant's products would comply with the applicable law relating to labeling and licensing. * * *

The issue before us is whether to recognize an exception to the traditional rules governing employment at will so as to permit a cause of action for wrongful discharge where the discharge contravenes a clear mandate of public policy. In addressing that claim, we must clarify what is not at stake in this litigation. The plaintiff does not challenge the general proposition that contracts of permanent employment, or for an indefinite term, are terminable at will. Nor does he argue that contracts terminable at will permit termination only upon a showing of just cause for dismissal. Some statutes do impose limitations of just cause upon the power to terminate some contracts; but the legislature has recently refused to interpolate such a requirement into contracts of employment. There is a significant distinction between a criterion of just cause and what the plaintiff is seeking. "Just cause" substantially limits employer discretion to terminate, by requiring the employer, in all instances, to proffer a proper reason for dismissal, by forbidding the employer to act arbitrarily or capriciously. By contrast, the plaintiff asks only that the employer be responsible in damages if the former employee can prove a demonstrably *improper* reason for dismissal, a reason whose impropriety is derived from some important violation of public policy. [Emphasis in original.—Eds.]

The argument that contract rights which are inherently legitimate may yet give rise to liability in tort if they are exercised improperly is not a novel one. Although private persons have the right not to enter into contracts, failure to contract under circumstances in which others are seriously misled gives rise to a variety of claims sounding in tort. The development of liability in contract for action induced by reliance upon a promise, despite the absence of common-law consideration normally required to bind a promisor, rests upon principles derived at least in part from the law of tort. By way of analogy, we have long recognized abuse of process as a cause of action in tort whose gravamen is the misuse or misapplication of process, its use "in an improper manner or to accomplish a purpose for which it was not designed."

It would be difficult to maintain that the right to discharge an employee hired at will is so fundamentally different from other contract rights that its exercise is never subject to judicial scrutiny regardless of how outrageous, how violative of public policy, the employer's conduct may be. The defendant does not seriously contest the propriety of cases in other jurisdictions that have found wrongful and actionable a discharge in retaliation for the exercise of an employee's right to: (1) refuse to commit perjury; (2) file a workmen's compensation claim; (3) engage in union activity; (4) perform jury duty. While it may be true that these cases are supported by mandates of public policy derived directly from the applicable state statutes and constitutions, it is equally true that they serve at a minimum to establish the principle that public policy imposes some limits on unbridled discretion to terminate the employment of someone hired at will. No case has been called to our attention in which, despite egregiously outrageous circumstances, the employer's contract rights have been permitted to override competing claims of public policy, although there are numerous cases in which the facts were found not to support the employee's claim.

The issue then becomes the familiar common-law problem of deciding where and how to draw the line between claims that genuinely involve the mandates of public policy and are actionable, and ordinary disputes between employee and employer that are not. We are mindful that courts should not lightly intervene to impair the exercise of managerial discretion or to foment unwarranted litigation. We are, however, equally mindful that the myriad of employees without the bargaining power to command employment contracts for a definite term are entitled to a modicum of judicial protection when their conduct as good citizens is punished by their employers.

The central allegation of the plaintiff's complaint is that he was discharged because of his conduct in calling to his employer's attention repeated violations of the Connecticut Uniform Food, Drug and Cosmetic Act. This act prohibits the sale of mislabeled food. General Statutes §§ 19–213,[4] 19–222.[5] The act, in § 19–215,[6] imposes criminal penalties

---

4. "[General Statutes] Sec. 19–213. PROHIBITED ACTS. The following acts and the causing thereof shall be prohibited: (a) The sale in intrastate commerce of any food, drug, device or cosmetic that is adulterated or misbranded; (b) the adulteration or misbranding of any food, drug, device or cosmetic in intrastate commerce. . . ."

5. Section 19–222 provides in relevant part: "MISBRANDED FOOD. A food shall be deemed to be misbranded: (a) If its labeling is false or misleading in any particular."

6. Section 19–215 provides in relevant part: "PENALTIES: (A) Any person who violates any provision of section 19–213 shall, on conviction thereof, be imprisoned not more than six months or fined not more than five hundred dollars or both. . . . (b) Notwithstanding the provisions of subsection (a) of this section, any person who violates any provision of section 19–213, with intent to defraud or mislead, shall be imprisoned not more than one year or fined not more than one thousand dollars or both.

upon anyone who violates § 19–213; subsection (b) of § 19–215 makes it clear that criminal sanctions do not depend upon proof of intent to defraud or mislead, since special sanctions are imposed for intentional misconduct. The plaintiff's position as quality control director and operations manager might have exposed him to the possibility of criminal prosecution under this act. The act was intended to "safeguard the public health and promote the public welfare by protecting the consuming public from injury by product use and the purchasing public from injury by merchandising deceit ..." General Statutes § 19–211.

It is useful to compare the factual allegations of this complaint with those of other recent cases in which recovery was sought for retaliatory discharge. In Geary v. United States Steel Corporation [456 Pa. 171, 319 A.2d 174 (1974)], in which the plaintiff had disputed the safety of tubular steel casings, he was denied recovery because, as a company salesman, he had neither the expertise nor the corporate responsibility to "exercise independent, expert judgment in matters of product safety." Id., 319 A.2d 178. By contrast, this plaintiff unless his title is meaningless, did have responsibility for product quality control. Three other recent cases in which the plaintiff's claim survived demurrer closely approximate the claim before us. In Trombetta v. Detroit, Toledo & Ironton R. Co., 81 Mich.App. 489, 496, 265 N.W.2d 385 (1978), a cause of action was stated when an employee alleged that he had been discharged in retaliation for his refusal to manipulate and alter sampling results for pollution control reports required by Michigan law. There as here falsified reports would have violated state law. In Harless v. First National Bank in Fairmont, 246 S.E.2d 270, 276 (W.Va.1978), an employee stated a cause of action when he alleged that he had been discharged in retaliation for his efforts to ensure his employer's compliance with state and federal consumer credit protection laws. There as here the legislature had established a public policy of consumer protection. In Pierce v. Ortho Pharmaceutical Corporation, 166 N.J.Super. 335, 399 A.2d 1023, 1026–1027 (1979), the plaintiff was entitled to a trial to determine whether she had been wrongfully discharged for refusing to pursue clinical testing of a new drug containing a high level of saccharin; the court noted that the plaintiff's status as a physician entitled her to invoke the Hippocratic Oath as well as state statutory provisions governing the licensing and the conduct of physicians. There as here the case might have been dismissed as a conflict in judgment.

In the light of these recent cases, which evidence a growing judicial receptivity to the recognition of a tort claim for wrongful discharge, the trial court was in error in granting the defendant's motion to strike. The plaintiff alleged that he had been dismissed in retaliation for his insistence that the defendant comply with the requirements of a state statute, the Food, Drug and Cosmetic Act. We need not decide whether violation of a state statute is invariably a prerequisite to the conclusion that a challenged discharge violates public policy. Certainly when there is a relevant state statute, we should not ignore the statement of public policy that it represents. For today, it is enough to decide that an employee should not be put to an election whether to risk criminal sanction or to jeopardize his continued employment.

There is error and the case is remanded for further proceedings.

COTTER, C.J. (dissenting)

* * * The majority by seeking to extend a "modicum" of judicial protection to shield employees from retaliatory discharges instead offers them a sword with which to coerce employers to retain them in their employ. In recognizing an exception to the traditional rules governing employment at will and basing a new cause of action for retaliatory discharge on the facts of this case, the majority is necessarily led to the creation of an overly broad new cause of action whose nuisance value alone may impair employers' ability to hire and retain employees who are best suited to their requirements. Other jurisdictions which have recognized a cause of action for retaliatory discharge have done so on the basis of a much clearer and more direct contravention of a mandate of public policy. * * *

In contrast, the purposes of the statute the majority would rely on, the Connecticut Uniform Food, Drug and Cosmetic Act, General Statutes §§ 19–211 through 19–239, can only be considered as, at most, marginally affected by an allegedly retaliatory discharge of an employee who observed the supposed sale of shortweight frozen entrees and the use of U.S. Government Certified "Grade B" rather than "Grade A" vegetables. A retaliatory discharge in the present case would not necessarily thwart or inhibit the Connecticut Uniform Food, Drug and Cosmetic Act's purpose of protecting the consumer. The plaintiff, if he desired to protect the consumer, could have communicated, even anonymously, to the commissioner of consumer affairs his concerns that his employer was violating the Food, Drug and Cosmetic Act so as to invoke the statute's enforcement mechanisms. To further and comply with the public policy expressed in Connecticut's Uniform Food, Drug and Cosmetic Act and to avoid the exceedingly remote possibility of criminal sanctions,[1] the plaintiff need not have jeopardized his continued employment. There is no indication that the plaintiff has either, before or after his discharge, informed or even attempted to inform the commissioner of consumer protection of violations the plaintiff claims to have first noted in his fourth month as its operations manager. Unlike those cases where an employer allegedly discharged employees for engaging in union activities or filing workmen's compensation claims and the discharge itself contravened a statutory mandate, in the present case the discharge itself at most only indirectly impinged on the statutory mandate.

Consequently, the majority seemingly invites the unrestricted use of an allegation of almost any statutory or even regulatory violation by an

---

1. There is no allegation in the plaintiff's amended complaint that he was exposed to criminal liability by the defendant's alleged violations and it should be noted that those presumed violations could well fall within the Uniform Food, Drug and Cosmetic Act's provisions for minor violations which the commissioner of consumer protection is not required to report to the state's attorney for possible institution of criminal proceedings. General Statutes § 19–218.

employer as the basis for a cause of action by a discharged employee hired for an indefinite term. By establishing a cause of action, grounded upon "intentionally tortious conduct," for retaliatory discharges which do not necessarily in and of themselves directly contravene statutory mandates, the majority is creating an open-ended arena for judicial policy making and the usurpation of legislative functions. To base this new cause of action on a decision as to whether an alleged reason for discharge "is derived from some important violation of public policy" is not to create adequate and carefully circumscribed standards for this new cause of action but is to invite the opening of a Pandora's box of unwarranted litigation arising from the hope that the judicial estimate of derivation, importance, and public policy matches that of the plaintiff.

Moreover, this is policy making that the Connecticut legislature recently declined to undertake. In 1974, the Connecticut General Assembly considered and rejected a bill which would have provided that "[a]ny employee [including private sector employees] hired for an indefinite term, may be dismissed only for just cause or because of the employer's reduction in work force for business reasons." Representative Francis J. Mahoney, the bill's sponsor, gave examples of the kind of discharges he intended the bill to cover: discharges for overlooking violations of building codes or for campaigning for the wrong political party.[2] Thus, "just cause" in the overwhelmingly rejected 1974 bill was meant to encompass the kinds of retaliatory discharge that the majority approves as a new cause of action. Furthermore, the most recent legislature enacted a statute protecting "whistle blowing" state employees [and] addressed the problem of retaliatory dismissals of building officials. The legislature is thus adopting appropriate remedies for certain types of retaliatory discharges at its own considered pace and there appears to be no urgency for this court to violate that measured momentum by creating a broadly based new cause of action. In these circumstances, this court should consider itself precluded from substituting its own ideas of what might be wise policy in place of a clear expression of legislative will.

THE CONCERN ABOUT PUBLIC POLICY

What criteria did Justice Peters identify as relevant when a wage earner is dismissed?

If his supervisor fired Sheets for attending the ballet on his day off, would Sheets have a basis for claiming wrongful discharge? It is unlikely that there is a statute that specifically prohibits discharge in such circumstances, and equally unlikely that a court would overturn the discharge. But how is attending the ballet—or viewing an X-rated

---

2. As the trial court points out in its memorandum of decision, the 1974 bill was just one of four bills introduced in recent years that the General Assembly has failed to pass which were aimed at providing a remedy for employees who claimed unjust discharges. * * *

movie—relevant to the ability to do a job? Would you limit the public policy exception to employment at will to those terminations that offend a significant societal interest derived from the Constitution or a statute? Or would you forbid any discharge that is not job related?

Sheets raises a more fundamental question. Do we condemn a discharge because it is wrong to discharge a satisfactory employee for engaging in an act of civic virtue? Or are we protecting the worker primarily because we want to promote compliance with public policy?

b. *Implied–In–Law Good Faith and Fair Dealing*

FORTUNE v. NATIONAL CASH REGISTER

The Supreme Judicial Court of Massachusetts, 1977.
373 Mass. 96, 364 N.E.2d 1251.

ABRAMS, JUSTICE.

Orville E. Fortune (Fortune), a former salesman of The National Cash Register Company (NCR), brought a suit to recover certain commissions allegedly due as a result of a sale of cash registers to First National Stores Inc. (First National) in 1968. Counts 1 and 2 of Fortune's amended declaration claimed bonus payments under the parties' written contract of employment. The third count sought recovery in quantum meruit for the reasonable value of Fortune's services relating to the same sales transaction. Judgment on a jury verdict for Fortune was reversed by the Appeals Court, and this court granted leave to obtain further appellate review. We affirm the judgment of the Superior Court. We hold, for the reasons stated herein, there was no error in submitting the issue of "bad faith" termination of an employment at will contract to the jury.

The issues before the court are raised by NCR's motion for directed verdicts. Accordingly, we summarize the evidence most favorable to the plaintiff.

Fortune was employed by NCR under a written "salesman's contract" which was terminable at will, without cause, by either party on written notice. The contract provided that Fortune would receive a weekly salary in a fixed amount plus a bonus for sales made within the "territory" (i.e., customer accounts or stores) assigned to him for "coverage or supervision," whether the sale was made by him or someone else. The amount of the bonus was determined on the basis of "bonus credits," which were computed as a percentage of the price of products sold. Fortune would be paid a percentage of the applicable bonus credit as follows: (1) 75% if the territory was assigned to him at the date of order, (2) 25% if the territory was assigned to him at the date of delivery and installation, or (3) 100% if the territory was assigned to him at both times. The contract further provided that the "bonus interest" would terminate if shipment of the order was not made within eighteen months from the date of the order unless (1) the territory was assigned to him for coverage at the date of delivery and installation, or (2) special engineering was required to fulfill the contract. In addition, NCR reserved the right to sell products in the salesman's territory without paying a bonus. However, this right could be exercised only on written notice.

In 1968, Fortune's territory included First National. The account had been part of his territory for the preceding six years; he had been successful in obtaining several orders from First National, including a million dollar order in 1963. Sometime in late 1967 or early 1968, NCR introduced a new model cash register, Class 5. Fortune corresponded with First National in an effort to sell the machine. He also helped to arrange for a demonstration of the Class 5 to executives of First National on October 4, 1968. NCR had a team of men also working on this sale.

On November 27, 1968, NCR's manager of chain and department stores, and the Boston branch manager, both part of NCR's team, wrote to First National regarding the Class 5. The letter covered a number of subjects, including price protection, trade-ins, and trade-in protection against obsolescence. While NCR normally offered price protection for only an eighteen-month term, apparently the size of the proposed order from First National caused NCR to extend its price protection terms for either a two-year or four-year period. On November 29, 1968, First National signed an order for 2,008 Class 5 machines to be delivered over a four-year period at a purchase price of approximately $5,000,000. Although Fortune did not participate in the negotiation of the terms of the order, his name appeared on the order form in the space entitled "salesman credited." The amount of the bonus credit as shown on the order was $92,079.99.

On January 6, 1969, the first working day of the year, Fortune found an envelope on his desk at work. It contained a termination notice addressed to his home dated December 2, 1968. Shortly after receiving the notice, Fortune spoke to the Boston branch manager with whom he was friendly. The manager told him, "You are through," but, after considering some of the details necessary for the smooth operation of the First National order, told him to "stay on," and to "(k)eep on doing what you are doing right now." Fortune remained with the company in a position entitled "sales support." In this capacity, he coordinated and expedited delivery of the machines to First National under the November 29 order as well as servicing other accounts.

Commencing in May or June, Fortune began to receive some bonus commissions on the First National order. Having received only 75% of the applicable bonus due on the machines which had been delivered and installed, Fortune spoke with his manager about receiving the full amount of the commission. Fortune was told "to forget about it." Sixty-one years old at that time, and with a son in college, Fortune concluded that it "was a good idea to forget it for the time being."

NCR did pay a systems and installations person the remaining 25% of the bonus commissions due from the First National order although contrary to its usual policy of paying only salesmen a bonus.

Approximately eighteen months after receiving the termination notice, Fortune, who had been with NCR for almost twenty-five years, was asked to retire. When he refused, he was fired in June of 1970. Fortune did not receive any bonus payments on machines which were delivered to First National after this date.

At the close of the plaintiff's case, the defendant moved for a directed verdict, arguing that there was no evidence of any breach of contract, and adding that the existence of a contract barred recovery under the quantum meruit count. Ruling that Fortune could recover if the termination and firing were in bad faith, the trial judge, without specifying on which count, submitted this issue to the jury. NCR then rested and, by agreement of counsel, the case was sent to the jury for special verdicts on two questions:

"1. Did the Defendant act in bad faith ... when it decided to terminate the Plaintiff's contract as a salesman by letter dated December 2, 1968, delivered on January 6, 1969?

"2. Did the Defendant act in bad faith ... when the Defendant let the Plaintiff go on June 5, 1970?"

The jury answered both questions affirmatively, and judgment entered in the sum of $45,649.62.

The central issue on appeal is whether this "bad faith" termination constituted a breach of the employment at will contract. Traditionally, an employment contract which is "at will" may be terminated by either side without reason.

The contract at issue is a classic terminable at will employment contract. It is clear that the contract itself reserved to the parties an explicit power to terminate the contract without cause or written notice. It is also clear that under the express terms of the contract, Fortune has received all the bonus commissions to which he is entitled. Thus, NCR claims that it did not breach the contract, and that it has no further liability to Fortune. According to a literal reading of the contract, NCR is correct.

However, Fortune argues that, in spite of the literal wording of the contract, he is entitled to a jury determination on NCR's motives in terminating his services under the contract and in finally discharging him. We agree. We hold that NCR's written contract contains an implied covenant of good faith and fair dealing, and a termination not made in good faith constitutes a breach of the contract.

We do not question the general principles that an employer is entitled to be motivated by and to serve its own legitimate business interests; that an employer must have wide latitude in deciding whom it will employ in the face of the uncertainties of the business world; and that an employer needs flexibility in the face of changing circumstances.

We recognize the employer's need for a large amount of control over its work force. However, we believe that where, as here, commissions are to be paid for work performed by the employee, the employer's decision to terminate its at will employee should be made in good faith. NCR's right to make decisions in its own interest is not, in our view, unduly hampered by a requirement of adherence to this standard.

On occasion, some courts have avoided the rigidity of the "at will" rule by fashioning a remedy in tort. We believe, however, that in this case there is remedy on the express contract. In so holding, we are merely recognizing the general requirement in this Commonwealth that parties to contracts and commercial transactions must act in good faith toward one another. Good faith and fair dealing between parties are pervasive requirements in our law; it can be said fairly that parties to contracts or commercial transactions are bound by this standard.

In the instant case, we need not pronounce our adherence to so broad a policy [as described in other states' courts' opinions cited by the court] nor need we speculate as to whether the good faith requirement is implicit in every contract for employment at will. It is clear, however, that on the facts before us, a finding is warranted that a breach of the contract occurred. Where the principal seeks to deprive the agent of all compensation by terminating the contractual relationship when the agent is on the brink of successfully completing the sale, the principal has acted in bad faith and the ensuing transaction between the principal and the buyer is to be regarded as having been accomplished by the agent. The same result obtains where the principal attempts to deprive the agent of any portion of a commission due the agent. Courts have often applied this rule to prevent overreaching by employers and the forfeiture by employees of benefits almost earned by the rendering of substantial services.

We think that NCR's conduct in June, 1970 permitted the jury to find bad faith.

Questions

1. In general, contract law assumes an implied promise of good faith and fair dealing. Why should there be an exception to that generalization, as there is in almost all states, when the contract is one of employment?

2. Is the *Fortune* court holding that, like contracts generally, all employment contracts have an implied promise of good faith?

3. What does "good faith" mean in a context where the employer is assumed to have the right to run its business?

4. In holding that the jury could properly and reasonably find the employer acted in bad faith, the court also suggested the jury, instead, could have properly found good faith. In so stating, the court observed (in a part of the opinion not reproduced) that the jury could have found the employer was motivated by a desire to keep the bonus to a minimum ("bad faith") or

motivated by the knowledge the plaintiff had little or nothing to do with the sale ("good faith"). How does a jury decide such an issue?

KUMPF v. STEINHAUS

United States Court of Appeals, Seventh Circuit, 1985.
779 F.2d 1323.

EASTERBROOK, CIRCUIT JUDGE.

From 1973 until August 1983, William A. Kumpf was the president and chief executive officer of Lincoln National Sales Corp. of Wisconsin (Lincoln Wisconsin). He owned 20% of Lincoln Wisconsin's stock. Lincoln National Sales Corp. (Lincoln Sales) owned the other 80% of the stock, and two of the three members of Lincoln Wisconsin's board of directors were employees of Lincoln Sales. Lincoln Sales is in turn a subsidiary of Lincoln National Life Insurance Co. (Lincoln Life). Lincoln Sales is the marketing arm of Lincoln Life; Lincoln Wisconsin was the Wisconsin agency of Lincoln Sales.

In April 1981, Orin A. Steinhaus became an executive vice-president of Lincoln Life, leaving a post as head of Lincoln's sales agency in Columbus, Ohio. The president of Lincoln Life gave Steinhaus and other employees the task of revising the firm's sales structure, which was losing money. Lincoln Life closed 25 sales agencies and decided to consolidate others. In August 1983, Steinhaus decided to consolidate five midwestern sales agencies into a single agency. (Doubtless other officers of Lincoln Life concurred in these decisions, but for simplicity we write as if Steinhaus made all decisions himself.) He instructed Lincoln Sales's directors on the board of Lincoln Wisconsin to approve a merger of Lincoln Wisconsin into Lincoln Chicago Corp. (Lincoln Chicago); Lincoln Wisconsin's board approved the merger by a vote of two to one, over Kumpf's dissent. Lincoln Wisconsin disappeared, and so did Kumpf's job. This litigation is the residue.

* * * [T]he initial question is whether Kumpf has identified an unsupportable consideration that led to his dismissal. The only one Kumpf presses on us is Steinhaus's self-interest (Kumpf calls it "greed"). * * *

The managers of the firm at the apex of the structure have an obligation to manage the whole structure in the interests of investors. Kumpf and Lincoln Wisconsin knew that when they started—when Kumpf took the risks associated with owning 20% of the stock, and holding one of three seats on the board, in a subsidiary of Lincoln Life. The superior managers in such a structure try to serve the interests of investors and other participants as a whole, and these interests will not always be congruent with the interests of managers of subsidiaries. Corporate reorganizations may reduce the costs of operation and put the structure in the hands of better managers, though this may be costly to existing managers.

If Kumpf had directly challenged the wisdom of a business decision of the managers of Lincoln Life, he would have been rebuffed with a reference to the business judgment doctrine—a rule of law that insulates business decisions from most forms of review. Courts recognize that managers have both better information and better incentives than they. The press of market forces—managers at Lincoln Life must continually attract new employees and capital, which they cannot do if they exploit existing participants or perform poorly—will more effectively serve the interests of all participants than will an error-prone judicial process.

The privilege to manage corporate affairs is reinforced by the rationale of employment at will. Kumpf had no tenure of office. The lack of job security gave him a keen motive to do well. Security of position may diminish that incentive. See Richard A. Epstein, In Defense of the Contract at Will, 51 U.Chi.L.Rev. 947 (1984). Employment at will, like the business judgment doctrine, also keeps debates about business matters out of the hands of courts. People who enter a contract without a fixed term know there is some prospect that their business partners may try to take advantage of them or simply make a blunder in deciding whether to continue the relationship. Yet people's concern for their reputation and their ability to make other advantageous contracts in the future leads them to try to avoid both mistakes and opportunistic conduct. Contracting parties may sensibly decide that it is better to tolerate the risk of error—to leave correction to private arrangements— than to create a contractual right to stay in office in the absence of a "good" reason. The reason for a business decision may be hard to prove, and the costs of proof plus the risk of mistaken findings of breach may reduce the productivity of the employment relation.

Many people have concluded otherwise; contracts terminable only for cause are common. But in Wisconsin, courts enforce whichever solution the parties select. A contract at will may be terminated for any reason (including bad faith) or no reason, without judicial review; the only exception is a termination that violates "a fundamental and well-defined public policy as evidenced by existing law." Brockmeyer v. Dun & Bradstreet, 113 Wis.2d 561, 335 N.W.2d 834, 840 (1983). Greed—the motive Kumpf attributes to Steinhaus—does not violate a "fundamental and well-defined public policy" of Wisconsin. Greed is the foundation of much economic activity, and Adam Smith told us that each person's pursuit of his own interests drives the economic system to produce more and better goods and services for all. "It is not from the benevolence of the butcher, the brewer, or the baker, that we expect our dinner, but from their regard to their own interest. We address ourselves, not to their humanity but to their self-love, and never talk to them of our own necessities but of their advantages." The Wealth of Nations 14 (1776; Modern Library ed.).

The reasons that led Wisconsin to hold in Brockmeyer that it is "unnecessary and unwarranted for the courts to become arbiters of any termination that may have a tinge of bad faith attached" (335 N.W.2d at 838) also establish that greed is not the sort of prohibited motive that will support Kumpf's tort action. In [another case] the court stated that majority shareholders possess a privilege "to take whatever action they deem advisable to further the interests of the corporation." The court then quoted with approval from a text stating that a person enjoys no privilege "if his object is to put pressure upon the plaintiff and coerce him into complying with the defendant's wishes in some collateral matter."

If Steinhaus got rid of Kumpf because Kumpf would not marry Steinhaus's daughter, that would have been pressure in a "collateral matter." It is quite another thing to say that a jury must determine whether Steinhaus installed himself as head of Lincoln Chicago "predominantly" because he thought that would be good for Lincoln Life or "predominantly" because Steinhaus would enjoy the extra income. The decision to consolidate agencies and change managers is not "collateral" to the business of Lincoln Life, and the rationale of the business judgment rule interdicts any attempt to look behind the decision to determine whether Steinhaus is an astute manager.

Often corporations choose to align the interests of investors and managers by giving the managers a share of the firm's revenue or profits. Commissions, the ownership of stock or options, and bonuses all make managers and investors do well or poorly together. Lincoln Life chose to give managers a financial stake in each agency's revenues. Steinhaus was privileged to act with that incentive in mind. Suppose a major auto manufacturer decides to pay its chief executive officer $1 per year plus a percentage of the firm's profit. The officer then closes an unprofitable subsidiary (owned 80% by the firm), discharging its employees. Under Kumpf's theory any of the employees would be entitled to recover from the executive if the jury should estimate that in the executive's mind making money for himself predominated over making money for the firm. Yet since the two are the same thing, that would be a bootless investigation, and one with great potential to stifle the executive's vigorous pursuit of the firm's best interests. We do not think this is the law in Wisconsin or anywhere else.

Kumpf presents one last argument. He asked the judge to charge the jury that it should consider "recognized ethical codes or standards for a particular area of business activity" and "concepts of fair play" in deciding whether the defendants' acts were privileged. This "business ethics" instruction, Kumpf contends, would have allowed the jury to supplement the rules of tort and contract with " 'the rules of the game' " in business. Although language of this sort appears in the Restatement (Second) of Torts § 767 comment j at p. 37 (1979), it was not designed to be given to a jury. It would leave the jury at sea, free to impose a brand of ethics for which people may not have bargained. No case in Wisconsin has required an instruction even remotely like this one.

The "rules of the game" are important in deciding what sorts of acts are privileged. If Lincoln Life had assured Kumpf that his agency would not be obliterated without his being given an opportunity to take a new job within the firm, that might cast a different light on his claim for interference with contract. But Kumpf does not say that he received such assurance or that any other understood "rule" has been breached. He therefore had to be content with the rules reflected in the definition of privileged acts.

The contention that businesses should be more considerate of their officers should be addressed to the businesses and to legislatures. Some firms will develop reputations for kind treatment of executives, some will be ruthless. Some will seek to treat executives well but find that the exigencies of competition frustrate their plans. The rule of this game is that Kumpf was an employee at will and had no right to stay on if his board wanted him gone. His board was dominated by people who answered to Lincoln Sales, which answered to Lincoln Life. Kumpf did not bargain for legal rights against Lincoln Life, and the judge properly declined to allow the jury to convert moral and ethical claims into legal duties.

Affirmed.

Questions and Notes

How would Judge Easterbrook have dealt with his own hypothetical about Kumpf not marrying Steinhaus' daughter? Would that be an example of a termination not in good faith?

How would the *Fortune* court have resolved the *Kumpf* case?

Judge Easterbrook's approach is illustrative of a solicitude for managerial decisions that presumptively enhance the profitability of the enterprise; these decisions are essentially unreviewable, he says, per the "business judgment doctrine." Is that a euphemism for "might makes right?" Or, a rationalization to avoid second-guessing employers who have fired their employees for reasons we might deem not just? Does Judge Easterbrook's view reflect any interest in the rational expectations of one of the parties to the contract, the employee? Consider the following observation by Professor Clyde Summers:

CLYDE SUMMERS, THE CONTRACT OF EMPLOYMENT AND THE RIGHTS OF INDIVIDUAL EMPLOYEES: FAIR REPRESENTATION AND EMPLOYMENT AT WILL
52 Fordham L.Rev. 1082, 1106 (1984).

* * * Spelling out all of the terms in advance is impossible, for the [employment] relationship changes, often in an evolutionary process that reshapes rights and duties without explicit recognition. Also, the employer must have a measure of freedom to change the understanding that each will show respect for the other's interests and that the employer will not arbitrarily change the rules so as to change the character of the relationship. [The obligation must reach beyond gross misappropriation or considerations like] the longevity of service, the expressed policy of the employer, the adoption of procedures for adjudicating disputes, and

the lack of good cause for termination. In many respects the duty of good faith and fair dealing expresses the basic contract principle that the employer is bound to act as he has led the employee to believe he will act. This principle, in turn, may be informed by how reasonable employers act and what is considered to meet community standards of fairness. An employer ought not be able to escape obligations to his employees by asserting, after the fact, that his employees know he is unfair and is not to be trusted.

c. *Implied–In–Fact Promises of Job Security*

PUGH v. SEE'S CANDIES, INC.

Court of Appeal, First District, Division 1, California, 1981.
116 Cal.App.3d 311, 171 Cal.Rptr. 917.

GRODIN, J.

After 32 years of employment with See's Candies, Inc., in which he worked his way up the corporate ladder from dishwasher to vice president in charge of production and member of the board of directors, Wayne Pugh was fired. Asserting that he had been fired in breach of contract and for reasons which offend public policy, he sued his former employer seeking compensatory and punitive damages for wrongful termination, and joined as a defendant a labor organization which, he alleged, had conspired in or induced the wrongful conduct. The case went to trial before a jury, and upon conclusion of the plaintiff's case-in-chief, the trial court granted the defendants' motions for nonsuit, and this appeal followed.

SUMMARY OF THE EVIDENCE

We summarize the evidence presented to the jury. The defendant employer is in the business of manufacturing fresh candy at its plants in Los Angeles and South San Francisco and marketing the candy through its own retail outlets.

Pugh began working for See's at its Bay Area plant (then in San Francisco) in January 1941 washing pots and pans. From there he was promoted to candy maker, and held that position until the early part of 1942, when he entered the Air Corps. Upon his discharge in 1946, he returned to See's and his former position. After a year, he was promoted to the position of production manager in charge of personnel, ordering raw materials and supervising the production of candy. When, in 1950, See's moved into a large plant in San Francisco, Pugh had responsibility for laying out the design of the plant, taking bids, and assisting in the construction. While working at this plant, Pugh sought to increase his value to the company by taking three years of night classes in plant layout, economics and business law. When See's moved its San Francisco plant to its present location in South San Francisco in 1957, Pugh was given responsibilities for the new location similar to those which he undertook in 1950. By this time, See's business and its number of production employees had increased substantially, and a new position of assistant production manager was created under Pugh's supervision.

In 1971, Pugh was again promoted, this time as vice president in charge of production and was placed upon the board of directors of See's northern California subsidiary, "in recognition of his accomplishments." In 1972, he received a gold watch from See's "in appreciation of 31 years of loyal service."

In May 1973, Pugh traveled with Charles Huggins, then president of See's, and their respective families to Europe on a business trip to visit candy manufacturers and to inspect new equipment. Mr. Huggins returned in early June to attend a board of director's meeting while Pugh and his family remained in Europe on a planned vacation.

Upon Pugh's return from Europe on Sunday, June 25, 1973, he received a message directing him to fly to Los Angeles the next day and meet with Mr. Huggins.

Pugh went to Los Angeles expecting to be told of another promotion. The preceding Christmas season had been the most successful in See's history, the Valentine's Day holiday of 1973 set a new sales record for See's, and the March 1973 edition of See's Newsletter, containing two pictures of Pugh, carried congratulations on the increased production.

Instead, upon Pugh's arrival at Mr. Huggins' office, the latter said, "Wayne, come in and sit down. We might as well get right to the point. I have decided your services are no longer required by See's Candies. Read this and sign it." Huggins handed him a letter confirming his termination and directing him to remove that day "only personal papers and possessions from your office," but "absolutely no records, formulas or other material"; and to turn in and account for "all keys, credit cards, et cetera." The letter advised that Pugh would receive unpaid salary, bonuses and accrued vacation through that date, and the full amount of his profit sharing account, but "No severance pay will be granted." Finally, Pugh was directed "not to visit or contact Production Department employees while they are on the job."

The letter contained no reason for Pugh's termination. When Pugh asked Huggins for a reason, he was told only that he should "look deep within [him]self" to find the answer, that "Things were said by people in the trade that have come back to us." Pugh's termination was subsequently announced to the industry in a letter which, again, stated no reasons.

When Pugh first went to work for See's, Ed Peck, then president and general manager, frequently told him: "If you are loyal to [See's] and do a good job, your future is secure." Laurance See, who became president of the company in 1951 and served in that capacity until his death in 1969, had a practice of not terminating administrative personnel except for good cause, and this practice was carried on by his brother, Charles B. See, who succeeded Laurance as president.

During the entire period of his employment, there had been no formal or written criticism of Pugh's work. No complaints were ever raised at the annual meetings which preceded each holiday season, and he was never denied a raise or bonus. He received no notice that there was a problem which needed correction, nor any warning that any disciplinary action was being contemplated.

Pugh's theory as to why he was terminated relates to a contract which See's at that time had with the defendant union. Prior to 1971, the union represented employees of See's as well as employees of certain other candy manufacturers in a multiemployer bargaining unit, and there existed a collective bargaining agreement between the union and an employer association representing those manufacturers. In addition, there existed for many years prior to 1971 a supplemental agreement between the union and See's which contained provisions applicable to See's only.

In 1968, the supplemental agreement contained a new rate classification which permitted See's to pay its seasonal employees at a lower rate. At a company meeting prior to the 1968 negotiations, Pugh had objected to the proposed new seasonal classification on the grounds that it might make it more difficult to recruit seasonal workers, and create unrest among See's regular seasonal workers who had worked previously for other manufacturers at higher rates. Huggins overruled Pugh's objection and (unknown to Pugh) recommended his termination for "lack of cooperation" as to which Pugh's objection formed "part of the reason." His recommendation was not accepted.

The 1968 association and supplemental agreements expired in 1971. Thereafter, See's negotiated with the union separately, and not as a part of any employer association.

The 1971 agreement expired in 1973. In April of that year, Huggins asked Pugh to be part of the negotiating team for the new union contract. Pugh responded that he would like to, but he was bothered by the possibility that See's had a "sweetheart contract" with the union. In response, someone banged on the table and said, "You don't know what the hell you are talking about." Pugh said, "Well, I think I know what I am talking about. I don't know whether you have a sweetheart contract, but I am telling you if you do, I don't want to be involved because they are immoral, illegal and not in the best interests of my employees." At the trial, Pugh explained that to him, a "sweetheart contract" was "a contract whereby one employer would get an unfair competitive advantage over a competitor by getting a lower wage rate, would be one version of it." He also felt, he testified, that "if they in fact had a sweetheart contract that it wouldn't be fair to my female employees to be getting less money than someone would get working in the same industry under the same manager."

The union's alleged participation in Pugh's termination was in the form of a statement attributed to Mr. Button (the individual who succeeded Pugh as production manager) at a negotiating meeting between the company and the union in June 1973. According to one witness, Mr. Button stated at the commencement of the meeting, "Now we've taken care of Mr. Pugh. What are you going to do for us."

DISCUSSION

A. Historical Background.

The law of the employment relationship has been, and perhaps still is, in the process of continuing evolution. The old law of master and servant, which held sway through the 18th century and to some extent beyond, viewed the relationship as primarily one of status rather than of contract. While agreement gave rise to the relationship and might establish certain of its terms, it was "custom and public policy, not the will of the parties, [which] defined the implicit framework of mutual rights and obligations."

The essence of the relationship as so defined drew its contours from the model of the household in which, typically, the servant worked, the master had general authority to discipline the servant, and it was the servant's duty to obey. At the same time, the master had certain responsibilities for the servant's general welfare. The relationship was thus in a sense paternalistic. And it was not terminable at will; rather, there existed a presumption (in the absence of contrary agreement) that employment was for a period of one year.

With the industrial revolution in the 19th century, the law of master and servant underwent a gradual remodeling, primarily at the hands of the judiciary. Primary emphasis came to be placed, through contract doctrine, upon the freedom of the parties to define their own relationship. "The emphasis shifted from obligation to freedom of choice." The terms of the contract were to be sought in voluntary agreement, express or implied, the employee being presumed to have assented to the rules and working conditions established by the employer.

In light of the generally superior bargaining power of the employer, "the employment contract became [by the end of the nineteenth century] a very special sort of contract—in large part a device for guaranteeing to management unilateral power to make rules and exercise discretion." And management's unilateral power extended, generally, to the term of the relationship as well. The new emphasis brought with it a gradual weakening of the traditional presumption that a general hiring (i.e., one without a specific term) was for a year, and its replacement by the converse presumption that "a general or indefinite hiring is prima facie a hiring at will. In California, this presumption is reflected in Labor Code section 2922, which provides: "An Employment, having no specified term, may be terminated at the will of either party on notice to the other. Employment for a specified term means an employment for a period greater than one month."

The recognized inequality in bargaining power between employer and individual employee undergirded the rise of the labor unions and the institutionalization of collective bargaining. And through collective bargaining, unions have placed limitations on the employer's unilateral right of termination. Under most union contracts, employees can only be dismissed for "just cause," and disputes over what constitutes cause for dismissal are typically decided by arbitrators chosen by the parties. Collective bargaining agreements, however, cover only a small fraction of the nation's work force, and employees who either do not or (as in the case of managerial employees such as Mr. Pugh) cannot form unions are left without that protection.

In recent years, there have been established by statute a variety of limitations upon the employer's power of dismissal. Employers are precluded, for example, from terminating employees for a variety of reasons, including union membership or activities, race, sex, age or political affiliation. Legislatures in this country have so far refrained, however, from adopting statutes, such as those which exist in most other industrialized countries, which would provide more generalized protection to employees against unjust dismissal. And while public employees may enjoy job security through civil service rules and due process, the legal principles which give rise to these protections are not directly applicable to employees in private industry.

Even apart from statute or constitutional protection, however, the employer's right to terminate employees is not absolute. "The mere fact that a contract is terminable at will does not give the employer the absolute right to terminate it in all cases." Two relevant limiting principles have developed, one of them based upon public policy and the other upon traditional contract doctrine. The first limitation precludes dismissal "when an employer's discharge of an employee violates fundamental principles of public policy," the second when the discharge is contrary to the terms of the agreement, express or implied. Appellant relies upon both these principles in contesting his termination here.

B. Public Policy Limitation.

[The court's analysis of the plaintiff's public policy arguments is omitted.]

We conclude that appellant did not establish a prima facie and cognizable case of wrongful termination based upon the public policy theories which he advanced.

C. Contract Limitations.

The presumption that an employment contract is intended to be terminable at will is subject, like any presumption, to contrary evidence. This may take the form of an agreement, express or implied, that the relationship will continue for some fixed period of time. Or, and of greater relevance here, it may take the form of an agreement that the employment relationship will continue indefinitely, pending the occurrence of some event such as the employer's dissatisfaction with the employee's services or the existence of some "cause" for termination. Sometimes this latter type of agreement is characterized as a contract for "permanent" employment, but that characterization may be misleading. In one of the earliest California cases on this subject, the Supreme Court interpreted a contract for permanent employment as meaning "that plaintiffs' employment . . . was to continue indefinitely, and until one or the other of the parties wish, for some good reason, to sever the relation."

A contract which limits the power of the employer with respect to the reasons for termination is no less enforceable because it places no equivalent limits upon the power of the employee to quit his employment. "If the requirement of consideration is met, there is no additional requirement of . . . equivalence in the values exchanged, or 'mutuality of obligation.' "

Moreover, while it has sometimes been said that a promise for continued employment subject to limitation upon the employer's power of termination must be supported by some "independent consideration," i.e., consideration other than the services to be rendered, such a rule is contrary to the general contract principle that courts should not inquire into the adequacy of consideration. "A single and undivided consideration may be bargained for and given as the agreed equivalent of one promise or of two promises or of many promises." Thus there is no analytical reason why an employee's promise to render services, or his actual rendition of services over time, may not support an employer's promise both to pay a particular wage (for example) and to refrain from arbitrary dismissal.

The most likely explanation for the "independent consideration" requirement is that it serves an evidentiary function: it is more probable that the parties intended a continuing relationship, with limitations upon the employer's dismissal authority, when the employee has provided some benefit to the employer, or suffers some detriment, beyond the usual rendition of service.

In determining whether there exists an implied-in-fact promise for some form of continued employments, courts have considered a variety of factors in addition to the existence of independent consideration. These have included, for example, the personnel policies or practices of the employer, the employee's longevity of service, actions or communications by the employer reflecting assurances of continued employment, and the practices of the industry in which the employee is engaged.

Here, there were facts in evidence from which the jury could determine the existence of such an implied promise: the duration of appellant's employment, the commendations and promotions he received, the apparent lack of any direct criticism of his work, the assurances he was given, and the employer's acknowledged policies. While oblique language will not, standing alone, be sufficient to establish agreement, it is appropriate to consider the totality of the parties' relationship: Agreement may be "shown by the acts and conduct of the parties, interpreted in the light of the subject matter and of the surrounding circumstances." We therefore conclude that it was error to grant respondents' motions for nonsuit as to See's.

Since this litigation may proceed toward yet uncharted waters, we consider it appropriate to provide some guidance as to the questions which the trial court may confront on remand. We have held that appellant has demonstrated a prima facie case of wrongful termination in violation of his contract of employment. The burden of coming forward with evidence as to the reason for appellant's termination now shifts to the employer. Appellant may attack the employer's offered explanation, either on the ground that it is pretextual (and that the real reason is one prohibited by contract or public policy), or on the ground that it is insufficient to meet the employer's obligations under the contract or applicable legal principles. Appellant bears, however, the ultimate burden of proving that he was terminated wrongfully. By what standard that burden is to be measured will depend, in part, upon what conclusions the jury draws as to the nature of the contract between the parties. The terms "just cause" and "good cause," "as used in a variety of contexts ... have been found to be difficult to define with precision and to be largely relative in their connotation, depending upon the particular circumstances of each case." Essentially, they connote "a fair and honest cause or reason, regulated by good faith on the part of the party exercising the power." Care must be taken, however, not to interfere with the legitimate exercise of managerial discretion. "Good cause" in this context is quite different from the standard applicable in determining the propriety of an employee's termination under a contract for a specified term. And where, as here, the employee occupies a sensitive managerial or confidential position, the employer must of necessity be allowed substantial scope for the exercise of subjective judgment.

THE CASE AGAINST THE UNION.

[The court's discussion of this issue is omitted.]

Questions

1. How can a trier of fact determine, from a contract that is silent on the issue, whether the employer promised "permanency," or the employer needs to prove "cause" to terminate lawfully an employee? Are there presumptions that dictate one answer rather than another? If so, are these presumptions a relic of the times, referred to in *Pugh*, when contract law was based on status rather than on the parties' motives?

2. Are these presumptions, as well as the concepts of status and motive, nothing more than a reflection of judicial values and preferences?

3. Does the court opine that an implied promise—to employ a standard of "cause" to justify a discharge—is the same as an explicit promise, like that found in a collective bargaining agreement, to employ a standard of "cause?" If the implied standards are less rigorous than the explicit standards, what are they?

4. According to the court, what facts (in *Pugh* or in other cases) imply a promise that employment will end only for cause? How does each of these facts give rise to the implication?

5. Have employees, as a class, gained anything significant from *Pugh* and the many opinions like it written by courts throughout the country? Or, are decisions like *Pugh* merely traps for the unwary employer? That is, unlike the implied (by law) promise of fair dealing, which probably cannot be waived by the parties, the implied promise of job security can be waived by more explicit language that makes clear that the employment is at-will.

DAMAGES AND ATTORNEY'S FEES

In general, courts have moved wrongful dismissal from the tort arena, where the plaintiff can show emotional distress or persuade a court in a particularly egregious case to award punitive damages, to contract, where damages are traditionally limited to lost wages. The possibility of large damage awards is the usual engine that induces the private bar to represent these plaintiffs. Examine in the reference supplement the provisions for damages in the Model Employment Termination Act. Professor Theodore St. Antoine, the spiritual force behind this statute, has suggested that contract damages make the model statute attractive to employers. St. Antoine, A Seed Germinates: Unjust Discharge Reform Heads Toward Full Flower, 67 Neb.L.Rev. 56, 69 (1988). A cynic might say that the interests of employees (and their lawyers?) have been compromised in order to make the model statute politically attractive.

On the other hand, by providing for counsel fees for successful plaintiffs, the Model Act provides a further incentive for lawyers to take on these cases. The recovery, however, hinges on the plaintiff's success. Without a statutory award of attorney's fees, the plaintiff's lawyer can take her fee only out of the client's recovery under a contingency arrangement. Thus the Model Termination Act shifts the costs of counsel fees from the plaintiff to the defendant. But both the statutory and the contingent fee arrangements create a fee only if the plaintiff is successful. Thus, employees with debatable or close-to-call claims have no effective access to the courts.

Awards of punitive damages in unjust dismissal cases based on tort theories are not unusual. A survey of such cases tried before juries between 1980 and 1982 in California found that in 32 of 41 cases plaintiffs prevailed and received general damages. Of the 32 victories, 17 included awards of punitive damages; and juries assessed more than $600,000 in each of six of the 17 cases. See Ad Hoc Committee on Termination at Will and Wrongful Discharge, State Bar of California Labor and Employment Law Section, To Strike A New Balance 5 (1984). By way of comparison, in arbitration a successful grievant will be limited to an award of back pay to compensate for lost earnings (including fringe benefits) and of reinstatement to permit the resumption of a productive working life. In breach of contract actions, damage awards are similarly intended only to make the employee whole. In both contract and arbitration awards, mitigation of damages is expected; in neither are punitive damages allowed.

In connection with various civil rights statutes, Congress and state legislatures have supplanted the traditional rule on fees by authorizing courts to award reasonable fees to the prevailing party. See, e.g., the Civil Rights Attorney's Fees Awards Act, 42 U.S.C. § 1988, and § 706(k) of Title VII in the statutory supplement. Should jurisdictions that recognize actions for unlawful discharge authorize courts to award counsel fees to prevailing plaintiffs, but deny all such plaintiffs any right to punitive damages?

To many, the most persuasive ground for assessing punitive damages against wrongdoers is the deterrence effect of costly mistakes. According to this theory, the higher a company's potential liability, the more careful management will be to observe the rights of all workers and to refrain from employment practices of dubious validity. Consider what effect the fear of a lawsuit and punitive damages might have on the decision-making process of a manager. Might the effect be management's over-indulgence of poor workers? Even if high monetary awards serve a desirable prophylactic purpose, why should the plaintiff receive an amount far in excess of any actual damages suffered? Awards for emotional distress respond to the plaintiff's psychological strains associated with unjust dismissal and the lengthy litigation process. Are punitive damages nothing more than a windfall for successful plaintiffs? On what grounds is such a windfall justified?

STATUTORY LAW

a.   ASSIGNMENT: Read with care the New Jersey Conscientious Employee Protection Act and the Model Employment Termination Act (META) in the statutory supplement.

Then test your understanding of the New Jersey Act, assuming the facts in *Sheets* arose in New Jersey. How do the provisions apply? Test your understanding of META by assuming the facts in *Fortune* and in *Pugh* arose in a jurisdiction that had adopted META. How do the provisions apply?

Finally, as a state legislator, would you vote for or against META, and why? What amendments, deletions or redrafting would you favor? Is the old common law of employment-at-will a better regulatory device than the new common law of employment-at-will or META?

b.   THE WORLD OF LEGISLATION

To this point, with few exceptions, the book has presented the law as written by judges. Of course, you know full well that an increasingly significant and copious source of the law is to be found in the legislatures of this country. The field of employment relations has not been immune from this development. Indeed, legislation regarding employment finds its beginnings in the late nineteenth century, picked up some steam (despite opposition from the courts, which were inclined to declare much of it unconstitutional) in the early twentieth century. By mid-century, legislation affecting the workplace was voluminous and still growing. As the twentieth century faded into the twenty-first, every state legislature and the United States Congress, as well as most cities' and large townships' legislative bodies, had written laws that were addressed directly to the workplace and to the employment relationship. It should not be surprising to learn that much of that legislation has directly affected the employment at-will doctrine.

First, there are general "whistle blower" statutes, adopted by several states, including (as you know) New Jersey, which purport to protect employees from discipline or discharge simply because those employees have disclosed information to a governmental agency of a violation of law (e.g., California) or, to one's own employer, as well as a governmental agency (e.g., Maine and New York). In Pennsylvania, at least, protection of the law is invoked by the employee's reporting either violations of law or "of a code of conduct or ethics designed to protect the interest of the public or the employer." "Whistleblower" laws vary as to how correct the employees must be: some statutes require the employees to be in "good faith;" others require that there be a "reasonable" basis for the report; while at least one state, Michigan, protects the employee "unless the employee knows that the report is false."

In addition, there are many federal and state laws that protect employees from discipline or discharge because the employees have taken advantage of the opportunities offered by the laws. Under federal law, for example, serving on a jury is protected from employer retaliation; so, too, are complaints about safety in a variety of contexts, such as railroads, motor vehicles, mines, and atomic facilities. State laws typically protect employees from retaliation for taking advantage of laws like workers compensation. Many states protect employees in voting or holding political office.

Finally, both Congress and many state legislatures have passed laws that have as their primary objective a rearrangement of the at-will doctrine. In the first part of the twentieth century, thanks to the United States Supreme Court's decisions, the Congress had a stop-and-start experience with efforts to protect from employer retaliation employees who wished to join labor unions or persuade others to do the same. In the late 1930s, the Supreme Court accepted the legitimacy of Congress's efforts. In a similar fashion, during the last third of the twentieth century, Congress enacted several laws that almost entirely precluded employers from refusing to hire or from discharging employees because of their race, sex, national origin, religion, age, or disability. In each of the relevant federal statutes, there is also a provision that protects complaining employees from employer punishment based on the fact the employees did make the complaints. In Part III of this Chapter, we shall examine some of the federal laws that have limited the at-will doctrine in the ways described. You should know that, in addition to these federal laws, the states and many municipalities have passed similar legislation which, sometimes, is broader in its protection than the comparable federal enactments. Often, rather than preempting the state law, the federal legislation expressly requires individuals first to seek relief under the parallel state law.

As you approach Part III, read somewhat casually (for the time being) Title VII of the Civil Rights Act of 1964, the Age Discrimination in Employment Act, and the Americans with Disabilities Act, all of which are in the supplement. The reading will give you a sense of what Congress has done. And, probably, the reading won't hurt.

III. AN OVERVIEW OF EQUAL EMPLOYMENT OPPORTUNITY LAW

Hypothetical

A.   PROBLEM: THE ATTORNEY WHO DOES NOT MAKE PARTNER

Commission on Human Rights
and Opportunities
   The State of Flux
Frances Kennedy, COMPLAINANT   Complaint No. 555–1212
         against
Hungadunga Hungadunga &
McCormick, RESPONDENT

REASONABLE CAUSE DECISION

Pursuant to its statutory authority to defer to the decisions of approved state agencies, the United States Equal Employment Opportunity Commission authorized this agency to undertake investigation of this complaint and to make a reasonable cause determination.

SUMMARY OF CHARGE

On May 29, 1998, a complaint was filed against the above-named law firm by Ms. Frances Kennedy, then an attorney in her seventh year of employment by respondent, alleging that said respondent had discriminated against her in violation of Title VII of the Civil Rights Act of 1964 (Title VII), as amended in 1991, 42 U.S.C. § 2000e et seq. by denying her advancement to the position of partner because of her sex. Complainant alleges that respondent's pattern of employment of partners and permanent associates and the refusal to consider complainant for partnership on the same basis as male attorneys tends to deprive her of employment opportunities open to men and to discriminate against her with respect to terms, conditions and privileges of employment because of her sex.

SUMMARY OF INVESTIGATION

(1) Respondent is a law firm in general corporate practice. As of November 1998, the firm consisted of 210 attorneys; 105 partners and 105 associates. During the summer respondent also employs second year law students as summer interns.

(2) Complainant was hired by respondent as an associate attorney on a partnership track in July 1990 and was assigned to the firm's litigation department. She had graduated in the top third of her class from the Flux University School of Law in 1988 and then worked at a small law firm in southern Flux. Before entering law school, complainant had accumulated five years of administrative and legislative experience, first as an assistant to Senator Rodmund Luskie, then as Administrator of the Office of a Special Prosecutor of the Flux Department of Justice.

At the time respondent hired complainant, respondent hired nine associates, all of whom were male except for complainant. An examination of complainant's resume shows her qualifications to be equal to and no less than the male associates hired in 1990.

(3) On November 16, 1997, after seven years of employment by respondent, Executive Committee Chairman Charles Nelson met with complainant and informed her that she had not been recommended for partnership. Nelson informed complainant of an opening in respondent's domestic relations department and promised her that if she agreed to work in this department, she would be made a partner in one year. Complainant rejected the offer and this action ensued.

(4) During the first six years of her employment by respondent, complainant along with all associates hired in 1990 were considered non-senior associates and were subjected to semi-annual reviews. Senior associates within two years of partnership consideration are evaluated annually.

The possible grades on the evaluations are as follows:

—DISTINGUISHED: Outstanding, exceptional; consistently demonstrates extraordinary adeptness and quality; star.

—GOOD: Displays particular merit on a consistent basis; effective work product and performance; able; talented.

—ACCEPTABLE: Satisfactory; adequate; displays neither particular merit nor any serious defects or omissions; dependable.

—MARGINAL: Inconsistent work product and performance; sometimes below the level of what you expect from Associates who are acceptable at this level.

—UNACCEPTABLE: Fails to meet minimum standard of quality expected by you of an associate at this level; frequently below level of what you expect.

At the first six reviews as a non-senior associate, 1991 to 1993, complainant received evaluations of "distinguished." At the next six reviews, 1994 to 1996, complainant received a grade of "acceptable" on all but one of the evaluations, the one differing being a grade of "good." At complainant's annual evaluation as senior associate in 1997, she also received a grade of "acceptable."

(5) During the reviews beginning in 1994, complainant was told that her evaluations declined because it had become apparent that her skills in the category of legal analysis did not meet the firm's standards. She was informed, however, that respondent believed her able to deal competently with clients and in the courtroom. Therefore, complainant was offered a position in the domestic relations department in 1997, as respondent believes that area does not require the same complex analysis as the firm's litigation department.

(6) In early November 1994, just as complainant got ready to leave for the day, George Hilder, a partner, called telling her that she would have to work all night on an important project. Complainant, who had two children at home, told him that she may have difficulty with the kids, but that she would see what she could do. Complainant was unable to make arrangements on such short notice and informed Hilder that she would be unable to do the project. Complainant's second semi-annual evaluation in 1994 indicated that she refused to do the project.

(7) In June 1994, complainant took a ten-week maternity leave to give birth to her third child. When she returned from leave she negotiated with respondent for a four-day, extended hours work week. After some initial reluctance, this schedule was approved by respondent, on a "trial basis."

(8) During the second semi-annual review in 1994, complainant was told that she would not receive the maximum salary increase because the number of billable hours she submitted was substantially below those recorded by her peers. Nevertheless, complainant received a rating of acceptable on the basis of the professional services she provided and because of the unusually large decrease in the liability payouts of one of her defense insurance clients.

(9) Complainant's second 1995 evaluation indicated that she had spent too much time on issues within the firm which did not pertain to her work. Complainant admits that she was actively involved in women's issues within the firm. Complainant had been specifically concerned about the firm's treatment of paralegals. Her perception was that the firm mistreated its paralegals by overworking and underpaying them and that treatment would not have occurred but for the fact that they were predominantly women.

(10) Complainant alleges that during a conversation with Jay Lewis, a managing partner, concerning her 1995 evaluations Lewis said something like, "Your dedication to this firm has been questionable. I know these things are more difficult for a woman."

(11) Complainant received a rating of good, one rank below distinguished, in her second 1996 review. Managing partner Jay Lewis told complainant that although her legal work "could not be faulted," respondent was concerned about complainant's failure "to generate new business and to cultivate existing clients."

(12) This Commission has examined respondent's pattern of promotion and advancement. Since 1955, respondent has had twelve female partners. Five of its one hundred-five present partners are female and there is only one woman among the twenty-eight partners in the litigation department in which complainant had sought partnership. Of the seventeen female attorneys employed by respondent as associates since 1978, two have become partners. For male attorneys, the average time between being hired as an associate and becoming a partner is seven years. The most senior female now at the firm graduated from law school and was hired by respondent in June 1974. She became a partner in 1986 after twelve years as an associate. All eight of the male attorneys who joined the firm in 1974 as associates have been partners since 1981.

(13) A specific comparative analysis of the allegedly "more favored group," in this case males in the class of 1990, was conducted.

At the time the firm refused complainant admission to the partnership, it offered partnership status to six of the eight male associates who joined the firm along with complainant in 1990. Complainant's law school credentials equaled those of the male associates. A comparison of the evaluations of complainant and of the male associates who made partner shows that for her first three years at the firm, complainant received equal or better evaluations than did the men. The subsequent evaluations of all six of the male associates who made partner show that each received some negative comments about work habits, writing ability, the number of billable hours during periods of illness or personal stress, and ability to increase the firm's client base. One of these male associates received negative comments equal to complainant's in the category of legal analysis.

Of the two remaining male associates who joined the firm along with complainant in 1990, one was killed in an automobile accident; and the other left respondent to run for political office and is currently a state senator.

(14) Complainant alleges that one of the six male associates in the class of 1986 who was recommended for partnership had a pattern of sexual harassment of female employees at the firm. Complainant alleges that the behavior was seen as insignificant by the evaluating partners and not worthy of mention to the Associate Committee in its consideration of that male associate for partnership.

(15) The pattern of hiring was examined. From 1972 to November 1993, respondent hired twenty-one female associates. During the same period, the firm hired 168 male associates. The number of women graduated from law schools in 1972 was 1,541, or 7% of all graduates that year. Twenty years later the number was 14,797, or 43% of all

graduates, a growth rate in absolute numbers of nearly 1,000 percent. By comparison, the growth rate of all persons entering law school during that same period was 157 percent. Respondent's pattern of hiring did not reflect the increased availability of female law students.

FINDING: [omitted]

ISSUES TO THINK ABOUT

The plaintiff's case:

Assuming the state agency cannot settle Kennedy's case and issues a right to sue letter, and that Kennedy decides to file a Title VII claim against the law firm, what must her complaint allege to survive a motion to dismiss? And what must she prove in order to prevail? The cases we have chosen, *Griggs v. Duke Power* and *McDonnell Douglas v. Green*, present different theories of liability, based on different subsections of § 703. As you read these cases, and the notes that follow them, compare Kennedy's claim to those in *Griggs* and *McDonnell Douglas*. You should also think about which theory of liability you would prefer to use—and whether you have a choice. Finally, what facts support your theories and how will you prove these "facts."

The defendant's case:

What evidence, if any, must the firm present to defend its decision? Should the firm rely on the line of defense advanced by its managing partner in the following deposition?

> The decision whether to make an offer of partnership is a most complicated and difficult decision. By definition the individuals are all qualified. If they were not they would not have been kept on as associates for six years or more. The record of each associate is, of course, a starting point; but in every case the final decision is also predicated on subjective factors such as collegiality, ability to work with attorneys and clients, appearance, poise, and the willingness and ability to fit into the firm's image. Among one of the most important considerations is whether the person will be completely dedicated to the firm. This dedication includes whether the person is willing to "go the extra mile" to accomplish what needs to be done. Oftentimes that means extra hours for that person.
>
> In addition to the above-mentioned factors, the firm must weigh such intangibles as the likelihood of continued, sustained performance at the level established for associates. Legal analytical skills are an important guide, of course, but more as a reason to exclude than a reason to admit, particularly where the associate's performance has been erratic or uneven. The worst thing we as a firm can do is to bring into the partnership a person who, being assured a good income and status, allows his or her primary skills to falter.

This consideration has gained importance over the years as firms such as ours face an increasingly competitive climate. A wrong decision could severely damage our firm's reputation as a highly skilled firm.

Another important consideration is whether the person will be a magnet for clients. As is true of most law firms, much of our work comes to us because of personal relationships and fortuity. We began our practice in employment law, for example, as an accommodation to General Datatronics. At the time GD was a relatively new client, brought to us because one of our partners married the daughter of GD's president. When GD began to have labor problems in the early 1990s, we agreed to help the company fight off an organizing campaign. Now we have twelve partners in the labor group.

Similar story with our specialty of municipal bond placement. Conner has been a sailing buddy of the director of the Capital City Symphony ever since the two were in law school. When the symphony needed legal help, Conner offered the firm's service pro bono, even though Capital City is over in the western part of the state. That led to Conner's joining the symphony's board of directors and getting to know the mayor. When Capital City came very close to defaulting on a lot of its obligations, the mayor called Conner. We did a good rescue job for them and earned a reputation as specialists in municipal bond placement. Frankly, many firms could have done just as good a job for Capital City. But because of an old sailing friendship we had the chance to show what we could accomplish.

In the end, the firm must rely on its collective good judgment. Some people stand out. There is no way of quantifying it, but they are better qualified than their colleagues to be partners in our firm. Having worked with associates for a number of years, you learn to sense when a person has the dedication, the intellectual ability and the personality to contribute to the firm. The selection process is at best an imperfect method of distinguishing among exceptionally qualified young men and women.

WOMEN AS RAINMAKERS
—Litigation—.
(Spring 1991).

[At a panel discussion on women litigators as rainmakers, Louise A. LaMothe of Irell & Manella (Los Angeles) and Jean Maclean Snyder of D'Ancona & Pflaun (Chicago) commented on the barriers for women trying to rise beyond the middle range of the partnership. Here are some edited excerpts from that discussion.—Eds.]

LaMothe: What we are seeing is a collision of the demographics of law practice. A great many more women are entering the profession while, due to economic conditions affecting law practice, there is an increasingly strong emphasis on the bottom line. That emphasis is not just on working harder, spending more time at the office, and generating more billable hours. The professional climate is changing, becoming much more oriented to achieving short-term results, increasing pressure on all lawyers to generate business. It used to be said in my own firm that it didn't make any difference whether you generated business; the important thing was that you were a good lawyer. That was enough to make partner. Although that is still said and may be true for people at the lower levels of the partnership, it is no longer true if you want to make it out of that range, much less to the top. Given a flat economy, clients who no longer feel married to one law firm, and tremendous competition for business, women are feeling the pressure of their law firms' looking to them and saying, "If you want to progress, you're going to have to bring in business." And that's a fact of life. I don't think it's something we should run from. All of us know that many firms have two tiers of associates. All of us probably also know that a number of law firms have two tiers of partners.

One west-coast firm recently restructured its partnership. It had 10 women partners when it started. When it finished that restructuring, 9 of them had become non-equity partners. There is one reason for that: Those 9 women were not bringing in business.

Snyder: One reason women are in this position is that women have been shut out of the traditional networks from which people get business. One obvious area is sports. Sports have been and continue to be a great source of business for men. They are the focus for all sorts of male bonding. Every October several men in our firm get their guns and their permits and go hunting. I can't imagine anything worse. They don't invite me, and I don't want to be invited. But this kind of traditional activity has gone on and still goes on, and women don't have an equal activity. How many women play golf? Again, the 19th hole is the scene of many a business transaction. And when men aren't playing sports, a lot of times they are watching them. They go to basketball games and football games. And sports are an area that many women as adults just haven't been interested in.

Another traditional area of business-getting that many women have been shut out of until now is business clubs. The doors of clubs like the Union League Club, where we had lunch today, have just been slammed in the faces of women up until recently. And I remember at the Union League Club in Chicago 15 years ago being escorted to the back door. Everyone remarked on how silly and cute it was, but indeed you could go to lunch—if you entered through the back door. And today the fact that the Union League Club and others are opened up doesn't mean that suddenly 20 percent or 50 percent of the membership is women, as I am sure anyone could have noted by walking through the Union League Club on the first floor. The only woman I saw was obviously somebody's daughter and not an early entrant to law school.

Even one-on-one socializing in the evening is often hard for women, but easier for men. Men take clients out. They take their wives, and the clients—almost always men—take their wives. Women have to renegotiate all of that, right from picking up the phone to say, "Would you like to go out to dinner?" Or maybe, "Could I take you out to dinner?" Or, "Shall we go to the theater?" You must decide how to do all that. Is the woman going to bring her husband with her? Does the client bring his wife? When the woman and the client talk about business, does her husband talk with his wife about—well—about what? What if she doesn't have a husband? Then the "Would you like to go out to dinner?" question is even harder. And the quasi-social nature of the evening at dinner or at the theater becomes even more difficult.

Also, there haven't been the women counterparts as clients. Women have to strategize in many cases about how to develop clients who are men, because the women are just not out there. If they are in corporations, they are very likely so far down that they are not in a position to give business. We are here talking about breaking through the glass ceiling for lawyers, but the glass ceiling is even farther down in business. It's a pretty gloomy picture, Louise.

LaMothe: Let me point the finger at some of the men who lead law firms. You know, mentoring is something that many of us think about and a lot of us value, and a lot of us are sorry for the fact that we haven't had it. Just to give you a few rather stark examples, when I went to law school, I never had a woman professor. I never knew a woman lawyer. There was no woman, of course, ahead of me in my law firm whom I could lean on or learn the ropes or anything else from. And even now, where I went to law school, there still are not very many women professors. I daresay you could probably go straight through law school and avoid them entirely.

And I think that even in my law firm, there are plenty of women associates who worked for quite a while before they ever came across another woman to work with—certainly in the role of a senior lawyer. I think law firms have neglected their women. And I can understand, by the way, that this idea of mentoring women makes a lot of men uncomfortable. Much as in the area of socializing with clients, there is the possibility of sexual overtones that makes the men very uncomfortable.

It's clear to us women that we need the access to mentors that men have had. Men pass business to younger men. Indeed, one of the functions of mentoring is showing younger people the ropes in dealing with clients. Men also pass the mantle of authority to younger men. Mentoring is much less available to younger women.

The problem may be even greater for women who have entered law later in life, as many have done now that the doors are open. They need mentoring, too. Yet often that does not occur to anyone. And it may be hard for men their age—or even younger—to feel comfortable playing mentor to them.

I also think that the decisions men make about whom they will work with in the law firm are often based on whom they feel comfortable working with. And it isn't surprising that those may be the people they golf with, for example, or with whom they play tennis, racquetball, handball, or poker. Institutionally, there is a tendency to create opportunities for people who are like the people already in power. That automatically forecloses opportunities for people who are different. And that includes us. So I think that the law firms need to look very critically at the ways they set up their mentoring networks—both formal and informal. And a real effort needs to be made by men to mentor women.

I spend a lot of time mentoring the women in my law firm. And there is not enough of me to go around. The other women partners feel the same way.

Snyder: A male partner of mine says: "The reason you women have trouble getting business is you never, when you were growing up, had to ask anyone for a date. We did. We learned how to do it. We learned how to get rejected. You haven't had the experience." And there is a lot of wisdom in what he says. Women are not used to being explicit about their needs. They are not in the habit of picking up the phone and saying, "Hello, I'd like to meet with you" and having the implicit message be that they eventually want to have a transaction that involves this person's giving something in return. I also think that women are not used to speaking up about their abilities. They have to stand up for themselves or explicitly ensure that the men in the firm—other people—will stand up and say they're good. Because, after all, the reason somebody gives somebody business isn't just that it was fun playing golf. It's also that the person has confidence. And I think traditionally women have shied away from using certain terms about themselves, talking about their cases in a way that says, "I'm a presence."

One specific example that shows how women haven't used their power is this: A lot of business is generated in relationships that people build in political campaigns, in charities, by being on a board of a charity, and so on. Certainly the men in my firm do this all the time. Now I know the women could write a check as easily because they are earning a lot of money. But they don't. Women do not contribute. They don't use their money to get the kind of power that men do, and that's something that women can do to turn things around quickly. It's a lot easier to do that than to try to persuade a country club that it ought to accept women or to try to become a member there and feel comfortable when there aren't any other women. And I think that women have to take on this responsibility for themselves.

Another thing some women have not been so good about is networking with other women to get business. One woman I know who has been a lawyer for some time says that women don't understand the rules. They want to be loved for themselves alone. They are romantics, and they don't understand or feel comfortable with the rules that say, "We're going to have a relationship in which I give business to you and you give business to me, and we like each other for that—and all that's okay." Women view that as being false. But women have to start learning the rules of the man's world if they want to participate in business because this is still a man's world. Louise, I know you have a caution about networking with women.

LaMothe: Well, I do. We have to be very careful in sending business to another woman. It's one thing when a woman refers business to a man, and let's say it doesn't turn out all that well. She's not likely to be castigated for it. But if she sends business to another woman, there is the implicit feeling that she has done so for an unjustified reason. So if the woman who handles that business doesn't do very well, you can be assured that it's also not going to go very well for the woman who sent her the business. So I think we do understand that here is another arena in which we are being held to a higher standard, and we might as well accept it.

Snyder: Let me just mention one last part of the problem: When success comes and a woman gets business, we should all congratulate her. But because men may feel threatened when women get business, too often, instead of congratulations, you hear, "Oh, that's a fluke."

LaMothe: How about this one from a senior partner about five years ago when I told him I brought in a good matter: "Well, everybody brings in business now and then."

Snyder: Or else, one that I've heard, "Oh, that's really my business. I met that guy's third cousin ten years ago." But the final thing I would have to say is that when we do bring in business, let's all have a drink of champagne. Because when anyone brings business into a firm, the whole firm benefits. For that reason alone, law firms should invest in helping women litigators to become successful rainmakers.

B. TWO MODELS OF PROOF

1. DISPARATE IMPACT OR DISPROPORTIONALITY

GRIGGS v. DUKE POWER CO.

Supreme Court of the United States, 1971.
401 U.S. 424, 91 S.Ct. 849, 28 L.Ed.2d 158.

MR. CHIEF JUSTICE BURGER delivered the opinion of the Court.

We granted the writ in this case to resolve the question whether an employer is prohibited by the Civil Rights Act of 1964, Title VII, from requiring a high school education or passing of a standardized general intelligence test as a condition of employment in or transfer to jobs when (a) neither standard is shown to be significantly related to successful job performance, (b) both requirements operate to disqualify Negroes at a substantially higher rate than white applicants, and (c) the jobs in question formerly had been filled only by white employees as part of a longstanding practice of giving preference to whites.

Congress provided, in Title VII of the Civil Rights Act of 1964, for class actions for enforcement of provisions of the Act and this proceeding was brought by a group of incumbent Negro employees against Duke Power Company. All the petitioners are employed at the Company's Dan River Steam Station, a power generating facility located at Draper, North Carolina. At the time this action was instituted, the Company had 95 employees at the Dan River Station, 14 of whom were Negroes; 13 of these are petitioners here.

The District Court found that prior to July 2, 1965, the effective date of the Civil Rights Act of 1964, the Company openly discriminated on the basis of race in the hiring and assigning of employees at its Dan River plant. The plant was organized into five operating departments: (1) Labor, (2) Coal Handling, (3) Operations, (4) Maintenance, and (5) Laboratory and Test. Negroes were employed only in the Labor Department where the highest paying jobs paid less than the lowest paying jobs in the other four "operating" departments in which only whites were employed.[2] Promotions were normally made within each department on the basis of job seniority. Transferees into a department usually began in the lowest position.

In 1955, the Company instituted a policy of requiring a high school education for initial assignment to any department except Labor, and for transfer from the Coal Handling to any "inside" department (Operations, Maintenance, or Laboratory). When the Company abandoned its policy of restricting Negroes to the Labor Department in 1965, completion of high school also was made a prerequisite to transfer from Labor to any other department. From the time the high school requirement

2. A Negro was first assigned to a job in an operating department in August 1966, five months after charges had been filed with the Equal Employment Opportunity Commission. The employee, a high school graduate who had begun in the Labor Department in 1953, was promoted to a job in the Coal Handling Department.

was instituted to the time of trial, however, white employees hired before the time of the high school education requirement continued to perform satisfactorily and achieve promotions in the "operating" departments. Findings on this score are not challenged.

The Company added a further requirement for new employees on July 2, 1965, the date on which Title VII became effective. To qualify for placement in any but the Labor Department it became necessary to register satisfactory scores on two professionally prepared aptitude tests, as well as to have a high school education. Completion of high school alone continued to render employees eligible for transfer to the four desirable departments from which Negroes had been excluded if the incumbent had been employed prior to the time of the new requirement. In September 1965, the Company began to permit incumbent employees who lacked a high school education to qualify for transfer from Labor or Coal Handling to an "inside" job by passing two tests—the Wonderlic Personnel Test, which purports to measure general intelligence, and the Bennett Mechanical Comprehension Test. Neither was directed or intended to measure the ability to learn to perform a particular job or category of jobs. The requisite scores used for both initial hiring and transfer approximated the national median for high school graduates.[3]

The District Court had found that while the Company previously followed a policy of overt racial discrimination in a period prior to the Act, such conduct had ceased. The District Court also concluded that Title VII was intended to be prospective only and, consequently, the impact of prior inequities was beyond the reach of corrective action authorized by the Act.

The Court of Appeals was confronted with a question of first impression, as are we, concerning the meaning of Title VII. After careful analysis a majority of that court concluded that a subjective test of the employer's intent should govern, particularly in a close case, and that in this case there was no showing of a discriminatory purpose in the adoption of the diploma and test requirements. On this basis, the Court of Appeals concluded there was no violation of the Act.

The Court of Appeals reversed the District Court in part, rejecting the holding that residual discrimination arising from prior employment practices was insulated from remedial action.[4] The Court of Appeals noted, however, that the District Court was correct in its conclusion that there was no showing of a racial purpose or invidious intent in the

---

3. The test standards are thus more stringent than the high school requirement, since they would screen out approximately half of all high school graduates.

4. The Court of Appeals ruled that Negroes employed in the Labor Department at a time when there was no high school or test requirement for entrance into the higher paying departments could not now be made subject to those requirements, since whites hired contemporaneously into those departments were never subject to them. The Court of Appeals also required that the seniority rights of those Negroes be measured on a plant-wide, rather than a departmental, basis. However, the Court of Appeals denied relief to the Negro employees without a high school education or its equivalent who were hired into the Labor Department after institution of the educational requirement.

adoption of the high school diploma requirement or general intelligence test and that these standards had been applied fairly to whites and Negroes alike. It held that, in the absence of a discriminatory purpose, use of such requirements was permitted by the Act. In so doing, the Court of Appeals rejected the claim that because these two requirements operated to render ineligible a markedly disproportionate number of Negroes, they were unlawful under Title VII unless shown to be job related.[5] We granted the writ on these claims. 399 U.S. 926, 90 S.Ct. 2238, 26 L.Ed.2d 791.

The objective of Congress in the enactment of Title VII is plain from the language of the statute. It was to achieve equality of employment opportunities and remove barriers that have operated in the past to favor an identifiable group of white employees over other employees. Under the Act, practices, procedures, or tests neutral on their face, and even neutral in terms of intent, cannot be maintained if they operate to "freeze" the status quo of prior discriminatory employment practices.

The Court of Appeals' opinion, and the partial dissent, agreed that, on the record in the present case, "whites register far better on the Company's alternative requirements" than Negroes.[6] This consequence would appear to be directly traceable to race. Basic intelligence must have the means of articulation to manifest itself fairly in a testing process. Because they are Negroes, petitioners have long received inferior education in segregated schools and this Court expressly recognized these differences in Gaston County v. United States, 395 U.S. 285 (1969). There, because of the inferior education received by Negroes in North Carolina, this Court barred the institution of a literacy test for voter registration on the ground that the test would abridge the right to vote indirectly on account of race. Congress did not intend by Title VII, however, to guarantee a job to every person regardless of qualifications. In short, the Act does not command that any person be hired simply because he was formerly the subject of discrimination, or because he is a member of a minority group. Discriminatory preference for any group, minority or majority, is precisely and only what Congress has proscribed. What is required by Congress is the removal of artificial, arbitrary, and unnecessary barriers to employment when the barriers operate invidiously to discriminate on the basis of racial or other impermissible classification.

Congress has now provided that tests or criteria for employment or promotion may not provide equality of opportunity merely in the sense of the fabled offer of milk to the stork and the fox. On the contrary, Congress has now required that the posture and condition of the job

5. One member of that court disagreed with this aspect of the decision, maintaining, as do the petitioners in this Court, that Title VII prohibits the use of employment criteria that operate in a racially exclusionary fashion and do not measure skills or abilities necessary to performance of the jobs for which those criteria are used.

6. In North Carolina, 1960 census statistics show that, while 34% of white males

had completed high school, only 12% of Negro males had done so.

Similarly, with respect to standardized tests, the EEOC in one case found that use of a battery of tests, including the Wonderlic and Bennett tests used by the Company in the instant case, resulted in 58% of whites passing the tests, as compared with only 6% of the blacks.

seeker be taken into account. It has—to resort again to the fable—provided that the vessel in which the milk is proffered be one all seekers can use. The Act proscribes not only overt discrimination but also practices that are fair in form, but discriminatory in operation. The touchstone is business necessity. If an employment practice which operates to exclude Negroes cannot be shown to be related to job performance, the practice is prohibited.

On the record before us, neither the high school completion requirement nor the general intelligence test is shown to bear a demonstrable relationship to successful performance of the jobs for which it was used. Both were adopted, as the Court of Appeals noted, without meaningful study of their relationship to job-performance ability. Rather, a vice president of the Company testified, the requirements were instituted on the Company's judgment that they generally would improve the overall quality of the work force.

The evidence, however, shows that employees who have not completed high school or taken the tests have continued to perform satisfactorily and make progress in departments for which the high school and test criteria are now used.[7] The promotion record of present employees who would not be able to meet the new criteria thus suggests the possibility that the requirements may not be needed even for the limited purpose of preserving the avowed policy of advancement within the Company. In the context of this case, it is unnecessary to reach the question whether testing requirements that take into account capability for the next succeeding position or related future promotion might be utilized upon a showing that such long-range requirements fulfill a genuine business need. In the present case, the Company has made no such showing.

The Court of Appeals held that the Company had adopted the diploma and test requirements without any "intention to discriminate against Negro employees." We do not suggest that either the District Court or the Court of Appeals erred in examining the employer's intent; but good intent or absence of discriminatory intent does not redeem employment procedures or testing mechanisms that operate as "built-in headwinds" for minority groups and are unrelated to measuring job capability.

The Company's lack of discriminatory intent is suggested by special efforts to help the undereducated employees through Company financing of two-thirds the cost of tuition for high school training. But Congress directed the thrust of the Act to the consequences of employment practices, not simply the motivation. More than that, Congress has placed on the employer the burden of showing that any given requirement must have a manifest relationship to the employment in question.

The facts of this case demonstrate the inadequacy of broad and general testing devices as well as the infirmity of using diplomas or degrees as fixed measures of capability. History is filled with examples of men and women who rendered highly effective performance without the conventional badges of accomplishment in terms of certificates, diplo-

---

7. For example, between July 2, 1965, and November 14, 1966, the percentage of white employees who were promoted but who were not high school graduates was nearly identical to the percentage of non-graduates in the entire white work force.

mas, or degrees. Diplomas and tests are useful servants, but Congress has mandated the commonsense proposition that they are not to become masters of reality.

The Company contends that its general intelligence tests are specifically permitted by § 703(h) of the Act.[8] That section authorizes the use of "any professionally developed ability test" that is not "designed, * * * intended or *used* to discriminate because of race * * *." (Emphasis added.)

The Equal Employment Opportunity Commission, having enforcement responsibility, has issued guidelines interpreting § 703(h) to permit only the use of job-related tests.[9] The administrative interpretation of the Act by the enforcing agency is entitled to great deference. Since the Act and its legislative history support the Commission's construction, this affords good reason to treat the guidelines as expressing the will of Congress.

Section 703(h) was not contained in the House version of the Civil Rights Act but was added in the Senate during extended debate. For a period, debate revolved around claims that the bill as proposed would prohibit all testing and force employers to hire unqualified persons simply because they were part of a group formerly subject to job discrimination.[10] Proponents of Title VII sought throughout the debate to assure the critics that the Act would have no effect on job-related tests. Senators Case of New Jersey and Clark of Pennsylvania, co-managers of the bill on the Senate floor, issued a memorandum explaining that the proposed Title VII "expressly protects the employer's right to insist that any prospective applicant, Negro or white, *must meet the applicable job qualifications*. Indeed, the very purpose of title VII is to promote hiring on the basis of job qualifications, rather than on the basis of race or color."[11] (Emphasis added.) Despite these assurances, Senator

8. Section 703(h) applies only to tests. It has no applicability to the high school diploma requirement.

9. EEOC Guidelines on Employment Testing Procedures, issued August 24, 1966, provide:

"The Commission accordingly interprets 'professionally developed ability test' to mean a test which fairly measures the knowledge or skills required by the particular job or class of jobs which the applicant seeks, or which fairly affords the employer a chance to measure the applicant's ability to perform a particular job or class of jobs. The fact that a test was prepared by an individual or organization claiming expertise in test preparation does not, without more, justify its use within the meaning of Title VII."

The EEOC position has been elaborated in the new Guidelines on Employee Selection Procedures, 29 CFR § 1607, 35 Fed.Reg. 12333 (Aug. 1, 1970). These guidelines demand that employers using tests have available "data demonstrating that the test is

predictive of or significantly correlated with important elements of work behavior which comprise or are relevant to the job or jobs for which candidates are being evaluated."

10. The congressional discussion was prompted by the decision of a hearing examiner for the Illinois Fair Employment Commission in Myart v. Motorola Co. (The decision is reprinted at 110 Cong.Rec. 5662.) That case suggested that standardized tests on which whites performed better than Negroes could never be used. The decision was taken to mean that such tests could never be justified even if the needs of the business required them. A number of Senators feared that Title VII might produce a similar result.

11. The Court of Appeals majority, in finding no requirement in Title VII that employment tests be job related, relied in part on a quotation from an earlier Clark–Case interpretative memorandum addressed to the question of the constitutionality of Title VII. The Senators said in that memorandum:

"There is no requirement in title VII that employers abandon bona fide qualifica-

Tower of Texas introduced an amendment authorizing "professionally developed ability tests." Proponents of Title VII opposed the amendment because, as written, it would permit an employer to give any test, "whether it was a good test or not, so long as it was professionally designed. Discrimination could actually exist under the guise of compliance with the statute." 110 Cong.Rec. 13504 (remarks of Sen. Case).

The amendment was defeated and two days later Senator Tower offered a substitute amendment which was adopted verbatim and is now the testing provision of § 703(h). Speaking for the supporters of Title VII, Senator Humphrey, who had vigorously opposed the first amendment, endorsed the substitute amendment, stating: "Senators on both sides of the aisle who were deeply interested in title VII have examined the text of this amendment and have found it to be in accord with the intent and purpose of that title." The amendment was then adopted.[12] From the sum of the legislative history relevant in this case, the conclusion is inescapable that the EEOC's construction of § 703(h) to require that employment tests be job related comports with congressional intent.

Nothing in the Act precludes the use of testing or measuring procedures; obviously they are useful. What Congress has forbidden is giving these devices and mechanisms controlling force unless they are demonstrably a reasonable measure of job performance. Congress has not commanded that the less qualified be preferred over the better qualified simply because of minority origins. Far from disparaging job qualifications as such, Congress has made such qualifications the controlling factor, so that race, religion, nationality, and sex become irrelevant. What Congress has commanded is that any tests used must measure the person for the job and not the person in the abstract.

The judgment of the Court of Appeals is, as to that portion of the judgment appealed from, reversed.

MR. JUSTICE BRENNAN took no part in the consideration or decision of this case.

tion tests where, because of differences in background and education, members of some groups are able to perform better on these tests than members of other groups. An employer may set his qualifications as high as he likes, he may test to determine which applicants have these qualifications, and he may hire, assign, and promote on the basis of test performance." 110 Cong. Rec. 7213.

However, nothing there stated conflicts with the later memorandum dealing specifically with the debate over employer testing, 110 Cong.Rec. 7247 (quoted from in the text above), in which Senators Clark and Case explained that tests which measure "applicable job qualifications" are permissible under Title VII. In the earlier memorandum Clark and Case assured the Senate

that employers were not to be prohibited from using tests that determine *qualifications*. Certainly a reasonable interpretation of what the Senators meant, in light of the subsequent memorandum directed specifically at employer testing, was that nothing in the Act prevents employers from requiring that applicants be fit for the job.

12. Senator Tower's original amendment provided in part that a test would be permissible "if ... in the case of any individual who is seeking employment with such employer, such test is designed to determine or predict whether such individual is suitable or trainable with respect to his employment in the particular business or enterprise involved...." This language indicates that Senator Tower's aim was simply to make certain that job-related tests would be permitted. * * *

Questions and Notes

1.   What subsection of § 703(a) is the Court applying in *Griggs*? If you cannot tell from the opinion itself, because the Court doesn't say, are you able to determine which subsection supports the Court's analysis?

2.   Is Fran Kennedy, and the other women associates who might complain about unequal opportunities at the Hungadunga firm, similar to the black employees in *Griggs*, in terms of the women's education, access to entry level-jobs, ability—or inability—to find better employment elsewhere? Should the differences, if any, affect a court's using the disparate theory in the Fran Kennedy case (assuming, of course, that the facts fit the theory)?

3.   Following a series of cases limiting the application of *Griggs*, the Supreme Court virtually undid the entire disparate impact basis for a cause of action pursuant to Title VII. *Wards Cove v. Atonio*, 490 U.S. 642, 109 S.Ct. 2115, 104 L.Ed.2d 733 (1989). Congress responded quickly. In the Civil Rights Act of 1991, Congress amended Title VII to codify the disparate impact claim (see Section 703(k)) and the employer's affirmative defense (see Sections 701(m) and 703(k)) that the challenged practice causing the disparate impact be "business related ... and consistent with business necessity."

Given the language of the amended statute, do you think that an employment practice with a disparate impact on women's opportunities is legally justified if the practice is "business related," whether or not it is "consistent with business necessity?" Or, does the use of the word "and" require that the employer show more than the practice is business related, that is, the practice is also a necessity? Of course, to read the statute in this literal manner lends credence to the complaint that the law is being interpreted to subsidize the employment of women. Is that complaint accurate?

4.   How does one measure "disparateness?" That question has at least two parts. First, one must ask: between what and what is there a disparity? In *Griggs*, should one of the categories being compared have been, for example, high school graduates in the county where the company's business was, in the entire state of North Carolina, or in the United States? Should the comparative category have been the general population (of where?), qualified people in the relevant area, applicants for the job, people who were offered the job, or people who held the job? The same kind of questions could be asked about the use of the pen-and-paper test the company used. Perhaps, all of these comparisons are valid, depending on the context. What other factors would be relevant?

Second, how great does the disparity have to be for one to conclude that the disparity is "too much?" If blacks graduated from high school half the time and whites 60% of the time, would that fact be sufficient to prove disparate impact? Do you think the differences should be greater in order to invoke the statute successfully? Or, do you think the differences could be less and still justify a finding of disparate impact? Would you care about the disparity in high school graduation statistics if the company had a proportional number of blacks (as compared with whatever statistic you thought appropriate like, for example, the general population)?

5. Is it accurate, or at least fair, to characterize *Griggs* as an affirmative action, or quota-demanding, decision?

2. DISPARATE TREATMENT OR INTENTIONAL DISCRIMINATION

McDONNELL DOUGLAS v. GREEN

Supreme Court of the United States, 1973.
411 U.S. 792, 93 S.Ct. 1817, 36 L.Ed.2d 668.

MR. JUSTICE POWELL delivered the opinion of the Court.

The case before us raises significant questions as to the proper order and nature of proof in actions under Title VII of the Civil Rights Act of 1964, 78 Stat. 253, 42 U.S.C. § 2000e et seq.

Petitioner, McDonnell Douglas Corp., is an aerospace and aircraft manufacturer headquartered in St. Louis, Missouri, where it employs over 30,000 people. Respondent, a black citizen of St. Louis, worked for petitioner as a mechanic and laboratory technician from 1956 until August 28, 1964 when he was laid off in the course of a general reduction in petitioner's work force.

Respondent, a long-time activist in the civil rights movement, protested vigorously that his discharge and the general hiring practices of petitioner were racially motivated.[2] As part of this protest, respondent and other members of the Congress on Racial Equality illegally stalled their cars on the main roads leading to petitioner's plant for the purpose of blocking access to it at the time of the morning shift change. The District Judge described the plan for, and respondent's participation in, the "stall-in" as follows:

> "[F]ive teams, each consisting of four cars would 'tie up' five main access roads into McDonnell at the time of the morning rush hour. The drivers of the cars were instructed to line up next to each other completely blocking the intersections or roads. The drivers were also instructed to stop their cars, turn off the engines, pull the emergency brake, raise all windows, lock the doors, and remain in their cars until the police arrived. The plan was to have the cars remain in position for one hour.
>
> "Acting under the 'stall in' plan, plaintiff [respondent in the present action] drove his car onto Brown Road, a McDonnell access road, at approximately 7:00 a.m., at the start of the morning rush hour. Plaintiff was aware of the traffic problems that would result. He stopped his car with the intent to block traffic. The police arrived

---

2. The court of appeals noted that respondent then "filed formal complaints of discrimination with the President's Commission on Civil Rights, the Justice Department, the Department of the Navy, the Defense Department, and the Missouri Commission on Human Rights." 463 F.2d 337 (8 Cir., 1972).

shortly and requested plaintiff to move his car. He refused to move his car voluntarily. Plaintiff's car was towed away by the police, and he was arrested for obstructing traffic. Plaintiff pleaded guilty to the charge of obstructing traffic and was fined." 318 F.Supp. 846.

On July 2, 1965, a "lock-in" took place wherein a chain and padlock were placed on the front door of a building to prevent the occupants, certain of petitioner's employees, from leaving. Though respondent apparently knew beforehand of the "lock-in," the full extent of his involvement remains uncertain.[3]

Some three weeks following the "lock-in," on July 25, 1965, petitioner publicly advertised for qualified mechanics, respondent's trade, and respondent promptly applied for re-employment. Petitioner turned down respondent, basing its rejection on respondent's participation in the "stall-in" and "lock-in." Shortly thereafter, respondent filed a formal complaint with the Equal Employment Opportunity Commission, claiming that petitioner had refused to rehire him because of his race and persistent involvement in the civil rights movement, in violation of §§ 703(a)(1) and 704(a) of the Civil Rights Act of 1964, 42 U.S. §§ 2000e–2(a)(1) and 2000e–3(a). The former section generally prohibits racial discrimination in any employment decision while the latter forbids discrimination against applicants or employees for attempting to protest or correct allegedly discriminatory conditions of employment.

The Commission made no finding on respondent's allegation of racial bias under § 703(a)(1), but it did find reasonable cause to believe petitioner had violated § 704(a) by refusing to rehire respondent because of his civil rights activity. After the Commission unsuccessfully attempted to conciliate the dispute, it advised respondent in March 1968, of his right to institute a civil action in federal court within 30 days.

On April 15, 1968, respondent brought the present action, claiming initially a violation of § 704(a) and, in an amended complaint, a violation of § 703(a)(1) as well. The District Court, 299 F.Supp. 1100, dismissed the latter claim of racial discrimination in petitioner's hiring procedures on the ground that the Commission had failed to make a determination

---

3. The "lock-in" occurred during a picketing demonstration by ACTION, a civil rights organization, at the entrance to a downtown office building which housed a part of petitioner's offices and in which certain of petitioner's employees were working at the time. A chain and padlock were placed on the front door of the building to prevent ingress and egress. Although respondent acknowledges that he was chairman of ACTION at the time, that the demonstration was planned and staged by his group, that he participated in and indeed was in charge of the picket line in front of the building, that he was told in advance by a member of ACTION "that he was planning to chain the front door," and that he "approved of" chaining the door, there is

no evidence that respondent personally took part in the actual "lock-in," and he was not arrested.

The Court of Appeals majority, however, found that the record did "not support the trial court's conclusion that Green 'actively cooperated' in chaining the doors of the downtown St. Louis building during the 'lock-in' demonstration." Judge Johnsen, in dissent, agreed with the District Court that the "chaining and padlocking [were] carried out as planned, [and that] Green had in fact given it ... approval and authorization."

In view of respondent's admitted participation in the unlawful "stall-in," we find it unnecessary to resolve the contradictory contentions surrounding this "lock-in."

of reasonable cause to believe that a violation of that section had been committed. The District Court also found that petitioner's refusal to rehire respondent was based solely on his participation in the illegal demonstrations and not on his legitimate civil rights activities. The court concluded that nothing in Title VII or § 704 protected "such activity as employed by the plaintiff in the 'stall in' and 'lock in' demonstrations." 318 F.Supp., at 850.

On appeal, the Eighth Circuit affirmed that unlawful protests were not protected activities under § 704(a), but reversed the dismissal of respondent's § 703(a)(1) claim relating to racially discriminatory hiring practices, holding that a prior Commission determination of reasonable cause was not a jurisdictional prerequisite to raising a claim under that section in federal court. The court ordered the case remanded for trial of respondent's claim under § 703(a)(1).

In remanding, the Court of Appeals attempted to set forth standards to govern the consideration of respondent's claim. The majority noted that respondent had established a prima facie case of racial discrimination; that petitioner's refusal to rehire respondent rested on "subjective" criteria which carried little weight in rebutting charges of discrimination; that, though respondent's participation in the unlawful demonstrations might indicate a lack of a responsible attitude toward performing work for that employer, respondent should be given the opportunity to demonstrate that petitioner's reasons for refusing to rehire him were mere pretext. In order to clarify the standards governing the disposition of an action challenging employment discrimination, we granted certiorari.

I

We agree with the Court of Appeals that absence of a Commission finding of reasonable cause cannot bar suit under an appropriate section of Title VII and that the District Judge erred in dismissing respondent's claim of racial discrimination under § 703(a)(1). Respondent satisfied the jurisdictional prerequisites to a federal action (i) by filing timely charges of employment discrimination with the Commission and (ii) by receiving and acting upon the Commission's statutory notice of the right to sue, 42 U.S.C. §§ 2000e–5(a) and 2000e–5(e). The Act does not restrict a complainant's right to sue to those charges as to which the Commission has made findings of reasonable cause, and we will not engraft on the statute a requirement which may inhibit the review of claims of employment discrimination in the federal courts. The Commission itself does not consider the absence of a "reasonable cause" determination as providing employer immunity from similar charges in a federal court, and the courts of appeal have held that, in view of the large volume of complaints before the Commission and the nonadversary character of many of its proceedings, "court actions under Title VII are de novo proceedings and ... a Commission 'no reasonable cause' finding does not bar a lawsuit in the case." Robinson v. Lorillard Corp., 444 F.2d 791, 800 (C.A.4 1971).

Petitioner argues, as it did below, that respondent sustained no prejudice from the trial court's erroneous ruling because in fact the issue of racial discrimination in the refusal to re-employ "was tried thoroughly" in a trial lasting four days with "at least 80% of the questions relating to the issue of race." Petitioner, therefore, requests that the judgment below be vacated and the cause remanded with instructions that the judgment of the District Court be affirmed. We cannot agree that the dismissal of respondent's § 703(a)(1) claim was harmless error. It is not clear that the District Court's findings as to respondent's § 704(a) contentions involved the identical issues raised by his claim under § 703(a)(1). The former section relates solely to discrimination against an applicant or employee on account of his participation in legitimate civil rights activities or protests, while the latter section deals with the broader and centrally important question under the Act of whether for any reason, a racially discriminatory employment decision has been made. Moreover, respondent should have been accorded the right to prepare his case and plan the strategy of trial with the knowledge that the § 703(a)(1) cause of action was properly before the District Court. Accordingly, we remand the case for trial of respondent's claim of racial discrimination consistent with the views set forth below.

II

The critical issue before us concerns the order and allocation of proof in a private, non-class action challenging employment discrimination. The language of Title VII makes plain the purpose of Congress to assure equality of employment opportunities and to eliminate those discriminatory practices and devices which have fostered racially stratified job environments to the disadvantage of minority citizens. Griggs v. Duke Power Co., 401 U.S. 424, 429, 91 S.Ct. 849, 852, 28 L.Ed.2d 158 (1971). As noted in *Griggs*, supra:

"Congress did not intend by Title VII, however, to guarantee a job to every person regardless of qualifications. In short, the Act does not command that any person be hired simply because he was formerly the subject of discrimination, or because he is a member of a minority group. Discriminatory preference for any group, minority or majority, is precisely and only what Congress has proscribed. What is required by Congress is the removal of artificial, arbitrary, and unnecessary barriers to employment when the barriers operate invidiously to discriminate on the basis of racial or other impermissible classification." Id., 401 U.S., at 430–431, 91 S.Ct., at 853.

There are societal as well as personal interests on both sides of this equation. The broad, overriding interest, shared by employer, employee, and consumer, is efficient and trustworthy workmanship assured through fair and racially neutral employment and personnel decisions. In the implementation of such decisions, it is abundantly clear that Title VII tolerates no racial discrimination, subtle or otherwise.

In this case respondent, the complainant below, charges that he was denied employment "because of his involvement in civil rights activities" and "because of his race and color." Petitioner denied discrimination of any kind, asserting that its failure to re-employ respondent was based upon and justified by his participation in the unlawful conduct against it. Thus, the issue at the trial on remand is framed by those opposing factual contentions. The two opinions of the Court of Appeals and the several opinions of the three judges of that court attempted, with a notable lack of harmony, to state the applicable rules as to burden of proof and how this shifts upon the making of a prima facie case. We now address this problem.

The complainant in a Title VII trial must carry the initial burden under the statute of establishing a prima facie case of racial discrimination. This may be done by showing (i) that he belongs to a racial minority; (ii) that he applied and was qualified for a job for which the employer was seeking applicants; (iii) that, despite his qualifications, he was rejected and (iv) that, after his rejection, the position remained open and the employer continued to seek applicants from persons of complainant's qualifications.[13] In the instant case, we agree with the Court of Appeals that respondent proved a prima facie case. Petitioner sought mechanics, respondent's trade, and continued to do so after respondent's rejection. Petitioner, moreover, does not dispute respondent's qualifications and acknowledges that his past work performance in petitioner's employ was "satisfactory."

The burden then must shift to the employer to articulate some legitimate, nondiscriminatory reason for the employee's rejection. We need not attempt in the instant case to detail every matter which fairly could be recognized as a reasonable basis for a refusal to hire. Here petitioner has assigned respondent's participation in unlawful conduct against it as the cause for his rejection. We think that this suffices to discharge petitioner's burden of proof at this stage and to meet respondent's prima facie case of discrimination.

The Court of Appeals intimated, however, that petitioner's stated reason for refusing to rehire respondent was a "subjective" rather than objective criterion which "carr[ies] little weight in rebutting charges of discrimination," 463 F.2d., at 343. This was among the statements which caused the dissenting judge to read the opinion as taking "the position that such unlawful acts as Green committed against McDonnell would not legally entitle McDonnell to refuse to hire him, even though no racial motivation was involved...." Id., at 355. Regardless of whether this was the intended import of the opinion, we think the court below seriously underestimated the rebuttal weight to which petitioner's reasons were entitled. Respondent admittedly had taken part in a carefully planned "stall-in," designed to tie up access to and egress from petition-

13. The facts necessarily will vary in Title VII cases, and the specification above of the prima facie proof required from respondent is not necessarily applicable in every respect to differing factual situations.

er's plant at peak traffic hour.[16] Nothing in Title VII compels an employer to absolve and rehire one who has engaged in such deliberate, unlawful activity against it.[17] In upholding, under the National Labor Relations Act, the discharge of employees who had seized and forcibly retained an employer's factory buildings in an illegal sit-down strike, the Court noted pertinently:

> "We are unable to conclude that Congress intended to compel employers to retain persons in their employ regardless of their unlawful conduct,—to invest those who go on strike with an immunity from discharge for acts of trespass or violence against the employer's property ... Apart from the question of the constitutional validity of an enactment of that sort, it is enough to say that such a legislative intention be found in some definite and unmistakable expression." NLRB v. Fansteel Corp., 306 U.S. 240, 255, 59 S.Ct. 490, 496, 83 L.Ed. 627 (1939).

Petitioner's reason for rejection thus suffices to meet the prima facie case, but the inquiry must not end here. While Title VII does not, without more, compel rehiring of respondent, neither does it permit petitioner to use respondent's conduct as a pretext for the sort of discrimination prohibited by § 703(a)(1). On remand, respondent must, as the Court of Appeals recognized, be afforded a fair opportunity to show that petitioner's stated reason for respondent's rejection was in fact pretext. Especially relevant to such a showing would be evidence that white employees involved in acts against petitioner of comparable seriousness to the "stall-in" were nevertheless retained or rehired. Petitioner may justifiably refuse to rehire one who has engaged in unlawful, disruptive acts against it, but only if this criterion is applied alike to members of all races.

Other evidence that may be relevant to any showing of pretext includes facts as to the petitioner's treatment of respondent during his prior term of employment; petitioner's reaction, if any, to respondent's legitimate civil rights activities, and petitioner's general policy and practice with respect to minority employment.[18] On the latter point, statistics as to petitioner's employment policy and practice may be

---

16. The trial judge noted that no personal injury or property damage resulted from the "stall-in" due "solely to the fact that law enforcement officials had obtained notice in advance of plaintiff's [here respondent's] demonstration and were at the scene to remove plaintiff's car from the highway."

17. The unlawful activity in this case was directed specifically against petitioner. We need not consider or decide here whether, or under what circumstances, unlawful activity not directed against the particular employer may be a legitimate justification for refusing to hire.

18. We are aware that some of the above factors were, indeed, considered by

the District Judge in finding under § 704(a), that "defendant's [here petitioner's] reasons for refusing to rehire the plaintiff was motivated solely and simply by the plaintiff's participation in the 'stall in' and 'lock in' demonstrations." We do not intimate that this finding must be overturned after consideration on remand of respondent's § 703(a)(1) claim. We do, however, insist that respondent under § 703(a)(1) must be given a full and fair opportunity to demonstrate by competent evidence that whatever the stated reasons for his rejection, the decision was in reality racially premised.

helpful to a determination of whether petitioner's refusal to rehire respondent in this case conformed to a general pattern of discrimination against blacks. Jones v. Lee Way Motor Freight, Inc. 431 F.2d 245 (C.A.10 1970); Blumrosen, Strangers in Paradise: Griggs v. Duke Power Co., and the Concept of Employment Discrimination, 71 Mich.L.Rev. 59, 91–94 (1972).[19] In short, on the retrial respondent must be given a full and fair opportunity to demonstrate by competent evidence that the presumptively valid reasons for his rejection were in fact a coverup for a racially discriminatory decision.

The court below appeared to rely on upon Griggs v. Duke Power Co., supra, in which the Court stated: "If an employment practice which operates to exclude Negroes cannot be shown to be related to job performance, the practice is prohibited." 401 U.S., at 431, 91 S.Ct., at 853, 28 L.Ed.2d 158. But *Griggs* differs from the instant case in important respects. It dealt with standardized testing devices which, however neutral on their face, operated to exclude many blacks who were capable of performing effectively in the desired position. *Griggs* was rightly concerned that childhood deficiencies in the education and background of minority citizens, resulting from forces beyond their control, not be allowed to work a cumulative and invidious burden on such citizens for the remainder of their lives. Id., at 430, 91 S.Ct., at 853. Respondent, however, appears in different clothing. He had engaged in a seriously disruptive act against the very one from whom he now seeks employment. And petitioner does not seek his exclusion on the basis of a testing device which overstates what is necessary for competent performance, or through some sweeping disqualification of all those with any past record of unlawful behavior, however remote, insubstantial, or unrelated to applicant's personal qualifications as an employee. Petitioner assertedly rejected respondent for unlawful conduct against it and, in the absence of proof of pretext or discriminatory application of such a reason, this cannot be thought the kind of "artificial, arbitrary, and unnecessary barriers to employment" which the Court found to be the intention of Congress to remove.[21]

19. The District Court may, for example, determine, after reasonable discovery that "the [racial] composition of defendant's labor force is itself reflective of restrictive or exclusionary practices." See Blumrosen, supra, at 92. We caution that such general determinations, while helpful, may not be in and of themselves controlling as to an individualized hiring decision, particularly in the presence of an otherwise justifiable reason for refusing to re-hire.

21. It is, of course, a predictive evaluation, resistant to empirical proof, whether "an applicant's past participation in unlawful conduct directed at his prospective employer might indicate the applicant's lack of a responsible attitude toward performing work for that employer." 463 F.2d., at 353. But in this case, given the seriousness and harmful potential of respondent's partic-

ipation in the "stall-in" and the accompanying inconvenience to other employees, it cannot be said that petitioner's refusal to employ lacked a rational and neutral business justification. As the Court has noted elsewhere: "Past conduct may well relate to present fitness; past loyalty may have a reasonable relationship to p resent and future trust." Garner v. Board of Public Works of Los Angeles, 341 U.S. 716, 720, 71 S.Ct. 909, 912, 95 L.Ed. 1317 (1951). [In *Garner* the Supreme Court upheld a city ordinance requiring city employees to swear they had not previously been affiliated with any group that advocated violent overthrow of the government. Prof. Laurence Tribe comments "the *Garner* oath would today be deemed violative of the first amendment freedom of association." L. Tribe, American Constitutional Law 489 n. 33 (1979).—Eds.]

III

In sum, respondent should have been allowed to pursue his claim under § 703(a)(1). If the evidence on retrial is substantially in accord with that before us in this case, we think that respondent carried his burden of establishing a prima facie case of racial discrimination and that petitioner successfully rebutted that case. But this does not end the matter. On retrial, respondent must be afforded a fair opportunity to demonstrate that petitioner's assigned reason for refusing to re-employ was a pretext or discriminatory in its application. If the District Judge so finds, he must order a prompt and appropriate remedy. In the absence of such a finding, a petitioner's refusal to rehire must stand.

The cause is hereby remanded to the District Court for reconsideration in accordance with this opinion.

Notes and Questions

1. The *McDonnell Douglas* formula, a formula that has evolved from Justice Powell's exemplary suggestion of how a case may be proved into a standard for virtually all disparate treatment cases, has been subjected to a long series of Supreme Court interpretations and clarifications. At this point in time, we believe it is safe to describe the law in the following way: (1) the burden of proving unlawful discrimination, including the employer's bad motive, remains on the plaintiff throughout the litigation; (2) once the plaintiff establishes a *prima facie* case, which is fairly easy in most cases, the employer must respond adequately or suffer a defeat on the merits of the case; (3) the burden on the employer—to articulate an adequate defense—is, like the plaintiff's *prima facie* case, easily satisfied; the employer has to prove nothing, only respond; (4) once the employer has so responded, the legal significance of the *prima facie* case evaporates; (5) at this stage of the proceedings, the parties are in positions to present their respective cases, which include any evidence that may have been relevant to making the plaintiff's *prima facie* case or to articulating the employer's defense; in addition, the plaintiff may attempt to show that the employer's defense is a pretext or, in some cases, that the employer had a reasonable alternative to accomplishing its objectives without imposing the challenged action upon the plaintiff; (6) proof that the employer's defense is a hoax is evidence to support the plaintiff's claim, but it is not conclusive that the employer violated Title VII; and (7) all of the foregoing evidence and arguments are presented to the trier of fact, who shall determine whether or not the employer violated the law. See Reeves v. Sanderson Plumbing Products, Inc., 530 U.S. 133, 120 S.Ct. 2097, 147 L.Ed.2d 105 (2000).

2. Is there such a thing as "motive?" How can we know someone else's? Is the requirement of motive a smokescreen for what finders of fact really do?

3. *McDonnell Douglas* and its progeny have as their bottom the unreal premise that people or institutions act on the basis of singular motives or catalysts. Assuming "motive" really exists, do you think people or institutions ever act on the basis of a single motive? If you believe that multiple motives explain actions, how does the *McDonnell Douglas* analysis help resolve whether or not an employer, in any given case, has intentionally violated the law? Consider the following case.

MOUNT HEALTHY CITY SCHOOL DISTRICT BOARD OF EDUCATION v. DOYLE

Supreme Court of the United States, 1977.
429 U.S. 274, 97 S.Ct. 568, 50 L.Ed.2d 471.

MR. JUSTICE REHNQUIST delivered the opinion of the Court.

Respondent Doyle sued petitioner Mt. Healthy Board of Education in the United States District Court for the Southern District of Ohio. Doyle claimed that the Board's refusal to renew his contract in 1971 violated his rights under the First and Fourteenth Amendments to the United States Constitution. After a bench trial the District Court held that Doyle was entitled to reinstatement with back pay. The Court of Appeals for the Sixth Circuit affirmed the judgment, 529 F.2d 524, and we granted the Board's petition for certiorari, 425 U.S. 933, 96 S.Ct. 1662, 48 L.Ed.2d 174 * * *.

Doyle was first employed by the Board in 1966. He worked under one-year contracts for the first three years, and under a two-year contract from 1969 to 1971. In 1969, he was elected president of the Teachers' Association, in which position he worked to expand the subjects of direct negotiation between the Association and the Board of Education. During Doyle's one-year term as president of the Association, and during the succeeding year when he served on its executive committee, there was apparently some tension in relations between the Board and the Association.

Beginning early in 1970, Doyle was involved in several incidents not directly connected with his role in the Teachers' Association. In one instance, he engaged in an argument with another teacher which culminated in the other teacher's slapping him. Doyle subsequently refused to accept an apology and insisted upon some punishment for the other teacher. His persistence in the matter resulted in the suspension of both teachers for one day, which was followed by a walkout by a number of other teachers, which in turn resulted in the lifting of the suspensions.

On other occasions, Doyle got into an argument with employees of the school cafeteria over the amount of spaghetti which had been served him; referred to students, in connection with a disciplinary complaint, as "sons of bitches"; and made an obscene gesture to two girls in connection with their failure to obey commands made in his capacity as cafeteria supervisor. Chronologically, the last in the series of incidents which respondent was involved in during his employment by the Board was a telephone call by him to a local radio station. It was the Board's consideration of this incident which the court below found to be a violation of the First and Fourteenth Amendments.

In February 1971, the principal circulated to various teachers a memorandum relating to teacher dress and appearance, which was apparently prompted by the view of some in the administration that there was a relationship between teacher appearance and public support for bond issues. Doyle's response to the receipt of the memorandum—on a subject which he apparently understood was to be settled by joint teacher-administration action—was to convey the substance of the memorandum to a disc jockey at WSAI, a Cincinnati radio station, who promptly announced the adoption of the dress code as a news item. Doyle subsequently apologized to the principal, conceding that he should have made some prior communication of his criticism to the school administration.

Approximately one month later, the superintendent made his customary annual recommendations to the Board as to the rehiring of nontenured teachers. He recommended that Doyle not be rehired. The same recommendation was made with respect to nine other teachers in the district, and in all instances, including Doyle's, the recommendation was adopted by the Board. Shortly after being notified of this decision, respondent requested a statement of reasons for the Board's actions. He received a statement citing "a notable lack of tact in handling professional matters which leaves much doubt as to your sincerity in establishing good school relationships." That general statement was followed by references to the radio station incident and to the obscene-gesture incident.[1]

The District Court found that all of these incidents had in fact occurred. It concluded that respondent Doyle's telephone call to the radio station was "clearly protected by the First Amendment," and that because it had played a "substantial part" in the decision of the Board not to renew Doyle's employment, he was entitled to reinstatement with back pay. The District Court did not expressly state what test it was applying in determining that the incident in question involved conduct protected by the First Amendment, but simply held that the communication to the radio station was such conduct. The Court of Appeals affirmed in a brief per curiam opinion. 529 F.2d 524.

Doyle's claims under the First and Fourteenth Amendments are not defeated by the fact that he did not have tenure. Even though he could

---

1. "I. You have shown a notable lack of tact in handling professional matters which leaves much doubt as to your sincerity in establishing good school relationships.

"A. You assumed the responsibility to notify W.S.A.I. Radio Station in regards to the suggestion of the Board of Education that teachers establish an appropriate dress code for professional people. This raised much concern not only within this community, but also in neighboring communities.

"B. You used obscene gestures to correct students in a situation in the cafeteria causing considerable concern among those students present.

"Sincerely yours,

"Rex Ralph

"Superintendent"

have been discharged for no reason whatever, and had no constitutional right to a hearing prior to the decision not to rehire him, Board of Regents v. Roth, 408 U.S. 564, 92 S.Ct. 2701, 33 L.Ed.2d 548 (1972), he may nonetheless establish a claim to reinstatement if the decision not to rehire him was made by reason of his exercise of constitutionally protected First Amendment freedoms. Perry v. Sindermann, 408 U.S. 593, 92 S.Ct. 2694, 33 L.Ed.2d 570 (1972).

That question of whether speech of a government employee is constitutionally protected expression necessarily entails striking "a balance between the interests of the teacher, as a citizen, in commenting upon matters of public concern and the interest of the State, as an employer, in promoting the efficiency of the public services it performs through its employees." Pickering v. Board of Education, 391 U.S. 563, 568, 88 S.Ct. 1731, 1734, 20 L.Ed.2d 811 (1968). There is no suggestion by the Board that Doyle violated any established policy, or that its reaction to his communication to the radio station was anything more than an ad hoc response to Doyle's action in making the memorandum public. We therefore accept the District Court's finding that the communication was protected by the First and Fourteenth Amendments. We are not, however, entirely in agreement with that court's manner of reasoning from this finding to the conclusion that Doyle is entitled to reinstatement with back pay.

The District Court made the following "conclusions" on this aspect of the case:

"1) If a non-permissible reason, e.g., exercise of First Amendment rights, played a substantial part in the decision not to renew— even in the face of other permissible grounds—the decision may not stand (citations omitted).

"2) A non-permissible reason did play a substantial part. That is clear from the letter of the Superintendent immediately following the Board's decision, which stated two reasons—the one, the conversation with the radio station clearly protected by the First Amendment. A court may not engage in any limitation of First Amendment rights based on 'tact'—that is not to say that the 'tactfulness' is irrelevant to other issues in this case."

At the same time, though, it stated that "[i]n fact, as this Court sees it and finds, both the Board and the Superintendent were faced with a situation in which there did exist in fact reason . . . independent of any First Amendment rights or exercise thereof, to not extend tenure."

Since respondent Doyle had no tenure, and there was therefore not even a state-law requirement of "cause" or "reason" before a decision could be made not to renew his employment, it is not clear what the District Court meant by this latter statement. Clearly, the Board legally could have dismissed respondent had the radio station incident never come to its attention. One plausible meaning of the court's statement is that the Board and the Superintendent not only could, but in fact would have reached that decision had not the constitutionally protected incident of the telephone call to the radio station occurred. We are thus brought to the issue whether, even if that were the case, the fact that the protected conduct played a "substantial part" in the actual decision not to renew would necessarily amount to a constitutional violation justifying remedial action. We think that it would not.

A rule of causation which focuses solely on whether protected conduct played a part, "substantial" or otherwise, in a decision not to rehire, could place an employee in a better position as a result of the exercise of constitutionally protected conduct than he would have occupied had he done nothing. The difficulty with the rule enunciated by the District Court is that it would require reinstatement in cases where a dramatic and perhaps abrasive incident is inevitably on the minds of those responsible for the decision to rehire, and does indeed play a part in that decision—even if the same decision would have been reached had the incident not occurred. The constitutional principle at stake is sufficiently vindicated if such an employee is placed in no worse a position than if he had not engaged in the conduct. A borderline or marginal candidate should not have the employment question resolved against him because of constitutionally protected conduct. But that same candidate ought not to be able, by engaging in such conduct, to prevent his employer from assessing his performance record and reaching a decision not to rehire on the basis of that record, simply because the protected conduct makes the employer more certain of the correctness of its decision.

This is especially true where, as the District Court observed was the case here, the current decision to rehire will accord "tenure." The long-term consequences of an award of tenure are of great moment both to the employee and to the employer. They are too significant for us to hold that the Board in this case would be precluded, because it considered constitutionally protected conduct in deciding not to rehire Doyle, from attempting to prove to a trier of fact that quite apart from such conduct Doyle's record was such that he would not have been rehired in any event.

* * *

Initially, in this case, the burden was properly placed upon respondent to show that his conduct was constitutionally protected, and that this conduct was a "substantial factor"—to put it in other words, that it was a "motivating factor" in the Board's decision not to rehire him. Respondent having carried that burden, however, the District Court should have gone on to determine whether the Board had shown by a preponderance of the evidence that it would have reached the same decision as to respondent's re-employment even in the absence of the protected conduct.

We cannot tell from the District Court opinion and conclusions, nor from the opinion of the Court of Appeals affirming the judgment of the District Court, what conclusion those courts would have reached had they applied this test. The judgment of the Court of Appeals is therefore vacated, and the case remanded for further proceedings consistent with this opinion.

Notes and Questions

Reasoning virtually identical to that of *Mount Healthy* was read into Title VII by the Supreme Court in *Price Waterhouse v. Hopkins*, 490 U.S. 228, 109 S.Ct. 1775, 104 L.Ed.2d 268 (1989). Subsequently, Congress amended Title VII to declare that these so-called "mixed motive" cases did violate the Act, see Section 703(m), but also to declare that the remedy in such cases, where the employer would have taken the disputed action for lawful reasons even if there had been no unlawful motive, is limited to injunctive or declaratory relief. See Section 706(g)(2)(B).

If you were a party in an employment discrimination case in which employer motivation was a disputed issue, how would you reconcile and comply with the formulas presented both in *McDonnell Douglas* and in *Mount Healthy*? How could you forecast which formula applies?

When we talk of the "motive" of a large, multi-person institution, what do we mean? How do we prove it? Does it even exist, at least, does it exist in the same sense that we speak of when we identify an individual's motive?

C. WHEN DIFFERENCES MATTER (OR NOT)

1. THE BONA FIDE OCCUPATIONAL QUALIFICATION (BFOQ)

Both Title VII and the Age Discrimination in Employment Act (ADEA) have specific provisions that allow an employer in very limited situations to explicitly take gender or age into account. Both use the same buzzwords, bona fide occupational qualification (BFOQ). See the definitions of the BFOQ in your statutory supplement: the ADEA provision is Sec. 4(f)(1) and the Title VII provision is Sec. 703(e).

The Supreme Court has explained the BFOQ under the ADEA in Western Air Lines, Inc. v. Criswell, 472 U.S. 400, 105 S.Ct. 2743, 86 L.Ed.2d 321 (1985), a small portion of which is excerpted below. Bear in mind this case involved the safety of air passengers, and it is entirely possible the justices were thinking of themselves as passengers on Western Air Lines or on another airline. The key to understanding the BFOQ defense is recognition that an employer may not take generalized truths about aging and apply them to specific employees unless the employer is unable to adopt or discover a reasonable way to test for the trait on an individual basis; a statistically higher incidence of vulnerability in older workers is not enough to support a BFOQ finding. Not surprisingly, but for the ADEA, many employers would always argue that it is too inefficient to make individual determinations regarding ability to do the work, and that age is the best and most legitimate basis for employment decisions.

In *Criswell*, the plaintiffs challenged Western's rule requiring flight engineers on commercial aircraft to retire on reaching age 60. Western's flight engineers monitored instrument panels during flights, and "the evidence at trial established the flight engineer's 'normal duties are less critical to the safety of flights than those of the pilot'" (quoting the district court). Under the rules of the Federal Aviation Administration and Western Air Lines, no one over the age of 60 could serve as a pilot or first officer on commercial flights. Western's engineers took over the controls only if both the pilot and first officer became incapacitated. A jury determined that Western's mandatory retirement of flight engineers at age 60 violated the ADEA. Western objected to the instruction informing the jury that (a) the "BFOQ defense is available only if it is reasonably necessary to the normal operation of or essence of defendant's business," that (b) "the essence of Western's business is the safe transportation of their passengers," and that (c)

"One method by which defendant Western may establish a BFOQ in this case is to prove:

"(1) That in 1978, when these plaintiffs were retired, it was highly impractical for Western to deal with each second officer over age 60 on an individualized basis to determine his particular ability to perform his job safely; and

"(2) That some second officers over age 60 possess traits of a physiological, psychological or other nature which preclude safe and efficient job performance that cannot be ascertained by means other than knowing their age.

"In evaluating the practicability to defendant Western of dealing with second officers over age 60 on an individualized basis, with respect to the medical testimony, you should consider the state of the medical art as it existed in July 1978."

On review, the Supreme Court opined,

"Western relied on two different kinds of job qualifications to justify its mandatory retirement policy. First, it argued that flight engineers should have a low risk of incapacitation or psychological and physiological deterioration. At this vague level of analysis the plaintiffs have not seriously disputed—nor could they—that the qualification of good health for a vital crew member is reasonably necessary to the essence of the airline's operations. Instead, they have argued that age is not a necessary proxy for that qualification.

"On a more specific level, Western argues that flight engineers must meet the same stringent qualifications as pilots, and that it was therefore quite logical to extend to flight engineers the FAA's age—60 retirement rule for pilots. Although the FAA's rule for pilots, adopted for safety reasons, is relevant evidence in the airline's BFOQ defense, it is not to be accorded conclusive weight. The extent to which the rule is probative varies with the weight of the evidence supporting its safety rationale and 'the congruity between the ... occupations at issue.' In this case, the evidence clearly established that the FAA, Western, and other airlines all recognized that the qualifications for a flight engineer were less rigorous than those required for a pilot.

"In the absence of persuasive evidence supporting its position, Western nevertheless argues that the jury should have been instructed to defer to 'Western's selection of job qualifications for the position of [flight engineer] that are reasonable in light of the safety risks.' This proposal is plainly at odds with Congress' decision, in adopting the ADEA, to subject such management decisions to a test of objective justification in a court of law. The BFOQ standard adopted in the statute is one of 'reasonable necessity,' not reasonableness.

"In adopting that standard, Congress did not ignore the public interest in safety. That interest is adequately reflected in instructions that track the language of the statute. When an employer establishes that a job qualification has been carefully formulated to respond to documented concerns for public safety, it will not be overly burdensome to persuade a trier of fact that the qualification is 'reasonably necessary' to safe operation of the business. The uncertainty implicit in the concept of managing safety risks always makes it 'reasonably necessary' to err on the side of caution in a close case. The employer cannot be expected to establish the risk of an airline accident 'to a certainty, for certainty would require running the risk until a tragic accident would prove that the judgment was sound.' Usery v. Tamiami Trail Tours, Inc., 531 F.2d, at 238. When the employer's argument has a credible basis in the record, it is difficult to believe that a jury of lay persons—many of whom no doubt have flown or could expect to fly on commercial air carriers— would not defer in a close case to the airline's judgment. Since the instructions in this case would not have prevented the airline from raising this contention to the jury in closing argument, we are satisfied that the verdict is a consequence of a defect in Western's proof rather than a defect in the trial court's instructions. * * * "

The Court rejected Western's contention that the ADEA requires the employer to show only a "rational basis in fact" for its belief that older employees were at risk. The Court continued:

> "It might well be 'rational' to require mandatory retirement at any age ... but that result would not comply with Congress' direction that employers must justify the rationale for the age chosen. Unless an employer can establish a substantial basis for believing that all or nearly all employees above an age lack the qualifications required for the position, the age selected for mandatory retirement ... must be an age at which it is highly impractical for the employer to insure by individual testing that its employees will have the necessary qualifications for the job."

Another aspect of the BFOQ defense discussed by the Court is that it must concern the essential parts of the job. The Court cited approvingly the earlier decision of Diaz v. Pan American World Airways, Inc., 442 F.2d 385 (5th Cir.1971), which held that Pan Am couldn't have a female-only requirement for cabin attendants; the quest for a "pleasant environment" and "cosmetic effect" that female attendants were thought to provide was "tangential" to the essence of the business, which was identified by the Court as safe transportation.

The courts have construed the BFOQ exception quite narrowly under Title VII, lest the exception swallow up the rule. The Court may have nodded in one case, Dothard v. Rawlinson, 433 U.S. 321, 97 S.Ct. 2720, 53 L.Ed.2d 786 (1977), in which it upheld an Alabama prison system rule that women could not serve as correctional counselors in the male sections of a maximum security penitentiary. This prompted a classic dissent by Justice Marshall that observed that the pedestal upon which women have been placed has once again been revealed as a cage.

What gender based BFOQ's would you endorse? Title VII doesn't allow for the BFOQ in cases of race discrimination. Why? Should it? Consider the following.

AUGUST WILSON, I WANT A BLACK DIRECTOR

The New York Times.
7/22/90, A25.

"I don't want to hire nobody just 'cause they're black." Eddie Murphy said that to me. We were discussing the possibility of Paramount Pictures purchasing the rights to my play "Fences." I said I wanted a black director for the film. My response [to his remark] was immediate. "Neither do I," I said.

What Mr. Murphy meant I am not sure. I meant I wanted to hire somebody talented, who understood the play and saw the possibilities of the film, who would approach my work with the same amount of passion and measure of respect with which I approach it, and who shared the cultural responsibilities of the characters.

That was more than three years ago. I have not talked to Mr. Murphy about the subject since. Paramount did purchase rights to make the film in 1987. What I thought of as a straightforward, logical request has been greeted by blank, vacant stares and the pious shaking of heads as if in response to my unfortunate naivete.

I usually have had to repeat my request, "I want a black director," as though it were a complex statement in a foreign tongue. I have often heard the same response: "We don't want to hire anyone just because they are black." What is being implied is that the only qualification any black has is the color of his skin.

In the film industry, the prevailing attitude is that a black director couldn't do the job, and to insist upon one is to make the film "unmakeable," partly because no one is going to turn a budget of $15 million over to a black director. That this is routinely done for novice white directors is beside the point.

The ideas of ability and qualification are not new to blacks. The skills of black lawyers, doctors, dentists, accountants and mechanics are often greeted with skepticism, even from other blacks. "Man, you sure you know what you doing?"

At the time of my last meeting with Paramount, in January 1990; a well-known, highly respected white director wanted very much to direct the film. I don't know his work, but he is universally praised for sensitive and intelligent direction. I accept that he is a very fine film director. But he is not black. He is not a product of black American culture—a culture that was honed out of the black experience and fired in the kiln of slavery and survival—and he does not share the sensibilities of black Americans.

I have been asked if I am not, by rejecting him on the basis of his race, doing the same thing Paramount is doing by not hiring a black director. That is a fair, if shortsighted, question which deserves a response.

I am not carrying a banner for black directors. I think they should carry their own. I am not trying to get work for black directors. I am trying to get the film of my play made in the best possible way.

As Americans of various races, we share a broad cultural ground, a commonality of society that links its diverse elements into a cohesive whole that can be defined as "American."

We share certain mythologies. A history. We share political and economic systems and a rapidly developing, if suspect, ethos. Within these commonalities are specifics. Specific ideas and attitudes that are not shared on the common cultural ground. These remain the property and possession of the people who develop them, and on that "field of manners and rituals of intercourse" (to use James Baldwin's eloquent phrase) lives are played out.

At the point where they intercept and link to the broad commonality of American culture, they influence how that culture is shared and to what purpose.

White American society is made up of various European ethnic groups which share a common history and sensibility. Black Americans are a racial group which do not share the same sensibilities. The specifics of our cultural history are very much different.

We are an African people who have been here since the early 17th century. We have a different way of responding to the world. We have different ideas about religion, different manners of social intercourse. We have different ideas about style, about language. We have different esthetics.

Someone who does not share the specifics of a culture remains an outsider, no matter how astute a student or how well-meaning their intentions.

I declined a white director not on the basis of race but on the basis of culture. White directors are not qualified for the job. The job requires someone who shares the specifics of the culture of black Americans.

Webster's "Third New International Dictionary" gives the following character definitions listed under black and white.

White: free from blemish, moral stain or impurity: outstandingly righteous; innocent; not marked by malignant influence; notably pleasing or auspicious; fortunate; notably ardent; decent; in a fair upright manner; a sterling man; etc.

Black: outrageously wicked; a villain; dishonorable; expressing or indicating disgrace, discredit or guilt; connected with the devil; expressing menace; sullen; hostile; unqualified; committing a violation of public regulation, illicit, illegal; affected by some undesirable condition; etc.

No wonder I had been greeted with incredulous looks when I suggested a black director for "Fences." I sat in the offices of Paramount suggesting that someone who was affected by an undesirable condition, who was a violator of public regulations, who was sullen, unqualified and marked by a malignant influence, direct the film.

While they were offering a sterling man, who was free from blemish, notably pleasing, fair and upright, decent and outstandingly righteous—with a reputation to boot!

Despite such a linguistic environment, the culture of black Americans has emerged and defined itself in strong and effective vehicles that have become the flag-bearers for self-determination and self-identity.

In the face of such, those who are opposed to the ideas of a "foreign" culture permeating the ideal of an American culture founded on the icons of Europe seek to dilute and control it by setting themselves up as the assayers of its value and the custodians of its offspring.

Therein lies the crux of the matter as it relates to Paramount and the film "Fences"—whether we as blacks are going to have control over our own culture and its products.

Some Americans, black and white, do not see any value to black American lives that do not contribute to the leisure or profit of white America. Some Americans, black and white, would deny that a black American culture even exists. Some Americans, black and white, would say that by insisting on a black director for "Fences" I am doing irreparable harm to the efforts of black directors who have spent the last 15 years trying to get Hollywood to ignore the fact that they are black. The origins of such ideas are so very old and shallow that I am amazed to see them so vividly displayed in 1990.

What to do? Let's make a rule. Blacks don't direct Italian films. Italians don't direct Jewish films. Jews don't direct black American films. That might account for about 3 percent of the films that are made in this country. The other 97 percent—the action-adventure, horror, comedy, romance, suspense, western, or any combination thereof, that the Hollywood and independent mills grind out—let it be every man for himself.

[August Wilson, reached yesterday, said through a spokeswoman: "Paramount agreed in principle in March to hire a black director. They have not done so, although just prior to publication of the Spin article they broached the subject and began suggesting names. I consider their agreement a small victory. I will consider their actually hiring a black director a greater victory."]

2. AFFIRMATIVE ACTION

PETER T. KILBORN, A COMPANY RECASTS ITSELF TO ERASE DECADES OF BIAS

New York Times.
10/4/90, A1.

Corning, N.Y.—When a black job candidate comes here to Corning Inc. for interviews, managers have a real incentive to hire him. Raises and bonuses for the executives, most of whom are white men, depend largely on recruiting blacks and women and on their success in training and promoting them.

Not only that. One interviewer is a black from the department where the recruit would start work. The interviewer helps put the candidate at ease, and afterward joins in assessing the candidate to guard against intrusions of racism. Once hired, most black recruits and many women are assigned a "coach," someone from another department who shows them the ways of Corning and steers them around the pitfalls that can thwart promotions.

Corning, the giant family-controlled maker of Pyrex, Corning Ware and Steuben Crystal, is engaged in one of corporate America's most ambitious experiments in cultural engineering. The company accommodates women and blacks in a score of ways, all ultimately intended to assure them of a good crack at the top jobs in the company. Eventually, the company wants to do the same for other minority members, who are fewer around Corning.

Pressed by advocacy groups and Government, and above all by their own economic self-interest, many big companies nowadays are trying to make affirmative action work better than it did five and 10 years ago. Corning, like many others, managed to hire women and blacks quite easily then, but many promptly fled, blaming entrenched, if often subtle, discrimination.

A few prominent companies have learned to retain women, and fewer still have done well by blacks. The advocates for women and blacks call Corning a rarer case of a company that has adopted effective ways to help both groups, even to the extent of luring black barbers and hairdressers to the area around Corning, where white barbers would not learn to cut blacks' hair.

"The corporation has been very receptive to just about everything that women and blacks have said they need to be able to do their work better," said Gail Baity, a black woman who started in industrial relations at Corning 14 years ago. She now conducts an intensive two-day course to purge employees of racist attitudes. This course and one on sexism are required for thousands of managers and professional employees.

Sybil Mobley, dean of the predominantly black business school at Florida A & M University in Tallahassee, said: "Our experience with them is very good, across the board. Our students have found that it's a very good place to work." Catalyst, a women's advocacy group in New York, has granted only four companies special awards for commitment to women: Gannett, Du Pont, Avon Products and Corning.

CURIOSITY AND A BACKLASH

The director of Corning's cultural diversity program, Dawn M. Cross, said, "During the course of a week, we get 20 to 25 calls from companies that are just beginning to deal with these issues."

But Corning's anti-discrimination efforts have fostered something of a backlash among the 3,000 white, male managers, professionals and technicians. Their generation is being asked to pay for all the earlier generations' discrimination in keeping the big, best-paid jobs for themselves.

White men still far outnumber other groups at Corning, and they still get most promotions. But more are by-passed than ever, too, and there is little the company intends to do about it. "A backlash is one of the prices you pay," said J. Edwin O'Brien Jr., director of education, training and recruiting. "Not that we like it or want it. It's a price of progress."

Some white men assert that management has set lower job standards for women and blacks, but Mr. O'Brien flatly denies it.

"It wouldn't work," he said. "Women and blacks would be the first to complain. And the people would fail. They wouldn't get salary increases. They wouldn't get promotions. And they'll look at their counterparts and quit."

GAINS FOR WORKERS

Once Scorned, Now a Mentor

A beneficiary of Corning's affirmative action policies is LeRoy E. Hambrick, a black who is consumer products marketing manager for Asia. Corning hired him 17 years ago, when he was 22, and dispatched him to a factory here as a foreman.

"One guy wrote a slur on a machine, 'Nigger, go home,' " he recalled, and he said he ignored it. He said he never encountered such blatant bigotry any more and rarely its subtler forms. "I play tennis with vice presidents," he said. "Some white males even gravitate toward me as a mentor."

Another is Lina M. Echeverria. She and her husband, both Ph.D. scientists from Stanford, joined the company's research laboratories in the early 1980s. A couple of years ago, as part of a team exploring new ceramic materials, Ms. Echeverria said, she proposed a novel research procedure derived from her doctoral work in geology. None of the others on the team, white men, had studied geology, and in their ignorance, she said, they belittled her.

"My ability to do something was questioned," Ms. Echeverria said. "I raised my voice and said, 'I'm not going to take this any more.' It was a difficult point in my career." To hold on to Ms. Echeverria, management transferred her to what she said was a far better assignment in materials research.

For its efforts, the company has begun to show some real gains. It says 52 percent of the salaried employees it has hired over the past three years are women, and 16 percent are black. Three years ago, the roughly 150 top managers included four white women and one black man. Today the same group has seven women and five blacks, including a black woman who is double counted.

Of 5,365 salaried personnel, the source of the top managers of 20 or 30 years from now, the percentage of women has climbed to 33.6 percent from 17.4 percent. Among blacks, the gain has been much smaller, to 5.5 percent from 5.1 percent. But that is well above the levels of most companies, and the percentage of blacks who quit the company has dropped to 10.9 percent last year from 15.1 percent in 1987.

MOTIVES FOR COMPANIES

Self–Interest
Amid Change

All big companies, Corning included, still have a long way to go in bringing women and minority members to the highest level of management. At the pinnacle of American corporations, women and minority members fill less than one percent of the jobs, and at Corning they hold none.

All the secretaries in the headquarters' glistening ninth-floor executive chambers are women. All the executives—the chairman, James R. Houghton, and six others—are white men. The culture there is starkly male, too. All but one of the seven smoke cigars.

Yet the "Seven Ups," as their underlings know them, say they are committed to seeing that the next generations of Seven Ups will be a richer mix. "It's the right thing to do," Mr. Houghton said. But more to the point, he said, it is a critical business thing to do.

To prosper and grow in the next decades, Corning says it needs competent managers, scientists and engineers, and irreversible demographic trends oblige the company to turn to women and blacks.

FEWER WHITE MALE WORKERS

The Bureau of Labor Statistics predicts that by the end of the 1990s, 39 percent of all workers will be white men, a decline from almost half 15 years ago, and that white males will account for just 20 percent of all the people entering the labor force by the end of the decade.

For companies like Corning, heavily oriented to technological advances, the competition for workers will be especially stiff because of a paucity of blacks who have the doctoral degrees that the company needs for its labs. Blacks account for 12 percent of the population but only 2 percent of the nation's scientists and engineers. (A little over 4 percent at Corning are black.)

"What happened to me was that about 1986, I got concerned," Mr. Houghton said. "We had been doing our equal opportunity, affirmative action bit for a long time, and we'd gone up every year as a percent in hiring." Yet Mr. Houghton found that around 15 percent of the company's women and blacks were quitting the company's salaried ranks each year, about triple the rate of white men.

BLOCKED FROM THE TOP

Management wondered if women and blacks left because competitors were poaching on Corning's recruits, or if the town was just too dull. Corning, an old-fashioned company town, is tucked amid the pastures of western New York State, an hour's drive from the closest real city, the minor metropolis of Ithaca.

But in their departure interviews, women and blacks said their biggest gripe was evidence that their progress up the ranks was restricted. "We found the reason was not the town but the perceived opportunities," Mr. Houghton said.

"I put a few things together," Mr. Houghton said, "and said this has to be a major corporate initiative."

Civil rights laws and the Bush Administration's new promises to use its power of Federal contracting to open up the executive suite have little relevance to this. Nor has the White House's opposition to the civil rights bill in Congress on the ground that it might force employers to set hiring quotas for women and blacks.

Mr. Houghton says he doesn't like numerical goals either. "But I don't know of any way around them."

GAME PLAN FOR CORNING

Encouraging
Ethnic Pride

Mr. Houghton has set two goals for Corning: one, the better mix of women and blacks in the company's management and professional ranks, and two, making a virtue of the mix. He says he wants a salad, not a purée-blacks who are proud to be black and women who are proud to be mothers and engineers. The melting pot is a delusion, black executives here say, and Corning's emphasis on it a decade ago led to the exclusion of both blacks and women and to their flight from the company.

Early in the company's affirmative action efforts, Ms. Baity said, blacks and women were encouraged to adopt not only the company's basic values—like integrity, hard work and a commitment to profits and growth—but also its white male cultural values, including dress and social activities. Women tried to look like men, donning gray flannel suits and neckties.

In meetings, people were expected to repress views they were passionate about and save disputes for private offices. Even now, Ms. Echeverria said, "you don't display aggressive behavior, even if you have to push a project very fast."

But such gentlemanliness can thwart the progress of women, she said, because in meetings, white male managers sometimes ignore women unless they demand attention. Inevitably, too, women and blacks who tried to be like white men couldn't, and they were denied opportunities and fled.

"The goal was assimilation so that we would come out with a homogenized mix," Ms. Cross said. "Today people are encouraged to maintain their cultural identity and ethnic heritage, and managers are encouraged to value that richness and to see that it adds value to the corporation."

Ms. Baity said: "We want people to recognize race. I want people to look at me as a black female who is competent in her job."

Some things the company has done might not seem like much to a white man who can find basic amenities even in a town of 12,000 like Corning. But Corning's blacks could not find programs they liked on radio or television, just as they could not find barbers.

So the company prevailed on the cable television outlet to pipe in a black radio station from Rochester and the Black Entertainment Network from Washington. The company has also helped recruit black teachers for the public schools and an assistant principal who is black.

RECRUITING THEM EARLY

To recruit women and blacks to Corning, the company offers well-paid internships to undergraduates more readily than it offers them to white male students. Blacks and women, much more than white men, tend to drop out of advanced science and engineering courses, and Kurt R. Fischer, human resources manager for the company's research and development operations, says the internships help keep them on course.

The 17 colleges that Corning calls its key recruiting campuses are mostly science and engineering schools, but they include just as many predominantly black schools—Howard, Florida A & M, and North Carolina A & T—as Ivy League schools—Cornell, the University of Pennsylvania and Mr. Houghton's alma mater, Harvard.

More than most companies, Corning also goes to great lengths to find jobs at Corning for recruits' spouses or "significant others," as one official puts it. Several hundred couples work for the company, all subject to only one firm rule—that one spouse not work for the other. In hundreds of other cases, Corning has helped recruits' spouses get jobs around town, including many in businesses that deal primarily with Corning.

ADJUSTMENTS FOR EVERYONE

Resentment,
And Praise

Blacks and women say the company could do still more. Corning operates a day care center for children 3 to 5 years old, for example, but young parents say they have just as much need for one for infants and toddlers. Some also want paid paternity leave. The company permits unpaid leave for fathers, and so far only one has taken it.

Blacks say Corning could do more in the community, using its influence to draw a few black merchants and still more black teachers.

The economics of Corning's accommodations are hard to gauge. The classes, the day care center, the personnel who manage the affirmative action efforts all cost something, but far less than the $4 million a year that Mr. Houghton says the company was spending a few years ago to recruit and train women and blacks to replace those who were quitting. And of course, people who do not anguish over racial and sexual abuse tend to work harder and more happily, helping Corning make money.

Many white men say they accept the change, but many also say they know of others who are resentful and bristling. One who says he accepts the new competition for the top jobs is James N. Nagel, 33, whose wife, like him, is a middle-level manufacturing executive. "The competition for me will be more difficult," Mr. Nagel said. "Corning has quotas. I don't resent it. It's a fact of life."

With the change in Corning's personnel mix, a change in the company's gentlemanly ways seems well under way. White men must now contend with women like Wendy E. Luce, 35, who as operations manager of a factory here is the highest-ranking woman in the overwhelmingly male manufacturing side of the company. Ms. Luce says she has no compunctions about yelling when she sees fit. "I'd rather see people get excited," she said.

Roy A. Farr, 60, her deputy at the plant, called her a good boss, but different. "Wendy really feels for people," he said. "She is kinder than men, more considerate, but not to the point where it gets in the way of the business. She knows what she wants to do. She leads. Men demand. She seems to be setting the tone of where Corning wants to go."

Question

Assume the facts in the Kilborn article on Corning to be accurate. Has Corning violated any anti-discrimination laws?

THE SUPREME COURT SPEAKS,
OFTEN AND VARIOUSLY

The Supreme Court has dealt with the validity of affirmative action programs in a number of cases in the past two decades. Its position has varied over the years, and there are clear opposing factions on the Court. The outcome of a given case seems to depend on whether the facts are such that one faction or the other can pick up the critical "swing" votes to make a majority. The case below, Johnson v. Transportation Agency, takes a position fairly consistent with the one 15 years earlier in Steelworkers v. Weber, which is discussed in *Johnson*. Bear in mind that *Johnson* is decided as a Title VII case, as was *Weber*. Since *Johnson* involved a state agency, the validity of the affirmative action program could have been determined under the Constitution, but that issue was not litigated. As you read the decision you should consider whether there would have been a different result under the Constitution.

JOHNSON v. TRANSPORTATION AGENCY,
SANTA CLARA COUNTY, CAL.

Supreme Court of the United States, 1987.
480 U.S. 616, 107 S.Ct. 1442, 94 L.Ed.2d 615.

JUSTICE BRENNAN delivered the opinion of the Court.

Respondent, Transportation Agency of Santa Clara County, California, unilaterally promulgated an Affirmative Action Plan applicable, inter alia, to promotions of employees. In selecting applicants for the promotional position of road dispatcher, the Agency, pursuant to the Plan, passed over petitioner Paul Johnson, a male employee, and promoted a female employee applicant, Diane Joyce. The question for decision is whether in making the promotion the Agency impermissibly took into account the sex of the applicants in violation of Title VII of the Civil Rights Act of 1964, 42 U.S.C. § 2000e et seq. The District Court for the Northern District of California, in an action filed by petitioner following receipt of a right-to-sue letter from the Equal Employment Opportunity Commission (EEOC), held that respondent had violated Title VII. The Court of Appeals for the Ninth Circuit reversed. We granted certiorari. We affirm.[2]

I

A

In December 1978, the Santa Clara County Transit District Board of Supervisors adopted an Affirmative Action Plan (Plan) for the County Transportation Agency. The Plan implemented a County Affirmative Action Plan, which had been adopted, declared the County, because "mere prohibition of discriminatory practices is not enough to remedy the effects of past practices and to permit attainment of an equitable representation of minorities, women and handicapped persons."[3] Relevant to this case, the Agency Plan provides that, in making promotions to positions within a traditionally segregated job classification in which women have been significantly under-represented, the Agency is authorized to consider as one factor the sex of a qualified applicant.

In reviewing the composition of its work force, the Agency noted in its Plan that women were represented in numbers far less than their proportion of the county labor force in both the Agency as a whole and in five of seven job categories. Specifically, while women constituted 36.4% of the area labor market, they composed only 22.4% of Agency employees. Furthermore, women working at the Agency were concentrated largely in EEOC job categories traditionally held by women: women made up 76% of Office and Clerical Workers, but only 7.1% of Agency Officials and Administrators, 8.6% of Professionals, 9.7% of Technicians, and 22% of Service and Maintenance workers. As for the job classification relevant to this case, none of the 238 Skilled Craft Worker positions was held by a woman. The Plan noted that this under-representation of women in part reflected the fact that women had not traditionally been employed in these positions, and that they had not been strongly motivated to seek training or employment in them "because of the limited opportunities that have existed in the past for them to work in such classifications." The Plan also observed that, while the proportion of ethnic minorities in the Agency as a whole exceeded the proportion of such minorities in the county work force, a smaller percentage of minority employees held management, professional, and technical positions.

2. No constitutional issue was either raised or addressed in the litigation below. We therefore decide in this case only the issue of the prohibitory scope of Title VII. Of course, where the issue is properly raised, public employers must justify the adoption and implementation of a voluntary affirmative action plan under the Equal Protection Clause. See Wygant v. Jackson Board of Education, 476 U.S. 267, 106 S.Ct. 1842, 90 L.Ed.2d 260 (1986).

3. The Plan reaffirmed earlier County and Agency efforts to address the issue of employment discrimination, dating back to the County's adoption in 1971 of an Equal Employment Opportunity Policy.

The Agency stated that its Plan was intended to achieve "a statistically measurable yearly improvement in hiring, training and promotion of minorities and women throughout the Agency in all major job classifications where they are under-represented." As a benchmark by which to evaluate progress, the Agency stated that its long-term goal was to attain a work force whose composition reflected the proportion of minorities and women in the area labor force. Thus, for the Skilled Craft category in which the road dispatcher position at issue here was classified, the Agency's aspiration was that eventually about 36% of the jobs would be occupied by women.

The Plan acknowledged that a number of factors might make it unrealistic to rely on the Agency's long-term goals in evaluating the Agency's progress in expanding job opportunities for minorities and women. Among the factors identified were low turnover rates in some classifications, the fact that some jobs involved heavy labor, the small number of positions within some job categories, the limited number of entry positions leading to the Technical and Skilled Craft classifications, and the limited number of minorities and women qualified for positions requiring specialized training and experience. As a result, the Plan counseled that short-range goals be established and annually adjusted to serve as the most realistic guide for actual employment decisions. * * *

The Agency's Plan thus set aside no specific number of positions for minorities or women, but authorized the consideration of ethnicity or sex as a factor when evaluating qualified candidates for jobs in which members of such groups were poorly represented. One such job was the road dispatcher position that is the subject of the dispute in this case.

B

On December 12, 1979, the Agency announced a vacancy for the promotional position of road dispatcher in the Agency's Roads Division. * * *

Twelve County employees applied for the promotion, including Joyce and Johnson. Joyce had worked for the County since 1970, serving as an account clerk until 1975. She had applied for a road dispatcher position in 1974, but was deemed ineligible because she had not served as a road maintenance worker. In 1975, Joyce transferred from a senior account clerk position to a road maintenance worker position, becoming the first woman to fill such a job. During her four years in that position, she occasionally worked out of class as a road dispatcher.

Petitioner Johnson began with the county in 1967 as a road yard clerk, after private employment that included working as a supervisor and dispatcher. He had also unsuccessfully applied for the road dispatcher opening in 1974. In 1977, his clerical position was downgraded, and he sought and received a transfer to the position of road maintenance worker. He also occasionally worked out of class as a dispatcher while performing that job.

Nine of the applicants, including Joyce and Johnson, were deemed qualified for the job, and were interviewed by a two-person board. Seven of the applicants scored above 70 on this interview, which meant that they were certified as eligible for selection by the appointing authority. The scores awarded ranged from 70 to 80. Johnson was tied for second with a score of 75, while Joyce ranked next with a score of 73. A second interview was conducted by three Agency supervisors, who ultimately recommended that Johnson be promoted. Prior to the second interview, Joyce had contacted the County's Affirmative Action Office because she feared that her application might not receive disinterested review.[5] The Office in turn contacted the Agency's Affirmative Action Coordinator, whom the Agency's Plan makes responsible for, inter alia, keeping the Director informed of opportunities for the Agency to accomplish its objectives under the Plan. At the time, the Agency employed no women in any Skilled Craft position, and had never employed a woman as a road dispatcher. The Coordinator recommended to the Director of the Agency, James Graebner, that Joyce be promoted.

Graebner, authorized to choose any of the seven persons deemed eligible, thus had the benefit of suggestions by the second interview panel and by the Agency Coordinator in arriving at his decision. After deliberation, Graebner concluded that the promotion should be given to Joyce. As he testified: "I tried to look at the whole picture, the combination of her qualifications and Mr. Johnson's qualifications, their test scores, their expertise, their background, affirmative action matters, things like that ... I believe it was a combination of all those."

The certification form naming Joyce as the person promoted to the dispatcher position stated that both she and Johnson were rated as well-qualified for the job. The evaluation of Joyce read: "Well qualified by virtue of 18 years of past clerical experience including 3½ years at West Yard plus almost 5 years as a [road maintenance worker]." The evaluation of Johnson was as follows: "Well qualified applicant; two years of [road maintenance worker] experience plus 11 years of Road Yard Clerk. Has had previous outside Dispatch experience but was 13 years ago." Graebner testified that he did not regard as significant the fact that

---

5. Joyce testified that she had had disagreements with two of the three members of the second interview panel. One had been her first supervisor when she began work as a road maintenance worker. In performing arduous work in this job, she had not been issued coveralls, although her male co-workers had received them. After ruining her pants, she complained to her supervisor, to no avail. After three other similar incidents, ruining clothes on each occasion, she filed a grievance, and was issued four pair of coveralls the next day. Joyce had dealt with a second member of the panel for a year and a half in her capacity as chair of the Roads Operations Safety Committee, where she and he "had

several differences of opinion on how safety should be implemented." In addition, Joyce testified that she had informed the person responsible for arranging her second interview that she had a disaster preparedness class on a certain day the following week. By this time about ten days had passed since she had notified this person of her availability, and no date had yet been set for the interview. Within a day or two after this conversation, however, she received a notice setting her interview at a time directly in the middle of her disaster preparedness class. This same panel member had earlier described Joyce as a "rebel-rousing, skirt-wearing person."

Johnson scored 75 and Joyce 73 when interviewed by the two-person board. * * *

The assessment of the legality of the Agency Plan must be guided by our decision in *Weber* [United Steelworkers v. Weber, 443 U.S. 193, 99 S.Ct. 2721, 61 L.Ed.2d 480 (1979)]. In that case, the Court addressed the question whether the employer violated Title VII by adopting a voluntary affirmative action plan designed to "eliminate manifest racial imbalances in traditionally segregated job categories." Id., 443 U.S., at 197, 99 S.Ct. at 2724. The respondent employee in that case challenged the employer's denial of his application for a position in a newly established craft training program, contending that the employer's selection process impermissibly took into account the race of the applicants. The selection process was guided by an affirmative action plan, which provided that 50% of the new trainees were to be black until the percentage of black skilled craftworkers in the employer's plant approximated the percentage of blacks in the local labor force. Adoption of the plan had been prompted by the fact that only 5 of 273, or 1.83%, of skilled craftworkers at the plant were black, even though the work force in the area was approximately 39% black. Because of the historical exclusion of blacks from craft positions, the employer regarded its former policy of hiring trained outsiders as inadequate to redress the imbalance in its work force.

We upheld the employer's decision to select less senior black applicants over the white respondent, for we found that taking race into account was consistent with Title VII's objective of "break[ing] down old patterns of racial segregation and hierarchy." As we stated:

> "It would be ironic indeed if a law triggered by a Nation's concern over centuries of racial injustice and intended to improve the lot of those who had 'been excluded from the American dream for so long' constituted the first legislative prohibition of all voluntary, private, race-conscious efforts to abolish traditional patterns of racial segregation and hierarchy."

We noted that the plan did not "unnecessarily trammel the interests of the white employees," since it did not require "the discharge of white workers and their replacement with new black hirees." Nor did the plan create "an absolute bar to the advancement of white employees," since half of those trained in the new program were to be white. Finally, we observed that the plan was a temporary measure, not designed to maintain racial balance, but to "eliminate a manifest racial imbalance." As Justice Blackmun's concurrence made clear, *Weber* held that an employer seeking to justify the adoption of a plan need not point to its own prior discriminatory practices, nor even to evidence of an "arguable violation" on its part. Rather, it need point only to a "conspicuous ... imbalance in traditionally segregated job categories." Our decision was grounded in the recognition that voluntary employer action can play a crucial role in furthering Title VII's purpose of eliminating the effects of discrimination in the workplace, and that Title VII should not be read to thwart such efforts.

In reviewing the employment decision at issue in this case, we must first examine whether that decision was made pursuant to a plan prompted by concerns similar to those of the employer in *Weber*. Next, we must determine whether the effect of the plan on males and non-minorities is comparable to the effect of the plan in that case.

The first issue is therefore whether consideration of the sex of applicants for skilled craft jobs was justified by the existence of a "manifest imbalance" that reflected under-representation of women in "traditionally segregated job categories." In determining whether an imbalance exists that would justify taking sex or race into account, a comparison of the percentage of minorities or women in the employer's work force with the percentage in the area labor market or general population is appropriate in analyzing jobs that require no special expertise, or training programs designed to provide expertise. Where a job requires special training, however, the comparison should be with those in the labor force who possess the relevant qualifications. The requirement that the "manifest imbalance" relate to a "traditionally segregated job category" provides assurance both that sex or race will be taken into account in a manner consistent with Title VII's purpose of eliminating the effects of employment discrimination, and that the interests of those employees not benefitting from the plan will not be unduly infringed.

A manifest imbalance need not be such that it would support a prima facie case against the employer, as suggested in Justice O'Connor's concurrence, since we do not regard as identical the constraints of Title VII and the federal constitution on voluntarily adopted affirmative action plans. Application of the "prima facie" standard in Title VII cases would be inconsistent with *Weber*'s focus on statistical imbalance, and could inappropriately create a significant disincentive for employers to adopt an affirmative action plan. A corporation concerned with maximizing return on investment, for instance, is hardly likely to adopt a plan if in order to do so it must compile evidence that could be used to subject it to a colorable Title VII suit.

It is clear that the decision to hire Joyce was made pursuant to an Agency plan that directed that sex or race be taken into account for the purpose of remedying under-representation. The Agency Plan acknowledged the "limited opportunities that have existed in the past," for women to find employment in certain job classifications "where women have not been traditionally employed in significant numbers." As a result, observed the Plan, women were concentrated in traditionally female jobs in the Agency, and represented a lower percentage in other job classifications than would be expected if such traditional segregation had not occurred.

* * * The Plan stressed that such goals "should not be construed as 'quotas' that must be met," but as reasonable aspirations in correcting

the imbalance in the Agency's work force. These goals were to take into account factors such as "turnover, layoffs, lateral transfers, new job openings, retirements and availability of minorities, women and handicapped persons in the area work force who possess the desired qualifications or potential for placement."

* * * Given the obvious imbalance in the Skilled Craft category, and given the Agency's commitment to eliminating such imbalances, it was plainly not unreasonable for the Agency to determine that it was appropriate to consider as one factor the sex of Ms. Joyce in making its decision.[14] The promotion of Joyce thus satisfies the first requirement enunciated in *Weber,* since it was undertaken to further an affirmative action plan designed to eliminate Agency work force imbalances in traditionally segregated job categories.

We next consider whether the Agency Plan unnecessarily trammeled the rights of male employees or created an absolute bar to their advancement. In contrast to the plan in *Weber,* which provided that 50% of the positions in the craft training program were exclusively for blacks, * * * the Plan sets aside no positions for women. * * * [T]he Plan merely authorizes that consideration be given to affirmative action concerns when evaluating qualified applicants. As the Agency Director testified, the sex of Joyce was but one of numerous factors he took into account in arriving at his decision. * * * [T]he Agency Plan requires women to compete with all other qualified applicants. No persons are automatically excluded from consideration; all are able to have their qualifications weighed against those of other applicants.

In addition, petitioner had no absolute entitlement to the road dispatcher position. Seven of the applicants were classified as qualified and eligible, and the Agency Director was authorized to promote any of the seven. Thus, denial of the promotion unsettled no legitimate firmly rooted expectation on the part of the petitioner. Furthermore, while the petitioner in this case was denied a promotion, he retained his employment with the Agency, at the same salary and with the same seniority, and remained eligible for other promotions.

Finally, the Agency's Plan was intended to attain a balanced work force, not to maintain one. * * *

The Agency acknowledged the difficulties that it would confront in remedying the imbalance in its work force, and it anticipated only gradual increases in the representation of minorities and women. It is thus unsurprising that the Plan contains no explicit end date, for the Agency's flexible, case-by-case approach was not expected to yield success in a brief period of time. Express assurance that a program is only

---

14. In addition, the Agency was mindful of the importance of finally hiring a woman in a job category that had formerly been all-male. The Director testified that, while the promotion of Joyce "made a small dent, for sure, in the numbers," nonetheless "philo- sophically it made a larger impact in that it probably has encouraged other females and minorities to look at the possibility of so-called 'non-traditional' jobs as areas where they and the agency both have samples of a success story."

temporary may be necessary if the program actually sets aside positions according to specific numbers. * * *

III

* * *

We * * * hold that the Agency appropriately took into account as one factor the sex of Diane Joyce in determining that she should be promoted to the road dispatcher position. The decision to do so was made pursuant to an affirmative action plan that represents a moderate, flexible, case-by-case approach to effecting a gradual improvement in the representation of minorities and women in the Agency's work force. Such a plan is fully consistent with Title VII, for it embodies the contribution that voluntary employer action can make in eliminating the vestiges of discrimination in the workplace. Accordingly, the judgment of the Court of Appeals is

Affirmed.

[The concurring opinions of JUSTICES STEVENS and O'CONNOR are omitted. The dissenting opinion of JUSTICE WHITE is omitted.]

JUSTICE SCALIA, with whom THE CHIEF JUSTICE joins, and with whom JUSTICE WHITE joins in Parts I and II, dissenting.

With a clarity which, had it not proven so unavailing, one might well recommend as a model of statutory draftsmanship, Title VII of the Civil Rights Act of 1964 declares:

"It shall be an unlawful employment practice for an employer

"(1) to fail or refuse to hire or to discharge any individual, or otherwise to discriminate against any individual with respect to his compensation, terms, conditions, or privileges of employment, because of such individual's race, color, religion, sex, or national origin; or

"(2) to limit, segregate, or classify his employees or applicants for employment in any way which would deprive or tend to deprive any individual of employment opportunities or otherwise adversely affect his status as an employee, because of such individual's race, color, religion, sex, or national origin." 42 U.S.C. § 2000e–2(a).

The Court today completes the process of converting this from a guarantee that race or sex will not be the basis for employment determinations, to a guarantee that it often will. Ever so subtly, without even alluding to the last obstacles preserved by earlier opinions that we now push out of our path, we effectively replace the goal of a discrimination-free society with the quite incompatible goal of proportionate representation by race and by sex in the workplace. Part I of this dissent will describe the nature of the plan that the Court approves, and its effect upon this petitioner. Part II will discuss prior holdings that are tacitly overruled, and prior distinctions that are disregarded. Part III will describe the engine of discrimination we have finally completed.

* * *

II

The most significant proposition of law established by today's decision is that racial or sexual discrimination is permitted under Title VII when it is intended to overcome the effect, not of the employer's own discrimination, but of societal attitudes that have limited the entry of certain races, or of a particular sex, into certain jobs. Even if the societal attitudes in question consisted exclusively of conscious discrimination by other employers, this holding would contradict a decision of this Court rendered only last Term. Wygant v. Jackson Board of Education held that the objective of remedying societal discrimination cannot prevent remedial affirmative action from violating the Equal Protection Clause. While Mr. Johnson does not advance a constitutional claim here, it is most unlikely that Title VII was intended to place a lesser restraint on discrimination by public actors than is established by the Constitution. * * *

In fact, however, today's decision goes well beyond merely allowing racial or sexual discrimination in order to eliminate the effects of prior societal *discrimination*. The majority opinion often uses the phrase "traditionally segregated job category" to describe the evil against which the plan is legitimately (according to the majority) directed. As originally used in Steelworkers v. Weber, that phrase described skilled jobs from which employers and unions had systematically and intentionally excluded black workers—traditionally segregated jobs, that is, in the sense of conscious, exclusionary discrimination. But that is assuredly not the sense in which the phrase is used here. It is absurd to think that the nationwide failure of road maintenance crews, for example, to achieve the Agency's ambition of 36.4% female representation is attributable primarily, if even substantially, to systematic exclusion of women eager to shoulder pick and shovel. It is a "traditionally segregated job category" *not* in the *Weber* sense, but in the sense that, because of longstanding social attitudes, it has not been regarded by *women themselves* as desirable work. Or as the majority opinion puts the point, quoting approvingly the Court of Appeals: " 'A plethora of proof is hardly necessary to show that women are generally under-represented in such positions and that strong social pressures weigh against their participation.' " Given this meaning of the phrase, it is patently false to say that "[t]he requirement that the 'manifest imbalance' relate to a 'traditionally segregated job category' provides assurance that sex or race will be taken into account in a manner consistent with Title VII's purpose of eliminating the effects of employment discrimination." There are, of course, those who believe that the social attitudes which cause women themselves to avoid certain jobs and to favor others are as nefarious as conscious, exclusionary discrimination. Whether or not that is so (and there is assuredly no consensus on the point equivalent to our national consensus against intentional discrimination), the two phenomena are certainly distinct. And it is the alteration of social attitudes, rather than the elimination of discrimination, which today's decision approves as justification for state-enforced discrimination. This is an enormous expansion, undertaken without the slightest justification or analysis.

* * *

Today's decision does more, however, than merely reaffirm *Weber*, and more than merely extend it to public actors. It is impossible not to be aware that the practical effect of our holding is to accomplish de facto what the law—in language even plainer than that ignored in *Weber*, see 42 U.S.C. § 2000e–2(j)—forbids anyone from accomplishing *de jure*: in many contexts it effectively *requires* employers, public as well as private, to engage in intentional discrimination on the basis of race or sex. This Court's prior interpretations of Title VII, especially the decision in *Griggs v. Duke Power Co.*, subject employers to a potential Title VII suit whenever there is a noticeable imbalance in the representation of minorities or women in the employer's work force. Even the employer who is confident of ultimately prevailing in such a suit must contemplate the expense and adverse publicity of a trial, because the extent of the imbalance, and the "job relatedness" of his selection criteria, are questions of fact to be explored through rebuttal and counter-rebuttal of a "prima facie case" consisting of no more than the showing that the employer's selection process "selects those from the protected class at a 'significantly' lesser rate than their counterparts." B. Schlei & P. Grossman, Employment Discrimination Law 91 (2d ed. 1983). If, however, employers are free to discriminate through affirmative action, without fear of "reverse discrimination" suits by their nonminority or male victims, they are offered a threshold defense against Title VII liability premised on numerical disparities. Thus, after today's decision the failure to engage in reverse discrimination is economic folly, and arguably a breach of duty to shareholders or taxpayers, wherever the cost of anticipated Title VII litigation exceeds the cost of hiring less capable (though still minimally capable) workers. (This situation is more likely to obtain, of course, with respect to the least skilled jobs—perversely creating an incentive to discriminate against precisely those members of the nonfavored groups least likely to have profited from societal discrimination in the past.) It is predictable, moreover, that this incentive will be greatly magnified by economic pressures brought to bear by government contracting agencies upon employers who refuse to discriminate in the fashion we have now approved. A statute designed to establish a color-blind and gender-blind workplace has thus been converted into a powerful engine of racism and sexism, not merely permitting intentional race- and sex-based discrimination, but often making it, through operation of the legal system, practically compelled.

It is unlikely that today's result will be displeasing to politically elected officials, to whom it provides the means of quickly accommodating the demands of organized groups to achieve concrete, numerical improvement in the economic status of particular constituencies. Nor will it displease the world of corporate and governmental employers (many of whom have filed briefs as *amici* in the present case, all on the side of Santa Clara) for whom the cost of hiring less qualified workers is often substantially less—and infinitely more predictable—than the cost of litigating Title VII cases and of seeking to convince federal agencies by nonnumerical means that no discrimination exists. In fact, the only losers in the process are the Johnsons of the country, for whom Title VII has been not merely repealed but actually inverted. The irony is that these individuals—predominantly unknown, unaffluent, unorganized— suffer this injustice at the hands of a Court fond of thinking itself the champion of the politically impotent. I dissent.

Questions and Observations

The contest between Ms. Joyce and Mr. Johnson came down to a judgment call by their supervisor about their respective qualifications and potential to do a good job (unless you believe that the two point difference in their interview scores was an objective factor that made a critical difference). The initial determination favored Mr. Johnson. We assume that the members of the interview panel were all males, given the statistical pattern discussed in the opinion and the information provided in footnote 5. Assuming we are correct, and that the panel had never seen a female occupy this job, isn't there a good chance their subjective judgment about things like leadership, firmness, and confidence, and their notions that these are appropriate criteria for the job, would lead them to prefer the male candidate? Could such a subjective basis for making a decision be challenged under *Griggs*, after the 1991 amendments to Title VII? What if Ms. Joyce didn't get the job and claimed intentional discrimination because she was female, citing the remark near the end of footnote 5. Do you think she'd prevail? Does the difficulty of proving discrimination suggest that the plan in Johnson can be viewed as a way of remedying and avoiding likely discrimination against women? Yet, if the employer is innocent, has not Johnson been victimized, as Justice Scalia opines?

We mentioned at the top of this section that the Court has come out on different sides of the affirmative action issue. The details of the different twists and turns taken in the evolution of affirmative action doctrine must be saved for a separate course. You should be aware, though, that as a very general proposition the Court will come down harder on an affirmative action program if it actually knocks somebody, for example, a white male, out of a job rather than gives an adder to one of several candidates seeking a job. Note how Justice Brennan deals with this point in his opinion. Perhaps the *Weber* plan met with Court approval because it involved a new program, with skills training that could benefit blacks and whites without damaging any existing employment expectations. Compare Wygant v. Jackson Bd. of Education, 476 U.S. 267, 106 S.Ct. 1842, 90 L.Ed.2d 260 (1986), where the Court struck down under the Equal Protection Clause (but did not face the Title VII issue) a layoff provision that would have eliminated more senior, white teachers in favor of recently hired, junior black teachers. This is a particularly knotty problem, because under affirmative action steps taken in recent years to improve minority hiring, minority employees tend to be the last hired and the lowest on the seniority list. They would then be the most vulnerable to layoff in a shrinking economy. That's what the parties were trying to avoid in *Wygant*, for it would have undone all their affirmative action efforts.

Affirmative remedies giving positions to victims of the involved employer's prior discrimination get a more hospitable reception when the victims are identifiable. See *Wygant* above at Part IV. Where there are no specific victims of past discrimination who can be the actual beneficiaries of an affirmative action program, the Court is less tolerant of an affirmative action program that lessens employment opportunities for non-minorities.

Consider the text of the 1991 amendments to Title VII, particularly sections 703(m) and 706(g)(2)(B), and section 116 of the 1991 Act, which reads, "Nothing in the amendments made by this title shall be construed to affect court-ordered remedies, affirmative action, or conciliation agreements, that are in accordance with the law." Consider, also, the observation of economist Lester Thurow, below.

Several cases, including the aforementioned *Wygant* decision, have addressed the constitutional ramifications of the use of affirmative action plans by governmental entities. Insofar as such plans are aimed at aiding minority racial groups, the Supreme Court has increasingly made clear that such plans must satisfy the Court's so-called "strict scrutiny" test, which is the most difficult Supreme Court standard for a government to meet in justifying the constitutionality of its laws. See Adarand Constructors, Inc. v. Pena, 515 U.S. 200, 115 S.Ct. 2097, 132 L.Ed.2d 158 (1995). This test demands that the government meet two conditions to justify its affirmative action plan: first, the discrimination must be "identified" [as distinguished from being societal or general]; and, second, there must be a "strong basis in evidence" for the state to believe that the affirmative action was necessary. See Shaw v. Hunt, 517 U.S. 899, 116 S.Ct. 1894, 135 L.Ed.2d 207 (1996).

While these cases are founded on constitutional equal protection jurisprudence, how likely is it that, per Title VII, the courts would hold lawful private employers' affirmative action plans that are more aggressive than those a government can impose upon itself? Put differently, in light of *Adarand*, do you think the interpretation of Title VII that is articulated in *Johnson* can survive? If not, what does one do with the consequences described in the following excerpt written by Lester Thurow?

LESTER THUROW, POLICY RECOMMENDATIONS CONCERNING THE SECOND DRAFT OF THE PASTORAL LETTER

5 St. Louis U.Pub.L.Rev. 281, 288–89 (1986).

* * * In American history we think every game starts with a starting score of zero-zero, but of course every game does not. For the last 110 years, Oxford has had an annual boat race where the boats begin where they left off the year before. If you were twenty-five lengths

behind at the end last year, you start off twenty-five lengths behind this year. The race never stops and starts over. An economy can be organized where it never stops and starts over, or, it can be organized like an American football game in which you start each game with a new score of zero-zero. If we played the British-type of game, Notre Dame would still be winning. The rules of football are written down, they are not axiomatic. It is the same thing with the economy. How do you acquire skills? How do you get to use those skills? Can you create a monopoly or can you not create a monopoly? All those decisions have to be made. Depending on how you make decisions about where to start, how wide the field is and what the rules are, you will get a different team to win. Of course, no matter what the rules are, some teams will win more than others. The Boston Celtics win more often than the Indiana Pacers. If the Boston Celtics won every game for five years in a row, we would change the rules of basketball. We would say that it is unfair that the Boston Celtics win all the time. We do the same thing in our market economy. If somebody is winning all the time and it becomes too inegalitarian, like the Rockefellers in the 1890s, we change the rules to stop this kind of behavior just as we would stop the Boston Celtics. * * *

Question

Antipathy towards affirmative action programs continues. Why? Consider the following observations by Professor Jerome Culp.

JEROME CULP, WATER BUFFALO AND DIVERSITY: NAMING NAMES AND RECLAIMING THE RACIAL DISCOURSE

26 Conn.L.Rev. 209,232–233.
(1993).

I am one of the relatively small number of black people who, through measures of luck, hard work, and government policy, have "made it." I teach law at one of this country's major law schools, and one of the courses I teach is Employment Discrimination. I have a nice salary, and in these economically awkward times my tenured position provides me with a kind of job security that is fast becoming obsolete in this country. In short, I have what David Duke tells whites they have lost to affirmative action. The unstated premise is that except for affirmative action, David Duke, or one of his white followers, would be sitting in my chair and looking at his pictures on the wall of my office (no doubt replacing my picture of Billie Holiday with one of Marilyn Monroe).

David Duke has come to this belief honestly. Former President Bush consistently called civil rights legislation of the 1990s a "quota bill," and important liberal and conservative commentators have attacked the results of race conscious public policy that helped to change for a time the economic position of black people and women. When David Duke uses quotas, affirmative action, and welfare as code words that equal blacks, he finds that many white Americans agree.

Why is it that, as the nightly news commentators have intimated, many white Americans believe they have legitimate complaints against black people? The reason for this belief is that there are two assumptions that people have made about public policy that are not supported by any empirical or other support but that have become mythic.

The first assumption is that all that black people have gained in the last twenty years, they gained through some unfair racial preference. I experience this assumption almost every day. My favorite, most recent example was a visit to a new white young female dentist this summer. My former dentist had retired, and I went in to have a front tooth cap replaced by his successor. My new dentist wondered whether I was a student. I said no, that I taught law. She then asked where I went to law school. (At this point I know the implicit question is, how did you become a law professor, but I also know that some of you will view this insight as a product of an overactive imagination.) I responded that I went to Harvard Law School. My dentist then asked the question that proves my point. She asked, "[Did you go to law school] on a scholarship?" I said no, that I had worked my way through law school. She asked that question because the persistent myth among many white Americans is that all blacks have gotten through school on the basis of the vast amount of scholarships available to black people but not white students.

I come up on this myth whenever I talk to law students or my colleagues about legal education. Indeed, despite the fact that we do not provide full scholarships to most black students, my colleagues have been known in arguments about affirmative action to make that assumption. One of my faculty colleagues during a recent meeting stated that affirmative action meant that he, the son of European immigrants, could not get a scholarship to our law school today (he had gone to a law school 30 years ago on such a full scholarship). The truth is that most scholarship money goes to white students, and people like him still have a better chance of getting into our law school and getting a scholarship than does the average black person in our country. My dentist assumed that I could not have gotten to where I am without that "unfair" help of scholarships that whites didn't get. This is not true, and more importantly, the real assumption is that black people are unworthy, so that they cannot have gained anything important unless it was gotten unfairly. Many white Americans make this assumption (even the well educated and the people who like to think of themselves as non-discriminatory). Some people want to blame this belief held by white people on the few race conscious remedies that have taken place in America (what is called affirmative action). Affirmative action, however, simply has not been extensive enough to bear the burden of such a racial present. Like the Duke supporters who claim to have black friends, the people who hold this negative view of black people are not bad—they are just American and racist.

3. REASONABLE ACCOMMODATION

TRANS WORLD AIRLINES, INC. v. HARDISON

Supreme Court of the United States, 1977.
432 U.S. 63, 97 S.Ct. 2264, 53 L.Ed.2d 113.

JUSTICE WHITE delivered the opinion of the Court.

* * * The issue in this case is the extent of the employer's obligation under Title VII to accommodate an employee whose religious beliefs prohibit him from working on Saturdays.

I

* * *

Petitioner Trans World Airlines (TWA) operates a large maintenance and overhaul base in Kansas City, Mo. On June 5, 1967, respondent Larry G. Hardison was hired by TWA to work as a clerk in the Stores Department at its Kansas City base. Because of its essential role in the Kansas City operation, the Stores Department must operate 24 hours per day, 365 days per year, and whenever an employee's job in that department is not filled, an employee must be shifted from another department, or a supervisor must cover the job, even if the work in other areas may suffer.

Hardison, like other employees as the Kansas City base, was subject to a seniority system contained in a collective-bargaining agreement that TWA maintains with petitioner International Association of Machinists and Aerospace Workers (IAM). The seniority system is implemented by the union steward through a system of bidding by employees for particular shift assignments as they become available. The most senior employees have first choice for job and shift assignments, and the most junior employees are required to work when the union steward is unable to find enough people willing to work at a particular time or in a particular job to fill TWA's needs.

In the spring of 1968, Hardison began to study the religion known as the Worldwide Church of God. One of the tenets of that religion is that one must observe the Sabbath by refraining from performing any work from sunset on Friday until sunset on Saturday. The religion also proscribes work on certain specified religious holidays.

When Hardison informed Everett Kussmann, the manager of the Stores Department, of his religious conviction regarding observance of the Sabbath, Kussman agreed that the union steward should seek a job swap for Hardison or a change of days off; that Hardison would have his religious holidays off whenever possible if Hardison agreed to work the traditional holidays when asked; and that Kussman would try to find Hardison another job that would be more compatible with his religious beliefs. The problem was temporarily solved when Hardison transferred to the 11 p.m.—7 a.m. shift. Working this shift permitted Hardison to observe his Sabbath.

The problem soon reappeared when Hardison bid for and received a transfer from Building 1, where he had been employed, to Building 2, where he would work the day shift. The two buildings had entirely separate seniority lists; and while in Building 1, Hardison had sufficient seniority to observe the Sabbath regularly, he was second from the bottom on the Building 2 seniority list.

In Building 2, Hardison was asked to work Saturdays when a fellow employee went on vacation. TWA agreed to permit the union to seek a change of work assignments for Hardison, but the union was not willing to violate the seniority provisions set out in the collective-bargaining contract, and Hardison had insufficient seniority to bid for a shift having Saturdays off.

A proposal that Hardison work only four days a week was rejected by the company. Hardison's job was essential, and on weekends he was the only available person on his shift to perform it. To leave the position empty would have impaired supply shop functions, which were critical to airline operations; to fill Hardison's position with a supervisor or an employee from another area would simply have undermanned another operation; and to employ someone not regularly assigned to work Saturdays would have required TWA to pay premium wages.

When an accommodation was not reached, Hardison refused to report for work on Saturdays. A transfer to the twilight shift proved unavailing since that schedule still required Hardison to work past sundown on Fridays. After a hearing, Hardison was discharged on grounds of insubordination for refusing to work during his designated shift.

Hardison * * * brought this action * * * against TWA and IAM, claiming that his discharge by TWA constituted religious discrimination in violation of Title VII. * * *

[After a bench trial, the district court ruled in favor of TWA and the union. The Eighth Circuit affirmed the judgment for the union, but reversed the judgment for TWA.]

* * *

III

The Court of Appeals held that TWA had not made reasonable efforts to accommodate Hardison's religious needs under the 1967 EEOC guidelines in effect at the time the relevant events occurred. In its view, TWA had rejected three reasonable alternatives, any one of which would have satisfied its obligation without undue hardship. First, within the framework of the seniority system, TWA could have permitted Hardison to work a four-day week, utilizing in his place a supervisor or another worker on duty elsewhere. That this would have caused other shop functions to suffer was insufficient to amount to undue hardship in the opinion of the Court of Appeals. Second—according to the Court of Appeals, also within the bounds of the collective-bargaining contract— the company could have filled Hardison's Saturday shift from other available personnel competent to do the job, of which the court said there were at least 200. That this would have involved premium over-time pay was not deemed an undue hardship. Third, TWA could have arranged a "swap between Hardison and another employee either for another shift or for the Sabbath days." In response to the assertion that this would have involved a breach of the seniority provisions of the contract, the court noted that it had not been settled in the courts whether the required statutory accommodation to religious needs stopped short of transgressing seniority rules, but found it necessary to decide the issue because, as the Court of Appeals saw the record, TWA had not sought, and the union had therefore not declined to entertain, a possible variance from the seniority provisions of the collective-bargain-ing agreement. The company had simply left the entire matter to the union steward who the Court of Appeals said "likewise did nothing."

We disagree with the Court of Appeals in all relevant respects. It is our view that TWA made reasonable efforts to accommodate and that each of the Court of Appeals' suggested alternatives would have been an undue hardship within the meaning of the statute as construed by the EEOC guidelines.

A

It might be inferred from the Court of Appeals' opinion and from the brief of the EEOC in this Court that TWA's efforts to accommodate were no more than negligible. The findings of the District Court, supported by the record, are to the contrary. In summarizing its more detailed findings, the District Court observed:

> TWA established as a matter of fact that it did take appropriate action to accommodate as required by Title VII. It held several meetings with plaintiff at which it attempted to find a solution to plaintiff's problems. It did accommodate plaintiff's observance of his special religious holidays. It authorized the union steward to search for someone who would swap shifts, which apparently was normal procedure.

It is also true that TWA itself attempted without success to find Hardison another job. The District Court's view was that TWA had done all that could reasonably be expected within the bounds of the seniority system.

The Court of Appeals observed, however, that the possibility of a variance from the seniority system was never really posed to the union. This is contrary to the District Court's findings and to the record. The District Court found that when TWA first learned of Hardison's religious observances in April 1968, it agreed to permit the union's steward to seek a swap of shifts or days off but that "the steward reported that he was unable to work out scheduling changes and that he understood that no one was willing to swap days with the plaintiff." Later, in March 1969, at a meeting held just two days before Hardison first failed to report for his Saturday shift, TWA again "offered to accommodate plaintiff's religious observance by agreeing to any trade of shifts or change of sections that plaintiff and the union could work out * * *. Any shift or change was impossible within the seniority framework and the union was not willing to violate the seniority provisions set out in the contract to make s shift or change." As the record shows, Hardison himself testified that Kussman was willing, but the union was not, to work out a shift or job trade with another employee.

We shall say more about the seniority system, but at this juncture it appears to us that the system itself represented a significant accommodation to the needs, both religious and secular, of all of TWA's employees. As will become apparent, the seniority system represents a neutral way of minimizing the number of occasions when an employee must work on a day that he would prefer to have off. Additionally, recognizing that weekend work schedules are the least popular, the company made further accommodations by reducing its work force to a bare minimum on those days.

B

We are also convinced, contrary to the Court of Appeals, that TWA itself cannot be faulted for having failed to work out a shift or job swap for Hardison. Both the union and TWA had agreed to the seniority system; the union was unwilling to entertain a variance over the objections of men senior to Hardison; and for TWA to have arranged unilaterally for a swap would have amounted to a breach of the collective-bargaining agreement.

(1)

Hardison and the EEOC insist that the statutory obligation to accommodate religious needs takes precedence over both the collective-bargaining contract and the seniority rights of TWA's other employees. We agree that neither a collective-bargaining contract nor a seniority system may be employed to violate the statute, but we do not believe that the duty to accommodate requires TWA to take steps inconsistent with the otherwise valid agreement. Collective bargaining, aimed at effecting workable and enforceable agreements between management and labor, lies at the core of our national labor policy, and seniority provisions are universally included in these contracts. Without a clear and express indication from Congress, we cannot agree with Hardison and the EEOC that an agreed-upon seniority system must give way when necessary to accommodate religious observances. The issue is important and warrants some discussion.

Any employer who, like TWA, conducts an around-the-clock operation is presented with the choice of allocating work schedules either in accordance with the preferences of its employees or by involuntary assignment. Insofar as the varying shift preferences of its employees complement each other, TWA could meet its manpower needs through voluntary work scheduling. In the present case, for example, Hardison's supervisor foresaw little difficulty in giving Hardison his religious holidays off since they fell on days that most other employees preferred to work, while Hardison was willing to work on the traditional holidays that most other employees preferred to have off.

Whenever there are not enough employees who choose to work a particular shift, however, some employees must be assigned to that shift even though it is not their first choice. Such was evidently the case with regard to Saturday work; even though TWA cut back its weekend work force to a skeleton crew, not enough employees chose those days off to staff the Stores Department through voluntary scheduling. In these circumstances, TWA and IAM agreed to give first preference to employees who had worked in a particular department the longest.

Had TWA nevertheless circumvented the seniority system by relieving Hardison of Saturday work and ordering a senior employee to replace him, it would have denied the latter his shift preference so that Hardison could be given his. The senior employee would also have been deprived of his contractual rights under the collective-bargaining agreement.

It was essential to TWA's business to require Saturday and Sunday work from at least a few employees even though most employees preferred those days off. Allocating the burdens of weekend work was a matter for collective bargaining. In considering criteria to govern this allocation, TWA and the union had two alternatives: adopt a neutral system, such as seniority, a lottery, or rotating shifts; or allocate days off in accordance with the religious needs of its employees. TWA would have had to adopt the latter in order to assure Hardison and others like him of getting the days off necessary for strict observance of their religion, but it would have done so only at the expense of others who had strong, but perhaps nonreligious, reasons for not working on weekends. There were no volunteers to relieve Hardison on Saturdays, and to give Hardison Saturdays off, TWA would have had to deprive another employee of his shift preference at least in part because he did not adhere to a religion that observed the Saturday Sabbath.

Title VII does not contemplate such unequal treatment. The repeated, unequivocal emphasis of both the language and the legislative history of Title VII is on eliminating discrimination in employment, and such discrimination is proscribed when it is directed against majorities as well as minorities. Indeed, the foundation of Hardison's claim is that TWA and IAM engaged in religious *discrimination* in violation of § 703(a)(1) when they failed to arrange for him to have Saturdays off. It would be anomalous to conclude that by "reasonable accommodation" Congress meant that an employer must deny the shift and job preference of some employees, as well as deprive them of their contractual rights, in order to accommodate or prefer the religious needs of others, and we conclude that Title VII does not require an employer to go that far.

(2)

Our conclusion is supported by the fact that seniority systems are afforded special treatment under Title VII itself. Section 703(h) provides in pertinent part:

> Notwithstanding any other provision of this subchapter, it shall not be an unlawful employment practice for an employer to apply different standards of compensation, or different terms, conditions, or privileges of employment pursuant to a bona fide seniority or merit system * * * provides that such differences are not the result of an intention to discriminate because of race, color, religion, sex, or national origin. * * *

"[T]he unmistakable purpose of § 703(h) was to make clear that the routine application of a bona fide seniority system would not be unlawful under Title VII." Teamsters v. United States, 431 U.S. 324, 352, 97 S.Ct. 1843, 1863, 52 L.Ed.2d 396 (1977). Section 703(h) is "a definitional provision; as with the other provisions of § 703, subsection (h) delineates which employment practices are illegal and thereby prohibited and which are not." Franks v. Bowman Transp. Co., 424 U.S. 747, 758, 96 S.Ct. 1251, 1261, 47 L.Ed.2d 444 (1976). Thus, absent a discriminatory purpose, the operation of a seniority system cannot be an unlawful employment practice even if the system has some discriminatory consequences.

There has been no suggestion of discriminatory intent in this case. "The seniority system was not designed with the intention to discriminate against religion nor did it act to lock members of any religion into a pattern wherein their freedom to exercise their religion was limited. It was coincidental that in plaintiff's case the seniority system act to compound his problems in exercising his religion." The Court of Appeals' conclusion that TWA was not limited by the terms of its seniority system was in substance nothing more than a ruling that operation of the seniority system was itself an unlawful employment practice even though no discriminatory purpose had been shown. That ruling is plainly inconsistent with the dictates of § 703(h), both on its face and as interpreted in the recent decision of this Court.

As we have said, TWA was not required by Title VII to carve out a special exception to its seniority system in order to help Hardison to meet his religious obligations.

C

The Court of Appeals also suggested that TWA could have permitted Hardison to work a four-day week if necessary in order to avoid working on his Sabbath. Recognizing that this might have left TWA short-handed on the one shift each week that Hardison did not work, the court still concluded that TWA would suffer no undue hardship if it were required to replace Hardison either with supervisory personnel or with qualified personnel from other departments. Alternatively, the Court of Appeals suggested that TWA could have replaced Hardison on his Saturday shift with other available employees through the payment of premium wages. Both of these alternatives would involve costs to TWA, either in the form of lost efficiency in other jobs or higher wages.

To require TWA to bear more than a *de minimis* cost in order to give Hardison Saturdays off is an undue hardship.[15] Like abandonment of the seniority system, to require TWA to bear additional costs when no such costs are incurred to give other employees the days off that they want would involve unequal treatment of employees on the basis of their religion. By suggesting that TWA should incur certain costs in order to give Hardison Saturdays off, the Court of Appeals would in effect require TWA to finance an additional Saturday off and then to choose the employee who will enjoy it on the basis of his religious beliefs. While incurring extra costs to secure a replacement for Hardison might remove the necessity of compelling another employee to work involuntarily in Hardison's place, it would not change the fact that the privilege of having Saturdays off would be allocated according to religious beliefs.

As we have seen, the paramount concern of Congress in enacting Title VII was the elimination of discrimination in employment. In the absence of clear statutory language or legislative history to the contrary, we will not readily construe the statute to require an employer to discriminate against some employees in order to enable others to observe their Sabbath.

JUSTICE MARSHALL, with whom JUSTICE BRENNAN joins, dissenting.

* * *

Today's decision deals a fatal blow to all efforts under Title VII to accommodate work requirements to religious practices. The Court holds, in essence, that although the EEOC regulations and the Act state that an employer must make reasonable adjustments in his work demands to take account of religious observances, the regulation and Act do not really mean what they say. An employer, the Court concludes, need not grant even the most minor special privilege to religious observers to enable them to follow their faith. As a question of social policy, this result is deeply troubling, for a society that truly values religious pluralism cannot compel adherents of minority religions to make the cruel choice of surrendering their religion or their job. And as a matter of law today's result is intolerable, for the Court adopts the very position that Congress expressly rejected in 1972, as if we were free to disregard

---

15. The dissent argues that "the costs to TWA of either paying overtime or not replacing respondent would [not] have been more than *de minimis*." This ignores, however, the express finding of the District Court that "[b]oth of these solutions would have created an undue burden on the conduct of TWA's business" and it fails to take account of the likelihood that a company as large as TWA may have many employees whose religious observances, like Hardison's, prohibit them from working on Saturdays or Sundays.

congressional choices that a majority of this Court thinks unwise. I therefore dissent.

With respect to each of the proposed accommodations to respondent Hardison's religious observances that the Court discusses, it ultimately notes that the accommodation would have required "unequal treatment," in favor of the religious observer. That is quite true. But if an accommodation can be rejected simply because it involves preferential treatment, then the regulation and the statute, while brimming with "sound and fury," ultimately "signif[y] nothing."

* * *

What makes today's decision most tragic, however, is not that respondent Hardison has been needlessly deprived of his livelihood simply because he chose to follow the dictates of his conscience. Nor is the tragedy exhausted by the impact it will have on thousands of Americans like Hardison who could be forced to live on welfare as the price they must pay for worshiping their God. The ultimate tragedy is that despite Congress's best efforts, one of this Nations's pillars of strength—our hospitality to religious diversity—has been seriously eroded. All Americans will be a little poorer until today's decision is erased.

Notes and Questions

1. By defining "religion" as it does, Section 701(j) of Title VII requires an employer, to avoid a successful complaint of discrimination based on religion, to demonstrate that it is "unable to reasonably accommodate to" the relevant employee's religious practice. *Hardison* made clear that an employer has to demonstrate very little to prove it has reasonably accommodated within the meaning of Section 701(j). But, must an employer reasonably accommodate in the manner proposed by the employee? In Ansonia Board of Education v. Philbrook, 479 U.S. 60, 107 S.Ct. 367, 93 L.Ed.2d 305 (1986), the Supreme Court responded, "By its very terms the statute directs that any reasonable accommodation by the employer is sufficient ... [W]here the employer has already reasonably accommodated the employee's religious needs, the statutory inquiry is at an end. The employer need not further show that each of the employee's alternative accommodations would result in undue hardship ... [T]he extent of undue hardship on the employer's business is at issue only where the employer claims that it is unable to offer any reasonable accommodation without such hardship."

2. Why do you think the Court, in both *Hardison* and *Philbrook*, interpreted the phrase, "to reasonably accommodate," so narrowly?

3. The Americans with Disabilities Act specifically encourages reasonable accommodation. Moreover, the ADA defines the required accommodation in a far more demanding manner than *Hardison* does. See ADA Sections 101(8), (9), and (10). Why would Congress want employers to accommodate disabled employees more than religious ones?

4. HARASSING BEHAVIOR

HARRIS v. FORKLIFT SYSTEMS, INC.

Supreme Court of the United States, 1993.
510 U.S. 17, 114 S.Ct. 367, 126 L.Ed.2d 295.

JUSTICE O'CONNOR delivered the opinion of the Court.

In this case we consider the definition of a discriminatorily "abusive work environment" (also known as a "hostile work environment") under Title VII of the Civil Rights Act of 1964.

I

Teresa Harris worked as a manager at Forklift Systems, Inc., an equipment rental company, from April 1985 until October 1987. Charles Hardy was Forklift's president.

The Magistrate found that, throughout Harris' time at Forklift, Hardy often insulted her because of her gender and often made her the target of unwanted sexual innuendos. Hardy told Harris on several occasions, in the presence of other employees, "You're a woman, what do you know" and "We need a man as the rental manager;" at least once, he told her she was a "dumb ass woman." Again in front of others, he suggested that the two of them "go to the Holiday Inn to negotiate [Harris'] raise." Hardy occasionally asked Harris and other female employees to get coins from his front pants pocket. He threw objects on the ground in front of Harris and other women, and asked them to pick the objects up. He made sexual innuendos about Harris' and other women's clothing.

In mid-August 1987, Harris complained to Hardy about his conduct. Hardy said he was surprised that Harris was offended, claimed he was only joking, and apologized. He also promised he would stop, and based on this assurance Harris stayed on the job. But in early September, Hardy began anew: While Harris was arranging a deal with one of Forklift's customers, he asked her, again in front of other employees, "What did you do, promise the guy * * * some [sex] Saturday night?" On October 1, Harris collected her paycheck and quit.

Harris then sued Forklift, claiming that Hardy's conduct had created an abusive work environment for her because of her gender. The United States District Court for the Middle District of Tennessee, adopting the report and recommendation of the Magistrate, found this to be "a close case," but held that Hardy's conduct did not create an abusive environment. The court found that some of Hardy's comments "offended [Harris], and would offend the reasonable woman," but that they were not

> so severe as to be expected to seriously affect [Harris'] psychological well-being. A reasonable woman manager under like circumstances would have been offended by Hardy, but his conduct would not have

risen to the level of interfering with that person's work performance.

Neither do I believe that [Harris] was subjectively so offended that she suffered injury * * *. Although Hardy may at times have genuinely offended [Harris], I do not believe that he created a working environment so poisoned as to be intimidating or abusive to [Harris].

In focusing on the employee's psychological well-being, the District Court was following Circuit precedent. *See* Rabidue v. Osceola Refining Co., 805 F.2d 611, 620 (6th Cir.1986), *cert. denied*, 481 U.S. 1041, 107 S.Ct. 1983, 95 L.Ed.2d 823 (1987). The United States Court of Appeals for the Sixth Circuit affirmed in a brief unpublished decision.

We granted certiorari, to resolve a conflict among the Circuits on whether conduct, to be actionable as "abusive work environment" harassment (no *quid pro quo* harassment issue is present here), must "seriously affect [an employee's] psychological well-being" or lead the plaintiff to "suffe[r] injury."

II

* * * When the workplace is permeated with "discriminatory intimidation, ridicule, and insult" that is "sufficiently severe or pervasive to alter the conditions of the victim's employment and create an abusive working environment," Title VII is violated.

This standard, which we reaffirm today, takes a middle path between making actionable any conduct that is merely offensive and requiring the conduct to cause a tangible psychological injury. As we pointed out in *Meritor,* [Meritor Savings Bank v. Vinson, 477 U.S. 57, 106 S.Ct. 2399, 91 L.Ed.2d 49 (1986)] "mere utterance of an * * * epithet which engenders offensive feelings in an employee," does not sufficiently affect the conditions of employment to implicate Title VII. Conduct that is not severe or pervasive enough to create an objectively hostile or abusive work environment—an environment that a reasonable person would find hostile or abusive—is beyond Title VII's purview. Likewise, if the victim does not subjectively perceive the environment to be abusive, the conduct has not actually altered the conditions of the victim's employment, and there is no Title VII violation.

But Title VII comes into play before the harassing conduct leads to a nervous breakdown. A discriminatorily abusive work environment, even one that does not seriously affect employees' psychological well-being, can and often will detract from employees' job performance, discourage employees from remaining on the job, or keep them from advancing in their careers. Moreover, even without regard to these tangible effects, the very fact that the discriminatory conduct was so severe or pervasive that it created a work environment abusive to employees because of their race, gender, religion, or national origin offends Title VII's broad rule of workplace equality. The appalling conduct alleged in *Meritor*, and the reference in that case to environments " 'so heavily polluted with discrimination as to destroy completely the emotional and psychological stability of minority group workers,' " *id.* at 66, 106 S.Ct. At 2405 (quoting Rogers v. EEOC, 454 F.2d 234, 238 (5th Cir.1971), *cert. denied,* 406 U.S. 957, 92 S.Ct. 2058, 32 L.Ed.2d 343 (1972)), merely present some especially egregious examples of harassment. They do not mark the boundary of what is actionable.

We therefore believe the District Court erred in relying on whether the conduct "seriously affected plaintiff's psychological well-being" or led her to "suffe[r] injury." Such an inquiry may needlessly focus the factfinder's attention on concrete psychological harm, an element Title VII does not require. Certainly Title VII bars conduct that would seriously affect a reasonable person's psychological well-being, but the statute is not limited to such conduct. So long as the environment would reasonably be perceived, and is perceived, as hostile or abusive, there is no need for it also to be psychologically injurious.

This is not, and by nature cannot be, a mathematically precise test. We need not answer today all the potential questions it raises, nor specifically address the [EEOC's] new regulations on this subject. But we can say that whether an environment is "hostile" or "abusive" can be determined only by looking at all the circumstances. These may include the frequency of the discriminatory conduct, its severity; whether it is physically threatening or humiliating, or a mere offensive utterance; and whether it unreasonably interferes with an employee's work performance. The effect on the employee's psychological well-being is, of course, relevant to determining whether the plaintiff actually found the environment abusive. But while psychological harm, like any other relevant factor, may be taken into account, no single factor is required.

III

Forklift, while conceding that a requirement that the conduct seriously affect psychological well-being is unfounded, argues that the District Court nonetheless correctly applied the *Meritor* standard. We disagree. Though the District Court did conclude that the work environment was not "intimidating or abusive to [Harris]," it did so only after finding that the conduct was not "so severe as to be expected to seriously affect plaintiff's psychological well-being," and that Harris was not "subjectively so offended that she suffered injury." The District Court's application of these incorrect standards may well have influenced its ultimate conclusion, especially given that the court found this to be a "close case."

We therefore reverse the judgment of the Court of Appeals, and remand the case for further proceedings consistent with this opinion.

JUSTICE SCALIA, concurring.

* * *

"Abusive" (or "hostile," which in this context I take to mean the same thing) does not seem to me a very clear standard—and I do not think clarity is at all increased by adding the adverb "objectively" or by appealing to a "reasonable person['s]" notion of what the vague word means. Today's opinion does list a number of factors that contribute to abusiveness, but since it neither says how much of each is necessary (an impossible task) nor identifies any single factor as determinative, it thereby adds little certitude. As a practical matter, today's holding lets virtually unguided juries decide whether sex-related conduct engaged in (or permitted by) an employer is egregious enough to warrant an award of damages. One might say that what constitutes "negligence" (a traditional jury question) is not much more clear and certain than what constitutes "abusiveness." Perhaps so. But the class of plaintiffs seeking to recover from negligence is limited to those who have suffered harm, whereas under this statute "abusiveness" is to be the test of whether legal harm has been suffered, opening more expansive vistas of litigation.

Be that as it may, I know of no alternative to the course the Court today has taken. One of the factors mentioned in the Court's nonexhaustive list—whether the conduct unreasonably interferes with an employees work performance—would, if it were made an absolute test, provide greater guidance to juries and employers. But I see no basis for such a limitation in the language of the statute. Accepting *Meritor's* interpretation of the term "conditions of employment" as the law, the test is not whether work has been impaired, but whether working conditions have been discriminatorily altered. I know of no test more faithful to the inherently vague statutory language than the one the Court today adopts. For these reasons, I join the opinion of the Court.

JUSTICE GINSBURG, concurring.

Today, the Court reaffirms the holding of *Meritor Savings Bank v. Vinson:* "[A] plaintiff may establish a violation of Title VII by proving that discrimination based on sex has created a hostile or abusive work environment." The critical issue, Title VII's text indicates, is whether members of one sex are exposed to disadvantageous terms or conditions of employment to which members of the other sex are not exposed. As the Equal Employment Opportunity Commission emphasized, the adjudicator's inquiry should center, dominantly, on whether the discriminatory conduct has unreasonably interfered with the plaintiff's work performance. To show such interference, "the plaintiff need not prove that his or her tangible productivity has declined as a result of the harassment." Davis v. Monsanto Chemical Co., 858 F.2d 345, 349 (6th Cir. 1988). It suffices to prove that a reasonable person subjected to the discriminatory conduct would find, as the plaintiff did, that the harassment so altered working conditions as to "ma[k]e it more difficult to do the job." *See id. Davis* concerned race-based discrimination, but that difference does not alter the analysis; except in the rare case in which a bona fide occupational qualification is shown, Title VII declares discriminatory practices based on race, gender, religion, or national origin equally unlawful.

* * *

Questions and Notes

1. How does one interpret Title VII to outlaw sexual harassment of any kind?

2. If Title VII requires an employer, in order to avoid Title VII liability, to discipline an employee who harasses a fellow-employee by creating a so-called hostile environment via tasteless jokes, stated innuendoes about the fellow-employee's appearance or private life, and the like, is a legitimate issue raised by the First Amendment's protection of speech?

3. More egregious than the conduct described in *Harris* is the so-called *quid pro quo* harassment which typically involves a manager or supervisor expressing to a subordinate something like, If you want the promotion, you have to go to bed with me. Given the decision in *Harris,* you should not be surprised that the Supreme Court has held, in the context of imposing vicarious liability upon an employer, that such conduct violates Title VII. See, Burlington Industries, Inc. v. Ellerth, 524 U.S. 742, 118 S.Ct. 2257, 141 L.Ed.2d 633 (1998) ("... When a plaintiff proves that a tangible employment action resulted from a refusal to submit to a supervisor's sexual demands," the employer is strictly liable.).

4. In the *Ellerth* case, 524 U.S. 742, 118 S.Ct. 2257, 141 L.Ed.2d 633 (1998), cited in the previous note, the Supreme Court also said the following regarding the vicarious liability of am employer for its supervisor's unlawful harassment of an employee in a case where there was no tangible employment action taken against the employee:

> "An employer is subject to vicarious liability to a victimized employee for an actionable hostile environment created by a supervisor with immediate (or successively higher) authority over the employee. When no tangible employment action is taken, a defendant employer may raise an affirmative defense to liability or damages, subject to proof by a preponderance of the evidence. The defense comprises two necessary elements: (a) that the employer exercised reasonable care to prevent and correct promptly any sexually harassing behavior, and (b) that the plaintiff employee unreasonably failed to take advantage of any preventive or corrective opportunities provided by the employer or to avoid harm otherwise. While proof that an employer had promulgated an anti-harassment policy with complaint procedure is not necessary in every instance as a matter of law, the need for a stated policy suitable to the employment circumstances may appropriately be addressed in any case when litigating the first element of defence ... No affirmative defense is available, however, when the supervisor's harassment culminates in a tangible employment action, such as discharge, demotion, or undesirable reassignment."

ONCALE v. SUNDOWNER OFFSHORE SERVICES, INC.

Supreme Court of the United States, 1998
523 U.S. 75, 118 S.Ct. 998, 140 L.Ed.2d 201

JUSTICE SCALIA delivered the opinion of the Court.

This case presents the question whether workplace harassment can violate Title VII's prohibition against "discriminat[ion] ... because of

... sex," Section 703(a)(1), when the harasser and the harassed employee are of the same sex.

I

The District Court having granted summary judgment for respondents, we must assume the facts to be as alleged by petitioner Joseph Oncale. The precise details are irrelevant to the legal point we must decide, and in the interest of both brevity and dignity we shall describe them only generally. In late October 1991, Oncale was working for respondent Sundowner Offshore Services, Inc., on a Chevron U.S.A., Inc., oil platform in the Gulf of Mexico. He was employed as a roustabout on an eight-man crew which included respondents John Lyons, Danny Pippen, and Brandon Johnson. Lyons, the crane operator, and Pippen, the driller, had supervisory authority. On several occasions, Oncale was forcibly subjected to sex-related, humiliating actions against him by Lyons, Pippen, and Johnson in the presence of the rest of the crew. Pippen and Lyons also physically assaulted Oncale in a sexual manner, and Lyons threatened him with rape.

Oncale's complaints to supervisory personnel produced no remedial action; in fact, the company's Safety Compliance Clerk, Valent Hohen, told Oncale that Lyons and Pippen "picked [on] him all the time too," and called him a name suggesting homosexuality. Oncale eventually quit—asking that his pink slip reflect that he "voluntarily left due to sexual harassment and verbal abuse." When asked at his deposition why he left Sundowner, Oncale stated: "I felt that if I didn't leave my job, that I would be raped or forced to have sex."

II

Title VII of the Civil Rights Act of 1964 provides, in relevant part, that "[i]t shall be an unlawful employment practice for an employer ... to discriminate against any individual with respect to his compensation, terms, conditions, or privileges of employment, because of such individual's race, color, religion, sex, or national origin." Section 703(a)(1). We have held that this not only covers "terms" and "conditions" in the narrow contractual sense, but "evinces a congressional intent to strike at the entire spectrum of disparate treatment of men and women in employment." Meritor Savings Bank, FSB v. Vinson, 477 U.S. 57, 64, 106 S.Ct. 2399, 2404, 91 L.Ed.2d 49 (1986) (citations and internal quotation marks omitted). "When the workplace is permeated with discriminatory intimidation, ridicule, and insult that is sufficiently severe or pervasive to alter the conditions of the victim's employment and create an abusive working environment, Title VII is violated." Harris v. Forklift Systems, Inc., 510 U.S. 17, 21, 114 S.Ct. 367, 370, 126 L.Ed.2d 295 (1993)(citations and internal quotation marks omitted).

If our precedents leave any doubt on the question, we hold today that nothing in Title VII necessarily bars a claim of discrimination "because of ... sex" merely because the plaintiff and the defendant (or the person charged with acting on behalf of the defendant) are of the same sex.

Courts have had little trouble with that principle in cases where an employee claims to have been passed over for a job or promotion. But when the issue arises in the context of a "hostile environment" sexual harassment claim, the state and federal courts have taken a bewildering variety of stances ... Some, like the Fifth Circuit in this case, have held that same-sex sexual harassment claims are never cognizable under Title VII. See also, *e.g., Goluszek v. H.P. Smith,* 697 F.Supp. 1452 (N.D.Ill. 1988). Other decisions say that such claims are actionable only if the plaintiff can prove that the harasser is homosexual (and thus presumably motivated by sexual desire). Compare *McWilliams v. Fairfax County Board of Supervisors,* 72 F.3d 1191 (C.A.4 1996), with *Wrightson v. Pizza Hut of America,* 99 F.3d 138 (C.A.4 1996). Still others suggest that workplace harassment that is sexual in content is always actionable, regardless of the harasser's sex, sexual orientation, or motivations. See *Doe v. Belleville,* 119 F.3d 563 (C.A.7 1997).

We see no justification in the statutory language or our precedents for a categorical rule excluding same-sex harassment claims from the coverage of Title VII. As some courts have observed, male-on-male sexual harassment in the workplace was assuredly not the principal evil Congress was concerned with when it enacted Title VII. But statutory prohibitions often go beyond the principal evil to cover reasonably comparable evils, and it is ultimately the provisions of our laws rather than the principal concerns of our legislators by which we are governed. Title VII prohibits "discriminat[ion] ... because of ... sex" in the "terms" or "conditions" of employment. Our holding that this includes sexual harassment must extend to sexual harassment of any kind that meets the statutory requirements.

Respondents and their *amici* contend that recognizing liability for same-sex harassment will transform Title VII into a general civility code for the American workplace. But that risk is no greater for same-sex than for opposite-sex harassment, and is adequately met by careful attention to the requirements of the statute. Title VII does not prohibit all verbal or physical harassment in the workplace; it is directed only at "*discriminat[ion]* ... because of ... sex." We have never held that workplace harassment, even harassment between men and women, is automatically discrimination because of sex merely because the words used have sexual content or connotations. "The critical issue, Title VII's text indicates, is whether members of one sex are exposed to disadvantageous terms or conditions of employment to which members of the other sex are not exposed." *Harris, supra,* at 25, 114 S.Ct., at 372 (GINSBURG, J., concurring).

Courts and juries have found the inference of discrimination easy to draw in most male-female sexual harassment situations, because the challenged conduct typically involves explicit or implicit proposals of sexual activity; it is reasonable to assume those proposals would not have been made to someone of the same sex. The same chain of inference would be available to a plaintiff alleging same-sex harassment, if there were credible evidence that the harasser was homosexual. But harassing conduct need not be motivated by sexual desire to support an inference of discrimination on the basis of sex. A trier of fact might reasonably find such discrimination, for example, if a female victim is harassed in such sex-specific and derogatory terms by another woman as to make it clear that the harasser is motivated by general hostility to the presence of women in the workplace. A same-sex harassment plaintiff may also, of course, offer direct comparative evidence about how the alleged harasser treated members of both sexes in a mixed-sex workplace. Whatever evidentiary route the plaintiff chooses to follow, he or she must always prove that the conduct at issue was not merely tinged with offensive sexual connotations, but actually constituted *"discrimina[tion]* ... because of ... sex."

And there is another requirement that prevents Title VII from expanding into a general civility code: As we emphasized in *Meritor* and *Harris,* the statute does not reach genuine but innocuous differences in the ways men and women routinely interact with members of the same sex and of the opposite sex. The prohibition of harassment on the basis of sex requires neither asexuality nor androgyny in the workplace; it forbids only behavior so objectively offensive as to alter the "conditions" of the victim's employment. "Conduct that is not severe or pervasive enough to create an objectively hostile or abusive work environment—an environment that a reasonable person would find hostile or abusive—is beyond Title VII's purview." *Harris,* 510 U.S., at 21, 114 S.Ct., at 370, citing *Meritor,* 477 U.S., at 67, 106 S.Ct., at 2405–2406. We have always regarded that requirement as crucial, and as sufficient to ensure that courts and juries do not mistake ordinary socializing in the workplace— such as male-on-male horseplay or intersexual flirtation—for discriminatory "conditions of employment."

We have emphasized, moreover, that the objective severity of harassment should be judged from the perspective of a reasonable person in the plaintiff's position, considering "all the circumstances." *Harris, supra,* at 23, 114 S.Ct., at 371. In same-sex (as in all) harassment cases, that inquiry requires careful consideration of the social context in which particular behavior occurs and is experienced by its target. A professional football player's working environment is not severely or pervasively abusive, for example, if the coach smacks him on the buttocks as he heads onto the field—even if the same behavior would reasonably be experienced as abusive by the coach's secretary (male or female) back at the office. The real social impact of workplace behavior often depends on a constellation of surrounding circumstances, expectations, and relationships which are not fully captured by a simple recitation of the words used or the physical acts performed. Common sense, and an appropriate sensitivity to social context, will enable courts and juries to distinguish between simple teasing or roughhousing among members of the same sex, and conduct which a reasonable person in the plaintiff's position would find severely hostile or abusive.

III

Because we conclude that sex discrimination consisting of same-sex sexual harassment is actionable under Title VII, the judgment of the Court of Appeals for the Fifth Circuit is reversed, and the case is remanded for further proceedings consistent with this opinion.

It is so ordered.

[The concurring opinion of Justice Thomas is omitted.]

Questions

1. After *Oncale,* how does one prove same-sex harassment?

2. If an employer sexually harasses men and women in a similar fashion, has the employer violated the law?

3. Is a refusal to hire an openly gay man a violation of Title VII? If not, why does Title VII deem same-sex harassment discriminatory but not employment policies based on sexual orientation?

5. PREGNANCY

NEWPORT NEWS SHIPBUILDING AND DRY DOCK CO. v. E.E.O.C.

Supreme Court of the United States, 1983.
462 U.S. 669, 103 S.Ct. 2622, 77 L.Ed.2d 89

JUSTICE STEVENS delivered the opinion of the Court.

In 1978 Congress decided to overrule our decision in *General Electric Co. v. Gilbert,* 429 U.S. 125, 97 S.Ct. 401, 50 L.Ed.2d 343 (1976), by amending Title VII of the Civil Rights Act of 1964 "to prohibit sex discrimination on the basis of pregnancy." On the effective date of the act, petitioner amended its health insurance plan to provide its female employees with hospitalization benefits for pregnancy-related conditions to the same extent as for other medical conditions. The plan continued, however, to provide less favorable pregnancy benefits for spouses of male employees. The question presented is whether the amended plan complies with the amended statute.

Petitioner's plan provides hospitalization and medical-surgical coverage for a defined category of employees and a defined category of dependents. Dependents covered by the plan include employees' spouses, unmarried children between 14 days and 19 years of age, and some older dependent children. Prior to April 29, 1979, the scope of the plan's coverage for eligible dependents was identical to its coverage for employees. All covered males, whether employees or dependents, were treated alike for purposes of hospitalization coverage. All covered females, whether employees or dependents, also were treated alike. Moreover, with one relevant exception, the coverage for males and females was identical. The exception was a limitation on hospital coverage for pregnancy that did not apply to any other hospital confinement.

After the plan was amended in 1979, it provided the same hospitalization coverage for male and female employees themselves for all medical conditions, but it [continued the limitations on hospital coverage for pregnancy of male employees' spouses].

On September 20, 1979, one of petitioner's male employees filed a charge with the EEOC alleging that petitioner had unlawfully refused to provide full insurance coverage for his wife's hospitalization caused by pregnancy; a month later the United Steelworkers filed a similar charge on behalf of other individuals.

Ultimately, the question we must decide is whether petitioner has discriminated against its male employees with respect to their compensation, terms, conditions, or privileges of employment because of their sex within the meaning of § 703(a)(1) of Title VII. Although the Pregnancy Discrimination Act has clarified the meaning of certain terms in this section, neither that Act nor the underlying statute contains a definition of the word "discriminate." In order to decide whether petitioner's plan discriminates against male employees because of *their* sex, we must therefore go beyond the bare statutory language. Accordingly, we shall consider whether Congress, by enacting the Pregnancy Discrimination Act, not only overturned the specific holding in *General Electric v. Gilbert, supra,* but also rejected the test of discrimination employed by the Court in that case. We believe it did. Under the proper test petitioner's plan is unlawful, because the protection it affords to married male employees is less comprehensive than the protection it affords to married female employees.

I

At issue in *General Electric v. Gilbert* was the legality of a disability plan that provided the company's employees with weekly compensation during periods of disability resulting from non-occupational causes. Because the plan excluded disabilities arising from pregnancy, the District Court and the Court of Appeals concluded that it discriminated against female employees because of their sex. This Court reversed.

When Congress amended Title VII in 1978, it unambiguously expressed its disapproval of both the holding and the reasoning of the Court in the *Gilbert* decision. It incorporated a new subsection in the "definitions" applicable "[f]or the purposes of this subchapter." The first clause of the Act states, quite simply: "The terms 'because of sex' or 'on the basis of sex' include, but are not limited to, because of or on the basis of pregnancy, childbirth, or related medical conditions." Section 701(k).

As petitioner argues, congressional discussion focused on the needs of female members of the work force rather than spouses of male employees. This does not create a "negative inference" limiting the scope of the act to the specific problem that motivated its enactment. See *United States v. Turkette,* 452 U.S. 576, 591, 101 S.Ct. 2524, 2532, 69 L.Ed.2d 246 (1981). Cf. *McDonald v. Santa Fe Trail Transp. Co.,* 427 U.S. 273, 285–296, 96 S.Ct. 2574, 2581–2586, 49 L.Ed.2d 493 (1976). Congress apparently assumed that existing plans that included benefits for dependents typically provided no less pregnancy-related coverage for the wives of male employees than they did for female employees. When the question of differential coverage for dependents was addressed in the Senate Report, the Committee indicated that it should be resolved "on the basis of existing title VII principles." The legislative context makes it clear that Congress was not thereby referring to the view of Title VII reflected in this Court's *Gilbert* opinion. Proponents of the legislation stressed throughout the debates that Congress had always intended to protect *all* individuals from sex discrimination in employment—including but not limited to pregnant women workers. Against this background we review the terms of the amended statute to decide whether petitioner has unlawfully discriminated against its male employees.

II

Section 703(a) makes it an unlawful employment practice for an employer to "discriminate against any individual with respect to his compensation, terms, conditions, or privileges of employment, because of such individual's race, color, religion, sex, or national origin...." Health insurance and other fringe benefits are "compensation, terms, conditions, or privileges of employment." Male as well as female employees are protected against discrimination. Thus, if a private employer were to provide complete health insurance coverage for the dependents of its female employees, and no coverage at all for the dependents of its male employees, it would violate Title VII. Such a practice would not pass the simple test of Title VII discrimination that we enunciated in *Los Angeles Department of Water & Power v. Manhart,* 435 U.S. 702, 711, 98 S.Ct. 1370, 1377, 55 L.Ed.2d 657 (1978), for it would treat a male employee with dependents "in a manner which but for that person's sex would be different." The same result would be reached even if the magnitude of the discrimination were smaller. For example, a plan that provided complete hospitalization coverage for the spouses of female employees but did not cover spouses of male employees when they had broken bones would violate Title VII by discriminating against male employees.

Petitioner's practice is just as unlawful. Its plan provides limited pregnancy-related benefits for employees' wives, and affords more extensive coverage for employees' spouses for all other medical conditions requiring hospitalization. Thus the husbands of female employees receive a specified level of hospitalization coverage for all conditions; the wives of male employees receive such coverage except for pregnancy-related conditions. Although *Gilbert* concluded that an otherwise inclusive plan that singled out pregnancy-related benefits for exclusion was nondiscriminatory on its face, because only women can become pregnant, Congress has unequivocally rejected that reasoning. The 1978 Act makes clear that it is discriminatory to treat pregnancy-related conditions less favorably than other medical conditions. Thus petitioner's plan unlawfully gives married male employees a benefit package for their dependents that is less inclusive than the dependency coverage provided to married female employees.

There is no merit to petitioner's argument that the prohibitions of Title VII do not extend to discrimination against pregnant spouses because the statute applies only to discrimination in employment. A two-step analysis demonstrates the fallacy in this contention. The Pregnancy Discrimination Act has now made clear that, for all Title VII purposes, discrimination based on a woman's pregnancy is, on its face, discrimination because of her sex. And since the sex of the spouse is always the opposite of the sex of the employee, it follows inexorably that discrimination against female spouses in the provision of fringe benefits is also discrimination against male employees. By making clear that an employer could not discriminate on the basis of an employee's pregnancy, Congress did not erase the original prohibition against discrimination on the basis of an employee's sex.

In short, Congress' rejection of the premises of *General Electric v. Gilbert* forecloses any claim that an insurance program excluding pregnancy coverage for female beneficiaries and providing complete coverage to similarly situated male beneficiaries does not discriminate on the basis of sex. Petitioner's plan is the mirror image of the plan at issue in *Gilbert*. The pregnancy limitation in this case violates Title VII by discriminating against male employees.

The judgment of the Court of Appeals is

Affirmed.

[JUSTICE REHNQUIST'S dissenting opinion is omitted.]

Note

1. The irony of *Newport News Shipbuilding*, that it interpreted Section 701(k) (the Pregnancy Discriminatory Act) to help male employees, is not to be lost on even the most casual reader. Yet, while it is hardly clear whether Congress contemplated and consciously resolved situations like the one presented in *Newport News Shipbuilding*, can you think of any good reason why Congress might have written the statute to accomplish a result different than the one the Court reached?

2. In cases subsequent to *Newport News*, courts have interpreted Section 701(k) to declare lawful a refusal to employ a woman because of her pregnancy (Marafino v. St. Louis County Circuit Court, 707 F.2d 1005 (8th Cir.1983) (The pregnant applicant would have needed a leave of absence shortly after initial employment and the employer would not hire anyone who would need to be absent shortly after starting work.), or to discharge her because of her absences due to her pregnancy (Dormeyer v. Comerica Bank–Illinois, 223 F.3d 579 (7th Cir.2000) ("The plaintiff was fired because of her absenteeism, not because of her pregnancy. ... It might seem that a

company's policy on absenteeism might be attacked from the direction of disparate impact ... but such an argument would not succeed. The concept of disparate impact was developed and is intended for cases in which employers impose eligibility requirements that are not really necessary for the job. ... The argument ... that the employer should be required to excuse pregnant employees from having to satisfy the *legitimate* require-ments of their job ... is an argument for subsidizing a class of workers ...'') (emphasis in original). Do you agree with the court's concern for subsidizing women? Consider the following.

3. Pregnancy and related matters reflect a real difference between the sexes. No matter how society reacts to the burdens created by pregnancy, there is an unavoidable difference in treatment of the sexes. If we protect pregnant people from the costs of pregnancy, women benefit; men do not. If we do not protect the women, they bear a burden that men do not. Do you agree with the norms that serve as the foundation for the Pregnancy Discriminatory Act (Section 701(k))?

6. AGE

Most of us, if we survive long enough, will encounter the changes in our work ability brought about by age. That singular fact, however, does not make discrimination based on age necessarily fair or acceptable to society. Individuals "age" at different speeds and in different ways. In the face of information that people often had been discriminated against in employment because of their age and regardless of their ability to do the job, Congress enacted a separate law prohibiting discrimination on the basis of age, the Age Discrimination in Employment Act (ADEA).

Although patterned closely on Title VII, the ADEA deals with age, which is somewhat different than race or sex. First, all of us are or were young once and, thus, the beneficiaries of the discrimination the law prohibits. Second, if we are lucky, all of us will become old. Third, most of us believe that there are changes that occur in us as we grow older. All of us have witnessed in ourselves or in some others that, as we age, we slow down, are weaker, are more forgetful, are less creative. We may suspect that there are greater health risks. We may be uncomfortable, for example, if—as we board a plane—we are greeted by a doddering, gray-haired pilot. We might think: are we safe in his hands? Doesn't he carry a higher risk that he will become fatigued during a long journey, or even more likely than a younger person to have a heart attack? To be fair, though, we also are likely to be nervous if the pilot is a young kid. Suddenly, in our minds, experience may outweigh youth. Are you pre-pared to accept as legitimate any generalizations made about women in the Fran Kennedy problem? Can you think of any employment distinc-tions based on race that may be legitimate? Should we be more willing to act on generalizations about the aging process? If so, in what ways?

Just what does it mean to discriminate on the basis of age? Some-times we make distinctions on the basis of factors that we do not think are age discrimination. But, are these factors really nothing but surro-

gates for age? For example, on average older workers have greater
seniority, higher wages, less up-to-date training, less endurance, less
strength, and more experience. May an employer terminate or reduce the
wages of an employee because his salary is too high relative to his
productivity and compared to other, younger employees? Or, because he
lacks the high tech training of a more recent graduate? Are these
employer actions responses to factors *other* than age, or are they precisely what age discrimination is all about?

HAZEN PAPER CO. v. BIGGINS

Supreme Court of the United States, 1993
507 U.S. 604, 113 S.Ct. 1701, 123 L.Ed.2d 338.

[In addition to its discussion of liability, which follows, the Court
considered whether the employer willfully violated the Act. Under the
Act, a willful violation results in liquidated damages. The Court reaffirmed prior law on this point, that an employer's violation of the Act is
willful where it either knew its conduct was prohibited by the statute or
showed reckless disregard about the matter. This portion of the opinion
is omitted.—Eds.]

JUSTICE O'CONNOR delivered the opinion of the Court.

In this case, we clarify the standards for liability and liquidated
damages under the Age Discrimination in Employment Act of 1967
(ADEA).

I

Petitioner Hazen Paper Company manufactures coated, laminated,
and printed paper and paperboard. The company is owned and operated
by two cousins, petitioners Robert Hazen and Thomas N. Hazen. The
Hazens hired respondent Walter F. Biggins as their technical director in
1977. They fired him in 1986, when he was 62 years old.

Respondent brought suit against petitioners in the United States
District Court for the District of Massachusetts, alleging a violation of
the ADEA. He claimed that age had been a determinative factor in
petitioners' decision to fire him. Petitioners contested this claim, asserting instead that respondent had been fired for doing business with
competitors of Hazen Paper. The case was tried before a jury, which
rendered a verdict for respondent on his ADEA claim and also found
violations of the Employee Retirement Income Security Act of 1974
(ERISA), 88 Stat. 895, § 510, 29 U.S.C. § 1140, and state law. On the
ADEA count, the jury specifically found that petitioners "willfully"
violated the statute. Under § 7(b) of the ADEA, 29 U.S.C. § 626(b), a
"willful" violation gives rise to liquidated damages. * * *

In affirming the judgments of liability, the Court of Appeals relied
heavily on the evidence that petitioners had fired respondent in order to
prevent his pension benefits from vesting. That evidence, as construed
most favorably to respondent by the court, showed that the Hazen Paper

pension plan had a 10–year vesting period and that respondent would have reached the 10–year mark had he worked "a few more weeks" after being fired. There was also testimony that petitioners had offered to retain respondent as a consultant to Hazen Paper, in which capacity he would not have been entitled to receive pension benefits. The Court of Appeals found this evidence of pension interference to be sufficient for ERISA liability, and also gave it considerable emphasis in upholding ADEA liability. After summarizing all the testimony tending to show age discrimination, the court stated:

> "Based on the foregoing evidence, the jury could reasonably have found that Thomas Hazen decided to fire [respondent] before his pension rights vested and used the confidentiality agreement [that petitioners had asked respondent to sign] as a means to that end. The jury could also have reasonably found that age was inextricably intertwined with the decision to fire [respondent]. If it were not for [respondent's] age, sixty-two, his pension rights would not have been within a hairbreadth of vesting. [Respondent] was fifty-two years old when he was hired; his pension rights vested in ten years."

II

A

The courts of appeals repeatedly have faced the question whether an employer violates the ADEA by acting on the basis of a factor, such as an employee's pension status or seniority, that is empirically correlated with age.... We now clarify that there is no disparate treatment under the ADEA when the factor motivating the employer is some feature other than the employee's age.

We long have distinguished between "disparate treatment" and "disparate impact" theories of employment discrimination.

The disparate treatment theory is of course available under the ADEA, as the language of that statute makes clear. "It shall be unlawful for an employer ... to fail or refuse to hire or to discharge any individual or otherwise discriminate against any individual with respect to his compensation, terms, conditions, or privileges of employment, *because of such individual's age*." 29 U.S.C. § 623(a)(1) (emphasis added). By contrast, we have never decided whether a disparate impact theory of liability is available under the ADEA, see *Markham v. Geller*, 451 U.S. 945, 101 S.Ct. 2028, 68 L.Ed.2d 332 (1981) (Rehnquist, J., dissenting from denial of certiorari), and we need not do so here. Respondent claims only that he received disparate treatment.

In a disparate treatment case, liability depends on whether the protected trait (under the ADEA, age) actually motivated the employer's decision. The employer may have relied upon a formal, facially discriminatory policy requiring adverse treatment of employees with that trait. Or the employer may have been motivated by the protected trait on an ad hoc, informal basis. Whatever the employer's decision making process, a disparate treatment claim cannot succeed unless the employee's protected trait actually played a role in that process and had a determinative influence on the outcome.

Disparate treatment, thus defined, captures the essence of what Congress sought to prohibit in the ADEA. It is the very essence of age discrimination for an older employee to be fired because the employer believes that productivity and competence decline with old age. As we explained in EEOC v. Wyoming, 460 U.S. 226, 103 S.Ct. 1054, 75 L.Ed.2d 18 (1983), Congress' promulgation of the ADEA was prompted by its concern that older workers were being deprived of employment on the basis of inaccurate and stigmatizing stereotypes.

"Although age discrimination rarely was based on the sort of animus motivating some other forms of discrimination, it was based in large part on stereotypes unsupported by objective fact.... Moreover, the available empirical evidence demonstrated that arbitrary age lines were in fact generally unfounded and that, as an overall matter, the performance of older workers was at least as good as that of younger workers." Id., at 231, 103 S.Ct., at 1057–1058.

Thus the ADEA commands that "employers are to evaluate [older] employees ... on their merits and not their age." *Western Air Lines, Inc. v. Criswell*, 472 U.S. 400, 422, 105 S.Ct. 2743, 2756, 86 L.Ed.2d 321 (1985). The employer cannot rely on age as a proxy for an employee's remaining characteristics, such as productivity, but must instead focus on those factors directly.

When the employer's decision is wholly motivated by factors other than age, the problem of inaccurate and stigmatizing stereotypes disappears. This is true even if the motivating factor is correlated with age, as pension status typically is. Pension plans typically provide that an employee's accrued benefits will become nonforfeitable, or "vested," once the employee completes a certain number of years of service with the employer. On average, an older employee has had more years in the work force than a younger employee, and thus may well have accumulated more years of service with a particular employer. Yet an employee's age is analytically distinct from his years of service. An employee who is younger than 40, and therefore outside the class of older workers as defined by the ADEA, see 29 U.S.C. § 631(a), may have worked for a particular employer his entire career, while an older worker may have been newly hired. Because age and years of service are analytically distinct, an employer can take account of one while ignoring the other, and thus it is incorrect to say that a decision based on years of service is necessarily "age-based."

The instant case is illustrative. Under the Hazen Paper pension plan, as construed by the Court of Appeals, an employee's pension benefits vest after the employee completes 10 years of service with the company. Perhaps it is true that older employees of Hazen Paper are more likely to be "close to vesting" than younger employees. Yet a decision by the company to fire an older employee solely because he has nine-plus years of service and therefore is "close to vesting" would not constitute discriminatory treatment on the basis of age. The prohibited stereotype ("Older employees are likely to be __") would not have figured in this decision, and the attendant stigma would not ensue. The decision would not be the result of an inaccurate and denigrating generalization about age, but would rather represent an *accurate* judgment about the employee—that he indeed is "close to vesting."

We do not mean to suggest that an employer *lawfully* could fire an employee in order to prevent his pension benefits from vesting. Such conduct is actionable under § 510 of ERISA, as the Court of Appeals rightly found in affirming judgment for respondent under that statute. But it would not, without more, violate the ADEA. That law requires the employer to ignore an employee's age (absent a statutory exemption or defense); it does not specify *further* characteristics that an employer must also ignore. Although some language in our prior decisions might be read to mean that an employer violates the ADEA whenever its reason for firing an employee is improper *in any respect*, see *McDonnell Douglas Corp. v. Green*, 411 U.S. 792, 802, 93 S.Ct. 1817, 1824, 36 L.Ed.2d 668 (1973) (creating proof framework applicable to ADEA) (employer must have "legitimate, nondiscriminatory reason" for action against employee), this reading is obviously incorrect. For example, it cannot be true that an employer who fires an older black worker because the worker is black thereby violates the ADEA. The employee's race is an improper reason, but it is improper under Title VII, not the ADEA.

We do not preclude the possibility that an employer who targets employees with a particular pension status on the assumption that these employees are likely to be older thereby engages in age discrimination. Pension status may be a proxy for age, not in the sense that the ADEA makes the two factors equivalent, cf. *Metz*, 828 F.2d, at 1208 (using "proxy" to mean statutory equivalence), but in the sense that the employer may suppose a correlation between the two factors and act accordingly. Nor do we rule out the possibility of dual liability under ERISA and the ADEA where the decision to fire the employee was motivated both by the employee's age and by his pension status. Finally, we do not consider the special case where an employee is about to vest in pension benefits as a result of his *age*, rather than years of service, and the employer fires the employee in order to prevent vesting. That case is not presented here. Our holding is simply that an employer does not violate the ADEA just by interfering with an older employee's pension benefits that would have vested by virtue of the employee's years of service.

Besides the evidence of pension interference, the Court of Appeals cited some additional evidentiary support for ADEA liability. Although there was no direct evidence of petitioners' motivation, except for two isolated comments by the Hazens, the Court of Appeals did note the following indirect evidence: Respondent was asked to sign a confidentiality agreement, even though no other employee had been required to do so, and his replacement was a younger man who was given a less onerous agreement. In the ordinary ADEA case, indirect evidence of this kind may well suffice to support liability if the plaintiff also shows that the employer's explanation for its decision—here, that respondent had been disloyal to Hazen Paper by doing business with its competitors—is " 'unworthy of credence.' " *Aikens*, 460 U.S., at 716, 103 S.Ct., at 1482 (quoting *Burdine*, 450 U.S., at 256, 101 S.Ct., at 1095). But inferring age-motivation from the implausibility of the employer's explanation may be problematic in cases where other unsavory motives, such as pension interference, were present.

* * *

[Justice Kennedy's concurring opinion is omitted.]

Questions

What arguments can you make for and against the Court's recognizing a disparate impact claim pursuant to ADEA? Take a look at the relevant statutory language. Consider also that Congress amended Title VII in 1991 to codify the disparate impact theory after the Supreme Court tried in 1989 to read disparate impact out of that statute. Congress did not amend ADEA at that time to codify disparate impact for age discrimination claims. What of the purposes of the two statutes? What else?

7. DISABILITY

As it became more and more clear that employers discriminated against people with noticeable disabilities, regardless of whether or not the disability was relevant to the individual's capacity to do the job, Congress was moved to limit some of this apparently irrational employer behavior. In 1973, the Vocational Rehabilitation Act (29 U.S.C. Sections 701 *et seq.*) was passed. That law precluded federal employers and contractors who did business with the federal government from engaging in employment discrimination based on individuals' "handicaps." In addition, the law required federal agencies and contractors doing business with the federal government to have affirmative action programs to increase the employment of handicapped persons. In 1990, Congress passed the Americans With Disabilities Act (ADA), thereby extending the limits on employer freedom to discriminate against disabled persons to all medium-sized and large businesses that affect interstate commerce (See 42 U.S.C. Section 101(5)).

The ADA reflects a great deal of what appears in, or has developed under, the other civil rights statutes regulating the employment relationship. Partly because of this incorporation of ideas from other experiences in the employment discrimination field and partly because of the many considerations and counter-considerations that appear to be relevant to the matter of outlawing irrational discrimination against disabled persons, on the one hand, and partly because of the desire to protect employers in their capacity to function efficiently, on the other hand, the ADA is remarkably complicated and opaque. Read, in particular, Sections

2, 3, and 101–103. One of the difficult issues presented by the ADA (as well as by the Vocational Rehabilitation Act) is the definition of the class of persons protected by the Act. Under the ADA, such a person is referred to as "a qualified individual with a disability" (See Section 102(a)). But, what is a "disability?" Section 3(2) provides a definition. In the following case, the Supreme Court put some meat on the statutory bones (although some observers might opine the Court stripped the flesh of the Act from its body).

SUTTON v. UNITED AIR LINES, INC.

Supreme Court of the United States, 1999.
527 U.S. 471, 119 S.Ct. 2139, 144 L.Ed.2d 450

JUSTICE O'CONNOR delivered the opinion of the Court.

The Americans with Disabilities Act of 1990 (ADA or Act) prohibits certain employers from discriminating against individuals on the basis of their disabilities. Petitioners challenge the dismissal of their ADA action for failure to state a claim upon which relief can be granted. We conclude that the complaint was properly dismissed. In reaching that result, we hold that the determination of whether an individual is disabled should be made with reference to measures that mitigate the individual's impairment, including, in this instance, eyeglasses and contact lenses. In addition, we hold that petitioners failed to allege properly that respondent "regarded" them as having a disability within the meaning of the ADA.

I

Petitioners are twin sisters, both of whom have severe myopia. Each petitioner's uncorrected visual acuity is 20/200 or worse in her right eye and 20/400 or worse in her left eye, but "[w]ith the use of corrective lenses, each ... has vision that is 20/20 or better." Consequently, without corrective lenses, each "effectively cannot see to conduct numerous activities such as driving a vehicle, watching television or shopping in public stores," but with corrective measures, such as glasses or contact lenses, both "function identically to individuals without a similar impairment."

In 1992, petitioners applied to respondent for employment as commercial airline pilots. They met respondent's basic age, education, experience, and FAA certification qualifications. After submitting their applications for employment, both petitioners were invited by respondent to an interview and to flight simulator tests. Both were told during their interviews, however, that a mistake had been made in inviting them to interview because petitioners did not meet respondent's minimum vision requirement, which was uncorrected visual acuity of 20/100 or better. Due to their failure to meet this requirement, petitioners' interviews were terminated, and neither was offered a pilot position.

II

The ADA prohibits discrimination by covered entities, including private employers, against qualified individuals with a disability. Specifically, it provides that no covered employer "shall discriminate against a qualified individual with a disability because of the disability of such individual in regard to job application procedures, the hiring, advancement, or discharge of employees, employee compensation, job training, and other terms, conditions, and privileges of employment." ("The term 'covered entity' means an employer, employment agency, labor organization, or joint labor-management committee"). A "qualified individual with a disability" is identified as "an individual with a disability who, with or without reasonable accommodation, can perform the essential functions of the employment position that such individual holds or desires." In turn, a "disability" is defined as:

"(A) a physical or mental impairment that substantially limits one or more of the major life activities of such individual;

"(B) a record of such an impairment; or

"(C) being regarded as having such an impairment." Section 3(2).

Accordingly, to fall within this definition one must have an actual disability (subsection (A)), have a record of a disability (subsection (B)), or be regarded as having one (subsection (C)).

III

With this statutory and regulatory framework in mind, we turn first to the question whether petitioners have stated a claim under subsection (A) of the disability definition, that is, whether they have alleged that they possess a physical impairment that substantially limits them in one or more major life activities. Because petitioners allege that with corrective measures their vision "is 20/20 or better," they are not actually disabled within the meaning of the Act if the "disability" determination is made with reference to these measures. Consequently, with respect to subsection (A) of the disability definition, our decision turns on whether disability is to be determined with or without reference to corrective measures.

Petitioners maintain that whether an impairment is substantially limiting should be determined without regard to corrective measures.

Respondent, in turn, maintains that an impairment does not substantially limit a major life activity if it is corrected.

Looking at the Act as a whole, it is apparent that if a person is taking measures to correct for, or mitigate, a physical or mental impairment, the effects of those measures—both positive and negative—must be taken into account when judging whether that person is "substantially limited" in a major life activity and thus "disabled" under the Act. The dissent relies on the legislative history of the ADA for the contrary proposition that individuals should be examined in their uncorrected state. Because we decide that, by its terms, the ADA cannot be read in this manner, we have no reason to consider the ADA's legislative history.

Three separate provisions of the ADA, read in concert, lead us to this conclusion. The Act defines a "disability" as "a physical or mental impairment that *substantially limits* one or more of the major life activities" of an individual. Because the phrase "substantially limits" appears in the Act in the present indicative verb form, we think the language is properly read as requiring that a person be presently—not potentially or hypothetically—substantially limited in order to demonstrate a disability. A "disability" exists only where an impairment "substantially limits" a major life activity, not where it "might," "could," or "would" be substantially limiting if mitigating measures were not taken. A person whose physical or mental impairment is corrected by medication or other measures does not have an impairment that presently "substantially limits" a major life activity. To be sure, a person whose physical or mental impairment is corrected by mitigating measures still has an impairment, but if the impairment is corrected it does not "substantially limi[t]" a major life activity.

The definition of disability also requires that disabilities be evaluated "with respect to an individual" and be determined based on whether an impairment substantially limits the "major life activities of such individual." Thus, whether a person has a disability under the ADA is an individualized inquiry.

The [EEOC's] guidelines' directive that persons be judged in their uncorrected or unmitigated state runs directly counter to the individualized inquiry mandated by the ADA. The agency approach would often require courts and employers to speculate about a person's condition and would, in many cases, force them to make a disability determination based on general information about how an uncorrected impairment usually affects individuals, rather than on the individual's actual condition. For instance, under this view, courts would almost certainly find all diabetics to be disabled, because if they failed to monitor their blood sugar levels and administer insulin, they would almost certainly be substantially limited in one or more major life activities. A diabetic whose illness does not impair his or her daily activities would therefore be considered disabled simply because he or she has diabetes. Thus, the guidelines approach would create a system in which persons often must be treated as members of a group of people with similar impairments, rather than as individuals. This is contrary to both the letter and the spirit of the ADA.

The guidelines approach could also lead to the anomalous result that in determining whether an individual is disabled, courts and employers could not consider any negative side effects suffered by an individual resulting from the use of mitigating measures, even when those side effects are very severe. This result is also inconsistent with the individualized approach of the ADA.

Finally, and critically, findings enacted as part of the ADA require the conclusion that Congress did not intend to bring under the statute's protection all those whose uncorrected conditions amount to disabilities. Congress found that "some 43,000,000 Americans have one or more physical or mental disabilities, and this number is increasing as the population as a whole is growing older." Section 2(a)(1). This figure is inconsistent with the definition of disability pressed by petitioners.

[T]he 43 million figure reflects an understanding that those whose impairments are largely corrected by medication or other devices are not "disabled" within the meaning of the ADA. The estimate is consistent with the numbers produced by studies performed during this same time period that took a similar functional approach to determining disability.

By contrast, nonfunctional approaches to defining disability produce significantly larger numbers. As noted above, the 1986 National Council on Disability report estimated that there were over 160 million disabled under the "health conditions approach."

Because it is included in the ADA's text, the finding that 43 million individuals are disabled gives content to the ADA's terms, specifically the term "disability." Had Congress intended to include all persons with corrected physical limitations among those covered by the Act, it undoubtedly would have cited a much higher number of disabled persons in the findings. That it did not is evidence that the ADA's coverage is restricted to only those whose impairments are not mitigated by corrective measures.

The dissents suggest that viewing individuals in their corrected state will exclude from the definition of "disab[led]" those who use prosthetic limbs (opinion of STEVENS, J.), (opinion of BREYER, J.), or take medicine for epilepsy or high blood pressure (opinion of STEVENS, J.). This suggestion is incorrect. The use of a corrective device does not, by itself, relieve one's disability. Rather, one has a disability under subsection (A) if, notwithstanding the use of a corrective device, that individual is substantially limited in a major life activity. For example, individuals who use prosthetic limbs or wheelchairs may be mobile and capable of functioning in society but still be disabled because of a substantial limitation on their ability to walk or run. The same may be true of individuals who take medicine to lessen the symptoms of an impairment so that they can function but nevertheless remain substantially limited. Alternatively, one whose high blood pressure is "cured" by medication may be regarded as disabled by a covered entity, and thus disabled under subsection (C) of the definition. The use or nonuse of a corrective device does not determine whether an individual is disabled; that determination depends on whether the limitations an individual with an impairment *actually* faces are in fact substantially limiting.

Applying this reading of the Act to the case at hand, we conclude that the Court of Appeals correctly resolved the issue of disability in respondent's favor. As noted above, petitioners allege that with corrective measures, their visual acuity is 20/20, and that they "function identically to individuals without a similar impairment." In addition, petitioners concede that they "do not argue that the use of corrective lenses in itself demonstrates a substantially limiting impairment." Accordingly, because we decide that disability under the Act is to be determined with reference to corrective measures, we agree with the courts below that petitioners have not stated a claim that they are substantially limited in any major life activity.

IV

Our conclusion that petitioners have failed to state a claim that they are actually disabled under subsection (A) of the disability definition does not end our inquiry. Under subsection (C), individuals who are "regarded as" having a disability are disabled within the meaning of the ADA. Subsection (C) provides that having a disability includes "being regarded as having a physical or mental impairment that substantially limits one or more of the major life activities of such individual." There are two apparent ways in which individuals may fall within this statutory definition: (1) a covered entity mistakenly believes that a person has a physical impairment that substantially limits one or more major life activities, or (2) a covered entity mistakenly believes that an actual, nonlimiting impairment substantially limits one or more major life activities. In both cases, it is necessary that a covered entity entertain misperceptions about the individual—it must believe either that one has a substantially limiting impairment that one does not have or that one has a substantially limiting impairment when, in fact, the impairment is not so limiting. These misperceptions often "resul[t] from stereotypic assumptions not truly indicative of . . . individual ability." See 42 U.S.C. § 3(a)(7).

There is no dispute that petitioners are physically impaired. Petitioners do not make the obvious argument that they are regarded due to their impairments as substantially limited in the major life activity of seeing. They contend only that respondent mistakenly believes their physical impairments substantially limit them in the major life activity of working. To support this claim, petitioners allege that respondent has a vision requirement, which is allegedly based on myth and stereotype. Further, this requirement substantially limits their ability to engage in the major life activity of working by precluding them from obtaining the job of global airline pilot, which they argue is a "class of employment." In reply, respondent argues that the position of global airline pilot is not a class of jobs and therefore petitioners have not stated a claim that they are regarded as substantially limited in the major life activity of working.

Standing alone, the allegation that respondent has a vision requirement in place does not establish a claim that respondent regards petitioners as substantially limited in the major life activity of working. By its terms, the ADA allows employers to prefer some physical attributes over others and to establish physical criteria. An employer runs afoul of the ADA when it makes an employment decision based on a physical or mental impairment, real or imagined, that is regarded as substantially limiting a major life activity. Accordingly, an employer is free to decide that physical characteristics or medical conditions that do not rise to the level of an impairment—such as one's height, build, or singing voice—are preferable to others, just as it is free to decide that some limiting, but not *substantially* limiting, impairments make individuals less than ideally suited for a job.

Considering the allegations of the amended complaint in tandem, petitioners have not stated a claim that respondent regards their impairment as *substantially limiting* their ability to work. The ADA does not define "substantially limits," but "substantially" suggests "considerable" or "specified to a large degree."

When the major life activity under consideration is that of working, the statutory phrase "substantially limits" requires, at a minimum, that plaintiffs allege they are unable to work in a broad class of jobs. To be substantially limited in the major life activity of working, then, one must be precluded from more than one type of job, a specialized job, or a particular job of choice. If jobs utilizing an individual's skills (but perhaps not his or her unique talents) are available, one is not precluded from a substantial class of jobs. Similarly, if a host of different types of jobs are available, one is not precluded from a broad range of jobs.

Because the parties accept that the term "major life activities" includes working, we do not determine [whether they are correct.]

Assuming without deciding that working is a major life activity, petitioners have failed to allege adequately that their poor eyesight is regarded as an impairment that substantially limits them in the major life activity of working. They allege only that respondent regards their poor vision as precluding them from holding positions as a "global airline pilot." Because the position of global airline pilot is a single job, this allegation does not support the claim that respondent regards petitioners as having a *substantially limiting* impairment. Indeed, there are a number of other positions utilizing petitioners' skills, such as regional pilot and pilot instructor to name a few, that are available to them.

JUSTICE GINSBURG, concurring.

I agree that 42 U.S.C. § 3(2)(A) does not reach the legions of people with correctable disabilities. The strongest clues to Congress' perception of the domain of the Americans with Disabilities Act (ADA), as I see it, are legislative findings that "some 43,000,000 Americans have one or more physical or mental disabilities," § 2(a)(1), and that "individuals with disabilities are a discrete and insular minority," persons "subjected to a history of purposeful unequal treatment, and relegated to a position of political powerlessness in our society," § 2(a)(7). These declarations are inconsistent with the enormously embracing definition of disability petitioners urge. As the Court demonstrates, the inclusion of correctable disabilities within the ADA's domain would extend the Act's coverage to far more than 43 million people. And persons whose uncorrected eyesight is poor, or who rely on daily medication for their well-being, can be found in every social and economic class; they do not cluster among the politically powerless, nor do they coalesce as historical victims of discrimination. In short, in no sensible way can one rank the large numbers of diverse individuals with corrected disabilities as a "discrete and insular minority." I do not mean to suggest that any of the constitutional presumptions or doctrines that may apply to "discrete and insular" minorities in other contexts are relevant here; there is no constitutional dimension to this case. Congress' use of the phrase, however, is a telling indication of its intent to restrict the ADA's coverage to a confined, and historically disadvantaged, class.

JUSTICE STEVENS, with whom JUSTICE BREYER joins, dissenting.

When it enacted the Americans with Disabilities Act in 1990, Congress certainly did not intend to require United Air Lines to hire unsafe or unqualified pilots. Nor, in all likelihood, did it view every person who wears glasses as a member of a "discrete and insular minority." Indeed, by reason of legislative myopia it may not have foreseen that its definition of "disability" might theoretically encompass, not just "some 43,000,000 Americans," but perhaps two or three times that number. Nevertheless, if we apply customary tools of statutory construction, it is quite clear that the threshold question whether an individual is "disabled" within the meaning of the Act—and, therefore, is entitled to the basic assurances that the Act affords—focuses on her past or present physical condition without regard to mitigation that has resulted from rehabilitation, self-improvement, prosthetic devices, or medication. One might reasonably argue that the general rule should not apply to an impairment that merely requires a nearsighted person to wear glasses. But I believe that, in order to be faithful to the remedial purpose of the Act, we should give it a generous, rather than a miserly, construction.

There are really two parts to the question of statutory construction presented by this case. The first question is whether the determination of disability for people that Congress unquestionably intended to cover should focus on their unmitigated or their mitigated condition. If the correct answer to that question is the one provided by eight of the nine Federal Courts of Appeals to address the issue, and by all three of the Executive agencies that have issued regulations or interpretive bulletins construing the statute—namely, that the statute defines "disability" without regard to ameliorative measures—it would still be necessary to decide whether that general rule should be applied to what might be characterized as a "minor, trivial impairment."

I

"As in all cases of statutory construction, our task is to interpret the words of [the statute] in light of the purposes Congress sought to serve." Congress expressly provided that the "purpose of [the ADA is] to provide a clear and comprehensive national mandate for the elimination of discrimination against individuals with disabilities." 42 U.S.C. § 2(b)(1). To that end, the ADA prohibits covered employers from "discriminat[ing] against a qualified individual *with a disability* because of the disability" in regard to the terms, conditions, and privileges of employment. 42 U.S.C. § 3(a) (emphasis added).

The three prongs of the statute, rather, are most plausibly read together not to inquire into whether a person is currently "functionally" limited in a major life activity, but only into the existence of an impairment—present or past—that substantially limits, or did so limit, the individual before amelioration. This reading avoids the counterintuitive conclusion that the ADA's safeguards vanish when individuals make themselves more employable by ascertaining ways to overcome their physical or mental limitations.

II

If a narrow reading of the term "disability" were necessary in order to avoid the danger that the Act might otherwise force United to hire pilots who might endanger the lives of their passengers, it would make good sense to use the "43,000,000 Americans" finding to confine its coverage. There is, however, no such danger in this case. If a person is "disabled" within the meaning of the Act, she still cannot prevail on a claim of discrimination unless she can prove that the employer took action "because of" that impairment, and that she can, "with or without reasonable accommodation, . . . perform the essential functions" of the job of a commercial airline pilot. See § 2(8). Even then, an employer may avoid liability if it shows that the criteria of having uncorrected visual acuity of at least 20/100 is "job-related and consistent with business necessity" or if such vision (even if correctable to 20/20) would pose a health or safety hazard. §§ 4(a) and (b).

This case, in other words, is not about whether petitioners are genuinely qualified or whether they can perform the job of an airline pilot without posing an undue safety risk. The case just raises the threshold question whether petitioners are members of the ADA's protected class. It simply asks whether the ADA lets petitioners in the door in the same way as the Age Discrimination in Employment Act of 1967 does for every person who is at least 40 years old, and as Title VII of the Civil Rights Act of 1964 does for every single individual in the work force. Inside that door lies nothing more than basic protection from irrational and unjustified discrimination because of a characteristic that is beyond a person's control. Hence, this particular case, at its core, is about whether, assuming that petitioners can prove that they are "qualified," the airline has any duty to come forward with some legitimate explanation for refusing to hire them because of their uncorrected eyesight, or whether the ADA leaves the airline free to decline to hire petitioners on this basis even if it is acting purely on the basis of irrational fear and stereotype.

I think it quite wrong for the Court to confine the coverage of the Act simply because an interpretation of "disability" that adheres to Congress' method of defining the class it intended to benefit may also provide protection for "significantly larger numbers" of individuals than estimated in the Act's findings. It has long been a "familiar canon of statutory construction that remedial legislation should be construed broadly to effectuate its purposes." Congress sought, in enacting the ADA, to "provide a . . . comprehensive national mandate for the discrimination against individuals with disabilities."

When faced with classes of individuals or types of discrimination that fall outside the core prohibitions of anti-discrimination statutes, we have consistently construed those statutes to include comparable evils within their coverage, even when the particular evil at issue was beyond Congress' immediate concern in passing the legislation. Congress, for instance, focused almost entirely on the problem of discrimination against African–Americans when it enacted Title VII of the Civil Rights Act of 1964. See, *e.g., United Steelworkers of America v. Weber,* 443 U.S. 193, 202–203, 99 S.Ct. 2721, 61 L.Ed.2d 480 (1979). But that narrow focus could not possibly justify a construction of the statute that excluded Hispanic–Americans or Asian–Americans from its protection—or as we later decided (ironically enough, by relying on legislative history and according "great deference" to the EEOC's "interpretation"), Caucasians. See McDonald v. Santa Fe Trail Transp. Co., 427 U.S. 273, 279–280, 96 S.Ct. 2574, 49 L.Ed.2d 493 (1976).

We unanimously applied this well-accepted method of interpretation last Term with respect to construing Title VII to cover claims of same-sex sexual harassment. *Oncale v. Sundowner Offshore Services, Inc.,* 523 U.S. 75, 118 S.Ct. 998, 140 L.Ed.2d 201 (1998). We explained our holding as follows:

> "As some courts have observed, male-on-male sexual harassment in the workplace was assuredly not the principal evil Congress was concerned with when it enacted Title VII. But statutory prohibitions often go beyond the principal evil to cover reasonably comparable evils, and it is ultimately the provisions of our laws rather than the principal concerns of our legislators by which we are governed. Title VII prohibits 'discriminat[ion] . . . because of . . . sex' in the 'terms' or 'conditions' of employment. Our holding that this includes sexual harassment must extend to sexual harassment of any kind that meets the statutory requirements."

I do not mean to suggest, of course, that the ADA should be read to prohibit discrimination on the basis of, say, blue eyes, deformed fingernails, or heights of less than six feet. Those conditions, to the extent that they are even "impairments," do not substantially limit individuals in any condition and thus are different in kind from the impairment in the case before us. While not all eyesight that can be enhanced by glasses is substantially limiting, having 20/200 vision in one's better eye is, without treatment, a significant hindrance. Only two percent of the population suffers from such myopia. Such acuity precludes a person from driving, shopping in a public store, or viewing a computer screen from a reasonable distance. Uncorrected vision, therefore, can be "substantially limiting" in the same way that unmedicated epilepsy or diabetes can be. Because Congress obviously intended to include individuals with the latter impairments in the Act's protected class, we should give petitioners the same protection.

III

The Court's mantra regarding the Act's "individualized approach," however, fails to support its holding. I agree that the letter and spirit of the ADA is designed to deter decision making based on group stereotypes, but the agencies' interpretation of the Act does not lead to this result. Nor does it require courts to "speculate" about people's "hypothetical" conditions. Viewing a person in her "unmitigated" state simply requires examining that individual's abilities in a different state, not the abilities of every person who shares a similar condition. It is just as easy individually to test petitioners' eyesight with their glasses on as with their glasses off.

Ironically, it is the Court's approach that actually condones treating individuals merely as members of groups. That misdirected approach permits any employer to dismiss out of hand every person who has uncorrected eyesight worse than 20/100 without regard to the specific qualifications of those individuals or the extent of their abilities to overcome their impairment. In much the same way, the Court's approach would seem to allow an employer to refuse to hire every person who has epilepsy or diabetes that is controlled by medication, or every person who functions efficiently with a prosthetic limb.

Under the Court's reasoning, an employer apparently could not refuse to hire persons with these impairments who are substantially limited even with medication, see *ante,* at 2148–2149, but that group-based "exception" is more perverse still. Since the purpose of the ADA is to dismantle employment barriers based on society's accumulated myths and fears, it is especially ironic to deny protection for persons with substantially limiting impairments that, when corrected, render them fully able and employable. Insofar as the Court assumes that the majority of individuals with impairments such as prosthetic limbs or epilepsy will still be covered under its approach because they are substantially limited "notwithstanding the use of a corrective device," I respectfully disagree as an empirical matter. Although it is of course true that some of these individuals are substantially limited in any condition, Congress enacted the ADA in part because such individuals are *not* ordinarily substantially limited in their mitigated condition, but rather are often the victims of "stereotypic assumptions not truly indicative of the individual ability of such individuals to participate in, and contribute to, society." 42 U.S.C. § 2(a)(7).

It has also been suggested that if we treat as "disabilities" impairments that may be mitigated by measures as ordinary and expedient as wearing eyeglasses, a flood of litigation will ensue. The suggestion is misguided. Although vision is of critical importance for airline pilots, in most segments of the economy whether an employee wears glasses—or uses any of several other mitigating measures—is a matter of complete indifference to employers. It is difficult to envision many situations in which a qualified employee who needs glasses to perform her job might be fired—as the statute requires—"because of," 42 U.S.C. § 102, the fact that she cannot see well without them. Such a proposition would be ridiculous in the garden-variety case. On the other hand, if an accounting firm, for example, adopted a guideline refusing to hire any incoming accountant who has uncorrected vision of less than 20/100—or, by the same token, any person who is unable without medication to avoid having seizures—such a rule would seem to be the essence of invidious discrimination.

In this case the quality of petitioners' uncorrected vision is relevant only because the airline regards the ability to see without glasses as an employment qualification for its pilots. Presumably it would not insist on such a qualification unless it has a sound business justification for doing so (an issue we do not address today). But if United regards petitioners as unqualified because they cannot see well without glasses, it seems eminently fair for a court also to use uncorrected vision as the basis for evaluating petitioners' life activity of seeing.

IV

Occupational hazards characterize many trades. The farsighted pilot may have as much trouble seeing the instrument panel as the near sighted pilot has in identifying a safe place to land. The vision of appellate judges is sometimes subconsciously obscured by a concern that their decision will legalize issues best left to the private sphere or will magnify the work of an already-overburdened judiciary. Although these concerns may help to explain the Court's decision to chart its own course—rather than to follow the one that has been well marked by Congress, by the overwhelming consensus of circuit judges, and by the Executive officials charged with the responsibility of administering the ADA—they surely do not justify the Court's crabbed vision of the territory covered by this important statute.

Accordingly, although I express no opinion on the ultimate merits of petitioners' claim, I am persuaded that they have a disability covered by the ADA. I therefore respectfully dissent.

[The dissenting opinion of Justice Breyer is omitted.]

Questions

1. Which opinion has the better of the disagreement regarding the literal words of the statute? Is it possible to give meaning to the literal words without reference to what it was Congress wished to accomplish? What was that purpose?

2. Should the plaintiffs have relied on section 3(2)(B), which defines "disability" to include "a record of such impairment?"

3. Assume, for the moment, that the Suttons could perform the job well. Why would Congress, which prohibited employment discrimination based on irrelevant concerns relating to disabilities, want to give an airline the freedom to refuse to employ someone because of her bad eyesight, when that bad eyesight was irrelevant to performance of the job?

4. It takes little imagination to conjure up the airline's real concerns, which almost surely had to do with the safety of having virtually blind people fly a plane, with or without glasses, lenses, or other temporary and not wholly stable corrective devices. If that supposition is correct, should not the case have been decided differently? That is, the airline's concern had to do with the ability of the plaintiffs to perform the "essential functions" of the job. See Section 101(8). Isn't that where the horserace in this case should have been? Why do you think the Court's majority held otherwise? Are its explanations persuasive?

5. Because the parties were not in dispute about the matter, the Court assumed, without deciding, that working is a "major life activity" within the meaning of Section 3(2). Is it? If so, does an employer who discriminates on the basis of, say, blindness, have a "defense" by pointing out that there are lots of employers who do not discriminate against blind people, therefore the plaintiff can easily find another job, and thus she does not have an impairment that limits her major life activity? Can it be that Congress meant to exempt from coverage the employer who has a unique bias against people with certain physical or mental impairments?

6. Are you persuaded that the majority and Justice Ginsburg are correct because of Section 2(a)(1)'s reference to forty-three million people with disabilities and by Section 2(a)(7)'s reference to people with disabilities being a "discrete and insular minority?" Assuming that the majority and Ginsburg are correct that Congress had in mind a discrete and insular minority of approximately forty-three million, and assuming further that they were also correct that such a number could not have included the many millions more who would suffer from disabilities but for corrective techniques (like eye glasses), does it follow that those many millions more are not covered by the statute? If so, should Title VII be read not to protect men? Or, Caucasians? Or, Protestants? Or, women from sexual harassment? Or, men from same sex harassment? If so, should the Pregnancy Discriminatory Act (Section 701(k) of Title VII) be read not to protect male employees?

IV. SHALL WE SWALLOW EMPLOYEES, THEIR FREEDOM, AND THEIR STATUTORY RIGHTS INTO THE WORLD OF CONTRACTS AND ARBITRATION?

A. VIA COVENANTS NOT TO COMPETE, CAN A FORMER EMPLOYER PRECLUDE AN EMPLOYEE FROM WORKING? IF IT IS THE EMPLOYER WHO TERMINATES THE CONTRACT, IS THE COVENANT NOT TO COMPETE STILL EFFECTIVE?

ROBERT S. WEISS AND ASSOCIATES, INC. v. WIEDERLIGHT

Supreme Court of Connecticut, 1988.
208 Conn. 525, 546 A.2d 216.

Glass, Associate Justice.

The plaintiff, Robert S. Weiss and Associates, Inc., instituted an action against Michael E. Wiederlight for breach of a restrictive covenant of employment and theft of trade secrets. In an amended complaint, the plaintiff added Insurance Associates of Connecticut, Inc. (IAC), as a defendant, alleging interference with a business enterprise and theft of trade secrets with Wiederlight acting as its agent. The trial court ruled in favor of the plaintiff on the issues of breach of the restrictive covenant and interference with a business enterprise and awarded damages, but found that the plaintiff had failed to sustain its burden of proof on the issue of theft of trade secrets. The plaintiff appealed. . . .

On appeal, the plaintiff claims that the trial court erred: (1) in failing to conclude that the plaintiff's customer lists and related insurance information constituted trade secrets and that Wiederlight had committed a theft of trade secrets; (2) in failing to award damages beyond the 1983–1984 period for Wiederlight's solicitation of the plaintiff's accounts in breach of the covenant; and (3) in failing to award damages for other accounts written in the area restricted by the covenant after the court found that the covenant was valid and that Wiederlight had breached it. The defendants on cross appeal argue that the trial court erred in finding that the restrictive covenant was reasonable and valid and in finding that IAC tortiously interfered with the plaintiff's contract.

The facts may be summarized as follows. The plaintiff is an independent insurance agency in Stamford, that was doing business throughout Fairfield County and in New York at the time of the events underlying this case. . . . [The plaintiff originally employed the defendant in 1975.]

In April 1979, the plaintiff's principal, Robert S. Weiss, and Wiederlight entered into a new four year employment agreement. Wiederlight expressed dissatisfaction with certain provisions of the 1979 contract, which reduced his status and commission rates and omitted a buy-in option that was set forth in the 1975 agreement. When the 1979 agreement was negotiated, Wiederlight's sole source of income was derived from his employment with Weiss. Wiederlight signed the agreement after he had read it and discussed it with his wife. He understood all the terms and conditions and voluntarily entered into the agreement.

The 1979 employment agreement contained three paragraphs pertinent to this case. Paragraph seven identified the agency's business records, including those produced by Wiederlight, as its exclusive property, and forbade Wiederlight from removing such records on termination of his employment. Paragraphs nine and ten barred Wiederlight, for two years from the date the agreement terminated, from soliciting accounts held by the plaintiff at the time the employment agreement terminated, and from working within Stamford and within ten miles from the outer borders of Stamford.

In March 1983, Weiss told Wiederlight that his employment agreement would not be renewed upon expiration. Immediately thereafter, Wiederlight was hired by IAC, then located in Southport, and began to solicit and sell commercial insurance policies to customers he had dealt with while working for Weiss. Before hiring Wiederlight, the principals of IAC had reviewed his employment agreement with Weiss and were aware of the terms of the restrictive covenant.

During his employment at IAC from April 1983 to March 1985, Wiederlight sold insurance to a number of accounts that belonged to the plaintiff when Wiederlight's employment there ceased. Wiederlight also sold commercial insurance to other customers within the restricted Stamford area. The commissions generated by Wiederlight during his employment at IAC inured to the financial benefit of his employer. The principals of IAC encouraged and induced Wiederlight to sell insurance to customers of the plaintiff and others in the Stamford area despite their knowledge of the restrictive covenant in Wiederlight's 1979 employment agreement with Weiss.

I

We first consider the defendants' claim on cross appeal that the trial court erred in concluding that the restrictive covenant in Wiederlight's 1979 employment agreement was reasonable and therefore valid. We find no error in the trial court's conclusion.

The defendants' first claim is that the trial court's conclusion was erroneous because it applied the wrong criteria to evaluate the reasonableness of the restrictive covenant. We disagree. *Scott v. General Iron & Welding Co.*, 171 Conn. 132, 368 A.2d 111 (1976), sets forth the criteria relevant to an evaluation of the reasonableness of a covenant not to compete ancillary to an employment agreement.[2]

The defendants next claim that the trial court erred in upholding the covenant because: (1) it contained time and geographic constraints that were unreasonable; (2) it unreasonably restrained Wiederlight from any employment in the commercial insurance business; (3) it unfairly protected the plaintiff's interests and interfered with the public's interest in open competition; and (4) it never became operative under the terms of the contract. We are unpersuaded.

Paragraph nine of the employment agreement barred Wiederlight from selling, soliciting or otherwise engaging in commercial insurance for himself or any other firm in Stamford or within a ten mile radius, excluding Long Island, New York, and areas north of Stamford, for two years following termination of the agreement. Paragraph ten prohibited him from soliciting or selling commercial insurance to customers of the plaintiff, existing when Wiederlight's employment terminated, for two years following termination.

The trial court's conclusion that this restrictive covenant was reasonable is consistent with other cases where we have held that time and geographic restrictions in a covenant not to compete are valid if they are reasonably limited and fairly protect the interests of both parties.

In the present case, the two year limitation fairly protected the plaintiff's interests in the commercial insurance business in the Stamford area while ensuring that Wiederlight could return to commercial insurance in that area within a definite period of time. In addition, the restricted geographical area was narrowly tailored to the plaintiff's business situation in the Stamford area. The provision of paragraph nine allowing Wiederlight to work in areas north of Stamford and in Long Island, New York, demonstrated the plaintiff's caution in avoiding an overly broad geographic restriction.

Further, we are not persuaded by the defendants' theory that paragraph ten is unreasonable because it lacks a geographic limitation. Paragraph ten barred Wiederlight from soliciting the plaintiff's accounts that existed when Wiederlight left. Upon the termination of the agreement, the clause fixed the geographical scope of the covenant to a definite and limited area. Such a restriction was reasonable in view of the plaintiff's business situation, and by its own terms did not protect the employer in areas where it did not do business.

The defendants assert that the scope of prohibited employment failed to protect Wiederlight's interests, especially since Wiederlight did nothing to cause the severance of his employment. ... Although the

2. The five factors to be considered in evaluating the reasonableness of a restrictive covenant ancillary to an employment agreement are: (1) the length of time the restriction operates; (2) the geographical area covered; (3) the fairness of the protection accorded to the employer; (4) the extent of the restraint on the employee's opportunity to pursue his occupation; and (5) the extent of interference with the public's interests.

covenant precluded Wiederlight from any employment in a commercial insurance business, the restriction only operated for two years and only applied to the greater Stamford area. Moreover, the reasonableness of a restrictive covenant of employment does not turn on whether the employee subject to the covenant left his position voluntarily or was dismissed by the employer. Similarly, we disagree with the defendants' theory that, because paragraph ten protects the plaintiff's interest in customers, the only result of paragraph nine was to prevent Wiederlight from working in the Stamford area. The fact that an employer seeks to protect his interest in potential new customers in a reasonably limited market area as well as his existing customers at the time the employee leaves does not render the covenant unreasonable.

The defendants further contend that the plaintiff's self-interest in protecting the Stamford commercial insurance market is outweighed by the public's interest in competitive insurance pricing and competition within the market place. We have stated that "[w]hen the character of the business and the nature of the employment are such that the employer requires protection for his established business against competitive activities by one who has become familiar with it through employment therein, restrictions are valid when they appear to be reasonably necessary for the fair protection of the employer's business or rights.... Especially if the employment involves ... [the employee's] contacts and associations with clients or customers it is appropriate to restrain the use, when the service is ended, of the knowledge and acquaintance, so acquired, to injure or appropriate the business which the party was employed to maintain and enlarge."

In the present case, Wiederlight's position as a commercial insurance salesman required him to maintain extensive contacts and associations with the plaintiff's customers. The trial court's conclusion that the covenant was reasonable was consistent with evidence that the plaintiff sought to protect information regarding current and potential customers in the Stamford area. Moreover, the defendants offer no explanation for their summary suggestion that the covenant impairs the public's interest in competitive insurance pricing. There is nothing in the findings to suggest that enforcement of the restrictive covenant in paragraph nine will interfere with the public's legitimate interest in open competition.

The defendants finally argue that the restrictive covenant in the 1979 agreement never became operative because Wiederlight's employment agreement was not "terminated" as required by the covenant. They assert that the meaning of "termination" is derived from paragraph six of the agreement, which states that the agreement shall "not be terminated except by mutual [consent] of both parties or for cause." Since Wiederlight's agreement lapsed at the end of the four year term, they argue that the agreement was not "terminated" and therefore the restrictions in paragraphs nine and ten could not operate.

The trial court found that the contract was unambiguous and rejected the defendant's contention that the word "termination" in paragraphs nine and ten only meant termination by mutual consent or for cause. " 'The intention of the parties is to be ascertained from the language used in the contract and that language must be given its common meaning and usage where it can be sensibly applied to the subject matter of the contracts.' The word terminate "means to 'come to a limit in time; to end.' " Because the ordinary meaning of "termination" may include lapse or expiration, the trial court was correct in ruling that the covenant became operative when Wiederlight's contract expired.

IV

Finally, we address the plaintiff's claims on the issue of damages. The trial court concluded that the plaintiff had sustained the burden of proof of damages for net profits lost in 1983 and 1984 through Wiederlight's sales to the plaintiff's accounts in breach of the restrictive covenant. In assessing damages, the court used certain tables, supplied by the plaintiff, that provided data on the accounts. The information included the account's name, the year the plaintiff obtained the account, and the claimed actual and projected losses for the years 1983 through 1991. To arrive at the damage figure, the trial court reduced the total amount of losses for the years 1983 and 1984 by 44 percent. The reduction included 27 percent for Wiederlight's salary compensation, 11 percent for the plaintiff's average annual loss of customers, and a 6 percent overhead factor. The court, however, found that there was no credible evidence that the plaintiff's customers would have renewed their accounts after 1984, and denied damages for the period following 1984. The plaintiff argues that because the trial court awarded damages for Wiederlight's sales to its accounts in 1983–1984 based on the plaintiff's tables, it implicitly accepted that loss of renewals in future years was compensable, and therefore could not logically deny damages for the years following 1984. We are unpersuaded.

The trial court has broad discretion in determining whether damages are appropriate.

At trial, Weiss testified that the plaintiff annually lost 11½ percent of its customers. Weiss also testified, however, that all of the plaintiff's accounts that Wiederlight sold had been accounts he had produced while working at the agency. Wiederlight testified that many of the disputed customer accounts had contacted him and sought his services after learning that he had left the plaintiff. Although other agents were assigned to contact these customers after Wiederlight left, Weiss did not know the extent of the plaintiff's subsequent contacts with the accounts.

On the basis of the evidence, the trial court could reasonably have found that the plaintiff failed to establish that it would have obtained renewals of the accounts after 1984. The trial court's conclusion that the plaintiff failed to prove damages for lost profits for the period after 1984 was not a clear abuse of discretion.

The plaintiff also contests the trial court's denial of damages for Wiederlight's breach of that part of the covenant barring him from working in the Stamford area for two years after termination of employment with it. The trial court found that there was no evidence that the plaintiff would have written any of the accounts in the restricted area had Wiederlight not breached the covenant. It concluded that the plaintiff's damage claim was speculative.

At trial, the plaintiff introduced a list of customers in the Stamford area that Wiederlight successfully had solicited during the restricted period. The data, which was supplied to the plaintiff by IAC, gave each account's name and date of inception, the total commission earned, the profit on the commission, and Wiederlight's share in the commission.

The proper measure of damages for breach of a covenant not to compete is the nonbreaching party's losses rather than the breaching party's gains. The plaintiff seeks to establish its lost profits by reference to the undisputed fact that Wiederlight sold commercial insurance to customers in the restricted area during the covenant's operation. To permit the plaintiff to recover damages merely by proving that the defendant breached the covenant, however, would ignore the well established rule that damages are essential to the plaintiff's proof and must be shown with reasonable clarity.

Questions

1. Did the Weiss court correctly resolve the damages issues? Given what the *Weiss* court did with the damages issues, which party "won?"

2. When an employer and its employees enter into employment contracts, the words of the contracts reflect, we hope accurately, the desires of the parties to the extent the parties have addressed matters. Of course, if the contract is silent about a matter, the courts must determine whether the particular contract will be read to address the unexpressed issue or whether the court will concede (what is usually the truth) that the parties did not address the issue. If the court acknowledges the parties did not address the issue in question, the court may still resolve the issue by adopting what is often called the "default" position. To a great extent, the employment-at-will cases and their common law exceptions reflect the sort of analysis suggested in this paragraph. For example, as you know, the black leather law in most American courts is that, in the absence of an explicitly defined period of employment and in the absence of explicit language that rejects the at-will doctrine, employment contracts are at-will. How should courts deal with silence in employment contracts?

3. How free is an employee to work for someone else after the relationship with the first employer is terminated? Clearly, if presented with the issue, the *Weiss* court would hold that the ex-employer cannot prevent an ex-employee from working ever again. Is there anything in the nature of things that dictates that conclusion? Conversely, the *Weiss* court was not prepared to hold that an ex-employee is free to do whatever he or she wants,

regardless of the previous contract with the ex-employer. Is there anything in the nature of things that dictates that conclusion?

4.   Rather than adopting either of the two extreme positions described in the immediately previous paragraph, the Court appears to have adopted the notion that an employer and its employee can contract to limit the employee's future employment with others, but can limit that future employment only in a "reasonable" manner. What does that mean? Are you persuaded that the Court's articulated standard is a good one?

5.   Why might not the court have held that, absent a compelling need for limitations on the ex-employee's future opportunities, the contract limiting the ex-employee is not enforceable? Or, conversely, why might not the court have held that, since employees have many opportunities to do many things in our complicated but thriving marketplace (shades of *Sutton*), employers ought to be able to preclude any future employment of the ex-employee by competitors?

6.   Implicit in the court's reasoning, it appears, is the thought that in the absence of a covenant not to compete, the "default" position of the parties would be that the ex-employee could work wherever and for whomever the ex-employee chose. What justifies that default position? Given the fact that an employer can insist, as a condition of employment, upon a covenant not to compete, does the default position matter? Sometimes? Never?

7.   Was the court correct when it held that it mattered not that the employer, not the employee, terminated the contract; and that the not-to-compete clause was still binding on the employee?

B.   THE "CONFLICT" OF STATUTE AND CONTRACT

OUBRE v. ENTERGY OPERATIONS

Supreme Court of the United States, 1998.
522 U.S. 422, 118 S.Ct. 838, 139 L.Ed.2d 849.

JUSTICE KENNEDY delivered the opinion of the Court.

An employee, as part of a termination agreement, signed a release of all claims against her employer. In consideration, she received severance pay in installments. The release, however, did not comply with specific federal statutory requirements for a release of claims under the Age Discrimination in Employment Act of 1967 (ADEA), 29 U.S.C. § 621 *et seq.* After receiving the last payment, the employee brought suit under the ADEA. The employer claims the employee ratified and validated the nonconforming release by retaining the monies paid to secure it. The employer also insists the release bars the action unless, as a precondition to filing suit, the employee tenders back the monies received. We disagree and rule that, as the release did not comply with the statute, it cannot bar the ADEA claim.

Petitioner Dolores Oubre worked as a scheduler at a power plant in Killona, Louisiana, run by her employer, respondent Entergy Operations, Inc. In 1994, she received a poor performance rating. Oubre's supervisor met with her on January 17, 1995 and gave her the option of either improving her performance during the coming year or accepting a voluntary arrangement for her severance. She received a packet of information about the severance agreement and had 14 days to consider her options, during which she consulted with attorneys. On January 31, Oubre decided to accept. She signed a release in which she "agree[d] to waive, settle, release, and discharge any and all claims, demands, damages, actions, or causes of action ... that I may have against Entergy...." In exchange, she received six installment payments over the next four months, totaling $6,528.

The Older Workers Benefit Protection Act (OWBPA) imposes specific requirements for releases covering ADEA claims. OWBPA, sections 626(f)(1)(B), (F), (G). In procuring the release, Entergy did not comply with the OWBPA in at least three respects: (1) Entergy did not give Oubre enough time to consider her options; (2) Entergy did not give Oubre seven days after she signed the release to change her mind; and (3) the release made no specific reference to claims under the ADEA.

II

The employer rests its case upon general principles of state contract jurisprudence. As the employer cites the rule, contracts tainted by mistake, duress, or even fraud are voidable at the option of the innocent party. The employer maintains, however, that before the innocent party can elect avoidance, she must first tender back any benefits received under the contract. If she fails to do so within a reasonable time after learning of her rights, the employer contends, she ratifies the contract and so makes it binding. The employer also invokes the doctrine of equitable estoppel. As a rule, equitable estoppel bars a party from shirking the burdens of a voidable transaction for as long as she retains the benefits received under it. Applying these principles, the employer claims the employee ratified the ineffective release (or faces estoppel) by retaining all the sums paid in consideration of it. The employer, then, relies not upon the execution of the release but upon a later, distinct ratification of its terms.

These general rules may not be as unified as the employer asserts. And in equity, a person suing to rescind a contract, as a rule, is not required to restore the consideration at the very outset of the litigation. Even if the employer's statement of the general rule requiring tender back before one files suit were correct, it would be unavailing. The rule cited is based simply on the course of negotiation of the parties and the alleged later ratification. The authorities cited do not consider the question raised by statutory declaration making non-conforming releases ineffective. It is the latter question we confront here.

In 1990, Congress amended the ADEA by passing the OWBPA. The OWBPA provides: "An individual may not waive any right or claim under [the ADEA] unless the waiver is knowing and voluntary.... [A] waiver may not be considered knowing and voluntary unless at a minimum" it satisfies certain enumerated requirements, including the three listed above. 29 U.S.C. § 626(f)(1).

The statutory command is clear: An employee "may not waive" an ADEA claim unless the waiver or release satisfies the OWBPA's requirements. The policy of the Older Workers Benefit Protection Act is likewise clear from its title: It is designed to protect the rights and benefits of older workers. The OWBPA implements Congress' policy via a strict, unqualified statutory stricture on waivers, and we are bound to take Congress at its word. Congress imposed specific duties on employers who seek releases of certain claims created by statute. Congress delineated these duties with precision and without qualification: An employee "may not waive" an ADEA claim unless the employer complies with the statute. Courts cannot with ease presume ratification of that which Congress forbids.

The OWBPA sets up its own regime for assessing the effect of ADEA waivers, separate and apart from contract law. The statute creates a series of prerequisites for knowing and voluntary waivers and imposes affirmative duties of disclosure and waiting periods. The OWBPA governs the effect under federal law of waivers or releases on ADEA claims and incorporates no exceptions or qualifications. The text of the OWBPA forecloses the employer's defense, notwithstanding how general contract principles would apply to non-ADEA claims.

The rule proposed by the employer would frustrate the statute's practical operation as well as its formal command. In many instances, a discharged employee likely will have spent the monies received and will lack the means to tender their return. These realities might tempt employers to risk non-compliance with the OWBPA's waiver provisions, knowing it will be difficult to repay the monies and relying on ratification. We ought not to open the door to an evasion of the statute by this device.

Oubre's cause of action arises under the ADEA, and the release can have no effect on her ADEA claim unless it complies with the OWBPA. In this case, both sides concede the release the employee signed did not comply with the requirements of the OWBPA. Since Oubre's release did not comply with the OWBPA's stringent safeguards, it is unenforceable against her insofar as it purports to waive or release her ADEA claim. As a statutory matter, the release cannot bar her ADEA suit, irrespective of the validity of the contract as to other claims.

In further proceedings in this or other cases, courts may need to inquire whether the employer has claims for restitution, recoupment, or setoff against the employee, and these questions may be complex where a release is effective as to some claims but not as to ADEA claims. We need not decide those issues here, however.

[The concurring opinion of Justice Breyer and the dissenting opinions of Justices Scalia and Thomas are omitted.]

Note and Questions

1. The prerequisites for a voluntary and knowing waiver in section 626(f) apply to the ADEA only. Of course, through settlements, at the very least, waivers are used in all employment litigation. Some courts have adopted the requirements of section 626(f) for Title VII, ADA, and other employment cases. Other courts apply a totality of the circumstances test to determine whether the waiver was voluntary and knowing. Like section 626(f), the totality of the circumstances test focuses on procedural regularity; the amount of time between offer and required acceptance, the opportunity to speak with an advisor, the level of education of the employee, and even the reasonableness or fairness of the settlement itself. When courts use the totality of the circumstances test for Title VII and ADA cases, the same waiver may be found enforceable as to Title VII and ADA claims because the circumstances seem reasonable to the court, but unenforceable as to ADEA claims because the waiver form did not comply with what may prove to be, in some cases, the stricter ADEA requirements.

2. Do you understand the *Oubre* opinion to preclude an employment contract that waives generally future violations of an employee's rights to be free of race, sex, age, or disability discrimination?

3. Are these rights, perhaps because they are statutory, to be treated differently than an employee's promise not to exercise his freedom to work (after he leaves the employment of the present employer)?

4. Regardless of *Oubre*, should employees be able to waive any of the foregoing rights, insofar as the waivers purport to waive generally future enforcement of those rights? Are settlements of specific, past disputes different? If you think an employee cannot waive rights generally regarding the unknown future, how do you reconcile that conclusion with the following Supreme Court decision?

GILMER v. INTERSTATE/JOHNSON LANE

Supreme Court of the United States, 1991.
500 U.S. 20, 111 S.Ct. 1647, 114 L.Ed.2d 26.

JUSTICE WHITE delivered the opinion of the Court.

The question presented in this case is whether a claim under the Age Discrimination in Employment Act of 1967 (ADEA), can be subjected to compulsory arbitration pursuant to an arbitration agreement in a securities registration application. The Court of Appeals held that it could, and we affirm.

I

Respondent Interstate/Johnson Lane Corporation (Interstate) hired petitioner Robert Gilmer as a Manager of Financial Services in May 1981. As required by his employment, Gilmer registered as a securities representative with several stock exchanges, including the New York Stock Exchange (NYSE). His registration application, entitled "Uniform

Application for Securities Industry Registration or Transfer," provided, among other things, that Gilmer "agree[d] to arbitrate any dispute, claim or controversy" arising between him and Interstate "that is required to be arbitrated under the rules, constitutions or by-laws of the organizations with which I register." Of relevance to this case, NYSE Rule 347 provides for arbitration of "[a]ny controversy between a registered representative and any member or member organization arising out of the employment or termination of employment of such registered representative."

Interstate terminated Gilmer's employment in 1987, at which time Gilmer was 62 years of age. After first filing an age discrimination charge with the Equal Employment Opportunity Commission (EEOC), Gilmer subsequently brought suit in the United States District Court for the Western District of North Carolina, alleging that Interstate had discharged him because of his age, in violation of the ADEA. In response to Gilmer's complaint, Interstate filed in the District Court a motion to compel arbitration of the ADEA claim. In its motion, Interstate relied upon the arbitration agreement in Gilmer's registration application, as well as the Federal Arbitration Act (FAA). The District Court denied Interstate's motion, based on this Court's decision in *Alexander v. Gardner–Denver Co.,* and because it concluded that "Congress intended to protect ADEA claimants from the waiver of a judicial forum." The United States Court of Appeals for the Fourth Circuit reversed, finding "nothing in the text, legislative history, or underlying purposes of the ADEA indicating a congressional intent to preclude enforcement of arbitration agreements." We granted certiorari, to resolve a conflict among the Courts of Appeals regarding the arbitrability of ADEA claims.

II

The FAA was originally enacted in 1925, and then reenacted and codified in 1947 as Title 9 of the United States Code. Its purpose was to reverse the longstanding judicial hostility to arbitration agreements that had existed at English common law and had been adopted by American courts, and to place arbitration agreements upon the same footing as other contracts. Its primary substantive provision states that "[a] written provision in any maritime transaction or a contract evidencing a transaction involving commerce to settle by arbitration a controversy thereafter arising out of such contract or transaction ... shall be valid, irrevocable, and enforceable, save upon such grounds as exist at law or in equity for the revocation of any contract." 9 U.S.C. § 2. The FAA also provides for stays of proceedings in federal district courts when an issue in the proceeding is referable to arbitration, § 3, and for orders compelling arbitration when one party has failed, neglected, or refused to comply with an arbitration agreement, § 4. These provisions manifest a "liberal federal policy favoring arbitration agreements." *Moses H. Cone Memorial Hospital v. Mercury Construction Corp.,* 460 U.S. 1, 24, 103

S.Ct. 927, 941, 74 L.Ed.2d 765 (1983).[2]

It is by now clear that statutory claims may be the subject of an arbitration agreement, enforceable pursuant to the FAA. Indeed, in recent years we have held enforceable arbitration agreements relating to claims arising under the Sherman Act, § 10(b) of the Securities Exchange Act of 1934, the civil provisions of the Racketeer Influenced and Corrupt Organizations Act (RICO), and § 12(2) of the Securities Act of 1933. In these cases we recognized that "[b]y agreeing to arbitrate a statutory claim, a party does not forgo the substantive rights afforded by the statute; it only submits to their resolution in an arbitral, rather than a judicial, forum." *Mitsubishi, Motors Corp. v. Soler Chrysler–Plymouth, Inc.*, 473 U.S. 614, at 628, 105 S.Ct. 3346, at 3354.

Although all statutory claims may not be appropriate for arbitration, "[h]aving made the bargain to arbitrate, the party should be held to it unless Congress itself has evinced an intention to preclude a waiver of judicial remedies for the statutory rights at issue." *Ibid.* In this regard, we note that the burden is on Gilmer to show that Congress intended to preclude a waiver of a judicial forum for ADEA claims. If such an intention exists, it will be discoverable in the text of the ADEA, its legislative history, or an "inherent conflict" between arbitration and the ADEA's underlying purposes. See McMahon, 482 U.S., at 227, 107 S.Ct., at 2337–2338. Throughout such an inquiry, it should be kept in mind that "questions of arbitrability must be addressed with a healthy regard for the federal policy favoring arbitration." *Moses H. Cone,* 460 U.S., at 24, 103 S.Ct., at 941.

III

Gilmer concedes that nothing in the text of the ADEA or its legislative history explicitly precludes arbitration. He argues, however, that compulsory arbitration of ADEA claims pursuant to arbitration

---

2. Section 1 of the FAA provides that "nothing herein contained shall apply to contracts of employment of seamen, railroad employees, or any other class of workers engaged in foreign or interstate commerce." 9 U.S.C. § 1. Several *amici curiae* in support of Gilmer argue that that section excludes from the coverage of the FAA *all* "contracts of employment." Gilmer, however, did not raise the issue in the courts below, it was not addressed there, and it was not among the questions presented in the petition for certiorari. In any event, it would be inappropriate to address the scope of the § 1 exclusion because the arbitration clause being enforced here is not contained in a contract of employment. The FAA requires that the arbitration clause being enforced be in writing. See 9 U.S.C. §§ 2, 3. The record before us does not show, and the parties do not contend, that Gilmer's employment agreement with Interstate contained a written arbitration clause. Rather,

the arbitration clause at issue is in Gilmer's securities registration application, which is a contract with the securities exchanges, not with Interstate. The lower courts addressing the issue uniformly have concluded that the exclusionary clause in § 1 of the FAA is inapplicable to arbitration clauses contained in such registration applications. We implicitly assumed as much in *Perry v. Thomas,* 482 U.S. 483, 107 S.Ct. 2520, 96 L.Ed.2d 426 (1987), where we held that the FAA required a former employee of a securities firm to arbitrate his statutory wage claim against his former employer, pursuant to an arbitration clause in his registration application. Unlike the dissent, see *post,* at 1659–1660, we choose to follow the plain language of the FAA and the weight of authority, and we therefore hold that § 1's exclusionary clause does not apply to Gilmer's arbitration agreement. Consequently, we leave for another day the issue raised by *amici curiae.*

agreements would be inconsistent with the statutory framework and purposes of the ADEA. Like the Court of Appeals, we disagree.

A

Congress enacted the ADEA in 1967 "to promote employment of older persons based on their ability rather than age; to prohibit arbitrary age discrimination in employment; [and] to help employers and workers find ways of meeting problems arising from the impact of age on employment." 29 U.S.C. § 621(b). To achieve those goals, the ADEA, among other things, makes it unlawful for an employer "to fail or refuse to hire or to discharge any individual or otherwise discriminate against any individual with respect to his compensation, terms, conditions, or privileges of employment, because of such individual's age." § 623(a)(1). This proscription is enforced both by private suits and by the EEOC. In order for an aggrieved individual to bring suit under the ADEA, he or she must first file a charge with the EEOC and then wait at least 60 days. § 626(d). An individual's right to sue is extinguished, however, if the EEOC institutes an action against the employer. § 626(c)(1). Before the EEOC can bring such an action, though, it must "attempt to eliminate the discriminatory practice or practices alleged, and to effect voluntary compliance with the requirements of this chapter through informal methods of conciliation, conference, and persuasion." § 626(b).

As Gilmer contends, the ADEA is designed not only to address individual grievances, but also to further important social policies. We do not perceive any inherent inconsistency between those policies, however, and enforcing agreements to arbitrate age discrimination claims. It is true that arbitration focuses on specific disputes between the parties involved. The same can be said, however, of judicial resolution of claims. Both of these dispute resolution mechanisms nevertheless also can further broader social purposes. The Sherman Act, the Securities Exchange Act of 1934, RICO, and the Securities Act of 1933 all are designed to advance important public policies, but, as noted above, claims under those statutes are appropriate for arbitration. "[S]o long as the prospective litigant effectively may vindicate [his or her] statutory cause of action in the arbitral forum, the statute will continue to serve both its remedial and deterrent function." *Mitsubishi, supra,* 473 U.S., at 637, 105 S.Ct., at 3359.

We also are unpersuaded by the argument that arbitration will undermine the role of the EEOC in enforcing the ADEA. An individual ADEA claimant subject to an arbitration agreement will still be free to file a charge with the EEOC, even though the claimant is not able to institute a private judicial action. Indeed, Gilmer filed a charge with the EEOC in this case. In any event, the EEOC's role in combating age discrimination is not dependent on the filing of a charge; the agency may receive information concerning alleged violations of the ADEA "from any source," and it has independent authority to investigate age discrimination. See 29 CFR §§ 1626.4, 1626.13 (1990). Moreover, nothing in the ADEA indicates that Congress intended that the EEOC be involved in all employment disputes. Such disputes can be settled, for example, without any EEOC involvement.[3] Finally, the mere involvement of an administrative agency in the enforcement of a statute is not sufficient to preclude arbitration. For example, the Securities Exchange Commission is heavily involved in the enforcement of the Securities Exchange Act of 1934 and the Securities Act of 1933, but we have held that claims under both of those statutes may be subject to compulsory arbitration.

Gilmer also argues that compulsory arbitration is improper because it deprives claimants of the judicial forum provided for by the ADEA. Congress, however, did not explicitly preclude arbitration or other nonjudicial resolution of claims, even in its recent amendments to the ADEA. "[I]f Congress intended the substantive protection afforded [by the ADEA] to include protection against waiver of the right to a judicial forum, that intention will be deducible from text or legislative history." *Mitsubishi*, 473 U.S., at 628, 105 S.Ct., at 3354. Moreover, Gilmer's argument ignores the ADEA's flexible approach to resolution of claims. The EEOC, for example, is directed to pursue "informal methods of conciliation, conference, and persuasion," 29 U.S.C. § 626(b), which suggests that out-of-court dispute resolution, such as arbitration, is consistent with the statutory scheme established by Congress. In addition, arbitration is consistent with Congress' grant of concurrent jurisdiction over ADEA claims to state and federal courts, see 29 U.S.C. § 626(c)(1) (allowing suits to be brought "in any court of competent jurisdiction"), because arbitration agreements, "like the provision for concurrent jurisdiction, serve to advance the objective of allowing [claimants] a broader right to select the forum for resolving disputes, whether it be judicial or otherwise." *Rodriguez de Quijas*, 490 U.S., at 483, 109 S.Ct., at 1921.

B

In arguing that arbitration is inconsistent with the ADEA, Gilmer also raises a host of challenges to the adequacy of arbitration procedures. Initially, we note that in our recent arbitration cases we have already rejected most of these arguments as insufficient to preclude arbitration of statutory claims. Such generalized attacks on arbitration "res[t] on suspicion of arbitration as a method of weakening the protections afforded in the substantive law to would-be complainants," and as such, they are "far out of step with our current strong endorsement of the federal statutes favoring this method of resolving disputes." *Rodriguez de Quijas, supra,* at 481, 109 S.Ct., at 1920. Consequently, we address these arguments only briefly.

Gilmer first speculates that arbitration panels will be biased. However, "[w]e decline to indulge the presumption that the parties and

---

3. In the recently enacted Older Workers Benefit Protection Act, Pub.L. 101–433, 104 Stat. 978, Congress amended the ADEA to provide that "[a]n individual may not waive any right or claim under this Act unless the waiver is knowing and voluntary." See § 201. Congress also specified certain conditions that must be met in order for a waiver to be knowing and voluntary. *Ibid.*

arbitral body conducting a proceeding will be unable or unwilling to retain competent, conscientious and impartial arbitrators." *Mitsubishi, supra,* 473 U.S. at 634, 105 S.Ct., at 3357–3358. In any event, we note that the NYSE arbitration rules, which are applicable to the dispute in this case, provide protections against biased panels. The rules require, for example, that the parties be informed of the employment histories of the arbitrators, and that they be allowed to make further inquiries into the arbitrators' backgrounds. In addition, each party is allowed one peremptory challenge and unlimited challenges for cause. Moreover, the arbitrators are required to disclose "any circumstances which might preclude [them] from rendering an objective and impartial determination." 2 CCH N.Y.S.E. Guide, at ¶ 2610, p. 4315 (Rule 610). The FAA also protects against bias, by providing that courts may overturn arbitration decisions "[w]here there was evident partiality or corruption in the arbitrators." 9 U.S.C. § 10(b). There has been no showing in this case that those provisions are inadequate to guard against potential bias.

Gilmer also complains that the discovery allowed in arbitration is more limited than in the federal courts, which he contends will make it difficult to prove discrimination. It is unlikely, however, that age discrimination claims require more extensive discovery than other claims that we have found to be arbitrable, such as RICO and antitrust claims. Moreover, there has been no showing in this case that the NYSE discovery provisions, which allow for document production, information requests, depositions, and subpoenas, will prove insufficient to allow ADEA claimants such as Gilmer a fair opportunity to present their claims. Although those procedures might not be as extensive as in the federal courts, by agreeing to arbitrate, a party "trades the procedures and opportunity for review of the courtroom for the simplicity, informality, and expedition of arbitration." *Mitsubishi, supra,* at 628, 105 S.Ct., at 3354. Indeed, an important counterweight to the reduced discovery in NYSE arbitration is that arbitrators are not bound by the rules of evidence.

A further alleged deficiency of arbitration is that arbitrators often will not issue written opinions, resulting, Gilmer contends, in a lack of public knowledge of employers' discriminatory policies, an inability to obtain effective appellate review, and a stifling of the development of the law. The NYSE rules, however, do require that all arbitration awards be in writing, and that the awards contain the names of the parties, a summary of the issues in controversy, and a description of the award issued. In addition, the award decisions are made available to the public. Furthermore, judicial decisions addressing ADEA claims will continue to be issued because it is unlikely that all or even most ADEA claimants will be subject to arbitration agreements. Finally, Gilmer's concerns apply equally to settlements of ADEA claims, which, as noted above, are clearly allowed.[4]

---

4. Gilmer also contends that judicial review of arbitration decisions is too limited. We have stated, however, that "although judicial scrutiny of arbitration awards nec-

It is also argued that arbitration procedures cannot adequately further the purposes of the ADEA because they do not provide for broad equitable relief and class actions. As the court below noted, however, arbitrators do have the power to fashion equitable relief. Indeed, the NYSE rules applicable here do not restrict the types of relief an arbitrator may award, but merely refer to "damages and/or other relief." 2 N.Y.S.E. Guide ¶ 2627(e), p. 4321 (Rule 627(e)). The NYSE rules also provide for collective proceedings. But "even if the arbitration could not go forward as a class action or class relief could not be granted by the arbitrator, the fact that the [ADEA] provides for the possibility of bringing a collective action does not mean that individual attempts at conciliation were intended to be barred." *Nicholson v. CPC Int'l Inc.,* 877 F.2d 221, 241 (C.A.3 1989) (Becker, J., dissenting). Finally, it should be remembered that arbitration agreements will not preclude the *EEOC* from bringing actions seeking classwide and equitable relief.

C

An additional reason advanced by Gilmer for refusing to enforce arbitration agreements relating to ADEA claims is his contention that there often will be unequal bargaining power between employers and employees. Mere inequality in bargaining power, however, is not a sufficient reason to hold that arbitration agreements are never enforceable in the employment context. Relationships between securities dealers and investors, for example, may involve unequal bargaining power, but we nevertheless held in *Rodriguez de Quijas* and *McMahon* that agreements to arbitrate in that context are enforceable. As discussed above, the FAA's purpose was to place arbitration agreements on the same footing as other contracts. Thus, arbitration agreements are enforceable "save upon such grounds as exist at law or in equity for the revocation of any contract." 9 U.S.C. § 2. "Of course, courts should remain attuned to well-supported claims that the agreement to arbitrate resulted from the sort of fraud or overwhelming economic power that would provide grounds 'for the revocation of any contract.' " *Mitsubishi,* 473 U.S., at 627, 105 S.Ct., at 3354. There is no indication in this case, however, that Gilmer, an experienced businessman, was coerced or defrauded into agreeing to the arbitration clause in his registration application. As with the claimed procedural inadequacies discussed above, this claim of unequal bargaining power is best left for resolution in specific cases.

IV

In addition to the arguments discussed above, Gilmer vigorously asserts that our decision in *Alexander v. Gardner–Denver Co.,* 415 U.S. 36, 94 S.Ct. 1011, 39 L.Ed.2d 147 (1974), and its progeny—*Barrentine v. Arkansas–Best Freight System, Inc.,* 450 U.S. 728, 101 S.Ct. 1437, 67 L.Ed.2d 641 (1981), and *McDonald v. City of West Branch,* 466 U.S. 284,

---

essarily is limited, such review is sufficient to ensure that arbitrators comply with the requirements of the statute" at issue.

Shearson/American Express Inc. v. McMahon, 482 U.S. 220, 232, 107 S.Ct. 2332, 2340, 96 L.Ed.2d 185 (1987).

104 S.Ct. 1799, 80 L.Ed.2d 302 (1984)—preclude arbitration of employment discrimination claims. Gilmer's reliance on these cases, however, is misplaced.

In *Gardner–Denver,* the issue was whether a discharged employee whose grievance had been arbitrated pursuant to an arbitration clause in a collective-bargaining agreement was precluded from subsequently bringing a Title VII action based upon the conduct that was the subject of the grievance. In holding that the employee was not foreclosed from bringing the Title VII claim, we stressed that an employee's contractual rights under a collective-bargaining agreement are distinct from the employee's statutory Title VII rights:

> "In submitting his grievance to arbitration, an employee seeks to vindicate his contractual right under a collective-bargaining agreement. By contrast, in filing a lawsuit under Title VII, an employee asserts independent statutory rights accorded by Congress. The distinctly separate nature of these contractual and statutory rights is not vitiated merely because both were violated as a result of the same factual occurrence." 415 U.S., at 49–50.

We also noted that a labor arbitrator has authority only to resolve questions of contractual rights. The arbitrator's "task is to effectuate the intent of the parties" and he or she does not have the "general authority to invoke public laws that conflict with the bargain between the parties." *Id.,* at 53, 94 S.Ct. at 1022. By contrast, "in instituting an action under Title VII, the employee is not seeking review of the arbitrator's decision. Rather, he is asserting a statutory right independent of the arbitration process." *Id.,* at 54, 94 S.Ct., at 1022. We further expressed concern that in collective-bargaining arbitration "the interests of the individual employee may be subordinated to the collective interests of all employees in the bargaining unit." *Id.,* at 58, n. 19, 94 S.Ct., at 1024, n. 19.[5]

Barrentine and *McDonald* similarly involved the issue whether arbitration under a collective-bargaining agreement precluded a subsequent statutory claim. In holding that the statutory claims there were not precluded, we noted, as in *Gardner–Denver,* the difference between contractual rights under a collective-bargaining agreement and individual statutory rights, the potential disparity in interests between a union and an employee, and the limited authority and power of labor arbitrators.

There are several important distinctions between the *Gardner–Denver* line of cases and the case before us. First, those cases did not

5. The Court in *Alexander v. Gardner–Denver Co.,* 415 U.S. 36, 94 S.Ct. 1011, 39 L.Ed.2d 147 (1974), also expressed the view that arbitration was inferior to the judicial process for resolving statutory claims. *Id.,* at 57–58, 94 S.Ct., at 1024–1025. That "mistrust of the arbitral process," however, has been undermined by our recent arbitration decisions. *McMahon,* 482 U.S., at 231– 232, 107 S.Ct., at 2340. "[W]e are well past the time when judicial suspicion of the desirability of arbitration and of the competence of arbitral tribunals inhibited the development of arbitration as an alternative means of dispute resolution." *Mitsubishi Motors Corp. v. Soler Chrysler–Plymouth, Inc.,* 473 U.S. 614, 626–627, 105 S.Ct. 3346, 3354, 87 L.Ed.2d 444 (1985).

182

222222222222

involve the issue of the enforceability of an agreement to arbitrate statutory claims. Rather, they involved the quite different issue whether arbitration of contract-based claims precluded subsequent judicial resolution of statutory claims. Since the employees there had not agreed to arbitrate their statutory claims, and the labor arbitrators were not authorized to resolve such claims, the arbitration in those cases understandably was held not to preclude subsequent statutory actions. Second, because the arbitration in those cases occurred in the context of a collective-bargaining agreement, the claimants there were represented by their unions in the arbitration proceedings. An important concern therefore was the tension between collective representation and individual statutory rights, a concern not applicable to the present case. Finally, those cases were not decided under the FAA, which, as discussed above, reflects a "liberal federal policy favoring arbitration agreements." *Mitsubishi,* 473 U.S., at 625, 105 S.Ct., at 3353. Therefore, those cases provide no basis for refusing to enforce Gilmer's agreement to arbitrate his ADEA claim.

V

We conclude that Gilmer has not met his burden of showing that Congress, in enacting the ADEA, intended to preclude arbitration of claims under that Act. Accordingly, the judgment of the Court of Appeals is

Affirmed.

JUSTICE STEVENS, with whom JUSTICE MARSHALL joins, dissenting.

Section 1 of the Federal Arbitration Act (FAA) states:

"[N]othing herein contained shall apply to contracts of employment of seamen, railroad employees, or any other class of workers engaged in foreign or interstate commerce." 9 U.S.C. § 1.

The Court today, in holding that the FAA compels enforcement of arbitration clauses even when claims of age discrimination are at issue, skirts the antecedent question of whether the coverage of the Act even extends to arbitration clauses contained in employment contracts, regardless of the subject matter of the claim at issue. In my opinion, arbitration clauses contained in employment agreements are specifically exempt from coverage of the FAA, and for that reason respondent Interstate/Johnson Lane Corporation cannot, pursuant to the FAA, compel petitioner to submit his claims arising under the Age Discrimination in Employment Act of 1967 (ADEA), to binding arbitration.

I

Petitioner did not, as the majority correctly notes, raise the issue of the applicability of the FAA to employment contracts at any stage of the proceedings below. Nor did petitioner raise the coverage issue in his petition for writ of certiorari before this Court. It was *amici* who first raised the argument in their briefs in support of petitioner prior to oral argument of the case.

Notwithstanding the apparent waiver of the issue below, I believe that the Court should reach the issue of the coverage of the FAA to employment disputes because resolution of the question is so clearly antecedent to disposition of this case....

II

The Court, declining to reach the issue for the reason that petitioner never raised it below, nevertheless concludes that "it would be inappropriate to address the scope of the § 1 exclusion because the arbitration clause being enforced here is not contained in a contract of employment.... Rather, the arbitration clause at issue is in Gilmer's securities registration application, which is a contract with the securities exchanges, not with Interstate." In my opinion, the Court too narrowly construes the scope of the exclusion contained in § 1 of the FAA.

* * *

Given that the FAA specifically was intended to exclude arbitration agreements between employees and employers, I see no reason to limit this exclusion from coverage to arbitration clauses contained in agreements entitled "Contract of Employment." In this case, the parties conceded at oral argument that Gilmer had no "contract of employment" as such with respondent. Gilmer was, however, required as a condition of his employment to become a registered representative of several stock exchanges, including the New York Stock Exchange (NYSE). Just because his agreement to arbitrate any "dispute, claim or controversy" with his employer that arose out of the employment relationship was contained in his application for registration before the NYSE rather than in a specific contract of employment with his employer, I do not think that Gilmer can be compelled pursuant to the FAA to arbitrate his employment-related dispute. Rather, in my opinion the exclusion in § 1 should be interpreted to cover any agreements by the employee to arbitrate disputes with the employer arising out of the employment relationship, particularly where such agreements to arbitrate are conditions of employment.

* * *

III

Not only would I find that the FAA does not apply to employment-related disputes between employers and employees in general, but also I would hold that compulsory arbitration conflicts with the congressional purpose animating the ADEA, in particular. As this Court previously has noted, authorizing the courts to issue broad injunctive relief is the cornerstone to eliminating discrimination in society. The ADEA, like Title VII, authorizes courts to award broad, class-based injunctive relief to achieve the purposes of the Act. 29 U.S.C. § 626(b). Because commercial arbitration is typically limited to a specific dispute between the particular parties and because the available remedies in arbitral forums generally do not provide for class-wide injunctive relief, see Shell, ERISA and Other Federal Employment Statutes: When is Commercial Arbitration an "Adequate Substitute" for the Courts?, 68 Texas L.Rev. 509, 568 (1990), I would conclude that an essential purpose of the ADEA is frustrated by compulsory arbitration of employment discrimination claims. Moreover, as Chief Justice Burger explained:

> "Plainly, it would not comport with the congressional objectives behind a statute seeking to enforce civil rights protected by Title VII to allow the very forces that had practiced discrimination to contract away the right to enforce civil rights in the courts. For federal courts to defer to arbitral decisions reached by the same combination of forces that had long perpetuated invidious discrimination would have made the foxes guardians of the chickens." *Barrentine v. Arkansas–Best Freight System, Inc.,* 450 U.S. 728, 750, 101 S.Ct. 1437, 1449–1450, 67 L.Ed.2d 641 (1981) (Burger, C.J., dissenting).

In my opinion the same concerns expressed by Chief Justice Burger with regard to compulsory arbitration of Title VII claims may be said of claims arising under the ADEA. The Court's holding today clearly eviscerates the important role played by an independent judiciary in eradicating employment discrimination.

IV

When the FAA was passed in 1925, I doubt that any legislator who voted for it expected it to apply to statutory claims, to form contracts between parties of unequal bargaining power, or to the arbitration of disputes arising out of the employment relationship.

In recent years, however, the Court "has effectively rewritten the statute", and abandoned its earlier view that statutory claims were not appropriate subjects for arbitration. See *Mitsubishi Motors v. Soler Chrysler–Plymouth, Inc.,* 473 U.S. 614, 646–651, 105 S.Ct. 3346, 3363–3367, 87 L.Ed.2d 444 (1985) (Stevens, J., dissenting). Although I remain persuaded that it erred in doing so, the Court has also put to one side any concern about the inequality of bargaining power between an entire industry, on the one hand, and an individual customer or employee, on the other. Until today, however, the Court has not read § 2 of the FAA as broadly encompassing disputes arising out of the employment relationship. I believe this additional extension of the FAA is erroneous. Accordingly, I respectfully dissent.

Notes and Questions

1. Can you reconcile *Oubre* and *Gilmer?*

2. Can you reconcile *Alexander,* referred to and distinguished in *Gilmer,* and *Gilmer?* If Mr. Gilmer lost his right to file an age discrimination suit in the courts only because he signed an agreement to arbitrate all disputes when he was first hired, why shouldn't Mr. Alexander also be held to his choice? One answer, attempted by the *Gilmer* Court in trying to distinguish the two cases, is that Mr. Gilmer made his own choice to

relinquish the judicial forum, while Mr. Alexander's fate was cast by his union, probably long before he ever arrived on the scene. (Does this suggest Mr. Alexander agreed to the union's waiver?) In assessing that distinction, you should ask whether Mr. Gilmer really had much of a choice in the matter. Had he refused to sign, he wouldn't have been employed. What choice would anyone have made under the circumstances? Compare the safeguards provided to older workers under the Older Workers Benefit Protection Act, which is in your reference supplement, and which was the subject in *Oubre*. Should similar safeguards also apply to a worker like Mr. Gilmer? Would they have helped him? In distinguishing Alexander v. Gardner–Denver, is the *Gilmer* Court saying that it trusts the union even less than the individual to make such a choice? Consider these counter-thoughts: (1) unions usually have more bargaining leverage than individuals; and (2) unions are uniquely expert in pursuing arbitration.

3. One of the questions left unresolved in *Gilmer* was answered in *Circuit City Stores v. Adams*,532 U.S. 105, 121 S.Ct. 1302, 149 L.Ed.2d 234 (2001). In that case, the Supreme Court held, by a vote of 5 to 4, that Section 1 of the Federal Arbitration Act, which excludes from the reach of the Act "contracts of employment of seamen, railroad employees, or any other class of workers engaged in Foreign or interstate commerce," does not exclude all the employment contracts of all employers whose businesses affect interstate commerce; rather, the Court held, the exclusion excludes only contracts of employment of transportation workers. If the court had held otherwise, all employment contracts with employers whose businesses affected interstate commerce would have been exempted from the Federal Arbitration Act and from the *Gilmer* holding.

The Differences Between Arbitration and Litigation.

There is a terrific article that goes into great detail on the differences between arbitration and litigation: David S. Schwartz, *Enforcing Small Print To Protect Big Business: Employee and Consumer Rights Claims in an Age of Compelled Arbitration*, 1997 Wisconsin L.Rev. 33. The information for the first part of this note is taken primarily, and often *verbatim*, from that article.

"*Public v. private process.* Arbitration is usually a product of a contractual commitment between two parties to use a private means of dispute resolution rather than the courts. In the employment context, arbitration gained prominence through its utilization in collective bargaining agreements negotiated by employers and the labor organizations representing the employers' employees, with virtually all collectively negotiated agreements containing clauses requiring employees to submit grievances and to resolve disputes through 'final and binding' arbitration proceedings. The description of arbitration as speedy and efficient as compared to litigation arises from the collective bargaining context. Consistent with *Gilmer,* increasingly, employers are requiring individual employees to submit to arbitration disputes 'arising out of or relating to employment.'

"*Rules and procedures.* Arbitration has few legally required rules or procedures. Parties structure their arbitration agreements to meet their needs, being able to limit by contract the issues they will arbitrate and to specify the contract rules under which the arbitration will be conducted. So, for example, an employer may condition employment on an employee's agreeing to have disputes resolved using the resources of private arbitration organizations, such as the American Arbitration Association (AAA) and the Judicial Arbitration and Mediation Services/Endispute (JAMS/Endispute). The notes that follow use the AAA procedures and rules for illustrative purposes; the AAA has no official powers to dictate rules to parties procedures.''

Costs. The AAA procedures for employment disputes include minimum process guarantees: the rights to counsel, to "reasonable" discovery of relevant information held by the employer, to "appropriate" remedies, to arbitrators with substantive knowledge of employment law. The AAA requires the claimant to pay filing and administrative fees up front: if the claim is for $50,000 to $100,000 the filing fee is $1,250; $100,000 to $250,000, the fee is $2,000; $250,000 to $500,000, the fee is $3,500; $500,000 to $1 million, the fee is $5,000. By comparison, the filing fee in federal court is $150 to pursue a claim of violation of employment rights guaranteed by statute. The administrative fee for a two-day arbitration would be $3,200, representing advance payment for half the per diem expenses and estimated arbitrator's compensation; arbitrators fees range from $350 to $700 a day, including charges for study time—reading the relevant contract language, researching the issues, writing the award. There is no administrative fee associated with a hearing in court.

Who decides. The AAA provides the parties with a list of five arbitrators. Although their current employment is identified, e.g. corporate litigator, no biographical data is released except for information that shows clear conflicts of interest. If arbitrators have authorized their awards for publication, the diligent attorney can find some evidence of the arbitrators' approaches (*see,* the series entitled Labor Arbitration (LA) in the BNA multi-volume and database); but the public record is far less complete than the record of opinions issued by judges, particularly federal judges who must provide findings of fact and conclusions of law. Selection of the arbitrator is according to the AAA's selection/ranking procedures: each party is allowed to strike up to three arbitrators and to rank their preferences among the remaining arbitrators. If the parties reject all five arbitrators, the AAA appoints a sixth individual.

Discovery. AAA employment rules give the arbitrator discretion to schedule a pre-hearing exchange of "relevant documents and other information," including witness identities. This is a change from the pre–1996 regime when the rules did not provide for any discovery whatsoever. The standard of "reasonable access" to "reasonably relevant" information, or information that is "necessary to a full and fair exploration of the issues" will probably be interpreted far more strictly than the federal courts' standard of "reasonably calculated to lead to the discovery of admissible evidence," particularly in light of arbitration being viewed as a superior proceeding precisely because it avoids the expense and time-eating nature of discovery. Arbitrators will probably place a heavy burden on claimants' attorneys to convince the arbitrator of the relevance of the sought-after information.

The hearing itself. Arbitration being a product of the agreement of the parties, there is no right for public access to observe the proceedings, as there is in federal court. The AAA's Guide for Employment Arbitrators emphasize that one of the reasons parties opt for arbitration is "their desire for privacy. You should therefore maintain the privacy of proceedings. . . ." There is no legal requirement that the hearings be on the record. Under AAA rules, a party may have the proceedings transcribed at her own expense.

Formal evidence rules do not apply to arbitrations, and the law does not require that witnesses be sworn (although some states may impose this requirement). The Federal Arbitration Act provides that a court may vacate an arbitration award "where the arbitrators were guilty of misconduct . . . in refusing to hear evidence pertinent and material to the controversy," so most arbitrators tend to let in all or almost all proffered evidence to avoid judicial vacation of their awards. Admission of hearsay material would be grounds to vacate the award only if the hearsay evidence made the hearing "fundamentally unfair." No law requires arbitrators to explain their decisions orally or in writing. Indeed, many arbitrators decline to explain their reasoning in writing in order to shield their awards from possible judicial review. The AAA's new rules for employment arbitrators depart from this practice by requiring written statements of reasons.

Unless the arbitration agreement provides otherwise, arbitrators may allocate arbitration fees and costs among the parties as part of the award. By way of comparison, there are no judicial administrative fees and costs, and most employment-related statutes make some provision for recovery of attorneys' fees, with the practice being that prevailing plaintiffs almost always receive fees and costs while prevailing defendants secure fees and costs only if the plaintiff's pursuit of the litigation is deemed frivolous.

Judicial review. An arbitration award may be vacated by a reviewing court if it was "procured by corruption, fraud or undue means"; if the arbitrator showed "evident partiality or corruption" or unreasonably refused to postpone the hearing on good cause shown or to hear evidence pertinent and material to the controversy; or if the arbitrator exceeded her or his powers or failed to make a definitive award. The courts typically state that these grounds must be construed very narrowly.

An arbitration award is not subject to judicial review for mere errors of law. Instead, the award must be vacated for "manifest disregard" of the law, meaning that the award will be vacated only if it is clear from the record that the arbitrator recognized the applicable law—and then ignored it. Arbitration awards confirmed as judgments in federal court are no different from ordinary judgments and are entitled to full preclusive effect; arguably unconfirmed awards have a similar preclusive effect but the issue is open.

The bottom line. Finally, although studies are inconclusive, random results, coupled with employers' stampede to substitute arbitration for litigation, suggest a pro-employer bias in arbitration as compared to civil litigation. For example, a study of nearly 1,000 cases decided by juries in California state and federal courts between 1981 and 1995 found that plaintiffs won one or more of their claims in 57.6% of the cases; the average award to a prevailing plaintiff was $661,200; punitive damages were awarded in 18.2% of the cases. The contrast with employment arbitrations in the securities industry is striking. In a survey of 62 arbitration awards in employment disputes issues by the industry's arbitrators between 1989 and 1994, employees won some damages in 53.2% of the cases. The average was $124,500. Punitive damages awards, as measured in a different study, were granted in 0.4% to 2.1% of the cases.

On the Other Side . . .

In *In Defense of Mandatory Arbitration of Employment Disputes: Saving the Baby, Tossing out the Bath Water, and Constructing a New Sink in the Process*, 2 U.PA. JOURNAL OF LABOR AND EMPLOYMENT LAW 73 (1999), David Sherwyn, J. Bruce Tracey and Zev. J. Eigen acknowledge some of the criticisms of the arbitral forum for resolving statutory employment claims, but insist that arbitration is preferable to the current scheme in which parties rely on lawyers, the EEOC and the federal courts. Because the administrative and court system is expensive for employers—anywhere from $50,000 to a million dollars to litigate a single case, plus loss of productivity and adverse publicity—employers are induced to settle cases, regardless of the merits. Employees, on the other hand, often file baseless claims with the expectation their employers often pay a nominal amount—the equivalent of two weeks' to six months pay—to avoid the aggravation, costs, and losses of time, productivity and morale that arise in defending against the alleged statutory violations. Additionally, the EEOC has a policy which gives priority to cases with national or local significance, because they are class actions or because they address new areas of law. In practice, this means that garden variety factual cases and those deemed dead are never even investigated. Thus many potentially meritorious claims are ignored, and plaintiffs' attorneys do not have the benefit of an EEOC investigation. Against this background, Sherwyn *et al* argue that mandatory arbitration is preferable, particularly for workers earning low wages. They also propose a model arbitration act, reproduced here for your consideration.

1. FILING OF CLAIMS

All employers with arbitration policies must submit copies of such policies to the EEOC within fifteen days of their enactment. Prior to submitting their cases to arbitration, employees may file their claims with the EEOC. The EEOC will have thirty days to determine if the case fits within its national enforcement plan. If so, and if the employee wishes the Agency to be involved in the case, the EEOC may litigate on behalf of the plaintiff(s) or class. If the employee does not wish the EEOC to be involved, or if the case does not fit into the EEOC's national enforcement plan, the case will be deferred to arbitration.

2. THE LAW AND DAMAGES

The arbitrators must follow the applicable federal and state substantive law. Arbitrators must comply with the statutorily prescribed damage provisions.

3. ESTABLISHMENT OF A BODY TO LICENSE, SELECT, AND MONITOR ARBITRATORS

Congress shall create or empower an agency that serves three functions: licensing, selecting, and monitoring arbitrators.

a. *Licensing*

Unlike labor arbitrators, employment discrimination arbitrators need to be trained in the law of the land, not the law of the shop. The agency will establish criteria that all discrimination arbitrators must meet. These criteria will include education and practical experience in the field. A mandatory licensing exam will ensure that the arbitrators are knowledgeable in the applicable law. From those that are licensed, the agency will establish a panel of a limited number of arbitrators for each geographic area.

b. *Selection*

When a case is set for arbitration, the agency will randomly select seven arbitrators from its panel. The arbitrators will be submitted to the parties. Each party will have one peremptory challenge and unlimited challenges for cause. An arbitrator will be randomly selected from those who are not disqualified.

c. *Monitoring Arbitrators*

Arbitrators will be required to file written opinions with the agency and the EEOC. The arbitrators will delete the names of the employer and the employee from the opinion. These opinions must describe: (1) the facts of the case; (2) the applicable legal standards; and (3) the application of the law to the facts so that the conclusion drawn can be understood. The agency will continually employ experts in the field to review the cases of the arbitrators to ensure that they are qualified to remain on the panel. The EEOC can use these opinions to ensure that arbitrators are applying the law correctly. If not, the EEOC can draft new regulations, propose new legislation to Congress, or make the issue part of its national enforcement plan.

V. AN INTRODUCTION TO ANOTHER EXCEPTION TO EMPLOYMENT AT WILL—UNION AND CONCERTED ACTIVITIES

Sections 7, 8(a)(1) and 8(a)(3) of the National Labor Relations Act protect certain activities undertaken by employees acting together. Take a look at those provisions now. As you will see, courts and the National Labor Relations Board, which administers the law, pay close attention to the statutory language, at least some of the time. Protected employee activities usually have as their end the establishment of a collective bargaining relationship. But the law protects concerted activity even if it falls short of that goal, as these materials will show.

As you examine the materials in this section, ask yourself why the law protects two or more individuals who jointly seek to improve their lot, while it ignores the individual who acts alone. Is it because the underlying goal of the NLRA is to foster collective bargaining, and the interests of the solitary employee are just too far removed from that objective? Or are collective dreams forged from individual challenges? Or, perhaps, Congress was considering unions and their activities and not joint action in which a union was uninvolved. See if you agree with the distinctions drawn in the materials.

In Chapter II, we will look at systems of worker participation that are alternatives to the traditional union relationship. We will examine whether workers who wish to speak out together, but are not interested in union representation, are also protected from reprisal by their employer. Read these materials with that question in mind.

There is some historical basis for the special protection in the law for concerted activity. Consider Recorder Levy's charge to the jury in Commonwealth v. Pullis, Philadelphia Mayor's Court (1806), popularly known as the Philadelphia Cordwainer's Case:

It is adopted by Blackstone, and laid down as the law by Lord Mansfield 1973, that an act innocent in an individual, is rendered criminal by a confederacy to effect it.

A combination of workmen to raise their wages may be considered a twofold point of view: one is to benefit themselves * * * the other is to injure those who do not join in their society. The rule of law condemns both.

Reprinted in 3J. Commons, U. Phillips, E. Gilmore, H. Sumner and J. Andrews, eds., A Documentary History of American Industrial Society 59 (1910).

The sentiment expressed by Recorder Levy, like other condemnations of concerted action by labor, gave way in the twentieth century to official acceptance of some types of collective activity. Since 1914, federal legislation has repeatedly affirmed the legality of workers acting in concert in order to change the terms and conditions of their employment. For example: Section 6 of the Clayton Act of 1914, 15 U.S.C. §§ 12–27, exempts labor organizations from antitrust provisions, in part because "the labor of a human being is not a commodity or article of commerce." The Norris LaGuardia Act of 1932, 29 U.S.C. §§ 101–115, withdraws the jurisdiction of federal courts to issue injunctions in labor disputes, except to the extent necessary to curtail violence or fraud, because, in the words of section 2, "the individual unorganized worker is commonly helpless to exercise actual liberty of contract and to protect his freedom of labor, and thereby to obtain acceptable terms and conditions of employment." The Railway Labor Act of 1926, 45 U.S.C. §§ 151–188—one of whose purposes is "to forbid any limitation upon freedom of association among employees or any denial, as a condition of employment or otherwise, of the right of employees to join a labor organization"—affirmatively requires railway and airline companies to bargain with labor organizations when a majority of company workers have chosen collective representation. Similarly, the National Labor Relations Act of 1935, 29 U.S.C. §§ 141 et seq., as amended, imposes a bargaining obligation on employers in private industry and, in section 7, recognizes for workers "the right to self-organization, to form, join or assist labor organizations, to bargain collectively through representatives of their own choosing, and to engage in concerted activities for the purpose of collective bargaining and other mutual aid and protection"; in 1947, section 7 was amended to add the right to refrain from these activities.

A. THE REQUIREMENT OF CONCERTEDNESS

NLRB v. CITY DISPOSAL SYSTEMS

Supreme Court of the United States, 1984.
465 U.S. 822, 104 S.Ct. 1505, 79 L.Ed.2d 839.

[The Court, per Justice Brennan, held that any time an employee invokes a right grounded in a collective bargaining agreement, he is engaged in concerted activity.]

The invocation of a right rooted in a collective-bargaining agreement is unquestionably an integral part of the process that gave rise to the agreement. That process—beginning with the organization of a union, continuing into the negotiation of a collective-bargaining agreement, and extending through the enforcement of the agreement—is a single, collective activity. Obviously, an employee could not invoke a right grounded in a collective-bargaining agreement were it not for the prior negotiating activities of his fellow employees. Nor would it make sense for a union to negotiate a collective-bargaining agreement if individual employees could not invoke the rights thereby created against their employer. Moreover, when an employee invokes a right grounded in the collective-bargaining agreement, he does not stand alone. Instead, he brings to bear on his employer the power and resolve of all his fellow employees. When, for instance, James Brown refused to drive a truck he believed to be unsafe, he was in effect reminding his employer that he and his fellow employees, at the time their collective-bargaining agreement was signed, had extracted a promise from City Disposal that they would not be asked to drive unsafe trucks. He was also reminding his employer that if it persisted in ordering him to drive an unsafe truck, he could reharness the power of that group to ensure the enforcement of that promise. It was just as though James Brown was reassembling his fellow union members to reenact their decision not to drive unsafe trucks. A lone employee's invocation of a right grounded in his collective-bargaining agreement is, therefore, a concerted activity in a very real sense.

Furthermore, the acts of joining and assisting a labor organization, which section 7 explicitly recognizes as concerted, are related to collective action in essentially the same way that the invocation of a collectively bargained right is related to collective action. When an employee joins or assists a labor organization, his actions may be divorced in time, and in location as well, from the actions of fellow employees. Because of the integral relationship among the employees' actions, however, Congress viewed each employee as engaged in concerted activity. The lone employee could not join or assist a labor organization were it not for the related organizing activities of his fellow employees. Conversely, there would be limited utility in forming a labor organization if other employees could not join or assist the organization once it is formed. Thus, the formation of a labor organization is integrally related to the activity of joining or assisting such an organization in the same sense that the negotiation of a collective-bargaining agreement is integrally related to the invocation of a right provided for in the agreement. In each case, neither the individual activity nor the group activity would be complete without the other.

Questions

Does the Court's reasoning make any sense? Can one answer that question without answering a more fundamental question—why does the statute require concertedness?

Assuming concertedness as a prerequisite for statutory protection, the usual case raises factual questions such as—Did more than one employee act? Was the action planned? Did the planning involve more than one employee?

B.   THE BRIGHT, ELUSIVE LINE BETWEEN CONCERTED ACTIVITY THAT IS PROTECTED AND THAT IS NOT PROTECTED

Two-ness is usually necessary to secure the protections of the NLRA, but it is not enough. The employees' activities must also have some nexus to "mutual aid and protection," presumably in the workplace. The *Washington Aluminum* case, which follows, involved a group of employees who walked off the job to protest conditions of extreme cold. Note that the Court protected them even if their act was unwise and even though they were not represented by a union. In Chapter II, we'll see what implications this has for protecting union as well as nonunion workers.

NLRB v. WASHINGTON ALUMINUM CO.

Supreme Court of the United States 1962.
370 U.S. 9, 82 S.Ct. 1099, 8 L.Ed.2d 298.

Mr. Justice Black delivered the opinion of the Court.

The Court of Appeals for the Fourth Circuit, with Chief Judge Soboleff dissenting, refused to enforce an order of the National Labor Relations Board directing the respondent Washington Aluminum Company to reinstate and make whole seven employees whom the company had discharged for leaving their work in the machine shop without permission on claims that the shop was too cold to work in.

* * * The machine shop in which the seven discharged employees worked was not insulated and had a number of doors to the outside that had to be opened frequently. An oil furnace located in an adjoining building was the chief source of heat for the shop, although there were two gas-fired space heaters that contributed heat to a lesser extent. The heat produced by these units was not always satisfactory and, even prior to the day of the walkout involved here, several of the eight machinists who made up the day shift at the shop had complained from time to time to the company's foreman "over the cold working conditions."

January 5, 1959 was an extraordinarily cold day for Baltimore, with unusually high winds and a low temperature of 11 degrees followed by a high of 22. When the employees on the day shift came to work that morning, they found the shop bitterly cold, due not only to the unusually harsh weather, but also to the fact that the large oil furnace had broken down the night before and had not as yet been put back into operation. As the workers gathered in the shop just before the starting hour of 7:30, one of them, a Mr. Caron, went into the office of Mr. Jarvis, the foreman, hoping to warm himself but, instead, found the foreman's quarters as uncomfortable as the rest of the shop. As Caron and Jarvis sat in Jarvis' office discussing how bitingly cold the building was, some of the other machinists walked by the office window "huddled" together in a fashion that caused Jarvis to exclaim that "[i]f those fellows had any guts at all, they would go home." When the starting buzzer sounded a few moments later, Caron walked back to his working place in the shop and found all the other machinists "huddled there, shaking a little, cold." Caron then said to these workers, "* * * Dave [Jarvis] told me if we had any guts, we would go home. * * * I am going home, it is too damned cold to work." Caron asked the other workers what they were going to do and, after some discussion among themselves, they decided to leave with him. One of these workers, testifying before the Board, summarized their entire discussion this way: "And we had all got together and thought it would be a good idea to go home; maybe we could get some heat brought into the plant that way." As they started to leave, Jarvis approached and persuaded one of the workers to remain at the job. But Caron and the other six workers on the day shift left practically in a body in a matter of minutes after the 7:30 buzzer.

* * * The company's president came in at approximately 8:20 a.m. and, upon learning of the walkout, immediately said to the foreman, "... if they have all gone, we are going to terminate them." * * *

On these facts, the Board found that the conduct of the workers was a concerted activity to protest the company's failure to supply adequate heat in its machine shop, that such conduct is protected under the provision of section 7 of the National Labor Relations Act which guarantees that "Employees shall have the right ... to engage in ... concerted activities for the purpose of collective bargaining or other mutual aid or protection," and that the discharge of these workers by the company amounted to an unfair labor practice under § 8(a)(1) of the Act, which forbids employers "to interfere with, restrain, or coerce employees in the exercise of the rights guaranteed in section 7." * * * [T]he Board then ordered the company to reinstate the discharged workers to their previous positions and to make them whole * * *.

In denying enforcement of this order, the majority of the Court of Appeals took the position that because the workers simply "summarily left their place of employment" without affording the company an "opportunity to avoid the work stoppage by granting a concession to a demand," their walkout did not amount to a concerted activity protected by § 7 of the Act. On this basis, they held that there was no justification for the conduct of the workers in violating the established rules of the plant by leaving their jobs without permission and that the Board had therefore exceeded its power in issuing the order involved here because § 10(c) declares that the Board shall not require reinstatement or back pay for an employee whom an employer has suspended or discharged "for cause."

We cannot agree that employees necessarily lose their right to engage in concerted activities under § 7 merely because they do not present a specific demand upon their employer to remedy a condition they find objectionable. The language of § 7 is broad enough to protect concerted activities whether they take place before, after, or at the same time such a demand is made. To compel the Board to interpret and apply that language in the restricted fashion suggested by the respondent here would only tend to frustrate the policy of the Act to protect the right of workers to act together to better their working conditions. Indeed, as indicated by this very case, such an interpretation of § 7 might place burdens upon employees so great that it would effectively nullify the right to engage in concerted activities which that section protects. The seven employees here were part of a small group of employees who were wholly unorganized.

* * * Having no bargaining representative and no established procedure by which they could take full advantage of their unanimity of opinion in negotiations with the company, the men took the most direct course to let the company know that they wanted a warmer place in which to work. So, after talking among themselves, they walked out together in the hope that this action might spotlight their complaint and bring about some improvement in what they considered to be the "miserable" conditions of their employment. This we think was enough to justify the Board's holding that they were not required to make any more specific demand than they did to be entitled to the protection of § 7.

Although the company contends to the contrary, we think that the walkout involved here did grow out of a "labor dispute" within the plain meaning of the definition of that term in § 2(9) of the Act, which declares that it includes 'any controversy concerning terms, tenure or conditions of employment....' The findings of the Board, which are supported by substantial evidence and which were not disturbed below, show a running dispute between the machine shop employees and the company over the heating of the shop on cold days—a dispute which culminated in the decision of the employees to act concertedly in an effort to force the company to improve that condition of their employment. The fact that the company was already making every effort to repair the furnace and bring heat into the shop that morning does not change the nature of the controversy that caused the walkout. At the very most, that fact might tend to indicate that the conduct of the men in leaving was unnecessary and unwise, and it has long been settled that the reasonableness of workers' decisions to engage in concerted activity is irrelevant to the determination of whether a labor dispute exists or not. Moreover, the evidence here shows that the conduct of these workers was far from unjustified under the circumstances. The company's own foreman expressed the opinion that the shop was so cold that the men should go home. This statement by the foreman but emphasizes the obvious—that is, that the conditions of coldness about which complaint had been made before had been so aggravated on the day of the walkout that the concerted action of the men in leaving their jobs seemed like a perfectly natural and reasonable thing to do.

Nor can we accept the company's contention that because it admittedly had an established plant rule which forbade employees to leave their work without permission of the foreman, there was justifiable "cause" for discharging these employees, wholly separate and apart from any concerted activities in which they engaged in protest against the poorly heated plant. Section 10(c) of the Act does authorize an employer to discharge employees for "cause" and our cases have long recognized this right on the part of an employer. But this, of course, cannot mean that an employer is at liberty to punish a man by discharging him for engaging in concerted activities which § 7 of the Act protects. And the plant rule in question here purports to permit the company to do just that for it would prohibit even the most plainly protected kinds of concerted work stoppages until and unless the permission of the company's foreman was obtained.

It is of course true that § 7 does not protect all concerted activities, but that aspect of the section is not involved in this case. The activities engaged in here do not fall within the normal categories of unprotected concerted activities such as those that are unlawful, violent or in breach of contract. Nor can they be brought under this Court's more recent pronouncement which denied the protection of § 7 to activities characterized as "indefensible" because they were there found to show a disloyalty to the workers' employer which this Court deemed unnecessary to carry on the workers' legitimate concerted activities. The activities of these seven employees cannot be classified as "indefensible" by any recognized standard of conduct. Indeed, concerted activities by employees for the purpose of trying to protect themselves from working conditions as uncomfortable as the testimony and Board findings showed them to be in this case are unquestionably activities to correct conditions which modern labor-management legislation treats as too bad to have to be tolerated in a humane and civilized society like ours.

We hold therefore that the Board correctly interpreted and applied the Act to the circumstances of this case and it was error for the Court of Appeals to refuse to enforce its order. The judgment of the Court of Appeals is reversed and the cause is remanded to that court with directions to enforce the order in its entirety.

Reversed and remanded.

Questions and Notes

Despite the *Washington Aluminum* opinion's tolerance for concerted activity that is not entirely "nice" behavior, that is, the Court protects a so-called "quickie" strike, there is no question that the Court is prepared to second-guess the propriety of the means used by employees to accomplish their goals. As you already know, some kinds of activity, like the lock-in and the stall-in employed in *McDonnell Douglas v. Green*, are deemed activities not protected by the NLRA. What factors other than the justices' own sensibilities do you think should educate the courts in deciding whether certain activity should or should not be protected? For example, does the NLRA protect employees who publicly mock the apparent pettiness of an employer's gift of ice cream to the employees? What of employees who concertedly slow down their work so that they produce only half of what they typically do? What of employees who concertedly engage in short, intermittent quickie strikes, say two or three unannounced fifteen minute strikes each day?

It is also clear from reading *City Disposal* and *Washington Aluminum* that the objective of the concerted activity must be for the mutual aid and protection of employees regarding their working conditions. A freezing workplace, or an unsafe truck, pretty comfortably fits that requirement. But, what of prices of food at a cafeteria in the employer's place of business? Should it matter whether the employer has subcontracted the catering to someone else? What of annual bonuses that are given at the employer's discretion? Of a plan of employees to make a bid to own the company? Or, whether the employer is going to automate? Of the quality of the product that the employer and employees give the public? Of the fact that the employer uses raw products from a nation that indulges the practice of slavery? Of the fact that the employer disgorges carbon dioxide into the air and, thereby, increases global warming?

C. MOTIVE (REVISITED) IN AN ANTI–UNION SETTING

The following case, a collector's item, shows the outer limits of an employer's claim that its motive had nothing to do with collective activity. Reconsider what you've already learned about competing claims of motive in the *Mount Healthy* case. The NLRB adopted the Mount Healthy formulation for use in NLRA, Section 8(a)(3) cases. See Wright Line, 251 NLRB 1083 (1980) enforced 662 F.2d 899 (1st Cir.1981). The Supreme Court approved the Board's standards in NLRB v. Transportation Management, 462 U.S. 393, 103 S.Ct. 2469, 76 L.Ed.2d 667 (1983). How would Weigand, the dischargee in the following case, fare under the Board's and the Court's current test for determining illegal motive?

EDWARD G. BUDD MANUFACTURING CO. v. NLRB

United States Court of Appeals, Third Circuit, 1943.
138 F.2d 86, cert. denied 321 U.S. 778, 64 S.Ct. 619, 88 L.Ed. 1071 (1944).

BIGGS, CIRCUIT JUDGE.

On charges filed by International Union, United Automobile, Aircraft and Agricultural Workers of America, an affiliate of the Congress of Industrial Organizations, with the National Labor Relations Board, a complaint issued dated November 26, 1941, alleging that the petitioner was engaging in unfair labor practices within the meaning of Section 8(1), (2), (3) of the National Labor Relations Act, 49 Stat. 449, 29 U.S.C.A. § 158(1), (2), (3). The complaint, as subsequently amended, alleges that the petitioner, in September, 1933, created and foisted a labor organization, known as the Budd Employee Representation Association, upon its employees and thereafter contributed financial support to the Association and dominated its activities. The amended complaint also alleges that in July, 1941, the petitioner discharged an employee, Walter Weigand, because of his activities on behalf of the union, and in October of that year refused to reinstate another employee, Milton Davis, for similar reasons. The petitioner denies these charges as does the Association, which was permitted to intervene. After extensive hearings before a trial examiner the Board on June 10, 1942 issued its decision and order, requiring the disestablishment of the Association and the reinstatement of Weigand and Davis. * * *

The case of Walter Weigand is extraordinary. If ever a workman deserved summary discharge it was he. He was under the influence of liquor while on duty. He came to work when he chose and he left the plant and his shift as he pleased. In fact, a foreman on one occasion was agreeably surprised to find Weigand at work and commented upon it. Weigand amiably stated that he was enjoying it. He brought a woman (apparently generally known as the "Duchess") to the rear of the plant yard and introduced some of the employees to her. He took another employee to visit her and when this man got too drunk to be able to go home, punched his time-card for him and put him on the table in the representatives' meeting room in the plant in order to sleep off his intoxication. Weigand's immediate superiors demanded again and again that he be discharged, but each time higher officials intervened on Weigand's behalf because as was naively stated he was "a representative." In return for not working at the job for which he was hired, the petitioner gave him full pay and on five separate occasions raised his wages. One of these raises was general; that is to say, Weigand profited by a general wage increase throughout the plant, but the other four raises were given Weigand at times when other employees in the plant did not receive wage increases.

The petitioner contends that Weigand was discharged because of cumulative grievances against him. But about the time of the discharge it was suspected by some of the representatives that Weigand had joined the complaining CIO union. One of the representatives taxed him with this fact and Weigand offered to bet a hundred dollars that it could not be proved. On July 22, 1941, Weigand did disclose his union membership to the vice-chairman (Rattigan) of the Association and to another representative (Mullen) and apparently tried to persuade them to support the union. Weigand asserts that the next day he with Rattigan and Mullen, were seen talking to CIO organizer Reichwein on a street corner. The following day, according to Weigand's testimony, Mullen came to Weigand at the plant and stated that Weigand, Rattigan and himself had been seen talking to Reichwein and that he, Mullen, had just had an interview with Personnel Director McIlvain and Plant Manager Mahan. According to Weigand, Mullen said to him, "Maybe you didn't get me in a jam." And, "We were seen down there." The following day, Weigand was discharged.

As this court stated in National Labor Relations Board v. Condenser Corp., 3 Cir., 128 F.2d at page 75, an employer may discharge an employee for a good reason, a poor reason or no reason at all so long as the provisions of the National Labor Relations Act are not violated. It is, of course, a violation to discharge an employee because he has engaged in activities on behalf of a union. Conversely an employer may retain an employee for a good reason, a bad reason or no reason at all and the reason is not a concern of the Board. But it is certainly too great a strain on our credulity to assert, as does the petitioner, that Weigand was discharged for an accumulation of offenses. We think that he was discharged because his work on behalf of the CIO had become known to the plant manager. That ended his sinecure at the Budd plant. The Board found that he was discharged because of his activities on behalf of the union. The record shows that the Board's finding was based on sufficient evidence.

The order of the Board will be enforced.

Note

Assuming that a case like *Budd* would be decided today in favor of a modern-day Weigand, what remedy can the National Labor Relations Board (the NLRB) reasonably impose upon the employer?

Chapter Two

PARTICIPATION IN WORKPLACE GOVERNANCE

A. TWO MODELS OF WORKPLACE PARTICIPATION

INTRODUCTORY DIALOGUE

Nan Stevens is a Nurse Practitioner at Mercy Hospital, a private, not-for-profit hospital in Center City. Mercy Hospital employs about 200 nurses on a 24–hour basis 7 days a week, performing all varieties of patient care. 20 of these nurses have been trained and certified as Nurse Practitioners. This means they may treat patients and prescribe medication, under the supervision of a physician. The other nurses are Registered Nurses (RN's) and Licensed Professional Nurses (LPN's), who have less formal training than the nurse practitioners and who perform more limited tasks under close direction and supervision by doctors. Mercy Hospital assigns the Nurse Practitioners to more responsible duties with much more independent responsibility.

Relations between all three groups of nurses and the Hospital administration, as well as with the physicians, have been strained. The nurses feel that their services are not valued. They are the ones who provide the most immediate patient care and understand most directly how medical services may be delivered effectively. Yet the Administration seldom involves them in planning or in decisions about delivery of services. Quite the opposite, the Administration makes changes in working assignments without consulting the nurses. The nurses are especially upset with recent staffing assignments in which nurses are sent to cover on floors that are understaffed, and are moved off the floors on which they are most accustomed to working. The Hospital recently made a change in the pension program, which favors newer staff members at the expense of senior nurses.

The nurses believe they are underpaid in light of the services they perform, especially relative to the salaries of doctors, who are paid much more, and other, less trained personnel, who are paid almost as much. They are also concerned about the impact health insurance companies are having and will have on their work. They fear that financial constraints under the rules of HMO's and other insurance programs will force hospitals to cut back on essential services, to substitute poorly trained nurses' aides for LPN's and RN's, and to use part time employees in lieu of full-timers to cut back on the cost of benefits. The nurses want to make sure they have a voice in preventing these and other changes from happening. The nurses also feel they are treated in a less than professional manner by the doctors, who often minimize the nurses' contributions and fail to give them credit for their work.

The administration has acknowledged this situation. It recently hired a new director of personnel, Delores McClean. McClean has been trained in some of the new methods of worker participation, and is convinced that a systematic opening of channels of communication among nurses, doctors, other staff, and the administration will bring about a more efficient and fair working environment. McClean wants to establish "Professional Care Circles," groupings of nurses, doctors, other staff, and administration within each area of service delivery, for example, the operating room, the critical care area, pediatrics, and other similar units. The Circles would meet periodically to discuss problems and come up with solutions for improving the delivery of services and for resolving issues. Each Circle would be given a budget to tackle the most pressing problems.

McClean has asked Stevens to serve as Chair of the Critical Care Circle, a team that would consist of some ten persons in the above categories. Other nurses, including fellow Nurse Practitioners, RN's and LPN's, have urged Stevens to accept this position. Stevens is well respected, and the nurses in the other two categories think it is a good idea to entrust leadership to a Nurse Practitioner, who enjoys a little more respect because of her training.

But other employees of the Hospital have asked Stevens not to serve. These employees have been in touch with the Unified Medical Care Association (UMCA), a union that specializes in the organization of hospital workers. They want to embark upon an organizing drive that will lead to the certification of the union as representative of all staff at the Hospital. These workers think that the only way that hospital workers can achieve the voice, dignity and benefits they deserve is through the formal structure of collective bargaining. They believe that the Professional Care Circles are really intended by the Hospital to give the staff the illusion that they have a voice, without giving them any of the tools that go along with collective bargaining, such as the right to compel discussions and to use economic weapons in support of their position. Even if McClean is acting with the best of intentions, as many believe is the case, these staff members think that the Professional Care

Circles will serve as a palliative, and divert staff members from pursuing the only true way they can serve their best interests.

Nan Stevens is not sure which way to turn. Fortunately she had a colleague in nursing, Paul Torres, who gave up the practice to go to law school to develop expertise in health law. Paul practices in Center City and has some experience with workplace issues. Paul met Nan for supper one evening and discussed some of the advantages and disadvantages of each system. He had put together a packet of materials on the subject, which he loaned to Nan.

We ask you to study the same materials that Nan read. Then we'll join Nan and Paul in a discussion several weeks later in which they talk about some of the articles.

CONCORD VS. DISCORD: IS THIS THE CHOICE?

IRVING BERNSTEIN, THE LEAN YEARS: A HISTORY OF THE AMERICAN WORKER, 1920–1933

145–146 (1960) (Penguin Books Inc.).

[The author is discussing the attitude of employers towards labor in the decade of the '20's].

1

This decade constituted a transitional stage in the development of American industry, one in which enterprises were growing rapidly in size, in which improved technology and rational methods were being applied to production and distribution, in which management was separating from ownership and becoming both professionalized and "scientific," and in which employers groped uncertainly in dealing with the serious labor problems their productive endeavors were largely instrumental in creating. Businessmen were far more comfortable handling units of production and dollars of profit than they were dealing with the people who were their employees. As a consequence, labor was a question to which they seldom addressed themselves. "The real difficulty of labor relations," industrialist Sam A. Lewisohn wrote, "has been one of neglect."

* * *

At bottom, this negligence stemmed from a fundamental uncertainty over the place of labor in the business system. Employers did not know whether to clutch workers to their breasts as partners in a great cooperative adventure in production or to keep them at arm's length as potential, if not present, enemies of capitalism. They would refer patronizingly to the worker as a pillar of society ("There is no better American citizen ... than the average American worker," Charles M. Schwab declared) and proceed promptly to truss him up. Employers could not decide whether their interests were better served simply by keeping labor disorganized or by putting it into organizations under their control. A general theme at management meetings was "the harmony of interests" between employers and employees. By this phrase the speakers meant that workers were to harmonize themselves with the goals and methods of management, and, failing that, employers had the obligation to use harmonious coercion. At a time when autocratic statements had become taboo, autocratic methods were widespread. Employers were unsure whether to regard the worker as a displaceable cog in the productive machine or as an indispensable consumer of industry's rising output, his wage as a cost item to be kept low or as an income factor to be pushed high. Finally, there was a general tendency within management to consider labor as an exclusively intra-firm problem at the very moment when industry-wide and interindustry forces were becoming decisive.

This ambivalence manifested itself most dramatically in the extraordinary shift in the labor policy of employers that occurred during the decade. At the outset management launched the so-called American Plan, a full-scale direct attack on trade unionism with the panoply of hostile techniques. In the latter part of the twenties employers veered sharply to the gentler methods of paternalistic welfare capitalism.

This schizophrenia contributed to those "astonishing contrasts in organization and disorganization" that President Hoover's Committee on Social Trends found so marked a feature of American society. "Not all parts of our organization are changing at the same speed or at the same time.... These unequal rates of change ... make zones of danger and points of tension." In the twenties, employers, when they were aware of them at all, were inclined to sweep these dangers and tensions under the rug.

Paul: Bernstein writes at some length about John D. Rockefeller, Jr. Look at Rockefeller's views of that period.

J.D. ROCKEFELLER, JR., LABOR AND CAPITAL–PARTNERS
Atlantic Monthly, p. 101, January 1916.

Labor and Capital are rather abstract words with which to describe those vital forces which working together become productively useful to mankind. Reduced to their simplest terms, Labor and Capital are men with muscle and men with money—human beings, imbued with the same weaknesses and virtues, the same cravings and aspirations. * * *

Are the interests of these human beings with labor to sell and with capital to employ necessarily antagonistic or necessarily mutual? Must the advance of one retard the progress of the other? Should their attitude toward each other be that of enemies or of partners? The answer one makes to these fundamental questions must constitute the basis for any consideration of the relationship of Labor and Capital. * * *

Much of the reasoning on this subject proceeds upon the theory that the wealth of the world is absolutely limited, and that if one man gets more, another necessarily gets less. Hence there are those who hold that if Labor's wages are increased or its working conditions improved, Capital suffers because it must deprive itself of the money needed to pay the bill. Some employers go so far as to justify themselves in appropriating from the product of industry all that remains after Labor has received the smallest amount which it can be induced or forced to accept; while, on the other hand, there are men who hold that Labor is the producer of all wealth, hence is entitled to the entire product, and that whatever is taken by Capital is stolen from Labor.

If this theory is sound, it might be maintained that the relation between Labor and Capital is fundamentally one of antagonism, and that each should consolidate and arm its forces, dividing the products of industry between them in proportion as their selfishness is enforced by their power.

But all such counsel loses sight of the fact that the riches available to man are practically without limit, that the world's wealth is constantly being developed and undergoing mutation, and that to promote this process both Labor and Capital are indispensable. If these great forces cooperate, the products of industry are steadily increased; whereas, if they fight, the production of wealth is certain to be either retarded or stopped altogether and the wellsprings of material progress choked.

The problem of promoting the cooperation of Labor and Capital may well be regarded, therefore, as the most vital problem of modern civilization. Peace may be established among the nations of the world; but if the underlying factors of material growth within each nation are themselves at war, the foundations of all progress are undermined.

Nan: I wonder, Paul, if Bernstein isn't wrong in concluding that we're merely reinventing an old system when we go for these worker participation systems. I think that the reality of the workplace has changed. We've been through a long testing period for unions, and that system has managed to create the very discord he deplores. The vocabulary and structure of the system are very adversarial. And when all is said and done, in today's economy the strike weapon is meaningless, and so you don't get anywhere when you finally roll out your weapons. If a unionized company gives its employees a raise, it simply loses business to nonunion competitors, both here and offshore. What's the point of being contentious if you don't have the muscle to back you up in the end, or if the use of those weapons turns out to be self-defeating? I think we are now beginning to see that the only way to work through these problems is by mutual discussions that are not confrontational. I think that when people work together they unlock all sorts of creative energy.

1. MODES OF WORKER PARTICIPATION

OUT WITH THE OLD WAYS: REINVENTING
THE WORKPLACE?

———

Paul: Whenever I see the term "reinvent," I get nervous. We think
we are reinventing the concord that employers dreamed about
in the '20's and '30's. It is the same with "reinventing government," that with-it phrase they used to describe Al Gore's
reform of the bureaucracy during the Clinton administration.
I'm afraid that what we're really reinventing is language, creating a newspeak as Orwell did in 1984. It is a language of peace,
harmony, joint goals, win-win. Well, language has a way of
trapping you, because when you don't have the vocabulary to
express your needs, you can't articulate them. This new vocabulary of togetherness is missing some words. I don't see the
words "rights," or "entitled," or "protection," or "enforcement," or "equality." I don't see anyone "demanding," as
unions used to do. I'm afraid that with these Circles you'll end
up with a system that is fine as long as you agree with
management. But when harder choices have to be made, when
it is a question of where you put your resources, whether
doctors should work harder or you should work harder, whether
the hospital should build another wing or raise your salaries,
then I think your voice will be silenced. You'll have no way to
back up your position.

You should think about the kinds of things that management might
be willing to talk about under this system. You'll have discussions about the general direction of hospital care, the desirability of more staffing, but do you think the hospital will actually
involve you in these decisions? What if the hospital decides to
merge with another hospital and combine resources and eliminate duplicative functions? Will they consult with you or seek
your approval? What about the hard bread and butter issues,
like salaries, and pensions and time off? Sure, the hospital may
take a survey of employee preferences and dissatisfactions. Non-
union employers often do this. But will they ask you directly
about your salary, and whether you need more, and how you are
paid in comparison with other employees? Suppose there is a
concern about diversity—hiring and advancing of minorities. Or
a problem about accommodating the special needs of a person
with a disability, who wants to transfer to a less physically
demanding job held by somebody else? Do you think the hospital
will involve the team in these discussions?

But keep in mind that the system of union representation may not
be ideally suited for some of these discussions either. Ironically,

some of the issues that go to the heart of how the hospital is run—mergers, the kinds of services provided—may not be mandatory subjects of bargaining under the NLRA, and the union may not have a legal right to press those issues at the bargaining table [this topic is discussed later in this chapter—Eds]. And the issues involving competing employee claims—diversity, disability—may also be ill suited for collective bargaining. After all, the union is charged with representing everyone in the bargaining unit. How will it reconcile the claims of minority employees, who seek rapid advancement, with the seniority rights of other employees who might be impacted by such advancement? Same question with regard to disabilities.

But getting back to the tension between workers' needs and management's interests, while this may seem to come from another age, it is wise to recall the Preamble to the IWW Constitution (From Paul Le Blanc, A Short History of the U.S. Working Class 67):

"The working class and the employing class have nothing in common" and that "between these two classes a struggle must go on until the workers of the world organize as a class, take possession of the earth and the machinery of production, and abolish the wage system."

Now, I realize that is stuff from a radical movement that has long since faded away, but it should remind us that in the last analysis the interests of labor and capital are antagonistic. This is something Judge Holmes reminded us of in his dissent in the famous Vegelahn v. Guntner [which appears in Chapter One—Eds.]

For example, John Case observes in his article, John Case, A Company of Businesspeople, Inc. 79-93, that workers and management used to count on the rules of the unionized plant to stabilize the workplace, "curbing arbitrary authority and providing for the expression of grievances." What takes the place of the union to provide stability and rights in the newer systems?

I like the way Freeman and Medoff put it. They say that individual exit and voice work fine for the employee at the margin, the one who is strong enough or good enough to make his or her views known and who has the wherewithal to leave if he or she doesn't get what he needs. But the employees in the middle, the majority, I would suppose, who are replaceable, need a better way to be heard.

PARTICIPATION WITH EMPOWERMENT— COLLECTIVE BARGAINING

R. FREEMAN AND J. MEDOFF, WHAT DO UNIONS DO?

pp. 7–11 (Basic Books, 1984).

[S]ocieties have two basic mechanisms for dealing with social or economic problems. The first is the classic market mechanism of exit-and-entry, in which individuals respond to a divergence between desired and actual social conditions by exercising freedom of choice or mobility: the dissatisfied consumer switches products; the diner whose soup is too salty seeks another restaurant; the unhappy couple divorces. In the labor market, exit is synonymous with quitting, while entry consists of new hires by the firm. By leaving less desirable for more desirable jobs, or by refusing bad jobs, individuals penalize the bad employer and reward the good, leading to an overall improvement in the efficiency of the economic system. The basic theorem of neoclassical economics is that, under well-specified conditions, the exit and entry of persons (the hallmark of the free-market system) produces a situation in which no individual can be made better off without making someone worse off. Much economic analysis can be viewed as a detailed study of the implications of this kind of adjustment and of the extent to which it works out in real economies. As long as the exit-entry market mechanism is viewed as the only adjustment mechanism, institutions like unions are invariably seen as impediments to the optimal operation of the economy.

The second mode of adjustment is the political mechanism that Hirschman termed "voice." [A. Hirschman, Exit, Voice and Loyalty (1970)] "Voice" refers to the use of direct communication to bring actual and desired conditions closer together. It means talking about problems: complaining to the store about a poor product rather than taking business elsewhere; telling the chef that the soup had too much salt; discussing marital problems rather than going directly to the divorce court. In a political context, "voice" refers to participation in the democratic process, through voting, discussion, bargaining, and the like.

The distinction between the two mechanisms is best illustrated by a specific situation—for instance, concern about the quality of schools in a given locality. The exit solution to poor schools would be to move to a different community or to enroll one's children in a private school, thereby "taking one's business elsewhere." The voice solution would involve political action to improve the school system through schoolboard elections, Parent Teacher Association meetings, and other channels of communication.

In the job market, voice means discussing with an employer conditions that ought to be changed, rather than quitting the job. In modern industrial economies, and particularly in large enterprises, a trade union is the vehicle for collective voice—that is, for providing workers as a group with a means of communicating with management.

Collective rather than individual bargaining with an employer is necessary for effective voice at the workplace for two reasons. First, many important aspects of an industrial setting are "public goods," that is, goods which will affect the well-being (negatively or positively) of every employee in such a way that one individual's partaking of the good does not preclude someone else from doing so. Safety conditions, lighting, heating, the speed of the production line, the firm's formal grievance procedure, pension plan, and policies on matters such as layoffs, work-sharing, cyclical wage adjustment, and promotion all obviously affect the entire workforce in the same way that defense, sanitation, and fire protection affect the community at large. One of the most important economic theorems is that competitive markets will not provide enough of such goods; some form of collective decision making is needed. Without a collective organization, the incentive for the individual to take into account the effects of his or her actions on others, or to express his or her preferences, or to invest time and money in changing conditions, is likely to be too small to spur action. Why not "let Harry do it" and enjoy the benefits at no cost? This classic "free-rider" problem lies at the heart of the so-called "union-security" versus "right-to-work" debate.

A second reason why collective action is necessary is that workers who are tied to a firm are unlikely to reveal their true preferences to an employer, for fear the employer may fire them. In a world in which workers could find employment at the same wages immediately, the market would offer adequate protection for the individual, but that is not the world we live in. The danger of job loss makes expression of voice by an individual risky. Collective voice, by contrast, is protected both by the support of all workers and by the country's labor law: "It shall be an unfair labor practice for an employer by discrimination in regard to hire or tenure or employment or any term or condition of employment to encourage or discourage membership in any labor organization." (National Labor Relations Act, Section 7a [sic; 8(3)—Eds.] of the 1935 law). * * *

The collective nature of trade unionism fundamentally alters the operation of a labor market and, hence, the nature of the labor contract. In a nonunion setting, where exit-and-entry is the predominant form of adjustment, the signals and incentives to firms depend on the preferences of the "marginal" worker, the one who might leave because of (or be attracted by) small changes in the conditions of employment. The firm responds primarily to the needs of this marginal worker, who is generally young and marketable; the firm can to a considerable extent ignore the preferences of typically older, less marketable workers, who— for reasons of skill, knowledge, rights that cannot be readily transferred to other enterprises, as well as because of other costs associated with changing firms—are effectively immobile. In a unionized setting, by contrast, the union takes account of *all* workers in determining its demands at the bargaining table, so that the desires of workers who are highly unlikely to leave the enterprise are also represented. With respect to public goods at the workplace, the union can add up members' preferences in much the same manner as a government can add up voters' preferences for defense, police protection, and the like to determine social demand for them. In sum, because unions are political institutions with elected leaders, they are likely to respond to a different set of preferences from those that prevail in a competitive labor market.

In a modern economy, where workers tend to be attached to firms for many years, younger and older workers are likely to have different preferences (for instance, regarding pension or health insurance plans versus take-home pay, or layoffs ordered inversely to seniority versus cuts in wage growth or work sharing). The change from an approach that focuses only on workers at the coming-or-going margin to one that considers all employees is likely to lead to a very different labor contract. Under some conditions, the union contract—by taking account of all workers and by appropriately considering the sum of preferences for work conditions that are common to all workers—can be economically more efficient than the contract that would result in the absence of unions.

Finally, as a collective voice unions also fundamentally alter the social relations of the workplace. The essence of the employment relationship under capitalism—as stressed by such diverse analysts as Karl Marx, Herbert Simon, and Ronald Coase—is the payment of money by the employer to the employee in return for the employer's control over a certain amount of the employee's time. The employer seeks to use his employee's time in a way that maximizes the profitability of the enterprise. Even in the case of piece rates, employers monitor employee activity to assure the quality of output, prevent the wastage of materials, and protect the stock of capital. As a result, the way in which the time purchased is utilized must be determined by some interaction between workers and their employer. In the absence of unionism, the worker has limited responses to orders that he feels are unfair: the worker can quit, or he can perhaps engage in quiet sabotage or shirking, neither of which is likely to alter the employer's actions. In the union setting, by contrast, the union constitutes a source of worker power, diluting managerial authority and offering members protection through both the "industrial jurisprudence" system, under which many workplace decisions are based on rules (such as seniority) instead of supervisory judgment or whim, and the grievance and arbitration system, under which disputes over proper managerial decision making on work issues can be resolved. As a result, management power within enterprises is curtailed by unionism, so that workers' rights are likely to be better enforced. Consider, for example, a firm that decides to fire senior workers immediately before they become eligible for pension rights. In the nonunion setting, a firm may be able to get away with such a maneuver; in the union setting, it is unlikely to have such power. Economic theorists of all persuasions have increasingly recognized that unions' ability to enforce labor agreements, particularly those with deferred claims, creates the possibility for improved labor contracts and arrangements and higher economic efficiency.

Nan: But the traditional, collective model seems to have gotten out of hand. As John Case explains it, collective bargaining assumes conflicting interests of worker and management, separate spheres of concern, and a rigid hierarchy where everything is done top down. That creates tension, which throttles initiative and productivity. I wonder if unions made a mistake by historically disavowing any interest in helping to run the company, and only reacting to decisions that they didn't like.

ONE PERSON'S VIEW OF THE UNION MODEL

JACK METZGAR, STRIKING STEEL: SOLIDARITY REMEMBERED

32–39 (Temple University Press 2000).

[Jack Metzgar's book is about his father, Johnny Metzgar, who worked for four decades in the steel mills in Johnstown, Pennsylvania. The book is also a history of the 1959 steel strike, the largest strike in U.S. history. Space permits only a few short excerpts, which we hope give you a feeling for what a union can do for a worker. Jack Metzgar is Professor of Humanities at Roosevelt University in Chicago.]

He learned the molder's trade from a friend and second cousin of his father's, Runt Espey, and enjoyed the work at first along with the camaraderie among the men, though not the dusty conditions that left you "still coughing two or three hours after you left work." He transferred out of molding in 1940 to the Lower Ship, where he eventually worked as a machinist making rolls for U.S.S. rolling mills. He remained in the Lower Ship until he retired in 1969, at the age of fifty-six. In good times, when there was lots of work, he was a machinist; when work was slack, he bumped down several job classifications to become a "hooker," the person who attached things to an overhead crane for delivery elsewhere in the mill.

He joined the union at his first opportunity in 1936, having been signed up by Runt Espey and in turn signing up others among the younger men, including my Uncle Stan. Runt, who was short and cocky, like my father, had some job security and not a little shop-floor power through his craft skills. There were certain molds that only Runt knew how to do correctly, and many others that benefitted from his skills and knowledge. In addition, in my father's words, he was a "crafty bugger" who "had something on everybody, or could make you think he did," and most foremen or superintendents had to solicit Runt's cooperation if they were to get production. Runt, therefore, could openly advocate for the union without fear of losing his job. Others could not. * * *

I once asked my father if he had thought, when he first joined, that the union would accomplish all that it had. Without hesitating, he answered "No. That's not why I joined. I didn't really think it would do any good. But I didn't care. I was young, single, and I hated my job, and ... I just couldn't live with the fear. I was just rebelling. I knew the company hated the union, so I joined. I don't know what I'd have done if I'd had a family then." The fear, he explained, was the fear of losing your job, and some foremen used that fear like a whip. He told numerous stories to illustrate how this worked, none of which involved him directly. "I was young, and I really didn't care if they fired me or not—I hated the mill—and they knew that. It [not caring] protected me. They went after the guys with families, the guys who couldn't afford to lose their jobs. If you let them know you were afraid for your job, they owned you. They owned your job, and that meant they owned *you*." The worst of these stories, which he and others told me several times over the years, went like this.

When work was slack during the depression, before the union, foremen were in control of who worked and who didn't on any given day. To get work, workers would vie with each other to curry favor with foremen and superintendents. One fellow who had a reputation as a particularly good worker had been employed steadily during one period; to ensure his employment, he cut his foreman's grass in the summer and shoveled snow for him in the winter without pay; he also brought homemade kielbasa and other goodies to the foreman on a regular basis. One day the foreman ran into this worker while the worker was with his sixteen-year-old daughter, a particularly beautiful young woman, as the story goes. The next day at work the foreman, a married man with a family and himself only slightly younger than his employee, asked the worker if he could arrange a "date" with his daughter. The worker said he'd see and would let the foreman know the next day. The next day the worker arrived with a particularly large supply of freshly made kielbasa, but told the foreman he would be unable to arrange the date. At this point he was summarily fired and was subsequently without work for the better part of a year—at a time when there was no unemployment compensation and "relief" was a breadline.

This story got told and retold because it was so extreme. Most foremen would not dream of doing anything like this. Most foremen were people you could reason with. But they all had this power over your life and the life of your family, and most of them used it in both big and little ways, sometimes with a purpose, sometimes just out of meanness, but always with the same humiliating result. The worst part of this story, for my father, was not the man's being without work for so long. The worst part was that he didn't, that he couldn't, just say no—that even in refusing the foreman's request, he couldn't "stand up to him," couldn't maintain his dignity.

As my father used to say, "If the union didn't do anything else, it put an end to that." Though it didn't happen all at once, the union eventually stripped not only the foreman but even the company itself of this arbitrary power.

At first, in 1937, it just gave a guy like Runt Espey something additional to work with, a way to extend to others some of the protections he enjoyed based on his craft skills. The grievance procedure in those early years didn't take away much of the foreman's formal power, but it meant that a union griever could go over his head to a superintendent, and then the union could go over a department superintendent's head if a complaint seemed justified. This immediately eliminated the worst excesses of foremen, which (as in the story above) violated existing company policy. And, with a little imagination, a crafty bugger like Runt, who was the molders' first grievance man, could use the formal power of the union contract to extend his informal power in the labor process. Pretty soon the guys on the molding floor were going to Runt asking "Can he [the foreman] do that?" and Runt almost uniformly would say, "Hell no!" and then go have a talk with the foreman. The foreman needed Runt's craft skills, and now his leadership, to get production; besides, many foremen, like most rank-and-file workers, were none too sure what the new system required of them. In this context, Runt was able to give the union a power and a presence on the molding floor all out of proportion to what had been agreed upon in March 1937 by John L. Lewis and U.S.S. head Myron Taylor in a hotel in New York City. To my father, who was 25 then, it was indescribably exhilarating to observe this process. * * *

Runt, in today's jargon, was my father's role model. But nobody's perfect, even role models, and that's why the union wouldn't really be a union if it had to depend on the consistent righteousness of the Runt Espeys. The idea was to eliminate arbitrary power itself, not just shift it from one person to another. Though it didn't happen all at once, that's exactly what the union contract eventually achieved.

Assigning work, firing, disciplining, even warning a steelworker—by the 1950's nobody—not the foreman, the company, nor any union leader, from the shop floor to international headquarters—had much discretion in doing any of these things. The rules laid out in the union contract determined who got laid off and who worked during bad times, who got overtime and who worked night shift, who worked in Job Classification 10 and who worked in Job Classification 15. If you had the seniority and could do the job, it was yours by right. Nobody *gave* it you. It was yours according to the rules everybody had agreed to. Though you needed the union to ensure that the rules were followed and, indeed, to get the rules written down and agreed to in the first place, you didn't need to be in anybody's good graces; you didn't need to bring anyone kielbasa, not even the union.

This system of rule-making and rule-observing is the essence of bureaucracy, and it has its disadvantages for both workers and managers. But it is also the essence of industrial democracy in the American system. Today, as labor historian David Brody had shown so clearly, both the left and right attack this "workplace rule of law" with little sense of its role in liberating workers from arbitrary authority and all the indignities, the humiliation, and the fear that come with being directly subject to the unlimited authority of another human being. Bureaucratic work rules, and the legalistic grievance system designed to interpret and enforce them, take away a lot of management discretion that may be desirable for competing in a more fiercely competitive world. They also bind workers as well as managers, restricting them from taking things into their own hands with wildcat strikes and other spontaneous job actions that might oppose injustices allowable under the contract; in the long run, this may undermine worker militancy and the very capacity for concerted action. Both the right and the left have a point. But the easy use of "bureaucracy" as a broad pejorative with rich negative connotations allows them to avoid the issue of what the alternatives to living by impersonal rules might be. * * *

In my father's view of things, the very impersonality of the labor contract as a binding document was the foundation of his freedom and dignity, and a great deal of peace of mind as well. He believed in what was called then "the sanctity of the contract": "You have to live by the contract. It binds us as well as them [management or the company]. But it's *our* contract. We were bound together before. They weren't." The union itself, not anything that it did or didn't do; the contract itself, not anything that was in it; these were the fundamentals, "the big thing," as he said. The rest was gravy. * * *

Specific work rules and working conditions were crucial to him, and he had a way of dividing them from wages and benefits, a way that coincided with the split between work and family that was so much a part of 1950s culture. The wages and benefits were for the family; the working conditions, for him alone. The money for both "came out of the put," he would say, and we should not expect him to degrade his working conditions (or fail to improve them) so that he could bring a little more home to us. * * *

Into the 1960's, the Steelworkers' wage-and-benefit package was always bargained and reported in cents, not in percentage-increase terms. This was done to benefit the lower pay grades, but it also had the effect of making the impact of wage bargaining more clear and meaningful to Steelworker families like mine. Through ten sets of negotiations and five strikes from 1946 to 1956, the steel companies fought every advance the union sought—and did so in a highly public way. It was pretty simple to figure out that without the union we wouldn't have gotten eight and a half of those eighteen and a half cents in 1946, and only a little more complicated to reason that without the union the companies would never have offered that dime in the first place.

From the time my father joined the union in 1936 until the 1959 strike, the average *real* wage of steelworkers increased 110 percent, with the bulk of the increase coming after the war. Think of that a minute. Think of what it does for a family's well-being to have more real spending power year after year, to experience a steady, relentless improvement in your standard of living for more than two decades. And, though they were often in the forefront, it wasn't just the steelworkers who experienced these benefits: the average real wage of all manufacturing workers increased 89 percent during the same period. This was not gravy. This was the very basis of life for a wage worker in a capitalist society. It meant you had something very few workers had ever had up until then—discretionary income, income that in a sense you didn't need, income that you could *decide* how to spend. Eventually, and this had happened by 1959, it meant an upgrading in what counted as necessities. In 1946, we did not have a car, a television set, or a refrigerator. By 1952 we had all those things, and I can remember vividly the excitement of the day when each arrived. And by 1959 these were all necessities, without which we could not have imagined living.

But the real wage increase doesn't cover the half of it. In 1949, the Steelworkers struck the companies for forty-two days in order to get them to fund a pension plan and to partially fund health insurance. These were nothing to brag about at first. The pension formula committed the companies to supplement Social Security so that a steelworker with enough service could receive $100 a month in retirement (at a time when it took at least $250 a month to live.) Likewise, health insurance only covered certain hospital costs and major procedures by doctors, and the company only paid half the premium. But they were a big deal at the time, and the companies at first resisted them on principle as "un-American and contrary to the most cherished ideals of self-reliance and personal initiative." After forty two days, the companies gave up on that principle, and the union then improved on the substance with each negotiation in the 1950s. * * *

And the pension eventually turned out to be a wonder. The idea of retiring at the age of 56 and being able to live comfortably, if frugally, was unimaginable in 1946. * * *

The perception and remembrance of the 1950s as a time of repressive conformism and spiritless materialism might relate to the middle-class organization man, the white-collar professional and managerial worker of the time. It did not relate to us. All the discretion that the foreman and the company were losing was flowing right into our homes. There were choices. There were prospects. There were possibilities. Few of these had been there before. Now they were. And because they came slowly, year by year, contract by contract, strike by bitter strike, they gave a lilting, liberating feeling to life—a sense that no matter what was wrong today, it could be changed, it could get better—in fact, by the late 1950s, that it was quite likely that it *would* get better. Hang in there. Stick with it. These moral injunctions to daily fortitude made so much more sense than when there were so many visible payoffs for doing so. And as my father would find out, my mother, my sister and I—like nearly everybody else in American society—were learning to tolerate less and less repression from anybody of anything, including him. If what we lived through in the 1950s was not liberation, then liberation never happens in real human lives.

UNIONS AND THE MARKET

MILTON AND ROSE FRIEDMAN, WHO PROTECTS THE WORKER?

Free to Choose 232–243 (1980).

... Given that members of strong unions are highly paid, the obvious question is: are they highly paid because their unions are strong, or are their unions strong because they are highly paid? Defenders of the unions claim that the high pay of their members is a tribute to the strength of union organization, and that if only all workers were members of unions, all workers would be highly paid.

The situation is, however, much more complex ... [T]he ability of unions to raise the wages of some workers does not mean that universal unionism could raise the wages of all workers. On the contrary, and this is a fundamental source of misunderstanding, *the gains that strong unions win for their members are primarily at the expense of other workers.*

The key to understanding the situation is the most elementary principle of economics: the law of demand—the higher the price of anything, the less of it people will be willing to buy. Make labor of any kind more expensive and the number of jobs of that kind will be fewer. Make carpenters more expensive, and fewer houses than otherwise will be built, and those houses that are built will tend to use materials and methods requiring less carpentry. Raise the wage of airline pilots, and air travel will become more expensive. Fewer people will fly, and there will be fewer jobs for airline pilots. Alternatively, reduce the number of carpenters or pilots, and they will command higher wages. Keep down the number of physicians, and they will be able to charge higher fees.

A successful union reduces the number of jobs available of the kind it controls. As a result, some people who would like to get such jobs at the union wage cannot do so. They are forced to look elsewhere. A greater supply of workers for other jobs drives down the wages paid for those jobs. Universal unionization would not alter the situation. It could mean higher wages for the persons who get jobs, along with more unemployment for others. * * *

Higher wages to one group of workers must come primarily from other workers. * * *

All of us, including the highly unionized, have indirectly been harmed as consumers by the effect of high union wages on the prices of consumer goods. Houses are unnecessarily expensive for everyone, including the carpenters. Workers have been prevented by unions from using their skills to produce the most highly valued items; they have been forced to resort to activities where their productivity is less. The total basket of goods available to all of us is smaller than it would have been.

The Source of Union Power

How can unions raise the wages of their members? What is the basic source of their power? The answer is: the ability to keep down the number of jobs available, or equivalently, to keep down the number of persons available for a class of jobs. Unions have been able to keep down the number of jobs by enforcing a high wage rate, generally with assistance from government. They have been able to keep down the number of persons available primarily through licensure, again with government aid. * * *

[H]ow can a union enforce a high wage rate? One way is violence or the threat of violence: threatening to destroy the property of employers, or to beat them up if they employ nonunion workers or if they pay union members less than the union-specified rate; or to beat up workers, or destroy their property, if they agree to work for a lower wage. That is the reason union wage arrangements and negotiations have so often been accompanied by violence.

An easier way is to get the government to help. That is the reason union headquarters are clustered around Capitol Hill in Washington, why they devote so much money and attention to politics. In his study of the airline pilots' union, Hopkins notes that "the union secured enough federal protective legislation to make the professional airline pilots practically a ward of the state."

A major form of government assistance to construction unions is the Davis–Bacon Act, a federal law that requires all contractors who work on a contract in excess of $2,000 to which the U.S. government or the District of Columbia is a party to pay wage rates no less than those "prevailing for the corresponding classes of laborers and mechanics" in the neighborhood in question, as "determined by the Secretary of Labor." In practice the "prevailing" rates have been ruled to be union wage rates in "an overwhelming proportion of wage determinations * * * regardless of area or type of construction." * * * The effect of these acts is that the government enforces union wage rates for much of construction activity. * * *

Another set of government measures enforcing wage rates are minimum wage laws. These laws are defended as a way to help low-income people. In fact, they hurt low-income people. The source of pressure for them is demonstrated by the people who testify before Congress in favor of a higher premium wage. They are mostly representatives of organized labor, of the AFL–CIO and other labor organizations. No member of their unions works for a wage anywhere close to the legal minimum. Despite all the rhetoric about helping the poor, they favor an ever higher minimum wage as a way to protect the members of their unions from competition. * * *

An alternative to enforcing a wage rate is to restrict directly the number who may pursue an occupation. That technique is particularly attractive when there are many employers—so that enforcing a wage rate is difficult. Medicine is an excellent example, since much of the activity of organized medicine has been directed toward restricting the number of physicians in practice.* * *

Licensure is widely used to restrict entry, particularly for occupations like medicine that have many individual practitioners dealing with a large number of individual customers. As in medicine, the boards that administer the licensure provisions are composed primarily of members of the occupation licensed—whether they be dentists, lawyers, cosmetologists, airline pilots, plumbers, or morticians. There is no occupation so remote that an attempt has not been made to restrict its practice by licensure.* * *

Labor unions can and often do provide useful services for their members—negotiating the terms of their employment, representing them with respect to grievances, giving them a feeling of belonging and participating in a group activity, among others. As believers in freedom, we favor the fullest opportunity for voluntary organization of labor unions to perform whatever services their members wish, and are willing to pay for, provided they respect the rights of others and refrain from using force.

However, unions and comparable groups such as the professional associations have not relied on strictly voluntary activities and membership with respect to their major proclaimed objective—improving the wages of their members. They have succeeded in getting government to grant them special privileges and immunities, which have enabled them to benefit some of their members and officials at the expense of other workers and all consumers. In the main, the persons benefited have decidedly higher incomes than the persons harmed.

KENNETH G. DAU–SCHMIDT—A BARGAINING ANALYSIS OF AMERICAN LABOR LAW AND THE SEARCH FOR BARGAINING EQUITY AND INDUSTRIAL PEACE

91 Mich. L. Rev. 419, 468–473 (1992).

C. A CRITIQUE OF THE MONOPOLY MODEL FROM AN ECONOMIC PERSPECTIVE

As previously discussed, in resolving the three issues presented in the primer on labor economics, the traditional monopoly model of unions and collective bargaining combines the first of the various possible assumptions presented with respect to each issue. The monopoly analysis assumes that the source of union benefits is a labor cartel, that employers respond to union wage increases by moving up their labor demand curve, and that the costs of collective bargaining should be treated as ordinary transaction costs. The choice of each of these three assumptions is questionable on grounds of both logical arguments and empirical evidence.

1. The Assumption of a Labor Cartel as the Source of Union Wage Increases

It seems very doubtful that cartelization of the labor market is the sole, or even the primary, source of union wage increases in the American economy. The establishment of a labor cartel in any market without licensure would seem very difficult. Workers are the consummate atomistic competitors. Moreover, if labor cartel power were the only source of union wage increases, an organizing campaign that proceeded to organize one competitive employer at a time would get nowhere because there would be only costs of unionization, but no benefits, to show employees until the requisite number of employers was organized. A labor cartel in a competitive product market without employer rents or productivity increases associated with unionism would have to be simultaneously organized across many employers in order to survive—like Athena springing full-grown from Zeus' head.

Employer product market power rents, Ricardian rents, and quasi-rents constitute much more likely sources of union wage increases.* If the requisite barriers to entry to a product market exist, the employers would be more likely to exploit them than would a labor cartel. The employers are much more concentrated than individual employees; moreover, normal economic profits sustain employers while they organize their cartel or increase their grasp on market share through expansion or merger. Indeed, when significant economies of scale exist in an industry, the employers, as producers, will naturally gravitate toward oligopoly or monopoly. No such anticompetitive gravity compels the workers to combination. Finally, it seems much more plausible that unions could organize employers who enjoy monopoly rents, Ricardian rents, or quasi-rents, because such organization could be undertaken on a more manageable basis, one employer at a time.

The arguments for the existence of at least some productivity increases associated with unionism also seem compelling. The argument that long-term implicit contracts yield benefits in monitoring and firm-specific human capital investment is intuitively appealing and well established in the economics literature. Without unions, workers are left with only the uncertain and inefficient discipline of reputation to prevent employers from breaching such contracts. Similarly, public goods dominate the conditions of employment in most employment contracts and pose a serious problem for the negotiation of efficient individual contracts. It seems quite plausible that collective bargaining could help

* Editor's note: An employer's product market power rents are profits in excess of the competitive rate of return that the employer enjoys because he or she has a monopoly or shares in an oligopoly in the product market. Ricardian rents are profits in excess of the competitive rate of return that the employer enjoys because the employer or employees employ some particularly productive and limited resource, for example a particularly rich vein of ore or the basketball skills of Michael Jordan. Quasi-rents are profits that the employer enjoys from a resource that is not easily transported or transformed into another use, for example a specialized steel mill.

rectify this problem, as well as lower worker turnover, by giving employees a superior means of expressing their concerns.

Several authors have argued that union productivity increases cannot be real or substantial because, if they were, employers would encourage unionism and split the proceeds from these productivity increases with employees. This argument ignores the fact that many employers are anxious to organize employees in committees or associations for the purposes of communication. Perhaps not coincidentally, the decline of unions in the United States has been accompanied by a rash of cases testing the legal bounds of employer efforts to organize employees despite the National Labor Relations Act's prohibition against company unions. What employers are not interested in is organizing independent unions that could vie for a share of employer rents and interfere with management prerogatives. Even though such independent organization would yield greater productivity increases due to effective enforcement of long-term implicit contracts, greater accuracy in the assessment of employee preferences with respect to collective goods, and more effective monitoring of management efficiency, employers do not want independent organization because sharing rents with employees decreases profits, and managers prefer not to be effectively monitored. Furthermore, employers can realize some of the productivity increases associated with independent employee organization by free riding on the information obtained by observing the production and employment practices of their organized competitors.

Empirical evidence also suggests that labor cartel power is less important than other sources of union wage increases. Based on available statistics, there seem to be few product markets in the United States that contain a percentage of organized workers that might even be imagined a labor cartel. Nationally, the proportion of private sector employees represented by a union is currently about 14%. Among industry groups and occupations for which such statistics are collected by the Bureau of Labor Statistics, the highest representation in any industry group on a national basis is 39%, while the highest representation in any particular occupation on a national basis is 42%. Although the percent organized in particular industries, such as automobiles or steel, is undoubtedly higher, typically such industries suffered from product market concentration prior to organization. Similarly, the highest percentage organized in any state is 36%, although variations undoubtedly exist among local product markets.

Direct empirical evidence of the source of union wage increases is difficult to produce due to the strategic incentives of employers in labor negotiations. Product price increases may be associated with the negotiation of a union contract even if the union wage increase will be paid out of employer monopoly rents, because the employer has incentive to underprice and plead poverty during negotiations and then adjust prices up after negotiation of the contract. However, the best available evidence suggests that union wage increases come largely at the expense of employers and are strongly associated with the market power of the employing firm. Most empirical models, and even many modern presentations of the monopoly theory of unions, depend on employer product market power, Ricardian rents, or quasi-rents as the source of union wage increases.

Finally, studies have found convincing evidence that some industries enjoy significant productivity increases from unionism. Perhaps the best of these studies was conducted by Kim Clark, who compared the physical output of cement plants before and after organization and between different organized and unorganized plants, finding statistically significant productivity increases with organization that ranged from 6% to 10%. However, other studies suggest that not all industries enjoy such productivity gains and that productivity increases associated with employee organization can evaporate if labor relations turn sour. Although further work needs to be done in identifying the sources of union wage increases in particular industries and over the American economy as a whole, it now appears to be a gross oversimplification and mischaracterization to assume that labor cartelization is the sole or even the dominant source of union wage increases in the American economy.

A BRIDGE BETWEEN THE UNION
AND NON–UNION MODELS?

WEINGARTEN RIGHTS IN THE NON–UNION WORKPLACE

The worker in the non-union workplace enjoys some legal protections, as you saw in Chapter One. Few of those statutory rights protect the worker's voice in the workplace. However, the NLRA confers the right to engage in concerted activity to workers who are not represented by a union. We saw that in Chapter One in the *Washington Aluminum* case, where the Court held that unrepresented workers were protected against discharge when they walked off the job to protest unreasonably cold conditions.

The NLRB recently issued a decision called *Epilepsy Foundation*, that gives workers in a non-union workplace the right to seek the help of a co-worker if the employer summons the worker to an investigation or interview about a matter that might lead to discipline. *Epilepsy Foundation* builds on a Supreme Court decision, *NLRB v. J. Weingarten*, 420 U.S. 251, 95 S.Ct. 959, 43 L.Ed.2d 171 (1975), which holds that employees in a unionized workplace are entitled to have their union representative present during a disciplinary interview or investigation. In either setting, union or not, if the employer doesn't want the representative to participate, it can do away with the interview altogether. Both *Weingarten* and *Epilepsy Foundation* say, simply, that if the employer insists on holding an investigatory interview it must allow the employee to have a representative if she chooses.

The *Epilepsy Foundation* decision follows, and it contains references to *Weingarten*. Do you think *Epilepsy Foundation* is a reasonable extension of *Weingarten*? Has the Board articulated an adequate rationale for the decision to be upheld in court? Will *Epilepsy Foundation* rights, if upheld by the courts, have any practical value for the unrepresented worker?

In our experience, the reality is that employers comply with *Weingarten* in the union sector by involving the union representative in the discussion, rather than by foregoing the interview altogether. The explanation is simple. If a worker in a unionized workplace is fired, she may challenge her discharge through binding arbitration under principles of just cause. The company wants to convince the arbitrator that it made a full investigation of the case, and the company will better accomplish this objective if it does not bypass the union representative. Some collective bargaining agreements may expressly allow for such representation, and some arbitrators may require it as an element of just cause. Further, because the union representative is experienced, he or she will often be able to resolve the matter during that interview. Will any of this happen in the non-union workplace?

EPILEPSY FOUNDATION OF NORTHEAST OHIO

National Labor Relations Board, 2000.
331 NLRB No. 92.

BY CHAIRMAN TRUESDALE AND MEMBERS FOX, LIEBMAN, HURTGEN, AND BRAME

Introduction

The General Counsel excepts to the [Administrative Law Judge's] finding that the Respondent did not violate Section 8(a)(1) of the Act by discharging employees Arnis Borgs and Ashraful Hasan. The General Counsel contends that both Borgs and Hasan were discharged for engaging in protected concerted activity. In arguing that the discharge of Borgs is unlawful, the General Counsel requests the Board to once again consider the question of whether the principles set forth by the Supreme Court in *NLRB v. J. Weingarten* should be extended to employees in nonunionized workplaces, to afford them the right to have a co-worker present at an investigatory interview which the employee reasonably believes might result in disciplinary action. The General Counsel contends that affording nonunionized employees this right is consistent with the Court's decision. We agree with the General Counsel's contentions, including those concerning *Weingarten*, and for the reasons set forth below, find that the discharges of both Borgs and Hasan are unlawful.

The Discharge of Arnis Borgs

The essential facts pertaining to Borgs' discharge are not in dispute. The Respondent provides services to persons affected by epilepsy. One of its programs involves a research project concerning school-to-work transition for teenagers with epilepsy. Borgs worked on this project as an employment specialist, and Ashraful Hasan was the Respondent's transition specialist on this project.

[Borgs and Hasan prepared a memo that was critical of their supervisor, Berger, and sent that memo to the Company's Executive Director, Loehrke. When Loehrke summoned Borgs to a meeting with her and Berger, Borgs requested that Hasan be present. Loehrke refused that request, and Borgs declined to meet with Loehrke and Berger.]

The following day, Borgs met with Loehrke and Jim Wilson, the Respondent's Director of Administration. Loehrke told Borgs that his refusal to meet the previous day constituted gross insubordination and that he was terminated. Loehrke then gave Borgs a letter of termination.

The judge found that the Respondent discharged Borgs for his persistent refusal to comply with Loehrke's directive to meet alone with her and Berger. The judge noted that, under *Weingarten*, employees in unionized work forces are entitled to representation in investigatory interviews which the employee reasonably believes could result in disciplinary action, but under current Board precedent, employees in nonunionized workplaces do not have the right to have a coworker present in similar circumstances, *E. I. DuPont & Co.*, 289 NLRB 627 (1988).

Accordingly, the judge found that Borgs had no statutory right to condition his attendance at the meeting on the presence of Hasan, and thus the Respondent's discharge of Borgs for refusing to attend the meeting did not violate Section 8(a)(1) of the Act.

We agree with the judge's finding that Borgs was discharged for refusing to attend the meeting with Loehrke and Berger. We also agree that the judge accurately applied the relevant Board precedent. After careful consideration, however, we find that precedent to be inconsistent with the rationale articulated in the Supreme Court's *Weingarten* decision, and with the purposes of the Act. Consequently, we shall overrule that precedent today and find that the Respondent's termination of Borgs for his attempt to have a coworker present at the meeting was unlawful.

Our examination of this issue begins with the Supreme Court's seminal *Weingarten* decision. There, as noted above, the Court held that an employer violated Section 8(a)(1) by denying an employee's request that a union representative be present at an investigatory interview which the employee reasonably believed might result in disciplinary action. The Court, in upholding the Board's finding of a violation, found that the employee's action in seeking representation in such circumstances "falls within the literal wording of Section 7 of the Act that '[e]mployees shall have the right ... to engage in ... concerted activities for the purpose of mutual aid or protection.'" The Court explained further as follows:

> The union representative whose participation he seeks is however safeguarding not only the particular employee's interest, but also the interests of the entire bargaining unit by exercising vigilance to

make certain that the employer does not initiate or continue a practice of imposing punishment unjustly.

Read together, these statements explain that the right to the presence of a representative is grounded in the rationale that the Act generally affords employees the opportunity to act together to address the issue of an employer's practice of imposing unjust punishment on employees.

Because the facts at issue in *Weingarten* involved a request for the presence of a union representative, the Court's decision did not specifically refer to circumstances involving the request for a coworker representative in nonunion settings. The Board, however, has addressed this precise issue on several occasions. In *Materials Research Corp.*, 262 NLRB 1010 (1982), the Board found that the *Weingarten* right includes the right to request the presence of a coworker at an investigatory interview in a nonunion setting. In that case, the Board relied on the fact that *Weingarten* emphasized that the right to the assistance of a representative is derived from the Section 7 protection afforded to concerted activity, rather than from a union's right pursuant to Section 9 to act as the employee's representative for the purpose of collective bargaining. Consequently, the Board found that the ability to avail oneself of this protection does not depend on whether the employees are represented by a union.

The Board overruled *Materials Research Corp.*, however, in *Sears, Roebuck & Co.*, 274 NLRB 230 (1985), and held there that *Weingarten* principles do not apply in circumstances where there is no certified or recognized union. In that case, the Board specifically rejected the prior decision's reliance on the fact that the *Weingarten* rights are based on Section 7, stating that "[t]he scope of Section 7's protections may vary depending on whether employees are represented or unrepresented...." The Board also expressed the view that extending *Weingarten* rights to employees not represented by a union is inconsistent with the Act because it infringes upon an employer's right to deal with employees on an individual basis when no union is present.

The Board modified the *Sears* rationale in *E. I. DuPont & Co.*, 289 NLRB 627 (1988). In that case, the Board adhered to its position that *Weingarten* rights are not applicable in nonunion settings, but acknowledged that "the statute might be amenable to other interpretations." Thus, the Board specifically disavowed *Sears* insofar as it held that the Act compels a finding that *Weingarten* rights are applicable only in unionized workplaces. The Board, however, declined to return to the rule of *Materials Research* for several reasons.* * *

We disagree with the Board's holdings in *Sears* and *Dupont*, and find that a return to the rule set forth in *Materials Research*, i.e., that *Weingarten* rights are applicable in the nonunionized workplace as well as the unionized workplace, is warranted. *Sears* and *Dupont* misconstrue the language of *Weingarten* and erroneously limit its applicability to the unionized workplace. In our view, the Board was correct in *Materials*

Research to attach much significance to the fact that the Court's *Weingarten* decision found that the right was grounded in the language of Section 7 of the Act, specifically the right to engage in "concerted activities for the purpose of mutual aid or protection." This rationale is equally applicable in circumstances where employees are not represented by a union, for in these circumstances the right to have a coworker present at an investigatory interview also greatly enhances the employees' opportunities to act in concert to address their concern "that the employer does not initiate or continue a practice of imposing punishment unjustly." Thus, affording *Weingarten* rights to employees in these circumstances effectuates the policy that "Section 7 rights are enjoyed by all employees and are in no wise dependent on union representation for their implementation." *Glomac Plastics, Inc.*, 234 NLRB 1309, 1311 (1978).

We find no merit to the contention raised in *Sears*, and subsequently disavowed in *Dupont*, that the imposition of *Weingarten* rights in these circumstances "wreaks havoc" with the provisions of the Act that enable an employer to deal with employees on an individual basis when no union is present. The Act clearly protects the right of employees—whether unionized or not—to act in concert for mutual aid or protection. Further, as noted above, the right to have a coworker present at the investigatory interview affords unrepresented employees the opportunity to act in concert to prevent a practice of unjust punishment. While an employer is generally free to deal with employees individually in the absence of union representation, an employer may not mask the obstruction of employee efforts to exercise Section 7 rights by asserting a right to deal on an individual basis. See generally, *Ontario Knife Co. v. NLRB*, 637 F.2d 840, 844–850 (2d Cir. 1980).

Member Brame contends that, by granting a nonunionized employee the right to have a coworker present in an investigatory interview, we are forcing the employer to "deal with" the equivalent of a labor organization, and that this conflicts with the exclusivity principle embodied in Section 9(a) of the Act. This contention was squarely addressed and soundly rejected by the Third Circuit Court of Appeals in *Slaughter v. NLRB*, 794 F.2d 120 (1986). * * *

In other words, even assuming that the role of an employee representative in an investigatory interview is equivalent to "dealing with" the employer, the argument advanced by Member Brame is irrelevant. "Dealing" is not equivalent to "collective bargaining," and the employer is not required to "bargain collectively" with the *Weingarten* representative. As the Third Circuit held, the Section 9(a) exclusivity principle does not limit the Section 7 rights of nonunionized employees.* * *

We also find that the concerns raised by the Board in *Dupont* do not warrant allowing an employer to prohibit the exercise of *Weingarten* rights in nonunionized workplaces. Specifically, we take issue with *Dupont's* reliance on the notions that the coworker has "no obligation" to represent the interests of fellow employees, and that the nonunionized coworker is less likely to have the skills necessary to provide representation comparable to that provided by a shop steward or some other union representative. The notion that employees in such circumstances would not be motivated to act in the interests of their fellow workers, or that employees might lack the abilities to offer constructive assistance to the interviewed employee, is wholly speculative. It also misses the point that the employee is free to choose whether to request or forego representation. What is important is the availability of the option. Moreover, Section 7 rights do not turn on either the skills or the motives of the employee's representative. Thus, these supposed concerns do not legitimately warrant foreclosing employees from the opportunity to avail themselves of the protections of the Act.

We also cannot agree with the statement in *Dupont* that extending *Weingarten* rights to the nonunion workplace will actually work to the detriment of employees by encouraging employers to forego the investigatory interview and thus leave the aggrieved employee without an opportunity to tell his or her side of the story. This too is based wholly on speculation, and assumes the worst in employer motives. In addition, such rationale ignores the fact that employees are not *obligated* to request the presence of a *Weingarten* representative, and—as in the unionized workplace—can freely evaluate the strategic merits of any particular course of action in this regard.* * *

Accordingly, for all these reasons, we find that by discharging Arnis Borgs for demanding that a coworker accompany him at an investigatory interview, the Respondent violated Section 8(a)(1) of the Act as alleged.

SOME OBSERVATIONS AND QUESTIONS TO GUIDE YOU THROUGH THIS CHAPTER

In this set of stories and articles about the workplace, we have sketched for you two competing visions of workplace governance. We have deliberately used the word "governance," not "participation," because we want to pay attention to how much control rather than mere input workers actually have.

As you read these materials, you should start to think about the workplace values that a civilized society should embrace. What do workers have a right to expect from their employers? What do employers have a right to expect in return? Then, as you study the various models and stories, ask yourself whether each satisfies your criteria for a just workplace.

For example, how important is it that a program of workplace governance put the worker and management on an equal footing? Which of the examples accomplishes this? Are workers sufficiently empowered under these systems that they can achieve the goals they think important, or is it up to management to decide what may be done? What assurances does each system give that the benefits that are promised employees will be delivered? What makes sure that management will listen sympathetically to the opinions of its workers? How important is it for workers to have a form of ownership? How critical is information sharing?

Does the system insure that those with special needs are not submerged by a larger majority? For example, a disabled worker may require a transfer to a different job as an accommodation. But that may go against a seniority system that awards those jobs on the basis of longevity rather than need. Does the system take account of a variety of worker interests? Does the system protect workers from reprisals for stating strong opinions?

In the succeeding sections of this chapter we will identify certain areas of workplace governance where we can compare the approaches of the two systems in securing the goals we value. These topics include how the relationship between worker and management is established, how inclusive its coverage is of employees, whether it leaves out employees who ought to have a role in governance, how it draws lines between the managers and the managed and whether it perpetuates or breaks down those distinctions, what rights employees have to speak without reprisal, how discussions between workers and management are structured and channeled, how rights are established and secured, including rights that arise from various statutes, and how economic forces may be used to obtain and enforce rights.

A detailed set of rules has developed for worker participation in the unionized sector, mostly as a result of some 60 years of experience under the National Labor Relations Act, the principal statute that regulates collective bargaining. There is very little law governing the worker in a non union setting, much less providing a systematic way for those workers to have their voices heard.

As you read these materials, you will notice from time to time reference to the decline in the number of workers who are represented by unions. While unions once represented more than 30% of the work-force, the percentage of union representation today is in the low teens at best, and much of it is in the public sector, where there is usually less resistance by the employer to unionization. Lots of reasons are given for this decline, and nobody seems to be able to measure the precise causes. Some suggest that the NLRA is not enforced with enough vigor to protect employees in organizing campaigns and in the enforcement of their collective agreements; others say that in a highly competitive economy a union can do little to enhance employees' wages and conditions, so unionization is futile and even counter productive; some of us will argue that in today's culture of individual achievement the idea of group support is unappealing. You will have to come up with your own answers as we go along. Whatever the causes, it is important to remember that given the low density (that's the buzz word) of union representation, society cannot rely exclusively on unions and the law governing collective bargaining to secure the workplace values it thinks important.

2. DOES THE LAW DISCOURAGE INFORMAL WORKER REPRESENTATION?

The Impact of Section 8(a)(2)

Nan is discouraged about the prospects of unionization, because she thinks it is a very divisive process that can be long and drawn out. The union does not seem to enjoy overwhelming worker support at Mercy Hospital, and Nan thinks that if the union loses the election there will be long standing divisions among those employees who support the union and who oppose it. She asks Paul for more information about the Quality Care Circles that Director of Personnel McClean is pushing.

> *Nan:* Is the Quality Care Circle model really a realistic possibility now that we have an organizing drive under way?

> *Paul:* If there is a union in the picture seeking representation, it is virtually impossible for you to set up a non union system of employee representation. The problem is Section 8(a)(2) of the NLRA, which says the employer may not "dominate or interfere with the formation or administration of any labor organization." Section 2(5) defines "labor organization" quite broadly, and focuses on the concept of "dealing with employers," a term that takes in a wider range of activity than what is covered by the technical term "bargaining." Taking all this together, your quality circle arrangement would be viewed as employer domination of a labor organization, even though you might not think of yourself as part of a union.

> *Nan:* What's the point of that provision of the law? Doesn't it go against what everyone is trying to do these days?

> *Paul:* Some people agree with you on that. Section 8(a)(2) appeared in the original Act as a response to company unions, an arrangement in which the company would install a weak union, sympathetic to management's needs, in an effort to forestall formation of a stronger union. It is sometimes called a "sweetheart" union. Bernstein describes that in his wonderful book, *The Lean Years*. I have a section for you to look at. Many argue that the modern worker participation systems are merely old wine in new bottles, and the law should still prevent them.

IRVING BERNSTEIN, THE LEAN YEARS: A HISTORY OF THE AMERICAN WORKER

pp. 163–164 (Penguin Books Inc. 1960).

In 1924 the Russell Sage Foundation published an exhaustive investigation of the plan. Failings in the wage area, of course, received emphasis. The responsibility of employee representatives for grievances was found to be "uncertain and variable." Representatives, fearing discharge, seldom pressed complaints. "Many of the miners' representatives were timid, untrained, and ill-prepared to argue the grievances of the miners...." Interest in the plan among the men, never great, declined over the years and the company had to resort to pressure to get even half of them to vote in elections. The tangible gains made were in welfare: medical care, housing, schools, churches, and recreation facilities. But this was entirely due to the initiative of management. "Neither in the written plan nor in practice do the employees' representatives have responsibility for decisions." As the study concluded, "The experiment which Mr. King planned and which Mr. Rockefeller has ... so effectively interpreted ... is as yet incomplete.... An 'industrial constitution' ... it has not yet become."

The Rockefeller Plan at CF & I, launched with such good intentions, was destined never to become anything more than a halfway house. It limped through the twenties. In 1933, in one of the first free elections conducted by the National Labor Board under Section 7(a), the miners voted 877 to 273 for the UMW over the representation plan. Late that year CF & I abandoned the Rockefeller Plan and negotiated its first genuine collective bargaining agreement with the United Mine Workers of America.

Although the employee-representation plan had little success with the coal miners in Colorado, its sponsor's philosophy and policies were to have a great impact upon management thinking in the twenties. Rockefeller, at the expense of a personal aversion to public appearances, conscientiously broadcast his ideas, speaking to audiences of the YMCA, the universities, the Chamber of Commerce, as well as to congressional committees and President Wilson's industrial conference. In his own mind he was merely applying his deep-seated Christian principles to the employer-employee relation. Rockefeller urged that "every man is his brother's keeper," that there exists in industry as elsewhere a "kinship of humanity," that "right principles ... effect right relations," that "the letter killeth but the spirit giveth life." Employer spokesmen in the twenties followed him in laying stress upon the Christian ethic.

The heart of the Rockefeller philosophy was what he labeled "human relations," understanding by managers that their employees were "human beings" and by workmen that managers and investors were "also human beings." Conflict, as he saw it, was both undesirable and wicked. He found it "wantonly wasteful"; both parties and the innocent public were losers. "To say that there is no way out except through constant warfare between Labor and Capital is an unthinkable counsel of despair."

The alternative in his view was a "harmony of interests," that employer and employee must "join hands and recognize that their interest is a common interest." Each was indispensable to the other in the development and sharing of the earth's riches. "Co-operation of Labor and Capital may well be regarded ... as the most vital problem of modern civilization."

Since he assumed "the fundamental fairness of men's purposes," the major impediment to achieving harmony was poor communication. "When men get together and talk over their differences candidly, much of the ground for dispute vanishes." In an earlier era enterprise was so small that direct contact between employer and employee was inescapable. Large industry, however, "has of necessity erected barriers ... thus making it more difficult for them to understand each other." Since human needs had not changed with advancing technology, it was necessary to devise machinery to improve communication. The means lay in the more perfect organization of capital and labor. The former organized itself in the corporation; the latter was to be organized in employee representation, the company union. Whether the trade union could serve the same purpose was uncertain. Although Rockefeller never spoke in derogation of organized labor, he carefully omitted it from his scheme of a better industrial society.

———

Nan: But why worry about these things? What harm is done if that's what employees want? Can't employees replace a sweetheart union with a real one if they are dissatisfied?

Paul: It is very hard to dislodge a union that is already in place, because Board law provides for an election to take place only at limited times. If a new union comes along to seek representation, or if an individual seeks to decertify a union, an existing collective bargaining agreement will serve as a bar to a new election for up to three years, except during a very brief window in which a rival union can file a challenge. Sec. 8(a)(2) does have the salutary effect of knocking out the sweetheart union as a bar to an election. In the face of a current union drive, I don't think the Hospital is going to take the trouble to set up professional circles, because that will invite a Sec. 8(a)(2) Charge. Further, if there is an election, and the Hospital wins, the union will point to the existence of the professional circles as an unlawful act that affected the outcome of the election. This could result in setting aside the election and starting all over. If the Hospital does beat the union in the election, it doesn't want to have its victory knocked out and have to start all over with another election, so it won't take a chance on setting up these circles now.

But if there were no prospect of a union election, the Hospital might be a little more willing to take a chance on a worker participation system, because the Act doesn't provide any real remedy or any real deterrent against a violation of Sec. 8(a)(2). I'd face a real ethical dilemma, though, if an employer asked me if it was okay to set up an employee participation program and I knew it violated Sec. 8(a)(2). Would I tell the employer to go ahead anyway, since there are no real consequences, unless another union happens to be in the picture?

Let me show you what is currently the Board's latest word on how Sec. 8(a)(2) works. The Board decided a series of 8(a)(2) cases, the most well known of which is the first one, called Electromation. The Board cases on 8(a)(2) are awfully long-winded, and I thought you'd get a better idea of the issues by looking at the Court of Appeals case that upheld Electromation. Of course, as you'll see in Electromation, the Supreme Court visited this question years ago in a case called Cabot Carbon, which focused on the definition of a "labor organization" and on the term "dealing with" in Section 2(5) of the Act, and that sort of set the course for the Board decisions.

ELECTROMATION, INC. v. NLRB

United States Court of Appeals, Seventh Circuit, 1994.
35 F.3d 1148.

WILL, DISTRICT JUDGE.

In this appeal, we consider a petition to set aside and a cross-petition to enforce an order of the National Labor Relations Board (the "NLRB" or "Board"), which found that the petitioner employer, Electromation, Inc. (the "company"), violated Section 8(a)(2) and (1) of the National Labor Relations Act (the "Act") through its establishment and administration of "action committees" consisting of employees and management. Believing that this case potentially raised the rather novel and important issue whether modern "employee involvement" or "employee participation" organizations are unlawful under Section 8(a)(2) and (1) of the Act, numerous amici have filed supporting and opposing briefs in this appeal. * * * As explained below, we find it unnecessary to address this much broader issue. For the reasons stated, we simply order that the Board's order in this case be enforced.

I.

BACKGROUND

Electromation manufactures at its plant in Elkhart, Indiana, small electrical and electronic components and related products, such as seat belt restraint solenoids, solenoids for outboard engines and chainsaws, switches and harnesses, primarily for the automobile industry and for power equipment manufacturers. At the time of the events, which gave rise to this suit, Electromation's approximately 200 employees, most of whom were women, were not represented by any labor organization. To minimize the financial losses it was experiencing at the time, the company in late 1988 decided to cut expenses by revising its employee attendance policy and replacing the 1989 scheduled wage increases with lump sum payments based on the length of each employee's service at the company. Electromation informed its employees of these changes at the 1988 employee Christmas party.

In January 1989, the company received a handwritten request signed by 68 employees expressing their dissatisfaction with and requesting reconsideration of the revised attendance bonus/wage policy. After meeting with the company's supervisors, the company President, John Howard, decided to meet directly with employees to discuss their concerns. Accordingly, on January 11, 1989, the company met with eight employees—three randomly selected high-seniority employees, three randomly selected low-seniority employees, and two additional employees who had requested that they be included—to discuss a number of matters, including wages, bonuses, incentive pay, tardiness, attendance programs, and bereavement and sick leave policy, all normal collective bargaining issues.

Following this meeting, Howard met again with the supervisors and concluded that management had "possibly made a mistake in judgment in December in deciding what we ought to do." Because Howard concluded that "it was very unlikely that further unilateral management action to resolve these problems was going to come anywhere near making everybody happy ... [and] that the better course of action would be to involve the employees in coming up with solutions to these issues," the company determined that "action committees" would be an appropriate way to involve employees in the process. Accordingly, on January 18, 1989, the company met again with the same eight employees and Howard explained that the management had distilled the employees' complaints, which had addressed approximately 20–25 areas of concern, into five categories and proposed the creation of action committees to "meet and try to come up with ways to resolve these problems; and that if they came up with solutions that ... we believed were within budget concerns and they generally felt would be acceptable to the employees, that we would implement these suggestions or proposals. * * * "

[While employee reaction to the committees was initially negative, the employees ultimately agreed to participate. The company set up five action committees, and selected employees to serve on them. All committees meetings took place on company time. The company provided necessary supplies]

On February 13, 1989, the International Brotherhood of Teamsters, Local Union No. 1049 (the "union") demanded recognition from the company. Until then, the company was unaware that any organizing efforts had occurred at the plant. In late February, Howard informed Dickey of the union's demand for recognition. Upon the advice of counsel, Dickey announced at the next meeting of each committee that, due to the union demand, the company could no longer participate in the committees, but that the employee members could continue to meet if they so desired. * * *

The union election took place on March 31, 1989; the employees voted 95 to 82 against union representation. On April 24, 1989, a regional director of the Board issued a complaint alleging that Electromation had violated the Act. * * *

The Board issued its final Decision and Order on December 17, 1992. The Board also found that the action committees constituted labor organizations within the meaning of Section 2(5) of the Act, and that the company had dominated and assisted them within the meaning of Section 8(a)(2) and (1). Specifically, the Board determined that the only purpose of the committees, which were created in direct response to employee disaffection concerning changes in conditions of employment, was to deal with those conditions through a bilateral process involving both employees and management. * * *

The Board also concluded that the employee committee members acted in a representational capacity within the meaning of the Act. Noting that (1) the employer initiated the idea to create the committees, (2) the employer unilaterally drafted the written purposes and goals statements of the committees, (3) the employer unilaterally determined how many members would compose each committee and that an employee could serve on only one committee at a time, and (4) the employer appointed management representatives to the committees to facilitate the discussions, the Board found that the company had violated Section 8(a)(2) and (1) of the Act by dominating the formation and administration of, and contributing financial and other support to, the action committees. In support of its findings, the Board also noted that the employer permitted the employees to conduct committee activities on paid time within a structure wholly designed by the employer.

The Board concluded on this evidence that the committees were the creation of the employer and * * * that the company did not effectively disestablish the committees upon receipt of the union's bargaining demand. The Board found that the purpose of the action committees was not to enable management and employees to cooperate to improve quality or efficiency, but rather to create in employees the impression that their disagreements with management had been resolved bilaterally, where in fact the employer had imposed on its employees a unilateral form of bargaining in violation of Sections 8(a)(2) and (1). [Two members of the Board wrote separate opinions]. * * *

II.

STANDARD OF REVIEW

* * * We must uphold the Board's determinations if its factual findings are supported by substantial evidence and its legal conclusions have a reasonable basis in the law. * * *

We must also consider whether the Board's construction of the Act is reasonable in light of its language and purposes, as determined by controlling decisions of the Supreme Court.

In reaching our determination in this case, we recall the Supreme Court's observation in *Beth Israel Hospital v. NLRB,* 437 U.S. 483, 500–

01, (1978) (citation omitted): "[i]t is the Board on which Congress conferred the authority to develop and apply fundamental national labor policy. . . . 'The function of striking [the balance between conflicting legitimate interests] to effectuate national labor policy is often a difficult and delicate responsibility, which the Congress committed primarily to the National Labor Relations Board, subject to limited judicial review.'"

III.

Discussion

As several *amici* have pointed out, in an effort to succeed in an increasingly competitive global marketplace, many United States companies have developed employee involvement structures which encourage employee participation in the design of workplace policies and procedures to improve the efficiency and effectiveness of the corporate organization and to create a workplace environment which is satisfactory to employees. These employee participation programs are premised on management's recognition that employees are capable of contributing far more to their companies than the mere performance of tasks assigned to them by the management.

We recognize the growing importance of such employee involvement organizations. In fact, we applaud the application of such employee participation structures in appropriate situations. Because the Board found no basis to conclude that the purposes of the action committees were limited to achieving increased productivity, quality, or efficiency, or that they were designed to function solely as communication devices to promote generally the interests of quality or efficiency, it did not reach the question of whether employer-initiated programs that exist for such purposes, as described by amici, may constitute labor organizations which violate Section 8(a)(2) and (1). * * *

The Board reasonably and properly declined to attempt to issue an opinion addressing all possible employee involvement programs. Rather, exercising its discretion to construe the Act in light of the legislative history, applicable Supreme Court precedent, and the underlying policies of the Act, the Board found that the company's actions here fell within the statutory proscriptions and did not implicate changing industrial realities that might be relevant to construction of the statute in other circumstances. * * *

Instead, it simply observed that it does not have latitude to change a particular construction of the statute based on changing industrial realities where congressional intent to the contrary is absolutely clear, or where the Supreme Court has decreed that a particular reading of the statute is required, or both. Nor was it necessary to do so in this case.

There are some serious policy arguments that suggest that today's evolving industrial environment may require reconsideration of Section 8(a)(2) of the Act, or at least its interpretation and application to certain modern employee organizations. However, this case fails to provide the proper forum for such re-analysis and re-interpretation. In any event, any substantial changes should more properly be considered by Congress. *See, e.g.,* H.R. 1529 (Representative Steven Gunderson, R–WI).* * * We emphasize that our reasoning and ruling in this case is limited to the action committees, which are at issue here. It is clear that a finding of a Section 8(a)(2) and (1) violation in this case does not foreclose the lawful use of legitimate employee participation organizations, especially those which are independent, which do not function in a representational capacity, and which focus solely on increasing company productivity, efficiency, and quality control, in appropriate settings. We agree with amici that the loss of these programs would not only be injurious to United States companies' ability to compete globally, but also that it would deprive employees of valuable mechanisms by which they can assist in the formation of a healthy and productive work environment. * * *

An allegation that Electromation has violated Section 8(a)(2) and (1) of the Act raises two distinct issues: first, whether the action committees in this case constituted "labor organizations" within the meaning of Section 2(5); and second, whether the employer dominated, influenced, or interfered with the formation or administration of the organization or contributed financial or other support to it, in violation of Section 8(a)(2) and (1) of the Act. Each issue will be examined in turn.

A. *The Action Committees Constituted Labor Organizations*

Section 2(5) of the Act defines a labor organization as:

> any organization of any kind, or any agency or employee representation committee or plan, in which employees participate and which exists for the purpose, in whole or in part, of dealing with employers concerning grievances, labor disputes, wages, rates of pay, hours of employment, or conditions of work.

29 U.S.C. § 152(5). Under this statutory definition, the action committees would constitute labor organizations if: (1) the Electromation employees participated in the committees; (2) the committees existed, at least in part, for the purpose of "dealing with" the employer; and (3) these dealings concerned "grievances, labor disputes, wages, rates of pay, hours of employment, or conditions of work."

In reaching its decision in this case, the Board also noted that "if the organization has as a purpose the representation of employees, it meets the statutory definition of 'employee representation committee or plan' under Section 2(5) and will constitute a labor organization if it also meets the criteria of employee participation and dealing with conditions of work or other statutory subjects." Because the Board found that the employee members of the action committees had acted in a representational capacity, it did not decide whether an employee group could ever be found to constitute a labor organization in the absence of a finding that it acted as a representative of the other employees. * * *

With respect to the first factor, there is no question that the Electromation employees participated in the action committees. Turning to the second factor, which is the most seriously contested on appeal, the Board found that the activities of the action committees constituted "dealing with" the employer.* * * The company argues in favor of a narrow construction of "labor organization" under the Act. However, as the Board noted, Congress phrased the statutory definition of labor organizations "very broadly." *See* S.Rep. No. 573, 74th Cong., 1st Sess. 7 (1935), *reprinted in* 2 NLRB, *Legislative History of the National Labor Relations Act, 1935* at 2306 (1959, reprinted 1985) (hereinafter "*NLRA Leg. Hist.*"). * * *

Moreover, an organization may satisfy the statutory requirement that it exist for the purpose in whole or in part of dealing with employers even if it has not engaged in actual bargaining or concluded a bargaining agreement. *NLRB v. Cabot Carbon Co.,* 360 U.S. 203, 210–14, (1959).

In *Cabot Carbon,* the Supreme Court expressly rejected the contention that "dealing with" means "bargaining with," noting that Congress had declined to accept a proposal to substitute the phrase "bargaining with" for "dealing with" under Section 2(5). * * *

Relying in large part on these principles, the Board here explained that "dealing with" is a bilateral mechanism involving proposals from the employee organization concerning the subjects listed in Section 2(5), coupled with real or apparent consideration of those proposals by management. While the Board further suggested that unilateral mechanisms such as suggestion boxes, brainstorming conferences, and other information exchanges do not constitute dealing, it is not necessary for us to reach that question.

Given the Supreme Court's holding in *Cabot Carbon* that "dealing with" includes conduct much broader than collective bargaining, the Board did not err in determining that the Electromation action committees constituted labor organizations within the meaning of Sections 2(5) and 8(a)(2) of the Act.* * *

B.   *The Company Violated Section 8(a)(2) and (1) of the Act*

Having concluded that each of the action committees constituted a labor organization under Section 2(5) of the Act, we must next consider whether, through their creation and administration of the action committees, the company acted unlawfully in violation of Section 8(a)(2) and (1) of the Act.

Section 8(a)(2) declares that it shall be an unfair labor practice for an employer:

> to dominate or interfere with the formation or administration of any labor organization or contribute financial or other support to it: *Provided,* That subject to rules and regulations made and published by the Board pursuant to [Section 6], an employer shall not be prohibited from permitting employees to confer with him during working hours without loss of time or pay.
> * * *

Electromation argues that the Board wrongly interpreted Section 8(a)(2) solely from the perspective of an employer's conduct and incorrectly attempted to develop an objective list of employer actions which constitute illegal domination or interference under the Act. According to the company, the Board's ruling in this case implies that an employer violates Section 8(a)(2) whenever it proposes a structure whereby the employees and employer "cooperate," or meet together to discuss topics of mutual concern. Electromation observes that Congress enacted Section 8(a)(2) primarily to ensure that employees remain free to decide for themselves how to deal with their employer, and reasons that the proper focus of that section should therefore be the subjective will of the employees against their preference. The company thus asserts that the Board may find a violation of Section 8(a)(2) only where it finds that the employer has actually undermined the free and independent choice of the employees.* * *

1. *Statutory Construction*

Both sides concede that the analysis of Section 8(a)(2) cannot be limited to the statutory language since its terms are not all self-defining. However, the company argues that the statutory language of Section 8(a)(2) supports its contention that the proper focus of the Board's inquiry should be the subjective will of the employees. * * *

Relying especially on the proviso, the company argues that, in adopting Section 8(a)(2), Congress plainly did not mean to prohibit all contacts or cooperation between employers and employees. Without a doubt, this is true. However, * * * the Board found that the activities of the company in this case constituted more than mere cooperation. ("There can be no doubt that the Respondent's conduct vis a vis the Action Committees constituted 'domination' in their formation and administration.... [The] employees essentially were presented with the Hobson's choice of accepting the status quo, which they disliked, or undertaking a bilateral 'exchange of ideas' within the framework of the Action Committees, as presented by the Respondent."). * * *

2. *Legislative History*

The Board found that the legislative history * * * supports its interpretation and application of Section 8(a)(2) to the facts of this case. We agree. While it is true that the thrust of Section 8(a)(2) is designed to protect the free will of the employees, the legislative history reveals that the coverage of that section is broad indeed. As Senator Wagner emphasized throughout the Senate's deliberations on the Act, "[c]ollective bargaining becomes a sham when the employer sits on both sides of the table or pulls the strings behind the spokesman of those with whom he is dealing."

Moreover, the legislative history reflects that Congress was well aware of both the usefulness and the popularity of employee committees at the time that it drafted the provisions of the Wagner Act. Before enacting the Wagner Act, Congress heard extensive testimony from employees who expressed great satisfaction with their employee representation plans and committees.

Congress nonetheless enacted a broad proscription of employer conduct in Section 8(a)(2).* * *

3. *Congressional Policies*

In further support of its position, the company identifies two congressional policies underlying Section 8(a)(2): first, the protection of employees' freedom of choice; and second, the promotion of cooperation between employers and employees. We agree that both constitute legitimate goals of this section. Electromation argues that no violation of Section 8(a)(2) can be found based on "mere cooperation" between employer and employee. Indeed, as we observed in *Chicago Rawhide Mfg. Co. v. NLRB,* 221 F.2d 165, 167 (7th Cir.1955): A line must be drawn ... between support and cooperation. Support, even though innocent, can be identified because it constitutes at least some degree of control or influence. Cooperation only assists the employees or their bargaining representatives in carrying out their independent intention. If this line between cooperation and support is not recognized, the employer's fear of accusations of domination may defeat the principal purpose of the Act, which is cooperation between management and labor. * * *

[The court then discusses and distinguishes cases that found the arrangement was merely cooperative, and not a violation of the Act.]

The company played a pivotal role in establishing both the framework and the agenda for the action committees. Electromation unilaterally selected the size, structure, and procedural functioning of the committees; it decided the number of committees and the topic(s) to be addressed by each. The company unilaterally drafted the action committees' purposes and goal statements, which identified from the start the focus of each committee's work. Also, as was pointed out during oral argument, despite the fact that the employees were seriously concerned about the lack of a wage increase, no action committee was designated to consider this specific issue. In this way, Electromation actually controlled which issues received attention by the committees and which did not.

Although the company acceded to the employees' request that volunteers form the committees, it unilaterally determined how many could serve on each committee, decided that an employee could serve on only one committee at a time, and determined which committee certain employees would serve on, thus exercising significant control over the employees' participation and voice at the committee meetings. * * *

Also, the company designated management representatives to serve on the committees. Employee Benefits Manager Dickey was assigned to coordinate and serve on all committees. * * *

Finally, the company paid the employees for their time spent on committee activities, provided meeting space, and furnished all necessary supplies for the committees' activities. While such financial support is clearly not a violation of Section 8(a)(2) by itself, in the totality of the circumstances in this case such support may reasonably be characterized to be in furtherance of the company's domination of the action committees. We therefore conclude that there is substantial evidence to support the Board's finding of unlawful employer domination and interference in violation of Section 8(a)(2) and (1).

IV.

CONCLUSION

The Supreme Court has explained that domination of a labor organization exists where the employer controls the form and structure of a labor organization such that the employees are deprived of complete freedom and independence of action as guaranteed to them by Section 7 of the Act, and that the principal distinction between an independent labor organization and an employer-dominated organization lies in the unfettered power of the independent organization to determine its own actions. The Electromation action committees, which were wholly created by the employer, whose continued existence depended upon the employer, and whose functions were essentially determined by the employer, lacked the independence of action and free choice guaranteed by Section 7.* * * Even assuming they acted from good intentions, their procedure in establishing the committees, their control of the subject matters to be considered or excluded, their membership and participation on the committees, and their financial support of the committees all combined to make the committees labor organizations dominated by the employer in violation of the Act.

Accordingly, because we find that substantial evidence supports the Board's factual findings and that its legal conclusions have a reasonable basis in the law, we affirm the Board's findings and enforce the Board's order.

ENFORCED.

Note that the issue of dealing with an employee group in a workplace in which there is already a recognized union raises additional issues under Section 8(a)(5) of the Act. Much of the analysis is the same as under 8(a)(2), since the employer must clear that hurdle as well. The Board treated this issue in E.I. du Pont de Nemours & Co., 311 NLRB 893, 143 LRRM 1121, 1993 WL 191471 (1993).

Nan: I would think such committees are extremely valuable in non union settings and ought to be allowed. We certainly have had such arrangements in hospital settings. The law seems to be foolish on this question. Can anything be done to change it?

Paul: Well, first of all the current Board approach seems inconsistent with some of the ideas under another federal statute, the Occupational Safety and Health Act (OSHA). That statute relies heavily upon employee involvement in securing a safe workplace. For example, OSHA Sec. 8 provides for inspections of workplaces by the Secretary of Labor. Subpart (3) of Sec. 8 requires the employer to monitor the exposure of employees to toxic substances, and gives "employees or their representatives" the opportunity to observe this monitoring and grants them access to the records of the monitoring. This seems to mean that in a non-union setting, Congress is content to give employees a significant role in making sure they aren't exposed to toxic substances.

By the same token, the outgoing OSHA administration in the last year of the Clinton presidency, in 2000, promulgated a standard that would deal with ergonomic hazards in the workplace. That standard required employers to have ergonomics programs in place that would identify and correct ergonomic hazards. The employer was required to ensure employee participation in the program. Employees and their representatives had to be given ways to promptly report ergonomics hazards, and "have ways to be involved in the development, implementation, and evaluation of your ergonomics program." "Employee representative" was defined to be, "where appropriate, a recognized or certified collective bargaining agent." This is all found in 65 FR 50017 and 29 CFR Part 1911, especially 1910.900. The standard was rescinded by a Republican Congress in 2001, but the lessons are instructive. The Agency, interpreting the will of Congress, thought that employee participation was essential to protect workers' health and safety. Where a union was in place, the agency gave the baton of worker representation to the existing unions. But where there was no union, the OSHA regulations appeared to contemplate some system of employee representation anyway. So there is a tension between the approach of the NLRA and OSHA on worker representation in the non union workplace.

STATUTORY REFORM?

In 1995 Congress enacted something called the TEAM Act, a nice acronym for a statute that would have allowed a certain degree of employee participation under Section 8(a)(2). The key provision was that employee participation programs would be allowed as long as the organization in question did not purport to actually bargain with the employer. President Clinton vetoed the proposed amendment.

THE "SATURN" ADVICE MEMO AND
BERNHARD–ALTMANN

In the next few pages we set out an abbreviated version of Bernhard–Altman, a Supreme Court case on premature recognition, and then excerpts from the Saturn Advice Memo, which shows you how and why the Board's General Counsel was prepared to conclude that the Saturn arrangement did not violate the Act. The analysis rests in part upon an ingenious argument that GM and the UAW were engaged in "impact bargaining" to protect displaced workers from the impact of closing down existing plants in order to shift work to the new Saturn facility. In reality, the decision may reflect the Administration's reluctance to interfere with a bold experiment that might heighten American competitiveness. In between the two decisions we present two articles on employee representation.

Bear in mind that the Saturn arrangement was set up "top down" in a deal between General Motors and the UAW. It was not a cooperative arrangement of the sort that is normally challenged under Section 8(a)(2). One may conclude that there is a bit of hypocrisy here—the law may allow worker participation programs, but only when they are union-driven.

The Board document that you will read with reference to Saturn is known as an "advice memorandum." Under the Board's rules, when a party files a Charge, as some objecting groups did in the Saturn situation, the Board doesn't proceed to a hearing until it determines that the Charge has possible merit. This initial screening is done by the Board's General Counsel. The General Counsel is an independent branch of the agency, entirely separate from the Board, which performs an adjudicatory function. The determination not to proceed is entirely unreviewable in the courts, for this is an exercise of the General Counsel's administrative discretion. So the bottom line is that when the General Counsel determines that the hiring arrangement in Saturn doesn't violate Section 8(a)(2), that's it. There is no procedure for the courts to determine that the General Counsel is wrong.

The Saturn advice memo has a section on "Premature Recognition," in which the General Counsel does an end run around the rule that a company may not grant recognition before a majority of the workers actually select the union to represent them. The Saturn memo rewrites the GM–UAW agreement to require that before recognition is actually granted, a majority of the workers must sign authorization cards designating the union to represent them. The memo builds on a Board case called Kroger, Co., which in turn is based on the key Supreme Court case on this subject, ILGWU v. NLRB, 366 U.S. 731, 81 S.Ct. 1603, 6 L.Ed.2d 762 (1961) (known among cognoscenti and referred to earlier as Bernhard–Altmann).

In Bernhard–Altmann, the union was conducting an organizing drive. While it was attempting to gain employee support, a group of workers went out on strike to protest a wage reduction. The strike was not related to the union organizing campaign. However, the pressure of the strike was enough to drive the employer to negotiate a "memorandum of understanding" with the union that would end the strike and lead to a final collective bargaining agreement. The parties mistakenly believed that the union at the time of the memo of understanding had obtained authorization cards from a majority of the workers. The union did in fact have such a majority when it finally signed a collective bargaining agreement a few weeks later. The Court concluded that the collective agreement was invalid because it was the product of recognition of a union that did not enjoy majority support at the time. Here is the heart of the Court's opinion:

INTERNATIONAL LADIES' GARMENT WORKERS' UNION v. NATIONAL LABOR RELATIONS BOARD

Supreme Court of the United States, 1961.
366 U.S. 731, 81 S.Ct. 1603, 6 L.Ed.2d 762..

On October 10, 1957, a formal collective bargaining agreement, embodying the terms of the August 30 memorandum, was signed by the parties. The bargaining unit description set out in the formal contract, although more specific, conformed to that contained in the prior memorandum. It is not disputed that as of execution of the formal contract the union in fact represented a clear majority of employees in the appropriate unit. In upholding the complaints filed against the employer and union by the General Counsel, the Board decided that the employer's good-faith belief that the union in fact represented a majority of employees in the unit on the critical date of the memorandum of understanding was not a defense, 'particularly where, as here, the Company made no effort to check the authorization cards against its payroll records.' Noting that the union was 'actively seeking recognition at the time such recognition was granted,' and that 'the Union was (not) the passive recipient of an unsolicited gift bestowed by the Company,' the Board found that the union's execution of the August 30 agreement was a 'direct deprivation' of the nonconsenting majority employees' organizational and bargaining rights. Accordingly, the Board ordered the employer to withhold all recognition from the union and to cease giving effect to agreements entered into with the union; the union was ordered to cease acting as bargaining representative of any of the employees until such time as a Board conducted election demonstrated its majority status, and to refrain from seeking to enforce the agreements previously entered.* * *

At the outset, we reject as without relevance to our decision the fact that, as of the execution date of the formal agreement on October 10, petitioner represented a majority of the employees. As the Court of Appeals indicated, the recognition of the minority union on August 30, 1957, was 'a fait accompli depriving the majority of the employees of

their guaranteed right to choose their own representative.' It is, therefore, of no consequence that petitioner may have acquired by October 10
the necessary majority if, during the interim, it was acting unlawfully.
Indeed, such acquisition of majority status itself might indicate that the
recognition secured by the August 30 agreement afforded petitioner a
deceptive cloak of authority with which to persuasively elicit additional
employee support.* * *

In their selection of a bargaining representative, Sec. 9(a) of the
Wagner Act guarantees employees freedom of choice and majority rule.
J. I. Case Co. v. National Labor Relations Board, 321 U.S. 332, 339. In
short, as we said in *Brooks v. National Labor Relations Board, 348 U.S.
96, 103,* the Act placed 'a nonconsenting minority under the bargaining
responsibility of an agency selected by a majority of the workers.' Here,
however, the reverse has been shown to be the case. Bernhard–Altmann
granted exclusive bargaining status to an agency selected by a minority
of its employees, thereby impressing that agent upon the nonconsenting
majority. There could be no clearer abridgment of Sec. 7 of the Act,
assuring employees the right 'to bargain collectively through representatives of their own choosing' or 'to refrain from' such activity. It follows,
without need of further demonstration, that the employer activity found
present here violated Sec. 8(a)(1) of the Act which prohibits employer
interference with, and restraint of, employee exercise of Sec. 7 rights.
Section 8(a)(2) of the Act makes it an unfair labor practice for an
employer to 'contribute * * * support' to a labor organization. The law
has long been settled that a grant of exclusive recognition to a minority
union constitutes unlawful support in violation of that section, because
the union so favored is given 'a marked advantage over any other in
securing the adherence of employees. * * *

The petitioner, while taking no issue with the fact of its minority
status on the critical date, maintains that both Bernhard–Altmann's and
its own good-faith beliefs in petitioner's majority status are a complete
defense. To countenance such an excuse would place in permissibly
careless employer and union hands the power to completely frustrate
employee realization of the premise of the Act—that its prohibitions will
go far to assure freedom of choice and majority rule in employee
selection of representatives. We find nothing in the statutory language
prescribing scienter as an element of the unfair labor practices are
involved. The act made unlawful by Sec. 8(a)(2) is employer support of a
minority union. Here that support is an accomplished fact. More need
not be shown, for, even if mistakenly, the employees' rights have been
invaded. It follows that prohibited conduct cannot be excused by a
showing of good faith.

This conclusion, while giving the employee only the protection
assured him by the Act, places no particular hardship on the employer or
the union. It merely requires that recognition be withheld until the
Board-conducted election results in majority selection of a representative. The Board's order here, as we might infer from the employer's
failure to resist its enforcement, would apparently result in similarly

slight hardship upon it. We do not share petitioner's apprehension that holding such conduct unlawful will somehow induce a breakdown, or seriously impede the progress of collective bargaining. If an employer takes reasonable steps to verify union claims, themselves advanced only after careful estimate—precisely what Bernhard–Altmann and petitioner failed to do here—he can readily ascertain their validity and obviate a Board election. We fail to see any onerous burden involved in requiring responsible negotiators to be careful, by cross-checking, for example, well-analyzed employer records with union listings or authorization cards. Individual and collective employee rights may not be trampled upon merely because it is inconvenient to avoid doing so.* * *

SUMMERS, EMPLOYEE VOICE AND EMPLOYER CHOICE

69 Chicago-Kent L.Rev. 129, 141–146 (1993).

III. THE OUTLINE OF A PROPOSAL

The core of my proposal, in simple terms, is to permit employers to establish employee representation plans free from the strictures of section 8(a)(2), if the plan met certain specified requirements. Those requirements would guarantee, so far as possible, that the employees' representatives had the independence necessary to speak freely on behalf of the employees, that they were the voice of the employees, not the echo of the employer. The suggested requirements, drawn largely from the German works councils, should be cast in general terms so as to provide flexibility. The central principles would be guaranteed independence from the employer and the guarantee of a meaningful voice.

This alternative should not be available to an employer which has interfered with its employee's free choice; its purpose is to provide a form of employee representation only where employees have freely chosen not to have a union. Therefore, an employer should not be allowed to establish such a plan when there was an active organizing campaign under way or a representation proceeding was pending. Nor should an employer be allowed to establish such a plan where an unfair labor practice proceeding against the employer was pending or there had been a final determination of an unfair labor practice against the employer in the preceding three years. The availability of an alternative should not provide the employer an incentive to interfere with an employee's freedom of choice.

The requirements which an employee representation plan should meet to be exempt from section 8(a)(2), I would suggest, include the following:

First, although the structure would be framed at the outset by the employer, the employees should be free to modify the structure by majority vote after consultation with the employer, so long as the structure is kept within the specified requirements. Once established, the plan could be abolished or disbanded only by the employees.

Second, supervisory and administrative employees should be represented separately from non-supervisory employees in order to insulate employee representatives from management influence or control. This should not preclude inclusion of first line foremen in the non-supervisory employee group where both agree, but the representatives of the non-supervisory groups must, themselves, be non-supervisory employees. The plan should call for joint meetings of representatives of all employee groups with representatives of management. But to assure continued independence, the representatives of the non-supervisory employees must retain the right to meet alone with representatives of management to deal with matters of their concern.

Third, the employee representatives should be elected by those they represent, free from outside influences. The elections should be at reasonable intervals and the nomination and election process should be subject to basic safeguards similar to those provided in Title IV of the Landrum–Griffin Act for election of union officers.

Most important, the choice must be that of the employees, uninfluenced by the employer. The employer should be barred from giving any support of any kind to any employee candidate, just as section 401(g) of Landrum–Griffin prohibits employers from promoting any candidate for union office.

Fourth, the employee representatives must be provided the resources needed for performing their functions. This would include paid time off for meetings with management, meetings with employees, handling of grievances, and internal discussions. The minimum amount could be fixed, as in Germany, by the number of employees covered. Employee representatives must also be provided office space and secretarial support, and have the right to hold employee meetings on company premises.

Most important, an employee representative plan must have guaranteed financial support for various organizational and educational purposes, and for hiring professional services and experts. This would include such costs as arbitration of grievances, enforcement of employees' legal rights, use of experts in health and safety matters and job evaluation programs. Again, the amount could be determined by some prescribed formula, to be paid by the employer. The employees should be free to supplement the amount with a check-off by majority vote.

Fifth, employee representatives should be protected from fear of retaliation for their activities. They should not be subject to dismissal or discipline, except upon employer proof of just cause, and they should not be subject to lay off so long as there was work available which they were qualified to perform. Prohibiting discrimination does not provide adequate protection because proving motive is too difficult. The representative should be able to enforce this right either by suit for dismissal contrary to public policy or by arbitration for dismissal without just cause, as well as by an unfair labor practice proceeding.

Sixth, the employer should have a duty to confer with the employee representatives on all matters which substantially affect the employees' working lives. Because the underlying principle of employee participation is to treat employees as members of the enterprise and give them a voice, there is no reason for drawing the troublesome and divisive line between bargainable subjects and management prerogatives. The only duty on management will be to confer; management will still retain the ultimate right to decide. The right of employees to strike would not be enlarged or reduced, for the only change in the National Labor Relations Act would be to provide an exemption from section 8(a)(2).

Employers would no doubt prefer to prescribe the subjects with which employee representatives could deal. This, however, would enable employers to limit the subjects and create a structure of elected representatives with no voice, a shell with no content. This is the kind of sham which section 8(a)(2) was designed to prevent. Any attempt to allow an employer to limit the subject matters to be discussed, but at the same time guarantee a substantial measure of participation would require line drawing which would generate uncertainty and controversy. The best test of whether a matter is of substantial interest to employees is their insistence on discussing it, and if it is of substantial interest to employees, the employer will undermine the purpose of participation if it insists that the subject is none of the employees' business.

The employer's duty should be to "confer" or "consult," not to "bargain," if for no other reason than to avoid the image of an adversarial process. But there would be a more fundamental difference; conferring or consulting would be a continuing process. Problems would be discussed and resolved as they arose, not bargained as a package and frozen for two or three year intervals. The duty on both sides would include, of course, the duty to meet, exchange views, and consider proposals and counter proposals for dealing with the problems in an effort to find a mutually acceptable solution. This solution would become the governing rule or principle to be followed by the parties until it was changed through the process of consultation.

Perhaps the most important aspect of the duty to confer would be the duty of the employer to provide the employee representatives all relevant information; they can not speak to a problem without all the relevant facts. This must include information which will enable them to make responsible judgments of the ability of the enterprise to bear the costs or burdens of potential solutions. The employees have as much concern as management with the continued viability of the enterprise. The scope of information required may be borrowed from the German Works Constitution Act. This includes giving information "in full and good time" of any plans concerning the construction, alteration or extension of the plant, work processes or jobs; matters relating to manpower planning such as manpower needs, staff movements and vocational training; and financial matters such as the economic and financial situation of the company, the production and investment programs, rationalization plans, introduction of new work methods, reduction of operations, and plan transfers or closures, or any "other circumstances and projects that may materially affect the interests of employees of the company.[44]

Finally, the employee representatives should have the authority and ability to aid employees in enforcing any statutory or other legal rights, including those arising under individual contracts of employment. Where the employer and the employee representatives have agreed upon any rules or benefits, whether stated in the form of employer policies or written agreements, these should be enforceable by any employee for whose benefit they are made as a part of their contract of employment, and also by the employee representatives. The plan should include a provision that disputes over rights under individual contracts of employment and under agreements between the employer and the employee representatives should be submitted to binding neutral arbitration.

These are the broadly stated standards which I believe an employer-created representation plan should meet to be entitled to exemption from section 8(a)(2). There remains the question of how such a proposal would be administered and enforced. If an employer-created plan, on its face, did not fully meet these standards, its creation would be an unfair labor practice and the order should be for the employer either to disestablish the plan or, if it met most of the standards, to amend it to meet the standards. If the plan, on its face, met the standards, but the employer in practice violated any of them, those violations would be unfair labor practices, leading to the usual order to cease and desist. If those violations were extensive or persistent, evidencing an unwillingness of the employer to observe the standards, then the plan should be disestablished.

The existence of such employee representation plans would not structurally change unionization or collective bargaining. Where the union represented some, but not all, of the employees in the establishment, the employee representation plan would include only those not covered by the union. The two forms of employee participation would coexist. This might well create some tension because their scope and functions would be different, but each could operate independently. Unions would retain all of their rights under the statute to organize, petition for elections, and to become an exclusive bargaining representative. If the majority in an appropriate unit voted for the union, this would demonstrate those employees' choice to be represented by the union rather than the employer-created plan and the union would become the statutory representative. The employer would then be barred from dealing with the plan's representatives on issues involving employees in the bargaining unit and would be required to bargain with the union. This might require a new election of representatives by those outside the bargaining unit, but the plan could continue for those not represented by the union.

44. Works Constitution Act 1972, Sec. 106.

All employees would retain all of their rights under the National Labor Relations Act, including their section 7 right to engage in concerted activity for mutual aid and protection. Any two or more employees who were dissatisfied with any of their terms and conditions of employment could, like the employees in *Washington Aluminum,* refuse to work until their demands were met. Certainly, the employee representatives should not be able to limit or surrender that right of employees to strike as a union may do in agreeing to a no-strike clause.

A substantial question is whether employee representatives could be barred by agreement or otherwise from calling a strike. German works councils are, by law, prohibited from engaging in "acts of industrial warfare," but they have the leverage of being able to demand arbitration on a number of issues. Employee representatives would have no such leverage. Their practical ability to call a strike would be very limited because they would have little or no resources to support a strike. Moreover, the very nature of their establishment and operation would not look toward use of economic force as a method of resolving differences. It seems to me that they should have available at least this limited instrument to encourage the employer to make serious efforts to reach mutually agreeable solutions.

WEILER AND MUNDLAK, NEW DIRECTIONS FOR THE LAW OF THE WORKPLACE
102 Yale L.J. 1907, 1922–23 (1993).

With respect to those employees who do not want to join a union, we recommend that the law—instead of regulating from the outside more and more aspects of the employment relationship—create a new alternative to union representation in which employees represent themselves on the job. Every American workplace above a certain size (say, for example, 25 or 50 employees) should have an "Employee Participation Committee" (EPC) that voices the interests of employees in dealings with senior management about a wide range of employment issues.

One of us has developed elsewhere the detailed case for this EPC concept. Suffice it here to say that committee members elected by both office and plant employees would have the right to be consulted before management could make material changes in workplace conditions (e.g., the introduction of new technology or the adoption of health care cost containment programs). Every EPC would be entitled to the relevant information necessary for performing its representational role on behalf of employees, analogous to the data that management now provides to boards of directors representing shareholders. The committee also would be entitled to a level of financial resources—contributed jointly by the firm and employees according to a statutory per capita formula—so that the committee could draw on the advice of people and organizations with experience and expertise in relevant subject matters. For larger firms with numerous committees representing employees at multiple locations, a "federal structure" to the EPC would ensure that firms take account of the interests of various groups in decisions that affect the broader enterprise. In order to ensure the representational value of these committees, elections of representatives would be conducted through a secret ballot process, and committee members would be protected from employer reprisals for defending the interests of fellow workers.

This brief sketch shows how the EPC model could provide a home-grown form of employee representation that is quite different from (though not incompatible with) what is now provided by labor unions and employment lawyers. A host of technical questions have to be confronted before the idea can be seriously entertained. Fortunately, we can draw upon considerable experience in this country with voluntary programs of employee involvement, and in other countries that have mandated such participation by law (most prominently, West Germany, whose workplace performance ranks high in both productivity and equity). However, as introducing a statutory model of EPC's would involve a major change in the industrial system of the United States, we suggest three incremental modes of implementation. Gradual experimentation with EPC's can provide a period of adjustment, assessment of their merits, and an opportunity to refine the structure of EPC's and the optimal role of the federal and state governments in mandating them.

NLRB GENERAL COUNSEL ADVICE MEMORANDUM: GM–UAW SATURN PROJECT

122 LRRM 1187 (1986).

These cases were submitted for advice as to: * * * whether General Motors Corp. (GM) and the United Auto Workers (UAW) could lawfully negotiate an agreement granting preference for employment at GM's new Saturn facility to current and laid off GM employees; and whether GM could lawfully extend, and the UAW lawfully accept, recognition at the Saturn facility, prior to the time any employees are actually transferred and/or hired.

FACTS: On November 9, 1983, GM announced its Project Saturn. Later that year, GM issued a joint press release with the UAW announcing "plans for a Joint Study Center aimed at achieving an unprecedented union-management partnership in the development and manufacture of a small car." In January, 1984, the monthly issue of "GM Today" announced "General Motors' plan to domestically build a new subcompact car [that would] include full employee participation and enhanced job security under terms of a partnership between the corporation and the United Auto Workers (UAW)." On September 21, 1984, GM and the UAW reached agreement on a national contract (National Agreement) which included the development of a JOBS (Job Opportunity Bank—Security) program to protect employees from layoff as a result of the introduction of technology and outsourcing, and which contained Document No. 10 on Job Security. That document made specific reference to the Saturn project as one of GM's efforts "to remain a viable domestic enterprise."

"The success of Saturn is fully dependent on its people. Hiring and retention of experienced, dedicated personnel is essential. It is recognized that the best source of such trained automotive workers is found in the existing GM–UAW workforce. Therefore, to insure a fully qualified workforce, a majority of the full initial complement of operating and skilled technicians in Saturn will come from GM–UAW units throughout the United States.

"During the period of organization and start-up, certain particular skilled personnel will be required, including operating technicians and skilled technicians, virtually all of whom will come from UAW-represented units; therefore, the UAW is recognized as the bargaining agent for the operating and skilled technicians in the Saturn manufacturing complex."

We conclude that GM did not violate the Act by according preferential hiring rights at Saturn to its own employees who are represented by the UAW.

Premature Recognition

The Charging Party argues that GM recognized the UAW at an inappropriate time, i.e., before any employees were hired at Saturn. We conclude that, in the current circumstances, the argument has no merit.

In Kroger Co., 219 NLRB 388, 89 LRRM 1641 (1978), the Board held that an employer could agree to grant recognition to a union at a future facility. In upholding this agreement, the Board said that it would assume that parties intended their agreement to be lawful and that it would read into the recognition agreement the condition that the union must in fact obtain majority status at the new facility. In the instant case, GM agreed to grant recognition to the UAW at Saturn, a future facility. Concededly, as in Kroger, there is nothing in the Saturn Agreement that expressly conditions recognition upon the UAW's attainment of a majority status at Saturn. As noted supra, however, the Board will read into the agreement the condition that the UAW must achieve majority status. Hence, the Saturn Agreement is, in law, an agreement to recognize the UAW at Saturn, in futuro, if and when the UAW achieves majority support there. As construed by Kroger, the agreement is lawful.

We have concluded that the preferential hire agreement is the product of legally required "effects" bargaining over an employer decision which has potential adverse consequences for unit employees, and that it does not discriminate unlawfully against employees. As discussed above, the case law requires that an employer bargain about the effect of a management decision that could affect the jobs of unit employees. Further, as discussed above, where the management decision involves the construction of a new facility, the bargaining will often involve the granting of preferential hiring rights at the new facility. It is clear that the agreement granting preferential hire rights at the Saturn facility to present and laid-off GM employees in units represented by the UAW was a legitimate product of such "effects" bargaining.

In the instant case, GM is granting a preference to its own employees. Employees are being transferred from one GM facility to another; they are not being newly hired. The preference they receive is based on their status as GM employees; it is not, as in the cases cited, based on experience with a wholly unrelated company merely because that company is signatory to a union contract. Stated simply, the Board cases do not prohibit an employer from preferring its own employees over "the rest of the world."

Prehire recognition has also been approved in NLRB v. Burns, 406 U.S. 272, 294–295, 80 LRRM 2225 (1972). Where a new employer takes over a unionized business and it is "perfectly clear" that the new employer "plans to retain" all or [sic] a sufficient number of the predecessor employees so that they will constitute a majority of the new employer's workforce, the new employer is privileged, and indeed obligated, to recognize the union as soon as it is apparent that the union will represent the workforce. This obligation arises whenever the intent to hire the predecessor employees becomes "perfectly clear", not necessarily only when there is actual hiring. Thus, it can arise before the workforce is hired.

In the instant case, it is "perfectly clear" that GM "plans," and has agreed, to give a hiring preference to employees now in GM–UAW units, and there is a strong likelihood that these employees will constitute a majority of the employees at the new facility. In this regard, we note that the Employer has agreed to extend offers of employment so that a majority of the Saturn workforce will come from the ranks of its own employees who are now represented by the UAW.

In light of all of the above, the instant charges should be dismissed, absent withdrawal. * * *

SOME QUESTIONS

Consider whether, in light of *Bernhard-Altmann,* the GC Saturn Advice Memo is a bit of a stretch. Why did the GC approve of the arrangement? Think of *Bernhard-Altmann* as addressing the principal problem that Section 8(a)(2) was designed to correct. Is the *Electromation* problem that we discussed earlier in this section of the same magnitude as the scenario dealt with in *Bernhard-Altmann*?

SAUL RUBINSTEIN, ET AL., "THE SATURN PARTNERSHIP: CO–MANAGEMENT AND THE REINVENTION OF THE LOCAL UNION," IN EMPLOYEE REPRESENTATION, BRUCE E. KAUFMAN AND MORRIS M. KLEINER, EDS.

(Industrial Relations Research Assoc. 1993) pp. 366–367.

Union-Management Relations and National Labor Policy

The labor-management partnership at Saturn is especially relevant to those concerned about the future of American industrial relations and worker representation, since it provides an approach for filling the void in worker representation that has resulted from the steady decline of traditional unions in the United States. Thus it adds another chapter to the research on alternative forms of worker representation, team-based work organization, employee involvement, and joint union-management participative structures.

It is interesting, however, that some of the most innovative aspects of this model may be inconsistent with doctrines embedded in current labor law. For example, the use of a joint study team such as the "Committee of 99" serves as one way of avoiding the adversarial conflicts that often accompany the question of union representation in new facilities. The UAW was recognized as the bargaining agent before the Spring Hill facility was constructed. By bringing the union in as a partner in the design process, a potentially difficult issue was taken off the table in a way that promoted innovation in the new organization and reinforced efforts to sustain worker and union participation in innovative efforts underway in existing GM plants. The National Right-to-Work Committee pursued an unsuccessful legal challenge to this arrangement, arguing that it was inconsistent with voting procedures contained in the current labor law.

Similarly, the co-management role the union plays at Saturn appears on its face to be inconsistent with the sharp separation of labor and management roles assumed to exist under the current law. In the 1980 *NLRB v. Yeshiva University* case, the U.S. Supreme Court determined that employees performing managerial work were not covered under the National Labor Relations Act. While the *Yeshiva* case related to academic faculties, Saturn represents an example of blue-collar industrial relations where large numbers of union members are performing work traditionally the responsibility of managerial employees. In this way it challenges the current statute and serves as another example of the need to update and transform current labor law so it encourages and facilitates rather than constrains innovation in American industrial relations.

A final dialogue

Paul: When you consider these readings, Nan, keep in mind that the Board and the courts may have gotten 8(a)(2) exactly right. We have to consider whether these programs aren't really an illusory form of worker participation and protection, and whether collective bargaining under the NLRA isn't the only meaningful way for workers to have a say.

Nan: Maybe that's so, Paul, but I think it is up to me and my fellow workers to decide whether we want to take a chance on being fooled.

B. THE BOUNDARIES, PERKS AND OB-LIGATIONS OF REPRESENTATION

INTRODUCTION

Nan meets with a group of Registered Nurses (RN's) to discuss whether she should accept the Hospital's invitation to work on the Critical Care Circle. The nurses urge her to abandon the worker participation system. They want to seek representation under the NLRA, and would like Nan's support. The nurses, through the Unified Medical Care Association, would petition for an election among all RN's who work for the hospital, including the Nurse Practitioners. They would also seek to represent other employees in other bargaining units.

The nurses explain that the process leading towards union representation usually begins with a small group of employees who are dissatisfied with the way things are. They generally seek the assistance of an outside organizer, a paid professional on the staff of a union. The film *Norma Rae,* starring Sally Fields, while quite dated, still gives you a very realistic picture of how this takes place, although in the context of a textile factory. The union organizer tries to persuade employees to authorize the union to represent them in collective bargaining, and to seek an election on their behalf. The employee's support of the union is usually manifested by a union authorization card, which you'll find a picture of in our reference supplement.

After gathering such cards from a solid majority of the employees, the union sends a demand letter to the Hospital, asking the Hospital to recognize the union for purposes of collective bargaining (a sample demand letter is contained in our reference supplement). The Hospital will probably refuse to recognize the union, and the question of representation will then have to be determined by an election conducted by the NLRB. That process is initiated by the filing of a Petition by the union seeking certification as the bargaining representative (a sample petition is also contained in our reference supplement). The process culminates in a proceeding to determine the appropriate bargaining unit, that is, the grouping of employees that is entitled to vote on whether to be represented by a union. The parties are often able to agree upon the appropriate unit. If they do not, the appropriate unit is determined through a hearing.

The process for unit determination in hospitals is a little different, for the Board has utilized a rule-making procedure to set out general rules for bargaining units in hospitals. In cases involving workplaces other than hospitals, the Board determines the appropriate unit on a case-by-case basis, although it has been criticized for not using rule-making in all unit determination questions. The statutory reference for determining the appropriate bargaining unit is NLRA Section 9(b), which you should consult as you study this topic.

The nurses understand that the Board will probably determine that the professional employees at the Hospital will fall into two units—one for RN's, the other for all other professional employees. A third professional unit would cover physicians, but the union has decided not to seek to represent them at this time. The placement of the Nurse Practitioners is somewhat in doubt, as the Board's cases on unit placement in hospitals have not dealt with this relatively new category of nurses.

Not only could the Nurse Practitioners find themselves in a bargaining unit where they are isolated from other staff members, but they might even be excluded from the coverage of the Act. This result, which Nan finds startling, is because Nurse Practitioners have some responsibility to direct other staff members. This may make them supervisors, as defined in the Act, and supervisors are not covered by the Act. We will give you a recent Supreme Court case on that point.

The Nurses Association would like to include the Nurse Practitioners in their unit, for they feel the Nurse Practitioners would provide leadership for the organizing drive. On a more cynical level, the nurses are concerned that if they don't include the Nurse Practitioners in their unit, and the Nurse Practitioners do not choose union representation, the Nurse Practitioners could be a threat to the nurses by continuing to work for the Hospital during a nurses' strike.

The Hospital too would like to include the Nurse Practitioners in the unit, because the Hospital has an opposite read on their support of the union. The Hospital believes that the Nurse Practitioners will not vote for the union, so the Hospital would like to include them in the voting unit to negate some of the votes for the union. This should tell you that this unit determination business sometimes has very little to do with what representational grouping makes the most sense, and very much to do with the politics of who will win the election.

Nan raises a series of questions with this group of nurses. Each issue, it seems to her, reveals deficiencies in the system of representation under the NLRA, and suggests that the cooperative employee care circle system may be a better alternative. Of course Nan realizes that under Section 8(a)(2) an informal system of representation may not be a realistic alternative as long as a union is in the picture. In this section of Chapter Two we will discuss some of the concerns Nan has about representation under the NLRA.

First, Nan is concerned about the adversarial nature of the recognition process. From her readings she learns that you write a letter asking for recognition and it is refused. You argue about the unit, and it is likely that both sides will give distorted descriptions of work responsibilities in order to prevail in the unit determination proceeding. Both sides confront each other in the campaign, each exaggerating the difference in interests between employee and employer. The employer may decide to play hardball and fire people who support the union. These employees may have weaker job performance records, but are still good employees, and they are victimized because of their views. Even if the terminations are honestly based on job performance, they are hotly litigated in proceedings that pit one employee against another. Management and workers start out as enemies. The scars are never healed.

Second, Nan is concerned about the principle of exclusivity, which is the foundation of the collective bargaining system of representation. One union speaks for all the employees that it represents. Its bargaining constituency may be defined very broadly. There is a good chance that not every interest will be heard or represented. Some voices will be drowned out. She wonders if the system of exclusivity, which is at the heart of the collective bargaining model, is such a good idea, and whether there shouldn't be multiple layers of representation.

Third, Nan is worried that the system of collective bargaining doesn't cover everyone, and has a caste of elitism. It excludes those at the top—supervisors and managers—and at least some of those who are perceived to be at the bottom—agricultural laborers or domestic servants (consult Section 2(3) of the NLRA). And even among those who are covered by the NLRA, those employees who don't have the same levels of training as nurses—aides, orderlies, and maintenance people—get put in a separate unit, suggesting that somehow they are not as important as their better educated counterparts.

Finally, Nan concludes from a previous discussion that because of the constraints of Section 8(a)(2) the law stacks the decks in favor of collective bargaining. It pretty much precludes an effective worker participation system that is not union-driven. Thus, the decision of workers to utilize unions and collective bargaining for a voice in workplace governance may not reflect their true choice between unionization and other forms of representation that don't involve unions.

1. EXCLUSIVITY: DOES THE UNITY OF THE MAJORITY SILENCE THE VOICES OF DISSENT?

As you will see from the cases that follow, the NLRA system of representation is based upon the principle of exclusivity. See Section 9(a) of the NLRA. The union that is chosen by the majority of employees to represent them has the power and obligation to represent everyone in that bargaining unit. This precludes any other representative from speaking for these employees. As you study these materials, consider whether exclusivity is a necessary system or a fair one, and what alternatives you might propose.

J.I. CASE v. NLRB

Supreme Court of the United States, 1944.
321 U.S. 332, 64 S.Ct. 576, 88 L.Ed. 762.

MR. JUSTICE JACKSON delivered the opinion of the Court.

This cause was heard by the National Labor Relations Board on stipulated facts which so far as concern present issues are as follows:

The petitioner, J.I. Case Company, at its Rock Island, Illinois, plant, from 1937 offered each employee an individual contract of employment. The contracts were uniform and for a term of one year. The Company agreed to furnish employment as steadily as conditions permitted, to pay a specified rate, which the Company might redetermine if the job changed, and to maintain certain hospital facilities. The employee agreed to accept the provisions, to serve faithfully and honestly for the term, to comply with factory rules, and that defective work should not be paid for. About 75% of the employees accepted and worked under these agreements.

According to the Board's stipulation and finding, the execution of the contracts was not a condition of employment, nor was the status of individual employees affected by reason of signing or failing to sign the contracts. It is not found or contended that the agreements were coerced, obtained by any unfair labor practice, or that they were not valid under the circumstances in which they were made.

While the individual contracts executed August 1, 1941 were in effect, a C.I.O. union petitioned the Board for certification as the exclusive bargaining representative of the production and maintenance employees. On December 17, 1941 a hearing was held, at which the Company urged the individual contracts as a bar to representation proceedings. The Board, however, directed an election, which was won by the union. The union was thereupon certified as the exclusive bargaining representative of the employees in question in respect to wages, hours, and other conditions of employment.

The union then asked the Company to bargain. It refused, declaring that it could not deal with the union in any manner affecting rights and obligations under the individual contracts while they remained in effect. It offered to negotiate on matters which did not affect rights under the individual contracts, and said that upon the expiration of the contracts it would bargain as to all matters. Twice the Company sent circulars to its employees asserting the validity of the individual contracts and stating the position that it took before the Board in reference to them.

The Board held that the Company had refused to bargain collectively, in violation of Sec. 8(5) of the National Labor Relations Act, 29 U.S.C.A. Sec. 158(5); and that the contracts had been utilized, by means of the circulars, to impede employees in the exercise of rights guaranteed by Sec. 7 of the Act, 29 U.S.C.A. Sec. 157, with the result that the Company had engaged in unfair labor practices within the meaning of Sec. 8(1) of the Act. It ordered the Company to cease and desist from giving effect to the contracts, from extending them or entering into new ones, from refusing to bargain and from interfering with the employees; and it required the Company to give notice accordingly and to bargain upon request.

The Circuit Court of Appeals, with modification not in issue here, granted an order of enforcement. The issues are unsettled ones important in the administration of the Act, and we granted certiorari. In doing so we asked counsel, in view of the expiration of the individual contracts and the negotiation of a collective contract, to discuss whether the case was moot. In view of the continuing character of the obligation imposed by the order we think it is not, and will examine the merits.

Contract in labor law is a term the implications of which must be determined from the connection in which it appears. Collective bargaining between employer and the representatives of a unit, usually a union, results in an accord as to terms which will govern hiring and work and pay in that unit. The result is not, however, a contract of employment except in rare cases; no one has a job by reason of it and no obligation to any individual ordinarily comes into existence from it alone. The negotiations between union and management result in what often has been called a trade agreement, rather than a contract of employment. Without pushing the analogy too far, the agreement may be likened to the tariffs established by a carrier, to standard provisions prescribed by supervising authorities for insurance policies, or to utility schedules of rates and rules for service, which do not of themselves establish any relationships but which do govern the terms of the shipper or insurer or customer relationship whenever and with whomever it may be established. Indeed, in some European countries, contrary to American practice, the terms of a collectively negotiated trade agreement are submitted to a government department and if approved become a governmental regulation ruling employment in the unit.

After the collective trade agreement is made, the individuals who shall benefit by it are identified by individual hirings. The employer, except as restricted by the collective agreement itself and except that he must engage in no unfair labor practice or discrimination, is free to select those he will employ or discharge. But the terms of the employment already have been traded out. There is little left to individual agreement except the act of hiring. This hiring may be by writing or by word of mouth or may be implied from conduct. In the sense of contracts of hiring, individual contracts between the employer and employee are not forbidden, but indeed are necessitated by the collective bargaining procedure.

But, however engaged, an employee becomes entitled by virtue of the Labor Relations Act somewhat as a third party beneficiary to all benefits of the collective trade agreement, even if on his own he would yield to less favorable terms. The individual hiring contract is subsidiary to the terms of the trade agreement and may not waive any of its benefits, any more than a shipper can contract away the benefit of filed tariffs, the insurer the benefit of standard provisions, or the utility customer the benefit of legally established rates. * * *

Individual contracts, no matter what the circumstances that justify their execution or what their terms, may not be availed of to defeat or delay the procedures prescribed by the National Labor Relations Act looking to collective bargaining, nor to exclude the contracting employee from a duly ascertained bargaining unit; nor may they be used to forestall bargaining or to limit or condition the terms of the collective agreement. "The Board asserts a public right vested in it as a public body, charged in the public interest with the duty of preventing unfair labor practices." National Licorice Co. v. National Labor Relations Board, 309 U.S. 350, 364, 60 S.Ct. 569, 577, 84 L.Ed. 799. Wherever private contracts conflict with its functions, they obviously must yield or the Act would be reduced to a futility.

It is equally clear since the collective trade agreement is to serve the purpose contemplated by the Act, the individual contract cannot be effective as a waiver of any benefit to which the employee otherwise would be entitled under the trade agreement. The very purpose of providing by statute for the collective agreement is to supersede the terms of separate agreements of employees with terms which reflect the strength and bargaining power and serve the welfare of the group. Its benefits and advantages are open to every employee of the represented unit, whatever the type or terms of his pre-existing contract of employment.

But it is urged that some employees may lose by the collective agreement, that an individual workman may sometimes have, or be capable of getting, better terms than those obtainable by the group and that his freedom of contract must be respected on that account. We are not called upon to say that under no circumstances can an individual enforce an agreement more advantageous than a collective agreement, but we find the mere possibility that such agreements might be made no ground for holding generally that individual contracts may survive or surmount collective ones. The practice and philosophy of collective bargaining looks with suspicion on such individual advantages. Of course, where there is great variation in circumstances of employment or capacity of employees, it is possible for the collective bargain to prescribe only minimum rates or maximum hours or expressly to leave certain areas open to individual bargaining. But except as so provided, advantages to individuals may prove as disruptive of industrial peace as disadvantages. They are a fruitful way of interfering with organization and choice of representatives; increased compensation, if individually deserved, is often earned at the cost of breaking down some other standard thought to be for the welfare of the group, and always creates the suspicion of being paid at the long-range expense of the group as a whole. Such discriminations not infrequently amount to unfair labor practices. The workman is free, if he values his own bargaining position more than that of the group, to vote against representation: but the majority rules, and if it collectivizes the employment bargain, individual advantages or favors will generally in practice go in as a contribution to the collective result. We cannot except individual contracts generally from the operation of collective ones because some may be more individually advantageous. Individual contracts cannot subtract from collective ones, and whether under some circumstances they may add to them in matters covered by the collective bargain, we leave to be determined by appropriate forums under the laws of contracts applicable, and to the Labor Board if they constitute unfair labor practices.

It also is urged that such individual contracts may embody matters that are not necessarily included within the statutory scope of collective bargaining, such as stock purchase, group insurance, hospitalization, or medical attention. We know of nothing to prevent the employees', because he is an employee, making any contract provided it is not inconsistent with a collective agreement or does not amount to or result from or is not part of an unfair labor practice. But in so doing the employer may not incidentally exact or obtain any diminution of his own obligation or any increase of those of employees in the matters covered by collective agreement.

Hence we find that the contentions of the Company that the individual contracts precluded a choice of representatives and warranted refusal to bargain during their duration were properly overruled. It follows that representation to the employees by circular letter that they had such legal effect was improper and could properly be prohibited by the Board.

[The Court modified the Board's cease and desist order to the employer because a] party is entitled to a definition as exact as the circumstances permit of the acts which he can perform only on pain of contempt of court. Nor should he be ordered to desist from more on the theory that he may violate the literal language and then defend by resort to the Board's construction of it. * * * Where, as here, the literal language of the order goes beyond what the Board admits was intended, correction should be made. Paragraphs 1(a) and 2(a) of the decree of the court below are hereby modified, by adding the words in italics, to read as follows:

"1. Cease and desist from:

(a) Giving effect to the individual contracts of employment or any modification, continuation, extension, or renewal thereof *to forestall collective bargaining or deter self-organization,* or entering into any similar form of contract with its employees for any period subsequent to the date of this Decree *for such purpose or with such effect.*

"2. Take the following affirmative action which the Board finds will effectuate the policies of the Act:

(a) Give separate written notice to each of its employees who signed an individual contract of employment or any modification, continuation, extension, or renewal thereof, or any similar form of contract for any period subsequent to the date of this Decree, that such contract will not in any manner be enforced or attempted to be enforced *to forestall collective bargaining or deter self-organization,* that the employee is not required or expected by virtue of such contract to deal with respondent individually *in respect to rates of pay, wages, hours of employment, or other conditions of employment,* and that such discontinuance of the contract is without prejudice to the assertion of any legal rights the employee may have acquired under such contract *or to any defenses thereto by the employer."*

As so modified the decree is

Affirmed.

MR. JUSTICE ROBERTS is of opinion that the judgment should be reversed.

EMPORIUM CAPWELL CO. v. WESTERN ADDITION COMMUNITY ORGANIZATION

Supreme Court of the United States, 1975.
420 U.S. 50, 95 S.Ct. 977, 43 L.Ed.2d 12.

Opinion of the Court by MR. JUSTICE MARSHALL, announced by MR. CHIEF JUSTICE BURGER.

This litigation presents the question whether, in light of the national policy against racial discrimination in employment, the National Labor Relations Act protects concerted activity by a group of minority employees to bargain with their employer over issues of employment discrimination. * * *

I

The Emporium Capwell Co. (Company) operates a department store in San Francisco. At all times relevant to this litigation it was a party to the collective-bargaining agreement negotiated by the San Francisco Retailer's Council, of which it was a member, and the Department Store Employees Union (Union) which represented all stock and marking area employees of the Company. The agreement, in which the Union was recognized as the sole collective-bargaining agency for all covered employees, prohibited employment discrimination by reason of race, color, creed, national origin, age, or sex, as well as union activity. It had a no-strike or lockout clause, and it established grievance and arbitration machinery for processing any claimed violation of the contract, including a violation of the antidiscrimination clause.[1]

---

1. Section 5B provided:

"Any act of any employer, representative of the Union, or any employe that is interfering with the faithful performance of this agreement, or a harmonious relationship between the employers and the UNION, may be referred to the Adjustment Board for such action as the Adjustment Board

deems proper, and is permissive within this agreement."

Section 36B established an Adjustment Board consisting of three Union and three management members. Section 36C provided that if any matter referred to the Adjustment Board remained unsettled after seven

On April 3, 1968, a group of Company employees covered by the agreement met with the secretary-treasurer of the Union, Walter Johnson, to present a list of grievances, including a claim that the Company was discriminating on the basis of race in making assignments and promotions. The Union official agreed to take certain of the grievances and to investigate the charge of racial discrimination. He appointed an investigating committee and prepared a report on the employees' grievances, which he submitted to the Retailer's Council and which the Council in turn referred to the Company. The report described "the possibility of racial discrimination" as perhaps the most important issue raised by the employees and termed the situation at the Company as potentially explosive if corrective action were not taken. It offered as an example of the problem the Company's failure to promote a Negro stock employee regarded by other employees as an outstanding candidate but a victim of racial discrimination.

Shortly after receiving the report, the Company's labor relations director met with Union representatives and agreed to "look into the matter" of discrimination and see what needed to be done. Apparently unsatisfied with these representations, the Union held a meeting in September attended by Union officials, Company employees, and representatives of the California Fair Employment Practices Committee (FEPC) and the local anti-poverty agency. The secretary-treasurer of the Union announced that the Union had concluded that the Company was discriminating, and that it would process every such grievance through to arbitration if necessary. Testimony about the Company's practices was taken and transcribed by a court reporter, and the next day the Union notified the Company of its formal charge and demanded that the joint union-management Adjustment Board be convened "to hear the entire case."

At the September meeting some of the Company's employees had expressed their view that the contract procedures were inadequate to handle a systemic grievance of this sort; they suggested that the Union instead begin picketing the store in protest. Johnson explained that the collective agreement bound the Union to its processes and expressed his view that successful grievants would be helping not only themselves but all others who might be the victims of invidious discrimination as well. The FEPC and antipoverty agency representatives offered the same advice. Nonetheless, when the Adjustment Board meeting convened on October 16, James Joseph Hollins, Tom Hawkins, and two other employees whose testimony the Union had intended to elicit refused to participate in the grievance procedure. Instead, Hollins read a statement objecting to reliance on correction of individual inequities as an approach to the problem of discrimination at the store and demanding that the president of the Company meet with the four protestants to work out a

days, either party could insist that the dispute be submitted to final and binding arbitration] broader agreement for dealing with the issue as they saw it. The four employees then walked out of the hearing.

Hollins attempted to discuss the question of racial discrimination with the Company president shortly after the incidents of October 16. The president refused to be drawn into such a discussion but suggested to Hollins that he see the personnel director about the matter. Hollins, who had spoken to the personnel director before, made no effort to do so again. Rather, he and Hawkins and several other dissident employees held a press conference on October 22 at which they denounced the store's employment policy as racist, reiterated their desire to deal directly with "the top management" of the Company over minority employment conditions, and announced their intention to picket and institute a boycott of the store. On Saturday, November 2, Hollins, Hawkins, and at least two other employees picketed the store throughout the day and distributed at the entrance handbills urging consumers not to patronize the store.[2] Johnson encountered the picketing employees, again urged them to rely on the grievance process, and warned that they might be fired for their activities. The pickets, however, were not dissuaded, and they continued to press their demand to deal directly with the Company president[3]

On November 7, Hollins and Hawkins were given written warnings that a repetition of the picketing or public statements about the Company could lead to their discharge[4] When the conduct was repeated the following Saturday, the two employees were fired.

2. The full text of the handbill read:

" * * BEWARE * * * * BEWARE
 * * * * BEWARE * *
"EMPORIUM SHOPPERS
" 'Boycott Is On' 'Boycott Is On'
'Boycott Is On'

"For years at The Emporium black, brown, yellow and red people have worked at the lowest jobs, at the lowest levels. Time and time again we have seen intelligent, hard working brothers and sisters denied promotions and respect.

"The Emporium is a 20th Century colonial plantation. The brothers and sisters are being treated the same way as our brothers are being treated in the slave mines of Africa.

"Whenever the racist pig at The Emporium injures or harms a black sister or brother, they injure and insult all black people. THE EMPORIUM MUST PAY FOR THESE INSULTS. Therefore, we encourage all of our people to take their money out of this racist store, until black people have full employment, and are promoted justly through out The Emporium.

"We welcome the support of our brothers and sisters from the churches, unions, sororities, fraternities, social clubs, Afro–

American Institute, Black Panther Party, W.A.C.O. and the Poor Peoples Institute."

3. Johnson testified that Hollins "informed me that the only one they wanted to talk to was Mr. Batchelder [the Company president] and I informed him that we had concluded negotiations in 1967 and I was a spokesman for the union and represented a few thousand clerks and I have never met Mr. Batchelder...."

4. The warning given to Hollins read:

"On October 22, 1968, you issued a public statement at a press conference to which all newspapers, radio, and TV stations were invited. The contents of this statement were substantially the same as those set forth in the sheet attached. This statement was broadcast on Channel 2 on October 22, 1968 and Station KDIA.

"On November 2nd you distributed copies of the attached statement to Negro customers and prospective customers, and to other persons passing by in front of The Emporium.

"These statements are untrue and are intended to and will, if continued injure the reputation of The Emporium.

"There are ample legal remedies to correct any discrimination you may claim to

Western Addition Community Organization (hereinafter respondent), a local civil rights association of which Hollins and Hawkins were members, filed a charge against the Company with the National Labor Relations Board. The Board's General Counsel subsequently issued a complaint alleging that in discharging the two the Company had violated § 8(a)(1) of the National Labor Relations Act, as amended, 61 Stat. 140, 29 U.S.C. Sec. 158(a)(1). After a hearing, the NLRB Trial Examiner found that the discharged employees had believed in good faith that the Company was discriminating against minority employees, and that they had resorted to concerted activity on the basis of that belief. He concluded, however, that their activity was not protected by Sec. 7 of the Act and that their discharges did not, therefore, violate Sec. 8(a)(1).

The Board, after oral argument, adopted the findings and conclusions of its Trial Examiner and dismissed the complaint. 192 N.L.R.B. 173. Among the findings adopted by the Board was that the discharged employees' course of conduct

"was no mere presentation of a grievance but nothing short of a demand that the [Company] bargain with the picketing employees for the entire group of minority employees.[5]

The Board concluded that protection of such an attempt to bargain would undermine the statutory system of bargaining through an exclusive, elected representative, impede elected unions' efforts at bettering the working conditions of minority employees, "and place on the Employer an unreasonable burden of attempting to placate self-designated representatives of minority groups while abiding by the terms of a valid bargaining agreement and attempting in good faith to meet whatever demands the bargaining representative put forth under that agreement.[6]

exist. Therefore, we view your activities as a deliberate and unjustified attempt to injure your employer.

"This is to inform you that you may be discharged if you repeat any of the above acts or make any similar public statement."

That given to Hawkins was the same except that the first paragraph was not included.

5. "192 N.L.R.B., at 185. The evidence marshaled in support of this finding consisted of Hollins' meeting with the Company president in which he said that he wanted to discuss the problem perceived by minority employees; his statement that the pickets would not desist until the president treated with them; Hawkins' testimony that their purpose in picketing was to "talk to the top management to get better conditions"; and his statement that they wanted to achieve their purpose through "group talk and through the president if we could talk to him," as opposed to use of the grievance-arbitration machinery.

6. The Board considered but stopped short of resolving the question of whether the employees' invective and call for a boycott of the Company bespoke so malicious an attempt to harm their employer as to deprive them of the protection of the Act. The Board decision is therefore grounded squarely on the view that a minority group member may not bypass the Union and bargain directly over matters affecting minority employees, and not at all on the tactics used in this particular attempt to obtain such bargaining.

Member Jenkins dissented on the ground that the employees' activity was protected by § 7 because it concerned the terms and conditions of their employment. Member Brown agreed but expressly relied upon his view that the facts revealed no attempt to bargain "but simply to urge [the Company] to take action to correct conditions of racial discrimination which the employees reasonably believed existed at the Emporium." 192 N.L.R.B., at 179.

On respondent's petition for review the Court of Appeals reversed and remanded. The court was of the view that concerted activity directed against racial discrimination enjoys a "unique status" by virtue of the national labor policy against discrimination, as expressed in both the NLRA, and in Title VII of the Civil Rights Act of 1964, and that the Board had not adequately taken account of the necessity to accommodate the exclusive bargaining principle of the NLRA to the national policy of protecting action taken in opposition to discrimination from employer retaliation[7] The court recognized that protection of the minority-group concerted activity involved in this case would interfere to some extent with the orderly collective-bargaining process, but it considered the disruptive effect on that process to be outweighed where protection of minority activity is necessary to full and immediate realization of the policy against discrimination. In formulating a standard for distinguishing between protected and unprotected activity, the majority held that the "Board should inquire, in cases such as this, whether the union was actually remedying the discrimination to the *fullest extent possible, by the most expedient and efficacious means*. Where the union's efforts fall short of this high standard, the minority group's concerted activities cannot lose [their] section 7 protection.[8] Accordingly, the court remanded the case for the Board to make this determination and, if it found in favor of the employees, to consider whether their particular tactics were so disloyal to their employer as to deprive them of Sec. 7 protection under our decision in NLRB v. Electrical Workers, 346 U.S. 464, 74 S.Ct. 172, 98 L.Ed. 195 (1953).[9]

II

Before turning to the central questions of labor policy raised by these cases, it is important to have firmly in mind the character of the

---

7. Section 9(a) of the NLRA, 29 U.S.C. § 159(a), provides in part:

"Representatives designated or selected for the purposes of collective bargaining by the majority of the employees in a unit appropriate for such purposes, shall be the exclusive representatives of all the employees in such unit for the purposes of collective bargaining in respect to rates of pay, wages, hours of employment, or other conditions of employment...."

Section 704(a) of Title VII, 42 U.S.C. § 2000e–3(a) (1970 ed., Supp. III), provides:

"It shall be an unlawful employment practice for an employer to discriminate against any of his employees or applicants for employment, for an employment agency or joint labor-management committee controlling apprenticeship or other training or retraining, including on-the-job training programs, to discriminate against any individual; or for a labor organization to discriminate against any member thereof or applicant for membership, because he has opposed any practice made an unlawful employment practice by this subchapter, or because he has made a charge, testified, assisted, or participated in any manner in an investigation, proceeding, or hearing under this subchapter."

8. "485 F.2d at 931 (emphasis in original). We hasten to point out that it had never been determined in any forum, at least as of the time that Hollins and Hawkins engaged in the activity for which they were discharged, that the Company had engaged in any discriminatory conduct. The Board found that the employees believed that the Company had done so, but that no evidence introduced in defense of their resort to self-help supported this belief.

9. Judge Wyzanski dissented insofar as the Board was directed on remand to evaluate the adequacy of the Union's efforts in opposing discrimination. He was of the view that minority concerted activity against discrimination would be protected regardless of the Union's efforts.

underlying conduct to which we apply them. As stated, the Trial Examiner and the Board found that the employees were discharged for attempting to bargain with the Company over the terms and conditions of employment as they affected racial minorities. Although the Court of Appeals expressly declined to set aside this finding, respondent has devoted considerable effort to attacking it in this Court, on the theory that the employees were attempting only to present a grievance to their employer within the meaning of the first proviso to Sec. 9(a).[12] We see no occasion to disturb the finding of the Board. Universal Camera Corp. v. NLRB, 340 U.S. 474, 491, 71 S.Ct. 456, 466, 95 L.Ed. 456 (1951). The issue, then, is whether such attempts to engage in separate bargaining are protected by Sec. 7 of the Act or proscribed by Sec. 9(a).

A

Section 7 affirmatively guarantees employees the most basic rights of industrial self-determination, "the right to self-organization, to form, join, or assist labor organizations, to bargain collectively through representatives of their own choosing, and to engage in other concerted activities for the purpose of collective bargaining or other mutual aid or protection," as well as the right to refrain from these activities. These are, for the most part, collective rights, rights to act in concert with one's fellow employees; they are protected not for their own sake but as an instrument of the national labor policy of minimizing industrial strife "by encouraging the practice and procedure of collective bargaining." 29 U.S.C. § 151.

Central to the policy of fostering collective bargaining, where the employees elect that course, is the principle of majority rule. See NLRB v. Jones & Laughlin Steel Corp., 301 U.S. 1, 57 S.Ct. 615, 81 L.Ed. 893 (1937). * * * In establishing a regime of majority rule, Congress sought to secure to all members of the unit the benefits of their collective strength and bargaining power, in full awareness that the superior strength of some individuals or groups might be subordinated to the interest of the majority. As a result, "[t]he complete satisfaction of all

---

12. That proviso states:

"That any individual employee or a group of employees shall have the right. at any time to present grievances to their employer and to have such grievances adjusted, without the intervention of the bargaining representative, as long as the adjustment is not inconsistent with the terms of a collective-bargaining contract or agreement then in effect...."

Respondent clearly misapprehends the nature of the "right" conferred by this section. The intendment of the proviso is to permit employees to present grievances and to authorize the employer to entertain them without opening itself to liability for dealing directly with employees in derogation of the duty to bargain only with the exclusive bargaining representative, a violation of § 8(a)(5). The Act nowhere protects this "right" by making it an unfair labor practice for an employer to refuse to entertain such a presentation, nor can it be read to authorize resort to economic coercion. This matter is fully explicated in Black–Clawson Co. v. Machinists, 313 F.2d 179 (C.A.2 1962). See also Republic Steel v. Maddox, 379 U.S. 650, 85 S.Ct. 614, 13 L.Ed.2d 580 (1965). If the employees' activity in the present litigation is to be deemed protected, therefore, it must be so by reason of the reading given to the main part of § 9(a), in light of Title VII and the national policy against employment discrimination, and not by burdening the proviso to that section with a load it was not meant to carry.

who are represented is hardly to be expected." Ford Motor Co. v. Huffman, 345 U.S. 330, 338, 73 S.Ct. 681, 686, 97 L.Ed. 1048 (1953).

The Court most recently had occasion to re-examine the underpinnings of the majoritarian principle in NLRB v. Allis–Chalmers Mfg. Co., 388 U.S. 175, 87 S.Ct. 2001, 18 L.Ed.2d 1123 (1967). In that case employees in two local unions had struck their common employer to enforce their bargaining demands for a new contract. In each local at least the two-thirds majority required by the constitution of the international union had voted for the strike, but some members nonetheless crossed the picket lines and continued to work. When the union later tried and fined these members, the employer charged that it had violated § 8(b)(1)(A) by restraining or coercing the employees in the exercise of their Sec. 7 right to refrain from concerted activities. In holding that the unions had not committed an unfair labor practice by disciplining the dissident members, we approached the literal language of Sec. 8(b)(1)(A) with an eye to the policy within which it must be read:

> "National labor policy has been built on the premise that by pooling their economic strength and acting through a labor organization freely chosen by the majority, the employees of an appropriate unit have the most effective means of bargaining for improvements in wages, hours, and working conditions. The policy therefore extinguishes the individual employee's power to order his own relations with his employer and creates a power vested in the chosen representative to act in the interests of all employees. 'Congress has seen fit to clothe the bargaining representative with powers comparable to those possessed by a legislative body both to create and restrict the rights of those whom it represents....' Steele v. Louisville & N.R. Co., 323 U.S. 192, 202, 65 S.Ct. 226, 232, 89 L.Ed. 173. Thus only the union may contract the employee's terms and conditions of employment, and provisions for processing his grievances; the union may even bargain away his right to strike during the contract term...." 388 U.S., at 180, 87 S.Ct., at 2006 (footnotes omitted).[14]

In vesting the representatives of the majority with this broad power Congress did not, of course, authorize a tyranny of the majority over minority interests. First, it confined the exercise of these powers to the context of a " 'unit appropriate' for the purposes of collective bargaining," i.e., a group of employees with a sufficient commonality of circumstances to ensure against the submergence of a minority with distinctively different interests in the terms and conditions of their employment. Second, it undertook in the 1959 Landrum–Griffin amendments, to assure that minority voices are heard as they are in the functioning of a democratic institution. Third, we have held, by the very nature of the exclusive bargaining representative's status as representative of *all* unit

---

14. The Union may not, of course, bargain away the employees' statutory right to choose a new, or to have no, bargaining representative. See NLRB v. Magnavox Co., 415 U.S. 322, 94 S.Ct. 1099, 39 L.Ed.2d 358 (1974).

employees, Congress implicitly imposed upon it a duty fairly and in good faith to represent the interests of minorities within the unit. And the Board has taken the position that a union's refusal to process grievances against racial discrimination, in violation of that duty, is an unfair labor practice. Hughes Tool Co., 147 N.L.R.B. 1573 (1964); see Miranda Fuel Co., 140 N.L.R.B. 181 (1962), enforcement denied, 326 F.2d 172 (C.A.2 1963). Indeed, the Board has ordered a union implicated by a collective-bargaining agreement in discrimination with an employer to propose specific contractual provisions to prohibit racial discrimination. See Local Union No. 12, United Rubber Workers of America v. NLRB, 368 F.2d 12 (C.A.5 1966) (enforcement granted).

B

Against this background of long and consistent adherence to the principle of exclusive representation tempered by safeguards for the protection of minority interests, respondent urges this Court to fashion a limited exception to that principle: employees who seek to bargain separately with their employer as to the elimination of racially discriminatory employment practices peculiarly affecting them should be free from the constraints of the exclusivity principle of Sec. 9(a). Essentially because established procedures under Title VII or, as in this case, a grievance machinery, are too time consuming, the national labor policy against discrimination requires this exception, respondent argues, and its adoption would not unduly compromise the legitimate interests of either unions or employers[16]

Plainly, national labor policy embodies the principles of nondiscrimination as a matter of highest priority, Alexander v. Gardner–Denver Co., 415 U.S. 36, 47, 94 S.Ct. 1011, 39 L.Ed.2d 147 (1974), and it is a commonplace that we must construe the NLRA in light of the broad national labor policy of which it is a part. These general principles do not aid respondent, however, as it is far from clear that separate bargaining is necessary to help eliminate discrimination. Indeed, as the facts of this litigation demonstrate, the proposed remedy might have just the opposite effect. The collective-bargaining agreement involved here prohibited without qualification all manner of invidious discrimination and made any claimed violation a grievable issue. The grievance procedure is directed precisely at determining whether discrimination has occurred.[17]

16. Our analysis of respondent's argument in favor of the exception makes it unnecessary either to accept or reject its factual predicate, *viz.*, that the procedures now established for the elimination of discrimination in employment are too cumbersome to be effective. We note, however, that the present record provides no support for the proposition. Thus, while respondent stresses the fact that Hollins and Hawkins had brought their evidence of discrimination to the Union in April 1968 but did not resort to self-help until the following October, it overlooks the fact that although they had been in contact with the state FEPC they did not file a charge with that agency or the Equal Employment Opportunity Commission (EEOC). Further, when they abandoned the procedures to which the Union was bound because they thought "the Union was sort of putting us off and on and was going into a lot of delay that we felt was unnecessary," it was at the very moment that the Adjustment Board had been convened to hear their testimony.

17. The Union in this case had been "prepared to go into arbitration" to enforce its position, but was advised by its attorney

That orderly determination, if affirmative, could lead to an arbitral award enforceable in court.[18] Nor is there any reason to believe that the processing of grievances is inherently limited to the correction of individual cases of discrimination. Quite apart from the essentially contractual question of whether the Union could grieve against a "pattern or practice" it deems inconsistent with the nondiscrimination clause of the contract, one would hardly expect an employer to continue in effect an employment practice that routinely results in adverse arbitral decisions.[19]

The decision by a handful of employees to bypass the grievance procedure in favor of attempting to bargain with their employer, by contrast, may or may not be predicated upon the actual existence of discrimination. An employer confronted with bargaining demands from each of several minority groups would not necessarily, or even probably, be able to agree to remedial steps satisfactory to all at once. Competing claims on the employer's ability to accommodate each group's demands, e.g., for reassignments and promotions to a limited number of positions, could only set one group against the other even if it is not the employer's intention to divide and overcome them. Having divided themselves, the minority employees will not be in position to advance their cause unless it be by recourse seriatim to economic coercion, which can only have the effect of further dividing them along racial or other lines.[20] Nor is the situation materially different where, as apparently happened here, self-designated representatives purport to speak for all groups that might consider themselves to be victims of discrimination. Even if in actual bargaining the various groups did not perceive their interests as divergent and further subdivide themselves, the employer would be bound to bargain with them in a field largely pre-empted by the current collective-bargaining agreement with the elected bargaining representative. In this instance we do not know precisely what form the demands advanced by Hollins, Hawkins, et al. would take, but the nature of the grievance that motivated them indicates that the demands would have included the transfer of some minority employees to sales areas in which higher commissions were paid. Yet the collective-bargaining agreement provided that no employee would be transferred from a higher-paying to a lower-

that it would be difficult to do so without the dissident members' testimony.

18. Even if the arbitral decision denies the putative discriminatee's complaint his access to the processes of Title VII and thereby to the federal courts is not foreclosed. Alexander v. Gardner–Denver Co., 415 U.S. 36, 94 S.Ct. 1011, 39 L.Ed.2d 147.

19. * * * The remarks of Union Secretary-Treasurer Johnson in response to the suggestion that the Union abandon the grievance-arbitration avenue in favor of economic coercion are indicative. " 'I informed them,' " he testified, " ' what an individual wanted to do on their own, they could do, but I wasn't going to engage in

any drama, but I wanted some orderly legal procedures that would have some long lasting effect.' " 192 N.L.R.B., at 182.

20. The Company's Employer Information Report EEO–1 to the EEOC for the period during which this dispute arose indicates that it had employees in every minority group for which information was required. Among sales workers alone it recorded male and female employees who were Negro, Oriental, and Spanish surnamed. In addition, the Union took the position that older employees were also being discriminated against.

paying classification except by consent or in the course of a layoff or reduction in force. The potential for conflict between the minority and other employees in this situation is manifest. With each group able to enforce its conflicting demands-the incumbent employees by resort to contractual processes and the minority employees by economic coercion-the probability of strife and deadlock, is high; the likelihood of making headway against discriminatory practices would be minimal.

What has been said here in evaluating respondent's claim that the policy against discrimination requires § 7 protection for concerted efforts at minority bargaining has obvious implications for the related claim that legitimate employer and union interests would not be unduly compromised thereby. The court below minimized the impact on the Union in this case by noting that it was not working at cross-purposes with the dissidents, and that indeed it could not do so consistent with its duty of fair representation and perhaps its obligations under Title VII. As to the Company, its obligations under Title VII are cited for the proposition that it could have no legitimate objection to bargaining with the dissidents in order to achieve full compliance with that law.

This argument confuses the employees' substantive right to be free of racial discrimination with the procedures available under the NLRA for securing these rights. Whether they are thought to depend upon Title VII or have an independent source in the NLRA, they cannot be pursued at the expense of the orderly collective-bargaining process contemplated by the NLRA. The elimination of discrimination and its vestiges is an appropriate subject of bargaining, and an employer may have no objection to incorporating into a collective agreement the substance of his obligation not to discriminate in personnel decisions; the Company here has done as much, making any claimed dereliction a matter subject to the grievance-arbitration machinery as well as to the processes of Title VII. But that does not mean that an employer may not have strong and legitimate objections to bargaining on several fronts over the implementation of the right to be free of discrimination for some of the reasons set forth above. Similarly, while a union cannot lawfully bargain for the establishment or continuation of discriminatory practices, see Steele v. Louisville & N.R. Co., 323 U.S. 192, 65 S.Ct. 226, 89 L.Ed. 173, 42 U.S.C. § 2000e–2(c)(3), it has a legitimate interest in presenting a united front on this as on other issues and in not seeing its strength dissipated and its stature denigrated by sub-groups within the unit separately pursuing what they see as separate interests. When union and employer are not responsive to their legal obligations, the bargain they have struck must yield *pro tanto* to the law, whether by means of conciliation through the offices of the EEOC, or by means of federal-court enforcement at the instance of either that agency or the party claiming to be aggrieved.
* * *

[Respondent also claimed that Section 704(a) of Title VII protected Hollins and Hawkins from discharge; therefore, "if the discharges did not also violate Section 8(a)(1) of the NLRA, then the integrity of section 704(a) will be seriously undermined." Without deciding whether the discharges violated section 704(a), the Court rejected the respondent's analysis, noting that the NLRA and Title VII are independent sources to protect conduct that may but need not be protected by both. The Court also addressed respondent's claim] that reliance on the remedies provided by Title VII is inadequate effectively to secure the rights conferred by Title VII. There are indeed significant differences between proceedings initiated under Title VII and an unfair labor practice proceeding. Congress chose to encourage voluntary compliance with Title VII by emphasizing conciliatory procedures before federal coercive powers could be invoked. Even then it did not provide the EEOC with the power of direct enforcement, but made the federal courts available to the agency or individual to secure compliance with Title VII. See Alexander v. Gardner–Denver Co., 415 U.S., at 44–45, 94 S.Ct. 1011. By contrast, once the General Counsel of the NLRB decides to issue a complaint, vindication of the charging party's statutory rights becomes a public function discharged at public expense, and a favorable decision by the Board brings forth an administrative order. As a result of these and other differences, we are told that relief is typically available to the party filing a charge with the NLRB in a significantly shorter time, and with less risk, than obtains for one filing a charge with the EEOC.

Whatever its factual merit, this argument is properly addressed to the Congress and not to this Court or the NLRB. In order to hold that employer conduct violates § 8(a)(1) of the NLRA *because* it violates § 704(a) of Title VII, we would have to override a host of consciously made decisions well within the exclusive competence of the Legislature. This obviously, we cannot do.

Reversed.

Mr. Justice Douglas, dissenting.

The Court's opinion makes these Union members—and others similarly situated—prisoners of the Union. The law, I think, was designed to prevent that tragic consequence. Hence, I dissent. * * *

The Board has held that the employees were unprotected because they sought to confront the employer outside the grievance process, which was under Union control. The Court upholds the Board, on the view that this result is commanded by the principle of "exclusive representation" embodied in § 9 of the NLRA. But in the area of racial discrimination the Union is hardly in a position to demand exclusive control, for the employee's right to nondiscriminatory treatment does not depend upon Union demand but is based on the law.

The law should facilitate the involvement of unions in the quest for racial equality in employment, but it should not make the individual a prisoner of the union. While employees may reasonably be required to approach the union first, as a kind of "exhaustion" requirement before resorting to economic protest, cf. NLRB v. Tanner Motor Livery, 419 F.2d 216 (CA9), they should not be under continued inhibition when it becomes apparent that the union response is inadequate. The Court of Appeals held that the employees should be protected from discharge unless the Board found on remand that the Union had been prosecuting their complaints "to the *fullest extent possible, by the most expedient and efficacious means.*" 485 F.2d 917, 931. I would not disturb this standard. Union conduct can be oppressive even if not made in bad faith. The inertia of weak-kneed, docile union leadership can be as devastating to the cause of racial equality as aggressive subversion. Continued submission by employees to such a regime should not be demanded.

I would affirm the judgment below.

Dissenting Union Members, Their Employer, and Their Union

As Justice Marshall noted in *Emporium Capwell*, workers dissatisfied with the terms negotiated or positions taken by their union have alternatives other than picketing and attempting to bargain with their employers. This note explores whether these are realistic alternatives. Are they preferable to allowing separate bargaining by frustrated interest groups?

1. *Title VII and other statutory redress.* If the interest group consists of persons protected by Title VII or some other workplace statute, such as the American With Disabilities Act, they can use that statute to challenge company and union policies. For example, in *Emporium Capwell* the pattern of promotions and transfers might well have revealed unlawful preferences for white employees. To have a court reach such a conclusion, however, the parties would face long and expensive litigation. If a court found a violation of Title VII, it could order the company to change its policies, place victims of discrimination in the jobs they sought, and order retroactive pay and seniority credits to some or all members of the interest group, especially identifiable victims of the challenged policies. See Franks v. Bowman Transportation Co., Inc., 424 U.S. 747, 96 S.Ct. 1251, 47 L.Ed.2d 444 (1976). A company that is ordered to change its practices to comply with Title VII, may find that it is now in violation of its collective bargaining agreement. For example, an order to place certain minority applicants into job openings in order to redress discrimination, may affect the rights of other employees in the bargaining unit who would be entitled to those openings under contractual rules of seniority. The Supreme Court has acknowledged that an employer may face dual liability in such a situation, and concluded that the employer could face two sets of monetary obligations. See W.R. Grace and Co. v. Local Union 759, 461 U.S. 757, 103 S.Ct. 2177, 76 L.Ed.2d 298 (1983).

Alternatively, to avoid the litigation costs, delays and burdensome remedial awards, the parties could settle the lawsuit, with the company, the complainants and the union agreeing, for example, that qualified minorities will receive a proportion of the next opportunities for promotion and transfer. If Title VII allows a group of minority workers to settle a lawsuit on terms that may adversely affect interests of others in the workplace, should the NLRA also permit "separate bargaining" by dissatisfied minority employees?

2. *The grievance-arbitration process.* As *Emporium Capwell* demonstrates, under most collective bargaining agreements union officials and not the grieving employees control the right to demand arbitration of issues that remain unresolved after passing through the steps of the grievance process. This means that grievants whose positions differ from any advanced by the union leadership may not obtain relief under the contract. And even if the union agrees to go forward with the claim of the minority employees, those employees will be unable to control the nature of the claim. For example, the union may not choose to cast the issue in terms of a group grievance with greater potential for class-wide relief. What is more, the arbitration proceedings will be controlled by the employer and the union, not by the grievants. The complaining workers in *Emporium Capwell* questioned the tactics of their union. Is such a process an adequate mechanism for protecting the special interests of minority employees? Why do you think collective bargaining agreements reserve to unions the right to initiate and control arbitration?

Later in this chapter we will study the question whether an individual or a group with a statutory claim can be forced to resolve that question through arbitration rather than by going through the courts. We will see that this is an unanswered question when it comes up in a union setting. This makes all the more important the question here of whether the grievance-arbitration process is an adequate avenue for the dissident employees in *Emporium Capwell*.

3. *The duty of fair representation.* The duty of fair representation requires a union to treat all employees it represents fairly and without malice or discrimination. If disgruntled workers can prove that their bargaining representative treated them differently because of their race, relief under a fair representation theory is virtually assured.

Do you think the union in *Emporium Capwell* met its obligation to represent the dissidents fairly? The union will say it negotiated a nondiscrimination clause, pledged to take every grievance charging employment discrimination to arbitration if necessary, held membership meetings to discuss the charges of discriminatory employment practices, and called in the state equal employment opportunities office to aid in the investigation. The union even warned Hollins and Hawkins that continued agitation could lead to their discharges. And there is no evidence that the union intentionally treated Hollins and Hawkins differently because of their race or because they differed with the union on its policies. On the other hand, the union did not treat the original grievances as a group grievance, nor did it expedite the grievance process. In light of these facts, was there sufficient evidence of wrongly motivated, racially discriminatory acts by the union? The union did not later file a grievance or a civil action challenging the discharges of Hollins and Hawkins; is that omission evidence of unfair, arbitrary or malicious treatment? We will see in Chapter III that it is very hard for a complaining employee to establish that the union had violated its duty of fair representation.

The opinion in *Emporium Capwell* stressed that giving minority interests separate bargaining rights would inhibit the union's ability to speak with one voice in negotiations with the company. In a somewhat contradictory vein, however, the Court noted that dissenting employees could vindicate their interests by suing the union. Does a lawsuit challenging the union's competence and its policies have a less hobbling effect on union solidarity than a process that allows separate bargaining?

4. *The political process within the union.* The Labor–Management Reporting and Disclosure Act of 1959 (LMRDA or Landrum–Griffin) is designed to insulate workers from overreaching by their unions. (The LMRDA is a further amendment to the original NLRA and to the amended LMRA. Among other provisions, the LMRDA requires unions to hold periodic elections for national and local officers. Some of these contests are well fought, and changes in the identities of union officers can lead to changes in policy. Dissatisfied members can sometimes pressure the bargaining unit as a whole to discuss what the union's policy should be and, perhaps, affect the policy. For example, Hollins and Hawkins could have campaigned within their local to make elimination of employment discrimination a top priority in upcoming contract negotiations, or they could have demanded that the membership endorse contract language giving the next ten promotions to qualified minority employees. If Hollins and Hawkins reflected only a dissident view, however, is it likely they would succeed in their efforts within the union? From the union's perspective, is such use of the internal political process consistent with the need to present a united front in negotiations? Who gains more from a bruising political battle within the union over priorities at upcoming negotiations—the workers, the union or the employer?

5. *Decertification.* Section 9 of the NLRA sets out election procedures to determine whether a union has majority support of the workers it wants to represent. Section 9(c)(3) provides for removal by majority vote of an incumbent bargaining representative. An interest group backed by a majority of workers rarely will need to resort to decertification because union officials are likely to be sensitive to the demands of their constituents. If the minority can't muster enough support to influence union policy, how likely is it to command the votes necessary to get rid of the union?

Even if worker sentiment against the union is strong, decertification may not be a realistic solution. Unions of any significance in the private sector are members of the AFL–CIO, which is a federation of domestically-based national and international labor organizations. An Article of the AFL–CIO Constitution, the "no raiding" provision, prohibits member unions from challenging the representational status of other member unions where an established bargaining relationship exists. In decertification elections, therefore, the choice is frequently between retaining the incumbent labor organization as bargaining representative or having no representative at all. Disenchanted as some employees may be with their union's policies or local enforcement of those policies, workers may not want to exchange their collective bargaining representative for the right to deal only as individuals with their employer.

NOTE ON TWO CONFLICTING DIRECTIVES
IN THE NLRA

After discussing the principle of majority rule, Justice Marshall goes on to say in Part II B that employees may not bargain separately with their employer, for that violates the principle of exclusivity. On the other hand, Section 9(a) of the Act (which you should consult right now), after setting out the principle of exclusive representation provides that individual employees have the right to present grievances to their employer and have them adjusted "without the intervention of the bargaining representative, as long as the adjustment is not inconsistent with the terms of a collective-bargaining contract or agreement then in effect." A further proviso says the union must be given the opportunity to be present at such adjustment. The further proviso says nothing about a union's veto power over the adjustment, but that may be implied by the previous sentence. You might read the proviso to give the individual the absolute right to raise a grievance with the employer. But the proviso has been interpreted merely to protect the employer against a charge by the union should the employer decide to deal with the individual employee (see footnote 12 in the *Emporium Capwell* decision.)

Justice Marshall goes on to say the complaining employees in *Emporium Capwell* "bypassed the grievance procedure" in favor of bargaining with their employer. How does Justice Marshall draw the line between individual employees expressing their demands through the grievance process, which is okay, and bargaining separately with their employer, which is not? Is the difference that in pursuing a grievance the employees merely seek to apply the existing terms of an agreement, while in bargaining they seek to change that agreement? You'll see as you study collective agreements further that there may be little difference between applying the existing terms of an agreement and altering the terms of the agreement. Some would say that most grievances about the meaning of the contract arise because the contract is not clear, and that any resolution of the grievance is really a change in the contract itself. Professor Theodore St. Antoine has suggested as much in his characterization of the arbitrator as the parties' designated "reader" of the contract. Theodore St. Antoine, A Second Look at Enterprise Wheel & Progeny, 75 Michigan Law Review 1137 (1977). Why does the Act tolerate fine tuning of the agreement by individuals, but not wholesale changes?

2. EXCLUSIVITY AND THE DUTY OF FAIR REPRESENTATION

FORD MOTOR CO. v. HUFFMAN

Supreme Court of the United States, 1953.
345 U.S. 330, 73 S.Ct. 681, 97 L.Ed. 1048.

MR. JUSTICE BURTON delivered the opinion of the Court.

In these cases we sustain the validity of collective-bargaining agreements whereby an employer, in determining relative seniority of employment among its employees, gives them credit for pre-employment military service as well as the credit required by statute for post-employment military service.

These proceedings were begun in the United States District Court for the Western District of Kentucky by respondent Huffman, acting individually and on behalf of a class of about 275 fellow employees of the Ford Motor Company, petitioner in Case No. 193 (here called Ford). * * *

The pleadings state that Huffman entered the employ of Ford September 23, 1943, was inducted into military service November 18, 1944, was discharged July 1, 1946, and, within 30 days, was reemployed by Ford with seniority dating from September 23, 1943, as provided by statute.[5] It does not appear whether the other members of his class are veterans but, like him, all have seniority computed from their respective dates of employment by Ford.

The pleadings allege further that Huffman and the members of his class all have been laid off or furloughed from their respective employments at times and for periods when they would not have been so laid off or furloughed except for the provisions complained of in the collective-bargaining agreements. Those provisions state, in substance, that after July 30, 1946, in determining the order of retention of employees, all veterans in the employ of Ford "shall receive seniority credit for their period of service, subsequent to June 21, 1941 in the land or naval forces or Merchant Marine of the United States or its allies, upon completion of their probationary period" of six months.

---

5. "Sec. 8. * * *

"(b) In the case of any such person who, in order to perform such training and service, has left or leaves a position, other than a temporary position, in the employ of any employer and who (1) receives such certificate [of satisfactory completion of his period of training and service], (2) is still qualified to perform the duties of such position, and (3) makes application for reemployment within ninety days after he is relieved from such training and service.

* * *

"(B) if such position was in the employ of a private employer, such employer shall restore such person to such position or to a position of like seniority, status, and pay unless the employer's circumstances have so changed as to make it impossible or unreasonable to do so; * * *." 54 Stat. 890, 58 Stat. 798, 50 U.S.C.App. § 308(b)(B), 50 U.S.C.A. Appendix, § 308.

The effect of these provisions is that whereas Huffman's seniority, and that of the members of his class, is computed from their respective dates of employment by Ford and they have been credited with their subsequent military service, if any, yet in some instances they are now surpassed in seniority by employees who entered the employ of Ford after they did but who are credited with certain military service which they rendered before their employment by Ford.[7]

[On cross-motions for summary judgment, the federal district court dismissed the action. The Court of Appeals reversed, with one judge dissenting.]

Respondent contended in the Court of Appeals that allowance of credit for pre-employment military service was invalid because it went beyond the credit prescribed by the Selective Training and Service Act of 1940. That argument was rejected unanimously. It has not been pressed here. There is nothing in that statute which prohibits allowing such a credit if the employer and employees agree to do so. The statutory rights of returning veterans are subject to changes in the conditions of their employment which have occurred in regular course during their absence in military service, where the changes are not hostile devices discriminating against veterans.

On the other hand, the second objection raised by respondent was sustained by a majority of the members of the Court of Appeals. This objection was that the authority of International, as a certified bargaining representative, was limited by statute and was exceeded when International agreed to the provisions that are before us.

The authority of every bargaining representative under the National Labor Relations Act, as amended, is stated in broad terms:

> "Sec. 7. Employees shall have the right to self-organization, to form, join, or assist labor organizations, to bargain collectively through representatives of their own choosing, and to engage in other concerted activities for the purpose of *collective bargaining or other mutual aid or protection.** * *

> "Sec. 9. (a) Representatives designated or selected for the purposes of collective bargaining by the majority of the employees in a unit appropriate for such purposes, shall be the exclusive represen-

---

7. On Huffman's return to Ford in July, 1946, his employment seniority, including his military service, dated from September 23, 1943. It totaled about 33 months, including about 14 months of pre-service company employment and 19 of post-employment military service. An example of a veteran who, due to the agreements before us, outranks Huffman in employment seniority is one who entered military service July 1, 1943, without any prior employment, served honorably until discharged March 1, 1945, and, thereafter, has been employed continuously by Ford, including six months of satisfactory probationary employment. His seniority dates from July 1, 1943. By July 1, 1946, it totaled 36 months, including 20 months of pre-employment military service, and 16 of post-service company employment. However, except for the collective-bargaining agreements. Huffman would then have outranked such a veteran by about 17 months, although Huffman's military service totaled one month less, his employment by Ford two months less and his combined military service and company employment three months less than that of such a veteran.

tatives of all the employees in such unit for the purposes of *collective bargaining in respect to rates of pay, wages, hours of employment, or other conditions of employment: * * * "* (Emphasis supplied.)

In the absence of limiting factors, the above purposes, including "mutual aid or protection" and "other conditions of employment", are broad enough to cover terms of seniority. The National Labor Relations Act, as passed in 1935 and as amended in 1947, exemplifies the faith of Congress in free collective bargaining between employers and their employees when conducted by freely and fairly chosen representatives of appropriate units of employees. That the authority of bargaining representatives, however, is not absolute is recognized in Steele v. Louisville & N.R. Co., 323 U.S. 192, 198–199, 65 S.Ct. 226, 230, 89 L.Ed. 173, in connection with comparable provisions of the Railway Labor Act. Their statutory obligation to represent all members of an appropriate unit requires them to make an honest effort to serve the interests of all of those members, without hostility to any.

Any authority to negotiate derives its principal strength from a delegation to the negotiators of a discretion to make such concessions and accept such advantages as, in the light of all relevant considerations, they believe will best serve the interests of the parties represented. A major responsibility of negotiators is to weigh the relative advantages and disadvantages of differing proposals. A bargaining representative, under the National Labor Relations Act, as amended, often is a labor organization but it is not essential that it be such. The employees represented often are members of the labor organization which represents them at the bargaining table, but it is not essential that they be such. The bargaining representative, whoever it may be, is responsible to, and owes complete loyalty to, the interests of all whom it represents. In the instant controversy, International represented, with certain exceptions not material here, all employees at the Louisville works, including both the veterans with, and those without, prior employment by Ford, as well as the employees having no military service. Inevitably differences arise in the manner and degree to which the terms of any negotiated agreement affect individual employees and classes of employees. The mere existence of such differences does not make them invalid. The complete satisfaction of all who are represented is hardly to be expected. A wide range of reasonableness must be allowed a statutory bargaining representative in serving the unit it represents, subject always to complete good faith and honesty of purpose in the exercise of its discretion.

Compromises on a temporary basis, with a view to long range advantages, are natural incidents of negotiation. Differences in wages, hours and conditions of employment reflect countless variables. Seniority rules governing promotions, transfers, layoffs and similar matters may, in the first instance, revolve around length of competent service. Variations acceptable in the discretion of bargaining representatives, however, may well include differences based upon such matters as the unit within which seniority is to be computed, the privileges to which it shall relate, the nature of the work, the time at which it is done, the fitness, ability or age of the employees, their family responsibilities, injuries received in course of service, and time or labor devoted to related public service, whether civil or military, voluntary or involuntary. See, e.g., Hartley v. Brotherhood of Clerks, 283 Mich. 201, 277 N.W. 885.

The National Labor Relations Act, as amended, gives a bargaining representative not only wide responsibility but authority to meet that responsibility. * * *

The public policy and fairness inherent in crediting employees with time spent in military service in time of war or national emergency is so clear that Congress, in the Selective Training and Service Act of 1940, required some credit to be given for it in computing seniority both in governmental and in private employment. Congress there prescribed that employees who left their private civilian employment to enter military service should receive seniority credit for such military service, provided their prior civilian employment, however brief, was bona fide and not on a temporary basis. There is little that justifies giving such a substantial benefit to a veteran with brief prior civilian employment that does not equally justify giving it to a veteran who was inducted into military service before having a chance to enter any civilian employment, or to a veteran who never worked for the particular employer who hired him after his return from military service. The respective values of all such veterans, as employees, are substantially the same. From the point of view of public policy and industrial stability, there is much to be said, especially in time of war or emergency, for allowing credit for all military service. Any other course adopts the doubtful policy of favoring those who stay out of military service over those who enter it.

The above considerations took concrete form in the Veterans' Preference Act of 1944 which added the requirement that credit for military service be given by every civilian federal agency, whether the military service preceded or followed civilian employment. Apparently recognizing the countless variations in conditions affecting private employment, Congress, however, did not make credit for such pre-employment military service compulsory in private civilian employment. A little later, the Administrator of the Retraining and Reemployment Administration of the United States Department of Labor assembled a representative committee to recommend principles to serve as guides to private employers in their employment of veterans and others. Among 15 principles developed by that committee, and "wholeheartedly" endorsed by the Secretary of Labor, in 1946, were the following:

"8. All veterans having reemployment rights under Federal statutes should be accorded these statutory rights *as a minimum.* * * *

"13. Newly hired veterans who have served a probationary period and qualified for employment should be allowed seniority credit, at least for purposes of job retention, equal to time spent in the armed services plus time spent in recuperation from service-connected injuries or disabilities either through hospitalization or vocational training."

The provisions before us reflect such a policy. It is not necessary to define here the limits to which a collective-bargaining representative may go in accepting proposals to promote the long range social or economic welfare of those it represents. Nothing in the National Labor Relations Act, as amended, so limits the vision and action of a bargaining representative that it must disregard public policy and national security. Nor does anything in that Act compel a bargaining representative to limit seniority clauses solely to the relative lengths of employment of the respective employees. * * *

The provisions before us are within reasonable bounds of relevancy. They extended but slightly, during a period of war and emergency, the acceptance of credits for military service under circumstances where comparable credit already was required, by statute, in favor of all who had been regularly employed by Ford before entering military service. These provisions conform to the recommendation of responsible Government officials and round out a statutory requirement which, unless so rounded out, produces discriminations of its own. A failure to adopt these provisions might have resulted in more friction among employees represented by International than did their adoption. * * *

We hold that International, as a collective-bargaining representative, had authority to accept these provisions. Accordingly, we find no ground sufficient to establish the invalidity of the provisions before us or to sustain an injunction against either petitioner. * * *

THE DUTY OF FAIR REPRESENTATION AFTER FORD MOTOR CO.

Ford Motor gives unions enormous leeway in negotiating the terms of a collective agreement. You might try to explain *Ford* by the Court's solicitude for returning veterans, which assured that the union's decision to protect their interests would be upheld. Indeed, our colleague Professor Laura Cooper has uncovered the union's brief in the Ford Motor case. It says this in support of the credit for time served in the armed forces: "Furthermore, during World War II, a considerable number of married women and other older persons were hired by employers engaged in war production. It was the belief of the petitioner that in the face of the predicted decrease in employment during the immediate postwar period, veterans should be given preference in job security over such persons who in all probability were in smaller actual need of remunerative employment." How would that argument fly today?

In any event, many years later in Air Line Pilots Ass'n v. O'Neill, 499 U.S. 65, 111 S.Ct. 1127, 113 L.Ed.2d 51 (1991,) the Court reviewed a challenge by airline pilots to a contract negotiated by their union which resulted in many loyal union pilots being permanently replaced by strikebreaking pilots. The Court characterized this as about as bad a deal as a union could make, but it held that the union didn't violate its duty of fair representation toward the pilots. While one can argue that the union could not have done much better with the difficult Continental Airlines, and thus the agreement is not as bad as it seems, the Court treats the union's conduct as quite deficient, and yet its language pretty well insulates union decisions in bargaining from challenge under the fair representation doctrine. The Court said,

> The Court of Appeals placed great stress on the fact that the deal struck by ALPA was worse than the result the union would have obtained by unilateral termination of the strike. Indeed, the court held that a jury finding that the settlement was worse than surrender could alone support a judgment that the union had acted arbitrarily and irrationally. *See* 886 F.2d at 1445–1446. This holding unduly constrains the "wide range of reasonableness," 345 U.S., at 338, 73 S.Ct., at 686, within which unions may act without breaching their fair representation duty.

> For purposes of decision, we may assume that the Court of Appeals was correct in its conclusion that, if ALPA had simply surrendered and voluntarily terminated the strike, the striking pilots would have been entitled to reemployment in the order of seniority. Moreover, we may assume that Continental would have responded to such action by rescinding its assignment of all of the 85–5 bid positions to working pilots. After all, it did rescind about half of those assignments pursuant to the terms of the settlement. Thus, we assume that the union made a bad settlement—one that was even worse than a unilateral termination of the strike.

> Nevertheless, the settlement was by no means irrational. A settlement is not irrational simply because it turns out *in retrospect* to have been a bad settlement. Viewed in light of the legal landscape at the time of the settlement, ALPA's decision to settle rather than give up was certainly not illogical. At the time of the settlement, Continental had notified the union that all of the 85–5 bid positions had been awarded to working pilots and was maintaining that none of the strikers had any claim on any of those jobs.

Some commentators had suggested that the latitude *Ford* gave unions to set the terms of an agreement should not be as broad when the union applies those terms to pending grievances. However, the ALPA Court says that the standards in both situations are the same, 499 U.S. 68 at 77. We will take a closer look at this proposition in Chapter III, when we examine the union's duty to represent separate interests in the grievance and arbitration process.

COMMUNICATIONS WORKERS OF AMERICA v. BECK
Supreme Court of the United States, 1988.
487 U.S. 735, 108 S.Ct. 2641, 101 L.Ed.2d 634.

JUSTICE BRENNAN delivered the opinion of the Court.

Section 8(a)(3) of the National Labor Relations Act of 1935 (NLRA), permits an employer and an exclusive bargaining representative to enter into an agreement requiring all employees in the bargaining unit to pay periodic union dues and initiation fees as a condition of continued employment, whether or not the employees otherwise wish to become union members. Today we must decide whether this provision also permits a union, over the objections of dues-paying nonmember employees, to expend funds so collected on activities unrelated to collective bargaining, contract administration, or grievance adjustment, and, if so, whether such expenditures violate the union's duty of fair representation or the objecting employees' First Amendment rights.

In accordance with § 9 of the NLRA, a majority of the employees of American Telephone and Telegraph Company and several of its subsidiaries selected petitioner Communications Workers of America (CWA) as their exclusive bargaining representative. As such, the union is empowered to bargain collectively with the employer on behalf of all employees in the bargaining unit over wages, hours, and other terms and conditions of employment, and it accordingly enjoys "broad authority ... in the negotiation and administration of [the] collective bargaining contract." Humphrey v. Moore, 375 U.S. 335, 342, 84 S.Ct. 368, 367, 11 L.Ed.2d 370 (1964). This broad authority, however, is tempered by the union's "statutory obligation to serve the interests of all members without hostility or discrimination toward any," Vaca v. Sipes, 386 U.S. 171, 177, 87 S.Ct. 903, 910, 17 L.Ed.2d 842 (1967), a duty that extends not only to the negotiation of the collective-bargaining agreement itself but also to the subsequent enforcement of that agreement, including the administration of any grievance procedure the agreement may establish. CWA chartered several local unions, copetitioners in this case, to assist it in discharging these statutory duties. In addition, at least in part to help defray the considerable costs it incurs in performing these tasks, CWA negotiated a union-security clause in the collective-bargaining agreement under which all represented employees, including those who do not wish to become union members, must pay the union "agency fees" in "amounts equal to the periodic dues" paid by union members. Under the clause, failure to tender the required fee may be grounds for discharge.

In June 1976, respondents, 20 employees who chose not to become union members, initiated this suit challenging CWA's use of their agency fees for purposes other than collective bargaining, contract administration, or grievance adjustment (hereinafter "collective-bargaining" or "representational" activities). Specifically, respondents alleged that the union's expenditure of their fees on activities such as organizing the employees of other employers, lobbying for labor legislation, and participating in social, charitable, and political events violated petitioners' duty of fair representation, § 8(a)(3) of the NLRA, the First Amendment, and various common-law fiduciary duties. In addition to declaratory relief, respondents sought an injunction barring petitioners from exacting fees above those necessary to finance collective-bargaining activities, as well as damages for the past collection of such excess fees.

The District Court concluded that the union's collection and disbursement of agency fees for purposes other than bargaining unit representation violated the associational and free speech rights of objecting nonmembers, and therefore enjoined their future collection. Applying a "clear and convincing" evidentiary standard, the District Court concluded that the union had failed to show that more than 21% of its funds were expended on collective-bargaining matters. The court ordered reimbursement of all excess fees respondents had paid since January 1976, and directed the union to institute a recordkeeping system to segregate accounts for representational and noncollective-bargaining activities.

A divided panel of the United States Court of Appeals for the Fourth Circuit agreed that respondents stated a valid claim for relief under the First Amendment, but, preferring to rest its judgment on a ground other than the Constitution, concluded that the collection of nonmembers' fees for purposes unrelated to collective bargaining violated § 8(a)(3). [776 F.2d 1187 (1985).] Turning to the specific activities challenged, the majority noted that the District Court's adoption of a "clear and convincing" standard of proof was improper, but found that for certain categories of expenditures, such as lobbying, organizing employees in other companies, and funding various community services, the error was harmless inasmuch as the activities were indisputably unrelated to bargaining unit representation. The majority remanded the case for reconsideration of the remaining expenditures, which the union claimed were made in connection with valid collective-bargaining activities. Chief Judge Winter dissented. He concluded that § 8(a)(3) authorized exaction of fees in amounts equivalent to full union dues, including fees expended on nonrepresentational activities, and that the negotiation and enforcement of agreements permitting such exactions was private conduct incapable of violating the constitutional rights of objecting nonmembers.

On rehearing, the en banc court vacated the panel opinion and by a 6–to–4 vote again affirmed in part, reversed in part, and remanded for further proceedings. The court explained in a brief *per curiam* opinion that five of the six majority judges believed there was federal jurisdiction over both the § 8(a)(3) and the duty-of-fair-representation claims, and that respondents were entitled to judgment on both. Judge Murnaghan, casting the deciding vote, concluded that the court had jurisdiction over only the duty-of-fair-representation claim; although he believed that § 8(a)(3) permits union-security clauses requiring payment of full union dues, he concluded that the collection of such fees from Nonmembers to finance activities unrelated to collective bargaining violates the union's duty of fair representation. All six of these judges agreed with the panel's resolution of the specific allocations issue and accordingly remanded the action. Chief Judge Winter, joined by three others, again dissented for the reasons set out in his earlier panel dissent.

A

Both the structure and purpose of § 8(a)(3) are best understood in light of the statute's historical origins. Prior to the enactment of the Taft–Hartley Act of 1947, § 8(a)(3) of the Wagner Act of 1935 (NLRA) permitted majority unions to negotiate "closed shop" agreements requiring employers to hire only persons who were already union members. By 1947, such agreements had come under increasing attack, and after extensive hearings Congress determined that the closed shop and the abuses associated with it "create[d] too great a barrier to free employment to be longer tolerated." S.Rep. No. 105, 80th Cong., 1st Sess., 6 (1947) (S.Rep.), Legislative History of Labor Management Relations Act, 1947. The 1947 Congress was equally concerned, however, that without such agreements, many employees would reap the benefits that unions negotiated on their behalf without in any way contributing financial support to those efforts. As Senator Taft, one of the authors of the 1947 legislation, explained, "the argument . . . against abolishing the closed shop . . . is that if there is not a closed shop those not in the union will get a free ride, that the union does the work, gets the wages raised, then the man who does not pay dues rides along freely without any expense to himself." 93 Cong.Rec. 4887 (1947), Leg. Hist. 1422.[5] Thus, the Taft–Hartley Act was

> "intended to accomplish twin purposes. On the one hand, the most serious abuses of compulsory unionism were eliminated by abolishing the closed shop. On the other hand, Congress recognized that in the absence of a union-security provision 'many employees sharing the benefits of what unions are able to accomplish by collective bargaining will refuse to pay their share of the cost.'"
> NLRB v. General Motors Corp., 373 U.S., at 740–741, 83 S.Ct., at 1458.

---

5. This sentiment was repeated throughout the hearings and lengthy debate that preceded passage of the bill. See, *e.g.*, 93 Cong.Rec. 3557 (1947), Leg.Hist. 740 (remarks of Rep. Jennings) (because members of the minority "would get the benefit of that contract made between the majority of their fellow workmen and the management . . . it is not unreasonable that they should go along and contribute dues like the others"); 93 Cong.Rec. 3558, Leg.Hist. 741 (remarks of Rep. Robison) ("If [union-negotiated] benefits come to the workers all alike, is it not only fair that the beneficiaries, whether the majority or the minority, contribute their equal share in securing these benefits?"); 93 Cong.Rec. 3837, Leg. Hist. 1010 (remarks of Sen. Taft) ([T]he legislation, "in effect, . . . say[s], that no one can get a free ride in such a shop. That meets one of the arguments for a union shop. The employee has to pay the union dues"); S.Rep., at 6, Leg.Hist. 412 ("In testifying before this Committee, . . . leaders of organized labor have stressed the fact that in the absence of [union-security] provisions many employees sharing the benefits of what unions are able to accomplish by collective bargaining will refuse to pay their share of the cost"). See also H.R.Rep. No. 245, 80th Cong., 1st Sess., 80 (1947) (H.R.Rep.), Leg.Hist. 371 ("[Closed shop] agreements prevent nonunion workers from sharing in the benefits resulting from union activities without also sharing in the obligations").

The legislative solution embodied in § 8(a)(3) allows employers to enter into agreements requiring all the employees in a given bargaining unit to become members 30 days after being hired as long as such membership is available to all workers on a nondiscriminatory basis, but it prohibits the mandatory discharge of an employee who is expelled from the union for any reason other than his or her failure to pay initiation fees or dues. As we have previously observed, Congress carefully tailored this solution to the evils at which it was aimed:

> "Th[e] legislative history clearly indicates that Congress intended to prevent utilization of union security agreements for any purpose other than to compel payment of union dues and fees. Thus Congress recognized the validity of unions' concerns about 'free riders,' *i.e.,* employees who receive the benefits of union representation but are unwilling to contribute their *fair share* of financial support to such union, and gave unions the power to contract to meet *that problem* while withholding from unions the power to cause the discharge of employees for any other reason." *Radio Officers v. NLRB,* 347 U.S. 17 (1954) (emphasis added).

Indeed, "Congress' decision to allow union-security agreements *at all* reflects its concern that ... the parties to a collective bargaining agreement be allowed to provide that there be no employees who are getting the benefits of union representation without paying for them." *Oil Workers v. Mobil Oil Corp.,* 426 U.S. 407, 416, 96 S.Ct. 2140, 2144, 48 L.Ed.2d 736 (1976) (emphasis added).

This same concern over the resentment spawned by "free riders" in the railroad industry prompted Congress, four years after the passage of the Taft–Hartley Act, to amend the RLA. As the House Report explained, 75 to 80% of the 1.2 million railroad industry workers belonged to one or another of the railway unions. These unions, of course, were legally obligated to represent the interests of all workers, including those who did not become members thus nonunion workers were able, at no expense to themselves, to share in all the benefits the unions obtained through collective bargaining. Noting that the "principle of authorizing agreements for the union shop and the deduction of union dues has now become firmly established as a national policy for all industry subject to the Labor Management Relations Act of 1947," the House Report concluded that "[n]o sound reason exists for continuing to deny to labor organizations subject to the Railway Labor Act the right to negotiate agreements with railroads and airlines of a character permitted in the case of labor organizations in the other large industries of the country." H.R. No. 2811, 81st Cong., 2d Sess., 4 (1950).

In drafting what was to become § 2, Eleventh, Congress did not look to § 8(a)(3) merely for guidance. Rather, as Senator Taft argued in support of the legislation, the amendment "inserts in the railway mediation law almost the exact provisions, so far as they fit, of the Taft–Hartley law, so that the conditions regarding the union shop and the check-off are carried into the relations between railroad unions and the

railroads." 96 Cong.Rec. 16267 (1950)[6] This was the universal understanding, among both supporters and opponents, of the purpose and
effect of the amendment. Indeed, railroad union representatives themselves proposed the amendment that incorporated in § 2, Eleventh,
§ 8(a)(3)'s prohibition against the discharge of employees who fail to
obtain or maintain union membership for any reason other than nonpay-
ment of periodic dues; in offering this proposal the unions argued, in
terms echoing the language of the Senate Report accompanying the
Taft–Hartley Act, that such a prohibition "remedies the alleged abuses
of compulsory union membership . . ., yet makes possible the elimination
of the 'free rider' and the sharing of the burden of maintenance by all of
the beneficiaries of union activity." Hearings on H.R. 7789 before the
House Committee on Interstate and Foreign Commerce, 81st Cong., 2d
Sess., 253 (1950).

In *Street* [Machinists v. Street, 367 U.S. 740, 81 S.Ct. 1784, 6
L.Ed.2d 1141 (1961)] we concluded "that § 2, Eleventh contemplated
compulsory unionism to force employees to share the costs of negotiating
and administering collective agreements, and the costs of the adjustment
and settlement of disputes," but that Congress did not intend "to
provide the unions with a means for forcing employees, over their
objection, to support political causes which they oppose." 367 U.S., at
764, 81 S.Ct., at 1798. Construing the statute in light of this legislative
history and purpose, we held that although § 2, Eleventh on its face
authorizes the collection from nonmembers of "periodic dues, initiation
fees, and assessments . . . *uniformly required* as a condition of acquiring
or retaining membership" in a union, 45 U.S.C. § 152, Eleventh (b)
(emphasis added), this authorization did not "ves[t] the unions with
unlimited power to spend exacted money." 367 U.S., at 768, 81 S.Ct., at
1800. We have since reaffirmed that "Congress' essential justification for
authorizing the union shop" limits the expenditures that may properly
be charged to nonmembers under § 2, Eleventh to those "necessarily or
reasonably incurred for the purpose of performing the duties of an
exclusive [bargaining] representative." *Ellis v. Railway Clerks,* 466 U.S.,
at 447–448, 104 S.Ct., at 1892. Given the parallel purpose, structure, and
language of § 8(a)(3), we must interpret that provision in the same
manner.[7] Like § 2, Eleventh, § 8(a)(3) permits the collection of "periodic
dues and initiation fees uniformly required as a condition of acquiring or

---

6. Although Senator Taft qualified his
comparison by explaining that the provisions of the Taft–Hartley law were incorporated into the RLA "so far as they fit," this
qualification merely reflected the fact that
the laws were not identical in all respects,
their chief difference inhering in their
preemptive effect, or lack thereof, on all
state regulation of union-security agreements. See n. 3, *supra.* This difference, of
course, does not detract from the near identity of the provisions insofar as they confer
on unions and employers authority to enter
into union-security agreements, nor does it
in any way undermine the force of Senator

Taft's comparison with respect to this authority. Indeed, Taft himself explained that
he initially "objected to some of the original
terms of the bill, but when the [bill's] proponents agreed to accept amendments
which made the provisions *identical* with
the Taft–Hartley law," he decided to support the law. 96 Cong.Rec. 16267 (1950)
(emphasis added).

7. We note that the NLRB, at least for a
time, also took the position that the uniform "periodic dues and initiation fees"
required by § 8(a)(3) were limited by the
congressional concern with free riders to

retaining membership" in the union and like its counterpart in the RLA, § 8(a)(3) was designed to remedy the inequities posed by "free riders" who would otherwise unfairly profit from the Taft–Hartley Act's abolition of the closed shop. In the face of such statutory congruity, only the most compelling evidence could persuade us that Congress intended the nearly identical language of these two provisions to have different meanings. Petitioners have not proffered such evidence here.

We conclude that § 8(a)(3), like its statutory equivalent, § 2, Eleventh of the RLA, authorizes the exaction of only those fees and dues necessary to "performing the duties of an exclusive representative of the employees in dealing with the employer on labor-management issues." Ellis, 466 U.S., at 448, 104 S.Ct., at 1892. Accordingly, the judgment of the Court of Appeals is

Affirmed.

JUSTICE KENNEDY took no part in the consideration or decision of this case.

JUSTICE BLACKMUN, with whom JUSTICE O'CONNOR and JUSTICE SCALIA join, concurring in part and dissenting in part.

———

The Court has given further guidance on the scope of mandatory fair share charges in the public sector in Lehnert v. Ferris Faculty Association, 500 U.S. 507, 111 S.Ct. 1950, 114 L.Ed.2d 572 (1991).

those fees necessary to finance collective-bargaining activities. In *Teamsters Local No. 959,* 167 N.L.R.B. 1042, 1045 (1967), the Board explained:

"[T]he right to charge 'periodic dues' granted unions by the proviso to Section 8(a)(3) is concerned exclusively with the concept that those enjoying the benefits of collective bargaining should bear their fair share of the costs incurred by the collective-bargaining agent in representing them. But it is manifest that dues that do not contribute, and are not intended to contribute, to the cost of operation of a union in its capacity as collective-bargaining agent cannot be justified as necessary for the elimination of 'free riders.'"

The Board, however, subsequently repudiated that view. See *Detroit Mailers Union No. 40,* 192 N.L.R.B. 951, 952 (1971).

Notwithstanding this unequivocal language, the dissent advises us, *post,* at 2660, n. 5, that we have misread *Teamsters Local.* Choosing to ignore the above-quoted passage, the dissent asserts that the Board never "embraced ... the view," *ibid.,* that "periodic dues and initiation fees" are limited to those that finance the union in its capacity as collective-bargaining agent, because in *Teamsters Local* itself the Board concluded that the dues in question "were

actually 'special purpose funds,'" and were thus "'assessments' not contemplated by the proviso to § 8(a)(3)." *Post,* at 2660, n. 5 (quoting *Teamsters Local, supra,* at 1044). This observation, however, avails the dissent nothing; obviously, once the Board determined that the dues were not used for collective-bargaining purposes, the conclusion that they were not dues within the meaning of § 8(a)(3) followed automatically. Under the dissent's reading, had the union simply built the increase into its dues base, rather than initially denominating it as a "special assessment," it would have been entitled to exact the fees as "periodic dues" and spend them for precisely the same purposes without running afoul of § 8(a)(3). The Board made entirely clear, however, that it was the *purpose* of the fee, not the manner in which it was collected, that controlled, and thus explained that "[m]onies collected for a credit union or building fund even if regularly recurring, as here, are obviously not 'for the maintenance of the' [union] as an organization, but are for a 'special purpose' and could be terminated without affecting *the continued existence of [the union] as the bargaining representative.*" * * *

3. SHARING THE COSTS OF EXCLUSIVE REPRESENTATION

NOTE ON WORKERS' VOICE AND UNION DUES ON JOINING THE UNION

On the Meaning of Membership

The Beck decision introduces you to two separate but related ideas. First is the notion that a worker does not have to join a union in order to work in a unionized workplace. One of the prevalent myths in workplace lore and law is that an employee has to join a union in order to work a job at a unionized workplace. The myth is well founded, as you will see when you now look at Section 8(a)(3) of the NLRA, especially the first Proviso. It says that a union lawfully may make an agreement with an employer that requires membership in the union after 30 days of employment as a condition of employment. Prior to the enactment of the NLRA, unions had been allowed to insist on a "closed shop" arrangement, in which the employer could only hire existing union members. But this was thought to be inimical to the right of employee choice. So the existing rule is characterized as the "union shop": a worker needn't be a union member to be hired—in fact, under 8(a)(3) it is unlawful for the employer to take union membership into account in hiring—but after hiring he or she may be required to join the union, if the employer has agreed to a union security clause.

However, the Supreme Court has interpreted the Proviso to require not membership, but only the payment to the union of the equivalent of union dues and initiation fees. This reading, not at all obvious, derives from the "Provided Further" portion of Section 8(a)(3), part (B), which can be interpreted to mean that all the union may require is payment of dues and initiation fees. As the Court said in NLRB v. General Motors, 373 U.S. 734, 83 S.Ct. 1453, 10 L.Ed.2d 670 (1963), " 'membership' as a condition of employment, is whittled down to its financial core." You'll encounter that language again in footnote 16 of the Patternmakers case, later in this chapter. Perhaps you can appreciate that an interpretation of the statute that required membership in a union might violate the First Amendment, and the Court's analysis simply follows the well trodden maxim that statutes should be interpreted in a way that avoids a possibly unconstitutional result. By the way, where's the state action that gives rise to the potential constitutional claim?

We are told that in most organized workplaces the union and the personnel staff will advise new employees that they must join the union within 30 days. Right to work advocates have mounted a campaign to make it unlawful to say this, given the gloss placed on the statute by the Court. Unions respond, how can it be unlawful to tell the worker exactly what the Act says? What do you think? Should the Act be amended to avoid this situation?

The NLRB has recently held, in California Saw and Knife Works, 320 NLRB 224 (1995), that the union's duty of fair representation requires it to disclose to a would-be member that the law does not require actual membership, but only the payment of the amount of union dues that covers the services provided by the union. We'll have more on that later.

But even if the NLRA does not require union membership, most workers find it to their advantage to join the union that represents them in the workplace. After all, the union speaks for them and has the exclusive right to set terms and administer the agreement, so the worker might as well have a voice in what the union does. The worker who does not join the union, has absolutely no say in its affairs, nor can he participate in elections for union officers. Internal union affairs are regulated by the Landrum–Griffin Act. If the collective agreement requires the worker to participate in the financial support of the union, the worker might as well get one's money's worth by participating in the governance of the union. Incidentally, a union has no obligation under the NLRA to admit a person to membership. This seems an entirely anachronistic and wrong notion, given the union's power over the bargaining unit. However, as a practical matter, a union seldom excludes anyone from membership these days.

On paying for the union's services

The power of exclusive representation granted to the union obliges it to represent everyone in the bargaining unit. We often hear people slip into the misusage that the union must represent all union members. But actually, the union must represent everyone in the bargaining unit, member or not. This means that the worker who does not join the union, but who nevertheless reaps the benefits of representation, must pay for those services. This is the second part of the message in *Beck*. It is an aspect of the notion that one who uses public goods must pay for them.

So while *Beck* allows workers to refrain from joining the union, if there is a clause in the collective bargaining agreement requiring membership in the union, the non-joining employee must pay the equivalent of union dues related to collective bargaining purposes. This is known as the "fair share" obligation. The "fair share" is not necessarily the full shot of union dues. In a number of decisions the Court has held that a person who does not wish to join a union need pay only that portion of union dues that is germane to collective bargaining at her workplace. The Beck case explains all this. However, in its preoccupation with finding a doctrinal basis to require the payment of a fair share, the Court pays little attention to what the scope of that fair share should be, simply endorsing without any discussion the finding of the lower court, which was that almost 80% of the union's dues were not germane to the costs of representation. What did the union do with that money? Did it squander it?

As you think about *Beck*, ask whether the Court draws its lines too narrowly. The modern union does an enormous amount of work in the legislative arena and in politics. In Chapter One we saw a host of statutes that benefit workers in both unionized and non-union workplaces. Who do you suppose lobbied for enactment of those laws? In Chapter Three we'll look at the regulation of health and safety in the workplace. We'll see that it is much more efficient for unions to pool their resources and lobby for protective laws that set a floor for safety and health conditions than to tackle them in each individual workplace. Indeed, the union can only gain effective worker health and safety protection if it secures these benefits across the board. The workplace that is required by its union to have tougher standards than its non-union competitor is not going to compete very effectively. We will also notice in Chapter Three that the plaintiff in one of the important cases on workers rights with respect to health and safety (*Johnson Controls*) was a union. So "voice" in the workplace includes voice in the enactment of legislation that benefits workers. It also involves politics, in supporting those candidates who are most likely to favor a workers' agenda. Why shouldn't the law require the objecting non-member to pay for that representation?

One answer may be that the Beck decision built upon an earlier Railway Labor Act case, *Street*, which seemed to have some Constitutional concerns, Machinists v. Street, 367 U.S. 740, 81 S.Ct. 1784, 6 L.Ed.2d 1141 (1961). Beck has made a wholesale adoption of the principles of Street. Yet, as the Beck decision reveals, the Court (and the lower courts as well) did not conclude that there necessarily is state action in the union dues situation. The Board in California Knife and Saw, discussed earlier, tackled the tough question that was finessed in Beck of whether the union is really a governmental actor by virtue of the power granted to it under the NLRA's exclusivity provision. That is, without the blessing granted by the statutory grant of exclusivity, the union would not be able to negotiate a provision in the collective bargaining agreement that requires membership (or at least its dues-paying equivalent) as a condition of employment. It remains to be seen whether the reconstituted Board during the Bush administration agrees with this conclusion, and whether it is accepted by the courts. If there is no state action in the negotiation of an agency fee clause, then there should be no Constitutional impediment to the union using a portion of those dues to lobby and support political causes.

The NLRB has recently taken the position that a union may charge a non-member for the costs of organizing a competitor. This conclusion was reversed by the Ninth Circuit in United Food and Commercial Workers v. NLRB, 249 F.3d 1115 (9th Cir. 2001). The court based its decision on the key Supreme Court case under the Railway Labor Act, Ellis v. Railway, Airline and Steamship Clerks, 466 U.S. 435, 104 S.Ct. 1883, 80 L.Ed.2d 428 (1984), which said a nonmember may be charged only for union activities related to collective bargaining, contract administration and grievance adjustment. In its decision in *Beck*, the Supreme

Court relied heavily upon *Ellis* in determining the scope of expenditures that may properly be charged to a nonmember, even though the two cases arise under different statutes.

The Board attempted to distinguish the two statutes. Is that a promising approach? Or would the Board be better off presenting empirical evidence that shows that the expenditures for organizing a competitor are a proper part of the costs of collective bargaining? What evidence would you marshal to try to establish that point? If a union does not organize the other companies in its industry, what chance does it have of negotiating a meaningful economic package for the employees it represents?

The Court has given further guidance on the scope of mandatory fair share charges in the public sector in Lehnert v. Ferris Faculty Association, 500 U.S. 507, 111 S.Ct. 1950, 114 L.Ed.2d 572 (1991).

The observation in this note must be qualified in right-to-work states. You may be aware of Section 14(b) of the NLRA, known as the "right-to-work" provision. It preserves the laws of those states that do not allow unions to require membership as a condition of work. This is said to preserve the rights of individuals to choose not to join unions. But with the gloss placed on the NLRA in *Beck,* there is little or no significance to the right to work provision, for the result is the same in all states. A number of right to work states allow a company and union to require the non-member to pay his fair share of the union dues (this is often known as the "agency fee," as it is usually called in the public sector).

4. THE COLLECTIVE BARGAINING COMMUNITY: INCLUSIVE OR DIVISIVE?

Nan meets with Eulah Blair, the organizer for the UMCA who is assisting the RN's in the organization of Mercy Hospital. They have the following conversation:

Nan: Eulah, I'm not sure where I stand on having a union represent me, but one of the things that concerns me is that I feel that nurse practitioners have different needs, different interests than the RN's in your group. As you know, we have taken additional training, we work independently, though under the supervision of physicians, we are allowed to write prescriptions, and occasionally to supervise other nurses. I'm afraid that if we're in a unit with RN's, where we're a distinct numerical minority, you just aren't going to look after our interests. You'll seek wage increases for the RN's at the expense of the nurse practitioners, you'll seek to upgrade the professional status of RN's by closing the gap with us, and in general not worry very much about our very small group.

Eulah: I hear you, but I think you have to realize that for the union movement to succeed we have to demonstrate unity among a wide range of employees. We can only convince the Hospital of our resolve if we are all in this together. We can't be effective if every special group looks after only its own interests. That's a two way street. I'm not asking you to abandon your needs as a nurse practitioner; rather, I'm telling you that the RN's will look after your interests because we need your help to succeed.

Nan: That is all well and good as long as we can agree on what needs to be worked out. But if we disagree, and inevitably we must because there are jealousies among the various groups of our profession, then we're simply outvoted by the larger body of RN's, and we lose out. Can't we form our own bargaining unit and work side by side with the RN's? That way we have some strength when we try to accommodate our needs with yours.

Eulah: I don't think that's possible, Nan. Now in many election situations, where hospitals are not involved, the NLRB holds a hearing to determine who goes together, and that is decided on a case-by-case basis. Even there the question is not whether we've picked the most appropriate unit, but whether the union has petitioned for "an appropriate unit." This means that although there may be several possibilities, the Board will defer to the union's choice, if it is reasonable. Of course, at the same time, and in a somewhat inconsistent message, the Act says in Section 9(c)(5) that "the extent to which the employees have been organized shall not be controlling." I suppose this means that we can't just pick as our unit the one with all the workers that we've managed to sign up. But in a non-hospital setting, you might be able to carve out a separate unit for the nurse-practitioners.

However, Congress has treated the health care industry somewhat differently under the NLRA (consult NLRA Sec. 2(2) and (14)— Eds.). The Board has determined the appropriate hospital units by a rule-making, rather than by individual case determinations. In its 1974 Amendments, Congress extended coverage under the Act to nonprofit hospitals, which had been previously excluded from the Act's coverage. During the hearings leading to these amendments, Congress expressed the concern that the Board might establish bargaining units for hospitals that are too fragmented, that is, too many separate units, and this might lead to labor disputes and disruptions that would affect patient care. So by way of its legislative history, Congress instructed the Board to avoid "undue proliferation" of bargaining units in health care institutions. The Board initially attempted to implement this mandate on a case-by-case basis. But after a number of fits and starts, with the appellate courts often striking the Board down, the Board decided to establish through rule making a basic set of 8 bargaining units. The Board had seldom used rule-making before, and its departure from its normal course was upheld by the Supreme Court in American Hospital Association v. NLRB, 499 U.S. 606, 111 S.Ct. 1539, 113 L.Ed.2d 675 (1991).

Anyway, here's a set of the Board's rules on units for hospitals. You'll see that there are really only two places for us to put Nurse Practitioners. We can either claim that they are simply specialized RN's, and thus belong in the first unit for RN's, or else they must be included in the residual professional unit for all professionals except RN's and doctors. I don't suppose you'd want to include yourselves in a unit with doctors, for you are always telling us that the doctors don't respect your work, and in the residual unit your voice would be drowned out even more.

Subpart C—Appropriate Bargaining Units

§ 103.30 Appropriate bargaining units in the health care industry.

(a) This portion of the rule shall be applicable to acute care hospitals, as defined in paragraph (f) of this section: Except in extraordinary circumstances and in circumstances in which there are existing non-conforming units, the following shall be appropriate units, and the only appropriate units, for petitions filed pursuant to section 9(c)(1)(A)(i) or 9(c)(1)(B) of the National Labor Relations Act, as amended, except that, if sought by labor organizations, various combinations of units may also be appropriate:

(1) All registered nurses.

(2) All physicians.

(3) All professionals except for registered nurses and physicians.

(4) All technical employees.

(5) All skilled maintenance employees.

(6) All business office clerical employees.

(7) All guards.

(8) All nonprofessional employees except for technical employees, skilled maintenance employees, business office clerical employees, and guards. *Provided That* a unit of five or fewer employees shall constitute an extraordinary circumstance.

(b) Where extraordinary circumstances exist, the Board shall determine appropriate units by adjudication.

(c) Where there are existing non-conforming units in acute care hospitals, and a petition for additional units is filed pursuant to sec. 9(c)(1)(A)(i) or 9(c)(1)(B), the Board shall find appropriate only units which comport, insofar as practicable, with the appropriate unit set forth in paragraph (a) of this section.

(d) The Board will approve consent agreements providing for elections in accordance with paragraph (a) of this section, but nothing shall preclude regional directors from approving stipulations not in accordance with paragraph (a), as long as the stipulations are otherwise acceptable.

(e) This rule will apply to all cases decided on or after May 22, 1989.

Nan: Isn't there any way we can create a separate bargaining unit for nurse practitioners?

Eulah: Not under the present regs. I suppose you could form your own union and then intervene in our election proceeding, which is what happens in conventional elections, or you could move the Board to amend its regs and carve out a separate unit for you. I doubt that the Board would go for that, given Congress' marching orders not to proliferate units. One thing to remember is that the Board is not required to pick the most appropriate unit, but simply an appropriate unit. If the choice is between our proposed unit, which includes NP's, and yours, which creates two separate units for these two groups, I suspect the Board will go for the former.

Besides, Nan, we've already agreed with the Hospital that we'd have an election in a unit of RN's which would include nurse practitioners.

Nan: I can't believe that! You mean the union has pulled us into this unit without our consent, and the Hospital has gone along with you?

Eulah: Well, maybe we should have talked this over with you, but we thought this is what you wanted. As I told you, we need the nurse practitioners in our unit to give it some clout. And this way we have some control over you if you try to do our work should we have to strike. The hospital is banking on you voting against us, that's why it is anxious to throw you into our unit. In these elections, nobody is thinking very much about the long run, about how the bargaining will actually work. They're only gerrymandering to get the best election district.

Nan: And the law encourages that? This is really a bad way for us to start out our relationship with you and with the hospital. You've dragged us in without giving us a say. Who speaks for me while you and the hospital are trying to decide whether there will be a union here?

Eulah: Let me repeat what I said earlier. We two groups need each other. We have more in common than you think. We'll work out ways to convince you that we'll protect your interests. Now what else do you want to talk about?

Nan: When I talked this through with my lawyer friend, he told me that the NLRA isn't a very democratic statute. In fact it is quite elitist. It excludes a whole bunch of people, like agricultural workers and domestics (see NLRA Sec. 2(2)—Ed.), for not very good reasons. And it provides no coverage for supervisors and confidential employees. Don't those workers need protection too?

Eulah: They certainly do. But there has always been the sense that a supervisor, a person who acts on behalf of management, faces an inherent conflict of interest if she is also represented by the union. This has never been a problem in the public sector, where we often find school principals having bargaining rights at the same time as the teachers whom they supervise. The Supreme Court has taken a tough stand on this exclusion of supervisors, even going against the Board's own determination, in a recent case involving nurses. It is very likely that your duties here at Mercy will take you right out of the statute! We will have to see when we move to the election hearing.

Nan: I think that is a very strange result, although it may be one I will applaud if it keeps me from being submerged in the larger unit. I still think the collective bargaining system makes little sense if it picks and chooses who belongs. I think the non union systems of worker participation are much more egalitarian.

Eulah: I know all about that. That may be the kind of all-inclusive team that you want to join, but when you operate without a union, it really doesn't matter who is on the team, as the group has no real power. Now I'm not defending the way it's done under the NLRA. I think some of the exclusions are arbitrary and some of the unit determination lines pretty hard to explain. But you have to understand that these determinations are made in cases where the union and the employer don't really care very much about who ultimately belongs in the bargaining unit. What they are trying to do is gerrymander the election district so their side can win. For example, when a union attempts to organize a workplace, it relies on the efforts of some key employees, usually outspoken leaders. If the employer wants to silence those key people, it can simply define their job duties so they are supervisors and exempt from the Act. This probably cannot be done for the purpose of altering the election outcome, but we know that motive is hard to prove, and if the employer can establish that the person in fact performs supervisory duties, then she may be excluded from the Act and from a vote in the election.

NATIONAL LABOR RELATIONS BOARD v. KENTUCKY RIVER COMMUNITY CARE, INC.

Supreme Court of the United States, 2001.
532 U.S. 706, 121 S.Ct. 1861, 149 L.Ed.2d 939.

JUSTICE SCALIA delivered the opinion of the Court.

Under the National Labor Relations Act, employees are deemed to be "supervisors" and thereby excluded from the protections of the Act if, *inter alia*, they exercise "independent judgment" in "responsibly . . . direct[ing]" other employees "in the interest of the employer." This case presents two questions: which party in an unfair-labor-practice proceeding bears the burden of proving or disproving an employee's supervisory status; and whether judgment is not "independent judgment" to the extent that it is informed by professional or technical training or experience.

I

In Pippa Passes, Kentucky, respondent Kentucky River Community Care, Inc., operates a care facility for residents who suffer from mental retardation and mental illness. The facility, named the Caney Creek Developmental Complex (Caney Creek), employs approximately 110 professional and nonprofessional employees in addition to roughly a dozen concededly managerial or supervisory employees. In 1997, the Kentucky State District Council of Carpenters (a labor union that is co-respondent here, supporting petitioner) petitioned the National Labor Relations Board to represent a single unit of all 110 potentially eligible employees at Caney Creek. See National Labor Relations Act (Act) § 9(c).

At the ensuing representation hearing, respondent objected to the inclusion of Caney Creek's six registered nurses in the bargaining unit, arguing that they were "supervisors" under § 2(11) of the Act, and therefore excluded from the class of "employees" subject to the Act's protection and includable in the bargaining unit. See § 2(3). The Board's Regional Director, to whom the Board has delegated its initial authority to determine an appropriate bargaining unit, see § 3(b), placed the burden of proving supervisory status on respondent, found that respondent had not carried its burden, and therefore included the nurses in the bargaining unit. The Regional Director accordingly directed an election to determine whether the union would represent the unit. See § 9(c)(1). The Board denied respondent's request for review of the Regional Director's decision and direction of election, and the union won the election and was certified as the representative of the Caney Creek employees.

Because direct judicial review of representation determinations is unavailable, *AFL v. NLRB,* 308 U.S. 401, 409–411, 60 S.Ct. 300, 84 L.Ed. 347 (1940), respondent sought indirect review by refusing to bargain with the union, thereby inducing the General Counsel of the Board to file an unfair labor practice complaint under §§ 8(a)(1) and 8(a)(5) of the Act. The Board granted summary judgment to the General Counsel pursuant to regulations providing that, absent newly developed evidence, the propriety of a bargaining unit may not be relitigated in an unfair labor practice hearing predicated on a challenge to the representation determination. 29 CFR § 102.67(f) (2000).* * *

II

The Act expressly defines the term "supervisor" in § 2(11), which provides:

> "The term 'supervisor' means any individual having authority, in the interest of the employer, to hire, transfer, suspend, lay off,

recall, promote, discharge, assign, reward, or discipline other employees, or responsibly to direct them, or to adjust their grievances, or effectively to recommend such action, if in connection with the foregoing the exercise of such authority is not of a merely routine or clerical nature, but requires the use of independent judgment."

The Act does not, however, expressly allocate the burden of proving or disproving a challenged employee's supervisory status. The Board therefore has filled the statutory gap with the consistent rule that the burden is borne by the party claiming that the employee is a supervisor.* * *

The Board argues that the Court of Appeals for the Sixth Circuit erred in not deferring to its resolution of the statutory ambiguity, and we agree. The Board's rule is supported by "the general rule of statutory construction that the burden of proving justification or exemption under a special exception to the prohibitions of a statute generally rests on one who claims its benefits." *FTC v. Morton Salt Co.,* 334 U.S. 37, 44–45, 68 S.Ct. 822, 92 L.Ed. 1196 (1948). The Act's definition of "employee," § 2(3), "reiterate[s] the breadth of the ordinary dictionary definition" of that term, so that it includes "any 'person who works for another in return for financial or other compensation,'" *NLRB v. Town & Country Elec., Inc.,* 516 U.S. 85, 90, 116 S.Ct. 450, 133 L.Ed.2d 371 (1995). Supervisors would fall within the class of employees, were they not expressly excepted from it. The burden of proving the applicability of the supervisory exception, under *Morton Salt,* should thus fall on the party asserting it. In addition, it is easier to prove an employee's authority to exercise 1 of the 12 listed supervisory functions than to disprove an employee's authority to exercise any of those functions, and practicality therefore favors placing the burden on the party asserting supervisory status. We find that the Board's rule for allocating the burden of proof is reasonable and consistent with the Act, and we therefore defer to it.* * *

III

The text of § 2(11) of the Act that we quoted above, sets forth a three-part test for determining supervisory status. Employees are statutory supervisors if (1) they hold the authority to engage in any 1 of the 12 listed supervisory functions, (2) their "exercise of such authority is not of a merely routine or clerical nature, but requires the use of independent judgment," and (3) their authority is held "in the interest of the employer." *NLRB v. Health Care & Retirement Corp. of America,* 511 U.S. 571, 573–574, 114 S.Ct. 1778, 128 L.Ed.2d 586 (1994). The only basis asserted by the Board, before the Court of Appeals and here, for rejecting respondent's proof of supervisory status with respect to directing patient care was the Board's interpretation of the second part of the test—to wit, that employees do not use "independent judgment" when they exercise "ordinary professional or technical judgment in directing less-skilled employees to deliver services in accordance with employer-specified standards." The Court of Appeals rejected that interpretation, and so do we.

Two aspects of the Board's interpretation are reasonable, and hence controlling on this Court. First, it is certainly true that the statutory term "independent judgment" is ambiguous with respect to the *degree* of discretion required for supervisory status. Many nominally supervisory functions may be performed without the "exercis[e of] such a degree of . . . judgment or discretion . . . as would warrant a finding" of supervisory status under the Act. It falls clearly within the Board's discretion to determine, within reason, what scope of discretion qualifies. Second, as reflected in the Board's phrase "in accordance with employer-specified standards," it is also undoubtedly true that the degree of judgment that might ordinarily be required to conduct a particular task may be reduced below the statutory threshold by detailed orders and regulations issued by the employer. * * *

The Board, however, argues further that the judgment even of employees who are permitted by their employer to exercise a sufficient *degree* of discretion is not "independent judgment" if it is a particular *kind* of judgment, namely, "ordinary professional or technical judgment in directing less-skilled employees to deliver services." The first five words of this interpretation insert a startling categorical exclusion into statutory text that does not suggest its existence. The text, by focusing on the "clerical" or "routine" (as opposed to "independent") nature of the judgment, introduces the question of degree of judgment that we have agreed falls within the reasonable discretion of the Board to resolve. But the Board's categorical exclusion turns on factors that have nothing to do with the degree of discretion an employee exercises. Let the judgment be significant and only loosely constrained by the employer; if it is "professional or technical" it will nonetheless not be independent. The breadth of this exclusion is made all the more startling by virtue of the Board's extension of it to judgment based on greater "experience" as well as formal training. What supervisory judgment worth exercising, one must wonder, does not rest on "professional or technical skill or experience"? If the Board applied this aspect of its test to every exercise of a supervisory function, it would virtually eliminate "supervisors" from the Act. Cf. *NLRB v. Yeshiva Univ.*, 444 U.S. 672, 687, 100 S.Ct. 856, 63 L.Ed.2d 115 (1980*)* (Excluding "decisions . . . based on . . . professional expertise" would risk "the indiscriminate recharacterization as covered employees of professionals working in supervisory and managerial capacities").

As it happens, though, only one class of supervisors would be eliminated in practice, because the Board limits its categorical exclusion with a qualifier: Only professional judgment that is applied "in directing less-skilled employees to deliver services" is excluded from the statutory category of "independent judgment." This second rule is no less striking than the first, and is directly contrary to the text of the statute. *Every* supervisory function listed by the Act is accompanied by the statutory requirement that its exercise "requir[e] the use of independent judgment" before supervisory status will obtain, but the Board would apply its restriction upon "independent judgment" to just 1 of the 12 listed functions: "responsibly to direct." There is no apparent textual justification for this asymmetrical limitation, and the Board has offered none. Surely no conceptual justification can be found in the proposition that supervisors exercise professional, technical, or experienced judgment only when they direct other employees. Decisions "to hire, . . . suspend, lay off, recall, promote, discharge, . . . or discipline" other employees, must often depend upon that same judgment, which enables assessment of the employee's proficiency in performing his job. Yet in no opinion that we were able to discover has the Board held that a supervisor's judgment in hiring, disciplining, or promoting another employee ceased to be "independent judgment" because it depended upon the supervisor's professional or technical training or experience. When an employee exercises one of these functions with judgment that possesses a sufficient degree of independence, the Board invariably finds supervisory status.

The Board's refusal to apply its limiting interpretation of "independent judgment" to any supervisory function other than responsibly directing other employees is particularly troubling because just seven years ago we rejected the Board's interpretation of part three of the supervisory test that similarly was applied only to the same supervisory function. See *NLRB v. Health Care & Retirement Corp. of America,* 511 U.S. 571, 114 S.Ct. 1778, 128 L.Ed.2d 586 (1994). In *Health Care,* the Board argued that nurses did not exercise their authority "in the interest of the employer," as § 152(11) requires, when their "independent judgment [was] exercised incidental to professional or technical judgment" instead of for "disciplinary or other matters, *i.e.,* in addition to treatment of patients." It did not escape our notice that the target of this analysis was the supervisory function of responsible direction. "Under § 2(11)," we noted, "an employee who in the course of employment uses independent judgment to engage in 1 of the 12 listed activities, including responsible direction of other employees, is a supervisor. Under the Board's test, however, a nurse who in the course of employment uses independent judgment to engage in responsible direction of other employees is not a supervisor." We therefore rejected the Board's analysis as "inconsistent with . . . the statutory language," because it "rea[d] the responsible direction portion of § 2(11) out of the statute in nurse cases." It is impossible to avoid the conclusion that the Board's interpretation of "independent judgment," applied to nurses for the first time after our decision in *Health Care,* has precisely the same object. This interpretation of "independent judgment" is no less strained than the interpretation of "in the interest of the employer" that it has succeeded.* * *

The Board contends, however, that Congress incorporated the Board's categorical restrictions on "independent judgment" when it first added the term "supervisor" to the Act in 1947. We think history shows the opposite. The Act as originally passed by Congress in 1935 did not mention supervisors directly. It extended to "employees" the "right to self-organization, to form, join, or assist labor organizations, [and] to bargain collectively through representatives of their own choosing... ." Act of July 5, 1935, § 7, 49 Stat. 452, and it defined "employee" expansively (if circularly) to "include any employee," § 2(3). We therefore held that supervisors were protected by the Act. *Packard Motor Car Co. v. NLRB,* 330 U.S. 485, 67 S.Ct. 789, 91 L.Ed. 1040 (1947). Congress in response added to the Act the exemption we had found lacking. The Labor Management Relations Act of 1947 (Taft–Hartley Act) expressly excluded "supervisors" from the definition of "employees" and thereby from the protections of the Act. § 2(3).

Well before the Taft–Hartley Act added the term "supervisor" to the Act, however, the Board had already been defining it, because while the Board agreed that supervisors were protected by the 1935 Act, it also determined that they should not be placed in the same bargaining unit as the employees they oversaw. To distinguish the two groups, the Board defined "supervisors" as employees who "supervise or direct the work of [other] employees ..., *and* who have authority to hire, promote, discharge, discipline, or otherwise effect changes in the status of such employees." The "and" bears emphasis because it was a true conjunctive: The Board consistently held that employees whose only supervisory function was directing the work of other employees were not "supervisors" within its test. * * *

When the Taft–Hartley Act added the term "supervisor" to the Act in 1947, it largely borrowed the Board's definition of the term, with one notable exception: Whereas the Board required a supervisor to direct the work of other employees *and* perform another listed function, the Act permitted direction alone to suffice. "The term 'supervisor' means any individual having authority ... to hire, transfer, suspend, lay off, recall, promote, discharge, assign, reward, or discipline other employees, *or* responsibly to direct them, or to adjust their grievances." Moreover, the Act assuredly did *not* incorporate the Board's current interpretation of the term "independent judgment" as applied to the function of responsible direction, since the Board had not yet developed that interpretation. It had had no reason to do so, because it had limited the category of supervisors more directly, by requiring functions *in addition* to responsible direction. It is the Act's alteration of precisely that aspect of the Board's jurisprudence that has pushed the Board into a running struggle to limit the impact of "responsibly to direct" on the number of employees qualifying for supervisory status—presumably driven by the policy concern that otherwise the proper balance of labor-management power will be disrupted.

It is upon that policy concern that the Board ultimately rests its defense of its interpretation of "independent judgment." In arguments that parallel those expressed by the dissent in *Health Care,* see 511 U.S., at 588–590, 114 S.Ct. 1778 (GINSBURG, J., dissenting), and which are adopted by Justice STEVENS in this case, see *post,* at 1874–1875, the Board contends that its interpretation is necessary to preserve the inclusion of "professional employees" within the coverage of the Act. See

§ 2(12). Professional employees by definition engage in work "involving the consistent exercise of discretion and judgment." § 152(12)(a)(ii). Therefore, the Board argues (enlisting dictum from our decision in *NLRB v. Yeshiva Univ.*, 444 U.S., at 690, and n. 30, 100 S.Ct. 856, that was rejected in *Health Care,* see 511 U.S., at 581–582, 114 S.Ct. 1778), if judgment of that sort makes one a supervisor under § 152(11), then Congress's intent to include professionals in the Act will be frustrated, because "many professional employees (such as lawyers, doctors, and nurses) customarily give judgment-based direction to the less-skilled employees with whom they work," Brief for Petitioner 33. The problem with the argument is not the soundness of its labor policy (the Board is entitled to judge that without our constant second-guessing). It is that the policy cannot be given effect through this statutory text. See *Health Care, supra,* at 581, 114 S.Ct. 1778 ("[T]here may be 'some tension between the Act's exclusion of [supervisory and] managerial employees and its inclusion of professionals,' but we find no authority for 'suggesting that that tension can be resolved' by distorting the statutory language in the manner proposed by the Board"). Perhaps the Board could offer a limiting interpretation of the supervisory function of responsible direction by distinguishing employees who direct the manner of others' performance of discrete *tasks* from employees who direct other *employees,* as § 152(11) requires. Certain of the Board's decisions appear to have drawn that distinction in the past. We have no occasion to consider it here, however, because the Board has carefully insisted that the proper interpretation of "responsibly to direct" is not at issue in this case.

What is at issue is the Board's contention that the policy of covering professional employees under the Act justifies the categorical exclusion of professional judgments from a term, "independent judgment," that naturally includes them. And further, that it justifies limiting this categorical exclusion to the supervisory function of responsibly directing other employees. These contentions contradict both the text and structure of the statute, and they contradict as well the rule of *Health Care* that the test for supervisory status applies no differently to professionals than to other employees.* * *

We may not enforce the Board's order by applying a legal standard the Board did not adopt, and as we noted above, the Board has not asked us to do so. Hence, the Board's error in interpreting "independent judgment" precludes us from enforcing its order. Our decision in *Health Care,* where the Board similarly had not asserted that its decision was correct on grounds apart from the one we rejected, simply affirmed the judgment of the Court of Appeals denying enforcement. Since that same condition applies here, and since neither party has suggested that *Health Care*'s method for determining the propriety of a remand should not apply here, we take the same course. * * *

[Justices Souter, Stevens, Ginsberg and Breyer dissented with respect to the Court's definition of supervisor. They would have deferred to the Board's interpretation of the statutory term "independent judgment," given its ambiguity. The dissenters were concerned that the majority's broad definition of "supervisor" would unduly narrow the Act's coverage of professional employees.]

Two strikes—Can the Board ever get it Right?

The Board seems to be trying to acknowledge, not just in the nurse cases, that in today's work world, where employees are more skilled, many employees direct the work of others as part of their routine tasks. The Board's attempt to modify the definition of supervisor would keep more employees under the coverage of the Act. As *Kentucky River* points out, the Board got it wrong in the *Health Care* case when it tried to construe narrowly the statutory phrase "in the interest of the employer." The Board got it wrong again in *Kentucky River* when it put a gloss on the statutory phrase "independent judgment." Yet, the Court in *Kentucky River* suggests that the Board may still be able to accomplish the result it seeks. Is this so? What path is still open to the Board?

FUTURE DIRECTIONS IN UNION REPRESENTATION

NLRB v. TOWN & COUNTRY ELECTRIC, INC.

Supreme Court of the United States, 1995.
516 U.S. 85, 116 S.Ct. 450, 133 L.Ed.2d 371.

JUSTICE BREYER delivered the opinion of the Court.

Can a worker be a company's "employee," within the terms of the National Labor Relations Act, if, at the same time, a union pays that worker to help the union organize the company? We agree with the National Labor Relations Board that the answer is "yes."

I

The relevant background is the following: Town & Country Electric, Inc., a nonunion electrical contractor, wanted to hire several licensed Minnesota electricians for construction work in Minnesota. Town & Country (through an employment agency) advertised for job applicants, but it refused to interview 10 of 11 union applicants (including two professional union staff) who responded to the advertisement. Its employment agency hired the one union applicant whom Town & Country interviewed, but he was dismissed after only a few days on the job.

The members of the International Brotherhood of Electrical Workers, Locals 292 and 343 (Union), filed a complaint with the National Labor Relations Board claiming that Town & Country and the employment agency had refused to interview (or retain) them because of their union membership. An Administrative Law Judge ruled in favor of the Union members, and the Board affirmed that ruling.

In the course of its decision, the Board determined that all 11 job applicants (including the two Union officials and the one member briefly hired) were "employees" as the Act defines that word. The Board recognized that under well-established law, it made no difference that the 10 members who were simply applicants were never hired. See *Phelps Dodge Corp. v. NLRB,* 313 U.S. 177, 185–186, (1941) (statutory word "employee" includes job applicants, for otherwise the Act's prohibition of " 'discrimination in regard to hire' " would "serve no function"). Neither, in the Board's view, did it matter (with respect to the meaning of the word "employee") that the Union members intended to try to organize the company if they secured the advertised jobs, nor that the Union would pay them while they set about their organizing. The Board then rejected the company's fact-based explanations for its refusals to interview or to retain these 11 "employees" and held that the company had committed "unfair labor practices" by discriminating on the basis of union membership.

II

The Act seeks to improve labor relations ("eliminate the causes of certain substantial obstructions to the free flow of commerce," in large part by granting specific sets of rights to employers and to employees. This case grows out of a controversy about rights that the Act grants to "employees," namely, rights "to self-organization, to form, join, or assist labor organizations, to bargain collectively . . . and to engage in other concerted activities for the purpose of collective bargaining or other mutual aid or protection." § 157. We granted certiorari to decide only that part of the controversy that focuses upon the meaning of the word "employee," a key term in the statute, since these rights belong only to those workers who qualify as "employees" as that term is defined in the Act.

The relevant statutory language is the following:

> "The term 'employee' shall include any employee, and shall not be limited to the employees of a particular employer, unless this subchapter explicitly states otherwise, and shall include any individual whose work has ceased as a consequence of, or in connection with, any current labor dispute or because of any unfair labor practice, and who has not obtained any other regular and substantially equivalent employment, but shall not include any individual employed as an agricultural laborer, or in the domestic service of any family or person at his home, or any individual employed by his parent or spouse, or any individual having the status of an independent contractor, or any individual employed as a supervisor, or any individual employed by an employer subject to the Railway Labor Act, as amended from time to time, or by any other person who is not an employer as herein defined." (emphasis added).

We must specifically decide whether the Board may lawfully interpret this language to include company workers who are also paid union organizers.

We put the question in terms of the Board's lawful authority because this Court's decisions recognize that the Board often possesses a degree of legal leeway when it interprets its governing statute, particularly where Congress likely intended an understanding of labor relations to guide the Act's application. We add, however, that the Board needs very little legal leeway here to convince us of the correctness of its decision.

Several strong general arguments favor the Board's position. For one thing, the Board's decision is consistent with the broad language of the Act itself—language that is broad enough to include those company workers whom a union also pays for organizing. The ordinary dictionary definition of "employee" includes any "person who works for another in return for financial or other compensation." The phrasing of the Act seems to reiterate the breadth of the ordinary dictionary definition, for it says "[t]he term 'employee' shall include *any* employee." (emphasis added). Of course, the Act's definition also contains a list of exceptions, for example, for independent contractors, agricultural laborers, domestic workers, and employees subject to the Railway Labor Act; but no exception applies here.

For another thing, the Board's broad, literal interpretation of the word "employee" is consistent with several of the Act's purposes, such as protecting "the right of employees to organize for mutual aid without employer interference," and "encouraging and protecting the collective-bargaining process." And, insofar as one can infer purpose from congressional reports and floor statements, those sources too are consistent with the Board's broad interpretation of the word. It is fairly easy to find statements to the effect that an "employee" simply "means someone who works for another for hire," H.R.Rep. No. 245, 80th Cong., 1st Sess., 18 (1947), and includes "every man on a payroll," 79 Cong. Rec. 9686 (1935). At the same time, contrary statements, suggesting a narrow or qualified view of the word, are scarce, or nonexistent—except, of course, those made in respect to the specific (here inapplicable) exclusions written into the statute.

Further, a broad, literal reading of the statute is consistent with cases in this Court such as, say, *Sure-Tan, Inc. v. NLRB, supra* (the Act covers undocumented aliens), where the Court wrote that the "breadth of § 2(3)' s definition is striking: the Act squarely applies to 'any employee.'"

Finally, at least one other provision of the 1947 Labor Management Relations Act seems specifically to contemplate the possibility that a company's employee might also work for a union. This provision forbids an employer (say, the company) to make payments to a person employed by a union, but simultaneously exempts from that ban wages paid by the company to "any . . . employee of a labor organization, who is also an employee" of the company (emphasis added). If Town & Country is right, there would not seem to be many (or any) human beings to which this last phrase could apply.

III

Town & Country believes that it can overcome these general considerations, favoring a broad, literal interpretation of the Act, through an argument that rests primarily upon the common law of agency. It first argues that our prior decisions resort to common-law principles in defining the term "employee." And it also points out that the Board itself, in its decision, found "no bar to applying common law agency principles to the determination whether a paid union organizer is an 'employee.'"

Town & Country goes on to argue that application of common-law agency principles requires an interpretation of "employee" that excludes paid union organizers. It points to a section of the Restatement (Second) of Agency (dealing with respondeat superior liability for torts), which says:

> "Since ... the relation of master and servant is dependent upon the right of the master to control the conduct of the servant in the performance of the service, giving service to two masters at the same time normally involves a breach of duty by the servant to one or both of them.... [A person] cannot be a servant of two masters in doing an act as to which an intent to serve one necessarily excludes an intent to serve the other."

It argues that, when the paid union organizer serves the union—at least at certain times in certain ways—the organizer is acting adversely to the company. Indeed, it says, the organizer may stand ready to desert the company upon request by the union, in which case, the union, not the company, would have "the right ... to control the conduct of the servant." Thus, it concludes, the worker must be the servant (i.e., the "employee") of the union alone.

As Town & Country correctly notes, in the context of reviewing lower courts' interpretations of statutory terms, we have said on several occasions that when Congress uses the term "employee" in a statute that does not define the term, courts interpreting the statute " 'must infer, unless the statute otherwise dictates, that Congress means to incorporate the established meaning of th[at] ter[m].... In the past, when Congress has used the term "employee" without defining it, we have concluded that Congress intended to describe the conventional master-servant relationship as understood by common-law agency doctrine.' " At the same time, when reviewing the Board's interpretation of the term "employee" as it is used in the Act, we have repeatedly said that "[s]ince the task of defining the term 'employee' is one that 'has been assigned primarily to the agency created by Congress to administer the Act,' ... the Board's construction of that term is entitled to considerable deference...." In some cases, there may be a question about whether the Board's departure from the common law of agency with respect to particular questions and in a particular statutory context, renders its interpretation unreasonable. But no such question is presented here since the Board's interpretation of the term "employee" is consistent with the common law.

Town & Country's common-law argument fails, quite simply, because, in our view, the Board correctly found that it lacks sufficient support in common law. The Restatement's hornbook rule (to which the quoted commentary is appended) says that a

> "person *may* be the servant of two masters . . . *at one time as to one act*, if the service to one does not involve *abandonment* of the service to the other." (emphasis added).

The Board, in quoting this rule, concluded that service to the union for pay does not "involve abandonment of . . . service" to the company.

And, that conclusion seems correct. Common sense suggests that as a worker goes about his or her ordinary tasks during a working day, say, wiring sockets or laying cable, he or she is subject to the control of the company employer, whether or not the union also pays the worker. The company, the worker, the union, all would expect that to be so. And, that being so, that union and company interests or control might sometimes differ should make no difference. As Prof. Seavey pointed out many years ago, "[o]ne can be a servant of one person for some acts and the servant of another person for other acts, even when done at the same time," for example, where "a city detective, in search of clues, finds employment as a waiter and, while serving the meals, searches the customer's pockets." W. Seavey, Handbook of the Law of Agency § 85, p. 146 (1964). The detective is the servant both "of the restaurateur" (as to the table waiting) and "of the city" (as to the pocket searching). How does it differ from Prof. Seavey's example for the company to pay the worker for electrical work, and the union to pay him for organizing? Moreover, union organizers may limit their organizing to nonwork hours. If so, union organizing, when done for pay but during nonwork hours, would seem equivalent to simple moonlighting, a practice wholly consistent with a company's control over its workers as to their assigned duties.

Town & Country's "abandonment" argument is yet weaker insofar as the activity that constitutes an "abandonment," i.e., ordinary union organizing activity, is itself specifically protected by the Act. This is true even if a company perceives those protected activities as disloyal. After all, the employer has no legal right to require that, as part of his or her service to the company, a worker refrain from engaging in protected activity.

Neither are we convinced by the practical considerations that Town & Country adds to its agency law argument. The company refers to a Union resolution permitting members to work for nonunion firms, which, the company says, reflects a union effort to "salt" nonunion companies with union members seeking to organize them. Supported by amici curiae, it argues that "salts" might try to harm the company, perhaps quitting when the company needs them, perhaps disparaging the company to others, perhaps even sabotaging the firm or its products.

Therefore, the company concludes, Congress could not have meant paid union organizers to have been included as "employees" under the Act.

This practical argument suffers from several serious problems. For one thing, nothing in this record suggests that such acts of disloyalty were present, in kind or degree, to the point where the company might lose control over the worker's normal workplace tasks. Certainly the Union's resolution contains nothing that suggests, requires, encourages, or condones impermissible or unlawful activity. For another thing, the argument proves too much. If a paid union organizer might quit, leaving a company employer in the lurch, so too might an unpaid organizer, or a worker who has found a better job, or one whose family wants to move elsewhere. And if an overly zealous union organizer might hurt the company through unlawful acts, so might another unpaid zealot (who may know less about the law), or a dissatisfied worker (who may lack an outlet for his or her grievances). This does not mean they are not "employees."

Further, the law offers alternative remedies for Town & Country's concerns, short of excluding paid or unpaid union organizers from all protection under the Act. For example, a company disturbed by legal but undesirable activity, such as quitting without notice, can offer its employees fixed-term contracts, rather than hiring them "at will" as in the case before us; or it can negotiate with its workers for a notice period. A company faced with unlawful (or possibly unlawful) activity can discipline or dismiss the worker, file a complaint with the Board, or notify law enforcement authorities. See, e.g., *NLRB v. Electrical Workers,* 346 U.S. 464, 472–478 (1953); *Willmar Elec. Service v. NLRB,* 968 F.2d, at 1330. See also *Budd Mfg. Co. v. NLRB,* 138 F.2d 86, 89–90 (C.A.3 1943) (worker who was intoxicated while on duty, "came to work when he chose and . . . left the plant and his shift as he pleased," and utterly failed to perform his assigned duties is still an "employee" protected under the Act). And, of course, an employer may as a rule limit the access of non employee union organizers to company property. *Lechmere, Inc. v. NLRB,* 502 U.S. 527, 538 (1992).

This is not to say that the law treats paid union organizers like other company employees in every labor law context. For instance, the Board states that, at least sometimes, a paid organizer may not share a sufficient "community of interest" with other employees (as to wages, hours, and working conditions) to warrant inclusion in the same bargaining unit. See, e.g., *NLRB v. Hendricks County Rural Elec. Membership Corp.,* 454 U.S., at 190, 102 S.Ct., at 228–229 (some confidential workers, although "employees," may be excluded from bargaining unit). We need not decide this matter. Nor do we express any view about any of the other matters Town & Country raised before the Court of Appeals, such as whether or not Town & Country's conduct (in refusing to interview, or to retain, "employees" who were on the union's payroll) amounted to an unfair labor practice. We hold only that the Board's construction of the word "employee" is lawful; that term does not exclude paid union organizers.

NOTE ON TOWN AND COUNTRY
AND ITS IMPLICATIONS

This very concise opinion settles no issue of overwhelming concern. Yet it is useful for several reasons:

1.   It reminds us that the source of Board law is the statute itself. Justice Breyer uses traditional tools of statutory interpretation to point out that the term "employee" is defined broadly, while the exclusions are narrow and discrete. Of course, a court will depart from the plain text of the language and rely upon legislative history and other considerations when it suits it. The best example may be the starkly contrasting case of NLRB v. Bell Aerospace, 416 U.S. 267 (1974), in which the Court found a broad exclusion from the Act's coverage for "managerial employees", that is, those employees, in this case buyers, who exercise independent judgment in making managerial decisions on behalf of the employer. Despite the breadth of the statutory definition of employees, and the absence of any exclusion for managerial employees, in the face of a specific exclusion for supervisors and of specific definitions regarding placement of professional employees, the Court concluded that the Act embraced a long-standing (though not so clear!) policy of the Board excluding managerial employees. The Court also thought the exclusion of managerial employees was sound for policy reasons. It would be surprising to find the modern Court, which relies so heavily upon statutory text rather than context, coming up with the same result as Bell Aerospace.

2.   Justice Breyer recites the well established rules of deference to the decisions of administrative agencies. You will see other places in the casebook where these rules are not followed. For it is quite easy for a court to turn around the rules stated by Justice Breyer and conclude that the agency went outside the authority prescribed by Congress.

3.   The decision rejects a claim by the employer that the salts would be disloyal to the employer because they served two bosses. It underscores the notion that a worker can be a loyal union member and still fulfill his obligations as an employee.

4.   The decision makes you wonder what the world of work has come to when the union must rely upon paid operatives to help organize a plant. Rather than concluding that the union movement must be moribund, the tactic may suggest that the union needs to bring paid union organizers into the plant to help get its message across. For we'll see in the next section of this chapter that under the current rules of the game a union has great difficulty in securing access to workers in an organizing campaign.

MEDICAL STUDENTS AND GRADUATE STUDENTS

In 1999, in Boston Medical Center, 330 NLRB No. 30, the Board ruled that residents and interns who are part of house staff are employees under the Act, even though they are required to do this work as part of their course of study. The opinion points out that even though the residents and interns are students, the work they do fits the traditional employment relationship. The Board relied heavily upon the broad definition of "employee" in the Act, citing Town and Country, among other decisions. The Board also concluded that there were no policy considerations militating against coverage of these employees, even though the Center suggested that it would be inappropriate for the union to bargain over aspects of the students' medical education.

One difference between Boston Medical Center and Town and Country is that the Board had for years taken the position that medical students are not employees under the Act. Should this switch in the Board's position make a difference when a court considers whether to uphold the decision?

A year later the Board applied Boston Medical Center to hold that graduate students at NYU who are teaching assistants are also employees under the Act, New York University, 332 NLRB No. 111. To avoid a challenge by NYU to the outcome, in which NYU said that unionization would bring the union into the inappropriate realm of bargaining about educational matters, the union said it would not bargain in those areas. We will discuss this question of appropriate topics for bargaining in a later section of this chapter.

Boston Medical and NYU remind us that the nature of work is ever changing, and that there are many new areas in which there is a potential for union representation. Consider the following article.

KATHERINE V.W. STONE, THE NEW PSYCHOLOGICAL CONTRACT: IMPLICATIONS OF THE CHANGING WORKPLACE FOR LABOR AND EMPLOYMENT LAW

48 UCLA L. Rev. 519, 621–624 (2001)

Roughly one hundred years ago, the employment relationship underwent a transformation that persisted throughout most of the twentieth century. Now we are witnessing another such change. The changes are as much in the implicit understandings that both employees and employers bring to the relationship as in the institutional arrangements that formally govern them. By understanding both the previous and the current transformations, we can identify the institutional and policy choices that are available for shaping employment relations into the next century.

In nineteenth-century America, skilled workers had a monopoly of knowledge about production. With their exclusive skills, knowledge, and expertise, nineteenth-century craft workers ensured themselves jobs and exerted considerable bargaining power vis-a-vis the manufacturers. By controlling skill, they controlled the choice of production process, the pace of work, and the distribution of revenues. Skilled workers transmitted their skills to others through elaborate apprenticeship systems that limited access to skill and ensured that it remained in the possession of the workers.

Toward the end of the century, the manufacturers set out to break the skilled workers' monopoly of knowledge about production. Once they succeeded, they enlisted the help of a group of industrial engineers to design a means to transfer skills and knowledge about production from the workers to management. Numerous systems of work rationalization were devised in that period, of which the most famous was Frederick Winslow Taylor's system called scientific management.

Throughout the twentieth century, scientific management and its close relative, Fordism, came to characterize the labor relations policies of most large manufacturing firms. While the methods were not implemented universally, the theory and practices of scientific management have shaped the dominant employment practices throughout the economy. They have also shaped ideas in society more generally about the meaning and value of efficiency. In addition, scientific management formed the dominant template against which American labor organizations strategized and American policymakers regulated. Thus the assumptions of scientific management have shaped the goals and conduct of twentieth-century labor unions, as well as the content and interpretation of the labor laws.

One of the key teachings of scientific management was that employers should construct employment structures comprised of hierarchical job ladders and limited ports of entry—a form of job structure known today as an internal labor market. The internal labor market involved employers giving their workers an implicit promise of long-term employment—a tacit promise that if they did their job and refrained from disruptive oppositional conduct, they would have a job for life. The implicit contract for long-term job security has been a central feature of employment relations in large U.S. firms for most of the past century.

In the past decade, many of the most dynamic firms in the American economy have again radically transformed their employment practices. They have abandoned Taylorism, dismantled their internal labor market modes of organization, and instead have attempted to substitute more flexible forms of work. Employers have discovered the value of having workers who possess a variety of skills that can be deployed on many different job assignments.

The effort to redefine work within large organizations has many names, including Total Quality Management, high-commitment work practices, and competency-based organization. These new organizational behavior theories and practices aim to inculcate knowledge and skill in the worker at every level. They also aim to build a high-commitment work force. A related aspect of the new employment practices is that firms have abandoned or renounced the implicit promises of job security that were embedded in the internal labor market setting. By making these changes, firms have had to create a new system of job structures, with new bases for motivation, incentives for skill acquisition, sources of morale, and inducements for loyalty. Yet, there is a paradox: How can employers motivate employees to build their skills and give employers high commitment when employers no longer give employees any promise of job security or prospect of promotion? The resolution of this paradox is what management practitioners and organizational theorists refer to as "the new *psychological* contract." * * *

C. THE ROAD TO REPRESENTATION

In this section we take a closer look at the process of representation under the NLRA. The "road" that we refer to in our title can be a long one. The process is more difficult and potentially contentious than setting up an informal system of employee representation of the sort we discussed earlier in the chapter. As we explained earlier, union representation begins with a drive to secure authorization cards. Typically, these cards are then used as the basis for a letter asking the employer to recognize the union. When the employer gives the usual response of declining to recognize the union, the union must petition for an election. The Board will move quickly to set up a conference in which the parties may agree upon the procedures for the election. But these procedures will move expeditiously only if the parties can agree upon the appropriate bargaining unit, an issue that we discussed in Part B of this chapter. If the employer doesn't accept the unit proposed by the union, the matter must be set down for a hearing on the appropriate unit. The NLRB makes some effort to streamline the time frame from the time a petition is filed until an election is held, and its success varies with each administration. It is probably safe to say that an election in which the unit placement is contested can take as long as six months from petition to election.

This may not be an optimal timeline for determining true employee choice. Union organizers tell us that even if the employer mounts a perfectly lawful campaign, employee support of the union diminishes with time even though it may increase at points in the campaign. After all, it is not an easy thing for workers to turn to a union to represent them. If they have a sense of loyalty to their employer they may be reluctant to repudiate their boss by bringing in an outside representative. If workers are having second thoughts about this course, those thoughts may prevail as time wears on. The union is trying to demonstrate to its prospective supporters that it can make a difference and that it can get things done. But if the union can't even bring about an election for half a year, workers may lose confidence in the ability of the union to make any kind of impact, and may discern that the employer has all the tools for getting its way.

The employer may go beyond a lawful campaign and engage in conduct that violates the Act. For example, as you will learn from the reading that follows, the employer may fire union supporters or threaten plant closings, which may create a climate of fear. If you pointed out to an employer client that time is on the employer's side, what would be the employer's instructions to you about whether to challenge the union's proposed election unit? What ethical constraints apply to your giving advice on this point?

The delay in holding an election gives the employer plenty of time to tell its side of the story, and the advantages of unionization will seem less rosy to the employee. One may suggest that this is all to the good, and no employee should make a binding choice until she has heard both sides of the story. But if the employer's presentation often includes coercive tactics such as threats that the worker will be out of a job if the union comes in, then the case for additional time is less compelling.

Further, the employer has the great advantage during this campaign period of having almost unlimited opportunities to get its message to its employees. It may hold general employee meetings at which it presents its message. Since these meetings are held on company time and the employee is on the clock, employees will normally attend these meetings. The employer can also get its message across by conversations by supervisors with smaller groups of employees and even with individual employees. And the employer has an easy means of distributing literature to the employees. In contrast, the union's professional organizers are usually prohibited from any access to or activity within the plant or its parking areas, and have to confine their face-to-face contact with employees to public property outside the plant, where traffic and location may make effective communication impossible. We will look at this issue in the Lechmere case in this section. We will see that the professional union staff must limit its contacts to off-premises, where it may have difficulty locating and reaching employees. As a result, the union must rely on its in-house organizing team to get its message across. These employees are not nearly as sophisticated and experienced as most management representatives. You may have your doubts about the need for more time in order to have a fair debate if the union doesn't have the same kind of access to the workers as the employer has.

Finally, during this extended period the employer may be able to remove some key union people from the workforce. That's what happens in the Ptolemy problem, which we study later in this section.

We first give you Professor Weiler's landmark article in which he discusses how delay operates to the employer's advantage. He advocates the use of the Canadian card model, which calls for prompt recognition on the basis of authorization cards. After that you will look at the law, with the *Gissel* case. This opinion is a goldmine of information and insight into the organizing process. It describes several typical organizing campaigns, and gives you in great detail one employer's response. It is followed by the *Lechmere* case, which discusses union access for organizing purposes.

PAUL WEILER, PROMISES TO KEEP: SECURING WORKERS' RIGHTS TO SELF–ORGANIZATION UNDER THE NLRA

96 Harv.L.Rev. 1769, 1769–71, 1776–81, 1794–95, 1805–06, 1811–12, 1817–19 (1983).

Contemporary American labor law more and more resembles an elegant tombstone for a dying institution. While administrators, judges, lawyers, and scholars busy themselves with sophisticated jurisprudential refinements of the legal framework for collective bargaining, the fraction of the work force actually engaged in collective bargaining is steadily declining. A major factor in this decline has been the skyrocketing use of coercive and illegal tactics—discriminatory discharges in particular—by employers determined to prevent unionization of their employees. The core of the legal structure must bear a major share of the blame for providing employers with the opportunity and the incentives to use these tactics, which have had such a chilling effect on worker interest in trade union representation. * * *

No feature of contemporary labor-management relations in the United States is more significant than the diminishing reach of collective bargaining. * * * When the NLRA was enacted in 1935, union density— the ratio of union membership to the nonagricultural work force—was only 13%. In just one decade, union density nearly tripled, reaching 35%. After a short postwar dip, union membership returned in 1954 to near the 35% level. Then began the slide—to less than 30% by 1965, and to just over 20% by 1980.

* * * By itself, this trend is a neutral statistical fact, reflecting within the NLRB certification procedure the decline in unionism. To a dispassionate observer, the simplest explanation for the drop in the union victory rate would be that it represents a corresponding drop in interest in collective bargaining among American workers. My thesis, however, is that the decline in union success in representation campaigns is in large part attributable to deficiencies in the law: evidence suggests that the current certification procedure does not effectively insulate employees from the kinds of coercive antiunion employer tactics that the NLRA was supposed to eliminate.

It is the time lag between the filing of a representation petition and the vote, usually about two months, that gives the employer the opportunity to attempt to turn its workers against the union. Typically, the firm will mount a vigorous campaign to fend off the threat of collective bargaining. It will emphasize to its workers how risky and troubled life might be in the uncharted world of collective bargaining: the firm might have to tighten up its supervisory and personnel practices and reconsider existing, expensive special benefits; the union would likely demand hefty dues, fines, and assessments, and might take the employees out on a long and costly strike with no guarantee that there would be jobs at the end if replacements had been hired in the meantime; if labor costs and labor unrest became too great, the employer might have to relocate.

The employees might well dismiss this message as mere bluffing were it not that a determined antiunion employer has at its disposal a potent weapon with which to demonstrate its power over the lives of its employees: the dismissal of selected union activists, in violation of section 8(a)(3) of the NLRA. Dismissal has the immediate effect of rendering these union supporters unable to vote—a consequence that by itself might tip the balance in a close election—and also excludes the discharged employees from the plant, the setting in which they could have campaigned most effectively among their fellow employees. Even more importantly, the dismissal of key union adherents gives a chilling edge to the warning that union representation is likely to be more trouble for the employees than it is worth.

Perhaps the most remarkable phenomenon in the representation process in the past quarter-century has been an astronomical increase in unfair labor practices by employers. One would not have anticipated such an increase at this stage in the life of a law like the NLRA. For the half-century before the enactment of the Wagner Act, American industrial employers fought bitterly against unionism, with little legal restraint. In 1935, the legal setting was drastically transformed by the Wagner Act, which many considered the most radical legislation of the New Deal. Not surprisingly, there was massive defiance of the new regime by employers determined not to give up their prerogatives. The discriminatory discharge, the most powerful weapon in the employer's arsenal, was heavily used in the years just after the NLRA's passage: in 1939 alone, the NLRB reinstated 7738 employees who had been illegally fired. One would have assumed, however, that once the basic principle of workers' rights to self-organization had become woven into the social and legal fabric, employer noncompliance would naturally have declined. And indeed, by 1957 only 922 illegally dismissed employees had to be offered reinstatement by the Board.

* * * In 1980, the NLRB secured reinstatement for more than 10,000 employees who had been discriminatorily discharged. A majority of these workers, though not all, were discharged during representation campaigns. Furthermore, the Board obtained backpay for another 5000 employees who had suffered some form of illegal treatment; many of these employees had also been fired but had settled for monetary relief in lieu of reinstatement. One can surmise as well that an additional but indeterminate number of workers were actually discharged in violation of the law but did not file or were unable to substantiate unfair labor practice complaints. A reasonable estimate, therefore, is that about 10,000 employees were fired in 1980 for involvement in representation campaigns. One would suppose that union supporters are most at risk from such employer reprisal. Unions obtained approximately 200,000 votes in representation elections in 1980. Astoundingly, then, the current odds are about one in twenty that a union supporter will be fired for

exercising rights supposedly guaranteed by federal law a half-century ago. Such a widespread pattern of employer intimidation has ramifications that reach far beyond the units in which discharges actually occur. It fosters an environment in which employees will take very seriously even subtle warnings about the consequences of joining a union.

* * * The vigorous debate about matters of high principle that still rages over the legitimacy of using bargaining orders in place of secret ballot elections is really beside the point. A bargaining order is an effort by an outside agency to construct a lasting collective bargaining relationship between a trade union and an employer whose antiunion behavior has been so egregious that the Board is prepared to bypass the normal secret ballot election. What can the union do with the bargaining order? Although the order requires the employer to sit down at the negotiating table and go through the motions of trying to reach an agreement, the governing principle of freedom of contract under the NLRA means that the employer is not required to consent to any significant changes in working conditions. The Board cannot direct the employer to make a reasonable contract offer.

If a decent employment package is to be extracted from a recalcitrant employer, it must come through the efforts of the workers themselves—that is, through the threat of strike action. Here lies the catch–22 of *Gissel*. The bargaining order has been issued because the employer's behavior is thought to have so thoroughly cowed the employees that they cannot express their true desires about collective bargaining even within the secrecy of the voting booth. But all the order can do is license the union to bring negotiations to the point at which its leadership must ask those same employees to put their jobs on the line by going on strike.

Again, timing is crucial. If a bargaining order is granted within a few weeks (or even months) of the organizing drive, while the attraction of collective bargaining remains strong among the employees, it might still be effective. But as time passes, employee interest wanes. Normal turnover will deprive the union of some key supporters, and to many of the replacements the union will seem a remote outsider that caused some trouble in the distant past. It is highly unlikely, therefore, that an order issued by the NLRB after protracted legal proceedings will actually produce a viable and enduring collective bargaining relationship. * * *

The key feature of the current regime is that after a union has initially organized a group of employees, it must still pass through a formal certification procedure. Even if the union can present incontrovertible evidence that the vast majority of employees have signed cards authorizing the union to represent them, the employer is not required to deal with the union. Instead, the employer can insist that the union face an NLRB-conducted secret ballot vote to test, after a prolonged campaign, the true majority will about collective bargaining. The time required for the formal certification procedure gives the employer a chance to reverse the initial employee enthusiasm for union representation and presents the employer with a strong temptation to use illegal coercion for this purpose.

There is an evident solution to this problem. Rather than encourage a certification election that will be preceded by a lengthy campaign, the law could simply base the award of bargaining rights on the results of the union's organizing drive. This could be accomplished by certifying a union when it presents signed authorization cards from a majority of the employees in the unit or, preferably, by holding an election immediately upon a union's presentation of enough cards to indicate substantial employee interest. Relying on cards or instant elections is by no means a novel or untried notion. Indeed, precisely such an approach is embodied in Canadian labor law, which otherwise emulates the American system of establishing the union as the exclusive bargaining agent once it has been selected by a majority of the employees. * * *

A Canadian Model: Cards

The most typical version of the Canadian model relies on union authorization cards. Once the provincial labor relations board confirms that a majority of the employees in a unit have signed cards authorizing a union to bargain on their behalf, it certifies the union as the bargaining agent. The aim of this approach is most clearly reflected in the British Columbia statute, which stipulates that the union's cards are to be counted as of the date of the application for certification. Thus, when the union surfaces with a majority of the bargaining unit signed up, the statutory condition for certification is satisfied. The employer is afforded no opportunity to campaign against the union. The antidote to employer intimidation, then, is not a heavy battery of regulations and sanctions, but rather a simple change in the legal environment—a change that, by making coercive tactics fruitless, eliminates the temptation to use them. * * *

After administering a card-based system for five years, I am satisfied that it not only rests on a more realistic appreciation of the tangible value of legal certification, but also permits a true reading of employees' sentiments about union representation. The system does, however, have one major drawback. Although both the union and the labor board may know that the union has the real support of the employees, the employer—who is prone to genuine self-deception on this score—often remains unconvinced on the basis of cards alone. A secret ballot vote has a symbolic value that a card check can never have. It clears the air of any doubts about the unions' majority and also confers a measure of legitimacy on the union's bargaining authority, especially among minority pockets of employees who were never contacted in the initial organizational drive.

The Province of Nova Scotia has devised a procedure—the "instant vote"—that achieves these values while still avoiding the trauma of the bitter representation battle. The Nova Scotia Labour Board must conduct an election no more than five days after it receives a certification petition. In this highly compressed interval, it is nearly impossible for the employer to mount a sustained offensive aimed at turning employee sentiments around through intimidation and discrimination. * * * *

In British Columbia and Ontario, the annual increase in union density produced by newly certified units is nearly three times as high as that in the United States. Even more striking is the impact on unfair labor practices of abolishing the representation campaign. In 1980, the number of discriminatory discharge complaints per election in Ontario was one-sixth, and in British Columbia just one twenty-fifth, the number in the United States.

This is the story within the representation process. Additional data suggest that these patterns have influenced the relative levels of unionization in the two countries. * * * For thirty years, the Canadian level tracked the American, although it was usually a few percentage points lower. In the mid–1960's, however, the two lines diverged. For the next fifteen years, the density of unions in Canada grew steadily, to a level fully one-third higher in 1980 than in 1964. The growth was primarily a result of the receptivity to collective bargaining of employees (and employers) in the public sector and, to a lesser extent, a result of favorable indicators in the business cycle. But although each of these background features was also present in the United States, the overall level of unionization in this country dropped by one-quarter in the same period. The crucial difference between the representation processes in the two countries is the intense representation campaigns that occur in the United States.

NLRB v. GISSEL PACKING CO.

Supreme Court of the United States, 1969.
395 U.S. 575, 89 S.Ct. 1918, 23 L.Ed.2d 547.

MR. CHIEF JUSTICE WARREN delivered the opinion of the Court.

These cases involve the extent of an employer's duty under the National Labor Relations Act to recognize a union that bases its claim to representative status solely on the possession of union authorization cards and the steps an employer may take, particularly with regard to the scope and content of statements he may make, in legitimately resisting such card-based recognition. The specific questions facing us here are whether the duty to bargain can arise without a Board election under the Act; whether union authorization cards, if obtained from a majority of employees without misrepresentation or coercion, are reliable enough generally to provide a valid, alternate route to majority status; whether a bargaining order is an appropriate and authorized remedy where an employer rejects a card majority while at the same time committing unfair practices that tend to undermine the union's majority and make a fair election an unlikely possibility; and whether certain specific statements made by an employer to his employees constituted such an election-voiding unfair labor practice and thus fell outside the protection of the First Amendment and § 8(c) of the Act, 49 Stat. 452, as amended, 29 U.S.C. § 158(c). For reasons given below, we answer each of these questions in the affirmative. * * *

No. 585

In No. 585, the factual pattern was quite similar. The petitioner, a producer of mill rolls, wire, and related products at two plants in Holyoke, Massachusetts, was shut down for some three months in 1952 as the result of a strike over contract negotiations with the American Wire Weavers Protective Association, the representative of petitioner's journeymen and apprentice wire weavers from 1933 to 1952. The Company subsequently reopened without a union contract, and its employees remained unrepresented through 1964, when the Company was acquired by an Ohio corporation, with the Company's former president continuing as head of the Holyoke, Massachusetts, division. In July 1965, the International Brotherhood of Teamsters, Local Union No. 404, began an organizing campaign among petitioner's Holyoke employees and by the end of the summer had obtained authorization cards from 11 of the Company's 14 journeymen wire weavers choosing the Union as their bargaining agent. On September 20, the Union notified petitioner that it represented a majority of its wire weavers, requested that the Company bargain with it, and offered to submit the signed cards to a neutral third party for authentication. After petitioner's president declined the Union's request a week later, claiming, *inter alia,* that he had a good faith doubt of majority status because of the cards' inherent unreliability, the Union petitioned, on November 8, for an election that was ultimately set for December 9.

When petitioner's president first learned of the Union's drive in July, he talked with all of his employees in an effort to dissuade them from joining a union. He particularly emphasized the results of the long 1952 strike, which he claimed "almost put our company out of business," and expressed worry that the employees were forgetting the "lessons of the past." He emphasized, secondly, that the Company was still on "thin ice" financially, that the Union's "only weapon is to strike," and that a strike "could lead to the closing of the plant," since the parent company had ample manufacturing facilities elsewhere. He noted, thirdly, that because of their age and the limited usefulness of their skills outside their craft, the employees might not be able to find re-employment if they lost their jobs as a result of a strike. Finally, he warned those who did not believe that the plant could go out of business to "look around Holyoke and see a lot of them out of business." The president sent letters to the same effect to the employees in early November, emphasizing that the parent company had no reason to stay in Massachusetts if profits went down.

During the two or three weeks immediately prior to the election on December 9, the president sent the employees a pamphlet captioned: "Do you want another 13–week strike?" stating, *inter alia,* that: "We have no doubt that the Teamsters Union can again close the Wire Weaving Department and the entire plant by a strike. We have no hopes that the Teamsters Union Bosses will not call a strike. * * * The Teamsters Union is a strike happy outfit." Similar communications followed in late November, including one stressing the Teamsters' "hoodlum control." Two days before the election, the Company sent out another pamphlet that was entitled: "Let's Look at the Record," and that purported to be an obituary of companies in the Holyoke–Springfield, Massachusetts, area that had allegedly gone out of business because of union demands, eliminating some 3,500 jobs; the first page carried a large cartoon showing the preparation of a grave for the Sinclair Company and other headstones containing the names of other plants allegedly victimized by the unions. Finally, on the day before the election, the president made another personal appeal to his employees to reject the Union. He repeated that the Company's financial condition was precarious; that a possible strike would jeopardize the continued operation of the plant; and that age and lack of education would make re-employment difficult. The Union lost the election 7–6, and then filed both objections to the election and unfair labor practice charges which were consolidated for hearing before the trial examiner.

The Board agreed with the trial examiner that the president's communications with his employees, when considered as a whole, "reasonably tended to convey to the employees the belief or impression that selection of the Union in the forthcoming election could lead [the Company] to close its plant, or to the transfer of the weaving production, with the resultant loss of jobs to the wire weavers." Thus, the Board found that under the "totality of the circumstances" petitioner's activities constituted a violation of § 8(a)(1) of the Act. The Board further agreed with the trial examiner that petitioner's activities, because they "also interfered with the exercise of a free and untrammeled choice in the election," and "tended to foreclose the possibility" of holding a fair election, required that the election be set aside. The Board also found that the Union had a valid card majority when it demanded recognition initially and that the Company declined recognition, not because of a good faith doubt as to the majority status, but, as the § 8(a)(1) violations indicated, in order to gain time to dissipate that status-in violation of § 8(a)(5). Consequently, the Board set the election aside, entered a cease-and-desist order, and ordered the Company to bargain on request.

On appeal, the Court of Appeals for the First Circuit sustained the Board's findings and conclusions and enforced its order in full. 397 F.2d 157. The court rejected the Company's proposition that the inherent unreliability of authorization cards entitled an employer automatically to insist on an election, noting that the representative status of a union may be shown by means other than an election; the court thus reaffirmed its stance among those circuits disavowing the Fourth Circuit's approach to authorization cards. Because of the conflict among the circuits on the card issues and because of the alleged conflict between First Amendment freedoms and the restrictions placed on employer speech by § 8(a)(1) in *Sinclair,* No. 585, we granted certiorari to consider both questions. 393 U.S. 997, 89 S.Ct. 482, 21 L.Ed.2d 462 (1968). For reasons given below, we reverse the decisions of the Court of Appeals for the Fourth Circuit and affirm the ruling of the Court of Appeals for the First Circuit.

II.

In urging us to reverse the Fourth Circuit and to affirm the First Circuit, the National Labor Relations Board contends that we should approve its interpretation and administration of the duties and obligations imposed by the Act in authorization card cases. The Board argues (1) that unions have never been limited under § 9(c) of either the Wagner Act or the 1947 amendments to certified elections as the sole route to attaining representative status. Unions may, the Board contends, impose a duty to bargain on the employer under § 8(a)(5) by reliance on other evidence of majority employee support, such as authorization cards. Contrary to the Fourth Circuit's holding, the Board asserts, the 1947 amendments did not eliminate the alternative routes to majority status. The Board contends (2) that the cards themselves, when solicited in accordance with Board standards which adequately insure against union misrepresentation, are sufficiently reliable indicators of employee desires to support a bargaining order against an employer who refuses to recognize a card majority in violation of § 8(a)(5). The Board argues (3) that a bargaining order is the appropriate remedy for the § 8(a)(5) violation, where the employer commits other unfair labor practices that tend to undermine union support and render a fair election improbable.

Relying on these three assertions, the Board asks us to approve its current practice, which is briefly as follows. When confronted by a recognition demand based on possession of cards allegedly signed by a majority of his employees, an employer need not grant recognition immediately, but may, unless he has knowledge independently of the cards that the union has a majority, decline the union's request and insist on an election, either by requesting the union to file an election petition or by filing such a petition himself under § 9(c)(1)(B). If, however, the employer commits independent and substantial unfair labor practices disruptive of election conditions, the Board may withhold the election or set it aside, and issue instead a bargaining order as a remedy for the various violations. A bargaining order will not issue of course, if the union obtained the cards through misrepresentation or coercion or if the employer's unfair labor practices are unrelated generally to the representation campaign. Conversely, the employers in these cases urge us to adopt the views of the Fourth Circuit.

C.

Remaining before us is the propriety of a bargaining order as a remedy for a § 8(a)(5) refusal to bargain where an employer has committed independent unfair labor practices which have made the holding of a fair election unlikely or which have in fact undermined a union's majority and caused an election to be set aside. We have long held that the Board is not limited to a cease-and-desist order in such cases, but has the authority to issue a bargaining order without first requiring the union to show that it has been able to maintain its majority status. And we have held the Board has the same authority even where it is clear that the union, which once had possession of cards from a majority of the employees, represents only a minority when the bargaining order is entered. We see no reason now to withdraw this authority from the Board. If the Board could enter only a cease-and-desist order and direct an election or a rerun, it would in effect be rewarding the employer and allowing him "to profit from [his] own wrongful refusal to bargain," while at the same time severely curtailing the employees' right freely to determine whether they desire a representative. The employer could continue to delay or disrupt the election processes and put off indefinitely his obligation to bargain[30] and any election held under these circumstances would not be likely to demonstrate the employees' true, undistorted desires.[31]

The employers argue that the Board has ample remedies, over and above the cease-and-desist order, to control employer misconduct. The Board can, they assert, direct the companies to mail notices to employees, to read notices to employees during plant time and to give the union access to employees during working time at the plant, or it can seek a court injunctive order under § 10(j) (29 U.S.C. § 160(j)) as a last resort. In view of the Board's power, they conclude, the bargaining order is an unnecessarily harsh remedy that needlessly prejudices employees' § 7 rights solely for the purpose of punishing or restraining an employer. Such an argument ignores that a bargaining order is designed as much to remedy past election damage[32] as it is to deter future misconduct. If

30. The Board indicates here that its records show that in the period between January and June 1968, the median time between the filing of an unfair labor practice charge and a Board decision in a contested case was 388 days. But the employer can do more than just put off his bargaining obligation by seeking to slow down the Board's administrative processes. He can also affect the outcome of a rerun election by delaying tactics, for figures show that the longer the time between a tainted election and a rerun, the less are the union's chances of reversing the outcome of the first election. See n. 31, infra.

31. A study of 20,153 elections held between 1960 and 1962 shows that in the 267 cases where rerun elections were held over 30% were won by the party who caused the election to be set aside. See Pollitt, NLRB Re–Run Elections: A Study, 41 N.C.L.Rev. 209, 212 (1963). The study shows further that certain unfair labor practices are more effective to destroy election conditions for a longer period of time than others. For instance, in cases involving threats to close or

transfer plant operations, the union won the rerun only 29% of the time, while threats to eliminate benefits or refuse to deal with the union if elected seemed less irremediable with the union winning the rerun 75% of the time. Finally, time appears to be a factor. The figures suggest that if a rerun is held too soon after the election before the effects of the unfair labor practices have worn off, or too long after the election when interest in the union may have waned, the chances for a changed result occurring are not as good as they are if the rerun is held sometime in between those periods. Thus, the study showed that if the rerun is held within 30 days of the election or over nine months after, the chances that a different result will occur are only one in five; when the rerun is held within 30–60 days after the election, the chances for a changed result are two in five.

32. The employers argue that the Fourth Circuit correctly observed that, "in the great majority of cases, a cease and desist order with the posting of appropriate an employer has succeeded in undermining a union's strength and destroying the laboratory conditions necessary for a fair election, he may see no need to violate a cease-and-desist order by further unlawful activity. The damage will have been done, and perhaps the only fair way to effectuate employee rights is to reestablish the conditions as they existed before the employer's unlawful campaign.[33] There is, after all, nothing permanent in a bargaining order, and if, after the effects of the employer's acts have worn off, the employees clearly desire to disavow the union, they can do so by filing a representation petition. For, as we pointed out long ago, in finding that a bargaining order involved no "injustice to employees who may wish to substitute for the particular union some other ... arrangement," a bargaining relationship "once rightfully established must be permitted to exist and function for a reasonable period in which it can be given a fair chance to succeed," after which the "Board may, ... upon a proper showing, take steps in recognition of changed situations which might make appropriate changed bargaining relationships."

Before considering whether the bargaining orders were appropriately entered in these cases, we should summarize the factors that go into such a determination. Despite our reversal of the Fourth Circuit below in Nos. 573 and 691 on all major issues, the actual area of disagreement between our position here and that of the Fourth Circuit is not large as a practical matter. While refusing to validate the general use of a bargaining order in reliance on cards, the Fourth Circuit nevertheless left open the possibility of imposing a bargaining order, without need of inquiry into majority status on the basis of cards or otherwise, in "exceptional" cases marked by "outrageous" and "pervasive" unfair labor practices. Such an order would be an appropriate remedy for those practices, the court noted, if they are of "such a nature that their coercive effects cannot be eliminated by the application of traditional remedies, with the result that a fair and reliable election cannot be had." The Board itself, we should add, has long had a similar policy of issuing a bargaining order, in the absence of a § 8(a)(5) violation or even a bargaining demand, when that was the only available, effective remedy for substantial unfair labor practices.

notices will eliminate any undue influences upon employees voting in the security of anonymity." NLRB v. S.S. Logan Packing Co., 386 F.2d at 570. It is for the Board and not the courts, however, to make that determination, based on its expert estimate as to the effects on the election process of unfair labor practices of varying intensity. In fashioning its remedies under the broad provisions of § 10(c) of the Act (29 U.S.C. 160(c)), the Board draws on a fund of knowledge and expertise all its own, and its choice of remedy must therefore be given special respect by reviewing courts. * * *

33. It has been pointed out that employee rights are affected whether or not a bargaining order is entered, for those who

desire representation may not be protected by an inadequate rerun election, and those who oppose collective bargaining may be prejudiced by a bargaining order if in fact the union would have lost an election absent employer coercion. Any effect will be minimal at best, however, for there "is every reason for the union to negotiate a contract that will satisfy the majority, for the union will surely realize that it must win the support of the employees, in the face of a hostile employer, in order to survive the threat of a decertification election after a year has passed." Bok, The Regulation of Campaign Tactics in Representation Elections Under the National Labor Relations Act, 78 Harv.L.Rev. 38, 135 (1964).

The only effect of our holding here is to approve the Board's use of the bargaining order in less extraordinary cases marked by less pervasive practices which nonetheless still have the tendency to undermine majority strength and impede the election processes. The Board's authority to issue such an order on a lesser showing of employer misconduct is appropriate, we should reemphasize, where there is also a showing that at one point the union had a majority; in such a case, of course, effectuating ascertainable employee free choice becomes as important a goal as deterring employer misbehavior. In fashioning a remedy in the exercise of its discretion, then, the Board can properly take into consideration the extensiveness of an employer's unfair practices in terms of their past effect on election conditions and the likelihood of their recurrence in the future. If the Board finds that the possibility of erasing the effects of past practices and of ensuring a fair election (or a fair rerun) by the use of traditional remedies, though present, is slight and that employee sentiment once expressed through cards would, on balance, be better protected by a bargaining order, then such an order should issue.

We emphasize that under the Board's remedial power there is still a third category of minor or less extensive unfair labor practices, which, because of their minimal impact on the election machinery, will not sustain a bargaining order. There is, the Board says, no *per se* rule that the commission of any unfair practice will automatically result in a § 8(a)(5) violation and the issuance of an order to bargain.

With these considerations in mind, we turn to an examination of the orders in these cases. In *Sinclair,* No. 585, the Board made a finding, left undisturbed by the First Circuit, that the employer's threats of reprisal were so coercive that, even in the absence of a § 8(a)(5) violation, a bargaining order would have been necessary to repair the unlawful effect of those threats. The Board therefore did not have to make the determination called for in the intermediate situation above that the risks that a fair rerun election might not be possible were too great to disregard the desires of the employees already expressed through the cards. The employer argues, however, that its communications to its employees were protected by the First Amendment and § 8(c) of the Act (29 U.S.C. § 158(c)), whatever the effect of those communications on the union's majority or the Board's ability to ensure a fair election; it is to that contention that we shall direct our final attention in the next section.

[The Court remanded the three cases in Nos. 573 and 691 from the Fourth Circuit for findings on "whether a bargaining order would have been necessary in the absence of an unlawful refusal to bargain" and on whether an election would be "a more reliable test of the employees' desires than the card count taken before the unfair labor practices occurred." * * *]

IV.

We consider finally petitioner Sinclair's First Amendment challenge to the holding of the Board and the Court of Appeals for the First

Circuit. At the outset we note that the question raised here most often arises in the context of a nascent union organizational drive, where employers must be careful in waging their antiunion campaign. As to conduct generally, the above-noted gradations of unfair labor practices, with their varying consequences, create certain hazards for employers when they seek to estimate or resist unionization efforts. But so long as the differences involve conduct easily avoided, such as discharge, surveillance, and coercive interrogation, we do not think that employers can complain that the distinctions are unreasonably difficult to follow. Where an employer's antiunion efforts consist of speech alone, however, the difficulties raised are not so easily resolved. The Board has eliminated some of the problem areas by no longer requiring an employer to show affirmative reasons for insisting on an election and by permitting him to make reasonable inquiries. We do not decide, of course, whether these allowances are mandatory. But we do note that an employer's free speech right to communicate his views to his employees is firmly established and cannot be infringed by a union or the Board. Thus, § 8(c) (29 U.S.C. § 158(c)) merely implements the First Amendment by requiring that the expression of "any views, argument, or opinion" shall not be "evidence of an unfair labor practice," so long as such expression contains "no threat of reprisal or force or promise of benefit" in violation of § 8(a)(1). Section 8(a)(1), in turn, prohibits interference, restraint or coercion of employees in the exercise of their right to self-organization.

Any assessment of the precise scope of employer expression, of course, must be made in the context of its labor relations setting. Thus, an employer's rights cannot outweigh the equal rights of the employees to associate freely, as those rights are embodied in § 7 and protected by § 8(a)(1) and the proviso to § 8(c). And any balancing of those rights must take into account the economic dependence of the employees on their employers, and the necessary tendency of the former, because of that relationship, to pick up intended implications of the latter that might be more readily dismissed by a more disinterested ear. Stating these obvious principles is but another way of recognizing that what is basically at stake is the establishment of a nonpermanent, limited relationship between the employer, his economically dependent employee and his union agent, not the election of legislators or the enactment of legislation whereby that relationship is ultimately defined and where the independent voter may be freer to listen more objectively and employers as a class freer to talk. Cf. New York Times Co. v. Sullivan, 376 U.S. 254, 84 S.Ct. 710, 11 L.Ed.2d 686 (1964).

Within this framework, we must reject the Company's challenge to the decision below and the findings of the Board on which it was based. The standards used below for evaluating the impact of an employer's statements are not seriously questioned by petitioner and we see no need to tamper with them here. Thus, an employer is free to communicate to his employees any of his general views about unionism or any of his specific views about a particular union, so long as the communications do not contain a "threat of reprisal or force or promise of benefit." He may even make a prediction as to the precise effects he believes unionization will have on his company. In such a case, however, the prediction must be carefully phrased on the basis of objective fact to convey an employer's belief as to demonstrably probable consequences beyond his control or to convey a management decision already arrived at to close the plant in case of unionization. See Textile Workers v. Darlington Mfg. Co., 380 U.S. 263, 274, n. 20, 85 S.Ct. 994, 13 L.Ed.2d 827 (1965). If there is any implication that an employer may or may not take action solely on his own initiative for reasons unrelated to economic necessities and known only to him, the statement is no longer a reasonable prediction based on available facts but a threat of retaliation based on misrepresentation and coercion, and as such without the protection of the First Amendment. We therefore agree with the court below that "[c]onveyance of the employer's belief, even though sincere, that unionization will or may result in the closing of the plant is not a statement of fact unless, which is most improbable, the eventuality of closing is capable of proof." As stated elsewhere, an employer is free only to tell "what he reasonably believes will be the likely economic consequences of unionization that are outside his control," and not "threats of economic reprisal to be taken solely on his own volition."

Equally valid was the finding by the court and the Board that petitioner's statements and communications were not cast as a prediction of "demonstrable 'economic consequences,' " but rather as a threat of retaliatory action. The Board found that petitioner's speeches, pamphlets, leaflets, and letters conveyed the following message: that the company was in a precarious financial condition; that the "strike-happy" union would in all likelihood have to obtain its potentially unreasonable demands by striking, the probable result of which would be a plant shutdown, as the past history of labor relations in the area indicated; and that the employees in such a case would have great difficulty finding employment elsewhere. In carrying out its duty to focus on the question: "[W]hat did the speaker intend and the listener understand?" (A. Cox, Law and the National Labor Policy 44 (1960)), the Board could reasonably conclude that the intended and understood import of that message was not to predict that unionization would inevitably cause the plant to close but to threaten to throw employees out of work regardless of the economic realities. In this connection, we need go no further than to point out (1) that petitioner had no support for its basic assumption that the union, which had not yet even presented any demands, would have to strike to be heard, and that it admitted at the hearing that it had no basis for attributing other plant closings in the area to unionism; and (2) that the Board has often found that employees, who are particularly sensitive to rumors of plant closings, take such hints as coercive threats rather than honest forecasts.

Petitioner argues that the line between so-called permitted predictions and proscribed threats is too vague to stand up under traditional First Amendment analysis and that the Board's discretion to curtail free speech rights is correspondingly too uncontrolled. It is true that a reviewing court must recognize the Board's competence in the first instance to judge the impact of utterances made in the context of the employer-employee relationship, see NLRB v. Virginia Electric & Power Co., 314 U.S. 469, 479, 62 S.Ct. 344, 349, 86 L.Ed. 348 (1941). But an employer, who has control over that relationship and therefore knows it best, cannot be heard to complain that he is without an adequate guide for his behavior. He can easily make his views known without engaging in " 'brinkmanship' " when it becomes all too easy to "overstep and tumble [over] the brink." At the least he can avoid coercive speech simply by avoiding conscious overstatements he has reason to believe will mislead his employees.

For the foregoing reasons, we affirm the judgment of the Court of Appeals for the First Circuit in No. 585, and we reverse the judgments of the Court of Appeals for the Fourth Circuit in Nos. 573 and 691 insofar as they decline enforcement of the Board's orders to bargain and remand those cases to that court with directions to remand to the Board for further proceedings in conformity with this opinion.

It is so ordered.

QUESTIONS AND NOTES ABOUT *GISSEL*

In addition to the issue of the circumstances under which a bargaining order should issue, *Gissel* involves a second, vital issue about the appropriate limitations upon an employer's ability to express its position during a union organizing campaign. In our concern for the first issue, we should not lose sight of the second.

The issue of employer free speech occupies Part IV of the opinion. How does Chief Justice Warren, a leading defender of the First Amendment, manage to take such a restrictive view of the employer's right of free speech in an organizing campaign? One of the premises of *Gissel* articulated by the Chief Justice is that the employee is economically dependent upon the employer. This makes the representation election very different from the typical political election. The employer's economic power may cast its words in a different light than in a political election.

An analogous approach—*Exchange Parts*

A similar observation was made by Justice Harlan, a Justice at a different end of the ideological spectrum, in a case in which an employer was held to violate the Act during an election campaign by improving certain employee benefits. In NLRB v. Exchange Parts, 375 U.S. 405, 84 S.Ct. 457, 11 L.Ed.2d 435 (1964), as part of its message in a letter to all employees urging them to oppose unionization, the employer listed the benefits that the company had granted in recent years. The letter included reference to two new benefits that the employer planned to grant, one involving increased overtime, the other more flexible scheduling of vacations. The Board found that these proposed improvements in benefits were timed with the purpose of persuading employees to vote against the union.

The employer argued that the new benefits were conferred unconditionally, and that there was no suggestion that they would be withdrawn if the union won the election.

The Court held that the grant of the new benefits violated Section 8(a)(1).

"We have no doubt that [8(a)(1)] prohibits not only intrusive threats and promises but also conduct immediately favorable to employees which is undertaken with the express purpose of impinging upon their freedom of choice for or against unionization and is reasonably calculated to have that effect.... The danger inherent in well-timed increases in benefits is the suggestion of a fist inside the velvet glove. Employees are not likely to miss the inference that the source of benefits now conferred is also the source from which future benefits must flow and which may dry up if it is not obliged. The danger may be diminished if, as in this case, the benefits are conferred permanently and unconditionally. But the absence of conditions or threats pertaining to the particular benefits conferred would be of no controlling significance only if it could be presumed that no question of additional benefits or renegotiation of existing benefits would arise in the future; and, of course, no such presumption is tenable."

Do you think that *Gissel* and *Exchange Parts,* each in its own way, take too paternalistic a role in regulating the organizing process? Do the approaches sell workers short? Would the union movement (and workers) be happier or better off if employers could grant benefits to workers during an organizing campaign without violating 8(a)(1)? If employers could do that, would workers have an incentive to mount an organizing campaign, gain short-term benefits, and then vote against the union to avoid paying union dues? Could avoidance of that result be the real explanation of the *Exchange Parts* decision?

Exchange Parts puts the employer in something of a dilemma during an organizing campaign. The employer does not violate 8(a)(1) if it truthfully advises employees of benefits it has granted in the past. It may not be a violation of 8(a)(1) for the employer to suggest that the pattern of benefits is likely to continue. Nor may it be a violation for the employer to announce a future benefit that had been planned before the organizing campaign began. On the other hand, if the employer had planned to implement a benefit and now holds back for fear of violating 8(a)(1) under the *Exchange Parts* rule, there is a danger that the employer will be held in violation of 8(a)(1) for denying workers a planned benefit as a reprisal for their initiating an organizing campaign.

Return to the use of authorization cards, which occupies most of the *Gissel* opinion. What are the down sides of using authorization cards as an alternative to the election? One concern is that they are often signed by the employee before she has heard the employer's position, and therefore may not be a reliable indicator of the employee's preferences. If the authorization cards are not a reliable indicator of employee choice, workers are deprived of the basic Section 7 right to decide whether they want union representation. *Gissel* of course upholds the imposition of the bargaining order only in extreme cases, where the employer's unlawful conduct has so poisoned the atmosphere that the authorization cards become a more reliable indicator of employee choice than the election itself.

What level of employer misconduct do you think it should take for the Board to issue a bargaining order? Do you think the standards should change from one political administration to the next? Later in this section we work on a problem involving the discharge of a union supporter. Do you think the discharge of an employee in violation of Section 8(a)(3) is enough to support a bargaining order? What about the threats of plant closings involved in *Gissel*?

You have to wonder if the bargaining order is a realistic deterrent to unlawful employer conduct. If a union cannot win an election, how much support do you think that union will have if it secures bargaining rights through authorization cards? Will it be strong enough to support its demands at the bargaining table? If not, is there any practical reason for the employer to be careful not to cross the line to the point where a bargaining order is imposed?

If the bargaining order is not effective, is it worth the potential interference with employee choice represented by the ballot box?

Bear in mind that an election may also be set aside as a result of conduct that does not rise to the level that would support an unfair labor practice finding, let alone a bargaining order. In Part II–C of *Gissel*, the Court talks about "a third category of minor or less extensive unfair labor practices" that do not warrant a bargaining order. In fact, there are a host of employer actions (and union actions too) that are not necessarily a violation of the Act, yet still are grounds to set the election aside. The rules include a prohibition on the company holding a "captive audience" speech within 24 hours of the election, that is, a speech on company time, on the theory that it has an unsettling effect so close to the election (Peerless Plywood Co., 107 NLRB 427 (1953); a requirement that the company provide the union with the names and addresses of employees eligible to vote in the election (Excelsior Underwear Inc., 156 NLRB 1236 (1966); prohibition of inflammatory racial appeals (Sewell Mfg. Co., 138 NLRB 66 (1962); and a prohibition against interrogating employees about their sentiments towards the union (NLRB v. Lorben Corp., 345 F. 2d 346 (2d Cir.1965). While these actions may not be unfair labor practices, and will not support a bargaining order, they will be grounds to set the election aside. This is true of both union and employer misconduct. On the employer's side, the employer would certainly like a victory against the union to be final, and this may provide an incentive for the employer to run a lawful election campaign.

On the other hand, misrepresentations of fact by either the company or the union are not grounds to set the election aside, although the rule used to be otherwise, Shopping Kart Food Market, 228 NLRB 1311 (1977), overruling the opposite rule established in Hollywood Ceramics, 140 NLRB 221 (1962). The premise of the Board's hands-off approach to misrepresentations seems to be that employees can sort out fact from fiction. Is this approach inconsistent with *Gissel* and *Exchange Parts*?

LECHMERE v. NLRB

Supreme Court of the United States, 1992.
502 U.S. 527, 112 S.Ct. 841, 117 L.Ed.2d 79.

JUSTICE THOMAS delivered the opinion of the Court.

This case requires us to clarify the relationship between the rights of employees under § 7 of the National Labor Relations Act, 49 Stat. 452, as amended, 29 U.S.C. § 157, and the property rights of their employers.

I.

This case stems from the efforts of Local 919 of the United Food and Commercial Workers Union, AFL–CIO, to organize employees at a retail store in Newington, Connecticut, owned and operated by petitioner Lechmere, Inc. The store is located in the Lechmere Shopping Plaza, which occupies a roughly rectangular tract measuring approximately 880 feet from north to south and 740 feet from east to west. Lechmere's store is situated at the Plaza's south end, with the main parking lot to its north. A strip of 13 smaller "satellite stores" not owned by Lechmere runs along the west side of the Plaza, facing the parking lot. To the Plaza's east (where the main entrance is located) runs the Berlin Turnpike, a four-lane divided highway. The parking lot, however, does not abut the Turnpike; they are separated by a 46–foot-wide grassy strip, broken only by the Plaza's entrance. The parking lot is owned jointly by Lechmere and the developer of the satellite stores. The grassy strip is public property (except for a four-foot-wide band adjoining the parking lot, which belongs to Lechmere).

The union began its campaign to organize the store's 200 employees, none of whom was represented by a union, in June 1987. After a full-page advertisement in a local newspaper drew little response, non-employee union organizers entered Lechmere's parking lot and began placing handbills on the windshields of cars parked in a corner of the lot used mostly by employees. Lechmere's manager immediately confronted the organizers, informed them that Lechmere prohibited solicitation or handbill distribution of any kind on its property,[1] and asked them to

---

1. Lechmere had established this policy several years prior to the union's organizing efforts. The store's official policy statement provided, in relevant part:

"Non-associates [*i.e.,* nonemployees] are prohibited from soliciting and distributing literature at all times anywhere on Company property, including parking lots. Non-leave. They did so, and Lechmere personnel removed the handbills. The union organizers renewed this handbilling effort in the parking lot on several subsequent occasions; each time they were asked to leave and the handbills were removed. The organizers then relocated to the public grassy strip, from where they attempted to pass out handbills to cars entering the lot during hours (before opening and after closing) when the drivers were assumed to be primarily store employees. For one month, the union organizers returned daily to the grassy strip to picket Lechmere; after that, they picketed intermittently for another six months. They also recorded the license plate numbers of cars parked in the employee parking area; with the cooperation of the Connecticut Department of Motor Vehicles, they thus secured the names and addresses of some 41 nonsupervisory employees (roughly 20% of the store's total). The union sent four mailings to these employees; it also made some attempts to contact them by phone or home visits. These mailings and visits resulted in one signed union authorization card.

Alleging that Lechmere had violated the National Labor Relations Act by barring the nonemployee organizers from its property, the union filed an unfair labor practice charge with respondent National Labor Relations Board (Board). Applying the criteria set forth by the Board in *Fairmont Hotel Co.,* an administrative law judge (ALJ) ruled in the union's favor. He recommended that Lechmere be ordered, among other things, to cease and desist from barring the union organizers from the parking lot and to post in conspicuous places in the store signs proclaiming in part:

> "WE WILL NOT prohibit representatives of Local 919, United Food and Commercial Workers, AFL–CIO ("the Union") or any other labor organization, from distributing union literature to our employees in the parking lot adjacent to our store in Newington, Connecticut, nor will we attempt to cause them to be removed from our parking lot for attempting to do so." 295 N.L.R.B. No. 15, ALJ slip op. (1988).

The Board affirmed the ALJ's judgment and adopted the recommended order, applying the analysis set forth in its opinion in *Jean Country,* which had by then replaced the short-lived *Fairmont Hotel* approach.

II

A

Section 7 of the NLRA provides in relevant part that "[e]mployees shall have the right to self-organization, to form, join, or assist labor

associates have no right of access to the non-working areas and only to the public and selling areas of the store in connection with its public use."

On each door to the store Lechmere had posted a 6 in. by 8 in. sign reading: "TO THE PUBLIC. No Soliciting, Canvassing, Distribution of Literature or Trespassing by Non–Employees in or on Premises." App. 115–116. Lechmere consistently enforced this policy inside the store as well as on the parking lot (against, among others, the Salvation Army and the Girl Scouts).

organizations." 29 U.S.C. § 157. Section 8(a)(1) of the Act, in turn, makes it an unfair labor practice for an employer "to interfere with, restrain, or coerce employees in the exercise of rights guaranteed in [§ 7]." 29 U.S.C. § 158(a)(1). By its plain terms, thus, the NLRA confers rights only on *employees,* not on unions or their nonemployee organizers. In *NLRB v. Babcock & Wilcox Co.,* 351 U.S. 105, 76 S.Ct. 679, 100 L.Ed. 375 (1956), however, we recognized that insofar as the employees' "right of self-organization depends in some measure on [their] ability ... to learn the advantages of self-organization from others," *id.,* at 113, 76 S.Ct., at 384, § 7 of the NLRA may, in certain limited circumstances, restrict an employer's right to exclude nonemployee union organizers from his property. It is the nature of those circumstances that we explore today.

Babcock arose out of union attempts to organize employees at a factory located on an isolated 100–acre tract. The company had a policy against solicitation and distribution of literature on its property, which it enforced against all groups. About 40% of the company's employees lived in a town of some 21,000 persons near the factory; the remainder were scattered over a 30–mile radius. Almost all employees drove to work in private cars and parked in a company lot that adjoined the fenced-in plant area. The parking lot could be reached only by a 100–yard–long driveway connecting it to a public highway. This driveway was mostly on company-owned land, except where it crossed a 31–foot-wide public right-of-way adjoining the highway. Union organizers attempted to distribute literature from this right-of-way. The union also secured the names and addresses of some 100 employees (20% of the total), and sent them three mailings. Still other employees were contacted by telephone or home visit.

The union successfully challenged the company's refusal to allow nonemployee organizers onto its property before the Board. While acknowledging that there were alternative, nontrespassory means whereby the union could communicate with employees, the Board held that contact at the workplace was preferable. "[T]he right to distribute is not absolute, but must be accommodated to the circumstances. Where it is impossible or unreasonably difficult for a union to distribute organizational literature to employees entirely off of the employer's premises, distribution on a nonworking area, such as the parking lot and the walkways between the parking lot and the gate, may be warranted." *The Babcock & Wilcox Co.,* 109 N.L.R.B. 485, 493–494 (1954). Concluding that traffic on the highway made it unsafe for the union organizers to distribute leaflets from the right-of-way, and that contacts through the mails, on the streets, at employees' homes, and over the telephone would be ineffective, the Board ordered the company to allow the organizers to distribute literature on its parking lot and exterior walkways.

The Court of Appeals for the Fifth Circuit refused to enforce the Board's order, and this Court affirmed. While recognizing that "the Board has the responsibility of 'applying the Act's general prohibitory language in the light of the infinite combinations of events which might be charged as violative of its terms,' " 351 U.S., at 111–112, we explained that the Board had erred by failing to make the critical distinction between the organizing activities of employees (to whom § 7 guarantees the right of self-organization) and nonemployees (to whom § 7 applies only derivatively). Thus, while "[n]o restriction may be placed on the employees' right to discuss self-organization *among themselves,* unless the employer can demonstrate that a restriction is necessary to maintain production or discipline," 351 U.S., at 113, 76 S.Ct., at 684 (emphasis added), "no such obligation is owed nonemployee organizers," 351 U.S., at 113, 76 S.Ct., at 684. As a rule, then, an employer cannot be compelled to allow distribution of union literature by nonemployee organizers on his property. As with many other rules, however, we recognized an exception. Where "the location of a plant and the living quarters of the employees place the employees beyond the reach of reasonable union efforts to communicate with them," *ibid.,* employers' property rights may be "required to yield to the extent needed to permit communication of information on the right to organize," *id.,* at 112, 76 S.Ct., at 684.

Although we have not had occasion to apply *Babcock's* analysis in the ensuing decades, we have described it in cases arising in related contexts. Two such cases, *Central Hardware Co. v. NLRB,* (1972), and *Hudgens v. NLRB,* (1976), involved activity by union supporters on employer-owned property. The principal issue in both cases was whether, based upon *Food Employees v. Logan Valley Plaza, Inc.,* the First Amendment protected such activities. In both cases we rejected the First Amendment claims, and in *Hudgens* we made it clear that *Logan Valley* was overruled. Having decided the cases on constitutional grounds, we remanded them to the Board for consideration of the union supporters' § 7 claims under *Babcock.* In both cases, we quoted approvingly *Babcock's* admonition that accommodation between employees' § 7 rights and employers' property rights "must be obtained with as little destruction of the one as is consistent with the maintenance of the other," 351 U.S., at 112, 76 S.Ct., at 684.

There is no hint in *Hudgens* and *Central Hardware,* however, that our invocation of *Babcock's* language of "accommodation" was intended to repudiate or modify *Babcock's* holding that an employer need not accommodate nonemployee organizers unless the employees are otherwise inaccessible. Indeed, in *Central Hardware* we expressly noted that nonemployee organizers cannot claim even a limited right of access to a nonconsenting employer's property until "[a]fter the requisite need for access to the employer's property has been shown." 407 U.S., at 545, 92 S.Ct., at 2241.

If there was any question whether *Central Hardware* and *Hudgens* changed § 7 law, it should have been laid to rest by *Sears, Roebuck & Co. v. San Diego County District Council of Carpenters,* 436 U.S. 180, 98 S.Ct. 1745, 56 L.Ed.2d 209 (1978). As in *Central Hardware* and *Hudgens,* the substantive § 7 issue in *Sears* was a subsidiary one; the case's primary focus was on the circumstances under which the NLRA pre-empts state law. Among other things, we held in *Sears* that arguable § 7 claims do not pre-empt state trespass law, in large part because the trespasses of nonemployee union organizers are "far more likely to be unprotected than protected," 436 U.S., at 205, 98 S.Ct., at 1761; permitting state courts to evaluate such claims, therefore, does not "create an unacceptable risk of interference with conduct which the Board, and a court reviewing the Board's decision, would find protected," *ibid.* This holding was based upon the following interpretation of *Babcock:*

> "While *Babcock* indicates that an employer may not always bar nonemployee union organizers from his property, his right to do so remains the general rule. To gain access, *the union has the burden of showing that no other reasonable means of communicating its organizational message to the employees exists* or that the employer's access rules discriminate against union solicitation. That the burden imposed on the union is a heavy one is evidenced by the fact that the balance struck by the Board and the courts under the *Babcock* accommodation principle has rarely been in favor of trespassory organizational activity." 436 U.S., at 205, 98 S.Ct., at 1761 (emphasis added; footnotes omitted).

We further noted that, in practice, non-employee organizational trespassing had generally been prohibited except where "unique obstacles" prevented nontrespassory methods of communication with the employees. *Id.,* at 205–206, n. 41, 98 S.Ct., at 1761–1762, n. 41.

B

Jean Country, as noted above, represents the Board's latest attempt to implement the rights guaranteed by § 7. It sets forth a three-factor balancing test:

> "[I]n all access cases our essential concern will be [1] the degree of impairment of the Section 7 right if access should be denied, as it balances against [2] the degree of impairment of the private property right if access should be granted. We view the consideration of [3] the availability of reasonably effective alternative means as especially significant in this balancing process." 291 N.L.R.B., at 14.

The Board conceded that this analysis was unlikely to foster certainty and predictability in this corner of the law, but declared that "as with other legal questions involving multiple factors, the 'nature of the problem, as revealed by unfolding variant situations, inevitably involves an evolutionary process for its rational response, not a quick, definitive formula as a comprehensive answer.' "

* * *

Citing its role "as the agency with responsibility for implementing national labor policy," the Board maintains in this case that *Jean Country* is a reasonable interpretation of the NLRA entitled to judicial deference.

* * * It is certainly true, and we have long recognized, that the Board has the "special function of applying the general provisions of the Act to the complexities of industrial life." *NLRB v. Erie Resistor Corp.,* 373 U.S. 221, 83 S.Ct. 1139, 10 L.Ed.2d 308 (1963).

* * * Like other administrative agencies, the NLRB is entitled to judicial deference when it interprets an ambiguous provision of a statute that it administers.

Before we reach any issue of deference to the Board, however, we must first determine whether *Jean Country*-at least as applied to nonemployee organizational trespassing-is consistent with our past interpretation of § 7. "Once we have determined a statute's clear meaning, we adhere to that determination under the doctrine of *stare decisis,* and we judge an agency's later interpretation of the statute against our prior determination of the statute's meaning." *Maislin Industries, U.S., Inc. v. Primary Steel, Inc.,* 497 U.S. 116, ___, 110 S.Ct. 2759, 2768, 111 L.Ed.2d 94 (1990).

In *Babcock,* as explained above, we held that the Act drew a distinction "of substance," 351 U.S., at 113, 76 S.Ct., at 684, between the union activities of employees and nonemployees. In cases involving *employee* activities, we noted with approval, the Board "balanced the conflicting interests of employees to receive information on self-organization on the company's property from fellow employees during nonworking time, with the employer's right to control the use of his property." *Id.,* at 109–110, 76 S.Ct., at 682–683. In cases involving *nonemployee* activities (like those at issue in *Babcock* itself), however, the Board was not permitted to engage in that same balancing (and we reversed the Board for having done so). By reversing the Board's interpretation of the statute for failing to distinguish between the organizing activities of employees and nonemployees, we were saying, in *Chevron* terms, that § 7 speaks to the issue of nonemployee access to an employer's property. *Babcock's* teaching is straightforward: § 7 simply does not protect nonemployee union organizers *except* in the rare case where "the inaccessibility of employees makes ineffective the reasonable attempts by nonemployees to communicate with them through the usual channels," 351 U.S., at 112, 76 S.Ct., at 684. Our reference to "reasonable" attempts was nothing more than a commonsense recognition that unions need not engage in extraordinary feats to communicate with inaccessible employees—*not* an endorsement of the view (which we expressly rejected) that the Act protects "reasonable" trespasses. Where reasonable alternative means of access exist, § 7's guarantees do not authorize trespasses by nonemployee organizers, *even* (as we noted in *Babcock, id.,* at 112, 76 S.Ct., at 684) "under . . . reasonable regulations" established by the Board.

Jean Country, which applies broadly to "all access cases," 291 N.L.R.B., at 14, misapprehends this critical point. Its principal inspiration derives not from *Babcock,* but from the following sentence in *Hudgens:* "[T]he locus of th[e] accommodation [between § 7 rights and private property rights] may fall at differing points along the spectrum depending on the nature and strength of the respective § 7 rights and private property rights asserted in any given context." 424 U.S., at 522, 96 S.Ct., at 1037. From this sentence the Board concluded that it was appropriate to approach every case by balancing § 7 rights against property rights, with alternative means of access thrown in as nothing more than an "especially significant" consideration. As explained above, however, *Hudgens* did not purport to modify *Babcock*, much less to alter it fundamentally in the way *Jean Country* suggests. To say that our cases require accommodation between employees' and employers' rights is a true but incomplete statement, for the cases also go far in establishing the *locus* of that accommodation where nonemployee organizing is at issue. So long as nonemployee union organizers have reasonable access to employees outside an employer's property, the requisite accommodation has taken place. It is *only* where such access is infeasible that it becomes necessary and proper to take the accommodation inquiry to a second level, balancing the employees' and employers' rights as described in the *Hudgens* dictum.

* * * At least as applied to nonemployees, *Jean Country* impermissibly conflates these two stages of the inquiry-thereby significantly eroding *Babcock's* general rule that "an employer may validly post his property against nonemployee distribution of union literature," 351 U.S., at 112, 76 S.Ct., at 684. We reaffirm that general rule today, and reject the Board's attempt to recast it as a multi-factor balancing test.

C

The threshold inquiry in this case, then, is whether the facts here justify application of *Babcock's* inaccessibility exception. The ALJ below observed that "the facts herein convince me that reasonable alternative means [of communicating with Lechmere's employees] *were* available to the Union," 295 N.L.R.B. No. 15, ALJ slip op., at 9 (emphasis added).[2] Reviewing the ALJ's decision under *Jean Country,* however, the Board reached a different conclusion on this point, asserting that "there was no reasonable, effective alternative means available for the Union to communicate its message to [Lechmere's] employees." 295 N.L.R.B. No. 15, Board slip op., at 4–5.

We cannot accept the Board's conclusion, because it "rest[s] on erroneous legal foundations," *Babcock,* 351 U.S., at 112, 76 S.Ct. at 684.

* * * As we have explained, the exception to *Babcock's* rule is a narrow one. It does not apply wherever nontrespassory access to employees may be cumbersome or less-than-ideally effective, but only where

---

2. Under the (pre-*Jean Country*) *Fairmont Hotel* analysis applied by the ALJ, it was only where the employees' § 7 rights and an employer's property rights were deemed "relatively equal in strength," *Fairmont Hotel Co.,* 282 N.L.R.B. 139, 142 (1986), that the adequacy of nontrespassory means of communication became relevant. Because the ALJ found that the § 7 rights involved here outweighed Lechmere's property rights, he had no need to address the latter issue. He did so, he explained, only because of the possibility that his evaluation of the relative weights of the rights might not be upheld. 295 N.L.R.B. No. 15, ALJ slip op., at 9.

"the *location of a plant and the living quarters of the employees* place the employees *beyond the reach* of reasonable union efforts to communicate with them," 351 U.S., at 113, 76 S.Ct., at 684 (emphasis added). Classic examples include logging camps, * * * mining camps, * * * and mountain resort hotels, * * * *Babcock's* exception was crafted precisely to protect the § 7 rights of those employees who, by virtue of their employment, are isolated from the ordinary flow of information that characterizes our society. The union's burden of establishing such isolation is, as we have explained, "a heavy one," *Sears, supra,* 436 U.S., at 205, and one not satisfied by mere conjecture or the expression of doubts concerning the effectiveness of nontrespassory means of communication.

The Board's conclusion in this case that the union had no reasonable means short of trespass to make Lechmere's employees aware of its organizational efforts is based on a misunderstanding of the limited scope of this exception. Because the employees do not reside on Lechmere's property, they are presumptively not "beyond the reach," *Babcock, supra,* 351 U.S., at 113, 76 S.Ct. at 684, of the union's message. Although the employees live in a large metropolitan area (Greater Hartford), that fact does not in itself render them "inaccessible" in the sense contemplated by *Babcock*. Their accessibility is suggested by the union's success in contacting a substantial percentage of them directly, via mailings, phone calls, and home visits. Such direct contact, of course, is not a necessary element of "reasonably effective" communication; signs or advertising also may suffice. In this case, the union tried advertising in local newspapers; the Board said that this was not reasonably effective because it was expensive and might not reach the employees. 295 N.L.R.B. No. 15, Board slip op., at 4–5. Whatever the merits of that conclusion, other alternative means of communication were readily available. Thus, signs (displayed, for example, from the public grassy strip adjoining Lechmere's parking lot) would have informed the employees about the union's organizational efforts. (Indeed, union organizers picketed the shopping center's main entrance for months as employees came and went every day.) *Access* to employees, not *success* in winning them over, is the critical issue-although success, or lack thereof, may be relevant in determining whether reasonable access exists. Because the union in this case failed to establish the existence of any "unique obstacles," *Sears,* 436 U.S., at 205–206, n. 41, 98 S.Ct., at 1761–1762, n. 41, that frustrated access to Lechmere's employees, the Board erred in concluding that Lechmere committed an unfair labor practice by barring the nonemployee organizers from its property. * * *

The judgment of the First Circuit is therefore reversed, and enforcement of the Board's order denied.

It is so ordered.

JUSTICE WHITE, with whom JUSTICE BLACKMUN joins, dissenting.

"We will uphold a Board rule so long as it is rational and consistent with the Act, ... even if we would have formulated a different rule had we sat on the Board." *NLRB v. Curtin Matheson Scientific, Inc.,* 494 U.S. 775, 787, 110 S.Ct. 1542, 108 L.Ed.2d 801 (1990). The judicial role is narrow: The Board's application of the rule, if supported by substantial evidence on the record as a whole, must be enforced. *Beth Israel Hospital v. NLRB,* 437 U.S. 483, 501, 98 S.Ct. 2463, 2473, 57 L.Ed.2d 370 (1978).* * *

NOTE ON ACCESS

Lechmere raises some important questions about administrative law generally, and particularly about judicial review of agency actions. The Court has told us in the context of another statute, in *Chevron, U.S.A., Inc. v. NRDC,* 467 U.S. 837 (relegated to a "cf." in *Lechmere*), that it is the agency's task to make the policy judgments that determine the application of a statute whose meaning is unclear. Section 8(a)(1), which prohibits an employer from interfering with Section 7 rights, would seem to be precisely that sort of statute, for it requires an accommodation of organizing rights with property rights. In the years shortly before *Lechmere,* the Board had worked out a careful accommodation of those rights in cases culminating with *Jean Country,* 282 NLRB 139 (1986). The Board revisited that accommodation in a post-*Lechmere* case in Pay Less Drug Stores, 312 NLRB No. 144, 145 LRRM 1096, 1993 WL 402920 (1993).

But the other half of the *Chevron* rule is that the agency's reading of the statute must be a permissible one. Justice Thomas concluded that many years earlier in the *Babcock & Wilcox* decision the Court had read the statute to allow solicitation on private property only in extreme situations such as an isolated lumber camp. Critics of the *Lechmere* decision say Justice Thomas read far too much into *Babcock and Wilcox,* which appeared to leave it to the Board to decide where on the spectrum the various interests lie.

Lechmere, you will note, arises in an organizing campaign. It remains to be seen how *Lechmere* will be applied in cases that involve not the solicitation of employees, for whom alternative means may be available, but appeals to consumers and suppliers in cases where economic pressure is brought to bear to support collective bargaining demands. *Lechmere* gives no hint as to how that accommodation will be worked out.

Consider Professor Getman's observations on the importance of union access.

GETMAN, RUMINATIONS ON UNION ORGANIZING IN THE PRIVATE SECTOR
53 U.Chi.L.Rev. 45, 71–73 (1986).

Employers have easy and instant access to their employees during an organizing campaign. Although the Supreme Court recognized quite

early that the right to consider the pros and cons of organization is included under section 7 of the NLRA, unions do not have a comparable opportunity to state the case for representation, and the trend of the law is toward limiting their opportunities still further. The two leading cases dealing with union access are NLRB v. Babcock & Wilcox Co.[72] and NLRB v. United Steelworkers of America (NuTone, Inc.).[73] In *Babcock & Wilcox,* the Court held that an employer could normally "post his property against nonemployee[s]," which meant that professional union organizers could be kept off the premises. In *NuTone,* the Court held that employers who engage in anti-union solicitation are not thereby required to permit unions to solicit on the premises. While the Court in both cases recognized the propriety of granting the union greater access if the Board found a significant imbalance in informational opportunities, the Board has only rarely exercised this power. Both liberal and conservative Boards have denied union claims for access whenever the union had any possibility of reaching the employees through other means. Even during periods in which the Board has been quite sensitive to the possibility of employer coercion, it has not granted unions greater access to the employees as a means of overcoming the coercive impact deemed to be inherent in the employees' economic dependence upon the employer. They have instead sought to provide protection through the extension of Board doctrines limiting employer campaign statements and tactics. Yet it seems clear that greater access would be a much more effective way to permit unions to overcome whatever coercive advantage the employer obtains from its position. It makes far more sense to permit unions to make an immediate response to employer threats than for the Board to respond by setting aside an election or issuing a bargaining order long after the election has been held or postponed.
* * *

The law relating to access is generally explained in terms of the courts' protectiveness of property rights. But this cannot be the entire story. Behind the law's almost total unwillingness to grant access must rest an unstated quid pro quo: since campaign regulation prevents employers from stating their most effective arguments, it is fair to require unions to scramble to get their messages heard.

Every union organizer to whom I have put the question acknowledges that this is a poor trade. When I interviewed Vicki Saporta, Director of Organizing for the Teamsters, she politely but firmly accused me of understating the potency of employer coercion. But when I asked her if she would be willing to give up Board regulation of employer speech in return for equal access, she did not hesitate for a moment before answering in the affirmative. Her response was the same as that of every other major figure in union organizing to whom I have put the question. Yet the theme of employer coercion is constantly struck by

72. 351 U.S. 105 (1955). **73.** 357 U.S. 357 (1958).

unions and their academic supporters while the claim for equal access is rarely made. * * *

FURTHER COMPLICATIONS—OFFSITE AND OFF DUTY WORKERS

Lechmere and the earlier *Babcock and Wilcox,* make a critical distinction between the access rights of employees and non-employees. Union organizers, fitting the latter category, enjoy fewer access rights than do the regular employees of the company. What are the rights of employees who are off duty, or who work for another branch of the company? Technically, they are employees under the Act, and an argument may be made that they enjoy the full access rights of the employees who are working on a particular shift at a particular location.

The question was recently raised in a case involving access rights of employees of a company who were employed at a different work site (known as off-site employees) and who attempted to handbill at the employee parking lot of a site where the Auto Workers were attempting to organize, ITT Industries v. NLRB, 251 F.3d 995 (D.C.Cir.2001).

Chief Judge Harry Edwards wrote that it is an open question whether the NLRA extends greater access rights to off-site workers than to non-employee union organizers. Judge Edwards indicated that while a court might defer to the Board's view on this question as a reasonable interpretation of the Act, the Board had failed to explain the basis for its decision, hence it was not entitled to deference.

"Because it is by no means obvious that [Section 7] extends nonderivative access rights to off-site employees, particularly given the considerations set forth in the Court's access cases, the Board was obliged to engage in considered analysis and explain its chosen interpretation."

What should the Board have done? What rationale should it develop to support the view that employees from other plants have a right of access to help in an organizing campaign at the targeted plant? What about the rights of off-duty employees to come on to plant property to assist in organizing? Should they be limited to the parking lots or allowed to enter the plant? Do you agree with the employer's argument in the ITT case that the Supreme Court meant by the term "non employee" in Babcock anyone who is trespassing? How does that square with the statutory definition of "employee?"

NOTE ON ORGANIZING ISSUES IN AN ELECTRONIC WORKPLACE

The general rule is that during their non-working hours employees are allowed to solicit other employees to support the union drive. This may take place anywhere on company premises. As we saw in *Lechmere,* this rule applies only to employees, and, quite possibly, only to employees who are on duty. Off duty employees generally are not entitled to access to the premises. The Board's rules on permissible limitations upon solicitation are reviewed by the Court in Beth Israel Hospital v. NLRB, 437 U.S. 483, 98 S.Ct. 2463, 57 L.Ed.2d 370(1978), in the context of a claimed need for tighter restrictions in a hospital setting. Employees are allowed to distribute literature, but not in working areas. Any employer policy limiting solicitation or distribution must not be applied on a discriminatory basis. That is, there may not be one rule for union activity and another rule for other forms of activity. Suppose that an employer has a broad ban against solicitation, but makes a narrow exception permitting solicitation for charities? Does this exception show that the employer is hostile to union organizing (and discriminates on the basis of union activity) or merely that the employer does not insist on a blanket rule and is willing to make some exceptions that have nothing to do with union activity?

How do these rules apply in the electronic age? May an employer bar employees from using e-mail to persuade workers to join the union? Probably not, unless the use of company e-mail is limited strictly to company business. And even then, there is some question whether an employer may prohibit all non business use of e-mail, since that would shut down one important channel of employee communication during an organizing drive, and constrain Section 7 rights. The Board's General Counsel addressed this in a 1998 Advice Memorandum, NLRB Office of General Counsel Advice Memorandum (Pratt & Whitney), Nos. 12–CA–18446, 18745 and 18863, 1998 NLRB GCM Lexis 40 (1998). The advice memo basically extended the Board's general rules about solicitation and distribution to employer e-mail policy. It concluded that e-mail is often more like a solicitation than a distribution of literature, more of an instantaneous communication, which cannot be barred outside of working hours. Some e-mails, however, are viewed as distributions of literature and may be prohibited in working areas. May the employer prohibit the use of e-mails for organizing purposes on the ground that the employee is utilizing company property? Not if the employer permits workers to use the e-mail system for other non business uses. And how should the law handle the employer's right to monitor employee use of e-mails to make sure they are not abusing the system? Will monitoring compromise employees' Section 7 rights?

But what about e-mail that is sent to employees from outside organizers? Recall that the rules for access to employees are different for outside organizers, who are not considered employees, than for workers in the plant. What if the employer blocks all incoming e-mails except those that pass some system of clearance? Again, the validity of any employer rule would turn in part on whether it is applied evenhandedly to all communications, not just those involving organizing. Assuming the employer's ban is total, should it validity be governed by the principles of *Lechmere*?

Another electronic issue age concerns the union's right to the names and addresses of those employees in the voting unit. Under the Board's *Excelsior Underwear* rule, the employer must disclose names and addresses after the union files it petition. Unions have argued that in a world of telecommuting, where employees don't show up at a place where they may be organized, the union is entitled to names and addresses prior to filing its petition. How should this controversy be resolved?

Some of the issues raised by the electronic workplace are discussed in a pair of articles, Susan S. Robfogel, Electronic Communication and the NLRA: Union Access and Employer Rights, 16 Labor Lawyer 231 (2000), and Gwynne A. Wilcox, Section 7 Rights of Employees and Union Access to Employees: Cyber Organizing, 16 Labor Lawyer 253 (2000). See also M. Malin and H. Perritt, The NLRA in Cyberspace: Union Organizing in Electronic Workplaces, 49 U. Kan. L. Rev. 1 (2000).

REVIEW PROBLEM

A hypothetical regulation for organizing campaigns

The Board does not like the stark alternative of issuing bargaining orders, whose enforcement is resisted by the courts and which raise problems of majority rule, or imposing no meaningful remedy at all. The Board proposes the following new rule on the conduct of elections, and asks for rule-making input from interested parties:

The Board establishes the following "Campaign and Election Protocol." This protocol will be placed in effect whenever an election is set aside and the Board concludes that there have been violations of the Act by the employer that have a substantial effect on the fairness of a subsequent election:

1.   After a Petition has been filed, the Board will arrange for an expedited conference between the employer and the union to resolve such issues as an appropriate bargaining unit and exclusion of supervisors and others. The Board will expedite any hearing to resolve open issues, and will expedite the holding of the election.

2.   The employer will grant the union access to the employer's facilities for limited periods of time and in restricted locations for the purpose of allowing the union to distribute literature and meet with employees.

3.   The employer shall be free to state to employees reasons to vote against the union. However, the employer shall not state that it opposes the employees' selection of a union.

4.   Employer communications with employees shall be limited to written distributions and to addresses and general meetings with groups of at least 10 employees. Meetings with smaller groups are prohibited because of their inherently coercive nature.

5. If the employer commits substantial violations of the Act during this second election, it shall agree to recognize the union based on a union showing of a majority of authorization cards.

6. If the union wins the election, or is recognized under the preceding paragraph, the employer agrees to commence negotiations promptly and to bargain in good faith. If agreement is not reached within six months, the dispute shall be submitted to binding interest arbitration.

What arguments should be made for and against this proposal by union and employer interest groups, and by other interests?

If this rule is promulgated as written here, what is the likelihood that it will be upheld in the courts? What portions of it are most vulnerable to judicial reversal, and for what reasons?

PROBLEM 2–1: THE OUTSPOKEN TECHNICIAN

Professor Weiler's article suggests that one out of 20 workers is fired during a union organizing campaign. The following problem deals with such a discharge. Consider the impact of this discharge upon the union's organizing campaign, and consider the remedy that should be imposed if the Board and courts agree that the firing violates the Act.

Hugh Ptolemy is employed as a lab assistant at Mercy Hospital. He has worked there five years and has a generally good work record overall. But Hugh has been an outspoken critic of the Hospital's practices, especially with regard to safety and sanitary conditions within the Hospital. He has filed several complaints with OSHA about the failure adequately to dispose of medical clothing and equipment that might be contaminated, and OSHA has responded favorably to his complaints. Ptolemy thinks that as a result of his activities the Hospital has targeted him as an employee to watch carefully. He fears that if he makes any mistakes in his job, the Hospital will seize upon this as an excuse to get rid of him.

Ptolemy has been active in the union's organizing drive at Mercy Hospital. Under the Board's rules for Hospital unit determinations, he would probably be in a bargaining unit consisting of all technical employees. The local newspaper and TV stations have done a couple of features on Ptolemy as one of the leaders of the union's campaign. In a recent feature in the paper on Ptolemy's efforts to link the union campaign to workers' health and safety concerns, Ptolemy was quoted as saying:

"I am very concerned that Mercy Hospital hasn't developed a good set of procedures for controlling and disposing of contaminated garments and equipment. You know, in this age of AIDS this is extremely dangerous. I've tried very hard to protect my fellow workers from exposure and I've gone to OSHA several times. I've finally come to believe that the only way we are going to get anywhere with worker protection is by having a strong union to represent us. A union would help us improve our benefits too. This Hospital cuts corners with our wages just like it does with its health and safety practices. If I were a patient I'd think twice about coming here for treatment. The other two hospitals in the area have much better safety practices."

The morning that this article appeared, the Hospital terminated Ptolemy. In a letter to Ptolemy signed by Matthew Crickboom, vice president for personnel, the Hospital simply stated "we are terminating you for conduct unbecoming a Mercy employee."

Ptolemy filed a Charge with the NLRB claiming that his discharge violated the Act. A copy of the charge is found in the reference supplement. Max Kafka, a representative of the Regional Office of the NLRB, has begun an investigation to determine if there is probable cause to issue a Complaint based on the Charge. Kafka has already interviewed Ptolemy and taken an affidavit from him. Kafka has now asked for an appointment with Crickboom to obtain the Hospital's explanation for the termination. Crickboom in turn referred the matter to his lawyers, Hungadunga, Hungadunga and McCormick.

Charles Hungadunga then called the Regional Office and asked for more information. "The Charge doesn't tell us a whole lot about Ptolemy's complaint. Surely he signed an affidavit. We would be better prepared to help in your investigation if we knew its contents." Kafka refused to supply Hungadunga with the affidavit or to discuss Ptolemy's claim prior to the conference with Crickboom.

Hungadunga will now prepare for the conference with Kafka. His goal is to convince Kafka that the Charge is without merit and should be dismissed. If the NLRB Regional Office doesn't issue a Complaint, that is the end of Ptolemy's claim under the NLRA. The Board's decision not to go ahead with a Complaint is virtually unreviewable, see Patrick Hardin, The Developing Labor Law, 1879 (3rd Ed., 1992). Hungadunga is certainly anxious to see that a Complaint not issue, because the Board's involvement behind Ptolemy's claim would lend credence to the union's organizing drive. And the union is much weaker without Ptolemy around to lead it.

The employees of Mercy Hospital are not represented by a labor organization, although a petition for representation has been filed. Mercy has issued all its employees a personnel manual. The manual has the following section on discipline:

"Mercy Hospital believes in treating all its employees fairly. If you are not performing your job satisfactorily, we will make every effort to guide you in correcting your performance. However, the Hospital must be the ultimate judge of your work performance, and reserves the right to terminate you when it is deemed necessary, as this manual does not create any contractual right to job security. Among the grounds for termination are

(1) unsatisfactory work performance

(2) poor attendance

(3) conduct unbecoming an employee of Mercy Hospital. Unbe-coming conduct of an egregious sort is grounds for immediate termination."

Depending on the preferences of your instructor, this problem may be the subject of a simulated exercise. The exercise may cover the following grounds:

A.   Two students, as associates in the Hungadunga firm, will interview Crickboom and prepare him for the conference with Kaf-ka.

B.   Two students, as associates of Board investigator Kafka, will conduct the conference with Crickboom.

C.   The investigators will then present to the Regional Director their recommendations as to whether a complaint should be issued. The Regional Director will determine whether to issue a complaint.

During the course of the exercise, we will discuss possibilities for settlement.

This exercise tests your ability to identify the facts and theories necessary to establish or resist Ptolemy's claim. It will also let you see the impact of the treatment of a discharge upon a union organizing campaign. Consider the next case and the notes that follow.

NATIONAL LABOR RELATIONS BOARD v. LOCAL UNION NO. 1229, INTERNATIONAL BROTH-ERHOOD OF ELECTRICAL WORKERS

Supreme Court of the United States, 1953.
346 U.S. 464, 74 S.Ct. 172, 98 L.Ed. 195.

MR. JUSTICE BURTON delivered the opinion of the Court.

The issue before us is whether the discharge of certain employees by their employer constituted an unfair labor practice, within the meaning of §§ 8(a)(1) and 7 of the Taft–Hartley Act, justifying their reinstate-ment by the National Labor Relations Board. For the reason that their discharge was 'for cause' within the meaning of § 10(c) of that Act, we sustain the Board in not requiring their reinstatement.

In 1949, the Jefferson Standard Broadcasting Company (here called the company) was a North Carolina corporation engaged in interstate commerce. Under a license from the Federal Communications Commis-sion, it operated, at Charlotte, North Carolina, a 50,000–watt radio station, with call letters WBT. It broadcast 10 to 12 hours daily by radio and television. The television service, which it started July 14, 1949, representing an investment of about $500,000, was the only such service in the area. Less than 50% of the station's programs originated in Charlotte. The others were piped in over leased wires, generally from New York, California or Illinois from several different networks. * * *

The company employed 22 technicians. In December 1948, negotiations to settle the terms of their employment after January 31, 1949, were begun between representatives of the company and of the respondent Local Union No. 1229, International Brotherhood of Electrical Workers, American Federation of Labor (here called the union). The negotiations reached an impasse in January 1949, and the existing contract of employment expired January 31. The technicians, nevertheless, continued to work for the company and their collective-bargaining negotiations were resumed in July, only to break down again July 8. The main point of disagreement arose from the union's demand for the renewal of a provision that all discharges from employment be subject to arbitration and the company's counter-proposal that such arbitration be limited to the facts material to each discharge, leaving it to the company to determine whether those facts gave adequate cause for discharge.

July 9, 1949, the union began daily peaceful picketing of the company's station. Placards and handbills on the picket line charged the company with unfairness to its technicians and emphasized the company's refusal to renew the provision for arbitration of discharges. The placards and handbills named the union as the representative of the WBT technicians. The employees did not strike. They confined their respective tours of picketing to their off-duty hours and continued to draw full pay. There was no violence or threat of violence and no one has taken exception to any of the above conduct.

But on August 24, 1949, a new procedure made its appearance. Without warning, several of its technicians launched a vitriolic attack on the quality of the company's television broadcasts. Five thousand handbills were printed over the designation 'WBT Technicians.' These were distributed on the picket line, on the public square two or three blocks from the company's premises, in barber shops, restaurants and busses. Some were mailed to local businessmen. The handbills made no reference to the union, to a labor controversy or to collective bargaining. They read:

'Is Charlotte A Second–Class City?

'You might think so from the kind of Television programs being presented by the Jefferson Standard Broadcasting Co. over WBTV. Have you seen one of their television programs lately? Did you know that all the programs presented over WBTV are on film and may be from one day to five years old? There are no local programs presented by WBTV. You cannot receive the local baseball games, football games or other local events because WBTV does not have the proper equipment to make these pickups. Cities like New York, Boston, Philadelphia, Washington receive such programs nightly. Why doesn't the Jefferson Standard Broadcasting Company purchase the needed equipment to bring you the same type of programs enjoyed by other leading American cities? Could it be that they consider Charlotte a second-class community and only entitled to the pictures now being presented to them?

'WBT Technicians'

This attack continued until September 3, 1949, when the company discharged ten of its technicians, whom it charged with sponsoring or distributing these handbills. The company's letter discharging them tells its side of the story.[4]

September 4, the union's picketing resumed its original tenor and, September 13, the union filed with the Board a charge that the company, by discharging the above-mentioned ten technicians, had engaged in an unfair labor practice. * * * The Board found that one of the discharged men had neither sponsored nor distributed the 'Second–Class City' handbill and ordered his reinstatement with back pay. It then found that the other nine had sponsored or distributed the handbill and held that the company, by discharging them for such conduct, had not engaged in an unfair labor practice. The Board, accordingly, did not order their reinstatement. * * *

In its essence, the issue is simple. It is whether these employees, whose contracts of employment had expired, were discharged 'for cause.' They were discharged solely because, at a critical time in the initiation of the company's television service, they sponsored or distributed 5,000 handbills making a sharp, public, disparaging attack upon the quality of the company's product and its business policies, in a manner reasonably

---

4. 'Dear Mr. * * *,

'When you and some of our other technicians commenced early in July to picket against this Company, we felt that your action was very ill-considered. We were paying you a salary of * * * per week, to say nothing of other benefits which you receive as an employee of our Company, such as time-and-a-half pay for all work beyond eight hours in any one day, three weeks vacation each year with full pay, unlimited sick leave with full pay, liberal life insurance and hospitalization, for you and your family, and retirement and pension benefits unexcelled anywhere. Yet when we were unable to agree upon the terms of a contract with your Union, you began to denounce us publicly as 'unfair.'

'And ever since early July while you have been walking up and down the street with placards and literature attacking us, you have continued to hold your job and receive your pay and all the other benefits referred to above.

'Even when you began to put out propaganda which contained many untruths about our Company and great deal of personal abuse and slander, we still continued to treat you exactly as before. For it has been our understanding that under our labor laws, you have a very great latitude in trying to make the public believe that your employer is unfair to you.

'Now, however, you have turned from trying to persuade the public that we are unfair to you and are trying to persuade the public that we give inferior service to them. While we are struggling to expand into and develop a new field, and incidentally losing large sums of money in the process, you are busy trying to turn customers and the public against us in every possible way, even handing out leaflets on the public streets advertising that our operations are 'second-class,' and endeavoring in various ways to hamper and totally destroy our business. Certainly we are not required by law or common sense to keep you in our employment and pay you a substantial salary while you thus do your best to tear down and bankrupt our business.

'You are hereby discharged from our employment. Although there is nothing requiring us to do so, and the circumstances certainly do not call for our doing so, we are enclosing a check payable to your order for two weeks' advance or severance pay.

'Very truly yours,

'Jefferson Standard Broadcasting Company

'By: Charles H. Crutchfield

'Vice President

'Enclosure'

calculated to harm the company's reputation and reduce its income. The attack was made by them expressly as 'WBT Technicians.' It continued ten days without indication of abatement. The Board found that—

'It (the handbill) occasioned widespread comment in the community, and caused Respondent to apprehend a loss of advertising revenue due to dissatisfaction with its television broadcasting service.

'In short, the employees in this case deliberately undertook to alienate their employer's customers by impugning the technical quality of his product. As the Trial Examiner found, they did not misrepresent, at least willfully, the facts they cited to support their disparaging report. And their ultimate purpose—to extract a concession from the employer with respect to the terms of their employment—was lawful. That purpose, however, was undisclosed; the employees purported to speak as experts, in the interest of consumers and the public at large. They did not indicate that they sought to secure any benefit for themselves, as employees, by casting discredit upon their employer.'

The company's letter shows that it interpreted the handbill as a demonstration of such detrimental disloyalty as to provide 'cause' for its refusal to continue in its employ the perpetrators of the attack. We agree.

Section 10(c) of the Taft–Hartley Act expressly provides that 'No order of the Board shall require the reinstatement of any individual as an employee who has been suspended or discharged, or the payment to him of any back pay, if such individual was suspended or discharged for cause.' There is no more elemental cause for discharge of an employee than disloyalty to his employer. It is equally elemental that the Taft–Hartley Act seeks to strengthen, rather than to weaken, that cooperation, continuity of service and cordial contractual relation between employer and employee that is born of loyalty to their common enterprise.

Congress, while safeguarding, in § 7, the right of employees to engage in 'concerted activities for the purpose of collective bargaining or other mutual aid or protection,' did not weaken the underlying contractual bonds and loyalties of employer and employee. The conference report that led to the enactment of the law said:

'(T)he courts have firmly established the rule that under the existing provisions of section 7 of the National Labor Relations Act, employees are not given any right to engage in unlawful or other improper conduct.

' * * * Furthermore, in section 10(c) of the amended act, as proposed in the conference agreement, it is specifically provided that no order of the Board shall require the reinstatement of any individual or the payment to him of any back pay if such individual was suspended or discharged for cause, and this, of course, applies with equal force whether or not the acts constituting the cause for discharge were committed in connection with a concerted activity.' H.R.Rep.No. 510, 80th Cong., 1st Sess. 38–39. * * *

The legal principle that insubordination, disobedience or disloyalty is adequate cause for discharge is plain enough. The difficulty arises in determining whether, in fact, the discharges are made because of such a separable cause or because of some other concerted activities engaged in for the purpose of collective bargaining or other mutual aid or protection, which may not be adequate cause for discharge.

In the instant case the Board found that the company's discharge of the nine offenders resulted from their sponsoring and distributing the 'Second–Class City' handbills of August 24—September 3, issued in their name as the 'WBT Technicians.' Assuming that there had been no pending labor controversy, the conduct of the 'WBT Technicians' from August 24 through September 3 unquestionably would have provided adequate cause for their disciplinary discharge within the meaning of § 10(c). Their attack related itself to no labor practice of the company. It made no reference to wages, hours or working conditions. The policies attacked were those of finance and public relations for which management, not technicians, must be responsible. The attack asked for no public sympathy or support. It was a continuing attack, initiated while off duty, upon the very interests, which the attackers were being paid to conserve and develop. Nothing could be further from the purpose of the Act than to require an employer to finance such activities. Nothing would contribute less to the Act's declared purpose of promoting industrial peace and stability.[12]

The fortuity of the coexistence of a labor dispute affords these technicians no substantial defense. While they were also union men and leaders in the labor controversy, they took pains to separate those categories. In contrast to their claims on the picket line as to the labor controversy, their handbill of August 24 omitted all reference to it. The handbill diverted attention from the labor controversy. It attacked public policies of the company, which had no discernible relation to that controversy. The only connection between the handbill and the labor controversy was an ultimate and undisclosed purpose or motive on the part of some of the sponsors that, by the hoped-for financial pressure, the attack might extract from the company some future concession. A disclosure of that motive might have lost more public support for the employees than it would have gained, for it would have given the handbill more the character of coercion than of collective bargaining. Referring to the attack, the Board said 'In our judgment, these tactics, in the circumstances of this case, were hardly less 'indefensible' than acts of physical sabotage.' In any event, the findings of the Board effectively separate the attack from the labor controversy and treat it solely as one

---

12. ' * * * An employee cannot work and strike at the same time. He cannot continue in his employment and openly or secretly refuse to do his work. He can not collect wages for his employment, and, at the same time, engage in activities to injure or destroy his employer's business.'

made by the company's technical experts upon the quality of the company's product. As such, it was as adequate a cause for the discharge of its sponsors as if the labor controversy had not been pending. The technicians, themselves, so handled their attack as thus to bring their discharge under § 10(c).

The Board stated 'We * * * do not decide whether the disparagement of product involved here would have justified the employer in discharging the employees responsible for it, had it been uttered in the context of a conventional appeal for support of the union in the labor dispute.' This underscored the Board's factual conclusion that the attack of August 24 was not part of an appeal for support in the pending dispute. It was a concerted separable attack purporting to be made in the interest of the public rather than in that of the employees.

We find no occasion to remand this cause to the Board for further specificity of findings. Even if the attack were to be treated, as the Board has not treated it, as a concerted activity wholly or partly within the scope of those mentioned in § 7, the means used by the technicians in conducting the attack have deprived the attackers of the protection of that section, when read in the light and context of the purpose of the Act.

MR. JUSTICE FRANKFURTER, whom MR. JUSTICE BLACK and MR. JUSTICE DOUGLAS join, dissenting.

The Court, relying on § 10(c) which permits discharges 'for cause,' points to the 'disloyalty' of the employees and finds sufficient 'cause' regardless of whether the handbill was a 'concerted activity' within § 7. Section 10(c) does not speak of discharge 'for disloyalty.' If Congress had so written that section, it would have overturned much of the law that had been developed by the Board and the courts in the twelve years preceding the Taft-Hartley Act. The legislative history makes clear that Congress had no such purpose but was rather expressing approval of the construction of 'concerted activities' adopted by the Board and the courts. Many of the legally recognized tactics and weapons of labor would readily be condemned for 'disloyalty' were they employed between man and man in friendly personal relations. In this connection it is significant that the ground now taken by the Court, insofar as it is derived from the provision of § 10(c) relating to discharge 'for cause,' was not invoked by the Board in justification of its order.

To suggest that all actions which in the absence of a labor controversy might be 'cause'—or, to use the words commonly found in labor agreements, 'just cause'—for discharge should be unprotected, even when such actions were undertaken as 'concerted activities for the purpose of collective bargaining', is to misconstrue legislation designed to put labor on a fair footing with management. Furthermore, it would disregard the rough and tumble of strikes, in the course of which loose and even reckless language is properly discounted.

'Concerted activities' by employees and dismissal 'for cause' by employers are not dissociated legal criteria under the Act. They are like the two halves of a pair of shears. Of course, as the Conference Report on the Taft–Hartley Act said, men on strike may be guilty of conduct 'in connection with a concerted activity' which properly constitutes 'cause' for dismissal and bars reinstatement. But § 10(c) does not obviate the necessity for a determination whether the distribution of the handbill here was a legitimate tool in a labor dispute or was so 'improper,' as the Conference Report put it, as to be denied the protection of § 7 and to constitute a discharge 'for cause.' It is for the Board, in the first instance, to make these evaluations, and a court of appeals does not travel beyond its proper bounds in asking the Board for greater explicitness in light of the correct legal standards for judgment.

The Board and the courts of appeals will hardly find guidance for future cases from this Court's reversal of the Court of Appeals, beyond that which the specific facts of this case may afford. More than that, to float such imprecise notions as 'discipline' and 'loyalty' in the context of labor controversies, as the basis of the right to discharge, is to open the door wide to individual judgment by Board members and judges. One may anticipate that the Court's opinion will needlessly stimulate litigation.

Section 7 of course only protects 'concerted activities' in the course of promoting legitimate interests of labor. But to treat the offensive handbills here as though they were circulated by the technicians as interloping outsiders to the sustained dispute between them and their employer is a very unreal way of looking at the circumstances of a labor controversy. Certainly there is nothing in the language of the Act or in the legislative history to indicate that only conventional placards and handbills, headed by a trite phrase such as 'Unfair To Labor,' are protected. In any event, on a remand the Board could properly be asked to leave no doubt whether the technicians, in distributing the handbills, were, so far as the public could tell, on a frolic of their own or whether this tactic, however unorthodox, was no more unlawful than other union behavior previously found to be entitled to protection. * * *

Read NLRA Sections 7, 8(a)(1), (3) and (4). Read the Washington Aluminum case in Chapter 1. 193

NOTE ON THE PTOLEMY PROBLEM

The Ptolemy problem involves two distinct issues. The first is a question of motive. Did Mercy Hospital fire Ptolemy because of his union activities, or because he spoke out against the Hospital? How do you determine which motive prevailed? You should be familiar with this issue from your study of motive in Chapter One. The employer will not admit that it fired a worker because of his union activity, but will assert that it had legitimate reasons that had nothing to do with unionization. Thus, we must ask whether the worker was treated differently because of his union activity. Or was he fired because of his disparagement of the company (which disparagement itself may or may not be protected apart from whether the response is tied to union activity)?

Since the early '80's, the Board has followed an approach to sorting out motive contained in its Wright Line decision (Wright Line, 251 NLRB 1083 (1980)). The Wright Line approach was upheld in NLRB v. Transportation Management Corp., 462 U.S. 393 (1983). The basic rule is that the General Counsel bears the burden of persuading the Board that antiunion animus contributed to the employer's decision. Assuming the General Counsel meets that burden, the employer may avoid any violation of the Act by showing by a preponderance of the evidence that the worker would have been fired anyway, even if he had not been involved with the union. Does this approach remind you of Mt. Healthy in Chapter I? The Court relied upon its decision in that case in upholding the Board's allocation of burdens.

Compare the statutory treatment of burdens of proof under Title VII in Sections 703(m) and 706 (g)(2)(B)(both 1991 amendments) in your statutory supplement.

ON CONCERTEDNESS

A second requirement in order for Ptolemy to be protected is that his activity must be in concert with other employees; he is not protected if he acts alone. Concertedness should be easy to establish in the Ptolemy situation, since Ptolemy is leading an organizing drive and his comments clearly make reference to that collective activity.

Section 7 of the Act protects "other concerted activities" for the purpose of mutual aid or protection. The "other" indicates that the Act protects activities that are not necessarily connected with unionization, as in Washington Aluminum, in Chapter I. The "concerted" requirement reminds us that this is a statute that protects collective activity, not individual action. If you ponder on that, you might conclude that since the statute is primarily aimed at protecting unionization, it is only concerned with activities that are at least a prelude to collective representation. Workers acting in concert, as in Washington Aluminum, may be leading up to union organization; at least the exercise there may give them that idea. In contrast, the worker acting alone may be too far from that collective objective to warrant protection of the Act. After all, this is not a statute designed to protect workers' rights in general, but only the right to seek improvement through collective means.

The Supreme Court's City Disposal decision (NLRB v. City Disposal Systems, Inc., 465 U.S. 822 (1984) makes some important distinctions about concertedness. When a lone worker in a unionized workplace takes a stand, there is a presumption of concertedness. That is because his position is usually grounded in the collective bargaining agreement. Justice Brennan wrote, "when an employee invokes a right grounded in the collective bargaining agreement, he does not stand alone. Instead, he brings to bear on his employer the power and resolve of all his fellow employees.'' City Disposal involved the discharge of a truck driver who refused to take out his truck when he thought it was unsafe. Justice Brennan continued that in that context the employee ''was in effect reminding his employer that he and his fellow employees, at the time their collective-bargaining agreement was signed, had extracted a promise from City Disposal that they would not be asked to drive unsafe trucks. * * * It was as though [he] was reassembling his fellow union members to reenact their decision not to drive unsafe trucks.''

The Brennan image of all those workers standing behind the sole driver may be a bit much, but that's what we have. In contrast, the lone worker who complains in a non union workplace enjoys no presumption that he or she is speaking for everyone else. That is so even in the context of a safety issue, where you might argue that the worker is invoking a statutory right that Congress enacted for the benefit of the individual worker as well as everyone else. The Board took that position in *Meyers Industries,* 281 NLRB 882 (1986).

The Board has more recently given a more expansive reading to concertedness in *Mike Yurosek and Son,* 306 NLRB 1037 (1992), when it read in to some similar but isolated activities of several workers a common resolve to react to provocation by management, thus making the action concerted and protected.

ON PROTECTED REMARKS

Finally, even if you assume that the Hospital fired Ptolemy because of what he said, and not because he was active in the union, there is a further question whether an employer may fire an employee for those remarks. That is the question raised by *Jefferson Standard.* Are these comments protected because they are an aspect of the worker's Section 7 rights, or is protection lost because the words fit the rather generalized term of ''disloyalty?'' Recall the *Emporium Capwell* case earlier in this chapter. Those employees made some very disparaging remarks about their employer. While *Emporium Capwell* turned on a different issue— that the fired employees had gone against their own union, thus forfeiting their Section 7 rights because of the doctrine of exclusivity—the Court also discussed in footnote 6 whether their conduct was unprotected because it disparaged the employer. The Court ultimately ducked that point.

In Part E of these materials, on the use of economic weapons, we will explore an analogous issue. At what point are the economic tactics of union members so ''indefensible'' that they lose the protection of the Act?

PROTECTION IN A NON–UNION WORKPLACE

Protections against discharge

At the outset of this chapter we looked at alternative forms of representation for employees who choose not or are unable to secure representation under the NLRA. One of the criteria we suggested for evaluating such a system is whether it protects the right of such a worker to speak out. How would Ptolemy have fared if he made these comments in a workplace where there was no union activity going on?

We saw in Chapter One that the law has carved out a number of protections for employees who would otherwise be vulnerable to termination under employment-at-will. Would Ptolemy have any protection under the public policy doctrines that we studied? Would the employee manual give him any rights? What if the state had adopted the Model Employee Termination Statute we discussed in Chapter One? If Ptolemy worked for a public hospital, would he be protected under the First Amendment? Would Ptolemy have any recourse under OSHA? We will see in Chapter III that under that statute an employee may not be fired for filing a complaint with OSHA. Would that help Ptolemy here?

What would it cost Ptolemy to retain a lawyer to represent him under one of these approaches? Would a lawyer be willing to take his case on a contingent fee basis? Would the lawyer be entitled to counsel fees if Ptolemy prevailed? How long would it take Ptolemy to see his case through to completion? What relief would he get if he wins, and how would he eat in the meantime?

In the Ptolemy problem, and particularly in the simulated exercise, we see how the NLRA protects employees who are terminated. Consider whether the Board's procedures are well designed to make factual and legal determinations. Do the NLRA procedures give Ptolemy a better hope of relief than if he hires a private attorney to pursue some other cause of action?

If Ptolemy had been represented by a union and a collective bargaining agreement were in place, Ptolemy could challenge his termination under the "just cause" provision of his Agreement. Consider the representative just cause arbitration award in Chapter One. Remember that the burden is on the company in such cases to justify the termination. What would the company have to prove in an arbitration in order to sustain its discharge of Ptolemy?

But even in a non-union workplace, Ptolemy's activities may also be protected under Section 7 of the NLRA. This basic principle was established years ago in the *Washington Aluminum* case back in Chapter 1 (NLRB v. Washington Aluminum Co., 370 U.S. 9 (1962)). The Court protected workers in a non-union shop who walked off the job to protest unusually cold working conditions. Despite the lack of a bargaining representative to whom the workers could turn, the Court held this was a "labor dispute" as defined in the Act. Presumably this reasoning also applies where workers in an employee participation system are fired or disciplined because of a position they take in dealing with their employer. Do you think the drafters of Section 7 contemplated that the Act would apply to a non-union workplace? Should a worker have the protection of Section 7 even where the employee participation program violates Section 8(a)(2)?

The worker in the non-union setting has an additional hurdle to clear before securing protection under Section 7: the activity in question must be concerted. Look again at the text of Section 7. This means that an individual employee looking out only for his own interests is not protected under Section 7. It does not matter that the employee is asserting a right or trying to make a change that will benefit his fellow workers. There has to be some showing that the worker is acting in concert with his or her fellow workers. That was easy to show in *Washington Aluminum*. It is generally presumed in a case where the workers are organized and working under a collective bargaining agreement. In the Ptolemy problem we worked on in class, the jointness of Ptolemy's activities was clear, because he was leading a union organizing drive. But if Ptolemy were not involved in an organizing campaign, he would have some difficulty in showing that his remarks to the newspaper about health and safety conditions at Mercy Hospital fit the requirements for concertedness.

WEINGARTEN RIGHTS IN THE
NON-UNION WORKPLACE

In the 1975 *Weingarten* decision, the Supreme Court held that a worker in a unionized workplace has the right to have his or her union representative present if the employer wishes to conduct an interview or meeting where that employee is a potential target for discipline. That right was extended by the Board to the worker in a non-union situation in *Epilepsy Foundation,* a case we discussed earlier in the chapter. Would the *Weingarten/Epilepsy* right have helped Ptolemy in any way in this problem?

D. WHAT DO WE TALK ABOUT WHEN WE TALK ABOUT WORK?—THE LAW THAT REGULATES COLLECTIVE BARGAINING

INTRODUCTION

We come back to the heart of this chapter. It is about how employees secure a meaningful voice in the governance of the workplace. We have described some of the ways this happens in the nonunion setting. There are not very many rules about the way people talk in the nonunion worker participation system. When the employer allows it, they simply get together and do it.

But we've raised some questions as to whether that voice is an effective one. Is worker participation just one big suggestion box? The employer isn't required to listen. If it does listen, it may not take the workers' ideas seriously. Can you think of other situations in which those who are not empowered may be marginalized in discussion? The employer is certainly not required to agree. In fact, the employer can call the whole thing off. And the workers have little they can do to get the employer to agree with them. If the workers reach agreements with the employer, it may be theoretically possible to reduce those agreements to a written contract that is enforceable. Of course, any such agreement would probably violate Section 8(a)(2), and might very well be unenforceable as a result.

In contrast, a complex set of rules governs the way employers and unions must talk to each other. The law begins with the command in Sections 8(b)(3) and 8(a)(5) that the parties must bargain with each other. Section 8(d) spells out an "obligation to confer in good faith with respect to wages, hours, and other terms and conditions of employment." The obligation under the NLRA to bargain in good faith is in sharp contrast with the approach that courts take in most other forms of bargaining, for example, in the law of commercial contracts. We will provide you with some case law on the subject of good faith bargaining under the NLRA and ask you to consider whether the duty to bargain in good faith really helps the union gain the ear of the employer. Is this truly a means of encouraging constructive talking, or is it just a legal device that gets in the way, whose only use is manipulation?

THE POWER BASE OF BARGAINING AND THE LAW RELATING TO USE OF ECONOMIC WEAPONS

The student should have no illusion that bargaining is simply about the ability of each side to persuade the other. The effectiveness of bargaining turns at least in part on the ability of each party to bring economic pressure to bear in support of its positions. For the union this is the right and ability to withhold the services of the employees—the right to strike—and to persuade other would be workers, suppliers and customers not to deal with the company. For the employer, this is the right and ability to carry out the operations with other workers such as replacements and supervisors, to transfer work elsewhere, or shut down until the union comes to terms. We will consider the use of these weapons in the next section, especially whether the law has come down in an even handed way in regulating their use.

Thus the law relating to collective bargaining operates in the shadow of the various economic weapons available to the parties. The student as well as the practicing lawyer must appreciate that the constraints of Sections 8(a)(5) and 8(b)(3) of the NLRA may have far less effect on the conduct of bargaining than the ability of each side to use its economic power.

As we will see when we study the rules about bargaining, the law does not provide very strong direct remedies if a party fails to carry out its bargaining obligation. This makes us question whether the whole endeavor of regulating bargaining is worth the effort. However, we must alert you that a party that fails to comply with the bargaining duties imposed by law may forfeit its right to use some of its critical economic weapons. The most significant consequence is that if an employer bargains in bad faith in violation of Section 8(a)(5), it may lose its ability to permanently replace strikers. By the same token, employees who engage in certain kinds of conduct condemned by the Board or courts may forfeit their rights as workers under the statute. The interplay between the rules of bargaining and the rights of parties to use certain economic weapons may in the last analysis make meaningful and effective the rules of bargaining that we will now study.

And even if the bargaining obligations don't have all the force we might like, they apparently have some impact on shaping the way people behave at the bargaining table. After all, lawyers tend to comply with the rituals imposed by the law.

We also remind the student that the bargainer usually has the ultimate goal of reaching a mutually acceptable agreement. So the rules may be less important than the practical drive to reach a settlement. As you study these materials, keep in mind that your contribution as a lawyer involved in negotiations may well be your ability to marshall information and data in support of your position, to build the other party's trust in your word, to see and understand the needs of the other side, and to propose creative solutions that advance the interests of both sides. This dimension of your work may be far more important than your ability to comport with the rules of bargaining.

Let's begin with the basic command of the NLRA that the parties must bargain in good faith. What does that mean? Consider the following problem:

PROBLEM 2–2: PREPARING FOR BARGAINING

As a result of the unit determination procedures discussed earlier, an election was held at Mercy Hospital among employees in each of seven units. Only in unit (2), physicians, was no election held. The nurse practitioners were included in unit (1) with the RN's. The Unified Medical Care Association has been certified to represent all employees at Mercy Hospital in those units in which elections were held. The union has written a letter to Mercy demanding that the parties begin bargaining for their first collective bargaining agreement. It requests coordinated bargaining for all seven units.

With the assistance of a law firm that specializes in counselling companies to resist union organizing drives, Mercy had waged a stiff campaign against the union and committed several violations of the NLRA. Mercy has decided that it would create an unproductive atmosphere for bargaining if that law firm continued to represent Mercy in the bargaining process. Your firm has a reputation for constructive approaches to collective bargaining, and you have been retained to conduct the negotiations. Matthew Crickboom, Mercy's vice president for human resources, has sent you the following memo in preparation for his initial strategy meeting with you:

"As you know from studying the election file that I sent you, the union won a very narrow victory, by a margin of 220–195. A number of employees, particularly the nurse practitioners, and a group of technical employees in the lab, were strongly opposed to the union, and have established dissident groups. The union's overall support is lukewarm, and I doubt very much that the union could muster the necessary support to call a strike in support of its bargaining demands.

"Under those circumstances, I don't see why we should agree to any substantial improvements in economic benefits, or to any terms that give the union significant power in the hospital. I would like to propose a single, modest wage increase of about 2%, which would then stay frozen for two years. I do not want to agree to binding arbitration of grievances. As I understand the law, we're not required to agree to arbitration, and since the union won't strike to get it, why should we give it?

"I don't have any problem reaching an agreement we can live with, along the above lines. However, it seems to me that if we can drag these negotiations out, the union supporters will lose heart. If we insist on our terms, the union may not agree to them. And if it does agree, the workers will not be very impressed with the contract. I predict the union will be decertified after the first contract expires. The workers will see the union can't do them any good.

"In our first meeting next week I'd like to discuss this approach with you. Am I missing anything? And what can the NLRB do to us if they conclude this is bargaining in bad faith?"

Please be prepared to respond to this memo. In addition to the legal issues that it raises, consider whether it presents any ethical issues for you in your representation of Mercy.

SURFACE BARGAINING—A CASE STUDY IN BARGAINING STRATEGIES AND ECONOMIC WEAPONS

TEAMSTERS LOCAL v. NLRB (REICHHOLD CHEMICALS)

United States Court of Appeals, District of Columbia Circuit, 1990.
906 F.2d 719.

[Editors' note: We utilize this D.C. Circuit decision as a case study that illustrates a range of issues that can come up in a bargaining situation. We will discuss Reichhold Chemicals at a couple of points in this section, and later when we consider the unfair labor practice strike and the right to replace strikers. The author of the opinion, Judge Harry T. Edwards, taught labor law at the University of Michigan Law School before going on the bench, and is the author of a number of articles and books on labor law. We begin with his description of the bargaining:]

A. Factual History

* * * In January 1983, Reichhold Chemicals, Inc. and Teamsters Local Union No. 515, the collective bargaining representative for the

production and maintenance employees at Reichhold's Kensington, Georgia, plant, commenced bargaining on an initial contract. During 29 bargaining meetings held between January 18, 1983, and February 15, 1984, the parties exchanged proposals and counterproposals. They reached agreement on a number of matters but were unable to agree on a management rights provision or on a no-strike clause, both of which the Union had identified as strike issues. As part of its proposed no-strike clause, Reichhold sought a waiver of the employees' statutory right to strike in protest against unfair labor practices and a waiver of certain statutory rights held by employees to seek redress from the Board and other governmental agencies.

The Union conducted two strike votes: one in August 1983, and one in April 1984. During the August 1983 strike-vote meeting, Union President Logan discussed the Company's proposals on management rights, the grievance procedure, the no-strike clause and various other provisions. Logan did not specifically mention the no-access provision, but he did tell the employees that the Company's proposals would seriously restrict the employees' rights to challenge employer conduct during the term of the agreement. At the urging of the Union leadership, the employees voted unanimously to authorize a strike. Eight months later, on April 1, 1984, Union President Logan again met with the bargaining unit employees to conduct a second strike vote. In discussing the Company's demands, the Union President told the employees that there were items in the proposed management rights provision and the no-strike clause that were unreasonable, outrageous and unlike any he had seen before, and that if the Union agreed to those items it would not have a significant labor agreement. See Reichhold Chemicals, Inc., 288 N.L.R.B. No. 8, slip op. at 12, 1987–1988 NLRB Dec. (CCH) & 19,308 at 33,353 (1988) ("Reichhold II"). At the close of the meeting the Reichhold employees voted to strike. It is undisputed that the Company's inclusion of a no-access provision was a principal reason for the Union's objection to the no-strike clause.

Members of the Union struck Reichhold from April 1, 1984, to April 6, 1984, at which time the striking employees made an unconditional offer to return to work. Twenty-nine members of the Union were informed that they had been permanently replaced during the strike but would be given preferential hiring rights at the Reichhold facility. As of the date of the unfair labor practice hearing, twenty-seven employees had not been recalled.

[As you can see from the summary of the negotiations, the sticking points were a couple of management proposals that would have weakened the union's role in its day to day representation of the union. One was an expanded management rights clause that allows the employer to take certain actions without being challenged by the union under the grievance and arbitration procedure. The second not only barred the union from striking during the life of the agreement, not an unusual provision in itself, but also said the employees could not strike in protest over any management unfair labor practices and waived their right to seek relief from the Board and other administrative agencies. Later on we will discuss why some of those provisions standing alone violate Section 8(a)(5), while others are perfectly okay under that section. Here we address the union's argument that the cumulative impact of these provisions showed that the employer had no intention of reaching an agreement, but was putting forward provisions that no self respecting union could accept. The issue is very close to the one in Problem 2–2. Judge Edwards responded as follows:]

C. The Union's Challenges to Alleged Surface Bargaining

The Union argues that the substance of the Company's proposals, the Company's failure to concede on any of the terms and conditions of employment encompassed within the management rights clause, and the negotiation to impasse on a provision that was not a mandatory subject are inconsistent with a determination that the Company engaged in good-faith bargaining.

Accordingly, the Union claims that the Board erred in concluding that the Company's "overall conduct establishes that it engaged in lawful hard bargaining, rather than unlawful surface bargaining," Reichhold II, 288 NLRB No. 8, slip op. at 2, 1987–1988 and urges the court to find that the Board's determination lacks substantial support in the record. Because we find no infirmity with the Board's determination on this point, we deny the Union's petition.

While parties to a negotiation are "not required to make concessions or to yield any position fairly maintained," "[r]igid adherence to disadvantageous proposals may provide a basis for inferring bad faith." NLRB v. Blevins Popcorn Co., 659 F.2d 1173, 1187 (emphasis added).

* * * "If a company insists on terms that 'no "self-respecting union" could brook,' Vanderbilt Products, Inc. v. NLRB, 297 F.2d 833, it may not be fulfilling its obligation to bargain." Id. at 1188. But the decision regarding "good faith" turns on

> "whether it is to be inferred from the totality of the employer's conduct that he went through the motions of negotiation as an elaborate pretense with no sincere desire to reach an agreement if possible, or that it bargained in good faith but was unable to arrive at an acceptable agreement with the union."

Soule Glass & Glazing Co. v. NLRB, 652 F.2d 1055, "Adamant insistence on a bargaining position ... is not in itself a refusal to bargain in good faith." Chevron Oil Co. v. NLRB, 442 F.2d 1067, 1072. And " '[i]f the insistence is genuinely and sincerely held, if it is not mere window dressing, it may be maintained forever though it produce a stalemate.' " McCourt v. California Sports, Inc., 600 F.2d 1193, 1201. An inference of bad faith from substantive terms of a proposal always must be drawn with caution. " '[T]he Board may not, either directly or indirectly, compel concessions or otherwise sit in judgment upon the substantive terms of collective bargaining agreements.' " H.K. Porter Co. v. NLRB, 397 U.S. 99, 106.

Under this legal standard, we conclude that the Board's determination regarding the Company's "good faith" bargaining is supported by the record. The Board found, and the Union does not dispute, that the Company "was willing at all times to meet and bargain with the Union, attended all scheduled meetings, fulfilled its procedural obligations, exchanged proposals, and shortly after the last meeting notified a Federal mediator that it was willing to bargain with the Union in March." Reichhold II, 288 NLRB No. 8, slip op. at 5, 1987–1988. We must uphold the Board's determination that there has been no violation of the Act unless it has no rational basis.

NOTE ON SURFACE BARGAINING

KENNETH G. DAU–SCHMIDT: A BARGAINING ANALYSIS OF AMERICAN LABOR LAW AND THE SEARCH FOR BARGAINING EQUITY AND INDUSTRIAL PEACE

91 Mich. L. Rev. 419, 442–443, 449–450, 483–487 (1992).

THE COSTS OF COLLECTIVE BARGAINING AS POSITIONAL EXTERNALITIES

[O]ne [can] explicitly account for the strategic nature of collective bargaining in modeling its costs. I define strategic behavior as any activity undertaken by one party to an agreement to increase its benefit from the agreement at the expense of the other party to the agreement. Examples of such activity include firing productive prounion employees, lying in negotiations, and intransigence or "hard bargaining" in negotiations or enforcement of the agreement. This type of activity results in costs, such as search and retraining to replace productive employees and strikes due to lying or intransigence in bargaining or enforcement. Thus, although these activities may increase one side's expected benefit from the agreement, they decrease the total expected value of the agreement to both parties. Moreover, to the extent that the division of the benefits from the agreement depends on the relative performance of the parties in collective bargaining, both sides may have incentives to act strategically. If one party decides to act strategically, the other side must either respond in like manner or forfeit the contest over the benefits of the agreement. In such a case, the costs incurred in attempting to gain the upper hand in the agreement are known as a positional externality. This is because the parties are competing for a relative position in undertaking the strategic behavior, for example who can be the most intransigent in bargaining, and the costs of responding to strategic behavior are external to the original decision to undertake such behavior. Due to this externality, the individual interests of the parties in pursuing strategic behavior diverge from their collective interest in avoiding it, and the conflict tends to escalate in cost even though the parties succeed only in wasting a portion of the benefit of the agreement.
* * *

I do not argue that unregulated collective negotiations inevitably degenerate into a strike. Both the employer and the union should recognize their dilemma and, to their mutual benefit, often be able to curb the temptation to bargain in an intransigent manner. The parties will be aided in this effort by the fact that, unlike some other dilemma games, employer-union negotiations often involve an established relationship and communication. Particularly in mature collective bargaining relationships where the parties have a history of cooperative bargaining and can foresee future negotiations that could be jeopardized by present strategic behavior, the parties usually will be able to avoid the costs of intransigent bargaining. My point is that, despite the parties' common incentive and frequent success at solving the dilemma game of collective negotiations to their mutual benefit, at the heart of the game lie individual incentives that tend to escalate the game and sometimes produce suboptimal solutions that waste a portion of the cooperative surplus.

Similar dilemma games can be constructed for organizing campaigns and enforcement of the collective agreement. With respect to organizing, the cooperative or low-cost strategy might correspond to the mere publicity of pro-or antiunion views in an employee election on union representation, while the recalcitrant or high-cost strategies might correspond to organizational strikes and discriminatory discharges. It seems reasonable to assume that a party's payoff in organizing depends on its relative performance, because resort to the recalcitrant or high-cost strategy by only one party will increase that party's chances of prevailing, while if both parties resort to the recalcitrant or high-cost strategy their efforts will tend to cancel each other out with respect to resolving the conflict. Thus, one would expect that organizational campaigns would have a tendency to escalate into costly affairs, wasting a portion of the cooperative surplus, in much the same way that negotiation conflicts can escalate. The parties are probably less likely to arrive at the mutually beneficial armistice of confining themselves to the cooperative or low-cost strategy in the case of the organizing game than in the case of the negotiations game, because in an organizing campaign the parties have not yet established a constructive relationship or steady communication and are probably quite hostile to one another.

With respect to enforcement of the collective agreement, the cooperative or low-cost strategy is to resolve disputes over interpretation of the agreement through arbitration, while the recalcitrant or high-cost strategy is to resort to more costly litigation or strikes to resolve contract disputes. Again, it seems reasonable to assume that a party's payoff in enforcement depends on its relative performance, because resort to the recalcitrant or high-cost strategy by only one party will increase that party's chances of prevailing, while if both parties resort to the recalcitrant or high-cost strategy their efforts will tend to cancel each other out with respect to resolving the conflict. Thus, one would expect that enforcement conflicts have a tendency to escalate, wasting a portion of the cooperative surplus, in much the same way that negotiation conflicts tend to escalate. In the enforcement game, it would seem very likely that the parties would achieve a mutually beneficial armistice by agreeing to confine their contract disputes to the cooperative or low-cost strategies because they have an established relationship and communication, and indeed have already successfully negotiated a collective agreement. It is thus not surprising that the vast majority of collective bargaining agreements provide arbitration as the means of resolving contract disputes.* * *

THE GOVERNMENT'S ROLE IN REGULATING
COLLECTIVE BARGAINING

The [fact] * * * that collective bargaining is a strategic endeavor and that many of its associated costs are positional externalities, suggests the need for extensive regulation of the conduct of labor relations. * * * Escalation of conflicts between employers and employees is not desirable from a societal perspective because it wastes the cooperative surplus produced by the parties. Therefore, it makes sense for the government to undertake reasonable measures to regulate labor relations to avoid such waste and promote the efficient resolution of such disputes.

There are two basic methods by which the government can seek to avoid such escalation and promote more efficient solutions to conflicts involving positional externalities. First, the government can change the expected payoffs of the game by penalizing or prohibiting the wasteful high-cost strategies so that it becomes individually rational for each party to confine itself to the efficient low-cost strategies. For example, in the bargaining game presented earlier, if the government prohibited intransigent bargaining and enforced this prohibition with an expected penalty of [sufficient magnitude] ..., both the employer and the union would decide to bargain cooperatively. Second, the government can enact measures that promote the parties' ability to recognize and follow their collective interest in not escalating the conflict and to observe an explicit or implicit private armistice that confines the resolution of their conflicts to the efficient low-cost strategies. Through logical arguments and empirical studies, social scientists have identified the following measures as promoting cooperative or low-cost solutions to dilemma games like those found in industrial relations: promoting homogeneity among the constituencies of the players of the game; limiting the number of players; requiring exchanges of information among the players; prohibiting certain bargaining strategies, including lying, committing to third parties, or cutting off negotiations; promoting repeated play of the dilemma game; and enforcing explicit private agreements to refrain from undertaking the high-cost strategies. Promoting homogeneity and reducing the number of players simplifies the game so that the players are more likely to see their collective interest in cooperation. Reducing the number of players also prevents a few uncooperative players from free riding on the cooperative efforts of the rest. Requiring exchanges of information on the game allows the parties to see their collective interest in avoiding escalation and promotes trust. Bargaining strategies such as lying, committing to third parties, and cutting off negotiations are themselves strategic acts that can jeopardize the larger game. Repeated play increases the costs of strategic behavior by making such behavior a threat not only to current negotiations but also to future negotiations. Finally, making explicit private armistices enforceable encourages the parties to negotiate such armistices and changes the payoffs of the game to make cooperation individually rational.

Which of the two solutions the government should employ in a particular situation depends on their relative costs and benefits in that situation. For example, in conflicts over employee organization, the high-cost strategies of discriminatory discharges and strikes are relatively easy to identify and monitor, and the chance of a voluntary armistice between the two unfamiliar, hostile parties seems remote. In such a situation, the efficient government policy to promote cooperative or low-cost solutions in industrial relations would be to rely primarily on penalties and prohibitions to regulate organizing conflicts. As a counterexample, in conflicts over collective negotiations, the high-cost strategy of intransigence may be harder to identify and monitor, while the probability of a voluntary armistice between two parties with an established relationship is significant. In this circumstance, the efficient government policy to regulate labor relations would be to rely more heavily on measures that promote voluntary armistices in regulating collective negotiations. Finally, in conflicts over enforcement of the collective agreement, the parties have a working relationship, having successfully negotiated a contract, and they have had the opportunity to agree explicitly to a voluntary armistice. Because so many employers and unions seem willing to include the armistice of final binding arbitration in their collective agreements voluntarily, it seems adequate to confine government efforts in regulating enforcement conflicts to the strategy of promoting such agreements and making them enforceable, even though the high-cost strategies of strikes and litigation are easy to identify and monitor. * * *

Reichhold Chemicals deals with the pervasive tactic that the courts term "surface bargaining," that is, going through the motions of bargaining without genuinely intending to reach agreement. The court upheld the Board's determination that Reichhold's conduct was proper. One way to look at a case of this sort is that the Board should be slow to intervene if the employer engages in dilatory bargaining. If the union wants an agreement it should use whatever economic weapons it has at its disposal. If the union doesn't have the economic strength to make the employer come around, the law should not supply the missing clout. On the other hand, Congress has declared that the policy of the Act is to encourage the practice and procedures of collective bargaining. Does this justify Board intervention when a party engages in dilatory tactics?

As you saw in *Reichhold Chemicals,* it is very difficult to tell the difference between approaching bargaining with no genuine intention of reaching agreement, and taking an adamant stand to obtain the best possible agreement. To get into the good faith of the parties' positions, the Board is tempted to look at the substance of their proposals. For example, if an employer makes a proposal that no self respecting union would accept, that may indicate that the employer's purpose is to frustrate bargaining. But the proviso to Section 8(d) says that neither party is required to make a concession or counter-proposal. In theory, then, the employer may take as firm a position as it wishes. This tension between these two views is illustrated by *Reichhold Chemicals.* It may tell us that it is unwise for the Board and courts to try to impose an obligation of good faith.

But you might reach a different conclusion if you thought that management representatives were using the technique of surface bargaining to avoid reaching an agreement. If you think that sort of tactic should be curbed, what sort of remedy would you impose?

———

A CASE STUDY ON BARGAINING UNDER THE NLRA

The decision and the bargaining

This is a story about the Carrier Corporation, the manufacturer of air conditioners. Carrier had been a stalwart corporate citizen of Syracuse, NY for decades. It was the naming contributor of Syracuse University's sports dome. In the mid–80's Carrier was taken over by United Technologies (UTC). Both before and after the UTC takeover, labor relations between Carrier and the Sheet Metal Workers Union had been rough. There had been strikes in 1979 and 1982, with the '79 strike running 13 weeks. Bruce Evans, the Union business agent, described the 1985 contract with UTC, the first after the takeover, as "the absolute worst contract we ever had," because of the monetary and language concessions it contained. But in the aftermath of the earlier two strikes, the union was "scared to death" to risk a strike in 1985.

In the fall of 1997 the union negotiated another contract with Carrier. Just a short four months later, the company came to the union and asked to negotiate a new contract, an "addendum", they called it, a separate set of provisions for the workers in TR–1, a huge facility that builds rotary chillers to cool large buildings.

The company threatened to move the factory elsewhere unless the union agreed to a new set of work rules for the TR–1 workers. The union was not about to do that. It was incensed that management had negotiated the 1997 contract without even mentioning that it was thinking about moving the chiller plant.

The union looked to the legal system for help. It filed charges with the NLRB, contending that the company had failed to bargain in good faith. It said that in the negotiations leading to the current agreement, the company had failed to notify the union of its impending plans, and that later it improperly tried to reopen a contract that had already been settled. These are the key passages of its Charge:

> The employer has failed "to engage in good faith, honest and forthright negotiations for a collective bargaining agreement covering the employees employed in building TR–1.* * *Since on or about April 1, 1998, * * * the employer has refused to bargain in good faith with the charging party over the decision to contract out bargaining unit work and the decision to relocate bargaining unit work, from building TR–1."

THE LEGAL CONSTRAINTS

What are the legal constraints upon a company's ability to close down and relocate part of its business? Compare the situation in the *Local 1330* case in Chapter One. While those workers were represented by a union, the legal theories that were advanced on their behalf were outside the collective bargaining relationship. They were based on contract theory, and failed to carry the day.

In the unionized workplace, the union has two main sources of legal restrictions upon the employer's actions. First, the collective bargaining agreement may contain some restriction upon the company's ability to terminate work and move it elsewhere. However, it is rare to find a provision in a collective bargaining agreement that expressly prevents a company from doing this. A company is not likely to agree to restraints on its ability to get the work done as economically as possible. If anything, the collective bargaining agreement will come down on management's side on this point. Look at the management rights provision in the sample collective bargaining agreement in our statutory supplement.

The union's best hope in a situation like Carrier is to make an argument for an implied restriction, using the recognition and wage clauses of the collective bargaining agreement. For example, in the sample agreement in our supplement, the company recognizes the union as the "exclusive bargaining representative" for workers in certain job categories. It goes on to list wage rates for those jobs. The union argues that those provisions imply that if certain work is performed at all by the company, it must be performed by workers in the specified categories and the established job rates.

A union would present this position by filing a grievance under the collective bargaining agreement, taking it to arbitration, and hoping that the arbitrator will rule in its favor. As you will learn later, the arbitrator's award is generally final, and binding on both parties. As you might expect, a whole body of arbitration awards has developed dealing with the issue of terminating and removing work. Because these decisions involve an implied restriction on the one hand (the recognition and wage clauses) and an implied permission on the other (the management rights clause), the outcome of these cases is mixed. It is fair to conclude that the union in the Carrier situation did not think a challenge under the collective bargaining agreement was very promising.

The other restraint on the employer comes from the NLRA. Section 8(a)(5) requires the employer to bargain with the union over wages, hours and other terms of employment, and Section 8(d) defines the bargaining obligation. A corollary of this requirement is that the company may not make a change in working conditions without satisfying its bargaining obligation. You should consult the text of both statutory provisions right now. As you saw in *Reichhold Chemicals,* theoretically the NLRA places no substantive restrictions upon the bargain the parties make. It is concerned only with process, with insuring that the parties bargain in good faith about the issues. In the *Reichhold Chemical* case, you saw some tension between the command, on the one hand, that the parties bargain in good faith, and the statement, on the other hand, that neither party need agree to the other's positions.

As you read through the description of the bargaining in Carrier, ask yourself what theory the union could present (through the General Counsel of the Board) that Carrier had not bargained in good faith.

THE STORY CONTINUES

The basis for the union's claim in Carrier is presented in the following articles that appeared in the local Syracuse papers.

Union Challenges Carrier's N.C. Move. By Charley Hannagan, Syracuse Post–Standard, September 29, 1998.

The Herald Company © 1998. The Post–Standard. All rights reserved. Reprinted with permission.

Local 527 of the Sheet Metal Workers International Association has asked the National Labor Relations Board to seek an injunction to halt, at least temporarily, Carrier's plans to move one of its town of DeWitt plants to North Carolina.

The action takes place amid mounting evidence that Carrier was quietly looking for a new factory even as it negotiated a contract last fall with Local 527, the union representing 2,100 workers on its East Syracuse campus.

The union filed an unfair labor practice charge against Carrier, arguing the company should have made it clear during negotiations in October that it was considering subcontracting work and moving the TR–1 plant, which makes roof-top chillers that cool high-rise buildings.

The union didn't learn of the proposed move until March, five months after it agreed to a new contract.

Carrier officials say they were scouting for new locations as an option to fix the company's ailing roof-top chiller business.* * *

The union claims the company was unfair during those contract talks because it didn't reveal its plans to subcontract work and move the plant. The company signed a three-year contract with the union in November.

"There was absolutely nothing mentioned about closing or moving," said Local 527 Business Manager Bruce Evans, who took part in the talks. * * *

In March, Carrier returned to the union. It wanted changes to the contract just for the TR–1 building. If the company got what it wanted, the town of DeWitt would be considered as a site for a new, more efficient factory replacing TR–1.

If not, the company told union officials, Carrier would move TR–1 out.

The company's proposed addendum to the contract would have carved the TR–1 workers off from the rest of the union. They would have different work rules, a different contract length and be required to cross picket lines if the rest of the union went on strike.

The union offered to negotiate the changes within the current agreement. The company said no. The talks went nowhere.

On May 1, the union filed an unfair labor practice charge. Later that month Carrier announced it would move the plant. In September it said it was going to North Carolina. * * *

The local NLRB region has reviewed the union's charge and sent it to the general counsel in Washington, D.C., for consideration, said the NLRB's [Regional Director Sandra] Dunbar.

The case carries complex issues that muddy the waters, she said. Carrier plans to subcontract work out, stop making some products and to relocate. Some of those issues are subject to bargaining; others aren't, Dunbar said.

"We have to look at how they bargain. It's not as clear as it might seem," she said. * * *

The two sides, for now, have an uneasy truce. They will begin soon to negotiate the effect the plant closing will have on workers. The union could ask for a better severance package, retraining, or even a chance for workers to move to North Carolina with their jobs.

Evans said he must work to protect the jobs and workers who will remain when TR–1 closes: "Our main goal is to keep the lights on."

The NLRB Regional office investigated the union's charge and issued a complaint. In a subsequent Petition for an injunction against Carrier under Section 10(j) of the Act, The NLRB summarized its Complaint as follows:

> There is reasonable cause to believe that Respondent is failing and refusing to bargain collectively and in good faith with the Union ... by insisting, as a condition of agreeing not to relocate certain Unit work, that the Union agree to separate terms and conditions for certain Unit employees, effectively removing those employees from the Unit; by insisting to impasse in bargaining, in support of such condition; by deciding to relocate certain Unit work, notwithstanding the fact that it had failed to reach a bona fide impasse in bargaining about the relocation decision; and by commencing the implementation of its decision to relocate certain Unit work.

THE 10(j) INJUNCTION

While the union's charge was pending before the NLRB, the Regional Director moved in Federal District Court for an injunction under NLRA Section 10(j) to prohibit the Company from making the move, pending the outcome of the NLRA litigation. The gist of the NLRB's claim was that Carrier would have spent so much money on the move if it went ahead that it could not be reversed through the bargaining process. Indeed, as Carrier's own lawyer said, in the arguments to the judge hearing the injunction claim, Carrier has spent so much, "no one will order it to bring the work back." Carrier attempted to convince the judge that it had indeed bargained in good faith with the union, and therefore had not violated the NLRA:

Plant Workers Await Injunction Decision. By Charles Hannagan.
Syracuse Post Standard, February 3, 1999

The Herald Company, © 1998. The Post–Standard.
All rights reserved. Reprinted with permission.

The company was willing to bargain with the union when it asked for the changes last March, [company Lawyer Louis D.] DiLorenzo said. It reserved hotel rooms for 15 days in anticipation of bargaining, he said. Carrier also responded to the union's request for proof of the plant's financial position with 1,300 pages of information, he said.

The rooms went empty because the union steadfastly refused to negotiate an addendum to the contract it signed four months earlier, DiLorenzo said.

Union leaders refused to discuss the addendum because it carved TR–1 workers out from the rest of union, Israel said. The addendum limited the rights of TR–1 workers to strike and restricted their rights to transfer to other jobs on the Dewitt campus.

The company told union leaders they had bargaining room, DiLorenzo said. For example, on the no strike clause, "maybe that could have been removed," he said. "We'll never know because the union wouldn't negotiate."

Carrier led union negotiators to believe there was no room to bargain, [NLRB attorney Charles] Israel said.

"Carrier said it's the addendum or nothing," he said. "It has to be the addendum or TR–1 will be an empty plant."

As the company makes plans to move the chiller business, DiLorenzo said Carrier is hopeful most of TR–1's workers will be able to transfer to other jobs on campus. However, he said some workers, not a significant number will lose their jobs when the plant closes later this year.

NEGOTIATIONS RESUME

The District Court judge issued a 10(j) injunction against the move, which was stayed by the Court of Appeals pending a hearing on appeal. With the legal process now in limbo, the parties used the uncertain cloud of litigation as a spur to negotiating a deal:

Union Settles on Carrier's Move. By James T. Mulder.
Syracuse Post Standard, March 9, 1999

The Herald Company, © 1998. The Post–Standard.
All rights reserved. Reprinted with permission.

A union's year long battle to keep Carrier Corp. from moving a 543–employee factory out of the town of Dewitt is over.

TR–1, a plant that makes rotary chillers to cool large buildings, is going to Huntersville, N.C., in a deal announced Monday by Carrier and Local 527 of the Sheet Metal Workers International Association.

Carrier agreed to pay $3.2 million to the union's membership to settle the dispute.

Carrier and the union said Monday the settlement resolves a federal lawsuit seeking to stop the move as well as unfair labor practice charges filed against the company by the National Labor Relations Board.

As part of the deal, each of the union's 2,031 members employed at Carrier on April 1, 1998, will get a lump-sum payment of $1,336. Carrier will go ahead with its plan to shut down TR–1 and relocate that operation to a new plant in Huntersville later this year. The move is expected to eliminate 543 of the 4,100 jobs at the East Syracuse campus.

Bruce Evans, Local 527 business manager, said the union decided to settle after it became "painfully clear" Carrier would never reconsider its decision to close TR–1.

"They (Carrier) came to us and wanted to know what it would take to make this thing go away," Evans said. "We're never going to get over the fact we're losing the business and 543 jobs. But we also feel the only way to really settle it in our favor was to reach the settlement we reached. It was like a business decision we had to make."

———

ANOTHER CRISIS

Only a little more than half a year went by before Carrier presented the union with yet another ultimatum. It was going to close the TR–2 unit, a warehouse that employs some 300 people, putting them all out of work. Bruce Evans had learned some lessons from the TR–1 debacle. This time he didn't want to see a unit closed. If TR–2 went, there would be little else to save. The following article tells you what finally happened:

Why Carrier Kept 2. By Charlie Hannagan. Syracuse Post–Standard, November 9, 1999

The Herald Company, © 1998. The Post–Standard. All rights reserved. Reprinted with permission.

In September, Carrier Corp. managers delivered the bad news: Barring a miracle, they planned to close the TR–2 parts warehouse in DeWitt, putting more than 300 local people out of work.

Monday the union and the company produced a miracle, but not without a price, one that some workers say is too high.

Carrier Corp.'s TR–2 and TR–19 parts warehouses will remain open at least through 2003, preserving the jobs of 438 hourly and salaried workers.

"We saved the jobs. We saved the business. We saved the building," said Bruce Evans, business manager for Local 527. * * *

The union hopes the laid-off workers will take jobs left by others who take the company's incentive to retire early or leave the company, said Dawson Minsch, local 527's recording secretary.

Local 527 has agreed to create a new job classification for the warehouses. It limits the top pay there to $12.35 per hour and workers there would not receive incentives or bonuses.

Union workers now at the warehouses make about $19 per hour, union and company officials said.

The company will give current warehouse workers three options: Stay and accept the wage cut, move to another job on the campus and keep their current pay, or accept an early retirement/severance package.

Those warehouse workers with seniority who choose to move to other jobs in the plant could "bump" less senior workers back into the lower paying warehouse jobs.

The retirement/severance packages also will be offered to workers elsewhere on campus [who meet stated eligibility requirements of age and years of service.]

"This is a win-win situation for all involved, and is a great example of what can happen when labor and management strip away the rhetoric and work toward a common goal," said Carrier President John R. Lord. * * *

The deal between the company and the union received mixed reviews from workers already reeling from job losses resulting from the closing of the TR–1 chiller assembly plant. * * *

"I think the union has the people's best interests in mind" [said one worker], but added "I don't see how you can make it on $10 an hour with no overtime and no bonuses."

———

After all this turmoil, the union and Carrier negotiated another three year agreement, running from the beginning of 2001. Under the previous deal, the TR–2 work is secure for the life of this agreement. Here's what the union's vice president, Dawson Minsch, said about the lessons he had learned from the concessions of the past few years:

Personally, [the closing] was a very disheartening event. The big building that closed was where I started, twenty years ago. Most of my life was spent there, working in that building. To walk through it now, to see it dark and empty, is not a good feeling. From a union guy, what I saw happen there, was that unfortunately there's two schools of thoughts for dealing with companies that make threats that they're going to close the building. One is you tell them to stick it, and draw a line in the sand. And you say go ahead and move it, and they go ahead and move it. All you've got is your pride. But you lost jobs. The other school is that you sit down in a back room and somehow try to come up with some kind of agreement that saves as many jobs as you can and reduces the pay cut as much as you can. That's concessionary bargaining. I'm not comfortable with either one of those, and I don't think we need to get locked into that.

From this experience, this is what I'm learning. If we were to organize better internally, and were to be prepared and showed real unity, and I really qualify that unity to be something that's thought out and prepared, and given some goal, if we work out that unity, and also if we have a clear understanding who we are dealing with, we can come at them with an agenda of our own. That is what we need to do to stay out of these other two schools of thoughts, because usually when you draw a line in the sand it is because they are coming at you. I think we need to enter into negotiations, for example, this fall, with us coming at them. We need to show that we can push some buttons and make everybody move the right way.

If we're mobilized and organized internally and if we have this real good education as to who is saying things in UTC, you've gotta go beyond the personnel directors here . * * * Having an in-depth understanding of the company that owns the company you're working with is critical. That's the approach that we need to stay out of those other two tracks. You get painted into a corner when its either draw the line in the sand or concessionary bargaining. Those aren't good places to be. That's what we learned.

What power do you have? When they see that in fact if we say everybody wears a red shirt on Thursday, and everyone wears a red shirt on Thursday, that has an effect on the immediate front-line supervision. They react to that, that begins to erode away at their control. Because their control isn't that they have more of them than us, their control is that they have us divided. They can talk one-on-one. People are out on the floor. You know, you need to think this way about this. Because this is really better for you. When we have that control, we get an in mass reaction, it really has that effect, certainly on the front-line supervisors, and that begins to shake things up. So when the company says we're gonna do this and we're gonna do that, they need to know that they're going to have resistance. Because often they say, well, we know what the workers really want. When they're discussing things with us, now we can begin to say we know what they really want because we get that reaction from them. We can show you that unity that we have. That has a really dramatic impact.

The second piece is that if you know the why of what they're saying, and the where of where the money is, and who is in control of the money, then when we sit down to have these talks with them, we can say, we know you have a warehouse there in Texas, and we know how much it will cost to move this business there, and we know that so and so in Connecticut would rather that this business be over there because they're not always on the same page. In fact, they're seldom on the same page. And if we begin to get a little clue of what is on the same page, and begin talking to them, it begins to take their arguments apart. Then you have an opportunity to not necessarily take over anything, but certainly you have an opportunity to make a solid argument for your position.

[The quoted comments of Dawson Minsch, and those of Bruce Evans that are not in the newspaper account, are taken from interviews that Bob Rabin conducted with Messrs. Minsch and Evans (complete transcript on file with author)].

Questions

1. Did the union do the right thing when it dug in its heels on the first closing, involving the chiller plant? Should it have agreed to the addendum?

2. Did the union do the right thing when it cut a deal to allow the warehouse work to remain?

3. Assuming these decisions are made by the leadership and not by the membership, what is the leadership's responsibility to make a correct decision?

4.   Recall that Carrier did not disclose to the union during negotiations in the fall of 1997 that it was planning to relocate the chiller operations the following spring. Assuming that Carrier had indeed moved its investigation along to the point that it was seriously considering this move, do you think the NLRA requires the company to advise the union of its plans? Under what theory? Is your answer affected by the fact that when the existing contract expires, and before a new one is negotiated, the union has the right to strike over Carrier's proposed move? However, once the union signs the successor agreement with Carrier (as it did here), that contract contains a broad no-strike clause which seems to prohibit all strikes during the life of the agreement. Consult the sample agreement in the statutory supplement, and see if that no-strike clause would apply to a union in a situation like this. Do you think that a no-strike agreement in the Carrier contract should be interpreted to bar a strike that is called to protest what the union thinks was an unfair labor practice committed by Carrier in refusing to disclose its move in advance? Look at the *Reichhold Chemicals* case for the company's demand there for a no-strike clause during the life of the contract.

If you conclude that the no-strike clause prohibits the union from striking over Carrier's decision to move the work, isn't this a further reason to require the company to disclose the potential move during negotiations, when the union could have utilized its right to strike to bring pressure against the move?

5.   Suppose that the union at Carrier decided to strike, during the effective period of the collective agreement, over Carrier's removal of the chiller work. Would Carrier be able to enjoin the strike, which, after all, is prohibited under the collective bargaining agreement? Section 7 of the Norris–LaGuardia Act prohibits the issuance of an injunction in a peaceful labor dispute. Does that mean a court may not enjoin a breach of a contractual no-strike provision? In an important case that we present in Chapter IV, Boys Markets v. Retail Clerks Union, 398 U.S. 235, 90 S.Ct. 1583, 26 L.Ed.2d 199 (1970), the Court held that an injunction to enforce a no-strike clause generally does not violate Norris–LaGuardia. The Court's thinking was that the underlying dispute in *Boys Markets,* over which the union struck, was one that could be resolved through arbitration. The injunction was not so much against the strike as in support of the arbitration process. That is, the union was required to utilize the arbitration process to which it had agreed, as the agreed upon alternative to the strike.

However, the text of *Boys Markets* suggests, and a later case (Buffalo Forge v. Steelworkers) explicitly holds, that the *Boys Markets* injunction may issue only if the underlying issue is one that is appropriate for arbitration. In other words, the *Boys Markets* exception to Norris–LaGuardia is designed to protect the integrity of the arbitration process, which is an integral part of the parties' bargain. But Norris–LaGuardia continues to apply if the strike is over a matter that cannot be arbitrated.

In Buffalo Forge v. Steelworkers, 428 U.S. 397, 96 S.Ct. 3141, 49 L.Ed.2d 1022 (1976), the company sought to enjoin a sympathy strike by a group of employees who were supporting the strike of fellow employees in another bargaining unit. The contract contained a no-strike clause. The Court held that the workers' strike was not over any issue that was subject to arbitration, hence could not be enjoined. The union in the Carrier situation might argue that there is no contractual bar on the company's removal of work, and therefore nothing for the union to arbitrate, so the *Boys Markets* exception doesn't apply and NOLA prevents the court from issuing an injunction. The employer will respond that the question of its removal of work is arbitrable; the fact that the union might lose the arbitration is not the same thing as saying the matter is not subject to arbitration. Which argument do you think should prevail?

6. When all is said and done, what role did the law play in the removal of the chiller plant to North Carolina?

7. An ironic footnote. About a year after we prepared this case study, and just as we were about to go to press, the local paper reported that the membership of the Sheet Metal Workers' union at Carrier Corporation had voted to replace Bruce Evans as the business manager. You will recall that Evans had engineered the compromise that induced Carrier to keep its warehouse work in Syracuse. The article, by Charley Hannagan, is entitled "Labor, management dynamic sees change," Syracuse Post—Standard, September 3, 2001, A1 and A8. The theme of the article is that union leaders say that unions must be partners with management and not adversaries. The article explains Evans' ouster as follows: "Even though it saved 438 union and salaried jobs, the deal was unpopular with members because it cut salaries, and because the leaders made the decision without putting it to a vote by the membership."

So, what have we learned from all this?

MORE LAW—MANDATORY SUBJECTS OF BARGAINING

You learned about the contours of the duty to bargain in good faith from the text of the NLRA and the *Reichhold Chemicals* case. However, there are some areas that are in effect roped off from the bargaining process altogether. Go back to the description of the Carrier dispute in which the Regional Director comments in the September 29, 1998 article that there was some uncertainty over whether the company had to bargain at all about certain issues, let alone bargain in good faith.

You might question the Regional Director's reservations in light of the fairly broad language of Section 8(d), which requires bargaining about "wages, hours and other terms and conditions of employment." This is a pretty broad definition, and you would think that the question of whether there is going to be any work at all for the chiller plant employees is certainly a term and condition of employment.

Carrier took the position that a decision to close down the chiller plant and relocate the work in a new facility was beyond the scope of the duty to bargain. If it was correct, this would mean that Carrier need not bargain at all about this decision; it could act unilaterally, it need not go through the rigamarole of appearing to bargain in good faith, and it need not provide the union with requested information. It would, however, still be required to give the union advance notice of its decision, under a rule which we will discuss shortly that requires the employer to give notice and bargain about the impact of decisions that might otherwise be exempt from the bargaining duty. You will note that in the Carrier story, in the September 29 article, Carrier had agreed to bargain with the union about the effects of its decision, even as it was challenging the union's charge that it had to bargain about the decision itself.

The Supreme Court has defined the scope of the duty to bargain in two cases, Fibreboard and First National Maintenance. The test of First National Maintenance follows:

FIRST NATIONAL MAINTENANCE CORPORATION v. NATIONAL LABOR RELATIONS BOARD

Supreme Court of the United States, 1981.
452 U.S. 666, 101 S.Ct. 2573, 69 L.Ed.2d 318.

JUSTICE BLACKMUN delivered the opinion of the Court.

Must an employer, under its duty to bargain in good faith "with respect to wages, hours, and other terms and conditions of employment," § § 8(d) and 8(a)(5) of the National Labor Relations Act (Act), * * * negotiate with the certified representative of its employees over its decision to close a part of its business? In this case, the National Labor Relations Board (Board) imposed such a duty on petitioner with respect to its decision to terminate a contract with a customer, and the United States Court of Appeals, although differing over the appropriate rationale, enforced its order.

I

Petitioner, First National Maintenance Corporation (FNM), is a New York corporation engaged in the business of providing housekeeping, cleaning, maintenance, and related services for commercial customers in the New York City area. It supplies each of its customers, at the customer's premises, contracted-for labor force and supervision in return for reimbursement of its labor costs (gross salaries, FICA and FUTA taxes, and insurance) and payment of a set fee. It contracts for and hires personnel separately for each customer, and it does not transfer employees between locations.

During the spring of 1977, petitioner was performing maintenance work for the Greenpark Care Center, a nursing home in Brooklyn. Its written agreement dated April 28, 1976, with Greenpark specified that Greenpark "shall furnish all tools, equiptment [sic], materials, and supplies," and would pay petitioner weekly "the sum of five hundred dollars plus the gross weekly payroll and fringe benefits." Its weekly fee, however, had been reduced to $250 effective November 1, 1976. The contract prohibited Greenpark from hiring any of petitioner's employees during the term of the contract and for 90 days thereafter. Petitioner employed approximately 35 workers in its Greenpark operation.

Petitioner's business relationship with Greenpark, seemingly, was not very remunerative or smooth. In March 1977, Greenpark gave petitioner the 30 days' written notice of cancellation specified by the contract, because of "lack of efficiency." This cancellation did not become effective, for FNM's work continued after the expiration of that 30–day period. Petitioner, however, became aware that it was losing money at Greenpark. On June 30, by telephone, it asked that its weekly fee be restored at the $500 figure and, on July 6, it informed Greenpark in writing that it would discontinue its operations there on August 1 unless the increase were granted. By telegram on July 25, petitioner gave final notice of termination.

While FNM was experiencing these difficulties, District 1199, National Union of Hospital and Health Care Employees, Retail, Wholesale and Department Store Union, AFL–CIO (union), was conducting an organization campaign among petitioner's Greenpark employees. On March 31, 1977, at a Board-conducted election, a majority of the employees selected the union as their bargaining agent. On July 12, the union's vice president, Edward Wecker, wrote petitioner, notifying it of the certification and of the union's right to bargain, and stating: "We look forward to meeting with you or your representative for that purpose. Please advise when it will be convenient." Petitioner neither responded nor sought to consult with the union.

On July 28, petitioner notified its Greenpark employees that they would be discharged three days later. Wecker immediately telephoned petitioner's secretary-treasurer, Leonard Marsh, to request a delay for the purpose of bargaining. Marsh refused the offer to bargain and told Wecker that the termination of the Greenpark operation was purely a matter of money, and final, and that the 30 days' notice provision of the Greenpark contract made staying on beyond August 1 prohibitively expensive. Wecker discussed the matter with Greenpark's management that same day, but was unable to obtain a waiver of the notice provision. Greenpark also was unwilling itself to hire the FNM employees because of the contract's 90–day limitation on hiring. With nothing but perfunctory further discussion, petitioner on July 31 discontinued its Greenpark operation and discharged the employees.

The union filed an unfair labor practice charge against petitioner, alleging violations of the Act's § § 8(a)(1) and (5). After a hearing held upon the Regional Director's complaint, the Administrative Law Judge made findings in the union's favor. Relying on *Ozark Trailers, Inc.*, 161 N.L.R.B. 561 (1966), he ruled that petitioner had failed to satisfy its duty to bargain concerning both the decision to terminate the Greenpark contract and the effect of that change upon the unit employees. The judge reasoned:

> "That the discharge of a man is a change in his conditions of employment hardly needs comment. In these obvious facts, the law is clear. When an employer's work complement is represented by a union and he wishes to alter the hiring arrangements, be his reason lack of money or a mere desire to become richer, the law is no less clear that he must first talk to the union about it.... If Wecker had

been given an opportunity to talk, something might have been worked out to transfer these people to other parts of [petitioner's] business.... Entirely apart from whether open discussion between the parties—with the Union speaking on behalf of the employees as was its right—might have persuaded [petitioner] to find a way of continuing this part of its operations, there was always the possibility that Marsh might have persuaded Greenpark to use these same employees to continue doing its maintenance work, either as direct employees or as later hires by a replacement contractor."

The Administrative Law Judge recommended an order requiring petitioner to bargain in good faith with the union about its decision to terminate its Greenpark service operation and its consequent discharge of the employees, as well as the effects of the termination. He recommended, also, that petitioner be ordered to pay the discharged employees backpay from the date of discharge until the parties bargained to agreement, or the bargaining reached an impasse, or the union failed timely to request bargaining, or the union failed to bargain in good faith.

The National Labor Relations Board adopted the Administrative Law Judge's findings without further analysis, and additionally required petitioner, if it agreed to resume its Greenpark operations, to offer the terminated employees reinstatement to their former jobs or substantial equivalents; conversely, if agreement was not reached, petitioner was ordered to offer the employees equivalent positions, to be made available by discharge of subsequently hired employees, if necessary, at its other operations.

The United States Court of Appeals for the Second Circuit, with one judge dissenting in part, enforced the Board's order, although it adopted an analysis different from that espoused by the Board. The Court of Appeals reasoned that no *per se* rule could be formulated to govern an employer's decision to close part of its business. Rather, the court said, § 8(d) creates a *presumption* in favor of mandatory bargaining over such a decision, a presumption that is rebuttable "by showing that the purposes of the statute would not be furthered by imposition of a duty to bargain," for example, by demonstrating that "bargaining over the decision would be futile," or that the decision was due to "emergency financial circumstances," or that the "custom of the industry, shown by the absence of such an obligation from typical collective bargaining agreements, is not to bargain over such decisions."

The Court of Appeals' decision in this case appears to be at odds with decisions of other Courts of Appeals, some of which decline to require bargaining over any management decision involving "a major commitment of capital investment" or a "basic operational change" in the scope or direction of an enterprise, and some of which indicate that bargaining is not mandated unless a violation of § 8(a)(3) (a partial closing motivated by antiunion animus) is involved. * * * The Board itself has not been fully consistent in its rulings applicable to this type of management decision. * * *

II

A fundamental aim of the National Labor Relations Act is the establishment and maintenance of industrial peace to preserve the flow of interstate commerce. Central to achievement of this purpose is the promotion of collective bargaining as a method of defusing and channeling conflict between labor and management. § 1 of the Act, as amended. Congress ensured that collective bargaining would go forward by creating the Board and giving it the power to condemn as unfair labor practices certain conduct by unions and employers that it deemed deleterious to the process, including the refusal "to bargain collectively." §§ 3 and 8.

Although parties are free to bargain about any legal subject, Congress has limited the mandate or duty to bargain to matters of "wages, hours, and other terms and conditions of employment." A unilateral change as to a subject within this category violates the statutory duty to bargain and is subject to the Board's remedial order. *NLRB v. Katz*, 369 U.S. 736, 82 S.Ct. 1107, 8 L.Ed.2d 230 (1962). Conversely, both employer and union may bargain to impasse over these matters and use the economic weapons at their disposal to attempt to secure their respective aims. *NLRB v. American National Ins. Co.*, 343 U.S. 395, 72 S.Ct. 824, 96 L.Ed. 1027 (1952). Congress deliberately left the words "wages, hours, and other terms and conditions of employment" without further definition, for it did not intend to deprive the Board of the power further to define those terms in light of specific industrial practices.

Nonetheless, in establishing what issues must be submitted to the process of bargaining, Congress had no expectation that the elected union representative would become an equal partner in the running of the business enterprise in which the union's members are employed. Despite the deliberate open-endedness of the statutory language, there is an undeniable limit to the subjects about which bargaining must take place:

> "Section 8(a) of the Act, of course, does not immutably fix a list of subjects for mandatory bargaining.... But it does establish a limitation against which proposed topics must be measured. In general terms, the limitation includes only issues that settle an aspect of the relationship between the employer and the employees."

Some management decisions, such as choice of advertising and promotion, product type and design, and financing arrangements, have only an indirect and attenuated impact on the employment relationship. See *Fibreboard*, 379 U.S., at 223, 85 S.Ct., at 409 (STEWART, J., concurring). Other management decisions, such as the order of succession of layoffs and recalls, production quotas, and work rules, are almost exclusively "an aspect of the relationship" between employer and employee. The present case concerns a third type of management decision, one that had a direct impact on employment, since jobs were inexorably eliminated by the termination, but had as its focus only the economic profitability of the contract with Greenpark, a concern under these facts wholly apart from the employment relationship. This decision, involving a change in the scope and direction of the enterprise, is akin to the decision whether to be in business at all, "not in [itself] primarily about conditions of employment, though the effect of the decision may be necessarily to terminate employment." *Fibreboard*, 379 U.S., at 223, 85 S.Ct., at 409 (STEWART, J., concurring). Cf. *Textile Workers v. Darlington Co.*, 380 U.S. 263, 268, 85 S.Ct. 994, 998, 13 L.Ed.2d 827 (1965) ("an employer has the absolute right to terminate his entire business for any reason he pleases"). At the same time, this decision touches on a matter of central and pressing concern to the union and its member employees: the possibility of continued employment and the retention of the employees' very jobs.

Petitioner contends it had no duty to bargain about its decision to terminate its operations at Greenpark. This contention requires that we determine whether the decision itself should be considered part of petitioner's retained freedom to manage its affairs unrelated to employment. The aim of labeling a matter a mandatory subject of bargaining, rather than simply permitting, but not requiring, bargaining, is to "promote the fundamental purpose of the Act by bringing a problem of vital concern to labor and management within the framework established by Congress as most conducive to industrial peace," *Fibreboard*, 379 U.S., at 211. The concept of mandatory bargaining is premised on the belief that collective discussions backed by the parties' economic weapons will result in decisions that are better for both management and labor and for society as a whole. This will be true, however, only if the subject proposed for discussion is amenable to resolution through the bargaining process. Management must be free from the constraints of the bargaining process to the extent essential for the running of a profitable business.

It also must have some degree of certainty beforehand as to when it may proceed to reach decisions without fear of later evaluations labeling its conduct an unfair labor practice. Congress did not explicitly state what issues of mutual concern to union and management it intended to exclude from mandatory bargaining. Nonetheless, in view of an employer's need for unencumbered decisionmaking, bargaining over management decisions that have a substantial impact on the continued availability of employment should be required only if the benefit, for labor-management relations and the collective-bargaining process, outweighs the burden placed on the conduct of the business.

The Court in *Fibreboard* implicitly engaged in this analysis with regard to a decision to subcontract for maintenance work previously done by unit employees. Holding the employer's decision a subject of mandatory bargaining, the Court relied not only on the "literal meaning" of the statutory words, but also reasoned:

> "The Company's decision to contract out the maintenance work did not alter the Company's basic operation. The maintenance work still had to be performed in the plant. No capital investment was

contemplated; the Company merely replaced existing employees with those of an independent contractor to do the same work under similar conditions of employment. Therefore, to require the employer to bargain about the matter would not significantly abridge his freedom to manage the business."

The Court also emphasized that a desire to reduce labor costs, which it considered a matter "peculiarly suitable for resolution within the collective bargaining framework," was at the base of the employer's decision to subcontract: "It was induced to contract out the work by assurances from independent contractors that economies could be derived by reducing the work force, decreasing fringe benefits, and eliminating overtime payments. These have long been regarded as matters peculiarly suitable for resolution within the collective bargaining framework, and industrial experience demonstrates that collective negotiation has been highly successful in achieving peaceful accommodation of the conflicting interests."

The prevalence of bargaining over "contracting out" as a matter of industrial practice generally was taken as further proof of the "amenability of such subjects to the collective bargaining process."

With this approach in mind, we turn to the specific issue at hand: an economically motivated decision to shut down part of a business.

III

A

Both union and management regard control of the decision to shut down an operation with the utmost seriousness. As has been noted, however, the Act is not intended to serve either party's individual interest, but to foster in a neutral manner a system in which the conflict between these interests may be resolved. It seems particularly important, therefore, to consider whether requiring bargaining over this sort of decision will advance the neutral purposes of the Act.

A union's interest in participating in the decision to close a particular facility or part of an employer's operations springs from its legitimate concern over job security. The Court has observed: "The words of [§ 8(d)] ... plainly cover termination of employment which ... necessarily results" from closing an operation. *Fibreboard*, 379 U.S., at 210. The union's practical purpose in participating, however, will be largely uniform: it will seek to delay or halt the closing. No doubt it will be impelled, in seeking these ends, to offer concessions, information, and alternatives that might be helpful to management or forestall or prevent the termination of jobs. It is unlikely, however, that requiring bargaining over the decision itself, as well as its effects, will augment this flow of information and suggestions. There is no dispute that the union must be given a significant opportunity to bargain about these matters of job security as part of the "effects" bargaining mandated by § 8(a)(5). See, e. g., *NLRB v. Royal Plating & Polishing Co.*, 350 F.2d 191, 196 (C.A.3 1965); *NLRB v. Adams Dairy, Inc.*, 350 F.2d 108 (C.A.8 1965), cert.

denied, 382 U.S. 1011, 86 S.Ct. 619, 15 L.Ed.2d 256 (1966). And, under § 8(a)(5), bargaining over the effects of a decision must be conducted in a meaningful manner and at a meaningful time, and the Board may impose sanctions to insure its adequacy. A union, by pursuing such bargaining rights, may achieve valuable concessions from an employer engaged in a partial closing. It also may secure in contract negotiations provisions implementing rights to notice, information, and fair bargaining. See BNA, Basis Patterns in Union Contracts 62–64 (9th ed., 1979).

Moreover, the union's legitimate interest in fair dealing is protected by § 8(a)(3), which prohibits partial closings motivated by antiunion animus, when done to gain an unfair advantage. *Textile Workers v. Darlington Co.*, 380 U.S. 263, 85 S.Ct. 994, 13 L.Ed.2d 827 (1965). Under § 8(a)(3) the Board may inquire into the motivations behind a partial closing. An employer may not simply shut down part of its business and mask its desire to weaken and circumvent the union by labeling its decision "purely economic."

Thus, although the union has a natural concern that a partial closing decision not be hastily or unnecessarily entered into, it has some control over the effects of the decision and indirectly may ensure that the decision itself is deliberately considered. It also has direct protection against a partial closing decision that is motivated by an intent to harm a union.

Management's interest in whether it should discuss a decision of this kind is much more complex and varies with the particular circumstances. If labor costs are an important factor in a failing operation and the decision to close, management will have an incentive to confer voluntarily with the union to seek concessions that may make continuing the business profitable. Cf. U.S. News & World Report, Feb. 9, 1981, p. 74; BNA, Labor Relations Yearbook—1979, p. 5 (UAW agreement with Chrysler Corp. to make concessions on wages and fringe benefits). At other times, management may have great need for speed, flexibility, and secrecy in meeting business opportunities and exigencies. It may face significant tax or securities consequences that hinge on confidentiality, the timing of a plant closing, or a reorganization of the corporate structure. The publicity incident to the normal process of bargaining may injure the possibility of a successful transition or increase the economic damage to the business. The employer also may have no feasible alternative to the closing, and even good-faith bargaining over it may both be futile and cause the employer additional loss.

There is an important difference, also, between permitted bargaining and mandated bargaining. Labeling this type of decision mandatory could afford a union a powerful tool for achieving delay, a power that might be used to thwart management's intentions in a manner unrelated to any feasible solution the union might propose. * * *

While evidence of current labor practice is only an indication of what is feasible through collective bargaining, and not a binding guide, see *Chemical Workers*, 404 U.S., at 176, 92 S.Ct., at 396, that evidence supports the apparent imbalance weighing against mandatory bargaining. We note that provisions giving unions a right to participate in the decisionmaking process concerning alteration of the scope of an enterprise appear to be relatively rare. Provisions concerning notice and "effects" bargaining are more prevalent.

Further, the presumption analysis adopted by the Court of Appeals seems ill-suited to advance harmonious relations between employer and employee. An employer would have difficulty determining beforehand whether it was faced with a situation requiring bargaining or one that involved economic necessity sufficiently compelling to obviate the duty to bargain. If it should decide to risk not bargaining, it might be faced ultimately with harsh remedies forcing it to pay large amounts of backpay to employees who likely would have been discharged regardless of bargaining, or even to consider reopening a failing operation. Also, labor costs may not be a crucial circumstance in a particular economically based partial termination. And in those cases, the Board's traditional remedies may well be futile. If the employer intended to try to fulfill a court's direction to bargain, it would have difficulty determining exactly at what stage of its deliberations the duty to bargain would arise and what amount of bargaining would suffice before it could implement its decision. * * * A union, too, would have difficulty determining the limits of its prerogatives, whether and when it could use its economic powers to try to alter an employer's decision, or whether, in doing so, it would trigger sanctions from the Board.

We conclude that the harm likely to be done to an employer's need to operate freely in deciding whether to shut down part of its business purely for economic reasons outweighs the incremental benefit that might be gained through the union's participation in making the decision, and we hold that the decision itself is *not* part of § 8(d)'s "terms and conditions," see n. 12, *supra*, over which Congress has mandated bargaining.

B

In order to illustrate the limits of our holding, we turn again to the specific facts of this case. First, we note that when petitioner decided to terminate its Greenpark contract, it had no intention to replace the discharged employees or to move that operation elsewhere. Petitioner's sole purpose was to reduce its economic loss, and the union made no claim of antiunion animus. In addition, petitioner's dispute with Greenpark was solely over the size of the management fee Greenpark was willing to pay. The union had no control or authority over that fee. The most that the union could have offered would have been advice and concessions that Greenpark, the third party upon whom rested the success or failure of the contract, had no duty even to consider. These facts in particular distinguish this case from the subcontracting issue presented in *Fibreboard*. Further, the union was not selected as the bargaining representative or certified until well after petitioner's economic difficulties at Greenpark had begun. We thus are not faced with an employer's abrogation of ongoing negotiations or an existing bargaining agreement. Finally, while petitioner's business enterprise did not involve the investment of large amounts of capital in single locations, we do not believe that the absence of "significant investment or withdrawal of capital," *General Motors Corp., GMC Truck & Coach Div.*, 191 N.L.R.B., at 952, is crucial. The decision to halt work at this specific location represented a significant change in petitioner's operations, a change not unlike opening a new line of business or going out of business entirely.

The judgment of the Court of Appeals, accordingly, is reversed, and the case is remanded to that court for further proceedings consistent with this opinion.

It is so ordered.

JUSTICE BRENNAN, with whom JUSTICE MARSHALL joins, dissenting.

Section 8(d) of the National Labor Relations Act, as amended, requires employers and employee representatives "to meet at reasonable times and confer in good faith with respect to wages, hours, and other terms and conditions of employment." 29 U.S.C. § 158(d). The question in this case is whether First National Maintenance Corporation's decision to terminate its Greenpark Care Center operation and to discharge the workers employed in that operation was a decision with respect to "terms and conditions of employment" within the meaning of the Act, thus rendering its failure to negotiate with the union unlawful.

As this Court has noted, the words "terms and conditions of employment" plainly cover termination of employment resulting from a management decision to close an operation. *Fibreboard Paper Products Corp. v. NLRB*, 379 U.S. 203, 210, 85 S.Ct. 398, 402, 13 L.Ed.2d 233 (1964). As the Court today admits, the decision to close an operation "touches on a matter of central and pressing concern to the union and its member employees." Moreover, as the Court today further concedes, Congress deliberately left the words "terms and conditions of employment" indefinite, so that the NLRB would be able to give content to those terms in light of changing industrial conditions. In the exercise of its congressionally delegated authority and accumulated expertise, the Board has determined that an employer's decision to close part of its operations affects the "terms and conditions of employment" within the meaning of the Act, and is thus a mandatory subject for collective bargaining. *Ozark Trailers, Inc.*, 161 N.L.R.B. 561 (1966). Nonetheless, the Court today declines to defer to the Board's decision on this sensitive question of industrial relations, and on the basis of pure speculation reverses the judgment of the Board and of the Court of Appeals. I respectfully dissent.

The Court bases its decision on a balancing test. It states that "bargaining over management decisions that have a substantial impact on the continued availability of employment should be required only if the benefit, for labor-management relations and the collective-bargaining process, outweighs the burden placed on the conduct of the business." I cannot agree with this test, because it takes into account only the interests of *management*; it fails to consider the legitimate employment interests of the workers and their union. Cf. *Brockway Motor Trucks v. NLRB*, 582 F.2d 720, 734–740 (C.A.3 1978) (balancing of interests of workers in retaining their jobs against interests of employers in maintaining unhindered control over corporate direction). This one-sided approach hardly serves "to foster in a neutral manner" a system for resolution of these serious, two-sided controversies. * * *

FNM AND FIBREBOARD—TWO DIFFERENT COURTS?

You saw in *First National Maintenance* numerous references to the Court's *Fibreboard* decision of almost two decades earlier (Fibreboard Paper Products Corp. v. NLRB, 379 U.S. 203 (1964)). That case, as the *FNM* court points out, required the employer to bargain about a decision to contract out janitorial work that was done on the premises. The decision to subcontract was based primarily on cost-cutting; in prior negotiations the company had asked the union for some relief in cutting maintenance costs. The Court upheld the Board order requiring the company to reinstitute the maintenance operation, reinstate employees who lost jobs as a result of the subcontracting, and provide back pay for a specified period. The Court reasoned that contracting out was within the statutory language ("the words even more plainly cover termination of employment which, as the facts of this case indicate, necessarily results from the contracting out of work performed by members of the established bargaining unit."), and that negotiation over this decision carried out a fundamental purpose of the Act "by bringing a problem of vital concern to labor and management within the framework established by Congress as most conducive to industrial peace." The Court also looked at industrial bargaining practices, as revealed by an examination of existing contract provisions in various industries, that showed that "contracting out in one form or another has been brought, widely and successfully, within the collective bargaining framework."

The *Fibreboard* Court stressed that the decision to contract out janitorial work did not alter the company's basic operation; the maintenance work was still done in the plant, no capital investment was involved, and the work continued to be done as before. "Therefore, to require the employer to bargain about the matter would not significantly abridge his freedom to manage the business."

Justice Stewart's concurrence picked up on the ideas in the previous paragraph. Concerned with the potential breadth of the majority decision, Justice Stewart joined only on the understanding that the majority decision was limited to the factual decision involved. He stated that while many management decisions could have an impact on employees, the duty to bargain should be limited to those that have a direct effect; decisions involving advertising, product design, financing and sales, should not be part of the bargaining rubric, nor should decisions about the direction of the enterprise. Justice Stewart wrote, "Nothing the

Court holds today should be understood as imposing a duty to bargain collectively regarding such managerial decisions, which lie at the core of entrepreneurial control. Decisions concerning the commitment of investment capital and the basic scope of the enterprise are not in themselves primarily about conditions of employment, though the effect of the decision may be necessarily to terminate employment.''

Courts of Appeals in the intervening years between *Fibreboard* and *FNM* picked up many of the reservations in Justice Stewart's concurrence, and those limitations appear to drive the later *FNM* decision. Factually, it is hard to imagine a situation more conducive to bargaining than *Fibreboard*—replacement of workers on the premises where costs were a factor and where there was a bargaining history—and one less conducive to bargaining than *FNM*—a newly organized bargaining unit, with no history of bargaining, where the company lost its contract to provide services for the nursing home, although some of the reasons for losing that contract may have had to do with labor costs. The union was much more likely to contribute to a resolution of the problem in *Fibreboard* than in *FNM*. So you have to decide whether *FNM* represents a significant retreat from the principles of *Fibreboard*, or is simply an application of the same rules to a different situation. The Board's *Dubuque Packing* decision, which we summarize shortly, is an attempt to synthesize the approaches of the two Supreme Court decisions.

Note the Court's concern in *FNM* with the secrecy needed by the employer in shutting down a business as a reason not to require bargaining. However, the *FNM* Court confirms that an employer is required to bargain about the *effects* of such a decision. Depending on how soon the effects-bargaining obligation requires the employer to notify the union when it is contemplating the decision, how does that square with the Court's concern for secrecy in *FNM*? Apply *FNM* to the Carrier situation.

In an important Board case known in the trade as Dubuque Packing, the Board attempted to clarify its thinking about the scope of the duty to bargain in light of *Fibreboard* and *First National Maintenance.* Its earlier decisions had been a hodge-podge of views, and the Board was criticized for not taking a unified position. There was a faint hope that the Supreme Court would resolve some unanswered questions by granting certiorari in *Dubuque Packing*. Alas, that was not to be.

Still, the Board's opinion in *Dubuque Packing* continues to be its current approach. We give you some excerpts from the D.C. Circuit Court opinion that affirms *Dubuque Packing.*

UNITED FOOD AND COMMERCIAL WORKERS v. NLRB

United States Court of Appeals, D.C.Cir., 1993.
1 F.3d 24.

BUCKLEY, CIRCUIT JUDGE,

* * * In these proceedings, the Board set out to enunciate a new legal test "guided by the principles set forth in First National Maintenance." Dubuque Packing, 303 N.L.R.B. at 390. It adopted the following standard for determining whether "a decision to relocate [bargaining] unit work," Id., is a mandatory subject of bargaining:

> Initially, the burden is on the [NLRB] General Counsel to establish that the employer's decision involved a relocation of unit work unaccompanied by a basic change in the nature of the employer's operation. If the General Counsel successfully carries his burden in this regard, he will have established prima facie that the employer's relocation decision is a mandatory subject of bargaining. At this juncture, the employer may produce evidence rebutting the prima facie case by establishing that the work performed at the new location varies significantly from the work performed at the former plant, establishing that the work performed at the former plant is to be discontinued entirely and not moved to the new location, or establishing that the employer's decision involves a change in the scope and direction of the enterprise. Alternatively, the employer may proffer a defense to show by a preponderance of the evidence: (1) that labor costs (direct and/or indirect) were not a factor in the decision, or (2) that even if labor costs were a factor in the decision, the union could not have offered labor cost concessions that could have changed the employer's decision to relocate.

Id. at 391. * * *

Viewing the Board's test through the lens of this interpretation, we find it sufficiently protective of an employer's prerogative to manage its business. Under First National Maintenance, employers may be required to negotiate management decisions where "the benefit, for labor-management relations and the collective-bargaining process, outweighs the burden placed on the conduct of the business." First National Maintenance, 452 U.S. at 679. The Board's test exempts from the duty to negotiate relocations that, viewed objectively, are entrepreneurial in nature. It exempts decisions that, viewed subjectively, were motivated by something other than labor costs. And it explicitly excuses employers from attempting to negotiate when doing so would be futile or impossible. What is left are relocations that leave the firm occupying much the same entrepreneurial position as previously, that were taken because of the cost of labor, and that offer a realistic hope for a negotiated settlement. The Board's determination that bargaining over such decisions promises benefits outweighing the "burden[s] placed on the conduct of [an employer's] business" was in no way unreasonable.

Similarly, the Board was also justified in finding that its test accords with Supreme Court precedent. A relocation satisfying the three layers of the Board's test will resemble the subcontracting decision held subject to a mandatory bargaining duty in Fibreboard in three distinct ways: Because of the new test's objective component, such a relocation will not "alter the Company's basic operation," Fibreboard, 379 U.S. at 213, in a way that implicates the employer's "core of entrepreneurial control," id. at 223, (Stewart, J., concurring); because of the new test's subjective component, "a desire to reduce labor costs" will lie "at the base of the employer's decision," see First National Maintenance, 452 U.S. at 680; and because of the new test's exclusion of situations in which bargaining would be futile, there will be some prospect of resolving the relocation dispute "within the collective bargaining framework." Fibreboard, 379 U.S. at 213–14. Like its balancing of burdens and benefits, the Board's finding that its test accords with precedent is fully defensible.

Dubuque counters that relocation decisions should not be treated the same as the subcontract considered in Fibreboard because they will differ from that arrangement on a crucial point-relocations involve the expenditure of capital.

The Board's test exempts from the duty to bargain relocations in which "the work performed at the new location varies significantly from the work performed at the former plant." Dubuque Packing, 303 N.L.R.B. at 391. Under this standard, relocations involving a sufficiently altered pattern of fixed-capital use (such as a shift from a labor-intensive production line to a fully automated factory) would appear exempt from the bargaining duty. Second, many "terms and conditions of employment" over which employers are plainly bound to bargain involve the expenditure of "capital." Unless management rights are impermissibly invaded every time a union bargains for a breakroom water-cooler or shop-floor safety equipment, the realm of mandatory bargaining must include at least some decisions involving capital expenditures. Third, while First National Maintenance did reflect the influence of Justice Stewart's Fibreboard opinion, it did not reiterate that opinion's specific concerns with management's prerogative over the expenditure of capital, or otherwise indicate that a line protecting all decisions to expend capital must be drawn. Given this, and the deference owed the Board's policy choices, see UFCW I, 880 F.2d at 1429, we find that the Board's test does not impermissibly fail to protect management's prerogatives over capital investment.

Dubuque's final contention is that the test is so imprecise that employers are denied the degree of certainty or guidance that it believes the Supreme Court mandated in First National Maintenance. While we can agree that First National Maintenance affirms management's need for "some degree of certainty" so that it "may proceed to reach decisions without fear of later evaluations labeling its conduct an unfair labor practice," see 452 U.S. at 679, 101 S.Ct. at 2581 (emphasis added), this does not require that the Board establish standards devoid of ambiguity at the margins. The test announced in Dubuque Packing provides more than the "some" degree of certainty required by the Supreme Court. It establishes rules on which management may plan with a large degree of confidence; and while the test undoubtedly leaves areas of uncertainty between relocation decisions that are clearly within the exclusive prerogatives of management and those that are equally clearly subject to negotiation, these will in time be narrowed through future adjudications.

We therefore conclude that the standard adopted by the Board was a reasonable policy choice and that its decision to proceed by adjudication, not rulemaking, was also within its discretion. * * *

NOTES ON THE SCOPE OF THE DUTY TO BARGAIN

The issue of the scope of the duty to bargain can arise in two distinct ways. In *Reichhold Chemicals,* as in Problem 2–2, one party presents a demand at the bargaining table that is challenged as beyond the scope of the duty to bargain. That is, it has no place at the bargaining table. A similar issue could have been raised by certain union demands. Suppose, for example, that the union in our Mercy Hospital situation in Problem 2–2 sought to restrict the Hospital's right to make arrangements with other hospitals for care arrangements for services normally performed at Mercy. Mercy could refuse to consider the demand on the ground it is outside the scope of mandatory subjects, relying on some of the employer's arguments put forth in *Dubuque Packing.* Mercy would violate the Act if it was wrong in its assessment, and the contracting out of health care arrangements turned out to be a mandatory subject of bargaining. By the same token, the union would violate the Act if it insisted on that point to impasse when it was ultimately held not a mandatory subject of bargaining.

The other way it comes up is illustrated in *First National Maintenance* and *Fibreboard,* as well as *Dubuque Packing.* If an employer is under a duty to bargain about a particular matter, the corollary is that the employer may not take unilateral action. By taking work away from the bargaining unit in FNM, the employer deprived the union of its voice in making such decisions, even if the bargaining wouldn't have necessarily produced agreement that the employer could not place the work elsewhere. In all three of these cases the courts expressed some concern about shielding the company from any obligation to bargain because that might compromise the speed, flexibility or secrecy that are needed in such a situation. You might think about whether this philosophy of protecting the employer's interests is at odds with and therefore undermined by the later national policy expressed in the WARN statute, which we discussed in Chapter I. That statute requires advance notice of company shutdowns and work dislocations. However, it makes an exception to the extent of a proven need to maintain secrecy in order to raise new capital or obtain new business. Should Section 8(d) be construed more in line with WARN?

Do you think these concerns for protecting management's ability to act quickly are valid? The German system of co-determination brings employee representatives into the decisional process. However, it imposes a duty of confidentiality on all board members. Does the concern for secrecy have the same force when the issue is not whether management has a unilateral right to act, but whether the union has a right to seek contract provisions that limit that right to act? After all, the Act also encourages the parties to resolve their difficulties through agreement. Why should the law intervene to cut off union demands for job security through a variety of restrictions against removal of work? Can't the company just say no? Perhaps the answer is that the strike weapon may force the employer to give in to a restriction that it might not wish to accept. But isn't that part of the bargaining struggle?

SOME PHILOSOPHICAL OBSERVATIONS ABOUT THE DUTY TO BARGAIN

There is a paradox in the way the law of collective bargaining monitors the conduct of the parties. On the one hand, in imposing an obligation of good faith, it may require more of the parties than the law does in other negotiating situations. But in sharp contrast, it takes a restrictive view as to the range of subjects covered by the duty to bargain. As to covered subjects, the parties have an obligation to approach the problem in good faith, which means addressing seriously the other party's concerns. But if a subject is not mandatory, one may turn a deaf ear to the other's demands. Why would a party do this if it is interested in genuine, constructive dialogue? Isn't this set of rules at odds with the more open approach taken to discussions in the cooperative model? By treating some subjects as nonmandatory, the law permits the employer to act unilaterally, without consulting the union. It is insulated from economic pressure or legal redress. This further undermines employee voice.

We suggest these distinctions between mandatory and non mandatory subjects of bargaining may actually inhibit constructive collective bargaining. First, the doctrine permits either party to take refuge in a legal doctrine and to avoid an issue that may be of importance to one if not both parties. Second, by carving out some areas as within the exclusive domain of the employer, we may send a message that the parties to the discussion are not equal partners. Is this bad? In our readings about the cooperative, non union workplace, we saw just the opposite approach. All issues of importance were fully discussed and none were exempt on account of a label.

You should also see that negotiators face the dilemma that they often can't be sure at the time of bargaining whether the subject on which they dig in their heels is or is not within the scope of mandatory bargaining. You might question whether it makes good practical sense to make the distinction with heavy consequences between mandatory and non mandatory subjects of bargaining where the lines of demarcation are not clear.

You might even question whether such line drawing is a permissible reading of the Act. Section 8(d) of the NLRA requires the parties to bargain in good faith with respect to "wages, hours, and other terms and conditions of employment." The last phrase is quite broad, and could be construed to encompass virtually any issue the parties raise at the bargaining table. After all, if it is important enough to be a bargaining issue, it must involve a term and condition of work.

Further, by removing certain subjects denominated "non-mandatory" from the arena of required joint determination, and ultimately, as we shall see, from the pressure of economic weapons, isn't the Board, with approval from the courts, regulating the substance of bargaining agreements? And isn't that exactly what the NLRA says shouldn't happen?

Justice Harlan suggested as much in his partial dissent to NLRB v. Wooster Division of Borg–Warner Corp., 356 U.S. 342, 78 S.Ct. 718, 2 L.Ed.2d 823 (1958). The company proposed two clauses to which the union objected. Both went to questions of how the union conducted its internal affairs: one clause required the union to present the company's last contract offer to the bargaining unit membership before calling a strike; the other clause recognized the local affiliate as the exclusive bargaining agent, instead of the International Union which had been certified by the NLRB. The Supreme Court majority agreed with the NLRB that both proposals were lawful. The Court held, however, that insistence on either of the two clauses as a precondition to signing an agreement constituted a refusal to bargain because neither was a mandatory subject of bargaining. Justice Harlan, joined by Justices Clark, Whittaker and Frankfurter, protested:

> Preliminarily, I must state that I am unable to grasp a concept of "bargaining" which enables one to "propose" a particular point, but not to "insist" on it as a condition to agreement. The right to bargain becomes illusory if one is not free to press a proposal in good faith to the point of insistence. Surely adoption of so inherently vague and fluid a standard is apt to inhibit the entire bargaining process because of a party's fear that strenuous argument might shade into forbidden insistence and thereby produce a charge of an unfair labor practice. This watered-down notion of "bargaining" which the Court imports into the Act with references to matters not within the scope of Sec. 8(d) appears as foreign to the labor field as it would to the commercial world. To me all of this adds up to saying that the Act limits *effective* "bargaining" to subjects within the three fields referred to in Sec. 8(d), that is "wages, hours, and other terms and conditions of employment." * * *

356 U.S. at 352, 78 S.Ct. at 724.

TO REITERATE

If a subject is outside the scope of the duty to bargain (that is, it is not a mandatory subject of bargaining), several consequences follow.

First, the company need not bargain about its decision. It may take unilateral action. That is one of the arguments made by Carrier. Carrier's other argument was that even assuming it had the duty to bargain, it fulfilled that obligation.

Second, if the union makes a demand in negotiations about a subject that is outside the scope of mandatory bargaining, the employer need not respond to that demand, bargain about it, or provide requested information with respect to it. For example, if the union in Carrier demanded a contract provision that prohibited the company from relocating bargaining unit work during the life of the contract, the company might take the position that this is not a mandatory subject of bargaining, and might refuse to discuss it at all. Of course, whether the employer is correct in that position depends on how the Board and courts read the *First National Maintenance* decision. What advantage does the company gain by refusing to discuss a subject that is of concern to the union? Is there a benefit in addressing the subject even if it is not a mandatory subject? What is the downside for the company if it chooses to bargain over a non-mandatory subject?

Third, another variation of the duty to bargain scenario is where the company raises a demand that is resisted by the union as outside the scope of bargaining. This is well illustrated by *Reichhold Chemicals,* where the company sought a contract provision that would limit the right of employees to file certain claims with the NLRB. The analysis turns not so much on the motivation of the party making the demand (which was another piece of *Reichhold Chemicals),* but on the notion that the subject is inappropriate. You can look at the decision in *Reichhold* as a statement that it was none of the employer's business as to whether its employees seek to vindicate their statutory rights; or you can see it as a rule that an employer may not use the bargaining process to cut off employees' access to an administrative agency. Other examples of company demands that may lie outside the scope of bargaining are a demand that the union submit any proposed contract to the membership for a vote, and that any strike decision be subject to a vote of the membership. In general, matters of internal union governance are thought to be none of the employer's business and therefore beyond the scope of mandatory bargaining.

SOME OTHER WAYS OF LOOKING AT THE CARRIER CASE STUDY

The two courses of action for the union that we have discussed in these materials do not quite exhaust the possible avenues of redress for the workers under the NLRA (we put to one side the WARN Act limitations discussed in Chapter I.)

First, the union might argue that Carrier's decision to remove the work to a non-union plant discriminates against the Carrier workers based on their union activity. That is, it is an attempt to get out from under a union contract. In theory, a move by an employer to avoid its obligations under a collective agreement would violate Section 8(a)(3), and the courts have held so, for example, in ILGWU v. NLRB (Garwin Corp), 374 F.2d 295 (D.C.Cir.1967), cert. den. 387 U.S. 942, 87 S.Ct. 2074, 18 L.Ed.2d 1328 (1967), characterizing such conduct as a "runaway shop." But usually the employer is able to show that the removal of the work is based on cost considerations and not on unionization.

Though the correlation between the two factors may be high, courts generally have accepted this employer explanation and found no violation of 8(a)(3), e.g. NLRB v. Rapid Bindery, 293 F.2d 170 (2d Cir.1961).

In the rare case where the employer openly admits that it has moved or shut down in order to avoid a union, the law is somewhat schizophrenic. The Court held in Textile Workers v. Darlington Mfg. Co., 380 U.S. 263, 85 S.Ct. 994, 13 L.Ed.2d 827 (1965), that an employer may shut down its business in its entirety in order to be free of a union. In the face of statutory language that would appear to prohibit such a move, Justice Harlan wrote that "a proposition that a single businessman cannot choose to go out of business if he wants to would represent such a startling innovation that it should not be entertained without the clearest manifestation of legislative intent or unequivocal judicial precedent so construing the Labor Act. We find neither." Justice Harlan contrasted the situation of the total shutdown with the runaway shop, where the employer would transfer the work to another facility. There, if the motivation were clearly anti-union, the move would violate Section 8(a)(3). But even in those cases the courts appear to be reluctant to order the work to be returned to its original location.

Darlington sets out a different rule where the employer shuts down one facility, as it did in *Darlington,* and continues to operate its other facilities (with no evidence that the work from the shut plant has been moved to the remaining plants). There, the test is whether the partial closing is "motivated by a purpose to chill unionism in any of the remaining plants of the single employer and if the employer may reasonably have foreseen that such closing will likely have that effect."

Do you think that either or both branches of the *Darlington* rule are too easy on the employer? Are they true to the language of 8(a)(3)?

WHAT IS AN IMPASSE, AND WHY IS IT IMPORTANT?

As you saw from the preceding materials, if a subject is within the mandatory realm of bargaining, an employer may not act unilaterally, but must first satisfy its bargaining obligation towards the union. (In the Carrier story, Carrier contended that it had offered to bargain with the union, but the union itself cut the talks short). The corollary of this is that once the company satisfies its bargaining obligation, it is free to act. For example, suppose Carrier proposes to close the chiller plant unless the union offered concessions. The union makes a proposal for a wage cut, but the cut is not enough to satisfy Carrier. Carrier asks for deeper cuts and the union rejects them. Eventually, the two sides run out of moves and it is clear that they won't reach agreement. At that point, the law says, the company is free to implement the proposal it had on the table.

The company may not implement a better proposal than it had offered to the union. To take an example in a different context, suppose that there is a dispute over wages. The company offers a 3% increase, but the union insists on 10%. The parties reach a stalemate. The company may now implement its 3% proposal; in a strike situation that might be an important inducement to hire replacement workers. But the company may not implement a 5% wage increase. To implement 5% while only offering 3% would suggest that its original bargaining position of a 3% maximum was not taken in good faith.

There are some problems with this impasse doctrine. For one thing, it is hard to determine when the parties have arrived at an impasse. In a bargaining situation with multiple issues on the table, the party seeking to avoid impasse (the union, in the wage example as well as in the Carrier situation) can easily make a modest modification in its package of proposals and contend that the bargaining has not yet run its course.

QUESTIONING THE IMPASSE DOCTRINE

Professors Ellen J. Dannin and Terry H. Wagar criticize the impasse doctrine in their article, Lawless Law? The Subversion of the National Labor Relations Act, 34 Loyola L.A. L. Rev. 197 (2000). The authors contend that the Board decisions allow the employer to reach impasse too readily, and that impasse becomes a tool for the employer to weaken and ultimately remove the union. An excerpt follows. If you agree with the authors' conclusions, what changes should be made in the law? Would you eliminate the impasse doctrine and say that the employer may never make a change in terms and conditions without the agreement of the union through bargaining?

ELLEN J. DANNIN AND TERRY H. WAGAR, LAWLESS LAW? THE SUBVERSION OF THE NATIONAL LABOR RELATIONS ACT

34 Loy. L.A. L.Rev. 197 (2000).

[The authors are summarizing a study they had conducted.] These employer losses were not the only financial costs. Although it did not suffer personally, trying and deciding a case lasting sixty days was enormously expensive for the government. The back pay was so great the employers risked being put out of business. The workers lost homes, had marriages broken, and suffered mental distress as a result of the employers' use of implementation upon impasse. All these losses were suffered despite the fact that the employers' purpose was not to gain important business ends: they wrecked lives and risked their own businesses to destroy workplace codetermination and worker participation in the decisions that affect workers' lives—rights guaranteed in the NLRA—just so the employers could have unilateral control of their businesses. As bad as all this is, the worst that could have happened from the union and workers' point of view did not occur—the workers did not strike and were not permanently replaced. The union was also able to hang on as the workers' representative and fight to regain what was taken from them. Other workers have not been as lucky. * * *

Indeed, the doctrine of implementation upon impasse offers almost no downside for the employer. Demanding deep concessions and demanding unilateral control over working conditions not only get you to an impasse, but once there, the employer is in a position to impose the very terms it wants. If the union strikes, the employer may permanently replace the strikers, and eventually the replacements will vote the union out, or the union will walk away. All through bargaining, an employer can use the threat of replacement to force the union to agree to its terms, because the union does not dare strike. The employer can threaten this or remind the union of the law, but it does not even need to mention it; the union will know it is in a very weak position.

It does not even matter if the workers strike or not; if they stay on the job, the employer can implement its final offer and enter an uneasy situation with increasing employee dissatisfaction with the union because it cannot improve their working conditions. In the end, this may lead to de-unionization.* * *

Such a doctrine does nothing to promote collective bargaining, an express purpose of the NLRA. Indeed, almost nothing could be better designed to undermine authentic negotiating. Yet, we contend, this is the way the NLRA works and has been working, particularly since the mid–1980s when the Board increasingly allowed employers to come to the table with proposals that were predictably unacceptable to unions and workers and, once there, make no movement. Since the mid–1980s, Board cases have forbidden the decision-maker from examining the content of employer proposals to determine whether the employer is advancing them in good faith, rather than as a ploy to create an impasse. In addition, the NLRA does not require employers to make any concessions or take any steps to reach agreement.

Indeed, during the mid–1980s the Board issued a number of decisions which made it easier to reach a bona fide impasse and thus for employers to implement their final offers. None of these decisions has been overruled by the Board, so they continue to affect future decisions as to whether a bona fide impasse exists and whether implementation is legal. Through these decisions, the Board has given employers freer rein to seek concessions without justifying the need for them; to seek total discretion in setting wages; and to have less obligation to provide information to the union upon the employer's making a plea of poverty. The Board also became more lenient in allowing an employer to re-implement an offer which had been implemented prior to reaching impasse rather than having to restore the status quo ante and lowering the number of bargaining sessions necessary to find an impasse existed. Employers were even allowed to "schedule" impasse rather than having to reach a real deadlock, a point at which, despite the parties' best efforts, movement is not possible. Finally, the Board reclassified subjects as mandatory or permissive in a way that made impasse easier. Indeed, the Board's view during this period was summed up by its statement in E.I. duPont de Nemours & Co. that the Board should have "no undue reluctance to find that an impasse existed."

As a result, an employer today can do no real bargaining and still not violate the law by bargaining in bad faith. The best unions can do is make successive concessions in an effort to show that the parties are not yet at impasse. They know that if the workers strike, the employer cannot fire them but can permanently replace them. As labor law professors are fond of asking rhetorically: "Query. Would you rather be fired or permanently replaced?"

It is our contention that allowing employers to implement their final offers makes a tremendous difference in how U.S. collective bargaining works and also limits how effective U.S. unions can be. It does this in many ways, including offering a legal tool to de-unionize, rewarding employers who do not engage in real bargaining, and ensuring that unions have less to offer workers and are thus less attractive to workers. * * *

The preliminary analysis of these data lead to the conclusion that labor law doctrine has advanced far down the wrong road, with disastrous consequences for unions and workers. Certainly, developing Board law so that impasse was a mere description that says the parties have reached a hard point in negotiations rather than making it a goal to be achieved would go far to promote good faith bargaining and achieve the purposes and policies of the NLRA. There are important consequences to preventing the use of impasse as a tool to de-unionize and to avoid the NLRA's bargaining obligation. Put another way, if it were more difficult to reach impasse and if employers who reached impasse were not rewarded by being allowed to implement their final offers, employers might find it more attractive to negotiate an agreement. At the least, they would be less likely to see negotiations as an anti-union tool as opposed to a means of codetermining workplace conditions and defusing worker discontent. At a minimum, to the extent it is more difficult to reach a bona fide impasse, more strikes would be unfair labor practice strikes and employers could not permanently replace the strikers. And at best, there would be greater workplace harmony, increased productivity, and improved wages and working conditions—the very goals the NLRA was enacted to achieve. * * *

A BRIEF EXERCISE ON IMPASSE

You represent Mercy Hospital and are hard at bargaining for a first union contract, but getting nowhere. Mercy's employees are covered by a health insurance program that has become increasingly expensive for you. The union has demanded an improvement in health insurance benefits, but you have insisted on no changes and perhaps even a roll back. Now your insurance carrier hits Mercy with a 38% increase in premiums. Mercy shops around and finds another insurance carrier that will charge it the same premiums as it is now paying, but will provide a somewhat lower level of benefits to its employees, primarily by imposing a higher annual deductible for each employee and requiring each employee to pay a slightly higher proportion of each bill that is covered by the plan (known as a co-pay arrangement). You approach the union at the bargaining table and ask it to agree to the new carrier. The union says it will not agree to a reduction in insurance benefits, and certainly not until all the other terms of the contract are agreed upon. You go back and forth on this point in a series of meetings, but the union won't budge and neither will you.

Next week is your deadline for renewing the old policy or replacing it with a new one. Are you free under the NLRA to make the change?

SOME PRACTICAL ALTERNATIVES—A DIALOGUE ON EFFECTS BARGAINING

Suppose that the Unified Medical Care Association has placed on the bargaining table a demand for Quality Care Circles, somewhat similar to the proposal that personnel director McLean had made before the union came onto the scene, back in our dialogue in Section A. The Hospital, somewhat miffed that it couldn't make the Circles concept work on its own, would like to put the whole project on the back burner, perhaps in the hope that it can raise it anew if the union ever goes away. The Hospital doesn't want to be put in the embarrassing position of having to reject portions of a demand that is based on its own proposal, so it decides not to discuss the subject at all. It asserts that this is a matter of management prerogative and not a mandatory subject of bargaining.

The union's chief negotiator reports on this development to its lawyer, David Diamond. Diamond takes the matter up with his boss, union general counsel Sam Gompers.

Diamond: I don't know where the NLBR is going on this, and maybe it will come around and see that worker participation is here to stay and these demands should be considered mandatory. It would be whacky if the Board would turn its back on the current trend of labor relations, the very thing it encouraged with Saturn.

Gompers: That's true, my boy, but do you want to spin your wheels litigating whether this is a mandatory subject of bargaining? Why not propose a trade? A discount in your wage demand in exchange for this worker participation program?

Diamond: You taught me early on that collective bargaining has always meant horse trading. But the Board's tight view of mandatory subjects gives something like worker participation an inflated value as a bargaining chip. I have to pay an awful lot to be able to talk about something I should be able to talk about all along.

Gompers: Oh, this mandatory-permissive business is worse than that. For example, if Mercy demands wage concessions and the union walks, strikers can't be discharged, under sections 13 and 2(3) of the Act. But Mercy could claim employees have no section 13 rights if they strike over demands the company is not legally required to discuss, like organizing production around teams with decisionmaking responsibility.

Diamond: You mean that if the NLRA doesn't protect workers who strike over permissive subjects, their fate depends on market factors, like the company's need to maintain production and the availability of an alternative source of labor?

Gompers: You hit the nail on the head. More than any of this legal mumbo jumbo about mandatory or permissive, the economic realities of a strike will determine whether there is going to be any meaningful discussion of our production team proposal. So let's try to think of another way to get the production team idea on the table.

Diamond: Kind of ironic, isn't it? All I read about lately is the move to a cooperative model of labor relations, adoptions of the Japanese approach. And here we are trying to figure out how to force the companies to get on the bandwagon.

Gompers: It's one thing for management to implement a new idea. Quite something else when they have to share control with the union. Of course, if a company implemented the team approach on its own, they'd have to bargain with us about the working conditions involved and, as to the rest, about the effects-whatever that means. But . . .

Diamond: Boss, you're a genius! Effects bargaining. That's our ace. Most companies demand a broad management functions clause, including the right to select, hire, promote, assign and determine the work schedules of employees. When Mercy insists on the clause, we respond with a proposal for production teams and claim the proposal deals with the "effects" of the management functions clause.

Gompers: Nice idea. But you'd better think it through carefully. I'm still concerned about the question of a strike.

ENTER Eulah Blair.

Blair: If you're talking about our people striking over the team concept, forget it. Down at Mercy, they're angry enough to strike over concessions, layoffs, raises. But not control on the shop floor.

Gompers: Not to worry. The workers can strike over Mercy's demand for concessions. They won't lose their section 13 protection against discharge, as long as the picket signs protest the company's position and Eulah's public comments mention only the demands for concessions.

Diamond: But where does that get us?

Gompers: The company would know that agreement on the production team concept could end resistance to their money demands *and* end the strike.

Diamond: So much for collective bargaining as a way to find reasoned solutions to problems of mutual concern. Is this kind of thing legal?

Blair: Legality is not the problem. For this to work, my people have to believe the strike is over the demand for concessions. You're asking me to lie to our members.

Gompers: Eulah, the company can settle the strike by giving in on the demand for concessions *or* the production teams, so there's no misrepresentation. Even if some members are confused about the union's priorities, it's the dumb law that's responsible for the union having to resort to this sleight of hand.

Diamond: But why should the members trust us next time?

Blair: And what do I tell them at the ratification vote?

THE RIGHT TO INFORMATION

The duty to bargain under the NLRA also entails the obligation of the employer (and the union too, for that matter) to provide information relevant to the bargaining process. For example, the union is entitled to data about current levels of wages and benefits. If the employer resists the union's demands because they are too costly, the employer is required to provide data to support its claim that it is unable to afford more, see NLRB v. Truitt Mfg. Co., 351 U.S. 149, 76 S.Ct. 753, 100 L.Ed. 1027 (1956). This often results in silly jockeying at the bargaining table over whether the company has pleaded an inability to pay.

The union may have legitimate need for test scores and other information regarding employees granted and denied promotions, in order to monitor the employer's affirmative action progress, or to assess whether the employer has complied with contractual provisions regarding entitlement to promotions based on seniority. However, such information often runs into defenses of confidentiality, see Detroit Edison Co. v. NLRB, 440 U.S. 301, 99 S.Ct. 1123, 59 L.Ed.2d 333 (1979). Similarly, while health and safety information may be relevant, the employer may plead that it cannot turn the data over because of trade secret concerns, see OCAW v. NLRB, 711 F.2d 348 (D.C.Cir.1983). We'll discuss this further in Chapter III, where we see that the right to information also stems from OSHA and related statutes.

The employer must exercise caution in this area. An unjustified refusal to provide information is as much a violation of the Act as bad faith bargaining through surface bargaining, unilateral changes or a refusal to bargain over a mandatory subject of bargaining.

How does the treatment of information by the parties, the Board and the courts under the NLRA differ from the approach in the cooperative, non-union setting? Recall the Company of Business people article that opened this chapter.

REMEDIES

What relief will the NLRB provide if it concludes that Mercy bargained in bad faith in any of the ways we have discussed in this section? It may order Mercy to cease and desist its unlawful conduct, and to return to the table and bargain in good faith. What will this buy for the union? If the order is issued two years or more after the initial bargaining (a very quick decision by today's standards), the union's position at the bargaining table will be even weaker. What will it gain through this second round of bargaining? Should the Board require Mercy to give the union what it would have obtained had Mercy bargained in good faith? Who is to say what that is? Is a "fair" agreement nothing more than what the union is able to achieve through the economic pressure it is able to bring to the table?

And from Mercy's perspective, what does such an order to bargain in good faith mean? How must Mercy change its tune so that it doesn't again fall into the snare of bad faith bargaining this time around? If it has to offer more to the union than the last time, isn't this inconsistent with the provision in Section 8(d) of the NLRA that neither party must agree to a proposal or make a concession?

The courts have from time to time urged the Board to fashion more inventive remedies for breaches of the duty to bargain in good faith, see Electrical Workers v. NLRB (Tiidee Products), 502 F.2d 349 (D.C.Cir. 1974). In one bout on this issue the Board agreed that its current remedies are inadequate: "A mere affirmative order that an employer bargain upon request does not eradicate the effects of an unlawful delay of 2 or more years in the fulfillment of a statutory bargaining obligation. It does not put the employees in the position of bargaining strength they would have enjoyed if the employer had immediately recognized and bargained with their chosen representative. It does not dissolve the inevitable employee frustration or protect the Union from the loss of employee support attributable to such delay." Ex–Cell–O Corporation, 185 NLRB 107 (1970). Having said all that, the Board wouldn't fashion a more meaningful remedy. *Ex-Cell–O* is an unusual case in that the employer had refused to bargain at all, claiming the union wasn't properly certified. The Board's refusal to grant a stronger remedy rested in part on its conclusion that the Employer's position, though ultimately wrong, was taken in good faith and was the only method by which the employer could challenge the Board's certification through judicial review.

Later in this chapter we'll suggest that the real deterrent to bad faith bargaining is that it may convert a strike into an unfair labor practice strike. This protects the workers who go on strike from being permanently replaced by the employer.

What do you think should be done? As a legislator, would you vote for an amendment to the NLRA that gives the Board authority:

(a) to fine an employer or labor organization for refusing to bargain in good faith;

(b) to charge attorneys fees and costs against the party that did not bargain in good faith;

(c) to order retroactive application of contract terms negotiated after a finding of bad faith bargaining;

(d) to set contract terms, based on those prevailing in the employing industry or on some other standard, after a finding of bargaining in bad faith.

SOME CONSIDERATIONS IN CONCLUSION

What should be the postmodern view about the duty to bargain? The NLRA allows employers to resist sharing control with unions on certain subjects, usually those that go to the heart of the matter, even to the point of not discussing such matters. Isn't this at odds with the picture painted at the outset of this chapter of the company so anxious to involve workers in decision making? Isn't this observation true with respect to the sharing of information too? There is an irony in that under *DuPont* there may not be a violation of 8(a)(2) if the parties talk about things that are beyond the scope of 8(a)(5). The irony, like a bad joke, is that the important things may not be talked about at the bargaining table, but they are fine in a nonunion setting; indeed, perhaps the only meaningful things that can be talked about there. Which branch of the statute is more responsive to the needs of today's workers?

E.   NEGOTIATING IN THE SHADOW OF ECONOMIC WEAPONS

INTRODUCTION

We lawyers, trained in the art of persuasion, would like to think that the process of reaching a collective agreement is merely the rational search for an acceptable solution. Each side makes its best case, whether for greater job security or more employer flexibility, higher wages or better competitive position, and the more compelling argument but-tressed by the most convincing data will prevail. The accounts you read of cooperative bargaining suggest that sometimes it works this way.

Yet, while we continue to encourage lawyers to work on constructive solutions, to engage in "win/win" bargaining in which both sides gain, we must acknowledge a harsher reality. Not all issues are subject to win-win solutions. There may be an irreconcilable tension between the claims of employees and of owners, investors and managers for a share of the profits. A union's desire to make seniority a controlling factor in job advancement may be inconsistent with management's need for greater flexibility in making assignments.

Sometimes mutual gain compromises can be made on these issues, but often it is not apparent that competing interests can be wholly accommodated. When that happens, each side must keep in mind a bottom line: what economic pressure can it bring to bear to make sure the other party yields to its demands? For the union, the primary weapon until recently has been the ability to strike; to withhold the services of the workforce so that the employer cannot produce. For the employer, it is the resiliency to operate efficiently even if the workers strike, for example, by hiring replacements, having the work done elsewhere, or simply riding out the storm where the employer has greater resources for survival than the union. The actual use of weapons probably does not matter as much as the potential for use. As you ponder the role of weapons in bargaining, consider that in the public sector strikes are often prohibited, yet parties routinely reach agreement on terms that are not too different than in the private sector. However, there are some statutory procedures in the public sector resolving impasses, as we will illustrate later in the chapter. What does this say about the importance of economic weapons in the bargaining process?

In these materials we look at the law's constraints on the use of economic weapons. As you'll see, while the law professes neutrality in the oversight of economic weapons, it has not taken a hands-off approach. As the law weighs in, you'll have to decide whether its belly on the scale tips too far in favor of one side or the other.

The title of this section is a deliberate knock off of a well known title in the literature of dispute resolution, Robert Mnookin, Negotiating in the Shadow of the Law. That work reminds us that when people negotiate marital or consumer disputes, for example, they keep an eye on the solution the law would impose if they cannot agree. The parties must calculate whether they are better off with the agreement made through negotiations than the outcome likely to be imposed by the law. In labor negotiations they keep in mind the outcome that would be dictated by economic strength. Is this a better backdrop?

We remind you that the potential arsenal of economic weapons is a feature that distinguishes the collective bargaining approach from the cooperative model. There is little or no mention in the materials you read of the use of economic weapons in the non-union setting. Perhaps that is because workers who do not choose to make the commitment to union representation can hardly be expected to rely on one another to support economic activity such as a strike. Or could it be that the law does not give the unorganized worker quite the range of economic weapons or protection as a worker who is represented by a union?

1. DEFINING THE BOUNDS OF JUDICIAL INTERVENTION: THE STRIKE, ITS LIMITATIONS, AND PROPOSALS FOR REFORM

NLRB v. MACKAY RADIO & TELEGRAPH CO.

Supreme Court of the United States, 1938.
304 U.S. 333, 58 S.Ct. 904, 82 L.Ed. 1381.

MR. JUSTICE ROBERTS, delivered the opinion of the Court.* * *

The respondent, a California corporation, is engaged in the transmission and receipt of telegraph, radio, cable, and other messages between points in California and points in other states and foreign countries. It maintains an office in San Francisco for the transaction of its business wherein it employs upwards of sixty supervisors, operators and clerks, many of whom are members of Local No. 3 of the American Radio Telegraphists Association, a national labor organization; the membership of the local comprising "point-to-point" or land operators employed by respondent at San Francisco. Affiliated with the national organization also were locals whose members are exclusively marine operators who work upon ocean-going vessels. The respondent, at its San Francisco office, dealt with committees of Local No. 3; and its parent company, whose headquarters were in New York, dealt with representatives of the national organization. Demand was made by the latter for the execution of agreements respecting terms and conditions of employment of marine and point-to-point operators. On several occasions when representatives of the union conferred with officers of the respondent and its parent company the latter requested postponement of discussion of the proposed agreements and the union acceded to the requests. In September, 1935, the union pressed for immediate execution of agreements and took the position that no contract would be concluded by the one class of operators unless an agreement were simultaneously made with the other. Local No. 3 sent a representative to New York to be in touch with the negotiations and he kept its officers advised as to what there occurred. The local adopted a resolution to the effect that if satisfactory terms were not obtained by September 23 a strike of the San Francisco point-to-point operators should be called. The national officers determined on a general strike in view of the unsatisfactory state of the negotiations. This fact was communicated to Local No. 3 by its representative in New York and the local officers called out the employees of the San Francisco office. At midnight Friday, October 4, 1935, all the men there employed went on strike. The respondent, in order to maintain service, brought employees from its Los Angeles office and others from the New York and Chicago offices of the parent company to fill the strikers' places.

Although none of the San Francisco strikers returned to work Saturday, Sunday, or Monday, the strike proved unsuccessful in other parts of the country and, by Monday evening, October 7th, a number of the men became convinced that it would fail and that they had better return to work before their places were filled with new employees. One of them telephoned the respondent's traffic supervisor Monday evening to inquire whether the men might return. He was told that the respondent would take them back and it was arranged that the official should meet the employees at a downtown hotel and make a statement to them. Before leaving the company's office for this purpose the supervisor consulted with his superior, who told him that the men might return to work in their former positions but that, as the company had promised eleven men brought to San Francisco they might remain if they so desired, the supervisor would have to handle the return of the striking employees in such fashion as not to displace any of the new men who desired to continue in San Francisco. A little later the supervisor met two of the striking employees and gave them a list of all the strikers together with their addresses, and the telephone numbers of those who had telephones, and it was arranged that these two employees should telephone the strikers to come to a meeting at the Hotel Bellevue in the early hours of Tuesday, October 8th. In furnishing this list the supervisor stated that the men could return to work in a body but he checked off the names of eleven strikers who he said would have to file applications for reinstatement which applications would be subject to the approval of an executive of the company in New York. Because of this statement the two employees, in notifying the strikers of the proposed meeting, with the knowledge of the supervisor, omitted to communicate with the eleven men whose names had been checked off. Thirty-six men attended the meeting. Some of the eleven in question heard of it and attended. The supervisor appeared at the meeting and reiterated his statement that the men could go back to work at once but read from a list the names of the eleven who would be required to file applications for reinstatement to be passed upon in New York. Those present at the meeting voted on the question of immediately returning to work and the proposition was carried. Most of the men left the meeting and went to the respondent's office Tuesday morning, October 8th, where on that day they resumed their usual duties. Then or shortly thereafter six of the eleven in question took their places and resumed their work without challenge. It turned out that only five of the new men brought to San Francisco desired to stay.

Five strikers who were prominent in the activities of the union and in connection with the strike, whose names appeared upon the list of eleven, reported at the office at various times between Tuesday and Thursday. Each of them was told that he would have to fill out an application for employment; that the roll of employees was complete, and that his application would be considered in connection with any vacancy that might thereafter occur. These men not having been reinstated in the course of three weeks, the secretary of Local No. 3 presented a charge to the National Labor Relations Board that the respondent had violated section 8(1) and (3) of the National Labor Relations Act. Thereupon the Board filed a complaint charging that the respondent had discharged and was refusing to employ the five men who had not been reinstated to their positions for the reason that they had joined and assisted the labor organization known as Local No. 3 and had engaged in concerted activities with other employees of the respondent for the purpose of collective bargaining and other mutual aid and protection; that by such discharge respondent had interfered with, restrained, and coerced the employees in the exercise of their rights guaranteed by section 7 of the National Labor Relations Act and so had been guilty of an unfair labor practice within the meaning of section 8(1) of the Act. The complaint further alleged that the discharge of these men was a discrimination in respect of their hire and tenure of employment and a discouragement of membership in Local No. 3, and thus an unfair labor practice within the meaning of section 8(3) of the Act. * * *

Second. Under the findings the strike was a consequence of, or in connection with, a current labor dispute as defined in section 2(9) of the Act, 29 U.S.C.A. § 152(9). That there were pending negotiations for the execution of a contract touching wages and terms and conditions of employment of point-to-point operators cannot be denied. But it is said the record fails to disclose what caused these negotiations to fail or to show that the respondent was in any wise in fault in failing to comply with the union's demands; and, therefore, for all that appears, the strike was not called by reason of fault of the respondent. The argument confuses a current labor dispute with an unfair labor practice defined in section 8 of the Act. True, there is no evidence that respondent had been guilty of any unfair labor practice prior to the strike, but within the intent of the Act there was an existing labor dispute in connection with which the strike was called. The finding is that the strike was deemed "advisable in view of the unsatisfactory state of the negotiations" in New York. It was unnecessary for the Board to find what was in fact the state of the negotiations in New York when the strike was called, or in so many words that a labor dispute as defined by the Act existed. The wisdom or unwisdom of the men, their justification or lack of it, in attributing to respondent an unreasonable or arbitrary attitude in connection with the negotiations, cannot determine whether, when they struck, they did so as a consequence of, or in connection with, a current labor dispute.

Third. The strikers remained employees under section 2(3) of the Act, which provides: "The term 'employee' shall include . . . any individual whose work has ceased as a consequence of, or in connection with, any current labor dispute or because of any unfair labor practice, and who has not obtained any other regular and substantially equivalent employment. . . ." Within this definition the strikers remained employees for the purpose of the Act and were protected against the unfair labor practices denounced by it.

Fourth. It is contended that the Board lacked jurisdiction because respondent was at no time guilty of any unfair labor practice. Section 8 of the Act denominates as such practice action by an employer to interfere with, restrain, or coerce employees in the exercise of their rights to organize, to form, join, or assist labor organizations, and to engage in concerted activities for the purpose of collective bargaining or other mutual aid or protection, or "by discrimination in regard to . . . tenure of employment or any term or condition of employment to encourage or discourage membership in any labor organization. . . ." There is no evidence and no finding that the respondent was guilty of any unfair labor practice in connection with the negotiations in New York. On the contrary, it affirmatively appears that the respondent was negotiating with the authorized representatives of the union. Nor was it an unfair labor practice to replace the striking employees with others in an effort to carry on the business. Although section 13 of the Act, provides, "Nothing in this Act [chapter] shall be construed so as to interfere with or impede or diminish in any way the right to strike," it does not follow that an employer, guilty of no act denounced by the statute, has lost the right to protect and continue his business by supplying places left vacant by strikers. And he is not bound to discharge those hired to fill the places of strikers, upon the election of the latter to resume their employment, in order to create places for them. The assurance by respondent to those who accepted employment during the strike that if they so desired their places might be permanent was not an unfair labor practice, nor was it such to reinstate only so many of the strikers as there were vacant places to be filled. But the claim put forward is that the unfair labor practice indulged by the respondent was discrimination in reinstating striking employees by keeping out certain of them for the sole reason that they had been active in the union. As we have said, the strikers retained, under the Act, the status of employees. Any such discrimination in putting them back to work is, therefore, prohibited by section 8.

Fifth. The Board's findings as to discrimination are supported by evidence. We shall not attempt a discussion of the conflicting claims as to the proper conclusions to be drawn from the testimony. There was evidence, which the Board credited, that several of the five men in question were told that their union activities made them undesirable to their employer; and that some of them did not return to work with the great body of the men at 6 o'clock on Tuesday morning because they understood they would not be allowed to go to work until the superior officials had passed upon their applications. When they did apply at times between Tuesday morning and Thursday they were each told that the quota was full and that their applications could not be granted in any event until a vacancy occurred. This was on the ground that five of the eleven new men remained at work in San Francisco. On the other hand, six of the eleven strikers listed for separate treatment who reported for work early Tuesday morning, or within the next day or so, were permitted to go back to work and were not compelled to await the approval of their applications. It appears that all of the men who had been on strike signed applications for re-employment shortly after their resumption of work. The Board found, and we cannot say that its finding is unsupported, that, in taking back six of the eleven men and excluding five who were active union men, the respondent's officials discriminated against the latter on account of their union activities and that the excuse given that they did not apply until after the quota was full was an afterthought and not the true reason for the discrimination against them.

As we have said, the respondent was not bound to displace men hired to take the strikers' places in order to provide positions for them. It might have refused reinstatement on the grounds of skill or ability, but the Board found that it did not do so. It might have resorted to any one of a number of methods of determining which of its striking employees would have to wait because five men had taken permanent positions during the strike, but it is found that the preparation and use of the list, and the action taken by respondent, was with the purpose to discriminate against those most active in the union. There is evidence to support these findings. * * *

NOTE ON THE SIGNIFICANCE OF MACKAY RADIO

Mackay Radio presents the employer with its most powerful antidote to the strike. That is the right to permanently replace workers who strike over economic issues. As we shall see shortly, if the employer makes a commitment to replacement workers that they will not only take the place of the striker but will keep the striker's job at the end of the strike, that representation may ripen into a legal obligation to retain the replacement worker. Once that happens, the striker knows that he or she may be in trouble, because if the strike doesn't succeed and the striker wants her job back, she may find it has been taken by the permanent replacement. The striker is not removed from the coverage of the Act, and she can get her old job if the replacement departs or if an equivalent vacancy arises. But this is small comfort to a long-term employee who strikes in difficult economic times.

The dilemma for the striker is compounded when she realizes that other strikers may be tempted to give up the strike and return to work before the employer hires permanent replacements. A junior employee will be especially tempted to do this, because when the strike ends reinstatement may be in the order of seniority, and the junior person will be at the end of the line. But if she can cross the picket line early in the game, she gains the favorable status of a replacement, and can beat out her brothers and sisters whom she originally joined in the strike. Better yet, she can improve her seniority position. Once this begins to occur it is like a chain reaction, for each striker who comes back to work makes the plight of the remaining strikers that much more precarious, as the union's support begins to wane. If the union wins the strike, it may be able to negotiate a settlement in which all the strikers get their jobs back. But if a number of strikers begin to defect, the union is unlikely to prevail.

Economic and Unfair Labor Practice Strikers

Mackay presages a very important distinction in the portion of the decision headed "second." There Justice Roberts speculated about strikes that are caused "by reason of fault" of the employer. This has evolved to mean strikes that are called in response to unfair labor practices committed by the employer. An unfair labor practice strike is contrasted to one that is purely about economic issues, that is, an economic strike. *Mackay's* replacement rule is limited to economic strikers. An unfair labor practice striker, on the other hand, can get her job back at any time, whether or not a replacement appears to stand in her way. The modern Supreme Court talks about this distinction in *Belknap v. Hale,* which comes up shortly.

This distinction means that the battle lines in a strike depend critically on whether the strikers are economic strikers or unfair labor practice strikers. If the latter, they gain (or regain, critics of *Mackay* would argue) the power to return to work at any time they choose to accept the employer's terms. Since they don't strike under the specter of permanent replacement, they may be more willing to hold out for an acceptable settlement. However, as we shall see, it is not easy to determine whether a particular strike falls into one category or the other, so both the union and the employer may have to make tactical decisions at the great peril of being wrong in their assessment of whether the strike is an unfair labor practice strike or an economic strike.

The Mystical Conversion of Strikers

A strike often starts its life as an economic strike, over some bread and butter issue like wages. Then, while the strike is in progress, the employer commits an unfair labor practice, like refusing to give the union information that it is lawfully entitled to have. Does this move the striker to remain on strike? Does it strengthen her resolve? Is it an accurate factual description to say that the strike has now become one in protest of the employer's unfair labor practices, or is that a fiction? Is it a good fiction? Consider how this all works in another portion of the *Reichhold Chemical* case, the case we have been using in this chapter as a case study of the strike and the bargaining process. You'll recall that we studied this case when we were examining what constitutes bad faith bargaining. You might go back to that opinion to remember the facts. In this portion of the case the court discusses how the employer's unfair labor practices may convert what started out as an economic strike into an unfair labor practice strike (Teamsters v. NLRB, 906 F.2d 719, 723 (D.C.Cir.1990)).

> * * * If an unfair labor practice committed by the employer is a "contributing cause" of a strike, then, as a matter of law, the strike must be considered an unfair labor practice strike ("ULP strike").

> * * * "The employer's unfair labor practice need not be the sole or even the major cause or aggravating factor of the strike; it need only

be a contributing factor." NLRB v. Moore Business Forms, Inc., 574 F.2d 835, 840 (5th Cir.1978). "The dispositive question is whether the employees, in deciding to go on strike, were motivated in part by the unfair labor practices committed by their employer, not whether, without that motivation, the employees might have struck for some other reason." Northern Wire Corp. v. NLRB, 887 F.2d 1313, 1319–20 (7th Cir.1989).[1] The significance of this causation determination is that, unlike employees who strike for economic reasons, unfair labor practice strikers are entitled to reinstatement with back pay, even when they have been replaced.

It is clear from the record in this case that Reichhold negotiated to impasse on a no-strike clause that included an unlawful no-access provision. Reichhold's original proposal provided, in relevant part, that, if an employee engages in any unauthorized strike, slowdown, walk-out or other cessation of work, "the Company shall have the unrestricted right to replace any and all such participants and they shall have no further rights under this Agreement and no action in law or equity or before any administrative agency, including the National Labor Relations Board." Reichhold's proposal of October 13, 1983, similarly provided that participants in activities prohibited by the work stoppage article "shall have no further rights under this Agreement and no action in law or equity or before any administrative agency, including the National Labor Relations Board." Reichhold continued to insist on the no-access provision through the final four bargaining meetings.

It is uncontested that the Union President indicated at the bargaining table that the no-access provision was a strike issue. It is also undisputed that at the strike vote meeting the Union President told employees that Reichhold's proposals were "unreasonable and outrageous," and that "there were items in the management rights clause and the no-strike clause that he had never seen proposed before. He told those present that if the Union agreed to these proposals they would not have a significant labor agreement."

The Board concluded, however, that "[i]n the absence of any evidence that the strikers even knew about the [Company's] proposal regarding a waiver of access to the Board, we are unwilling to infer from the record evidence in this case that one of the reasons for the strike was the strikers' desire to protest that particular proposal." Id. at 13, 1987–1988. [See Reichhold II, 288 N.L.R.B. No. 8, slip op. at 10, 1987–1988 NLRB Dec. (CCH) at 33,353.] The Board explained that

The information on which the employees acted when they voted to strike is what is crucial in determining if there is a causal connection between the [Company's] insistence on a waiver of employees' rights to go to the Board and the determination to strike. In light of

---

1. An employer's failure to reinstate unfair labor practice strikers violates sections 8(a)(1) and (3) of the Act, 29 U.S.C. § 158(a)(1), (3).

our finding that this proposal was never discussed with employees at either of the strike-vote meetings, we decline to find that this proposal played any part in the employees' decision to strike.

Id., 1987–1988.

The obvious flaw in the Board's reasoning is that it simply ignores the evidence that proves the point on causation. The dispositive criterion in a case of this sort is the "real and actuating motivation" for the strike. NLRB v. Pope Maintenance Corp., 573 F.2d 898, 906 (5th Cir.1978). In this case, because the matter of the no-access provision was not specifically discussed at the strike meeting, it is crucial to inquire whether the Union's reasons for recommending a strike can be imputed to the employees who voted for the strike. That inquiry is relatively easy on this record, for it is unrefuted that the employees voted to strike solely pursuant to the Union President's recommendations.

At the hearing before the ALJ, the Company successfully objected to the admission of any evidence from employees as to why they struck. Having excluded this evidence, the Board was constrained to consider only what the employees were told by the Union President in assessing causation. Thus, if the Union leader urged a strike because he thought the Company's demands were "outrageous," and the employees then voted to strike, the question of causation is tied directly to the reasons that prompted the Union President to call for a strike. It is undisputed that one of those reasons was the inclusion of a no-access provision in the no-strike clause.

In short, there is no doubt that the concerns of the Union President posed a strike issue from the outset of negotiations. Indeed, the Board specifically found that, with respect to the first strike vote, "[t]he union president's feelings were clearly communicated when he told those present that no self-respecting union would sign such a contract. Convinced by the president's arguments in this regard, the employees voted unanimously to strike at that meeting." Id. Reichhold II, 288 N.L.R.B. No. 8, slip op. at 12. Furthermore, the evidence in this record plainly reveals that the employees struck because the Union President told them that the Company's demands (which included the no-access provision) were unreasonable and outrageous, that their labor agreement would be meaningless if they acceded to the Company's demands, and that a strike was necessary to break the deadlock in negotiations. On this record, it must be found that, when the employees voted to strike, they impliedly endorsed their Union President's strong opposition to the no-access provision.

Well, you've read the opinion. Do you buy it? Did the workers strike in protest against the employer's unfair labor practices?

THE ANTIDOTE TO MACKAY? THE STRIKER REPLACEMENT BILL

Early in the Clinton Presidency, in the first Democratic administration in 12 years, one of the burning legislative issues in labor law was a bill that would prevent an employer from permanently replacing striking workers. Labor saw this bill as its modern Magna Carta, for the employer's present right to permanently replace striking workers robs labor of its most potent weapon.

The striker replacement bill never reached fruition, so we don't have a draft version for your consideration. But if you were a member of Congress inclined to change the rule of *Mackay,* what would be the key features of the bill you would draft? Would a bill that simply gives the striker the right to go back to work at any time tip the balance too far the other way? Would this be unfair to the replacement worker who may have in good faith relied on the employer's assurance of permanent employment? What about a bill that simply says that any person hired to replace a striker is treated as a temporary replacement only, subject to being bumped by the returning striker?

Later on in the Clinton administration, when the President realized his bill was going nowhere, the President decided to issue an Executive Order prohibiting government contractors from permanently replacing strikers.

Some readers may recall the Steel seizure fiasco during President Harry Truman's days, when Truman took over the steel mills during a strike (to show the employers a thing or two) rather than seeking an injunction against the strike under Taft–Hartley. The Supreme Court shut Harry down, rather than the mills, in the famous case on Presidential powers of Youngstown Sheet and Tube v. Sawyer, 343 U.S. 579, 72 S.Ct. 863, 96 L.Ed. 1153 (1952). The Court held that whatever residual claim to power the President might have, that power was foreclosed since Congress had already spoken on the subject by setting out the rules for dealing with strikes that create national emergencies.

President Clinton's EO was challenged under an analogous theory. The argument was that Congress has set out the groundrules for dealing with strikers (we might add that those groundrules were articulated largely by judicial fiat in Mackay), and therefore the President's action was preempted. Chamber of Commerce v. Reich, 74 F.3d 1322 (D.C.Cir. 1996).

THE AUTHORS AND FRIEND GO TO CONGRESS

Representatives Cameron, Dau–Schmidt, Rabin, Silverstein and Schatzki are sitting around the House caucus room discussing the upcoming floor debate on the striker replacement bill. They wax nostalgically about Mackay.

Bob: I've often wondered why so many legal scholars point to *Mackay Radio* as almost the paradigm example of how the

Court's decisions are so value-laden. *Mackay* is cited as a pro-employer decision. But I think of it as a perfectly neutral decision that simply allows each party to make use of whatever economic weapons it chooses. I surely don't see it as permitting the employer to punish employees for exercising their right to strike, so it doesn't distort 8(a)(3); and as an 8(a)(1) case it sets a reasonable balance between protected employee rights and legitimate employer interests.

George: I disagree. Allowing the company to recruit strikebreakers and to retain them instead of reinstating strikers should be considered a per se violation of 8(a)(3).

Ken: Do we have to go that far? Couldn't you argue that the facts in *Mackay* show discrimination with an intent to discourage? The Court said an employer does not lose "the right to protect and continue" the business by filling places left vacant by strikers. In *Mackay* that meant transferring nonstriking personnel to San Francisco to do the struck work. That's a legitimate response to economic pressure on the part of the union. But the company did not stop at merely insuring continuity of operations; it went further, guaranteeing transferees the right to remain in San Francisco once the strike was over. There was no evidence in *Mackay* that the employer needed to offer permanent employment *in San Francisco* in order to induce transferees to cross picket lines.

Eileen: I think that observation is correct, and it gives the *Mackay* doctrine a very broad reach. The right to continue operations now means that, absent any showing of need, the company can replace strikers with strangers off the street; and, absent any showing of need, the company can offer the new hires permanent employment. An empirical study on the subject done by the Wharton School of Business found that employers are generally able to carry on operations during a strike without hiring replacements, [A. Perry, E. Kramer and T. Schneider, Operating During Strikes: Company Experience, NLRB Policies, and Government Regulations 63–65 (1982).] When employers overrespond, particularly by favoring strikebreakers over unionists, 8(a)(3) is violated.

Bob: I'll grant you that much. The employer shouldn't be allowed to permanently replace employees unless it can demonstrate that this is the only way it can induce nonstriking personnel to work during the strike.

Ken: What an evidentiary nightmare! A finding on the company's need to hire permanent replacements would be made after the strike ended and the outcome would be largely speculative. What would a management lawyer tell her clients?

Eileen: The same thing she does now. We already know how difficult it is to make a clean or meaningful distinction between economic strikers and unfair labor practice strikers. The effectiveness of the employer's right to replace depends so heavily on that fact, but it's hard both to understand the basis of the legal distinction and to see how it may be shown in practice. Bob's proposal just shifts the point at which the risk arises, and I'll bet most companies will be able to make enough of a factual showing to prevail.

Bob: Well, let me make a further concession. Suppose we simply let the employer hire replacements for the duration of the strike, but when the strike ends the replacements must yield to the original workforce. In other words, give all strikers the rights of unfair labor practice strikers.

George: What's the justification for that retreat, or its limits? Once you take the step of restricting the employer's replacement rights, you undercut your original proposition that the law should take a laissez-faire approach to the parties' use of economic weapons.

Bob: I'm simply responding to the arguments about administrative feasibility and the difficulty of drawing lines. I'm saying, let's presume that most employers do not need to promise permanent status in order to operate during a strike. Some may, but the administrative benefits of a clean rule outweigh the unfairness in isolated cases. Do you still maintain that this limited right to replace is inconsistent with the premises of the Act? You mean that under your view a union can call a strike and the employer may not respond in any fashion by hiring replacements?

George and *Eileen:* Yes.

Eileen: Even a qualified right to replace strikers denies employees the right to strike guaranteed by the Act. Workers control only one economic weapon, the ability to withhold their labor. Companies have a lot of ways to respond to strikes: they use supervisors and administrators to do struck work; or they subcontract the work or have it done at their own nonunion facilities; or they stockpile in anticipation of a strike; or they rely on increasingly automated processes to carry on temporarily without replacements. Some companies even control the timing of the work stoppage by locking out the employees. So it's the unusual situation where a company absolutely cannot maintain operations without employing strangers temporarily. In such cases the strikers are central to the functioning of the enterprise. The *law* shouldn't blunt the power of such workers to force contract terms reflecting the value of their labor.

Chris: Wait a second. Strikers can also earn money during the strike by taking other jobs. That's the real equivalent of a company's maintaining operations. And strikers who take jobs elsewhere don't lose their status as employees of the struck employer. In fact, the employer has innumerable obligations towards the strikers. If the business expands or a replacement leaves, the employer must recall qualified strikers. [NLRB v. Fleetwood Trailer Co., 389 U.S. 375, 88 S.Ct. 543, 19 L.Ed.2d 614 (1967); Laidlaw Corp., 171 NLRB 1366, affirmed 414 F.2d 99 (7th Cir.1969).] There's some authority, though the point is unsettled, that if the striker's job is filled by a permanent replacement the employer must recall the striker to another job for which he is qualified. [Arlington Hotel Co., Inc. v. NLRB, 785 F.2d 249 (8th Cir.1986), cert. denied 479 U.S. 914, 107 S.Ct. 314, 93 L.Ed.2d 288 (1986).] Once recalled the striker gets all his seniority [Globe Molded Plastic Co., 204 NLRB 1041 (1973)], which gives him a competitive edge over any replacement. Since employees can protect their own economic well-being during the strike, why can't their employer take steps to protect its financial viability?

Bob: And aren't you concerned that unions will strike more frequently if employees know their jobs are safe and the company can't even replace them temporarily?

Eileen: Unions may strike over principles, workers don't. Mortgage payments and grocery bills don't stop because there's a strike. Workers also know that contract gains rarely make up for pay lost while on strike. They won't let their unions act irresponsibly.

George and *Chris:* Please note our disagreements with Eileen's assumptions.

Bob: Surely you don't contend that the language of the Act compels your conclusion, or that the legislative history supports your position. Section 13 just says "Nothing in this Act * * * shall be construed so as to interfere with or impede or diminish in any way the right to strike * * *." That section should be understood as a response to judicial regulation of labor disputes through criminal conspiracy charges and injunctions; Congress was only making sure that the NLRB and courts couldn't enjoin strikes, fine and jail strikers, or uphold an employer's decision to discharge strikers. Isn't that enough? In the public sector, employees often aren't even allowed to strike. Private sector employees have it good.

George: Nobody's saying any language in the Act compels anything, but you're looking at the wrong section of the statute. Sections 7 and 8(a)(1) expressly protect the right to strike, to join or assist labor organizations, and to engage in concerted activity for mutual aid and protection, free from employer interference, restraint or coercion. Moreover, section 8(a)(3) pretty clearly makes it unlawful to discriminate against employees for being good union members. It would seem all that language at least is a solid foundation from which to begin analysis.

Bob: That reasoning does lead to the conclusion that hiring replacements is per se a violation of section 8(a)(1) or (3). But doesn't it also suggest that any preparation for the strike that might tend to restrain employees from actually striking would be unlawful under, at least, section 8(a)(1)?

Eileen: I have to agree with Bob. Some critics of *Mackay* are absolutists, arguing that any rule that diminishes the effectiveness of a strike amounts to a denial of the right to strike. Others point out that the statute doesn't recognize a company's right to maintain operations, and they say an "inherent right" can't override express statutory rights. [See, e.g., J. Atleson, Values and Assumptions In American Labor Law (1983) and Klare, Judicial Deradicalization of the Wagner Act and the Origins of Modern Legal Consciousness, 62 Minn.L.Rev. 256 (1978).] But both propositions prove too much.

Bob: Then aren't you also agreeing with my original proposition, that an employer has the right to respond to a strike with whatever economic measures it needs?

Chris: And with my point about employers and employees having equal rights to maintain income and to survive a strike?

Eileen: No. I'm responding to the limited question of a qualified right to replace strikers. The Act tolerates economic pressure because economic hardship forces the parties to compromise. Too great an imbalance in weapons means the process won't work. Given all the options management has, it doesn't need the additional one of hiring strangers to do the struck work on the company's premises.

Bob: Why draw the line at temporary replacements? Contracting out struck work is just another way to get the work done.

Eileen: And that's another example of what's wrong with *Mackay.* Every decision on the legitimacy of a company's use of economic pressure begins with the proposition that a company has the right to maintain operations even to the point of permanently replacing economic strikers. Alternatives like contracting out look mild in comparison precisely because they don't deprive strikers of access to their jobs once the strike is over. So no court ever has to ask whether the right to contract out gives employers overwhelming economic advantages, or whether a company chooses a particular economic response because it needs to maintain production, because it's only trying to reduce the strikers' morale, or is intent on killing off the union. I guess I reach the same conclusion as George, but by a different route.

George: In the end, this entire discussion misses the point. The justification for *Mackay* is that it is the sole effective sanction to make companies bargain in good faith. If employers bargain without breaking the law, management gets a "perk", the unconditional right to hire permanent replacements. The vice, of course, is that in order to get management to bargain with the union, the Court imposes on workers, union supporters and strikebreakers, the need to compete for the same jobs. As ever, the Court sacrifices the interests of some employees by pitting them against one another in order to achieve a "public good"; this time it's collective bargaining.

2. DO REPLACEMENT WORKERS HAVE RIGHTS TOO?

A Problem to focus on the issues

To: Associate

From: Partner

Our firm is labor counsel to Enderby Enterprises, a manufacturer of talc products. I have been working on the following matter, and need your assistance.

The United Factory Workers recently won an election to represent the Enderby workers. The union's victory was extremely narrow. The President of Enderby instructed me to take an extremely aggressive position in negotiations. He said there was no reason, given the union's narrow majority, to make a generous offer. The union would take whatever it could get. If the members didn't like it, perhaps they'd decertify. I told the President I was uncomfortable with these directions, and that I was obliged to bargain in good faith with the union. I said I would go ahead on that understanding.

At the bargaining table we proposed a two-year agreement, with a 2% wage increase the first year and a wage freeze the second year. The union made the usual demand for a standard clause for binding arbitration. We rejected that. I said we'd agree instead to advisory, non-binding arbitration, but there was no way we'd turn our disputes over to a third party for binding resolution. At least not for our first contract.

The negotiations dragged along for about 8 months, when the union called a strike and pulled out all of the workers. Its picket signs said, "UFW protesting the lack of a meaningful contract and the employer's bad faith bargaining." Frankly, we were surprised. We didn't think the union had that kind of support.

Before the strike, Enderby had a work force of about 120 active employees. All 120 workers went out on strike. Enderby was able to hire 40 replacements. Each replacement worker signed an application that said:

"I understand that to the extent permitted by law I am a permanent replacement for striking employees."

During the next month 20 strikers "crossed over" and began to work for Enderby. These were for the most part employees with very low seniority at Enderby. Enderby now had 60 workers (the 40 new hires and 20 cross-overs). 100 workers were now on strike (the 120 original strikers minus the 20 cross-overs).

Eventually Enderby could not operate with a production staff of just 60 employees. So we made an offer to the union to end the strike. This included a more generous wage increase and binding rather than advisory arbitration. The union said it would agree to settle the strike, but only on condition that Enderby restore all the strikers to their jobs. Enderby insisted that it could not restore all the strikers because it had a contractual commitment to all the striker replacements it hired. We had a standoff.

Then the union lawyer made another suggestion. She said the union didn't care which of the current workers Enderby let go, so long as we brought back the 100 people presently on strike. This meant we could let go 20 of the cross-over employees, and 20 of the replacement employees, or whatever combination we wished.

We now have 160 workers competing for 120 jobs (100 strikers, 40 new hires as replacements and 20 cross-overs). In order to settle the strike, we must remove 40 of the current workers from the active payroll.

I must advise Enderby how to settle the strike. What are our alternatives, and what is our liability to each group of employees (replacements, cross-overs and strikers) who are not brought back to active employment status?

The following case will be very helpful in working through this problem. But it doesn't answer all the questions. When a replacement worker is promised a permanent job by the employer, does she gain any legal rights in her job? Recall our discussion of the erosion of the employment at will doctrine in Chapter I. Ask yourself which of the doctrines that you studied there confers rights in the job upon the replacement workers in this problem and in the next case. Can you give the client an answer without first analyzing state law?

If the employer attracts permanent replacements, and the union is still able to settle the strike and insist on the reinstatement of the original strikers, how do the union and employer resolve the competing claims of too many workers, strikers and their replacements, for too few jobs? Since the union has a duty to represent all employees in the bargaining unit, must it protect the interests of the strike replacements? If they are loathed by the strikers, how can the union represent the replacement's interests? If there was an established system of seniority before the strike, does that provide a neutral principle to guide union representation? Or is that too simple a solution, for it will almost always favor the strikers over their replacements? Does the Belknap decision make it easier or harder for the parties to settle a strike?

BELKNAP, INC. v. HALE

Supreme Court of the United States, 1983.
463 U.S. 491, 103 S.Ct. 3172, 77 L.Ed.2d 798.

JUSTICE WHITE delivered the opinion of the Court.

The federal labor relations laws recognize both economic strikes and strikes to protest unfair labor practices. Where employees have engaged in an economic strike, the employer may hire permanent replacements whom it need not discharge even if the strikers offer to return to work unconditionally. If the work stoppage is an unfair labor practice strike, the employer must discharge any replacements in order to accommodate returning strikers. In this case we must decide whether the National Labor Relations Act (NLRA or Act) pre-empts a misrepresentation and breach-of-contract action against the employer brought in state court by strike replacements who were displaced by reinstated strikers after having been offered and accepted jobs on a permanent basis and assured they would not be fired to accommodate returning strikers.

I

Petitioner Belknap, Inc., is a corporation engaged in the sale of hardware products and certain building materials. A bargaining unit consisting of all of Belknap's warehouse and maintenance employees selected International Brotherhood of Teamsters Local No. 89 (Union) as their collective-bargaining representative. In 1975, the Union and Belknap entered into an agreement which was to expire on January 31, 1978. The two opened negotiations for a new contract shortly before the expiration of the 1975 agreement, but reached an impasse. On February 1, 1978, approximately 400 Belknap employees represented by the Union went out on strike. Belknap then granted a wage increase, effective February 1, for union employees who stayed on the job.

Shortly after the strike began, Belknap placed an advertisement in a local newspaper seeking applicants to "permanently replace striking warehouse and maintenance employees."[1] A large number of people responded to the offer and were hired. After each replacement was hired, Belknap presented to the replacement the following statement for his signature:

1. The advertisement said:

"PERMANENT EMPLOYEES WANTED

"BELKNAP, INC.

"111 EAST MAIN STREET LOUISVILLE, KENTUCKY

"OPENINGS AVAILABLE FOR QUALIFIED PERSONS LOOKING FOR EMPLOYMENT TO PERMANENTLY REPLACE STRIKING WAREHOUSE AND MAINTENANCE EMPLOYEES.

"EXCELLENT EARNINGS, FRINGE BENEFITS AND WORKING CONDITIONS WITH STEADY YEAR-ROUND EMPLOYMENT.

"MINIMUM STARTING RATE $4.55 PER HOUR. TOP RATE $5.85, DEPENDING ON SKILL, ABILITY AND EXPERIENCE. PLUS INCENTIVE EARNINGS OVER HOURLY RATE FOR MOST JOBS.

"APPLY IN PERSON AT THE BELKNAP OFFICE LOCATED AT 111 EAST MAIN STREET BETWEEN 9:00 A.M. AND 2:30 P.M., MONDAY THRU FRIDAY. PARK IN COMPANY LOT AT 1st AND MAIN.

"WE ARE AN EQUAL OPPORTUNITY EMPLOYER"

"I, the undersigned, acknowledge and agree that I as of this date have been employed by Belknap, Inc. at its Louisville, Kentucky, facility as a regular full time permanent replacement to permanently replace _____ in the job classification of _____."

On March 7, the Union filed unfair labor practice charges against petitioner Belknap. The charge was based on the unilateral wage increase granted by Belknap. Belknap countered with charges of its own. On April 4, the company distributed a letter which said, in relevant part:

"TO ALL PERMANENT REPLACEMENT EMPLOYEES

* * *

"We recognize that many of you continue to be concerned about your status as an employee. The Company's position on this matter has not changed nor do we expect it to change. You will continue to be permanent replacement employees so long as you conduct yourselves in accordance with the policies and practices that are in effect here at Belknap.

* * *

"We continue to meet and negotiate in good faith with the Union. It is our hope and desire that a mutually acceptable agreement can be reached in the near future. However, we have made it clear to the Union that we have no intention of getting rid of the permanent replacement employees just in order to provide jobs for the replaced strikers if and when the Union calls off the strike."

On April 27, the Regional Director issued a complaint against Belknap, asserting that the unilateral increase violated §§ 8(a)(1), 8(a)(3), and 8(a)(5) of the Act. Also on April 27, the company again addressed the strike replacements:

"We want to make it perfectly clear, once again, that there will be no change in your employment status as a result of the charge by the National Labor Relations Board, which has been reported in this week's newspapers."

"We do not believe there is any substance to the charge and we feel confident we can prove in the courts satisfaction that our intent and actions are completely within the law."

A hearing on the unfair labor practice charges was scheduled for July 19. The Regional Director convened a settlement conference shortly before the hearing was to take place. He explained that if a strike settlement could be reached, he would agree to the withdrawal and dismissal of the unfair labor practice charges and complaints against both the company and the Union. During these discussions the parties made various concessions, leaving one major issue unresolved, the recall of the striking workers. The parties finally agreed that the company would, at a minimum, reinstate 35 strikers per week. The settlement agreement was then reduced to writing. Petitioner laid off the replacements, including the 12 respondents, in order to make room for the returning strikers.

Respondents sued Belknap in the Jefferson County, Ky., Circuit Court for misrepresentation and breach of contract. Belknap, they alleged, had proclaimed that it was hiring permanent employees, knowing both that the assertion was false and that respondents would detrimentally rely on it. The alternative claim was that Belknap was liable for breaching its contracts with respondents by firing them as a result of its agreement with the Union. Each respondent asked for $250,000 in compensatory damages, and an equal amount in punitive damages.

Belknap, after unsuccessfully seeking to remove the suit to federal court, moved for summary judgment, on the ground that respondents' causes of action were preempted by the NLRA. * * *

II

Our cases have announced two doctrines for determining whether state regulations or causes of action are preempted by the NLRA. Under the first, set out in San Diego Building Trades Council v. Garmon, 359 U.S. 236, 79 S.Ct. 773, 3 L.Ed.2d 775 (1959), state regulations and causes of action are presumptively preempted if they concern conduct that is actually or arguably either prohibited or protected by the Act. The state regulation or cause of action may, however, be sustained if the behavior to be regulated is behavior that is of only peripheral concern to the federal law or touches interests deeply rooted in local feeling and responsibility. In such cases, the State's interest in controlling or remedying the effects of the conduct is balanced against both the interference with the National Labor Relations Board's ability to adjudicate controversies committed to it by the Act, and the risk that the State will sanction conduct that the Act protects. The second preemption doctrine, set out in Machinists v. Wisconsin Employment Relations Comm'n, 427 U.S. 132, 96 S.Ct. 2548, 49 L.Ed.2d 396 (1976), proscribes state regulation and state-law causes of action concerning conduct that Congress intended to be unregulated, conduct that was to remain a part of the self-help remedies left to the combatants in labor disputes.

Petitioner argues that the action was preempted under both Garmon and Machinists. * * *

III

It is asserted that Congress intended the respective conduct of the Union and Belknap during the strike beginning on February 1 " 'to be controlled by the free play of economic forces,' " and that entertaining the action against Belknap was an impermissible attempt by the Kentucky courts to regulate and burden one of the employer's primary weapons during an economic strike, that is, the right to hire permanent replacements. To permit the suit filed in this case to proceed would upset the delicate balance of forces established by the federal law. Subjecting the employer to costly suits for damages under state law for entering into settlements calling for the return of strikers would also conflict with the federal labor policy favoring the settlement of labor disputes. These arguments, it is urged, are valid whether or not a strike is an economic strike.

We are unpersuaded. It is true that the federal law permits, but does not require, the employer to hire replacements during a strike, replacements that it need not discharge in order to reinstate strikers if it hires the replacements on a "permanent" basis within the meaning of the federal labor law. But when an employer attempts to exercise this very privilege by promising the replacements that they will not be discharged to make room for returning strikers, it surely does not follow that the employer's otherwise valid promises of permanent employment are nullified by federal law and its otherwise actionable misrepresentations may not be pursued. We find unacceptable the notion that the federal law on the one hand insists on promises of permanent employment if the employer anticipates keeping the replacements in preference to returning strikers, but on the other hand forecloses damages suits for the employer's breach of these very promises. Even more mystifying is the suggestion that the federal law shields the employer from damages suits for misrepresentations that are made during the process of securing permanent replacements and are actionable under state law.

Arguments that entertaining suits by innocent third parties for breach of contract or for misrepresentation will "burden" the employer's right to hire permanent replacements are no more than arguments that "this is war," that "anything goes," and that promises of permanent employment that under federal law the employer is free to keep, if it so chooses, are essentially meaningless. It is one thing to hold that the federal law intended to leave the employer and the union free to use their economic weapons against one another, but is quite another to hold that either the employer or the union is also free to injure innocent third parties without regard to the normal rules of law governing those relationships. We cannot agree with the dissent that Congress intended such a lawless regime.

The argument that entertaining suits like this will interfere with the asserted policy of the federal law favoring settlement of labor disputes fares no better. This is just another way of asserting that the employer need not answer for its repeated assurances of permanent employment or for its otherwise actionable misrepresentations to secure permanent replacements. We do not think that the normal contractual rights and other usual legal interests of the replacements can be so easily disposed of by broad-brush assertions that no legal rights may accrue to them during a strike because the federal law has privileged the "permanent" hiring of replacements and encourages settlement. * * *

An employment contract with a replacement promising permanent employment, subject only to settlement with its employees' union and to a Board unfair labor practice order directing reinstatement of strikers, would not in itself render the replacement a temporary employee subject to displacement by a striker over the employer's objection during or at the end of what is proved to be a purely economic strike. The Board suggests that such a conditional offer "might" render the replacements only temporary hires that the employer would be required to discharge at the conclusion of a purely economic strike. But the permanent-hiring requirement is designed to protect the strikers, who retain their employee status and are entitled to reinstatement unless they have been permanently replaced. That protection is unnecessary if the employer is ordered to reinstate them because of the commission of unfair labor practices. It is also meaningless if the employer settles with the union and agrees to reinstate strikers. But the protection is of great moment if the employer is not found guilty of unfair practices, does not settle with the union, or settles without a promise to reinstate. In that eventuality, the employer, although it has prevailed in the strike, may refuse reinstatement only if it has hired replacements on a permanent basis. If it has promised to keep the replacements on in such a situation, discharging them to make way for selected strikers whom it deems more experienced or more efficient would breach its contract with the replacements. Those contracts, it seems to us, create a sufficiently permanent arrangement to permit the prevailing employer to abide by its promises.

We perceive no substantial impact on the availability of settlement of economic or unfair labor practice strikes if the employer is careful to protect itself against suits like this in the course of contracting with strike replacements.[9] Its risk of liability if it discharges replacements pursuant to a settlement or to a Board order would then be minimal.
* * *

There is still another variant or refinement of the argument that the employer and the Union should be privileged to settle their dispute and provide for striker reinstatement free of burdensome lawsuits such as this. It is said that respondent replacements are employees within the bargaining unit, that the Union is the bargaining representative of petitioner's employees, and the replacements are thus bound by the terms of the settlement negotiated between the employer and "their" representative.[10] The argument is not only that as a matter of federal law the employer cannot be foreclosed from discharging the replacements

---

9. If, as we hold, an employer may condition his offer to replacements and hence avoid conflicting obligations to strikers and replacements in the event of a settlement providing for reinstatement, the employer will very likely do so. Hence, there will be little occasion for replacements to bring suits for breach of contract or misrepresentation. The employer that nevertheless makes unconditional commitments to replacements and wants to discharge them after settlement with the union will be in much the same position as the employer in W.R. Grace & Co. v. Rubber Workers, 461 U.S. 757, 103 S.Ct. 2177, 76 L.Ed.2d 298 (1983). There the employer signed a conciliation agreement with the Equal Employment Opportunity Commission that conflicted with its collective-bargaining agreement with the union. We recognized the employer's dilemma, but because it was of the employer's own making we unanimously refused to relieve the employer of either obligation.

10. The AFL–CIO disavows this argument. It suggests that replacements are bound only by those agreements that a union makes, as the exclusive bargaining agent for the struck employer's workers, regarding the terms and conditions of employment for the employer's workforce after the termination of the strike.

pursuant to a contract with a bargaining agent, but also that by virtue of the agreement with the Union it is relieved from responding in damages for its knowing breach of contract, that is, that the contracts are not only not specifically enforceable but also may be breached free from liability for damages. We need not address the former issue, the issue of specific performance, since the respondents ask only damages. As to the damages issue, as we have said above, such an argument was rejected in J.I. Case.

If federal law forecloses this suit, more specific and persuasive reasons than those based on *Machinists* must be identified to support any such result. Belknap insists that the rationale of the Garmon decision, properly construed and applied, furnishes these reasons.

IV

The complaint issued by the Regional Director alleged that on or about February 1, Belknap unilaterally put into effect a 50 per-hour wage increase, that such action constituted unfair labor practices under §§ 8(a)(1), 8(a)(3), and 8(a)(5), and that the strike was prolonged by these violations. If these allegations could have been sustained, the strike would have been an unfair labor practice strike almost from the very start. From that time forward, Belknap's advertised offers of permanent employment to replacements would arguably have been unfair labor practices since they could be viewed as threats to refuse to reinstate unfair labor practice strikers. Furthermore, if the strike had been an unfair labor practice strike, Belknap would have been forced to reinstate the strikers rather than keep replacements on the job. Belknap submits that its offers of permanent employment to respondents were therefore arguably unfair labor practices, the adjudication of which were within the exclusive jurisdiction of the Board, and that discharging respondents to make way for strikers was protected activity since it was no more than the federal law required in the event the unfair labor practices were proved. * * *

Belknap contends that the misrepresentation suit is pre-empted because it related to the offers and contracts for permanent employment, conduct that was part and parcel of an arguable unfair labor practice. It is true that whether the strike was an unfair labor practice strike and whether the offer to replacements was the kind of offer forbidden during such a dispute were matters for the Board. The focus of these determinations, however, would be on whether the rights of strikers were being infringed. Neither controversy would have anything in common with the question whether Belknap made misrepresentations to replacements that were actionable under state law. The Board would be concerned with the impact on strikers not with whether the employer deceived replacements. * * * The strikers cannot secure reinstatement, or indeed any relief, by suing for misrepresentation in state court. The state courts in no way offer them an alternative forum for obtaining relief that the Board can provide. * * * Hence, it appears to us that maintaining the misrepresentation action would not interfere with the Board's determination of matters within its jurisdiction and that such an action is of no more than peripheral concern to the Board and the federal law. At the same time, Kentucky surely has a substantial interest in protecting its citizens from misrepresentations that have caused them grievous harm. * * *

[JUSTICE BLACKMUN concurred. JUSTICES BRENNAN, MARSHALL and POWELL dissented.]

SOME PRACTICAL QUESTIONS ABOUT *BELKNAP*

The employer is hit with a strike and must operate with replacements. The employer's ads for replacements qualify its offer in the manner suggested in footnote 9 in *Belknap*. Would any responsible lawyer ignore Justice White's free legal advice in *Belknap*? But think about this: If every offer of permanent replacement is qualified in the manner suggested by Justice White, is there any such thing as a truly permanent replacement? Don't all such offers carry the contingency that the replacement will lose his job if the strike is settled or the employer commits unfair labor practices? Does this suggest that the premise behind *Mackay Radio,* that an employer needs the right to permanently replace, is all wrong? (The *Belknap* Court considers this suggestion, but is not moved to overturn *Mackay.*)

Now suppose that the employer isn't having much success in hiring permanent replacement workers. Interviews with applicants reveal that the striker replacements are unwilling to come to work at the going rate of pay because their employment may turn out to be temporary, and because they will have to endure a tremendous amount of emotional pressure and perhaps physical danger as they cross the picket line each day. The employer decides that it can attract a sufficient number of replacements if it offers them a salary 15% higher than what it was paying at the time of the strike. This figure is considerably higher than any salary the employer had offered the union at the bargaining table. Go back to the materials in the last section on good faith bargaining and impasse, and consider whether and how this may be done. What are the consequences if the employer does it wrong?

Another tactic: Suppose the employer also determines through these interviews that in order to attract replacements it must offer them a "seniority adder." This means that each replacement will start out with credit for a fictional period of time served with Enderby, say five years. This is done to neutralize the impact of present strikers returning to work, as most of them will have greater seniority than the replacements. This is a problem for the replacements, because normally when a workforce is downsized the least senior employees are the first to be let go. Without this additional seniority, the strike replacements would be vulnerable to layoff.

The Supreme Court in NLRB v. Erie Resistor Corp., 373 U.S. 221, 83 S.Ct. 1139, 10 L.Ed.2d 308 (1963) struck down a somewhat similar system, known as "super-seniority", in which the employer gave striker replacements twenty years of seniority. The Court upheld the Board's conclusion that this weapon crossed the permissible line for several reasons:

> "The Board made a detailed assessment of super-seniority and, to its experienced eye, such a plan had the following characteristics:

> (1) Super-seniority affects the tenure of all strikers whereas permanent replacement, proper under *Mackay,* affects only those who are, in actuality, replaced. It is one thing to say that a striker is subject to loss of his job at the strike's end but quite another to hold that in addition to the threat of replacement, all strikers will at best return to their jobs with seniority inferior to that of the replacements and of those who left the strike.

> (2) A super-seniority award necessarily operates to the detriment of those who participated in the strike as compared to non-strikers.

> (3) Super-seniority made available to striking bargaining unit employees as well as to new employees is in effect offering individual benefits to the strikers to induce them to abandon the strike.

> (4) Extending the benefits of super-seniority to striking bargaining unit employees as well as to new replacements deals a crippling blow to the strike effort. At one stroke, those with low seniority have the opportunity to obtain the job security which ordinarily only long years of service can bring, while conversely, the accumulated seniority of older employees is seriously diluted. This combination of threat and promise could be expected to undermine the strikers' mutual interest and place the entire strike effort in jeopardy. The history of this strike and its virtual collapse following the announcement of the plan emphasize the grave repercussions of super-seniority.

> (5) Super-seniority renders future bargaining difficult, if not impossible, for the collective bargaining representative. Unlike the replacement granted in *Mackay* which ceases to be an issue once the strike is over, the plan here creates a cleavage in the plant continuing long after the strike is ended. Employees are henceforth divided into two camps: those who stayed with the union and those who returned before the end of the strike and thereby gained extra seniority. This breach is reemphasized with each subsequent layoff and stands as an ever-present reminder of the dangers connected with striking and with union activities in general."

In the course of the opinion in *Erie Resistor,* Justice White makes some revealing observations about the way the Court determines whether the employer was motivated by unlawful considerations:

"Though the intent necessary for an unfair labor practice may be shown in different ways, proving it in one manner may have far different weight and far different consequences than proving it in another. When specific evidence of a subjective intent to discriminate or to encourage or discourage union membership is shown, and found, many otherwise innocent or ambiguous actions which are normally incident to the conduct of a business may, without more, be converted into unfair labor practices. * * *

The outcome may well be the same when intent is founded upon the inherently discriminatory or destructive nature of the conduct itself. The employer in such cases must be held to intend the very consequences which foreseeably and inescapably flow from his actions and if he fails to explain away, to justify or to characterize his actions as something different than they appear on their face, an unfair labor practice charge is made out. *Radio Officers Union of Commercial Telegraphers Union, A.F.L. v. National Labor Relations Board,* 347 U.S. 17, 74 S.Ct. 323, 98 L.Ed. 455 (1954). But, as often happens, the employer may counter by claiming that his actions were taken in the pursuit of legitimate business ends and that his dominant purpose was not to discriminate or to invade union rights but to accomplish business objectives acceptable under the Act. Nevertheless, his conduct *does* speak for itself—it *is* discriminatory and it *does* discourage union membership and whatever the claimed overriding justification may be, it carries with it unavoidable consequences which the employer not only foresaw but which he must have intended. As is not uncommon in human experience, such situations present a complex of motives and preferring one motive to another is in reality the far more delicate task, reflected in part in decisions of this Court, of weighing the interests of employees in concerted activity against the interest of the employer in operating his business in a particular manner and of balancing in the light of the Act and its policy the intended consequences upon employee rights against the business ends to be served by the employer's conduct. This essentially is the teaching of the Court's prior cases dealing with this problem and, in our view, the Board did not depart from it.

The *Erie Resistor* opinion concludes with a paragraph that suggests that the *Mackay* rule remains intact. But go back to the reasons given by the Court above in striking down the 20 year super-seniority provision and ask whether they apply with equal force to the permanent replacement tool approved in dictum in *Mackay.*

3. UNION ATTEMPTS TO REDRESS THE BALANCE

Unions understand that in the current economic climate the employer's right to replace may be fatal to a strike. What other pressures can take the place of the union's strike weapon?

What about slowdowns at work by working in strict accordance with the rules, calling brief strikes of an hour or two duration on an intermittent basis, or appealing to the public not to deal with the employer until the labor dispute is settled? Unions are looking for a "safe" approach to economic warfare, and the literature is replete with articles detailing these tactics. But weapons short of the full blown strike also carry a high risk for the union. The Board or the courts may conclude that any other tactics are unprotected under Section 7 of the Act. If so, the workers may not only be replaced, but since they become non-persons under the Act, the employer may terminate them for good.

Unions and employers have a difficult time in knowing how to draw the lines between protected and unprotected activity. The union can be sure only that the fullblown strike is protected under Section 7 or under the explicit protection of the right to strike in Section 13. At the other extreme, unlawful acts such as physical sabotage are clearly unprotected, as stated in the *Jefferson Standard* case set out earlier in this chapter. The cases are less clear when it comes to activity that isn't clearly a violation of some other law. We saw this in *Jefferson Standard*, when union conduct that disparaged the company was held unprotected because it amounted to "disloyalty." That case may have rested on the fact that the union made no attempt to link its criticisms of the company to a labor dispute. Still, it casts a large shadow on union activity. Footnote 6 of *Emporium Capwell*, earlier in this chapter, indicates that there is some uncertainty about what is protected activity.

One area of union conduct that is not fully resolved is the use of intermittent or "quickie" strikes. We saw in *Washington Aluminum* in Chapter I that employees were protected when they walked off the job to protest an abnormally cold workplace. It is not clear whether that decision rests on the safety and health issue that was involved, or if it is a broader statement that one-shot withdrawals of service are protected. The cases seem to allow employees to make one such mistake, if that is the right way to put it, but that an ongoing refusal to fully carry out one's work obligation, especially if the employer has ordered the workers to continue to work, deprives the employee of the protection of the Act. Why should that be the consequence? Shouldn't a refusal to work on a regular basis be treated as the equivalent of the strike, with the employer limited to permanently replacing the recalcitrant worker, as in Mackay?

There is some suggestion at the Supreme Court level that the intermittent strike is unprotected. In the next case, *Insurance Agents*, you will find a reference to *Automobile Workers v. Wisconsin Employers Relations Board*, a case sometimes known as *Briggs-Stratton*, 336 U.S. 245, 69 S.Ct. 516, 93 L.Ed. 651 (1949), holding such conduct unprotected. But since that case comes up as a preemption question of whether a state could regulate that activity, the Court may not have faced the underlying NLRA issue squarely. In the *Insurance Agents* case the Court treats the *Briggs-Stratton* result as an "arguendo," rather than embracing it wholeheartedly. For a discussion of the courts' [and Board's] treatment of the two lines of cases, disloyalty and intermittent strikes, see Calvin Sharpe, "By Any Means Necessary"—Unprotected Conduct and Decisional Discretion Under the NLRA, 20 Berkeley J. Employment & Lab.L. 203 (1999).

4. THE WISDOM OF JUDICIAL AND ADMINISTRATIVE INTERVENTION

The scorecard shows that the Court has come down only once against the employer's use of an economic weapon, the superseniority device in *Erie Resistor*. The right to replace was upheld in *Mackay*, and the right to lock out has also been upheld, in *American Ship Building v. NLRB,* 380 U.S. 300, 85 S.Ct. 955, 13 L.Ed.2d 855 (1965), a case that appears shortly, although there has been no definitive Court ruling on whether the lockout may lawfully be combined with the *Mackay* right to permanently replace the employees who were locked out.

Unions have fared less well in their use of weapons, particularly the campaigns that involve disparagement and intermittent strikes. You might ask whether the whole arena of economic weapons is better left unregulated. That is, each party may bring to bear whatever weapons it wishes, unless their conduct violates some other law. Of course, the worker starts out with the legally protected right to strike, tempered by the *Mackay* right to replace.

We now give you two cases which show the Court's approach to the use of economic weapons. In the first, *Insurance Agents*, the Board held that the union's use of certain work tactics while negotiations were in progress violated its duty to bargain in good faith. The Court held that the Board had gone too far in regulating the use of economic weapons. In the second, *American Shipbuilding*, the Board condemned the employer's use of the lockout. The Court again overturned the Board, saying once again that the Board had gone too far in its regulation of economic weapons. Are the two decisions consistent? Should the Board be given more leeway in assessing the impact of economic weapons, or should the parties be given more leeway to use the weapons they chose? If you fall into the latter camp, you'll have to ask whether the balance has been drawn properly in the cases in Section 5, on the union's ability to control and persuade members and workers who don't support the union's position. The same question may be asked about union activity that falls short of a full-blown strike, as in the following case.

NLRB v. INSURANCE AGENTS' INTERNATIONAL UNION, AFL–CIO

Supreme Court of the United States, 1960.
361 U.S. 477, 80 S.Ct. 419, 4 L.Ed.2d 454.

MR. JUSTICE BRENNAN delivered the opinion of the Court.

This case presents an important issue of the scope of the National Labor Relations Board's authority under § 8(b)(3) of the National Labor Relations Act, which provides that "It shall be an unfair labor practice for a labor organization or its agents . . . to refuse to bargain collectively

with an employer, provided it is the representative of his employees...."
The precise question is whether the Board may find that a union, which
confers with an employer with the desire of reaching agreement on
contract terms, has nevertheless refused to bargain collectively, thus
violating that provision, solely and simply because during the negotiations it seeks to put economic pressure on the employer to yield to its
bargaining demands by sponsoring on-the-job conduct designed to interfere with the carrying on of the employer's business.

Since 1949 the respondent Insurance Agents' International Union
and the Prudential Insurance Company of America have negotiated
collective bargaining agreements covering district agents employed by
Prudential in 35 States and the District of Columbia. The principal
duties of a Prudential district agent are to collect premiums and to
solicit new business in an assigned locality known in the trade as his
"debit." He has no fixed or regular working hours except that he must
report at his district office two mornings a week and remain for two or
three hours to deposit his collections, prepare and submit reports, and
attend meetings to receive sales and other instructions. He is paid
commissions on collections made and on new policies written; his only
fixed compensation is a weekly payment of $4.50 intended primarily to
cover his expenses.

In January 1956 Prudential and the union began the negotiation of
a new contract to replace an agreement expiring in the following March.
Bargaining was carried on continuously for six months before the terms
of the new contract were agreed upon on July 17, 1956. It is not
questioned that, if it stood alone, the record of negotiations would
establish that the union conferred in good faith for the purpose and with
the desire of reaching agreement with Prudential on a contract.

However, in April 1956, Prudential filed a § 8(b)(3) charge of refusal
to bargain collectively against the union. The charge was based upon
actions of the union and its members outside the conference room,
occurring after the old contract expired in March. The union had
announced in February that if agreement on the terms of the new
contract was not reached when the old contract expired, the union
members would then participate in a "Work Without a Contract"
program-which meant that they would engage in certain planned, concerted on-the-job activities designed to harass the company.

A complaint of violation of § 8(b)(3) issued on the charge and
hearings began before the bargaining was concluded. It was developed in
the evidence that the union's harassing tactics involved activities by the
member agents such as these: refusal for a time to solicit new business,
and refusal (after the writing of new business was resumed) to comply
with the company's reporting procedures; refusal to participate in the
company's "May Policyholders' Month Campaign"; reporting late at
district offices the days the agents were scheduled to attend them, and
refusing to perform customary duties at the offices, instead engaging
there in "sit-in-mornings," "doing what comes naturally" and leaving at

noon as a group; absenting themselves from special business conferences arranged by the company; picketing and distributing leaflets outside the various offices of the company on specified days and hours as directed by the union; distributing leaflets each day to policyholders and others and soliciting policyholders' signatures on petitions directed to the company; and presenting the signed policyholders' petitions to the company at its home office while simultaneously engaging in mass demonstrations there. * * *

First. The bill which became the Wagner Act included no provision specifically imposing a duty on either party to bargain collectively. Senator Wagner thought that the bill required bargaining in good faith without such a provision. However, the Senate Committee in charge of the bill concluded that it was desirable to include a provision making it an unfair labor practice for an employer to refuse to bargain collectively in order to assure that the Act would achieve its primary objective of requiring an employer to recognize a union selected by his employees as their representative. It was believed that other rights guaranteed by the Act would not be meaningful if the employer was not under obligation to confer with the union in an effort to arrive at the terms of an agreement. * * *

However, the nature of the duty to bargain in good faith thus imposed upon employers by § 8(5) of the original Act was not sweepingly conceived. The Chairman of the Senate Committee declared: "When the employees have chosen their organization, when they have selected their representatives, all the bill proposes to do is to escort them to the door of their employer and say, 'Here they are, the legal representatives of your employees.' What happens behind those doors is not inquired into, and the bill does not seek to inquire into it."

The limitation implied by the last sentence has not been in practice maintained-practically, it could hardly have been—but the underlying purpose of the remark has remained the most basic purpose of the statutory provision. That purpose is the making effective of the duty of management to extend recognition to the union; the duty of management to bargain in good faith is essentially a corollary of its duty to recognize the union. Decisions under this provision reflect this. * * *

But at the same time, Congress was generally not concerned with the substantive terms on which the parties contracted. Obviously there is tension between the principle that the parties need not contract on any specific terms and a practical enforcement of the principle that they are bound to deal with each other in a serious attempt to resolve differences and reach a common ground. And in fact criticism of the Board's application of the "good-faith" test arose from the belief that it was forcing employers to yield to union demands if they were to avoid a successful charge of unfair labor practice. Thus, in 1947 in Congress the fear was expressed that the Board had "gone very far, in the guise of determining whether or not employers had bargained in good faith, in setting itself up as the judge of what concessions an employer must make and of the proposals and counterproposals that he may or may not make." Since the Board was not viewed by Congress as an agency which should exercise its powers to arbitrate the parties' substantive solutions of the issues in their bargaining, a check on this apprehended trend was provided by writing the good-faith test of bargaining into § 8(d) of the Act. * * *

Second. At the same time as it was statutorily defining the duty to bargain collectively, Congress, by adding § 8(b)(3) of the Act through the Taft–Hartley amendments, imposed that duty on labor organizations. Unions obviously are formed for the very purpose of bargaining collectively; but the legislative history makes it plain that Congress was wary of the position of some unions, and wanted to ensure that they would approach the bargaining table with the same attitude of willingness to reach an agreement as had been enjoined on management earlier. It intended to prevent employee representatives from putting forth the same "take it or leave it" attitude that had been condemned in management. 93 Cong.Rec. 4135, 4363, 5005.

Third. It is apparent from the legislative history of the whole Act that the policy of Congress is to impose a mutual duty upon the parties to confer in good faith with a desire to reach agreement, in the belief that such an approach from both sides of the table promotes the overall design of achieving industrial peace. See National Labor Relations Board v. Jones & Laughlin Steel Corp., 301 U.S. 1, 45, 57 S.Ct. 615, 628, 81 L.Ed. 893. Discussion conducted under that standard of good faith may narrow the issues, making the real demands of the parties clearer to each other, and perhaps to themselves, and may encourage an attitude of settlement through give and take. The mainstream of cases before the Board and in the courts reviewing its orders, under the provisions fixing the duty to bargain collectively, is concerned with insuring that the parties approach the bargaining table with this attitude. But apart from this essential standard of conduct, Congress intended that the parties should have wide latitude in their negotiations, unrestricted by any governmental power to regulate the substantive solution of their differences.

We believe that the Board's approach in this case—unless it can be defended, in terms of § 8(b)(3), as resting on some unique character of the union tactics involved here—must be taken as proceeding from an erroneous view of collective bargaining. It must be realized that collective bargaining, under a system where the Government does not attempt to control the results of negotiations, cannot be equated with an academic collective search for truth—or even with what might be thought to be the ideal of one. The parties—even granting the modification of views that may come from a realization of economic interdependence—still proceed from contrary and to an extent antagonistic viewpoints and concepts of self-interest. The system has not reached the ideal of the philosophic notion that perfect understanding among people would lead to perfect agreement among them on values. The presence of economic weapons in reserve, and their actual exercise on occasion by the parties, is part and parcel of the system that the Wagner and Taft–Hartley Acts have recognized. Abstract logical analysis might find inconsistency between the command of the statute to negotiate toward an agreement in good faith and the legitimacy of the use of economic weapons, frequently having the most serious effect upon individual workers and productive enterprises, to induce one party to come to the terms desired by the other. But the truth of the matter is that at the present statutory stage of our national labor relations policy, the two factors-necessity for good-faith bargaining between parties, and the availability of economic pressure devices to each to make the other party incline to agree on one's terms—exist side by side. One writer recognizes this by describing economic force as "a prime motive power for agreements in free collective bargaining."[14] Doubtless one factor influences the other; there may be less need to apply economic pressure if the areas of controversy have been defined through discussion; and at the same time, negotiation positions are apt to be weak or strong in accordance with the degree of economic power the parties possess. A close student of our national labor relations laws writes: "Collective bargaining is curiously ambivalent even today. In one aspect collective bargaining is a brute contest of economic power somewhat masked by polite manners and voluminous statistics. As the relation matures, Lilliputian bonds control the opposing concentrations of economic power; they lack legal sanctions but are nonetheless effective to contain the use of power. Initially it may be only fear of the economic consequences of disagreement that turns the parties to facts, reason, a sense of responsibility, a responsiveness to government and public opinion, and moral principle; but in time these forces generate their own compulsions, and negotiating a contract approaches the ideal of informed persuasion." Cox, The Duty to Bargain in Good Faith, 71 Harv.L.Rev. 1401, 1409.

For similar reasons, we think the Board's approach involves an intrusion into the substantive aspects of the bargaining process—again, unless there is some specific warrant for its condemnation of the precise tactics involved here. The scope of § 8(b)(3) and the limitations on Board power which were the design of § 8(d) are exceeded, we hold, by inferring a lack of good faith not from any deficiencies of the union's performance at the bargaining table by reason of its attempted use of economic pressure, but solely and simply because tactics designed to exert economic pressure were employed during the course of the good-faith negotiations. Thus the Board in the guise of determining good or bad faith in negotiations could regulate what economic weapons a party might summon to its aid. And if the Board could regulate the choice of economic weapons that may be used as part of collective bargaining, it would be in a position to exercise considerable influence upon the substantive terms on which the parties contract. As the parties' own devices became more limited, the Government might have to enter even more directly into the negotiation of collective agreements. Our labor policy is not presently erected on a foundation of government control of

14. G.W. Taylor, Government Regulation of Industrial Relations, p. 18.

the results of negotiations. Nor does it contain a charter for the National Labor Relations Board to act at large in equalizing disparities of bargaining power between employer and union.

Fourth. The use of economic pressure, as we have indicated, is of itself not at all inconsistent with the duty of bargaining in good faith. But in three cases in recent years, the Board has assumed the power to label particular union economic weapons inconsistent with that duty. The Board freely (and we think correctly) conceded here that a "total" strike called by the union would not have subjected it to sanctions under § 8(b)(3), at least if it were called after the old contract, with its no-strike clause, had expired. The Board's opinion in the instant case is not so unequivocal as this concession (and therefore perhaps more logical). But in the light of it and the principles we have enunciated, we must evaluate the claim of the Board to power, under § 8(b)(3), to distinguish among various economic pressure tactics and brand the ones at bar inconsistent with good-faith collective bargaining. We conclude its claim is without foundation.

(a) The Board contends that the distinction between a total strike and the conduct at bar is that a total strike is a concerted activity protected against employer interference by §§ 7 and 8(a)(1) of the Act, while the activity at bar is not a protected concerted activity. We may agree arguendo with the Board that this Court's decision in the Briggs–Stratton case, [Automobile Workers] v. Wisconsin Employers Relations Board, 336 U.S. 245, 69 S.Ct. 516, 93 L.Ed. 651, establishes that the employee conduct here was not a protected concerted activity. On this assumption the employer could have discharged or taken other appropriate disciplinary action against the employees participating in these "slow-down," "sit-in," and arguably unprotected disloyal tactics. But surely that a union activity is not protected against disciplinary action does not mean that it constitutes a refusal to bargain in good faith. The reason why the ordinary economic strike is not evidence of a failure to bargain in good faith is not that it constitutes a protected activity but that, as we have developed, there is simply no inconsistency between the application of economic pressure and good-faith collective bargaining. The Board suggests that since (on the assumption we make) the union members' activities here were unprotected, and they could have been discharged, the activities should also be deemed unfair labor practices, since thus the remedy of a cease-and-desist order, milder than mass discharges of personnel and less disruptive of commerce, would be available. The argument is not persuasive. There is little logic in assuming that because Congress was willing to allow employers to use self-help against union tactics, if they were willing to face the economic consequences of its use, it also impliedly declared these tactics unlawful as a matter of federal law. Our problem remains that of construing § 8(b)(3)'s terms, and we do not see how the availability of self-help to the employer has anything to do with the matter.

(b) The Board contends that because an orthodox "total" strike is "traditional" its use must be taken as being consistent with § 8(b)(3);

but since the tactics here are not "traditional" or "normal," they need not be so viewed. Further, the Board cites what it conceives to be the public's moral condemnation of the sort of employee tactics involved here. But again we cannot see how these distinctions can be made under a statute which simply enjoins a duty to bargain in good faith. Again, these are relevant arguments when the question is the scope of the concerted activities given affirmative protection by the Act. But as we have developed, the use of economic pressure by the parties to a labor dispute is not a grudging exception to some policy of completely academic discussion enjoined by the Act; it is part and parcel of the process of collective bargaining. On this basis, we fail to see the relevance of whether the practice in question is time-honored or whether its exercise is generally supported by public opinion. It may be that the tactics used here deserve condemnation, but this would not justify attempting to pour that condemnation into a vessel not designed to hold it. The same may be said for the Board's contention that these activities, as opposed to a "normal" strike, are inconsistent with § 8(b)(3) because they offer maximum pressure on the employer at minimum economic cost to the union. One may doubt whether this was so here, but the matter does not turn on that. Surely it cannot be said that the only economic weapons consistent with good-faith bargaining are those which minimize the pressure on the other party or maximize the disadvantage to the party using them. The catalog of union and employer weapons that might thus fall under ban would be most extensive.

Fifth. These distinctions essayed by the Board here, and the lack of relationship to the statutory standard inherent in them, confirm us in our conclusion that the judgment of the Court of Appeals, setting aside the order of the Board, must be affirmed. For they make clear to us that when the Board moves in this area, with only § 8(b)(3) for support, it is functioning as an arbiter of the sort of economic weapons the parties can use in seeking to gain acceptance of their bargaining demands. It has sought to introduce some standard of properly "balanced" bargaining power, or some new distinction of justifiable and unjustifiable, proper and "abusive" economic weapons into the collective bargaining duty imposed by the Act. The Board's assertion of power under § 8(b)(3) allows it to sit in judgment upon every economic weapon the parties to a labor contract negotiation employ, judging it on the very general standard of that section, not drafted with reference to specific forms of economic pressure. We have expressed our belief that this amounts to the Board's entrance into the substantive aspects of the bargaining process to an extent congress has not countenanced. * * *

AMERICAN SHIP BUILDING COMPANY, PETITIONER, v. NLRB

Supreme Court of the United States, 1965.
380 U.S. 300, 85 S.Ct. 955, 13 L.Ed.2d 855.

MR. JUSTICE STEWART delivered the opinion of the Court.

The American Ship Building Company seeks review of a decision of the United States Court of Appeals for the District of Columbia enforcing an order of the National Labor Relations Board which found that the company had committed an unfair labor practice under §§ 8(a)(1) and 8(a)(3) of the National Labor Relations Act. The question presented is that expressly reserved in National Labor Relations Board v. Truck Drivers Local Union, etc., 353 U.S. 87, 93, 77 S.Ct. 643, 646, 1 L.Ed.2d 676; namely, whether an employer commits an unfair labor practice under these sections of the Act when he temporarily lays off or 'locks out' his employees during a labor dispute to bring economic pressure in support of his bargaining position. To resolve an asserted conflict among the circuits upon this important question of federal labor law we granted certiorari, 379 U.S. 814, 85 S.Ct. 69, 13 L.Ed.2d 27.

The American Ship Building Company operates four shipyards on the Great Lakes—at Chicago, at Buffalo, and at Toledo and Lorain, Ohio. The company is primarily engaged in the repairing of ships, a highly seasonal business concentrated in the winter months when the freezing of the Great Lakes renders shipping impossible. What limited business is obtained during the shipping season is frequently such that speed of execution is of the utmost importance to minimize immobilization of the ships.

Since 1952 the employer has engaged in collective bargaining with a group of eight unions. Prior to the negotiations here in question, the employer had contracted with the unions on five occasions, each agreement having been preceded by a strike. The particular chapter of the collective bargaining history with which we are concerned opened shortly before May 1, 1961, when the unions notified the company of their intention to seek modification of the current contract, due to expire on August 1.* * *

[O]n August 9, after extended negotiations, the parties separated without having resolved substantial differences on the central issues dividing them and without having specific plans for further attempts to resolve them—a situation which the trial examiner found was an impasse. Throughout the negotiations, the employer displayed anxiety as to the unions' strike plans, fearing that the unions would call a strike as soon as a ship entered the Chicago yard or delay negotiations into the winter to increase strike leverage. The union negotiator consistently insisted that it was his intention to reach an agreement without calling a strike; however, he did concede incomplete control over the workers—a fact borne out by the occurrence of a wildcat strike in February 1961. Because of the danger of an unauthorized strike and the consistent and deliberate use of strikes in prior negotiations, the employer remained apprehensive of the possibility of a work stoppage.

In light of the failure to reach an agreement and the lack of available work, the employer decided to lay off certain of his workers. On August 11 the employees received a notice which read: 'Because of the labor dispute which has been unresolved since August 1, 1961, you are laid off until further notice.' The Chicago yard was completely shut down and all but two employees laid off at the Toledo yard. A large force was retained at Lorain to complete a major piece of work there and the employees in the Buffalo yard were gradually laid off as miscellaneous tasks were completed. Negotiations were resumed shortly after these layoffs and continued for the following two months until a two-year contract was agreed upon on October 27. The employees were recalled the following day.

Upon claims filed by the unions, the General Counsel of the Board issued a complaint charging the employer with violations of §§ 8(a)(1), (a)(3), and (a) (5). The trial examiner found that although there had been no work in the Chicago yard since July 19, its closing was not due to lack of work. Despite similarly slack seasons in the past, the employer had for 17 years retained a nucleus crew to do maintenance work and remain ready to take such work as might come in. The examiner went on to find that the employer was reasonably apprehensive of a strike at some point. Although the unions had given assurances that there would be no strike, past bargaining history was thought to justify continuing apprehension that the unions would fail to make good their assurances. It was further found that the employer's primary purpose in locking out his employees was to avert peculiarly harmful economic consequences which would be imposed on him and his customers if a strike were called either while a ship was in the yard during the shipping season or later when the yard was fully occupied. * * *

A three-to-two majority of the Board rejected the trial examiner's conclusion that the employer could reasonably anticipate a strike. Finding the unions' assurances sufficient to dispel any such apprehension, the Board was able to find only one purpose underlying the layoff: a desire to bring economic pressure to secure prompt settlement of the dispute on favorable terms. The Board did not question the examiner's finding that the layoffs had not occurred until after a bargaining impasse had been reached. Nor did the Board remotely suggest that the company's decision to lay off its employees was based either on union hostility or on a desire to avoid its bargaining obligations under the Act. The Board concluded that the employer 'by curtailing its operations at the South Chicago yard with the consequent layoff of the employees, coerced employees in the exercise of their bargaining rights in violation of Section 8(a)(1) of the Act, and discriminated against its employees within the meaning of Section 8(a)(3) of the Act.'

The difference between the Board and the trial examiner is thus a narrow one turning on their differing assessments of the circumstances which the employer claims gave it reason to anticipate a strike. Both the Board and the examiner assumed, within the established pattern of Board analysis, that if the employer had shut down its yard and laid off its workers solely for the purpose of bringing to bear economic pressure to break an impasse and secure more favorable contract terms, an unfair labor practice would be made out. 'The Board has held that, absent special circumstances, an employer may not during bargaining negotiations either threaten to lock out or lock out his employees in aid of his bargaining position. Such conduct the Board has held presumptively infringes upon the collective-bargaining rights of employees in violation of Section 8(a)(1) and the lockout, with its consequent layoff, amounts to discrimination within the meaning of Section 8(a)(3). In addition, the Board has held that such conduct subjects the Union and the employees it represents to unwarranted and illegal pressure and creates an atmosphere in which the free opportunity for negotiation contemplated by Section 8(a)(5) does not exist.' *Quaker State Oil Refining Corp.,* 121 N.L.R.B. 334, 337.

The Board has, however, exempted certain classes of lockouts from proscription. 'Accordingly, it has held that lockouts are permissible to safeguard against * * * loss where there is reasonable ground for believing that a strike was threatened or imminent.' Ibid. Developing this distinction in its rulings, the Board has approved lockouts designed to prevent seizure of a plant by a sitdown strike, to forestall repetitive disruptions of an integrated operation by 'quickie' strikes, to avoid spoilage of materials which would result from a sudden work stoppage, and to avert the immobilization of automobiles brought in for repair. In another distinct class of cases the Board has sanctioned the use of the lockout by a multiemployer bargaining unit as a response to a whipsaw strike against one of its members.

In analyzing the status of the bargaining lockout under §§ 8(a)(1) and (3) of the National Labor Relations Act, it is important that the practice with which we are here concerned be distinguished from other forms of temporary separation from employment. No one would deny that an employer is free to shut down his enterprise temporarily for reasons of renovation or lack of profitable work unrelated to his collective bargaining situation. Similarly, we put to one side cases where the Board has concluded on the basis of substantial evidence that the employer has used a lockout as a means to injure a labor organization or to evade his duty to bargain collectively. [sic What we are here concerned with is the use of a temporary layoff of employees solely as a means to bring economic pressure to bear in support of the employer's bargaining position, after an impasse has been reached. This is the only issue before us, and all that we decide.[8]

To establish that this practice is a violation of § 8(a)(1), it must be shown that the employer has interfered with, restrained, or coerced employees in the exercise of some right protected by § 7 of the Act. The Board's position is premised on the view that the lockout interferes with two of the rights guaranteed by § 7: the right to bargain collectively and the right to strike. In the Board's view, the use of the lockout 'punishes' employees for the presentation of and adherence to demands made by

8. Contrary to the views expressed in a concurring opinion filed in this case, we intimate no view whatever as to the consequences which would follow had the employer replaced its employees with permanent replacements or even temporary help. Cf. *National Labor Relations Board v. Mackay Radio & Telegraph Co.,* 304 U.S. 333, 58 S.Ct. 904, 82 L.Ed. 1381.

their bargaining representatives and so coerces them in the exercise of their right to bargain collectively. It is important to note that there is here no allegation that the employer used the lockout in the service of designs inimical to the process of collective bargaining. There was no evidence and no finding that the employer was hostile to its employees' banding together for collective bargaining or that the lockout was designed to discipline them for doing so. It is therefore inaccurate to say that the employer's intention was to destroy of frustrate the process of collective bargaining. What can be said is that it intended to resist the demands made of it in the negotiations and to secure modification of these demands. We cannot see that this intention is in any way inconsistent with the employees' rights to bargain collectively.

Moreover, there is no indication, either as a general matter or in this specific case, that the lockout will necessarily destroy the unions' capacity for effective and responsible representation. The unions here involved have vigorously represented the employees since 1952, and there is nothing to show that their ability to do so has been impaired by the lockout. Nor is the lockout one of those acts which are demonstrably so destructive of collective bargaining that the Board need not inquire into employer motivation, as might be the case, for example, if an employer permanently discharged his unionized staff and replaced them with employees known to be possessed of a violent antiunion animus. Cf. *National Labor Relations Board v. Erie Resistor Corp.*, 373 U.S. 221, 83 S.Ct. 1139, 10 L.Ed.2d 308. The lockout may well dissuade employees from adhering to the position which they initially adopted in the bargaining, but the right to bargain collectively does not entail any 'right' to insist on one's position free from economic disadvantage. Proper analysis of the problem demands that the simple intention to support the employer's bargaining position as to compensation and the like be distinguished from a hostility to the process of collective bargaining which could suffice to render a lockout unlawful.

The Board has taken the complementary view that the lockout interferes with the right to strike protected under §§ 7 and 13 of the Act in that it allows the employer to pre-empt the possibility of a strike and thus leave the union with 'nothing to strike against.' Insofar as this means that once employees are locked out, they are deprived of their right to call a strike against the employer because he is already shut down, the argument is wholly specious, for the work stoppage which would have been the object of the strike has in fact occurred. It is true that recognition of the lockout deprives the union of exclusive control of the timing and duration of work stoppages calculated to influence the result of collective bargaining negotiations, but there is nothing in the statute which would imply that the right to strike 'carries with it' the right exclusively to determine the timing and duration of all work stoppages. The right to strike as commonly understood is the right to cease work—nothing more. No doubt a union's bargaining power would be enhanced if it possessed not only the simple right to strike but also the power exclusively to determine when work stoppages should occur, but the Act's provisions are not indefinitely elastic, content-free forms to be shaped in whatever manner the Board might think best conforms to the proper balance of bargaining power.

Thus, we cannot see that the employer's use of a lockout solely in support of a legitimate bargaining position is in any way inconsistent with the right to bargain collectively or with the right to strike. Accordingly, we conclude that on the basis of the findings made by the Board in this case, there has been no violation of § 8(a)(1).

Section 8(a)(3) prohibits discrimination in regard to tenure or other conditions of employment to discourage union membership. Under the words of the statute there must be both discrimination and a resulting discouragement of union membership. It has long been established that a finding of violation under this section will normally turn on the employer's motivation. Thus when the employer discharges a union leader who has broken shop rules, the problem posed is to determine whether the employer has acted purely in disinterested defense of shop discipline or has sought to damage employee organization. It is likely that the discharge will naturally tend to discourage union membership in both cases, because of the loss of union leadership and the employees' suspicion of the employer's true intention. But we have consistently construed the section to leave unscathed a wide range of employer actions taken to serve legitimate business interests in some significant fashion, even though the act committed may tend to discourage union membership. See, e.g., National Labor Relations Board v. Mackay Radio & Telegraph Co., 304 U.S. 333, 347, 58 S.Ct. 904, 911, 82 L.Ed. 1381. Such a construction of § 8(a)(3) is essential if due protection is to be accorded the employer's right to manage his enterprise. See Textile Workers' Union v. Darlington Mfg. Co., 380 U.S. 263, 85 S.Ct. 994.

This is not to deny that there are some practices which are inherently so prejudicial to union interests and so devoid of significant economic justification that no specific evidence of intent to discourage union membership or other antiunion animus is required. In some cases, it may be that the employer's conduct carries with it an inference of unlawful intention so compelling that it is justifiable to disbelieve the employer's protestations of innocent purpose. Radio Officers' Union v. National Labor Relations Board, supra, 347 U.S. at 44–45, 74 S.Ct. at 337–338; National Labor Relations Board v. Erie Resistor Corp., supra. Thus where many have broken a shop rule, but only union leaders have been discharged, the Board need not listen too long to the plea that shop discipline was simply being enforced. In other situations, we have described the process as the 'far more delicate task * * * of weighing the interests of employees in concerted activity against the interest of the employer in operating his business in a particular manner * * *.' *National Labor Relations Board v. Erie Resistor Corp., supra,* 373 U.S. at 229, 83 S.Ct. at 1145.

But this lockout does not fall into that category of cases arising under § 8(a)(3) in which the Board may truncate its inquiry into employer motivation. As this case well shows, use of the lockout does not carry with it any necessary implication that the employer acted to discourage union membership or otherwise discriminate against union members as such. The purpose and effect of the lockout were only to bring pressure upon the union to modify its demands. Similarly, it does not appear that the natural tendency of the lockout is severely to discourage union membership while serving no significant employer interest. In fact, it is difficult to understand what tendency to discourage union membership or otherwise discriminate against union members was perceived by the Board. There is no claim that the employer locked out only union members, or locked out any employee simply because he was a union member; nor is it alleged that the employer conditioned rehiring upon resignation from the union. It is true that the employees suffered economic disadvantage because of their union's insistence on demands unacceptable to the employer, but this is also true of many steps which an employer may take during a bargaining conflict, and the existence of an arguable possibility that someone may feel himself discouraged in his union membership or discriminated against by reason of that membership cannot suffice to label them violations of § 8(a)(3) absent some unlawful intention. The employer's permanent replacement of strikers *(National Labor Relations Board v. Mackay Radio & Telegraph Co., supra)*, his unilateral imposition of terms *(National Labor Relations Board v. Tex–Tan, Inc.,* 5 Cir., 318 F.2d 472, 479–482), or his simple refusal to make a concession which would terminate a strike—all impose economic disadvantage during a bargaining conflict, but none is necessarily a violation of § 8(a)(3).

To find a violation of § 8(a)(3), then, the Board must find that the employer acted for a proscribed purpose. Indeed, the Board itself has always recognized that certain 'operative' or 'economic' purposes would justify a lockout. But the Board has erred in ruling that only these purposes will remove a lockout from the ambit of § 8(a)(3), for that section requires an intention to discourage union membership or otherwise discriminate against the union. There was not the slightest evidence and there was no finding that the employer was actuated by a desire to discourage membership in the union as distinguished from a desire to affect the outcome of the particular negotiations in which it was involved. * * * However, there is nothing in the Act which gives employees the right to insist on their contract demands, free from the sort of economic disadvantage which frequently attends bargaining disputes. Therefore, we conclude that where the intention proven is merely to bring about a settlement of a labor dispute on favorable terms, no violation of § 8(a)(3) is shown.* * *

Although neither § 8(a)(1) nor § 8(a)(3) refers specifically to the lockout, various other provisions of the National Labor Relations Act do refer to the lockout, and these references can be interpreted as a recognition of the legitimacy of the device as a means of applying economic pressure in support of bargaining positions. Thus 29 U.S.C. § 158(d)(4) (1958 ed.) prohibits the use of a strike or lockout unless requisite notice procedures have been complied with; 29 U.S.C. § 173(c) (1958 ed.) directs the Federal Mediation and Conciliation Service to seek voluntary resolution of labor disputes without resort to strikes or lockouts; and 29 U.S.C. §§ 176, 178 (1958 ed.) authorize procedures whereby the President can institute a board of inquiry to forestall certain strikes or lockouts. The correlative use of the terms 'strike' and 'lockout' in these sections contemplates that lockouts will be used in the bargaining process in some fashion. This is not to say that these provisions serve to define the permissible scope of a lockout by an employer. That, in the context of the present case, is a question ultimately to be resolved by analysis of §§ 8(a)(1) and (3).

The Board has justified its ruling in this case and its general approach to the legality of lockouts on the basis of its special competence to weigh the competing interests of employers and employees and to accommodate these interests according to its expert judgment. 'The Board has reasonably concluded that the availability of such a weapon would so substantially tip the scales in the employer's favor as to defeat the Congressional purpose of placing employees on a par with their adversary at the bargaining table.' To buttress its decision as to the balance struck in this particular case, the Board points out that the employer has been given other weapons to counterbalance the employees' power of strike. The employer may permanently replace workers who have gone out on strike, or, by stockpiling and subcontracting, maintain his commercial operations while the strikers bear the economic brunt of the work stoppage. Similarly, the employer can institute unilaterally the working conditions which he desires once his contract with the union has expired. Given these economic weapons, it is argued, the employer has been adequately equipped with tools of economic self-help.

There is of course no question that the Board is entitled to the greatest deference in recognition of its special competence in dealing with labor problems. In many areas its evaluation of the competing interests of employer and employee should unquestionably be given conclusive effect in determining the application of §§ 8(a)(1), (3), and (5). However, we think that the Board construes its functions too expansively when it claims general authority to define national labor policy by balancing the competing interests of labor and management.

While a primary purpose of the National Labor Relations Act was to redress the perceived imbalance of economic power between labor and management, it sought to accomplish that result by conferring certain affirmative rights on employees and by placing certain enumerated restrictions on the activities of employers. The Act prohibited acts which interfered with, restrained, or coerced employees in the exercise of their rights to organize a union, to bargain collectively, and to strike; it proscribed discrimination in regard to tenure and other conditions of employment to discourage membership in any labor organization. The central purpose of these provisions was to protect employee self-organization and the process of collective bargaining from disruptive interferences by employers. Having protected employee organization in countervailance to the employers' bargaining power, and having established a system of collective bargaining whereby the newly coequal adversaries might resolve their disputes, the Act also contemplated resort to economic weapons should more peaceful measures not avail. Sections 8(a)(1) and (3) do not give the Board a general authority to assess the relative economic power of the adversaries in the bargaining process and to deny weapons to one party or the other because of its assessment of that party's bargaining power. *National Labor Relations Board v. Brown,* 380 U.S. 278, 85 S.Ct. 980. In this case the Board has, in essence, denied the use of the bargaining lockout to the employer because of its conviction that use of this device would give the employer 'too much power.' In so doing, the Board has stretched §§ 8(a)(1) and (3) far beyond their functions of protecting the rights of employee organization and collective bargaining. What we have recently said in a closely related context is equally applicable here:

> '(W)hen the Board moves in this area * * * it is functioning as an arbiter of the sort of economic weapons the parties can use in seeking to gain acceptance of their bargaining demands. It has sought to introduce some standard of properly 'balanced' bargaining power, or some new distinction of justifiable and unjustifiable, proper and 'abusive' economic weapons into * * * the Act. * * * We have expressed our belief that this amounts to the Board's entrance into the substantive aspects of the bargaining process to an extent Congress has not countenanced.' *National Labor Relations Board v. Insurance Agents' International Union,* 361 U.S. 477, 497–498, 80 S.Ct. 419, 431.

We are unable to find that any fair construction of the provisions relied on by the Board in this case can support its finding of an unfair labor practice. Indeed, the role assumed by the Board in this area is fundamentally inconsistent with the structure of the Act and the function of the sections relied upon. The deference owed to an expert tribunal cannot be allowed to slip into a judicial inertia which results in the unauthorized assumption by an agency of major policy decisions properly made by Congress. Accordingly, we hold that an employer violates neither § 8(a)(1) nor § 8(a)(3) when, after a bargaining impasse has been reached, he temporarily shuts down his plant and lays off his employees for the sole purpose of bringing economic pressure to bear in support of his legitimate bargaining position.

Reversed.

[The concurring opinions are omitted.]

TO THE CYNICS AMONG US

Insurance Agents tells us that whatever we may think of the tactics of the insurance agents—reporting late, working to rule and all that—these tactics have no bearing in assessing the union's behavior at the bargaining table. "Here are the parties," says the legislative history, and we don't inquire much about what goes on behind closed doors.

Is this a great victory for unions? Would it have mattered very much if the union's tactics were found to be evidence of bad faith bargaining?

Isn't the real worry for unions not whether tactics like those used in *Insurance Agents* would be condemned under Section 8(b)(3), but whether the employees' conduct is protected under the Act? The union might consider a whole arsenal of weapons other than a strike, all of which may involve lesser risks to its members. For example, it might engage in a slowdown, a "work to rule," frequent trips to the restrooms, or intermittent work stoppages. A union can be confident only that the pure strike will be considered protected activity under the Act. The striker cannot be discharged or disciplined for engaging in the strike, although we know that the replacement route under *Mackay* may amount to the same thing.

Compare the treatment of the economic weapon used in *Local 1229* (the "Jefferson Standard" case). The "disloyal" activities of the WBT technicians were held to be "indefensible," and, therefore, not entitled to the protection of the Act. Specifically, the Court held their discharges were "for cause" under Section 10(c), adding that their "tactics were hardly less indefensible than physical sabotage."

If you take *Local 1229* to set physical sabotage as the worst case of indefensible conduct, how do you decide where other kinds of worker action fit on the scale? Is the worker at risk any time he engages in economic activity other than the pure strike? The cases indicate this may be so.

For example, employees who engage in a violent sit-down strike in protest of their employer's unfair labor practices are not protected by the Act, NLRB v. Fansteel Metallurgical Corp., 306 U.S. 240, 59 S.Ct. 490, 83 L.Ed. 627 (1939). On the other hand a peaceful sit-down strike that ended at the request of the police was protected although the activity violated state law, NLRB v. Pepsi–Cola Bottling Co. of Miami, 449 F.2d 824 (5th Cir.1971), cert. denied 407 U.S. 910, 92 S.Ct. 2434, 32 L.Ed.2d 683 (1972). Employees who violate the federal mutiny laws by striking are not protected, Southern S.S. Co. v. NLRB, 316 U.S. 31, 62 S.Ct. 886, 86 L.Ed. 1246 (1942). Nor, as we have seen, are employees who engage in unfair labor practices, National Packing Co. v. NLRB, 377 F.2d 800 (10th Cir.1967). Employees who engage in activities to force the employer to violate the NLRA or another law are also unprotected, Hoover Co. v. NLRB, 191 F.2d 380 (6th Cir.1951); American News Co., 55 NLRB 1302 (1944).

What is the justification for depriving employees of the protection of the Act when they use these tactics? Presumably they resort to them because they are more effective than the strike and entail less cost to the worker (except for the risk of discharge). Do you think it wise for courts, without more detailed guidance from Congress, to draw these lines? Consider the dissent in *Local 1229*.

5. UNION CONTROL OVER AND PERSUASION OF THOSE WHO DO NOT HONOR ITS ECONOMIC ACTIVITIES

In the past unions had success with the strike and the picket line because workers respected them. Members of the union that called the strike and strangers to the dispute understood that the union was making an appeal, and most honored the strike and picket line and refused to take jobs with the struck company. But as the economy has weakened and the lessons of history have been forgotten, workers appear to be much more willing to cross picket lines and take the place of strikers. In contemporary history the change may show up most dramatically in the use of replacements for football and baseball players in recent strikes in both those national pasttimes, and in President Ronald Reagan's firing of air traffic controllers who slowed down their activities. The following two cases, both heavily edited, show how unions attempt to control such behavior and the more restrictive approach of the law to their efforts.

CLEAR PINE MOULDINGS, INC.

Decision of the National Labor Relations Board, 1984.
268 NLRB 1044, 115 LRRM 1113, 1984 WL 36067, affirmed sub nom. Clear
Pine Mouldings, Inc. v. NLRB, 765 F.2d 148 (9th Cir.1985), cert.
denied 474 U.S. 1105, 106 S.Ct. 893, 88 L.Ed.2d 926 (1986).

DOTSON, CHAIRMAN; ZIMMERMAN, HUNTER, and DENNIS, MEMBERS.

The present proceeding is concerned with issues of reinstatement and backpay calculation under the terms of the Board's Decision and Order reported at 238 NLRB 69 (1978), enfd. 632 F.2d 721 (9th Cir. 1980). We agree with the judge's determination as to the amount of backpay due to all claimants except Rodney Sittser and Robert Anderson, who shall be denied reinstatement and backpay. * * * Contrary to the judge, we conclude that Sittser and Anderson engaged in conduct justifying the Respondent's refusal to reinstate them. * * *

THE FACTS

Testimony revealed that Rodney Sittser physically threatened one employee who showed reluctance to join the strike and that Sittser made several threatening phone calls to the same employee. Additionally, a witness testified that Sittser made a phone call to the Union Business Agent suggesting that physical force be used against certain union members who were reluctant to strike. Finally, Sittser threatened a female employee who had resigned from the Union at the start of the strike by telling her that she was "taking her life in her hands by crossing the picket line and would live to regret it." * * *

Several employees testified that Robert Anderson was seen using physical force against nonstriking employees. Anderson was seen using a two-foot-long club to beat on two separate trucks and a car of nonstriking employees and, later, to chase after an employee on a motorcycle. Anderson also said "I am going to kill you." * * *

The Administrative Law Judge found that Sittser's and Anderson's misconduct were not sufficiently serious to disqualify the two strikers from reinstatement. * * *

ANALYSIS

Section 7 of the Act gives employees the right to peacefully strike, picket, and engage in other concerted activities for the purpose of collective bargaining or other mutual aid or protection. Section 7 also grants employees the equivalent right to "refrain from" these activities.

Previously, the Board has held that "not every impropriety committed in the course of a strike deprives an employee of the protective mantle of the Act" and that "minor acts of misconduct must have been in the contemplation of Congress when it provided for the right to strike...." However, the Board has also acknowledged that "serious acts of misconduct which occur in the course of a strike may disqualify a striker from the protection of the Act."

The difficulty lies in deciding whether particular strike misconduct results in the loss of statutory protection the employees otherwise would have. In the past, the Board has held that verbal threats by strikers, "not accompanied by any physical acts or gestures that would provide added emphasis or meaning to [the] words," do not constitute serious strike misconduct warranting an employer's refusal to reinstate the strikers. On the other hand, the Board has held that verbal threats which are accompanied by physical movements or contacts, such as hitting cars, do constitute serious strike misconduct. The Board summarized its standard for finding strike misconduct based on verbal threats in Coronet Casuals [207 NLRB 304, 84 LRRM 304, 1973 WL 4603 (1973)], where it stated that "absent violence ... a picket is not disqualified from reinstatement despite ... making abusive threats against nonstrikers...."

We disagree with this standard because actions such as the making of abusive threats against nonstriking employees equate to "restraint and coercion" prohibited elsewhere in the Act and are not privileged by Section 8(c) of the Act. Although we agree that the presence of physical gestures accompanying a verbal threat may increase the gravity of verbal conduct, we reject the per se rule that words alone can never warrant a denial of reinstatement in the absence of physical acts. Rather, we agree with the United States Court of Appeals for the First Circuit that "[a] serious threat may draw its credibility from the surrounding circumstances and not from the physical gestures of the speaker." We also agree with the United States Court of Appeals for the Third Circuit that an employer need not "countenance conduct that amounts to intimidation and threats of bodily harm." In McQuaide [NLRB v. W.C. McQuaide, Inc., 552 F.2d 519 (3d Cir.1977)], the Third Circuit applied the following objective test for determining whether verbal threats by strikers directed at fellow employees justify an employer's refusal to reinstate: " 'whether the misconduct is such that, under the circumstances existing, it may reasonably tend to coerce or intimidate employees in the exercise of rights protected under the Act.' " We believe this is the correct standard and we adopt it.

The legislative history of the Labor Management Relations Act supports the adoption of such a standard. Although the Act specifically recognizes the right to strike, and although any strike which involves picketing may have a coercive aspect, it is clear that Congress never intended to afford special protection to all picket line conduct, whatever the circumstances. The legislative history of the Labor Management Relations Act clearly indicates that Congress intended to impose limits on the types of employee strike conduct that would be considered protected. The right to strike embodied in Section 13 of the Act was modified with the passage of the Taft–Hartley Act in 1947. The amendments to Section 13 included a provision that nothing in the Act shall be construed "to affect the limitations [or] qualifications on" the right to strike. The legislative history of this amendment indicates that it was designed, inter alia, to incorporate into the Act the restrictions on the scope of protected strike activities found by the Supreme Court in Fansteel Metallurgical Corp. v. NLRB. In Fansteel, although the specific type of striker misconduct was different from that presented in the instant case, the reasoning of the Court is nevertheless applicable here. There, striking employees had seized their employer's plant. The Court held:

> The seizure and holding of the building was itself a wrong apart from any acts of sabotage. But in its legal aspect the ousting of the owner from lawful possession is not essentially different from an assault upon the officers of an employing company . . . or other unlawful acts in order to force compliance with demands. To justify such conduct because of the existence of a labor dispute or of an unfair labor practice would be to put a premium on resort to force instead of legal remedies and to subvert the principles of law and order which lie at the foundations of society.

Interpreting Section 13 (even before modification of that section by Taft–Hartley), the Court held that "this recognition of 'the right to strike' plainly contemplates a lawful strike, the exercise of the unquestioned right to quit work." The Court went on to state:

> There is not a line in the statute to warrant the conclusion that it is any part of the policies of the Act to encourage employees to resort to force and violence in defiance of the law of the land. On the contrary, the purpose of the Act is to promote peaceful settlements of disputes by providing legal remedies for the invasion of the employees' rights.

There is also evidence in the legislative history of the Taft–Hartley Act that Congress was acutely aware of, and concerned with curbing, picket line violence in general.

We believe it is appropriate, at this point, to state our view that the existence of a "strike" in which some employees elect to voluntarily withhold their services does not in any way privilege those employees to engage in other than peaceful picketing and persuasion. They have no right, for example, to threaten those employees who, for whatever reason, have decided to work during the strike, to block access to the employer's premises, and certainly no right to carry or use weapons or other objects of intimidation. As we view the statute, the only activity the statute privileges in this context, other than peaceful patrolling, is the nonthreatening expression of opinion, verbally or through signs and pamphleteering, similar to that found in Section 8(c). * * *

PATTERN MAKERS' LEAGUE OF NORTH AMERICA, AFL–CIO v. NLRB

Supreme Court of the United States, 1985.
473 U.S. 95, 105 S.Ct. 3064, 87 L.Ed.2d 68.

JUSTICE POWELL delivered the opinion of the Court.

The Pattern Makers' League of North America, AFL–CIO (the League), a labor union, provides in its constitution that resignations are not permitted during a strike or when a strike is imminent. The League fined 10 of its members who, in violation of this provision, resigned during a strike and returned to work. The National Labor Relations Board held that these fines were imposed in violation of § 8(b)(1)(A) of the National Labor Relations Act, 29 U.S.C. § 158(b)(1)(A). We granted a petition for a writ of certiorari in order to decide whether § 8(b)(1)(A) reasonably may be construed by the Board as prohibiting a union from fining members who have tendered resignations invalid under the union constitution.

I

The League is a national union composed of local associations (locals). In May 1976, its constitution was amended to provide that:

> "No resignation or withdrawal from an Association, or from the League, shall be accepted during a strike or lockout, or at a time when a strike or lockout appears imminent."

This amendment, known as League Law 13, became effective in October 1976, after being ratified by the League's locals. On May 5, 1977, when a collective-bargaining agreement expired, two locals began an economic strike against several manufacturing companies in Rockford, Illinois and Beloit, Wisconsin. Forty-three of the two locals' members participated. In early September 1977, after the locals formally rejected a contract offer, a striking union member submitted a letter of resignation to the Beloit association. He returned to work the following day. During the next three months, 10 more union members resigned from the Rockford and Beloit locals and returned to work. On December 19, 1977, the strike ended when the parties signed a new collective-bargaining agreement. The locals notified 10 employees who had resigned that their resignations had been rejected as violative of League Law 13. The locals further informed the employees that, as union members, they were subject to sanctions for returning to work. Each was fined approximately the equivalent of his earnings during the strike.

II

A

Section 7 of the Act, 29 U.S.C. § 157, grants employees the right to "refrain from any or all [concerted] ... activities...." This general right is implemented by § 8(b)(1)(A). The latter section provides that a union commits an unfair labor practice if it "restrain[s] or coerce[s] employees in the exercise" of their § 7 rights. When employee members of a union refuse to support a strike (whether or not a rule prohibits returning to work during a strike), they are refraining from "concerted activity." Therefore, imposing fines on these employees for returning to work "restrain[s]" the exercise of their § 7 rights. Indeed, if the terms "refrain" and "restrain or coerce" are interpreted literally, fining employees to enforce compliance with any union rule or policy would violate the Act.

Despite this language from the Act, the Court in NLRB v. Allis–Chalmers, 388 U.S. 175, 87 S.Ct. 2001, 18 L.Ed.2d 1123 (1967), held that § 8(b)(1)(A) does not prohibit labor organizations from fining current members. In NLRB v. Textile Workers 409 U.S. 213, 93 S.Ct. 385, 34 L.Ed.2d 422 (1972), and Machinists & Aerospace Workers v. NLRB, 412 U.S. 84, 93 S.Ct. 1961, 36 L.Ed.2d 764 (1973) (per curiam), the Court found as a corollary that unions may not fine former members who have resigned lawfully. Neither Textile Workers, supra, nor Machinists, supra, however, involved a provision like League Law 13, restricting the members' right to resign. We decide today whether a union is precluded from fining employees who have attempted to resign when resignations are prohibited by the union's constitution.

B

The Court's reasoning in Allis–Chalmers, supra, supports the Board's conclusion that petitioners in this case violated § 8(b)(1)(A). In Allis–Chalmers, the Court held that imposing court-enforceable fines against current union members does not "restrain or coerce" the workers in the exercise of their § 7 rights. In so concluding, the Court relied on the legislative history of the Taft–Hartley Act. It noted that the sponsor of § 8(b)(1)(A) never intended for that provision " 'to interfere with the internal affairs or organization of unions,' " and that other proponents of the measure likewise disclaimed an intent to interfere with unions'"internal affairs." From the legislative history, the Court reasoned that Congress did not intend to prohibit unions from fining present members, as this was an internal matter. The Court has emphasized that the crux of Allis–Chalmers' holding was the distinction between "internal and external enforcement of union rules...."

The Congressional purpose to preserve unions' control over their own "internal affairs" does not suggest an intent to authorize restrictions on the right to resign. Traditionally, union members were free to resign and escape union discipline. In 1947, union constitutional provisions restricting the right to resign were uncommon, if not unknown. Therefore, allowing unions to "extend an employee's membership obligation through restrictions on resignation" would "expan[d] the definition of internal action" beyond the contours envisioned by the Taft–Hartley Congress.

C

Language and reasoning from other opinions of this Court confirm that the Board's construction of § 8(b)(1)(A) is reasonable. In Scofield v. NLRB, 394 U.S. 423, 89 S.Ct. 1154, 22 L.Ed.2d 385 (1969), the Court upheld a union rule setting a ceiling on the daily wages that members working on an incentive basis could earn. The union members' freedom to resign was critical to the Court's decision that the union rule did not "restrain or coerce" the employees within the meaning of § 8(b)(1)(A). It stated that the rule was "reasonably enforced against union members who [were] free to leave the union and escape the rule." The Court deemed it important that if members were unable to take full advantage of their contractual right to earn additional pay, it was because they had "chosen to become *and remain* union members." (Emphasis added).

The decision in NLRB v. Textile Workers, 409 U.S. 213, 93 S.Ct. 385, 34 L.Ed.2d 422 (1972), also supports the Board's view that § 8(b)(1)(A) prohibits unions from punishing members not free to resign. There, 31 employees resigned their union membership and resumed working during a strike. We held that fining these former members "restrained or coerced" them, within the meaning of § 8(b)(1)(A). In reaching this conclusion, we said that "the vitality of § 7 requires that the member be free to refrain in November from the actions he endorsed in May." Restrictions on the right to resign curtail the freedom that the Textile Workers Court deemed so important. See also Machinists, supra.

III

Section 8(b)(1)(A) allows unions to enforce only those rules that "impai[r] no policy Congress has imbedded in the labor laws...." The Board has found union restrictions on the right to resign to be inconsistent with the policy of voluntary unionism implicit in § 8(a)(3). We believe that the inconsistency between union restrictions on the right to resign and the policy of voluntary unionism supports the Board's conclusion that League Law 13 is invalid.

Closed shop agreements, legalized by the Wagner Act in 1935, became quite common in the early 1940's. Under these agreements, employers could hire and retain in their employ only union members in good standing. Full union membership was thus compulsory in a closed shop; in order to keep their jobs, employees were required to attend union meetings, support union leaders, and otherwise adhere to union rules. Because of mounting objections to the closed shop, in 1947, after hearings and full consideration, Congress enacted the Taft–Hartley Act. Section 8(a)(3) of that Act effectively eliminated compulsory union membership by outlawing the closed shop. The union security agreements permitted by § 8(a)(3) require employees to pay dues, but an employee cannot be discharged for failing to abide by union rules or policies with which he disagrees.[16]

Full union membership thus no longer can be a requirement of employment. If a new employee refuses formally to join a union and subject himself to its discipline, he cannot be fired. Moreover, no employee can be discharged if he initially joins a union, and subsequently resigns. We think it noteworthy that § 8(a)(3) protects the employment rights of the dissatisfied member, as well as those of the worker who never assumed full union membership. By allowing employees to resign from a union at any time, § 8(a)(3) protects the employee whose views come to diverge from those of his union.

League Law 13 curtails this freedom to resign from full union membership. Nevertheless, the petitioners contend that League Law 13 does not contravene the policy of voluntary unionism imbedded in the Act. They assert that this provision does not interfere with workers' employment rights because offending members are not discharged, but only fined. We find this argument unpersuasive, for a union has not left a "worker's employment rights inviolate when it exacts [his entire] paycheck in satisfaction of a fine imposed for working." Wellington, Union Fines and Workers' Rights, 85 Yale L.J. 1022, 1023 (1976). Congress in 1947 sought to eliminate completely any requirement that the employee maintain full union membership. Therefore, the Board was justified in concluding that by restricting the right of employees to resign, League Law 13 impairs the policy of voluntary unionism.

IV

[The League made several other arguments under the language and legislative history of the Act].

---

16. Under § 8(a)(3), the only aspect of union membership that can be required pursuant to a union shop agreement is the payment of dues. See Radio Officers v. NLRB, 347 U.S. 17, 41, 74 S.Ct. 323, 336, 98 L.Ed. 455 (1954) (union security agreements cannot be used for "any purpose other than to compel payment of union dues and fees"). " 'Membership,' as a condition of employment, is whittled down to its financial core." NLRB v. General Motors Corp., 373 U.S. 734, 742, 83 S.Ct. 1453, 1459, 10 L.Ed.2d 670 (1963). See also Ellis v. Railway Clerks, 466 U.S. 435, 104 S.Ct. 1883, 80 L.Ed.2d 428 (1984) (under the Railway Labor Act, employees in a "union shop" cannot be compelled to pay dues to support certain union activities). Therefore, an employee required by a union security agreement to assume financial "membership" is not subject to union discipline. Such an employee is a "member" of the union only in the most limited sense.

VI

The Board found that by fining employees who had tendered resignations, the petitioners violated § 8(b)(1)(A) of the Act, even though League Law 13 purported to render the resignations ineffective. We defer to the Board's interpretation of the Act and so affirm the judgment of the Court of Appeals enforcing the Board's order.

[JUSTICE WHITE concurred. JUSTICES BLACKMUN, BRENNAN and MARSHALL dissented in an opinion by JUSTICE BLACKMUN. A brief excerpt from that opinion follows. JUSTICE STEVENS dissented separately.]

"[T]he principle of fidelity to one's word is an ancient one." C. Fried, Contract As Promise 2 (1991). The assumption that one's freedom has been limited by being held to one's freely made bargain is as misguided in the context of the labor law as when stated as a general principle. By focusing exclusively on the right to refrain from collective action, by assuming an arid and artificial conception of the proviso circumscribing that right, and by ignoring Congress' intentions in promulgating the NLRA in the first instance, the Board and the Court abandon their proper role as mediators between any conflicting interests protected by the labor laws. In the name of protecting individual workers' rights to violate their contractual agreements, the Court debilitates the right of all workers to take effective collective action. The conclusion that freedom under the NLRA means freedom to break a freely made promise to one's fellow workers after they have relied on that promise to their detriment is not only a notion at odds with the structure and purpose of our labor law, but is an affront to the autonomy of the American worker. I dissent.

A COUPLE OF QUESTIONS AND OBSERVATIONS

Clear Pine Mouldings and *Pattern Makers* both make it harder for a union to command solidarity during a strike. Are the decisions correct?

The analysis in *Clear Pine Mouldings* is somewhat easier to follow, and therefore perhaps easier to accept. If you represented the Woodworkers' Union, what would you argue on appeal? How do you overcome the natural aversion to threats of physical harm?

Does the Board's opinion in *Clear Pine Mouldings* adequately appreciate the fragile line between speech and conduct? Try to imagine the kinds of verbal appeals you as a striker might make to a person about to cross your picket line to replace you at work. Undoubtedly you would not go as far as Sittser and Anderson did, but would you inject some hint of menace in your verbal confrontation on the picket line? Wouldn't you want your replacement to feel badly about his decision? Does the Board's opinion place too great a burden on the striker and trench too closely upon the right of free speech protected in section 8(c)?

We suggest an analogy that may help you think about this question. Did you notice the Board's reference in *Clear Pine Mouldings* to picketing, in the discussion of Sittser's and Anderson's conduct? "Although the

Act specifically recognizes the right to strike, and although any strike which involves picketing may have a coercive aspect, it is clear that Congress never intended to afford special protection to all picket line conduct, whatever the circumstances."

Sittser and Anderson were operating on a picket line. Picketing has occupied an uneasy position in the constellation of economic weapons regulated (or not regulated) under the Act. The right to strike is expressly protected in section 13, but the Act doesn't explicitly provide safe harbor for picketing. To the contrary, picketing is singled out for special treatment in other sections of the Act. For example, section 8(b)(4) prohibits certain types of secondary activity—that is, activity directed at an employer not a direct party to the union's labor dispute. But a proviso to that section permits the union to truthfully advise the public, through publicity "other than picketing," that certain products are made by an employer with whom the union has a dispute. And section 8(b)(7), discussed later in this chapter, puts severe limits on a union's right to picket in order to secure recognition.

Why is picketing singled out for more restrictive treatment under both these sections? Picketing would seem to be part of a labor dispute and subject to the protections of section 7 ("to engage in other concerted activities") as well as to strict limits imposed on federal district courts by the Norris–LaGuardia Act, 29 U.S.C. §§ 101–15, when issuing injunctions in labor disputes.

Why, then, is picketing more closely regulated than other forms of communication? The answer seems to be twofold. One reason is that picketing serves as a signal to other workers, usually organized, that they are not to do business with the employer being picketed. The signal apparently short circuits the give-and-take normally incident to free speech. Second, the picket line carries with it the potential for violence.

The latter factor was pivotal in *Vegelahn v. Guntner*, which we read in Chapter I. You will recall that Justice Allen concluded in issuing an injunction that "the patrol * * * was one means of intimidation. * * * Intimidation is not limited to threats of violence or of physical injury to person or property. It has a broader signification, and there also may be a moral intimidation, which is illegal." To this Justice Holmes replied that any such intimidation would be reached by the injunction he proposed to issue, which would have expressly prohibited physical intimidation. What was objectionable to Justice Holmes was that the decree barred moral intimidation as well, even by peaceful means.

One can say that the difference between the majority and Justice Holmes was an assumption that the patrol necessarily carried a threat of bodily harm. Another way to look at the case, if one accepts Justice Holmes' characterization of the facts, is that the difference between the majority and the dissent has to do with whether the objectives of the picketing, rather than the means used, are acceptable to the court.

Justice Holmes' views on picketing have prevailed today. But do you see a parallel between the close regulation of picketing in cases like

Vegelahn v. Guntner and the tight scrutiny the Board gives to the words used by the strikers in *Clear Pine Mouldings?*

In *Pattern Makers* you see an oft-repeated refrain by the Court: "We're not saying we agree with the Board. We just think it was the Board's decision to make, and as long as its judgment is within its statutory authority, it's not our job to say that a different solution is better." However, we'll also read a number of cases in which the Court says that the Board's judgment is beyond its scope of discretion. You'll have some trouble distinguishing between those cases in which the Court defers to the Board's exercise of discretion and those in which the Court condemns it. You may even come to suspect that the mode of review depends on whether the Court agrees with the outcome of the Board's decision.

Take a closer look at *Pattern Makers*. Note that despite the plain language of section 8(a)(3), which allows a union and an employer to agree to make union membership a condition of employment, that isn't really the case. The most the parties can require of the employee is that she pay the equivalent of her union dues. There may even be a limit to what kinds of activities the union may properly include in assessing fees for non-member representation. That is the subject of Ellis v. Brotherhood of Railway, Airline and S.S. Clerks, 466 U.S. 435, 104 S.Ct. 1883, 80 L.Ed.2d 428 (1984) (Railway Labor Act), cited in note 16 of *Pattern Makers'*, and Communication Workers of America v. Beck, 487 U.S. 735, 108 S.Ct. 2641, 101 L.Ed.2d 634 (1988), which appears earlier in this chapter. Since the worker is not subject to compulsory membership, why shouldn't the Court treat a worker's voluntary decision to join a union as it would any other contract of association? If the employee accepts the union's terms, including a provision that the employee will not resign, why should the law intervene in that arrangement? Does your answer depend on whether the union has advised a prospective member that the NLRA and the contract language, which both say that a person must join the union to keep a job, don't mean what they say?

6. WHAT ABOUT THE ECONOMIC WEAPONS OF NON–UNION WORKERS?

We return to a question raised at the outset of this section. Why is it that we don't read about strike threats and other economic weapons in the non-union worker cooperation settings that opened this chapter? Some may suggest that it is almost an oxymoron to think of economic warfare driving a cooperative system. But in the two union examples of worker cooperation that we have seen, Xerox and Saturn, the strike is certainly part of the picture, if only in the background. Perhaps a system doesn't have to be wholly cooperative or wholly adversary. Xerox and Saturn may demonstrate such a mix, and the non-union situations might too except that the non represented workers can't get it together to make an effective show of force. Do you buy that? Was the reluctance of Nan, our Nurse Practitioner, to join a union because of her antipathy to collective interests? Or was she just fearful of the way group strength may be used and harnessed under the collective system?

In some respects the legal system offers as much protection and no more impediment to the economic activities of the non-union worker. *Washington Aluminum*, which we read in Chapter I, tells us that workers who are not represented enjoy the protection of Section 7 as long as their activity involves their working conditions. Those were the non-union workers, you'll recall, who walked out when their shop was too cold. As long as there is no majority union in the picture, the unrepresented worker doesn't have to deal with the strictures on minority union activity, as in *Emporium Capwell*.

One real deterrent to the unrepresented worker's use of economic weapons is that the Act, in Section 8(b)(7), pushes workers towards the representation and election route if they want to engage in picketing in support of their demands. Consult the text of NLRA 8(b)(7). It says that under certain circumstances a labor organization may not picket an employer where an object is to force the employer to bargain with it. One of those conditions, in part (C), is that a petition for an NLRB election must be filed within 30 days of the picketing. (The other two parts, (A) and (B), would apply equally to a union or non-union group picketing within twelve months of an election or where the employer has recognized another union).

We are not sure, for the precise question has to our knowledge never come up, whether a non-union group seeking to deal with its employer would come under 8(b)(7). We think that its disclaimer of being a labor organization would not speak as loudly as its deeds. And we think the broad definition of "dealing with" in the definition of a union in Section 2(5) could bring the employee group within the ambit of 8(b)(7). On the other hand, if the employee group resorted to a strike without picketing, or took its message to the public through handbills (we'll explore the picketing vs. handbilling distinction in the next section), Section 8(b)(7) would not stand in its way.

SECTION 8(b)(7) DISCUSSION ... AT A CAST PARTY

MAIN CLAUSE: Congress was wise to include Section 8(b)(7) in its 1959 amendments. Before we came along it was possible for a union which did not yet represent a majority of the employees to put economic pressure on the company through picketing. The company, afraid this would mess up deliveries, or at least be bad public relations, would agree to recognize the union, perhaps making sure first that the initial collective bargaining agreement was an easy one to live with. That kind of pressure is bad because it pressures employees to join a union without a chance to exercise their free choice in an election. Until § 8(b)(7) came along, this kind of activity was resolved by tort doctrines, in cases like Vegelahn v. Guntner. Of course, there were First Amendment questions, but the Supreme Court made clear in Teamsters v. Vogt [354 U.S. 284,

77 S.Ct. 1166, 1 L.Ed.2d 1347 (1957)] that overriding state concerns justified limitations on such picketing. Now, of course, § 8(b)(7) occupies the field, and any state efforts at regulation would run up against the preemption doctrine.

PROVIDED FURTHER: It's a good thing that I'm in the statute. I preserve the constitutional rights you would have taken away. All a union has to do is design its picket signs to make clear that the purpose of the picketing is to advise the public that the company is nonunion.

MAIN CLAUSE: That isn't so, Provided Further. As I read our statute you have a very limited role in labor relations. You apply, the words say, when "the purpose" of the picketing is to advise the public. Now most organizational picketing, as I see it, has a dual purpose: maybe to advise the public, but more critically, to force the employer to bargain with the union. So I think your section saves only the activity that has purely a publicity purpose.

PROVIDED FURTHER: You've had too many bloody literalisms at this party. If you think I apply only when the picketing is solely informational, then I'm superfluous.

MAIN CLAUSE: You said it, not I.

PROVIDED FURTHER: No, I'm serious. Picketing that is for the sole purpose of advising the public literally cannot at the same time have a recognitional object. Purely informational picketing, if there is such a thing, does not fit within the main clause of § 8(b)(7). Section 8(b)(7) would not apply at all, and the picketing would not need my protection to be immune from regulation. That is why I say that, unless Congress simply meant to add a few more meaningless words to an already convoluted statute, it must have meant for the "provided further" clause to operate in those situations in which the union seeks recognition, but also desires to advise the public that the company is nonunion. At the very least the consumer ought to have the information that the company has no union, so that he or she can refuse to deal with the company if he or she chooses.

MAIN CLAUSE: You are saying, then, that a union that pickets for recognition, as defined in the main clause of § 8(b)(7), may exempt its activity from regulation merely by giving it an informational aspect. Now that seems dishonest. Isn't it too easy for the union to manufacture a motive to save its picketing?

PROVIDED FURTHER: I assume the union can't make it all up, but must have a bona fide interest in advising the public.

MAIN CLAUSE: With all respect, you dissemble. I don't think unions are at all concerned with the publicity aspect of their picketing. They want to stop deliveries. Now what happens when a union asks its lawyer how to draft its signs to comply with § 8(b)(7)? Do you think the lawyer is going to say, "Now don't you engage in publicity appeals unless you really mean it?" Even if law students are taught that it is unethical to draw up a sign reflecting a phony motive, won't a lawyer feel silly telling this to his client? Won't he be afraid of losing the client?

PROVIDED FURTHER: You are a hard, cynical concatenation of words, but I suppose the triggering paragraph of a section like ours has to be tough, or else violators of the Act would escape our net. Now on the ethical question, let me tell you what the ABA Code of Professional Responsibility says:

"Canon 7

"A lawyer should represent a client zealously within the bounds of the law.

"Disciplinary Rule DR 7–102: (A) In his representation of a client a lawyer shall not:

* * *

"(6) Participate in the creation or preservation of evidence when he knows or it is obvious that the evidence is false."

The Model Rules say (Rule 3.4(b)) that a lawyer shall not "falsify evidence."

I have enjoyed meeting you on the grounds of logic and policy in figuring out how our section treats informational picketing, but the evening wears on, so I give you authority. Have a look at Smitley, d/b/a Crown Cafeteria v. NLRB, 327 F.2d 351 (9th Cir.1964). There you will find the court affirms a Board decision which gives me my due as a proviso. I'd rather recite Yeats at this party, but let me quote you a little Duniway, J., from the Smitley case:

> "Petitioners urge that if the picketing has as 'an object' recognition or organization, then it is still illegal, even though it has 'the purpose' of truthfully advising the public, etc., within the meaning of the second proviso to subparagraph (C). It seems to us, as it did to the Board, that to so construe the statute would make the proviso meaningless. The hard realities of union-employer relations are such that it is difficult, indeed almost impossible, for us to conceive of picketing falling within the terms of the proviso that did not also have as 'an object' obtaining a contract with the employer. This is normally the ultimate objective of any union in relation to an employer who has employees whose jobs fall within the categories of employment that are within the jurisdiction of the union, which is admittedly the situation here."

MAIN CLAUSE: Courts don't help us very much when they cut the heart out of a statute by giving effect to little provisos like you.

UNLESS ... : Watch your tongue, Main Clause. Thanks to "little provisos" like me, even though I don't go under that name, your job is much easier. We "unless" clauses like to hide in the thicket near the end of a statutory clause and turn the whole meaning around. Now look at me. I can undo in a sentence or so all the damage caused by Provided Further. You see, if "such picketing," that is, Provided Further's kind of tactics, has an effect of interfering with the employer's operations, say, by inducing employees not to work or suppliers not to deliver, then § 8(b)(7) is violated in spite of Provided Further.

PROVIDED FURTHER: Yes, you are a pernicious sort. No thanks to you, the statute is a tease. It promises protection of First Amendment rights through my proviso, but renders it an illusion when your clause comes into play.

UNLESS ... : Every student of labor law and constitutional law knows that there is speech and then there is something more than speech. The appeals that you would protect, especially when carried out with pickets, are not just an exchange in the marketplace of ideas. They are signals for action, unthinking action of the sort not encompassed by the rationale of the First Amendment. When I step in, it is only because speech has gone beyond its legitimate boundaries as pure speech.

PROVIDED FURTHER: Would you stop all activity protected under my clause simply because some truck driver working for a solitary supplier happens to respect the appeal?

UNLESS ...: You must think I'm unreasonable. Isolated instances won't trigger application of my clause. See Barker Bros. v. NLRB, 328 F.2d 431 (9th Cir.1964).

MAIN CLAUSE: Then, ladies and gentlemen, can we all agree that Provided Further and Unless give us a tidy accommodation between the kind of speech which appeals to the public and that which goes beyond pure speech and undercuts the lofty purposes of § 8(b)(7)?

ALL: Perhaps.

ATEBESEVENA § (8(b)(7)(A)): Thank goodness my sister Atebesevenbe § (8(b)(7)(B)) and I are pure and simple. We have no provisos, no unlesses, and care not for motives and ethics. We simply say that if a union has been recognized in such a manner that an election would be barred, or if a valid election has been held within the past 12 months, then all picketing is barred under § 8(b)(7). No further questions are asked. In this respect we are closely akin to our cousin Atebeforce § (8(b)(4)(C)), who deals with certified unions and sets up pretty much the same rule.

MAIN CLAUSE: You are too simple and not pure enough. Before we can deal with you we must face a threshold question. For whether we deal with the picketing under parts A, B, or C, it must first be established that the picketing is recognitional picketing and not something else.

ATEBESEVENBE: But everybody knows....

MAIN CLAUSE: No, everybody doesn't know that there is picketing that looks like recognitional picketing but really isn't. Now once upon a time, before we words went into the big statute book, the courts saw a distinction between organizational and recognitional picketing. The former was tolerated by most courts on the ground that it was sort of a prelude to a real push for recognition and didn't entail the dangers of recognitional picketing. Now that is a hard line to draw, and wisely our statute eliminates the distinction. Picketing which has recognition as its goal, whether immediately or ultimately, comes within the proscriptions of our section. Even so, unions have managed to escape our net by disclaiming any interest whatever in recognition, and by contending that they are interested rather in improving area standards or some noble sounding thing like that. It seems to me a big loophole was opened up in the Houston Building Case (Claude Everett), 136 NLRB 321 (1962), where a union was able to get away with using the following picket sign:

> "Houston Building and Construction Trades Council, AFL–CIO, protests substandard wages and conditions being paid on this job by Claude Everett Company. Houston Building and Construction Trades Council does not intend by this picket line to induce or encourage the employees of any other employer to engage in a strike or concerted refusal to work."

PROVIDED FURTHER: But don't you think that Congress was not concerned with such activity when it enacted § 8(b)(7)?

MAIN CLAUSE: Maybe not. But once again I think it is too easy for unions and their lawyers to fabricate a purpose which masks their true intent. Or perhaps the union will try to take advantage of the ill-chosen term "to picket" at the beginning of 8(b)(7) and will use other devices not literally proscribed, like handbilling, to achieve its goal. Fortunately, the Board and courts have treated such activity, where it has a coercive or "signal" effect rather than a persuasive one, as within the proscription of § 8(b)(7).

ATEBESEVENCE § (8(b)(7)(C)): What a dull party. Don't you realize that all the action is under § 8(b)(7)(C)? Most § 8(b)(7) cases don't involve prior recognition, certification, or elections. Rather, they deal with a union which pickets for recognition but fails to petition for an election. I'm not an unreasonable clause, and I effect a nice compromise. I give the unions a little leeway to do their thing, but I draw the line at too much picketing. At that point I insist they go to an election if they want to keep picketing.

PROVIDED: What a mischievous piece of legislation you are! You pronounce to the world that a union may picket for 30 days without filing a petition, but not if 30 days is unreasonably long. Is it 30 days or isn't it? Who is to say what is a reasonable time? How can a lawyer intelligently advise a client how the Board will handle picketing which runs 28 days?

ATEBESEVENCE: Well, we generally give the union 30 days unless the employer is hurting....

UNLESS: ... Ah.

PROVIDED FURTHER: More hypocrisy. We respect free speech until it becomes effective.

ATEBESEVENCE: I was about to say that we curtail the free period where improper means, such as intimidation, are used, or violence results.

PROVIDED: Well, you still give me trouble. I am supposed to set up an expedited election once "such a petition" has been filed. I really don't know what that means. Is "such a petition" one filed within the 30–day reasonable time period, or is it one filed outside it?

ATEBESEVENCE: We'd better go slowly. First of all, nothing happens under § 8(b)(7)(C) unless the employer files a charge. The Board does not police recognitional picketing on its own. This is not such a trivial point, for as a practical matter the employer may be reluctant to file such a charge, as we shall see in a moment.

PROVIDED: All right, but now let's suppose that on the 28th day of picketing the employer files a charge and that under the circumstances picketing for 28 days without filing a petition was not an unreasonable period of time.

ATEBESEVENCE: Now your expedited election machinery goes into effect.

PROVIDED: I have trouble seeing this. The union's conduct is still conduct which does not violate § 8(b)(7) for it has not exceeded the 30–day reasonable time marker.

ATEBESEVENCE: True, the union's conduct doesn't violate § 8(b)(7)(C). But the very next sentence says that when such a petition is filed, that is, one which is filed within the 30–day reasonable time frame, an expedited election shall be held. You see, we don't bar recognitional picketing of reasonable duration. But the price the union must pay for this concession is to move into an expedited election procedure if the employer files a charge.

PROVIDED: I guess I see all that. But where is the petition that triggers the expedited election? Don't you need one to invoke this machinery?

ATEBESEVENCE: Absolutely. But it can be an RM petition filed by the employer. Or the union, upon receipt of the § 8(b)(7) charge, may decide to file a petition within the 30–day reasonable time period.

PROVIDED: Why on earth would it do that?

ATEBESEVENCE: Because if it doesn't, the picketing will go beyond the 30–day reasonable time frame without a petition having been filed, the opportunity for an expedited election will have been lost, and the union will be enjoined from further picketing. In short, if the picketing goes beyond 30 days without a petition being filed, the effect of an § 8(b)(7) charge is to cause the picketing to be enjoined. If, on the other hand, the petition is filed within 30 days, the only effect of the § 8(b)(7) charge is to move the election into the expedited system.

UNLESS . . .: This means that a union can get perhaps 28 days of unlimited economic pressure on the employer, petition on the 29th day, and still be free of § 8(b)(7)'s restraints. This enables it to continue to picket until the election is held. At that point, if the union wins we don't worry about § 8(b)(7). And if the union loses, then the unqualified bar on picketing takes effect under § 8(b)(7)(B). But meanwhile, it seems to me, the union gets an awfully long period in which to picket as though § 8(b)(7) did not exist.

PROVIDED: That troubles me. It also troubles me that any union that is impatient with the timetable of union elections has only to picket for 30 days and file a petition, which would seem to mandate an expedited election. That seems a devious way to force a quick election.

ATEBESEVENCE: Maybe that suggests that the real problem is with our cumbersome election machinery. Perhaps if new labor legislation is enacted, the speed of the election process will do away with much of the need of expedited elections under § 8(b)(7). Anyway, a union can't get an expedited election merely by manipulating the statute that way. The expedited election machinery is triggered by the employer's filing of an § 8(b)(7)(C) charge, together with its RM petition or an RC petition filed by the union. This really leaves the use of the expedited election route up to the employer. If the employer needs the time that it takes to hold an ordinary election to mount an effective campaign against the union, then it will have to think twice about going to an expedited election as the price of containing the union's pressure.

MAIN CLAUSE: What you seem to be saying is that quicker routine election procedures would eliminate the need for the § 8(b)(7) expedited route. What do we lose by the expedited procedure? Does the Board ignore important unit determination questions?

PROVIDED: Of course not. We still must follow the mandate of section 9(a). But we save time by eliminating some of the procedural hassles, like showing of interest.

TENNEL § 10(l): Can I get an injunction against a union that pickets for, say, 25 days, if that is an unreasonable period of time?

MAIN CLAUSE: Who invited you?

TENNEL: No § 8(b)(7) party is complete without me. I provide the enforcement machinery. I can restrain § 8(b)(7) picketing. Indeed, I get priority over all other cases.

PROVIDED FURTHER: This is astonishing. You mean to tell me that if a union guesses wrong and pickets for 25 days without filing a petition, and 25 days turns out under the circumstances to be an unreasonable period of time, you can enjoin the picketing?

TENNEL: Certainly.

PROVIDED: But what happens to my expedited election?

TENNEL: Nothing. Because no petition has been filed. And if one finally is filed, it will be too late. Not within a reasonable period of time. So you don't have "such a petition" on which to act.

ATEBESEVENCE: The beauty of our section is that it leaves so much to chance. The union that pickets without a petition being filed cannot be sure that the employer will propel it into an expedited election. The employer who files an § 8(b)(7) charge will not know whether the union will simply cease picketing, or will accept the challenge and move to a quick election. And neither party can predict accurately whether a shorter period than 30 days will be applicable. But basically the section works well. See if you now understand the classic explanation, in Blinne Construction, 135 NLRB 1153 (1962). It's in all the casebooks, and it says:

"The expedited election procedure is applicable, of course, only in a § 8(b)(7)(C) proceeding, i.e., where an § 8(b)(7)(C) unfair labor practice charge has been filed. Congress rejected efforts to amend the provisions of § 9(c) of the Act so as to dispense generally with preelection hearings. Thus, in the absence of an § 8(b)(7)(C) unfair labor practice charge, a union will not be enabled to obtain an expedited election by the mere device of engaging in recognition or organization picketing and filing a representation petition. And on the other hand, a picketing union which files a representation petition pursuant to the mandate of § 8(b)(7)(C) and to avoid its sanctions will not be propelled into an expedited election, which it may not desire, merely because it has filed such a petition. In both the above situations, the normal representation procedures are applicable; the showing of a substantial interest will be required, and the preelection hearing directed in § 9(c)(1) will be held.

"This, in our considered judgment, puts the expedited election procedure prescribed in the first proviso to subparagraph C in its proper and intended focus. That procedure was devised to shield aggrieved employers and employees from the adverse effects of prolonged recognition or organizational picketing. Absent such a grievance, it was not designed either to benefit or to handicap picketing activity." * * *

Let's try it another way. Here's an excerpt from Morris, The Developing Labor Law, 1098–99 (2d ed. 1983):

"Section 8(b)(7)(C) establishes two routes for dealing with proscribed picketing, depending on whether a petition is filed. If a petition is filed, there will be no violation of subparagraph (C) and the picketing may continue during the processing of the petition. If a Section 8(b)(7)(C) charge is also filed by the employer, the petition may be processed by the expedited election procedure. However, the expedited election procedure may be invoked only by an employer's Section 8(b)(7)(C) charge; otherwise, unions could obtain expedited elections simply by picketing or perhaps by having sympathetic employees file Section 8(b)(7)(C) charges. If an election is directed, the Section 8(b)(7)(C) charge will be dismissed because the election resolves the representation question. If the union is not certified and it continues to picket for a proscribed object, Section 8(b)(7)(B) will be activated. If the union is certified, Section 8(b)(7) ceases to apply.

"For various reasons both the union and the employer may decide not to file a petition. The employer, for example, may not wish to risk calling an election which it might lose; or it may decide that activating the expedited election procedure by an RM petition and a Section 8(b)(7)(C) charge will not shorten the time during which proscribed picketing is permitted. Upon the expiration of 30 days of proscribed picketing without the filing of a petition, a Section 8(b)(7)(C) charge will proceed solely along the unfair labor practice route; a petition filed thereafter, or lingering Section 8(a)(1) or (3) violations, will not affect the issue. If the regional director 'has reasonable cause to believe the charge is true and that a complaint should issue,' he is required to petition a federal district court for an injunction."

PROVIDED FURTHER: One last point. Suppose a union gets propelled into an expedited election, but finds that the employer has committed certain unfair labor practices which might cause the union to lose the election. In a normal election the union can "block" the election; that is, hold it up until the charges are resolved. What happens in an expedited situation?

PROVIDED: If the union files its petition within 30 days or within a reasonable period of time, it can utilize the "blocking" technique as in any ordinary election. In that way the picketing continues, but the election may be delayed. But if the union goes beyond the 30–day mark without filing a petition, the pendency of those charges is not going to affect the Board's determination to seek a § 10(l) injunction.

MAIN CLAUSE: But suppose the union now argues that it was not picketing to gain recognition at all, but was picketing to protest the employer's unfair labor practices? Can't the union get the best of all possible worlds that way? Engage in picketing, avoid an expedited election, and put the employer to the task of defending unfair labor practice charges?

PROVIDED FURTHER: I think I'm going to have a hangover tomorrow. I'm going home.

7. IS THERE A SUBSTITUTE FOR ECONOMIC WEAPONS?

The public sector model. Most statutes regulating public sector bargaining prohibit unions from striking. Without the potential of a strike, something may have to take its place to encourage meaningful bargaining. Many states have adopted a procedure for binding arbitration of the terms of the collective agreement, as an alternative to the strike. This process is usually known as "interest arbitration." The dynamics of the process and the application of the relevant statutory criteria are illustrated by the following interest arbitration award in the State of Connecticut.

STATE OF CONNECTICUT INTEREST ARBITRATION AND DOMESTIC PARTNER BENEFITS

SEBAC Award: January 31, 2000
State Employees Bargaining
Agent Coalition

Arbitrator: Roberta Golick, Esq.

INTRODUCTION

The parties are the State of Connecticut and SEBAC, a coalition of unions representing a majority of State bargaining unit employees. This is a single-issue interest arbitration stemming from a reopener provision in the parties' 1997–2017 health and pension benefit agreement (SEBAC V).

SEBAC V is a twenty-year agreement. As negotiations for this agreement neared completion, all but two of approximately 200 issues were resolved. One was a Coalition proposal that the State extend health and pension benefits to the domestic partners of State employees and to their otherwise eligible children. The other was an early retirement issue. The State opposed the inclusion of any domestic partner benefit in SEBAC V, but when it became apparent that the entire deal was in jeopardy over this issue, the State agreed to a reopener to occur in 1999 on domestic partners' benefits. The reopener provided:

The issue of whether and how domestic partners should be covered by pension and welfare benefits shall be the subject of contract reopener negotiations and arbitration to begin on or about January 1, 1999. SEBAC shall contact the State thirty (30) days prior to the date it wishes to begin such negotiations. * * *

STATUTORY FRAMEWORK

This interest arbitration arises under Connecticut General Statutes §§ 5–276a (e)(5), which provides:

The factors to be considered by the arbitrator in arriving at a decision are: The history of negotiations between the parties including those leading to the instant proceeding; the existing conditions of employment of similar groups of employees; the wages, fringe benefits and working conditions prevailing in the labor market; the overall compensation paid to the employees involved in the arbitration proceedings, including direct wages compensation, overtime and premium pay, vacations, holidays and other leave, insurance, pensions, medical and hospitalization benefits, food and apparel furnished and all other benefits received by such employees; the ability of the employer to pay; changes in the cost of living; and the interests and welfare of the employees.

The process requires the selection of one or the other Last Best Offer.

THE ISSUE

As set forth in SEBAC V, the issue is:

Whether and how domestic partners should be covered by pension and welfare benefits.

THE LAST BEST OFFERS

The State:

The State's last best offer is:

No such provision.

SEBAC:

The Coalition's last best offer is:

"Domestic Partners

A. Couples covered: A couple shall be eligible for domestic partner status only if the couple is unable to marry in Connecticut because Connecticut's marriage provisions distinguish between same sex and opposite sex couples. Should eligibility to marry in Connecticut no longer be precluded on the basis of this distinction, the following provision shall cease to be effective on that date, except that coverage for couples having already achieved domestic partner status under the terms of this provision shall cease one year from that date.

B. The term "spouse" used anywhere in this Agreement shall be deemed to include a covered person's unmarried domestic partner who has executed an affidavit in accordance with this provision. An employee wishing to change his/her health or pension status based upon being in a domestic partnership must execute an affidavit with the employer, together with appropriate evidence of joint residency and mutual dependence. * * *"

THE COALITION'S ARGUMENTS

The Coalition begins its arguments with some general observations. First, it notes that health coverage is terribly important for every family, and the State's current benefit for employees' spouses and children is an important part of the State's compensation system. The Coalition argues that denial of health benefits to partners and dependent children of same-sex couples results in distinctions based solely upon domestic partners' legal bar to marriage. The failure to provide equal health benefits condones and perpetuates social discrimination against and devaluation of gays and lesbians. The Coalition states, "There can be no genuine disagreement that the facts show a real, live human problem, and no good reason not to fix it." * * *

Ability to pay, the Coalition continues, cannot be used as a shield by the State to avoid granting this benefit. This is a matter of "choosing" to pay, not "ability" to pay. The Coalition contends that the cost of providing this benefit is "tiny" and the State is well-positioned to fund it.

The next factor, changes in the cost of living, is also advanced to support the Coalition's LBO. The medical cost of living is rising substantially faster than the overall cost of living. State employees in domestic partner relationships are increasingly unable to provide adequate insurance for their families.

Finally, the overall compensation of affected bargaining unit employees is currently far lower than that of heterosexual married members who enjoy expanded health care coverage for their spouses and children. In this factor, as in the others, the Coalition maintains that the evidence supports its LBO. * * *

THE STATE'S ARGUMENTS

The State opens its arguments with the observation that domestic partner benefits coverage is not a matter of statutory discrimination, and neither state law nor federal law requires domestic partnership coverage. The State's overarching contention, though, is that domestic partner benefits coverage is a public policy issue that is more appropriately decided by the legislature. Arbitrators should not decide issues of public policy. Moreover, current policy in Connecticut does not support the extension of domestic partner health insurance and pension benefits to domestic partners.

As for the statutory factors guiding this issue, it is the State's contention that they strongly support its LBO, not the Coalition's. Most significant are the factors related to conditions of employment of similar groups of employees and conditions prevailing in the labor market, the ability of the employer to pay, the interests and welfare of the State's employees, and the overall compensation paid to employees.

The State notes that very few public employers at the state and municipal levels provide health benefits to domestic partners. In the private sector, both locally and nationally, the extension of such benefits remains rare. The statistics favor the State's position that no benefits of this nature should be granted at this time.* * *

DISCUSSION

Because of the emotional charge attached to gay/lesbian issues, it is critical at the outset to declare what this exercise is and what it is not. This is an interest arbitration over a benefit sought by the Coalition for a small, precisely defined group of bargaining unit members. Like every other interest arbitration over unresolved disputes, this labor is guided by the enumerated statutory factors. It is a balancing exercise—relevant evidence evaluated and measured against relevant standards. It is conducted with detachment.

What this is *not* is a commentary about the members of the class. It is not a voice in the religious, moral or political debate surrounding same-sex relationships. It neither advocates for nor preaches against gay rights.* * *

It also makes sense at the outset to address the roles, if any, that federal and state discrimination laws play in the selection of the more reasonable LBO. The short answer is that they play no appreciable role. This is not a grievance about unlawful discrimination. It is, rather, a negotiations conflict about what in most jurisdictions remains *lawful* discrimination, that is, legally sanctioned distinctions between married and unmarried couples. * * *

Finally, the State's public policy argument does not dispose of this case. For one thing, there is no persuasive evidence that an award granting the benefit in this matter would contravene public policy. The State extrapolates from tangential issues a view that domestic partner benefits would run counter to public policy, but that view is far from proof of an explicit, well-defined expression contained in State law or legal precedent. At best, the public policy of the State of Connecticut on this issue remains unsettled. Further, there can be no dispute that the matter of health and pension benefits for State employees is a mandatory subject of collective bargaining. Whether to extend health benefits to a particular group of employees is something the parties can and did bargain about, reach impasse about, and eventually agree to send to binding interest arbitration.* * *

THE STATUTORY FACTORS

*History of Negotiations * * **

The other relevant feature of the negotiations history pertains to the agreed-upon duration of the SEBAC V agreement. Unlike most every collective bargaining agreement in this country, the SEBAC V contract is a twenty-year settlement. Effective July 1, 1997, SEBAC V does not expire until June 30, 2017. Thus, factored into the assessment of the parties' respective LBO's must be the reality that the resolution of this issue carries for seventeen more years. The issue is not simply which LBO is more reasonable in the year 2000 but which LBO is more likely to endure as the more reasonable until the year 2017.

From that standpoint, the Coalition's LBO—with *some* benefit, as opposed to the State's LBO with *no* benefit—is more reasonable. The evidence points to an increase in the availability of domestic partner health benefits among employers. It appears more likely than not that these benefits will be widespread well before the end of the SEBAC V agreement.

Existing Conditions of Employment of Similar Groups of Employees; Wages, Fringe Benefits and Working Conditions Prevailing in the Labor Market

These factors invite a number of statistical constructs: numbers of public sector employers that provide the benefit; private sector employers; employers with more than 200 employees, municipalities, academic institutions, etc. They also invite discussion of what constitutes a "similar group" of employees—external comparisons and/or internal. There is no question that domestic partner health benefits are not commonplace today. * * *

On the other hand, there is also no question that as a benefit for employees, domestic partner health and pension coverage is appearing with increased frequency, particularly among larger employers. * * *

The fact is that when prevailing working conditions are viewed through the narrow lens of "today," it is undeniable that the list of those who do provide domestic partner benefits is dwarfed by the list of those who do not—in every category. However, when the lens is opened to permit a glimpse backward at the rate of growth and projection forward to the seventeen years remaining in the SEBAC V term, the figures suggest a course toward inclusion rather than exclusion of this benefit in employment benefit packages.

In the current labor market, moreover, the State of Connecticut must remain competitive to continue to attract a highly qualified and diverse workforce. Though the State argues that it does not wish to be a "leader" in this particular area, leadership is not measured in narrow increments. The State *is* a leader. In sheer size it presents a dominant force in Connecticut. Its compensation and benefit levels already serve as a beacon for recruitment and retention of talent. Its long-standing commitment to fairness and equity transcends this issue. Were it to provide domestic partner benefits, the State would not become a leader; it would merely ensure that its status as one is not jeopardized.* * *

From a labor employment perspective, there is no basis to justify the inequity between employees with spouses and those with spouse equivalents. The Coalition's LBO contains sufficient restrictions to warrant that participation in the benefit would be limited to just those unit members who, but for statutory constraints, *would* marry. Indeed, recognizing that not every couple who *can* marry *does* marry, the Coalition's LBO provides that should Connecticut's laws change to permit marriage between same sex individuals, the domestic partnership provision of SEBAC V would cease to be effective. * * *

Ability of the Employer to Pay

Prior to the submission of LBO's, the Coalition sought domestic partner benefits for both same sex and opposite sex couples. There is no dispute that when opposite sex couples are excluded, both the anticipated increase in health benefit enrollment and the overall cost to the employer drop dramatically.

At the hearings, the parties stated:

> State: The State has agreed to an assumption, for lack of a better term, that almost regardless of what definition is used for the term "domestic partner," and regardless of whether it is limited to same sex or opposite sex, it is equally unlikely that the total cost will exceed 2 percent of the total health insurance cost.

> Coalition: I indicated in an off-the-record discussion with counsel that SEBAC was prepared to agree that whatever the definition ultimately selected here, it is unlikely that the benefit will cost less

than half a percent of the health care—of the State's overall health care budget for actives who are always covered now, and then gradually that would increase to no less than half a percent of the overall cost for new retirees.* * *

There is no persuasive evidence that the State would be unable to pay for domestic partner health/pension benefits, nor that providing the benefits would pose a hardship. Arguments about ability to pay naturally centered upon costs in the context of the State's immediate financial condition. While even those arguments don't support a finding that the State cannot afford to provide the benefit today, it is notable that there is no evidence that the State would be unable to fund the benefit over the next 17 years.

As for the current fiscal year and the next, the record fails to demonstrate inability to pay, or ability to pay only at great sacrifice. The State does advance the spending cap—estimated expenditures cannot be greater than estimated revenues; the General Assembly will not adopt a budget greater than the growth in personal income or the growth in the CPI absent a 3/5 vote of both houses—in support of its claim that a costly benefit is unlikely to be welcomed by the legislature. But, as the Coalition argues, the existence of the spending cap in and of itself does not mean that the State would have to exceed the cap to fund the benefit.

The State is correct when it points out, "The fact that any public employer has the power to raise taxes on its residents does not justify an endless stream of benefits for those who are compensated with tax dollars." For that reason, ability to pay as a factor in an interest arbitration is not assessed in a vacuum. It is, rather, considered along a spectrum of reasonableness. Within that framework, the evidence here favors the Coalition in that the record discloses no tangible economic obstacle at present or reason to suspect the emergence of one as the term of the agreement progresses. * * *

On balance, then, the weight of the evidence supports an award that grants the benefit rather than an award that denies it. The Coalition in its LBO responded to the criticisms leveled at its earlier positions. It inserted "teeth" into the eligibility criteria and dramatically reduced the scope of eligible beneficiaries. After careful consideration of the record and arguments, I am persuaded that the Coalition's LBO is the more reasonable of the two.

AWARD

I hereby award the Last Best Offer of the Coalition.

Roberta Golick, Esq.
Arbitrator
Date: January 31, 2000

F. APPLYING AND ENFORCING THE COMPACT

1. AN OVERVIEW: TWO CONTRASTING MODELS

After we talk and talk about work, and finally reach some understanding, do we have an agreement that we can enforce? In the non-union worker participation programs that we have read about, we find no systematic way for employees and management to tie up their understandings. Nor is there a standard mechanism for them to resolve disputes about the scope of their agreement. Of course if the parties want to continue to have open, constructive discussions, they have a great practical incentive to follow whatever agreements they reach.

In marked contrast, the collective bargaining model under the NLRA provides a well-developed system for memorializing and enforcing agreements reached through bargaining. The bargaining obligation imposed by Sections 8(b)(3) and 8(a)(5), and defined in § 8(d), includes the obligation to execute "a written contract incorporating any agreement reached if requested by either party....." Section 301 goes on to provide that such an agreement is enforceable in the federal courts. Under well established case law, the agreement may also be enforced in state courts, although federal law governs the substantive issues that may arise. As we will see, the parties in collective bargaining usually choose the machinery of arbitration as the primary vehicle to interpret and enforce their agreement.

Of course there are enforceable contractual commitments in the non-union setting. There may be written promises, oral agreements, or representations that can be enforced under normal contract principles, or through a theory of promissory estoppel, as the plaintiffs attempted to do in the *Steelworkers* case in Chapter I. We know from our readings in Chapter I that employer commitments in the form of company handbooks or other representations may be enforceable in the courts. And the *Gilmer* case, which we studied in Chapter I, holds that an individual employee may make a binding commitment to arbitrate disputes with the company even if they arise under statutory provisions. The statutory basis for enforcing an agreement of the sort Mr. Gilmer made is the Federal Arbitration Act.

But these are for the most part individual contracts, presented to the employee by the company on a basis in which little negotiation may be possible. Some jobs in the workplace, whether managerial or highly competitive positions, may involve extensive contractual commitments, some negotiated with considerable give and take and competitive bargaining power, including those that prevent the employee from using trade secrets and other proprietary information if the employee leaves the company, and restricting the employee's ability to compete. However, the overall control of the non-union workplace is normally left in the hands of management and not governed by any sort of agreement, certainly not one negotiated on behalf of the employees collectively.

Indeed, an agreement that resulted from any kind of representational status of workers would undoubtedly violate Section 8(a)(2) of the NLRA under principles we discussed earlier in this chapter.

THE TYPICAL COLLECTIVE BARGAINING AGREEMENT

In contrast, the typical unionized workplace is regulated by a collective bargaining agreement that provides a detailed blueprint for workplace governance. You should consult the sample collective agreement in the reference supplement to get an idea of the scope of a typical collective agreement. It may cover such topics as the level of wages; fringe benefits, such as health insurance and pensions; time off for vacations, illness and personal matters; restrictions on the employer's ability to have work done outside the bargaining unit, for example, through subcontracting; provisions that determine which groups of employees have jurisdiction over certain types of work, provisions for allocating work opportunities on the basis of seniority and other factors, similar protections, usually based on seniority, when jobs shrink and workers have to be laid off or placed on other jobs; and protections against discipline and dismissal without just cause.

THE CENTRAL ROLE OF ARBITRATION

Section 301 of the LMRA explicitly provides that the collective bargaining agreement is enforceable in federal court and is governed by federal law. Textile Workers v. Lincoln Mills, 353 U.S. 448, 77 S.Ct. 912, 1 L.Ed.2d 972 (1957). Parallel avenues for enforcement are available in state court. Teamsters v. Lucas Flour Co., 369 U.S. 95, 82 S.Ct. 571, 7 L.Ed.2d 593 (1962). As you will see in the sample agreement, and in most contracts and cases you read, the parties do not provide for direct enforcement of their contract in court. That could be a very cumbersome procedure, given the number of disputes that arise under a collective bargaining agreement. Rather, they provide for binding arbitration to determine the meaning and application of the collective bargaining agreement. This means they entrust to an impartial arbitrator, usually selected by the parties, the task of deciding disputes that arise under the contract. This arbitration step is the culmination of a grievance procedure in which the parties have the opportunity if not the obligation, to attempt to resolve their dispute before it gets to arbitration.

We have chosen to deal with some of the attributes of arbitration in Chapter III, where you will have the opportunity to consider the general structure of arbitration in the specific context of health and safety disputes. As you will see in Chapter III, the arbitrator is given wide discretion to interpret and apply the contract. The courts undertake only very limited review of the arbitrator's award. In a nutshell, claimed errors in reading and applying the agreement, or failures in the fact-finding process, will fall on deaf judicial ears. The Supreme Court explains this by saying that the parties bargained for the arbitrator's judgment, and they are stuck with it. Only where the award violates a well established public policy or is tainted by arbitral bias will the reviewing court throw it out. By the same token, the agreement to arbitrate disputes is read broadly, so that there is a presumption that a dispute is covered by the arbitration clause unless it is expressly excluded. The cases that establish these propositions are found in Chapter III.

INDIVIDUAL AND UNION CHALLENGES TO MANAGEMENT ACTION

The powerful contractual statement of the parties' rights and obligations drives their day to day administration of the agreement. Normally, management makes a variety of decisions, and the union or the individual worker may challenge them through the filing of a grievance. Section 9(a) of the Act, which you should consult now, permits the individual employee to raise and adjust her own grievances with the employer, but provides that the union must be consulted and may object to an adjustment as inconsistent with the collective agreement. You might read Section 9(a) to give the employee an absolute right to take her grievance up with management. But Section 9(a) has not been interpreted as a sword for the individual employee to deal with management. Rather, it is a shield, which permits the employer to deal with the employee if it chooses to do so, without violating Section 8(a)(5)'s obligation to deal exclusively with the union.

ENFORCEMENT OF THE BARGAIN

Under the collective bargaining model, both sides are entitled to enforce their bargain. For example, if the parties are unable to resolve a dispute through the grievance process, the dissatisfied party may proceed to arbitration.

In most cases in which the union demands arbitration, management does not dispute the choice of forum, and is content to defend against the union's claim on the merits in arbitration. The presumption of arbitrability gives management little choice on this score. For if the employer does not agree to arbitrate, then the union may attempt to compel arbitration under Section 301. The law on this point is expressed most recently in A T & T Technologies v. CWA, 475 U.S. 643, 106 S.Ct. 1415, 89 L.Ed.2d 648 (1986), a case we'll examine in Chapter III. The case reaffirms doctrines of 25 years' standing, known as the Steelworkers Trilogy (you'll find references to those cases in A T & T Technologies, as well as in the Caesar Wright case, which we include in this section of the book). Basically, the Court recognizes arbitration as a consensual matter, and holds that a party cannot be required to arbitrate a matter that it has not agreed to submit to arbitration. But in deciding whether the parties have agreed to arbitrate a particular matter, the court will presume that the matter is arbitrable, thus furthering the national policy of peaceful resolution of labor disputes. In applying that presumption, the court will not look into the underlying merits of the dispute.

THE INDIVIDUAL'S RIGHT TO COMPEL ARBITRATION

Both parties, union and management, are usually entitled to compel arbitration, but that right does not extend to the individual employee. Most contracts provide that the union determines whether to take a case to arbitration. The union is in effect the gatekeeper of the process, deciding which claims to advance and which to drop or compromise for lack of merit or in order to advance the goals of the overall bargaining unit. This is one of the aspects of exclusivity that we discussed earlier in the chapter, one that Nan was most concerned about when she urged that the nurse practitioners have their own bargaining unit so that their interests would not be sacrificed for the larger group. The duty of fair representation, which we discuss in greater depth in Chapter III, serves as a very modest limit on the union's discretion to advance or turn down a grievance. The leading case, Vaca v. Sipes, which we study in Chapter III, has been intact for about 30 years. It holds that an employee does not have an absolute right to have his grievance submitted to arbitration. However, the union "may not arbitrarily ignore a meritorious grievance or process it in a perfunctory fashion," and must administer the grievance and arbitration machinery "in good faith and in a nonarbitrary manner." However, as we shall see, these phrases do not impose very stringent limits on the union's discretion to turn down a grievance.

TOO ADVERSARIAL?

Some may object that the system of grievance arbitration in the organized sector is too adversarial. It reinforces the hierarchy in which management acts and the union or worker reacts. Others may argue that the contractual approach is too rigid. It deprives the parties of needed flexibility to carry on day to day operations. As certain understandings in the way the plant is operated become elevated to rights, it becomes increasingly difficult for the union to make accommodations to management. Some of the approaches to cooperative labor relations in the organized sector attempt to soften the confrontational use of the grievance process, and this is attempted in some innovative collective bargaining relationships, such as the Saturn contract. Recall and contrast the day to day discussions in a non-union setting, such as the Company of Business People. There may be greater flexibility in the non-union context, but there is no enforceable set of standards or rights that serves to guide day to day communications.

ARBITRATION OF EXTERNAL RIGHTS

We saw in Chapter I that a wealth of statutes now confer rights upon individual employees whether or not a collective agreement is in force. These include the various laws that prohibit discrimination based on race, gender, age or disability, statutes that grant employees rights to time off, and judge-made exceptions to the employment at will doctrine. We use the term "external rights" simply as a shorthand for rights that exist independently of the collective bargaining agreement. For workers in a union setting, this presents the possibility of parallel claims, one under the collective agreement, another in the courts. In the non-union setting we have seen a pronounced expansion of arbitration with respect to claims that arise under statutory or judge-made law.

While we haven't made an empirical study of this proposition, it is probably undisputed that the vast majority of claims that are taken to arbitration under a collective bargaining agreement in a unionized workplace have nothing to do with any statutory rights. Rather, those disputes focus exclusively on the language of the collective agreement and the practices of the workplace.

One very common dispute that is submitted to arbitration involves the termination of an employee. Most collective agreements in the unionized workplace provide that the worker may not be terminated except for just cause. This means that the employer has the burden to establish in arbitration that it had good grounds to terminate the worker. In making this decision, an arbitrator may look at the deficiencies in the employee's work, whether the worker has had persistent problems, and whether the worker has been warned and been given an opportunity to correct these problems. The issue normally has nothing to do with any statutory rights.

But a discharge case under a collective bargaining agreement may involve statutory rights as well as contractual rights. A worker may claim she was terminated because of her race. Termination on that basis surely is not for just cause. But it also violates Title VII. When we studied *Gilmer* in Chapter I, we saw that an employee could agree to have the propriety of a termination resolved through arbitration, even if it involves a statutory claim that could otherwise be heard in court. The rules are different in the unionized workplace. The following case, in effect now for three decades, deals with the availability of multiple forums for employees represented by a union. It has been decried as giving the employee "two bites at the apple."

ALEXANDER v. GARDNER–DENVER CO.

Supreme Court of the United States, 1974.
415 U.S. 36, 94 S.Ct. 1011, 39 L.Ed.2d 147.

MR. JUSTICE POWELL delivered the opinion of the Court.

This case concerns the proper relationship between federal courts and the grievance-arbitration machinery of collective-bargaining agreements in the resolution and enforcement of an individual's rights to equal employment opportunities under Title VII of the Civil Rights Act of 1964. Specifically, we must decide under what circumstances, if any, an employee's statutory right to a trial de novo under Title VII may be foreclosed by prior submission of his claim to final arbitration under the nondiscrimination clause of a collective-bargaining agreement.

I

In May 1966, petitioner Harrell Alexander, Sr., a black, was hired by respondent Gardner–Denver Co. (the company) to perform maintenance work at the company's plant in Denver, Colorado. In June 1968, petitioner was awarded a trainee position as a drill operator. He remained at that job until his discharge from employment on September 29, 1969. The company informed petitioner that he was being discharged for producing too many defective or unusable parts that had to be scrapped.

On October 1, 1969, petitioner filed a grievance under the collective-bargaining agreement in force between the company and petitioner's union, Local No. 3029 of the United Steelworkers of America (the union). The grievance stated: "I feel I have been unjustly discharged and ask that I be reinstated with full seniority and pay." No explicit claim of racial discrimination was made.

Under Art. 4 of the collective-bargaining agreement, the company retained "the right to hire, suspend or discharge [employees] for proper cause." Article 5, § 2, provided, however, that "there shall be no discrimination against any employee on account of race, color, religion, sex, national origin, or ancestry," and Art. 23, § 6(a), stated that "[n]o employee will be discharged, suspended or given a written warning notice except for just cause." The agreement also contained a broad arbitration clause. * * *

The union processed petitioner's grievance through the above machinery. In the final pre-arbitration step, petitioner raised, apparently for the first time, the claim that his discharge resulted from racial discrimination. The company rejected all of petitioner's claims, and the grievance proceeded to arbitration. Prior to the arbitration hearing, however, petitioner filed a charge of racial discrimination with the Colorado Civil Rights Commission, which referred the complaint to the Equal Employment Opportunity Commission on November 5, 1969.

At the arbitration hearing on November 20, 1969, petitioner testified that his discharge was the result of racial discrimination and informed the arbitrator that he had filed a charge with the Colorado Commission because he "could not rely on the union." The union introduced a letter in which petitioner stated that he was "knowledgeable that in the same plant others have scrapped an equal amount and sometimes in excess, but by all logical reasoning I ... have been the target of preferential discriminatory treatment." The union representative also testified that the company's usual practice was to transfer unsatisfactory trainee drill operators back to their former positions.

On December 30, 1969, the arbitrator ruled that petitioner had been "discharged for just cause." He made no reference to petitioner's claim of racial discrimination. The arbitrator stated that the union had failed to produce evidence of a practice of transferring rather than discharging trainee drill operators who accumulated excessive scrap, but he suggested that the company and the union confer on whether such an arrangement was feasible in the present case. * * *

II

Congress enacted Title VII of the Civil Rights Act of 1964, to assure equality of employment opportunities by eliminating those practices and devices that discriminate on the basis of race, color, religion, sex, or national origin. Cooperation and voluntary compliance were selected as the preferred means for achieving this goal. To this end, Congress created the Equal Employment Opportunity Commission and established a procedure whereby existing state and local equal employment opportunity agencies, as well as the Commission, would have an opportunity to settle disputes through conference, conciliation, and persuasion before the aggrieved party was permitted to file a lawsuit. In the Equal Employment Opportunity Act of 1972 Congress amended Title VII to provide the Commission with further authority to investigate individual charges of discrimination, to promote voluntary compliance with the requirements of Title VII, and to institute civil actions against employers or unions named in a discrimination charge.

Even in its amended form, however, Title VII does not provide the Commission with direct powers of enforcement. The Commission cannot adjudicate claims or impose administrative sanctions. Rather, final responsibility for enforcement of Title VII is vested with federal courts. The Act authorizes courts to issue injunctive relief and to order such affirmative action as may be appropriate to remedy the effects of unlawful employment practices. Courts retain these broad remedial powers despite a Commission finding of no reasonable cause to believe that the Act has been violated. Taken together, these provisions make plain that federal courts have been assigned plenary powers to secure compliance with Title VII.

In addition to reposing ultimate authority in federal courts, Congress gave private individuals a significant role in the enforcement process of Title VII. Individual grievants usually initiate the Commission's investigatory and conciliatory procedures. And although the 1972 amendment to Title VII empowers the Commission to bring its own actions, the private right of action remains an essential means of obtaining judicial enforcement of Title VII. In such cases, the private litigant not only redresses his own injury but also vindicates the important congressional policy against discriminatory employment practices.

Pursuant to this statutory scheme, petitioner initiated the present action for judicial consideration of his rights under Title VII. The District Court and the Court of Appeals held, however, that petitioner was bound by the prior arbitral decision and had no right to sue under Title VII. Both courts evidently thought that this result was dictated by notions of election of remedies and waiver and by the federal policy favoring arbitration of labor disputes, as enunciated by this Court in

Textile Workers Union v. Lincoln Mills, 353 U.S. 448, 77 S.Ct. 912, 923, 1 L.Ed.2d 972 (1957), and the Steelworkers trilogy. We disagree.

III

Title VII does not speak expressly to the relationship between federal courts and the grievance-arbitration machinery of collective-bargaining agreements. It does, however, vest federal courts with plenary powers to enforce the statutory requirements; and it specifies with precision the jurisdictional prerequisites that an individual must satisfy before he is entitled to institute a lawsuit. In the present case, these prerequisites were met when petitioner (1) filed timely a charge of employment discrimination with the Commission, and (2) received and acted upon the Commission's statutory notice of the right to sue. There is no suggestion in the statutory scheme that a prior arbitral decision either forecloses an individual's right to sue or divests federal courts of jurisdiction.

In addition, legislative enactments in this area have long evinced a general intent to accord parallel or overlapping remedies against discrimination. In the Civil Rights Act of 1964, Congress indicated that it considered the policy against discrimination to be of the "highest priority." Consistent with this view, Title VII provides for consideration of employment-discrimination claims in several forums. And, in general, submission of a claim to one forum does not preclude a later submission to another. Moreover, the legislative history of Title VII manifests a congressional intent to allow an individual to pursue independently his rights under both Title VII and other applicable state and federal statutes. The clear inference is that Title VII was designed to supplement, rather than supplant, existing laws and institutions relating to employment discrimination. In sum, Title VII's purpose and procedures strongly suggest that an individual does not forfeit his private cause of action if he first pursues his grievance to final arbitration under the nondiscrimination clause of a collective-bargaining agreement.

In reaching the opposite conclusion, the District Court relied in part on the doctrine of election of remedies. That doctrine, which refers to situations where an individual pursues remedies that are legally or factually inconsistent, has no application in the present context. In submitting his grievance to arbitration, an employee seeks to vindicate his contractual right under a collective-bargaining agreement. By contrast, in filing a lawsuit under Title VII, an employee asserts independent statutory rights accorded by Congress. The distinctly separate nature of these contractual and statutory rights is not vitiated merely because both were violated as a result of the same factual occurrence. And certainly no inconsistency results from permitting both rights to be enforced in their respectively appropriate forums. The resulting scheme is somewhat analogous to the procedure under the National Labor Relations Act, as amended, where disputed transactions may implicate both contractual and statutory rights. Where the statutory right underlying a particular claim may not be abridged by contractual agreement, the Court has recognized that consideration of the claim by the arbitrator as a contractual dispute under the collective-bargaining agreement does not preclude subsequent consideration of the claim by the National Labor Relations Board as an unfair labor practice charge or as a petition for clarification of the union's representation certificate under the Act. There, as here, the relationship between the forums is complementary since consideration of the claim by both forums may promote the policies underlying each. Thus, the rationale behind the election-of-remedies doctrine cannot support the decision below.

We are also unable to accept the proposition that petitioner waived his cause of action under Title VII. To begin, we think it clear that there can be no prospective waiver of an employee's rights under Title VII. It is true, of course, that a union may waive certain statutory rights related to collective activity, such as the right to strike. These rights are conferred on employees collectively to foster the processes of bargaining and properly may be exercised or relinquished by the union as collective-bargaining agent to obtain economic benefits for union members. Title VII, on the other hand, stands on plainly different ground; it concerns not majoritarian processes, but an individual's right to equal employment opportunities. Title VII's strictures are absolute and represent a congressional command that each employee be free from discriminatory practices. Of necessity, the rights conferred can form no part of the collective-bargaining process since waiver of these rights would defeat the paramount congressional purpose behind Title VII. In these circumstances, an employee's rights under Title VII are not susceptible of prospective waiver.

The actual submission of petitioner's grievance to arbitration in the present case does not alter the situation. Although presumably an employee may waive his cause of action under Title VII as part of a voluntary settlement, mere resort to the arbitral forum to enforce contractual rights constitutes no such waiver. Since an employee's rights under Title VII may not be waived prospectively, existing contractual rights and remedies against discrimination must result from other concessions already made by the union as part of the economic bargain struck with the employer. It is settled law that no additional concession may be exacted from any employee as the price for enforcing those rights.

Moreover, a contractual right to submit a claim to arbitration is not displaced simply because Congress also has provided a statutory right against discrimination. Both rights have legally independent origins and are equally available to the aggrieved employee. This point becomes apparent through consideration of the role of the arbitrator in the system of industrial self-government.[16] As the proctor of the bargain, the

---

16. See Meltzer, Labor Arbitration and Overlapping and Conflicting Remedies for Employment Discrimination, 39 U.Chi. L.Rev. 30, 32–35 (1971); Meltzer, Ruminations About Ideology, Law, and Labor Arbitration, 34 U.Chi.L.Rev. 545 (1967). As the late Dean Shulman stated:

"A proper conception of the arbitrator's function is basic. He is not a public

arbitrator's task is to effectuate the intent of the parties. His source of authority is the collective-bargaining agreement, and he must interpret and apply that agreement in accordance with the "industrial common law of the shop" and the various needs and desires of the parties. The arbitrator, however, has no general authority to invoke public laws that conflict with the bargain between the parties:

> "[A]n arbitrator is confined to interpretation and application of the collective bargaining agreement; he does not sit to dispense his own brand of industrial justice. He may of course look for guidance from many sources, yet his award is legitimate only so long as it draws its essence from the collective bargaining agreement. When the arbitrator's words manifest an infidelity to this obligation, courts have no choice but to refuse enforcement of the award." United Steelworkers of America v. Enterprise Wheel & Car Corp., 363 U.S. 593, 597, 80 S.Ct. 1358, 1361, 4 L.Ed.2d 1424 (1960).

If an arbitral decision is based "solely upon the arbitrator's view of the requirements of enacted legislation," rather than on an interpretation of the collective-bargaining agreement, the arbitrator has "exceeded the scope of the submission," and the award will not be enforced. Ibid. Thus the arbitrator has authority to resolve only questions of contractual rights, and this authority remains regardless of whether certain contractual rights are similar to, or duplicative of, the substantive rights secured by Title VII.

IV

The District Court and the Court of Appeals reasoned that to permit an employee to have his claim considered in both the arbitral and judicial forums would be unfair since this would mean that the employer, but not the employee, was bound by the arbitral award. In the District Court's words, it could not "accept a philosophy which gives the employee two strings to his bow when the employer has only one." This argument mistakes the effect of Title VII. Under the Steelworkers trilogy, an arbitral decision is final and binding on the employer and employee, and judicial review is limited as to both. But in instituting an action under Title VII, the employee is not seeking review of the arbitrator's decision. Rather, he is asserting a statutory right independent of the arbitration process. An employer does not have "two strings to his bow" with respect to an arbitral decision for the simple reason that Title VII does not provide employers with a cause of action against employees. An employer cannot be the victim of discriminatory employment practices.

tribunal imposed upon the parties by superior authority which the parties are obliged to accept. He has no general charter to administer justice for a community which transcends the parties. He is rather part of a system of self-government created by and confined to the parties. He serves their pleasure only, to administer the rule of law established by their collective agreement." Shulman, Reason, Contract, and Law in Labor Relations, 68 Harv.L.Rev. 999, 1016 (1955).

The District Court and the Court of Appeals also thought that to permit a later resort to the judicial forum would undermine substantially the employer's incentive to arbitrate and would "sound the death knell for arbitration clauses in labor contracts." Again, we disagree. The primary incentive for an employer to enter into an arbitration agreement is the union's reciprocal promise not to strike. As the Court stated in Boys Markets, Inc. v. Retail Clerk's Union, 398 U.S., at 248, 90 S.Ct., at 1591, "a no-strike obligation, express or implied, is the quid pro quo for an undertaking by the employer to submit grievance disputes to the process of arbitration." It is not unreasonable to assume that most employers will regard the benefits derived from a no-strike pledge as outweighing whatever costs may result from according employees an arbitral remedy against discrimination in addition to their judicial remedy under Title VII. Indeed, the severe consequences of a strike may make an arbitration clause almost essential from both the employees' and the employer's perspective. Moreover, the grievance-arbitration machinery of the collective-bargaining agreement remains a relatively inexpensive and expeditious means for resolving a wide range of disputes, including claims of discriminatory employment practices. Where the collective-bargaining agreement contains a nondiscrimination clause similar to Title VII, and where arbitral procedures are fair and regular, arbitration may well produce a settlement satisfactory to both employer and employee. An employer thus has an incentive to make available the conciliatory and therapeutic processes of arbitration which may satisfy an employee's perceived need to resort to the judicial forum, thus saving the employer the expense and aggravation associated with a lawsuit. For similar reasons, the employee also has a strong incentive to arbitrate grievances, and arbitration may often eliminate those misunderstandings or discriminatory practices that might otherwise precipitate resort to the judicial forum.

V

Respondent contends that even if a preclusion rule is not adopted, federal courts should defer to arbitral decisions on discrimination claims where: (i) the claim was before the arbitrator; (ii) the collective-bargaining agreement prohibited the form of discrimination charged in the suit under Title VII; and (iii) the arbitrator has authority to rule on the claim and to fashion a remedy.[17] Under respondent's proposed rule, a court would grant summary judgment and dismiss the employee's action if the above conditions were met. The rule's obvious consequence in the present case would be to deprive the petitioner of his statutory right to attempt to establish his claim in a federal court.

* * * Respondent's deferral rule is necessarily premised on the assumption that arbitral processes are commensurate with judicial processes and that Congress impliedly intended federal courts to defer to arbitral decisions on Title VII issues. We deem this supposition unlikely.

---

17. Brief for Respondent 37. Respondent's proposed rule is analogous to the NLRB's policy of deferring to arbitral decisions on statutory issues in certain cases.

Arbitral procedures, while well suited to the resolution of contractual disputes, make arbitration a comparatively inappropriate forum for the final resolution of rights created by Title VII. This conclusion rests first on the special role of the arbitrator, whose task is to effectuate the intent of the parties rather than the requirements of enacted legislation. Where the collective-bargaining agreement conflicts with Title VII, the arbitrator must follow the agreement. To be sure, the tension between contractual and statutory objectives may be mitigated where a collective-bargaining agreement contains provisions facially similar to those of Title VII. But other facts may still render arbitral processes comparatively inferior to judicial processes in the protection of Title VII rights. Among these is the fact that the specialized competence of arbitrators pertains primarily to the law of the shop, not the law of the land. Parties usually choose an arbitrator because they trust his knowledge and judgment concerning the demands and norms of industrial relations. On the other hand, the resolution of statutory or constitutional issues is a primary responsibility of courts, and judicial construction has proved especially necessary with respect to Title VII, whose broad language frequently can be given meaning only by reference to public law concepts.

Moreover, the factfinding process in arbitration usually is not equivalent to judicial factfinding. The record of the arbitration proceedings is not as complete; the usual rules of evidence do not apply; and rights and procedures common to civil trials, such as discovery, compulsory process, cross-examination, and testimony under oath, are often severely limited or unavailable. And as this Court has recognized, "[a]rbitrators have no obligation to the court to give their reasons for an award." Indeed, it is the informality of arbitral procedure that enables it to function as an efficient, inexpensive, and expeditious means for dispute resolution. This same characteristic, however, makes arbitration a less appropriate forum for final resolution of Title VII issues than the federal courts.[19]

It is evident that respondent's proposed rule would not allay these concerns. Nor are we convinced that the solution lies in applying a more demanding deferral standard. * * * As respondent points out, a standard that adequately insured effectuation of Title VII rights in the arbitral forum would tend to make arbitration a procedurally complex, expensive, and time-consuming process. And judicial enforcement of such a standard would almost require courts to make de novo determinations of the employees' claims. It is uncertain whether any minimal savings in

19. A further concern is the union's exclusive control over the manner and extent to which an individual grievance is presented. In arbitration, as in the collective-bargaining process, the interests of the individual employee may be subordinated to the collective interests of all employees in the bargaining unit. Moreover, harmony of interest between the union and the individual employee cannot always be presumed, especially where a claim of racial discrimination is made. And a breach of the union's duty of fair representation may prove difficult to establish. In this respect, it is noteworthy that Congress thought it necessary to afford the protections of Title VII against unions as well as employers. See 42 U.S.C. § 2000e-2(c).

judicial time and expense would justify the risk to vindication of Title VII rights.

A deferral rule also might adversely affect the arbitration system as well as the enforcement scheme of Title VII. Fearing that the arbitral forum cannot adequately protect their rights under Title VII, some employees may elect to bypass arbitration and institute a lawsuit. The possibility of voluntary compliance or settlement of Title VII claims would thus be reduced, and the result could well be more litigation, not less.

We think, therefore, that the federal policy favoring arbitration of labor disputes and the federal policy against discriminatory employment practices can best be accommodated by permitting an employee to pursue fully both his remedy under the grievance-arbitration clause of a collective-bargaining agreement and his cause of action under Title VII. The federal court should consider the employee's claim de novo. The arbitral decision may be admitted as evidence and accorded such weight as the court deems appropriate.[21]

The judgment of the Court of Appeals is reversed.

Reversed.

Gardner-Denver has also been applied where the employer argued that an arbitration award that went against the employee blocked a subsequent section 1983 action, McDonald v. City of West Branch, Mich., 466 U.S. 284, 104 S.Ct. 1799, 80 L.Ed.2d 302 (1984). That decision was highly critical of the ability of the arbitral process adequately to protect statutory rights. The Court's concerns included the lack of arbitral expertise in resolving statutory issues, the weaknesses of arbitral fact finding, and the possible conflicts between the individual and group interests represented by the union.

But when the claim involves a prior administrative decision, as opposed to an arbitration award, the balance of interests may change in multiple forum litigation. For example, in Kremer v. Chemical Construction Corp., 456 U.S. 461, 102 S.Ct. 1883, 72 L.Ed.2d 262 (1982), the Court held that a litigant who lost a discrimination case before the state

---

21. We adopt no standards as to the weight to be accorded an arbitral decision, since this must be determined in the court's discretion with regard to the facts and circumstances of each case. Relevant factors include the existence of provisions in the collective-bargaining agreement that conform substantially with Title VII, the degree of procedural fairness in the arbitral forum, adequacy of the record with respect to the issue of discrimination, and the special competence of particular arbitrators. Where an arbitral determination gives full consideration to an employee's Title VII rights, a court may properly accord it great weight. This is especially true where the issue is solely one of fact, specifically addressed by the parties and decided by the arbitrator on the basis of an adequate record. But courts should ever be mindful that Congress, in enacting Title VII, thought it necessary to provide a judicial forum for the ultimate resolution of discriminatory employment claims. It is the duty of courts to assure the full availability of this forum.

agency, and then appealed the result in state court, was precluded by res judicata from bringing a Title VII action covering the same ground. The decision turned on the fact that the claimant took a judicial appeal, even though the Court acknowledged that the scope of review was very narrow. Even this scanty review, however, triggers the constitutional obligation of federal courts to give full faith and credit to judicial decisions of the states.

THE GILMER CASE

You studied the *Gilmer* case in Chapter I, along with a note on the recent *Circuit City* decision, which put to rest any question whether employment disputes are subject to mandatory arbitration under the FAA.

NOTE ON RECONCILING ALEXANDER AND GILMER

Are you able to reconcile *Alexander* and *Gilmer*? If Mr. Gilmer forfeits his right to file an age discrimination suit in the courts simply because he signed an agreement to arbitrate all disputes when he was first hired, why shouldn't Mr. Alexander also be held to his choice? One answer, attempted by the *Gilmer* Court in trying to distinguish the two cases, is that Mr. Gilmer made his own choice to relinquish the judicial forum, while Mr. Alexander's fate was cast by his union, probably long before he ever arrived on the scene. In assessing that distinction, you should ask whether Mr. Gilmer really had much more of a choice in the matter. Had he refused to sign, he wouldn't have been allowed to work for the stock exchange. What choice would you have made under the circumstances? Compare the safeguards provided to older workers under the Older Workers Benefit Protection Act in your reference supplement when they make important decisions about their employment. Consider the Oubre case in Chapter I as well. Should those safeguards also apply to a worker like Mr. Gilmer? Would they have helped him? In distinguishing *Alexander v. Gardner–Denver*, is the Court saying that it trusts the union even less than the individual to make such a choice?

Who would have a better shot of winning his case in arbitration, Mr. Alexander or Mr. Gilmer (putting aside that you know that Mr. Alexander lost his arbitration case)? Do you think the union in *Alexander v. Gardner–Denver*, which presumably had years of experience in handling discharge cases, could do a better job in arbitration for Mr. Alexander than Mr. Gilmer could do in arbitration without a union, either by himself or with a lawyer? Did the Court get the distinction backwards?

There are two other factors to consider in comparing *Alexander* and *Gilmer*. First, in the union situation, as in *Alexander*, the grievance belongs to the union, and in presenting it the union may advance interests of the group at the expense of those of the grievant. For example, an individual employee who seeks an accommodation because of a disability may be at odds with the worker whose job he wishes to take. This may put the union in an untenable conflict of interest. Compare the situation in *Emporium Capwell*, earlier in this Chapter. Second, the difference between the two cases may have nothing to do with whether the workplace is unionized. Rather, it may reflect a more embracing attitude of the Court towards arbitration in the present age. Just a comparison of the language of the two opinions tells you that the Court has changed its view about arbitration.

The Supreme Court had an opportunity to reconcile the two decisions, about which Justice Scalia says, with some understatement, "there is obviously some tension between these two lines of cases." Read his decision in the following case, *Wright v. Universal Maritime Service Corporation*, and see if you can predict how the Supreme Court would decide a case that squarely pitted the two decisions against each other.

WRIGHT v. UNIVERSAL MARITIME SERVICE CORPORATION ET AL.

Supreme Court of the United States, 2001.
525 U.S. 70, 119 S.Ct. 391, 142 L.Ed.2d 361.

JUSTICE SCALIA delivered the opinion of the Court.

This case presents the question whether a general arbitration clause in a collective-bargaining agreement (CBA) requires an employee to use the arbitration procedure for an alleged violation of the Americans with Disabilities Act of 1990(ADA), 104 Stat. 327, 42 U.S.C. § 12101 *et seq.*

I

In 1970, petitioner Ceasar Wright began working as a longshoreman in Charleston, South Carolina. He was a member of Local 1422 of the International Longshoremen's Association, AFL–CIO (Union), which uses a hiring hall to supply workers to several stevedore companies represented by the South Carolina Stevedores Association (SCSA). Clause 15(B) of the CBA between the Union and the SCSA provides in part as follows: "Matters under dispute which cannot be promptly settled between the Local and an individual Employer shall, no later than 48 hours after such discussion, be referred in writing covering the entire grievance to a Port Grievance Committee...." If the District Grievance Committee cannot reach a majority decision within 72 hours after meeting, then the committee must employ a professional arbitrator.

Clause 15(F) of the CBA provides as follows:

"The Union agrees that this Agreement is intended to cover all matters affecting wages, hours, and other terms and conditions of employment and that during the term of this Agreement the Employers will not be required to negotiate on any further matters affecting these or other subjects not specifically set forth in this Agreement. Anything not contained in this Agreement shall not be construed as being part of this Agreement. All past port practices being observed may be reduced to writing in each port."

Finally, Clause 17 of the CBA states: "It is the intention and purpose of all parties hereto that no provision or part of this Agreement shall be violative of any Federal or State Law."

Wright was also subject to the Longshore Seniority Plan, which contained its own grievance provision, reading as follows: "Any dispute concerning or arising out of the terms and/or conditions of this Agreement, or dispute involving the interpretation or application of this Agreement, or dispute arising out of any rule adopted for its implementation, shall be referred to the Seniority Board." The Seniority Board is equally divided between labor and management representatives. * * *

On February 18, 1992, while Wright was working for respondent Stevens Shipping and Terminal Company (Stevens), he injured his right heel and his back. He sought compensation from Stevens for permanent disability under the Longshore and Harbor Workers' Compensation Act, 44 Stat. 1424, as amended, 33 U.S.C. § 901 *et seq.,* and ultimately settled the claim for $250,000 and $10,000 in attorney's fees. Wright was also awarded Social Security disability benefits.

In January 1995, Wright returned to the Union hiring hall and asked to be referred for work. (At some point he obtained a written note from his doctor approving such activity.) Between January 2 and January 11, Wright worked for four stevedoring companies, none of which complained about his performance. When, however, the stevedoring companies realized that Wright had previously settled a claim for permanent disability, they informed the Union that they would not accept Wright for employment, because a person certified as permanently disabled (which they regarded Wright to be) is not qualified to perform longshore work under the CBA. The Union responded that the employers had misconstrued the CBA, suggested that the ADA entitled Wright to return to work if he could perform his duties, and asserted that refusing Wright employment would constitute a "lock-out" in violation of the CBA.

When Wright found out that the stevedoring companies would no longer accept him for employment, he contacted the Union to ask how he could get back to work. Wright claims that instead of suggesting the filing of a grievance, the Union told him to obtain counsel and file a claim under the ADA. Wright hired an attorney and eventually filed charges of discrimination with the Equal Employment Opportunity Commission (EEOC) and the South Carolina State Human Affairs Commission, alleging that the stevedoring companies and the SCSA had violated the ADA by refusing him work. In October 1995, Wright received a right-to-sue letter from the EEOC.

In January 1996, Wright filed a complaint against the SCSA and six individual stevedoring companies in the United States District Court for the District of South Carolina. Respondents' answer asserted various affirmative defenses, including Wright's failure to exhaust his remedies under the CBA and the Seniority Plan. * * *

II

In this case, the Fourth Circuit concluded that the general arbitration provision in the CBA governing Wright's employment was sufficiently broad to encompass a statutory claim arising under the ADA, and that such a provision was enforceable. The latter conclusion brings into question two lines of our case law. The first is represented by *Alexander v. Gardner–Denver Co.*, which held that an employee does not forfeit his right to a judicial forum for claimed discriminatory discharge in violation of Title VII of the Civil Rights Act of 1964, if "he first pursues his grievance to final arbitration under the nondiscrimination clause of a collective-bargaining agreement." In rejecting the argument that the doctrine of election of remedies barred the Title VII lawsuit, we reasoned that a grievance is designed to vindicate a "contractual right" under a CBA, while a lawsuit under Title VII asserts "independent statutory rights accorded by Congress." The statutory cause of action was not waived by the union's agreement to the arbitration provision of the CBA, since "there can be no prospective waiver of an employee's rights under Title VII." We have followed the holding of *Gardner-Denver* in deciding the effect of CBA arbitration upon employee claims under other statutes.

The second line of cases implicated here is represented by *Gilmer v. Interstate/Johnson Lane Corp.*, *supra*, which held that a claim brought under the Age Discrimination in Employment Act of 1967 (ADEA), 81 Stat. 602, as amended, 29 U.S.C. § 621 *et seq.*, could be subject to compulsory arbitration pursuant to an arbitration provision in a securities registration form. Relying upon the federal policy favoring arbitration embodied in the Federal Arbitration Act (FAA), 9 U.S.C. § 1 *et seq.*, we said that "statutory claims may be the subject of an arbitration agreement, enforceable pursuant to the FAA."

There is obviously some tension between these two lines of cases. Whereas *Gardner-Denver* stated that "an employee's rights under Title VII are not susceptible of prospective waiver," *Gilmer* held that the right to a federal judicial forum for an ADEA claim could be waived. Petitioner and the United States as *amicus* would have us reconcile the lines of authority by maintaining that federal forum rights cannot be waived in union-negotiated CBAs even if they can be waived in individually executed contracts—a distinction that assuredly finds support in the text of *Gilmer*. Respondents and their *amici*, on the other hand, contend that the real difference between *Gardner-Denver* and *Gilmer* is the radical change, over two decades, in the Court's receptivity to arbitration, leading *Gilmer* to affirm that "questions of arbitrability must be addressed with a healthy regard for the federal policy favoring arbitration,"; *Gilmer*, they argue, has sufficiently undermined *Gardner-Denver* that a union *can* waive employees' rights to a judicial forum. Although, as will appear, we find *Gardner-Denver* and *Gilmer* relevant for various purposes to the case before us, we find it unnecessary to resolve the question of the validity of a union-negotiated waiver, since it is apparent to us, on the facts and arguments presented here, that no such waiver has occurred.

III

In asserting the existence of an agreement to arbitrate the ADA claim, respondents rely upon the presumption of arbitrability this Court has found in § 301 of the Labor Management Relations Act 1947 (LMRA), 61 Stat. 156, 29 U.S.C. § 185. In collective-bargaining agreements, we have said, "there is a presumption of arbitrability in the sense that '[a]n order to arbitrate the particular grievance should not be denied unless it may be said with positive assurance that the arbitration clause is not susceptible of an interpretation that covers the asserted dispute.' " *AT & T Technologies, Inc. v. Communications Workers,* (quoting *Warrior & Gulf*).

That presumption, however, does not extend beyond the reach of the principal rationale that justifies it, which is that arbitrators are in a better position than courts *to interpret the terms of a CBA.* This rationale finds support in the very text of the LMRA, which announces that "[f]inal adjustment by a method agreed upon by the parties is declared to be the desirable method for settlement of grievance disputes arising *over the application or interpretation of an existing collective-bargaining agreement.*" 29 U.S.C. § 173(d) (emphasis added). The dispute in the present case, however, ultimately concerns not the application or interpretation of any CBA, but the meaning of a federal statute. The cause of action Wright asserts arises not out of contract, but out of the ADA, and is distinct from any right conferred by the collective-bargaining agreement. To be sure, respondents argue that Wright is not qualified for his position as the CBA requires, but even if that were true he would *still* prevail if the refusal to hire violated the ADA.

Nor is the statutory (as opposed to contractual) focus of the claim altered by the fact that Clause 17 of the CBA recites it to be "the intention and purpose of all parties hereto that no provision or part of this Agreement shall be violative of any Federal or State Law." As we discuss below in Part IV, this does not incorporate the ADA by reference. Even if it did so, however—thereby creating a contractual right that is coextensive with the federal statutory right—the ultimate question for the arbitrator would be not what the parties have agreed to, but what federal law requires; and that is not a question which should be *presumed* to be included within the arbitration requirement. Application of that principle is unaffected by the fact that the CBA in this case, unlike the one in *Gardner-Denver*, does not expressly limit the arbitrator to interpreting and applying the contract. The *presumption* only extends that far, whether or not the text of the agreement is similarly limited. It may well be that ordinary textual analysis of a CBA will show that matters which go beyond the interpretation and application of contract terms are subject to arbitration; but they will not be *presumed* to be so.

IV

Not only is petitioner's statutory claim not subject to a presumption of arbitrability; we think any CBA requirement to arbitrate it must be particularly clear. In *Metropolitan Edison Co. v. NLRB,* 460 U.S. 693, 103 S.Ct. 1467, 75 L.Ed.2d 387 (1983), we stated that a union could waive its officers' statutory right under § 8(a)(3) of the National Labor Relations Act, 29 U.S.C. § 158(a)(3), to be free of antiunion discrimination, but we held that such a waiver must be clear and unmistakable. "[W]e will not infer from a general contractual provision that the parties intended to waive a statutorily protected right unless the undertaking is 'explicitly stated.' More succinctly, the waiver must be clear and unmistakable."

We think the same standard applicable to a union-negotiated waiver of employees' statutory right to a judicial forum for claims of employment discrimination. Although that is not a substantive right, see *Gilmer,* 500 U.S., at 26, 111 S.Ct. 1647, and whether or not *Gardner-Denver's* seemingly absolute prohibition of union waiver of employees' federal forum rights survives *Gilmer, Gardner–Denver* at least stands for the proposition that the right to a federal judicial forum is of sufficient importance to be protected against less-than-explicit union waiver in a CBA. The CBA in this case does not meet that standard. Its arbitration clause is very general, providing for arbitration of "[m]atters under dispute," which could be understood to mean matters in dispute under the contract. And the remainder of the contract contains no explicit incorporation of statutory antidiscrimination requirements. (Indeed, it does not even contain, as did the CBAs in *Austin* and *Gardner-Denver,* its own specific antidiscrimination provision.) The Fourth Circuit relied upon the fact that the equivalently broad arbitration clause in *Gilmer—* applying to "any dispute, claim or controversy"—was held to embrace federal statutory claims. But *Gilmer* involved an individual's waiver of his own rights, rather than a union's waiver of the rights of represented employees and hence the "clear and unmistakable" standard was not applicable.

Respondents rely upon Clause 15(F) of the CBA, which states that "this Agreement is intended to cover all matters affecting wages, hours, and other terms and conditions of employment." But even if this could, in isolation, be considered a clear and unmistakable incorporation of employment-discrimination laws (which is doubtful), it is surely deprived of that effect by the provision, later in the same paragraph, that "[a]nything not contained in this Agreement shall not be construed as being part of this Agreement." Respondents also rely upon Clause 17 of the CBA, which states that "[i]t is the intention and purpose of all parties hereto that no provision or part of this Agreement shall be violative of any Federal or State Law." They argue that this requires the arbitrator to "apply legal definitions derived from the ADA" in determining whether Wright is "qualified" for employment within the meaning of the CBA. Perhaps so, but that is not the same as making compliance with the ADA a contractual commitment that would be subject to the arbitration clause. This becomes crystal clear when one contrasts Clause 17 with the provision of the CBA which states that "[t]he requirements of the Occupations *[sic]* Safety and Health Administration shall be binding on both Parties." (Under respondents' interpretation of Clause 17, this OSHA provision would be superfluous.) Clause 17 seems to us nothing more than a recitation of the canon of construction which would in any event have been applied to the CBA—that an agreement should be interpreted in such fashion as to preserve, rather than destroy, its validity (*ut res magis valeat quam pereat*).

Finally, we do not find a clear and unmistakable waiver in the Longshore Seniority Plan. Like the CBA itself, the plan contains no antidiscrimination provision; and it specifically limits its grievance procedure to disputes related to the agreement.

We hold that the collective-bargaining agreement in this case does not contain a clear and unmistakable waiver of the covered employees' rights to a judicial forum for federal claims of employment discrimination. We do not reach the question whether such a waiver would be enforceable. The judgment of the Fourth Circuit is vacated, and the case is remanded for further proceedings consistent with this opinion.

QUESTIONS ABOUT WRIGHT

If you were house counsel to a union, what would you recommend that it do after *Wright*? Do you think a union violates its duty of fair representation towards those it represents if it negotiates a clause that, unlike the one in *Wright*, squarely puts all statutory claims into arbitration. Does the employee have a claim against the union for forcing her into arbitration?

Do you think a union, as an institutional matter, wants the responsibility for arbitrating statutory claims? An employee has to pay a large fee to an attorney for representing her in a statutory claim. Of course if she prevails, the employer pays her attorneys' fees. Can a union afford to provide representation in arbitration to all employees who may have a statutory claim?

If unions don't want to touch these cases, the tension between *Alexander* and *Gilmer* may never have to be reconciled.

One of the unanswered questions about arbitration of statutory rights in a unionized workplace is whether the courts will give any meaningful judicial review to the arbitrator's decision. As you will see in Chapter III, the prevailing view under the Steelworkers Trilogy (now represented by the *Eastern Coal* case in Chapter III) is for the courts to play an extremely limited role in reviewing arbitration awards, limited, in effect, to claims of fraud, or to a showing, hard to make, that the arbitrator exceeded his contractual authority. However, *Gilmer* suggests that the scope of judicial review may be more extensive in statutory cases. After all, one of the predicates of the *Gilmer* decision is that arbitration is not a second-best way of vindicating statutory rights, but is the equal of a judicial proceeding. For that to be true, it may be necessary to provide an equivalent scope of judicial review.

We have discussed some of these issues in Chapter I. They may be equally applicable to arbitrations in the union sector.

Finally, what should the courts' role be in compelling a party to arbitrate? Suppose that in a non-union setting the employer and employee have agreed to arbitrate all claims arising out of federal statutes. An employee requires leave time to care for an ailing parent. While he is on leave a promotional opportunity arises. The employee contends that under the Family and Medical Leave Act he is entitled to have the employer consider him for promotion. The employer responds that the Family and Medical Leave Act provides for no such thing, and that this employee is trying to get into arbitration to create rights that don't exist under the statute. Should the court follow the same presumption for compelling arbitration as it does under *AT & T Technologies* (which appears in Chapter III) in cases arising under collective bargaining agreements? If not, what justifies the difference in approach? Does the philosophy of encouraging arbitration under the NLRA apply with the same force to agreements to arbitrate in a non-union setting?

NOTE ON A DIFFICULT TECHNICAL
POINT: NLRB DEFERRAL

In the unionized workplace, some management actions that could be challenged through arbitration might also be the subject of a charge before the NLRB. Suppose, for example, the employer tries to relocate an operation while a collective bargaining agreement is in effect. The collective bargaining agreement may provide the answer, for example, by addressing the question of when the employer may have work performed outside the bargaining unit. The union should be able to challenge that move by filing a grievance and letting the arbitrator determine the outcome. If the union sought that route, a court would be inclined to compel arbitration in view of the presumption of arbitrability under Section 301 that we discussed earlier. A more detailed examination of this presumption is found in Chapter III. However, the termination and removal of work may also constitute a violation of Section 8(a)(5), if it is a mandatory subject of bargaining. You saw in the Carrier story earlier in this chapter that the union might have challenged the removal of the work through the collective bargaining agreement, but chose instead to file a Charge under the NLRA.

What is the appropriate forum for challenging management's action? A Charge filed with the Board under Section 8(a)(5), or an arbitration, claiming a violation of some provision of the collective agreement? The Board's current view is to "defer" such cases to arbitration, allowing the parties to attempt to resolve them first in that forum. Collyer Insulated Wire, 192 NLRB 837 (1971). The arbitrator's award binds the parties unless the grievance and arbitration procedures "have not been fair or regular" or the arbitrator has reached a result which is "repugnant" to the Act. In those limited circumstances, the Board will take jurisdiction and hear the case even though it has gone through arbitration, United Technologies and Machinists Union, 268 NLRB 557, 115 LRRM 1049, 1984 WL 36028 (1984).

This deferral route was not discussed in the account of the Carrier situation that we presented earlier.

The deferral doctrine has been accepted by the courts for the most part, but sometimes a bit grudgingly when it is not clear that the arbitrator has actually considered the statutory issue. There is more controversy over whether the Board should defer in cases that involve individual rights under the NLRA, as opposed to questions that turn on the reading of the collective bargaining agreement. The classic example is a worker who is fired for strongly advocating a grievance. The Board has taken the view, in the *United Technologies* case noted above, that this claim too must be deferred to arbitration, unless it appears that the union has taken a position at odds with the employee and can't effectively represent her in arbitration.

Some of these points will be amplified in Chapter III. We describe the NLRB's deferral system now because it offers an alternative approach to the problem of multiple forums. The Court could take the view that the parties should be required to arbitrate their dispute first, and then the courts would defer to the result if it isn't inconsistent with external law. But that approach was expressly advocated and rejected in *Gardner–Denver*.

G. USING MORE GLOBAL ECONOMIC WEAPONS

INTRODUCTION

In a previous section we saw the limits of the effective use of the traditional strike weapon and the response of operating with replacements. Those tactics, particularly on the union side, are becoming outmoded in a global economy.

To begin with, the strike is not the weapon it once was, given an economy of job scarcity and the decline of the union movement. Potential workers just do not take a picket line as seriously as before. They no longer have the linkages of family and friends in the labor movement and may have no sense of loyalty to the strikers. And even if they did, the economic pinch may force them to jump at the chance to gain solid employment even if it means displacing a striker.

But even if the strike weapon were effective at the work site, today's conglomerate employer can counter it by placing the affected work elsewhere in the enterprise, often overseas, or subcontracting it to other employers, or by simply closing down the struck facility and maintaining a revenue stream from other parts of the corporation.

The union's typical response is to bring economic pressure upon any other employer that assists the struck employer, or upon other subdivisions of the conglomerate. When the union does this, however, it runs up against a portion of the Act that is designed to isolate neutral employers and their employees from the economic pressures generated by a labor dispute.

The Section in question, 8(b)(4), is a real bear to read. We'll try to assist you by giving you a break out of the various provisions that are central to our discussion:

A TRIP THROUGH § 8(B)(4)

Unfair labor practice for a labor organization:

(i) To engage in,

or to induce or encourage any individual employed in commerce to engage in,

—a strike, or

—a refusal to use, manufacture, process, transport, or otherwise handle or work on any goods etc., or

(ii) to threaten, coerce, or restrain any person engaged in commerce,

Where in either case an object is:

    A.   Forcing or requiring any employer or self-employed person

—to join any labor organization, or

—to enter any agreement prohibited by 8(e)

    B.   Forcing or requiring any person

—to cease using, selling, handling etc. products of any other producer etc., or

—to cease doing business with any other person, or

forcing or requiring any other employer

—to recognize a labor organization not certified under Sec. 9

PROVIDED, Nothing in (B) shall be construed to make unlawful any primary strike or primary picketing.

PROVIDED, nothing in 8(b) shall be construed to make unlawful refusal of any person to enter premises of another employer where employees are on strike.

PROVIDED FURTHER, for 8(b)(4), nothing in 8(b)(4) shall be construed

to prohibit publicity, other than picketing,

—for the purpose of truthfully advising the public, including consumers and members of a labor organization,

that products are produced by an employer with whom union has primary dispute, and

are distributed by another employer

As long as such publicity does not have an effect

of inducing any individual employed by any person other than the primary employer

in the course of his employment to refuse to pick up etc. or not to perform any services.

This convoluted provision is known in the business as the "secondary boycott" section. Let's start with some terminology. The union usually has its basic dispute with one employer, referred to in the court decisions as the "primary" employer. Sometimes the union will try to influence the primary employer by putting pressure on another employer, perhaps one that supplies the primary employer. The union hopes this pressure will encourage (maybe that is too kind a word) the neutral employer to stop doing business with the employer. The design of the secondary boycott provision is to prevent the union from putting pressure on the neutral, or secondary, employer.

This is pretty easy to understand, although it has its difficult moments, when a union puts pressure on an employer that is truly neutral in the union's dispute with the primary. There we can understand the philosophy that where the union has no ax to grind with workers and their employers, the neutral employer should not be dragged into the union's problems with another employer. We will start our study with a typical arrangement that involves that scenario. But we will see that we run into problems in the modern economy, when it is less clear how to draw the lines between a truly neutral employer and one that is somehow connected with the labor dispute of the primary employer.

We will consider the various applicable doctrines by looking at an imaginary dialogue between Marcia Bell, a beginning lawyer who works in the office of the general counsel of the United Factory Workers' Union, and her boss, general counsel Sam Gompers. The Union for years had a collective bargaining agreement with Enderby Industries, a manufacturer of plastics. During the last contract, Enderby was taken over by Octopus Enterprises, a large conglomerate. Octopus was assisted in the takeover by First Fidelity Funding, which provided much of the financing for the takeover.

Octopus honored Enderby's collective bargaining agreement with the union. But that contract is now expiring. Octopus is taking a very hard line in negotiations. If it cannot secure a favorable contract, it is inclined to fold the Enderby division and place its resources elsewhere. Bell and Gompers discuss the union's potential responses should bargaining break down and Octopus attempt to carry out its threat.

1. THE TRADITIONAL DISTINCTION BETWEEN PRIMARY AND SECONDARY PRESSURE

The union would like to put up picket lines at the various enterprises that supply Enderby. It would also like to picket the bank, First

Fidelity Funding, urging patrons of the bank to withdraw their funds until Octopus bargains more productively with the union. It would also like to place picket lines in front of Enderby.

Bell: Am I correct in readings 8(b)(4) to allow me to picket at Enderby but not at any of its suppliers and not at the bank? I am not sure I see the sense in that distinction.

Gompers: Here's the key: If the union has a dispute with Enderby, then, in the jargon of the statute, Enderby is the primary employer. In order to put pressure on Enderby, the union goes to another employer with whom Enderby deals. That other employer is deemed a neutral in the union's dispute with Enderby. In the language of the trade it is the secondary employer. The NLRA prohibits the union to put pressure on the neutral, secondary employer to induce it to stop doing business with Enderby. That's the gist of the prohibition on secondary activity.

Bell: Well, I don't quite understand. Suppose my union has a dispute with Enderby and sets up a picket line around Enderby's plant. Along comes a truck owned by another company, driven by a member of the Teamsters union, bringing raw materials into Enderby. The driver sees the picket line and turns the truck around. Now, haven't we violated the statute? We've put up a picket line with the object of restraining the neutral trucking company from doing business with Enderby, the primary employer with whom we have the dispute. Violation?

Gompers: You're right, but you're wrong. If the statute went that far it would immunize Enderby from the unavoidable consequences of primary picketing. Look at the proviso that says "nothing … shall be construed to make unlawful, where not otherwise unlawful, any primary strike or primary picketing." Read the following case and you'll understand the philosophy and operation of this section:

LOCAL 761, ELECTRICAL WORKERS v. NLRB

Supreme Court of the United States, 1961.
366 U.S. 667, 81 S.Ct. 1285, 6 L.Ed.2d 592.

MR. JUSTICE FRANKFURTER delivered the opinion of the Court.

Local 761 of the International Union of Electrical, Radio and Machine Workers, AFL–CIO, was charged with a violation of § 8(b)(4)(A) of the National Labor Relations Act, as amended by the Taft–Hartley Act, 61 Stat. 136, 141, 29 U.S.C.A. § 158(b)(4)(A), upon the following facts.

General Electric Corporation operates a plant outside of Louisville, Kentucky, where it manufactures washers, dryers, and other electrical household appliances. The square-shaped, thousand-acre, unfenced plant is known as Appliance Park. A large drainage ditch makes ingress and egress impossible except over five roadways across culverts, designated as gates.

Since 1954, General Electric sought to confine the employees of independent contractors, described hereafter, who work on the premises of the Park, to the use of Gate 3–A and confine its use to them. The undisputed reason for doing so was to insulate General Electric employees from the frequent labor disputes in which the contractors were involved. Gate 3–A is 550 feet away from the nearest entrance available for General Electric employees, suppliers, and deliverymen. Although anyone can pass the gate without challenge, the roadway leads to a guardhouse where identification must be presented. Vehicle stickers of various shapes and colors enable a guard to check on sight whether a vehicle is authorized to use Gate 3–A. Since January 1958, a prominent sign has been posted at the gate which states: "Gate 3–A For Employees Of Contractors Only—G.E. Employees Use Other Gates." On rare occasions, it appears, a General Electric employee was allowed to pass the guardhouse, but such occurrence was in violation of company instructions. There was no proof of any unauthorized attempts to pass the gate during the strike in question.

The independent contractors are utilized for a great variety of tasks on the Appliance Park premises. Some do construction work on new buildings; some install and repair ventilating and heating equipment; some engage in retooling and rearranging operations necessary to the manufacture of new models; others do "general maintenance work." These services are contracted to outside employers either because the company's employees lack the necessary skill or manpower, or because the work can be done more economically by independent contractors. The latter reason determined the contracting of maintenance work for which the Central Maintenance department of the company bid competitively with the contractors. While some of the work done by these contractors had on occasion been previously performed by Central Maintenance, the findings do not disclose the number of employees of independent contractors who were performing these routine maintenance services, as compared with those who were doing specialized work of a capital-improvement nature.

The Union, petitioner here, is the certified bargaining representative for the production and maintenance workers who constitute approximately 7,600 of the 10,500 employees of General Electric at Appliance Park. On July 27, 1958, the Union called a strike because of 24 unsettled grievances with the company. Picketing occurred at all the gates, including Gate 3–A, and continued until August 9 when an injunction was issued by a Federal District Court. The signs carried by the pickets at all gates read: "Local 761 On Strike G.E. Unfair." Because of the picketing, almost all of the employees of independent contractors refused to enter the company premises.

Neither the legality of the strike or of the picketing at any of the gates except 3–A nor the peaceful nature of the picketing is in dispute.

The sole claim is that the picketing before the gate exclusively used by employees of independent contractors was conduct proscribed by § 8(b)(4)(A).

The Trial Examiner recommended that the Board dismiss the complaint. He concluded that the limitations on picketing which the Board had prescribed in so-called "common situs" cases were not applicable to the situation before him, in that the picketing at Gate 3–A represented traditional primary action which necessarily had a secondary effect of inconveniencing those who did business with the struck employer. He reasoned that if a primary employer could limit the area of picketing around his own premises by constructing a separate gate for employees of independent contractors, such a device could also be used to isolate employees of his suppliers and customers, and that such action could not relevantly be distinguished from oral appeals made to secondary employees not to cross a picket line where only a single gate existed.

The Board rejected the Trial Examiner's conclusion. It held that, since only the employees of the independent contractors were allowed to use Gate 3–A, the Union's object in picketing there was "to enmesh these employees of the neutral employers in its dispute with the Company," thereby constituting a violation of § 8(b)(4)(A) because the independent employees were encouraged to engage in a concerted refusal to work "with an object of forcing the independent contractors to cease doing business with the Company." * * *

I.

Section 8(b)(4)(A) of the National Labor Relations Act provides that it shall be an unfair labor practice for a labor organization

" * * * to engage in, or to induce or encourage the employees of any employer to engage in, a strike or a concerted refusal in the course of their employment to use, manufacture, process, transport, or otherwise handle or work on any goods, articles, materials, or commodities or to perform any services, where an object thereof is: (A) forcing or requiring * * * any employer or other person * * * to cease doing business with any other person * * *."

This provision could not be literally construed; otherwise it would ban most strikes historically considered to be lawful, so-called primary activity. "While § 8(b)(4) does not expressly mention 'primary' or 'secondary' disputes, strikes or boycotts, that section often is referred to in the Act's legislative history as one of the Act's 'secondary boycott sections.'" National Labor Relations Board v. Denver Building & Const. Trades Council, 341 U.S. 675, 686, 71 S.Ct. 943, 950, 95 L.Ed. 1284. "Congress did not seek by § 8(b)(4), to interfere with the ordinary strike * * *." National Labor Relations Board v. International Rice Milling Co., 341 U.S. 665, 672, 71 S.Ct. 961, 965, 95 L.Ed. 1277. The impact of the section was directed toward what is known as the secondary boycott whose "sanctions bear, not upon the employer who alone is a party to the dispute, but upon some third party who has no concern in it." Thus the section "left a striking labor organization free to use persuasion, including picketing, not only on the primary employer and his employees but on numerous others. Among these were secondary employers who were customers or suppliers of the primary employer and persons dealing with them * * * and even employees of secondary employers so long as the labor organization did not * * * 'induce or encourage the employees of any employer to engage, in a strike or a concerted refusal in the course of their employment' * * *."

But not all so-called secondary boycotts were outlawed in § 8(b)(4)(A). "The section does not speak generally of secondary boycotts. It describes and condemns specific union conduct directed to specific objectives. * * * Employees must be induced; they must be induced to engage in a strike or concerted refusal; an object must be to force or require their employer or another person to cease doing business with a third person. Thus, much that might argumentatively be found to fall within the broad and somewhat vague concept of secondary boycott is not in terms prohibited."

Important as is the distinction between legitimate "primary activity" and banned "secondary activity," it does not present a glaringly bright line. The objectives of any picketing include a desire to influence others from withholding from the employer their services or trade. See Sailors' Union of the Pacific (Moore Dry Dock), 92 N.L.R.B. 547. "[I]ntended or not, sought for or not, aimed for or not, employees of neutral employers do take action sympathetic with strikers and do put pressure on their own employers." Seafarers International Union, etc. v. National Labor Relations Board, 105 U.S.App.D.C. 211, 265 F.2d 585, 590. "It is clear that, when a union pickets an employer with whom it has a dispute, it hopes, even if it does not intend, that all persons will honor the picket line, and that hope encompasses the employees of neutral employers who may in the course of their employment (deliverymen and the like) have to enter the premises." Id., at page 591. "Almost all picketing, even at the situs of the primary employer and surely at that of the secondary, hopes to achieve the forbidden objective, whatever other motives there may be and however small the chances of success." National Labor Relations Board v. Local 294, International Brotherhood of Teamsters, 284 F.2d 887, 890 (2d Cir.1960). But picketing which induces secondary employees to respect a picket line is not the equivalent of picketing which has an object of inducing those employees to engage in concerted conduct against their employer in order to force him to refuse to deal with the struck employer. National Labor Relations Board v. International Rice Milling Co., supra.

However difficult the drawing of lines more nice than obvious, the statute compels the task. Accordingly, the Board and the courts have attempted to devise reasonable criteria drawing heavily upon the means to which a union resorts in promoting its cause. Although "[n]o rigid rule which would make * * * [a] few factors conclusive is contained in or deducible from the statute," "[i]n the absence of admissions by the union of an illegal intent, the nature of acts performed shows the intent.''

The nature of the problem, as revealed by unfolding variant situations, inevitably involves an evolutionary process for its rational response, not a quick, definitive formula as a comprehensive answer. And so, it is not surprising that the Board has more or less felt its way during the fourteen years in which it has had to apply § 8(b)(4)(A), and has modified and reformed its standards on the basis of accumulating experience. ''One of the purposes which lead to the creation of such boards is to have decisions based upon evidential facts under the particular statute made by experienced officials with an adequate appreciation of the complexities of the subject which is entrusted to their administration.'' Republic Aviation Corp. v. National Labor Relations Board, 324 U.S. 793, 800, 65 S.Ct. 982, 986, 89 L.Ed. 1372.

II.

The early decisions of the Board following the Taft–Hartley amendments involved activity which took place around the secondary employer's premises. For example, in Wadsworth Building Co., [United Brotherhood of Carpenters and Joiners of America, 81 N.L.R.B. 802 (1942)], the union set up a picket line around the situs of a builder who had contracted to purchase prefabricated houses from the primary employer. The Board found this to be illegal secondary activity.

In contrast, when picketing took place around the premises of the primary employer, the Board regarded this as valid primary activity. In Oil Workers International Union (Pure Oil Co.), 84 N.L.R.B. 315, Pure had used Standard's dock and employees for loading its oil onto ships. The companies had contracted that, in case of a strike against Standard, Pure employees would take over the loading of Pure oil. The union struck against Standard and picketed the dock, and Pure employees refused to cross the picket line. The Board held this to be a primary activity, although the union's action induced the Pure employees to engage in a concerted refusal to handle Pure products at the dock. The fact that the picketing was confined to the vicinity of the Standard premises influenced the Board not to find that an object of the activity was to force Pure to cease doing business with Standard, even if such was a secondary effect. * * *

In United Electrical Workers (Ryan Construction Corp.), 85 N.L.R.B. 417, Ryan had contracted to perform construction work on a building adjacent to the Bucyrus plant and inside its fence. A separate gate was cut through the fence for Ryan's employees which no employee of Bucyrus ever used. The Board concluded that the union on strike against Bucyrus could picket the Ryan gate, even though an object of the picketing was to enlist the aid of Ryan employees, since Congress did not intend to outlaw primary picketing.

''When picketing is wholly at the premises of the employer with whom the union is engaged in a labor dispute, it cannot be called 'secondary' even though, as is virtually always the case, an object of the picketing is to dissuade all persons from entering such premises for business reasons. It makes no difference whether 1 or 100 other employees wish to enter the premises. It follows in this case that the picketing of Bucyrus premises, which was primary because in support of a labor dispute with Bucyrus, did not lose its character and become 'secondary' at the so-called Ryan gate because Ryan employees were the only persons regularly entering Bucyrus premises at that gate.'' 85 N.L.R.B., at 418.

Thus, the Board eliminated picketing which took place around the situs of the primary employer-regardless of the special circumstances involved from being held invalid secondary activity under § 8(b)(4)(A).

However, the impact of the new situations made the Board conscious of the complexity of the problem by reason of the protean forms in which it appeared. This became clear in the "common situs" cases situations where two employers were performing separate tasks on common premises. The Moore Dry Dock case, supra, laid out the Board's new standards in this area. There, the union picketed outside an entrance to a dock where a ship, owned by the struck employer, was being trained and outfitted. Although the premises picketed were those of the secondary employer, they constituted the only place where picketing could take place; furthermore, the objectives of the picketing were no more aimed at the employees of the secondary employer—the dock owner—than they had been in the Pure Oil and Ryan cases. The Board concluded, however, that when the situs of the primary employer was "ambulatory" there must be a balance between the union's right to picket and the interest of the secondary employer in being free from picketing. It set out four standards for picketing in such situations which would be presumptive of valid primary activity: (1) that the picketing be limited to times when the situs of dispute was located on the secondary premises, (2) that the primary employer be engaged in his normal business at the situs, (3) that the picketing take place reasonably close to the situs, and (4) that the picketing clearly disclose that the dispute was only with the primary employer. These tests were widely accepted by reviewing federal courts. * * *

As is too often the way of law or, at least, of adjudications, soon the Dry Dock tests were mechanically applied so that a violation of one of the standards was taken to be presumptive of illegal activity. For example, failure of picket signs clearly to designate the employer against whom the strike was directed was held to be violative of § 8(b)(4)(A).

In Local 55 (PBM), 108 N.L.R.B. 363, the Board for the first time applied the Dry Dock test, although the picketing occurred at premises owned by the primary employer. There, an insurance company owned a tract of land that it was developing, and also served as the general contractor. A neutral subcontractor was also doing work at the site. The union, engaged in a strike against the insurance company, picketed the entire premises, characterizing the entire job as unfair, and the employees of the subcontractor walked off. The Court of Appeals for the Tenth Circuit enforced the Board's order which found the picketing to be illegal on the ground that the picket signs did not measure up to the Dry Dock standard that they clearly disclose that the picketing was directed against the struck employer only.

The Board's application of the Dry Dock standards to picketing at the premises of the struck employer was made more explicit in Retail Fruit & Vegetable Clerks (Crystal Palace Market), 116 N.L.R.B. 856. The owner of a large common market operated some of the shops within, and leased out others to independent sellers. The union, although given permission to picket the owner's individual stands, chose to picket outside the entire market. The Board held that this action was violative of § 8(b)(4)(A) in that the union did not attempt to minimize the effect of its picketing, as required in a common-situs case, on the operations of the neutral employers utilizing the market. "We believe ... that the foregoing principles should apply to all common situs picketing, including cases where, as here, the picketed premises are owned by the primary employer." [The Ryan case was overruled to the extent it implied the contrary.] The Court of Appeals for the Ninth Circuit, in enforcing the Board's order, specifically approved its disavowance of an ownership test. 249 F.2d 591. The Board made clear that its decision did not affect situations where picketing which had effects on neutral third parties who dealt with the employer occurred at premises occupied solely by him. "In such cases, we adhere to the rule established by the Board ... that more latitude be given to picketing at such separate primary premises than at premises occupied in part (or entirely) by secondary employers."

In rejecting the ownership test in situations where two employers were performing work upon a common site, the Board was naturally guided by this Court's opinion in Rice Milling, in which we indicated that the location of the picketing at the primary employer's premises was "not necessarily conclusive" of its legality. Where the work done by the secondary employees is unrelated to the normal operations of the primary employer, it is difficult to perceive how the pressure of picketing the entire situs is any less on the neutral employer merely because the picketing takes place at property owned by the struck employer. The application of the Dry Dock tests to limit the picketing effects to the employees of the employer against whom the dispute is directed carries out the "dual congressional objectives of preserving the right of labor organizations to bring pressure to bear on offending employers in primary labor disputes and of shielding unoffending employers and others from pressures in controversies not their own." National Labor Relations Board v. Denver Building & Const. Trades Council.

III.

From this necessary survey of the course of the Board's treatment of our problem, the precise nature of the issue before us emerges. With due regard to the relation between the Board's function and the scope of judicial review of its rulings, the question is whether the Board may apply the Dry Dock criteria so as to make unlawful picketing at a gate utilized exclusively by employees of independent contractors who work on the struck employer's premises. The effect of such a holding would not bar the union from picketing at all gates used by the employees, suppliers, and customers of the struck employer. Of course an employer may not, by removing all his employees from the situs of the strike, bar the union from publicizing its cause. The basis of the Board's decision in this case would not remotely have that effect, nor any such tendency for the future.

The Union claims that, if the Board's ruling is upheld, employers will be free to erect separate gates for deliveries, customers, and replacement workers which will be immunized from picketing. This fear is baseless. The key to the problem is found in the type of work that is being performed by those who use the separate gate. It is significant that the Board has since applied its rationale, first stated in the present case, only to situations where the independent workers were performing tasks unconnected to the normal operations of the struck employer-usually construction work on his buildings. In such situations, the indicated limitations on picketing activity respect the balance of competing interests that Congress has required the Board to enforce. On the other hand, if a separate gate were devised for regular plant deliveries, the barring of picketing at that location would make a clear invasion on traditional primary activity of appealing to neutral employees whose tasks aid the employer's everyday operations. The 1959 Amendments to the National Labor Relations Act, which removed the word "concerted" from the boycott provisions, included a proviso that "nothing contained in this clause (B) shall be construed to make unlawful, where not otherwise unlawful, any primary strike or primary picketing."

The proviso was directed against the fear that the removal of "concerted" from the statute might be interpreted so that "the picketing at the factory violates Section 8(b)(4)(A) because the pickets induce the truck drivers employed by the trucker not to perform their usual services where an object is to compel the trucking firm not to do business with the * * * manufacturer during the strike." Analysis of the bill prepared by Senator Kennedy and Representative Thompson, 105 Cong.Rec. 16589.

In a case similar to the one now before us, the Court of Appeals for the Second Circuit sustained the Board in its application of § 8(b)(4)(A) to a separate-gate situation. "There must be a separate gate marked and set apart from other gates; the work done by the men who use the gate must be unrelated to the normal operations of the employer and the work must be of a kind that would not, if done when the plant were engaged in its regular operations, necessitate curtailing those operations." United Steelworkers of America, AFL–CIO v. National Labor Relations Board, 2d Cir., 289 F.2d 591, 595. These seem to us controlling considerations.

IV.

The foregoing course of reasoning would require that the judgment below sustaining the Board's order be affirmed but for one consideration, even though this consideration may turn out not to affect the result. The legal path by which the Board and the Court of Appeals reached their decisions did not take into account that if Gate 3–A was in fact used by employees of independent contractors who performed conventional maintenance work necessary to the normal operations of General Electric, the use of the gate would have been a mingled one outside the bar of § 8(b)(4)(A). In short, such mixed use of this portion of the struck employer's premises would not bar picketing rights of the striking employees. While the record shows some such mingled use, it sheds no light on its extent. It may well turn out to be that the instances of these maintenance tasks were so insubstantial as to be treated by the Board as de minimis. We cannot here guess at the quantitative aspect of this problem. It calls for Board determination. For determination of the questions thus raised, the case must be remanded by the Court of Appeals to the Board.

Reversed.

THE CHIEF JUSTICE and MR. JUSTICE BLACK concur in the result.

———

Bell: I think I understand. I also think I see why it didn't do GE any good to set up "reserved gates" through which to funnel the subcontractors and suppliers. By isolating the subcontractors and suppliers, GE was able to argue that by picketing at those gates the union would be directing its action at the neutrals and not at the primary employer. However, the union was entitled to picket all aspects of the GE operation, even if that necessarily had an effect on neutrals.

But now what happens if the facts are reversed? Suppose that in the GE case another union had a dispute with one of GE's suppliers, say a trucking concern. Could that union follow the trucks to GE, then set up pickets? If I understand what I've read so far, that picketing might induce the employees of GE not to report to work.

Gompers: That might violate the statute. Think of it this way. It's usually considered permissible to picket at the location (sometimes we call it situs) of the employer with whom the union has a dispute (the primary employer), even if that has an impact on neutral, secondary employers. But once the picketing moves away from the primary employer's main location, then it becomes suspect, as it may unnecessarily involve a neutral. In that situation the reserved gate ploy tried in GE would work. If GE set aside gates for its suppliers, a union with a dispute with one of those suppliers would have to confine its picketing to the gate reserved for the supplier. If it goes beyond that reserved gate, it would be obvious that its purpose isn't to limit the dispute to the supplier but to involve the neutral, General Electric.

There are some very complicated and specialized rules that have to do with how you decide whether the union has gone too far in pursuing the primary employer to a neutral situs. Justice Frankfurter's discussion of this issue in the Local 761 case should give you enough of a basic understanding. You can follow up some of the case references in his decision, particularly Sailors' Union of the Pacific (Moore Dry Dock), 92 NLRB 547 (1950), if you are interested in pursuing this further.

There are also some specialized rules when the dispute occurs in the construction industry, where the primary employer may happen to work alongside the neutral employer. The rules to govern these disputes have been articulated in NLRB v. Denver Building & Construction Trades Council, 341 U.S. 675, 71 S.Ct. 943, 95 L.Ed. 1284 (1951), discussed briefly in the Local 761 opinion, and in Building and Construction Trades Council of New Orleans (Markwell & Hartz, Inc.), 155 NLRB 319 (1965). Basically, they allow the general contractor on a job to use reserved gates to isolate the various subcontractors on the job. A union that has a dispute with an offending subcontractor or supplier must confine its picketing to the entrance that sub or supplier uses. It also means that, unlike the result in Local 761, if the union's dispute is with the general contractor, it cannot apply pressure on the subcontractors if they are assigned a separate gate. Organized labor has criticized these decisions as failing to recognize that the construction site is one integrated job, and that it's proper for the union to picket the job site even if that pressure is felt by neutral subcontractors or a neutral general contractor. Legislative proposals have been made to change the outcome of these cases. For example, in the mid–1970's, Congress considered but failed to enact a "common situs" bill that, for picketing purposes, would have treated contractors and subcontractors at one construction site as single employers.

Now let's see how this applies to the union's dispute with Enderby and its efforts to picket the bank, Octopus' headquarters, and the other Octopus subsidiaries. The bank and Octopus will argue that the union's dispute is really with Enderby. The other Octopus subsidiaries, as well as the bank, are neutrals in this dispute. So any picketing undertaken by the union at these secondary sites would violate Section 8(b)(4).

2.   THE COURTS RELAX THE MEANING OF "COERCION"

Bell: The statute makes a distinction, between the (i) part and the (ii) part, about the kinds of tactics that are outlawed. A union may not induce or encourage an employee ("an individual employed in commerce") to do certain things. But when it comes to persons other than employees, say, members of the public, the rules seem to change. I take it that the reference in (ii) to "any person" is intended to go beyond employees. Now what is outlawed is not merely inducing or encouraging, but threats, coercion and restraint, something that sounds more onerous than merely inducing or encouraging.

But doesn't this statute come dangerously close to violating the First Amendment? I can understand how picketing historically has been associated with violence, and how perhaps you can view picketing as a form of coercion. The operative terms in Section 8(b)(4)(B) appears to be "forcing or requiring". But what about using an appeal other than picketing? How about newspaper and TV ads and leaflets. Wouldn't 8(b)(4)(B) be unconstitutional as a violation of free speech rights if it extended to those kinds of activities?

Gompers: I think you are right. Take a look at the DeBartolo case, which I happen to have right here. The Court interpreted the statute not to ban the use of handbills, for such a reading might violate the First Amendment. This opens up a whole new arena of economic pressure for us, although I have to question whether a handbill is as effective as a big sign on a stick. And I wonder how big a handbill has to be, or how aggressive the handbilling, before it becomes the equivalent of a picket sign.

EDWARD J. DEBARTOLO CORP. v. FLORIDA GULF COAST BUILDING AND CONSTRUCTION TRADES COUNCIL

Supreme Court of the United States, 1988.
485 U.S. 568, 108 S.Ct. 1392, 99 L.Ed.2d 645.

JUSTICE WHITE delivered the opinion of the Court.

This case centers around the respondent union's peaceful handbilling of the businesses operating in a shopping mall in Tampa, Florida, owned by petitioner, the Edward J. DeBartolo Corporation (DeBartolo). The union's primary labor dispute was with H.J. High Construction Company (High) over alleged substandard wages and fringe benefits. High was retained by the H.J. Wilson Company (Wilson) to construct a department store in the mall, and neither DeBartolo nor any of the other 85 or so mall tenants had any contractual right to influence the selection of contractors.

The union, however, sought to obtain their influence upon Wilson and High by distributing handbills asking mall customers not to shop at any of the stores in the mall "until the Mall's owner publicly promises that all construction at the Mall will be done using contractors who pay their employees fair wages and fringe benefits."[1] The handbills' message

1. The Handbill read:
"PLEASE *DON'T SHOP AT EAST LAKE SQUARE MALL* PLEASE
"The FLA. GULF COAST BUILDING TRADES COUNCIL, ALF–CIO, is request-

ing that you do not shop at the stores in the East Lake Square Mall because of The Mall ownership's contribution to substandard wages.

was that "[t]he payment of substandard wages not only diminishes the working person's ability to purchase with earned, rather than borrowed, dollars, but it also undercuts the wage standard of the entire community." The handbills made clear that the union was seeking only a consumer boycott against the other mall tenants, not a secondary strike by their employees. At all four entrances to the mall for about three weeks in December 1979, the union peacefully distributed the handbills without any accompanying picketing or patrolling.

After DeBartolo failed to convince the union to alter the language of the handbills to state that its dispute did not involve DeBartolo or the mall lessees other than Wilson and to limit its distribution to the immediate vicinity of Wilson's construction site, it filed a complaint with the National Labor Relations Board (Board), charging the union with engaging in unfair labor practices under § 8(b)(4) of the National Labor Relations Act (NLRA). The Board's General Counsel issued a complaint, but the Board eventually dismissed it, concluding that the handbilling was protected by the publicity proviso of § 8(b)(4). The Court of Appeals for the Fourth Circuit affirmed the Board, but this Court reversed in Edward J. DeBartolo Corp. v. NLRB, 463 U.S. 147, 103 S.Ct. 2926, 77 L.Ed.2d 535 (1983). There, we concluded that the handbilling did not fall within the proviso's limited scope of exempting "publicity intended to inform the public that the primary employer's product is 'distributed by' the secondary employer" because DeBartolo and the other tenants, as opposed to Wilson, did not distribute products of High. Since there had not been a determination below whether the union's handbilling fell within the prohibition of § 8(b)(4), and, if so, whether it was protected by the First Amendment, we remanded the case.

"The Wilson's Department Store under construction on these premises is being built by contractors who pay substandard wages and fringe benefits. In the past, the Mall's owner, The Edward J. DeBartolo Corporation, has supported labor and our local economy by insuring that the Mall and its stores be built by contractors who pay fair wages and fringe benefits. Now, however, and for no apparent reason, the Mall owners have taken a giant step backwards by permitting our standards to be torn down. The payment of substandard wages not only diminishes the working person's ability to purchase with earned, rather than borrowed, dollars, but it also undercuts the wage standard of the entire community. Since low construction wages at this time of inflation means decreased purchasing power, do the owners of East Lake Mall intend to compensate for the decreased purchasing power of workers of the community by en-couraging the stores in East Lake Mall to cut their prices and lower their profits?

"CUT–RATE WAGES ARE NOT FAIR UNLESS MERCHANDISE PRICES ARE ALSO CUT–RATE.

"We ask for your support in our protest against substandard wages. Please do not patronize the stores in the East Lake Square Mall until the Mall's owner publicly promises that all construction at the Mall will be done using contractors who pay their employees fair wages and fringe benefits.

"IF YOU MUST ENTER THE MALL TO DO BUSINESS, please express to the store managers your concern over substandard wages and your support of our efforts.

"We are appealing only to the public—the consumer. We are not seeking to induce any person to cease work or to refuse to make deliveries."

On remand, the Board held that the union's handbilling was proscribed by § 8(b)(4)(ii)(B). 273 N.L.R.B. 1431 (1985). It stated that under its prior cases "handbilling and other activity urging a consumer boycott constituted coercion." Id., at 1432. The Board reasoned that "[a]ppealing to the public not to patronize secondary employers is an attempt to inflict economic harm on the secondary employers by causing them to lose business," and "such appeals constitute 'economic retaliation' and are therefore a form of coercion." It viewed the object of the handbilling as attempting "to force the mall tenants to cease doing business with DeBartolo in order to force DeBartolo and/or Wilson's not to do business with High." Id., at 1432. The Board observed that it need not inquire whether the prohibition of this handbilling raised serious questions under the First Amendment, for "the statute's literal language and the applicable case law require[d]" a finding of a violation. Finally, it reiterated its longstanding position that "as a congressionally created administrative agency, we will presume the constitutionality of the Act we administer."

The Court of Appeals for the Eleventh Circuit denied enforcement of the Board's order. Because there would be serious doubts about whether § 8(b)(4) could constitutionally ban peaceful handbilling not involving nonspeech elements, such as patrolling, the court applied our decision in NLRB v. Catholic Bishop of Chicago, 440 U.S. 490, 99 S.Ct. 1313, 59 L.Ed.2d 533 (1979), to determine if there was a clear congressional intent to proscribe such handbilling. The language of the section, the court held, revealed no such intent, and the legislative history indicated that Congress, by using the phrase "threaten, coerce, or restrain," was concerned with secondary picketing and strikes rather than appeals to consumers not involving picketing. 796 F.2d, at 1336–1340. The court also concluded that the publicity proviso did not manifest congressional intent to ban all speech not coming within its terms because it was "drafted as an interpretive, explanatory section" and not as an exception to an otherwise-all-encompassing prohibition on publicity in § 8(b)(4). Id., at 1344. The court went on to construe the section as not prohibiting consumer publicity; DeBartolo petitioned for certiorari. Because this case presents important questions of federal constitutional and labor law, we granted the petition, 482 U.S. 913, 107 S.Ct. 3182, 96 L.Ed.2d 671 (1987), and now affirm.

The NLRB, the agency entrusted by Congress with the authority to administer the NLRA, has the "special function of applying the general provisions of the Act to the complexities of industrial life." NLRB v. Erie Resistor Corp., 373 U.S. 221, 236, 83 S.Ct. 1139, 1150, 10 L.Ed.2d 308 (1963); see Pattern Makers' League of North America v. NLRB, 473 U.S. 95, 114, 105 S.Ct. 3064, 3075, 87 L.Ed.2d 68 (1985); NLRB v. Steelworkers, 357 U.S. 357, 362–363, 78 S.Ct. 1268, 1271–1272, 2 L.Ed.2d 1383 (1958). Here, the Board has construed § 8(b)(4) of the Act to cover handbilling at a mall entrance urging potential customers not to trade with any retailers in the mall, in order to exert pressure on the proprietor of the mall to influence a particular mall tenant not to do business with a nonunion construction contractor. That statutory interpretation by the Board would normally be entitled to deference unless that construction were clearly contrary to the intent of Congress. Chevron U.S.A. Inc. v. National Resources Defense Council, Inc., 467 U.S. 837, 842–843, and n. 9, 104 S.Ct. 2778, 2781–2782, and n. 9, 81 L.Ed.2d 694 (1984).

Another rule of statutory construction, however, is pertinent here: where an otherwise acceptable construction of a statute would raise serious constitutional problems, the Court will construe the statute to avoid such problems unless such construction is plainly contrary to the intent of Congress. Catholic Bishop, supra, 440 at 499–501, 504, 99 S.Ct., at 1320–1321. This cardinal principle has its roots in Chief Justice Marshall's opinion for the Court in Murray v. The Charming Betsy, 2 Cranch 64, 118, 6 L.Ed.2d 1141 (1804), and has for so long been applied by this Court that it is beyond debate. As was stated in Hooper v. California, 155 U.S. 648, 657, 15 S.Ct. 207, 211, 39 L.Ed. 297 (1895), "[t]he elementary rule is that every reasonable construction must be resorted to, in order to save a statute from unconstitutionality." This approach not only reflects the prudential concern that constitutional issues not be needlessly confronted, but also recognizes that Congress, like this Court, is bound by and swears an oath to uphold the Constitution. The courts will therefore not lightly assume that Congress intended to infringe constitutionally protected liberties or usurp power constitutionally forbidden it.

We agree with the Court of Appeals and respondents that this case calls for the invocation of the Catholic Bishop rule, for the Board's construction of the statute, as applied in this case, poses serious questions of the validity of § 8(b)(4) under the First Amendment. The handbills involved here truthfully revealed the existence of a labor dispute and urged potential customers of the mall to follow a wholly legal course of action, namely, not to patronize the retailers doing business in the mall. The handbilling was peaceful. No picketing or patrolling was involved. On its face, this was expressive activity arguing that substandard wages should be opposed by abstaining from shopping in a mall where such wages were paid. Had the union simply been leafletting the public generally, including those entering every shopping mall in town, pursuant to an annual educational effort against substandard pay, there is little doubt that legislative proscription of such leaflets would pose a substantial issue of validity under the First Amendment. The same may well be true in this case, although here the handbills called attention to a specific situation in the mall allegedly involving the payment of unacceptably low wages by a construction contractor.

That a labor union is the leafletter and that a labor dispute was involved does not foreclose this analysis. We do not suggest that communications by labor unions are never of the commercial speech variety and thereby entitled to a lesser degree of constitutional protection. The handbills involved here, however, do not appear to be typical commercial speech such as advertising the price of a product or arguing its merits, for they pressed the benefits of unionism to the community and the dangers of inadequate wages to the economy and the standard of living of the populace. Of course, commercial speech itself is protected by the First Amendment, Virginia Pharmacy Bd. v. Virginia Citizens Consumer Council, Inc., 425 U.S. 748, 762, 96 S.Ct. 1817, 1826, 48 L.Ed.2d 346 (1976), and however these handbills are to be classified, the Court of Appeals was plainly correct in holding that the Board's construction would require deciding serious constitutional issues.

The Board was urged to construe the statute in light of the asserted constitutional considerations, but thought that it was constrained by its own prior authority and cases in the courts of appeals, as well as by the express language of the Act, to hold that § 8(b)(4) must be construed to forbid the handbilling involved here. Even if this construction of the Act were thought to be a permissible one, we are quite sure that in light of the traditional rule followed in Catholic Bishop, we must independently inquire whether there is another interpretation, not raising these serious constitutional concerns, that may fairly be ascribed to § 8(b)(4)(ii). This the Court has done in several cases.

In NLRB v. Drivers, 362 U.S. 274, 284, 80 S.Ct. 706, 712, 4 L.Ed.2d 710 (1960), for example, the Court rejected the Board's interpretation of the phrase "restrain or coerce" to include peaceful recognitional picketing and stated:

> "In the sensitive area of peaceful picketing Congress has dealt explicitly with isolated evils which experience has established flow from such picketing. Therefore, unless there is the clearest indication in the legislative history of § 8(b)(1)(A) supporting the Board's claim of power under that section, we cannot sustain the Board's order here. We now turn to an examination of the legislative history."

That examination of the legislative history failed to yield the requisite "clearest indication." Similarly, in NLRB v. Fruit Packers, 377 U.S. 58, 63, 84 S.Ct. 1063, 1066, 12 L.Ed. 129 (1964) (Tree Fruits), we disagreed with the Board's determination that § 8(b)(4)(ii)(B) prohibited all consumer picketing at a secondary establishment, no matter the economic consequences of that picketing, because our examination of the legislative history led us to "conclude that it does not reflect with the requisite clarity a congressional plan to proscribe all peaceful consumer picketing at secondary sites, and, particularly, any concern with peaceful picketing when it is limited, as here, to persuading" customers not to purchase a specific product of the secondary establishment. We once more looked for the "isolated evils" that Congress had focused on because "[b]oth the congressional policy and our adherence to this principle of interpretation reflect concern that a broad ban against peaceful picketing might collide with the guarantees of the First Amendment." Id., at 62–63, 84 S.Ct., at 1066; see id., at 67, 71, 84 S.Ct., at 1068–1069, 1070–1071. Because there was not the required "clearest indication in the legislative history," we rejected the Board's interpretation that limited expressive activities. Again, in Catholic Bishop, we independently determined whether the Board's jurisdiction extended to parochial schools in the face of a substantial First Amendment challenge, although the Board itself had previously considered the First Amendment challenge and presumably interpreted the statute cognizable of those limits. 440 U.S., at 497–499, 99 S.Ct., at 1317–1318.

We follow this course here and conclude, as did the Court of Appeals, that the section is open to a construction that obviates deciding whether a congressional prohibition of handbilling on the facts of this case would violate the First Amendment.

The case turns on whether handbilling such as involved here must be held to "threaten, coerce, or restrain any person" to cease doing business with another, within the meaning of § 8(b)(4)(ii)(B). We note first that "induc[ing] or encourag[ing]" employees of the secondary employer to strike is proscribed by § 8(b)(4)(i). But more than mere persuasion is necessary to prove a violation of § 8(b)(4)(ii): that section requires a showing of threats, coercion, or restraints. Those words, we have said, are "nonspecific, indeed vague," and should be interpreted with "caution" and not given a "broad sweep," Drivers, supra, at 290; and in applying § 8(b)(1)(A) they were not to be construed to reach peaceful recognitional picketing. Neither is there any necessity to construe such language to reach the handbills involved in this case. There is no suggestion that the leaflets had any coercive effect on customers of the mall. There was no violence, picketing, or patrolling and only an attempt to persuade customers not to shop in the mall.

The Board nevertheless found that the handbilling "coerced" mall tenants and explained in a footnote that "[a]ppealing to the public not to patronize secondary employers is an attempt to inflict economic harm on the secondary employers by causing them to lose business. As the case law makes clear, such appeals constitute 'economic retaliation' and are therefore a form of coercion." 273 N.L.R.B., at 1432, n. 6.[3] Our decision in Tree Fruits, however, makes untenable the notion that any kind of handbilling, picketing, or other appeals to a secondary employer to cease doing business with the employer involved in the labor dispute is "coercion" within the meaning of § 8(b)(4)(ii)(B) if it has some economic impact on the neutral. In that case, the union picketed a secondary

---

3. The Board cited two of its decisions that had been enforced by the Courts of Appeals as authority for its construction of § 8(b)(4)(ii)(B). The court in Honolulu Typographical Union No. 37 v. NLRB, 131 U.S.App.D.C. 1, 6, 401 F.2d 952, 957 (1968), enf'g 167 N.L.R.B. 1030 (1967), upheld the Board's determination that the handbilling there violated § 8(b)(4)(ii)(B), but that handbilling was part and parcel of a consumer picketing campaign in which the handbills were distributed at the edge of a line of picketers who were patrolling the entrance to the mall. The absence of picket-ing in the present case distinguishes it from Honolulu Typographical. In Great Western Broadcasting Corp. v. NLRB, 356 F.2d 434, 436 (CA9), cert. denied, 384 U.S. 1002, 86 S.Ct. 1924, 16 L.Ed.2d 1015 (1966), enf'g 150 N.L.R.B. 467 (1964), the court upheld the Board's determination that the handbilling there fell within the publicity proviso and thus was not unlawful, but it stated in dictum that § 8(b)(4)(ii)(B) covered the union activity. The court provided no analysis in support of the brief sentence and we find it unpersuasive.

employer, a retailer, asking the public not to buy a product produced by the primary employer. We held that the impact of this picketing was not coercion within the meaning of § 8(b)(4) even though, if the appeal succeeded, the retailer would lose revenue.[4]

NLRB v. Retail Store Employees, 447 U.S. 607, 100 S.Ct. 2372, 65 L.Ed.2d 377 (1980) (Safeco), * * * in turn, held that consumer picketing urging a general boycott of a secondary employer aimed at causing him to sever relations with the union's real antagonist was coercive and forbidden by § 8(b)(4). It is urged that Safeco rules this case because the union sought a general boycott of all tenants in the mall. But "picketing is qualitatively 'different from other modes of communication,' " Babbitt v. Farm Workers, 442 U.S. 289, 311, n. 17, 99 S.Ct. 2301, 2315, n. 17, 60 L.Ed.2d 895 (1979) (quoting Hughes v. Superior Court, 339 U.S. 460, 465, 70 S.Ct. 718, 721, 94 L.Ed. 985 (1950)), and Safeco noted that the picketing there actually threatened the neutral with ruin or substantial loss. As Justice Stevens pointed out in his concurrence in Safeco, supra, at 619, 100 S.Ct., at 2379, picketing is "a mixture of conduct and communication" and the conduct element "often provides the most persuasive deterrent to third persons about to enter a business establishment." Handbills containing the same message, he observed, are "much less effective than labor picketing" because they "depend entirely on the persuasive force of the idea." Similarly, the Court stated in Hughes v. Superior Court, supra, at 465, 70 S.Ct., at 721:

> "Publication in a newspaper, or by distribution of circulars, may convey the same information or make the same charge as do those patrolling a picket line. But the very purpose of a picket line is to exert influences, and it produces consequences, different from other modes of communication."

In Tree Fruits, we could not discern with the "requisite clarity" that Congress intended to proscribe all peaceful consumer picketing at secondary sites. There is even less reason to find in the language of § 8(b)(4)(ii), standing alone, any clear indication that handbilling, without picketing, "coerces" secondary employers. The loss of customers because they read a handbill urging them not to patronize a business, and not because they are intimidated by a line of picketers, is the result of mere persuasion, and the neutral who reacts is doing no more than what its customers honestly want it to do.

The Board argues that our first DeBartolo case goes far to dispose of this case because there we said that the only nonpicketing publicity "exempted from the prohibition is publicity intended to inform the public that the primary employer's product is 'distributed by' the secondary employer." 463 U.S., at 155, 103 S.Ct., at 2932. We also indicated that if the handbilling were protected by the proviso, the distribution requirement would be without substantial practical effect. Id., at 157,

---

4. The Board points out that *Tree Fruits* indicates urging customer boycotts can be coercion within the meaning of § 8(b)(4). See 377 U.S., at 72, 84 S.Ct., at 1071. But the Court was there talking about picketing and not mere handbilling.

103 S.Ct., at 2933. But we obviously did not there conclude or indicate that the handbills were covered by § 8(b)(4)(ii), for we remanded the case on this very issue. Id., at 157B158, 103 S.Ct., at 2933.

It is nevertheless argued that the second proviso to § 8(b)(4) makes clear that that section, as amended in 1959, was intended to proscribe nonpicketing appeals such as handbilling urging a consumer boycott of a neutral employer. That proviso reads as follows:

> "Provided further, That for the purposes of this paragraph (4) only, nothing contained in such paragraph shall be construed to prohibit publicity, other than picketing, for the purpose of truthfully advising the public, including consumers and members of a labor organization, that a product or products are produced by an employer with whom the labor organization has a primary dispute and are distributed by another employer, as long as such publicity does not have an effect of inducing any individual employed by any person other than the primary employer in the course of his employment to refuse to pick up, deliver, or transport any goods, or not to perform any services, at the establishment of the employer engaged in such distribution."

By its terms, the proviso protects nonpicketing communications directed at customers of a distributor of goods produced by an employer with whom the union has a labor dispute. Because handbilling and other consumer appeals not involving such a distributor are not within the proviso, the argument goes, those appeals must be considered coercive within the meaning of § 8(b)(4)(ii). Otherwise, it is said, the proviso is meaningless, for if handbilling and like communications are never coercive and within the reach of the section, there would have been no need whatsoever for the proviso.

This approach treats the proviso as establishing an exception to a prohibition that would otherwise reach the conduct excepted. But this proviso has a different ring to it. It states that § 8(b)(4) "shall not be construed" to forbid certain described nonpicketing publicity. That language need not be read as an exception. It may indicate only that without the proviso, the particular nonpicketing communication the proviso protects might have been considered to be coercive, even if other forms of publicity would not be. Section 8(b)(4), with its proviso, may thus be read as not covering nonpicketing publicity, including appeals to customers of a retailer as they approach the store, urging a complete boycott of the retailer because he handles products produced by non-union shops.[6]

---

6. Consumer picketing against the distributor of a struck manufacturer's product was the paradigm case considered in the debates. 105 Cong.Rec. 17904 (1959), 2 NLRB, Legislative History of the Labor–Management Reporting and Disclosure Act of 1959, p. 1437 (1959) (hereinafter Leg. Hist.) (Sen. Goldwater, discussing Conference agreement); 105 Cong.Rec. 15672–15673, 2 Leg.Hist. 1615 (Rep. Griffin); 105 Cong.Rec. 16591, 2 Leg.Hist. 1708 (analysis prepared by Rep. Thompson and Sen. Kennedy).

The Board's reading of § 8(b)(4) would make an unfair labor practice out of any kind of publicity or communication to the public urging a consumer boycott of employers other than those the proviso specifically deals with. On the facts of this case, newspaper, radio, and television appeals not to patronize the mall would be prohibited; and it would be an unfair labor practice for unions in their own meetings to urge their members not to shop in the mall. Nor could a union's handbills simply urge not shopping at a department store because it is using a nonunion contractor, although the union could safely ask the store's customers not to buy there because it is selling mattresses not carrying the union label. It is difficult, to say the least, to fathom why Congress would consider appeals urging a boycott of a distributor of a nonunion product to be more deserving of protection than nonpicketing persuasion of customers of other neutral employers such as that involved in this case.

Neither do we find any clear indication in the relevant legislative history that Congress intended § 8(b)(4)(ii) to proscribe peaceful handbilling, unaccompanied by picketing, urging a consumer boycott of a neutral employer. That section was one of several amendments to the NLRA enacted in 1959 and aimed at closing what were thought to be loopholes in the protections to which secondary employers were entitled. We recounted the legislative history in Tree Fruits and NLRB v. Servette, Inc., 377 U.S. 46, 84 S.Ct. 1098, 12 L.Ed.2d 121 (1964), and the Court of Appeals carefully reexamined it in this case and found "no affirmative intention of Congress clearly expressed to prohibit nonpicketing labor publicity." 796 F.2d, at 1346. For the following reasons, for the most part expressed by the Court of Appeals, we agree with that conclusion.

First, among the concerns of the proponents of the provision barring threats, coercion, or restraints aimed at secondary employers was consumer boycotts of neutral employers carried out by picketing. At no time did they suggest that merely handbilling the customers of the neutral employer was one of the evils at which their proposals were aimed. Had they wanted to bar any and all nonpicketing appeals, through newspapers, radio, television, handbills or otherwise, the debates and discussions would surely have reflected this intention. Instead, when asked, Congressman Griffin, co-sponsor of the bill that passed the House, stated that the bill covered boycotts carried out by picketing neutrals but would not interfere with the constitutional right of free speech.

Second, the only suggestions that the ban against coercing secondary employers would forbid peaceful persuasion of customers by means other than picketing came from the opponents of any proposals to close the perceived loopholes in § 8(b)(4). Among their arguments in both the House and the Senate was that picketing and handbilling a neutral employer to force him to cease dealing in the products of an employer engaged in labor disputes, appeals which were then said to be legal, would be forbidden by the proposal that became § 8(b)(4)(ii). The prohibition, it was said, "reaches not only picketing but leaflets, radio broadcasts, and newspaper advertisements, thereby interfering with freedom of speech." 105 Cong.Rec. 15540, 2 Leg.Hist. 1576.[8] The views of opponents of a bill with respect to its meaning, however, are not persuasive:

> "[W]e have often cautioned against the danger, when interpreting a statute, of reliance upon the views of its legislative opponents. In their zeal to defeat a bill, they understandably tend to overstate its reach. 'The fears and doubts of the opposition are no authoritative guide to the construction of legislation. It is the sponsors that we look to when the meaning of the statutory words is in doubt.' " Tree Fruits, 377 U.S., at 66, 84 S.Ct., at 1068 (quoting Schwegmann Bros. v. Calvert Distillers Corp., 341 U.S. 384, 394–395, 71 S.Ct. 745, 750–751, 95 L.Ed. 1035 (1951)).

Without more, the interpretation put on the words "threaten, coerce, or restrain" by those opposed to the amendment hardly settles the matter.

Third, § 8(b)(4)(ii) was one of the amendments agreed upon by a House–Senate Conference on the House's Landrum–Griffin bill and the Senate's Kennedy–Ervin bill. An analysis of the Conference bill was presented in the House by Representative Griffin and in the Senate by Senator Goldwater. With respect to appeals to consumers, the summary said that the House provision prohibiting secondary consumer picketing was adopted but "with clarification that other forms of publicity are not prohibited." The clarification referred to was the second proviso to § 8(b)(4). The Court of Appeals held that although the proviso was itself confined to advising the customers of an employer that the latter was distributing a product of another employer with whom the union had a labor dispute, the legislative history did not foreclose understanding the proviso as a clarification of the meaning of § 8(b)(4) rather than an exception to a general ban on consumer publicity. We agree with this view.

In addition to the summary presented by Senator Goldwater and Congressman Griffin, Senator Kennedy, the Chairman of the Conference Committee, in presenting the Conference Report on the Senate floor, stated that under the amendments as reported by the Conference Committee, a "union can hand out handbills at the shop, can place advertisements in newspapers, can make announcements over the radio, and can carry on all publicity short of having ambulatory picketing in front of a secondary site." And he assured Senator Goldwater that union

---

8. This statement was made in an analysis of the Landrum–Griffin Bill by Congressmen Thompson and Udall, two of its opponents. Shortly thereafter but prior to agreement on a Conference bill, this analysis on the secondary boycott provision was adopted almost verbatim in a report issued by Representative Thompson and Senator Kennedy, who also opposed the Landrum–Griffin Bill. 105 Cong.Rec. 16591, 2 Leg. Hist. 1708. Other members of the opposition made similar claims, most notably Senator Humphrey, who led the fight against amending § 8(b)(4) and urged that the limit on secondary boycotts proposed by Senator Goldwater would overturn settled law permitting leafletting of secondary businesses. He referred particularly to a decision of the Court of Appeals for the Ninth Circuit, the *Machinists* case discussed in n. 5, *supra*. 105 Cong.Rec. 6232, 2 Leg.Hist. 1037.

buy-America campaigns-that is, publicity requesting that consumers not buy foreign-made products, even though there is no ongoing labor dispute with the actual producer-would not be prohibited by the section.

Senator Kennedy included in his statement, however, the following:

"Under the Landrum–Griffin Bill it would have been impossible for a union to inform the customers of a secondary employer that that employer or store was selling goods which were made under racket conditions or sweatshop conditions, or in a plant where an economic strike was in progress. We were not able to persuade the House conferees to permit picketing in front of that secondary shop, but we were able to persuade them to agree that the union shall be free to conduct informational activity short of picketing."

The Board relies on this part of the Senator's exposition as an authoritative interpretation of the words "threaten, coerce, or restrain" and argues that except as saved by the express language of the proviso, informational appeals to customers not to deal with secondary employers are unfair labor practices. The Senator's remarks about the meaning of § 8(b)(4)(ii) echoed his views, and that of others, expressed in opposing and defeating in the Senate any attempts to give more protection to secondary employers from consumer boycotts, whether carried out by picketing or nonpicketing means. See n. 8, supra, and accompanying text. And if the proviso added in conference were an exception rather than a clarification, it surely would not follow, as the Senator said, that under the Conference bill, unions would be free to "conduct informational activity short of picketing" and could handbill, advertise in newspapers, and carry out all publicity short of ambulatory picketing in front of a secondary site. Nor would buy-America appeals be permissible, for they do not fall within the proviso's terms. At the very least, the Kennedy–Goldwater colloquy falls far short of revealing a clear intent that all nonpicketing appeals to customers urging a secondary boycott were unfair practices unless protected by the express words of the proviso. Nor does that exchange together with the other bits of legislative history relied on by the Board rise to that level.

In our view, interpreting § 8(b)(4) as not reaching the handbilling involved in this case is not foreclosed either by the language of the section or its legislative history. That construction makes unnecessary passing on the serious constitutional questions that would be raised by the Board's understanding of the statute. Accordingly, the judgment of the Court of Appeals is

Affirmed.

JUSTICE O'CONNOR and JUSTICE SCALIA concur in the judgment.

JUSTICE KENNEDY took no part in the consideration or decision of this case.

3. ON NEUTRALITY

Bell: The handbill gives us a neat way of avoiding the restrictions of § 8(b)(4)(B). But sometimes we need to get back to the good old-fashioned picket sign and the traditional picket line. Drivers, especially Teamster drivers, may still refuse to cross a picket line. And customers may be wary too. I assume that if the company we are picketing is not truly neutral in our dispute with Octopus, then all bets are off. We can use handbilling, picketing and whatever else we want. I would think that First Fidelity Funding is not really neutral in the union's dispute with Octopus. After all, the bank is a key player in Octopus' takeover of Enderby, and in these transactions the financial advisors usually call the shots. Fidelity has a real economic stake in the union's dispute with Octopus, so I don't see how it can be considered a neutral.

Gompers: This is an uphill battle. Courts seem reluctant to find diverse components of a corporation integrated, and are inclined to conclude that they are neutrals. A good example is Pet, Inc. v. NLRB, 641 F. 2d 545 (8th Cir., 1981). The union had a dispute in a plant that was a division of Hussmann, one of Pet's wholly owned subsidiaries. The Board found that the various Pet subdivisions were operationally independent entities. The union began a campaign urging consumers to boycott all Pet products. The court held that even though the profits in the Hussmann plant went to Pet, this didn't mean that Hussmann "produces" Pet's products. Thus, the union's activities did not fall within the publicity proviso that would have allowed it to advise the public that it had a dispute with Pet as a producer of these products. The leading Supreme Court case that finds some publicity protected is NLRB v. Servette, 377 U.S. 46 (1964), but the *Pet* court found Servette distinguishable.

ON FINER DISTINCTIONS REGARDING NEUTRALITY

Gompers: You know, Bell, if the law doesn't develop to accept our claim that Octopus and its other subsidiaries in the conglomerate are legitimate targets of our picketing, we may still have some traditional bases to justify picketing them. Under older law, cited in the opinions I gave you, if there were a strike against Enderby, and Enderby's work were shipped to another Octopus subsidiary, that subsidiary would be considered a so-called "ally" of Enderby and vulnerable to picketing and other economic pressure. In helping Enderby by taking the heat off it during a strike, the other entity loses its disinterested status and cannot claim the protections given a neutral under Section 8(b)(4). This is the "struck work" branch of what is known as the "ally" doctrine, and the classic case illustrating it is Royal

Typewriter [NLRB v. Business Machines and Office Union, 228 F.2d 553 (2d Cir.1955)].

I suppose it's possible to stretch that doctrine by claiming that if Enderby ceases operations in response to a strike and its personnel are used in other subsidiaries, or if corporate resources are shifted into those other components, they too become allies under this traditional doctrine. But this also gets us into frontier areas of the law.

Other branches of the traditional ally doctrine might allow the union to enmesh the so-called neutral on other theories. However, the law hasn't been hospitable to those arguments either. For example, in Sears, Roebuck & Co., 190 NLRB 143 (1971), the union had a dispute with a contractor that regularly installed carpets for Sears. The union argued that it was entitled to picket at Sears' stores, because the work of Sears and the contractor was so closely connected. The Board refused to find Sears an ally. I'm not sure, though, that the result would have been the same if the facts were flipped; that is, if the union had a dispute with Sears and picketed the independent installer that was installing Sears' product. Do you see a difference between the two situations?

The theory that seems to be behind the union's claim in a case like Sears is that the so called neutral really performs an integral part of the offending employer's manufacturing function. This has come to be known as the Board's "straight line operation" doctrine. However, the refusal to apply it in J.G. Roy & Sons Co. v. NLRB, 251 F.2d 771 (1st Cir.1958), seems to indicate that theory will not be very helpful to unions in avoiding charges of secondary activity.

Efforts to predicate ally status on joint ownership have been similarly unsuccessful. See, for example, Miami Newspaper Printing Pressmen's Local No. 46 v. NLRB, 322 F.2d 405 (D.C.Cir.1963).

With all that history, then, you can understand why it's an uphill fight for unions to reach other subsidiaries and lending institutions without running afoul of the § 8(b)(4) prohibitions.

In any event, I think eventually we'll need Congress' help. If we were to mount a legislative campaign to amend the secondary boycott provisions of the Act to reflect the new realities of conglomerate organizations, just what would you propose?

4. THE PUBLICITY PROVISO AND THE FIRST AMENDMENT

Bell: I think I follow everything so far. But I think that the union's most effective weapons continues to be picketing, and I'm not sure how Congress can outlaw this under the First Amendment. How can it single out picketing in the proviso if the purpose of the picketing is merely to advise the public in a truthful manner?

What's more, why did Congress give all this protection with one hand (may picket for the purpose of truthfully advising the public) and then take it away with the other (so long as such publicity doesn't have the effect of inducing others not to perform)? Isn't that hypocritical-and, even worse, inefficient? Why is it OK to exercise free speech rights only as long as they don't have the desired effects? Isn't that precisely why we allow people to have the right of free speech? To achieve something?

Gompers: Perhaps the following case will give you some answers. It explains generally why the Court treats picketing as a form of speech within the meaning of the first amendment.

NLRB v. FRUIT & VEGETABLE PACKERS & WAREHOUSEMEN, LOCAL 760 (TREE FRUITS)

Supreme Court of the United States, 1964.
377 U.S. 58, 84 S.Ct. 1063, 12 L.Ed.2d 129.

MR. JUSTICE BRENNAN delivered the opinion of the Court.

Under § 8(b)(4)(ii)(B) of the National Labor Relations Act, as amended, it is an unfair labor practice for a union "to threaten, coerce, or restrain any person," with the object of "forcing or requiring any person to cease using, selling, handling, transporting, or otherwise dealing in the products of any other producer ... or to cease doing business with any other person...." A proviso excepts, however, "publicity, *other than picketing*, for the purpose of truthfully advising the public ... that a product or products are produced by an employer with whom the labor organization has a primary dispute and are distributed by another employer, as long as such publicity does not have an effect of inducing any individual employed by any person other than the primary employer in the course of his employment to refuse to pick up, deliver, or transport any goods, or not to perform any services, at the establishment of the employer engaged in such distribution." (Italics supplied.) The question in this case is whether the respondent unions violated this section when they limited their secondary picketing of retail stores to an appeal to the customers of the stores not to buy the products of certain firms against which one of the respondents was on strike.

Respondent Local 760 called a strike against fruit packers and warehousemen doing business in Yakima, Washington. The struck firms sold Washington State apples to the Safeway chain of retail stores in and about Seattle, Washington. Local 760, aided by respondent Joint Council, instituted a consumer boycott against the apples in support of the strike. They placed pickets who walked back and forth before the customers' entrances of 46 Safeway stores in Seattle. The pickets-two at each of 45 stores and three at the 46th store-wore placards and distributed handbills which appealed to Safeway customers, and to the public generally, to refrain from buying Washington State apples, which were only one of numerous food products sold in the stores.[3] Before the pickets appeared at any store, a letter was delivered to the store manager informing him that the picketing was only an appeal to his customers not to buy Washington State apples, and that the pickets were being expressly instructed "to patrol peacefully in front of the consumer entrances of the store, to stay away from the delivery entrances and not to interfere with the work of your employees, or with deliveries to or pickups from your store." A copy of written instructions to the pickets-which included the explicit statement that "you are also forbidden to request that the customers not patronize the store", was enclosed with the letter. Since it was desired to assure Safeway employees that they were not to cease work, and to avoid any interference with pickups or deliveries, the pickets appeared after the stores opened for business and departed before the stores closed. At all times during the picketing, the store employees continued to work, and no deliveries or pickups were obstructed. Washington State apples were handled in normal course by both Safeway employees and the employees of other employers involved. Ingress and egress by customers and others was not interfered with in any manner.

A complaint issued on charges that this conduct violated § 8(b)(4) as amended. The case was submitted directly to the National Labor Relations Board on a stipulation of facts and the waiver of a hearing and proceedings before a Trial Examiner. The Board held, following its construction of the statute in Upholsterers Frame & Bedding Workers Twin City Local No. 61, 132 N.L.R.B. 40, that "by literal wording of the proviso [to Section 8(b)(4)] as well as through the interpretive gloss placed thereon by its drafters, consumer picketing in front of a secondary establishment is prohibited." 132 N.L.R.B. 1172, 1177. Upon respondents' petition for review and the Board's cross-petition for enforcement, the Court of Appeals for the District of Columbia Circuit set aside the Board's order and remanded. The court rejected the Board's construction

---

3. The placard worn by each picket stated: "To the Consumer: Non–Union Washington State apples are being sold at this store. Please do not purchase such apples. Thank you. Teamsters Local 760, Yakima, Washington."

A typical handbill read:

"DON'T BUY WASHINGTON STATE APPLES

THE 1960 CROP OF WASHINGTON STATE APPLES IS BEING PACKED BY NON-UNION FIRMS

Included in this non-union operation are twenty-six firms in the Yakima Valley with which there is a labor dispute. These firms are charged with being

UNFAIR

by their employees who, with their union, are on strike and have been replaced by

non-union strikebreaking workers employed under substandard wage scales and working conditions.

In justice to these striking union workers who are attempting to protect their living standards and their right to engage in good-faith collective bargaining, we request that you

DON'T BUY WASHINGTON STATE APPLES

TEAMSTERS UNION LOCAL 760
YAKIMA, WASHINGTON

This is not a strike against any store or market.

(P.S.—PACIFIC FRUIT & PRODUCE CO. is the only firm packing Washington State Apples under a union contract.)"

and held that the statutory requirement of a showing that respondents' conduct would "threaten, coerce, or restrain" Safeway could only be satisfied by affirmative proof that a substantial economic impact on Safeway had occurred, or was likely to occur as a result of the conduct. Under the remand the Board was left "free to reopen the record to receive evidence upon the issue whether Safeway was in fact threatened, coerced, or restrained."

The Board's reading of the statute—that the legislative history and the phrase "other than picketing" in the proviso reveal a congressional purpose to outlaw all picketing directed at customers at a secondary site—necessarily rested on the finding that Congress determined that such picketing always threatens, coerces or restrains the secondary employer. We therefore have a special responsibility to examine the legislative history for confirmation that Congress made that determination. Throughout the history of federal regulation of labor relations, Congress has consistently refused to prohibit peaceful picketing except where it is used as a means to achieve specific ends which experience has shown are undesirable. "In the sensitive area of peaceful picketing Congress has dealt explicitly with isolated evils which experience has established flow from such picketing." National Labor Relations Board v. Drivers etc. Local Union, 362 U.S. 274, 284, 80 S.Ct. 706, 712, 4 L.Ed.2d 710. We have recognized this congressional practice and have not ascribed to Congress a purpose to outlaw peaceful picketing unless "there is the clearest indication in the legislative history," ibid., that Congress intended to do so as regards the particular ends of the picketing under review. Both the congressional policy and our adherence to this principle of interpretation reflect concern that a broad ban against peaceful picketing might collide with the guarantees of the First Amendment.

We have examined the legislative history of the amendments to § 8(b)(4), and conclude that it does not reflect with the requisite clarity a congressional plan to proscribe all peaceful consumer picketing at secondary sites, and, particularly, any concern with peaceful picketing when it is limited, as here, to persuading Safeway customers not to buy Washington State apples when they traded in the Safeway stores. All that the legislative history shows in the way of an "isolated evil" believed to require proscription of peaceful consumer picketing at secondary sites was its use to persuade the customers of the secondary employer to cease trading with him in order to force him to cease dealing with, or to put pressure upon, the primary employer. This narrow focus reflects the difference between such conduct and peaceful picketing at the secondary site directed only at the struck product. In the latter case, the union's appeal to the public is confined to its dispute with the primary employer, since the public is not asked to withhold its patronage from the secondary employer, but only to boycott the primary employer's goods. On the other hand, a union appeal to the public at the secondary site not to trade at all with the secondary employer goes beyond the goods of the primary employer, and seeks the public's assistance in forcing the secondary employer to cooperate with the union in its primary dispute. This is not to say that this distinction was expressly alluded to in the debates. It is to say, however, that the consumer picketing carried on in this case is not attended by the abuses at which the statute was directed.

When major labor relations legislation was being considered in 1958 the closing of these loopholes was important to the House and to some members of the Senate. The Administration introduced such a bill, and it was supported by Senators Dirksen and Goldwater. Senator Goldwater, an insistent proponent of stiff boycott curbs, also proposed his own amendments. We think it is especially significant that neither Senator, nor the Secretary of Labor in testifying in support of the Administration's bill, referred to consumer picketing as making the amendments necessary. Senator McClellan, who also offered a bill to curb boycotts, mentioned consumer picketing but only such as was "pressure in the form of dissuading customers *from dealing with* secondary employers." (Emphasis supplied.) It was the opponents of the amendments who, in expressing fear of their sweep, suggested that they might proscribe consumer picketing. Senator Humphrey first sounded the warning early in April. Many months later, when the Conference bill was before the Senate, Senator Morse, a conferee, would not support the Conference bill on the express ground that it prohibited consumer picketing. But we have often cautioned against the danger, when interpreting a statute, of reliance upon the views of its legislative opponents. In their zeal to defeat a bill, they understandably tend to overstate its reach. "The fears and doubts of the opposition are no authoritative guide to the construction of legislation. It is the sponsors that we look to when the meaning of the statutory words is in doubt." Schwegmann Bros. v. Calvert Distillers Corp., 341 U.S. 384, 394–395, 71 S.Ct. 745, 750, 95 L.Ed. 1035. The silence of the sponsors of amendments is pregnant with significance since they must have been aware that consumer picketing as such had been held to be outside the reach of § 8(b)(4). We are faithful to our practice of respecting the congressional policy of legislating only against clearly identified abuses of peaceful picketing when we conclude that the Senate neither specified the kind of picketing here involved as an abuse, nor indicated any intention of banning all consumer picketing.

The House history is similarly beclouded, but what appears confirms our conclusion.* * *

Senator Kennedy presided over the Conference Committee. He and Congressman Thompson prepared a joint analysis of the Senate and House bills. This analysis pointed up the First Amendment implications of the broad language in the House revisions of § 8(b)(4) stating,

> "The prohibition [of the House bill] reaches not only picketing but leaflets, radio broadcasts and newspaper advertisements, thereby interfering with freedom of speech.

> " * * * one of the apparent purposes of the amendment is to prevent unions from appealing to the general public as consumers

for assistance in a labor dispute. This is a basic infringement upon freedom of expression."

This analysis was the first step in the development of the publicity proviso, but nothing in the legislative history of the proviso alters our conclusion that Congress did not clearly express an intention that amended § 8(b)(4) should prohibit all consumer picketing. Because of the sweeping language of the House bill, and its implications for freedom of speech, the Senate conferees refused to accede to the House proposal without safeguards for the right of unions to appeal to the public, even by some conduct which might be "coercive." The result was the addition of the proviso. But it does not follow from the fact that some coercive conduct was protected by the proviso, that the exception "other than picketing" indicates that Congress had determined that all consumer picketing was coercive.

No Conference Report was before the Senate when it passed the compromise bill, and it had the benefit only of Senator Kennedy's statement of the purpose of the proviso. He said that the proviso preserved "the right to appeal to consumers by methods other than picketing asking them to refrain from buying goods made by non-union labor *and* to refrain from trading with a retailer who sells such goods. * * * We were not able to persuade the House conferees to permit picketing in front of that secondary shop, but were able to persuade them to agree that the unions shall be free to conduct informational activity short of picketing. In other words, the union can hand out handbills at the shop ... and can carry on all publicity short of having ambulatory picketing...." (Italics supplied.) This explanation does not compel the conclusion that the Conference Agreement contemplated prohibiting any consumer picketing at a secondary site beyond that which urges the public, in Senator Kennedy's words, to "refrain from trading with a retailer who sells such goods." To read into the Conference Agreement, on the basis of a single statement, an intention to prohibit all consumer picketing at a secondary site would depart from our practice of respecting the congressional policy not to prohibit peaceful picketing except to curb "isolated evils" spelled out by the Congress itself.

Peaceful consumer picketing to shut off all trade with the secondary employer unless he aids the union in its dispute with the primary employer, is poles apart from such picketing which only persuades his customers not to buy the struck product. The proviso indicates no more than that the Senate conferees' constitutional doubts led Congress to authorize publicity other than picketing which persuades the customers of a secondary employer to stop all trading with him, but not such publicity which has the effect of cutting off his deliveries or inducing his employees to cease work. On the other hand, picketing which persuades the customers of a secondary employer to stop all trading with him was also to be barred.

In sum, the legislative history does not support the Board's finding that Congress meant to prohibit all consumer picketing at a secondary site, having determined that such picketing necessarily threatened, coerced or restrained the secondary employer. Rather, the history shows that Congress was following its usual practice of legislating against peaceful picketing only to curb "isolated evils."

This distinction is opposed as "unrealistic" because, it is urged, all picketing automatically provokes the public to stay away from the picketed establishment. The public will, it is said, neither read the signs and handbills, nor note the explicit injunction that "This is not a strike against any store or market." Be that as it may, our holding today simply takes note of the fact that Congress has never adopted a broad condemnation of peaceful picketing, such as that urged upon us by petitioners, and an intention to do so is not revealed with that "clearest indication in the legislative history," which we require. National Labor Relations Board v. Drivers, etc. Local Union, supra.

We come then to the question whether the picketing in this case, confined as it was to persuading customers to cease buying the product of the primary employer, falls within the area of secondary consumer picketing which Congress did clearly indicate its intention to prohibit under § 8(b)(4)(ii). We hold that it did not fall within that area, and therefore did not "threaten, coerce, or restrain" Safeway. While any diminution in Safeway's purchases of apples due to a drop in consumer demand might be said to be a result which causes respondents' picketing to fall literally within the statutory prohibition, "it is a familiar rule that a thing may be within the letter of the statute and yet not within the statute, because not within its spirit nor within the intention of its makers." Holy Trinity Church v. United States, 143 U.S. 457, 459, 12 S.Ct. 511, 512, 36 L.Ed. 226. When consumer picketing is employed only to persuade customers not to buy the struck product, the union's appeal is closely confined to the primary dispute. The site of the appeal is expanded to include the premises of the secondary employer, but if the appeal succeeds, the secondary employer's purchases from the struck firms are decreased only because the public has diminished its purchases of the struck product. On the other hand, when consumer picketing is employed to persuade customers not to trade at all with the secondary employer, the latter stops buying the struck product, not because of a falling demand, but in response to pressure designed to inflict injury on his business generally. In such case, the union does more than merely follow the struck product; it creates a separate dispute with the secondary employer.

We disagree therefore with the Court of Appeals that the test of "to threaten, coerce, or restrain" for the purposes of this case is whether Safeway suffered or was likely to suffer economic loss. A violation of § 8(b)(4)(ii)(B) would not be established, merely because respondents' picketing was effective to reduce Safeway's sales of Washington State apples, even if this led or might lead Safeway to drop the item as a poor seller.

The judgment of the Court of Appeals is vacated and the case is remanded with direction to enter judgment setting aside the Board's order. It is so ordered.

Judgment of Court of Appeals vacated and case remanded with directions.

MR. JUSTICE DOUGLAS took no part in the consideration or decision of this case.

SOME CONCLUDING OBSERVATIONS

The law regulating economic weapons has never taken the "all's fair in war" approach. Congress has mandated some intervention in the use of weapons. On the employer side, § 8(a)(3) prohibits the employer from discharging the employee who engages in a strike or other protected activity. This limitation loses much of its force, however, when the employer is allowed to replace a striker, and even more force where the employees' activity is unprotected, under doctrines we saw in section E, above.

The law has intervened on the union side by deeming some union conduct unprotected, as we saw in the previous section. It has gone further, and in the 1947 amendments in § 8(b) has outlawed certain union activity that affects neutral employers. Perhaps in 1947 and the next couple of decades that was a fair enough balance. But in the global economy, does § 8(a)(3) give unions enough protection to make § 8(b)(4) a fair trade? Or are some union leaders right that the union movement would be better off if neither section applied and the parties were left to the forces of the market?

Chapter Three

HEALTH AND SAFETY IN THE WORKPLACE

Introduction: Some Idea of the Problem and the Range of Solutions

NICHOLAS A. ASHFORD, CRISIS IN THE WORKPLACE
9–12 (1976).

Typical *health* hazards include toxic and carcinogenic chemicals and dusts, often in combination with noise, heat, and other forms of stress. Other health hazards include physical and biological agents. The interaction of health hazards and the human organism can occur either through the senses, by absorption through the skin, by intake into the digestive tract via the mouth, or by inhalation into the lungs. The results of these interactions can be respiratory disease, heart disease, cancer, neurological disorder, systemic poisoning, or a shortening of life expectancy due to general physiological deterioration. The disease or sickness can be acute or chronic, can require a long latency period even if the original exposure is brief, and can be difficult or impossible to diagnose early or with certainty. (It should also be noted that disease can give rise to accidents.)

The real world, unfortunately, does not offer isolated hazards. Chemical, physical, biological, and stress hazards are often found in combination, and their effects can be not merely additive but intensified (synergistic). Carbon monoxide and heat, amphetamines and over-crowding, asbestos and smoking, and promoters of cancer are all examples of agents whose effects can be synergistic. Most such combination effects are probably still to be recognized, and this recognition often occurs only after adverse effects are accidentally encountered (as in the case of barbiturates and alcohol).

Unlike safety hazards, the effects of health hazards may be slow, cumulative, irreversible, and complicated by nonoccupational factors. While an unguarded blade in a rotary saw may present a severe and imminent danger, it is often difficult to perceive the severity or imminent danger contained in a brief exposure to a potential carcinogen that can take years to cause a tumor or death. However, the probability of dying from cancer may be just as high as that of having an accident with the saw.

The failure of the nation's injury reporting system and workmen's compensation system to include occupational disease adequately has contributed to the failure of society to recognize the severity of occupational health hazards. The very nature of the differences between health and safety hazards has resulted in a pervasive safety bias that has affected legislation, the setting of standards, enforcement, manpower development, employer and employee education, and technology development. This relative overemphasis on safety has fostered complacency and has thus prevented much needed progress in the more neglected area of occupational health.

The Public Health Service estimates that 390,000 new cases of occupational disease appear annually. Epidemiological analyses of excess mortality among workers in several industries suggest that as many as 100,000 deaths occur each year as a result of occupational disease. Evidence from the insurance industry indicates that the *excess* risk of death, in actuarial terms, is substantial among certain occupational groups. The excess risk is on the order of magnitude of all the other risks of death we must face—in other words, the probability of death (given age, race, sex, etc.) facing members of certain hazardous occupations is in some cases greater than twice the norm for a matched cohort drawn from the general population.

Occupational factors may very well play a far more significant role than is presently realized in the causation of the major diseases and health problems that confront us. Two million people die every year in the United States. Heart disease, the leading cause of death (accounting for 38.7% or about 750,000 deaths), is only 25% "explained" by known physiological and environmental factors, such as excess weight, hypertension, serum cholesterol, and cigarette smoking. An unknown but quite possibly substantial proportion of the 75% of heart disease risk that is presently unaccounted for could be related to work and its attendant hazards, particularly stress.

Cancer is the second leading cause of death in the United States today, with an annual toll of 300,000. The incidence of cancer has risen rapidly with industrialization: in 1900, 3.7% of all deaths were attributable to cancer, but by 1968 the proportion of deaths from this cause was 16.5%. In part, improved diagnosis and longer life expectancy are responsible for this dramatic increase. Nevertheless, there are indications that the true incidence of cancer has been on the upswing.

Research in the United Kingdom indicates that more than 80% of cancer is of environmental origin and therefore, theoretically, preventable. This conclusion is based upon the observation that the variation in cancer incidence rates among geographic and occupational environments is enormous. Domestically, an HEW Task Force on Research Planning in Environmental Health Science reported that

> there is abundant evidence that the great majority of malignant neoplasms—probably over 90 percent of the total—are induced, maintained or promoted by specific environmental factors. Many of the known environmental causes of cancer are physical and chemical agents that directly concern the environmental health professions. *Carcinogenesis must therefore be regarded as one of the most significant potential consequences of environmental contamination.* (Emphasis added)

Although 80 or 90% of cancer could be environmentally caused, it is not presently known how much is occupationally related. There seems to be a general consensus among cancer researchers and environmentalists that probably one-half of all cases are complicated by occupational factors. The experiences of chemists, asbestos workers, underground uranium miners, and, most recently, rubber workers handling vinyl chloride, amply document the proposition that "excess" cancer of various types is indeed occupationally related.

Since the production of petrochemicals in the United States has doubled every five years since the end of World War II, the incidence of cancer characterized by long latency periods may be expected to rise significantly over the next twenty to thirty years. This expectation is reflected in the considerable legislative activity directed toward the regulation of chemicals—and especially of chemicals known to be carcinogenic.

Chronic diseases of the respiratory system have been reported with increasing frequency in the United States and have become major causes of death and disability. Chronic bronchitis and emphysema are the fastest-growing diseases in the country, doubling every five years since World War II, and account for the second highest number of disabilities under social security.

Much of the respiratory disease that plagues workers is known to be job-related. Both "specific" diseases such as coal workers' pneumoconiosis and general diseases such as emphysema and chronic bronchitis can be of occupational origin.

Even if only 5% of heart disease, cancer, and respiratory disease is in fact occupationally related, the number of deaths that could thereby be classified as "job-related" would exceed 60,000. Thus, the Public Health Service estimate of "as many as 100,000" may not be unreasonable. A recent study conducted for NIOSH by the University of Washington reported that 31% of over 1100 medical conditions found in 908 participants were of probable occupational origin, with an additional 10% manifesting "suggestive history." The probable incidence of occupational disease was 28.4 per hundred workers. Only 2% of these illnesses were reported on the employer's log required by OSHA, and only 3% were found in workmen's compensation records.

The risk of occupational illness is not shared equally by all members of the labor force. Miners, construction and transportation workers, and blue-collar and lower-level supervisory personnel in manufacturing industries experience the bulk of both occupational disease and injury. Further, the job illness and injury rate in agriculture is exceeded only by those in mining and construction.

Occupational health problems are not restricted, however, to the industrial or agricultural worker. They affect white-collar workers and corporate executives as well. Dentists are being studied for the possible effects of X-radiation, mercury, and anesthetics on their having the highest rate of suicide of any professional group and excess diseases of the nervous system, leukemia, and lymphatic malignancies. Operating-room nursing personnel suffer several times the miscarriage rates of other nurses and give birth to a larger proportion of children with congenital deformities. Cosmetologists (beauticians) display excess cancer and respiratory and cardiac disease. Administrators are far more likely to develop coronary disease than are scientists and engineers.

NICHOLAS A. ASHFORD AND CHARLES C. CALDERT, TECHNOLOGY, LAW, AND THE WORKING ENVIRONMENT

(1991) 29–32.

The passage of the Occupational Safety and Health Act (OSHAct) changed the basic institutional framework for addressing occupational health and safety problems in this country. One result has been a significant increase in union activity in the area of protecting worker health and safety. Yet, despite the creation of a health and safety infrastructure and the passage of other workplace health and safety-related laws since 1970, serious problems persist. Moreover, new problems have been identified and other new concerns have been created in emerging era of microelectronics based technologies.

(i) The Role of Unions. Unions have played an important role in the protection of health and safety on the job, despite their shrinking share of the work force. According to economist James Robinson, workers appear to turn to union representation as one strategy for dealing with unsafe and unhealthy working conditions. Union membership and pro-union sentiment are much higher in hazardous jobs than in safe jobs. Although there has been substantial erosion of union strength even in the most dangerous employments since the late 1970s, unions remain the one organization that can play an intervening role in occupational health and safety conflicts (Robinson 1988; Weil 1987, 1991a and 1991b).

The percentage of union contracts that contain clauses regarding safety equipment, the creation of joint safety committees, hazard pay, the right to refuse hazardous work, and other health and safety protections has risen steadily since the 1950s, accelerating in the 1970s and 1980s (Robinson 1988). Moreover, union representation makes a difference in the ability of any group of workers to advance health and safety protections. Organization and resources enable workers to force employers to take safety seriously. The Philadelphia Project on Occupational Safety and Health (PHILAPOSH) assembled a list of union-initiated interventions in the Philadelphia area that gives a sense of what is possible. The list includes campaigns by a variety of different union locals that resulted in improved spray booths at a pump plant, new handling procedures for PCBs, removal of asbestos from ceilings in a city clinic, reduced workloads to relieve stress of welfare department workers, an end to the use of a fiberglass-coated wire that was causing rashes and itching at an assembly plant, a new grievance procedure and health and safety training program at a large plant to address OSHA findings of excess levels of lead and other heavy metals, installation of a fan and hood after workers tested the air and found dangerously high vapor levels, and many other similar changes (Noble 1986, pp. 135–136).

Not only can union representation afford workers the resources and mechanisms necessary for a stronger negotiating position, union representation also increases the effectiveness of federal health and safety rules and regulations. Union representation is correlated with a greater probability of OSHA inspection, a higher number of citations per inspection, and, in manufacturing, greater monetary penalties per violation. According to a recent empirical study, "Unions in the manufacturing, construction, and service sectors increase both the quantity (number of inspections) and quality of inspections (measured in inspection duration and scope of inspection activity) over their nonunion counterparts. Additionally, unions reduce the time required to abate violations of OSHA standards and limit employer alterations of those abatement periods" (Weil 1987, p. 334). Unions create incentives for employers to improve health and safety conditions voluntarily by increasing the threat of regulatory enforcement. Given the inadequacy of OSHA's budget and staffing throughout its history and particularly since the deep cuts suffered during the Reagan years, union representation provides perhaps the best way for workers to improve their chances of working in a safe and healthy environment.

(ii) Continuing Problems. The enactment of a law and the creation of a bureaucracy does not make a problem disappear. And OSHA itself has provided only limited relief to America's workers, improving conditions significantly in some industries such as textiles and industries where explosions were common, but having little impact in many other dangerous and less dangerous trades. Not surprisingly, therefore, health and safety problems at work persist. According to the National Institute for Occupational Safety and Health the ten leading work-related diseases and injuries are:

1. Occupational lung diseases: asbestosis, byssinosis, silicosis, coal workers' pneumoconiosis, lung cancer, occupational asthma

2. Musculoskeletal injuries: disorders of the back, trunk, upper extremity, neck, lower extremity; traumatically induced Raynaud's phenomenon

3. Occupational cancers (other than lung): leukemia; mesothelioma; cancers of the bladder, nose, and liver

4. Amputations, fractures, eye loss, lacerations, and traumatic deaths

5. Cardiovascular diseases: hypertension, coronary artery disease, acute myocardial infarction

6. Disorders of reproduction: infertility, spontaneous abortion, teratogenesis

7. Neurotoxic disorders: peripheral neuropathy, toxic encephalitis, psychoses, extreme personality changes (exposure-related)

8. Noise-induced loss of hearing

9. Dermatologic conditions: dermatoses, burns (scaldings), chemical burns, contusions (abrasions)

10. Psychological disorders: neuroses, personality disorders, alcoholism, drug dependency

The conditions listed under each category are *selected examples,* not comprehensive definitions of the category (NIOSH 1983). Further, most suspect carcinogens still remain unregulated, as do reproductive hazards and neurotoxins. (The reader is referred to Levy and Wegman 1988 and Rom 1983 for extensive reviews of occupational disease.)

As in the earlier half of the century, the risk of illness and death on the job is not evenly distributed. Certain industries are far more dangerous than others (see Figure 1–4). Farm work is among the most dangerous. The National Safety Council has estimated that the death rate in agriculture is 66 per 100,000, far higher than the industrial average of 18 per 100,000. Although few statistics are available, one government estimate is that 80,000 to 90,000 field workers get sick and 800 to 1000 die each year from pesticide exposure (Pollack and Grozuczak 1984). Minorities are concentrated in the most dangerous industries, including dry cleaning, foundries, hospitals, farm work, textiles, and tobacco. Studies of occupational segregation in textile, steel, and other industries have shown that within those industries minorities hold the most dangerous jobs. The increased exposure to dangerous and unhealthy work has quite serious costs. While the life expectancy of the average American is over 70 years, the life expectancy of a migrant farmworker is only 49 years. Black workers face a 37 percent greater risk of illness and a 20 percent greater risk of death due to their jobs than white workers, according to the Urban Environmental Conference (Pollack and Grozuczak 1984). Black workers are one and a half times more likely to be severely disabled from job injuries and illnesses.

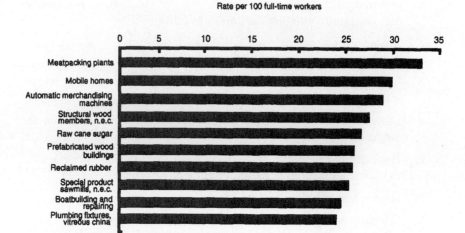

Figure 1-4. Injury and illness incidence rates, total cases, high-risk manufacturing industries, 1986 BLS Annual Survey, p. f-59. n.e.c. = not elsewhere classified.

[G17742]

In addition to the problems generated by the technologies of yesterday, emerging technologies in manufacturing and office work are generating a set of new problems that are only beginning to be addressed. Of course, new technology can eliminate dangerous work, as has often been the case in U.S. manufacturing. The use of robots to replace workers in auto paint shops is one good example. At the same time, though, new unintended problems are often created. Steven Deutsch (1988) notes five areas of concern emerging from the proliferation of microelectronics-based technologies. These are as follows:

1. **Chemical hazards.** The solvents and other chemicals used in the manufacture of semiconductors and computers have been associated with a host of skin diseases and other adverse effects including central nervous system problems.

2. **Musculoskeletal problems.** New equipment that is not ergonomically well designed can lead to problems such as "carpal tunnel syndrome," a nerve disorder in the wrist that has affected alarming proportions of grocery clerks, clerical workers, postal workers, and others. The National Institute for Occupational Safety and Health estimates that 15 to 20 percent of American workers are at risk from these ailments.

3. **Video display terminal hazards.** There is growing evidence of arm, back, wrist, and leg problems associated with VDT use. Vision problems due to poorly designed work stations are also common. In addition, there remain serious questions as to the possibility of radiation hazards of VDT work, particularly for pregnant women (Bureau of National Affairs 1987).

4. **Stress.** In recent years, there has been a noticeable rise in
    stress-related worker compensation claims and a general in-
    creased awareness of stress-related illness. Workers on micro-
    electronics-based equipment suffer increased stress resulting
    from the pacing of work, computer monitoring by employers,
    invasion of privacy, and pressure for production (OTA 1987).

5. **Job loss and fear of job loss.** It is well documented in the
    literature that job loss and fear of displacement manifest them-
    selves in increased levels of depression, alcohol and drug abuse,
    cardiovascular disease, gastrointestinal disorders and other
    physical problems. New technologies and the pace of technologi-
    cal change in the past decade have reduced the job security of
    tens of millions of Americans and have resulted in the elimina-
    tion of jobs for as many as a million employed workers per year
    since 1979 (Cyert and Mowery 1987). This increased instability
    is an occupational hazard that is becoming more widespread.

In addition to this list of new problems, widespread classical problems such as lead and other heavy metal poisoning, systemic toxicity,
and dust-induced respiratory disease persist. Chemical sensitivities causing allergy-like problems are also receiving increased attention (Ashford
and Miller 1991; Cullen 1987).

SOME UPDATED STATISTICS ABOUT INJURIES
AND ILLNESSES IN THE WORKPLACE

Employees continue to be killed, injured, or made ill while at the
workplace. According to the Bureau of Labor Statistics, over the period
from 1995 to 2000, the average number of workers killed per year on the
job in the United States was 6165. The number has been steadily
declining; in 2000, 5915 employees were killed on the job. The most
common cause of these deaths was related to vehicles. Significant numbers of fatalities also were caused by assaults, falls, contact with objects
and equipment, and exposure to harmful materials.

In 1999, 5.7 million employees suffered from injuries or illnesses
while on the job. This amounted to 6.3 employees out of every 100
fulltime-equivalent employees. That number (6.3) had steadily declined
since 1994. Of the 5.7 million employees who were injured or taken ill in
1999, 2.7 million lost work time because of their malady, and 1.7 million
lost more time than the remainder of the day in which they were injured
or taken ill. Carpal tunnel syndrome caused the longest average time of
absence from work of all illnesses or injuries (27 days). Carpal tunnel
syndrome and hearing loss made up nearly two-thirds of the causes of
illnesses (non-injuries) requiring time away from work.

Not surprisingly, employees involved in goods production were significantly more affected than employees involved in services. Perhaps
surprisingly, employees in mid-size companies were more likely to be
injured or taken ill than employees at either small or large companies.

The sources for this information are U.S. Department of Labor News Release 00–357, Tuesday, December 12, 2000 (Workplace Injuries and Illnesses in 1999), and U.S. Department of Labor News Release 01–261, Tuesday, August 14, 2001 (National Census of Fatal Occupational Injuries in 2000). Both documents are found on line at http://stats.bls.gov/oshhome.htm.

A. THE COMMON LAW RESPONSE TO EMPLOYEE INJURIES

FARWELL v. BOSTON AND WORCESTER RAIL ROAD CORPORATION

Supreme Judicial Court of Massachusetts, 1842.
45 Mass. 49.

SHAW, C.J. This is an action of new impression in our courts, and involves a principle of great importance. It presents a case, where two persons are in the service and employment of one company, whose business it is to construct and maintain a rail road, and to employ their trains of cars to carry persons and merchandize for hire. They are appointed and employed by the same company to perform separate duties and services, all tending to the accomplishment of one and the same purpose—that of the safe and rapid transmission of the trains; and they are paid for their respective duties, and the labor and skill required for their proper performance. The question is, whether, for damages sustained by one of the persons so employed, by means of the carelessness and negligence of another, the party injured has a remedy against the common employer. It is an argument against such an action, though certainly not a decisive one, that no such action has before been maintained.

It is laid down by Blackstone, that if a servant, by his negligence, does any damage to a stranger, the master shall be answerable for his neglect. * * *

But this does not apply to the case of a servant bringing his action against his own employer to recover damages for an injury arising in the course of that employment, where all such risks and perils as the employer and the servant respectively intend to assume and bear may be regulated by the express or implied contract between them, and which, in contemplation of law, must be presumed to be thus regulated.

* * *

The claim, therefore, is placed, and must be maintained, if maintained at all, on the ground of contract. As there is no express contract between the parties, applicable to this point, it is placed on the footing of an implied contract of indemnity, arising out of the relation of master and servant. It would be an implied promise, arising from the duty of the master to be responsible to each person employed by him, in the conduct of every branch of business, where two or more persons are employed, to pay for all damage occasioned by the negligence of every other person employed in the same service. If such a duty were established by law— like that of a common carrier, to stand to all losses of goods not caused by the act of God or of a public enemy—or that of an innkeeper, to be responsible, in like manner, for the baggage of his guests; it would be a rule of frequent and familiar occurrence, and its existence and application, with all its qualifications and restrictions, would be settled by judicial precedents. But we are of opinion that no such rule has been established, and the authorities, as far as they go, are opposed to the principle. *Priestley v. Fowler,* 3 Mees. & Welsb. 1. *Murray v. South Carolina Rail Road Company,* 1 McMullan, 385.

The general rule, resulting from considerations as well of justice as of policy, is, that he who engages in the employment of another for the performance of specified duties and services, for compensation, takes upon himself the natural and ordinary risks and perils incident to the performance of such services, and in legal presumption, the compensation is adjusted accordingly. And we are not aware of any principle which should except the perils arising from the carelessness and negligence of those who are in the same employment. These are perils which the servant is as likely to know, and against which he can as effectually guard, as the master. They are perils incident to the service, and which can be as distinctly foreseen and provided for in the rate of compensation as any others. To say that the master shall be responsible because the damage is caused by his agents, is assuming the very point which remains to be proved. They are his agents to some extent, and for some purposes; but whether he is responsible, in a particular case, for their negligence, is not decided by the single fact that they are, for some purposes, his agents. * * *

In considering the rights and obligations arising out of particular relations, it is competent for courts of justice to regard considerations of policy and general convenience, and to draw from them such rules as will, in their practical application, best promote the safety and security of all parties concerned. This is, in truth, the basis on which implied promises are raised, being duties legally inferred from a consideration of what is best adapted to promote the benefit of all persons concerned, under given circumstances. * * *

Where several persons are employed in the conduct of one common enterprise or undertaking, and the safety of each depends much on the care and skill with which each other shall perform his appropriate duty, each is an observer of the conduct of the others, can give notice of any misconduct, incapacity or neglect of duty, and leave the service, if the common employer will not take such precautions, and employ such agents as the safety of the whole party may require. By these means, the safety of each will be much more effectually secured, than could be done by a resort to the common employer for indemnity in case of loss by the negligence of each other. Regarding it in this light, it is the ordinary case of one sustaining an injury in the course of his own employment, in which he must bear the loss himself, or seek his remedy, if he have any, against the actual wrong-doer.

In applying these principles to the present case, it appears that the plaintiff was employed by the defendants as an engineer, at the rate of wages usually paid in that employment, being a higher rate than the plaintiff had before received as a machinist. It was a voluntary undertaking on his part, with a full knowledge of the risks incident to the employment; and the loss was sustained by means of an ordinary casualty, caused by the negligence of another servant of the company. Under these circumstances, the loss must be deemed to be the result of a pure accident, like those to which all men, in all employments, and at all times, are more or less exposed; and like similar losses from accidental causes, it must rest where it first fell, unless the plaintiff has a remedy against the person actually in default; of which we give no opinion.

It was strongly pressed in the argument, that although this might be so, where two or more servants are employed in the same department of duty, where each can exert some influence over the conduct of the other, and thus to some extent provide for his own security; yet that it could not apply where two or more are employed in different departments of duty, at a distance from each other, and where one can in no degree control or influence the conduct of another. But we think this is founded upon a supposed distinction, on which it would be extremely difficult to establish a practical rule. When the object to be accomplished is one and the same, when the employers are the same, and the several persons employed derive their authority and their compensation from the same source, it would be extremely difficult to distinguish, what constitutes one department and what a distinct department of duty. It would vary with the circumstances of every case. If it were made to depend upon the nearness or distance of the persons from each other, the question would immediately arise, how near or how distant must they be, to be in the same or different departments. In a blacksmith's shop, persons working in the same building, at different fires, may be quite independent of each other, though only a few feet distant. In a ropewalk, several may be at work on the same piece of cordage, at the same time, at many hundred feet distant from each other, and beyond the reach of sight and voice, and yet acting together.

Besides, it appears to us, that the argument rests upon an assumed principle of responsibility which does not exist. The master, in the case supposed, is not exempt from liability, because the servant has better means of providing for his safety, when he is employed in immediate connexion with those from whose negligence he might suffer; but because the *implied contract* of the master does not extend to indemnify the servant against the negligence of any one but himself; and he is not liable in tort, as for the negligence of his servant, because the person suffering does not stand towards him in the relation of a stranger, but is one whose rights are regulated by contract express or implied. The exemption of the master, therefore, from liability for the negligence of a fellow servant, does not depend exclusively upon the consideration, that the servant has better means to provide for his own safety, but upon other grounds. Hence the separation of the employment into different departments cannot create that liability, when it does not arise from express or implied contract, or from a responsibility created by law to third persons, and strangers, for the negligence of a servant.

In coming to the conclusion that the plaintiff, in the present case, is not entitled to recover, considering it as in some measure a nice question, we would add a caution against any hasty conclusion as to the application of this rule to a case not fully within the same principle. It may be varied and modified by circumstances not appearing in the present case, in which it appears, that no wilful wrong or actual negligence was imputed to the corporation, and where suitable means were furnished and suitable persons employed to accomplish the object in view. We are far from intending to say that there are no implied warranties and undertakings arising out of the relation of master and servant. * * *

Plaintiff nonsuit.

B. A CLASS DISCUSSION ABOUT WORKERS' COMPENSATION LAWS[1]

George: By the end of the nineteenth century, many believed that the common law that developed after *Farwell* was not working effectively. From the employees' view, the law was considered by many to be unfair. First, a plaintiff-employee had to prove negligence on the part of the defendant-employer. Many, perhaps most, injuries in the workplace have never been due, so far as anyone can discern, to the negligence of the employer or of any identifiable person. They are as likely to be due to worker exhaustion, ultrahazardous working conditions, or other faultless "error." Moreover, in those days, an employee suing her or his employer was hard pressed to get fellow employees to testify against their own employer. Thus, employees rarely could prove employer negligence. Even if the employees could make proof of this sort, however, they had to avoid the consequences of the assumption of risk and fellow servant doctrines, both of which had their foundation in the *Farwell* case, and contributory negligence, which in those times was a complete bar to recovery.

As a consequence, virtually no employee injuries were compensable in court. Even when a plaintiff did win a case, the litigation took a great deal of time and the delay often weighed heavily on the injured employee and her or his family. Employees thought the system unfair. So, too, increasingly did academics and politicians. Many were of the opinion that, regardless of fault, em-

1. A fascinating and thorough account of the evolution of law from tort to workers' compensation can be found in L. Friedman and J. Ladinsky, *Social Change and the Law of Industrial Accidents,* 67 Colum.L.Rev. 50 (1967).

ployee injuries were part of doing business and that employers or their customers, rather than employees, should bear the cost.

At the same time, employers were becoming concerned with common law developments affecting their relative immunity. While most employees could get no remedy for job injuries, in response to the increasing criticism and in recognition of some of the inequities of their own dogma, the courts were creating exceptions to the usual employer defenses. These exceptions, in combination with sometime sympathetic juries, constituted a system that was both episodic, unpredictable, and occasionally very generous to individual plaintiffs. As the common law became more complex, recoveries more frequent and sometimes larger, and society more industrialized, the number of lawsuits multiplied rapidly. The costs associated with employee injuries thereby increased, although not in a predictable or reasonable manner.

In 1902, Maryland passed the first workers' compensation law. In 1949, Mississippi became the last of the contiguous forty-eight states to have such a law. Today, all fifty states have workers' compensation laws.

First, let's get some basics out in the open. What characteristics are typical of virtually all workers' compensation laws?

Mimi: First, I think typically each state has established an administrative agency which provides hearings to determine whether there will be compensation and how much. I think the substantive standard for compensation is that an employee can recover without regard to fault if his or her injury, in the words of a typical statute, "arises out of and in the course of employment."

Boris: That sounds a lot like the no-fault automobile statutes we read in torts.

Mimi: I guess that's right. Even the workers' compensation statutes' *quid pro quo,* that is, no-fault in exchange for limited remedies, resembles the automobile-accident statutes. Workers' comp laws provide that remedies are limited to actual medical expenses plus a fraction (usually, two-thirds) of lost wages, and the latter has a cap or ceiling. Generally, there are no damages for pain and suffering or for punitive purposes.

Finally, the employer is immune to a suit brought by the employee for tort damages.

Hans: I thought those auto no-fault statutes weren't working out too well. How come workers' comp has survived all of this time?

Susannah: First, typical auto no-fault-laws apply only to relatively minor injury cases, so a plaintiff's lawyer can avoid the no-fault system by claiming excessive damages. Workers' comp applies to all job-related injuries. Second, from what I have read, I suspect that probably many employees are served better by the compensation system than they might be by the common law; many more employees recover under the compensation system than they did under the common law. We have yet to see the auto no-fault system accomplish the same kind of result.

Hans: Yes, but there could be other alternatives to the exclusive no-fault remedy. For example, retention of the common law with-out the three employer defenses (assumption of the risk, fellow-servant rule, and contributory negligence). I think that would serve employees better.

Susannah: I am not sure of that. While the potential of the remedies for employees would be greater, all plaintiffs would first need to prove employer negligence, which probably could not be done in the vast majority of work injury cases. Also, in any cases where potential damages are not great employees would not be able to get lawyers. We should worry, also, that the cost of tort litiga-tion is substantially more burdensome to society than worker comp's no-fault system.

Nedda: What of the idea of absolute liability, but with common law remedies?

Susannah: Do you think the cost of such a system could be accept-able?

Nedda: That's a political question. If no one tries for such a system, how will we know if it's acceptable?

Boris: On a slightly different tack regarding workers' comp reme-dies, does it make sense to limit recovery to a fraction of the employee's present salary? I am especially bothered that the payout to injured employees often is made up of periodic pay-ments over a number of years. Inflation reduces even further the value of what the employee receives. There has got to be a remedy for that phenomenon.

George: Before you reach the easy conclusion that workers should receive more in the way of compensation, should you not also consider what are the consequences of the present payouts and what are likely to be the consequences of greater remedies?

Mario: You're right. Common sense tells us—and I read somewhere there is some empirical evidence to support the thought—that as the cost of the compensation increases, the level of wages drops.

Boris: So? Do you know of a way for a legislature—or anyone—to assess accurately what is the appropriate tradeoff, higher comp benefits and lower wages versus the opposite? Hey, once one believes that probably there is that kind of tradeoff, one might reexamine the workers' compensation remedies to see if they should be even less generous. An exercise like that would really worry me.

Mario: Why? Maybe smaller comp rewards are sensible.

Hans: By not permitting employees to recover damages for pain and suffering, it's clear the law has been written to ignore what may be significant harm that negatively affects employees and their families, harm that the common law honors. That limitation distresses me.

Susannah: Yeah, but pain and suffering is so unknowable for a trier-of-fact. The cost of litigating a matter that is pure guesswork seems undesirable. And, that is not even raising the matter of potential plaintiff's fraud.

Hans: Well, changing the subject a little, the workers' comp law also does not permit punitive damages.

Susannah: It does not necessarily follow that the law has no deterrent purpose or effect. Remember, the money for workers' compensation is provided either by self-insuring employers or pooled "premiums" paid by employers to insurance or governmental institutions. The size of the contributions made by individual employers to the pool is determined, first, by the experience of the industry of which each employer is a part. To the extent the individual employer is large enough to have a significant experience with employee injuries, the rates of contribution are altered somewhat from the industrywide standard to reflect the individual employer's experience. I concede the evidence is hardly overwhelming, but there is some suggestion that workers' compensation laws do reduce deaths and serious injuries.

Hans: Even so, we could argue forever whether the resulting deterrence is enough. Any conclusion is empirically problematic and value laden.

Mario: Studies also suggest that as a workers' compensation system becomes more aggressive in protecting employees, more claims for less serious injuries are filed. I wonder if that reflects the fact that employees are lulled by the compensation system into being less careful in protecting themselves.

Boris: That's silly.

Mimi: Maybe, but it may also be that the more generous compensation system encourages the filing of more claims which are relatively small, doubtful, or dishonest.

George: If you assume that the system does encourage employers to prevent serious injuries at the workplace but also encourages small and/or fake claims, can you devise a system that would better deter and avoid the claims that we deem either inappropriate or not essential to a fair employment relationship?

Hans: You mean something like incentives for employers which avoid serious injuries in the workplace?

Violetta: I assume the system's justifications include the idea that workers' comp systems get money to injured workers substantially faster than the courtroom, common law system would. I'd guess that goal is often frustrated in those cases where employers challenge the decision of the workers' compensation board. I suspect the delay caused by court review can be substantial and defeat the effectiveness of workers' compensation law. If I represented employers, the delay would most likely occur in those cases the system is most concerned with, that is, the cases involving serious injuries and significant remedies.

Susannah: Listen, the "no fault" aspect of this whole system bothers me. I mean, what's going to stop a hypochondriac, sincere or fraudulent, from filing claims all the time? I read something that said a small percentage of workers are responsible for a vastly disproportionate number of worker compensation claims. It really doesn't matter to me whether these employees are "injury prone," have low tolerances for discomfort, or are less than honorable in the claims they make; employers should not have to tolerate such a problem.

Boris: I think it matters whether or not the claims are honest.

Susannah: Whatever. The employers ought to be able to protect themselves from employees who are "claims-prone." I just don't know how.

George: While there are many legal issues that arise out of the workers' compensation laws, the most ubiquitous and the most important is the interpretation given to the requirement that the injury "arise out of and in the course of employment." Aside from the line-drawing and somewhat artificial distinctions such a concept necessarily requires of the workers' compensation boards and the courts, all of you would ask why our society chooses to limit people's recoveries to work-related injuries. Would it make more sense to have a more universal system that addresses all injuries? Of course, that would take the subject out of this course and into one dealing with health care plans.

Mimi: A system like that, at least if it were written solely as a health care plan, would not reimburse employees for lost wages, let alone pain and suffering or punitive damages.

Boris: You could partially address that concern by allowing the injured worker to collect unemployment benefits while she's out of work.

Eva: It occurs to me that each state has its own workers' compensation system. In light of the mega-corporations that now dominate our economy, their presence in many states, and the interstate business of all of them and most other employers, I think it would make sense to nationalize the workers' compensation system. This is especially true if we believe that corporations, in deciding whether to move all or major parts of their businesses from one state to another, often factor the comparative costs of the workers' compensation systems into the equation. The unintended consequences might involve enormous dislocations and inefficiencies.

Nedda: But, nationalizing workers' comp law will have some unwanted costs, like losing the competition between states as to what kind of community each wishes to be, or like making uniform a lot of answers to issues that do not yet have clearly correct answers. Once we create a national answer, I fear we'll be locked in.

Susannah: Our concern for avoiding wrong answers is heightened today by foreign competition.

Boris: I read that, even if one assumes that workers' compensation systems do sufficiently deter injuries caused by accidents, no one believes that the workers' compensation model has any significant effect on injuries caused by exposure to toxins and dust and other conditions that produce disease and injury after long exposure or a long latency period.

Mimi: In fact, most compensation laws originally did not include disease as a compensable injury.

Boris: Well, today, most systems do call for compensation for disease, although the statutory conditions sometimes are quite confining. Not to mention, it is often almost impossible to prove that the workplace was the source of the cause of the employee's condition and that nothing else ought to be denominated the legal cause.

Eva: It's worse than that. Even before the legal system gets to hear the case, the employee has to be aware that workers' comp is a possibility. She may have forgotten altogether about the exposure, she may never have known of it, or she may never have understood the relationship between the exposure and her present problems.

Susannah: Wait up! Everything Eva just said is equally applicable to a tort action.

Mimi: Even if the employee understands all of what Eva just described, in some states she will unhappily learn that the remedy is not worth much because it will be limited to two-thirds of the salary she was receiving long ago, at the time she was exposed to the substance that caused her present illness. That's a joke. Thank goodness more states use relatively recent wages as a basis for compensation.

Eva: I guess, in cases where the state looks to the wage levels of many years ago, the health insurance system is probably a simpler and surer way for an employee to recover for her medical expenses, which are likely to constitute the lion's share of the money she might eventually receive from that workers' compensation system.

Violetta: Yeah, but be fair. That's not the only joke one discovers in the workers' comp field. For example, workers' comp is supposed to spare society and the parties a whole lot of litigation. Yet, employees more and more, in both toxic and accident cases, undermine that societal objective by filing tort lawsuits against the manufacturers, distributors, transporters, and retailers of substances or machinery and equipment that caused the ailment or injuries. The way things stand now, all too often the employee has an absolute right to limited recovery through workers' compensation *and* a chance at winning the big tort-lawsuit lottery at the same time. That seems to be a betrayal of the original understanding that made workers' comp possible, that is, workers benefit from legislated absolute liability and, at the same time, have limits or caps on the amount of money they can recover.

Eva: Betrayal? Are you kidding? If the employees were precluded from suing the manufacturers and other malfeasors who injured the workers, those manufacturers and others would get a windfall and feel free to be casual, or worse, about their products and services.

Mimi: I agree with Eva. Another problem I have is that the workers' compensation system fails to provide incentives for employers to reduce disease caused by working conditions. First, as you guys have suggested, whatever concerns, if any, employers may have about causing employee disease through working conditions, those concerns are largely independent of any deterrence caused by the workers' compensation system. On top of that, I suspect employers are naturally disinclined to spend lots of money to avoid far-off, uncertain diseases. I mean, what employer ten years ago could have even imagined that tuberculosis would come back? Employers and medical researchers do not know— or are not sufficiently certain—what working conditions are dangerous to the employees' health.

George: Many of the occupational diseases from which employees suffer have long latency periods—perhaps, fifteen to thirty years. Am I being impish in asking whether this suggests that certain jobs should be done only by older employees, a disproportionately large number of whom may never suffer from the diseases that younger employees would eventually contact? Would such a policy violate the Age Discrimination in Employment Act? What would such a policy do to attitudes about older people in the workplace?[2]

2. For some discussion of problems facing the workers' compensation system in the near future, see Maakestadt and Helin, *Protecting Workplace Safety and Health,* 17 N.Ky.L.Rev. 9 (1989), Larson, *Tensions of the Next Decade,* in New Perspectives in

C. OCCUPATIONAL SAFETY AND HEALTH ACT OF 1970

With the enactment of the Occupational Safety and Health Act in 1970 (OSHA), our nation became committed to a policy, so the statute says, of securing a safe and healthy work environment for every worker. The OSHA imposes two fundamental obligations upon the employer. The first, known as the "general duty" [Section 5(a)(1)], requires the employer to "furnish to each of his employees employment and a place of employment which are free from recognized hazards that are causing or are likely to cause death or serious physical harm to his employees." We will take a brief look at this obligation later in the chapter.

The other broad duty of the employer is to "comply with occupational safety and health standards promulgated under this chapter." Section 5(a)(2). The obligation is the subject of the *Benzene* case, which follows directly. That case will introduce you to the intricacies of the OSHA. One of the themes we explore in this chapter is the relationship between the standards set by the Secretary of Labor, under Section 5(a)(2), and attempts by unions to negotiate and enforce standards of health and safety at particular workplaces.

Enforcement of these statutory obligations is secured by abatement orders and a system of penalties, primarily fines, under Section 10 of the OSHA. There is no provision for an individual employee to enforce the statute. Another inquiry in this chapter concerns alternative means of enforcement, such as worker self-help and the use of the collective bargaining machinery.

Administration of a program of health and safety requires access to information. Section 8 of the OSHA provides for governmental inspection and investigation procedures, although the Supreme Court has held both that the OSHA does not authorize warrantless searches of the workplace and that a warrant is required under the Fourth Amendment. Marshall v. Barlow's, Inc., 436 U.S. 307, 98 S.Ct. 1816, 56 L.Ed.2d 305 (1978). The Act requires inspection and investigation procedures. It also requires the employer to maintain certain records and to share that information with employee representatives. Section 8(e) provides that employee representatives may accompany the government representative during a physical inspection of the facilities.

Is the OSHA model of direct governmental regulation the best way for society to address the problems of health and safety in the workplace? As you will see in the *Benzene* decision which follows this note, the costs of securing a safe and healthy workplace can be considerable. A uniform system of government regulation has the virtue of distributing relatively evenly the costs of obtaining information and eliminating workplace harms, although the costs of regulation may fall more disruptively and disproportionately upon smaller businesses. More significant-

Workers' Compensation (J. Burton, ed., 1988), and M. Fredenheim, *Costs Soar for*   *On–the–Job Injuries,* New York Times, April 11, 1991, p. D–1.

ly, perhaps, the regulation will not affect foreign competitors of domestic employers.

Federal regulation has the advantage of spurring a national debate about the trade-offs that must be made between worker health and safety, on the one hand, and economic success, on the other. There is a limit on the cost that can be imposed on industry before business becomes uneconomical or non-competitive. Even if it is true that injury and disease are more uneconomical for society than are the costs of providing safe work places, it is debatable that the costs should be shouldered by employers rather than the society as a whole.

Another serious limitation of the OSHA is the almost infinite number of work situations that may or may not pose serious safety (as distinguished from health) problems. Can a general rule deal fairly or efficiently with such a multitude of variables?

Should safety issues be left, generally, to workers' compensation and tort laws? That is the individual rights model. It recognizes that government cannot be the omnipresent regulator and relies upon the individual to look after her own rights. In addition to workers' compensation and tort laws, the Title VII and wrongful discharge cases studied in Chapter I are examples of this model, which suggests employees can be reimbursed for their individual losses and may not be disciplined for engaging in self-help and reporting violations to the government. Does this model protect employees who abuse the right to blow whistles or file claims? As we saw in Chapter I and the brief discussion of workers' compensation laws, government does not prescribe the conditions of employment under this model.

The worker participation model, which is discussed in Chapter II, has its strengths as well. It allows tailoring of workplace protections to each unique work situation. In recognition of the usefulness of worker-employer cooperation in the safety arena, workers' compensation statutes sometimes provide for worker-employer safety committees at the workplace. In the health and safety area, as perhaps in no other area we have studied, the worker often wants to become involved in problem-solving. But should the protection of worker interests in this important area be dependent on the ability of a union to marshal economic weapons in support of its position? If so, workers in some workplaces will receive less protection than society thinks is minimally necessary. In others, staunch union activity may make the employer noncompetitive, thus driving work to other companies or countries where the money addressed to health and safety is less.

In this chapter we shall explore some of the differences between securing rights through collective, individual, and governmental means. One recurring dilemma is the following: In negotiating collective rights the union may draw lines differently than would government or the individual employee. Sometimes the bargain gives the individual a relative advantage, sometimes not. To what extent may an individual repudiate the bargain struck by her union and rely upon individual rights and government standards?

1. ASSESSING RISKS AND BALANCING VALUES

INDUSTRIAL UNION DEPARTMENT, AFL–CIO v. AMERICAN PETROLEUM INSTITUTE (BENZENE CASE)

Supreme Court of the United States, 1980.
448 U.S. 607, 100 S.Ct. 2844, 65 L.Ed.2d 1010.

MR. JUSTICE STEVENS announced the judgment of the Court and delivered an opinion, in which THE CHIEF JUSTICE and MR. JUSTICE STEWART joined and in Parts I, II, III–A, III–B, III–C and III–E of which MR. JUSTICE POWELL joined.

The Occupational Safety and Health Act of 1970 (Act) was enacted for the purpose of ensuring safe and healthful working conditions for every working man and woman in the Nation. This litigation concerns a standard promulgated by the Secretary of Labor to regulate occupational exposure to benzene, a substance which has been shown to cause cancer at high exposure levels. The principal question is whether such a showing is a sufficient basis for a standard that places the most stringent limitation on exposure to benzene that is technologically and economically possible.

The Act delegates broad authority to the Secretary to promulgate different kinds of standards. The basic definition of an "occupational safety and health standard" is found in § 3(8), which provides:

> "The term 'occupational safety and health standard' means a standard which requires conditions, or the adoption or use of one or more practices, means, methods, operations, or processes, reasonably necessary or appropriate to provide safe or healthful employment and places of employment."

Where toxic materials or harmful physical agents are concerned, a standard must also comply with § 6(b)(5), which provides:

> "The Secretary, in promulgating standards dealing with toxic materials or harmful physical agents under this subsection, shall set the standard which most adequately assures, to the extent feasible, on the basis of the best available evidence, that no employee will suffer material impairment of health or functional capacity even if such employee has regular exposure to the hazard dealt with by such standard for the period of his working life. Development of standards under this subsection shall be based upon research, demonstrations, experiments, and such other information as may be appropriate. In addition to the attainment of the highest degree of health and safety protection for the employee, other considerations shall be the latest available scientific data in the field, the feasibility

of the standards, and experience gained under this and other health and safety laws."

Wherever the toxic material to be regulated is a carcinogen, the Secretary has taken the position that no safe exposure level can be determined and that § 6(b)(5) requires him to set an exposure limit at the lowest technologically feasible level that will not impair the viability of the industries regulated. In this case, after having determined that there is a causal connection between benzene and leukemia (a cancer of the white blood cells), the Secretary set an exposure limit on airborne concentrations of benzene of one part benzene per million parts of air (1 ppm), regulated dermal and eye contact with solutions containing benzene, and imposed complex monitoring and medical testing requirements on employers whose workplaces contain 0.5 ppm or more of benzene. 29 CFR §§ 1910.1028(c), (e) (1979).

* * *

We agree with the Fifth Circuit's holding that § 3(8) requires the Secretary to find, as a threshold matter, that the toxic substance in question poses a significant health risk in the workplace and that a new, lower standard is therefore "reasonably necessary or appropriate to provide safe or healthful employment and places of employment." Unless and until such a finding is made, it is not necessary to address the further question whether the Court of Appeals correctly held that there must be a reasonable correlation between costs and benefits, or whether, as the federal parties argue, the Secretary is then required by § 6(b)(5) to promulgate a standard that goes as far as technologically and economically possible to eliminate the risk. * * *

I

Benzene is a familiar and important commodity. It is a colorless, aromatic liquid that evaporates rapidly under ordinary atmospheric conditions. Approximately 11 billion pounds of benzene were produced in the United States in 1976. Ninety-four percent of that total was produced by the petroleum and petrochemical industries, with the remainder produced by the steel industry as a byproduct of coking operations. Benzene is used in manufacturing a variety of products including motor fuels (which may contain as much as 2% benzene), solvents, detergents, pesticides, and other organic chemicals.

The entire population of the United States is exposed to small quantities of benzene, ranging from a few parts per billion to 0.5 ppm, in the ambient air. Over one million workers are subject to additional low-level exposures as a consequence of their employment. The majority of these employees work in gasoline service stations, benzene production (petroleum refineries and coking operations), chemical processing, benzene transportation, rubber manufacturing, and laboratory operations.

Benzene is a toxic substance. Although it could conceivably cause harm to a person who swallowed or touched it, the principal risk of harm comes from inhalation of benzene vapors. When these vapors are inhaled, the benzene diffuses through the lungs and is quickly absorbed into the blood. Exposure to high concentrations produces an almost immediate effect on the central nervous system. Inhalation of concentrations of 20,000 ppm can be fatal within minutes; exposures in the range of 250 to 500 ppm can cause vertigo, nausea, and other symptoms of mild poisoning. Persistent exposures at levels above 25–40 ppm may lead to blood deficiencies and diseases of the blood-forming organs, including aplastic anemia, which is generally fatal.

Industrial health experts have long been aware that exposure to benzene may lead to various types of nonmalignant diseases. By 1948 the evidence connecting high levels of benzene to serious blood disorders had become so strong that the Commonwealth of Massachusetts imposed a 35 ppm limitation on workplaces within its jurisdiction. In 1969 the American National Standards Institute (ANSI) adopted a national consensus standard of 10 ppm averaged over an 8–hour period with a ceiling concentration of 25 ppm for 10–minute periods or a maximum peak concentration of 50 ppm. In 1971, after the Occupational Safety and Health Act was passed, the Secretary adopted this consensus standard as the federal standard, pursuant to 29 U.S.C. § 655(a).[3]

As early as 1928, some health experts theorized that there might also be a connection between benzene in the workplace and leukemia.

* * *

Between 1974 and 1976 additional studies were published which tended to confirm the view that benzene can cause leukemia, at least when exposure levels are high. In an August 1976 revision of its earlier recommendation, NIOSH stated that these studies provided "conclusive" proof of a causal connection between benzene and leukemia. Although it acknowledged that none of the intervening studies had provided the dose-response data it had found lacking two years earlier, NIOSH nevertheless recommended that the exposure limit be set low as possible. As a result of this recommendation, OSHA contracted with a consulting firm to do a study on the costs to industry of complying with the 10 ppm standard then in effect or, alternatively, with whatever standard would be the lowest feasible.

3. Section 6(a) of the Act, as set forth in 29 U.S.C. § 655(a), provides:

"Without regard to chapter 5 of Title 5 or to the other subsections of this section, the Secretary shall, as soon as practicable during the period beginning with the effective date of this chapter and ending two years after such date, by rule promulgate as an occupational safety or health standard any national consensus standard, and any established Federal standard, unless he determines that the promulgation of such a standard would not result in improved safety or

health for specifically designated employees. In the event of conflict among any such standards, the Secretary shall promulgate the standard which assures the greatest protection of the safety or health of the affected employees."

In this case the Secretary complied with the directive to choose the most protective standard by selecting the ANSI standard of 10 ppm, rather than the 25 ppm standard adopted by the American Conference of Government Industrial Hygienists.

[Subsequently, at the urging of NIOSH, OSHA proposed an emergency standard, and then a final standard, at 1 ppm.—Eds.]

* * *

In its published statement giving notice of the proposed permanent standard, OSHA did not ask for comments as to whether or not benzene presented a significant health risk at exposures of 10 ppm or less. Rather, it asked for comments as to whether 1 ppm was the minimum feasible exposure limit. As OSHA's Deputy Director of Health Standards, Grover Wrenn, testified at the hearing, this formulation of the issue to be considered by the Agency was consistent with OSHA's general policy with respect to carcinogens. Whenever a carcinogen is involved, OSHA will presume that no safe level of exposure exists in the absence of clear proof establishing such a level and will accordingly set the exposure limit at the lowest level feasible. The proposed 1 ppm exposure limit in this case thus was established not on the basis of a proven hazard at 10 ppm, but rather on the basis of "OSHA's best judgment at the time of the proposal of the feasibility of compliance with the proposed standard by the [a]ffected industries." Given OSHA's cancer policy, it was in fact irrelevant whether there was any evidence at all of a leukemia risk at 10 ppm. The important point was that there was no evidence that there was not some risk, however small, at that level. The fact that OSHA did not ask for comments on whether there was a safe level of exposure for benzene was indicative of its further view that a demonstration of such absolute safety simply could not be made.

* * *

Whenever initial monitoring indicates that employees are subject to airborne concentrations of benzene above 1 ppm averaged over an 8–hour workday, with a ceiling of 5 ppm for any 15–minute period, employers are required to modify their plants or institute work practice controls to reduce exposures within permissible limits. Consistent with OSHA's general policy, the regulation does not allow respirators to be used if engineering modifications are technologically feasible.[4] Employers in this category are also required to perform monthly monitoring so long as their workplaces remain above 1 ppm, provide semiannual medical examinations to exposed workers, post signs in and restrict access to "regulated areas" where the permissible exposure limit is exceeded, and conduct employee training programs where necessary. * * *

As presently formulated, the benzene standard is an expensive way of providing some additional protection for a relatively small number of employees. * * *

---

4. Indeed, in its explanation of the standard OSHA states that an employer is required to institute engineering controls (for example, installing new ventilation hoods) even if those controls are insufficient, by themselves, to achieve compliance and respirators must therefore be used as well. 43 Fed.Reg. 5952 (1978). OSHA's preference for engineering modifications is based on its opinion that respirators are rarely used properly (because they are uncomfortable, are often not properly fitted, etc.) and therefore cannot be considered adequate protective measures.

Compliance costs in [the rubber] industry are estimated to be rather low, with no capital costs and initial operating expenses estimated at only $34 million ($1,390 per employee); recurring annual costs would also be rather low, totalling less than $1 million. By contrast, the segment of the petroleum refining industry that produces benzene would be required to incur $24 million in capital costs and $600,000 in first-year operating expenses to provide additional protection for 300 workers ($82,000 per employee), while the petrochemical industry would be required to incur $20.9 million in capital costs and $1 million in initial operating expenses for the benefit of 552 employees ($39,675 per employee).[5]

Although OSHA did not quantify the benefits to each category of worker in terms of decreased exposure to benzene, it appears from the economic impact study done at OSHA's direction that those benefits may be relatively small. Thus, although the current exposure limit is 10 ppm, the actual exposures outlined in that study are often considerably lower. For example, for the period 1970–1975 the petrochemical industry reported that, out of a total of 496 employees exposed to benzene, only 53 were exposed to levels between 1 and 5 ppm and only 7 (all at the same plant) were exposed to between 5 and 10 ppm.

II

The critical issue at this point in the litigation is whether the Court of Appeals was correct in refusing to enforce the 1 ppm exposure limit on the ground that it was not supported by appropriate findings.

Any discussion of the 1 ppm exposure limit must, of course, begin with the Agency's rationale for imposing that limit. The written explanation of the standard fills 184 pages of the printed appendix. Much of it is devoted to a discussion of the voluminous evidence of the adverse effects of exposure to benzene at levels of concentration well above 10 ppm. This discussion demonstrates that there is ample justification for regulating occupational exposure to benzene and that the prior limit of 10 ppm, with a ceiling of 25 ppm (or a peak of 50 ppm) was reasonable. It does not, however, provide direct support for the Agency's conclusion that the limit should be reduced from 10 ppm to 1 ppm.

* * *

It is noteworthy that at no point in its lengthy explanation did the Agency quote or even cite § 3(8) of the Act. It made no finding that any of the provisions of the new standard were "reasonably necessary or appropriate to provide safe or healthful employment and places of

---

5. The high cost per employee in the latter two industries is attributable to OSHA's policy of requiring engineering controls rather than allowing respirators to be used to reduce exposures to the permissible limit. The relatively low estimated cost per employee in the rubber industry is based on OSHA's assumption that other solvents and adhesives can be substituted for those that contain benzene and that capital costs will therefore not be required.

employment." Nor did it allude to the possibility that any such finding might have been appropriate.

III

Our resolution of the issues in these cases turns, to a large extent, on the meaning of and the relationship between § 3(8), which defines a health and safety standard as a standard that is "reasonably necessary and appropriate to provide safe or healthful employment," and § 6(b)(5), which directs the Secretary in promulgating a health and safety standard for toxic materials to "set the standard which most adequately assures, to the extent feasible, on the basis of the best available evidence, that no employee will suffer material impairment of health or functional capacity. . . ." * * *

[We] think it is clear that § 3(8) does apply to all permanent standards promulgated under the Act and that it requires the Secretary, before issuing any standard, to determine that it is reasonably necessary and appropriate to remedy a significant risk of material health impairment. Only after the Secretary has made the threshold determination that such a risk exists with respect to a toxic substance, would it be necessary to decide whether § 6(b)(5) requires him to select the most protective standard he can consistent with economic and technological feasibility, or whether, as respondents argue, the benefits of the regulation must be commensurate with the costs of its implementation. Because the Secretary did not make the required threshold finding in these cases, we have no occasion to determine whether costs must be weighed against benefits in an appropriate case.

A

* * *

[We] think it is clear that the statute was not designed to require employers to provide absolutely risk-free workplaces whenever it is technologically feasible to do so, so long as the cost is not great enough to destroy an entire industry. Rather, both the language and structure of the Act, as well as its legislative history, indicate that it was intended to require the elimination, as far as feasible, of significant risks of harm.

B

By empowering the Secretary to promulgate standards that are "reasonably necessary or appropriate to provide safe or healthful employment and places of employment," the Act implies that, before promulgating any standard, the Secretary must make a finding that the workplaces in question are not safe. But "safe" is not the equivalent of "risk-free." There are many activities that we engage in every day—such as driving a car or even breathing city air—that entail some risk of accident or material health impairment; nevertheless, few people would consider these activities "unsafe." Similarly, a workplace can hardly be considered "unsafe" unless it threatens the workers with a significant risk of harm.

Therefore, before he can promulgate *any* permanent health or safety standard, the Secretary is required to make a threshold finding that a place of employment is unsafe—in the sense that significant risks are present and can be eliminated or lessened by a change in practices. This requirement applies to permanent standards promulgated pursuant to § 6(b)(5), as well as to other types of permanent standards. For there is no reason why § 3(8)'s definition of a standard should not be deemed incorporated by reference into § 6(b)(5). The standards promulgated pursuant to § 6(b)(5) are just one species of the genus of standards governed by the basic requirement. That section repeatedly uses the term "standard" without suggesting any exception from, or qualification of, the general definition; on the contrary, it directs the Secretary to select "*the* standard"—that is to say, one of various possible alternatives that satisfy the basic definition in § 3(8)—that is most protective. Moreover, requiring the Secretary to make a threshold finding of significant risk is consistent with the scope of the regulatory power granted to him by § 6(b)(5), which empowers the Secretary to promulgate standards, not for chemicals and physical agents generally, but for "*toxic* materials" and "*harmful* physical agents." * * *

In the absence of a clear mandate in the Act, it is unreasonable to assume that Congress intended to give the Secretary the unprecedented power over American industry that would result from the Government's view of §§ 3(8) and 6(b)(5), coupled with OSHA's cancer policy. Expert testimony that a substance is probably a human carcinogen—either because it has caused cancer in animals or because individuals have contracted cancer following extremely high exposures—would justify the conclusion that the substance poses some risk of serious harm no matter how minute the exposure and no matter how many experts testified that they regarded the risk as insignificant. That conclusion would in turn justify pervasive regulation limited only by the constraint of feasibility. In light of the fact that there are literally thousands of substances used in the workplace that have been identified as carcinogens or suspect carcinogens, the Government's theory would give OSHA power to impose enormous costs that might produce little, if any, discernible benefit.

If the Government was correct in arguing that neither § 3(8) nor § 6(b)(5) requires that the risk from a toxic substance be quantified sufficiently to enable the Secretary to characterize it as significant in an understandable way, the statute would make such a "sweeping delegation of legislative power" that it might be unconstitutional under the Court's reasoning in A.L.A. Schechter Poultry Corp. v. United States, 295 U.S. 495, 539, 55 S.Ct. 837, 847, 79 L.Ed. 1570, and Panama Refining Co. v. Ryan, 293 U.S. 388, 55 S.Ct. 241, 79 L.Ed. 446. A construction of the statute that avoids this kind of open-ended grant should certainly be favored.

* * *

D

Given the conclusion that the Act empowers the Secretary to promulgate health and safety standards only where a significant risk of harm exists, the critical issue becomes how to define and allocate the burden of proving the significance of the risk in a case such as this, where scientific knowledge is imperfect and the precise quantification of risks is therefore impossible. The Agency's position is that there is substantial evidence in the record to support its conclusion that there is no absolutely safe level for a carcinogen and that, therefore, the burden is properly on industry to prove, apparently beyond a shadow of a doubt, that there is a safe level for benzene exposure. The Agency argues that, because of the uncertainties in this area, any other approach would render it helpless, forcing it to wait for the leukemia deaths that it believes are likely to occur before taking any regulatory action.

We disagree. As we read the statute, the burden was on the Agency to show, on the basis of substantial evidence, that it is at least more likely than not that long-term exposure to 10 ppm of benzene presents a significant risk of material health impairment. Ordinarily, it is the proponent of a rule or order who has the burden of proof in administrative proceedings. See 5 U.S.C. § 556(d). In some cases involving toxic substances, Congress has shifted the burden of proving that a particular substance is safe onto the party opposing the proposed rule. The fact that Congress did not follow this course in enacting the Occupational Safety and Health Act indicates that it intended the Agency to bear the normal burden of establishing the need for a proposed standard.

In this case OSHA did not even attempt to carry its burden of proof. The closest it came to making a finding that benzene presented a significant risk of harm in the workplace was its statement that the benefits to be derived from lowering the permissible exposure level from 10 to 1 ppm were "likely" to be "appreciable." The Court of Appeals held that this finding was not supported by substantial evidence. Of greater importance, even if it were supported by substantial evidence, such a finding would not be sufficient to satisfy the Agency's obligations under the Act. * * *

Contrary to the Government's contentions, imposing a burden on the Agency of demonstrating a significant risk of harm will not strip it of its ability to regulate carcinogens, nor will it require the Agency to wait for deaths to occur before taking any action. First, the requirement that a "significant" risk be identified is not a mathematical straitjacket. It is the Agency's responsibility to determine, in the first instance, what it considers to be a "significant" risk. Some risks are plainly acceptable and others are plainly unacceptable. If, for example, the odds are one in a billion that a person will die from cancer by taking a drink of chlorinated water, the risk clearly could not be considered significant. On the other hand, if the odds are one in a thousand that regular inhalation of gasoline vapors that are 2% benzene will be fatal, a reasonable person might well consider the risk significant and take appropriate steps to decrease or eliminate it. Although the Agency has no duty to calculate the exact probability of harm, it does have an obligation to find that a significant risk is present before it can characterize a place of employment as "unsafe."

Second, OSHA is not required to support its finding that a significant risk exists with anything approaching scientific certainty. Although the Agency's findings must be supported by substantial evidence, 29 U.S.C. § 655(f), § 6(b)(5) specifically allows the Secretary to regulate on the basis of the "best available evidence." As several Courts of Appeals have held, this provision requires a reviewing court to give OSHA some leeway where its findings must be made on the frontiers of scientific knowledge. Thus, so long as they are supported by a body of reputable scientific thought, the Agency is free to use conservative assumptions in interpreting the data with respect to carcinogens, risking error on the side of overprotection rather than underprotection.

* * *

It should also be noted that, in setting a permissible exposure level in reliance on less-than-perfect methods, OSHA would have the benefit of a backstop in the form of monitoring and medical testing. Thus, if OSHA properly determined that the permissible exposure limit should be set at 5 ppm, it could still require monitoring and medical testing for employees exposed to lower levels. By doing so, it could keep a constant check on the validity of the assumptions made in developing the permissible exposure limit, giving it a sound evidentiary basis for decreasing the limit if it was initially set too high. Moreover, in this way it could ensure that workers who were unusually susceptible to benzene could be removed from exposure before they had suffered any permanent damage.

* * *

[JUSTICE REHNQUIST concurred on the ground that Congress had impermissibly delegated its legislative responsibility to the Secretary of Labor. A brief excerpt from his opinion follows—Eds.]

* * * The decision whether the law of diminishing returns should have any place in the regulation of toxic substances is quintessentially one of legislative policy. For Congress to pass that decision on to the Secretary in the manner it did violates, in my mind, John Locke's caveat-reflected in the cases cited earlier in this opinion—that legislatures are to make laws, not legislators. Nor, as I think the prior discussion amply demonstrates, do the provisions at issue or their legislative history provide the Secretary with any guidance that might lead him to his somewhat tentative conclusion that he must eliminate exposure to benzene as far as technologically and economically possible. Finally, I would suggest that the standard of "feasibility" renders meaningful judicial review impossible.

* * * It is difficult to imagine a more obvious example of Congress simply avoiding a choice which was both fundamental for purposes of the statute and yet politically so divisive that the necessary decision or compromise was difficult, if not impossible, to hammer out in the legislative force. Far from detracting from the substantive authority of Congress, a declaration that the first sentence of § 6(b)(5) of the Occupational Safety and Health Act constitutes an invalid delegation to the Secretary of Labor would preserve the authority of Congress. If Congress wishes to legislate in an area which it has not previously sought to enter, it will in today's political world undoubtedly run into opposition no matter how the legislation is formulated. But that is the very essence of legislative authority under our system. It is the hard choices, and not the filling in of the blanks, which must be made by the elected representatives of the people. When fundamental policy decisions underlying important legislation about to be enacted are to be made, the buck stops with Congress and the President insofar as he exercises his constitutional role in the legislative process.

* * *

[JUSTICE MARSHALL, speaking for four Justices, dissented. His opinion concluded that Congress had indeed instructed the Secretary to set the standard at the safest possible level. The policy considerations underlying the dissent are captured in the following excerpt.]

Unlike the plurality, I do not purport to know whether the actions taken by Congress and its delegates to ensure occupational safety represent sound or unsound regulatory policy. The critical problem in cases like the ones at bar is scientific uncertainty. While science has determined that exposure to benzene at levels above 1 ppm creates a definite risk of health impairment, the magnitude of the risk cannot be quantified at the present time. The risk at issue has hardly been shown to be insignificant; indeed, future research may reveal that the risk is in fact considerable. But the existing evidence may frequently be inadequate to enable the Secretary to make the threshold finding of "significance" that the Court requires today. If so, the consequence of the plurality's approach would be to subject American workers to a continuing risk of cancer and other fatal diseases, and to render the Federal Government powerless to take protective action on their behalf. Such an approach would place the burden of medical uncertainty squarely on the shoulders of the American worker, the intended beneficiary of the Occupational Safety and Health Act. It is fortunate indeed that at least a majority of the Justices reject the view that the Secretary is prevented from taking regulatory action when the magnitude of a health risk cannot be quantified on the basis of current techniques.

Because today's holding has no basis in the Act, and because the Court has no authority to impose its own regulatory policies on the Nation, I dissent.

SEVERAL YEARS LATER

In September, 1987, OSHA promulgated a new final standard for worker exposure to benzene, effective December 10, 1987. The agency reduced the existing exposure limit from 10 ppm to 1 ppm, the same limit struck down by the Court in the *Benzene* decision.

The agency's new standard was based on additional data showing risks of exposure to amounts greater than 1ppm. The new standard provides exemptions for certain industries, and allows compliance by such means as employee monitoring and medical surveillance, and by personal protective equipment. If these strategies keep employee exposure below the maximum level, the employer is not obligated to comply with some of the requirements of the standard.

The full text of the new standard, as well as the supporting date for the determination, may be found at 29 C.F.R. 1910.1028.

COST–BENEFIT ANALYSIS UNDER OSHA AND THE VALUE OF A LIFE

AMERICAN TEXTILE MANUFACTURERS INSTITUTE, INC. v. DONOVAN (COTTON DUST CASE)

Supreme Court of the United States, 1981.
452 U.S. 490, 101 S.Ct. 2478, 69 L.Ed.2d 185.

MR. JUSTICE BRENNAN delivered the opinion of the Court.

* * * In 1978, the Secretary [of Labor], acting through the Occupational Safety and Health Administration (OSHA), promulgated a standard limiting occupational exposure to cotton dust, an airborne particle byproduct of the preparation and manufacture of cotton products, exposure to which induces a "constellation of respiratory effects" known as "byssinosis." * * *

Petitioners in these consolidated cases, representing the interests of the cotton industry, challenged the validity of the "Cotton Dust Standard" in the Court of Appeals for the District of Columbia Circuit * * * They contend in this Court, as they did below, that the Act requires OSHA to demonstrate that its Standard reflects a reasonable relationship between the costs and benefits associated with the Standard. Respondents, the Secretary of Labor and two labor organizations, counter that Congress balanced the costs and benefits in the Act itself, and that the Act should therefore be construed not to require OSHA to do so. They interpret the Act as mandating that OSHA enact the most protective standard possible to eliminate a significant risk of material health impairment, subject to the constraints of economic and technological feasibility. The Court of Appeals held that the Act did not require OSHA to compare costs and benefits. * * * We granted certiorari * * * to resolve this important question. * * *

I

Byssinosis, known in its more severe manifestations as "brown lung" disease, is a serious and potentially disabling respiratory disease primarily caused by the inhalation of cotton dust. * * * Byssinosis is a "continuum * * * disease," * * * that has been categorized into four grades. In its least serious form, byssinosis produces both subjective symptoms, such as chest tightness, shortness of breath, coughing, and wheezing, and objective indications of loss of pulmonary functions. In its most serious form, byssinosis is a chronic and irreversible obstructive pulmonary disease, clinically similar to chronic bronchitis or emphysema, and can be severely disabling. At worst, as is true of other respiratory diseases including bronchitis, emphysema, and asthma, byssinosis can create an additional strain on cardiovascular functions and can contribute to death from heart failure. * * *

The Cotton Dust Standard promulgated by OSHA establishes mandatory PEL's over an 8–hour period of 200 mu g/m<3> for yarn manufacturing, 750 mug/m<3> for slashing and weaving operations, and 500 mu g/m<3> for all other processes in the cotton industry. * * * OSHA chose an implementation strategy for the Standard that depended primarily on a mix of engineering controls, such as installation of ventilation systems, and work practice controls, such as special floor-sweeping procedures. Full compliance with the PEL's is required within four years, except to the extent that employers can establish that the engineering and work practice controls are infeasible. * * *

In promulgating the Cotton Dust Standard, OSHA interpreted the Act to require adoption of the most stringent standard to protect against material health impairment, bounded only by technological and economic feasibility. OSHA therefore rejected the industry's alternative proposal for a PEL of 500 mu g/m<3> in yarn manufacturing, a proposal which would produce a 25% prevalence of at least Grade 1/2 byssinosis. The agency expressly found the Standard to be both technologically and economically feasible based on the evidence in the record as a whole. Although recognizing that permitted levels of exposure to cotton dust would still cause some byssinosis, OSHA nevertheless rejected the union proposal for a 100 mu g/m<3> PEL because it was not within the "technological capabilities of the industry." Similarly, OSHA set PEL's for some segments of the cotton industry at 500 mu g/m<3> in part because of limitations of technological feasibility. Finally, the Secretary found that "engineering dust controls in weaving may not be feasible even with massive expenditures by the industry," and for that and other reasons adopted a less stringent PEL of 750 mu g/m<3> for weaving and slashing. * * *

II

The principal question presented in these cases is whether the Occupational Safety and Health Act requires the Secretary, in promulgating a standard pursuant to § 6(b)(5) of the Act, 29 U.S.C. § 655(b)(5), to determine that the costs of the standard bear a reasonable relationship to its benefits. Relying on §§ 6(b)(5) and 3(8) of the Act, 29 U.S.C. §§ 655(b)(5) and 652(8), petitioners urge not only that OSHA must show that a standard addresses a significant risk of material health impairment, see *Industrial Union Dept.* v. *American Petroleum Institute, 448 U.S., at 639* (plurality opinion), but also that OSHA must demonstrate that the reduction in risk of material health impairment is significant in light of the costs of attaining that reduction.[26] Respondents on the other hand contend that the Act requires OSHA to promulgate standards that eliminate or reduce such risks "to the extent such protection is technologically and economically feasible."[27] To resolve this debate, we must turn to the language, structure, and legislative history of the Act.

A

The starting point of our analysis is the language of the statute itself. * * * Section 6(b)(5) of the Act, 29 U.S.C. § 655(b)(5) (emphasis added), provides:

> The Secretary, in promulgating standards dealing with toxic materials or harmful physical agents under this subsection, shall set the standard which most adequately assures, *to the extent feasible*, on the basis of the best available evidence, that no employee will suffer material impairment of health or functional capacity even if such

---

26. Petitioners ATMI et al. express their position in several ways. They maintain that OSHA "is required to show that a reasonable relationship exists between the risk reduction benefits and the costs of its standards." Petitioners also suggest that OSHA must show that "the standard is expected to achieve a *significant reduction in* [the significant risk of material health impairment]" based on "an assessment of the costs of achieving it." Allowing that "[this] does not mean that OSHA must engage in a rigidly formal cost-benefit calculation that places a dollar value on employee lives or health," petitioners describe the required exercise as follows:

"First, OSHA must make a responsible determination of the costs and risk reduction benefits of its standard. Pursuant to the requirement of Section 6(f) of the Act, this determination must be factually supported by substantial evidence in the record. The subsequent determination whether the reduction in health risk is 'significant' (based upon the factual assessment of costs and benefits) is a judgment to be made by the agency in the first instance."

Respondent Secretary disputes petitioners' description of the exercise, claiming that any meaningful balancing must involve "placing a [dollar] value on human life and freedom from suffering," ..., and that there is no other way but through formal cost-benefit analysis to accomplish petitioners' desired balancing,. Cost-benefit analysis contemplates "systematic enumeration of all benefits and all costs, tangible and intangible, whether readily quantifiable or difficult to measure, that will accrue to all members of society if a particular project is adopted." E. Stokey & R. Zeckhauser, A Primer for Policy Analysis 134 (1978). * * * Whether petitioners' or respondent's characterization is correct, we will sometimes refer to petitioners' proposed exercise as "cost-benefit analysis."

27. As described by the union respondents, the test for determining whether a standard promulgated to regulate a "toxic material or harmful physical agent" satisfies the Act has three parts:

"First, whether the 'place of employment is unsafe—in the sense that significant risks are present and can be eliminated or lessened by a change in practices.' [*Industrial Union Dept., supra*, at 642 (plurality opinion).] Second, whether of the possible available correctives the Secretary has selected '*the* standard ... that is most protective.' *Ibid.* Third, whether that standard is 'feasible.' " Brief for Union Respondents 40–41.

We will sometimes refer to this test as "feasibility analysis."

employee has regular exposure to the hazard dealt with by such standard for the period of his working life.

Although their interpretations differ, all parties agree that the phrase "to the extent feasible" contains the critical language in § 6(b)(5) for purposes of these cases. * * *

The plain meaning of the word "feasible" supports respondents' interpretation of the statute. According to Webster's Third New International Dictionary of the English Language 831 (1976), "feasible" means "capable of being done, executed, or effected." * * *

In effect then, as the Court of Appeals held, Congress itself defined the basic relationship between costs and benefits, by placing the "benefit" of worker health above all other considerations save those making attainment of this "benefit" unachievable. Any standard based on a balancing of costs and benefits by the Secretary that strikes a different balance than that struck by Congress would be inconsistent with the command set forth in § 6(b)(5). Thus, cost-benefit analysis by OSHA is not required by the statute because feasibility analysis is. * * *

B

Even though the plain language of § 6(b)(5) supports this construction, we must still decide whether § 3(8), the general definition of an occupational safety and health standard, either alone or in tandem with § 6(b)(5), incorporates a cost-benefit requirement for standards dealing with toxic materials or harmful physical agents. Section 3(8) of the Act, 29 U.S.C. § 652(8) (emphasis added), provides:

> The term 'occupational safety and health standard' means a standard which requires conditions, or the adoption or use of one or more practices, means, methods, operations, or processes, *reasonably necessary or appropriate* to provide safe or healthful employment and places of employment.

Taken alone, the phrase "reasonably necessary or appropriate" might be construed to contemplate some balancing of the costs and benefits of a standard. Petitioners urge that, so construed, § 3(8) engrafts a cost-benefit analysis requirement on the issuance of § 6(b)(5) standards, even if § 6(b)(5) itself does not authorize such analysis. We need not decide whether § 3(8), standing alone, would contemplate some form of cost-benefit analysis. For even if it does, Congress specifically chose in § 6(b)(5) to impose separate and additional requirements for issuance of a subcategory of occupational safety and health standards dealing with toxic materials and harmful physical agents: it required that those standards be issued to prevent material impairment of health *to the extent feasible*. Congress could reasonably have concluded that *health* standards should be subject to different criteria than *safety* standards because of the special problems presented in regulating them. See *Industrial Union Dept. v. American Petroleum Institute, 448 U.S., at 649, n. 54* (plurality opinion).

Agreement with petitioners' argument that § 3(8) imposes an additional and overriding requirement of cost-benefit analysis on the issuance of § 6(b)(5) standards would eviscerate the "to the extent feasible" requirement. Standards would inevitably be set at the level indicated by cost-benefit analysis, and not at the level specified by § 6(b)(5). * * *

We cannot believe that Congress intended the general terms of § 3(8) to countermand the specific feasibility requirement of § 6(b)(5). Adoption of petitioners' interpretation would effectively write § 6(b)(5) out of the Act. We decline to render Congress' decision to include a feasibility requirement nugatory, thereby offending the well-settled rule that all parts of a statute, if possible, are to be given effect. *E. g., Reiter v. Sonotone Corp.*, 442 U.S., at 339; *Weinberger v. Hynson, Westcott & Dunning, Inc.*, 412 U.S. 609, 633–634 (1973); *Jarecki v. G. D. Searle & Co.*, 367 U.S. 303, 307–308 (1961). Congress did not contemplate any further balancing by the agency for toxic material and harmful physical agents standards, and we should not " 'impute to Congress a purpose to paralyze with one hand what it sought to promote with the other.' " *Weinberger v. Hynson, Westcott & Dunning, Inc., supra*, at 631, quoting *Clark v. Uebersee Finanz–Korporation*, 332 U.S. 480, 489 (1947).[32] * * *

C

The legislative history of the Act, while concededly not crystal clear, provides general support for respondents' interpretation of the Act. The congressional Reports and debates certainly confirm that Congress meant "feasible" and nothing else in using that term. Congress was concerned that the Act might be thought to require achievement of absolute safety, an impossible standard, and therefore insisted that health and safety goals be capable of economic and technological accomplishment. Perhaps most telling is the absence of any indication whatsoever that Congress intended OSHA to conduct its own cost-benefit analysis before promulgating a toxic material or harmful physical agent standard. The legislative history demonstrates conclusively that Congress was fully aware that the Act would impose real and substantial costs of compliance on industry, and believed that such costs were part

---

32. This is not to say that § 3(8) might not require the balancing of costs and benefits for standards promulgated under provisions other than § 6(b)(5) of the Act. As a plurality of this Court noted in *Industrial Union Dept.*, if § 3(8) had no substantive content, "there would be no statutory criteria at all to guide the Secretary in promulgating either national consensus standards or permanent standards other than those dealing with toxic materials and harmful physical agents." 448 U.S., at 640, n. 45. Furthermore, the mere fact that a § 6(b)(5) standard is "feasible" does not mean that § 3(8)'s "reasonably necessary or appropriate" language might not impose additional restraints on OSHA. For example, all § 6(b)(5) standards must be addressed to "significant risks" of material health impairment. *Id.*, at 642. In addition, if the use of one respirator would achieve the same reduction in health risk as the use of five, the use of five respirators was "technologically and economically feasible," and OSHA thus insisted on the use of five, then the "reasonably necessary or appropriate" limitation might come into play as an additional restriction on OSHA to choose the one-respirator standard. In this case we need not decide all the applications that § 3(8) might have, either alone or together with § 6(b)(5).

of the cost of doing business. We thus turn to the relevant portions of the legislative history. * * *

The Senate Committee on Labor and Public Welfare, reporting on the Williams bill, included a provision virtually identical to the House version, except for the additional requirement that the Secretary set the standard "which most adequately *and feasibly assures* * * * that no employee will suffer any impairment of health." *Id.*, at 242 (the Senate provision was numbered § 6(b)(5)) (emphasis added). This addition to the Williams bill was offered by Senator Javits, who explained his amendment:

> "As a result of this amendment the Secretary, in setting standards, is expressly required to consider feasibility of proposed standards. This is an improvement over the Daniels bill [as reported out of the House Committee], which might be interpreted to require *absolute* health and safety in all cases, regardless of feasibility, and the Administration bill, which contains no criteria for standards at all." S. Rep. No. 91–1282, p. 58 (1970), Leg. Hist. 197 (emphasis added).

Thus the Senator's concern was that a standard might require "absolute health and safety" without any consideration as to whether such a condition was achievable. The full Senate Committee also noted that standards promulgated under this provision "shall represent feasible requirements," S. Rep. No. 91–1282, at 7, Leg. Hist. 147, and commented that "[such] standards should be directed at assuring, *so far as possible*, that no employee will suffer impaired health * * *," *ibid.* (emphasis added). * * *

Not only does the legislative history confirm that Congress meant "feasible" rather than "cost-benefit" when it used the former term, but it also shows that Congress understood that the Act would create substantial costs for employers, yet intended to impose such costs when necessary to create a safe and healthful working environment. Congress viewed the costs of health and safety as a cost of doing business. Senator Yarborough, a cosponsor of the Williams bill, stated: "We know the costs would be put into consumer goods but that is the price we should pay for the 80 million workers in America." 116 Cong. Rec., at 37345, Leg. Hist. 444. He asked:

> "One may well ask too expensive for whom? Is it too expensive for the company who for lack of proper safety equipment loses the services of its skilled employees? Is it too expensive for the employee who loses his hand or leg or eyesight? Is it too expensive for the widow trying to raise her children on meager allowance under workmen's compensation and social security? And what about the man—a good hardworking man—tied to a wheel chair or hospital bed for the rest of his life? That is what we are dealing with when we talk about industrial safety.

* * * "We are talking about people's lives, not the indifference of some cost accountants." 116 Cong. Rec., at 37625, Leg. Hist. 510.

Senator Eagleton commented that "[the] costs that will be incurred by employers in meeting the standards of health and safety to be established under this bill are, in my view, *reasonable and necessary costs of doing busines.*" 116 Cong. Rec., at 41764, Leg. Hist. 1150–1151 (emphasis added). * * *

Other Members of Congress voiced similar views. Nowhere is there any indication that Congress contemplated a different balancing by OSHA of the benefits of worker health and safety against the costs of achieving them. * * *

V

When Congress passed the Occupational Safety and Health Act in 1970, it chose to place pre-eminent value on assuring employees a safe and healthful working environment, limited only by the feasibility of achieving such an environment. We must measure the validity of the Secretary's actions against the requirements of that Act. For "[the] judicial function does not extend to substantive revision of regulatory policy. That function lies elsewhere—in Congressional and Executive oversight or amendatory legislation." *Industrial Union Dept. v. American Petroleum Institute*, 448 U.S., at 663 (BURGER, C.J., concurring); see *TVA v. Hill*, 437 U.S. 153, 185, 187–188, 194–195 (1978). Accordingly, the judgment of the Court of Appeals is affirmed in all respects except to the extent of its approval of the Secretary's application of the wage guarantee provision of the Cotton Dust Standard at 29 CFR § 1910.1043(f)(2)(v) (1980). To that extent, the judgment of the Court of Appeals is vacated and the case remanded with directions to remand to the Secretary for further proceedings consistent with this opinion.

It is so ordered.

JUSTICE POWELL took no part in the decision of these cases.

The dissent of Justice Stewart, jointed by the Justice Rehnquist, is omitted.

In a separate dissent, joined by the Chief Justice, Justice Rehnquist reiterated his arguments in his concurring opinion in the *Benzene* case that the Occupational Safety and Health Act position on standards amounts to an unconstitutional delegation of the Secretary of Labor of legislative power.

Questions:

1. What are the "feasibility" and "cost-benefit" criteria for promulgating an OSHA standard? What are the statutory bases for these criteria? How do they compare? Which is "better" for workers and which is "better" for employers?

2. Does the Supreme Court think that the same criterion necessarily applies to OSHA standards on "toxic substances and harmful physical agents" under § 6(b)(5) and to "general safety" standards? Does its position make sense?

3. In his dissent in *Cotton Dust* Justice Rehnquist stated:

As I read the Court's opinion, * * * the Act does not require the Secretary to engage in a cost-benefit analysis, which suggests of course that the Act *permits* the Secretary to undertake such an analysis if he so chooses.

Is this a good reading of the Court's opinion? According to the Court, who has the responsibility for making the cost-benefit analysis for OSHA under the "feasibility" criterion?

The appropriate role of cost-benefit analysis in the promulgation of health and safety regulations has been a bone of contention within the executive branch for over three decades. Since 1974, every president has issued at least one executive order encouraging or requiring some form of evaluation of the economic impact of OSHA regulations prior to their promulgation. The height of this effort was reached during the Reagan administration. Shortly after the *Cotton Dust* case was argued, but before it was decided, President Reagan issued Executive Order 12,291, 46 Fed. Reg. 13,193 (1981), which subjected all new and existing federal regulations to cost-benefit analysis and review by the Office of Management and Budget. Later, in 1985, President Reagan issued Executive Order 12,498, 50 Fed. Reg. 684 (1985), further expanding the Office of Management and Budget's role in reviewing regulations issued by OSHA and other agencies. The Clinton administration adopted a more moderate position on cost-benefit analysis. A portion of the current Executive Order on the subject is reproduced below:

EXECUTIVE ORDER 12866
Regulatory Planning and Review
(58 FR 51735)
September 30, 1993.

* * * With this Executive order, the Federal Government begins a program to reform and make more efficient the regulatory process. * * * In pursuing these objectives, the regulatory process shall be conducted so as to meet applicable statutory requirements and with due regard to the discretion that has been entrusted to the Federal agencies.

Accordingly, by the authority vested in me as President by the Constitution and the laws of the United States of America, it is hereby ordered as follows:

Section 1. *Statement of Regulatory Philosophy and Principles.*

(a) *The Regulatory Philosophy.* Federal agencies should promulgate only such regulations as are required by law, are necessary to interpret the law, or are made necessary by compelling public need, such as material failures of private markets to protect or improve the health and safety of the public, the environment, or the well-being of the American people. In deciding whether and how to regulate, agencies should assess all costs and benefits of available regulatory alternatives, including the alternative of not regulating. Costs and benefits shall be understood to include both quantifiable measures (to the fullest extent that these can be usefully estimated) and qualitative measures of costs and benefits that are difficult to quantify, but nevertheless essential to consider. Further, in choosing among alternative regulatory approaches, agencies should select those approaches that maximize net benefits (including potential economic, environmental, public health and safety, and other advantages; distributive impacts; and equity), unless a statute requires another regulatory approach.

(b) *The Principles of Regulation.* To ensure that the agencies' regulatory programs are consistent with the philosophy set forth above, agencies should adhere to the following principles, to the extent permitted by law and where applicable: * * *

(5) When an agency determines that a regulation is the best available method of achieving the regulatory objective, it shall design its regulations in the most cost-effective manner to achieve the regulatory objective. In doing so, each agency shall consider incentives for innovation, consistency, predictability, the costs of enforcement and compliance (to the government, regulated entities, and the public), flexibility, distributive impacts, and equity.

(6) Each agency shall assess both the costs and the benefits of the intended regulation and, recognizing that some costs and benefits are difficult to quantify, propose or adopt a regulation only upon a reasoned determination that the benefits of the intended regulation justify its costs.

---

1. Does Executive Order 12,866 encourage or require cost-benefit analysis in the promulgation of OSHA regulations? Would it be consistent with the Court's opinion in *Cotton Dust* to require cost benefit analysis?

2. How does Executive Order 12,866 deal with the problem of valuing human life in the economic evaluation of OSHA regulations?

3. If you were the Secretary of Labor, promulgating new safety regulations, how would you direct OHSA to comply with the requirements of the Act, as interpreted in *Cotton Dust* and Executive Order 12866? What sort of information would you have OSHA use and what sort of comparisons would you have them make? How would you evaluate the value of lives and limbs saved by a regulation? A recent example of OHSA's efforts is set forth below:

DEPARTMENT OF LABOR
OCCUPATIONAL SAFETYAND HEALTH ADMIN.
SAFETY STANDARDS FOR STEEL ERECTION

29 CFR Part 1926
Federal Register, Vol. 66, No. 12, p. 5196
January 18, 2001.

SUMMARY: By this notice the Occupational Safety and Health Administration (OSHA) revises the construction industry safety standards which regulate steel erection. The final rule enhances protections provided to workers engaged in steel erection and updates the general provisions that address steel erection. The final rule sets performance-oriented criteria, where possible, to protect employees from steel erection related hazards such as working under loads; hoisting, landing and placing decking; column stability; double connections; hoisting, landing and placing steel joists; and falls to lower levels. To effectuate this, the final rule contains requirements for hoisting and rigging, structural steel assembly, beam and column connections, joist erection, systems-engineered metal building erection, fall protection and training. * * *

V.   Summary of the Final Economic and Regulatory Flexibility Analysis

Introduction

This final standard is a significant regulatory action under Executive Order (EO) 12866 * * * Accordingly, OSHA has developed a final economic analysis * * * of the costs, benefits, and regulatory and non-regulatory alternatives of the rule, as required by the EO. * * * This section of OSHA's notice of final rulemaking summarizes the Agency's economic analysis of the final steel erection standard. * * *

Final Changes to OSHA's Steel Erection Standard

This final steel erection standard modifies and strengthens the steel erection standard it replaces in a number of areas. For example, the final standard includes a scope section that identifies the types of construction projects and activities subject to the rule. * * * The final rule also includes a new section addressing site layout, site-specific erection plans, and construction sequence. Other revisions to the existing standard include:

● Explicit requirements for hoisting and rigging and the protection of workers and the public from the hazards of overhead loads;

● Additional and strengthened requirements for the structural steel assembly of beams, columns, joists, decking, and systems-engineered metal buildings, including provisions for the protection of employees from tripping hazards and slippery surfaces on walking/working surfaces;

● Modified and clarified requirements for fall protection for connectors, decking assemblers, and other iron workers during the erection of structural steel; and

● New requirements for training in fall hazards, multiple lift rigging, connecting, and controlled decking zones.

Evaluation of Risk and Potential Benefits

For this final economic analysis, OSHA developed a profile of the risks facing iron workers who are performing steel erection operations. OSHA's risk profile for steel erection is based on data from the Bureau of Labor Statistics' National Census of Fatal Occupational Injuries, data from the Bureau's Survey of Occupational Injuries and Illnesses, and an analysis by a SENRAC workgroup of OSHA fatality/catastrophe inspection data obtained from the Agency's Integrated Management Information System.

OSHA anticipates that the final standard will significantly reduce the number of accidents and fatalities currently reported in the steel erection industry, particularly those accidents caused by falls from elevated levels and by objects such as dislodged structural members and building materials striking workers. OSHA believes that the more protective requirements for fall protection, structural stability, and training in the final standard will help to save lives and prevent injuries in the iron worker workforce. For accidents involving events or exposures potentially addressed by the final standard, OSHA estimates that approximately 35 fatalities and 2,279 lost-workday injuries currently occur annually among structural metal workers. * * * This is the current industry risk baseline used in this analysis. OSHA projects that full compliance with the final standard would prevent 30 of these fatalities and 1,142 of these lost-workday injuries. Eight of these fatalities and 303 serious injuries could be prevented if employers were currently in compliance with OSHA's existing steel erection standard. The final standard will thus prevent an additional 22 fatalities and 838 injuries that would not be prevented even by full compliance with the existing standard. * * *

In addition to saving lives and improving overall safety in the steel erection industry, OSHA believes that the final standard, once fully implemented by erection contractors, will yield substantial cost savings to parties within and connected with the industry and ultimately to society as a whole. These monetized benefits take the form of reductions in employer, employee, and insurer accident-related costs in several areas: the value of lost output associated with temporary total disabilities and permanent partial disabilities; reductions in accident-related medical costs; reductions in administrative expenses incurred by workers' compensation insurance providers (including employers who self-insure); and indirect costs related to productivity losses to other workers, work stoppages, and the conduct of accident investigations and reports. Applying data from the construction and insurance industries on the direct costs of accidents and data from the literature on the indirect costs of accidents and other tort-and administrative-related costs to OSHA's estimate of avoided injuries * * * the Agency has monetized the value of the cost savings employers and society will accrue by avoiding these injuries. The monetized benefits therefore underestimate the true benefits that will be realized by the standard. They also do not, in accordance with Agency policy, attempt to place a monetary value on the lives the final rule will save. These benefits estimates are thus gross underestimates of the true benefits that will be realized by the standard. OSHA estimates that annual cost savings of $10.4 million would result from full compliance with the current rule and an additional $29.1

million would be saved as a result of full compliance with the final rule.
* * *

Technological Feasibility and Compliance Costs

OSHA projects that full compliance with the final standard will, after deducting costs incurred to achieve compliance with the existing standard, result in net (or incremental) annualized costs of $78.4 million for affected establishments. Among incremental annualized costs, expenditures for slip-resistant coatings of skeletal structural steel are expected to total $29.5 million, or 38 percent of total costs; expenditures for the safe design and erection of steel joists required by the final standard account for $19.3 million, or 25 percent of total costs; fall arrest systems account for $14.4 million, or 18 percent of total costs; and expenditures for anchor bolts necessary for structural stability account for $11.0 million, or 14 percent of total costs. Other control costs associated with compliance with the final steel erection standard are those for guardrails ($2.9 million); recordkeeping associated with administrative controls (1.4 million); and training ($1.0 million). In addition, OSHA anticipates that the expanded use of fall arrest systems in bridge erection will eventually lead to a dramatic reduction in the use of personnel safety nets on those projects, resulting in estimated cost savings of $5.2 million.

Potential Economic Impacts

OSHA analyzed the potential impacts of these compliance costs on prices, profits, construction output and other economic indices in the steel erection industry. In particular, OSHA examined potential economic impacts on establishments in SIC 1791, Structural Steel Erection, where the majority of the 57,000 structural metal workers are employed. This analysis shows that the final standard is economically feasible for these firms.

OSHA examined the potential economic impacts of the final standard by making two assumptions used by economists to bound the range of possible impacts: the worst-case assumption of no-cost pass-through, i.e., that employers will be unable to pass any of the costs of compliance forward to their customers, and the worst-case assumption of full-cost pass-through, i.e., that employers will be able to pass all of the costs of compliance forward to their customers. * * * OSHA estimates that, if affected firms in SIC 1791 were forced to absorb these compliance costs entirely from profits (a highly unlikely scenario), profits would be reduced by an average of 6.5 percent. If, at the other extreme, affected firms were able to pass all of these compliance costs forward to general contractors and project owners, OSHA projects that the price (revenue) increase required to pay for these costs would be less than 1 percent (0.40 percent). A price increase of 0.40 percent would have little, if any, effect on the choice between steel erection and other forms of building.
* * *

OSHA believes that, prior to the generation of the cost savings projected to accrue from implementation of the standard, most steel erectors will handle the increase in direct costs by increasing their prices somewhat and absorbing the remainder from profits. * * * Although these minimal economic impacts would be felt by most affected employers after implementation of the standard, OSHA anticipates—based on testimony by members of SENRAC and other industry representatives whose current fall protection programs and other safety measures mirror those required by the final standard * * *—that offsetting cost savings will at least partially reverse any negative economic impacts. * * *

Questions:

1. How does OSHA apply cost-benefit analysis to justify the Steel Erection Regulations? Does OSHA put an explicit value on the lives saved by the regulation? Is this consistent with Executive Order 12,866? With *Cotton Dust?*

2. OSHA estimates that the new Steel Erection Regulations will prevent 22 fatalities and 838 injuries a year. OSHA also provides an "underestimate" of indirect cost savings (lost output, workers' compensation costs, medical expenses, etc.) of $29.1 million a year and an estimate of the direct costs of implementation of the new regulation of $78.4 million a year. If one assumes that the actual indirect cost savings of the regulation are one and a half times those listed ($43.65 million) and that ten injuries are worth a life, what is the implicit value on human life incorporated in the Steel Erection Regulations? Is this too much to ask firms and consumers to pay to save steelworkers' lives and limbs? Is it too little?

LAWRENCE S. BACOW, BARGAINING FOR JOB SAFETY AND HEALTH

12–14 (1980).

The Occupational Safety and Health Administration relies upon a system of standards, inspections, and fines to create incentives for making the workplace safe. The Labor Department has primary responsibility for promulgating and enforcing standards.

Most of the OSHA standards currently on the books were adopted during the years immediately following the enactment of the law (1971–1973). During this period Congress permitted the Secretary of Labor to promulgate as OSHA standards "any national consensus standards, and any established federal standards." The intent was to avoid duplicating the efforts of private organizations (such as the American National Standards Institute) that had been in the business of defining safe practices for years. About 4,400 standards were adopted under this procedure. Each standard attempts to address a different workplace hazard. Many of these regulations are very detailed, specifying the exact procedures that must be followed to abate a hazard. For example, ladder safety is covered by over 140 regulations. OSHA has since rescinded many of these consensus standards because they proved to be obsolete.

[The OSHA standard setting process] is slow and cumbersome. For example, since its inception OSHA has adopted only 23 new health standards, an average of fewer than 4 per year.

Responsibility for compliance with OSHA standards rests almost exclusively with employers. Although workers have a legal duty to comply with the terms of the act, there are no sanctions for employee noncompliance. Management compliance is monitored through workplace inspections, many of which are targeted at firms in high-risk industries. The remaining inspections are triggered by worker complaints or major accidents. Until 1978 OSHA inspectors performed these inspections by simply showing up at the workplace and demanding entrance, but in that year the Supreme Court ruled that employers could legally refuse to admit OSHA inspectors who failed to produce a search warrant on demand. Because OSHA must demonstrate that probable cause exists in order to obtain a warrant, random searches are no longer permitted.

OSHA's inspection force is small relative to the number of firms subject to regulation: 1,560 federal inspectors are available to inspect the nation's 5 million workplaces. This force is supplemented by an additional 1,500–1,800 state inspectors operating under the aegis of approved state occupational safety and health plans. Because of the size of the inspection force, inspections are infrequent; one study estimates that OSHA is capable of inspecting only 2 percent of the firms it regulates each year.

OSHA inspectors are required by law to issue citations for all standards violations observed. Citations typically result in modest fines. A Senate Oversight Committee reported that from July 1972 through March 1974 98 percent of all OSHA violations cited were minor. The average fine for these violations was $16. Serious violations made up only 1.2 percent of all violations, with fines averaging $648. The remaining violations were classified as "willful," "repeat," or "imminent danger," and fines averaged $1,104.

The regulatory approach mandated by the Occupational Safety and Health Act is striking in light of the number of separate problems that must be addressed as well as the diversity of the regulated institutions. Congress has given OSHA the enormous task of prescribing how every hazard in the nation's workplaces is to be abated. As if this were not a big enough job, OSHA must also write its standards so that they will work well in a wide variety of employment settings. OSHA's job is made even more difficult by the fact that the threats it has at its disposal to encourage compliance—infrequent inspections and modest fines—are unlikely to bring about expensive investments in job safety and health.

In effect, the existing regulatory structure requires OSHA to be omniscient and omnipresent. Congress has enacted a regulatory program that would work well if the occupational safety and health problem consisted of a few major hazards in a handful of homogeneous workplaces. Thus, it should not be surprising that OSHA has been intensely criticized for not promulgating standards quickly enough, for creating standards that do little to improve health and safety conditions and often create more problems than they solve, for imposing excessive costs on employers, and for failing to vigorously protect the health and safety of the American worker. Congress has given OSHA an impossible job, and OSHA has regarded it as possible. The judgment of both institutions is questionable.

[Editors' Note: In 1991, Congress authorized, but with one exception did not mandate, larger civil fines than those authorized at the time of the immediately preceding excerpt from Bacow's book. It is too soon to ascertain whether larger fines and greater deterrence will be the consequences of the statutory amendments.]

LYNN K. RHINEHART, WOULD WORKERS BE BETTER PROTECTED IF THEY WERE DECLARED AN ENDANGERED SPECIES? A COMPARISON OF CRIMINAL ENFORCEMENT UNDER THE FEDERAL WORKPLACE SAFETY AND ENVIRONMENTAL PROTECTION LAWS

31 American Criminal Law Review 351, 353–54 (1994).

* * * [M]ore than 9,000 workers [were] killed in 1991 from traumatic injuries caused by hazardous working conditions. While statistics on deaths due to occupational disease are more difficult to obtain, tens of thousands of workers are thought to die each year due to cancer and other illnesses caused by workplace exposure to toxic substances. Job hazards injure or make ill millions more workers each year. Despite willful violations of the law resulting in employee deaths, injury and illness, employers like American Bumper have, almost without exception, escaped criminal liability for their actions. In the twenty-three year history of the Occupational Safety and Health (OSH) Act, only two employers have gone to jail for violating the Act.

The dearth of criminal enforcement under the OSH Act contrasts sharply with the enforcement track record under environmental laws. Only twenty-three employers have been convicted of or have pleaded guilty to charges of violating the OSH Act since its passage in 1970. In contrast, since 1982, as many as 600 defendants have been convicted for violating environmental laws. In 1992 alone, nearly 100 defendants were convicted for environmental crimes, while only one defendant was convicted under the OSH Act. Moreover, the maximum penalty under environmental laws is thirty times greater than the maximum penalty for OSH Act violations.

This disparate treatment presents an anomaly. The OSH Act and the various environmental laws were enacted in the same era and share many common goals and purposes. All protect human health from harm and hold accountable those companies that place workers or the public at risk. Indeed, these statutes regulate many of the same toxic substances and dangerous processes. In practice, however, improper handling of toxic substances is far more likely to result in criminal prosecution when it threatens the environment—meaning natural resources or the general public—than when it threatens workers. Do the laws reflect a value judgment that environmental protection is more important than worker protection? Or has the OSH Act simply not kept pace with current attitudes toward corporate accountability?

2. LEARNING ABOUT RISKS AND HOW TO DEAL WITH THEM (OR: HOW I LEARNED TO STOP WORRYING AND TO LOVE MY JOB)

JAMES T. O'REILLY, DRIVING A SOFT BARGAIN: UNIONS, TOXIC MATERIALS, AND RIGHT TO KNOW LEGISLATION

9 Harv.Env.L.Rev. 307, 308 (1985).

The American workplace is undergoing a revolutionary change in information rights and obligations. Faced with the problem of worker exposure to toxic materials, unions have tried to create employer obligations to disclose to employees the identity and dangers of all hazardous chemicals used in the workplace. This information is a first step towards improved warnings, training, and safety procedures, all of which are required to reduce the number of injuries and diseases caused by toxic materials. Unions and their allies have addressed the problem of toxic information chiefly through state legislation, in the form of state "right to know" laws requiring employers to disclose information about toxic chemicals, and through federal regulation by the Occupational Safety and Health Administration ("OSHA"), in the form of OSHA's Hazard Communication standard, which goes into effect in 1985 and 1986. Unions have, at the same time, made little use of collective bargaining, either to obtain contract provisions requiring disclosure or to use the toxics information won under state law to bargain for workplace safety improvements.

The choice of collective bargaining representatives to seek workplace chemical identity information chiefly through legislation and regulation, rather than through collective bargaining, was noteworthy. That decision made lobbyists, not negotiators, predominant in achieving union goals. Employer disclosure obligations have become the "soft bargain" of the modern union movement, a victory won not with hard bargaining and concessions at the negotiating table but at a relatively low cost in state legislatures and before OSHA rulemakers.

[This] article draws three conclusions from the right to know experience. First, unions correctly decided that they should use legislation to establish an employer obligation to disclose. Second, unions have missed an opportunity, at the individual plant level, to interpret chemical data and press for the training, engineering controls, and monitoring that are necessary to realize real health and safety benefits from the raw information won through legislation. Third, unions must be prepared for the possibility that they may incur new legal liabilities along with the new information resources of right to know laws.

DELAWARE VALLEY TOXICS COALITION, WINNING THE RIGHT TO KNOW: A HANDBOOK FOR TOXICS ACTIVISTS

13–14 (1984).

DEVELOPING RIGHT TO KNOW LEGISLATION

Here are some issues to consider when developing Right to Know provisions for your area:

WORKER RIGHT TO KNOW OR PUBLIC-ACCESS LEGISLATION?

Since OSHA promulgated an industry-backed Right to Know standard which purports to give workers the Right to Know and attempts to preempt other Right to Know laws, the case for pushing public access legislation rather than laws giving only workers access to information is stronger than ever. Adoption of the OSHA regulation bolsters the industry argument against the necessity of local legislation giving workers the Right to Know, despite the fact that the standard is weak and coverage is limited. Public access legislation counters that argument by doing what OSHA never can—giving the public the right to toxics information.

In addition, public-access laws have several advantages over worker Right to Know laws that only provide employees with access to information about toxics in their own workplace. Under public-access laws, neighborhood residents, firefighters, health professionals, and land use planners, as well as workers can use Right to Know to reduce toxics problems. In addition, public-access laws enable non-union workers to get information about their own workplace without having to ask their employer, thus avoiding the risk of retaliation.

Proposing public-access Right to Know legislation also makes sense strategically. The greater the number of interest groups backing the Right to Know, the better the chances are for passage in the face of stiff business opposition. After passage, the greater the number of requests for information, the greater the chances are that the law will be implemented effectively. * * *

TYPES OF TOXICS INFORMATION

Information about substances released from the plant is most critical to residents, but workers are generally more concerned about labeling of toxics in the workplace. * * *

In order to provide information about the health hazards of a toxic, most Right to Know laws mandate completion of a Material Safety Data Sheet (MSDS) following the format of the U.S. Department of Labor form OSHA 20, for each chemical covered by Right to Know. Some Right to Know laws require each business to supply the MSDS for each toxic to be reported. Others mandate that a government agency complete the MSDS. An MSDS can also be required for mixtures that have been tested for adverse health effects. * * *

Unfortunately, MSDSs may often be incomplete, particularly concerning chronic health effects. But they do provide information that allows you to begin to learn about a material's adverse health effects. Right to Know laws may require additional information.

The AFL–CIO suggested in its critique of the OSHA proposal (before it was promulgated) that because MSDSs are so often incomplete, they should be accompanied by a supplemental data sheet. The supplemental data sheet would include information which is "not reflected in MSDS health effects section because of professional judgment . . .". The AFL–CIO suggests that the combined "material safety data sheet and supplemental data sheet reflect all information available in the relevant computer files of the National Library of Medicine . . .". Such a provision may also be valuable for local Right to Know laws.

a. *Under the NLRA*

OCAW v. NLRB

United States Court of Appeals District of Columbia Circuit, 1983.
711 F.2d 348.

HARRY T. EDWARDS, CIRCUIT JUDGE:

These consolidated petitions for review and applications for enforcement involve three decisions of the National Labor Relations Board ("NLRB" or "Board") in cases dealing with requests by unions for information concerning the health and safety of employees represented by the bargaining agents. In each instance, the company was found to have violated sections 8(a)(1) and 8(a)(5) of the National Labor Relations Act ("NLRA" or "Act") by failing to provide the unions with information, other than data constituting trade secrets or individually identifiable medical records, relevant to the health and safety of the employees.

* * * Each company argues that the requested information is not relevant to the unions' bargaining responsibilities and that, in any event, the inclusion of proprietary and trade secret data within the scope of the unions' requests for information legitimated the employers' refusal to comply with those requests. The employers, alone or in combination, also raise a number of other defenses premised, for example, on allegations pertaining to the confidentiality of employees' medical records, the burdensomeness of the unions' requests, and the unions' waivers of their

right to receive relevant information. We find no merit in any of these contentions.

The Board's decisions are attacked, from a different angle, by two locals of the Oil, Chemical & Atomic Workers International Union ("International") and one affiliated with the International Chemical Workers Union ("ICWU"). The unions, while satisfied with most aspects of the NLRB's decisions, argue that the Board ignored its statutory obligation to resolve unfair labor practice charges in failing to decide whether the employers' refusal to supply relevant information containing trade secrets violated the NLRA. We disagree. In our view, the Board's decisions, fairly read, reveal clearly its conclusion that the companies had not been shown to have contravened the Act by declining unconditionally to disclose the small part of the requested information constituting proprietary or trade secret material. As the Board found, however, the employers failed to satisfy their bargaining obligations concerning this information by wholly denying its relevance; accordingly, we approve the orders requiring them to bargain in good faith with the unions over the conditions under which trade secret information might appropriately be disclosed.

* * *

II. DISCUSSION

A. General Principles

The disposition of these petitions for review does not require the development of any novel legal principles. An employer's duty to bargain in good faith with a labor organization representing its employees has long been acknowledged to include a duty to supply a union with "requested information that will enable [the union] to negotiate effectively and to perform properly its other duties as bargaining representative." This fundamental obligation to furnish relevant information is "rooted in recognition that union access to such information can often prevent conflicts which hamper collective bargaining," and it undoubtedly extends to data requested in order properly to administer and police a collective bargaining agreement as well as to requests advanced to facilitate the negotiation of such contracts. In either instance, the employer's duty is predicated on the need of the union for information that will promote "intelligent representation of the employees."

The union's need and the employer's duty depend, in all cases, on the "probability that the desired information [is] relevant, and that it [will] be of use to the union in carrying out its statutory duties and responsibilities." It is a commonplace that "[e]ach case must turn upon its particular facts," NLRB v. Truitt Manufacturing Co., 351 U.S. 149, 153, 76 S.Ct. 753, 756, 100 L.Ed. 1027 (1956), but it is nevertheless also true that a dichotomy has developed between data bearing directly on mandatory bargaining subjects and other kinds of information. Information in the first category, pertaining to wages, hours or conditions of employment, is *presumptively* relevant, and must be disclosed unless the employer proves a lack of relevance. On the other hand, when information not ordinarily pertinent to collective bargaining, such as information concerning nonunit employees, is requested by a union, relevance is not assumed. Instead the union must affirmatively demonstrate relevance to bargainable issues.

The use of a presumption of relevance, of course, may substantially simplify the assessment of a union's request for information. But, when seeking information to which the presumption does not apply, a union "need not demonstrate that the information * * * is certainly relevant or clearly dispositive of the basic * * * issues between the parties. The fact that the information is of probable or potential relevance is sufficient to give rise to an obligation * * * to provide it." Under this "discovery-type standard," NLRB v. Acme Industrial Co., 385 U.S. at 437, 87 S.Ct. at 568, " 'relevant' is synonymous with 'germane' " and, in the absence of some valid countervailing interest, an employer must disclose information requested by a union as long as that information has a bearing on the bargaining process.

The application of this standard is, in the first instance, a matter for the NLRB, and the Board's conclusions are given great weight by the courts. But a finding of relevance does not ensure that the union will receive all of the desired information in the precise form it requested. This court has long recognized that particular circumstances sometimes warrant a refusal to disclose or the imposition of conditions upon the production of requested information. And the Supreme Court has clearly rejected "the proposition that union interests in arguably relevant information must always predominate over all other interests, however legitimate." Detroit Edison Co. v. NLRB, 440 U.S. 301, 318, 99 S.Ct. 1123, 1132, 59 L.Ed.2d 333 (1979).

In a decision necessarily resting heavily on the facts of the particular case, the *Detroit Edison* Court concluded that the NLRB's failure adequately to protect an employer's interest in the confidentiality of its aptitude test battery and answer sheets constituted an abuse of the Board's remedial authority. The Court also held that the employer satisfied its bargaining obligation by offering to disclose employees' test scores only upon receipt of consents from the affected individuals. In reaching these conclusions, the Court made clear that it frequently will be necessary to strike an appropriate balance between the legitimate interests of employers and unions.

When applied to the decisions currently under review, we believe, these governing principles justify enforcement in full.

* * *

B. *Relevance*

The right to relevant information, the previous section makes clear, validates requests for data reasonably necessary to enable unions effectively to administer and police collective bargaining agreements or intelligently to seek their modification. Employee health and safety indisputably are mandatory subjects of collective bargaining, about which the unions in each of these cases have insisted on negotiating. The resulting contractual health and safety provisions, of course, are not set in stone and may appropriately be modified in future negotiations. In the meantime, it is "the duty of union representatives * * * to see that * * * [the employers meet their] obligations under those clauses." * * *

In cases like those now before us, where the employees admittedly are exposed to a variety of potential hazards and have expressed growing and legitimate concerns over their health and safety, where the unions explained the rationales underlying their requests in considerable detail, and where the pertinent collective bargaining agreements obligate both management and the unions to take specified actions to safeguard employees' health and safety, the relevance of a wide range of information concerning the various elements of the working environment and employees' health experiences cannot be gainsaid.

* * *

C.   Trade Secrets

In defense of their refusal to disclose, the employers contend that some of the data encompassed within the unions' requests constitute trade secrets. As the NLRB found, however, this trade secret defense applies to only a small portion of the requested information and thus could not justify the companies' total noncompliance with the unions' requests. And, while *Detroit Edison* makes clear that a union's interest in relevant information will not always outweigh an employer's legitimate and substantial interests in maintaining the confidentiality of such information, that case certainly affords no support for the proposition that an employer is absolutely privileged from revealing relevant proprietary or trade secret information. Even a cursory examination of the NLRB's decisions in these cases reveals the Board's faithfulness to the accommodative philosophy espoused by the *Detroit Edison* Court.

In each of the cases under consideration, the NLRB concluded, explicitly or implicitly, that the General Counsel had not established that the refusal to disclose trade secret information violated the NLRA. The Board held, however, that the employers' blanket denials of relevance, which it rejected, had precluded meaningful bargaining over the conditions under which this proprietary information *might* be disclosed; accordingly, the employers were ordered to bargain in good faith on this point. This position, it seems clear, fully respects the legitimacy of the companies' interests in the confidentiality of their trade secrets, for, as we read the Board's orders, they express no view on whether trade secret information ultimately need be disclosed. If conditions can be devised to accommodate both the employers' confidentiality interests and the unions' interest in obtaining relevant information, a refusal to disclose under those conditions likely will be found to violate the Act. But if no such conditions can be created, the Board might be forced to sanction the companies' refusal to disclose trade secret information.

* * *

b. Under "Right to Know" Statutes

UNITED STEELWORKERS OF AMERICA, AFL–CIO v. AUCHTER

United States Court of Appeals, Third Circuit, 1985.
763 F.2d 728.

GIBBONS, CIRCUIT JUDGE:

* * *

I.

EVOLUTION OF THE STANDARD

Section 6 of the OSH Act directs the Secretary of Labor to promulgate occupational safety and health standards to further the purpose of the Act "to assure so far as possible every working man and woman in the Nation safe and healthful working conditions. * * *" 29 U.S.C. §§ 651(b) and 655(b)(1) (1982). Any standard promulgated by the Secretary

> shall prescribe the use of labels or other appropriate forms of warning as are necessary to insure that employees are apprised of all hazards to which they are exposed, relevant symptoms and appropriate emergency treatment, and proper conditions and precautions of safe use or exposure.

29 U.S.C. § 655(b)(7) (1982).

* * *

[Such a] standard was published in its final form on November 25, 1983. It requires that chemical manufacturers and importers "evaluate chemicals produced in their workplaces or imported by them to determine if they are hazardous." 29 C.F.R. § 1910.1200(d)(1) (1984). It refers to several compilations of toxic materials. These lists establish a floor of toxic substances which chemical manufacturers or importers must treat as hazardous. 29 C.F.R. § 1910.1200(d)(3) (1984). Chemicals not included in the designated compilations must be evaluated for hazardousness by reference to "available scientific evidence." 29 C.F.R. § 1910.1200(d)(2) (1984). A manufacturer or importer of chemicals found to be hazardous must "ensure that each container . . . leaving the workplace is labeled" with the chemical identity, with appropriate hazard warnings, and with the name and address of the source. 29 C.F.R. § 1910.1200(f)(1) (1984). Manufacturers or importers must also prepare a "material safety data sheet" (MSDS) containing the chemical common names of each hazardous ingredient, and information necessary for safe use of the product. 29 C.F.R. § 1910.1200(g) (1984). The MSDS must be provided to each employer in the manufacturing sector (Standard Industrial Classification Codes 20–39) purchasing a hazardous chemical. That employer must in turn make the MSDS available for employee inspection. 29 C.F.R. § 1910.1200(g)(8) (1984), and "shall provide employees with information and training on hazardous chemicals in their work area. * * * " 29 C.F.R. § 1910.1200(h) (1984).

The rule allows an exception from the labeling and MSDS ingredient disclosure requirements when a chemical manufacturer or importer claims that the chemical identity is a trade secret. 29 C.F.R. § 1910.1200(i) (1984). In such a case, the manufacturer or importer must provide a MSDS disclosing the hazardous properties of the chemical and suggesting appropriate precautions. In the case of a medical emergency, the manufacturer or importer must disclose the chemical identity to a treating physician or nurse, and may later require such a health professional to sign a confidentiality agreement. 29 C.F.R. § 1910.1200(i)(2) (1984). Absent a medical emergency, the manufacturer or importer may be required to disclose the chemical identity to a health professional who makes a written request detailing the occupational need for the information, and who is willing to sign a confidentiality agreement containing a liquidated damages clause. 29 C.F.R. § 1910.1200(i)(3) & (4) (1984). In no case is the manufacturer required to disclose the precise formula, as opposed to the identity of chemicals in the compound.

* * *

IV.

CHALLENGES TO THE VALIDITY OF THE STANDARD

[Petitioners challenged the Hazard Communication Standard on three grounds: (1) that its coverage was limited to the manufacturing sector, (2) that it failed to adopt the list of hazardous substances already compiled by NIOSH in its Registry of Toxic Effect of Chemical Substances (RTECS), and (3) that it contained an improper exemption for trade secrets.

As to the first issue, the court concluded that the Secretary of Labor had failed to carry the burden of showing that limitation to the manufacturing sector was proper. The court said, "once a standard has been promulgated * * * the Secretary may exclude a particular industry only if he informs the reviewing court, not merely that the sector selected for coverage presents greater hazards, but also why it is not feasible for the same standard to be applied in other sectors where workers are exposed to similar hazards." The Secretary was directed to reconsider application of the standard to other sectors and to apply it to those sectors "unless he can state reasons why such application would not be feasible."

The court's disposition of the other two issues follows:]

C. Failure to Incorporate the RTECS Hazard List

While the Hazard Communication Standard includes several lists of substances which chemical manufacturers and importers must treat as hazardous, the Standard places primary responsibility for determining which products are hazardous on the chemical manufacturer or importer. 29 C.F.R. § 1910.1200(d)(1) (1984). Petitioner Public Citizen urges that the Secretary should have adopted the RTECS list compiled by NIOSH. The agency found that the hazard determination procedure provided the most protective coverage possible by establishing standards to guide manufacturers in determining whether a substance is hazardous. 48 Fed.Reg. 53299. It rejected use of the RTECS list, finding that it was overinclusive because it encompasses "potential" as well as "identifiable" hazards, id. at 53298, and that it was underinclusive because no one list can remain suitably up-to-date, id. at 53296. These findings are supported by the Introduction to the RTECS list in which the editor explains that "[t]he absence of a substance from the Registry does not imply that the substance is non-toxic, and thus non-hazardous, any more than the presence of a substance in the Registry indicates that the substance is hazardous in common use." NIOSH, Registry of Toxic Effects of Chemical Substances (RTECS) Introduction xi (July 1984). Indeed the editor notes that the RTECS list includes substances that are common in everyday life and in nearly every household. Id. at x.

The Public Citizen contends that OSHA's determination that the RTECS list is inappropriate is belied by the Agency's use of that list in its Records Access rule, see Louisiana Chemical Association v. Bingham, 657 F.2d 777, 783 & n. 10 (5th Cir.1981). The Records Access rule, which merely requires that employers make available those records which are kept anyway, imposes a much lighter burden on employers than the Hazard Communication Standard. Because the purposes and requirements of the two rules are not identical, it was reasonable for the Secretary to conclude that the hazard determination procedure for each rule need not be identical. We conclude that the Secretary's rejection of the RTECS list as overinclusive is supported by substantial evidence and is consistent with the OSH Act's statutory purposes.

D. The Trade Secret Exemption

Several petitioners challenge the inclusion in the Hazard Communication Standard of a "trade secret" exception. 29 C.F.R. § 1910.1200(i) (1984). They contend that the agency has defined "trade secret" too broadly, and that the conditions under which workers may obtain information claimed to be a trade secret are unduly burdensome.

1. The Definition of Trade Secret

Trade secret protection may arise from two sources: state law or a federal statute. Ruckelshaus v. Monsanto Co., 467 U.S. 986, 1001, 104 S.Ct. 2862, 2872, 81 L.Ed.2d 815 (1984); Chevron Chemical Co. v. Costle, 641 F.2d 104, 115 (3d Cir.), cert. denied, 452 U.S. 961, 101 S.Ct. 3110, 69

L.Ed.2d 972 (1981). The OSH Act does not create substantive trade secret protection. * * *

Plainly the Secretary has provided greater protection for chemical manufacturers and importers than that afforded in those states utilizing the Restatement of Torts trade secret definition. Even the Restatement definition, moreover, goes beyond the protection afforded to trade secrets in other regulatory contexts. See Public Citizen Health Research Group v. Food and Drug Administration, 704 F.2d 1280, 1287 (D.C.Cir.1983) (Food and Drug Administration's adoption of Restatement of Torts trade secret definition inconsistent with Freedom of Information Act).

Section 15 deals only with disclosure by the agency or its employees, and section 6(b)(5) does not permit the Secretary to balance employee safety against competing economic concerns. No other statutory provision has been called to our attention which would justify enlarging trade secret protection beyond that afforded by state law. Indeed it seems plain that state law cannot prevent the implementation of section 6 safety standards that are otherwise feasible.

* * *

We agree that there is no legal justification for affording broader trade secret protection in the Hazard Communication Standard than state law affords. No petitioner urges that the Secretary's original proposal, which would have protected formula and process information but required disclosure of hazardous ingredients, is inadequate. That proposal was consistent with "[t]he general policy of OSHA ... that the interests of employee safety and health are best served by full disclosure of chemical identity information." 48 Fed.Reg. 53312 (1983). The petition for review will therefore be granted and the proceedings remanded to the Secretary for reconsideration of the definition of trade secrets, which definition shall not include chemical identity information that is readily discoverable through reverse engineering. * * *

THE RECORDS ACCESS RULE

OSHA has promulgated two separate rules dealing with the dissemination of information about the exposure of workers to toxic substances. The Hazard Communications Standard is the subject of the *Auchter* decision, above. In addition, there is an earlier Records Access Rule also discussed in *Auchter* by way of comparison.

The Records Access Rule, 29 C.F.R. § 1910.20, requires employers to provide OSHA and "employees and their designated representatives" access to records voluntarily created by employers which contain medical and exposure histories of employees exposed to toxic substances or harmful physical agents. The rule expressly protects existing "legal and ethical obligations concerning the maintenance and confidentiality of employee medical information," any existing duty to disclose information to an employee, the physician/patient relationship and trade secrets.

The rule makes clear that a "designated representative includes a certified or recognized collective bargaining agent," and that such an agent "shall be treated automatically as a designated representative without regard to written employee authorization." Section 1910.20(c)(3).

NOTE ABOUT EMPLOYEE KNOWLEDGE OF EMPLOYMENT DANGERS AND HAZARDS

1. In assessing whether notice-of-danger requirements work, consider the following assumptions.

a. The more employees fear the real or fancied dangers and hazards in their work environment, the more expense the employer will incur to run its business, at least in the short run. That is, the employer will be forced to raise wages, improve (or appear to improve) safety and health conditions, or face higher employee turnover. Each consequence will result in greater expense to the employer. An employer singularly dedicated to profits would have to assess the least expensive of these alternatives (or a combination of them) to deal with the employees' greater concerns about health and safety.

b. In light of that additional expense, it follows that the profit-maximizing employer will have a motive to have the employees believe, regardless of the truth, that the workplace is as safe as it conceivably can be. The employer's reticence to be wholly candid is reinforced by the fact that the expense may be great both to discover and to describe all the elements of the workplace that make for hazards. While modern tort law may give some manufacturers some incentive to warn users of the dangers of hazardous substances which may be used in the workplace, it is not clear that employers, protected by the workers' compensation limits, yet have a similar motive.

c. OSHA's Hazard Communication Standard places most of the onus on a manufacturer to decide for itself whether something it produces is hazardous and therefore must be identified as such for the users, along with a description of the product's ingredients. If a manufacturer does not determine that a product is hazardous, the standard's requirements do not apply. Why are the interests of users of the products left to the judgment of the manufacturer? Would it make more sense, for example, to require that all products be subject to the Standard's requirements? What would be gained or lost by such a change in the law?

2. The Hazard Communication Standard's primary readers are not the employees but the employers (really, their managers and technicians) who receive the information from the producers. The employers are then obliged by the standard to make the hazard communications available to

the employees and to train employees in the use of the products. There is a hope that, once being aware of the hazards, employers will change what they do. There is evidence that some employers, perhaps as many as 30 percent, substitute less toxic ingredients in some situations. It is also hoped that employers and employees will be more careful because of the Hazard Communications.

3.   Are employees in any position to understand a chemical description of a product? Will they be able to deal with the probability analysis? If they are so inclined, employees can sometimes get better understanding through advice from friends who are knowledgeable, their doctors, unions, or others. To the extent employees take advantage of such opportunities, they will not be relying entirely on the unilateral determination made by the manufacturer.

4.   To what use can a collective bargaining agent put the information? If a union is not the bargaining representative of the employees, would it be able to use the information for any legitimate purpose?

If employees are not represented by a union, does the NLRA permit employees and an employer to create a joint employer-employee committee to study, assess, design, and administer a safety and health program in the workplace? Review the materials in Chapter II regarding Section 8(a)(2) of the NLRA and the use of employee committees. If you are persuaded that the NLRA does not permit such committees, should the OSHA, the NLRA, or both be amended to permit them? If so, in what way should they be constructed? What authority should the law give the employee-members of such a committee?

CATHERINE RUCKELSHAUS AND FANETTE POLLACK, BOOK REVIEW, WOMEN'S HEALTH IN THE WORKPLACE

24 Legal Studies Forum 207 (2000).

We pay less attention to workers' health in this country than we do to attention-getters like AIDS and health insurance. * * * The subject of women's occupational health (which affects almost half of the workforce) is virtually a non-entity. * * *. [W]ithout more scientific and policy attention to the specific needs of women workers, they will continue to suffer unnecessary adverse health effects from workplace hazards.

* * *[W]ithout gender-specific research in occupational health, women will continue to fail to achieve equal opportunity in the workplace. Women will continue to have to explain to their doctors and to their employers the reason for the impact of their work on their health, why the debilitating pains in their wrists and hands from typing eight hours a day are not "all in their head," and why they need a transfer from an unsafe job during their pregnancy. From a legal standpoint, the systemic bias in research and policies in women's occupational health and in their "special physical organization" impacts on women's ability

to get and keep a job and to work for a living wage, all of which constitutes sex discrimination.

* * * [W]omen, who are concentrated in such jobs as clerical and data entry work, grocery store cashiers, and chicken processing, report disproportionate instances of repetitive stress injuries such as carpal tunnel syndrome. In addition, the biological make-up of women and the stresses they face as primary care-givers in the home may exacerbate their propensity to exhibit these symptoms as compared to males in the same jobs. This means that anyone looking at the issue of women's occupational health must take into account women's life on and off the job.

* * * [W]omen's reproductive health on the job is treated differently by employers, policy makers, and scientists if the health or safety issue involves a pregnancy (and, most importantly, a developing fetus).* * * While we agree that the health of a developing fetus merits close attention by the scientific community, lawmakers, and the courts if necessary, the extent to which this particular "women's" health issue eclipses all others is striking. This focus, to the exclusion of the non-reproductive concerns of women workers, reflects the attitude that reproduction is still women's grand purpose in life, even though women have shown that they intend to be a permanent part of the workforce. The legal system seems to be saying that women need protection in the workplace, as they did at the turn of the century, "to preserve the strength and vigor of the race."

Many studies * * * fail to take into account women's lives outside of the workplace, and undervalue such workplace stressors as sexual harassment and lack of control and their impact on the physiological systems of women workers. * * * Thus, articles appear in the popular press citing published scientific studies that dismiss repetitive stress claims by women, and argue that indoor air pollution and its supposed effects are the result of mass hysteria among women workers. Women are themselves blamed for their work-related ailments and some mental health professionals concentrate on characteristics of the worker rather than workplace conditions.

* * *

The Occupational Safety and Health Act, which covers most private-sector workplaces in this country and nominally requires that employers provide a healthy and safe workplace, is almost useless for workers without a union (and protections contained in a collective bargaining agreement) ... Unlike chemicals found in foods, drug, and some pesticides which must be carefully tested and approved before being introduced, workplace chemicals have no such requirement. * * *

Furthermore, chemical exposure is not the sole workplace health hazard. For the vast majority of non-chemical workplace hazards that affect women, there are no OSHA standards at all. * * *

D. PROBLEM 3–1

The Maria Perez Case

To: Hungadunga Law Firm

From: Vice–President Crickboom

Re: Pregnancy in the Computer Maintenance Shop

Maria Perez, one of our employees in the computer repair and maintenance shop, told me today that she is pregnant. She is deeply concerned about the possible impact computers and repair equipment may have on her next child, who is due in about seven and one-half months. As you know, the shop is a small room (approximately four hundred square feet) and has benches with bulky, expensive equipment which is shared by five or six employees at any given time during each of two shifts. Perez' obstetrician told her a number of medical experts believe that the computers and the testing equipment may emit waves that are dangerous to the fetus. Moreover, the doctor told her that her job requires her to sit more than is good for the position of the fetus. Perez thinks the chairs are badly designed and they are placed poorly in relation to the computer keyboard and screen. She says that both these deficiencies present ergonomics hazards, especially for a woman who is carrying a child and who can be stressed and fatigued by sitting in these positions. Perez is a good employee. Although I doubt her obstetrician's fears are very sensible, I am going to take her concern seriously.

I am in a quandary. I do not want the newborn child to be harmed. Moreover, I do not want to find the company liable to the parents or the newborn child for any birth defects.

I am considering transferring Perez to another department. Unfortunately, the only other jobs she can do are unskilled positions. We are presently overloaded with unskilled employees. Several who have more company seniority than Perez are on a layoff due to lack of work.

Then, I thought I might excuse Ms. Perez during the pregnancy. If I agreed to pay her for the time, she might be willing to take a leave. I doubt she would agree to a leave without pay. Can I require her to take a paid leave? An unpaid leave?

The leave possibility, alas, also poses problems for us. The employees in Perez's department are highly trained. A prolonged leave will put us in the position of hiring an additional high salaried employee whom we will have to train but we will not need permanently. In light of that expense, I am not sure I want to offer Perez a leave. Yet, she may decide that the only way to protect the fetus is to get away from the shop. I wonder if the company is required to give her a leave. Can I discharge her?

I could also respond to Ms. Perez' concerns about the ergonomics of her work station by investigating different seat designs and different placement of seats.

Before I do anything, please advise me whether any action I take will have legal ramifications.

[the Enderby—United Factory Workers Union collective bargaining contract has no provisions addressed explicitly to leaves with or without pay. The contract does have the following provisions:

1) An employee may be disciplined or discharged by the company only if there is good cause for the company to do so.

2) Neither the company nor the union will change any of the terms of this contract without negotiations with the other.

3) The company shall not discriminate against or for any employee because of union activity, concerted activity, race, sex, age, religion, nationality, national origin, disability, or sexual orientation.

4) Seniority shall be established on a plantwide basis. So long as the more senior employee is qualified, promotions, layoffs, and bumping shall be controlled by seniority.]

––––––

To: The Enderby—UFWU (Maria Perez) FILE

From: Hungadunga

Re: Outline of Possible Responses to Crickboom's Memorandum

We shall have to learn more about the possible causes and effects between her work and the future child's health. Assuming Perez has a reasonable basis to fear harm to her next child, I believe our client, Enderby, has four options. They are: (A) Require Perez to take a leave either with or without pay; (B) Assign Perez to another job which she can do, despite her relative lack of seniority; (C) Require Perez to continue her work; or (D) Permit Perez to choose between either taking a leave or staying at her present job. This memorandum begins an analysis of these options.

A. Is it lawful for Enderby to discharge Perez or suspend her with or without pay?

1. STATUTES

If Enderby does force Perez to be away from work during the remainder of her pregnancy because of the possible dangers the machines pose for the yet-to-be-born child and because of the company's fear of liability to the child, will the company violate either Title VII, OSHA, or the ADA? I think the *Johnson Controls* case, which follows, will set the parameters for any understanding of the Title VII issues. The *American Cyanamid* case, which I also reproduce in part, is dispositive I think of an OSHA claim, although it is from a Court of Appeals, merely. Finally, while it is too early to be certain about much regarding the ADA, I think we may have a problem. In any event, I quote a few of that statute's relevant provisions.

a. *Title VII—Johnson Controls*

INTERNATIONAL UNION, UAW
v. JOHNSON CONTROLS

The Supreme Court of the United States, 1991.
499 U.S. 187, 111 S.Ct. 1196, 113 L.Ed.2d 158.

JUSTICE BLACKMUN delivered the opinion of the Court.

In this case we are concerned with an employer's gender-based fetal-protection policy. May an employer exclude a fertile female employee from certain jobs because of its concern for the health of the fetus the woman might conceive?

I

Respondent Johnson Controls, Inc., manufactures batteries. In the manufacturing process, the element lead is a primary ingredient. Occupational exposure to lead entails health risks, including the risk of harm to any fetus carried by a female employee. * * *

Between 1979 and 1983, eight employees became pregnant while maintaining blood lead levels in excess of 30 micrograms per deciliter. This appeared to be the critical level noted by the Occupational Health and Safety Administration (OSHA) for a worker who was planning to have a family. See 29 CFR § 1910.1025 (1989). The company responded by announcing a broad exclusion of women from jobs that exposed them to lead:

" * * * [I]t is [Johnson Controls'] policy that women who are pregnant or who are capable of bearing children will not be placed into jobs involving lead exposure or which could expose them to lead through the exercise of job bidding, bumping, transfer or promotion rights." App. 85–86.

The policy defined "women ... capable of bearing children" as "[a]ll women except those whose inability to bear children is medically documented." *Id.*, at 81. It further stated that an unacceptable work station was one where, "over the past year," an employee had recorded a blood lead level of more than 30 micrograms per deciliter or the work site had yielded an air sample containing a lead level in excess of 30 micrograms per cubic meter. *Ibid.*

II

In April 1984, petitioners filed in the United States District Court for the Eastern District of Wisconsin a class action challenging Johnson Controls' fetal-protection policy as sex discrimination that violated Title VII of the Civil Rights Act of 1964, as amended, 42 U.S.C. § 2000e *et seq.* Among the individual plaintiffs were petitioners Mary Craig, who had chosen to be sterilized in order to avoid losing her job, Elsie Nason, a 50–year-old divorcee, who had suffered a loss in compensation when she was transferred out of a job where she was exposed to lead, and Donald Penney, who had been denied a request for a leave of absence for the purpose of lowering his lead level because he intended to become a father.

* * *

III

The bias in Johnson Controls' policy is obvious. Fertile men, but not fertile women, are given a choice as to whether they wish to risk their reproductive health for a particular job. Section 703(a) of the Civil Rights Act of 1964, prohibits sex-based classifications in terms and conditions of employment, in hiring and discharging decisions, and in other employment decisions that adversely affect an employee's status. Respondent's fetal-protection policy explicitly discriminates against women on the basis of their sex. The policy excludes women with childbearing capacity from lead-exposed jobs and so creates a facial classification based on gender. Respondent assumes as much in its brief before this Court. * * *

Nevertheless, the Court of Appeals assumed * * * that because the asserted reason for the sex-based exclusion (protecting women's unconceived offspring) was ostensibly benign, the policy was not sex-based discrimination. That assumption, however, was incorrect.

First, Johnson Controls' policy classifies on the basis of gender and childbearing capacity, rather than fertility alone. Respondent does not seek to protect the unconceived children of all its employees. Despite evidence in the record about the debilitating effect of lead exposure on the male reproductive system, Johnson Controls is concerned only with the harms that may befall the unborn offspring of its female employees. * * *

This Court faced a * * * conceptually similar situation in *Phillips v. Martin Marietta Corp.,* 400 U.S. 542, 91 S.Ct. 496, 27 L.Ed.2d 613 (1971), and found sex discrimination because the policy established "one hiring policy for women and another for men—each having pre-school-age children." Johnson Controls' policy is facially discriminatory because it requires only a female employee to produce proof that she is not capable of reproducing.

Our conclusion is bolstered by the Pregnancy Discrimination Act of 1978 (PDA), in which Congress explicitly provided that, for purposes of Title VII, discrimination "on the basis of sex" includes discrimination "because of or on the basis of pregnancy, childbirth, or related medical conditions." "The Pregnancy Discrimination Act has now made clear that, for all Title VII purposes, discrimination based on a woman's pregnancy is, on its face, discrimination because of her sex." *Newport News Shipbuilding & Dry Dock Co. v. EEOC,* 462 U.S. 669, 684, 103 S.Ct. 2622, 2631, 77 L.Ed.2d 89 (1983). In its use of the words "capable of bearing children" in the 1982 policy statement as the criterion for exclusion, Johnson Controls explicitly classifies on the basis of potential for pregnancy. Under the PDA, such a classification must be regarded, for Title VII purposes, in the same light as explicit sex discrimination. Respondent has chosen to treat all its female employees as potentially pregnant; that choice evinces discrimination on the basis of sex.

We concluded above that Johnson Controls' policy is not neutral because it does not apply to the reproductive capacity of the company's male employees in the same way as it applies to that of the females. Moreover, the absence of a malevolent motive does not convert a facially discriminatory policy into a neutral policy with a discriminatory effect. Whether an employment practice involves disparate treatment through explicit facial discrimination does not depend on why the employer discriminates but rather on the explicit terms of the discrimination. In *Martin Marietta, supra,* the motives underlying the employers' express exclusion of women did not alter the intentionally discriminatory character of the policy. Nor did the arguably benign motives lead to consideration of a business necessity defense. The question in that case was whether the discrimination in question could be justified under § 703(e) as a BFOQ. The beneficence of an employer's purpose does not undermine the conclusion that an explicit gender-based policy is sex discrimination under § 703(a) and thus may be defended only as a BFOQ.

* * *

IV

* * *

The BFOQ defense is written narrowly, and this Court has read it narrowly * * *. We have read the BFOQ language of § 4(f) of the Age Discrimination in Employment Act of 1967 (ADEA), which tracks the BFOQ provision in Title VII, just as narrowly. Our emphasis on the restrictive scope of the BFOQ defense is grounded on both the language and the legislative history of § 703.

The wording of the BFOQ defense contains several terms of restriction that indicate that the exception reaches only special situations. The statute thus limits the situations in which discrimination is permissible to "certain instances" where sex discrimination is "reasonably necessary" to the "normal operation" of the "particular" business. Each one of these terms—certain, normal, particular—prevents the use of general subjective standards and favors an objective, verifiable requirement. But the most telling term is "occupational"; this indicates that these objective, verifiable requirements must concern job-related skills and aptitudes.

The concurrence defines "occupational" as meaning related to a job. According to the concurrence, any discriminatory requirement imposed by an employer is "job-related" simply because the employer has chosen to make the requirement a condition of employment. In effect, the concurrence argues that sterility may be an occupational qualification for women because Johnson Controls has chosen to require it. This reading of "occupational" renders the word mere surplusage. "Qualification'' by itself would encompass an employer's idiosyncratic requirements. By modifying "qualification" with "occupational," Congress narrowed the term to qualifications that affect an employee's ability to do the job.

Johnson Controls argues that its fetal-protection policy falls within the so-called safety exception to the BFOQ. Our cases have stressed that discrimination on the basis of sex because of safety concerns is allowed only in narrow circumstances. In *Dothard v. Rawlinson,* [433 U.S. 321, 97 S.Ct. 2720, 53 L.Ed.2d 786 (1977)] this Court indicated that danger to a woman herself does not justify discrimination. We there allowed the employer to hire only male guards in contact areas of maximum-security male penitentiaries only because more was at stake than the "individual woman's decision to weigh and accept the risks of employment." We found sex to be a BFOQ inasmuch as the employment of a female guard would create real risks of safety to others if violence broke out because the guard was a woman. Sex discrimination was tolerated because sex was related to the guard's ability to do the job—maintaining prison security. We also required in *Dothard* a high correlation between sex and ability to perform job functions and refused to allow employers to use sex as a proxy for strength although it might be a fairly accurate one.

Similarly, some courts have approved airlines' layoffs of pregnant flight attendants at different points during the first five months of pregnancy on the ground that the employer's policy was necessary to ensure the safety of passengers.

We considered safety to third parties in *Western Airlines, Inc. v. Criswell,* [472 U.S. 400, 105 S.Ct. 2743, 86 L.Ed.2d 321 (1985)] in the context of the ADEA. We focused upon "the nature of the flight engineer's tasks," and the "actual capabilities of persons over age 60" in relation to those tasks. Our safety concerns were not independent of the individual's ability to perform the assigned tasks, but rather involved the possibility that, because of age-connected debility, a flight engineer might not properly assist the pilot, and might thereby cause a safety emergency. Furthermore, although we considered the safety of third parties in *Dothard* and *Criswell,* those third parties were indispensable to the particular business at issue. In *Dothard,* the third parties were the inmates; in *Criswell,* the third parties were the passengers on the plane. We stressed that in order to qualify as a BFOQ, a job qualification must relate to the "essence," or to the "central mission of the employer's business."

The concurrence ignores the "essence of the business" test and so concludes that "the safety to fetuses in carrying out the duties of battery manufacturing is as much a legitimate concern as is safety to third parties in guarding prisons (*Dothard*) or flying airplanes (*Criswell*)." By limiting its discussion to cost and safety concerns and rejecting the "essence of the business" test that our case law has established, the concurrence seeks to expand what is now the narrow BFOQ defense. Third-party safety considerations properly entered into the BFOQ analysis in *Dothard* and *Criswell* because they went to the core of the employee's job performance. Moreover, that performance involved the central purpose of the enterprise. *Dothard,* 433 U.S., at 335, 97 S.Ct., at 2729–2730 ("The essence of a correctional counselor's job is to maintain prison security"); *Criswell,* 472 U.S., at 413, 105 S.Ct., at 2751 (the central mission of the airline's business was the safe transportation of its passengers): The concurrence attempts to transform this case into one of customer safety. The unconceived fetuses of Johnson Controls' female employees, however, are neither customers nor third parties whose safety is essential to the business of battery manufacturing. No one can disregard the possibility of injury to future children; the BFOQ, however, is not so broad that it transforms this deep social concern into an essential aspect of batterymaking.

Our case law, therefore, makes clear that the safety exception is limited to instances in which sex or pregnancy actually interferes with the employee's ability to perform the job. This approach is consistent with the language of the BFOQ provision itself, for it suggests that permissible distinctions based on sex must relate to ability to perform the duties of the job. Johnson Controls suggests, however, that we expand the exception to allow fetal-protection policies that mandate particular standards for pregnant or fertile women. We decline to do so. Such an expansion contradicts not only the language of the BFOQ and the narrowness of its exception but the plain language and history of the Pregnancy Discrimination Act.

The PDA's amendment to Title VII contains a BFOQ standard of its own: unless pregnant employees differ from others "in their ability or inability to work," they must be "treated the same" as other employees "for all employment-related purposes." This language clearly sets forth Congress' remedy for discrimination on the basis of pregnancy and potential pregnancy. Women who are either pregnant or potentially pregnant must be treated like others "similar in their ability ... to work." In other words, women as capable of doing their jobs as their male counterparts may not be forced to choose between having a child and having a job.

The concurrence asserts that the PDA did not alter the BFOQ defense. The concurrence arrives at this conclusion by ignoring the second clause of the Act which states that "women affected by pregnancy, childbirth, or related medical conditions shall be treated the same for all employment-related purposes ... as other persons not so affected but similar in their ability or inability to work." * * *

With the PDA, Congress made clear that the decision to become pregnant or to work while being either pregnant or capable of becoming pregnant was reserved for each individual woman to make for herself.

We conclude that the language of both the BFOQ provision and the PDA which amended it, as well as the legislative history and the case law, prohibit an employer from discriminating against a woman because of her capacity to become pregnant unless her reproductive potential prevents her from performing the duties of her job. We reiterate our holdings in *Criswell* and *Dothard* that an employer must direct its concerns about a woman's ability to perform her job safely and efficiently to those aspects of the woman's job-related activities that fall within the "essence" of the particular business.[4]

V

We have no difficulty concluding that Johnson Controls cannot establish a BFOQ. Fertile women, as far as appears in the record, participate in the manufacture of batteries as efficiently as anyone else. Johnson Controls' professed moral and ethical concerns about the welfare of the next generation do not suffice to establish a BFOQ of female sterility. Decisions about the welfare of future children must be left to the parents who conceive, bear, support, and raise them rather than to the employers who hire those parents.

* * *

VI

A word about tort liability and the increased cost of fertile women in the workplace is perhaps necessary. One of the dissenting judges in this case expressed concern about an employer's tort liability and concluded that liability for a potential injury to a fetus is a social cost that Title VII does not require a company to ignore. It is correct to say that Title VII does not prevent the employer from having a conscience. The statute, however, does prevent sex-specific fetal-protection policies. These two aspects of Title VII do not conflict.

More than 40 States currently recognize a right to recover for a prenatal injury based either on negligence or on wrongful death.

According to Johnson Controls, however, the company complies with the lead standard developed by OSHA and warns its female employees about the damaging effects of lead. It is worth noting that OSHA gave the problem of lead lengthy consideration and concluded that "there is no basis whatsoever for the claim that women of childbearing age should be excluded from the workplace in order to protect the fetus or the course of pregnancy." 43 Fed.Reg. 52952, 52966 (1978). Instead, OSHA established a series of mandatory protections which, taken together, "should effectively minimize any risk to the fetus and newborn child." Without negligence, it would be difficult for a court to find liability on the part of the employer. If, under general tort principles, Title VII bans

4. The concurrence predicts that our reaffirmation of the narrowness of the BFOQ defense will preclude considerations of privacy as a basis for sex-based discrimination. We have never addressed privacy-based sex discrimination and shall not do so here because the sex-based discrimination at issue today does not involve the privacy interests of Johnson Controls' customers. Nothing in our discussion of the "essence of the business test," however, suggests that sex could not constitute a BFOQ when privacy interests are implicated. *See, e.g., Backus v. Baptist Medical Center,* 510 F.Supp. 1191 (E.D.Ark.1981), vacated as moot, 671 F.2d 1100 (C.A.8 1982) (essence of obstetrics nurse's business is to provide sensitive care for patient's intimate and private concerns).

sex-specific fetal-protection policies, the employer fully informs the woman of the risk, and the employer has not acted negligently, the basis for holding an employer liable seems remote at best.

Although the issue is not before us, the concurrence observes that "it is far from clear that compliance with Title VII will preempt state tort liability." The cases relied upon by the concurrence to support its prediction, however, are inappropriate. For example, in *California Federal S. & L. Assn. v. Guerra,* 479 U.S. 272, 107 S.Ct. 683, 93 L.Ed.2d 613 (1987), we considered a California statute that expanded upon the requirements of the PDA and concluded that the statute was not preempted by Title VII because it was not inconsistent with the purposes of the federal statute and did not require an act that was unlawful under Title VII. Here, in contrast, the tort liability that the concurrence fears will punish employers for *complying* with Title VII's clear command. When it is impossible for an employer to comply with both state and federal requirements, this Court has ruled that federal law pre-empts that of the States.

This Court faced a similar situation in *Farmers Union v. WDAY, Inc.,* 360 U.S. 525, 79 S.Ct. 1302, 3 L.Ed.2d 1407 (1959). In *WDAY,* it held that § 315(a) of the Federal Communications Act of 1934 barred a broadcasting station from removing defamatory statements contained in speeches broadcast by candidates for public office. It then considered a libel action which arose as a result of a speech made over the radio and television facilities of WDAY by a candidate for the 1956 senatorial race in North Dakota. It held that the statutory prohibition of censorship carried with it an immunity from liability for defamatory statements made by the speaker. To allow libel actions "would sanction the unconscionable result of permitting civil and perhaps criminal liability to be imposed for the very conduct the statute demands of the licensee." *Id.,* at 531, 79 S.Ct., at 1306. It concluded:

> "We are aware that causes of action for libel are widely recognized throughout the States. But we have not hesitated to abrogate state law where satisfied that its enforcement would stand 'as an obstacle to the accomplishment and execution of the full purposes and objectives of Congress.' " *Id.,* at 535, 79 S.Ct., at 1308, quoting *Bethlehem Steel Co. v. New York Labor Board,* 330 U.S. 767, 773, 67 S.Ct. 1026, 1030, 91 L.Ed. 1234 (1947).

If state tort law furthers discrimination in the workplace and prevents employers from hiring women who are capable of manufacturing the product as efficiently as men, then it will impede the accomplishment of Congress' goals in enacting Title VII. Because Johnson Controls has not argued that it faces any costs from tort liability, not to mention crippling ones, the pre-emption question is not before us. We therefore say no more than that the concurrence's speculation appears unfounded as well as premature.

The tort-liability argument reduces to two equally unpersuasive propositions. First, Johnson Controls attempts to solve the problem of reproductive health hazards by resorting to an exclusionary policy. Title VII plainly forbids illegal sex discrimination as a method of diverting attention from an employer's obligation to police the workplace. Second, the spectre of an award of damages reflects a fear that hiring fertile women will cost more. The extra cost of employing members of one sex, however, does not provide an affirmative Title VII defense for a discriminatory refusal to hire members of that gender. See *Manhart,* 435 U.S., at 716–718, and n. 32, 98 S.Ct., at 1379–1380, and n. 32. Indeed, in passing the PDA, Congress considered at length the considerable cost of providing equal treatment of pregnancy and related conditions, but made the "decision to forbid special treatment of pregnancy despite the social costs associated therewith." *Arizona Governing Committee v. Norris,* 463 U.S. 1073, 1084, n. 14, 103 S.Ct. 3492, 3499, n. 14, 77 L.Ed.2d 1236 (1983) (opinion of Marshall, J.). See *Price Waterhouse v. Hopkins,* 490 U.S. 228, 109 S.Ct. 1775, 104 L.Ed.2d 268 (1988).

We, of course, are not presented with, nor do we decide, a case in which costs would be so prohibitive as to threaten the survival of the employer's business. We merely reiterate our prior holdings that the incremental cost of hiring women cannot justify discriminating against them.

VII

Our holding today that Title VII, as so amended, forbids sex-specific fetal-protection policies is neither remarkable nor unprecedented. Concern for a woman's existing or potential offspring historically has been the excuse for denying women equal employment opportunities. Congress in the PDA prohibited discrimination on the basis of a woman's ability to become pregnant. We do no more than hold that the Pregnancy Discrimination Act means what it says.

It is no more appropriate for the courts than it is for individual employers to decide whether a woman's reproductive role is more important to herself and her family than her economic role. Congress has left this choice to the woman as hers to make.

The judgment of the Court of Appeals is reversed and the case is remanded for further proceedings consistent with this opinion.

It is so ordered.

JUSTICE WHITE, with whom THE CHIEF JUSTICE and JUSTICE KENNEDY join, concurring in part and concurring in the judgment.

The Court properly holds that Johnson Controls' fetal protection policy overtly discriminates against women, and thus is prohibited by Title VII unless it falls within the bona fide occupational qualification (BFOQ) exception. The Court erroneously holds, however, that the BFOQ defense is so narrow that it could never justify a sex-specific fetal protection policy. I nevertheless concur in the judgment of reversal because on the record before us summary judgment in favor of Johnson

Controls was improperly entered by the District Court and affirmed by the Court of Appeals.

I

* * *

For the fetal protection policy involved in this case to be a BFOQ, therefore, the policy must be "reasonably necessary" to the "normal operation" of making batteries, which is Johnson Controls' "particular business." Although that is a difficult standard to satisfy, nothing in the statute's language indicates that it could never support a sex-specific fetal protection policy.

On the contrary, a fetal protection policy would be justified under the terms of the statute if, for example, an employer could show that exclusion of women from certain jobs was reasonably necessary to avoid substantial tort liability. Common sense tells us that it is part of the normal operation of business concerns to avoid causing injury to third parties, as well as to employees, if for no other reason than to avoid tort liability and its substantial costs. This possibility of tort liability is not hypothetical; every State currently allows children born alive to recover in tort for prenatal injuries caused by third parties, * * * and an increasing number of courts have recognized a right to recover even for prenatal injuries caused by torts committed prior to conception.

* * *

Prior decisions construing the BFOQ defense confirm that the defense is broad enough to include considerations of cost and safety of the sort that could form the basis for an employer's adoption of a fetal protection policy.

* * *

Dothard and *Criswell* make clear that avoidance of substantial safety risks to third parties is *inherently* part of both an employee's ability to perform a job and an employer's "normal operation" of its business.

* * *

On the facts of this case, for example, protecting fetal safety while carrying out the duties of battery manufacturing is as much a legitimate concern as is safety to third parties in guarding prisons (*Dothard*) or flying airplanes (*Criswell*).[34]

---

34. I do not, as the Court asserts, reject the "essence of the business" test. Rather, I merely reaffirm the obvious—that safety to third parties is part of the "essence" of most if not all businesses. Of course, the BFOQ inquiry " 'adjusts to the safety factor.' " *Criswell,* 472 U.S., at 413, 105 S.Ct., at 2751 (quoting *Tamiami,* 531 F.2d, at 236). As a result, more stringent occupational qualifications may be justified for jobs involving higher safety risks, such as flying airplanes. But a recognition that the importance of safety varies among businesses does not mean that safety is completely irrelevant to the essence of a job such as battery manufacturing.

Dothard and *Criswell* also confirm that costs are relevant in determining whether a discriminatory policy is reasonably necessary for the normal operation of a business. In *Dothard,* the safety problem that justified exclusion of women from the prison guard positions was largely a result of inadequate staff and facilities.... If the cost of employing women could not be considered, the employer there should have been required to hire more staff and restructure the prison environment rather than exclude women. Similarly, in *Criswell* the airline could have been required to hire more pilots and install expensive monitoring devices rather than discriminate against older employees.

* * *

II

Despite my disagreement with the Court concerning the scope of the BFOQ defense, I concur in reversing the Court of Appeals because that court erred in affirming the District Court's grant of summary judgment in favor of Johnson Controls. First, the Court of Appeals erred in failing to consider the level of risk-avoidance that was part of Johnson Controls' "normal operation."

* * *

Second, even without more information about the normal level of risk at Johnson Controls, the fetal protection policy at issue here reaches too far. This is evident both in its presumption that, absent medical documentation to the contrary, all women are fertile regardless of their age, and in its exclusion of presumptively fertile women from positions that might result in a promotion to a position involving high lead exposure. There has been no showing that either of those aspects of the policy is reasonably necessary to ensure safe and efficient operation of Johnson Controls' battery-manufacturing business. Of course, these infirmities in the company's policy do not warrant invalidating the entire fetal protection program.

Third, it should be recalled that until 1982 Johnson Controls operated without an exclusionary policy, and it has not identified any grounds for believing that its current policy is reasonably necessary to its normal operations. Although it is now more aware of some of the dangers of lead exposure, it has not shown that the risks of fetal harm or the costs associated with it have substantially increased. Cf. *Manhart,* 435 U.S., at 716, n. 39, 98 S.Ct., at 1379, n. 30, in which we rejected a BFOQ defense because the employer had operated prior to the discrimination with no significant adverse effects.

Finally, the Court of Appeals failed to consider properly petitioners' evidence of harm to offspring caused by lead exposure in males. The court considered that evidence only in its discussion of the business necessity standard, in which it focused on whether *petitioners* had met their burden of proof. The burden of proving that a discriminatory qualification is a BFOQ, however, rests with the employer. Thus, the court should have analyzed whether the evidence was sufficient for petitioners to survive summary judgment in light of *respondent's* burden of proof to establish a BFOQ.

* * *

JUSTICE SCALIA, concurring in the judgment.

I generally agree with the Court's analysis, but have some reservations, several of which bear mention.

* * *

I am willing to assume, as the Court intimates, that any action required by Title VII cannot give rise to liability under state tort law. That assumption, however, does not answer the question whether an action is required by Title VII (including the BFOQ provision) even if it is subject to liability under state tort law. It is perfectly reasonable to believe that Title VII has *accommodated* state tort law through the BFOQ exception. However, all that need be said in the present case is that Johnson has not demonstrated a substantial risk of tort liability— which is alone enough to defeat a tort-based assertion of the BFOQ exception.

Last, the Court goes far afield, it seems to me, in suggesting that increased cost alone—short of "costs ... so prohibitive as to threaten survival of the employer's business," cannot support a BFOQ defense. I agree with Justice White's concurrence that nothing in our prior cases suggests this, and in my view it is wrong. I think, for example, that a shipping company may refuse to hire pregnant women as crew members on long voyages because the on-board facilities for foreseeable emergencies, though quite feasible, would be inordinately expensive. In the present case, however, Johnson has not asserted a cost-based BFOQ.

I concur in the judgment of the Court.

———

(i) May our client forbid Perez from working in the computer maintenance shop? *Johnson Controls* appears to preclude the company's justifying such action on the broad, reasonably unsubstantiated grounds that fertile women pose different potential risks to the employer than do other employees. *Johnson Controls* also appears to deem it irrelevant in assessing applicability of Title VII for the employer to take into account the welfare of the fetus. Yet, if we can prove that the dangers of the computer maintenance shop are unique to fetuses, that is, don't discriminate between non-sterile men and fertile women, will we be able to justify to a court that the company acted lawfully in requiring her to take a leave?

(ii) If we can establish that there is a likelihood of our being liable in tort to the Perez child or its parents if it is born with defects caused by the exposure to the computer maintenance room, can we establish a

Bona Fide Occupational Qualification (BFOQ) that would justify our requiring Perez to take a leave? Must we show that the potential tort liability will be substantial, perhaps "ruinous," in order to invoke successfully the BFOQ defense?

(iii) The preceding question assumes that, despite the *Johnson Controls* majority opinion's comments about preemption, there is a possibility that state tort law will apply to protect the newborn child, even in a case where Title VII has been interpreted to require the employer to continue employing an employee like Perez. As I understand preemption law, the Court will find preemption (a) if Congress expressly preempted (not this situation), (b) Congress so completely occupied the field that there was no appropriate "space" for state regulation, (In Title VII, Congress expressly provided for no preemption on this ground. See Section 708. See, also, Section 1104 of Title XI of the Civil Rights Act of 1964.), or (c) when state law required action deemed unlawful by federal law (Section 708 of Title VII authorizes preemption only for this purpose) or state law created some obstacles for implementing the purposes of the federal statute. Allowing Perez' child, after its birth, to sue Enderby in tort may create obstacles to Title VII purposes because an employer will be less likely to employ a fertile woman who may present a Perez-like problem for the employer. Assessing the likelihood of such an effect is highly problematic. Thus, it is uncertain whether the state tort action will be preempted by Title VII.

b. OSHA—American Cyanamid Case

OCAW v. AMERICAN CYANAMID CO.

United States Court of Appeals, District of Columbia Circuit, 1984.
741 F.2d 444.

Bork, Circuit Judge:

Petitioners Oil, Chemical and Atomic Workers International Union and Local 3–499, Oil, Chemical and Atomic Workers (together, "OCAW") seek reversal of an order by the Occupational Safety and Health Review Commission. The Commission held that respondent American Cyanamid Company's fetus protection policy "is not a hazard cognizable under the Occupational Safety and Health Act." That policy, adopted at the company's Willow Island, West Virginia plant, provided that women employees of childbearing age could not hold jobs that exposed them to toxic substances at levels considered unsafe for fetuses. An exception was made for women who could show that they had been surgically sterilized. The Secretary of Labor issued a citation alleging that Cyanamid's policy violated the general duty clause of the Occupational Safety and Health Act of 1970, 29 U.S.C. § 654(a)(1) (1982). The Administrative Law Judge vacated the citation, and the Commission affirmed on the ground that the policy in question was not cognizable under the Act. OCAW, an intervenor in the proceedings before the

Commission, brought this petition for review. The Secretary has not challenged the Commission's decision.

For reasons discussed below, we think the language of the Act cannot be stretched so far as to hold that the sterilization option of the fetus protection policy is a "hazard" of "employment" under the general duty clause. Consequently, we affirm.

I.

* * * In January and February of 1978, Glen Mercer, the plant Director of Industrial Relations, conducted a series of meetings for small groups of the Willow Island plant's female employees. At these meetings Mercer informed the women that hundreds of chemicals used at the plant were harmful to fetuses and that, consequently, the company had decided to exclude women of "childbearing capacity" from all departments of the plant where such chemicals were used. Mercer further declared that the company would deem any woman between the ages of 16 and 50 to be of childbearing capacity unless she presented proof that she had been surgically sterilized.

A company doctor and nurse accompanied Mercer to these meetings and addressed the women. They explained to the women that such "buttonhole surgery" was simple and that it could be obtained locally in several places. The women were also told that the company's medical insurance would pay for the procedure, and that sick leave would be provided to those undergoing the surgery.

Mercer told the women that once the fetus protection policy was fully implemented the plant would have only about seven jobs for fertile women in the entire facility. Approximately thirty women were then employed at the Willow Island plant. Apart from the women who obtained those seven positions, Mercer said that female employees who failed to undergo surgical sterilization by May 1, 1978, would be terminated. The company extended the May 1, 1978, deadline several times. In September, 1978, the company informed the women of changes in its policy. The deadline had been extended to October 2, 1978, the Inorganic Pigments Department was the only department affected, and the only material covered by the policy was lead. It is undisputed that lead poses a severe danger to fetuses. OSHA's lead standard states the agency's belief that "the fetus is at risk from exposure to lead throughout the gestation period . . ." and is "susceptible to neurological damage." 43 Fed.Reg. 54,422 (1978). OSHA concluded that "blood lead levels should be kept below 30 ug/100 g." That level is 30 micrograms of lead per 100 grams of whole blood. American Cyanamid was unable to reduce the lead hazard in its Inorganic Pigments Department to the level required to protect fetuses. The Administrative Law Judge ("ALJ") determined that it was economically infeasible to reduce ambient air lead levels to [an acceptable level.] * * *

American Cyanamid apparently concluded, after considering these facts, that the only realistic and clearly lawful possibility left open to it was to remove women capable of bearing children from the Inorganic Pigments Department.

Between February and July, 1978, five women employed in the Inorganic Pigments Department underwent surgical sterilization at a hospital not connected with the company. Two female employees in that department did not choose sterilization. The company transferred them into other departments and, after ninety days, lowered their rate of pay to correspond to the rates characteristic of their new jobs.

From January 4 through April 13, 1979, OSHA conducted an inspection of the Willow Island plant. On October 9, 1979, OSHA issued the citation that is the subject of this case. The citation alleged that American Cyanamid had violated section 5(a)(1) of the Act, 29 U.S.C. § 654(a)(1) (1982), the "general duty clause," as follows:

> The employer did not furnish employment and a place of employment which were free from recognized hazards that were causing or were likely to cause death or serious physical harm to employees, in that: The employer adopted and implemented a policy which required women employees to be sterilized in order to be eligible to work in the areas of the plant where they would be exposed to certain toxic substances:

(a) Inorganic Pigment Department—Buildings No. 85 and No. 86.

Classifying the violation as willful, the citation declared that it should be abated immediately and proposed a penalty of $10,000. * * *

II.

* * * The general duty clause of the Occupational Safety and Health Act of 1970 provides:

> (a) Each employer—
>
> (1) shall furnish to each of his employees employment and a place of employment which are free from recognized hazards that are causing or are likely to cause death or serious physical harm to his employees.

29 U.S.C. § 654(a)(1).

There is no doubt that the words of the general duty clause can be read, albeit with some semantic distortion, to cover the sterilization exception contained in American Cyanamid's fetus protection policy. As OCAW points out, the rule bears upon "employment," and may be described as a "condition of employment." The policy may be characterized as a "hazard" to female employees who opted for sterilization in order to remain in the Inorganic Pigments Department, though it requires some stretching to call the offering of a choice a "hazard" to the person who is given the choice. Sterilization can, of course, be a "serious physical harm." For these reasons, OCAW contends that the sterilization exception falls within the plain meaning of the statutory language. That conclusion is necessary, however, only if the words of the statute inescapably have the meaning petitioners find in them and are unaffected by precedent, usage, and congressional intent. The words of the statute—in particular, the terms "working conditions" and "hazards"—are not so plain that they foreclose all interpretation.

Indeed, these words have been interpreted by courts, and in a way that strongly suggests affirmance of the Commission. Corning Glass Workers v. Brennan, 417 U.S. 188, 94 S.Ct. 2223, 41 L.Ed.2d 1 (1974), though it involved the Equal Pay Act of 1963, spoke to the meaning of the phrase, "working conditions" and decided it should be given content by "the language of industrial relations." The language of industrial relations, of course, is as relevant to the OSH Act as to the Equal Pay Act. In *Corning Glass Workers,* the Supreme Court stated:

> [T]he element of working conditions encompasses two subfactors: "surroundings" and "hazards." "Surroundings" measures the elements, such as toxic chemicals or fumes, regularly encountered by a worker, their intensity, and their frequency. *"Hazard" takes into account the physical hazards regularly encountered, their frequency, and the severity of injury they can cause.* This definition of "working conditions" is ... well accepted across a wide range of American industry.

(emphasis added) (footnotes omitted). The narrowness of this definition is emphasized by the fact that, using it, the Court determined that the difference between a night shift and a day shift was not a "working condition."

This definition was applied by the Fourth Circuit to the OSH Act in Southern Ry. v. OSHRC, 539 F.2d 335, cert. denied, 429 U.S. 999, 97 S.Ct. 525, 50 L.Ed.2d 609 (1976):

> We think this aggregate of "surroundings" and "hazards" contemplates an area broader in its contours than ... "particular, discrete hazards" ... but something less than the employment relationship in its entirety.... *[W]e are of the opinion that the term "working conditions" as used in Section 4(b)(1) means the environmental area in which an employee customarily goes about his daily tasks.*

(emphasis added). Although a different section of the Act was involved in *Southern Ry.,* we can think of no reason why the definition given of "working conditions" should not apply to section 2(b) and hence influence the concept of "hazards" in the general duty clause. Congress may be presumed to have legislated about industrial relations with the "language of industrial relations" in mind. It follows, therefore, that the general duty clause does not apply to a policy as contrasted with a physical condition of the workplace.

We might rest the outcome of this case upon this case law, but petitioners advance an argument by analogy that should be discussed: "In this case, employees had in effect two choices: to undergo sterilization, or to quit. That such a 'choice' offends the Act can be seen from the fact that if, instead of a sterilization *policy,* the hazard at issue in this case had consisted of exposure to a sterilizing *chemical,* employees would have had the same choices: to undergo sterilization, or to quit. . . . [T]he Commission would not suggest that the presence of such factors would remove the sterilizing *chemical* from the ambit of the Act, and there is no logical basis for suggesting that the presence of such factors should remove the sterilization *policy* from the ambit of the Act." Brief for Petitioners (emphasis in original). To make the analogy complete, we should also suppose that in the hypothetical case, the employer could not possibly remove enough of the chemical to eliminate its sterilizing effect. We have no desire to decide this hypothetical case, so we will assume for the sake of the argument that an employer could not, under the OSH Act, permit workers to choose continued employment and sterilization by the chemical. It remains true, nonetheless, that the "hazards" in the two cases are not identical unless it can be said that anything, no matter what its nature or how it operates, is a "hazard" within the meaning of the general duty clause if it has a harmful effect. A chemical is not the same thing as a policy and a congressional decision to deal with one does not necessarily constitute a decision to deal with the other.

This, essentially, was the reasoning of the Review Commission. The Commission pointed out that the Act does not define the term "hazard" and turned to the legislative history for guidance. "Congressional floor debates, committee reports, and individual and minority views . . . are replete with discussions of air pollutants, industrial poisons, combustibles and explosives, noise, unsafe work practices and inadequate training and the like." From this, and other evidence of a similar nature, the Commission concluded that "Congress conceived of occupational hazards in terms of processes and materials which cause injury or disease by operating directly upon employees as they engage in work or work-related activities." The fetus protection policy, by contrast, does not affect employees while they are engaged in work or work-related activities. The decision to be sterilized "grows out of economic and social factors which operate primarily outside the workplace," and hence the fetus protection policy "is not a hazard within the meaning of the general duty clause." We agree with this conclusion. Were we to decide otherwise, we would have to adopt a broad principle of unforeseeable scope: any employer policy which, because of employee economic incentives, left open an option exercised outside the workplace that might be harmful would constitute a "hazard" that made the employer liable under the general duty clause. It might be possible to legislate limitations upon such a principle but that is a task for Congress rather than courts. As it now stands, the Act should not be read to make an employer liable for every employee reaction to the employer's policies. There must be some limit to the statute's reach and we think that limit surpassed by petitioners' contentions. The kind of "hazard" complained of here is not, as the Commission said, sufficiently comparable to the hazards Congress had in mind in passing this law. * * *

The case might be different if American Cyanamid had offered the choice of sterilization in an attempt to pass on to its employees the cost of maintaining a circumambient lead concentration higher than that permitted by law. But that is not this case. The company could not reduce lead concentrations to a level that posed an acceptable risk to fetuses. The sterilization exception to the requirement of removal from the Inorganic Pigments Department was an attempt not to pass on costs of unlawful conduct but to permit the employees to mitigate costs to them imposed by unavoidable physiological facts.

The women involved in this matter were put to a most unhappy choice. But no statute redresses all grievances, and we must decide cases according to law. Reasoning from precedent, congressional intent, and the unforeseeable consequences of a contrary holding, we conclude that American Cyanamid's fetus protection policy did not constitute a "hazard" within the meaning of the OSH Act.

Affirmed.

———

c. *The Americans with Disabilities Act*

Section 102 of the ADA defines "discrimination" in a manner that leaves little doubt, I believe, that if the state of pregnancy is a "disability" within the meaning of the Act, Enderby would violate the ADA by treating Perez differently because of her pregnancy. I suppose the company could argue that whatever it did to Perez, it did not act because of her pregnancy but because of concern for the future child or because of the fear of tort liability. I do not think one should rely heavily on such nice reasoning, however. After all, the Supreme Court has already rejected, for Title VII purposes, a similar argument. See *Johnson Controls*. The ADA's definition of "disability" seems to fit pregnancy like a glove. See Section 3, which defines the term. Yet, I am uncomfortable with reading pregnancy into the definition. First, in general, I am uncertain whether the ADA includes "temporary ailments" and the like within the meaning of "disability." Second, I am discomforted by the historical fact that many employers denied women opportunities because of pregnancy or even the potential for pregnancy. On the other hand, it is that very fact of past discrimination that makes it more plausible to view pregnancy as a "disability" under the ADA. The Equal Employment Commission (the EEOC) has stated in a regulation that pregnancy is not an "impairment" within the meaning of Section 3. To date, several federal district courts have struggled with this issue. Almost all of them have held that pregnancy alone, is not a "disability," but that a complication within the pregnancy may be. The issue will eventually reach higher and more authoritative courts, I am sure.

In the meantime, we should recognize that, regardless of what *Johnson Controls* dictates, the ADA poses its own difficulties.

First, as already mentioned, is pregnancy a "disability" within the ADA's definition found in Section 3(2)?

Second, if it is such a disability, may Enderby "reasonably accommodate" Perez by imposing a paid leave upon her? Consider ADA Section 101(9). Does one reach a different result if the leave is unpaid?

Third, is a paid leave an "undue hardship" upon Enderby, within the meaning of Section 101(10)? Might even an unpaid leave be such a hardship?

As to the last question regarding an unpaid leave, it is difficult to conclude such a leave would be deemed an "undue hardship" upon Enderby because another statute, the Family and Medical Leave Act, 29 U.S.C. § 2601 *et seq.* (1993), requires an employer to grant twelve weeks unpaid leave to an employee for, among other things, illness or the care of an ill child. That Act, which I shall address more directly in part C of this memo, is distinguishable on several grounds, but I wonder if any of the distinctions are compelling in understanding "undue hardship" in the ADA. Perhaps the Family and Medical Leave Act, by analogy, suggests that an unpaid leave for as much as twelve weeks is presumptively not an "undue hardship." Can one safely conclude that requiring a leave of more than twelve weeks is an "undue hardship?"

2. THE COLLECTIVE BARGAINING CONTRACT

(a) Arbitrability—Can we refuse to arbitrate?

It is axiomatic for management-labor lawyers that promises to arbitrate disputes arising under a collective bargaining contract are enforceable under § 301(a) of the 1947 Taft–Hartley amendments to the National Labor Relations Act. See United Steelworkers v. American Manufacturing Co., 363 U.S. 564, 80 S.Ct. 1343, 4 L.Ed.2d 1403 (1960) and United Steelworkers v. Warrior & Gulf Navigation Co., 363 U.S. 574, 80 S.Ct. 1347, 4 L.Ed.2d 1409 (1960). But, when is a matter a dispute arising under a collective bargaining contract? More to the point, if we were to impose a leave of absence upon Perez until the feared danger to the fetus had passed, would we be compelled to arbitrate a union grievance that she was disciplined for "cause?" And, who would answer these questions, an arbitrator or a judge?

AT & T TECHNOLOGIES, INC. v. COMMUNICATIONS WORKERS OF AMERICA

Supreme Court of the United States, 1986.
475 U.S. 643, 106 S.Ct. 1415, 89 L.Ed.2d 648.

JUSTICE WHITE delivered the opinion of the Court.

The issue presented in this case is whether a court asked to order arbitration of a grievance filed under a collective-bargaining agreement must first determine that the parties intended to arbitrate the dispute, or whether that determination is properly left to the arbitrator.

I

AT & T Technologies, Inc. (AT & T or the Company) and the Communications Workers of America (the Union) are parties to a collective-bargaining agreement which covers telephone equipment installation workers. Article 8 of this agreement establishes that "differences arising with respect to the interpretation of this contract or the performance of any obligation hereunder" must be referred to a mutually agreeable arbitrator upon the written demand of either party. This Article expressly does not cover disputes "excluded from arbitration by other provisions of this contract." Article 9 provides that, "subject to the limitations contained in the provisions of this contract, but otherwise not subject to the provisions of the arbitration clause," AT & T is free to exercise certain management functions, including the hiring and placement of employees and the termination of employment.[2] "When lack of work necessitates Layoff," Article 20 prescribes the order in which employees are to be laid off.[3]

On September 17, 1981, the Union filed a grievance challenging AT & T's decision to lay off 79 installers from its Chicago base location. The Union claimed that, because there was no lack of work at the Chicago location, the planned layoffs would violate Article 20 of the agreement. Eight days later, however, AT & T laid off all 79 workers, and soon thereafter, the Company transferred approximately the same number of installers from base locations in Indiana and Wisconsin to the Chicago base. AT & T refused to submit the grievance to arbitration on the ground that under Article 9, the Company's decision to lay off workers when it determines that a lack of work exists in a facility is not arbitrable.

The Union then sought to compel arbitration by filing suit in federal court pursuant to § 301(a) of the Labor Management Relations Act, 29 U.S.C. § 185(a).

* * *

II

The principles necessary to decide this case are not new. They were set out by this Court over 25 years ago in a series of cases known as the Steelworkers Trilogy: Steelworkers v. American Mfg. Co., supra; Steelworkers v. Warrior & Gulf Navigation Co., supra; and Steelworkers v.

---

2. Article 9 states:

"The Union recognizes the right of the Company (subject to the limitations contained in the provisions of this contract, but otherwise not subject to the provisions of the arbitration clause) to exercise the functions of managing the business which involve, among other things, the hiring and placement of Employees, the termination of employment, the assignment of work, the determination of methods and equipment to be used, and the control of the conduct of work."

3. Article 20 provides, in pertinent part, "[w]hen lack of work necessitates Layoff, Employees shall be Laid–Off in accordance with Term of Employment and by Layoff groups as set forth in the following [subparagraphs stating the order of layoff]." Article 1.11 defines the term "Layoff" to mean "a termination of employment arising out of a reduction in the force due to lack of work."

Enterprise Wheel & Car Corp., 363 U.S. 593, 80 S.Ct. 1358, 4 L.Ed.2d 1424 (1960). These precepts have served the industrial relations community well, and have led to continued reliance on arbitration, rather than strikes or lockouts, as the preferred method of resolving disputes arising during the term of a collective-bargaining agreement. We see no reason either to question their continuing validity, or to eviscerate their meaning by creating an exception to their general applicability.

The first principle gleaned from the *Trilogy* is that "arbitration is a matter of contract and a party cannot be required to submit to arbitration any dispute which he has not agreed so to submit." Warrior & Gulf, supra, 363 U.S., at 582, 80 S.Ct., at 1353. This axiom recognizes the fact that arbitrators derive their authority to resolve disputes only because the parties have agreed in advance to submit such grievances to arbitration.

The second rule, which follows inexorably from the first, is that the question of arbitrability—whether a collective-bargaining agreement creates a duty for the parties to arbitrate the particular grievance—is undeniably an issue for judicial determination. Unless the parties clearly and unmistakably provide otherwise, the question of whether the parties agreed to arbitrate is to be decided by the court, not the arbitrator.

* * *

The third principle derived from our prior cases is that, in deciding whether the parties have agreed to submit a particular grievance to arbitration, a court is not to rule on the potential merits of the underlying claims. Whether "arguable" or not, indeed even if it appears to the court to be frivolous, the union's claim that the employer has violated the collective-bargaining agreement is to be decided, not by the court asked to order arbitration, but as the parties have agreed, by the arbitrator. "The courts, therefore, have no business weighing the merits of the grievance, considering whether there is equity in a particular claim, or determining whether there is particular language in the written instrument which will support the claim. The agreement is to submit all grievances to arbitration, not merely those which the court will deem meritorious." *American Mfg. Co.,* 363 U.S., at 568, 80 S.Ct., at 1346 (footnote omitted).

Finally, where it has been established that where the contract contains an arbitration clause, there is a presumption of arbitrability in the sense that "[a]n order to arbitrate the particular grievance should not be denied unless it may be said with positive assurance that the arbitration clause is not susceptible of an interpretation that covers the asserted dispute. Doubts should be resolved in favor of coverage." *Warrior & Gulf,* 363 U.S., at 582–583, 80 S.Ct., at 1352–1353. See also Gateway Coal Co. v. Mine Workers, supra, 414 U.S., at 377–378, 94 S.Ct., at 636–637. Such a presumption is particularly applicable where the clause is as broad as the one employed in this case, which provides for arbitration of "any differences arising with respect to the interpretation of this contract or the performance of any obligation hereunder

* * *." In such cases, "[i]n the absence of any express provision excluding a particular grievance from arbitration, we think only the most forceful evidence of a purpose to exclude the claim from arbitration can prevail." *Warrior & Gulf,* supra, 363 U.S., at 584–585, 80 S.Ct., at 1353–1354.

This presumption of arbitrability for labor disputes recognizes the greater institutional competence of arbitrators in interpreting collective bargaining agreements, "furthers the national labor policy of peaceful resolution of labor disputes and thus best accords with the parties' presumed objectives in pursuing collective bargaining." The willingness of parties to enter into agreements that provide for arbitration of specified disputes would be "drastically reduced," however, if a labor arbitrator had the "power to determine his own jurisdiction...." Cox, Reflections Upon Labor Arbitration, 72 Harv.L.Rev. 1482, 1509 (1959). Were this the applicable rule, an arbitrator would not be constrained to resolve only those disputes that the parties have agreed in advance to settle by arbitration, but instead, would be empowered "to impose obligations outside the contract limited only by his understanding and conscience." Ibid. This result undercuts the longstanding federal policy of promoting industrial harmony through the use of collective-bargaining agreements, and is antithetical to the function of a collective-bargaining agreement as setting out the rights and duties of the parties.

With these principles in mind, it is evident that the Seventh Circuit erred in ordering the parties to arbitrate the arbitrability question. It is the court's duty to interpret the agreement and to determine whether the parties intended to arbitrate grievances concerning layoffs predicated on a "lack of work" determination by the Company. If the court determines that the agreement so provides, then it is for the arbitrator to determine the relative merits of the parties' substantive interpretations of the agreement. It was for the court, not the arbitrator, to decide in the first instance whether the dispute was to be resolved through arbitration.

* * *

(b) Arbitration—Is it the exclusive remedy?

Suppose we discharge Perez or require her to take a leave. Is there any basis for concluding there is "good cause" to discipline or discharge Perez? Would either a paid or an unpaid involuntary leave of absence be a form of "discipline?"

In addition to the relatively open-ended question—can the union treat this as discipline and, thereby, raise the "good cause" standard?—I wonder if a forced leave might be deemed sex or disability discrimination. If so, are the union and Perez limited to a single option, taking the claim through the grievance procedure to arbitration, as *Gilmer,* in Chapter II of the casebook, suggests? Whether or not she pursues arbitration, may she pursue her possible Title VII, ADA, or OSHA remedies? Consider, again, *Alexander v. Gardner–Denver* and *Wright v.*

Universal Maritime, in Chapter II, and *Gilmer* and *Circuit City* in Chapter I.

In *Alexander*, the Supreme Court held that individual Title VII remedies could not be preempted (or deemed waived by an individual employee) by a collective bargaining contract's no-discrimination and arbitration clauses. The *Gilmer* court did not overrule *Alexander,* although *Wright* acknowledges a tension between the two decisions. Rather, the Court wrote that the statutory forum for the Age Discrimination in Employment Act (ADEA) could be anticipatorily waived by an employee for disputes that would arise after an individual employment contract was signed, so long as the contract provided for arbitration; but that a union could not make a similar waiver for the employees in a collective bargaining contract. The distinction the Court drew between Gilmer's waiver of his ADEA rights and the union's waiving Alexander's Title VII rights may reflect the Court's or Congress' mistrust of unions, a mistrust that apparently outweighs whatever benefits a union might provide in arbitration to an individual worker who claims unlawful discrimination. I am not certain the implicit balance of the benefits and costs to the employee, the employer, or to the statutory purposes will justify future continuation of the distinction the Court drew in *Gilmer*.

(c) *Statutory Reference within Contract.*

If the union and Perez should end up in arbitration, can they establish "sex discrimination" within the meaning of the contract? The *Johnson Controls* case, which I have attached to this memo, will help us understand the issue. Regarding this issue, must the arbitrator follow the statutory law and its judicial gloss?

(d) *What does the collective bargaining contract mean?*

Since the contract does not address leaves, and I have not been informed of any practice or understanding between the company and the union regarding leaves, I would hazard the following:

(i) Forcing Perez to take an unpaid leave may run afoul of the "no-discipline-without-cause" language in the contract. Forcing her to take a paid leave may not violate that part of the contract, but the conclusion is hardly clear. The basic question appears to be whether requiring someone to take a leave-of-absence, paid or unpaid, can be considered discipline.

(ii) Yet, the contract also precludes discrimination based on sex or disability. If the company fails to accommodate Perez, there is the reasonably arguable position that the company has, therefore, discriminated in a manner prohibited by the contract. Arbitrators are not limited to statutory niceties. Thus, while it is unlikely that an arbitrator will interpret even slightly ambiguous contractual language in a manner that violates a statute (Why would the parties be understood to have contracted to break the law?), an arbitrator might well interpret the contract to demand of an employer even more than the statutes do.

This reasoning pushes in the direction of doing something to accommodate Perez. On the other hand, if the arbitrator, in effect, forces the company to grant preferential treatment based on sex, there is the risk that the arbitrator will force the company and union to run afoul of Title VII by discriminating against men.

(iii) The contract forbids unilateral changes by the employer. If the employer requires Perez to take a leave, with or without pay, there is the possibility an arbitrator will interpret the action as unilateral. That is only a possibility, however, because the contract does not address leaves, there appear to be no past practices or understandings, and federal law may require some kind of leave opportunity.

(iv) In reviewing the contract, I note it states, "Recognition. The company recognizes the union as the collective bargaining agent for all the employees covered by this contract regarding their wages, hours, and other terms and conditions of employment." Will the requirement of a leave violate an implicit promise to talk to the union about the matter? Is this idea independent of the clause forbidding unilateral action, or do the two clauses reinforce one another?

3. THE NLRB AND UNILATERAL ACTION

In order to avoid possible tort or ADA liability, may the company lawfully impose a leave upon Perez without first negotiating with the union about the policy underlying the employer's action? If there were no collective bargaining agreement, long-standing NLRA law, approved by the Supreme Court in NLRB v. Katz, 369 U.S. 736, 82 S.Ct. 1107, 8 L.Ed.2d 230 (1962), clearly precludes Enderby from adopting a new policy regarding employees like Perez without first negotiating with the union. With a contract and its arbitration clause in the problem, the analysis usually is different. I know there is a lot of law about the interaction of the collective bargaining contract and the NLRA. With virtually unanimous judicial approval, the NLRB has held that it will defer to the arbitration process in unilateral-action cases. See Collyer Insulated Wire, 192 NLRB 837 (1971).

Yet, given the facts that there are no provisions in the contract addressing leaves, that the parties apparently did not discuss the subject during negotiations, and that the contract expressly prohibits unilateral action addressed only to "terms of this contract" and not necessarily to conditions unmentioned by the contract, the Board or a court might adopt the view that the parties never reached an agreement about the matter and Section 8(a)(5) requires Enderby to bargain before it implements the new policy. See, for example, Johnson–Bateman Co., 295 NLRB No. 26 (1989). The safest thing for the company to do, if there is time, is to propose the leave for Perez to the union and impose the leave only after giving the union a shot at participating in and informing the decision.

B. Reassignment of Perez.

As already noted, a second option Enderby is considering is the reassignment of Perez to another position. For her to be reassigned to an unskilled job, the only other position for which she is qualified, the company will have to leapfrog Perez over other employees who are presently on layoff but who have more seniority than she. Is the employer permitted under the law to do this? Is it required by law to do this?

1. The earlier discussion of the law of the collective bargaining contract is relevant to understanding the effect of the contract on the employer's option to reassign Perez. The contract outlaws discrimination based on sex or disability; this may mean Perez can have no advantages because of her pregnancy, or it may mean she should suffer from no disadvantages because of her condition. Section 701(k) of Title VII was passed after two court decisions had interpreted the remainder of Title VII to permit the exclusion of pregnancy-related-costs from employee health insurance plans. Section 701(k) has been interpreted by the Supreme Court to permit affirmative action to protect pregnant women. In California Federal Savings & Loan Association v. Guerra, 479 U.S. 272, 107 S.Ct. 683, 93 L.Ed.2d 613 (1987), the Court held that Section 701(k)'s language, "women affected by pregnancy * * * shall be treated the same ... as other persons not so affected * * *" did not preclude the State of California from having a law that required employers to grant pregnant women four months unpaid leave.

I believe that, insofar as Title VII and, possibly, the ADA are concerned, the reasoning of *Guerra* is likely to prevail if Enderby, in order to accommodate Perez' concerns, decides to treat her better than the company ordinarily would treat an employee. Yet, that is hardly clear. *Guerra* involved a state's mandatory affirmative action, not the action of a private employer.

2. The real rub comes from the seniority provision of the contract which, on its face, would preclude the company from assigning Perez to an open unskilled job while other, more senior employees await assignment to the same opening. Does either Title VII or the ADA permit, or even require, the employer to override the seniority clause of the contract?

a. Title VII. Section 703(h) saves the applicability of a bona fide seniority system against some of the other commands of Title VII. That is, if the employer's actions are motivated by honoring a legitimate seniority provision in the collective bargaining contract and not by a desire to discriminate on the ground of sex, the employer is free to honor the collective bargaining contract. In Teamsters v. United States, 431 U.S. 324, 97 S.Ct. 1843, 52 L.Ed.2d 396 (1977), the Supreme Court upheld the application of a seniority ladder in the face of a Title VII, disparate-impact attack which argued the employer must override the seniority ladder. I assume that the same reasoning would apply to unintended sex discrimination in the Perez situation. I am aware of no case, however, that addresses directly whether, without violating Title VII, an employer may favor blacks or pregnant women in the face of a contrary seniority provision.

b.   Whatever *Teamsters* means, it may not apply to the ADA, which has no provision comparable to Title VII's Section 703(h)'s protection of seniority ladders. Moreover, the ADA has an express taboo on contracts, specifically even with labor unions, that "discriminate" against disabled persons in a way prohibited by the Act. Query whether a bona fide seniority ladder that interferes with reassignment of a disabled person is such discrimination. Under the Rehabilitation Act of 1973, 29 U.S.C. § 701 et seq., which was the model for the ADA, the courts held regularly either that there was no duty to reassign or that seniority provisions protected an employer from having to reassign a "handicapped" employee. Note that "reassignment to a vacant position" may be part of the reasonable accommodation that an employer may owe a disabled person. Section 101(9)(B). Yet, the language of Section 101(9) and of the remainder of the ADA hardly suggests that the existence of a possible reassignment is, by itself, dispositive.

Finally, at least at first blush, it seems strange if Congress has imposed upon employers (and unions) the duty to reassign, in the face of a countermanding seniority clause, a disabled person but not a minority or woman who was the victim of *Griggs*-like disparate impact. Why would Congress want to do that?

C. Is it lawful for Enderby to require Perez to continue working in the computer maintenance shop?

In light of OSHA, workers compensation laws, and possible common law addressed to protection of the newly born child, one would suppose that an employer with a concern either for the bottom line or for the larger social good would desire to have as safe a workplace as feasible. I wonder what impact the Americans with Disabilities Act of 1990 and the Family and Medical Leave Act of 1993 will have on this concern and on the alternative of requiring Perez to continue working on the job during her pregnancy. (In the following suggested analysis I am assuming, without having knowledge, that the fetus's exposure to the computer maintenance shop poses a serious risk for the child upon its birth.)

1.   On first reading, the ADA appears to be easily reconcilable with the primary importance other laws have placed upon safety in the workplace. Section 102(b) of the ADA specifically states, "The term 'qualification standards' may include a requirement that an individual shall not pose a direct threat to the health or safety of other individuals in the workplace." Yet, it is hardly clear that injury to the fetus is injury to "other individuals in the workplace." The national debate about abortion rights is based, in large part, on the definition of a fetus—is it "another individual" or is it part of the woman? In the context of the right of a woman to make her own choice about an abortion, the Supreme Court appears to have held that the fetus is not necessarily another individual. Even if that reading of the cases is correct, however,

it hardly determines the status of the fetus within the meaning of the ADA. It is possible that the ADA might be read to authorize preclusion of pregnant women from jobs that jeopardize the future health of the yet-to-be-born child. On the other hand, the *Johnson Controls* case suggests the contrary, even though it is an interpretation of Title VII.

If the ADA precludes Enderby from placing Perez on leave and the union contract lawfully precludes her reassignment, Perez' only option may be to stay at her job. The newborn child may be born with defects. Will the dictum in *Johnson Controls* survive to preempt tort law suits brought by the newborn? Should the Court's concern for preemption be so compelling if the potential risk to the employer is greater? Or less? Should it matter if the employer had alternatives that were permissible under the ADA? Should the nature of the injury to the child and the possible remedies available to it be of any relevance to the preemption issue? Given our ignorance of so much, any advice we give Enderby regarding any of this has to be largely qualified.

(2) The Family and Medical Leave Act of 1993 authorizes an employee to invoke a right to twelve weeks of unpaid leave under certain circumstances. If Perez' situation fits the Family Leave Act's "glove," I think Enderby will be well advised to grant her at least the twelve weeks leave. That period of time may well take her past the time of risk for the fetus.

Section 102 of the Act requires an employer to grant such a leave in four contexts, two of which are arguably relevant to Perez. That is, does she have a "serious health condition that makes [her] unable to perform?" Or, does she have to "care for * * * a son [or] daughter [who] has a serious health condition?"

Although a study of the legislative history may address the matter, I suspect Congress did not anticipate the case of the expectant mother who wishes to protect her fetus. On the one hand, if the child is born, all of us—Perez most of all—want it to be healthy. The purpose of giving leave to protect children would seem to apply equally to protection of the fetus. On the other hand, the perception of the law's treating a fetus as a child runs into, at least conceptually, some of the reasoning to be found in the aforementioned right-to-abortions cases. Moreover, and on much narrower footing, if Congress did not anticipate the issue and the most plausible reading of the statutory words would deny the right to an unpaid leave in Perez' situation, maybe Perez is not entitled to such a leave.

D.   Ergonomics issues.

Ms. Perez' concerns about the ergonomic design of the workplace may be the easiest to address. It may be possible, with modest changes, to make it easier for Ms. Perez and other workers to sit at their computer screens for longer periods of time without fatigue or discomfort. But before we embark upon what might be an expensive and time consuming overhaul of our workplace equipment and placement, I'd like to give a little more thought to whether we are obliged to do this by law.

There is literature indicating that the various injuries that employees suffer from repetitive workplace motions are now among the most numerous and insidious of workplace injuries. The U.S. Bureau of Labor Statistics reports repetitive motion problems as both injuries and illnesses. In its report for 1999 (BLS News, December 12, 2000, reported at http:// stats.bls.gov/oshhome.htm), BLS stated that "there were about 372,000 newly reported cases of occupational illnesses in private industry in 1999. Manufacturing accounted for three-fifths of these cases. Disorders associated with repeated trauma, such as carpal tunnel syndrome and noise-induced hearing loss, accounted for 4 percent of the 5.76 million total workplace injuries and illnesses. They were, however, the dominant type of illness reported, making up 66 percent of the 372,000 total illness cases. Seventy percent of the recent trauma cases were in manufacturing industries." For a graphic description of such hazards from a position strongly critical of government's failure to act, see Marc Linder, I Gave My Employer a Chicken That Had No Bone: Joint Firm—State Responsibility for Line—Speed Related Occupational Injuries, 46 Case W. Res. L. Rev. 33 (1995). See also Robert J. Rabin, The Role of Government in Regulating the Workplace, 13 Labor Lawyer 1–9 (1997).

I suppose that a worker who suffers from repeated workplace trauma and who is unable to work to her fullest capacity may claim that she is disabled under the ADA. But since this disability may only keep the worker from performing certain jobs, this is not a limitation of a major life activity. That is, the worker may still function in the work place in general. The Supreme Court will face this issue this Term, and those decisions will undoubtedly cast light on this question, if they don't answer it conclusively. Assuming such a worker is held to be disabled, Enderby would then presumably be required to make some sort of accommodation. If it were not too costly—not an "undue hardship", in the words of the statute—ergonomic redesign could be one such accommodation.

But what about OSHA? Is it unlawful under OSHA for an employer to maintain a workplace design that causes workplace trauma? OSHA has no standard in place under Section 6 that deals with repetitive motion hazards. During the Clinton administration, OSHA attempted to design such a standard, but a series of Congressional budget riders prohibited the agency from even doing research in this area (see the Rabin article, cited above, pages 6–7, and footnotes 35–47). Finally, in the waning days of the Clinton administration, OSHA promulgated the long-awaited (and, for some, long-dreaded) ergonomics standard. It was a rather cumbersome affair that relied upon employees to identify ergonomics hazards in their workplace, and then called upon the employer to establish a program to correct those hazards (the standard was initially found on the OSHA web site, www.osha.gov, under Ergonomics Program Standard 1910.900.) Whether that standard would have been workable, or would have withstood various legal challenges, became a moot point when the new Congress that came in with the Bush administration killed the ergonomics standard under an obscure fast-track provision for review of administrative rules (see 5 USCA § 801).

As I mentioned, the new standard would have relied heavily upon workers to identify hazards and work with their employer to eliminate them. Do you think that would have constituted unlawful dealing under NLRA § 8(a)(2) in non-union workplaces? Do you think that such a system of worker communication in a unionized workplace would have to be set up pursuant to the bargaining process?

The new Secretary of Labor has promised that she would revisit the question of ergonomics. Meanwhile, OSHA may have some authority under the general duty clause to sanction employers whose workplaces present ergonomic hazards. Look at the text of the general duty clause, Section 5(a)(1) of OSHA. What are the statutory hurdles to treating ergonomics issues as involving hazards that can be addressed under the general duty clause?

OSHA has taken the position in a couple of cases that the general duty clause does apply to ergonomics hazards; the key case is Pepperidge Farm, 17 OSH Cas. 1993 (BNA), 1997 OSHD Par. 31,301 (1997).

E.   THE WORKER WHO TAKES MATTERS INTO HER OWN HANDS—PROBLEM 3–2

D. NELKIN AND M. BROWN, WORKERS AT RISK

164, 106, 122 (1984).

EVE, SORTER, MANUFACTURING PLANT

The more the economy goes down, the more they lay off people. They no longer have the people to maintain equipment like they used to. We have to insist that they do. If the people would only refuse to work in dirty areas, they would have to clean them up. But some of them just say, "Oh well, they'll probably have it cleaned tonight." Well, don't wait until tonight. Tell them to clean it or else, because they can't fire you if you refuse to work in something that you know is hazardous. People talk about health problems but do nothing about it.

* * *

STEVE, RAILROAD TRACKMAN

Last September they started spraying 2, 4–D on the job I was working on. The smell was amazingly pungent. On the best information available on that chemical, I closed down a job involving 40 workers as soon as they started spraying. When it became clear that we were going to take a firm stand, they stopped spraying, making all kinds of phony apologies about not knowing what was going on. The moral of the story is that a job action is the only way to protect ourselves. That isn't easy. I personally had to conduct an on-the-spot education and agitation program on the subject, because I couldn't just walk down the track and tell everybody to pack up and go without them thinking that I was flipping my lid. I had to explain to them what the chemical was and what it had done to our members and to the Vietnam veterans. I put the issue in these terms: "Your welfare now and you and your family's welfare in the future are at stake. They have absolutely no need to expose you to this; there's absolutely no justification for doing it, and you have every right to stop them." There was a high degree of unanimity about the action that we took, and we won a modest victory. We got them to stop spraying near us; unfortunately we didn't get them to stop spraying it entirely so that innocent bystanders who aren't informed or organized will no doubt continue being needlessly exposed.

We got away with it. There were no repercussions and no one lost pay. However there's a problem in stopping work. You stop even one worker from doing one thing and you've done something very serious. If you don't do it right, you can expose someone to charges of insubordination. Often workers themselves don't want to go along. Believe it or not, in spite of what others might have you believe, workers come to work to work. Really. And they may resent having jobs stopped by the union unless it's very clear that their vital interests are at stake and there's no other way. That's a special problem when the risks are not immediate but long term.

PROBLEM 3–2

To: Assistant General Counsel Diamond

From: Eulah Blair, UFW Business Agent

Re: Maria Perez, Discharge for Refusal to Work

Enderby has fired one of the employees in the computer repair and maintenance shop. Her name is Maria Perez. She is pregnant. For the past two weeks, she has reported for work, asked her supervisor to assign her to another job, and left the shop when he refused her request and instructed her to do her usually assigned job. She will not work in the shop where many of the machines, her doctor says, pose a danger to the health of the fetus, the future child. She also says that the poor ergonomics design of her chair and its placement before the computer screen endanger her child. Her refusal of the past two weeks came only after she had advised Crickboom of her problem and he had explored alternative ways of dealing with the dilemma. He suggested to me that he might transfer her to another job. After consulting with other employees who have greater seniority than Perez, I made clear that if Crickboom ignored seniority, I would file a grievance protesting the violation of the seniority clause. To avoid liability for birth defects and, maybe, for the good of the child, Crickboom also thought about firing Perez or, at least, putting her on leave. Perez objected, and I threatened a grievance over those alternatives, also. So, the company did nothing and Perez has refused to work in the computer repair room. She got fired for refusing to work and has grieved. We have exhausted all the grievance steps with Crickboom but he will not budge.

Should we go to arbitration? Is there a better remedy? Or should I drop the matter?

————

To: The Enderby (Maria Perez discharge) file

From: Asst. GC Diamond

I have taken a quick look at this case. I do not have much confidence we can help Perez. The following sets out my tentative thoughts and some relevant materials.

1. Arbitration. Typically, arbitrators are not pleased with an employee who refuses to do the work she is assigned. It is viewed as almost the equivalent of a mutiny at sea. Arbitrators usually take the view that the employee should work and grieve later. The most singular exception to the work-and-grieve tenet is the situation where the employee can demonstrate imminent serious threat to her health and safety. It is not clear the exception applies to concern for a future baby's health. I am attaching some materials that talk about arbitrations and refusals to work.

I should add that Perez' situation is complicated by the fact that, prior to refusing work, she had spoken with management, which in turn spoke to us. We objected to the remedies the management was considering. How does that fact affect her chances?

2. National Labor Relations Act. We can file a charge alleging discharge for concerted activity. There are problems, however.

(a) We have the deferral problem. Unlike the unilateral action cases, which pretty much have found the Board and the courts agreeing on deferral, the discharge and discipline cases [the 8(a)(1) and/or (3) cases] have divided the Board, which wants to defer, see the excerpted *United Technologies Corp.* decision, from some (although not all) of the courts of appeals. See, for example, the excerpted *Taylor v. N.L.R.B.* decision.

I think the posture we took regarding the earlier proposals considered by management and Perez to work out the problem may help Perez argue against deferral.

(b) In the event that the Board will not defer, we still need to face up to the "concerted action" requirement. There is little doubt in my mind that if a group of employees had protested the danger of computers and their repair machines and had refused to work in the face of it, they would be engaged in "concerted activities" within the meaning of Section 7 of the NLRA. See, for example, the *Washington Aluminum* case, excerpts of which are in Chapter I. In Perez' situation, however, I see two problems. First, it is not evident to me that she was in concert with any other employees. Second, there is the collective bargaining contract. Can she unilaterally ignore it? Reconsider *City Disposal Systems,* Chapter I of the casebook. If it proves to be the case that she is being treated in violation of Title VII, OSHA, or the ADA, will that affect the analysis?

3. OSHA. Consider the *Whirlpool* case, parts of which are attached. I gather there is some question whether the computer repair shop does pose a risk for the child-to-be. It is not clear to me that the *Whirlpool* case can be used to protect the yet-to-be-born or to protect Perez, who has not complained on her own behalf. Moreover, the OSHA solution, if any, could take a long time to be realized. Perez needs work now.

4. Title VII. Is it possible that the danger of the computer room has a *Griggs*-type disparate impact on women, who are the people who get pregnant and, therefore, are the only ones faced with the possible dilemma of either working or protecting future children? One needs to review *Griggs,* Chapter I of the casebook, its progeny, Section 703(k) of the Act which defines "disparate impact" cases, and Section 701(k), which makes clear that discrimination "because of sex" includes discrimination because of pregnancy. In light of *Johnson Controls,* can an employer protect a future child by treating the future mother differently than it treats other employees? Reconsider the *Guerra* case (reproduced in Ch. 1 and referred to in part B of the Hungadunga memo in Problem 3–1), which implies that Title VII does not preclude discrimination, at least sometimes, in favor of women. If Enderby cannot lawfully favor a pregnant woman, on what basis does Enderby violate the law when the company refuses to treat Perez differently? I am reminded of the line of Supreme Court cases wrestling with Title VII's application to pregnant women. See, for example, General Electric v. Gilbert, 429 U.S. 125, 97 S.Ct. 401, 50 L.Ed.2d 343 (1976).

Even with Section 701(k), which was a Congressional reaction to *General Electric,* the problem of treating people equally when they are not the same (only women can have babies) seems to defy wholly logical or satisfactory responses.

5. Americans with Disabilities Act of 1990 (ADA). Will this statute be interpreted to include pregnancy within the meaning of "disability," as that word is used in the Act. At least literally, Section 3(2) fits. Yet I have strong doubts.

If the ADA includes pregnancy within the definition of "disability," Enderby will be faced with the need to "reasonably accommodate" Perez' status, unless such an accommodation will impose an "undue hardship" upon Enderby. See Section 102(b)(5)(A) of the ADA, and Sections 101(9) and (10) for definitions of the two quoted phrases. Since the ADA was largely modeled after the Rehabilitation Act of 1973, there must be cases under the 1973 statute that will inform us as to the meaning of the obligation to accommodate a disability, but a unique meaning will surely evolve for the ADA. Moreover, based on what we know about the facts of the shop at Enderby, it is not clear, one way or the other, what sorts of accommodation might be reasonably possible.

While the ADA route is worth pursuing, would it make any sense for pregnant women to get better protection under that Act than under Title VII, especially in light of the latter's express protection of pregnant women?

6.   In attempting to invoke rights for Perez under Title VII, the ADA, OSHA, or the NLRA, we must face the question whether she is limited solely to her arbitration remedies. I know that the *Gilmer* decision expressly refused to overrule the *Alexander* case (part A.2. of the Hungadunga memo in Problem 3–1), but I wonder if the distinction will survive. The *Wright* case, in Chapter II suggests the answer is still unclear.

7.   Something bothers me throughout this whole analysis. The foregoing ignores largely the role we, the union, have played in this vignette. Have we put Perez in an impossible position? If there is arbitration, may she understandably object to the role we usually play in that process? That is, should the union retain its usual control of the employee's case? How would the arbitration proceed if we did not keep control? Conversely, does Enderby have a legitimate gripe in that we have sided with the more senior employees to oppose a reassignment for Perez, we have sided with Perez to oppose the company's desire to lay her off until the baby is born, and now we are opposing her discharge. Should either Perez or the company have some recourse in response to our apparent opposition to anything the company does, regardless of the circumstances? See *Ford v. Huffman* in Chapter I, and consider the excerpts from the *Vaca v. Sipes* case and other materials which follow Problem 3–3, *infra*.

It also has occurred to me that, maybe, Perez may sue us for failing to assure, in some manner, the safety of her child-to-be. I think, probably, the union will not be liable. See *Steelworkers v. Rawson,* which I think will keep us pretty well protected. I have attached excerpts from that opinion.

1.   ARBITRATION AND REFUSALS TO WORK

JAMES A. GROSS AND PATRICIA A. GREENFIELD, ARBITRAL VALUE JUDGMENTS IN HEALTH AND SAFETY DISPUTES: MANAGEMENT RIGHTS OVER WORKERS' RIGHTS

34 Buff.L.Rev. 645–55 (1985).

The influence of personal beliefs and values on the judgments of judicial and quasi-judicial decision-makers, such as labor arbitrators, continues to be ignored almost totally in the literature of labor law and labor arbitration. The research that has been done on this subject, however, demonstrates that prevailing ideas about ethics, humanity, law, private property, economics and the nature of the employer-worker relationship not only condition the thinking of these decision-makers, but also provide them with the ultimate standards for judgment. These value judgments pre-position a decision-maker's approach to particular case situations, thereby exercising a powerful influence on the outcomes of those cases.

* * * This study focuses on health and safety disputes because the even more fundamental clash between management's rights to operate the enterprise and workers' rights to a safe and healthful workplace is most likely to evoke arbitral value judgments. * * *

[A]rbitral value judgments establish the standards of proof and presumptions that shape arbitrators' conceptions of health and safety cases by focusing on management rights rather than workers' rights. These value judgments constitute the current arbitral common law in this area.

A. REFUSAL TO WORK CASES

Almost forty years ago, distinguished arbitrator Harry Shulman set forth in *Ford Motor Company* [Ford Motor Co., 3 Lab.Arb. (BNA) 779 (1944) (Shulman, Arb.)] the principle of "work first, grieve later." In that case, a union representative countermanded a management order temporarily assigning employees to work in higher job classifications because that order was allegedly in violation of a long-standing practice of temporary assignments to lower but not higher classifications. Shulman ruled that "normally" an employee must obey a legitimate work order even if the employee is convinced the order is improper. According to Shulman, the employees should have worked in the higher classification and then protested by filing a grievance since "the grievance procedure would have provided them adequate recompense for the wrong." Otherwise, Shulman said, individual action would be substituted for collective action and the grievance procedure would be replaced with extra-contractual methods so that no enterprise could operate. * * *

Shulman allowed for exceptions to his rule: when obedience to a management order would require commission of a criminal or otherwise unlawful act or create an "unusual health hazard or other serious sacrifice." Shulman's "work first, grieve later" rule, reflecting the underlying value judgment that management has the right to direct and control the workforce, has become an axiom of labor relations as has his "threat to health or safety" exception to the rule.

Arbitrators, however, do not literally except health and safety from the "work first, grieve later" rule. Arbitral application of the rule in cases where employees refuse to obey management orders because of perceived or actual threats to health and safety reflects an insubordination mode of analysis. Management's right to direct and control the workplace becomes the analytic starting point, and the challenge to that right, i.e., a refusal to work, is insubordination. This approach relegates the safety and health claim to an affirmative defense to the insubordination charge. * * *

It is the employee who must carry the burden of ultimate persuasion by establishing the sufficiency of his or her reason for refusing the work assignment, thus proving to an arbitrator's satisfaction that a health or safety hazard justified disobedience. In only one out of the 154 refusal to work cases did the arbitrator also put a burden of ultimate persuasion on the employer to prove the existence of a safe and healthful workplace.
* * *

The effect of this mode of analysis on the outcome of these cases is even more severe for employees because arbitrators routinely place upon them the heaviest possible standards of proof. Standards of proof in these cases come in three weights: objective proof, reasonable belief, and good faith belief. In forty-two percent of the 120 refusal to work cases where the standard of proof could be identified, arbitrators required the employee (or the employee's union) to produce objective proof that a health or safety hazard existed—proof which is defined as objective evidence of abnormally dangerous conditions: "demonstrative, objective, or factual evidence," such as "scientific evidence," that there was "in fact an extremely hazardous situation," beyond the "normal hazards" involved in the disputed work. Examples ranged from proof that there was in fact ice on the ceiling and a water line freeze-up, an oil spill in the work area, to proof that there was hot, flying scale in the forge shop.
* * *

Although by definition "reasonable belief" would seem to require a lighter burden of proof, most often there is only a slight difference, if any, between what arbitrators require of employees under the objective proof and reasonable belief standards. Arbitrators emphasize the factual basis, if any, for the perceived danger under both standards and the facts required to substantiate a reasonable belief are often identical to those needed to demonstrate objective proof. In other words, some arbitrators find a grievant's belief reasonable only when it is supported by objective proof of a health or safety hazard. Thus, in twenty-four percent of the cases with identifiable standards of proof, arbitrators applying "reasonable belief standards" required factual bases essentially indistinguishable from those required under the standard of objective proof. In effect, therefore, in sixty-six percent of these cases objective proof was required.
* * *

By far both the lightest and least applied standard of proof is that of "good faith," belief defined by arbitrators as a fear that is "genuine," "sincere," "honest and not a subterfuge"—"an honest and sincere personal conviction that his life would be in danger" regardless of whether an unsafe or unhealthful condition actually existed. This honest conviction must pertain to a perceived hazard beyond "the normal hazard attendant upon the regular duties of the job." Arbitrators made reference to this standard of proof in approximately nine percent of the cases.

The actual use of this standard by arbitrators is so rare, however, that there was only one reported case where an employee's good faith belief was the sole, or even the primary, basis for barring a finding of insubordination for refusing to obey a work order for reasons of health or safety. A good faith belief is more often used as a basis for mitigating the penalty imposed for such an insubordination.

ROBERT J. RABIN, SOME COMMENTS ON OBSCENITIES, HEALTH AND SAFETY, AND WORKPLACE VALUES

34 Buff.L.Rev. 725, 728–30 (1985).

The seminal "obey now, grieve later" arbitration award of Harry Shulman is referred to at length * * *. Curious to learn more, I read the original case. Here is what happened:

Significantly, the grievance arose during World War II. Shulman says "it was desirable to keep the supercharger going in that building * * * because of the great need for that product in the war effort. * * * " He refers at the outset to the "blockade of Gates 9 and 10, * * * incident to the memorable disturbance in the aircraft building." This language is indicative of the cryptic nature of the decision (an inevitable price for the welcome brevity of Shulman's awards) so we're not sure exactly what was up. We can infer that, however, there was a special situation at this plant: work had been disrupted, and production was needed during wartime. Contrary to what one might think when reading an account of the arbitration award, it was not a rank and file worker who was disciplined here. Rather, it was a committeeman who had instructed other workers not to work outside their normal duties.

It was against the background of the war and other disruptions that Shulman delivered his stern lecture to the bargaining unit. He addressed the assumption that a committeeman could countermand orders: "That assumption is wrong. And it should be clearly understood that it is wrong." The famous sermon about an industrial plant not being a debating society followed. In dictum, he extended his position to rank and file workers as well as committeemen. I think Shulman's position should be understood as a firm rebuke for an act that was unacceptable given a special situation. Even at that, the committeeman received only a four-day suspension, although the mildness of the penalty may have been influenced by the company's past treatment of others for the same type of conduct.

I wondered how far Shulman intended to take his rule. I needed to look no further than the very next case in the reports. In that case, which came up two years later, after the war, glaziers had refused to accept a painting assignment because they claimed that it would make them ill. The glaziers were discharged. Shulman did not treat the refusal as a health and safety issue. Rather, he assumed that they refused the new job because it was not within their job description. Shulman reinstated the grievants with full back-pay! He said that his prior award should not be applied to skilled craft employees when the assignment clearly took them outside their regular classifications. In language presenting a stark contrast to today's insubordination cases, Shulman said: "[N]or was there any emergency or unusual reason for the assignment. . . . And supervision persisted in making the assignment over a period of time despite the aggrieved's protests and despite the clear difference in the two classifications."

Stunned, I did further research and found that Shulman himself read other exceptions and qualifications into his own "obey now, grieve later" rule. In one case, for example, the union had called three of its alternate committeemen to attend to a particular matter. Their supervisor ordered them to remain on the job. Shulman upheld their right to walk off the job to take care of union matters, but he did observe that their absence would not interfere with production. In another case, he refused to find that workers had engaged in a strike when they delayed their start of work for an hour and disputed management's work assignment. "The cause of the delay," said Shulman, "was plainly a failure in Management's duty of communication to the employees on a matter of considerable importance to them."

I didn't read any further. Perhaps some scholar, intrigued by these clues, will dig some more. But surely the wee evidence I've found indicates that the origins of the rule running through the modern cases are not nearly as pervasive and inflexible as today's arbitral awards suggest.

Maybe it is time to take another look at the foundations of the "obey now, grieve later" rule. By piecing together the exceptions and qualifications that have developed over the years, as I've done with just a few of Shulman's awards, we might arrive at a very different understanding of the rule. We would probably continue to agree with the general proposition that orders must be obeyed. We would get nowhere if each participant had to calculate whether the grounds of the refusal are more weighty than the need to get the job done immediately.

But by studying past decisions, perhaps a more detailed set of rules would emerge. Just as we say that health and safety cases are an exception to the obligation to obey now (although we may pay no more than lip service to this notion), we might be able to catalogue other exceptions, as Shulman did. We might say, as Shulman suggested in his decision involving the one-hour delay, that it is not proper to order a worker to carry out a task until he has an opportunity to say his piece, and that no penalty may be imposed until the employee has a chance to consult with a union representative. We might want to limit this exception to cases that do not seriously interfere with production. We might want to consider the events leading up to the refusal, and whether management provoked it.

We should also think about the flip side of the equation, whether the employee's rights can be adequately vindicated if he obeys now and grieves later. I heard a case in which a skilled tradesman had refused to continue digging a ditch, and the evidence showed that his task was useless and foolish. What remedy could an arbitrator impose if the worker complied and grieved? Order his supervisor to dig a ditch? One solution is to use a schedule of liquidated damages for employees who obey improper orders.

2. PROTECTED CONCERTED ACTIVITIES, THE NATIONAL LABOR RELATIONS BOARD AND DEFERRAL TO THE ARBITRAL PROCESS

UNITED TECHNOLOGIES CORP. AND INTERNATIONAL ASSOCIATION OF MACHINISTS & AEROSPACE WORKERS, AFL/CIO

National Labor Relations Board, 1984.
268 NLRB 557, 115 LRRM 1049, 1984 WL 36028.

The complaint * * * alleges that the Respondent violated Section 8(a)(1) by threatening employee Sherfield with disciplinary action if she persisted in processing a grievance to the second step. At the hearing, the Respondent denied that it had violated Section 8(a)(1) as alleged and argued that, in any event, since the dispute was cognizable under the grievance-arbitration provisions of the parties' collective-bargaining agreement, it should be resolved pursuant to those provisions. Accordingly, the Respondent urged the Board to defer the exercise of its jurisdiction in this matter to the grievance-arbitration machinery. * * *

On 6 November 1981 the Union filed a third-step grievance alleging that the Respondent, through its general foreman, Peterson, intimidated, coerced, and harassed shop steward Wilson and employee Sherfield at a first-step grievance meeting by threatening disciplinary action against Sherfield if she appealed her grievance to the second step.[2] The remedy the Union sought was that "the Company immediately stop these contract violations and General Foreman Roger Peterson be properly disciplined and reinstructed for his misuse, abuse, and violation of the contract." The Respondent denied the Union's grievance at the third step, and the Union withdrew it on 27 January 1982 "without prejudice." * * * Thereafter, the Union filed the charge * * *.

The Respondent and the Union were parties to a collective-bargaining agreement which was effective from 24 April 1978 through 24 April 1983. Article VII of the contract establishes a grievance procedure that

2. The grievance that was the subject of the first-step meeting alleged that Sherfield had been "repeatedly harassed, intimidated, and discriminated against" by her foreman, Cote, and that Cote had engaged in an "act of aggression" against her. The act of aggression referred to an incident in which Cote had responded to Sherfield's request for certain parts by allegedly tossing a bag of parts weighing approximately one-third of an ounce at her workbench. At some point during the first-step meeting, Cote apologized to Sherfield, whereupon General Foreman Peterson denied the grievance and urged everyone to return to work. Shop steward Wilson and Sherfield indicated that they would appeal the grievance to the second step. Peterson then told Sherfield that the Company had been nice to her and that they had not disciplined her in the past because of her rejects. Wilson stated that Peterson's statement could be construed as a threat. Peterson denied that he was threatening Sherfield; rather, he said he was merely telling Sherfield what could and would happen.

includes an oral step, four written steps, and an arbitration provision that calls for final and binding arbitration.

Arbitration as a means of resolving labor disputes has gained widespread acceptance over the years and now occupies a respected and firmly established place in Federal labor policy. The reason for its success is the underlying conviction that the parties to a collective-bargaining agreement are in the best position to resolve, with the help of a neutral third party if necessary, disputes concerning the correct interpretation of their contract. * * *

Similarly, the concept of judicial and administrative deference to the arbitral process and the notion that courts should support, rather than interfere with, this method of dispute resolution have become entrenched in American jurisprudence. * * *

The Board endowed this sound approach with renewed vigor in the seminal case of *Collyer Insulated Wire,* in which the Board dismissed a complaint alleging unilateral changes in wages and working conditions in violation of Section 8(a)(5) in deference to the parties' grievance-arbitration machinery. The *Collyer* majority articulated several factors favoring deferral: The dispute arose within the confines of a long and productive collective-bargaining relationship; there was no claim of employer animosity to the employees' exercise of protected rights; the parties' contract provided for arbitration in a very broad range of disputes; the arbitration clause clearly encompassed the dispute at issue; the employer had asserted its willingness to utilize arbitration to resolve the dispute; and the dispute was eminently well suited to resolution by arbitration. In these circumstances, deferral to the arbitral process merely gave full effect to the parties' agreement to submit disputes to arbitration. In essence, the *Collyer* majority was holding the parties to their bargain by directing them to avoid substituting the Board's processes for their own mutually agreed-upon method for dispute resolution.

The experience under *Collyer* was extremely positive. The *Collyer* deferral doctrine was endorsed by the courts of appeals and was quoted favorably by the Supreme Court. * * *

Despite the universal judicial acceptance of the *Collyer* doctrine, however, the Board in *General American Transportation* abruptly changed course and adopted a different standard for arbitral deferral, one that we believe ignores the important policy considerations in favor of deferral. Indeed, by deciding to decline to defer cases alleging violations of Sections 8(a)(1) and (3) and 8(b)(1)(A) and (2), the *General American Transportation* majority essentially emasculated the Board's deferral policy, a policy that had favorably withstood the tests of judicial scrutiny and of practical application. And they did so for reasons that are largely unsupportable. Simply stated, *Collyer* worked well because it was premised on sound legal and pragmatic considerations. Accordingly, we believe it deserves to be resurrected and infused with renewed life.

It is fundamental to the concept of collective bargaining that the parties to a collective-bargaining agreement are bound by the terms of their contract. Where an employer and a union have voluntarily elected to create dispute resolution machinery culminating in final and binding arbitration, it is contrary to the basic principles of the Act for the Board to jump into the fray prior to an honest attempt by the parties to resolve their disputes through that machinery. For dispute resolution under the grievance-arbitration process is as much a part of collective bargaining as the act of negotiating the contract. In our view, the statutory purpose of encouraging the practice and procedure of collective bargaining is ill-served by permitting the parties to ignore their agreement and to petition this Board in the first instance for remedial relief. * * *

[D]eferral is not akin to abdication. It is merely the prudent exercise of restraint, a postponement of the use of the Board's processes to give the parties' own dispute resolution machinery a chance to succeed. The Board's processes may always be invoked if the arbitral result is inconsistent with the standards of *Spielberg*.[18] * * *

The facts of the instant case make it eminently well suited for deferral. The dispute centers on a statement a single foreman made to a single employee and a shop steward during the course of a routine first-step grievance meeting allegedly concerning possible adverse consequences that might flow from a decision by the employee to process her grievance to the next step. The statement is alleged to be a threat violative of Section 8(a)(1). It is also, however, clearly cognizable under the broad grievance-arbitration provision of section VII of the collective-bargaining agreement.[20] Moreover, the Respondent has expressed its willingness, indeed its eagerness, to arbitrate the dispute.

In view of the foregoing, we believe it would best effectuate the purposes and policies of the Act to defer this case to the arbitral forum. * * *

MEMBER ZIMMERMAN, dissenting.

* * *

Employees' Section 7 rights are public rights charged to the Board's protection. * * * Therefore, by forcing employees to pursue the private adjudication of their public rights through the arbitration process rather than through the processes of the Board, my colleagues are actually repudiating, rather than applying, the relevant judicial precedent.

With respect to the putative supremacy of obligations flowing from the grievance and arbitration provision of a collective-bargaining agreement, my colleagues again overstate their case. Implicit in their reasoning is that an exclusive collective-bargaining representative may waive an individual employee's right to seek initial redress of interference with

---

18. Spielberg Mfg. Co., 112 NLRB 1080 (1955).

20. In this regard, we note that art. IV of the contract states that "the company and the union recognize that employees covered by this agreement may not be discriminated against in violation of the provisions of the Labor Management Relations Act, 1947 as amended...." It is manifest, therefore, that the parties contemplated that disputes such as the one here be resolved under the grievance-arbitration machinery.

Section 7 rights before the Board. A union may, of course, agree to waive some individual statutory rights. But in my view a union cannot waive an individual employee's right to choose a statutory forum in which to initiate and litigate an unfair labor practice issue. Even if it could, such a waiver would have to be a "clear and unmistakable" one. Here, however, the majority forces individual employees to litigate statutory rights in a contractual forum and does so without making any determination that there has been a "clear and unmistakable" waiver of the right to resort first and exclusively to the Board. My colleagues simply assume that the mere existence of a contractual grievance and arbitration procedure proves a waiver.

Finally, it is pure conceit that the deferral doctrine announced here is mere "prudent restraint" and that *Spielberg* is a catchall safety net for those individuals whose individual rights are not protected in grievance and arbitration. The arbitration process is not designed to and is not particularly adept at protecting employee statutory or public rights. First, a union, without breaching its duty of fair representation, might not vigorously support an employee's claim in arbitration inasmuch as the union, in balancing individual and collective interests, might trade off an employee's statutory right in favor of some other benefits for employees in the bargaining unit as a whole. Second, because arbitrators' competency is primarily in "the law of the shop, not the law of the land," they may lack the competency to resolve the statutory issue(s) involved in the dispute. Third, even if the arbitrator is conversant with the Act, he is limited to determining the dispute in accordance with the parties' intent under the collective-bargaining agreement. Finally, because the arbitrator's function is to effectuate the parties' intent rather than to enforce the Act, he may issue a ruling that is inimical to the public policies underlying the Act, thereby depriving an employee of his protected statutory rights.

TAYLOR v. NLRB

United States Court of Appeals, Eleventh Circuit, 1986.
786 F.2d 1516, cert. denied 493 U.S. 891, 110 S.Ct. 237, 107 L.Ed.2d 187 (1989).

LYNNE, SENIOR DISTRICT JUDGE:

Melvin D. Taylor challenges the National Labor Relations Board's deferral to the decision of a grievance committee to dismiss his unfair labor practice claim. We hold that deferral was not warranted and remand for further consideration by the Board.

FACTS

On December 2, 1982, Melvin D. Taylor was terminated from his job as a truck driver by Ryder Truck Lines, Inc., when he refused to drive a 1979 Ford tractor assigned to him by Ryder from its pool of vehicles. Taylor complained of several safety problems with the tractor but primarily objected to the Ford's telescoping steering column, which had frozen and could not be adjusted to accommodate his 240–pound frame.

Ryder's truckdrivers are parties to a collective bargaining agreement and are represented by the International Brotherhood of Teamsters, Chauffeurs, Warehousemen, and Helpers of America (the Union). The Agreement states that Ryder may not require employees to operate an unsafe vehicle and further provides that disputes shall be resolved through final and binding grievance and arbitration procedures.

After his termination, Taylor filed a grievance protesting his discharge. The grievance was submitted to a Southern Multi–State Grievance Committee (the Multi–State Committee) comprised of Union and Ryder representatives. This Committee held a hearing on January 25, 1983, and heard testimony from Ryder and from Taylor but was unable to reach a decision. The case was automatically appealed to the Southern Conference Joint Area Grievance Committee (the Area Committee). At this hearing, the transcript of the first grievance proceeding was made a part of the record and a Ryder representative made a brief statement. Taylor was not permitted to be present at this hearing; the Union representative made no statement on Taylor's behalf. The Area Committee denied the grievance with no discussion other than the following pronouncement: "DECISION: Case No. 15 DENIED, COST TO THE UNION."

On March 3, 1983, Taylor filed charges with the National Labor Relations Board, which issued a complaint against Ryder on April 11 of that year. After a hearing on July 28–29, 1983, an Administrative Law Judge (ALJ) issued a recommended decision and order on September 21, 1983. The ALJ declined to defer to the Area Committee's denial of Taylor's complaint, noting that Ryder had not offered the Area Committee decision or the Multi–State Committee transcript into evidence. Reaching the merits of Taylor's grievance, the ALJ held that Taylor's refusal to drive the Ford tractor was a protected "concerted activity" and that his termination by Ryder violated Section 8(a)(3) of the National Labor Relations Act.

Ryder filed numerous exceptions to the findings and order of the ALJ. While these exceptions were pending, the Board decided Olin Corp., 268 NLRB 573 (1984), in which it restated the Board's standard for deferral to arbitration procedures. On its own initiative, the Board remanded Taylor's case to the ALJ on the deferral issue alone, with instructions to reopen the record and reconsider that issue in light of *Olin*.

After reviewing the transcript of the Multi–State Committee hearing and the decision of the Area Committee, the ALJ issued on July 17, 1984, a supplemental decision finding that the "cursory" findings of the Area Committee provided no basis for deferral and reaffirming its original decision.

Relying on the *Olin* decision, the Board reversed the supplemental decision, holding that the General Counsel had not met its burden of affirmatively demonstrating that the unfair labor practice had not received adequate consideration by the Area Committee. This appeal followed.

DISCUSSION

Taylor contends that the ALJ's decision not to defer to the arbitral finding of the Area Committee was proper because it could not be determined from the Committee's decision whether Taylor's unfair labor practice claim had been considered. The Board responds by relying upon its new criteria for deferral as set forth in *Olin Corp.*, and its finding that the General Counsel did not affirmatively demonstrate that deferral was not warranted.

1. Background of NLRB's Deferral Policy

The NLRB's responsibility to prevent and penalize unfair labor practices historically has been pitted against a countervailing desire to encourage the private settlement of labor disputes. The tension between these competing concerns is readily apparent from Congressional directives to the Board. Section 10(a) of the National Labor Relations Act provides that the Board's power to prevent unfair labor disputes "shall not be affected by any other means of adjustment or prevention that has been or may be established by agreement, law, or otherwise." Section 203(d) of the Act, however, states that binding arbitration is "the desirable method of settlement of grievances arising over the application or interpretation of an existing collective bargaining agreement." 29 U.S.C. §§ 160(a), 173(d).

In the seminal case of Spielberg Mfg. Co., 112 NLRB 1080 (1955), the Board ruled that "recognition" of an arbitration award was justified because (1) the proceedings appeared to have been fair and regular; (2) all parties had agreed to be bound; and (3) the decision of the arbitration panel was not clearly repugnant to the purposes and policies of the Act. 112 NLRB at 1802. It soon became apparent, however, that a more exacting standard was required to ensure that unfair labor practice issues were in fact being addressed and resolved. See Raytheon Co., 140 NLRB 883, 886 (1963) (Board cannot neglect function of protecting rights of protected employees), enforcement denied on other grounds, 326 F.2d 471 (1st Cir.1964). Raytheon Co. added the further requirement that an unfair labor practice issue must have been "fully and fairly litigated" at the arbitration level to justify deferral by the Board. 140 NLRB at 887.

The Board deviated from the *Spielberg* and *Raytheon* policy of cautious deferral in Electronics Reproduction Service Corp., 213 NLRB 758 (1974), in which it ruled that arbitral findings would be given effect unless "special circumstances" precluded the grievant from a "full and fair *opportunity*" to present evidence of an unfair labor practice. 213 NLRB at 764 (emphasis supplied). Although not expressly stated, this standard in effect placed upon the grievant the burden of proving to the Board that such unusual circumstances existed at the arbitration level.

The Board's new criteria established in *Electronic Reproduction* decision drew sharp disapproval from courts and critics. In Suburban Motor Freight, 247 NLRB 146 (1980), the Board acknowledged criticisms that *Electronic Reproduction* represented an "unwarranted extension of the *Spielberg* doctrine and an impermissible delegation of the Board's exclusive jurisdiction under [the NLRA] to decide unfair labor practice issues." 247 NLRB at 146. The Board overruled *Electronic Reproduction,* even though its more liberal standard encouraged collective bargaining relationships, because it also "derogate[d] the equally important purpose of protecting employees in the exercise of their rights." Id. The *Suburban Motor Freight* panel explicitly ruled that it would "give no deference to an arbitration award which bears no indication that the arbitrator ruled on the statutory issue of discrimination in determining the propriety of an employer's disciplinary actions." Id. The Board also expressly restored the previous burden of proof allocations.

The Board's return to the traditional deferral criteria did not solve the difficult questions that confront Board members and courts in an effort to reconcile the opposing policies of private dispute resolution and statutory rights protection. The Supreme Court has observed that "the opinions of the Courts of Appeal strongly suggest that there is marked disagreement on the circumstances under which the policy of Board deferral must be exercised." Schaefer v. NLRB, 464 U.S. 945, 945, 104 S.Ct. 362, 364, 78 L.Ed.2d 323, 325 (1983) (O'Connor, J., dissenting).

2. *Olin Corp.'s New Deferral Standard*

The NLRB presumably attempted to address this need for uniformity in *Olin Corp.*, 268 NLRB 573 (1984), in which yet another approach to deferral was formulated. The Board cited infrequent deferral under *Suburban Motor Freight* as the primary reason for its new standard, concluding that *Olin Corp.* is more consistent with "the aims of the Act and American labor policy." 268 NLRB at 574. After expressly reaffirming the general *Spielberg* criteria, the *Olin* majority went on to state its new deferral standard:

> We would find that an arbitrator has adequately considered the unfair labor practice if (1) the contractual issue is factually parallel to the unfair labor practice issue, and (2) the arbitrator was presented generally with the facts relevant to resolving the unfair labor practice. In this respect, differences, if any, between the contractual and statutory standards of review should be weighed by the Board as part of its determination under the *Spielberg* standards of whether an award is "clearly repugnant" to the Act.

> * * * And, with respect to the inquiry into [*Spielberg's*] "clearly repugnant" standard, * * * unless the award is "palpably wrong," i.e., unless the arbitrator's decision is not susceptible to an interpretation consistent with the Act, we will defer.

Id. (footnotes omitted). *Olin Corp.* also modified the *Raytheon* "fully and fairly litigated" test by returning to the *Electronic Reproduction* rule placing the burden upon the General Counsel to demonstrate that deferral was not necessary. Id.

Taylor urges, however, that the *Olin Corp.* standard confers upon arbitral decisions a nearly preclusive effect that is inappropriate in many contexts in which contractual and statutory labor disputes may arise. Taylor contends that factual parallelism does not always guarantee legal parallelism and sets forth several instances in which *Olin's* "factually parallel" test will result in inadequate or no litigation of the unfair labor practice issue.[5]

As evidenced by the application of the *Olin Corp.* standard to Taylor's labor claim, the Board's latest attempt to formulate a consistent deferral policy has swung back too far in the direction of *Electronic Reproduction* and cannot pass muster. As noted above, the NLRB has a statutory duty to enforce the National Labor Relations Act and exclusive jurisdiction to decide unfair labor practices. The Board may not avoid this responsibility through a far-reaching deferral policy which apparently presumes that an unfair labor practice claim has been resolved through arbitration.

The Supreme Court has stated in Alexander v. Gardner–Denver Co., 415 U.S. 36, 94 S.Ct. 1011, 39 L.Ed.2d 147 (1974), that an employee whose grievance was dismissed at arbitration nevertheless could bring a Title VII claim arising from the same underlying facts. Recognizing that the arbitrator's competence lies in "the law of the shop, not the law of the land," the Court held that an employee may still assert statutory claims independent of any rights created by a collective bargaining agreement. 415 U.S. 36, 57, 94 S.Ct. 1011, 1024. Deferral to an arbitral finding is not justified when the arbitrator did not address or resolve a distinct statutory claim. Id.

Several Courts of Appeal have faced similar fact situations and ruled against deferral where the circumstances surrounding the arbitral process were unknown or unclear. * * *

In a closely analogous context, courts have grappled with similar concerns in applying standards for granting preclusive effect to an arbitral finding. In Barrentine v. Arkansas–Best Freight System, Inc.,

---

5. (1) The facts relevant to establishing a contract violation may differ from those facts relevant to unfair labor practice violations, although there may be some overlap. Example: An arbitrator's finding of just cause for an employee's termination may overlook a real underlying reason for discharge arising from some protected activity.

(2) The standard of review for a contract violation may differ from a Board for an analogous unfair labor practice claim. Example: The amount of allowable insubordination by an employee differs for Board and arbitral purposes.

(3) The interest of the union may be to establish a favorable interpretation of a contract, not to protect an employee from a specific unfair labor practice. Example: A group of cases may be resolved jointly on a compromise basis, despite the wishes of one grievant to proceed with an unfair labor practice complaint.

(4) A bipartite grievance committee issues a decision denying a grievance but giving no indication of whether, and if so what, evidence or issues were considered in reaching that decision. Example: The majority of Teamster grievance committee decisions do not include written explanations, as demonstrated in the decision to deny Taylor's grievance.

450 U.S. 728, 101 S.Ct. 1437, 67 L.Ed.2d 641 (1981), the Supreme Court rejected the contention that arbitration of wage claims precluded a later suit under the Fair Labor Standards Act based on the same underlying facts. 450 U.S. at 745–46, 101 S.Ct. at 1447–48. In McDonald v. City of West Branch, 466 U.S. 284, 104 S.Ct. 1799, 80 L.Ed.2d 302 (1984), the Court similarly held that an earlier arbitral finding did not preclude a civil rights action brought under 42 U.S.C. § 1983. The *McDonald* Court held that its limitation of deferral in *Alexander* and preclusion in *Barrentine* was "based in large part on our conclusion that Congress intended the statutes at issue in those cases to be judicially enforceable and that arbitration could not provide an adequate substitute for judicial proceedings in adjudicating claims under those statutes." 466 U.S. at 289, 104 S.Ct. at 1803, 80 L.Ed.2d at 308. This concern for individual rights has been expressed in refusals by other courts to give preclusive effect to arbitration in a later statutory action.

The Fifth Circuit has recognized the importance of maintaining a viable forum for the resolution of statutory rights as stated by the Supreme Court in *Alexander, Barrentine,* and *McDonald.* In McNair v. United States Postal Service, 768 F.2d 730 (5th Cir.1985), a case which ultimately upheld preclusion for an arbitral finding, the court first reviewed the principles of deferral and preclusion. *McNair* recognized the need for employees to be able to assert statutory rights independent of the arbitration process, citing four factors to support this conclusion.

(1) an arbitrator, schooled primarily in the law of the shop, may lack the expertise to resolve complex statutory questions; (2) "because an arbitrator's authority derives solely from the contract, an arbitrator may not have the authority to enforce" statutes; (3) the union, which generally controls the grievance process, because its interests are not necessarily identical to those of its employees, may not adequately protect their statutory rights; and (4) "arbitral factfinding generally is not equivalent to judicial factfinding."

768 F.2d at 736, note 7 (citing McDonald v. City of West Branch, supra).

Relying on the principles and interests stated in the above cases, it is apparent that the *Olin Corp.* standard—like its predecessor in *Electronic Reproduction*—does not protect sufficiently an employee's rights granted by the National Labor Relations Act. By presuming, until proven otherwise, that all arbitration proceedings confront and decide every possible unfair labor practice issue, *Olin Corp.* gives away too much of the Board's responsibility under the NLRA. The ALJ in this case was presented with two grievance committee proceedings. In his supplemental decision, the ALJ found that the statutory issue clearly was considered at the Multi–State Committee hearing. If that hearing had produced a dispositive result, then deferral to that result would have been proper under any of the many variations of the *Spielberg* standard. It is the Area Committee's decision, however, that is relevant for deferral purposes and the ALJ had no indication from the transcript of that proceeding whether the Area Committee considered any unfair labor practice claim.

This case does not present the court with the question of whether the facts and issues were sufficiently parallel to justify deferral, nor does it involve scrutinizing an arbitral finding for a result that is "clearly repugnant" to the Act. The overriding question in this case is whether the Area Committee ever considered any facts relevant to Taylor's statutory claim.

Under *Olin Corp.*, the Board essentially has decided that deferral is proper in all cases unless it is affirmatively demonstrated that some unusual circumstances require that the ALJ conduct an independent inquiry into a grievant's statutory claims. Such a result cannot be reconciled with the need to protect statutory rights, as expressed by the Supreme Court in *Alexander, Barrentine,* and *McDonald,* supra. *Olin Corp.* either overlooks or ignores those instances where contract and statutory issues may be factually parallel but involve distinct elements of proof and questions of factual relevance.

The new standard further ignores the practical reality of many bipartite proceedings, in which individual rights may be negotiated away in the interest of the collective good. The circumstances surrounding bipartite proceedings such as Taylor's Area Committee hearing hardly inspire confidence in the fairness of the process or the accuracy of the result. A recent survey of Teamster Grievance Committees casts doubt on the competence of union representatives, thoroughness of investigation, adequacy of preparation, and reliability of evidence. See generally Summers, The Teamster Grievance Committees: Grievance Disposal Without Adjudication, 37 Proc. of the Nat'l Acad. of Arb. 130 (1984); *Olin Corp.*'s standard appears on its face to represent an abdication of Board responsibility, and application of that standard to proceedings such as these fully supports this conclusion. *Spielberg*'s first requirement—that the proceedings below appear to have been fair and regular—can hardly be satisfied in this context. The Supreme Court has recognized that arbitration is valuable therapy for the complicated and troubled area of labor dispute resolution. There can be little therapeutic value, however, in a deferral policy so unmindful of the Board's statutory responsibility and of individual rights.

We therefore VACATE the Board's order deferring to the decision of the Area Grievance Committee, and REMAND the case for further consideration of Ryder's exceptions and the General Counsel's cross-exceptions to the decision of the ALJ.

3. COLLECTIVE ACTION WITHOUT REPRESENTATION

Re–Read *NLRB v. Washington Aluminum Co.,* in Chapter I.

4. OSHA AND REFUSALS TO WORK

WHIRLPOOL CORP. v. MARSHALL

Supreme Court of the United States, 1980.
445 U.S. 1, 100 S.Ct. 883, 63 L.Ed.2d 154.

MR. JUSTICE STEWART delivered the opinion of the Court.

The Occupational Safety and Health Act of 1970 (Act) prohibits an employer from discharging or discriminating against any employee who exercises "any right afforded by" the Act.[2] The Secretary of Labor (Secretary) has promulgated a regulation providing that, among the rights that the Act so protects, is the right of an employee to choose not to perform his assigned task because of a reasonable apprehension of death or serious injury coupled with a reasonable belief that no less drastic alternative is available.[3] The question presented in the case before us is whether this regulation is consistent with the Act.

The petitioner company maintains a manufacturing plant in Marion, Ohio, for the production of household appliances. Overhead conveyors transport appliance components throughout the plant. To protect employees from objects that occasionally fall from these conveyors, the

---

2. Section 11(c)(1) of the Act, 29 U.S.C. § 660(c)(1).

3. The regulation, 29 CFR § 1977.12 (1979), provides in full:

"(a) In addition to protecting employees who file complaints, institute proceedings, or testify in proceedings under or related to the Act, section 11(c) also protects employees from discrimination occurring because of the exercise 'of any right afforded by this Act.' Certain rights are explicitly provided in the Act; for example, there is a right to participate as a party in enforcement proceedings (sec. 10). Certain other rights exist by necessary implication. For example, employees may request information from the Occupational Safety and Health Administration; such requests would constitute the exercise of a right afforded by the Act. Likewise, employees interviewed by agents of the Secretary in the course of inspections or investigations could not subsequently be discriminated against because of their cooperation.

"(b)(1) On the other hand, review of the Act and examination of the legislative history discloses that, as a general matter, there is no right afforded by the Act which would entitle employees to walk off the job because of potential unsafe conditions at the workplace. Hazardous conditions which may be violative of the Act will ordinarily be corrected by the employer, once brought to his attention. If corrections are not accomplished, or if there is dispute about the

existence of a hazard, the employee will normally have opportunity to request inspection of the workplace pursuant to section 8(f) of the Act, or to seek the assistance of other public agencies which have responsibility in the field of safety and health. Under such circumstances, therefore, an employer would not ordinarily be in violation of section 11(c) by taking action to discipline an employee for refusing to perform normal job activities because of alleged safety or health hazards.

"(2) However, occasions might arise when an employee is confronted with a choice between not performing assigned tasks or subjecting himself to serious injury or death arising from a hazardous condition at the workplace. If the employee, with no reasonable alternative, refuses in good faith to expose himself to the dangerous condition, he would be protected against subsequent discrimination. The condition causing the employee's apprehension of death or injury must be of such a nature that a reasonable person, under the circumstances then confronting the employee, would conclude that there is a real danger of death or serious injury and that there is insufficient time due to the urgency of the situation, to eliminate the danger through resort to regular statutory enforcement channels. In addition, in such circumstances, the employee, where possible, must also have sought from his employer, and been unable to obtain, a correction of the dangerous condition."

petitioner has installed a horizontal wire-mesh guard screen approximately 20 feet above the plant floor. This mesh screen is welded to angle-iron frames suspended from the building's structural steel skeleton.

Maintenance employees of the petitioner spend several hours each week removing objects from the screen, replacing paper spread on the screen to catch grease drippings from the material on the conveyors, and performing occasional maintenance work on the conveyors themselves. To perform these duties, maintenance employees usually are able to stand on the iron frames, but sometimes find it necessary to step onto the steel mesh screen itself.

In 1973, the company began to install heavier wire in the screen because its safety had been drawn into question. Several employees had fallen partly through the old screen, and on one occasion an employee had fallen completely through to the plant floor below but had survived. A number of maintenance employees had reacted to these incidents by bringing the unsafe screen conditions to the attention of their foremen. The petitioner company's contemporaneous safety instructions admonished employees to step only on the angle-iron frames.

On June 28, 1974, a maintenance employee fell to his death through the guard screen in an area where the newer, stronger mesh had not yet been installed.[4] Following this incident, the petitioner effectuated some repairs and issued an order strictly forbidding maintenance employees from stepping on either the screens or the angle-iron supporting structure. An alternative but somewhat more cumbersome and less satisfactory method was developed for removing objects from the screen. This procedure required employees to stand on power-raised mobile platforms and use hooks to recover the material.

On July 7, 1974, two of the petitioner's maintenance employees, Virgil Deemer and Thomas Cornwell, met with the plant maintenance superintendent to voice their concern about the safety of the screen. The superintendent disagreed with their view, but permitted the two men to inspect the screen with their foreman and to point out dangerous areas needing repair. Unsatisfied with the petitioner's response to the results of this inspection, Deemer and Cornwell met on July 9 with the plant safety director. At that meeting, they requested the name, address, and telephone number of a representative of the local office of the Occupational Safety and Health Administration (OSHA). Although the safety director told the men that they "had better stop and think about what [they] were doing," he furnished the men with the information they

---

4. As a result of this fatality, the Secretary conducted an investigation that led to the issuance of a citation charging the company with maintaining an unsafe walking and working surface in violation of 29 U.S.C. § 654(a)(1). The citation required immediate abatement of the hazard and proposed a $600 penalty. Nearly five years following the accident, the Occupational Safety and Health Review Commission affirmed the citation, but decided to permit the petitioner six months in which to correct the unsafe condition. Whirlpool Corp., 1979 CCH OSHD ¶ 23,552. A petition to review that decision is pending in the United States Court of Appeals for the District of Columbia Circuit.

requested. Later that same day, Deemer contacted an official of the regional OSHA office and discussed the guard screen.

The next day, Deemer and Cornwell reported for the night shift at 10:45 p.m. Their foreman, after himself walking on some of the angle-iron frames, directed the two men to perform their usual maintenance duties on a section of the old screen.[6] Claiming that the screen was unsafe, they refused to carry out this directive. The foreman then sent them to the personnel office, where they were ordered to punch out without working or being paid for the remaining six hours of the shift.[7] The two men subsequently received written reprimands, which were placed in their employment files.

A little over a month later, the Secretary filed suit in the United States District Court for the Northern District of Ohio, alleging that the petitioner's actions against Deemer and Cornwell constituted discrimination in violation of § 11(c)(1) of the Act. As relief, the complaint prayed, *inter alia,* that the petitioner be ordered to expunge from its personnel files all references to the reprimands issued to the two employees, and for a permanent injunction requiring the petitioner to compensate the two employees for the six hours of pay they had lost by reason of their disciplinary suspensions.

Following a bench trial, the District Court found that the regulation in question justified Deemer's and Cornwell's refusals to obey their foreman's order on July 10, 1974. The court found that the two employees had "refused to perform the cleaning operation because of a genuine fear of death or serious bodily harm," that the danger presented had been "real and not something which [had] existed only in the minds of the employees," that the employees had acted in good faith, and that no reasonable alternative had realistically been open to them other than to refuse to work. The District Court nevertheless denied relief, holding that the Secretary's regulation was inconsistent with the Act and therefore invalid. * * *

The Act itself creates an express mechanism for protecting workers from employment conditions believed to pose an emergent threat of death or serious injury. Upon receipt of an employee inspection request stating reasonable grounds to believe that an imminent danger is present in a workplace, OSHA must conduct an inspection. 29 U.S.C. § 657(f)(1). In the event this inspection reveals workplace conditions or practices that "could reasonably be expected to cause death or serious physical harm immediately or before the imminence of such danger can be eliminated through the enforcement procedures otherwise provided by" the Act, 29 U.S.C. § 662(a), the OSHA inspector must inform the affected employees and the employer of the danger and notify them that he is recommending to the Secretary that injunctive relief be sought.

6. This order appears to have been in direct violation of the outstanding company directive that maintenance work was to be accomplished without stepping on the screen apparatus.

7. Both employees apparently returned to work the following day without further incident.

§ 662(c). At this juncture, the Secretary can petition a federal court to restrain the conditions or practices giving rise to the imminent danger. By means of a temporary restraining order or preliminary injunction, the court may then require the employer to avoid, correct, or remove the danger or to prohibit employees from working in the area. § 662(a).

To ensure that this process functions effectively, the Act expressly accords to every employee several rights, the exercise of which may not subject him to discharge or discrimination. An employee is given the right to inform OSHA of an imminently dangerous workplace condition or practice and request that OSHA inspect that condition or practice. 29 U.S.C. § 657(f)(1). He is given a limited right to assist the OSHA inspector in inspecting the workplace, §§ 657(a)(2), (e), and (f)(2), and the right to aid a court in determining whether or not a risk of imminent danger in fact exists. See § 660(c)(1). Finally, an affected employee is given the right to bring an action to compel the Secretary to seek injunctive relief if he believes the Secretary has wrongfully declined to do so. § 662(d).

In the light of this detailed statutory scheme, the Secretary is obviously correct when he acknowledges in his regulation that, "as a general matter, there is no right afforded by the Act which would entitle employees to walk off the job because of potential unsafe conditions at the workplace." By providing for prompt notice to the employer of an inspector's intention to seek an injunction against an imminently dangerous condition, the legislation obviously contemplates that the employer will normally respond by voluntarily and speedily eliminating the danger. And in the few instances where this does not occur, the legislative provisions authorizing prompt judicial action are designed to give employees full protection in most situations from the risk of injury or death resulting from an imminently dangerous condition at the worksite.

As this case illustrates, however, circumstances may sometimes exist in which the employee justifiably believes that the express statutory arrangement does not sufficiently protect him from death or serious injury. Such circumstances will probably not often occur, but such a situation may arise when (1) the employee is ordered by his employer to work under conditions that the employee reasonably believes pose an imminent risk of death or serious bodily injury, and (2) the employee has reason to believe that there is not sufficient time or opportunity either to seek effective redress from his employer or to apprise OSHA of the danger.

Nothing in the Act suggests that those few employees who have to face this dilemma must rely exclusively on the remedies expressly set forth in the Act at the risk of their own safety. But nothing in the Act explicitly provides otherwise. Against this background of legislative silence, the Secretary has exercised his rulemaking power under 29 U.S.C. § 657(g)(2) and has determined that, when an employee in good faith finds himself in such a predicament, he may refuse to expose himself to the dangerous condition, without being subjected to "subsequent discrimination" by the employer.

The question before us is whether this interpretative regulation constitutes a permissible gloss on the Act by the Secretary, in light of the Act's language, structure, and legislative history. Our inquiry is informed by an awareness that the regulation is entitled to deference unless it can be said not to be a reasoned and supportable interpretation of the Act.

A

The regulation clearly conforms to the fundamental objective of the Act—to prevent occupational deaths and serious injuries.

The Act does not wait for an employee to die or become injured. It authorizes the promulgation of health and safety standards and the issuance of citations in the hope that these will act to prevent deaths or injuries from ever occurring. It would seem anomalous to construe an Act so directed and constructed as prohibiting an employee, with no other reasonable alternative, the freedom to withdraw from a workplace environment that he reasonably believes is highly dangerous.

Moreover, the Secretary's regulation can be viewed as an appropriate aid to the full effectuation of the Act's "general duty" clause. That clause provides that "[e]ach employer ... shall furnish to each of his employees employment and a place of employment which are free from recognized hazards that are causing or are likely to cause death or serious physical harm to his employees." 29 U.S.C. § 654(a)(1). As the legislative history of this provision reflects, it was intended itself to deter the occurrence of occupational deaths and serious injuries by placing on employers a mandatory obligation independent of the specific health and safety standards to be promulgated by the Secretary. Since OSHA inspectors cannot be present around the clock in every workplace, the Secretary's regulation ensures that employees will in all circumstances enjoy the rights afforded them by the "general duty" clause.

The regulation thus on its face appears to further the overriding purpose of the Act, and rationally to complement its remedial scheme. In the absence of some contrary indication in the legislative history, the Secretary's regulation must, therefore, be upheld, particularly when it is remembered that safety legislation is to be liberally construed to effectuate the congressional purpose.

B

In urging reversal of the judgment before us, the petitioner relies primarily on two aspects of the Act's legislative history.

1

Representative Daniels of New Jersey sponsored one of several House bills that led ultimately to the passage of the Act. As reported to the House by the Committee on Education and Labor, the Daniels bill contained a section that was soon dubbed the "strike with pay" provision. This section provided that employees could request an examination by the Department of Health, Education, and Welfare (HEW) of the toxicity of any materials in their workplace. If that examination revealed a workplace substance that had "potentially toxic or harmful effects in such concentration as used or found," the employer was given 60 days to correct the potentially dangerous condition. Following the expiration of that period, the employer could not require that an employee be exposed to toxic concentrations of the substance unless the employee was informed of the hazards and symptoms associated with the substance, the employee was instructed in the proper precautions for dealing with the substance, and the employee was furnished with personal protective equipment. If these conditions were not met, an employee could "absent himself from such risk of harm for the period necessary to avoid such danger without loss of regular compensation for such period."

This provision encountered stiff opposition in the House. * * *

The bill that was reported to and, with a few amendments, passed by the Senate never contained a "strike with pay" provision. It did, however, give employees the means by which they could request immediate Labor Department inspections. These two characteristics of the bill were underscored on the floor of the Senate by Senator Williams, the bill's sponsor.

After passage of the Williams bill by the Senate, it and the Steiger [substitute] bill were submitted to a Conference Committee. There, the House acceded to the Senate bill's inspection request provisions.

The petitioner reads into this legislative history a congressional intent incompatible with an administrative interpretation of the Act such as is embodied in the regulation at issue in this case. The petitioner argues that Congress' overriding concern in rejecting the "strike with pay" provision was to avoid giving employees a unilateral authority to walk off the job which they might abuse in order to intimidate or harass their employer. Congress deliberately chose instead, the petitioner maintains, to grant employees the power to request immediate administrative inspections of the workplace which could in appropriate cases lead to coercive judicial remedies. As the petitioner views the regulation, therefore, it gives to workers precisely what Congress determined to withhold from them.

We read the legislative history differently. Congress rejected a provision that did not concern itself at all with conditions posing real and immediate threats of death or severe injury. The remedy which the rejected provision furnished employees could have been invoked only after 60 days had passed following HEW's inspection and notification that improperly high levels of toxic substances were present in the workplace. Had that inspection revealed employment conditions posing a threat of imminent and grave harm, the Secretary of Labor would presumably have requested, long before expiration of the 60–day period, a court injunction pursuant to other provisions of the Daniels bill.

Consequently, in rejecting the Daniels bill's "strike with pay" provision, Congress was not rejecting a legislative provision dealing with the highly perilous and fast-moving situations covered by the regulation now before us.

It is also important to emphasize that what primarily troubled Congress about the Daniels bill's "strike with pay" provision was its requirement that employees be paid their regular salary after having properly invoked their right to refuse to work under the section. It is instructive that virtually every time the issue of an employee's right to absent himself from hazardous work was discussed in the legislative debates, it was in the context of the employee's right to continue to receive his usual compensation.

When it rejected the "strike with pay" concept, therefore, Congress very clearly meant to reject a law unconditionally imposing upon employers an obligation to continue to pay their employees their regular paychecks when they absented themselves from work for reasons of safety. But the regulation at issue here does not require employers to pay workers who refuse to perform their assigned tasks in the face of imminent danger. It simply provides that in such cases the employer may not "discriminate" against the employees involved. An employer "discriminates" against an employee only when he treats that employee less favorably than he treats others similarly situated.

2

The second aspect of the Act's legislative history upon which the petitioner relies is the rejection by Congress of provisions contained in both the Daniels and the Williams bills that would have given Labor Department officials, in imminent-danger situations, the power temporarily to shut down all or part of an employer's plant. These provisions aroused considerable opposition in both Houses of Congress. The hostility engendered in the House of Representatives led Representative Daniels to delete his erosion of the provision in proposing amendments to his original bill. The Steiger bill that ultimately passed the House gave the Labor Department no such authority. The Williams bill, as approved by the Senate, did contain an administrative shutdown provision, but the Conference Committee rejected this aspect of the Senate bill.

The petitioner infers from these events a congressional will hostile to the regulation in question here. The regulation, the petitioner argues, provides employees with the very authority to shut down an employer's plant that was expressly denied a more expert and objective United States Department of Labor.

As we read the pertinent legislative history, however, the petitioner misconceives the thrust of Congress' concern. Those in Congress who prevented passage of the administrative shutdown provisions in the Daniels and Williams bills were opposed to the unilateral authority those provisions gave to federal officials, without any judicial safeguards, drastically to impair the operation of an employer's business. Congressional opponents also feared that the provisions might jeopardize the Government's otherwise neutral role in labor-management relations.

Neither of these congressional concerns is implicated by the regulation before us. The regulation accords no authority to Government officials. It simply permits private employees of a private employer to avoid workplace conditions that they believe pose grave dangers to their own safety. The employees have no power under the regulation to order their employer to correct the hazardous condition or to clear the dangerous workplace of others. Moreover, any employee who acts in reliance on the regulation runs the risk of discharge or reprimand in the event a court subsequently finds that he acted unreasonably or in bad faith. The regulation, therefore, does not remotely resemble the legislation that Congress rejected.

C

For these reasons we conclude that 29 CFR § 1977.12(b)(2) (1979) was promulgated by the Secretary in the valid exercise of his authority under the Act. Accordingly, the judgment of the Court of Appeals is affirmed.

5. THE UNION'S OBLIGATION TO PROVIDE A SAFE WORKPLACE

UNITED STEELWORKERS OF AMERICA v. RAWSON

Supreme Court of the United States, 1990.
495 U.S. 362, 110 S.Ct. 1904, 109 L.Ed.2d 362.

JUSTICE WHITE delivered the opinion of the Court.

* * *

I

This dispute arises out of an underground fire that occurred on May 2, 1972, at the Sunshine Mine in Kellogg, Idaho, and caused the deaths of 91 miners. Respondents, the survivors of four of the deceased miners, filed this state-law wrongful death action in Idaho state court. Their complaint alleged that the miners' deaths were proximately caused by fraudulent and negligent acts of petitioner United Steelworkers of America (Union), the exclusive bargaining representative of the miners working at the Sunshine Mine. As to the negligence claim, the complaint specifically alleged that the Union "undertook to act as accident prevention representative and enforcer of an agreement negotiated between [sic] [the Union] on behalf of the deceased miners," and "undertook to provide representatives who inspected [the Sunshine Mine] and pretended to enforce the contractual accident prevention clauses." Respondents' answers to interrogatories subsequently made clear that their suit was based on contentions that the Union had, through a collective bargaining agreement negotiated with the operator of the Sunshine Mine, caused to be established a joint management/labor safety committee intended to exert influence on management on mine safety measures; that members of the safety committee designated by the Union had been inadequately trained on mine safety issues; and that the Union, through its representatives on the safety committee, had negligently performed inspections of the mine that it had promised to conduct, failing to uncover obvious and discoverable deficiencies.

* * *

After extensive discovery, the trial court * * * granted summary judgment for the Union. * * *

The Idaho Supreme Court * * * concluded that respondents had stated a valid claim under Idaho law that was not pre-empted by federal labor law. [That decision was appealed to The United States Supreme Court, which remanded the case for further consideration in light of *Electrical Workers v. Hechler,* 481 U.S. 851, 107 S.Ct. 2161, 95 L.Ed.2d 791 (1987).]

On remand, the Supreme Court of Idaho "adhere[d] to [its] opinion as written." The court also distinguished *Hechler,* stressing that there we had considered a situation where the alleged duty of care arose from the collective-bargaining agreement, whereas in this case "the activity was concededly undertaken and the standard of care is imposed by state law without reference to the collective bargaining agreement." The court further stated that it was "not faced with looking at the Collective Bargaining Agreement to determine whether it imposes some new duty upon the union—rather it is conceded that the union undertook to inspect and, thus, the issue is solely whether that inspection was negligently performed under traditional Idaho tort law."

* * *

Over 30 years ago, this Court held that § 301 not only provides the federal courts with jurisdiction over controversies involving collective-bargaining agreements but also authorizes the courts to fashion "a body of federal law for the enforcement of these collective bargaining agreements." *Textile Workers v. Lincoln Mills of Alabama,* 353 U.S. 448, 451, 77 S.Ct. 912, 915, 1 L.Ed.2d 972 (1957). Since then, the Court has made clear that § 301 is a potent source of federal labor law, for though state courts have concurrent jurisdiction over controversies involving collective-bargaining agreements, *Charles Dowd Box Co. v. Courtney,* 368 U.S. 502, 82 S.Ct. 519, 7 L.Ed.2d 483 (1962), state courts must apply federal law in deciding those claims, *Teamsters v. Lucas Flour Co.,* 369 U.S. 95, 82 S.Ct. 571, 7 L.Ed.2d 593 (1962), and indeed any state-law cause of action for violation of collective-bargaining agreements is entirely displaced by federal law under § 301, see *Avco Corp. v. Machinists,* 390 U.S. 557, 88 S.Ct. 1235, 20 L.Ed.2d 126 (1968). State law is thus "pre-empted" by § 301 in that only the federal law fashioned by the courts under § 301 governs the interpretation and application of collective-bargaining agreements.

In recent cases, we have recognized that the pre-emptive force of § 301 extends beyond state-law contract actions. In *Allis–Chalmers Corp. v. Lueck,* 471 U.S. 202, 105 S.Ct. 1904, 85 L.Ed.2d 206 (1985), we held that a state-law tort action against an employer may be pre-empted by § 301 if the duty to the employee of which the tort is a violation is created by a collective-bargaining agreement and without existence independent of the agreement. Any other result, we reasoned, would "allow parties to evade the requirements of § 301 by relabeling their contract claims as claims for tortious breach of contract." *Id.,* at 211, 105 S.Ct., at 1911. We extended this rule of pre-emption to a tort suit by an employee against her union in *Electrical Workers v. Hechler, supra.* There Hechler alleged that her union had by virtue of its collective-bargaining agreement with the employer and its relationship with her assumed the duty to ensure that she was provided with a safe workplace, and that the union had violated this duty. As in *Allis–Chalmers,* the duty relied on by Hechler was one without existence independent of the collective-bargaining agreement (unions not, under the common law of Florida, being charged with a duty to exercise reasonable care in providing a safe workplace, see 481 U.S., at 859–860, 107 S.Ct. at 2167) but was allegedly created by the collective-bargaining agreement, of which Hechler claimed to be a third-party beneficiary, see *id.,* at 861, 107 S.Ct., at 2167–68. Because resolution of the tort claim would require a court to "ascertain, first, whether the collective-bargaining agreement in fact placed an implied duty of care on the Union . . ., and second, the nature and scope of that duty," *id.,* at 862, 107 S.Ct., at 2168, we held that the tort claim was not sufficiently independent of the collective-bargaining agreement to withstand the pre-emptive force of § 301.

At first glance it would not appear difficult to apply these principles to the instant case. Respondents alleged in their complaint that the Union was negligent in its role as "enforcer of an agreement negotiated between [*sic*] [the Union] on behalf of the deceased miners," a plain reference to the collective-bargaining agreement with the operator of the Sunshine Mine.

* * * Prior to our remand, the Supreme Court of Idaho evidently was of this view as well. The court noted then that the Union could be liable under state tort law because it allegedly had contracted to inspect, and had in fact inspected the mine "pursuant to the provisions of the collective bargaining agreement." 111 Idaho, at 638, 726 P.2d, at 750. Although the Idaho Supreme Court believed that resolution of the tort claim would not require interpretation of the terms of the collective-bargaining agreement, it acknowledged that the provisions of that agreement determined "the nature and scope of the Union's duty," *id.,* at 640, 726 P.2d, at 752.

The situation is complicated, however, by the Idaho Supreme Court's opinion after our remand. Although the court stated that it adhered to its prior opinion as written, 115 Idaho, at 788, 770 P.2d, at 797, it also rejected the suggestion that there was any need to look to the collective-bargaining agreement to discern whether it placed any implied duty on the union. Rather, Idaho law placed a duty of care on the Union because the Union did, in fact, actively inspect the mine, and the Union could be held liable for the negligent performance of that inspection. *Id.,* at 787, 770 P.2d, at 796. According to the Supreme Court of Idaho, the Union may be liable under state tort law because its duty to perform that inspection reasonably arose from the fact of the inspection itself rather than the fact that the provision for the Union's participation in mine inspection was contained in the labor contract.

As we see it, however, respondents' tort claim cannot be described as independent of the collective-bargaining agreement. This is not a situation where the Union's delegates are accused of acting in a way that might violate the duty of reasonable care owed to every person in society. There is no allegation, for example, that members of the safety committee negligently caused damage to the structure of the mine, an act that could be unreasonable irrespective of who committed it and could foreseeably cause injury to any person who might possibly be in the vicinity.

Nor do we understand the Supreme Court of Idaho to have held that any casual visitor in the mine would be liable for violating some duty to the miners if the visitor failed to report obvious defects to the appropriate authorities. Indeed, the court did not disavow its previous opinion, where it acknowledged that the Union's representatives were participating in the inspection process pursuant to the provisions of the collective-bargaining agreement and that the agreement determined the nature and scope of the Union's duty. If the Union failed to perform a duty in connection with inspection, it was a duty arising out of the collective-bargaining agreement signed by the Union as the bargaining agent for the miners. Clearly, the enforcement of that agreement and the remedies for its breach are matters governed by federal law. Accordingly, this suit, if it is to go forward at all, must proceed as a case controlled by federal rather than state law.

III

The Union insists that the case against it may not go forward even under federal law. It argues first that only the duty of fair representation governs the exercise of its representational functions under the collective-bargaining contract, and that a member may not sue it under § 301 for breach of contract. Second, the Union submits that even if it may be sued under § 301, the labor agreement contains no enforceable promise made by it to the members of the unit in connection with inspecting the mine. Third, the Union asserts that as the case now stands, it is charged with only negligence, which is insufficient to prove a breach of its duty of fair representation.

* * *

The Union's duty of fair representation arises from the National Labor Relations Act itself. The duty of fair representation is thus a matter of status rather than contract. We have never held, however, that as a matter of federal law, a labor union is *prohibited* from voluntarily assuming additional duties to the employees by contract. Although at one time it may have appeared most unlikely that unions would be called upon to assume such duties, see *Humphrey v. Moore,* 375 U.S. 335, 356–357, 84 S.Ct. 363, 375–376, 11 L.Ed.2d 370 (1964) (Goldberg, J., concurring in result), nonetheless "it is of the utmost importance that the law reflect the realities of industrial life and the nature of the collective bargaining process," *id.,* at 358, 84 S.Ct., at 376, and it may well be that if unions begin to assume duties traditionally viewed as the prerogatives of management, cf. *Breininger, supra,* [493 U.S.] at 87–88; *Electrical Workers v. Hechler,* 481 U.S., at 859–860, employees will begin to demand that unions be held more strictly to account in their carrying out those duties.

* * *

But having said as much, we also think it necessary to emphasize caution, lest the courts be precipitate in their efforts to find unions contractually bound to employees by collective-bargaining agreements. The doctrine of fair representation is an important check on the arbitrary exercise of union power, but it is a purposefully limited check, for a "wide range of reasonableness must be allowed a statutory bargaining representative in serving the unit it represents." *Ford Motor Co. v. Huffman,* 345 U.S. 330, 338, 73 S.Ct. 681, 686, 97 L.Ed. 1048 (1953). If an employee claims that a union owes him a more far-reaching duty, he must be able to point to language in the collective-bargaining agreement specifically indicating an intent to create obligations enforceable against the union by the individual employees. Cf. *Republic Steel Corp. v. Maddox,* 379 U.S. 650, 653, 85 S.Ct. 614, 616–17, 13 L.Ed.2d 580 (1965).

Applying this principle to the case at hand, we are quite sure that respondents may not maintain a § 301 suit against the Union. Nothing in the collective-bargaining agreement suggests that it creates rights directly enforceable by the individual employees against the Union.

* * *

Moreover, under traditional principles of contract interpretation, respondents have no claim, for with exceptions under federal labor law not relevant here, see *Lewis v. Benedict Coal Corp.,* 361 U.S. 459, 468–471, 80 S.Ct. 489, 494–496, 4 L.Ed.2d 442 (1960), third-party beneficiaries generally have no greater rights in a contract than does the promisee. For the respondents to have an enforceable right as third-party beneficiaries against the Union, at the very least the employer must have an enforceable right as promisee. But the provisions in the collective-bargaining agreement relied on by respondents are not promises by the Union to the employer. Cf. *Teamsters v. Lucas Flour Co.,* 369 U.S., at 104–106, 82 S.Ct., at 577–578. They are, rather, concessions made by the employer to the Union, a limited surrender of the employer's exclusive authority over mine safety. A violation by the employer of the provisions allowing inspection of the mine by Union delegates might form the basis of a § 301 suit against the employer, but we are not presented with such a case.

In performing its functions under the collective-bargaining agreement, the Union did, as it concedes, owe the miners a duty of fair representation, but we have already noted that respondents' allegation of mere negligence will not state a claim for violation of that duty. Indeed, respondents have never specifically relied on the federal duty of fair representation, nor have they alleged that the Union improperly discriminated among its members or acted in arbitrary and capricious fashion in failing to exercise its duties under the collective-bargaining agreement. Cf. *Vaca v. Sipes,* 386 U.S., at 177, 87 S.Ct. at 909–10.

* * *

It follows that the judgment of the Supreme Court of Idaho must be *Reversed.*

JUSTICE KENNEDY, with whom THE CHIEF JUSTICE and JUSTICE SCALIA join, dissenting.

* * *

Although we have inferred that Congress intended to impose a duty of fair representation in § 9(a), I see no justification for the further conclusion that Congress desired to grant unions an immunity from all state tort law. Nothing about a union's status as the exclusive representative of a bargaining unit creates a need to exempt it from general duties to exercise due care to avoid injuring others. At least to some extent, therefore, I would conclude that Congress "by silence indicate[d] a purpose to let state regulation be imposed." * * *

Idaho may hold the union liable for negligence in inspecting the mine. The strength and legitimacy of the State's interests in mine safety stand beyond question; the union's failure to exercise due care, according to the allegations, caused or contributed to the deaths of 91 Idaho miners. Allowing this case to proceed to trial, moreover, would pose little threat to the federal regulatory scheme. State courts long have held unions liable for personal injuries under state law. * * *

The Union presents no argument that this longstanding practice has interfered with federal labor regulation. Indeed, as the Court itself holds, nothing in the federal statutory scheme addresses the Union's conduct or provides redress for the injuries that it may have produced. See *ante,* at 1910–1913.

The Union's position also deviates from the well-established position of the courts of appeals. These courts have found preemption by the duty of fair representation in two situations. First, the courts have said that the duty of fair representation pre-empts state duties that depend on a collective-bargaining agreement or on the union's status as the exclusive collective bargaining agent. As noted above, however, the Union's duties in this case do not stem from a contract or from its status as a union. Second, other courts have found the federal duty of fair representation to supplant equivalent state law duties.... In this case, state law differs from federal law in that the duty of fair representation does not address the conduct in question. The Union, as a result, has shown no support for its contention that the duty of fair representation pre-empts the Idaho tort law. For these reasons, I dissent.

F. PROBLEM 3-3

The Individual Worker at Risk: The Union's Dilemma

The current collective bargaining agreement between Enderby Industries and the United Factory Workers is about to expire. Eulah Blair, the union negotiator, and Matthew Crickboom, Enderby's Vice President for Labor, traditionally meet just before the formal negotiations to hold an off-the-record exploratory session or two. We join them at two successive sessions.

Day 1

Blair: You know, you're killing us with this random drug testing. People who come in new, we don't care about them. Do what you want. But once they're hired and we represent them, then we have to deal with this problem. We are getting lots of complaints from our employees. They say not only do you get a blood test and urine analysis when you hire them, as well as a complete medical and family history, but you continue to do random testing and screening. They're afraid employment decisions are being made on the basis of medical information that is not shared with them and that often cannot be understood by them; in any event testing is an invasion of their privacy. The testing may show prior exposure, but not necessarily current performance impairment. My membership is demanding you put a stop to this.

Crickboom: I'm aware of how they feel. I don't think I'd like it either. But try to see what we're up against. Drug and alcohol abuse seems to be rampant. We have workers out there who mix batches of dangerous chemicals, work with hazardous machinery, pour hot plastic into molds, drive forklift trucks and so on. They are dangerous to themselves and others if they're on something. And what about our products? For instance, we make polyurethane seal for an aircraft engine to precise tolerances. What happens to us if an inspector who's high lets a substandard piece pass through? We can't take that kind of risk of product failure.

Oh I know. You'll say our only business is with how the worker behaves on the job. If we see a problem, then we can test. But I tell you that's too late. The only way to go is random drug testing.

Blair: It seems to me that there are plenty of impairments that a worker encounters and plenty of ways to sense trouble. Why must we perpetuate the notion that drug testing is the cure for all workplace ills? Typical tests include drugs that haven't been shown to impair performance. What is more, when you test you get a false sense of having made the workplace safer even though none of the tests cover a lot of substances that in fact impair performance, stuff like industrial solvents.

Crickboom: We have the right to make our own decisions about protecting our capital investment. We have the ultimate liability for workplace harms, and we have to do what we can to create a safe workplace. Even the public sector cases recognize the employer's interests.

As you know, OSHA already requires us to perform certain routine tests on employees to monitor for exposure to toxic substances. We may have to move employees out of extremely hazardous situations where they are especially at risk. But if we see a problem with drugs, we'll come down hard on the employee. We will of course take every precaution to make sure this information is kept confidential.

Blair: I always felt this testing for exposure is a cop-out. You won't spend a nickel on engineering controls. Instead, you spread the exposure among the workers. And think of the hypocrisy. When we say there's some danger from VDT exposure you tell us the evidence is inconclusive. But when you want to test for drugs, you say the risks are strong enough to act. What your tests really accomplish is the discouragement of workers' use of medications employees need to cope with the stresses of their jobs.

Crickboom: These are tough choices. You want it the other way? Even if we had the technology to make a safer work environment, we'd be killed competitively—and your people would be out of jobs.

Blair: Well, I'd better tell you that we're going to push for a clause that opposes all testing and screening except where the employer can show probable cause—that is, where the employee actually exhibits on the job symptoms of drug problems. As for screening for exposure, we're going to insist that any employee who is moved from a job because of exposure be placed on another job with no loss of pay.

Crickboom: Then you should understand that we'll resist both these demands. We have the ultimate responsibility for health and safety. Our insurance carriers insist on some of this testing. As for the wage guarantees, OSHA doesn't require them and we're not about to become noncompetitive by paying people for more than they do. For us this is a strike issue. I know these workers. They won't strike over this. It's not a bread and butter issue.

Blair: If your insurance carriers don't get their way, they may raise your premiums; but, believe me, the costs of these tests will be greater, and your injury rate isn't going to be changed because of the tests.

Day 2

Blair: I guess you were right. We're not going to strike over these testing issues. We'll rely on the existing just cause language as protection against unfair testing or improper use of test results.

We do need some protection for workers who are removed if they test positively on toxic workplace exposures. We'd like them to be able to bump into any other job for which they are qualified, on the basis of seniority, and retain their wage level.

You know, Matt, off the record, the rank and file response was very interesting. Some of our people actually favored testing. Especially for AIDS and other diseases they think are contagious. This put me in a tough spot. Should I give in to their wishes? I always felt it was our role to protect individual privacy and dignity. Yet here are the people I represent, with a very different set of values. I guess I weaken on principle too when I give in on testing for new employees. I don't represent them yet, so I don't protect them.

Crickboom: I sympathize with your position. Believe it or not, I like to see the worker get a fair shake. Consider the AIDS victim. Here's what we face: For a while the AIDS victim will be able to perform his job. But when he gets sick he misses more and more days of work, and that costs us. And the higher his experience ratings, the more our premium costs for his health insurance will be. That's one reason we're anxious to go along with the insurance company's request for HIV screening. If nobody tests positively, the rates may be lower. I'd like to see the AIDS victim stay on the job as long as he can, with dignity. But why is it my problem? The issue is played out at the workplace, but it belongs to all of society.

But now that we've both let our hair down, let's get some mileage out of this. You back off these wage protection provisions and I'll go along with the bumping proposal.

Day 223

The parties had formal negotiations after the discussion set out above. Eventually they went through a formal, on-the-record version of that dialogue, at much greater length and with more rancor. The union made and later withdrew a proposal barring drug testing, and said it would instead rely on existing contract language and external law. It made its wage protection demand; the company proposed the bumping proposal discussed above. The contract was signed with no provision at all for drug or AIDS testing or test consequences.

Subsequently, the following situation arose: Braveman was a forklift truck operator at Enderby. He was asked to submit to blood and urine tests not required by OSHA provisions and regulations. Believing strongly in his privacy, he refused to take the tests. The company did not discharge or suspend him for his refusal, but it did treat the refusal as the equivalent of a positive test result. Consistent with the bumping proposal it had made during negotiations, the company removed Braveman from the forklift operator's job and transferred him to a vacant cleaner's job, where the company claims there is less risk of injury or damage from an employee's being under the influence of drugs. The cleaner's job pays $1.75 less per hour than the forklift operator's job. The Company has refused to maintain Braveman's former wage level.

Claiming that the Company had no right to require him to submit to these tests, to transfer him, or to lower his wage, Braveman filed a grievance. In the grievance, Braveman and the union relied only on the contract provision that limited discipline to "good cause." Having exhausted the grievance procedure, is the union free to refuse to take the matter to arbitration? If the union goes to arbitration, what are its chances for success?

VACA v. SIPES

Supreme Court of the United States, 1967.
386 U.S. 171, 87 S.Ct. 903, 17 L.Ed.2d 842.

[Upon his return from sick leave, Owens, the grievant, was discharged for poor health. He filed a grievance. The union used the grievance process to try to have Owens reinstated. The medical evidence on Owens was conflicting. The union sent Owens to a doctor at union expense to try to get a favorable medical opinion. When this didn't come through, the union decided not to take the case to arbitration, as there wasn't sufficient medical evidence to support Owens.

Owens then brought suit against the union in state court in Missouri, alleging that the union had "arbitrarily, capriciously and without just or reasonable reason or cause" refused to take his case to arbitration. Owens also sued his employer, Swift, for breach of contract in discharging him. A jury awarded Owens $7,000 compensatory damages and $3,300 punitive damages in his suit against the union.

The union first argued that Owens' suit was preempted. The NLRB had already established that a union's breach of the duty of fair representation is an unfair labor practice. Thus, under doctrines you are familiar with, it was logical to assert that since the union's treatment of Owens was arguably an unfair labor practice, it was the Board's province alone to deal with the claim. But the Court concluded that the preemption doctrine did not apply here:

"[A] primary justification for the pre-emption doctrine—the need to avoid conflicting rules of substantive law in the labor relations area and the desirability of leaving the development of such rules to the administrative agency created by Congress for that purpose—is not applicable to cases involving alleged breaches of the union duty of fair representation. The doctrine was judicially developed in Steele and its progeny, and suits alleging breach of the duty remained judicially cognizable long after the NLRB was given unfair labor practice jurisdiction over union activities by the L.M.R.A. Moreover, when the Board declared in Miranda Fuel that a union's breach of its duty of fair representation would henceforth be treated as an unfair labor practice, the Board adopted and applied the doctrine as it had been developed by the federal courts. * * * Finally, as the dissenting Board members in Miranda Fuel have pointed out, fair representation duty suits often require review of the substantive positions taken and policies pursued by a union in its negotiation of a collective bargaining agreement and in its handling of the grievance machinery; as these matters are not normally within the Board's unfair labor practice jurisdiction, it can be doubted whether the Board brings substantially greater expertise to bear on these problems than do the courts, which have been engaged in this type of review since the Steele decision."

A second reason for the Court's conclusion that the suit is not preempted has to do with the peculiar theory of Owens' claim. Since it is not an obvious explanation, it bears a little amplification. This summary is taken from part II B of the *Vaca* decision.

You will recall that Owens' claim is at bottom a suit for breach of contract by his employer. That is, the employer breached its contractual promise not to discharge him except for cause. Had Owens sued his employer alone, the employer would have responded that Owens must exhaust his contractual remedy—file a grievance and proceed to arbitration: "Since the employee's claim is based upon breach of the collective bargaining agreement, he is bound by terms of that agreement which govern the manner in which contractual rights may be enforced. For this reason, it is settled that the employee must at least attempt to exhaust exclusive grievance and arbitration procedures established by the bargaining agreement."

This rule is easy to apply if the union takes the case to arbitration. Not only will the grievant have exhausted the agreed upon procedure, but under the Trilogy both the grievant and employer will be bound by the result. But what if the union refuses to take the case to arbitration? Since most collective agreements provide that arbitration is a matter between the union and the company, and confer on the individual no rights to pursue his own arbitration, the union's decision to drop the grievance could be said to both satisfy the exhaustion requirement and bar the individual. But, said the Court, "because these contractual remedies have been devised and are often controlled by the union and the employer, they may well prove unsatisfactory or unworkable for the individual grievant. The problem then is to determine under what circumstances the individual employee may obtain judicial review of his breach-of-contract claim despite his failure to secure relief through the contractual remedial procedures."

The key language of *Vaca* follows. As you pore over it, try to determine exactly what it is that constitutes a *wrongful* refusal by the union to carry the case to arbitration.]

* * *

III.

Petitioners contend, as they did in their motion for judgment notwithstanding the jury's verdict, that Owens failed to prove that the Union breached its duty of fair representation in its handling of Owens' grievance. Petitioners also argue that the Supreme Court of Missouri, in rejecting this contention, applied a standard that is inconsistent with governing principles of federal law with respect to the Union's duty to an individual employee in its processing of grievances under the collective bargaining agreement with Swift. We agree with both contentions.

A.   In holding that the evidence at trial supported the jury's verdict in favor of Owens, the Missouri Supreme Court stated:

"The essential issue submitted to the jury was whether the union * * * arbitrarily * * * refused to carry said grievance * * * through the fifth step.* * *

"We have concluded that there was sufficient substantial evidence from which the jury reasonably could have found the foregoing issue in favor of plaintiff. It is notable that no physician actually testified in the case. Both sides were content to rely upon written statements. Three physicians certified that plaintiff was able to perform his regular work. Three other physicians certified that they had taken plaintiff's blood pressure and that the readings were approximately 160 over 100. It may be inferred that such a reading does not indicate that his blood pressure was dangerously high. Moreover, plaintiff's evidence showed that he had actually done hard physical labor periodically during the four years following his discharge. We accordingly rule this point adversely to defendants." 397 S.W.2d, at 665.

Quite obviously, the question which the Missouri Supreme Court thought dispositive of the issue of liability was whether the evidence supported Owens' assertion that he had been wrongfully discharged by Swift, regardless of the Union's good faith in reaching a contrary conclusion. This was also the major concern of the plaintiff at trial: the bulk of Owens' evidence was directed at whether he was medically fit at the time of discharge and whether he had performed heavy work after that discharge.

A breach of the statutory duty of fair representation occurs only when a union's conduct toward a member of the collective bargaining unit is arbitrary, discriminatory, or in bad faith. There has been considerable debate over the extent of this duty in the context of a union's enforcement of the grievance and arbitration procedures in a collective bargaining agreement. See generally Blumrosen, The Worker and Three Phases of Unionism: Administrative and Judicial Control of the Worker–Union Relationship, 61 Mich.L.Rev. 1435, 1482–1501 (1963); Comment, Federal Protection of Individual Rights under Labor Contracts, 73 Yale L.J. 1215 (1964). Some have suggested that every individual employee should have the right to have his grievance taken to arbitration. Others have urged that the union be given substantial discretion (if the collective bargaining agreement so provides) to decide whether a grievance should be taken to arbitration, subject only to the duty to refrain from patently wrongful conduct such as racial discrimination or personal hostility.

Though we accept the proposition that a union may not arbitrarily ignore a meritorious grievance or process it in perfunctory fashion, we do not agree that the individual employee has an absolute right to have his grievance taken to arbitration regardless of the provisions of the applicable collective bargaining agreement. In L.M.R.A. § 203(d), 61 Stat. 154, 29 U.S.C. § 173(d), Congress declared that "Final adjustment by a method agreed upon by the parties is * * * the desirable method for settlement of grievance disputes arising over the application or interpretation of an existing collective-bargaining agreement." In providing for a grievance and arbitration procedure which gives the union discretion to supervise the grievance machinery and to invoke arbitration, the employer and the union contemplate that each will endeavor in good faith to settle grievances short of arbitration. Through this settlement process, frivolous grievances are ended prior to the most costly and time-consuming step in the grievance procedures. Moreover, both sides are assured that similar complaints will be treated consistently, and major problem areas in the interpretation of the collective bargaining contract can be isolated and perhaps resolved. And finally, the settlement process furthers the interest of the union as statutory agent and as coauthor of the bargaining agreement in representing the employees in the enforcement of that agreement. See Cox, Rights Under a Labor Agreement, 69 Harv.L.Rev. 601 (1956).

If the individual employee could compel arbitration of his grievance regardless of its merit, the settlement machinery provided by the contract would be substantially undermined, thus destroying the employer's confidence in the union's authority and returning the individual grievant to the vagaries of independent and unsystematic negotiation. Moreover, under such a rule, a significantly greater number of grievances would proceed to arbitration.[15] This would greatly increase the cost of the

---

15. Under current grievance practices, an attempt is usually made to keep the number of arbitrated grievances to a minimum. An officer of the National Union testified in this case that only one of 967 grievances filed at all of Swift's plants between September 1961 and October 1963 was taken to arbitration. And the AFL–CIO's *amicus* brief reveals similar performances at General Motors Corporation and United States Steel Corporation, two of the Nation's largest unionized employers: less than .05% of all written grievances filed during a recent period at General Motors required arbitration, while only 5.6% of the grievances processed beyond the first step at United States Steel were decided by an arbitrator.

grievance machinery and could so overburden the arbitration process as to prevent it from functioning successfully. It can well be doubted whether the parties to collective bargaining agreements would long continue to provide for detailed grievance and arbitration procedures of the kind encouraged by L.M.R.A. § 203(d), supra, if their power to settle the majority of grievances short of the costlier and more time-consuming steps was limited by a rule permitting the grievant unilaterally to invoke arbitration. Nor do we see substantial danger to the interests of the individual employee if his statutory agent is given the contractual power honestly and in good faith to settle grievances short of arbitration. For these reasons, we conclude that a union does not breach its duty of fair representation, and thereby open up a suit by the employee for breach of contract, merely because it settled the grievance short of arbitration.

For these same reasons, the standard applied here by the Missouri Supreme Court cannot be sustained. For if a union's decision that a particular grievance lacks sufficient merit to justify arbitration would constitute a breach of the duty of fair representation because a judge or jury later found the grievance meritorious, the union's incentive to settle such grievances short of arbitration would be seriously reduced. The dampening effect on the entire grievance procedure of this reduction of the union's freedom to settle claims in good faith would surely be substantial. Since the union's statutory duty of fair representation protects the individual employee from arbitrary abuses of the settlement device by providing him with recourse against both employer (in a § 301 suit) and union, this severe limitation on the power to settle grievances is neither necessary nor desirable. Therefore, we conclude that the Supreme Court of Missouri erred in upholding the verdict in this case solely on the ground that the evidence supported Owens' claim that he had been wrongfully discharged.

B. Applying the proper standard of union liability to the facts of this case, we cannot uphold the jury's award, for we conclude that as a matter of federal law the evidence does not support a verdict that the Union breached its duty of fair representation. As we have stated, Owens could not have established a breach of that duty merely by convincing the jury that he was in fact fit for work in 1960; he must also have proved arbitrary or bad-faith conduct on the part of the Union in processing his grievance. The evidence revealed that the Union diligently supervised the grievance into the fourth step of the bargaining agreement's procedure, with the Union's business representative serving as Owens' advocate throughout these steps. When Swift refused to reinstate Owens on the basis of his medical reports indicating reduced blood pressure, the Union sent him to another doctor of his own choice, at Union expense, in an attempt to amass persuasive medical evidence of Owens' fitness for work. When this examination proved unfavorable, the Union concluded that it could not establish a wrongful discharge. It then encouraged Swift to find light work for Owens at the plant. When this effort failed, the Union determined that arbitration would be fruitless and suggested to Owens that he accept Swift's offer to send him to a heart association for rehabilitation. At this point, Owens' grievance was suspended in the fourth step in the hope that he might be rehabilitated.

In administering the grievance and arbitration machinery as statutory agent of the employees, a union must, in good faith and in a nonarbitrary manner, make decisions as to the merits of particular grievances. See Humphrey v. Moore, 375 U.S. 335, 349–350, 84 S.Ct. 363, 371–372, 11 L.Ed.2d 370; Ford Motor Co. v. Huffman, 345 U.S. 330, 337–339, 73 S.Ct. 681, 685–687, 97 L.Ed. 1048. In a case such as this, when Owens supplied the Union with medical evidence supporting his position, the Union might well have breached its duty had it ignored Owens' complaint or had it processed the grievance in a perfunctory manner. See Cox, Rights under a Labor Agreement, 69 Harv.L.Rev., at 632–634. But here the Union processed the grievance into the fourth step, attempted to gather sufficient evidence to prove Owens' case, attempted to secure for Owens less vigorous work at the plant, and joined in the employer's efforts to have Owens rehabilitated. Only when these efforts all proved unsuccessful did the Union conclude both that arbitration would be fruitless and that the grievance should be dismissed. There was no evidence that any Union officer was personally hostile to Owens or that the Union acted at any time other than in good faith. Having concluded that the individual employee has no absolute right to have his grievance arbitrated under the collective bargaining agreement at issue, and that a breach of the duty of fair representation is not established merely by proof that the underlying grievance was meritorious, we must conclude that that duty was not breached here.

IV.

In our opinion, there is another important reason why the judgment of the Missouri Supreme Court cannot stand. Owens' suit against the Union was grounded on his claim that Swift had discharged him in violation of the applicable collective bargaining agreement. In his complaint, Owens alleged "that, as a direct result of said wrongful breach of said contract, by employer ... Plaintiff was damaged in the sum of Six Thousand, Five Hundred ($6,500.00) Dollars per year, continuing until the date of trial." For the Union's role in "preventing Plaintiff from completely exhausting administrative remedies," Owens requested, and the jury awarded, compensatory damages for the above-described breach of contract plus punitive damages of $3,000. We hold that such damages are not recoverable from the Union in the circumstances of this case.

The appropriate remedy for a breach of a union's duty of fair representation must vary with the circumstances of the particular breach. In this case, the employee's complaint was that the Union wrongfully failed to afford him the arbitration remedy against his employer established by the collective bargaining agreement. But the damages sought by Owens were primarily those suffered because of the employer's alleged breach of contract. Assuming for the moment that

Owens had been wrongfully discharged, Swift's only defense to a direct action for breach of contract would have been the Union's failure to resort to arbitration, and if that failure was itself a violation of the Union's statutory duty to the employee, there is no reason to exempt the employer from contractual damages which he would otherwise have had to pay. The difficulty lies in fashioning an appropriate scheme of remedies.

Petitioners urge that an employee be restricted in such circumstances to a decree compelling the employer and the union to arbitrate the underlying grievance. It is true that the employee's action is based on the employer's alleged breach of contract plus the union's alleged wrongful failure to afford him his contractual remedy of arbitration. For this reason, an order compelling arbitration should be viewed as one of the available remedies when a breach of the union's duty is proved. But we see no reason inflexibly to require arbitration in all cases. In some cases, for example, at least part of the employee's damages may be attributable to the union's breach of duty, and an arbitrator may have no power under the bargaining agreement to award such damages against the union. In other cases, the arbitrable issues may be substantially resolved in the course of trying the fair representation controversy. In such situations, the court should be free to decide the contractual claim and to award the employee appropriate damages or equitable relief.

A more difficult question is, what portion of the employee's damages may be charged to the union: in particular, may an award against a union include, as it did here, damages attributable solely to the employer's breach of contract? We think not. Though the union has violated a statutory duty in failing to press the grievance, it is the employer's unrelated breach of contract which triggered the controversy and which caused this portion of the employee's damages. The employee should have no difficulty recovering these damages from the employer, who cannot, as we have explained, hide behind the union's wrongful failure to act; in fact, the employer may be (and probably should be) joined as a defendant in the fair representation suit, as in Humphrey v. Moore, supra. It could be a real hardship on the union to pay these damages, even if the union were given a right of indemnification against the employer. With the employee assured of direct recovery from the employer, we see no merit in requiring the union to pay the employer's share of the damages.

The governing principle, then, is to apportion liability between the employer and the union according to the damage caused by the fault of each. Thus, damages attributable solely to the employer's breach of contract should not be charged to the union, but increases if any in those damages caused by the union's refusal to process the grievance should not be charged to the employer. In this case, even if the Union had breached its duty, all or almost all of Owens' damages would still be attributable to his allegedly wrongful discharge by Swift. For these reasons, even if the Union here had properly been found liable for a breach of duty, it is clear that the damage award was improper.

Reversed.

———

Three members of the Court concurred in the result in *Vaca,* but would have dismissed the state suit on the ground that the matter was preempted by the NLRA.

Justice Black dissented with characteristic pithiness:

> "The Court today opens slightly the courthouse door to an employee's incidental claim against his union for breach of its duty of fair representation, only to shut it in his face when he seeks direct judicial relief for his underlying and more valuable breach-of-contract claim against his employer * * *. Today's decision, while giving the worker an ephemeral right to sue his union for breach of its duty of fair representation, creates insurmountable obstacles to block his far more valuable right to sue his employer for breach of the collective bargaining agreement."

NOTE—THE DUTY OF FAIR REPRESENTATION

How do the doctrines developed in *Vaca v. Sipes* help you unravel the threads of the Braveman problem?

If you look at the problem as whether Braveman had a contractual right to refuse testing, and whether the contract entitled him to stay on his old job at his old level of wages, then the *Vaca* analysis fits well. The formulaic question is whether the union's refusal to pursue a claimed contractual right is "arbitrary, discriminatory, perfunctory, hostile, or in bad faith." As many have observed, these terms, which come out of the *Vaca* decision, aren't much help in resolving a specific factual question. See generally, The Changing Law of Fair Representation (J. McKelvey ed. 1985).

Should the allowable range of discretion the union enjoys in determining whether to take the grievance to arbitration depend on the strength of the contractual claim? Where the claim is solid (how many are?), Professor Clyde Summers argues that the union has virtually no discretion to refuse to take the case to arbitration. Once the union has negotiated a benefit for its members, he believes, it is obliged to take up the cudgels on any employee's behalf. What arguments can be made to refute Professor Summers?

WARNING: DAMAGES IN FAIR
REPRESENTATION SUITS

Whatever you tell the union about whether it had a duty to take Braveman's grievance to arbitration, you'd better warn the union that it faces stiff liability if a court concludes it acted improperly. A reading of the *Vaca* opinion will demonstrate to you that damages are to be apportioned between the employer and the union "according to the damage caused by the fault of each." The *Vaca* opinion emphasizes that if the employee was wrongfully discharged, his damages are attributable in large part to the employer's breach of contract. Said the Court, "With the employee assured of direct recovery from the employer, we see no merit in requiring the union to pay the employer's share of the damages."

In a more recent decision, however, Bowen v. United States Postal Service, 459 U.S. 212, 103 S.Ct. 588, 74 L.Ed.2d 402 (1983), the Court held that where the employee prevails in a fair representation claim, the employer is liable for back pay only up to the hypothetical date at which an arbitrator would have ordered the employee reinstated had the case gone to arbitration. The union is liable for all damages, including lost wages, beyond that point.

Think about that. When in doubt about whether a union is obliged to take a grievance to arbitration, what will you advise?

While a union faces potentially heavy damages under *Bowen* for its failure to carry a grievance to arbitration, it can take some comfort in the relatively short statute of limitations afforded an employee to pursue such a claim. While it might be thought that an employee's claim of unfair representation against his union is either a tort or a contract claim and, therefore, governed by the relatively long state statutes of limitations for such actions, the Court has adopted the six month statute of limitations for actions brought under the National Labor Relations Act. DelCostello v. International Broth. of Teamsters, 462 U.S. 151, 103 S.Ct. 2281, 76 L.Ed.2d 476 (1983).

This six month statute of limitations applies as well to fair representation cases in which the employee claims he was represented improperly in arbitration, a situation we shall look at shortly. Actions to set aside an arbitration award are typically governed by state statutes that impose a relatively short statute of limitations, for example, 90 days in New York State. The state's interest in arbitral finality yields, in such a jurisdiction, to the slightly longer period imposed under the uniform federal standard.

The duty of fair representation is useful in dealing with an isolated event involving single employees. For example, you can compare the way the employee was treated against the plain contract language and the treatment of other employees in the same boat. Or you can look at whether the union bore some political animosity towards the grievant, for example, because he opposed the incumbent president in the last election.

But what happens when the union must decide between large sets of different interests in the bargaining unit? For example, in the Braveman problem the screening programs may have had a heavier impact upon minority employees. Should the union oppose those programs in the interest of the younger employees? Or should it be concerned as well with the interests of others in the unit? Consider the proposed unit of registered nurses and nurse practitioners at Mercy Hospital in the problem in Chapter II. Can the nurse practitioners exempt themselves from the bargaining unit on the grounds that their interests are different than the registered nurses'? If they are included in the overall unit, does the duty of fair representation protect their interests from being submerged into the needs of the majority of employees? Or must you conclude that the duty of fair representation is simply inadequate to police the difficult political choices a union must make in choosing among conflicting interests in the workplace? Reconsider the *J.I. Case* and *Emporium Capwell* decisions in Chapter 2.

In order to decide whether it acted properly in not pressing for further restrictions against drug testing, and in not pursuing Braveman's grievance, the union has to know a little more about drug testing.

DALE M. FEINAUER, THE RELATIONSHIP BETWEEN WORKPLACE ACCIDENT RATES AND DRUG AND ALCOHOL ABUSE: THE UNPROVEN HYPOTHESIS
Winter 1990 Labor Studies Journal 3, 10–13.

[Professor Feinauer reviewed 31 reported research projects, which he believed were all the then-existing studies of the relationship of drug use and workplace accidents.]

SUMMARY OF AVAILABLE DATA

In summarizing data available in 1959 regarding the cost of alcohol abuse to industry, Observer noted,

> There is an appalling lack of concrete studies from which to make projections. * * * [T]he authoritativeness behind these statistics is specious. The fact is that these figures have found their way into rather wide acceptance more by virtue of repetition than anything else. They have been accepted without benefit of adequate scientific studies. This is not to say that these estimates are wide of the mark but rather to insist that it is not known how accurate or how wide of the mark they are.

Observer's comments from 1959 regarding the extent of our knowledge of the relationship between alcohol abuse and on-the-job accidents are still relevant today regarding both alcohol and drug use.

Commenting on the validity of presently available data, Mark Wright (director of the employee assistance program at the Adolph Coors Company) pointed out that statistics regarding the problems caused by drug and alcohol abuse are often provided by consultants and associations who treat and combat substance abuse. Hess, an official with the United Auto Workers, indicated that companies selling drug testing services are expected to grow significantly and that "these companies have shifted into high gear in order to promote their wares."

The absence of reliable data is exemplified by an article beginning with the question, "Drug abuse in industry—how does it affect safety?" and proceeded to assume there is a relationship without offering any supporting documentation. The widespread acceptance of a relationship between substance abuse and workplace accidents, even in the absence of supporting data, may be a result of its intuitive appeal and the well publicized and documented relationship between substance abuse and motor vehicle accident rates; alcohol alone is a factor in half of all traffic fatalities.

Several potential reasons why accident rates may not be higher for alcohol abusers have been suggested. Extra caution among drinking drivers was reported by Mulford and may be applicable to on-the-job accidents as well as driving. Absenteeism, when significantly under the influence of alcohol, and self selection into repetitive jobs that allow managing the effect of alcohol have also been suggested as reasons alcoholics would not have higher accident rates. Finally, but somewhat hard to accept, is the argument made by alcoholics that they are less likely to be involved in workplace accidents because they have a few drinks to steady themselves during working hours. All of these reasons appear equally relevant to the use of other drugs in the workplace as they are to the use of alcohol.

Importance of Empirically Testing the Hypothesis

As Observer noted, the absence of reliable data does not imply that a relationship does or does not exist; rather it is a call to empirically test the hypothesis that substance abuse is related to workplace accidents. In addition to our responsibility as scholars to ascertain truth, there are two practical reasons to determine the nature of the relationship between substance abuse and on-the-job accidents:

1. the assumed relationship has provided the legal/ethical rationale for drug testing and is the reason given to unions for accepting testing programs;

2. the nature of the relationship is important to the efficient use of firms' resources to promote employee health and combat workplace accidents.

Drug and alcohol tests are by their nature intrusive, and are viewed by many as demeaning and an invasion of individual privacy. However, numerous authors as well as former President Reagan have argued that the relationship between substance abuse and public safety is an overriding rationale for drug testing. Court rulings that support testing of workers have consistently emphasized public safety concerns as the rationale for testing.

Workplace safety concerns have also played a significant role in justifying testing. Rothstein indicated that showing "substantial danger" to workers themselves is an important legal component defending drug testing programs. Denenberg noted that arbitrators are likely to accept testing programs only if the programs promote a safe and productive workplace. In a survey of 10,000 members of The American Management Association, the most common reason cited for instituting drug testing was a concern for workplace safety; 72 percent of the respondents indicated this was part of their rationale, while only 42 percent cited concern for public safety.

In addition to convincing the courts of the desirability of substance testing, firms covered by the National Labor Relations Act must bargain with unions about testing policies and procedures for existing employees since these are mandatory bargaining topics and cannot be imposed unilaterally on unionized employees. In attempting to convince unions to accept testing programs, concern for co-worker safety is the prime rationale advanced by firms. By contrast the National Labor Relations Board allows firms to implement, without union consent, pre-employment screening based on the rationale that prospective employees are not yet members of the bargaining unit. The Supreme Court ruled that firms covered by the Railway Labor Act do not have to negotiate the addition of drug screening to routine physical exams; this was considered a minor change and only subject to arbitration.

Determining if a relationship exists is important not only to justify substance testing, but also to make the best use of safety and health promotion dollars. If substance abuse has a significant impact on employees' safety and health, then from both humanitarian and health care cost perspectives, firms should allocate resources to reduce substance abuse.

If the relationship between abuse and accidents is weaker than many have hypothesized, firms may not be utilizing their limited safety resources properly; other causes of accidents (stress, fatigue, lack of experience) may not be receiving sufficient attention. It has been suggested that by emphasizing the impact of substance abuse, firms may attempt to divert attention from the role of company safety violations in workplace accidents.

To specify the nature of the relationship between substance abuse and workplace accidents, it is desirable to identify research designs which will support empirical specification of the relationship.

———

SKINNER v. RAILWAY LABOR EXECUTIVES' ASS'N

Supreme Court of the United States, 1989.
489 U.S. 602, 109 S.Ct. 1402, 103 L.Ed.2d 639.

JUSTICE KENNEDY delivered the opinion of the Court.

The Federal Railroad Safety Act of 1970 authorizes the Secretary of Transportation to "prescribe, as necessary, appropriate rules, regulations, orders, and standards for all areas of railroad safety." 84 Stat. 971, 45 U.S.C. § 431(a). Finding that alcohol and drug abuse by railroad employees poses a serious threat to safety, the Federal Railroad Administration (FRA) has promulgated regulations that mandate blood and urine tests of employees who are involved in certain train accidents. The FRA also has adopted regulations that do not require, but do authorize, railroads to administer breath and urine tests to employees who violate certain safety rules. The question presented by this case is whether these regulations violate the Fourth Amendment.

* * *

III

* * *

For the Fourth Amendment does not proscribe all searches and seizures, but only those that are unreasonable.

* * *

The Government's interest in regulating the conduct of railroad employees to ensure safety, like its supervision of probationers or regulated industries, or its operation of a government office, school, or prison, "likewise presents 'special needs' beyond normal law enforcement that may justify departures from the usual warrant and probable-cause requirements." The Hours of Service employees covered by the FRA regulations include persons engaged in handling orders concerning train movements, operating crews, and those engaged in the maintenance and repair of signal systems. It is undisputed that these and other covered employees are engaged in safety-sensitive tasks.

An essential purpose of a warrant requirement is to protect privacy interests by assuring citizens subject to a search or seizure that such intrusions are not the random or arbitrary acts of government agents. A warrant assures the citizen that the intrusion is authorized by law, and that it is narrowly limited in its objectives and scope. A warrant also provides the detached scrutiny of a neutral magistrate, and thus ensures an objective determination whether an intrusion is justified in any given case. In the present context, however, a warrant would do little to further these aims. Both the circumstances justifying toxicological testing and the permissible limits of such intrusions are defined narrowly and specifically in the regulations that authorize them, and doubtless are well known to covered employees. Indeed, in light of the standardized nature of the tests and the minimal discretion vested in those charged with administering the program, there are virtually no facts for a neutral magistrate to evaluate.

We have recognized, moreover, that the Government's interest in dispensing with the warrant requirement is at its strongest when, as here, "the burden of obtaining a warrant is likely to frustrate the governmental purpose behind the search."

* * *

Our cases indicate that even a search that may be performed without a warrant must be based, as a general matter, on probable cause to believe that the person to be searched has violated the law.

* * * In limited circumstances, where the privacy interests implicated by the search are minimal, and where an important governmental interest furthered by the intrusion would be placed in jeopardy by a requirement of individualized suspicion, a search may be reasonable despite the absence of such suspicion. We believe this is true of the intrusions in question here.

By and large, intrusions on privacy under the FRA regulations are limited. To the extent transportation and like restrictions are necessary to procure the requisite blood, breath, and urine samples for testing, this interference alone is minimal given the employment context in which it takes place. Ordinarily, an employee consents to significant restrictions in his freedom of movement where necessary for his employment, and few are free to come and go as they please during working hours. Any additional interference with a railroad employee's freedom of movement that occurs in the time it takes to procure a blood, breath, or urine sample for testing cannot, by itself, be said to infringe significant privacy interests.

Our decision in *Schmerber v. California,* 384 U.S. 757, 86 S.Ct. 1826, 16 L.Ed.2d 908 (1966), indicates that the same is true of the blood tests required by the FRA regulations. In that case, we held that a State could direct that a blood sample be withdrawn from a motorist suspected of driving while intoxicated, despite his refusal to consent to the intrusion.

* * *

The breath tests authorized by Subpart D of the regulations are even less intrusive than the blood tests prescribed by Subpart C.

A more difficult question is presented by urine tests. Like breath tests, urine tests are not invasive of the body and, under the regulations, may not be used as an occasion for inquiring into private facts unrelated to alcohol or drug use.[7] We recognize, however, that the procedures for collecting the necessary samples, which require employees to perform an excretory function traditionally shielded by great privacy, raise concerns

---

7. When employees produce the blood and urine samples required by Subpart C they are asked by medical personnel to complete a form stating whether they have taken any medications during the preceding 30 days. The completed forms are shipped with the samples to the FRA's laboratory. This information is used to ascertain whether a positive test result can be explained by the employee's lawful use of medications. While this procedure permits the Government to learn certain private medical facts that an employee might prefer not to disclose, there is no indication that the Government does not treat this information as confidential, or that it uses the information for any other purpose. Under the circumstances, we do not view this procedure as a significant invasion of privacy.

not implicated by blood or breath tests. While we would not characterize these additional privacy concerns as minimal in most contexts, we note that the regulations endeavor to reduce the intrusiveness of the collection process. The regulations do not require that samples be furnished under the direct observation of a monitor, despite the desirability of such a procedure to ensure the integrity of the sample. The sample is also collected in a medical environment, by personnel unrelated to the railroad employer, and is thus not unlike similar procedures encountered often in the context of a regular physical examination.

More importantly, the expectations of privacy of covered employees are diminished by reason of their participation in an industry that is regulated pervasively to ensure safety, a goal dependent, in substantial part, on the health and fitness of covered employees.

* * *

We do not suggest, of course, that the interest in bodily security enjoyed by those employed in a regulated industry must always be considered minimal. Here, however, the covered employees have long been a principal focus of regulatory concern. As the dissenting judge below noted, "[t]he reason is obvious. An idle locomotive, sitting in the roundhouse, is harmless. It becomes lethal when operated negligently by persons who are under the influence of alcohol or drugs." 839 F.2d, at 593. Though some of the privacy interests implicated by the toxicological testing at issue reasonably might be viewed as significant in other contexts, logic and history show that a diminished expectation of privacy attaches to information relating to the physical condition of covered employees and to this reasonable means of procuring such information. We conclude, therefore, that the testing procedures contemplated by Subparts C and D pose only limited threats to the justifiable expectations of privacy of covered employees.

By contrast, the government interest in testing without a showing of individualized suspicion is compelling. Employees subject to the tests discharge duties fraught with such risks of injury to others that even a momentary lapse of attention can have disastrous consequences. Much like persons who have routine access to dangerous nuclear power facilities, employees who are subject to testing under the FRA regulations can cause great human loss before any signs of impairment become noticeable to supervisors or others.

* * *

By ensuring that employees in safety-sensitive positions know they will be tested upon the occurrence of a triggering event, the timing of which no employee can predict with certainty, the regulations significantly increase the deterrent effect of the administrative penalties associated with the prohibited conduct, concomitantly increasing the likelihood that employees will forgo using drugs or alcohol while subject to being called for duty.

The testing procedures contemplated by Subpart C also help railroads obtain invaluable information about the causes of major accidents, and to take appropriate measures to safeguard the general public.

* * *

A requirement of particularized suspicion of drug or alcohol use would seriously impede an employer's ability to obtain this information, despite its obvious importance. Experience confirms the Agency's judgment that the scene of a serious rail accident is chaotic. Investigators who arrive at the scene shortly after a major accident has occurred may find it difficult to determine which members of a train crew contributed to its occurrence. Obtaining evidence that might give rise to the suspicion that a particular employee is impaired, a difficult endeavor in the best of circumstances, is most impracticable in the aftermath of a serious accident.

* * *

Even if urine test results disclosed nothing more specific than the recent use of controlled substances by a covered employee, this information would provide the basis for further investigative work designed to determine whether the employee used drugs at the relevant times. The record makes clear, for example, that a positive test result, coupled with known information concerning the pattern of elimination for the particular drug and information that may be gathered from other sources about the employee's activities, may allow the Agency to reach an informed judgment as to how a particular accident occurred.

More importantly, the Court of Appeals overlooked the Agency's policy of placing principal reliance on the results of blood tests, which unquestionably can identify very recent drug use, see, *e.g.,* 49 Fed.Reg. 24291 (1984), while relying on urine tests as a secondary source of information designed to guard against the possibility that certain drugs will be eliminated from the bloodstream before a blood sample can be obtained. The court also failed to recognize that the FRA regulations are designed not only to discern impairment but also to deter it. Because the record indicates that blood and urine tests, taken together, are highly effective means of ascertaining on-the-job impairment and of deterring the use of drugs by railroad employees, we believe the Court of Appeals erred in concluding that the post-accident testing regulations are not reasonably related to the Government objectives that support them.[10]

We conclude that the compelling government interests served by the FRA's regulations would be significantly hindered if railroads were

10. The Court of Appeals also expressed concern that the tests might be quite unreliable, and thus unreasonable. The record compiled by the Agency after years of investigation and study does not support this conclusion. While it is impossible to guarantee that no mistakes will ever be made in isolated cases, respondents have challenged the administrative scheme on its face. We deal therefore with whether the tests contemplated by the regulations can *ever* be conducted. Respondents have provided us with no reason for doubting the Agency's conclusion that the tests at issue here are accurate in the overwhelming majority of cases.

required to point to specific facts giving rise to a reasonable suspicion of impairment before testing a given employee. In view of our conclusion that, on the present record, the toxicological testing contemplated by the regulations is not an undue infringement on the justifiable expectations of privacy of covered employees, the Government's compelling interests outweigh privacy concerns.

IV

The possession of unlawful drugs is a criminal offense that the Government may punish, but it is a separate and far more dangerous wrong to perform certain sensitive tasks while under the influence of those substances. Performing those tasks while impaired by alcohol is, of course, equally dangerous, though consumption of alcohol is legal in most other contexts. The Government may take all necessary and reasonable regulatory steps to prevent or deter that hazardous conduct, and since the gravamen of the evil is performing certain functions while concealing the substance in the body, it may be necessary, as in the case before us, to examine the body or its fluids to accomplish the regulatory purpose. The necessity to perform that regulatory function with respect to railroad employees engaged in safety-sensitive tasks, and the reasonableness of the system for doing so, have been established in this case.

Alcohol and drug tests conducted in reliance on the authority of Subpart D cannot be viewed as private action outside the reach of the Fourth Amendment. Because the testing procedures mandated or authorized by Subparts C and D effect searches of the person, they must meet the Fourth Amendment's reasonableness requirement. In light of the limited discretion exercised by the railroad employers under the regulations, the surpassing safety interests served by toxicological tests in this context, and the diminished expectation of privacy that attaches to information pertaining to the fitness of covered employees, we believe that it is reasonable to conduct such tests in the absence of a warrant or reasonable suspicion that any particular employee may be impaired. We hold that the alcohol and drug tests contemplated by Subparts C and D of the FRA's regulations are reasonable within the meaning of the Fourth Amendment. The judgment of the Court of Appeals is accordingly reversed.

It is so ordered.

[The concurring opinion of JUSTICE STEVENS is omitted.]

JUSTICE MARSHALL, with whom JUSTICE BRENNAN joins, dissenting.

The issue in this case is not whether declaring a war on illegal drugs is good public policy. The importance of ridding our society of such drugs is, by now, apparent to all. Rather, the issue here is whether the Government's deployment in that war of a particularly draconian weapon—the compulsory collection and chemical testing of railroad workers' blood and urine—comports with the Fourth Amendment. Precisely because the need for action against the drug scourge is manifest, the need for vigilance against unconstitutional excess is great. History teaches that grave threats to liberty often come in times of urgency, when constitutional rights seem too extravagant to endure. The World War II relocation-camp cases, *Hirabayashi v. United States,* 320 U.S. 81, 63 S.Ct. 1375, 87 L.Ed. 1774 (1943); *Korematsu v. United States,* 323 U.S. 214, 65 S.Ct. 193, 89 L.Ed. 194 (1944), and the Red Scare and McCarthy–Era internal subversion cases, *Schenck v. United States,* 249 U.S. 47, 39 S.Ct. 247, 63 L.Ed. 470 (1919); *Dennis v. United States,* 341 U.S. 494, 71 S.Ct. 857, 95 L.Ed. 1137 (1951), are only the most extreme reminders that when we allow fundamental freedoms to be sacrificed in the name of real or perceived exigency, we invariably come to regret it.

In permitting the Government to force entire railroad crews to submit to invasive blood and urine tests, even when it lacks any evidence of drug or alcohol use or other wrongdoing, the majority today joins those shortsighted courts which have allowed basic constitutional rights to fall prey to momentary emergencies. The majority holds that the need of the Federal Railroad Administration (FRA) to deter and diagnose train accidents outweighs any "minimal" intrusions on personal dignity and privacy posed by mass toxicological testing of persons who have given no indication whatsoever of impairment. In reaching this result, the majority ignores the text and doctrinal history of the Fourth Amendment, which require that highly intrusive searches of this type be based on probable cause, not on the evanescent cost-benefit calculations of agencies or judges. But the majority errs even under its own utilitarian standards, trivializing the raw intrusiveness of, and overlooking serious conceptual and operational flaws in, the FRA's testing program. These flaws cast grave doubts on whether that program, though born of good intentions, will do more than ineffectually symbolize the Government's opposition to drug use.

The majority purports to limit its decision to postaccident testing of workers in "safety-sensitive" jobs, much as it limits its holding in the companion case to testing of transferees to jobs involving drug interdiction or the use of firearms. *National Treasury Employees Union v. Von Raab,* 489 U.S. 656, 664, 109 S.Ct. 1384, 1390, 103 L.Ed.2d 685 (1989). But the damage done to the Fourth Amendment is not so easily cabined. The majority's acceptance of dragnet blood and urine testing ensures that the first, and worst, casualty of the war on drugs will be the precious liberties of our citizens. I therefore dissent.

* * *

IV

In his first dissenting opinion as a Member of this Court, Oliver Wendell Holmes observed:

"Great cases, like hard cases, make bad law. For great cases are called great, not by reason of their real importance in shaping the law of the future, but because of some accident of immediate overwhelming interest which appeals to the feelings and distorts the judgment. These immediate interests exercise a kind of hydraulic pressure which makes what previously was clear seem doubtful, and before which even well settled principles of law will bend." *Northern Securities Co. v. United States,* 193 U.S. 197, 400–401, 24 S.Ct. 436, 468, 48 L.Ed. 679 (1904).

A majority of this Court, swept away by society's obsession with stopping the scourge of illegal drugs, today succumbs to the popular pressures described by Justice Holmes. In upholding the FRA's plan for blood and urine testing, the majority bends time-honored and textually-based principles of the Fourth Amendment—principles the Framers of the Bill of Rights designed to ensure that the Government has a strong and individualized justification when it seeks to invade an individual's privacy. I believe the Framers would be appalled by the vision of mass governmental intrusions upon the integrity of the human body that the majority allows to become reality. The immediate victims of the majority's constitutional timorousness will be those railroad workers whose bodily fluids the Government may now forcibly collect and analyze. But ultimately, today's decision will reduce the privacy all citizens may enjoy, for, as Justice Holmes understood, principles of law, once bent, do not snap back easily. I dissent.

Note

In a companion case, the Supreme Court decided whether the federal government was constitutionally free to require urinalysis of United States Custom Service employees who sought to hold certain positions. National Treasury Employees Union v. Von Raab, 489 U.S. 656, 109 S.Ct. 1384, 103 L.Ed.2d 685 (1989). In the case, the agency had decreed that urinalysis was required of all employees who were involved in drug interdiction, who carried firearms, or who handled "classified" material. The Court held, 5–to–4, that "the suspicionless testing of employees who apply for promotion to positions directly involving the interdiction of illegal drugs, or to positions which require the incumbent to carry a firearm, is reasonable." The Court did not rule on the lawfulness of mandatory urinalysis for employees who will handle "classified" material. In one of the dissenting opinions, Justice Scalia wrote,

* * * Today, in Skinner, we allow a less intrusive bodily search of railroad employees involved in train accidents. I joined the Court's opinion there because the demonstrated frequency of drug and alcohol use by the targeted class of employees, and the demonstrated connection between such use and grave harm, rendered the search a reasonable means of protecting society. I decline to join the Court's opinion in the present case because neither frequency of use nor connection to harm is demonstrated or even likely. In my view the Customs Service rules are a kind of immolation of privacy and human dignity in symbolic opposition to drug use.

* * *

What is absent in the Government's justifications—notably absent, revealingly absent, and as far as I am concerned dispositively absent—is the recitation of even a single instance in which any of the speculated horribles actually occurred: an instance, that is, in which the cause of bribe-taking, or of poor aim, or of unsympathetic law enforcement, or of compromise of classified information, was drug use.

* * *

Today's decision would be wrong, but at least of more limited effect, if its approval of drug testing were confined to that category of employees assigned specifically to drug interdiction duties. Relatively few public employees fit that description. But in extending approval of drug testing to that category consisting of employees who carry firearms, the Court exposes vast numbers of public employees to this needless indignity. Logically, of course, if those who carry guns can be treated in this fashion, so can all others whose work, if performed under the influence of drugs, may endanger others—automobile drivers, operators of other potentially dangerous equipment, construction workers, school crossing guards. A similarly broad scope attaches to the Court's approval of drug testing for those with access to "sensitive information." Since this category is not limited to Service employees with drug interdiction duties, nor to "sensitive information" specifically relating to drug traffic, today's holding apparently approves drug testing for all federal employees with security clearances—or, indeed, for all federal employees with valuable confidential information to impart. Since drug use is not a particular problem in the Customs Service, employees throughout the government are no less likely to violate the public trust by taking bribes to feed their drug habit, or by yielding to blackmail. Moreover, there is no reason why this super-protection against harms arising from drug use must be limited to public employees; a law requiring similar testing of private citizens who use dangerous instruments such as guns or cars, or who have access to classified information would also be constitutional.

There is only one apparent basis that sets the testing at issue here apart from all these other situations—but it is not a basis upon which the Court is willing to rely. I do not believe for a minute that the driving force behind these drug-testing rules was any of the feeble justifications put forward by counsel here and accepted by the Court. The only plausible explanation, in my view, is what the Commissioner himself offered in the concluding sentence of his memorandum to Customs Service employees announcing the program: "Implementation of the drug screening program would set an important example in our country's struggle with this most serious threat to our national health and security."

* * *

SOME QUESTIONS ABOUT BRAVEMAN'S PROBLEM

1. Enderby's policy may not address the use and influence of alcohol. If that is true, is enforcement of the company's policy in jeopardy?

2. What is the purpose of the company's policy? One can imagine the company is concerned with efficiency, the individual employee's safety, the well-being of fellow-employees, the public's interest in having quality and safe products, morality, or a commitment to supporting the

drug laws. Depending on your assessment of the purpose of the policy, would your analysis of the problem change?

3. Should it matter what kind of job an employee has for an employer to impose a drug-testing policy like Enderby's?

4. In the context of most jobs, should there be a "triggering event" (like an accident or "spaced-out" appearance) to justify drug testing?

5. Is your answer to any of the foregoing questions affected by your assessment of the accuracy of the tests or of the selection of the drugs targeted by the tests?

6. In the Braveman problem, the union didn't succeed in obtaining additional protection against drug testing, but stated at the bargaining table that it was content to rely on existing contractual language and other protections outside the contract. Just what are those other protections, and may the union now rely upon them in an arbitration proceeding? Are these considerations relevant in the case of an employee not represented by a union? How would such an employee attempt to vindicate her rights?

In looking at other sources to inform the contractual language, one finds snippets of guidance in OSHA. It provides for medical screening and surveillance of workers, primarily to make sure they haven't been exposed to toxic substances. What use may an employer make of any information it learns about the employee's personal habits in the course of these permissible investigations? May OSHA be read to prohibit, at least by implication, any screening that is not expressly allowed?

On the other hand, the ADA clearly "washes its hands" of the drug-testing issue. Section 104(d) expressly provides that the Act not "be construed to encourage, prohibit, or authorize" drug testing.

Many argue that the public policy considerations embodied in constitutional protections apply as well to the private sector employment relationship. Surely a union could reasonably argue to an arbitrator that the basic notion of just cause includes freedom from unwarranted intrusion into privacy. If there were no union in the picture, an individual like Braveman might successfully argue, in those jurisdictions that recognize a just cause or good faith exception to the employment at will doctrine, that the discipline was unlawful.

For example, in Hennessey v. Coastal Eagle Point Oil Co., 129 N.J. 81, 609 A.2d 11 (1992), the New Jersey Supreme Court said, "Mandatory random urine testing by private employers can be an invasion of privacy sufficient to breach public policy, deriving from both the common law and New Jersey's Constitution ..." Yet, the Court further opined, "[W]e must also consider [and balance] the competing public interest [which is, in this case, public safety]." Finally, the Court said, "If the employee's duties are so fraught with hazard that his or her attempts to perform them while in a state of drug impairment would pose a threat to co-workers, to the workplace, or to the public at large, then the employer must prevail."

G. PROBLEM 3–4

Dealing With the Arbitration Award:
The Effect of External Law

The United Factory Workers' Union recently submitted to arbitration a grievance involving a worker who was transferred from his job because he tested positively for HIV.

You are a student "intern" working with the arbitrator in the case. She has asked you to critique her proposed decision, which follows. Please respond to her request with complete candor. In doing so, consider the materials that appear after the proposed decision: an excerpt from an article about AIDS, the *Arline* decision, a note about the Americans with Disabilities Act with which you are already familiar, and the *Eastern Coal* case.

Arbitration Between	)
United Factory Workers, AFL–	)
CIO, CLC	)
and	)
Enderby Industries, Inc.	)
(R. Axfell grievance)	)

Proposed Decision of Arbitrator

Marianne Just, Arbitrator,

The grievant, R. Axfell, worked in the employer's testing lab for some five years before this incident occurred. He was assigned to the lab "clean room," where he was responsible for cleaning and sterilizing all materials used in the lab.

As part of Enderby's routine testing procedures, Axfell was ordered to submit to a battery of tests, including a test designed to show whether the HIV virus is present in the body. Axfell objected to taking the tests, but was told to take the tests and challenge them later through a grievance. Fearing that he would be discharged for insubordination if he did not submit to the test, Axfell reluctantly agreed to be tested. The result of the test showed he had the HIV virus.

As a consequence, Enderby removed Axfell from his lab job and placed him in a custodial position. The custodial job paid $2 per hour less than the lab job, but the company refused to maintain Axfell's former level of wages.

The employer's vice president for labor, Matthew Crickboom, testified as to why the company transferred Axfell when he tested positively:

First, the company understood that while AIDS is contagious the means for transmittal of the disease are limited. Nevertheless, the company felt it could take no chances, given the current level of medical knowledge, with an employee who handles and is responsible for cleaning materials in which a variety of products are tested. Further, other employees in the lab would be unwilling to work with materials that Axfell has cleaned.

Second, while Axfell had no present symptoms of AIDS, given his vulnerability to the disease it was unwise to continue him in the lab job. The lab position is too important to assign to a person with the potential for a poor attendance record.

The union first argues that it was inappropriate for the company to test Axfell, and therefore the company cannot use the positive test results against him. It relies upon the union contract provision that "no employee may be terminated or otherwise disciplined except for just cause." The union argues that the company had no cause to administer this test to Axfell; he exhibited no symptoms of AIDS, and, although such information would be irrelevant, he was not known to be a homosexual, a user of intravenous drugs, or a hemophiliac.

The company responds that nothing in the agreement precludes it from administering tests, including the test for HIV. It asserts that, under its inherent right to run the business, and under the specific management rights clause in this agreement, the company has the right, and indeed the responsibility, to test and screen employees who might endanger themselves and others. The company points out that in the last round of negotiations the union at first sought contract language that would prevent the employer from testing and screening workers, except as required by OSHA. The employer refused to agree to such a provision, and insisted on its right to test and screen employees. The union withdrew this provision and was content to rely upon the existing just cause language, which says nothing about testing. The union may not obtain through arbitration what it could not achieve at the bargaining table.

The arbitrator agrees with the company on this issue. The potential for harm caused by employees under the influence of drugs or suffering from other conditions is so great that it is proper for a company to engage in screening. As a general matter, whether a company may engage in random testing, or must limit its testing to those cases in which it has reasonable grounds to believe there is an abuse, is a question I need not reach. For the parties had the opportunity to set out guidelines in negotiations, and the union withdrew language that would have limited management's rights. Thus it was permissible for the company to test Axfell.

As for the test results, I share the union's concern that people will react with panic to the AIDS epidemic and assume that the disease is contagious in a way it is not. In this regard I welcome the Supreme Court's *Arline* decision, which held that handicap laws prohibit an employer from discriminating against an employee with tuberculosis by assuming that the disease is contagious when it is not.

Unfortunately, *Arline* does not deal with the dilemma here. The best medical evidence indicates that AIDS is contagious. Even if it is not transmittable in the course of the lab work done by Axfell, other employees surely perceive it that way. Consequently, to allow Axfell to continue working in the testing lab will be to impair the ability of his coworkers to do lab work.

Federal disability law applies to Enderby. It prohibits discrimination against an employee on account of a disability. Even assuming that Axfell must be viewed as a disabled employee on account of the perception that his disease is contagious, the laws regarding disability discrimination require only that his employer make an accommodation by giving the employee other work. Transferring Axfell to a custodial job is a reasonable accommodation under the circumstances.

I conclude, however, that the employer must maintain Axfell's wages. The company is permitted to transfer Axfell only because doing so is a reasonable accommodation of his disability. But since Axfell was transferred through no fault of his own, he cannot be expected to suffer economic harm as well.

In opposition, the company points out that the union failed to obtain a clause in negotiations that would have preserved wage levels in the event an employee was transferred as the result of a positive HIV test. The company staunchly resisted that clause, and instead agreed only that the employee would be transferred to another job he was capable of performing. It argues that the union must not be allowed to recapture that demand through arbitration.

However, my conclusion that wage maintenance is required does not flow from the contract language, but rather from the company's independent obligation to make an accommodation towards handicapped employees. Therefore, Axfell must be paid at his former rate of pay for work as a custodian.

1. A LITTLE INFORMATION REGARDING AIDS

ARTHUR S. LEONARD, AIDS AND EMPLOYMENT LAW REVISITED

14 Hofstra L.Rev. 11.16–20, 27–29 (1985).

First, AIDS is the end stage of complications of infection by a retrovirus which will be referred to herein as HIV (Human Immunodeficiency Virus). The virus, which is bloodborne (specifically in white blood cells known as T–4 helper lymphocytes), is transmitted through the exchange of blood or semen during sexual intercourse, or by the use of tainted blood or blood products, including blood transfusions, shared intravenous needles, blood clotting medications, and prenatal or natal exposure. No other mode of transmittal from person to person has been documented, although HIV has been found in saliva, urine, and tears of some infected persons. HIV is not spread through casual physical contact, and does not live outside the body long enough in sufficient quantity to be spread by food, drinking fountains, utensils, or toilet facilities.

Once introduced into the body, HIV produces an enzyme which allows it to transcribe its genetic material onto the genetic material of the T–4 lymphocytes, thus altering the lymphocytes and impeding their growth and replication. The T–4 lymphocytes play an important role in triggering immune response to certain organisms which are already present in large portions of the population. Having performed its transcription function, HIV may remain "dormant" in the T–4 lymphocytes and never cause any further damage to the immune system. However, there is evidence that HIV sometimes crosses the blood-brain barrier and infects brain cells, resulting in dementia or meningitis, and also infects cells of the central nervous system in some individuals. The most significant and lethal activity of HIV, which seems to be triggered by unidentified cofactors, is the stimulated replication of infected T–4 lymphocytes, rapidly reproducing in the form of new HIV, which then attacks remaining healthy T–4 lymphocytes until there are few healthy ones left. During the intermediate stage of infection, when the number of healthy T–4 lymphocytes is reduced, the individual may experience various symptoms which are referred to as AIDS–Related Complex.

Infected T–4 lymphocytes are unable to perform their normal immune system functions, which results in proliferation of common (and usually harmless) parasites, producing lymphadenopathy (enlarged lymph nodes), *Kaposi's sarcoma* (a form of skin cancer), *pneumocystis carinii* pneumonia, and other opportunistic infections characteristic of end-stage AIDS. The CDC has defined AIDS, for epidemiological surveillance purposes, as a reliably diagnosed disease predictive of immune deficiency in a person with no known underlying cause of immune deficiency. However, as can be seen from this description, end-stage (or CDC-defined) AIDS is only one of several manifestations of HIV infection, which are lumped together in the public minds as AIDS.

One of the medical facts which makes AIDS a significant workplace issue is that a person may experience HIV infection in its various stages and be virtually asymptomatic, or have symptoms which, while uncomfortable, are not actually disabling. Indeed, some individuals with CDC-defined AIDS are, apart from such nondisabling conditions as early-stage *Kaposi's sarcoma,* in relatively good health and physically able to function at work, and there are some people who have lived and worked for months or years after a confirmed AIDS diagnosis. AIDS is a disability of the immune system, but not itself an overtly disabling illness; rather, symptoms produced by the body's reaction to organisms usually suppressed by the healthy immune system, such as weakness, fatigue, severe weight loss, and loss of respiratory and digestive function, are the overt physical disabilities linked to AIDS. These eventually lead to death in most CDC-defined AIDS cases.

[Professor Leonard sets out the typology of individual cases.]

Assuming that the statute is held to apply [to persons with AIDS], however, the issue of employer defenses is significant. Even though transmissibility is not normally a valid defense in an AIDS case, an argument could be made that a person with a compromised immune system should not be exposed to the variety of infectious agents found in the workplace for his or her own safety. This argument would be quite persuasive if AIDS were a disease involving generalized loss of immune function, or particular vulnerability to infectious agents found in some or all workplaces. But the medical evidence is that AIDS involves a loss of particularized immune function, and that the opportunistic infections associated with AIDS are caused by parasites that are normally present in most of the adult population. Consequently, medical authorities writing on AIDS have not suggested that persons with ARC or AIDS need to be excluded from the workplace to prevent them from contracting opportunistic infections. The medical evidence appears to indicate that they are just as likely to contract such infections sitting at home as attending a job.

The accommodation issue can also present serious problems in Type III and IV cases. It is likely that persons with ARC or AIDS will have problems maintaining good attendance, due to the occasional need for treatment for ARC systems or opportunistic infections. Furthermore, ARC and AIDS tend to be debilitating, lessening the individual's stamina and ability to maintain a high degree of effort throughout a full workday. Depending upon the nature of the job and the needs (and particularly the size) of the employer's operation, it may be that accommodating the person with ARC or AIDS will, in some circumstances, create an undue burden. This, however, will be a matter for the employer to prove objectively. Moreover, the defense will not be available prospectively, since speculation about long term future inability to meet work requirements is not normally a permissible basis for present discrimination under these statutes.

2. THE REHABILITATION ACT OF 1973

SCHOOL BOARD OF NASSAU COUNTY, FLORIDA v. ARLINE

Supreme Court of the United States, 1987.
480 U.S. 273, 107 S.Ct. 1123, 94 L.Ed.2d 307.

JUSTICE BRENNAN delivered the opinion of the Court.

Section 504 of the Rehabilitation Act of 1973 prohibits a federally funded state program from discriminating against a handicapped individual solely by reason of his or her handicap. This case presents the questions whether a person afflicted with tuberculosis, a contagious disease, may be considered a "handicapped individual" within the meaning of § 504 of the Act, and, if so, whether such an individual is "otherwise qualified" to teach elementary school.

From 1966 until 1979, respondent Gene Arline taught elementary school in Nassau County, Florida. She was discharged in 1979 after suffering a third relapse of tuberculosis within two years. After she was denied relief in state administrative proceedings, she brought suit in federal court, alleging that the School Board's decision to dismiss her because of her tuberculosis violated § 504 of the Act.

A trial was held in the District Court, at which the principal medical evidence was provided by Marianne McEuen, M.D., an assistant director of the Community Tuberculosis Control Service of the Florida Department of Health and Rehabilitative Services. According to the medical records reviewed by Dr. McEuen, Arline was hospitalized for tuberculosis in 1957. For the next twenty years, Arline's disease was in remission. Then, in 1977, a culture revealed that tuberculosis was again active in her system; cultures taken in March 1978 and in November 1978 were also positive.

The superintendent of schools for Nassau County, Craig Marsh, then testified as to the School Board's response to Arline's medical reports. After both her second relapse, in the Spring of 1978, and her third relapse in November 1978, the School Board suspended Arline with pay for the remainder of the school year. At the end of the 1978–1979 school year, the School Board held a hearing, after which it discharged Arline, "not because she had done anything wrong," but because of the "continued reoccurence [sic] of tuberculosis."

* * *

II

In enacting and amending the Act, Congress enlisted all programs receiving federal funds in an effort "to share with handicapped Americans the opportunities for an education, transportation, housing, health care, and jobs that other Americans take for granted." 123 Cong.Rec. 13515 (1977) (statement of Sen. Humphrey). To that end, Congress not only increased federal support for vocational rehabilitation, but also addressed the broader problem of discrimination against the handicapped by including § 504, an antidiscrimination provision patterned after Title VI of the Civil Rights Act of 1964. Section 504 of the Rehabilitation Act reads in pertinent part:

"No otherwise qualified handicapped individual in the United States, as defined in section 706(7) of this title, shall, solely by reason of his handicap, be excluded from participation in, be denied the benefits of, or be subjected to discrimination under any program or activity receiving Federal financial assistance...."

In 1974 Congress expanded the definition of "handicapped individual" for use in § 504 to read as follows:[3]

3. The primary focus of the 1973 Act was to increase federal support for vocational rehabilitation; the Act's original definition of the term "handicapped individual" reflected this focus by including only those whose disability limited their employability, and those who could be expected to benefit from vocational rehabilitation. After review-ing the Department of Health, Education, and Welfare's subsequent attempt to devise regulations to implement the Act, however, Congress concluded that the definition of "handicapped individual," while appropriate for the vocational rehabilitation provisions in Titles I and III of the Act, was too narrow to deal with the range of discrimi-

"[A]ny person who (i) has a physical or mental impairment which substantially limits one or more of such person's major life activities, (ii) has a record of such an impairment, or (iii) is regarded as having such an impairment." 29 U.S.C. § 706(7)(B).

The amended definition reflected Congress' concern with protecting the handicapped against discrimination stemming not only from simple prejudice, but from "archaic attitudes and laws" and from "the fact that the American people are simply unfamiliar with and insensitive to the difficulties confront[ing] individuals with handicaps." To combat the effects of erroneous but nevertheless prevalent perceptions about the handicapped, Congress expanded the definition of "handicapped individual" so as to preclude discrimination against "[a] person who has a record of, or is regarded as having, an impairment [but who] may at present have no actual incapacity at all." Southeastern Community College v. Davis, 442 U.S. 397, 405–406, n. 6, 99 S.Ct. 2361, 2366–2367, n. 6, 60 L.Ed.2d 980 (1979).

In determining whether a particular individual is handicapped as defined by the Act, the regulations promulgated by the Department of Health and Human Services are of significant assistance. As we have previously recognized, these regulations were drafted with the oversight and approval of Congress; they provide "an important source of guidance on the meaning of § 504." The regulations are particularly significant here because they define two critical terms used in the statutory definition of handicapped individual.[5] "Physical impairment" is defined as follows:

"[A]ny physiological disorder or condition, cosmetic disfigurement, or anatomical loss affecting one or more of the following body systems: neurological; musculoskeletal; special sense organs; skin; and endocrine." 45 CFR § 84–3(j)(2)(i) (1985).

In addition, the regulations define "major life activities" as:

"functions such as caring for one's self, performing manual tasks, walking, seeing, hearing, speaking, breathing, learning, and working." § 84.3(j)(2)(ii).

natory practices in housing, education, and health care programs which stemmed from stereotypical attitudes and ignorance about the handicapped.

5. In an appendix to these regulations, the Department of Health and Human Services explained that it chose not to attempt to "set forth a list of specific diseases and conditions that constitute physical or mental impairments because of the difficulty of ensuring the comprehensiveness of any such list." Nevertheless, the Department went on to state that "such diseases and conditions as orthopedic, visual, speech, and hearing impairments, cerebral palsy, epilepsy, muscular dystrophy, multiple sclerosis, cancer, heart disease, diabetes, mental retardation, [and] emotional illness" would be covered. The Department also reinforced what a careful reading of the statute makes plain, "that a physical or mental impairment does not constitute a handicap for purposes of section 504 unless its severity is such that it results in a substantial limitation of one or more major life activities." Although many of the comments on the regulations when first proposed suggested that the definition was unreasonably broad, the Department found that a broad definition, one not limited to so-called "traditional handicaps," is inherent in the statutory definition.

III

Within this statutory and regulatory framework, then, we must consider whether Arline can be considered a handicapped individual. According to the testimony of Dr. McEuen, Arline suffered tuberculosis "in an acute form in such a degree that it affected her respiratory system," and was hospitalized for this condition. Arline thus had a physical impairment as that term is defined by the regulations, since she had a "physiological disorder or condition * * * affecting [her] * * * respiratory [system]." This impairment was serious enough to require hospitalization, a fact more than sufficient to establish that one or more of her major life activities were substantially limited by her impairment. Thus, Arline's hospitalization for tuberculosis in 1957 suffices to establish that she has a "record of * * * impairment" within the meaning of 29 U.S.C. § 706(7)(B)(ii), and is therefore a handicapped individual.

Petitioners concede that a contagious disease may constitute a handicapping condition to the extent that it leaves a person with "diminished physical or mental capabilities," and concede that Arline's hospitalization for tuberculosis in 1957 demonstrates that she has a record of a physical impairment. Petitioners maintain, however, Arline's record of impairment is irrelevant in this case, since the School Board dismissed Arline not because of her diminished physical capabilities, but because of the threat that her relapses of tuberculosis posed to the health of others.

We do not agree with petitioners that, in defining a handicapped individual under § 504, the contagious effects of a disease can be meaningfully distinguished from the disease's physical effects on a claimant in a case such as this. Arline's contagiousness and her physical impairment each resulted from the same underlying condition, tuberculosis. It would be unfair to allow an employer to seize upon the distinction between the effects of a disease on others and the effects of a disease on a patient and use that distinction to justify discriminatory treatment.[7]

Nothing in the legislative history of § 504 suggests that Congress intended such a result. That history demonstrates that Congress was as concerned about the effect of an impairment on others as it was about its effect on the individual. Congress extended coverage, in 29 U.S.C. § 706(7)(B)(iii), to those individuals who are simply "regarded as having" a physical or mental impairment. The Senate Report provides as an

---

7. The United States argues that it is possible for a person to be simply a carrier of a disease, that is, to be capable of spreading a disease without having a "physical impairment" or suffering from any other symptoms associated with the disease. The United States contends that this [is] true in the case of some carriers of the Acquired Immune Deficiency Syndrome (AIDS) virus. From this premise the United States concludes that discrimination solely on the basis of contagiousness is never discrimination on the basis of a handicap. The argument is misplaced in this case, because the handicap here, tuberculosis, gave rise both to a physical impairment and to contagiousness. This case does not present, and we therefore do not reach, the questions whether a carrier of a contagious disease such as AIDS could be considered to have a physical impairment, or whether such a person could be considered, solely on the basis of contagiousness, a handicapped person as defined by the Act.

example of a person who would be covered under this subsection "a person with some kind of visible physical impairment which in fact does not substantially limit that person's functioning." Such an impairment might not diminish a person's physical or mental capabilities, but could nevertheless substantially limit that person's ability to work as a result of the negative reactions of others to the impairment.

Allowing discrimination based on the contagious effects of a physical impairment would be inconsistent with the basic purpose of § 504, which is to ensure that handicapped individuals are not denied jobs or other benefits because of the prejudiced attitudes or the ignorance of others. By amending the definition of "handicapped individual" to include not only those who are actually physically impaired, but also those who are regarded as impaired and who, as a result, are substantially limited in a major life activity, Congress acknowledged that society's accumulated myths and fears about disability and disease are as handicapping as are the physical limitations that flow from actual impairment. Few aspects of a handicap give rise to the same level of public fear and misapprehension as contagiousness. Even those who suffer or have recovered from such noninfectious diseases as epilepsy or cancer have faced discrimination based on the irrational fear that they might be contagious. The Act is carefully structured to replace such reflexive reactions to actual or perceived handicaps with actions based on reasoned and medically sound judgments: the definition of "handicapped individual" is broad, but only those individuals who are both handicapped *and* otherwise qualified are eligible for relief. The fact that *some* persons who have contagious diseases may pose a serious health threat to others under certain circumstances does not justify excluding from the coverage of the Act *all* persons with actual or perceived contagious diseases. Such exclusion would mean that those accused of being contagious would never have the opportunity to have their condition evaluated in light of medical evidence and a determination made as to whether they were "otherwise qualified." Rather, they would be vulnerable to discrimination on the basis of mythology—precisely the type of injury Congress sought to prevent.[14] We conclude that the fact that a person with a record of a physical impairment is also contagious does not suffice to remove that person from coverage under § 504.

---

14. Congress reaffirmed this approach in its 1978 amendments to the Act. There, Congress recognized that employers and other grantees might have legitimate reasons not to extend jobs or benefits to drug addicts and alcoholics, but also understood the danger of improper discrimination against such individuals if they were categorically excluded from coverage under the Act. Congress therefore rejected the original House proposal to exclude addicts and alcoholics from the definition of handicapped individual, and instead adopted the Senate proposal excluding only those alcoholics and drug abusers "whose current use of alcohol or drugs prevents such individual from performing the duties of the job in question or whose employment * * * would constitute a direct threat to property or the safety of others." 29 U.S.C. § 706(7)(B). See 124 Cong.Rec. 30322 (1978); Brief for Senator Cranston et al. as *Amici Curiae* 35–36; 43 Op.Atty.Gen. No. 12 (1977).

This approach is also consistent with that taken by courts that have addressed the question whether the Act covers persons suffering from conditions other than contagious diseases that render them a threat to the safety of others.

IV

The remaining question is whether Arline is otherwise qualified for the job of elementary school teacher. To answer this question in most cases, the District Court will need to conduct an individualized inquiry and make appropriate findings of fact. Such an inquiry is essential if § 504 is to achieve its goal of protecting handicapped individuals from deprivations based on prejudice, stereotypes, or unfounded fear, while giving appropriate weight to such legitimate concerns of grantees as avoiding exposing others to significant health and safety risks.[16] The basic factors to be considered in conducting this inquiry are well established.[17] In the context of the employment of a person handicapped with a contagious disease, we agree with amicus American Medical Association that this inquiry should include:

> "[findings of] facts, based on reasonable medical judgments given the state of medical knowledge, about (a) the nature of the risk (how the disease is transmitted), (b) the duration of the risk (how long is the carrier infectious), (c) the severity of the risk (what is the potential harm to third parties) and (d) the probabilities the disease will be transmitted and will cause varying degrees of harm."

In making these findings, courts normally should defer to the reasonable medical judgments of public health officials. The next step in the "otherwise-qualified" inquiry is for the court to evaluate, in light of these medical findings, whether the employer could reasonably accommodate the employee under the established standards for that inquiry.

Because of the paucity of factual findings by the District Court, we, like the Court of Appeals, are unable at this stage of the proceedings to resolve whether Arline is "otherwise qualified" for her job. The District Court made no findings as to the duration and severity of Arline's condition, nor as to the probability that she would transmit the disease. Nor did the court determine whether Arline was contagious at the time

---

16. A person who poses a significant risk of communicating an infectious disease to others in the workplace will not be otherwise qualified for his or her job if reasonable accommodation will not eliminate that risk. The Act would not require a school board to place a teacher with active, contagious tuberculosis in a classroom with elementary school children. Respondent conceded as much at oral argument.

17. "An otherwise qualified person is one who is able to meet all of a program's requirements in spite of his handicap." Southeastern Community College v. Davis, 442 U.S. 397, 406, 99 S.Ct. 2361, 2367, 60 L.Ed.2d 980 (1979). In the employment context, an otherwise qualified person is one who can perform "the essential functions" of the job in question. 45 CFR § 84.3(k) (1985). When a handicapped person is not able to perform the essential functions of

the job, the court must also consider whether any "reasonable accommodation" by the employer would enable the handicapped person to perform those functions. Ibid. Accommodation is not reasonable if it either imposes "undue financial and administrative burdens" on a grantee, Southeastern Community College v. Davis, supra, at 412, 99 S.Ct., at 2370, or requires "a fundamental alteration in the nature of [the] program" id., at 410. See 45 CFR § 84.12(c) (1985) (listing factors to consider in determining whether accommodation would cause undue hardship); 45 CFR pt. 84, App. A., p. 315 (1985) ("where reasonable accommodation does not overcome the effects of a person's handicap, or where reasonable accommodation causes undue hardship to the employer, failure to hire or promote the handicapped person will not be considered discrimination").

she was discharged, or whether the School Board could have reasonably accommodated her. Accordingly, the resolution of whether Arline was otherwise qualified requires further findings of fact.

* * *

We remand the case to the District Court to determine whether Arline is otherwise qualified for her position.

———

3. SOME QUESTIONS ABOUT THE AMERICANS WITH DISABILITIES ACT AND THE ARBITRATION AWARD

The ADA is largely modeled on the Rehabilitation Act, which serves as the bottom for the *Arline* case. The definition of "handicap" under the Rehabilitation Act is virtually identical to the definition of "disability" found in Section 3(2) of the ADA. In footnote 7 of the *Arline* decision, the Court left open whether or not it is a handicap (or, one assumes, disability) to be contagious (a carrier) while not suffering personally with any ailment. Is that a fact question that needs answering in the Axfell arbitration case on which you are working?

Section 102 of the ADA prohibits discrimination against qualified employees because of their disabilities in regard to their opportunities in the workplace. Has Enderby done that to Axfell? Consider Section 104(d)(1) and (4), which outlaws medical examinations of employees unless the exam is "job-related and consistent with business necessity." Can Enderby meet this statutory requirement?

The Act also requires the employer to make "reasonable accommodations" to enable otherwise qualified employees to do the job, although the accommodations need not be an "undue hardship" upon the employer. Section 102(b)(5). Is an employer justified in adopting an accommodation to serve its interests rather than those of an employee who may not need any accommodation? Put differently, are Enderby's concerns sufficient to justify its imposing the limitations on Axfel? Is Section 103, which provides a defense to an employer who demonstrates that an employee is "a direct threat to the health and safety of other individuals in the workplace," relevant?

If it is assumed that the employer's reasons for its actions are sufficient justification for some kind of imposed accommodation, who should decide what should be the content of that accommodation? Should Axfel have a voice in that decision? The union?

Was the arbitrator correct in holding that the change in positions was a reasonable accommodation? Was she correct in holding that the reduction in wages was not?

Finally, was she correct in awarding an ADA-type remedy (to wit, precluding the reduction in wages) when the contract language is not the basis for the award?

4. IS THE PROPOSED AXFEL AWARD
ENFORCEABLE IN THE COURTS?

EASTERN ASSOCIATED COAL CORPORATION
v. UNITED MINE WORKERS OF AMERICA

Supreme Court of the United States, 2000.
531 U.S. 57, 121 S.Ct. 462, 148 L.Ed.2d 354

JUSTICE BREYER delivered the opinion of the Court.

A labor arbitrator ordered an employer to reinstate an employee truck driver who had twice tested positive for marijuana. The question before us is whether considerations of public policy require courts to refuse to enforce that arbitration award. We conclude that they do not. The courts may enforce the award. And the employer must reinstate, rather than discharge, the employee.

I

Petitioner, Eastern Associated Coal Corp., and respondent, United Mine Workers of America, are parties to a collective-bargaining agreement with arbitration provisions. The agreement specifies that, in arbitration, in order to discharge an employee, Eastern must prove it has "just cause." Otherwise the arbitrator will order the employee reinstated. The arbitrator's decision is final.

James Smith worked for Eastern as a member of a road crew, a job that required him to drive heavy trucklike vehicles on public highways. As a truck driver, Smith was subject to Department of Transportation (DOT) regulations requiring random drug testing of workers engaged in "safety-sensitive" tasks.

In March 1996, Smith tested positive for marijuana. Eastern sought to discharge Smith. The union went to arbitration, and the arbitrator concluded that Smith's positive drug test did not amount to "just cause" for discharge. Instead the arbitrator ordered Smith's reinstatement, provided that Smith (1) accept a suspension of 30 days without pay, (2) participate in a substance-abuse program, and (3) undergo drug tests at the discretion of Eastern (or an approved substance-abuse professional) for the next five years.

Between April 1996 and January 1997, Smith passed four random drug tests. But in July 1997 he again tested positive for marijuana. Eastern again sought to discharge Smith. The union again went to arbitration, and the arbitrator again concluded that Smith's use of marijuana did not amount to "just cause" for discharge, in light of two mitigating circumstances. First, Smith had been a good employee for 17 years. And, second, Smith had made a credible and "very personal appeal under oath * * * concerning a personal/family problem which caused this one time lapse in drug usage."

The arbitrator ordered Smith's reinstatement provided that Smith (1) accept a new suspension without pay, this time for slightly more than three months; (2) reimburse Eastern and the union for the costs of both arbitration proceedings; (3) continue to participate in a substance abuse program; (4) continue to undergo random drug testing; and (5) provide Eastern with a signed, undated letter of resignation, to take effect if Smith again tested positive within the next five years.

Eastern brought suit in federal court seeking to have the arbitrator's award vacated, arguing that the award contravened a public policy against the operation of dangerous machinery by workers who test positive for drugs. The District Court, while recognizing a strong regulation-based public policy against drug use by workers who perform safety-sensitive functions, held that Smith's conditional reinstatement did not violate that policy. And it ordered the award's enforcement.

The Court of Appeals for the Fourth Circuit affirmed on the reasoning of the District Court. We granted certiorari in light of disagreement among the Circuits. We now affirm the Fourth Circuit's determination.

II

Eastern claims that considerations of public policy make the arbitration award unenforceable. In considering this claim, we must assume that the collective-bargaining agreement itself calls for Smith's reinstatement. That is because both employer and union have granted to the arbitrator the authority to interpret the meaning of their contract's language, including such words as "just cause." See *Steelworkers v. Enterprise Wheel & Car Corp.,* 363 U.S. 593, 599, 80 S.Ct. 1358, 4 L.Ed.2d 1424 (1960). They have "bargained for" the "arbitrator's construction" of their agreement. *Ibid.* And courts will set aside the arbitrator's interpretation of what their agreement means only in rare instances. *Id.,* at 596, 80 S.Ct. 1358. Of course, an arbitrator's award "must draw its essence from the contract and cannot simply reflect the arbitrator's own notions of industrial justice." *Paperworkers v. Misco, Inc.,* 484 U.S. 29, 38, 108 S.Ct. 364, 98 L.Ed.2d 286 (1987). "But as long as [an honest] arbitrator is even arguably construing or applying the contract and acting within the scope of his authority," the fact that "a court is convinced he committed serious error does not suffice to overturn his decision." *Ibid.;* see also *Enterprise Wheel, supra,* at 596, 80 S.Ct. 1358 (the "proper" judicial approach to a labor arbitration award is to "refus[e] ... to review * the merits"). Eastern does not claim here that the arbitrator acted outside the scope of his contractually delegated authority. Hence we must treat the arbitrator's award as if it represented an agreement between Eastern and the union as to the proper meaning of the contract's words "just cause." See St. Antoine, Judicial Review of Labor Arbitration Awards: A Second Look at *Enterprise Wheel* and Its Progeny, 75 Mich. L.Rev. 1137, 1155 (1977). For present purposes, the award is not distinguishable from the contractual agreement.

We must then decide whether a contractual reinstatement requirement would fall within the legal exception that makes unenforceable "a collective bargaining agreement that is contrary to public policy." *W.R.*

Grace & Co. v. Rubber Workers, 461 U.S. 757, 766, 103 S.Ct. 2177, 76 L.Ed.2d 298 (1983). The Court has made clear that any such public policy must be "explicit," "well defined," and "dominant." *Ibid.* It must be "ascertained 'by reference to the laws and legal precedents and not from general considerations of supposed public interests.' " *Ibid.* And, of course, the question to be answered is not whether Smith's drug use itself violates public policy, but whether the agreement to reinstate him does so. To put the question more specifically, does a contractual agreement to reinstate Smith with specified conditions, run contrary to an explicit, well-defined, and dominant public policy, as ascertained by reference to positive law and not from general considerations of supposed public interests?

III

Eastern initially argues that the District Court erred by asking, not whether the award is "contrary to" public policy "as ascertained by reference" to positive law, but whether the award "violates" positive law, a standard Eastern says is too narrow. We believe, however, that the District Court correctly articulated the standard set out in *W.R. Grace* and *Misco,* and applied that standard to reach the right result.

We agree, in principle, that courts' authority to invoke the public policy exception is not limited solely to instances where the arbitration award itself violates positive law. Nevertheless, the public policy exception is narrow and must satisfy the principles set forth in *W.R. Grace* and *Misco.* Moreover, in a case like the one before us, where two political branches have created a detailed regulatory regime in a specific field, courts should approach with particular caution pleas to divine further public policy in that area.

Eastern asserts that a public policy against reinstatement of workers who use drugs can be discerned from an examination of that regulatory regime, which consists of the Omnibus Transportation Employee Testing Act of 1991 and DOT's implementing regulations. The Testing Act embodies a congressional finding that "the greatest efforts must be expended to eliminate the * * * use of illegal drugs, whether on or off duty, by those individuals who are involved in [certain safety-sensitive positions, including] the operation of * * * trucks." Pub.L. 102–143, § 2(3), 105 Stat. 953. The Act adds that "increased testing" is the "most effective deterrent" to "use of illegal drugs." § 2(5). It requires the Secretary of Transportation to promulgate regulations requiring "testing of operators of commercial motor vehicles for the use of a controlled substance." 49 U.S.C. § 31306(b)(1)(A) (1994 ed., Supp. III). It mandates suspension of those operators who have driven a commercial motor vehicle while under the influence of drugs. 49 U.S.C. § 31310(b)(1)(A) (requiring suspension of at least one year for a first offense); § 31310(c)(2) (requiring suspension of at least 10 years for a second offense). And DOT's implementing regulations set forth sanctions applicable to those who test positive for illegal drugs. 49 CFR § 382.605 (1999).

In Eastern's view, these provisions embody a strong public policy against drug use by transportation workers in safety-sensitive positions and in favor of random drug testing in order to detect that use. Eastern argues that reinstatement of a driver who has twice failed random drug tests would undermine that policy—to the point where a judge must set aside an employer-union agreement requiring reinstatement.

Eastern's argument, however, loses much of its force when one considers further provisions of the Act that make clear that the Act's remedial aims are complex. The Act says that "rehabilitation is a critical component of any testing program," § 2(7), 105 Stat. 953, that rehabilitation "should be made available to individuals, as appropriate," *ibid.*, and that DOT must promulgate regulations for "rehabilitation programs," 49 U.S.C. § 31306(e). The DOT regulations specifically state that a driver who has tested positive for drugs cannot return to a safety-sensitive position until (1) the driver has been evaluated by a "substance abuse professional" to determine if treatment is needed, 49 CFR § 382.605(b) (1999); (2) the substance-abuse professional has certified that the driver has followed any rehabilitation program prescribed, § 382.605(c)(2)(i); and (3) the driver has passed a return-to-duty drug test, § 382.605(c)(1). In addition, (4) the driver must be subject to at least six random drug tests during the first year after returning to the job. § 382.605(c)(2)(ii). Neither the Act nor the regulations forbid an employer to reinstate in a safety-sensitive position an employee who fails a random drug test once or twice. The congressional and regulatory directives require only that the above-stated prerequisites to reinstatement be met.

Moreover, when promulgating these regulations, DOT decided not to require employers either to provide rehabilitation or to "hold a job open for a driver" who has tested positive, on the basis that such decisions "should be left to management/driver negotiation." 59 Fed.Reg. 7502 (1994). That determination reflects basic background labor law principles, which caution against interference with labor-management agreements about appropriate employee discipline.

We believe that these expressions of positive law embody several relevant policies. As Eastern points out, these policies include Testing Act policies against drug use by employees in safety-sensitive transportation positions and in favor of drug testing. They also include a Testing Act policy favoring rehabilitation of employees who use drugs. And the relevant statutory and regulatory provisions must be read in light of background labor law policy that favors determination of disciplinary questions through arbitration when chosen as a result of labor-management negotiation.

The award before us is not contrary to these several policies, taken together. The award does not condone Smith's conduct or ignore the risk to public safety that drug use by truck drivers may pose. Rather, the award punishes Smith by suspending him for three months, thereby depriving him of nearly $9,000 in lost wages, it requires him to pay the arbitration costs of both sides; it insists upon further substance-abuse treatment and testing; and it makes clear (by requiring Smith to provide a signed letter of resignation) that one more failed test means discharge.

The award violates no specific provision of any law or regulation. It is consistent with DOT rules requiring completion of substance-abuse treatment before returning to work, for it does not preclude Eastern from assigning Smith to a non-safety-sensitive position until Smith completes the prescribed treatment program. It is consistent with the Testing Act's 1–year and 10–year driving license suspension requirements, for those requirements apply only to drivers who, unlike Smith, actually operated vehicles under the influence of drugs. The award is also consistent with the Act's rehabilitative concerns, for it requires substance-abuse treatment and testing before Smith can return to work.

The fact that Smith is a recidivist—that he has failed drug tests twice—is not sufficient to tip the balance in Eastern's favor. The award punishes Smith more severely for his second lapse. And that more severe punishment, which included a 90–day suspension, would have satisfied even a "recidivist" rule that DOT once proposed but did not adopt—a rule that would have punished two failed drug tests, not with discharge, but with a driving suspension of 60 days. * * *

Regarding drug use by persons in safety-sensitive positions, then, Congress has enacted a detailed statute. And Congress has delegated to the Secretary of Transportation authority to issue further detailed regulations on that subject. Upon careful consideration, including public notice and comment, the Secretary has done so. Neither Congress nor the Secretary has seen fit to mandate the discharge of a worker who twice tests positive for drugs. We hesitate to infer a public policy in this area that goes beyond the careful and detailed scheme Congress and the Secretary have created.

We recognize that reasonable people can differ as to whether reinstatement or discharge is the more appropriate remedy here. But both employer and union have agreed to entrust this remedial decision to an arbitrator. We cannot find in the Act, the regulations, or any other law or legal precedent an "explicit," "well defined," "dominant" public policy to which the arbitrator's decision "runs contrary." *Misco,* 484 U.S., at 43, 108 S.Ct. 364; *W.R. Grace,* 461 U.S., at 766, 103 S.Ct. 2177. We conclude that the lower courts correctly rejected Eastern's public policy claim. The judgment of the Court of Appeals is

Affirmed.

JUSTICE SCALIA, with whom JUSTICE THOMAS joins, concurring in the judgment.

I concur in the Court's judgment, because I agree that no public policy prevents the reinstatement of James Smith to his position as a truck driver, so long as he complies with the arbitrator's decision, and with those requirements set out in the Department of Transportation's regulations. I do not endorse, however, the Court's statement that "[w]e agree, in principle, that courts' authority to invoke the public policy exception is not limited solely to instances where the arbitration award itself violates positive law." No case is cited to support that proposition, and none could be. There is not a single decision, since this Court washed its hands of general common-lawmaking authority, see *Erie R. Co. v. Tompkins*, 304 U.S. 64, 58 S.Ct. 817, 82 L.Ed. 1188 (1938), in which we have refused to enforce on "public policy" grounds an agreement that did not violate, or provide for the violation of, some positive law.

After its dictum opening the door to flaccid public policy arguments of the sort presented by petitioner here, the Court immediately posts a giant "Do Not Enter" sign. "[T]he public policy exception," it says, "is narrow and must satisfy the principles set forth in *W.R. Grace*," ante, at 467, which require that the applicable public policy be "explicit," "well defined," "dominant," and "ascertained 'by reference to the laws and legal precedents and not from general considerations of supposed public interests.'" It is hard to imagine how an arbitration award could violate a public policy, identified in this fashion, without actually conflicting with positive law. If such an award could ever exist, it would surely be so rare that the benefit of preserving the courts' ability to deal with it is far outweighed by the confusion and uncertainty, and hence the obstructive litigation, that the Court's Delphic "agree[ment] in principle" will engender.

Note: Lessons to be learned from *Eastern Associated Coal,* and other questions about Problem 3–4.

The issue that grabbed the Court's attention when it took the *Eastern Associated Coal* case was whether the arbitator's reinstatement of Mr. Smith violated public policy, and whether that was a basis to overturn the arbitration award. You saw that *Eastern* revisited an earlier case that dealt with public policy, *Paperworkers v. Misco.*

We chose to use *Eastern Associate Coal* in this portion of the materials because it repeats some venerated truths about the role of the courts in reviewing labor arbitration awards. See the discussion starting at Point II, where the Court reminds us that the parties have given the arbitrator the authority to interpret the meaning of their contract, and that they have "bargained for" the arbitrator's construction of the agreement. This interpretation, the Court says, will rarely be set aside. The arbitrator is on safe ground when her award draws its essence from the contract and not from her own notions of industrial justice. The arbitrator may not stray from her contractually delegated authority. Applying these principles, how much of Arbitrator Just's award is based on her interpretation of the contract, and how much on her own notions of industrial justice? Does she rely as well on statutory law? If so, does the award continue to draw its essence from the contract?

The arbitrator in the *Eastern Coal* case concluded that the company did not have just cause to discharge Smith on the basis of his testing positive for marijuana. We presume this means that the company concluded, and the arbitrator agreed, that Smith was at work while under the effects of marijuana. Why isn't this grounds for discharge? Does the opinion explain this to your satisfaction?

The arbitrator conditioned Smith's reinstatement upon his participation in a substance abuse program. He was to be subjected to continuing random drug testing. Does this suggest that the arbitrator approached Smith's condition as a disability, and allowed Smith to return to work only if he was able to successfully complete rehabilitation? Is this approach within the discretion of the arbitrator, or is she obliged to require the employer to reinstate the employee subject to rehabilitation? In short, is an employee who suffers from drug or alcohol abuse a disabled employee under the Americans with Disabilities Act? Consult Section 104 of the Americans with Disabilities Act in your statutory supplement. Section 104(a) provides that a person currently engaging in illegal use of drugs or alcohol is not a "qualified individual with a disability," hence not entitled to the protection of the ADA. But it carves out an exception in Section 104(b) for a person who has successfully completed a supervised drug rehabilitation program and is no longer using drugs. In the *Eastern Coal* case, the arbitrator required Mr. Smith to undergo drug rehabilitation as a condition of reemployment. This suggests that Mr. Smith was not in rehabilitation at the time he was fired. Do you think that an employee who has not yet undertaken rehabilitation at the time he was fired fits the shelter in Section 104(b)? Or does Section 104(b) apply only to the employee who has successfully completed a rehabilitation program and is drug free at the time he is fired? Would an employer have reason to fire an employee in that situation? What does that tell you about the likely intent of Section 104(b)?

ANOTHER EXCEPTION TO ARBITRAL FINALITY

In addition to the exceptions to arbitral finality set out in *Eastern Associated Coal,* one other should be mentioned: the award may be set aside if the aggrieved employee can show that the arbitration process was tainted by the union's failure to represent the employee fairly.

This rule was articulated by the Court in Hines v. Anchor Motor Freight, Inc., 424 U.S. 554, 96 S.Ct. 1048, 47 L.Ed.2d 231 (1976). In *Hines,* the employer, a trucking concern, fired several drivers because they allegedly padded their bills for reimbursement for overnight lodging. The drivers told their union that they put in for the correct amount, but that the motel clerk submitted a lower figure to his employer and pocketed the difference. This, said the drivers, accounted for the discrepancy between their figures and those of the motel. The union declined to pursue this suggested lead, and assured the drivers their case would be handled adequately in arbitration.

The union presented the drivers' grievance before a "joint committee," a common mechanism in the trucking industry for resolving grievances. Under this system a panel comprised of an equal number of employee and management representatives decides the grievance. If the panel is deadlocked, a neutral arbitrator will decide the case. In *Hines,* the joint committee found against the drivers. For purposes of the case, the Court treated the decision of the joint committee as if it were the same as the more typical decision of a single, neutral arbitrator. What arguments would you make that it is different?

The following brief excerpt explains why the Court thought the arbitration award was subject to judicial review, and why the union's performance didn't measure up to its duty of fair representation. Is the standard in *Hines* more or less stringent in scrutinizing the union's conduct than the standard applied in Vaca v. Sipes to a union's decision not to take a case to arbitration?

"It is true that *Vaca* dealt with a refusal by the union to process a grievance. It is also true that where the union actually utilizes the grievance and arbitration procedures on behalf of the employee, the focus is no longer on the reasons for the union's failure to act but on whether, contrary to the arbitrator's decision, the employer breached the contract and whether there is substantial reason to believe that a union breach of duty contributed to the erroneous outcome of the contractual proceedings. * * *

"But the burden on employees will remain a substantial one, far too heavy in the opinion of some. To prevail against either the company or the Union, petitioners must not only show that their discharge was contrary to the contract but must also carry the burden of demonstrating breach of duty by the Union. As the District Court indicated, this involves more than demonstrating mere errors in judgment.

"Petitioners are not entitled to relitigate their discharge merely because they offer newly discovered evidence that the charges against them were false and that in fact they were fired without cause. The grievance processes cannot be expected to be error-free. The finality provision has sufficient force to surmount occasional instances of mistake. But it is quite another matter to suggest that erroneous arbitration decisions must stand even though the employee's representation by the Union has been dishonest, in bad faith, or discriminatory; for in that event error and injustice of the grossest sort would multiply. The contractual system would then cease to qualify as an adequate mechanism to secure individual redress for damaging failure of the employer to abide by the contract. Congress has put its blessing on private dispute settlement arrangements provided in collective agreements, but it was anticipated, we are sure, that the contractual machinery would operate within some minimum levels of integrity. In our view, enforcement of the finality provision where the arbitrator has erred is conditioned upon the union's having satisfied its statutory duty fairly to represent the employee in connection with the arbitration proceedings. Wrongfully discharged employees would be left without jobs and without a fair opportunity to secure an adequate remedy. * * * "

Chapter Four

ECONOMIC SECURITY AND CAPITAL MOBILITY

The law of the workplace that we have been exploring in the preceding chapters is predicated on assumptions about efficiency, profits, fairness in decision-making, participation in workplace governance, and protection of safety and health. Another assumption, that the goals of capital and labor can be accommodated without an undue burden on either, has been severely tested by recent changes in the United States and international economies. In this chapter we look at workplace experiences involving significant re-allocations of resources and speculate a bit about the nature of future work arrangements. We also examine how the legal system has adjusted the short-term interests of labor in fairness, participation and protection and those of capital in efficiency and profits, on the one hand, with the long-term interests of society in sustained growth, on the other.

The readings in Section A describe some of the changes in the economy during the last three decades. They also raise questions about the choices made by the government, employers, entrepreneurs, labor organizations, workers, shareholders, taxpayers and consumers. One feature of the "new" economy is the accelerated speed at which capital moves: manufacturing firms shift physical capital from one location to another, and electronic transfers enable significant amounts of money to be moved from one place to another "in literally seconds."[1] We look at the consequences for the labor market and at the social costs accompanying this transformation of the economy.

In Section B we ask about the means to insure that the changes in the new economy are shared equitably by employees, shareholders, entrepreneurs, taxpayers. The inquiry about means is two-fold: how has

1. Barry Bluestone and Bennett Harrison call this the "hypermobility" of capital in books which analyze the phenomenon, The Deindustrialization of America (1982) and Growing Prosperity: The Battle for Growth with Equity in the Twenty–First Century (2000).

the law responded to the problems at the workplace associated with accelerated capital mobility and how could the law be used to address these problems. The inquiry covers a lot of ground. The primary vehicle for traversing this territory is a series of case studies involving profit-motivated business decisions and the effects of those decisions on workers, owners, shareholders and communities. For each case study we describe a transaction and its implications, offer examples of how adversely affected parties have used the law to challenge or to reshape the transaction, and then widen the inquiry to explore untried means that could accommodate the desire for unimpeded capital mobility and the continuing commitments to fairness, participation and protection. Throughout we turn for guidance to the four models for structuring the employment relationship that we explored in the preceding chapters—control through the market, protection for individual rights, meaningful exercise of collective rights, and statutory regulation through minimum standards.

We conclude our investigation into the relationship between capital mobility and economic security with an introduction to employment-related legal issues arising from doing business in the global economy. In this evolving area, policy questions dominate and, as sections C and D demonstrate, economic and political considerations structure the debate about legal resolutions.

A. INTRODUCTION

The readings in this section introduce labor and employment issues associated with the changing economy. We begin with two commentators who offer the traditional justifications for minimally regulated markets. We then present observations on how the economy and the labor market have changed and on how workers, communities and the government have coped with accelerated capital mobility. Finally, we look at where the work is and is likely to be found in the near future.

In the debate over unimpeded capital mobility and short-term economic security there is no obviously correct position. You may well conclude that the gains from minimally regulated markets amply justify the labor-and-employment-related costs; or you may question why the law should not redistribute some of the benefits and burdens.

1. FREE ENTERPRISE CAPITALISM: THEORY AND PRACTICE

THOMAS J. HAILSTONES

Basic Economics, 5th ed. 1976.
37–39.

Basic economic questions apply to any type of economic system. Decisions on what to produce, how much to produce, and what method to adopt in allocating goods and services are confronted by any society, but the questions are answered in different ways.* * *

A free enterprise capitalistic system, or market economy is distinguished from other types of economic systems by the fact that the decisions as to what and how much to produce, and the manner in which goods and services are to be allocated, are made primarily by the actions of individuals and firms in the economy. Both socialism and communism, on the other hand, advocate a considerable degree of government direction and control of the production and distribution functions of their economies.

Under our capitalistic system, capital goods are owned and used mainly by individuals and firms in the economy, rather than by governmental agencies. This capital may be in the form of machinery, equipment, and buildings, or it may be represented by money that can be used to purchase these capital goods. The institution of private property is essential to a capitalistic system. This implies more than the ownership of real estate. It means that individuals not only have the right to own, use, or sell machinery, equipment, and buildings, but that they also have the right to the ownership of the fruits of their productivity. Thus, when the farmer grows cotton on his land with the use of his labor and capital, the cotton becomes his property and he can dispose of it as he sees fit. In a similar fashion, a firm that produces shoes is entitled to the ownership of the shoes and can sell them if it desires. After compensating the owners of the other resources that have contributed to the production of the shoes, the firm is entitled to what is left of the total revenue. This residual return is called profit, and profit is the incentive for obtaining and using capital goods to produce goods and services that satisfy consumer needs.

Under the free enterprise system individuals may offer their services to someone else in exchange for a wage payment, let someone use their land in exchange for rent, or lend their money to another in exchange for an interest payment. On the other hand, instead of selling productive services to another, a person can combine several factors of production to produce goods and sell them at a profit. But to operate a business, one must produce goods or services that people want and must offer them at a price they are willing to pay. The farmer who grows cotton and sells it at a profit is benefitting not only himself but also the community by supplying a basic commodity that is needed or desired. Likewise, the shoe producer is satisfying people's wants for shoes in addition to making a profit. Since the cotton grower and shoe producer may use the labor, land, and capital of others, they provide jobs and income for other members of the community. Thus, in a model situation the producer, in the process of using property to make a profit, will increase the well-being of other people. To be successful, consumer demand must be satisfied. In some situations, however, the producer may suffer a loss or may exploit people by supplying them with an inferior product or by underpaying the factors of production that are utilized.

In the operation of our economic system, the ultimate use of our manpower and resources and the allocation of goods and services are determined primarily by consumer demand. Individuals express their demand in the prices they are willing to pay. Usually the stronger the demand, other things being equal, the higher the price that consumers will pay for a particular good or service. In an effort to make a profit, people in business cater to consumer demand. Through the prices we are willing to pay as consumers, businesses obtain the revenue necessary to purchase the manpower, resources, and capital goods necessary for producing the goods and services that are demanded. The opportunity to make profits serves as an incentive for businesses to produce these goods and services.

If the demand for a particular commodity is strong enough, it will be produced. Sometimes, however, there is such a large demand for total goods and services that we do not have sufficient manpower and capital to produce all of them. What, then, is produced? Once again, in a model system it is the consumers who decide. The firms and industries with the strongest demand for their products will have the revenues necessary to bid relatively scarce productive agents away from other uses. If consumer demand for a particular commodity is weak and the price offer is so low that it does not permit sufficient profit to the producer, few resources will be devoted to its production.

Free enterprise capitalism, resting as it does on the institution of private property and on the profit incentive, relies upon competition to make the system function. Business firms compete for shares of the consumer's dollar. In the markets for productive resources they compete for scarce resources. In a command economy, production quotas are assigned to firms by a political leader or a planning committee. Similarly, resources are directed to employment in various industries. When allocation decisions are decentralized, however, competition serves to regulate the volume of output and the allocation of resources.

If competition is effective, the economy functions efficiently without an overseer. Through competition consumers are protected against the marketing of shoddy products and the charging of exorbitant prices. The prospect that rival firms will offer a better product at the same price or a comparable product at a lower price forces each firm to maintain quality and restrict price increases. Resource owners are protected against exploitation by the opportunity of alternative employments made available by competitive firms. The possibility open to the resource owner of selling resource services to the highest bidder prevents any one firm from keeping resources in its own employ at depressed prices. In this way effective competition regulates the power of business firms, preventing any one firm from dominating the market. Each firm is free to pursue its own profit without direct concern for the overall allocation of resources and products in the economy. Yet the impersonal force of competition assures the regulation of production and the flow of resources toward the most efficient firms that can afford to offer the highest prices for the factors of production.

Of course, competition is not always effective, and it is seldom perfect. Sometimes business firms may be able to exclude others from the industry and thereby exercise almost unlimited control over price, industry output, and employment conditions. When this happens, it is deemed the responsibility of government to restore competitive conditions. Rather than taking control of the industry or assuming ownership of the means of production, the central political authority is expected to impose legal sanctions against restraint of competition or abuses that are defended in the name of competition.

The guiding principle of competitive capitalism is that privately owned business firms should produce the goods and services wanted by consumers in the quantities they wish to consume. So that firms may satisfy consumer wants by pursuing the immediate goal of profit, competition is relied upon as a mechanism for regulating trade. Only where it is believed that competition cannot be made to work effectively—such as police and fire protection or public utilities—does the government operate to influence or control production. Otherwise the government is expected to create and enforce laws which assure that at least minimal conditions of competition will prevail.

CHARLES E. LINDBLOM, UNIONS AND CAPITALISM

6–9 (1949).

The characteristic features of our economy can be read in the term "competitive price system." The essential fact about it is that order is produced through the instrumentality of price with a minimum of discretionary group control. It needs to be called a competitive price system to distinguish it from price systems built on other legal bases. In our society the fuel in the social engine is the self-interest of thousands of independent entrepreneurs. But one can also imagine a price system operated through government ownership of business enterprise or one composed solely of consumer cooperatives.

The concept of an economic system calls to mind a method of "doing business" or "earning a living." These impressions are inadequate for an understanding of the role of price in the American social-economic order. The system has to be seen as a social mechanism for performing certain functions necessary to the general welfare.

The main job of the economic system is to economize: that is, to use scarce resources so as to achieve the maximum satisfaction of human wants from them. Whose wants are to be satisfied, whether those of a minority or a majority, will depend upon the policies of the society. In a democracy the wants of the majority presumably set the society's goals. In any case the economic problem is given in the discrepancy between scarce resources, on the one hand, and the unlimited wants, on the other hand, of whatever group in a society can control the economizing process.

The difficulty of maintaining a prosperous economy inevitably directs the public's immediate attention to problems of monetary management and employment. The result is that we begin to talk and act as though the function of an economic system were to maintain itself in running order, avoid inflation, and create as many jobs as possible. But granted that these may be intelligent goals of public policy, they are not the goals of economic activity any more than it is the function of a locomotive not to burn out a bearing.

The essential talk in the economizing process is intelligent choice among alternative uses for the limited resources. For an individual and a society alike, the difference between a wise and foolish choice is logically clear cut. To sacrifice a greater value to gain a lesser one is senseless. And to refuse to sacrifice a lesser value for a greater one is no wiser. What is sacrificed to gain a commodity is, in familiar terms, its cost. A society chooses intelligently, then, when costs are minimized.

The economizing process therefore requires a systematic method for comparing values, for calculating costs, and for allocating resources in accordance with choices made. All this is done through price in our economy. Values and cost are measured in price, the enterprise is controlled through cost-price relationships, and the allocation of resources to the enterprise is governed by price.

The price system necessarily involves many particular operations, each intricate in itself. Wants or choices are indicated by consumers acting as they freely decide in purchasing at a price, and changes in consumer demands are reflected in price movements. An elaborate set of legal rules is required to make production respond to these consumer purchases. Specifically, production must be regulated by the requirement that price cover cost. Costs in turn are prices on resources, reflecting values of the resources in alternate uses. This is achieved by arrangements which set price on resources in any given use according to the value of increases in production which could be had by applying the resources to the best alternative use.

The distribution of income is determined as a by-product of the pricing of productive resources, since the wage income of a laborer is determined when his productive capacity is priced as a resource. Workers' preferences with regard to conditions of work are expressed through the terms of the wage bargain, just as consumer preferences are indicated in the market for consumer goods and services. If workers feel a strong desire for safe and comfortable conditions of work rather than remuneration solely in money income, employers competing for their services will take account of preferences.

In short, three characteristics distinguish the price system. Wants or choices are indicated by individuals or very small groups, acting independently, buying at a price; costs are calculated with reference to the value of resources in alternative uses; and production is governed by the rule that cost must not exceed price. The complexity and impersonality of the system are at once apparent.

Needless to say, the price system is by no means the perfectly competitive economy of the economists or anything closely approaching it. It is shot through with monopoly and other imperfections. But these do not destroy the major outlines of the structure any more than misrepresentation of the population through improper apportionment of legislators destroys the basic structure of political democracy. Great as these imperfections are, the society remains dependent upon the framework of the price system just as it does on the framework of political democracy.

It is therefore naive to say that the price system today is largely nonexistent. The objection is no more serious than that of college students who with the new learning of their first course in political science tell their less enlightened friends that the United States is not really a democracy.

When production is undertaken, it is largely at the instigation of profit-seeking businessmen; when production fails, it is because the opportunities for expansion are inadequate in their eyes; when there are maladjustments in the economy, it is because relative prices are improperly adjusted; when resources are not used aimlessly, it is because under the rules of a price system their owners can profit from their systematic allocation; when production is responsive to consumer wants, it is because the consumer may express his desires through the marketplace. For good or bad, when "things get done" in the economy it is largely through the pricing mechanism. Even the economic activities of government operate through it in the recruitment of labor, equipment, and raw materials.

PETER CAPPELLI,
THE NEW DEAL AT WORK

76 Chi–Kent L. Rev. 1169, 1175–78.
2000.

The world began to change for employers with the 1981–82 recession, the worst economic period since the Great Depression, which brought with it structural changes that went well beyond the usual cyclical downturn in product demand. A number of important changes in the economy and in the way business was conducted got underway in that period. They include the following:

A. Pressures to Increase Shareholder Value: The rising influence of institutional investors and legal decisions made maximizing shareholder value not only the singular goal for directors of public companies and the executives they managed, but also made shareholders the only stakeholder to whom companies were legally accountable. New financial institutions such as junk bonds made possible hostile takeovers of companies that were not maximizing shareholder value. Any resources that companies may have devoted to other causes, such as protecting employees from business risks, were quickly transferred to the goal of shareholder value. More important, investors and analysts seem to be persuaded that cutting jobs raises shareholder value even though the hard evidence on that point is decidedly mixed. New accounting techniques, such as economic value added to maximize shareholder value, punish fixed costs, including the fixed investments in employees.

B. Changes in the Boundaries of the Firm: Companies were persuaded that divesting unrelated businesses and acquiring new ones with appropriate synergies could raise shareholder value, and mergers and acquisitions rose to record levels year after year. Companies concerned about focusing on their core competencies learned to outsource functions that were not central to their capabilities and to pursue joint ventures as an alternative to internal development of capabilities. The consequence for employment was to disrupt long-term career paths and, more fundamentally, to make the security of all functions and jobs uncertain. Any operation could be divested if changing markets and changing patterns of competition align themselves, and all functions could be outsourced if a low-cost vendor comes along. One might say that the number of good jobs stays the same in this model and just moves around from company to company, but such movement and the constant uncertainty about movement undermines job security and any attempt to develop long-term careers.

C. Changes in the Speed of Competition: Shorter production cycles and more rapid change in business strategies associated with faster-paced competition makes skills obsolete more quickly. The examples here are like the change from physical chemistry to biotechnology in pharmaceuticals or from one market segment in insurance to another, where the skills needed are completely different. Employers simply do not have time to develop the new skills they need internally where dramatic changes in products and strategies happen quickly. So they turn to outside hiring to get those new skills. They also turn to outside hiring to get the managerial skills and experience to facilitate changes in their administrative operations. One way to think about these developments is that product life cycles have now become shorter than the expected career of an employee, as explained below.

D. Changes in Management Systems: Work systems that empower employees, such as cross-functional teams, break down traditional job ladders, eliminate supervisory positions, and widen spans of control. Information systems eliminate many of the internal control functions of middle management positions, and decentralizing operations through the creation of profit centers and similar arrangements further reduce the need for central administration. Flatter hierarchies and the sharp reduction in central administration reduces promotion prospects.

E. Policy Pressure: Public policy in the 1980s contributed to the pressures to unbundle employee protection provisions inside firms. The Reagan Administration explicitly argued for increasing employer discretion in employment decisions in an attempt to link economic competitiveness to the ability to shed redundant employees, a position that arguably had more influence on management than the decision to fire the striking Professional Air Traffic Controllers Organization workers. Various reports gave guidance as to the best ways to cut workforces. Even under a democratic administration, the U.S. Department of Labor had by 1995 accepted that companies would continue to restructure their operations in ways that cut jobs. It argued not for preventing such changes but for minimizing the damage to employees.

Coercive pressures from leaders in the employer community also reversed. IBM's announcement of its decision to abandon employment security and lay off employees was followed shortly thereafter by a wave of layoffs among other large employers. The business community organized itself to press for greater flexibility in employment. For example, the Labor Policy Association, an employer group concerned with public policy, produced a widely circulated study arguing that the key to improved corporate performance is greater management discretion in employment decisions, in other words, the end of administrative practices to protect jobs.

The requirements of employment legislation also created incentives to unravel the internalized employment structure, incentives that built as regulations increased. The vast array of federal legislation directed at employment has largely been tied to the traditional, internalized model of employment. Alternative arrangements, such as contracting out or contingent work, can mean that "employers" are no longer covered by the legislation, freeing them from its obligations.

F. Market Alternatives: An enormous market has developed to respond to these developments. Vendors who will take in every function that could be outsourced now exist. Staffing agencies will lease employees with any set of skills, even CEOs, so that labor costs can be transformed from fixed to variable costs. And, as noted below, corporate recruiters now offer a rich menu of available applicants to any employer willing to pursue outside hiring.

White-collar and managerial employees have experienced the most fundamental changes because they are the ones with the most protections to lose. First, they now face much the same increased insecurity and instability as production workers, a profound change as it undermines what has been the very basis of the distinction between white collar and blue collar. That distinction stems from the New Deal Era's Fair Labor Standards Act which was based on the assumption that production workers needed legislative protections that white-collar workers did not because the latter were already protected by the firm. Second, white-collar employees have seen internal careers evaporate as job ladders shrink, restructuring disrupts the promotion tracks that remain, and external hiring blocks advancement by filling more senior positions.
* * *

2. THE CHANGING LABOR MARKET AND ITS EFFECTS

The developments described above have profound consequences for labor and employment relations. Kenneth Dau–Schmidt compares the labor market as it functioned from the end of World War II (1945) through the 1990s. Vicki Schultz comments on the consequences for workers and communities. Maria Ontiveros discusses whether there is latent racism in the impact of markets.

KENNETH G. DAU–SCHMIDT, EMPLOYMENT IN THE NEW AGE OF TRADE AND TECHNOLOGY: IMPLICATIONS FOR LABOR AND EMPLOYMENT LAW

76 Ind. L. J. 1,1, 8–12.
2001.

Trade and technology have always dictated the nature of the employment relationship, and accordingly the issues that are important in labor and employment law. * * *

A. THE GOLDEN AGE OF LIFETIME EMPLOYMENT IN AMERICA

Lifetime employment, governed by an internal labor market, has been the dominant paradigm of employment relationships in America throughout the twentieth century. Although its roots go back to the employment practices of William Durant and Henry Ford in the 1910s and 1920s, the paradigm of lifetime employment reached the zenith of its reign in America during the decades just after World War II. During this period, international competition was of small concern to most American businesses. The United States emerged from the war as one of the few nations with its productive capacity intact. Indeed, American manufacturing had been greatly strengthened during the war due to government investments in technology and productive capacity. As a result, American manufacturing dominated world trade. Although some American industries were highly competitive, many, such as the auto, steel, and petroleum industries, settled into "comfortable" relations with their domestic competitors. Corporate strategies for increasing profits were based on vertical integration and growth. Following the lead of General Motor's William Durant, most firms saw vertical integration of production as necessary to ensure adequate quality and quantity of the requisite components of the finished product.

This environment proved fertile for the growth of lifetime employment and internal labor markets. The relative security of American firms in international and domestic competition made it easy for firms to accept the risk that fixed investments, such as investments in employees' skills would become obsolete and made flexibility in production methods a low priority. Moreover, the large vertically integrated corporate enterprises that evolved during this time lent themselves to governance by internal labor markets. The administrative staff necessary to run the internal labor market posed a relatively small addition to the managerial staff necessary to run these large vertically integrated operations, while the steps of the vertical operation proved amenable to the "career ladders" of promotion found in the internal labor market. Furthermore, tight labor markets in the postwar boom years encouraged employers to try to keep and to further develop skilled employees. Accordingly, during this period, lifetime employment governed by internal labor markets was viewed by many managers and academics as the "best" management practice, at least for large companies.

What did the lifetime employment relationship look like during this period? As an idealized example, we might examine the employment practices of IBM from 1950 to 1985. The concept of lifetime employment was first undertaken by IBM in the1950s with the adoption of distinctive criteria for hiring employees. Under the IBM plan, specific job skills were much less important than general aptitude, team work skills, and "character," because the company itself planned to develop the employees' particular job skills. Indeed, once hired, an employee was subjected to an extensive training regimen that never ended during the course of his or her career. This training included skills training at the firm's Armonk training center, on-the-job training in a variety of firm positions chosen for the employee's development, and generous programs to facilitate or pay for employee training at institutions of higher education. Every manager's performance appraisal included employee development as a goal. Because IBM was large, and had few competitors, it was relatively easy for the corporation to develop and follow long-term business plans. This long-term planning allowed IBM to develop the skills and talent it needed internally by promoting skills development among its employees and promoting successful employees up the corporate ladder. IBM managed demand swings internally by shifting employees from one production process to another and was "proud of the fact that it had never had a layoff in its forty-year history as a modern computer company"—a fact that it advertised to all potential new hires. IBM was rewarded for these efforts with a highly skilled workforce, thoroughly versed in the operations of the firm, motivated by internal promotions and rewards, and loyal to the company that had undertaken to invest in and guarantee their futures.

B.   THE NEW AGE OF TRADE AND TECHNOLOGY AND THE RISE OF SHORT-TERM AND CONTINGENT EMPLOYMENT

During the last three decades of the twentieth century, the conditions that fostered lifetime employment and internal labor markets began to change. First, international competition became a much more important factor for most American firms. The complete victory of the proponents of free trade, as represented in a variety of international treaties, has combined with a retooled Europe and Japan and with industrial development in previously third-world countries, to ensure that American companies across the entire breadth of our economy now feel the pressures of international competition. Indeed, the breadth of this change, in concert with a growth in American consumer demand for services, has caused the transformation of the American economy from one dominated by manufacturing to one dominated by its service sector. Together with the deregulation movement over the same period, the increase in international trade in the last quarter of the twentieth century has ensured that most American firms operate in a much more competitive environment than they previously did.

Second, new information technology has both facilitated the movement of capital from country to country and allowed new methods of managing firms and organizing production that bring the market inside the firm. Increased communication and information processing capabilities allow companies to keep track of and manage plants and investments in other countries. The increased mobility of capital in the international economy has meant that employees must now compete with workers in other countries merely to retain the allegiance of their employer. The improvements in information gathering and processing capabilities have also allowed employers to trim mid-level management positions and devolve some management responsibilities to lower-level employees. As a result, the managerial ranks are much leaner than in times past and some of the past distinctions between managers and the managed have disappeared. Furthermore, the new information technology has allowed employers to collect and manage data on rivals and potential suppliers and use this information as a "benchmark" for the performance of their own divisions and operations. As a result, individual departments and divisions within firms have been placed in direct competition with their rivals in a way not previously experienced in the modern corporation. Finally, the new information technology allows employers to collect and manage information on the current capabilities and capacities of component suppliers to an extent not previously possible outside a single firm. Thus, it is no longer necessary for firms to be vertically integrated to ensure the adequate quality and quantity of their component parts, and methods of production increasingly rely on the subcontracting of important production work.

The economic environment in the new age of trade and technology is much less hospitable to internal labor markets and lifetime employment. The increased level of competition to which firms are subject has increased the risk of fixed investments such as employee training, and caused firms to put new emphasis on flexibility in methods of production. As the level of competition has increased, firms have tended to focus on ever smaller areas of "core competency" in which they enjoy some competitive advantage. With the narrowing of corporate interests, fixed investments, such as specialized employee skills, run a greater risk of becoming useless to the firm.

Moreover, with greater competition, American firms are more subject to the dictates of the market place and want to remain flexible in order to respond to changes in demand. As a result, firms are less amenable to accepting the risk that employee skills will become obsolete and to locking themselves into long-term employment commitments.

In addition, the new information technology has allowed the reorganization of firms in leaner ways that are internally more subject to the machinations of the market and less integrated in their levels of production. The paring of mid-level managers from the operations of the firms and the availability of market-oriented management strategies such as benchmarking has made the administration necessary for internal labor markets relatively more expensive. Why maintain a large and costly human resources apparatus when the rest of your management tasks are being streamlined and reoriented to the market?

Finally, the disintegration of the firm allows for the subcontracting of work to various suppliers. Such subcontracting changes the firm's concerns back to payment for product and dismantles the larger corporate enterprises that served as vehicles for long-term careers. It is perhaps not surprising then that currently the "best" management practices identified by managers and academics are those that focus on flexibility and an immediate orientation to the market.

No single example demonstrates all of the many ways in which the employment relationship is changing in the new age of trade and technology, but perhaps the most talked about is the Volkswagen truck assembly plant in Resende, Brazil. Although most employers usually retain at least a core of "permanent" employees, supplementing them with temporary employees or subcontractors to handle particular components or seasonal variations in demand, the Volkswagen truck plant in Resende employs almost no permanent employees. Instead, truck production is undertaken in four "modules" which are produced by four different subcontractors within the Volkswagen plant. Once employees from one subcontractor assemble the chassis, it makes its way down the main assembly line as employees from other subcontractors assemble and attach their components. Yellow lines on the floor of the plant delineate the area in which each subcontractor is supposed to operate. Volkswagen's relationship with the subcontractors runs on a quarterly basis and the subcontractors accordingly make no commitment of long-term employment to their employees. Employees of the subcontractors earn about a third of the wage of unionized Volkswagen workers in São Paulo, Brazil. Although this "virtual Volkswagen" plant is still somewhat unique, there are plans to emulate its system of subcontracted modular production in the industry. General Motors is currently engaged in negotiations to undertake subcontracted modular production at four of its American plants, including the new Saturn plant, under its "project Yellowstone." * * *

The change in the American workplace from the paradigm of internal labor market and lifetime employment to the paradigm of international spot markets and short-term employment raises a number of important issues in labor and employment law: How will employers gain adequate information on prospective employees and monitor the work of those employees while not infringing the employees' freedom from defamation and right to privacy? How can we encourage employers to take an interest in adequately training short-term employees? How can we promote the expression of employees' collective voice in this market-driven atomistic environment? How do we ensure employees opportunities for benefits and promotions in multi employer careers? Finally, how can the nations preserve their national sovereignty and their ability to effectively regulate the employment relationship in a global economy? These are the questions that will dominate labor and employment law for the foreseeable future. * * *

VICKI SCHULTZ, LIFE'S WORK

100 Colum. L. Rev. 1881, 1924–1927.
November 2000.

According to many commentators, declining job security is one of the hallmarks of the new economic order. Both job stability (the tendency of workers to form long-term bonds with their employers) and job security (workers' ability to remain in their jobs so long as their performance is satisfactory) apparently have declined over the last two decades. Many employees now feel more insecure about their jobs, and for good reason: Involuntary job loss increased in the 1990s and impacted roughly ten percent of the population. Job displacement is not limited to low-skilled workers. The 1990s saw a significant increase in the risk of job loss for white-collar workers—including managers, whose rate of job loss due to "position abolished" more than doubled. Even in today's red-hot economy, displaced workers face a hard time finding new jobs. In a recent Economic Policy Institute study, more than one-third of displaced workers were still out of work when interviewed one to three years later. Those who did manage to find new jobs earned less and were less likely to retain health insurance.

The new economy forces everyone—even many once-secure workers—to live with increased insecurity and inestimable risk. In such a climate, the cultural imperative is to keep moving and taking risks: Those afraid to leap are said to deserve to be stuck. In this new organizational/cultural economy, advancing age is associated with fearfulness and fixity. Management argues that "older workers have inflexible mindsets and are risk-averse, as well as lacking in the sheer physical energy needed to cope with the demands of life in the flexible workplace." The notion that young workers are flexible, while older workers are rigid, provides an ideological justification for targeting older workers for devaluation and dismissal. Accumulated experience is no longer seen as something that deserves respect and value. Instead, it is a sign of worthlessness which will mark even well-off workers with the passage of time.

In addition to downsizing and eliminating clear internal career trajectories, many corporations have turned to various forms of nonstandard (sometimes called contingent) work. Many companies have converted full-time positions into part-time, temporary, contract, or on-call jobs, or outsourced them to "temp" agencies or subcontractors that offer lower wages and no benefits, and other firms are creating these forms of employment at rapid rates. Although some highly-educated workers may enjoy the flexibility that such forms of contracting entail, it is a return to Lochnerian formalism to refer to most of these contingent workers as free agents or entrepreneurs. As two recent studies by the Economic Policy Institute show, most forms of employment that do not involve full-time, year-round jobs are inferior to such standard jobs. Nonstandard jobs are significantly less likely to provide health insurance or a pension; they are more likely to be temporary, and they do not typically lead to regular employment, at least with the same firm.

Furthermore, most people who work in nonstandard jobs earn less than regular full-time workers. Both men and women in all types of nonstandard work (except contracting) are more likely to receive poverty-level hourly wages than workers with similar personal and job characteristics employed in regular full-time jobs. Although most people who work in nonstandard job arrangements are worse off than standard jobholders on a variety of dimensions, women of all races and minority men tend to occupy the lowest-paying types of nonstandard jobs.

A second major characteristic of the new economic order is increasing wage inequality. Despite some initial controversy about its existence, the growth in the earnings gap between the highest-and lowest-paid workers has by now been well-documented. Between 1979 and 1990, there was a sharp increase in the likelihood that a year-round, full-time worker would have annual earnings below the poverty-level; the same trend also held for all workers. This widening wage distribution occurred throughout the economy—at least among men—in virtually every occupation and industry and in both the manufacturing and service sectors. Among women, the picture was more complicated: For better-educated women, wages increased, as discrimination and job segregation by sex decreased. For less-skilled women, wages declined, although not as steeply as for their male counterparts (who had farther to fall).

According to recent research, the dramatic growth in wage inequality has continued into the 1990s, but its character has shifted. In the 1980s, there was a growing separation between top and middle earners versus middle and bottom earners. But in the 1990s, the inequality was generated by a divergence between the top and everyone else. The status of those in the middle deteriorated. According to the Economic Policy Institute study, male white-collar wages have stagnated or declined. Even "women workers in the middle and upper-middle part of the wage distribution, who saw real wages rise significantly in the 1980s, have experienced a sharp deceleration in the 1990s." Although a tight economy brought wage increases in the last few years of the 1990s, as of 1999, the improvements of 1997–98 had still left wage trends in the 1990s no better than they were for most workers in the 1980s. "To the extent that the typical American family has been able to hold its ground, the most important factor has been the large increase in the hours worked by family members."

Like other concerned scholars and activists, I believe these changes threaten the social order. Richard Sennett argues that a commitment to work performed over the course of a life is a precondition to a stable society and strong sense of self, and I think he is right. As the notion of a career that progresses through a few institutions is eroding, as the marshaling even of a singled bundle of skills through the course of a life are declining, as more and more people work harder and harder to have fleeting associations with strangers in short-term jobs in new locations, something vital is lost (and it is not simply wages). Working with one's peers in pursuit of common goals is the structure upon which a vibrant civic life rests. Stable work is the experience through which we create coherent life stores. We need work to sustain ourselves and our loved ones. We need to live free of the anxiety produced by not knowing when one's next project—and paycheck—are coming, or whether they will come at all.

MARIA L. ONTIVEROS
A VISION OF GLOBAL CAPITALISM THAT PUTS
WOMEN AND PEOPLE OF COLOR AT THE CENTER

3 Journal of Small and Emerging Business Law 27, 36–37.
Summer 1999.

[T]he growth of contingency in the white working class has been consciously used to fuel racism, in order to divert the workers' attention from their own exploitation. In the United States the rich are getting richer, the stock market is going through the roof, and corporate profits are skyrocketing. The white working class, however, is not sharing in this boom. In fact, the profits are coming at the expense of workers: the current record rise in profits is a direct result of a shift in income from wages to profits. In the United States, for example, had the shift from labor to capital not occurred, the current wage growth would be twice the actual rate. Seeing all the prosperity, while personally experiencing tough economic times, leads to cognitive dissonance in the working class. The economic and political right have capitalized on the dissonance and convinced this group that their problems are caused not by capitalist exploitation, but by immigrants coming in to take their jobs and by African Americans and women unjustly benefitting from affirmative action.

In a different variation racism, specifically the notion of a racial hierarchy, is reinforced when inhumane labor conditions are justified as appropriate for "other" workers. When child labor is described as the "best alternative" for Pakistani children or Vietnamese wage scales as sufficient for people in that situation, we accept inhumane situations for some workers that we would not accept for American workers. Feelings of racial superiority are also promoted when the white working class is told that at least they are doing better than the nonwhite workers.

The use of Indian engineers by the Silicon Valley computer industry illustrates many of these concepts. At the same time that companies are laying off thousands of middle-level engineers and managers, the companies are asking that immigration quotas on H–1B or temporary skilled worker visas be raised, ostensibly because there is a shortage of such workers. Others argue that these workers are hired because they can be more easily exploited. They are paid less, are hired as independent contractors without full employee benefits, and are temporary (either by contract or through visa design). They are also tied to their employer by the visa restrictions, which make them unable to move to other, more desirable jobs at other companies unless they get new work visas and pay hefty penalties to their original employers. Meanwhile, the white, male engineers are told that their jobs were eliminated either because the company had to save spots for "affirmative action" hires or because foreign competition—read as nonwhite, non-American workers—have taken their jobs. All this occurs as the companies experience record profits and their CEOs record salaries. * * *

B. LEGAL RESPONSES TO ACCELERATED CAPITAL MOBILITY

1. GOING OUT OF BUSINESS

> **CASE STUDY: LOCAL 1330 STEEL WORKERS v. U.S. STEEL REPRISED**
>
> As you no doubt recall, U.S. Steel, like most United States steel producers, lost its competitive position, and the board of directors decided to reassure investors by developing the non-steel lines of business and by stopping capital investments in steel production facilities. Long-time steel workers lost their jobs and a community lost its largest employer and tax payer. Let's assume that, having decided to shut down steel production facilities, the board of directors adopts a new name, like Natural Gas Inc. Shareholders have the option of holding onto or selling their shares.
>
> *Does the law allow the board of directors to close operations in order to maximize shareholder returns?*

a. The Law

Unprofitable or underperforming enterprises are likely targets for liquidation. So are profitable businesses whose owners (or shareholders and management) want to take their gains and pursue other ventures.

Unsurprisingly, state and federal laws impose few employment-related restrictions on the decision to go out of business. As we saw in *Local 1330, Steel Workers v. U.S. Steel* (in chapter one), judges may sympathize with the losses experienced by employees and communities, but the judiciary is bound by legal principles that reflect and reinforce the laissez-faire tradition of the United States economy. Indeed, even when employers terminate operations for societally condemned reasons, like closing to escape unionization, the law deplores but generally allows the action. For example, in Textile Workers Union v. Darlington Mfg. Co., 380 U.S. 263, 85 S.Ct. 994, 13 L.Ed.2d 827 (1965), the employer closed one of its many facilities and broadcast its anti-union animus to the remaining employees of the enterprise. The Supreme Court found a violation of § 8 (a) (3) because Darlington reaped the future benefit of employee reluctance to unionize or to press for better working conditions. Closing down unaccompanied by self-generated future benefits is legal. And the Supreme Court, having instructed how *not* to go out of business, employers rarely make the mistake that Darlington did. As we will see, it is not difficult to accomplish an illegal end through legal means.

Is this fair? Let's assume an economist could present a convincing case that it is socially desirable to continue marginal operations. Perhaps her argument is that some closings are too costly when the hidden expenses, like increased demand for unemployment benefits and social services and lost tax revenues, are included in the calculations. How could a law require a company to continue operations and to make the capital investments necessary for maintenance and new technology? To take the hypothetical a step further: If the law could require capital investments in failing companies, why not governmental oversight of healthy companies to insure investment decisions consistent with the companies' continuing viability? (You may recall from your property class one such experiment: In the 1960s judges ordered that residential rental properties meet standards of habitability; many landlords promptly abandoned buildings rather than make the investments deemed necessary by the judiciary. Is this example instructive for our purposes, or do you think business owners would respond differently to investment mandates than the landlords?)

In 1988 Congress enacted the Worker Adjustment and Retraining Notification Act (WARN), reproduced in the statutory supplement. One of WARN's express purposes was to cushion the impact of closings on working people and their communities. If WARN had been a part of the federal law when the Local 1330 events occurred, would its provisions have had a significant impact on U.S. Steel's decision to close steel-producing operations?

b. Does a Collective Bargaining Agreement Make a Difference?

LOCAL 461 v. SINGER CO.

United States District Court, Southern District of New Jersey, 1982.
540 F.Supp. 442.

STERN, DISTRICT JUDGE.

The Singer Company has announced its intention to close its sewing machine manufacturing facility in Elizabeth, New Jersey by the end of 1982. The company's employees now sue to compel Singer to keep the plant open. Plaintiffs contend that in exchange for millions of dollars in union "give-backs," the company agreed to keep the Elizabeth facility open for the length of the agreement by investing $2 million to restructure the plant and by using best efforts to keep the plant open, at least in part by securing defense contract work to supplement the manufacture of sewing machines. Plaintiffs claim that Singer has neither spent the $2 million nor used best efforts to secure defense work. Plaintiffs bring this action pursuant to section 301 of the National Labor Relations Act, 29 U.S.C. § 185, alleging that Singer has thereby breached its collective bargaining agreement with Local 461 of the International Union of Electrical, Radio and Machine Workers, AFL–CIO ("Local 461"). Plaintiffs, seeking specific performance of the agreement, ask the Court to enter a preliminary and permanent injunction restraining defendant from taking any steps to close the Elizabeth facility during the term of the contract or, at least, until Singer fulfills its contractual obligations. In addition, plaintiffs seek damages for defendant's alleged breach.

It is Singer's contention that the collective bargaining agreement imposes no obligation on the company to stay in business. Singer argues that while it was obligated to spend $2 million to restructure the Elizabeth plant to make it more efficient, it at no time surrendered what it characterizes as the prerogative of any company to go out of business when it so desires. Singer argues, in addition, that although it has admittedly breached its contract by failing to spend the $2 million, it should be excused from the payment of any damages because performance under the contract became impracticable by November 1981, less than five months after it was signed, due to an unexpected and severe decline in market demand. In other words, Singer wishes to close this plant and walk away from the situation, without incurring any damages, despite the fact that it has operated the Elizabeth plant since May 1981 with the benefit of substantial union "give-backs" that were extracted on the basis of promises which have now been breached.

The Court finds that the agreement, which is clear and unambiguous, contains no promise that Singer will refrain from discontinuing operations in Elizabeth. * * *

At the hearing on May 14, 1982, plaintiffs conceded in the following colloquy that Appendix Z [of the agreement] cannot be construed as a guarantee that the plant would be kept open:

THE COURT: * * * They never made you a promise. Show me a word in the contract that says they will keep open * * *

MR. LEWIS: Well, this appendix, they were committed—both sides were committed to make every effort—

THE COURT: Read the words to me.

MR. LEWIS: "Every effort to improve productivity of the plant."

THE COURT: Yes.

MR. LEWIS: And the company was to invest two million dollars in restructuring the facility to make more efficient the production facilities for the manufacture of industrial sewing machines.

THE COURT: Yes.

MR. LEWIS: And the company would continue to devote emphasized attention to the procurement of defense work compatible with the machine's capabilities.

Then they give us this stuff about Secretary of Defense Weinberger—

THE COURT: Yes.

MR. LEWIS: Who, you know, and this whole thing, that wasn't a little thing. They made—that was a real circus.

THE COURT: Show me the words where it says they are going to stay open.

MR. LEWIS: Well, of course I say that this has to be viewed in the context, really, of the entire negotiations between the parties.

THE COURT: You are a sophisticated lawyer. This is a big time operation. If a Union could have gotten a straight promise to keep open, they would have been foolhardy not to have achieved it. They didn't get it because they couldn't get it.

MR. LEWIS: But they got the next best thing. They got a promise to use best efforts.

THE COURT: I understand, but you will then agree with me that they did not get a promise to keep open.

MR. LEWIS: I don't think we said we got a promise to keep it open. We just got a promise that they would exert their best efforts.

* * *

Just as it is clear that Singer made no promise to stay in business, it is equally clear that defendant stands in breach of Appendix Z. * * * Indeed, Singer admits that it has breached its agreement with Local 461:

THE COURT: Did you violate this agreement or didn't you?

MR. RASIN: We did not spend the two million dollars, your Honor.

THE COURT: Does that mean yes?

MR. RASIN: Yes, it does. We breached it in that respect.

* * * Singer contends that had it complied with the contract the plant would still have been forced to close in any event due to decreased market demand and that plaintiffs would have been no better off then they are now. The Court finds Singer's position to be untenable.

* * * It is plain that this Court cannot now divine through some occult device what might have been had Singer fulfilled its obligations. This Court cannot measure damages in such a speculative manner.

The Court has determined therefore that an appropriate and ascertainable measure of damages should be either the value of the "give-backs" tendered by the union, a figure which will be determined at trial, or the $2 million Singer promised to spend on the plant, whichever is greater. In this way, the workers will be made whole; they will be no worse off than they would have been had they entered into a collective bargaining agreement without tendering "give-backs" and without extracting the promises contained in Appendix Z.

[The court subsequently approved a settlement of $3.5 million negotiated by the union and the company—eds.]

---

c. Some Consequences of Going Out of Business

Just because there are no direct legal restraints on decisions to close operations does not mean that going out of business is cost-free from a labor and employment law perspective. Companies and employees may sometimes agree (explicitly or implicitly) that the employees' wages will be less than market rate in exchange for the companies' commitment to provide pensions and health benefits to current and already retired employees. Or companies keep jittery employees from finding an employer with longer staying power by promising generous severance payments in the event of a closing. Are these promises enforceable? Is there a reason to treat these assurances differently than assurances of job security predicated on improved productivity? Why should it be up to employers to meet the needs of the elderly, the retired, or the unemployed who no longer contribute to their companies' success?

The subject of employee benefits is complicated. The federal statute that regulates most employee benefit plans in the private sector is the Employee Retirement Income Security Act of 1974 (ERISA), 29 U.S.C. §§ 29 U.S.C. § 1001 et seq. As its name suggests, the primary concern of the legislation is insuring that promises of retirement benefits will be enforceable. But ERISA also regulates employer-sponsored welfare benefit plans, like health and disability insurance.

i. Pension Plans

A pension plan is a form of deferred compensation. Employers make contributions during the employees' working years and once the workers retire the assets are distributed.

Employers are not obligated to offer their employees pension plans, but Congress has encouraged employers to establish them by providing favorable tax treatment for plans that comply with ERISA's requirements. This means, among other things, that once a company enrolls employees in a qualified pension plan federal law determines the criteria for funding, eligibility, and vesting; and federal law requires qualified plans to provide benefits to all classes of employees, not just those who are highly compensated.

Workers who meet statutorily-prescribed minimum eligibility requirements of a pension plan have nonforfeitable rights to a pension on reaching normal retirement age. The amount of the pension will depend on the number of years in service with the employer sponsoring the plan; some plans provide for reduced benefits on early retirement. The time at which an employee's right to a pension vests depends on the type of plan offered by the employer, anytime between 3 and 7 years from beginning employment.

ERISA regulation of pension plans is comprehensive and detailed. (Indeed, ERISA merits a course of its own!) Participants, beneficiaries, fiduciaries and the Secretary of Labor have enforcement responsibility for the various obligations set by ERISA. Penalties include imprisonment, fines and other civil remedies.

Pension plans are either defined benefit plans, in which workers are promised a fixed monthly payment on retirement, or defined contribution plans, in which an employer contributes to each employee's individual account with the total contributions in that account determining each employee's benefits on retirement.

One crucial distinction between defined benefit and defined contribution plans is the way in which they allocate risk. Because a worker is entitled to a promised monthly benefit under a defined benefit plan, the employer is responsible for making up the difference between the anticipated and the actual yield if investments do not produce enough money to meet obligations to all retired employees. (Of course, if investments do better than anticipated, employers are able to reduce some future contributions.) By way of contrast, under a defined contribution plan, the employer's obligation is completed once money is deposited in an employee's account. If, on retirement, the account does not produce the desired yield, the employee must accept the consequences. (Of course, if the investment does better than expected, the employee enjoys the windfall.)

ii. Welfare benefit plans

ERISA also regulates employee welfare benefit plans, such as plans for medical benefits, disability pay, life insurance, child care, vacation, unemployment and severance pay. Unlike pension benefits, which vest after a statutorily-mandated period, welfare benefits are governed by the terms of the plan establishing them. Employers that find continued coverage more costly than anticipated may modify or terminate benefits, such as health care coverage, as long as discretion to do so is reserved in the plan documents.

The closest Congress has come to requiring continuation of health insurance and other welfare benefits is a statutory obligation that companies offer departing employees the opportunity to purchase continued participation in the company's on-going health plan at the group rate. The Consolidated Omnibus Budget Reconciliation Act of 1985 (COBRA), 29 U.S.C. § 1161 (1986), implemented by amendments to ERISA and the Internal Revenue Code, allows most workers who lose or retire from their jobs to continue health care coverage for up to 18 months—as long as they can afford the premiums plus the administrative surcharge COBRA authorizes employers to collect—and assuming the company continues to offer group health insurance to its remaining employees. What effect should COBRA have on a company's decision to terminate operations?

Since ERISA does not require vesting or minimum funding of welfare benefit plans, you might expect states to fill the void. But section 514 of ERISA, 29 U.S.C. § 1144, expressly preempts state laws that "relate to" any employee benefit plan covered by ERISA. In the face of this expression of Congressional intention to establish uniform national standards governing the operation of employee benefits plans, states may regulate only the business of insurance companies (historically an area of state concern, *see Metropolitan Life Insurance Co. v. Massachusetts,* 471 U.S. 724, 105 S.Ct. 2380, 85 L.Ed.2d 728 (1985)) and benefits that involve a one-time payment and no administrative apparatus, such as a lump-sum severance payment (thereby falling outside the preemption provision because no "plan" attaches to the benefits, *see Fort Halifax Packing Co., Inc. v. Coyne,* 482 U.S. 1, 107 S.Ct. 2211, 96 L.Ed.2d 1 (1987)). The practical effect of ERISA's broad preemption provision is fairly rigorous federal regulation of pension plans and little oversight of welfare benefit plans by federal or state governments.

Are there distinctions between pensions on the one hand and health benefits on the other that explain the use of government standards to regulate one and market forces to regulate the other? As a company officer would you prefer welfare benefit plans to be subject to government funding and vesting standards, or to case-by-case evaluation of an employer's continuing responsibility to its employees and retirees?

d. Perspectives

Should the law even address the issues of continued employment or health benefits or pension plans?

i. The market model. John Langbein raises some pointed questions about government interference in the market, using ERISA's pension rules as his example while noting that his argument extends to any regulatory requirement.

> ERISA's vesting protection is so often described as a triumph of "reform" that one can forget to ask whether vesting rules are justifiable. Forfeiture sounds like a bad thing so protection against forfeiture sounds like a good thing. But another way to understand ERISA's vesting requirement (or indeed any other regulatory requirement) is as an interference with personal autonomy. ERISA forbids employers and employees to contract for a particular term in the compensation package. ERISA allows the parties to contract for no pension plan at all, but it forbids them to contract for a pension plan whose benefits are made contingent beyond ERISA's permitted forfeiture periods. Why forbid private parties to contract as they please? * * *

> Suppose the employer is willing to invest in training the employee for a higher paying job only if the employer can use the sanction of pension forfeiture to increase the period over which the employer can retain the employee and thereby recoup the firm's investment in training. In such a case, an employment arrangement that stipulates forfeitures of pension benefits might actually maximize the joint advantage of the parties. Should the federal government restrict the liberty of the parties to agree to that contract? * * *

> Consider the possibility of employee disdain as a factor explaining why many employees may not value pension rights enough to be willing to contract to bear the greater cost of more rapid vesting, in the absence of regulation forcing them to do so. If labor markets are reasonably competitive, an employer who offers a more desirable form of compensation would obtain an advantage in the competition to obtain the best workers at lowest cost. Thus, if many employees wanted greater pension security, we would expect firms to have offered [liberal vesting schedules]. The question arises, therefore, how much employees really care about pensions. * * *

JOHN H. LANGBEIN and BRUCE F. WOLK, PENSION AND EMPLOYEE BENEFIT LAW 90–93 (1990). *See* chapters 4–7 (1990).

ii. Minimum standards set by the government. Reflecting a different perspective, some commentators note that the social security program adopted in the 1930s already established government responsibility for assuring adequate retirement income. They would supplement social security through additional minimum standards legislation, such as a requirement that all employees and employers participate in pension plans. One proposal is for a Minimum Universal Pension System (MUPS) to be funded by employer contributions. Employers could administer their own pension plans or could send their contributions to a governmentally administered portability fund that would invest in the economy. In addition to supporting the retired population, mandatory funding of pensions could encourage capital investment, help the long run productive capabilities of the economy, and limit reliance on direct intergenerational income transfers from the working to the retired.

iii. The individual rights model. A third perspective is offered by Marleen O'Connor. She would redefine the scope and content of fiduciary duties to require corporate directors to defend employee interests during fundamental corporate changes and give employees a cause of action against directors who fail to meet these fiduciary obligations. Her discussion compares the fiduciary duty approach to a legislative solution that would set minimum requirements for providing job retraining, vesting of pensions, funding of health benefit plans and the like.

> [T]he choice between statutory relief and the fiduciary duty solution requires analysis of the costs and benefits of the legislature's prescribing a remedy ex ante or the court's determining the appropriate relief ex post. First, legislatures would find it difficult to anticipate all the problems that arise in plant closings and layoffs, leaving workers subject to opportunistic conduct. Statutes would be overinclusive in some cases and underinclusive in others. Conceivably, the federal government could create a highly structured set of rules to alleviate the consequences of job dislocation. Complex regulations, however, would impede directors' ability to respond to the situation severely. * * * Thus, external regulation is inadequate because it results in layer upon layer of rules that impose unnecessary costs. Further, statutes provide a blunt form of relief that cannot remedy opportunistic behavior effectively. Recognizing a fiduciary duty to displaced workers would allow for judicial monitoring to confront and evaluate transactions as they arise. Courts traditionally have played an important role in policing long-term relational contracts; from its ex post perspective, a court can determine if the more dominant party has taken advantage of the weaker party in the relationship unfairly. In addition, ex post settling-up provides a comparative benefit over ex ante adjustment because it measures compensation on a situation-specific basis.

> While the fiduciary duty solution provides a case-by-case remedy, its flexibility also creates uncertainty. Thus, it is necessary to respond to the contention that the costs of litigating and second-guessing business decisions may outweigh any social benefits derived from imposing a fiduciary duty. Professor Macey argues that the increase in shareholder uncertainty will deter investment and ultimately result in fewer workers being hired. In response, the current system that allows companies to close plants without showing concern for affected employees produces substantial uncertainty for displaced workers. As Professor Singer notes, the question is not only whether regulation creates more or less uncertainty, but how that uncertainty is distributed. Indeed, imposing a fiduciary duty on directors to prevent the corporation from externalizing the costs of displacement may prevent some socially inefficient transactions.

　　* * * [R]ecognizing a fiduciary duty to displaced workers may lead to greater uncertainty and litigation. Legislation avoids these problems by providing clear rules about the corporation's liability. Consequently, to take advantage of the benefits of both types of solutions, states may want to facilitate corporate planning by providing statutory safe harbors for directors to use in providing relief to displaced workers, while concurrently permitting judicial expansion of the director's fiduciary duties to displaced workers.

Marleen A. O'Connor, Restructuring the Corporation's Nexus of Contracts: Recognizing a Fiduciary Duty to Protect Displaced Workers, 69 No.Ca.L.Rev. 1189, 1258–59 (1991).

　　iv. Participation by workers in business decisions. Unions are credited with making employer-funded pension and welfare benefit plans a part of an employee's compensation package. *See* William C. Greenough & Francis P. King, Pension Plans and Public Policy (1973) (describing the strikes by mine workers, steelworkers and autoworkers from 1946 to 1950 to establish employer-funded pension plans). Even in the 1990s there was a high correlation between unionization and pension coverage. Although employees in collective bargaining units make up 9 percent of the private sector workforce, in 1999 70% of employees covered by a union contract were covered by a pension plan; 41% of employees not covered by a union contract were covered by a pension plan.

　　Unions and employees have little say, however, in how pension funds are invested. In LABOR'S CAPITAL: THE ECONOMICS AND POLITICS OF PRIVATE PENSIONS 176–78 (1992), Teresa Ghilarducci proposes "a gradual democratization and replacement of the voluntary private pension system."

　　　　* * * [F]ederal or state legislation that required all pension funds to allocate 10 percent of their funds into a "redevelopment" fund would begin the process of amassing capital designated for "socially" productive activity. * * * The pension-fund investment industry—banks, insurance companies, and money managers—would not necessarily lose its clients and the funds' performance would hardly be affected if only 10 percent were invested in the "social capital" redevelopment fund. This fund, like the thousands of community redevelopment funds and federal demonstration projects, would easily find and fund productive investments that were missed by traditional capital markets. A board directing the funds would represent a cross section of society. * * * Such a plan would shift emphasis away from property rights—as the reason pension funds should be controlled differently—to a social-needs criteria. In summary (and in the short run), the fund should

　　　　1.　require all single-employer funds to have worker trustees as investment advisors; and

　　　　2.　create a national strategic fund, composed of 10 percent of all private pension funds, that guarantees a fixed rate of return and is invested in projects that demonstrate the ability to enhance and stabilize the national economy.

In the medium run, the employer-based pension system, as well as the employer-based health insurance system, could gradually be eliminated for a nationalized and universal advance-funded scheme. Tax exemptions for employer-sponsored pension contributions could gradually be eliminated and replaced by a new tax structure that would support an advance-funded Social Security system.

Under a nationalized pension scheme, such as Social Security, pension credits are portable and benefits are based on a worker's entire work history rather than service with one employer—some pension plans are portable within an industry, TIAA–CREF (for university professors) and union multi employer plans. An advance-funded Social Security system would substitute the tens of thousands of employers' (tax-exempt) funds for national or regional Social Security funds. The Social Security system's small surplus could be invested in public ventures instead of government bonds. Unions may balk at this proposal because they would lose the advantages of negotiated employer-based pensions * * *—that pensions serve as a fudge factor in bargaining and as a leverage in organizing. Employers would lose all the benefits of a voluntary system—the personnel tool and the source of internal funds. The pension fund management industry would not survive in its current form. The losses are as apparent as the current benefits. However, the gains overall, compared to the current system, are considerable. * * *

2. REORGANIZATION UNDER CHAPTER 11 OF THE BANKRUPTCY CODE

CASE STUDY: DELACROIX PRESS

Delacroix Press' debts exceed its assets by $12 million. In addition, Delacroix faces immediate financial demands: Delacroix has a quarterly payment of $800,000 due on a bank loan, owes $200,000 to its supplier of office equipment, is behind three months on its rent, and has been sued by retirees for failing to maintain contributions to the health insurance fund.

Delacroix's vice president for financial affairs believes Delacroix can return to financial health if Delacroix's creditors can be persuaded to restructure Delacroix's debt load by stretching out payment schedules, reducing interest rates, and eliminating penalties. The few creditors the financial officer has approached have balked; each creditor wants to be sure it is not absorbing an excessive amount of Delacroix's losses, and all the creditors are suspicious of Delacroix's continuing ability to operate successfully. Indeed, Delacroix fears that the creditors most immediately affected by its current defaults—the bank, the supplier and the lessor—will sue, thereby alerting all other creditors and Delacroix's customers to Delacroix's precarious finances. The resulting loss in business and additional claims on Delacroix's meager resources would force Delacroix into liquidation.

An alternative to death at its creditors' hands is for Delacroix to seek protection from immediate claims by filing a petition for reorganization under Chapter 11 of the federal Bankruptcy Code. Filing the petition for reorganization means Delacroix loses considerable autonomy, since the bankruptcy court acquires jurisdiction over Delacroix's financial affairs. The bankruptcy court even has the power to replace Delacroix's existing management with a trustee, although in a chapter 11 reorganization the debtor, referred to as the debtor-in-possession, usually retains its assets and incumbent officers continue to run the business. In return for subjecting its decision-making to the bankruptcy court's veto, Delacroix is shielded from the claims of its creditors until either (a) it negotiates a plan that will enable it to reorganize so as to satisfy the creditors and to have an adequate financial plan to operate a successful business; or (b) until Delacroix must indeed liquidate. (The assumption of Delacroix management is that the company's value as an ongoing enterprise is greater than its value if assets are sold off piecemeal and that, therefore, a reorganization rather than a liquidation will be the outcome of the bankruptcy proceedings.)

Part of the reorganization plan includes reducing operating expenses. Delacroix proposes to cut wages of hourly employees by 5% and of salaried employees by 15%. Delacroix's written personnel policy designates salaried employees as employees-at-will and expressly retains Delacroix's right to adjust their wages and benefits at Delacroix's discretion and without notice. The wages and benefits due Delacroix's hourly employees are set out in a three-year collective bargaining agreement that includes a provision stating "wages and benefits shall be those as designated in this Agreement and shall not be reduced during the term of this Agreement without the consent of the Union."

What effect does filing a Chapter 11 petition have on Delacroix's employees?

a. Chapter 11 Reorganization and Labor Costs

Although there have been a few notorious cases of companies filing for reorganization in order to cut labor costs and avoid other obligations to workers, most companies do not invoke Chapter 11 solely because of labor relations concerns. Nonetheless even honestly motivated bankruptcies have severe consequences for employees.[2]

For all employees when their employer is in Chapter 11, questions arise about the company's ongoing obligation to pay wages, accrued vacation pay, severance benefits and the like. Employees are also con-

2. For a fascinating exploration of the ability of businesses to shield themselves from liability using, among other devices, the Bankruptcy Code, *see* Lynn M. LoPucki, The Death of Liability, 106 Yale L. J. 1 (1996); James J. White, Corporate Judg-ment Proofing: A Reply to Lynn LoPucki's The Death of Liability, 107 Yale L. J. 1363 (1998); and Lynn M. LoPucki, Virtual Judgment Proofing: A Rejoinder, 107 Yale L. J. 1413 (1998).

cerned about where they stand in the line of creditors, should the company's assets be insufficient to meet its outstanding obligations.

The questions of which claims get paid when and the status of claims is dealt with explicitly in the Bankruptcy Code. Under the Code secured creditors have the highest priority. Second priority for payment goes to administrative expenses. Administrative expenses are the actual, necessary costs of preserving the estate (that is, the total assets of the debtor). 11 U.S.C. § 507. Employee claims classified as administrative expenses include wages, salaries, commissions and vacation pay *earned after the company files for Chapter 11 protection*. These post-petition expenses have priority as administrative expenses because the employees' continued efforts are essential in enabling the reorganizing company to continue operating. By comparison, the Bankruptcy Code treats wages, vacation pay and severance pay earned (but not paid) within 90 days prior to the chapter 11 filing or the cessation of operations as lower priority claims *and* sets a cap on these claims, $4000 per employee in 1996. Amounts owed for pre-petition work or benefits in excess of the cap are treated as general, unsecured claims, that is, claims that will share the assets, if any, once all other claims have been paid. See *In re Ionosphere Clubs, Inc.,* 22 F.3d 403 (2d Cir.1994), for a discussion of these priorities.

The obligation of a company in a Chapter 11 reorganization to pay for work as it is performed is one thing. But is the Chapter 11 employer required to maintain the same compensation and conditions of employment that prevailed pre-petition? One fundamental goal of a reorganization is equality of distribution among creditors. If a lending institution must receive 20 cents on the dollar so that the debtor can reorganize successfully, should an employee see her position reduced similarly? In what way do employees differ from other creditors, like banks and suppliers? And who decides whether employees retain their pre-petition terms of employment—the company unilaterally; the company and employees in negotiation; the employees, other creditors and the company; the bankruptcy court? For employees, does it matter who decides, given the relative strengths of the contending parties?

b. Does a Collective Bargaining Agreement Make a Difference?

The issue begins with the puzzle that long-term contracts pose in bankruptcy. Suppose that the debtor has contracted to sell 100 pairs of jeans for $10 per pair to a retailer. Before performance, the market for jeans flourishes and the same jeans could be sold for $15 per pair. If there is no bankruptcy, the debtor must perform (deliver jeans worth $1500 for $1000) or breach and pay damages (the extra $500 that the retailer will have to pay to get the same jeans at current prices). In bankruptcy, however, the retailer should not be treated differently than other creditors. To achieve that result, the trustee is allowed to breach ("reject") the contract and treat the retailer the same as any other $500 creditor.

Will the debtors' contracts with its employees be treated as any other long-term contract, allowing the trustee to reject and transform employees into creditors of a bankruptcy estate that rarely pays over 20 cents on the dollar?

What about employees covered by a collective bargaining agreement? Are they in a better position than employees-at-will to protect extant wages and working conditions once a Chapter 11 petition is filed? And to what extent are non-monetary working conditions subject to renegotiation? For example, may Delacroix propose as necessary modifications not only the 5% cut of hourly employee wages but also elimination of the agreement's "last-hired, first-fired" clause and elimination of the union dues check-off provision by which management deducts dues from employee paychecks?

TRUCK DRIVERS LOCAL 807 v. CAREY TRANSP., INC.

United States Court of Appeals, Second Circuit, 1987.
816 F.2d 82.

ALTIMARI, CIRCUIT JUDGE:

This appeal involves the showing a debtor-employer must make in order to obtain Bankruptcy Court approval of the employer's application to reject a collective bargaining agreement in accordance with 11 U.S.C. § 1113. We agree with the conclusions and, for the most part, the analysis of the Bankruptcy Court for the Southern District of New York (Burton R. Lifland, J.). Therefore, we affirm the decision of the United States District Court for the Southern District of New York (Richard Owen, J.) upholding Judge Lifland's approval of Carey Transportation's application to reject two collective bargaining agreements with Truck Drivers Local 807 ("Local 807") or ("the union.")

FACTS AND PROCEEDINGS BELOW

Carey, a wholly owned subsidiary of Schiavone Carrier Corporation, commenced this litigation by filing a voluntary reorganization petition under Chapter 11 of the Bankruptcy Code in April 1985. Carey, both prior to and since that filing, has been engaged in the business of providing commuter bus service between New York City and Kennedy and LaGuardia Airports.

Local 807 has been the exclusive bargaining representative of Carey's bus drivers and station employees. Local 807 and Carey entered into collective bargaining agreements covering these two groups of employees on August 20, 1982, thereby settling a sixty-four day strike by union members. These two agreements were scheduled to expire on February 28, 1986.

Carey officials have blamed the strike for a subsequent 30% drop in ridership and the yearly revenue losses that preceded its filing for reorganization. Carey has operated at a loss since at least December 31,

1981, reporting annual losses of $750,000 for fiscal year 1983, $1,500,000 for fiscal year 1984, and $2,500,000 for fiscal year 1985.

In September 1983, Carey terminated fifty Local 807 members employed as station workers, although an arbitrator later directed that ten of them be rehired with back pay. The net result of these forty layoffs, according to Carey officials, has been an annual cost savings of approximately $1 million.

In 1984 and 1985, Carey sought and obtained concessions from a union representing Carey's mechanics and repair-shop workers. Those concessions led to layoffs of approximately eight workers and annual cost savings estimated at $144,000.

In June 1984, Carey proposed several modifications in its agreements with Local 807. After negotiations, Local 807 and Carey agreed on certain supplemental provisions applicable only to drivers hired after July 1, 1984. These "second-tier" drivers would not get any paid sick days, and they would receive significantly reduced wages, overtime pay, and benefits. These changes, according to Carey, yielded savings of only $100,000 prior to Carey's filing for bankruptcy. The reason given for the relatively small savings was that seasonal variations in industry business resulted in few drivers being hired after the effective date of the Supplement.

On January 31, 1985, counsel for Carey wrote to Local 807 representatives, requesting additional modifications of the two agreements. A series of meetings took place during February and March of 1985, with Carey warning that a failure to reach agreement could force the company to file a Chapter 11 petition and, most likely, apply for permission to reject the existing agreements. Near the end of these sessions, union negotiators agreed to present to union members a set of modifications affecting lunch periods, booking and check-out time, driver rotation rules, holidays, vacation days, sick days, fringe benefit contributions, supplemental unemployment compensation, and supplemental disability insurance. Those concessions, if approved and implemented, would have yielded approximately $750,000 in yearly savings.

On March 27th, however, management added to this proposed modification several additional terms, and described the resultant package as its final offer. In essence, this last set of modifications would have extended the expiration date of the contract for an additional two years, with wages and fringe benefits frozen at the proposed levels until April 1, 1987. At that time, a "reopener" provision would permit the union to bargain for increased wages and benefits during the final year of the extended contract. The union requested that there be binding arbitration if reopener negotiations proved unsuccessful, but management rejected this demand.

This final offer was submitted to the bargaining unit employees on March 29, 1985 and rejected by an 82–7 vote. According to Local 807's business agent, the union members were particularly adamant about not accepting the two-year contract extension and the freeze on wages and benefits.

Carey filed its Chapter 11 petition with the Bankruptcy Court on April 4, 1985, and one day later, delivered to Local 807 a proposal to modify its collective bargaining agreements pursuant to 11 U.S.C. § 1113(b)(1)(A). This post-petition proposal was designed to achieve annual savings of $1.8 million for each of the next three fiscal years.

Carey planned to achieve savings of this magnitude by (1) freezing all wages for second-tier drivers and reducing wages for first-tier drivers (those on the payroll prior to July 1, 1984) by $1.00 per hour; (2) reducing health and pension benefit contributions by approximately $1.50 per hour; (3) replacing daily overtime with weekly overtime; (4) eliminating all sick days and reducing the number of paid holidays; (5) eliminating supplemental workers' compensation and supplemental disability payments; (6) eliminating premium payments and reducing commissions paid to charter drivers; and (7) changing numerous scheduling and assignment rules. All terms were to be frozen for three years under this post-petition proposal.

When Carey presented this proposal to Local 807, company officers were projecting fiscal year 1986 losses of approximately $950,000. (Carey revised this estimate shortly thereafter, projecting losses of $746,000.) In a cover letter accompanying this proposal, Carey asserted that it needed to slash costs by considerably more than its projected losses in order to improve its long-term financial health by updating and expanding its bus fleet, operations, and maintenance facilities. Without savings of this magnitude, Carey explained, it would be unable to propose a feasible reorganization plan to creditors and resolve its indebtedness to them. Carey requested a meeting with Local 807 representatives "to discuss the proposals and to attempt to reach mutually satisfactory modifications of the agreement[s]."

Shortly after the Company submitted its post-petition proposal, dissension within Local 807 became obvious; in fact, virtually all union members formed a "Drivers Committee" and hired an attorney to represent them separately from Local 807 officials. The Drivers Committee then refused to participate in most post-petition negotiations, despite union officials' pleas that they reconsider that decision to "stonewall" these sessions.

In the meantime, Carey filed its section 1113 application to reject its bargaining agreements. The Bankruptcy Court scheduled and conducted five days of hearings on Carey's application, urging the parties to continue negotiations at the same time. After the third day of hearings, a Local 807 officer presented to Carey a counter-proposal designed to achieve annual cost savings of $776,000. The counter-proposal would have extended the expiration date of the existing agreements by fifteen months, and frozen wages and benefits except for a reopener, with binding arbitration, scheduled for June 24, 1986. Carey found the counter-proposal unacceptable, and the hearings continued.

The central issues at the hearing, as on this appeal, were whether the post-petition proposal contained only necessary modifications of the existing agreements, *see* 11 U.S.C. § 1113(b)(1)(A), whether that proposal treated all parties fairly and equitably, *see id.*, whether Local 807 lacked good cause for rejecting that proposal, *see* § 1113(c)(2), and whether the balancing of the equities clearly favored rejection of the bargaining agreements, see § 1113(c)(3).

On June 14, 1985, the bankruptcy court issued its decision approving Carey's application to reject the collective bargaining agreements. Bankruptcy Judge Lifland adopted, with certain modifications, a nine-step analysis of § 1113 first used in *In re American Provision Co.,* 44 B.R. 907 (Bankr.D.Minn.1984). Applying this analysis, he held that Carey had met its burden of proving compliance with the procedural and substantive standards set forth in the statute.

On appeal, the United States District Court for the Southern District of New York affirmed on the opinion below, in an Order dated August 14, 1986. The Union filed a timely notice of appeal on September 12, 1986.

Discussion

Congress enacted section 1113 of the Bankruptcy Code, 11 U.S.C. § 1113,[1] in response to *NLRB v. Bildisco & Bildisco,* 465 U.S. 513, 104 S.Ct. 1188, 79 L.Ed.2d 482 (1984), where the Court concluded that a debtor-in-possession could reject a collective bargaining agreement, subject to certain constraints.

Bildisco involved two key holdings. The first involved the proper substantive standard to be used by bankruptcy courts asked to approve rejections of collective bargaining agreements, while the second involved the procedural prerequisites to rejection. In defining the substantive standard, the Supreme Court declined to adopt this court's previous rule that rejection could be approved only after a finding that adherence to the agreement would "thwart efforts to save a failing [company] in bankruptcy from collapse." The Court instead endorsed the equitable

1. Section 1113 provides in pertinent part:

(b)(1) Subsequent to filing a petition and prior to filing an application seeking rejection of a collective bargaining agreement, the debtor in possession or trustee (hereinafter in this section 'trustee' shall include a debtor in possession), shall—

(A) make a proposal to the authorized representative of the employees covered by such agreement, based on the most complete and reliable information available at the time of such proposal, which provides for those necessary modifications in the employees benefits and protection that are necessary to permit the reorganization of the debtor and assures that all creditors, the debtor and all of the affected parties are treated fairly and equitably....

(c) The court shall approve an application for rejection of a collective bargaining agreement only if the court finds that—

(1) the trustee has, prior to the hearing, made a proposal that fulfills the requirements of subsection (b)(1);

(2) the authorized representative of the employees has refused to accept such proposal without good cause; and

(3) the balance of the equities clearly favors rejection of such agreement.

11 U.S.C. § 1113(b), (c).

standard set forth in *In re Brada Miller Freight System, Inc.*, 702 F.2d 890 (11th Cir.1983), and held that the debtor need only prove "that the collective-bargaining agreement burdens the estate, and that after careful scrutiny, the equities balance in favor of rejecting the labor contract."

On the procedural question, the *Bildisco* Court held that a reorganizing debtor did not have to engage in collective bargaining before modifying or rejecting provisions of the agreement, and that such unilateral alterations by a debtor would not violate either section 8(a)(5) or section 8(d) of the National Labor Relations Act. This procedural ruling intensified existing congressional concerns over reports that some companies were misusing the bankruptcy law in collective bargaining. Congressional response to *Bildisco* was swift, culminating within a few short months in the passage of section 1113.

Before addressing the question of whether Carey has proven its compliance with the requirements of the new statute, we must consider a preliminary issue raised by appellants.

I. Standard of Appellate Review [omitted]

II. Merits of the Decision Below

* * * [T]he statute permits the bankruptcy court to approve a rejection application only if the debtor, besides following the procedures set forth by Congress, makes three substantive showings. The first is that its post-petition proposal for modifications satisfies § 1113(b)(1), which in turn limits the debtor to proposing only "those necessary modifications in ... benefits and protections that are necessary to permit the reorganization of the debtor," and obliges the debtor to assure the court that "all creditors, the debtor and all affected parties are treated fairly and equitably." Second, the debtor must show that the union has rejected this proposal without good cause. Bankr.Code § 1113(c)(2). Third, the debtor must prove that "the balance of the equities clearly favors rejection of [the bargaining] agreement." Code § 1113(c)(3). The first two statutory requirements go beyond the substantive test adopted by the *Bildisco* Court, but the third requirement represents a codification of the equitable test adopted in *Bildisco*.

* * * We affirm the decision below because it substantially comports with our reading of the statute, and because Judge Lifland's factual findings are not clearly erroneous.

1. Compliance with § 1113(b)(1)

(a) Necessity of the modifications

* * * [T]his provision "emphasizes the requirement of the debtor's good faith in seeking to modify its existing labor contract." Although all courts appear to agree on that basic principle, a judicial controversy has arisen over two additional, related questions raised by this provision: (1) how necessary must the proposed modifications be, and (2) to what goal must those alterations be necessary?

In answer to the first of these questions, the Third Circuit concluded that "necessary" as used in subsection (b)(1)(A) is synonymous with "essential" in subsection (e), which authorizes the court to approve certain non-negotiated interim changes while the rejection application is pending. Thus, the court held, necessity must "be construed strictly to signify only modifications that the trustee is constrained to accept." *Wheeling–Pittsburgh Steel,* 791 F.2d at 1088. As to the second question, the Third Circuit concluded that the statute requires the bankruptcy court to focus its attention on "the somewhat shorter term goal of preventing ... liquidation ... rather than the longer term issue of the debtor's ultimate future."

Local 807 asks us to adopt the Third Circuit's reasoning, arguing that the post-petition proposal must fail because it sought more than break-even cost reductions, because the proposed three year term was too long in relation to the eight months remaining under the existing agreement, and because it did not provide for wages and benefits to "snap-back" in the event that Carey's financial performance improved.

First of all, the legislative history strongly suggests that "necessary" should not be equated with "essential" or bare minimum. Although the Third Circuit may be correct that the "necessary" language was viewed as a victory for organized labor because it approximated the "minimum modifications" language urged by Senator Packwood, Congress obviously did not adopt Senator Packwood's proposal. Instead, as the *Wheeling–Pittsburgh Steel* panel acknowledged, Congress settled on "a substitute for this clause." Congress' ultimate choice of this substitute clause suggests that it was uncomfortable with language suggesting that a debtor must prove that its initial post-petition proposal contained only bare-minimum changes.

Judge Lifland, in the decision below, properly pointed out a second reason for not reading "necessary" as the equivalent of "essential" or bare minimum. Because the statute requires the debtor to negotiate in good faith over the proposed modifications, an employer who initially proposed truly minimal changes would have no room for good faith negotiating, while one who agreed to any substantive changes would be unable to prove that its initial proposals were minimal. Thus, requiring the debtor to propose bare-minimum modifications at the outset would make it virtually impossible for the debtor to meet its other statutory obligations.

The Third Circuit's answer to the "necessary to what" question is also troubling. In our view, the *Wheeling–Pittsburgh* court did not adequately consider the significant differences between interim relief requests and post-petition modification proposals. Interim relief is available only until the hearing process is completed—normally within two months, *see* § 1113(d)(1), (2)—and only upon a showing that adherence to the agreement during that time could imperil "continuation of the debtor's business" or cause "irreparable damage to the estate." *Id.* § 1113(e). In the interim relief context, therefore, it is only proper that the court focus on the bare minimum requirements for short-term survival. In making the decision whether to permit the debtor to reject its bargaining agreement, however, the court must consider whether rejection would increase the likelihood of successful reorganization. A final reorganization plan, in turn, can be confirmed only if the court determines that neither liquidation nor a need for further reorganization is likely to follow. Thus, in virtually every case, it becomes impossible to weigh necessity as to reorganization without looking into the debtor's ultimate future and estimating what the debtor needs to attain financial health. As the *Royal Composing Room* court phrased it, "A debtor can live on water alone for a short time but over the long haul it needs food to sustain itself and retain its vigor."

Moreover, the length of Carey's proposal and the absence of a snapback provision likewise did not require rejection of the proposal. While the Third Circuit relied on a similar argument in finding a proposed modification not "necessary" for purposes of section 1113, this argument was not raised in either court below and may not be raised here for the first time. The only exception to this rule, avoidance of manifest injustice, is inapplicable here because Local 807 wholly failed to demonstrate that Carey's proposed three year term was unnecessary or exceeded either the prevailing industry practice or the parties' past experience.

In sum, we conclude that the necessity requirement places on the debtor the burden of proving that its proposal is made in good faith, and that it contains necessary, but not absolutely minimal, changes that will enable the debtor to complete the reorganization process successfully. Although Judge Lifland did not incorporate each of these factors into his discussion of necessity, he did reach each of these questions in the course of his decision. Thus we cannot conclude that the lower court either misread or misapplied the "necessary modifications" requirement as a matter of law.

Each of the findings pertinent to this inquiry, moreover, is supported by substantial evidence in the record. For instance, record evidence indicates that Carey was losing large sums of money, that its Local 807 labor costs (in contrast to other employees' salaries and benefits) were well above industry averages, and that Carey lacked sufficient assets to meet its current expenses. This well-documented testimony from Carey officials supports the court's finding that Carey had good faith reasons for seeking modifications in its Local 807 agreements. Moreover, record evidence also supports the view that Carey needed to upgrade its facilities and its vehicles in order to complete reorganization successfully. Therefore the bankruptcy court's conclusion that Carey needed to obtain modifications of the magnitude requested, and not merely break-even cost reductions as Local 807 argues, is not clearly erroneous.

(b) Fairness as to all parties

The requirement that the debtor assure the court that "all creditors, the debtor and all affected parties are treated fairly and equitably," Code

§ 1113(b)(1)(A), is a relatively straightforward one. The purpose of this provision, according to *Century Brass,* "is to spread the burden of saving the company to every constituency while ensuring that all sacrifice to a similar degree." Local 807 argues that the bankruptcy court erred as a matter of both law and fact in assessing the burdens imposed on management, non-union employees, the parent company, and Carey's creditors. We disagree.

The debtor is not required to prove, in all instances, that managers and non-union employees will have their salaries and benefits cut to the same degree that union workers' benefits are to be reduced. To be sure, such a showing would assure the court that these affected parties are being asked to shoulder a proportionate share of the burden, but we decline to hold that this showing must be made in every case.

Rather, a debtor can rely on proof that managers and non-union employees are assuming increased responsibilities as a result of staff reductions without receiving commensurate salary increases: this is surely a sacrifice for these individuals. Particularly where, as here, the court finds that only the employees covered by the pertinent bargaining agreements are receiving pay and benefits above industry standards, it is not unfair or inequitable to exempt the other employees from pay and benefit reductions.

Local 807 has consistently argued that Carey's managers and supervisors are more than adequately compensated, that Local 807 members are not paid substantially more than their counterparts working for Carey's competitors, and that non-union staffing levels have increased rather than decreased since Schiavone purchased Carey. But substantial record evidence supports each of the bankruptcy court's contrary conclusions. For instance, the record contains unrebutted testimony that Carey drivers' hourly wages and benefits exceeded those paid by other private carriers by several dollars per hour, while managers' and supervisors' compensation packages were described as "barely competitive." Carey also offered evidence of pre-petition reductions in its managerial staff (from twenty-four to fifteen people) and its non-union supervisory staff (from fifteen to twelve), achieved by increasing the remaining officials' responsibilities. In light of this record evidence, we cannot disturb the bankruptcy court's findings on this score.

The lower court also correctly looked to pre-petition concessions obtained from the mechanics' union and two of Carey's principal creditors—the MTA and the Port Authority—as proof that these parties were contributing fairly and equitably to the effort to keep Carey afloat. Because a section 1113 application will almost always be filed before an overall reorganization plan can be prepared, the debtor cannot be expected to identify future alterations in its debt structure. Local 807 argues that the lower court overlooked Schiavone's status as a substantial creditor of its subsidiary and Carey's failure to show that Schiavone would write off part of this debt. We reject the suggestion that the statutory requirement that "all creditors" be treated fairly and equitably, *see* § 1113(b)(1)(A), means that a creditor who is also an owner of the debtor must ordinarily take a smaller percentage dividend than other creditors on its bona fide claims. The mere fact that there have been intercompany transactions between a debtor and its owner is not a source of unfairness to other creditors unless the transactions themselves were financially unfair to the debtor. Local 807 has not called to our attention, nor has our own review of the record disclosed, any evidence to indicate that Schiavone's claims against Carey arise from transactions that were financially unfair to Carey. And were there an indication of such unfair dealing, it would not necessarily support the Union's argument that Carey's rejection of its labor contracts should be disapproved. The more appropriate response would seem to be to seek the equitable subordination of claims by the owner, *see* 11 U.S.C. § 510(c), or the appointment of a trustee who could seek recovery of any fraudulent conveyance, *see* 11 U.S.C. §§ 544, 548, 1104(a); these remedies would more fairly and equitably benefit all interested parties, not just the union members.

Finally, we note that even if a greater sacrifice is required of an owner-creditor than of other creditors, a write-off of outstanding debts is not the only way a creditor can assist its debtor. Here the record shows that Schiavone did not charge any interest on its loans to Carey, and that Schiavone otherwise subsidized Carey's day-to-day operations. By doing so, Schiavone made sacrifices that contributed significantly to Carey's survival.

In light of this evidence, we affirm the bankruptcy court's ruling that all parties were participating "fairly and equitably" in the attempt to save Carey from liquidation.

2. *Good Cause*

The debtor's obligation to prove that the union lacked good cause for refusing the post-petition proposal, like the necessity question, has been the subject of some debate among commentators and the courts. The bankruptcy court here reasoned that because the proposed modifications were necessary, fair, and equitable, the union's refusal to accept them was without good cause. This reasoning, of course, suggests that the good cause provision adds nothing to the other substantive requirements of the statute.

We conclude, nonetheless, that this analysis is proper where, as here, the union has neither participated meaningfully in post-petition negotiations nor offered any reason for rejecting the proposal other than its view that the proposed modifications were excessive. At least one commentator has noted that the statute appears to authorize conduct similar to what the Drivers Committee did here: "stonewalling" post-petition negotiations and hoping that the courts will find that the proposal does not comply with subsection (b)(1). This tactic is unacceptable and inconsistent with Congressional intent. This good cause requirement was " 'intended to ensure that a continuing process of good faith negotiations will take place before court involvement.'" (quoting remarks by Representative Morrison).

Thus, even though the debtor retains the ultimate burden of persuading the court that the union lacked good cause for refusing proposed modifications, the union must come forward with evidence of "its reason for declining to accept the debtor's proposal in whole or in part. If prehearing, a union has assigned no reason for its refusal to accept a debtor's proposal, it has perforce refused to accept the proposal without good cause under Code § 1113(e)(2)." We agree with the bankruptcy court that because the union engaged in such prehearing stonewalling here, it now cannot claim that it had good cause for refusing the proposal.

Local 807 insists that because it later counter-proposed modifications that would have yielded significant cost savings, it had good cause for rejecting the debtor's proposal. We find, however, that ample record evidence supports the bankruptcy court's conclusion that this counter-proposal did not have the backing of union members. In fact, the counter-proposal was virtually identical to a pre-petition request that the union members had rejected overwhelmingly. A union's presentation of a counter-offer that its members do not support does not satisfy the good cause requirement. Moreover, we have already upheld the lower court's finding that greater than break-even cost savings were necessary. Therefore, this is not a situation where a union's counterproposal of an equally effective set of modifications might justify its refusal to accept management's proposal. The union's manifest failure to participate meaningfully in the post-petition negotiations confirms its lack of justification for rejecting Carey's proposed modifications.

3. Balancing the Equities

This requirement, is a codification of the *Bildisco* standard. Therefore, the factors identified in *Bildisco* and other cases preceding section 1113's enactment remain applicable today. And although we do not seek to set outer limits on what courts may consider under this broad, flexible test, we note the *Bildisco* Court's reminder that bankruptcy courts "must focus on the ultimate goal of Chapter 11 when considering these equities. The Bankruptcy Code does not authorize freewheeling consideration of every conceivable equity, but rather only how the equities relate to the success of the reorganization."

The lower court's decision, for the most part, is consistent with still-vital case law applying this equitable balancing test. From *Bildisco* and the cases consistent with its analysis, we glean at least six permissible equitable considerations, many of which also factor into the other substantive requirements imposed by section 1113. Those are (1) the likelihood and consequences of liquidation if rejection is not permitted; (2) the likely reduction in the value of creditors' claims if the bargaining agreement remains in force; (3) the likelihood and consequences of a strike if the bargaining agreement is voided; (4) the possibility and likely effect of any employee claims for breach of contract if rejection is approved; (5) the cost-spreading abilities of the various parties, taking into account the number of employees covered by the bargaining agreement and how various employees' wages and benefits compare to those of others in the industry; and (6) the good or bad faith of the parties in dealing with the debtor's financial dilemma. The only analytical error we find in the lower court's balancing of the equities in this case was its insistence that an allegation of bad faith in initiating the Chapter 11 proceeding may not be raised in an objection to a section 1113 application. We agree with the *Brada Miller* court that equity would preclude a court from approving rejection if the debtor were misusing the entire Chapter 11 process. But the lower court's suggestion that this contention would better be raised in a motion to dismiss the entire proceeding or to have a receiver appointed is of no moment. This is because Judge Lifland alternatively found, with ample support in the record, that Carey had a good faith need for seeking protection under Chapter 11.

Substantial record evidence supports the lower court's other findings pertinent to this inquiry, despite the union's continued insistence that such support is lacking. For instance, documentary evidence in the record is consistent with the district court's findings that unionized labor costs were approximately 60% above the industry average, that 66% of Carey's employees are unionized, that managers, supervisors, and non-union workers were receiving less than average compensation while taking on increased workloads, and that Local 807, therefore, could fairly be expected to bear a substantial proportion of the needed cost-cutting measures. Record evidence also clearly shows that increasing losses in previous years, and continued but decreased projected losses in the then-current year, made liquidation a very real threat. The Union has not attempted to refute the evidence indicating that the company's low asset value, the secured creditors' existing claims, and the anticipated costs of administration and liquidation, would leave little or nothing for unsecured creditors and shareholders if the liquidation threat materialized. In view of this substantial and largely unrebutted evidence, we concur in the bankruptcy court's conclusion that the equities clearly favored rejection of the Local 807 agreements.

Conclusion

For these reasons, we affirm the judgment of the district court upholding the bankruptcy court's approval of Carey's section 1113 application to reject its bargaining agreements with Local 807.

Notes

i. *Section 1113*

Congress rejected the *Bildisco* Court's holding that authorized a Chapter 11 employer to treat a collective bargaining agreement like an executory contract and to reject the agreement unilaterally. Instead,

Congress authorized rejection of a bargaining agreement only after approval by the bankruptcy court. Section 1113 sets out the procedural and substantive prerequisites to rejection. Section 1113 was restated as a nine-part test in *In re American Provision Company,* 44 B.R. 907, 909 (Bkrtcy.Minn.1984), and some courts refer to this formulation rather than the loosely organized statutory language in reviewing applications for approval to reject bargaining agreements:

1. The debtor in possession must make a proposal to the Union to modify the collective bargaining agreement.

2. The proposal must be based on the most complete and reliable information available at the time of the proposal.

3. The proposed modifications must be necessary to permit the reorganization of the debtor.

4. The proposed modifications must assure that all creditors, the debtor and all of the affected parties are treated fairly and equitably.

5. The debtor must provide to the Union such relevant information as is necessary to evaluate the proposal.

6. Between the time of the making of the proposal and the time of the hearing on approval of the rejection of the existing collective bargaining agreement, the debtor must meet at reasonable times with the Union.

7. At the meetings the debtor must confer in good faith in attempting to reach mutually satisfactory modifications of the collective bargaining agreement.

8. The Union must have refused to accept the proposal without good cause.

9. The balance of the equities must clearly favor rejection of the collective bargaining agreement.

ii. Application of Section 1113

Christopher David Ruiz Cameron has astutely noted that section 1113 "alone among our labor laws appears to embrace government supervision of bargaining product as well as process." *See,* Christopher David Ruiz Cameron, How 'Necessary' Became The Mother Of Rejection: An Empirical Look At the Fate of Collective Bargaining Agreements On the Tenth Anniversary of Bankruptcy Code Section 1113(c), 34 Santa Clara L. Rev. 841, 904 (1993). How judges apply section 1113 may be some evidence of the fate of labor-management negotiations if a neutral party, the National Labor Relations Board or a federal judge, similarly evaluated the merit of bargaining proposals.

The opinion in *Carey Transportation* is typical of decisions reviewing a debtor's petition to reject a collective bargaining agreement: The "necessity" element of the statutory requirement looms large, and all elements of the test are reviewed in the light most favorable to the

Chapter 11 employer. (*Wheeling Pittsburgh* and the Court of Appeals for the Third Circuit, mentioned in *Carey,* is an exception.)

a.) Necessity. Section 1113 places the burden of meeting the statutory prerequisites on the debtor-in-possession. Courts following *Carey* look at the debtor's evidence of future need for financial health and of labor costs as contributing to financial weakness. How can a union respond to evidence that a proposed reduction in labor costs will increase the probability of a successful reorganization? Under what circumstances will retaining current labor costs increase the likelihood of a successful reorganization?

b.) Good cause. In 1974 a typesetters local union, recognizing that technology had made their skilled craft obsolete, obtained from their employer, the Daily News, lifetime job guarantees in exchange for consenting to automation. In 1992 Maxwell Newspapers (seller/debtor-in-possession dba the Daily News), Mortimer Zuckerman (purchaser/debtor-in-possession), and the union bargained about but could not reach agreement on a modification of the lifetime job guarantees. In essence, the union accepted Zuckerman's demand for a reduction of guaranteed employment (by limiting the number of shifts worked in a week), but insisted on a more gradual phase out and more generous incentives for early retirement. The parties could not agree on a formula, and Maxwell claimed the union lacked good cause to reject Zuckerman's final offer to the union, valued at approximately $30 million. The court of appeals upheld the finding of the bankruptcy court that the union lacked good cause to reject the offer and granted permission to reject the bargaining agreement, on condition that the debtor keep recently negotiated offers open. In re Maxwell Newspapers, 981 F.2d 85 (2d Cir.1992). The Court of Appeals for the Second Circuit explained the good cause requirement this way:

CARDAMONE, CIRCUIT JUDGE: * * *

What "good cause" means is difficult to answer in the abstract apart from the moorings of a given case. A more constructive and perhaps more answerable inquiry is why this term is in the statute. We think good cause serves as an incentive to the debtor trying to have its labor contract modified to propose in good faith only those changes necessary to its successful reorganization, while protecting it from the union's refusal to accept the changes without a good reason.

To that end, the entire thrust of § 1113 is to ensure that well-informed and good faith negotiations occur in the market place, not as part of the judicial process. Reorganization procedures are designed to encourage such a negotiated voluntary modification. Knowing that it cannot turn down an employer's proposal without good cause gives the union an incentive to compromise on modifications of the collective bargaining agreement, so as to prevent its complete rejection. Because the employer has the burden of proving its proposals are necessary, the union is protected from an employer whose proposals may be offered in bad faith.

Thus, for example, a union will not have good cause to reject an employer's proposal that contains *only* those modifications essential for the debtor's reorganization, that is, the union's refusal to accept it will be held to be without good cause. On the other hand, as we have noted, where the union makes compromise proposals during the negotiating process that meet its needs while preserving the debtor's savings, its rejection of the debtor's proposal would be with good cause. See Royal Composing Room, 848 F.2d at 349.

Whether or not the bankruptcy court may have misstated the good cause rule, its findings clearly were not wrong. For example, it found the debtor measures its workforce by calculating "full time equivalents" (FTEs) derived from dividing payroll expenses by five, which is the number of days in a week worked by a full-time employee. The bankruptcy judge further found that from September 1990 to August 1992, FTEs for debtor's employees declined as follows: for managers 58 percent, guild members 34 percent, drivers 46 percent, pressmen 47 percent, mailers 45 percent, paper-handlers 54 percent, machinists and electricians 21 percent, engravers and stereotypers 27 percent. In stark contrast, the Local 6 typographers workforce declined only 13 percent, and these employees are by far the highest hourly paid employees of the debtor. No other employees or unions suffered so small an FTE cut as Local No. 6.

Moreover, unsecured creditors, the bankruptcy court observed, are estimated to obtain only 13 to 18 cents on the dollar and the value of stockholders' equity is nearly worthless. Yet, the bankruptcy judge declared, the union did not offer an alternative that focused on the needs of its employer's reorganization, but instead adhered to its position that Local 6's excess employees had to be given an incentive to induce them to leave. Neither the debtor or purchaser could fund this demand. Where there is a plausible view of the evidence, considering the entire record, a fact finder's determination to adopt that view may not be held clearly erroneous. See Anderson v. City of Bessemer, 470 U.S. 564, 573–74 [37 FEP Cases 396] (1985).

[The Court also commented on the manner in which Zuckerman made his final offer to the union.] First, Local No. 6 did not complain that it had too little time to respond to the employer's proposal made on October 21. In addition, parties to collective bargaining agreements routinely negotiate for many hours under imperative deadlines. In that negotiating universe, ten hours is ample time to consider and respond to a proposal. Consequently, the bankruptcy court correctly concluded that Local No. 6 rejected the employer's proposal without good cause.

---

iii.   Section 1114: Retiree Insurance Benefits

In 1986 the LTV Corporation filed a Chapter 11 bankruptcy petition and immediately canceled the health and life insurance benefits of approximately 78,000 retirees. Thus prompted, Congress reviewed the effect of the reorganization process on retirees and enacted the Retiree Benefits Bankruptcy Protection Act of 1988, much of which is codified at 11 U.S.C. § 1114.

Section 1114 requires that medical, surgical or hospital care benefits or benefits payable in the event of sickness, accident, death or disability provided to retired employees, their spouses and dependents pursuant to a plan, fund or program in effect at the time a Chapter 11 proceeding is commenced will continue to be paid until or unless a modification is agreed to by the parties or ordered by the court. The section also authorizes the bankruptcy court to enter multiple modifications if warranted by the debtor's financial position; gives retiree benefits administrative status (unlike section 1113 which does not give collectively-negotiated employee benefits administrative status); and details the substantive and procedural prerequisites for court approval of modification of retiree benefits (these are modeled on section 1113 because the Senate committee believed "it is important to use a standard with which the courts are already familiar" (S.Rep.No. 119, 100th Cong., 2nd Sess. 6, reprinted in 1988 U.S.Code Cong. & Admin.News 683, 687)).

The effect of Section 1114 is not yet clear. A widely cited decision, *In re Chateaugay Corp.*, 945 F.2d 1205 (2d Cir.1991), *cert. denied* 502 U.S. 1093, 112 S.Ct. 1167, 117 L.Ed.2d 413 (1992), was withdrawn as part of a settlement. 17 E.B.C. 1102, 1993 WL 388809 (S.D.N.Y.1993). The reasoning of the majority and dissent in that case may be a guide to judicial thinking, however. Two members of the panel held that the Retiree Benefits Bankruptcy Protection Act does not require the debtor employer to pay health benefits after the expiration of a collective bargaining agreement. In this case the retiree health benefits were guaranteed through the collective bargaining agreement and through a Benefit Trust to which many employers contributed. The Benefit Trust sued to have the reorganizing company (LTV, by the way) continue health insurance contributions. But the majority looked to the "plan" in existence at the time of the Chapter 11 filing, found that Article XX of the bargaining agreement stated "h]ealth care benefits are guaranteed during the term of this Agreement," and held that the company's obligation ceased on the date the agreement terminated. The (financially distressed) Benefit Trust would be responsible for the lifetime insurance guarantees. (According to the majority: "There is no cessation of benefits, there is no termination of benefits. Whether the plan is able to fund fully the benefits is a separate issue." 945 F.2d at 1210.) In dissent, Judge Restani objected that Section 1114 should not be read so as to distinguish between retirees who were at-will employees and those whose health benefits were secured through collective bargaining. Neither decision relies on the legislative history, much of which could be read as requiring the company to continue retiree benefits beyond the date of the bargaining agreement.

As noted, the parties have settled this dispute and the opinion is theoretically of no precedential value. Yet the rationale of *In re Chateau-*

gay Corp. is that plan documents override Section 1114. Query: if the plan documents for at-will employees provide that health benefits "are guaranteed until the first of June of each year, unless extended," what force does Section 1114 have?

Congress expressly noted that Section 1114 deals exclusively with rejection or modification of retiree benefits of companies in Chapter 11 proceedings. What about active employees (anticipating continued health benefits after retirement) and retirees (already relying on such benefits) of companies that are in financial difficulty but have not yet petitioned, indeed may never petition, for reorganization under the Bankruptcy Code? Are such companies free, should they be free, to terminate or modify commitments regarding retirement benefits?

c. Perspectives

i.) Bankruptcy Law and Labor Law

Reorganization pursuant to Chapter 11 of the Bankruptcy Code has two fundamental purposes: equality of distribution of benefits and burdens, and preservation of going-concern value. The Code is not primarily concerned with regulating labor and employment relations; but, in establishing priorities for payment, Congress took into account the employees' dual roles as creditors of and contributors to the reorganizing enterprise. Congress has gone further with regard to collectively-negotiated agreements and retiree health benefits. In effect, Sections 1113 and 1114 tell other creditors and the officers of the reorganizing company that bargaining agreements and retiree health benefits must be examined apart from the established hierarchy of priorities for executory contracts.

Sections 1113 and 1114 have met resistance from judges. Are judges, as compared to legislators, less sympathetic to working people? Or is the problem the manner in which the concerns of working people are sometimes addressed by Congress—as adjustments which could nullify the underlying premises of the statutes to which they are appended?

ii.) The Perverse Consequences of Dealing With Labor and Employment Law Issues Through the Bankruptcy Code

Some observers argue that the cures of Sections 1113 and 1114 could prove worse than the diseases of unilateral rejection of bargaining agreements and termination of retiree benefits. Dan Keating, for example, argues that

[S]ection 1114 may make it less likely that companies with significant retiree benefits liabilities will be able to reorganize successfully. If retirees receive a greater relative entitlement in a Chapter 11 [reorganization] case than in a Chapter 7 [liquidation] case, other unsecured creditors will see their recovery in a Chapter 11 case reduced. Thus, these nonretiree unsecured creditors may have an incentive to block a company's Chapter 11 reorganization plan even when that company's going-concern value would be realized best in the Chapter 11 forum.

This rearrangement of nonbankruptcy entitlements, even though for the benefit of a sympathy-evoking class like retirees, undermines two of the most fundamental reorganization goals: equality of distribution and preservation of on-going concern value.

Probably the greatest weakness of the new retiree benefits legislation is that it fails to address the real problem behind crises like that in the LTV reorganization: the failure to prefund the corporate promise to provide insurance benefits to retirees. If a company has not set aside assets to cover its promise to retirees, a mere change in the Bankruptcy Code cannot overcome the void. The new benefits legislation is not broad enough to give any true protection to retirees, yet the legislation alters the nature of the Chapter 11 bargaining process significantly enough to make reorganization less likely for any company with large retiree benefits.

Dan Keating, Good Intentions, Bad Economics: Retiree Insurance Benefits in Bankruptcy, 43 VAND.L.REV. 161, 163 (1990).

How could the law preserve the fundamental goals of legislation like Chapter 11 of the Bankruptcy Code and allocate the costs of reorganization in a way that respects the special place of bargaining agreements and retiree health benefits? Is it easier to integrate society's concern about retirees and preference for reorganization over liquidation than it is to mesh the processes of collective bargaining and reorganization proceedings? Professor Keating suggests that Congress directly confront the problem of retiree health benefits by amending ERISA to require prefunding of plans (and repealing Section 1114 of the Bankruptcy Code). Companies with a weak commitment to retiree benefits would terminate plans, but employees would know in advance not to count on employers, any of which may, like LTV, treat retiree benefits as gratuities. No special rule would then be required in the event of a bankruptcy.

3. RESTRUCTURING TO CUT COSTS

CASE STUDY: PLAIN AND SIMPLE I

Plain & Simple, a Boise-based consumer products manufacturer, plans to reduce 13,000 positions worldwide over the next three to four years in a massive restructuring effort. Plain & Simple has set aside a $1.5 billion reserve, and expects to save $500 million within three years.

According to the company chair and CEO, as quoted in the New York Times: "The public has come to think of corporate restructuring as a sign of trouble, but this is definitely not our situation. We have a healthy, growing business, a strong balance sheet, and a well-stocked technology pipeline with plenty of opportunities for growth. However, we must slim down to lower prices and stay competitive.

"The company will have record earnings in fiscal 200___. Earnings are expected to exceed $2 billion after taxes for the first time, and Plain & Simple expects to report double-digit earnings growth for the full year."

The reductions will affect 12 percent of the worldwide workforce of 106,000. About 6500 positions will be eliminated over the next two years as a result of workplace reorganizations and changes in work processes at the company. About 4000 of these jobs are located in the United States.

Another 6500 positions will be affected when the company closes about 30 of its 147 manufacturing plants. Final decisions have not yet been made on which plants will close. The company plans to reassign as many of these employees as possible. Some of the Plain & Simple plants are unionized.

In addition to attrition, Plain & Simple's director of personnel proposes three ways to reduce the number of employees on the payroll: an involuntary reduction in force, that is, firing people who cost too much given their productivity; voluntary separation offers, including generous severance benefits, to roughly 15% of the workforce; an early retirement plan with enhanced pension benefits to eligible employees. Details about these three options as set out in a memorandum from the personnel director are developed below. Plain & Simple's director of financial affairs likes the just-fire-people option and sees no reason to incur the additional expenses associated with severance benefits and early retirement incentives. The director of personnel prefers to use all three methods believing that the morale of remaining employees will be better if they see their peers depart with severance and early retirement money. He is also concerned about the reputational effect on future employee recruitment if Plain & Simple is viewed as a company without compassion. In addition, he is concerned with applicable legal restraints. Your assignment is to assess the legality and fairness of each option, as described in company documents quoted below.

RESTRUCTURING BY ELIMINATING JOBS

a. *Just fire people*

"Many of the employees' jobs were created during the 1970s and 80s, when companies tried to do everything in-house, from financing to public relations to sensitivity training. Whole departments can be eliminated and the work contracted out at low cost. If a terminated employee is needed subsequently, she can be hired as a consultant or on a yearly contract. The restructuring is also an opportunity to merge jobs, eliminate duplicative positions, and consolidate programs. For example, the company has over 50 computer systems throughout the world. An internal study demonstrated that these can be merged into 5 systems, significantly reducing the need for programmers and support staff. In addition, many job classifications reflect outmoded technology. Job functions can be consolidated and only those employees with the skills, knowledge, and flexibility to handle all aspects of the new jobs retained. Since technologically unsophisticated employees tend to be older and better paid, discharge for not meeting job specifications will cut positions and generate significant savings. Finally, mistakes over the years in hiring and promotion can finally be remedied.

"To guard against favoritism, a consulting firm should evaluate positions and employees, then recommend the cuts."

What more would you need to know about the make-up of the workforce and their salary ranges before going ahead with this option? Wholesale discharges to cut costs means some employees lose their jobs not because of poor performance but because of working in the wrong location or having too high a salary. What federal and state statutes might limit Plain & Simple's freedom to fire unneeded, unwanted or underperforming employees? Does Plain & Simple need to worry about claims of breach of an implicit contract based on its personnel policies? In combining job functions does Plain & Simple need to pay special attention to accommodations for its disabled employees?

We could give you lots of cases illustrating that a company may discharge large numbers of people as long as the company follows its previously advertised procedures and avoids a pattern of firing members of protected groups. By now you will have developed your own checklist against which to test personnel decisions. One thing to remember though is that even the best planning can end up in litigation. Would it make more sense for the law to mandate a schedule of severance benefits for employees discharged in a restructuring and to eliminate all legal challenges to the reason for discharges or the manner in which those discharges were carried out? How would such a fund be financed and administered?

b. Voluntary Separations Combined With Generous Severance Benefits

"The theory behind this approach is that employees are compensated for the unanticipated loss of a job. Severance benefits equaling three to six months salary, depending on length and level of employment, will be offered. Severance benefits are in consideration for an employee signing a waiver of legal claims. The waiver is security against lawsuits filed by departed employees who change their minds. To insure an enforceable waiver, follow the guidelines for waivers set out in the Older Workers Benefit Protection Act of 1990, an amendment to the ADEA, on the theory that a waiver which is voluntary and knowing for ADEA purposes will be a voluntary and knowing waiver for all legal claims. As an additional disincentive to lawsuits, be sure to include an agreement committing the employee to pay any company attorneys' fees arising from the employee's decision to challenge the company over the severance agreement."

This option seems humane; is it? Are waivers of legal claims indeed assurances against lawsuits by disgruntled former employees? What would such a waiver need to contain?

i. Voluntariness

Financial incentives are a common feature of commercial relations, a familiar example being the over-booked airline's offer of cash and a seat on a later flight in exchange for your reserved seat on the about-to-depart plane. Intuitively, though, the "choice" offered to employees who know their company is undertaking a major restructuring effort seems different than the "choice" offered to the airline passenger. For one thing the employees' options are limited and the stakes are high: Take the money and run, or wait around to see if the ax (as it is wielded over and over again) falls on you. Older employees with higher salaries and longer lengths of service may feel they are the most vulnerable. In many cases their cost to the company is believed to exceed their productivity, making them likely targets for termination should they fail to accept the severance package. But members of traditionally excluded groups, like white women and people of color, may see the restructuring as a "neutral" way to thin their ranks, and they may consider acceptance of the severance package as the only realistic choice. Even individuals who do a good job but do not get along with their bosses may feel pushed into accepting separation with severance benefits.

In two celebrated cases the federal courts of appeals debated the "voluntariness" of incentive offers. For Judge Easterbrook and the Seventh Circuit, an incentive to end employment is an added opportunity:

> Providing the employee may decline the offer and keep working under lawful conditions, the offer makes him better off. He has an additional option, one that may be (as it was here) worth a good deal of money. * * * This may put him to a hard choice: he may think the offer too good to refuse; but it is not Don Corleone's "Make him an offer he can't refuse." "Your money or your life?" calls for a choice, but each option makes the recipient of the offer worse off. When one option makes the recipient better off and the other is the status quo, the offer is beneficial. That the benefits may overwhelm the recipient and dictate the choice cannot be dispositive. The question "Would you prefer $100,000 to $50,000" will elicit the same answer from everyone, but it does not on that account produce an "involuntary" response.

Henn v. National Geographic Society, 819 F.2d 824, 826 (7th Cir.1987), *cert. denied* 484 U.S. 964, 108 S.Ct. 454, 98 L.Ed.2d 394 (1987).

Starting from a different baseline, Judge Pettine observed in *Hebert v. Mohawk Rubber Co.,* 872 F.2d 1104, 1112–13 (1st Cir.1989):

> In our view, to accept the reasoning * * * that a person's acceptance of an early retirement package is voluntary when faced with a "choice" between the Scylla of forced retirement or the Charybdis of discharge * * * is to turn a blind eye upon the "take-it-or-leave-it" nature of such an "offer." * * * Absent the right to decline an employer's offer of early retirement and keep working under lawful conditions, the "decision" to take the early retirement "option" is no decision at all. A "choice" between not working with benefits and not working without benefits amounts to, in effect, compulsory retirement.

ii. Waivers and Releases

Just because an employee accepts a severance package, doesn't mean the employee will not sue the employer. Severance pay temporarily cushions the blow of unexpected unemployment, but decisions may come to be regretted if a weak economy means a long period of joblessness and if being without a paying job wreaks havoc on one's self-esteem. To try to ward off lawsuits challenging the legitimacy of separation agreements, employers routinely require employees to sign waivers and releases. Employees acknowledge the voluntariness of the separation and expressly give up any claims against the employer arising out of the soon-to-be terminated employment relationship, including a claim that the separation itself was unlawful or carried out in an unlawful manner. The severance package is identified as consideration for the waivers and release. These pre-dispute waivers are generally enforceable if found to be knowing and voluntary.

The OWBPA. In the Older Workers Benefit Protection Act (OWBPA), Congress detailed its understanding of a knowing and voluntary waiver, at least insofar as ADEA claims are concerned. The OWBPA, as codified at 29 U.S.C. 626(f)(3), appears in the reference supplement. Consult it now (or the rest of this section won't make sense!).

The waiver provisions of the OWBPA apply only to claims involving the ADEA. But employers want insurance against all employment-related claims, not just those arising under ADEA. Take a look at the following voluntary separation agreement and release and waiver of claims, adapted from a form used by IBM as part of a company-wide reduction-in-force pursuant to an enhanced benefits severance plan. *See Astor v. IBM,* 7 F.3d 533 (6th Cir.1993). Does it meet OWBPA requirements? Does it also protect the employer from other legal claims arising from the employment relationship?

GENERAL RELEASE AND COVENANT NOT TO SUE

_____

COMPANY ADVISES YOU TO CONSULT AN ATTORNEY BEFORE YOU SIGN THIS RELEASE

If you feel that you are being coerced to sign this release or that your signing would for any reason not be voluntary, or you believe the process by which you have been offered this release or the payment in exchange for this release is discriminatory, you are encouraged to discuss this with your management or Personnel before signing this release. You should thoroughly review and understand the effects of the release before signing it.

In exchange for the sums and benefits which you will receive pursuant to the terms of the Individual Transition Option Program, [employee name] (hereinafter "you") agrees to release Company from all claims, demands, actions or liabilities you may have against Company which are related to your employment with Company or the termination of that employment. You agree that this also releases from liability Company's agents, directors, officers, employees, representatives, successors and assigns (hereinafter "those associated with Company"). You agree that you have executed this release on your own behalf, and also on behalf of any heirs, agents, representatives, successors and assigns that you may have now or in the future. You also agree that this release covers, but is not limited to, claims arising from the Age Discrimination in Employment Act of 1967, as amended, Title VII of the Civil Rights Act of 1964, as amended, and any other federal or state law dealing with discrimination in employment on the basis of sex, race, national origin, religion, disability, or age. You also agree that this release includes claims based on theories of contract or tort, whether based on common law or otherwise. This release does not include your vested rights if any in the Company Retirement Plan, which survive unaffected by this release.

You agree that you will never institute a claim or charge of employment discrimination with any agency or sue Company, or those associated with Company, concerning any claim you may have relating to your employment with Company or the termination of that employment. If you violate this release by suing Company or those associated with Company, you agree that you will pay all costs and expenses of defending against the suit incurred by Company or those associated with Company, including reasonable attorneys' fees.

You acknowledge and agree that:

1. The benefits provided pursuant to the ITO Program constitute consideration for this release, in that they are benefits to which you would not have been entitled had you not signed this release.

2. You have been given a period of at least forty-five (45) days within which to consider this release.

3. This release does not waive any claims that you may have which arise after the date you sign the release.

4. You have not relied on any representations, promises, or agreements of any kind made to you in connection with your decision to accept the ITO Program except for those set forth in the ITO Summary Plan Description and other official plan documentation.

This release is not effective or enforceable for seven (7) days after you sign it and you may revoke it during that time.

Signed & dated_____

iii. What do severance benefits buy?

Recall the case of *Oubre v. Entergy Operations, Inc.*, 522 U.S. 422 (1998) in Chapter One, in which the Supreme Court stated that the statutory requirements of the OWBPA, and not common law doctrines, determine the validity of releases. You will recall that the employer provided an invalid release but argued unsuccessfully that the former employees were required to tender back the severance payments before suing the employer. Here are some more questions about *Oubre*.

1. Justice Breyer suggests that should the plaintiff prevail on her age discrimination claim, any recovery will be reduced by the amount of the employee-retained severance benefit. Fair enough. But what if the defendant prevails on the merits? Presumably, the plaintiff keeps the severance payments. Has the company received any benefit from its bargain?

2. How difficult would it have been for the company to give *Oubre* enough time to consider her options, to give her seven days after she signed the release to change her mind, or to include in the release a specific reference to claims under the ADEA? Did the company act out of negligence, stupidity, or guile?

3. If the waiver in *Oubre* had been valid, the company's motion for summary judgment would have been granted. Assume Plain and Simple's employees sign a valid waiver, which includes the information that the departing employees will be replaced with part-timers who will not receive benefits (and who are anticipated to be college students). What *public* policy is served by enforcing the waiver?

4. Can the courts develop a common law set of requirements like OWBPA as part of unconscionability?

c. *Early retirement incentives to eligible employees*

"The goal is to eliminate as many highly paid positions as possible and to consolidate existing managerial and supervisory functions. Under the retirement plan presently in effect, if eligible employees over age 57 retired or were fired now, they would receive roughly 60 percent of their retirement benefits on reaching normal retirement age of 65. To stimulate early retirement, offer eligible employees over age 57 100 percent of their pension benefits as of the date they retire if they retire during the first three months of the fiscal year. Employees who decline the early retirement incentives have no job security and no guarantees of enhanced benefits should they be terminated. Finally, include language giving discretion to managers to exclude from eligibility any otherwise qualified employees who the company can't afford to lose.

"In addition to the waivers of legal claims discussed in connection with severance benefits, the Voluntary Separation Agreement should include the employee's promise not to apply for a position with Plain & Simple during the five years following acceptance of early retirement.

The waivers and no application agreement are insurance against lawsuits by former employees who regret their decision to retire."

This option looks attractive because employees self-select to leave the workplace and because the costs to the employer are delayed, depending on the accounting rules in force with regard to funding pension and welfare benefit plans. But how can a company offer this retirement incentive to employees over 57 without violating ADEA? What about the 50–year-old, long-term employees who would be better off leaving through early retirement than through a separation with severance pay? And is the agreement not to apply for employment for five years enforceable?

And how can the employer protect against losing coveted employees with knowledge needed by the firm? May the employer exclude those employees from the group eligible for early retirement, or otherwise insure that Plain & Simple continues to benefit from their work?

i. *ADEA and early retirement incentives*

Early retirement benefits as age discrimination. The common sense answer to the question whether otherwise nondiscriminatory early retirement plans violate the ADEA because they exclude some age protected employees is presented in *Karlen v. City Colleges of Chicago,* 837 F.2d 314, 318 (7th Cir.1988), *cert. denied* 486 U.S. 1044, 108 S.Ct. 2038, 100 L.Ed.2d 622 (1988):

> An early retirement plan that treats you better the older you are is not suspect under the Age Discrimination in Employment Act. Title VII protects whites and men as well as blacks and women, but the Age Discrimination in Employment Act does not protect the young as well as the old, or even, we think, the younger against the older. The protected zone begins at age 40, but if on that account workers 40 or older but younger than the age of eligibility for early retirement could complain * * * early retirement plans would effectively be outlawed, and that was not the intent of the framers of the Age Discrimination in Employment Act. The *reductio ad absurdum* of the reasoning which views early retirement plans with suspicion would be to view permitting workers to retire when they reach the age of 65 as a form of discrimination against workers aged 40 to 64. Then the employer could be confident of escaping liability under the Age Discrimination in Employment Act only by allowing retirement at age 40!

When Congress amended the ADEA in 1990, through the Older Workers Benefit Protection Act (OWBPA), it intended to codify this common sense approach to early retirement incentives, by providing that it shall not be unlawful for an employer "to observe the terms of a bona fide employee benefit plan ... that is a voluntary early retirement plan consistent with the relevant purposes of this Act." 29 U.S.C. § 623(f)(2)(B)(ii).

ii. Restrictions on future employment as age discrimination

EEOC v. LOCAL 350, PLUMBERS

United States Court of Appeals, Ninth Circuit, 1992.
998 F.2d 641, rehearing en banc denied (1993).

FLETCHER, CIRCUIT JUDGE

The Equal Employment Opportunity Commission ("EEOC") appeals the district court's grant of summary judgment in favor of Local 350, Plumbers and Pipefitters ("Local 350"). The EEOC brought suit to challenge Local 350's policy of refusing to allow retired members to seek work through Local 350's hiring hall while the members continued to receive pension benefits. We reverse.

FACTS

Local 350 represents pipefitters and plumbers in Northern Nevada and parts of California. Together with industry employers, Local 350 operates a hiring hall. The hiring hall dispatcher keeps four "out of work lists," with different qualifications and priorities, from which members are hired. At issue in this case is list number 1, the "out of work list," reserved for persons who have been employed for at least 4,000 hours or more during the five years immediately preceding placement on the list. The dispatcher sends members out to jobs in the order in which they signed up.

Donald Pilot, a member of Local 350, retired in 1983. After retirement, he paid retired members' dues. In 1984, he decided to return to work, and signed onto the out of work list. Local 350 removed his name from the list, stating he was not eligible. In a letter dated April 20, 1984, Local 350 informed Pilot that, "as a 'retiree,' having applied for and been granted a pension, you are not presently eligible for dispatch through the UA Local 350 Hiring Hall." Local 350 informed Pilot that to be eligible to sign up for referral, he would have to cease receiving his pension. Pilot apparently continued to seek to sign up until as late as November 1987.

In June 1984, Pilot filed charges with the National Labor Relations Board ("NLRB") to challenge Local 350's policy. The NLRB refused to issue a complaint in the matter. A subsequent NLRB challenge filed by Pilot also did not result in NLRB action.

In December, 1987, Pilot filed a discrimination charge with the Nevada Equal Rights Commission and the EEOC. In June 1989, the EEOC filed an action under the Age Discrimination in Employment Act ("ADEA"), 29 U.S.C. § 621 *et seq.,* on behalf of Pilot and similarly situated union members, seeking equitable relief, back pay, and liquidated damages. In May 1990, the district court granted summary judgment in favor of Local 350. In August 1990, it denied the EEOC's motion for reconsideration. * * *

* * *

II. Does 29 U.S.C. § 623(f)(2) Bar Review of Local 350's Policy?

Local 350 argues that its policy is protected by the prior version of 29 U.S.C. § 623(f)(2), which provided that it shall not violate the ADEA:

> To observe the terms of a bona fide seniority system or any bona fide employee benefit plan such as a retirement, pension, or insurance plan, which is not a subterfuge to evade the purposes of this chapter, except that no such employee benefit plan shall excuse the failure to hire any individual, and no such seniority system or employee benefit plan shall require or permit the involuntary retirement of any individual specified by section 631(a) of this title because of the age of such individual;

29 U.S.C. § 623(f)(2). That section has been superseded by subsequent amendment.

We find the statute irrelevant in that it is the denial of employment opportunities, not Local 350's seniority system or benefits plan, that is at issue. Retired members of Local 350 are not allowed to sign the out of work list while they are receiving pension benefits from the union. This prohibition, although keyed to receipt of a pension, does not transform the Union's hiring hall policies into provisions of a pension plan. Local 350's argument in this regard is simply specious.

Thus, section 623(f)(2) does not bar review of Local 350's policy.

III. Does Local 350's Policy Violate 29 U.S.C. § 623(c)(2)?

The EEOC claims that Local 350's policy violates 29 U.S.C. § 623(c)(2) because it discriminates against older workers. The district court did not decide this issue, but rather found that even if the policy were discriminatory, Local 350 could successfully rely on the affirmative defense set forth in 29 U.S.C. § 623(f)(1).

Section 623(c)(2) provides:

It shall be unlawful for a labor organization—

> (2) to limit, segregate, or classify its membership, or to classify or fail or refuse to refer for employment any individual, in any way which would deprive or tend to deprive any individual of employment opportunities, or would limit such employment opportunities or otherwise adversely affect his status as an employee or as an applicant for employment, because of such individual's age[.]

29 U.S.C. § 623(c)(2).

"[A]n employer discriminates 'because of' age whenever age is a 'but for' cause of discrimination." *EEOC v. Borden's, Inc.,* 724 F.2d 1390, 1393 (9th Cir.1984). In *Borden's,* when the employer closed a plant, it gave severance pay to the plant's employees; however, employees who were eligible for retirement benefits were not given severance pay. This court held that "[a]ge was a 'but for' cause or necessary condition for the denial of severance pay to Borden's retireable employees since only employees 55 or older were eligible for retirement."

Under this analysis, Local 350's policy discriminates on the basis of age. On its face, it discriminates only against retired employees; however, only employees 55 or older are eligible to retire. There is thus a very close connection between age and the factor on which discrimination is based. *See, e.g., Borden's,* 724 F.2d at 1393; *EEOC v. Westinghouse Elec. Corp.,* 725 F.2d 211, 222 (3d Cir.1983) (discussing "close relationship" between early retirement and age), *cert. denied,* 469 U.S. 820, 105 S.Ct. 92, 83 L.Ed.2d 38 (1984); *cf. Leftwich v. Harris–Stowe State College,* 702 F.2d 686, 691 (8th Cir.1983) (employer's selection plan based on tenure status was discriminatory "because of the close relationship between tenure status and age").

Local 350 argues that the policy is not discriminatory because the "but for" cause of discrimination is not the retiree's age but his voluntary decision to retire and remain retired. This argument is unavailing. First, as *Borden's* suggests, we have been unwilling to draw so fine a line when determining causation. Moreover, the very "choice" Local 350 identifies is discriminatory. Only retired, older employees need decide whether to remain retired and forego alternative sources of income while they seek work as pipefitters; younger workers need not choose between receiving unemployment benefits or holding another job and placing their names on Local 350's list. Younger employees who have "chosen" not to work as pipefitters for some time for whatever reason are not penalized in the same way as retired workers.

Thus, Local 350's policy violates Section 623(c)(2) because it refuses to refer certain employees for work on the basis of a factor very closely related to age. Because the policy discourages retired employees from seeking to return to the workforce, it frustrates the ADEA's goal of promoting the employment of older persons based on their ability rather than age.

IV. Was Local 350's Policy Based on "Reasonable Factors Other Than Age" Within the Meaning of 29 U.S.C. § 623(f)(1)?

The district court awarded summary judgment in favor of Local 350 because the union had established an "exemption from liability" pursuant to 29 U.S.C. § 623(f)(1). That section provides:

It shall not be unlawful for an employer, employment agency, or labor organization—

   (1) to take any action otherwise prohibited under subsections (a), (b), (c), or (e) of this section where age is a bona fide occupational qualification reasonably necessary to the normal operation of the particular business, or where the differentiation is based on reasonable factors other than age. . . .

29 U.S.C. § 623(f)(1). The district court was wrong. Neither the proposed factors cited by the district court in its opinion, nor the additional
factors suggested by Local 350, are viable, non-age-based reasons for its
policy.

The district court reasoned:

Defendant's hiring hall policy is intended to help out-of-work members obtain employment. The policy does not bar retired members from
using the hall, rather, it bars retired members receiving a pension from
using the hall. These retired members may use the hiring hall for the
period that they elect not to receive pension benefits. In essence, the
defendant's policy merely states that retired members receiving a pension are not "out-of-work," and are therefore not eligible to use the
hiring hall.

This proposed justification fails because it rests on pension receipt, a
status closely related to age. "A retired member receiving a pension"—a
member necessarily aged 55 or older—is treated differently from other
members seeking employment, for example, from a member drawing
unemployment benefits or a member employed in another trade.

Local 350 proposes several additional supposedly non-age based
factors cited by Local 350 business manager George Foster in his
declaration. It argues that it needs to preserve work opportunities for its
members. It suggests that a flood of retirees returning to work would
result in long periods of unemployment for non-retired members who
would otherwise get work. However, it is hard to see why Local 350's
management of employment opportunities should be carried out by
requiring retirees to forego their pensions before being allowed to sign
up for work. Once again, the proposed factor seems to embody the very
discrimination that is the subject of this suit. If preventing retirees from
reentering the working force is the rationale (which it could not be,
under the ADEA), no retirees should be allowed to sign up. Moreover, as
the EEOC notes, the Local had fewer than 130 retired members in 1990
and since 1981 only a handful have sought to return to work.

Local 350 also argues that retirees who return to work would quit
after 39 hours of employment in a month to preserve their pension
benefits. It suggests this would cause problems for employers who want
to retain employees for the duration of the project for which they are
hired. However, this "no short term work" policy apparently applies
only to pensioned retirees seeking to return to work. Local 350 does not
suggest that other unemployed workers are required to commit to any
minimum time on the job. Moreover, if an employer is dissatisfied when
a retiree quits after working only a limited time on its job, it can refuse
to hire that retiree in the future.

Local 350 finally "points to the basic unfairness of allowing one
group of unemployed workers to collect a pension while on the 'out-of-
work' list while others go unsubsidized." Local 350 notes that, unlike
other unemployed workers, retirees may be eligible for both unemployment insurance and pension benefits, and are benefitting from a life-

time, not a limited, stipend. However, many retirees cannot simultaneously collect both unemployment and pension benefits. *See* Nev.Rev. Stat. § 612.375 ¶ 2 (reduction of unemployment benefits for certain persons receiving pension payments). As to the other part of the argument, it is hard to see how the "lifetime" versus "temporary" subsidy distinction justifies Local 350's policy. First, it is once again an age-related distinction: generally, only older workers will have "life-time" stipends. Moreover, if Local 350 believes it is unfair for "subsidized" workers to enjoy the benefits of its list, it should refuse to allow unemployed workers on the list for as long as they can draw unemployment benefits.

* * * Because neither the reason proposed by the district court nor the justifications presented by Local 350 satisfy the requirements of section 623(f)(1), we find the district court erred in concluding that this defense protected Local 350's policy. We thus reverse the grant of summary judgment in favor of Local 350.[1]

REVERSED.

---

1. Local 350 has requested that we hold the mandate and reconsider the denial of rehearing in this case in light of the Supreme Court's recent decision in *Hazen Paper Co. v. Biggins,* Local [507] U.S. [604], 113 S.Ct. 1701, 123 L.Ed.2d 338 (1993). *Hazen* sets forth the parameters of disparate treatment in the age discrimination context, while expressly leaving open the question whether disparate impact claims are cognizable under the ADEA. *See id.*507 U.S. at [609–610], 113 S.Ct. at 1706–07. We perceive no conflict between *Hazen* and our decision in this case. The EEOC does not specify in its pleadings or briefs on appeal whether it is proceeding under a disparate treatment or disparate impact theory of discrimination. Because in this circuit a plaintiff may challenge age discrimination under a disparate impact analysis, both theories were potentially available to the EEOC. *See EEOC v. Borden's Inc.,* 724 F.2d 1390, 1392 (9th Cir.1984). The EEOC's complaint concerns an employment practice that is "facially neutral … but that in fact fall[s] more harshly on one group than another and [assertedly] cannot be justified by business necessity," and seeks relief for an entire class of workers in addition to the named complainant. It is therefore cognizable as a disparate impact challenge. *Hazen,* [507] U.S. at [609], 113 S.Ct. at 1705 (quoting *Teamsters v. United States,* 431 U.S. 324, 335 n. 15, 97 S.Ct. 1843, 1854 n. 15, 52 L.Ed.2d 396 (1977)); *Borden's,* 724 F.2d at 1392.

The violation alleged by the EEOC may also fall within *Hazen's* definition of disparate treatment. A disparate treatment claim is made out where the plaintiff can show that an employer treated him differently because of his age. In such a case, "[p]roof of discriminatory motive is critical, although it can in some situations be inferred from the mere fact of differences in treatment." *Hazen,* [507] U.S. at [648], 113 S.Ct. at 1705 (quoting *Teamsters,* 431 U.S. at 335 n. 15, 97 S.Ct. at 1854 n. 15). As *Hazen* explains,

[i]n a disparate treatment case, liability depends on whether the protected trait … actually motivated the employer's decision.

* * *

We do not preclude the possibility that an employer who targets employees with a particular pension status on the assumption that these employees are likely to be older thereby engages in age discrimination. Pension status may be a proxy for age … in the sense that the employer may suppose a correlation between the two factors and act accordingly. [507] U.S. at [612–13], 113 S.Ct. at 1706, 1707.

On remand, the district court should direct the EEOC to articulate its theory or theories of discrimination in accordance with the principles set forth in *Hazen.*

1. After this decision Local 350 changed its policy. A retiree who wants to register on the out-of-work list must submit forms to the pension plans advising of the intent to register. The union registers the retiree immediately, and the pension plans take whatever action is appropriate. *See EEOC v. Local 350, Plumbers & Pipefitters,* 842 F.Supp. 417 (D.Nev.1994).

2. One pension plan dealt with the problem of "double dipping" by instituting a rule that requires state or local employees who accept subsequent state or local jobs to choose between not receiving benefits from the first job but accruing additional pension benefits from the second job, or receiving pension benefits from the first job but not accruing further benefits from the second job. See Connolly v. McCall, 254 F.3d 36 (2d Cir. 2001). The Court of Appeals for the Second Circuit, rejecting a due process complaint, accepted that the state's legitimate interest in saving money was not irrational.

iii. Can the employer pick and choose who is eligible for early retirement?

McNAB v. GENERAL MOTORS CORP.

United States Court of Appeals for the Seventh Circuit, 1998.
162 F.3d 959.

EASTERBROOK, CIRCUIT JUDGE.

Like many other firms, General Motors Corporation uses early-retirement programs to reduce its workforce without resorting to involuntary separation. One problem with early-retirement systems, however, is that the best employees may leap at the opportunity, knowing that they can add income from other jobs to their retirement packages; the firm wants to keep these superior employees while shedding those who are not up to snuff, but the sub-par workers are less willing to go, because they may value sinecures and do not expect to find comparable employment elsewhere. If the firm augments the early-retirement incentive to make it attractive to employees who lack prospects of finding other jobs, then the best employees have even more reason to take the offer. To overcome this problem of adverse selection, firms may limit early-retirement programs to employees chosen by management. Managers offer the package to the weakest members of the staff, simultaneously cutting their unit's budget and improving the average quality of its workers. But good workers may take exclusion poorly; why, they may ask, should rewards vary inversely with quality? Resentment may lead to litigation. In this case 13 employees at the Allison Gas Turbine division of General Motors, told that they were too valuable to let go, contend that the Employee Retirement Income Security Act (ERISA) forbids GM to implement an early-retirement system that leaves participation to the discretion of managers. Although they do not say that discretion is always forbidden, they do contend that it must be exercised so that every similar case company-wide is treated identically. Because this is impossible at any large company, their position is functionally equivalent to an argument that ERISA forbids discretionary early-retirement programs.

In January 1992 GM adopted what it called the "1992 Corporate Window Retirement Program" under which the early-retirement age was decreased from 55 to 53, and the retirement package was sweetened by computing benefits without reduction for the earlier age of retirement or earnings at other jobs. Later in 1992 GM dropped the minimum age from 53 to 50. Early retirement was particularly attractive to employees at the Allison Gas Turbine division, which GM was trying to sell. Some employees were uncertain about their future and perceived early retirement as a source of guaranteed income; others saw it as a means to increase their income, for they could "retire" from GM and draw a pension while remaining employed full time at the newly constituted Allison Engine Company (which was spun off as an independent firm late in 1993). But under the 1992 program early retirement was possible only if GM and the employee agreed, and GM reserved the right to choose according to "GM's best interest." Plant personnel directors sent lists of candidates to the Management Committee of GM's board, which made the final decision.

None of our plaintiffs was selected by Allison's management, which wanted to keep its best workers in order to facilitate the impending sale. Appeals to the Management Committee were unsuccessful. For example, plaintiff Michael Asher related that he was told "that the best employees were being kept because any prospective buyer of the Company needed an experienced workforce. Three times during the meeting, Dr. Wallace told me that I was 'invaluable to the Company.' I was considered to be 'a long term fit in the organization' and not considered to be 'excess to the needs of the organization.' " Plaintiff Nicholas Schmutte was not recommended because managers had been "told that any positions vacated by the incentive separation were not to be replaced. At the time the Contracts Department [in which Schmutte worked] was unable to meet all of the demands with the people on board, let alone with one [fewer]." The district court concluded that none of GM's choices could be called "arbitrary and capricious," the right standard for judicial review of an operational decision under a plan that expressly gives the administrator discretion.

Plaintiffs do not contend that GM's stated reasons were mistaken, let alone arbitrary and capricious. They do not argue that the Contracts Department was overstaffed or that they were "excess to the needs of" GM—that any reasonable decisionmaker at GM would have been bound to consider them deadwood. Instead they maintain that decisions under the programs were not strictly according to inverse rankings of performance. One employee was given early retirement to avoid a threat of litigation; another was allowed to retire so that he could stay home with his ill wife; another because he had hypertension; another was a manager so senior that he could put his own name on the list; still others were (as plaintiffs see things) as valuable to GM as plaintiffs themselves. Plaintiffs' reply brief sums up their position: managers "deviate[d] from the ... Plan's stated purpose [and] made selection decisions based upon cronyism, whimsy and personal notions of honor, duty and fairness. They also reversed nonselection decisions ... for hidden and undisclosed reasons e.g. threats of litigation, complaints of discrimination, cronyism, complaints of health problems."

It is more than a little difficult to see why plaintiffs, whose applications were correctly denied under the program's stated criteria, should be entitled to relief because GM was unduly generous with other employees. If this were a medical benefits program, would one decision to pay for an un-covered medical procedure (say, a dental implant in lieu of a bridge) entitle every other employee to reimbursement for that procedure? An employer is supposed to apply the plan's written terms, and departure from those terms on one occasion does not stop the employer to enforce them on others. See Frahm v. Equitable Life Assurance Society, 137 F.3d 955 (7th Cir.1998). Plaintiffs suggest that every divergence from a plan's criteria is an "amendment" of the plan entitling them to the same benefits, but that is a non-starter, rejected in Frahm. Amendments are accomplished through a formal process and produce a revised written instrument. Deviations from a plan are just that—deviations. The plan remains what it was, and claims for benefits continue to be evaluated in light of its written criteria.

But plaintiffs' position has a deeper problem. There's nothing wrong under ERISA with a system that gives plan administrators discretion. Subject to a few explicit rules in the statute, an employer may design a pension or welfare plan with features of its choosing, provided it is willing to pay the cost. Lockheed Corp. v. Spink, 517 U.S.882, 116 S.Ct. 1783, 135 L.Ed.2d 153 (1996); Johnson v. Georgia–Pacific Corp., 19 F.3d 1184 (7th Cir.1994); McGath v. Auto–Body North Shore, Inc., 7 F.3d 665 (7th Cir.1993). See also Henn v. National Geographic Society, 819 F.2d 824 (7th Cir.1987) (no problem under age discrimination laws either, provided early retirement is voluntary). Plaintiffs concede that GM is entitled to adopt an early-retirement plan under which the eligibility standard is the best interests of GM, as GM's board of directors sees those interests. This is exactly what GM did, having put up the extra money necessary to pay for the benefits. If it is lawful to adopt a plan that gives discretion to senior managers, it must be lawful to *use* that discretion to evaluate what the "best interests" of a firm are. Managers may conclude that it is in the best interest of a firm to allow employees to assist stricken family members or retire early when in ill health; benevolent employment policies make it easier for the firm to attract good workers, and to keep them at lower salaries than Simon Legree Mfg., Inc., must pay. Managers may conclude that it is cheaper (and hence in the best interest of the firm) to let a given worker retire early than to underwrite the costs of defending a lawsuit, for even weak suits may require steep attorneys' fees to achieve victory. (This suit is a good example of that fact.) Because GM is such a large corporation, different managers at different plants (even different managers at the same plant) are bound to interpret the "best interests" of the firm differently. That is the inevitable result of choosing a *standard* (such as "best interests of the firm") rather than a *rule* (such as "in the bottom 20% according to last year's performance evaluations"). Flexibility is doubtless the reason GM adopted a standard rather than a rule; flexible administration therefore cannot be the program's undoing, or we have simply used an under-the-table method to make discretion unlawful, contradicting the conclusion that ERISA permits discretionary plans.

Discretion might be curtailed and the results made more consistent by having a single decisionmaker. But that's not feasible for a large organization such as GM and at any event would not eliminate plaintiffs' beef. What might appear to GM's early-retirement czar as compassion (the health cases) or thrift (the litigation-settlement cases) might appear to plaintiffs as "cronyism"—for they might not be privy to the factors that influenced the decision or might weigh them differently from the plan administrator. "Cronyism" is just an epithet plaintiffs attach to decisions they do not understand or approve. Using a district judge as arbiter of such disputes would compromise the discretionary nature of the program or appoint the judge as the plan's real early-retirement czar. ERISA does not require the former and does not permit the latter. No surprise, then, that courts have invariably rejected challenges to discretionary decisions made under earlier versions of GM's early-retirement plan, Bair v. General Motors Corp., 895 F.2d 1094 (6th Cir.1990); Valz v. General Motors Corp., No. 88–1794, 1988 WL 150794 (8th Cir. Dec.22, 1988) (unpublished order); Friesen v. General Motors Corp., 759 F.Supp. 560 (E.D.Mo.1991); *Jewell v. Chevrolet Motors Division of General Motors Corp.*, Civ. No. 90–0689–B(CM) (S.D.Cal. Feb. 11, 1991), as well as under comparable plans at other firms. E.g., Averhart v. US WEST Management Pension Plan, 46 F.3d 1480, 1488 (10th Cir.1994); Berger v. Edgewater Steel Co., 911 F.2d 911, 918–19 (3d Cir.1990); Hlinka v. Bethlehem Steel Corp., 863 F.2d 279, 283–84 (3d Cir.1988). Our decision in Fletcher v. Kroger Co., 942 F.2d 1137 (7th Cir.1991), is in the same vein. Plaintiffs' protest to the 1992–93 edition of GM's plan meets the same fate.

EICHORN v. AT & T CORP.

United States Court of Appeals for the Third Circuit, 2001.
248 F.3d 131, *cert. denied* ___ U.S. ___, 122 S.Ct. 506, 151 L.Ed.2d 415 (2001).

Scirica, Circuit Judge.

In this appeal from the grant of summary judgment we must decide whether defendants AT & T Corp., NCR Corp., Lucent Technologies, and Texas Pacific Group's agreement to restrict the hiring of certain employees upon Lucent's sale of Paradyne Corp. was a violation of § 1 of the Sherman Antitrust Act. We also must decide whether this no-hire agreement which effectively cancelled the plaintiff employees' AT & T pension bridging rights violated § 510 of the Employee Retirement

Income Security Act. We hold the no-hire agreement was a valid covenant not to compete that was reasonable in scope and therefore not a violation of § 1 of the Sherman Act. But also we hold plaintiffs have presented sufficient prima facie evidence of AT & T and Lucent's specific intent to interfere with an ERISA funded employee pension fund to survive summary judgment on the ERISA § 510 claim.

I.

In July 1995, AT & T, a long distance telephone and wireless services provider, decided to sell one of its affiliates, Paradyne Corp., a manufacturer of network access products for the telecommunications industry. Contemplating the sale, AT & T wanted to ensure that Paradyne remained a viable entity because A T & T and its other affiliates, including Lucent Technologies, purchased many of the network access products Paradyne manufactured. To make Paradyne more attractive to buyers as an ongoing business, AT & T adopted a human resource plan that placed restrictions on Paradyne employees' ability to transfer to other divisions of AT & T ("the Preliminary Net"). Specifically, the Preliminary Net precluded an employee who voluntarily left Paradyne from being hired by any other division of AT & T. The premise for the hiring bar was AT & T's belief that one of Paradyne's most marketable assets was its skilled employees. The retention of Paradyne's employees, therefore, was considered essential for the sale of Paradyne.

Shortly after adopting the Preliminary Net, A T & T consummated a business reorganization plan resulting in three independent companies: AT & T, Lucent Technologies, and NCR Corp. (the "trivestiture"). As part of the trivestiture, AT & T transferred ownership of Paradyne to Lucent. Consistent with the Preliminary Net, the Paradyne employees, now employed by Lucent, were precluded from seeking re-employment at any other AT & T division or affiliate after the trivestiture.

On July 31, 1996, Lucent sold Paradyne to Texas Pacific Group. Before closing, Lucent agreed, on behalf of itself and the other former AT & T affiliates, that it would not hire, rehire, retain, or solicit the services of any Paradyne employee or consultant whose annual income exceeded $50,000. This "Pre Closing Net" was consistent with the understanding that Texas Pacific Group's interest in purchasing Paradyne was based on its desire to acquire the technical skills of Paradyne's employees for a sufficient period of time to ensure a successful transition of ownership.

Once the deal was closed, Lucent and Texas Pacific Group entered a post-closing agreement ("Post Closing Net") in which Lucent warranted on behalf of itself and the other AT & T affiliates that for 245 days (8 months) following the sale and the expiration of the Pre Closing Net, it would not seek to hire, solicit or rehire any Paradyne employee or consultant whose compensation exceeded $50,000. The eight month no-hire agreement had the practical effect of cancelling the Paradyne employees' accrued pension benefits under their former AT & T pension plans. Under the AT & T pension plan, employees were entitled to "bridging rights" which allowed them to retain their level of accrued pension benefits if they left AT & T and returned within six months. After six months, the bridging rights expired. Employees rehired after the six month period would need five years of employment to regain their previous pension levels. Because the Post Closing Net barred Paradyne employees from returning to an A T & T affiliate for eight months, these employees automatically lost the bridging rights they had acquired under their AT & T pensions.

Before the sale was consummated, Texas Pacific Group hired an outside consultant to determine the benefit package it could offer the Paradyne employees. Paradyne's Vice President of Human Resources, Sherril Claus Melio, who had previously held the same position when Paradyne was owned by AT & T and Lucent, assisted the consultant in drafting various benefit plan proposals. The consultant concluded that in order to make Paradyne financially competitive, Texas Pacific Group could not offer the same pension package AT & T had previously offered its employees. Although Melio's exact role in Texas Pacific Group's decision is disputed, Texas Pacific Group ultimately decided not to offer a defined pension benefits program to its new employees.

The plaintiffs are former Paradyne employees who allege the Preliminary Net, as well as the Pre and Post Closing Nets, collectively represent an unlawful group boycott in violation of § 1 of the Sherman Act. Additionally, they contend the defendants conspired to eliminate their pension benefits thereby engaging in an illegal price fixing scheme in violation of § 1 of the Sherman Act. Furthermore, they allege the no-hire agreement, which effectively cancelled Paradyne employees' bridging rights under their AT & T pensions, violated § 510 of the Employee Retirement Income Security Act.

In addressing these claims, the District Court held that plaintiffs failed to prove a violation of § 1 of the Sherman Act and failed to produce sufficient prima facie evidence of AT & T and Lucent's specific intent to interfere with an ERISA funded pension plan to support their § 510 claim. The court, therefore, granted defendants' motion for summary judgment. After the grant of summary judgment, plaintiffs filed a discovery motion in connection with an anticipated motion for class certification which the District Court denied. This appeal followed.

II.

* * * We exercise plenary review over the District Court's grant of summary judgment on plaintiffs' antitrust and ERISA claims. * * *

III.

Section 1 of the Sherman Act provides:

Every contract, combination in the form of trust or otherwise, or conspiracy, in restraint of trade or commerce among the several states, or with foreign nations, is hereby declared to be illegal. 15 U.S.C. § 1 (1994).

Under § 1, unreasonable restraints on trade are prohibited because they inhibit competition within the market. Bus. Elecs. Corp. v. Sharp Elecs. Corp., 485 U.S. 717, 723, 108 S.Ct. 1515, 99 L.Ed.2d 808 (1988). In order to assert a cause of action under S 1, plaintiffs must prove they have suffered an antitrust injury that is causally related to the defendants' allegedly illegal anti-competitive activity. Brunswick Corp. v. Pueblo Bowl–O–Mat, Inc., 429 U.S. 477, 489, 97 S.Ct. 690, 50 L.Ed.2d 701 (1977). Once there is the finding of antitrust injury, courts examine the alleged illegal conduct under one of two distinct tests: per se violation or rule of reason. Under the per se test, "agreements whose nature and necessary effect are so plainly anti-competitive that no elaborate study of the industry is needed to establish their illegality" are found to be antitrust violations. Nat'l Soc'y of Prof. Eng'rs v. United States, 435 U.S. 679, 692, 98 S.Ct. 1355, 55 L.Ed.2d 637 (1978). For those activities not within the per se invalidity category, courts employ the rule of reason test. Under this test, plaintiffs have the burden of establishing that, under all the circumstances, "the challenged acts are unreasonably restrictive of competitive conditions" in the relevant market. Standard Oil Co. of N.J. v. United States, 221 U.S. 1, 28, 31 S.Ct. 502, 55 L.Ed. 619 (1911). "An analysis of the reasonableness of particular restraints includes the consideration of the facts peculiar to the business in which the restraint is applied, the nature of the restraint and its effects, and the history of the restraint and the reasons for its adoption." United States v. Topco Assocs., Inc., 405 U.S. 596, 607, 92 S.Ct. 1126, 31 L.Ed.2d 515 (1972).

A.

We hold the AT & T Preliminary Net was not a violation of § 1 of the Sherman Act. The District Court found that "as of ... the date that the Preliminary Net was put into effect ..., Lucent was a wholly-owned subsidiary of A T & T, and accordingly, the two companies were a singular entity that could not conspire to violate the Antitrust laws." *Eichorn v. AT & T Corp.*, CA No. 96–3587, slip op. at *17 (D.N.J. September 10, 1999). In Copperweld Corp. v. Independence Tube Corp., 467 U.S. 752, 104 S.Ct. 2731, 81 L.Ed.2d 628 (1984), the Supreme Court held the coordinated acts of a parent and its wholly owned subsidiary cannot themselves give rise to § 1 antitrust violations. The Court reasoned, "[a] parent and its wholly owned subsidiary have a complete unity of interest. Their objectives are common, not disparate; their general corporate actions are guided or determined not by two separate corporate consciousnesses, but one." Because the Preliminary Net was an internal restriction between a single corporation, AT & T, and its wholly owned subsidiaries, Lucent and NCR, and not an agreement between separate corporate identities, it was not a violation of § 1 of the Sherman Act. ("An internal agreement to implement a single unitary firm's policies does not raise the antitrust dangers that § 1 was designed to police.'') Although plaintiffs assert A T & T and Lucent were not motivated by a single "corporate consciousness" because they were in the process of becoming separate entities, we believe that during the effective time period of the AT & T Preliminary Nct, AT & T and Lucent rctained a unified corporate interest for the purpose of antitrust analysis. It was not until AT & T divested all of its stock in Lucent and after the lapse of the Preliminary Net that the two companies became completely separate entities.* * *

We next turn to plaintiffs' claim that the Pre and Post Closing Nets, collectively referred to as the no-hire agreement, represent an illegal group boycott and a horizontal price fixing conspiracy under § 1 of the Sherman Act. Plaintiffs allege Lucent, AT & T and Texas Pacific Group horizontally competed for the plaintiff employees' technical skills and services. As competitors, they argue, the defendants conspired to suspend competition for plaintiffs' technical services with the purpose and the effect of locking them out of the labor market. By locking them out and effectively cancelling their entitlement to AT & T pension rights, plaintiffs argue the defendants conspired to fix the cost of labor in the market. In support, plaintiffs cite several Supreme Court cases that hold horizontal group boycotts and price fixing conspiracies are per se violations of the Sherman Antitrust Act. *See* FTC v. Super. Ct. Trial Lawyers Assoc., 493 U.S. 411, 422, 110 S.Ct. 768, 107 L.Ed.2d 851 (1990); Arizona v. Maricopa County Med. Soc'y, 457 U.S. 332, 344–45, 102 S.Ct. 2466, 73 L.Ed.2d 48 (1982); Broad. Music, Inc. v. Columbia Broad. Sys., Inc., 441 U.S. 1, 7–8, 99 S.Ct. 1551, 60 L.Ed.2d 1 (1979). * * *

[The court concluded that plaintiffs had standing to litigate their § 1 claims because the no-hire agreement directly impeded plaintiffs' ability to sell their labor to at least three companies within the competitive market and effectively cancelled their AT & T pension benefits; but found that there was no per se violation of the Sherman Act because per se analysis applied only to limited types of anti-competitive practices whose sole purpose was the stifling of competition and covenants not to compete, of which the no hire agreement was a species, had never been treated as a per se violation. The court then considered whether the company policies violated the Sherman Act's rule of reason.]

Under the rule of reason, we look at the totality of the circumstances surrounding an alleged anti-competitive activity, including facts peculiar to the relevant business, to determine the "nature or purpose" of the allegedly illegal restraint. * * *

We agree that the no-hire agreement was not an unreasonable restraint of trade under § 1 of the Sherman Act. Frackowiak v. Farmers Ins. Co., Inc., 411 F.Supp. 1309, 1318 (D.Kan.1976) ("Numerous Courts have recognized the general rule that agreements not to compete, entered into in conjunction with the termination of employment or sale of a business, do no offend the federal antitrust provisions if they are reasonable in duration and geographical limitation.") The primary purpose of the no-hire agreement was to ensure that Texas Pacific Group, as the purchaser of Paradyne, could retain the skilled services of Paradyne's employees. Although the no-hire agreement precluded the employees from seeking employment at an AT & T affiliate for 245 days, the primary purpose of the agreement was not anti-competitive. Contrary to plaintiffs' assertions, we can find no evidence to support their claim that the no-hire agreement was executed for the improper purpose of restraining trade and the cost of labor in the telecommunications industry. The primary purpose of the no-hire agreement was to ensure the successful sale of Paradyne to Texas Pacific Group which required workforce continuity.[3] Any restraint on plaintiffs' ability to seek employment at AT & T and any effect on their pension bridging rights was incidental to the effective sale of Paradyne.

Because the no-hire agreement was a legitimate ancillary restraint on trade, we must determine whether the eight-month restriction from employment at an A T & T affiliate was reasonable or whether it went further than necessary to ensure the successful transition of ownership. Cesnick, 490 F.Supp. at 868 (quoting Syntex Labs., 315 F.Supp. at 56) ("The question in every case [involving a covenant not to compete ancillary to the sale of a business] is whether the restraint is reasonably calculated to protect the legitimate interests of the purchaser in what he has purchased, or whether it goes so far beyond what is necessary as to provide a basis for the inference that its real purpose is the fostering of monopoly").

We do not think the eight month restriction on re-employment at an AT & T affiliate was unreasonably broad. It is reasonable to believe Texas Pacific Group would require the technical skills of these employees for at least this eight month period, if not longer, to ensure a successful transition of ownership from Lucent. Furthermore, the no-hire agreement only precluded the plaintiffs from working at Lucent or an A T & T affiliate. The employees were free to leave Texas Pacific Group and seek employment elsewhere within the telecommunications industry. Significantly, there is no evidence in the record to support plaintiffs' claim that AT & T was the only employer in the market to whom they could sell their services. As the District Court found, there are over twenty other telecommunications firms that compete for plaintiffs' technical services. Furthermore, the market for plaintiffs with more generalized educational and work backgrounds includes "a vast number of jobs" nationwide. *Eichorn*, CA No. 96–3587, slip op. at *27–28 n. 17.

Therefore, we hold the no-hire agreement was not an unreasonable restraint on trade. * * *

---

3. Plaintiffs contend the true motive of the no-hire agreement was not work force continuity but eliminating pension benefits to reduce Texas Pacific Group's costs. They argue that if work force continuity were really the motive, Texas Pacific Group could have offered enhanced benefits packages to entice the work force to remain with Paradyne rather then simply agreeing to cancel their AT & T pension benefits. But the existence of alternative means to achieve a legitimate business goal does not in itself mean the defendants chosen course of action was uncompetitive and improper.

IV.

We now turn to whether the no-hire agreement, which effectively cancelled plaintiffs' A T & T pension bridging rights, violated § 510 of ERISA. Section 510 of ERISA provides:

> It shall be unlawful for any person to discharge, fine, suspend, expel, discipline or discriminate against a participant or beneficiary for exercising any right to which he is entitled under the provisions of the employee benefit plan ... for the purpose of interfering with the attainment of any right to which such participant may become entitled under the plan.

29 U.S.C. § 1140 (1994).

Congress enacted § 510 "primarily to prevent unscrupulous employers from discharging or harassing their employees in order to keep them from obtaining vested pension benefits." Dewitt v. Penn–Del Directory Corp., 106 F.3d 514, 522 (3d Cir.1997). We have held an employer violates § 510 when it acts with the specific intent to interfere with an employee's right to benefits. DiFederico v. Rolm Co., 201 F.3d 200, 204–05 (3d Cir.2000). To prove a prima facie case under § 510 a plaintiff must show (1) that an employer took specific actions (2) for the purpose of interfering (3) with an employee's attainment of pension benefit rights. Gavalik v. Cont'l Can Co., 812 F.2d 834, 852 (3d. Cir.), *cert. denied*, 484 U.S. 979, 108 S.Ct. 495, 98 L.Ed.2d 492 (1987). We held in DiFederico that once a plaintiff makes a prima facie showing, the employer has the burden of articulating a legitimate non-discriminatory reason for his conduct. Then, the burden shifts back to the plaintiff to show that the employer's rationale was not pre-textual and that the cancellation of benefits was the "determinative influence" on the employer's actions.

The crucial threshold issue in this case is whether defendants AT & T and Lucent had the specific intent to interfere with the Paradyne employees' pension benefit rights or whether the cancellation of the bridging rights was merely an incidental by-product of the sale of Paradyne. Dewitt, 106 F.3d at 523 ("[E]mployee must show that the employer made a conscious decision to interfere with the employee's attainment of pension eligibility or additional benefits"). Plaintiffs allege the no-hire agreement and its eight month restriction on re-employment was enacted for "the direct and immediate objective and with the singular purpose of eliminating the Paradyne pensions." In support of their claim, plaintiffs argue the eight month restriction on re-employment is suspiciously close to the six month vesting period of the AT & T pension plan and that this temporal proximity provides circumstantial evidence that the cancellation of the benefits was a motivating factor in the timing of the no-hire agreement. Additionally, they point to the role of Paradyne's Vice–President of Human Resources in proposing Texas Pacific Group's ultimate pension package for the Paradyne employees. Plaintiffs also cite a confidential memorandum between Larry Knoch and Linda Roussau of Lucent Technologies, which acknowledges the eight month restriction in the no-hire agreement had the practical effect of cancelling the Paradyne employees' pension rights. Finally, plaintiffs point to the economic benefits that both Lucent and AT & T received from the no-hire agreement, specifically that neither defendant was required to pay for pension benefits, as evidence of specific intent to interfere with an ERISA pension plan in violation of § 510. Turner v. Schering–Plough Corp., 901 F.2d 335, 348 (3d. Cir.1990) (savings to an employer that result from employees' termination might be viewed as a motivating factor sufficient to satisfy the intent element of § 510 liability).

Although the District Court found this evidence insufficient to support a finding of specific intent to interfere with the plaintiffs' benefit plans, we believe at this stage of the proceedings plaintiffs have presented sufficient circumstantial evidence of intent to interfere with their pension rights to create a genuine issue of material fact. As we held in Dewitt, "[i]n most cases, . . . 'smoking gun' evidence of specific intent to discriminate does not exist. As a result, the evidentiary burden in these cases may also be satisfied by the introduction of circumstantial evidence." Of course we express no opinion whether plaintiffs will prevail at trial under the preponderance of evidence standard for § 510 claims. DiFederico, 201 F.3d at 205 ("[If] employer carries its burden, the plaintiff then must persuade the court by a preponderance of the evidence that the employer's legitimate reason is pre-textual.") Because plaintiffs have submitted sufficient prima facie evidence to withstand defendant's motion for summary judgment, we will reverse and remand for further proceedings.

* * *

d. Cost as a Factor in Decisions to Close Operations

So far we've looked at legal restraints on identifying individuals who will be terminated. But Plain & Simple won't meet its cost-cutting goals unless it closes down some of its facilities. What factors may Plain & Simple consider in deciding which operations to close? The cost of running a facility is an obvious consideration. What about the racial composition of the workforce? Would Plain & Simple violate Section 703(a)(2) of Title VII if it closed only those plants employing very high percentages of people of color? What about considering whether a plant is unionized? Would Plain & Simple violate Section 8(a)(3) of the NLRA if it closed plants because they are unionized? How likely is it, though, that the company, having lived with a diverse workforce and with unions all these years, will simply base its choices on the color of employees' skins or on the presence of unions? On the other hand, what if the deciding factor is cost? And what if the plants with diverse workforces or those that are unionized simply cost more to operate? And how can the law determine whether a wrong motive tainted a decision to close?

MARLEY WEISS, RISKY BUSINESS: AGE AND RACE DISCRIMINATION IN CAPITAL DEPLOYMENT DECISIONS

48 Maryland L.Rev. 901, 910–917 (1989).

Given the high rate of capital redeployment, one might predict that impermissible discrimination would play a role in a significant number of redeployment decisions. Verifying that hypothesis is difficult: corporations shroud in secrecy their decision making processes for matters such as site selection, plant relocation, and subcontracting. This lack of public information precludes direct estimates of the frequency of discrimination. Diverse sources, however, suggest that discrimination is widespread. [The details of Prof. Weiss' discussion of the impact of relocations on black and older workers is omitted.—Eds.]

The disproportionate adverse consequences for blacks an older workers resulting from transfers of operations, closures, and subcontracting decisions are some evidence that discrimination may be influencing corporate decision making. Information about the closure and site selection decision making process provides further evidence that many capital redeployment decisions include conscious or subconscious consideration of such factors as the age or race of existing or potential employees. * * *

A rare window on the corporate site-selection policies opened up in the course of discovery in the 1983 litigation over a land dispute involving Amoco Fabrics Company, a subsidiary of Standard Oil Company (Indiana). The company was forced to reveal correspondence evidencing a corporate policy against locating a new facility in an area with over thirty-three percent black population. When questioned by a reporter about the disclosure, industrial development specialists from several southern states, including some local government officials, acknowledged that numerous companies, working with these specialists to select new plant sites automatically had excluded from consideration areas where the black population exceeded a specified percentage. Other companies, these specialists stated, did not openly express such a policy, but had engaged in a pattern of site selection choices evidencing a desire to avoid or escape from locations with a high concentration of blacks. The industrial specialists identified the companies stated reasons for such practices: (1) a belief that black employees are less reliable and less skilled than whites; (2) the perception that blacks are easier to unionize than whites; (3) the desire to avoid problems with affirmative action programs; and (4) the wish to avoid racial issues in community relations. Amoco Fabrics officials, in court papers, explained the rationale for Amoco Fabrics race-based siting rule: "Our experiences are that the lower the concentration of minorities, the better we're able to perform and get a plant started up." * * *

ALLEN v. DIEBOLD, INC.

United States Court of Appeals, Sixth Circuit, 1994.
33 F.3d 674.

MERRITT, CIRCUIT JUDGE.

In this age discrimination appeal, the theory of the plaintiffs' case is that their employer replaced two unionized Ohio manufacturing plants with two non-union plants in Virginia and South Carolina in order to replace several hundred older Ohio workers with approximately 100 younger workers at the new plants. At the Ohio plant 80% of the workers were over 40, but 83% of the new workers at the new plants were under 40. * * *

[The defendant moved for summary judgment on the merits and on statute of limitations grounds. The district court granted the defendant's motion on statute of limitations grounds and did not address the merits. The Court of Appeals affirmed the grant of summary judgment, based on the merits, and did not address the statute of limitations issue.]

The Age Discrimination in Employment Act (ADEA) makes it unlawful for an employer to discriminate against an individual on the basis of age. In *Hazen Paper Co. v. Biggins,* 507 U.S. [604], 113 S.Ct. 1701, 123 L.Ed.2d 338 (1993), the Supreme Court clarified the scope of this prohibition. The Court held that the ADEA prohibits only actions actually motivated by age and does not constrain an employer who acts on the basis of other factors—pension status, seniority, wage rate—that are empirically correlated with age. Of course an employer may not use any of these factors as a proxy for age, but age itself must be the motivating factor behind the employment action in order to constitute an ADEA violation.

The purpose of the ADEA, according to the Supreme Court, is to protect older workers from being "deprived of employment on the basis of inaccurate and stigmatizing stereotypes" and to ensure that employers evaluate their employees on the basis of their merits and not their age. * * *

The ADEA was not intended to protect older workers from the often harsh economic realities of common business decisions and the hardships associated with corporate reorganizations, downsizing, plant closings and relocations. Unlike law and social policy in many European countries, the laws of the United States do not prohibit or seriously discourage these plant closing and relocation + activities and the attendant dislocation, unemployment and new employment. States and counties in the United States compete with each other for companies contemplating relocation. Labor laws like the National Labor Relations Act do not discourage such relocations or prohibit the closing of a unionized plant in one part of the country and the opening of a nonunion plant in another part of the country or in a foreign country. The North American Free Trade Agreement contemplates such relocations. Although the parties here do not cite any empirical studies or statistics on the number or effect on workers of such relocations, we know from experience and from history that such relocations have occurred frequently over the course of the last century. In the past several decades there has been a substantial movement of industry to the southern and border states, as well as to foreign countries. The plant relocations in this case follow that trend.

In order to state and support a claim then, plaintiffs must allege that Diebold discriminated against them because they were old, not because they were expensive. Specifically, plaintiffs must allege facts which, if true, would support a prima facie case of age discrimination. We have found no case that articulates the elements of a prima facie case of discrimination in the context of a plant closing where transfer or recall rights are not at issue. In *Barnes v. Gencorp Inc.,* this Court determined that when an employer reduces the size of its work force, a plaintiff may establish a prima facie case of discrimination by showing "direct, circumstantial or statistical evidence tending to indicate that the employer singled out the plaintiff for discharge for impermissible reasons." 896 F.2d 1457, 1465 (6th Cir.1990) (citations omitted), *cert. denied,* 498 U.S. 878, 111 S.Ct. 211, 112 L.Ed.2d 171 (1990). The Barnes panel noted that in a typical reduction in force case, the precise standard for a prima facie case of discrimination set forth in *McDonnell Douglas Corp. v. Green* is not particularly useful. Therefore the panel found it sufficient for a plaintiff to proffer evidence of a significant disparity in age between those employees who were discharged and those who were retained, so long as the plaintiff also eliminates the most common non-discriminatory explanations for the disparity. This latter requirement is essential because a prima facie case, by definition, creates an inference that the employer intentionally discriminated. A plaintiff must present evidence of actions taken by the employer which, if unexplained, are more likely than not based on consideration of impermissible factors.

Although plant closings and relocations are factually distinct from a reduction in force situation, we think the standard articulated in *Barnes* is somewhat helpful. Instead of showing direct, circumstantial or statistical evidence that older workers were discharged while younger workers were retained, plaintiffs in a plant closing case must show that an employer's decisions regarding which factories to close or downsize were based on consideration of the ages of the workers at those factories. In this case, plaintiffs must offer statistics relating to discharges and new hires which are so unusual that, absent explanation by defendant, we could permit a jury to infer age discrimination on that basis alone.

The statistics offered by plaintiffs do not appear unusual on their face. Eighty percent of the employees who were discharged due to Diebold's plant closing and reduction in force in Ohio were over 40. This figure was to be expected since Diebold had laid off workers according to seniority during previous cutbacks, effectively eliminating most of its younger workers. Plaintiffs make no showing that this figure is disproportionate in relation to the percentage of older Diebold workers in Ohio and indeed they could not, since almost all of the workers retained by

Diebold in Ohio are over the age of 40. Nor do we have reason to believe that it is at all unusual that eighty-three percent of the new workers hired in Virginia and South Carolina are under 40. Plaintiffs present no evidence that this figure is disproportionate to the hiring pool in those areas or that age played any role in Diebold's hiring processes at the new plants. Without more, these statistics are not really probative of anything and far from what is required before we could allow a factfinder to infer that the defendant intentionally discriminated.

Plaintiffs themselves acknowledge that the most common reasons for this type of relocation—reduced labor costs and favorable treatment by the host states—were the motivating factors behind Diebold's actions in this case. They present no evidence that Diebold acted pursuant to anything other than a business decision but contend that other evidence demonstrates Diebold's bad faith. Plaintiffs point out that none of the Ohio workers were offered transfers to the new plants at their Ohio wage and benefit rates but acknowledge that their contract did not provide for such transfers.[6] They also argue that the new plants are non-union, that Virginia and South Carolina subsidized some labor-related costs, that Diebold used subjective criteria in its hiring practices and that the relocation was not required by economic necessity. We do not see how any of these allegations relate to a claim of age discrimination.

Nor is there any evidence that Diebold engaged in a pattern of discriminatory conduct. Plaintiffs concede that Diebold discharged them according to seniority and that the company has acted pursuant to the governing collective bargaining agreement at all times.[7] These facts indicate that Diebold's past cutbacks and the recent downsizing have disproportionately affected younger workers in Ohio. Plaintiffs' evidence does not support a claim of age discrimination. After careful consideration of the entire record we are unable to find any additional evidence upon which a factfinder could rely in determining that Diebold acted with discriminatory intent.

The heart of plaintiffs' allegation—that defendant replaced them with younger workers because they were too costly—does not state a claim under the ADEA. Plaintiffs allege that Diebold downsized its Ohio operations and hired younger, cheaper, non-union employees in Virginia and South Carolina in order to increase its profitability. They argue that their salaries and benefits were a burden to the company whose management believed it could make more money by moving to a "right to work" state, hiring fewer workers and paying them lower wages. Plaintiffs even

6. Plaintiffs stipulated that none of them would have been willing to relocate to Virginia or South Carolina to work for Diebold for the wages and benefits the company offered at the new plants.

7. Plaintiffs suggest that the discharge of two salaried employees who were over forty and the retention of two younger, less senior, salaried employees at the Canton plant is evidence of a pattern of discrimination. We disagree. Management personnel testified that salaried persons were discharged when their jobs were eliminated and kept on when their jobs were retained. Plaintiffs have offered absolutely no evidence that this particular decision—regarding salaried employees not governed by the labor contract's seniority requirements—was at all improper or that the ages of the persons involved is anything but fortuitous.

proffer expert testimony regarding just how much money Diebold can be expected to save over the long term by virtue of its reorganization. This allegation—that Diebold's decision to restructure was driven by financial considerations based on the profit motive—does not state a claim under the ADEA. The ADEA does not bar the discharge of older employees but only prohibits employers from discriminating against them.

The basic problem with plaintiffs' case is that the Congress and the courts in interpreting our labor laws and our law of contract have made the social judgment, rightly or wrongly, that our capitalistic system, Darwinian though it may be, will not discourage companies from relocating on the basis of their own calculations of factors relating to efficiency and competitiveness. The rules of the marketplace govern. By so reflecting commercial interests, the institutions of government serve—according to current legal and economic theory—the long-term best interests of society as a whole. That is the basic social policy the country has opted to follow. Therefore we affirm the district court's grant of summary judgment for defendant on the basis that plaintiffs have failed to state or support a claim of age discrimination.

e. Does a collective bargaining agreement make a difference?

CASE STUDY: PLAIN AND SIMPLE II

The unionized plants at Plain & Simple operate under collective bargaining agreements that contain (1) a comprehensive no-strike clause, (2) a broad agreement to arbitrate any dispute arising under the agreement, (3) a management's rights clause reserving to the employer the rights to hire, fire and to determine the number of persons it will employ or retain as employees, and (4) a standard provision requiring just cause for dismissal.

Does the collective bargaining agreement give the unionized employees a lever against loss of employment due to plant closings not available to the nonunionized workforce?

As you no doubt have guessed, the no strike clause in the bargaining agreement will be violated if the bargaining unit members cease work in protest over the decision to terminate employees and close plants. What options are open to Plain & Simple if the employees, supported by their union, strike nonetheless?

---

i. Self–Help

The employer might fire the strikers, thus accomplishing the terminations and closings. Alternatively, the employer might want to retain some of the striking employees after the restructuring or might have a short-term, immediate need for the strikers' services, so that firing the entire group would be counterproductive. What the employer might want, then, is to stop the strike, get the employees back to work, and proceed with the restructuring on its own timetable.

ii. Cooperation

One way to end the work stoppage would be to negotiate a resolution with the union. What advantages could Plain & Simple gain through negotiations?

iii. The Courts

Another way to end the strike would be to secure an injunction. The statutory barrier to an injunction appears to be the 1932 Norris–LaGuardia Act, 29 U.S.C. §§ 102–115, which can be found in the statutory supplement. This law withdraws from federal courts the jurisdiction to issue injunctions in peaceful labor disputes (section 4) and imposes strict procedural prerequisites on federal courts in the limited circumstances where labor injunctions are permitted (section 7). Filing for an injunction in state court does not evade the barrier of Norris–LaGuardia, because some states have adopted baby Norris–LaGuardia Acts that impose anti-injunction restrictions on state courts and because suits initially brought in state court may be removed to federal court under the federal question removal jurisdiction of 28 U.S.C. § 1441.

If you were counsel to Plain & Simple, could you frame an argument that federal courts have jurisdiction to stop the concededly peaceful strike and enforce the agreement to arbitrate, notwithstanding the Norris–LaGuardia Act? Compare your argument to the rationale of the following case.

BOYS MARKETS, INC. v. RETAIL CLERKS UNION, LOCAL 770

Supreme Court of the United States, 1970.
398 U.S. 235, 90 S.Ct. 1583, 26 L.Ed.2d 199.

MR. JUSTICE BRENNAN delivered the opinion of the Court. * * *

I

In February 1969, at the time of the incidents that produced this litigation, petitioner and respondent were parties to a collective-bargaining agreement which provided, inter alia, that all controversies concerning its interpretation or application should be resolved by adjustment and arbitration procedures set forth therein and that, during the life of the contract, there should be "no cessation or stoppage of work, lock-out, picketing or boycotts * * *." The dispute arose when petitioner's frozen foods supervisor and certain members of his crew who were not members of the bargaining unit began to rearrange merchandise in the frozen food cases of one of petitioner's supermarkets. A union representative insisted that the food cases be stripped of all merchandise and be restocked by union personnel. When petitioner did not accede to the union's demand, a strike was called and the union began to picket petitioner's establishment. Thereupon petitioner demanded that the union cease the work stoppage and picketing and sought to invoke the grievance and arbitration procedures specified in the contract.

The following day, since the strike had not been terminated, petitioner filed a complaint in California Superior Court seeking a temporary restraining order, a preliminary and permanent injunction, and specific performance of the contractual arbitration provision. * * * Shortly thereafter, the union removed the case to the Federal District Court and there made a motion to quash the state court's temporary restraining order. * * * Concluding that the dispute was subject to arbitration under the collective-bargaining agreement and that the strike was in violation of the contract, the District Court ordered the parties to arbitrate the underlying dispute and simultaneously enjoined the strike, all picketing in the vicinity of petitioner's supermarket, and any attempts by the union to induce the employees to strike or to refuse to perform their services.

[Parts II & III omitted]

IV

* * *

The literal terms of § 4 of the Norris–LaGuardia Act must be accommodated to the subsequently enacted provisions of § 301(a) of the Labor Management Relations Act and the purposes of arbitration. Statutory interpretation requires more than concentration upon isolated words; rather, consideration must be given to the total corpus of pertinent law and the policies that inspired ostensibly inconsistent provisions.

The Norris–LaGuardia Act was responsive to a situation totally different from that which exists today. In the early part of this century, the federal courts generally were regarded as allies of management in its attempt to prevent the organization and strengthening of labor unions; and in this industrial struggle the injunction became a potent weapon that was wielded against the activities of labor groups. The result was a large number of sweeping decrees, often issued *ex parte,* drawn on an *ad hoc* basis without regard to any systematic elaboration of national labor policy.

In 1932 Congress attempted to bring some order out of the industrial chaos that had developed and to correct the abuses that had resulted from the interjection of the federal judiciary into union-management disputes on the behalf of management. See declaration of public policy, Norris–LaGuardia Act, § 2. Congress, therefore, determined initially to limit severely the power of the federal courts to issue injunctions "in any case involving or growing out of any labor dispute * * *." § 4. Even as initially enacted, however, the prohibition against federal injunctions was by no means absolute. See Norris–LaGuardia Act, §§ 7, 8, 9. Shortly thereafter Congress passed the Wagner Act, designed to curb various management activities that tended to discourage employee participation in collective action.

As labor organizations grew in strength and developed toward maturity, congressional emphasis shifted from protection of the nascent labor movement to the encouragement of collective bargaining and to administrative techniques for the peaceful resolution of industrial disputes. This shift in emphasis was accomplished, however, without extensive revision of many of the older enactments, including the anti-injunction section of the Norris–LaGuardia Act. Thus it became the task of the courts to accommodate, to reconcile the older statutes with the more recent ones. * * *

A leading example of this accommodation process is *Brotherhood of Railroad Trainmen v. Chicago River & Ind. R. Co.*, 353 U.S. 30, 77 S.Ct. 635, 1 L.Ed.2d 622 (1957). There we were confronted with a peaceful strike which violated the statutory duty to arbitrate imposed by the Railway Labor Act. The Court concluded that a strike in violation of a statutory arbitration duty was not the type of situation to which the Norris–LaGuardia Act was responsive, that an important federal policy was involved in the peaceful settlement of disputes through the statutorily mandated arbitration procedure, that this important policy was imperiled if equitable remedies were not available to implement it, and hence that Norris–LaGuardia's policy of nonintervention by the federal courts should yield to the overriding interest in the successful implementation of the arbitration process.

The principles elaborated in *Chicago River* are equally applicable to the present case. To be sure, *Chicago River* involved arbitration procedures established by statute. However, we have frequently noted, in such cases as *Lincoln Mills,* the *Steelworkers Trilogy,* and *Lucas Flour,* the importance that Congress has attached generally to the voluntary settlement of labor disputes without resort to self-help and more particularly to arbitration as a means to this end. Indeed, it has been stated that *Lincoln Mills,* in its exposition of § 301(a), "went a long way towards making arbitration the central institution in the administration of collective bargaining contracts."

* * * Clearly employers will be wary of assuming obligations to arbitrate specifically enforceable against them when no similarly efficacious remedy is available to enforce the concomitant undertaking of the union to refrain from striking. On the other hand, the central purpose of the Norris–LaGuardia Act to foster the growth and viability of labor organizations is hardly retarded—if anything, this goal is advanced—by a remedial device that merely enforces the obligation that the union freely undertook under a specifically enforceable agreement to submit disputes to arbitration. We conclude, therefore, that the unavailability of equitable relief in the arbitration context presents a serious impediment to the congressional policy favoring the voluntary establishment of a mechanism for the peaceful resolution of labor disputes, that the core purpose of the Norris–LaGuardia Act is not sacrificed by the limited use of equitable remedies to further this important policy, and consequently that the Norris–LaGuardia Act does not bar the granting of injunctive relief in the circumstances of the instant case.

V

Our holding in the present case is a narrow one. We do not undermine the vitality of the Norris–LaGuardia Act. We deal only with the situation in which a collective-bargaining contract contains a mandatory grievance adjustment or arbitration procedure. Nor does it follow from what we have said that injunctive relief is appropriate as a matter of course in every case of a strike over an arbitrable grievance. The dissenting opinion in *Sinclair* [*Refining Co. v. Atkinson,* 370 U.S. 195, 82 S.Ct. 1328, 8 L.Ed.2d 440 (1962)] suggested the following principles for the guidance of the district courts in determining whether to grant injunctive relief—principles that we now adopt:

> "A District Court entertaining an action under § 301 may not grant injunctive relief against concerted activity unless and until it decides that the case is one in which an injunction would be appropriate despite the Norris–LaGuardia Act. When a strike is sought to be enjoined because it is over a grievance which both parties are contractually bound to arbitrate, the District Court may issue no injunctive order until it first holds that the contract *does* have that effect; and the employer should be ordered to arbitrate, as a condition of his obtaining an injunction against the strike. Beyond this, the District Court must, of course, consider whether issuance of an injunction would be warranted under ordinary principles of equity— whether breaches are occurring and will continue, or have been threatened and will be committed; whether they have caused or will cause irreparable injury to the employer; and whether the employer will suffer more from the denial of an injunction than will the union from its issuance." 370 U.S., at 228, 82 S.Ct., at 1346. (Emphasis in original.)

In the present case there is no dispute that the grievance in question was subject to adjustment and arbitration under the collective-bargaining agreement and that the petitioner was ready to proceed with arbitration at the time an injunction against the strike was sought and obtained. The District Court also concluded that, by reason of respondent's violations of its no-strike obligation, petitioner "has suffered irreparable injury and will continue to suffer irreparable injury." Since we now overrule *Sinclair,* the holding of the Court of Appeals in reliance on *Sinclair* must be reversed. Accordingly, we reverse the judgment of the Court of Appeals and remand the case with directions to enter a judgment affirming the order of the District Court.

It is so ordered.

Mr. Justice Black, dissented.

Notes

i.) A few observations about *Boys Markets* injunctions. The Court emphasizes the narrowness of the *Boys Markets* holding. The factors identified in *Boys Markets* as entitling a federal court to grant a labor injunction against peaceful collective activity despite the strictures of Norris–LaGuardia are: a strike in breach of a no strike clause; an arbitrable grievance; an order to arbitrate as a condition for the employer receiving an injunction; evidence that breaches are occurring, continuing, or threatened; and findings that the breaches cause irreparable injury to the employer and that the balance of harms favors the employer. How difficult will it be for an employer to satisfy these factors when a union strikes over a dispute at the workplace in the face of a no strike clause?

(a) Consider the facts giving rise to the *Boys Markets* dispute. Why would the union strike over what seems to be a minor issue of who straightens out the stocks in a food freezer?

(b) As an employer, seeking a *Boys Markets* injunction, would you ever deny the grievance's arbitrability or refuse to take the grievance to arbitration?

(c) What was the irreparable injury suffered by the employer in *Boys Markets?* It cannot have been lost revenues attributable to the picketing because such revenues are compensable, that is, there is an adequate remedy at law for monetary losses. Will employers in the future have a difficult time establishing irreparable harm?

(d) Once a court makes a finding of irreparable harm from the strike, how can the balance of harms ever favor the union?

ii.) The reverse slam-dunk. Can a union invoke *Boys Markets* and seek an injunction pending arbitration against unilateral actions by an employer where the union claims the unilateral action is in breach of contract and the dispute is arbitrable?

Assume the unionized employees at Plain & Simple do not strike. Instead on learning which plants will be closed, they file a petition asking a federal district court to enjoin the planned closings. Assume also that you are a law clerk to the federal district court judge who will hear the case. She has scheduled a conference with counsel for this afternoon on the question of the injunction. She asks you to brief her on the factors the court must consider in deciding whether to issue an injunction. What are the arguments each side is likely to make and how should the court respond to them?

ALUMINUM WORKERS INTERN. v. CONSOLIDATED ALUMINUM CORP.

United States Court of Appeals, Sixth Circuit, 1982.
696 F.2d 437, rehearing denied 112 LRRM 3056, 1983 WL 31005 (1983).

MARTIN, CIRCUIT JUDGE.

Consolidated Aluminum Corporation appeals an order enjoining it from reorganizing job classifications pending arbitration. The district court found that the reorganization, which would eliminate sixteen jobs, would irreparably harm those left unemployed and that any subsequent award by an arbitrator would be inadequate to recompense the employees for their injuries. We stayed that portion of the order enjoining reclassification pending this appeal. We now vacate the injunction, the injunction bond, and the order to arbitrate and remand to the lower court for rehearing to determine Consolidated's damages.

Consolidated and Aluminum Workers International Union, AFL–CIO, Local 215 are parties to a collective bargaining agreement effective until July 18, 1984. Article 5 of the agreement is a broad grievance and arbitration provision which includes the following language: "Should any difference arise between the company and any employee, under and during the terms of this agreement, an attempt in good faith shall immediately be made to amicably adjust such matters in an orderly fashion and in the following manner." There follows a four-step dispute resolution procedure culminating, in step four, with arbitration.

On March 23, 1982, Consolidated notified the Union that it intended to restructure certain job classifications referred to in the agreement by reassigning duties from one job classification to another with the ultimate effect of eliminating sixteen employees. Consolidated maintained that article 3 of the agreement specifically authorized such unilateral action by management. Article 3 provides, in part: "Subject to the provisions of this Agreement, the management of the plant and the direction of the working forces are vested exclusively in the company (does not take precedence over the provisions of the labor agreement)."

In response, the Union asserted that article 3 was subject to article 10(D) which prohibits job reclassifications unless necessitated by plant expansion. Article 10(D) provides, in part:

> It is recognized by the parties that the Company's operation shall be divided into the departments as outlined in Appendix B of this agreement with the job classifications and wage grades included within and comprising each such department.

> As the Company's operations expand it may, from time to time, establish such further departments and job classifications as may be necessary. Before new departments or classifications or changes in existing classifications are established, the Company shall meet with the Union and explain the changes and reasons therefor. The Company shall give a written explanation of the changes and reasons to the Union. The Company and the Union shall mutually agree to the rates to be paid for each classification and the seniority of the employee effected.

> If no mutual agreement is made, the Union may file a grievance and arbitrate the matter.

That this was not the first time the parties disagreed over interpretation of 10(D) is clear from the inclusion in the agreement of article 34—"Letters of Understanding." That article provides, in part:

During the course of 1981 contract negotiations, Art.... 10(D) ... [was] ... discussed and no agreement reached except to return to current contract language. The agreement reached above recognizes that the parties do not agree upon interpretation of the 1978–81 contract language and that this memo simply recognizes and confirms each party's agreement to disagree and does not prejudice either party's position.

Consolidated was not persuaded. On April 4, it implemented its plan. On the following day, the Union filed its complaint. On April 6, after hearing, the court ordered Consolidated to reinstate the sixteen laid-off employees and to return to the *status quo ante* pending arbitration. The court found that "the changes effected by ... [Consolidated] ... appear to be in violation of [a]rticle 10(D)" and that the "apparent breach" had occurred and would continue unless enjoined. It also found that:

> [Consolidated] ... will suffer little or none from issuance of an injunction pending arbitration requiring it to continue the operations as it has in the past. While such an order will reinstate laid-off employees, ... [Consolidated] ... will have the benefit of production from those persons. On the other hand, denial of the injunction will irreparably harm employees represented by ... [the Union] ... in that job opportunities and wages will be lost. An arbitration award will not substantially return these persons to status quo ante.

The injunction bond was set at $1,000 and the parties were ordered to proceed to arbitration. The court specifically stated, however, that nothing in its order precluded Consolidated from reducing the size of its work force pursuant to article 12(A) of the agreement. Article 12(A) provides, in part: "the Company shall have the right to reduce the force of employees at any time."

Consolidated immediately filed a notice of appeal and a motion in the district court to stay the injunction pending appeal. That motion was denied. An identical motion filed in this court was granted.

Here, Consolidated raises several issues. First, it contends that its actions did not threaten the integrity of the arbitration process. Therefore, it continues, the lower court lacked jurisdiction to issue an injunction. Second, even if the court had jurisdiction, it exercised it improperly because it failed to make the requisite findings of fact necessary to both support the issuance of an injunction in these circumstances and to properly set the amount of the bond. Finally, it contests the scope of the injunction insofar as it orders the parties to arbitrate.

There is no more fundamental policy in our national labor laws than that which favors peaceful resolution of labor disputes through voluntary arbitration.

* * * Section 4 of the Norris–LaGuardia Act, 29 U.S.C. § 104 (1973), promotes that policy by severely limiting the jurisdiction of the federal courts to intercede in labor disputes. * * *

Despite the broad prohibitions of section 4, the Supreme Court has recognized a "narrow exception" to the anti-injunction policy of the Act. In *The Boys Markets v. Retail Clerks Union,* 398 U.S. 235, 90 S.Ct. 1583, 26 L.Ed.2d 199 (1970), the Court reconciled the narrow strictures of section 4 with the more permissive language of section 301(a) of the Labor–Management Relations Act, 29 U.S.C. § 185(a) (1973). * * *

Although *Boys Markets* involved employee violation of a no-strike clause, unilateral action by employers may have an equally pernicious effect on the arbitral process. Therefore, the courts have extended the *Boys Markets* exception to embrace employer behavior which has the effect of evading a duty to arbitrate or which would otherwise undermine the integrity of the arbitral process. To obtain an injunction, however, the union, like the employer, must establish that all of the *Boys Markets* criteria have been met. * * *

I.

A. *Arbitrability*

* * * The Union has no difficulty establishing arbitrability here. Consolidated concedes that fact and, we note, both parties are actively pursuing arbitration.

B. *Equitable bases for relief*

* * *

1. *Ongoing nature of the breach*

The Union encounters no difficulty in establishing the ongoing nature of Consolidated's alleged breach of the agreement. Reclassification and the attendant loss of jobs had occurred prior to the issuance of the *status quo* injunction. If it has not already been reimplemented following our stay of that injunction, it is clear Consolidated intends to do so if permitted.

2. *Irreparable harm*

Although the Union may easily meet other *Boys Markets* criteria, it has considerable and, ultimately, insurmountable difficulty demonstrating that it will suffer irreparable harm if Consolidated's reclassification plan is not enjoined. It is for this reason, therefore, that the Union's request for injunctive relief should have been denied.

Irreparable harm is injury so great that an arbitrator's award, if forthcoming, would be inadequate to fully recompense the injured party. It renders the award an "empty victory," *Brotherhood of Locomotive Engineers v. Missouri–Kansas–Texas Railroad,* 363 U.S. 528, 534, 80 S.Ct. 1326, 1330, 4 L.Ed.2d 1435 (1960), *quoted in Panoramic,* and thereby undermines the integrity of the arbitral process as thoroughly as did the union's violation of the no-strike clause in *Boys Markets.*

Because it is this very "frustration or vitiation of arbitration," which justified the "narrow exception" to the anti-injunction provision of the Norris–LaGuardia Act, the irreparability of the injury suffered by the union has in many cases become virtually the sole inquiry in those cases where injunctive relief is sought against an employer.

The injury complained of here is loss of employment for sixteen persons. The Union argues that loss of employment constitutes irreparable harm because awards of back pay and reinstatement, traditional remedies for such an injury, cannot fully compensate employees for the repossessions, foreclosures, and injury to credit stature which could accompany unemployment. We disagree insofar as loss of employment is, as it is here, solely the result of job eliminations by a solvent employer. Absent some indication of action on the part of the employer which could jeopardize its ability to reinstate affected employees or to pay them wages for the period of unemployment, we hold that loss of employment, even if occasioned by employer action which is subject to arbitration, is not irreparable harm and will not support a claim by the union for injunctive relief.

The Union refers us to two relatively recent Fourth Circuit cases, *Lever Brothers* and *Akers Motor Lines,* which purportedly support its position. We disagree. On the contrary, the rationale of those decisions supports our holding here.

In *Lever Brothers,* the employer advised the union that it was permanently closing its manufacturing plant in one state and transferring production to a facility in another state. The parties disagreed as to the proper characterization to be given such action and, therefore, whether the collective bargaining contract forbade the transfer. Finding that the dispute was one properly subject to arbitration and that the union had demonstrated a likelihood of prevailing upon the merits, the district court enjoined the transfer pending arbitration.

The appellate court, without addressing the issue of irreparable harm, but adopting the reasoning of *Greyhound* as it concerned the likelihood of prevailing upon the merits, affirmed the lower court. However, in an addendum to its opinion necessitated by the Ninth Circuit's reversal of *Greyhound,* the *Lever Brothers* court did reach the question of irreparable harm. It held that the district court properly issued an injunction to maintain the *status quo* because, absent such an order, the employees at the plant from which production was to be transferred *"would have been totally and permanently deprived of their employment."* (emphasis in original). In contrast, said the court, the union's grievance in *Greyhound* concerned a work schedule change. In that situation, the court continued, unlike in the situation before it, "the arbitrator *could* subsequently alter pay schedules or revise the work schedules depending on whether he found for the union or the company and return the parties to substantially the *status quo ante.*" (emphasis in original).

The Union also relies on *Akers Motor Lines.* In that case, the Fourth Circuit considered the propriety of *Boys Markets* injunctive relief against an employer who was partially liquidating his business. The court enjoined the liquidation pending arbitration, finding that:

> If Akers–Central is allowed to continue its process of liquidation and disposition of assets, any victory by the union at the arbitration table may be meaningless. If the remaining terminals and vehicles are sold, there will be *no jobs* for re-assignment to Local 71 employees. If assets from ongoing operations are encumbered, there will be *no fund* from which to pay vacation monies. "[T]he arbitral award when rendered could not return the parties substantially to the *status quo ante.*" (emphasis added).

We do not take issue with the decisions of the Fourth Circuit in *Lever Brothers* and *Akers*. However, the "compelling circumstances" of those two cases are not before us. Unlike the situation in those cases, there is no evidence in this record to suggest that Consolidated would be unable to comply fully with an order for back pay and reinstatement in the event the arbitrator found the company in violation of the agreement.

The Union nevertheless points to the possible "repossessions, foreclosures, and injury to credit status" which might befall the sixteen employees left jobless. While these are undeniably hardships which may be attendant upon unemployment, they do not represent the type of harm that, by its occurrence, threatens the integrity of the arbitral process.

First, they are speculative damages which will materialize only in select cases and only in the event the parties are unable or unwilling to commence arbitration in a timely manner. In this case, we note, Consolidated has repeatedly professed its willingness to commence arbitration at the earliest possible date. Were that not the case, the Union would be free to seek an order compelling arbitration.

Second, the availability of unemployment relief, health insurance, and, in certain situations, financial support from the union will help mitigate the financial pressures felt by the displaced employee awaiting arbitration. Moreover, in the event the employee prevails in arbitration, the arbitrator's award of back pay could, and realistically would, be used to repair any damage to credit stature or to repurchase goods repossessed in the interim.

Third, to affirm the injunction in this case where the sole injuries alleged are the consequence of temporary unemployment would be to invite virtually every employee laid-off or discharged in a manner which arguably contravened the collective bargaining contract to resort to the courts to stay the onset of joblessness. We cannot avoid the conclusion that such a situation would have as much, if not more, of a corrosive effect upon the arbitral process as Consolidated's actions allegedly will have here. In the words of the Supreme Court, the prospect of such potentially widespread judicial involvement in the area of labor relations "would cut deeply into the policy of the Norris–LaGuardia Act and make

the courts potential participants in a wide range of arbitrable disputes."
We refuse to foster such a situation.

There being no evidence in the record to suggest Consolidated's
inability to render back pay or to reinstate the sixteen employees in the
event of an arbitrator's decision for the Union, we hold that the Union
has failed to establish that it will suffer irreparable harm as a result of
Consolidated's actions. The injunction is vacated.

3. *Balance of hardships*

Because the Union's case for injunctive relief fails on the issue of
irreparable harm, it is unnecessary for us to deal with the third equitable principle specifically mentioned in *Boys Markets*—the balance of
hardships. In disposing of it in this manner, we do not intend to
diminish its importance in appropriate cases. Only in those cases where
the party seeking relief can demonstrate irreparable harm, however,
need a court go on to balance that harm against the harm to be suffered
by the party against whom relief is sought.

II.

Consolidated also argues that the court below ignored the procedural requirements of section 7 of the Norris–LaGuardia Act, 29 U.S.C.
§ 107 (1973), when it failed to make specific factual findings as to
irreparable injury. We reiterate that the inability of the Union to
demonstrate irreparable harm disposes of the question of the propriety
of the *status quo* injunction. Because we consider procedural compliance
a critical issue in *Boys Markets* cases, however, we address it here.

Section 7 states, in part, that no federal court confronted with a
labor dispute has jurisdiction to award injunctive relief unless it makes
"findings of fact" as to the ongoing or threatened nature of the act to be
enjoined, the irreparability of the harm suffered by the complainant, the
balance of hardships, and the lack of adequate legal remedy. Although
some courts have questioned the applicability of section 7 to suits
brought pursuant to section 301, this court, at least since our decision in
Detroit News, has recognized the vitality of section 7 procedural mandates in a section 301 suit. In *Detroit News,* we reversed an order
granting injunctive relief against an employer because we found both a
failure to make the required factual findings of irreparable injury and a
lack of evidentiary support for such a finding. Even if we were indisposed
to apply section 7 in suits such as this, however, its requirements are
essentially met in every case where the court properly complies with the
dictates of *Boys Markets.*

In this case, the court found that:

> [Consolidated] ... will suffer little or none from issuance of an
> injunction pending arbitration requiring it to continue the opera-
> tions as it has in the past. While such an order will reinstate laid-off
> employees, ... [Consolidated] ... will have the benefit of production
> from those persons. On the other hand, denial of the injunction will

irreparably harm employees represented by . . . [the Union] . . . in that job opportunities and wages will be lost. An arbitration award will not substantially return these persons to status quo ante.

We specifically take issue with the court's treatment of irreparable harm. While it finds that the sixteen employees will be irreparably harmed "in that job opportunities and wages will be lost," it fails to explain why loss of job opportunities and wages constitute irreparable harm. In other words, the court neglected to address the critical issue of why the injuries complained of cannot be adequately redressed by an arbitrator's award. Unless specifically addressed and resolved in favor of the complaining party, the entire premise for equitable relief in this context, carefully enunciated in *Boys Markets* and delimited in *Buffalo Forge*, is lacking.

III.

A related issue also raised by Consolidated here is the district court's treatment of the injunction bond required by section 7.

The Union correctly points out that the amount of an injunction bond is within the sound discretion of the district court. The exercise of that discretion, however, is constrained by the statutory language which authorizes it. Section 7 clearly states that a primary concern of the district court in setting the amount of the bond should be the sufficiency of the amount to recompense the party enjoined for "any loss, expense, or damages caused by the improvident or erroneous issuance of such order or injunction, including all reasonable costs (together with a reasonable attorney's fee) and expense of defense against the order." In its remarks accompanying the setting of the bond, however, the lower court expressly stated that its "only concern" was "to be sure that the Union can comply and whatever order it has entered is not frustrated by bond requirements." Limitation of the inquiry in this manner was error. The order setting the bond at $1,000 is therefore vacated and the case remanded for rehearing on the issue of Consolidated's damages.

IV.

Finally, Consolidated argues that the court's order should not have included a directive to arbitrate because the only evidence before the court showed that Consolidated would willingly and expeditiously proceed to arbitration. We agree.

* * *

Notes

i.) As the court in Consolidated Aluminum points out, the key inquiry in attempts to secure a Boys Markets injunction against employers is the nature of the injury suffered by the workers and the union. Unions have identified different types of harm as irreparable with varying degrees of success. A representative sample of decisions follows.

In *IBEW System Council U–4 v. Florida Power & Light,* 784 F.Supp. 854 (S.D.Fla.1991), the union sought an injunction, pending arbitration, against a reorganization plan that would eliminate 350 jobs. The court denied the injunction finding that the dispute was not arbitrable. And as a separate and independent ground the court held that the 350 layoffs and additional 650 position displacements that would result from a bumping provision in the contract did not amount to irreparable harm absent some indication of employer action that could jeopardize the employer's ability to reinstate affected workers. The court also noted the union's ability to avoid harm by not insisting on the contractual bumping procedure and accepting instead straight layoffs.

In *Amalgamated Local 813, International Union, Allied Industrial Workers of America v. Diebold Incorporated,* 605 F.Supp. 32 (N.D.Ohio 1984), the union sought to enjoin, pending arbitration, the closing of a facility and moving its operations to a second facility. The court denied the injunction finding that irreparable harm was possible absent a showing by employer that it could reassemble closed operations, BUT because the collective bargaining agreement was due to expire in 6 months and there is no requirement that employers keep a facility operating, arbitration could provide complete relief in the form of back pay up to and until the expiration of the bargaining agreement.

In International Brotherhood of Teamsters v. Almac's, Inc., 894 F.2d 464 (1st Cir.1990), the union sought to enjoin, pending arbitration, the layoff of 180 employees and the closing of the distribution center in anticipation of the sale of the center. The union wanted the arbitrator to rule on whether the intended sale would breach the successor clause in agreement. The trial court and the court of appeals found no irreparable harm in the imminent terminations and closing because the company president testified that the company could restock the distribution center if ordered to do so by an arbitrator. The court thus distinguished *Panoramic* (referred to in *Consolidated Aluminum*) as a case in which consummation of the sale was imminent and there was no opportunity for the arbitrator to rule on the effect of a successorship clause.

By contrast, in *Local 818, AFCSME v. Town of East Haven,* 42 Conn. Sup. 227, 614 A.2d 1260 (1992), the union sought an injunction, pending a hearing before the state labor board, against implementation of notices of termination that allegedly violated a job security clause. The court granted the injunction because of the irreparable injury to the credibility and efficacy of the union if the union was powerless to prevent repudiation of the collective bargaining agreement that furnished job security, in light of the fact that the union came into existence recently and explicitly to obtain job security for union members. Connecticut's anti-injunction statute was no bar, under the reasoning of *Boys Markets.*

ii.) Arbitrators rarely award monetary relief beyond the amount needed to remedy a specific financial loss, seldom add interest to back pay, and consider compensatory and expectation damages speculative. Elkouri & Elkouri, How Arbitration Works 401 (4th ed. 1985). Does this pattern lend support to the courts' tendency to find no irreparable injury to employees terminated in a reorganization?

f. Perspectives

i.) *The market model.* The law of the workplace leaves it up to management to decide when to reduce costs and whether to do so by eliminating jobs, departments, facilities or entire divisions. As long as an employer follows the procedures set up by statute or benefit plan documents or bargaining agreements, the labor and employment laws will not second-guess decisions about restructuring operations. The regulatory scheme seems to assume that well-counseled employers should be free to respond to market conditions with a minimum of governmental interference.

Do you agree that laws designed to govern at the workplace should address the consequences of restructuring solely by insuring compliance with statutory and contractual procedures? Perhaps it is inevitable that the pressures of capital mobility in a competitive economy will overwhelm all other concerns. On the other hand, laws directed at regulating workplace relations are enacted precisely because reliance on the market reaches inefficient or unfair results. Perhaps we need to think a bit more creatively about the kind of regulatory model relied on to accommodate the interests of owners, shareholders, managers, non-managerial employees, and communities.

Caveat: In proposing alternatives to the market model, we are not making normative judgments. It may be that after exploring the alternatives discussed below, and others that you will develop, we will favor retention of the market model. We may conclude that in a less than ideal world the market model delivers as much efficiency and fairness as it is reasonable to expect when companies undertake major restructuring plans.

ii.) Let's assume a consensus that restructuring as presently regulated imposes disproportionate costs on workers and communities. How can the labor and employment laws effectively reform restructuring practices to allocate costs more evenhandedly?

a.) *The individual rights model.* Congress could identify certain aspects of restructuring, like just firing people, as particularly devastating to workers and communities and could prohibit those practices, just as Title VII forbids certain types of discrimination. Federal courts or a federal agency could be given jurisdiction to hear claims of employees and communities injured by companies' unlawful restructuring practices. What defenses should be allowed? What remedies would be appropriate? Keep in mind that the goal is to cushion employees and communities from the harshest consequences of restructuring, not to halt economically-motivated responses to changes in the business environment.

b.) *Minimum standards through government regulation.* One problem faced by employees and communities following a major restructuring is loss of income. Perhaps Congress should require all companies that reduce the size of the workforce by certain percentages to set aside designated sums for worker retraining or for seed money for out-of-work people to start businesses. Companies could also be required to compensate local governments for lost tax revenues. What would the schedule of compensation look like?

Who would enforce compliance? What exceptions, if any, are appropriate? How would such added costs affect decisions to restructure?

c.) *Participation by workers and communities in restructuring decisions.* One obvious change in the law would be to abolish the distinction between mandatory and permissive subjects of bargaining so that unions could demand and strike over the right to participate meaningfully in strategic corporate decisions. Many states and the federal WARN law require companies to notify government agencies and to discuss impending changes that will effect the communities. Perhaps the laws could be strengthened to give local government the right to take over operations that a company wants to abandon. Perhaps money to finance a locally-controlled takeover could come from state and federal funds. See, Staughton Lynd, *Towards A Not–For–Profit Economy: Public Development Authorities For Acquisition And Use Of Industrial Property,* 22 HARV.CIV.R. & CIV.LIB.L.REV. 13 (1987).

(d) If you were a member of the House of Representatives or a state legislature would you support any of these approaches? What other options would you propose?

iii.) Looking beyond labor and employment laws.

Concerned workers and communities have looked beyond the confines of labor and employment laws for ways to ameliorate the worst ravages of corporate restructurings. The examples discussed below should tickle your imagination and stimulate you to assess the costs of enlarging the labor lawyer's toolbox.

a.) *The common law I*: Wickes Co. acquired $15 million of voting securities in Owens–Corning Fiberglass Corporation (OCF) and on August 6, 1986, announced its intention to acquire OCF. OCF fought off Wickes through a recapitalization plan that left OCF with a $2 billion debt. Wickes decided not to pursue OCF and sold all its OCF stock by September 2, 1986, making a profit of $30 million.

The plaintiff employees lost their jobs when OCF closed various operations in order to raise cash to service the $2 billion debt. The employees, along with their union (the Glass and Pottery Workers), filed a class action against Wickes, the would-be acquirer, for compensatory and punitive damages. They alleged state claims of tortious interference with a prospective economic relationship and negligence. The trial court refused to grant Wickes' motion to dismiss saying that "the novelty of a specific occasion for application of a principle * * * is no reason for according it a chilly reception [citation omitted]." *Glass and Pottery Workers v. Wickes Companies, Inc.,* 243 N.J.Super. 44, 578 A.2d 402, 404–05 (1990). Specifically, the judge found:

> * * * [P]laintiffs have, at the least, suggested facts which can bring relief under the cause of action "intentional and/or tortious interference" with a prospective economic relationship. Dealing with the four elements of a properly pleaded complaint I find as follows.
>
> 1. Plaintiffs have alleged facts showing some protectable right, a prospective economic relationship. For example, paragraph 4(c) of the complaint alleges that plaintiffs had a reasonable, quantifiable economic

advantage and benefit in their jobs, salary and benefits. This gives rise to some reasonable expectation of economic advantage.

2. The complaint has at least suggested facts claiming that the interference was done intentionally and with malice—malice defined to mean the interference was done intentionally and without justification or excuse. Plaintiffs allege facts showing that defendant Wickes attempted a hostile takeover of O.C.F.; that defendant intentionally violated federal laws and regulations in making certain purchases of O.C.F. stock without the required reporting and waiting period; that this intentional and illegal process was taken with the knowledge of plaintiff's relationship and interest with O.C.F. and that this intentional, illicit process would certainly cause harm to the existing future economic advantage plaintiffs have with O.C.F.

3. Plaintiffs have, at the least, suggested facts leading to the conclusion that the interference caused the loss of prospective gain. Additionally, they have alleged that O.C.F. was a leader in everything from home insulation to the manufacture of building materials for pleasure boat hulls and that, without the tortious interference, there was a reasonable probability that plaintiffs would have retained their future economic advantage.

4. Plaintiffs have alleged facts showing they have suffered actual damages as a result of Wickes' tortious interference.

Does the first count, dealing with the alleged negligence of defendant Wickes, state a claim upon which relief can be granted? Defendant Wickes argues that plaintiffs have failed because, first, defendant owed no duty to plaintiffs and, second, there is no "proximate cause," i.e., the ultimate consequence of the negligence act was so remote that there can be no recovery.

Plaintiffs reply by citing Justice Handler's opinion in *People Express Airlines, Inc. v. Consolidated Rail Corp.*,

> ... [a] defendant owes a duty of care to take reasonable measures to avoid the risk of causing economic damages, aside from physical injury, to particular plaintiffs or plaintiffs comprising an identifiable class with respect to whom defendant knows or has reason to know are likely to suffer such damages from its conduct. A defendant failing to adhere to this duty of care may be found liable for such economic damages proximately caused by its breach of duty.

Plaintiffs allege that defendant had a common-law duty to exercise "ordinary care not to injure" O.C.F. workers, that it was foreseeable that these workers would be injured, and that the violation of this duty proximately produced the economic damage.

I find that plaintiffs have factually suggested a cause of action in negligence. Since this motion is brought at the earliest stage of the litigation, and such motions, at this stage, should be granted in only the rarest of instances, I find this an inappropriate time to dismiss this count.* * *

[The court also rejected Wickes' preemption claims.]

Subsequently the court certified a class of nearly 2000 former OCF workers at four plants who had been terminated, downgraded or put on early retirement as a consequence of OCF's defense against Wickes. In May 1993 a $5 million settlement was reported. "5 Million Settlement Proposed In Union Lawsuit Against Wickes Co.," PR Newswire Associates, Financial News NEXIS 5/3/93.

(1.) *The lawyer's toolbox. Glass and Pottery Workers v. Wickes* is an example of creative lawyering. The union and the OCF employees had no way to stop Wickes from putting O.C.F. in play. Nor did the union or employees have an opportunity to influence the defense strategy adopted by OCF. Indeed, the union and employees might have been better off if Wickes had successfully executed the hostile takeover since Wickes may have continued production lines closed down by O.C.F. But O.C.F. management and directors thought they (and the shareholders?) were better off without Wickes. So the workers, their union and their lawyers applied garden variety tort claims in a novel context to try to recoup some of the workers' losses. (To labor lawyers with a sense of history, successful use against a corporation of the tort of intentional interference with a prospective economic relationship is ironic and satisfying. *See Vegelahn v. Guntner* in chapter one.)

(2.) *Allocating risk.* Do you think that the threat of lawsuits by displaced employees will chill takeover activity like Wickes' or the use of defensive maneuvers like O.C.F.'s? If a company must compensate employees for damages arising from takeover activity, who should bear the expense— the raider like Wickes or the target like O.C.F.? If the trial judge had dismissed the lawsuit, who would have borne the costs of job loss?

b.) *The common law II:* General Motors and the town of Ypsilanti, Michigan agreed repeatedly over a twelve-year period that the town would obtain tax abatements available under state law and requested by General Motors in order for GM to continue manufacturing certain car models at its Willow Run plant. When GM decided in 1992 to transfer these automobile assembly operations to a plant in Arlington, Texas, the town of Ypsilanti sued to enjoin the move or for damages.

The complaint alleged, among other bases for relief, breach of contract and promissory estoppel. The trial judge held that the statute enabling a municipality to seek tax abatements did not impose contractual obligations on the subsidized industries. However, the judge did grant a preliminary injunction based on the theory of promissory estoppel. *Charter Township of Ypsilanti v. GM*, 8 IER Cases (BNA) 385, 1993 WL 132385 (Mich.Cir.Ct. 1993). The trial judge distinguished our old friend *Steel Workers, Local 1330,* as a case in which "the corporation was simply closing a plant because it was economically necessary and the [court] concluded that the company never promised to operate a plant when there was no demand for its product. Here, General Motors has stipulated, as it must, that economic necessity is *not* a defense. Again, General Motors is not closing this plant because there is no demand for the cars which are made there. It simply has chosen to transfer the one shift of production of those cars at Willow Run to add a new third shift at another plant in Arlington, Texas."

A court of appeals dissolved the injunction and reversed the finding of promissory estoppel. 201 Mich.App. 128, 506 N.W.2d 556, 8 IER Cases 1165 (1993). The Ypsilanti plant closed in September 1993.

(1.) *The lawyer's toolbox.* GM announced the closing of Willow Run and expansion of operations at Arlington, Texas, in February 1992. The only basis for challenging GM's decision was the series of town applications for tax abatements for GM. The breach of contract theory foundered on the absence of a contract; the tax abatement statute simply did not create a contract between the state or its subdivisions and the subsidized industry. On appeal the promissory estoppel theory failed because "almost all of the statements the trial court cited as foundations for a promise were, instead, expressions of defendant's hopes or expectations of continued employment at Willow Run" and "even if the finding of a promise could have been sustained, reliance on the promise would not have been reasonable. * * * It has never been held that an abatement carries a promise of continued employment." 506 N.W.2d at 559, 561, 8 IER Cases at 1167, 1168.

These results were unsurprising. Indeed, the only surprise in the litigation was the willingness of the trial judge to find promissory estoppel and issue a preliminary injunction. Given the paucity of authority for its position and the precedents hostile to its claims, what was counsel for Ypsilanti really seeking from this lawsuit? Looking ahead, how can counsel for other towns in Michigan—or the other 30 states with similar tax abatement statutes— secure enforceable promises in exchange for tax abatements?

(2.) *Allocating risks.* Should tax abatements be conditioned on enforceable promises to continue operations for a certain period? Do you think that the threat of lawsuits by communities will chill applications for tax abatements or stop multi-state companies from transferring work from one location to another? If slowing down a planned transfer becomes one of the costs of restructuring, who bears the expense? If appellate courts in Michigan had upheld the injunction, what would GM have done?

c.) *State statutes.* Over one-half of the states have enacted legislation, known as stakeholder statutes, that give corporate directors some discretion to consider the effects of their decisions on the interests of non-shareholder constituencies, like employees, customers, suppliers, and residents of the local community. With two exceptions (Connecticut and Pennsylvania), stakeholder laws do not *require* consideration of non-shareholder interests, nor (except in Pennsylvania) do they put stakeholder concerns on a par with that of shareholders; indeed it is not clear whether stakeholders have standing to sue under these laws.

Exactly what are these stakeholder statutes intended to accomplish? Some commentators describe stakeholder statutes as recognition that ownership of the firm is separate from ownership of the capital invested in the firm. Accordingly, non-shareholders like employees are entitled, by virtue of long and loyal service, to have their interests considered by corporate directors who are making strategic decisions about a company's future. Within this school of thought there is a debate about the actual versus symbolic value of these laws and the weight to be given non-shareholder concerns. Other observers insist that the stakeholder statutes are really a defensive shield behind which corporate directors can hide when they resist unwanted overtures from a purchaser willing to pay a premium for stock. In other words, directors cannot refuse to maximize shareholder wealth because they want to remain in control of a company but they can turn down a high-priced offer because the gain for shareholders is inadequate given the cost to stakeholders. For lively and informative discussions of the issues, see *Symposium: Corporate Malaise—Stakeholder Statutes: Cause Or Cure?*, 21 Stetson L.Rev. 1 (1991) and Symposium: The Corporate Stakeholder Debate: The Classical Theory and its Critics, 63 U.Toronto L.J. 297 (1993).

4. TRANSFER OF OWNERSHIP

CASE STUDY: FROST AND SUNSHINE 1

Susan Frost and Ben Sunshine are negotiating the sale of Frost Company to Sunshine, Inc. Frost Company consists of 15 retail garden care centers in the tri-state area, a gardening catalogue published twice a year, and a modest mail order business; Sunshine, Inc. is a marketer of gardening and lawn care equipment, supplies and accessories. Sunshine intends to continue Frost as an ongoing concern and to retain many Frost employees with no loss of work time or salary.

Frost's corporate policy manual, which applies to all salaried employees except company officers (who have written contracts of employment), includes commitments from Frost to its employees, such as a provision limiting discharge to just cause and plans for severance pay and for nonpension, retirement-related benefits. Some of Frost's employees have made commitments to the company in the form of covenants not to compete, and all of the salaried employees have signed an agreement to submit to arbitration any dispute arising out of the employment relationship.

Frost intends to terminate its employees as of midnight on November 14 and Sunshine intends to employ those workers as of 12:01 a.m. on November 15. What happens to the promises of Frost and its employees? If Frost must pay severance benefits or if Sunshine must honor Frost's health-related benefits as they come due, seller and buyer want those obligations reflected in the purchase price. Can Frost assign the covenants not to compete to Sunshine? Can Sunshine hold disgruntled employees to their promise to use arbitration, instead of the courts, to resolve any employment-related disputes that arise after the transfer of ownership? Can employees hold Sunshine to Frost's promise of dismissal for just cause only?

Frost and Sunshine can negotiate terms that make Sunshine's intentions clear, along with a purchase price that reflects the value of Frost's employment-related commitments and contingent obligations. What role is there for the employees who will be affected by Sunshine's willingness or not to make good on Frost's promises and by Sunshine's insistence that employees comply with the arrangements originally made with Frost? And what if, as is likely, Frost and Sunshine ignore the pesky problem of commitments to and by the workforce; will the law step in to decide which obligations survive the transfer of ownership and which don't?

The cases that follow address some of the employment issues that arise in connection with transfers of company ownership. Although we have structured this transaction as a sale of assets in which Frost continues as an ongoing concern, the issues raised are applicable to other types of ownership changes, such as mergers, takeovers and spinoffs.

A BRIEF DETOUR INTO THE WORLD OF CORPORATE LAW

To better understand this material, a brief introduction to terms used in corporate law is necessary. First, it is important to understand the difference between a "purchaser of assets" and a "purchaser of stock." In American law, a corporation is a legal person. When the ownership of stock in a corporation is transferred, the corporation continues on as the same legal entity, and it will still be required to observe all the contracts it entered into under the previous ownership. Thus, when the stock of a corporation is transferred from one entity to another, all the corporation's "promises" survive the transfer.

The following cases deal not with the transfer of stock, but with the transfer of assets. Ownership of the corporation is not transferred, but rather ownership of some distinct asset of the corporation, for example, a manufacturing plant, is transferred to some other corporation or individual. Thus, the following cases discuss the question of whether and when a purchaser of assets is required to observe the obligations of its predecessor.

Many of the following cases also use the terms "branch" and "subsidiary." The distinction between the two terms may seem subtle, but it can have significant consequences for liability. A "branch" is simply an office, division, or unit of business located in a place other than that of the business's main office. In contrast, a "subsidiary" is a separate corporation whose stock (or, at least a controlling share) is held by another corporation, called the "Parent Corporation." Because a subsidiary is a separate corporation, the parent company is afforded the benefit of the limited liability rule that is normally afforded to shareholders in a corporation.[8] Thus, as we will see in the cases that follow, a parent corporation will usually not be held liable for obligations that its subsidiary has incurred.

A final important concept for this section is "piercing the corporate veil." This refers to the situation in which the court goes behind the limited liability rule and holds the corporation's shareholder(s) liable for the actions of the corporation (for example, a parent corporation might be held liable for the liabilities of its subsidiary). In order to succeed on a

---

8. In American corporate law, the liability of a shareholder in a corporation is limited to the amount of the shareholder's initial investment.

piercing the corporate veil theory a plaintiff must show that the corporation is really an "alter ego" of its shareholder. That is, it must be shown 1) that "the separate personalities" of the two corporations "no longer exist . . ." and 2) that observing the corporate form would work an injustice. *Minton v. Cavaney* 56 Cal.2d 576, 15 Cal.Rptr. 641, 364 P.2d 473 (1961). In general it is very difficult to pierce the corporate veil if all corporate formalities have been observed. It will be worth remembering as you read the following cases that it is not enough to simply show that an obligation will go unfulfilled if the corporate veil is not pierced: if that were the case then the limited liability rule would be meaningless.

BACK TO THE WORLD OF LABOR
AND EMPLOYMENT LAW

A word of caution: there is no unified "law of employment obligations across a transfer of ownership." There are just a lot of cases trying to figure out how the many laws that regulate the workplace should be applied in the context of a transfer of ownership. Rarely do judges step back to consider if one group—sellers, buyers, customers, employees, taxpayers—is systematically benefitting from or being burdened by the employment-related consequences of changes in ownership. If judges did consider the question, what would they find?

a. *Do Promises of Fidelity Survive Transfers of Ownership?*

i. *Covenants Not to Compete as a Limit on the Right to Work*

As we saw in chapter one, employers may require employees, as a condition of new or continued employment, to sign covenants not to compete for specified periods of time and geographic areas. Enforceability of these covenants is a matter of state law. Similarly, state law determines whether a successor employer may enforce covenants not to compete signed by its predecessor and the predecessor's employees. But certain general guidelines can be identified: First, in many jurisdictions a valid covenant made by the seller of a business is transferable to and enforceable by the buyer, on the theory that the mere transfer of ownership did not affect a change in the employing enterprise, as viewed from the employee's perspective. In contrast, some jurisdictions refuse to allow the buyer to enforce a covenant not to compete signed by an employee and the buyer's predecessor on the ground that an employment contract is a contract for personal services and, thus, not assignable. But even in those jurisdictions that hold personal service contracts not assignable, exceptions have been found. For example, a provision in a written employment contract stating that the contract is assignable or that the obligations runs to a successor may turn an unenforceable covenant into an express agreement; that is, if the predecessor and employee contract around the rule against assignability their written agreement may be enforced by the successor. Similarly, a successor may enforce a covenant not to compete if the employee's behavior manifests consent or ratification of the assignment; in these circumstances courts usually require evidence of assignment by the predecessor and knowledge of that assignment by the employee. Alternatively, some courts distinguish unenforceable personal service contracts which require performance from enforceable covenants not to compete which bar performance.

The opinion that follows illustrates the application of these general rules.

FREUND v. E.D. & F. MAN INTERNATIONAL, INC.

United States Court of Appeals, Seventh Circuit, 1999.
199 F.3d 382.

POSNER, CHIEF JUDGE.

This diversity suit for breach of contract was resolved against the plaintiff, David Freund, after a bench trial. The ground of the decision was that the key contractual provision on which Freund was suing was contrary to the common law of Illinois. The contract provides that it shall be interpreted in accordance with Illinois law and the parties agree, at least tacitly (and that's good enough), that Illinois law governs the enforceability as well as interpretation of the contract.

Freund is a commodities broker who in 1990 entered into a contract with Index Futures Group, Inc., a brokerage firm, to become an employee of Index and create a "Freund Division" within the firm—or rather continue it, since he had had a "Freund Division" in the previous brokerage firm that he had worked for. The contract, which either party could terminate on 30 days' notice, provided for a splitting of the brokerage fees paid by customers served by the Freund Division between the Division (meaning Freund) and Index. The following clause is the focus of the lawsuit: "All personnel hired by Freund will remain in the division until termination. Said personnel will not be offered or given employment with Index or its affiliates without prior approval by Freund. This provision will remain in effect until one year after Index and Freund part company."

Freund had brought with him to Index several brokers, including Walter and Mueller, and they became employees of Index. In 1996 Index sold its business to the defendant, Man, and the district court held that the sale included an assumption by Man of Index's contract with Freund. So Freund and the other brokers in the Freund Division became employees of Man. The following year, however, Man terminated Freund's employment contract after the required 30 days' notice, but retained Walter and Mueller in violation of the contractual provision that we quoted. Freund seeks damages for that violation.

The provision is a variant of an employee covenant not to compete. Instead of the employees' being the promisors, they were not parties to the contract that restricted their employment opportunities. The contractual promise was made by Index and assumed by Man, and it was a promise not to hire (more precisely, not to retain) rather than not to be hired. Illinois law is suspicious of employee covenants not to compete. But the district judge made no finding on whether, had Walter and Mueller promised not to work for Index—or for Man, which the judge held had stepped into Index's shoes in the contract—if Freund were fired, an Illinois court would have enforced the promise. The judge thought that in any event such a court would not enforce a promise that had not been made by, or at least known to, the employees affected by it.

At first glance it may seem bizarre indeed to seek to hold a person to a contract to which he was not a party and of which he had no knowledge. For not only did neither Walter nor Mueller sign a covenant not to remain with Index or its successor should Freund leave; they didn't know about the provision disabling them from remaining with the firm without Freund's consent. But neither Walter nor Mueller is a defendant. Freund is not seeking to "hold" them to this contractual provision to which they were not parties and of which they were not even aware. It is true that if he wins this suit the decision will be a precedent the practical effect of which will be to bind any future Walters and Muellers much as if they were defendants; but that is also a possible effect of legal doctrines that no one would question. Suppose another brokerage firm had induced Freund to break his contract with Index and bring his group with him to that firm, and Index had sued Freund for breach of contract and the firm for intentional interference with contract. The threat of such a suit would deter such a breach and by doing so would limit the practical employment opportunities of the other members of the Freund Division, such as Walter and Mueller; yet it would be a conventional tort suit.

Coming even closer to home, we find cases in which Illinois courts have enforced contracts in which one firm agrees not to "steal" the employees of another. In no case was the validity of the contract squarely in issue, but in both American Food Management and H & M Driver Leasing Services the court, in upholding the propriety of injunctive relief, clearly indicated its belief that the contract served a valid purpose. We infer that under Illinois law an employer who has made a substantial enough investment in the human capital of its employees to enforce a covenant by his employees not to compete with him (for a reasonable time and within a reasonable geographical and product space) can also enforce a promise by another employer not to hire away these employees, provided the contract does not unreasonably restrain competition between the two employers * * *.

But this case is different both because it required the employees to be fired rather than just foreclosed from alternative employment, and being fired is usually a greater hardship than not being hired, and because the employees were not employees of the covenantee, Freund. They were employees of Index, and later of Man. The situation was thus that one employee obtained a contract whereby fellow employees would lose their jobs if he lost his. It was the commercial equivalent of the discredited Hindu practice of suttee, whereby the widow is required to immolate herself on her husband's funeral bier. If Freund went, Walter and Mueller had to go too. And unlike the case of suttee, Walter and Mueller were not aware that they were "married" to Freund.

It is true that since they were employees at will they had no "right" to continued employment, and so the contractual provision in issue did not infringe their rights. Still, such provisions are sufficiently unusual that neither Walter nor Mueller would reasonably foresee such an impediment to their remaining with their employer. Given the hostility of Illinois courts to employee covenants not to compete, it strikes us as unlikely that such a court would enforce a covenant not to compete that the employees who would lose their job because of it had no knowledge of or reason to suspect—unless the promisee came up with a better reason for this unusual arrangement than anything that Freund has offered. Although the covenant was not onerous in scope and time—only one potential employer was excluded, and for only one year—scope and duration are not the only factors that the Illinois courts consider in deciding whether to enforce a covenant not to compete. Others include the purpose and business justification of the restraint. And we have no doubt that they would weigh the fact that this covenant requires the employee to be fired in deciding whether it was justified.

Yet we can imagine a valid purpose. If the Freund Division was essentially an independent business in 1990 when Freund joined Index Futures Group, then Freund would have wanted to capture its value ("goodwill") in a lump sum; but to induce Freund to keep working (this was a personal-services business, after all), Index would have preferred to pay out the value over a period of years, perhaps as an unusually large salary for Freund, so that he didn't just take the lump sum and run. But this scheme of deferred compensation created a strategic opportunity for Index and Man: woo away the business of the Freund Division (that is, redirect the customers' loyalty), then fire Freund and so avoid having to pay the deferred component of the payment for the 1990 acquisition of the Freund Division. One way to make that strategic conduct unattractive to Index in the initial contract would be to require Index or its successor to divest itself of the entire business of the Freund Division if it fired Freund, and the only practical way of doing that was to require Index or its successor to get rid of the employees who were handling the customers of the Freund Division—who *were* (with Freund) the Freund Division. But this theory of why the challenged clause was included in the initial contract is not argued; nor does it explain why the employees affected by it had to be kept in the dark. It would have been simple enough to condition the contract between Freund and Index on the affected employees' signing the noncompete provision. On this record, the concealment of the provision from the employees was gratuitous, and a gratuitous interference with employment is unenforceable in Illinois.

We are supported in this conclusion by Szabo Food Service, Inc. v. County of Cook, 160 Ill.App.3d 845, 112 Ill.Dec. 266, 513 N.E.2d 875, 877 (1987), which refused to enforce a promise by one firm to another not to deal with a third firm's employees whom the third firm had "stolen" from the second. The court distinguished American Food Management as a case in which the plaintiff was trying to restrict the actions of persons with whom it had a contractual relation; Freund, in parallel with Szabo, had no contract with Walter or Mueller.

AFFIRMED.

CAMPBELL v. POTASH CORP.
OF SASKATCHEWAN, INC.

United States Court of Appeals, Sixth Circuit, 2001.
238 F.3d 792.

BOGGS, CIRCUIT JUDGE.

The Potash Corporation of Saskatchewan, Inc. ("PCS") appeals from the district court's partial grant of summary judgment and its judgment after trial in favor of plaintiffs-appellees J.D. Campbell, Peter Kesser, and Alfred Williams, Jr., all former executives of the Arcadian Corporation.

Campbell (the former President and CEO), Kesser (the former Vice President and General Counsel), and Williams (the former Vice President and CFO) sued PCS for breach of contract approximately two months after its successful March 6, 1997 merger with Arcadian, because PCS refused to make severance payments to the executives triggered under those executives' employment agreements[1] by the change in corporate control of Arcadian and additional "good cause."

PCS moved to dismiss plaintiffs' charges for failure to join PCS Nitrogen (the merger subsidiary wholly owned by PCS into which Arcadian was absorbed) as an indispensable party. The district court denied that motion . * * *

I

PCS, a Saskatchewan fertilizer corporation, approached Arcadian, a Tennessee fertilizer corporation, about a possible merger in August 1996. The Arcadian board decided to pursue the overture on August 27, and heard a presentation on proposed severance plans at that time. Over Labor Day weekend, Arcadian and PCS negotiated the terms of the merger and the severance agreements. PCS's Executive Committee and the Arcadian board approved and executed the merger agreement at respective board meetings on September 2. After approving the agreement, the Arcadian board approved employment agreements for nine senior executives that included so-called golden parachutes. Campbell, Kesser, and Williams signed employment agreements containing these parachutes three days later. The "golden parachute" portion of the severance package provided a formula to compensate senior executives in

---

1. This opinion will follow the district court in using the terms "employment agreements" and "severance agreements" interchangeably to refer to the executives' agreement with Arcadian.

case of a change in corporate control accompanied by a material change in the executive's position at the new company. In such a circumstance, the executive could leave the company and receive an aggregate payment in one lump sum within 30 days of termination, totaling:

> an amount equal to the sum of (A) three (3) times Executive's Base Salary in effect at the time of [the Executive's] termination . . . , (B) three (3) times the average of all bonus, profit sharing and other incentive payments made by the Company to Executive in respect of the two (2) calendar years immediately preceding such termination, and (C) the pro-rata share of Executive's target bonus, profit sharing and other incentive payments for the calendar year in which such termination occurred. . . .

§ 4.3(c)(1)(ii) of the Employment Agreement.

Arcadian's compensation system historically emphasized incentives, enhancing an industry median base salary with supplemental incentive payments for meeting performance targets as well as profit-sharing payments and additional bonuses. Under the 1994 profit-sharing plan (only), appellees were also eligible for performance-based SARs (stock appreciation rights) and CESARs (cash equivalent SARs), which vested ratably over three years after they were granted. In addition to the formal plan, Arcadian distributed other stock options without regard to company performance. It also contributed 4% of each employee's annual compensation into an Employee Stock Ownership Plan (ESOP) and into a Supplemental Executive Retirement Plan (SERP) for certain higher-salaried employees whose income level precluded their full participation in an ESOP.

At PCS's insistence during the Labor Day weekend discussions, Arcadian reduced the number of secondary events that could trigger the golden parachutes following a change in corporate control, and devised a formula based on actual compensation for the two calendar years preceding termination rather than on expected compensation for the two years following termination. Ironically, the look-back formula was adopted in part because PCS felt a retrospective formula would be less contestable than a prospective one. PCS also requested that the multiplier be limited to salary and bonuses, but Arcadian indicated that its pay structure was too incentive-laden for that to be feasible. Bruce Jocz of Bracewell & Patterson, Kesser's former law firm, drafted the clause under Kesser's direction.[2] In Jocz's brief presentation to the board following approval of the merger, no mention was made of whether the "other incentive payments" in the multiplier formula included long-term incentives. Rather, Jocz's summary described the formula as 3 times base salary, plus 3 times prior years' average profit-sharing and bonus, plus a pro-

---

2. Jocz modeled the first iteration of the employment agreements after golden parachutes that had been devised for another client to ward off a hostile takeover. As such, the original draft proposal included more generous parachutes that could be triggered simply by a change in control. PCS rejected that draft and suggested using the golden parachute agreements it had with its own executives as an alternative model. Jocz then adapted PCS's model to Arcadian's needs.

rata share of current year's profit-sharing or bonus. Arcadian Executive Charles Lance presented slides suggesting that the multiplier totaled 36 months of salary and bonus. However, in a mid-September spreadsheet prepared for PCS and its outside benefits consultant (Richard Davenport of Deloitte & Touche) calculating the golden parachutes, Lance did include stock rights, stock options, and performance-based SARs and CESARs from the 1994 profit sharing plan in the multiplier formula (but, perhaps inadvertently, left other individual SARs out of it).[3] Lance sent PCS copies of all Arcadian benefit plans for due diligence purposes.

Several weeks later, Lance added the individual SARs, CESARs, ESOPs and SERPs to the spreadsheet, and Davenport added some other accidentally omitted long-term incentives to correct the spreadsheet. Lance drafted administrative guidelines interpreting the variable components of the multiplier clause. Arcadian's accounting department calculated potential severance payments based on a 1996 and a 1997 merger closing, which Arcadian's outside auditors Peat Marwick then reviewed. The compensation committee reviewed and approved the administrative guidelines on October 21 and reported its action to the full board the following day. In early November, Lance contacted his counterpart at PCS to call attention to the much higher severance benefit costs that would be entailed by a 1997 closing. Shortly thereafter, PCS told Lance it thought the severance packages should be limited to three times cash compensation, but Lance said that was inconsistent with both his understanding of the terms reached and the language of the employment agreements.

The agreements also contained a provision requiring Arcadian to obtain an assumption agreement from any "direct or indirect" successor agreeing "to expressly assume and agree to perform, by a written agreement in form and substance satisfactory to Executive, all of the obligations of the Company [Arcadian] under this Agreement." Failure by Arcadian to obtain such an agreement from a successor automatically triggered the golden parachutes upon a change in control. PCS and Arcadian filed a Joint Proxy Statement with the SEC on January 28, 1997, laying out the severance formula, including incentive payments, lump-sum pension benefits, and the tax gross-up feature whereby the company increased the golden parachutes to cover related taxes.

PCS continued to resist Arcadian's inclusion of long-term incentives in the formula. Plaintiffs' counsel thus recommended that plaintiffs engage Arthur Anderson to produce a report justifying plaintiffs' interpretation of the golden parachutes, to defend against a possible challenge by PCS. The audit confirmed that the employment agreements were "well within competitive practice." The compensation committee heard the report on February 24, but took no action. Then Arcadian's chair-

---

3. Arcadian occasionally granted non-performance-based SARs to employees as compensation. Campbell, for instance, ap- parently received some SARs as a kind of signing bonus when he came to Arcadian.

man refused to hear a report to the full board, stating that it was part of PCS's due diligence and "whatever it costs, it costs."

Two days before the March 6, 1997 closing, Kesser demanded that PCS and PCS Nitrogen expressly assume the golden parachute severance agreements signed by plaintiffs. PCS Senior Vice President and General Counsel John Hampton refused, saying PCS was not the successor to Arcadian's business or assets. Kesser threatened to delay closing on March 6, causing Hampton to have Barry Humphreys, PCS's Senior Vice President for Finance, sign the assumption agreement on behalf of PCS to avoid delaying closing and incurring difficulties with merger financing. Hampton himself signed on behalf of PCS Nitrogen as its Secretary.

Prior to closing, Campbell and Williams were offered jobs at PCS Nitrogen materially different from their previous ones with Arcadian, so both terminated at closing for good cause. Hampton released Kesser from the new company's employ at the closing. Though PCS acknowledged that it owed some amounts to Campbell, Kesser and Williams, it refused to pay even the undisputed portions of their severance packages within the allotted thirty days, thereby precipitating this suit.

[Sections II and III of the opinion, dealing with standards of review and PCS' rejected claims of duress and failure of consideration, are omitted.—Eds.]

IV

PCS next argues that the golden parachutes violate public policy, and therefore that the assumption agreement promising them is void.[4] PCS advances this argument even though it offers golden parachutes to its own top managers. Hypocrisy aside, PCS cites no circuit case law supporting its proposition. At most this court has frowned on golden parachutes in past dicta, but we have never held that such severance packages are *per se* unlawful. *See* Brown v . . Ferro Corp., 763 F.2d at 800–01. Nor does PCS provide much reason to equate this type of executive compensation with contracts prohibited by public policy, such as ones to perform illegal acts. PCS cites a Congressional committee report saying that golden parachutes should be discouraged and notes that there is a heavy excise tax on parachutes over a certain value (exceeded here), but, as Plaintiffs point out, Congress taxed golden parachutes, it did not prohibit them. PCS further argues that these particular golden parachutes violate public policy because they are

4. There is a rich, albeit somewhat dated, secondary literature discussing the pros and cons of golden parachutes. Whatever else might be gleaned from this material, golden parachutes are not uniformly condemned as offensive to public policy. *See, e.g.,* Kenneth Johnson, Note, Golden Parachutes and the Business Judgement Rule: Toward a Proper Standard of Review, 94 Yale L.J. 909 (1985); John C. Coffee, Jr., Shareholders Versus Managers: The Strain in the Corporate Web, 85 Mich.L.Rev. 1, 76 (1986); Ann Marie Hanrahan, Note, Koenings v. Joseph Schlitz Brewing Co.: The Wisconsin Supreme Court Addresses Executive Termination Benefits in a Golden Parachute Contract, 1987 Wis.L.Rev. 823; Richard P. Bress, Comment, Golden Parachutes: Untangling the Ripcords, 39 Stan.L.Rev. 955 (1987); Drew H. Campbell, Note, Golden Parachutes: Common Sense From the Common Law, 51 Ohio St. L.J. 279 (1990).

excessive and have a gross-up feature to compensate the recipient for any tax penalty. These features do not make the golden parachutes violative of public policy, and parachutes with such features have been upheld. *See* Tate & Lyle PLC v. Staley Continental, Inc., Civ. A. No. 9813, 1988 WL 46064, at *7 (Del.Ch.1988); Worth v. Huntington Bancshares, Inc., 43 Ohio St.3d 192, 540 N.E.2d 249, 255 (1989).

PCS further argues that these golden parachutes violate public policy because they were approved after the merger had been approved, and therefore served no legitimate corporate purpose.[5] Though adopted after the merger was approved, these golden parachutes were authorized later in the same meeting at which the approval occurred. Thus, PCS's argument that their adoption violated public policy because it came after approval of the merger is somewhat misleading. Moreover, the timing of the adoption of the golden parachute provision fits with the rationale given for their adoption in deposition testimony by Arcadian's then-directors. With a merger pending, the company feared that its top personnel might seek lucrative offers elsewhere. Not only would the company then be deprived of the services of key employees in the interim (and potentially receive less value from a merger if the firm suffered from poor management just prior to closing), but it also risked no longer having the managers who had brought so much profit to Arcadian in the event that the merger was never consummated. To ensure that neither of those situations occurred, Arcadian used golden parachutes to entice nine of its top executives to remain with the company until and unless there was both a change of corporate control and a decline in those executives' respective positions in the company. Five managers stayed with the company for a time after the merger. Four did not, including the three plaintiffs in this case. At least one court has embraced a similar rationale for golden parachutes in the past. *See* Koenings v. Joseph Schlitz Brewing Co., 126 Wis.2d 349, 377 N.W.2d 593, 603–04 (1985).[6]

Mixed with its argument about public policy, PCS argues against application of the business judgment rule to this case. Not only did the manner of the golden parachutes' adoption violate public policy, according to PCS, it also violated a duty of care prerequisite to applying the business judgment rule. * * *

---

5. Commentators originally objected to the use of golden parachutes as anti-takeover devices where they were crafted as poison pills and triggered automatically by the single trigger of a change in corporate control. More recently, commentators have noted the potential moral hazard entailed by golden parachutes, inasmuch as they may encourage inefficient management to induce a takeover that is lucrative for departing managers. The golden parachutes here were adopted after approval of the merger, so neither of these objections can be made against them. Moreover, they re-quired two triggering events, as termination or a role reduction had to accompany a change in control before the golden parachute could be demanded. Thus, activation of the parachutes was within PCS's control.

6. Golden parachutes have also been defended as a means of compensating managers for their investments in firm-specific skills. *See* Daniel R. Fischel, Organized Exchanges and the Regulation of Dual Class Common Stock, 54 U.Chi.L.Rev 119, 137–38 (1987); John C. Coffee, Jr., Shareholders Versus Managers, 85 Mich.L.Rev. at 76.

Even if we ourselves did not perceive a good rationale for these parachutes, courts should be loath to condemn a business practice simply because they do not perceive a good rationale for a given practice. Condemning poorly understood practices simply for lack of a clear rationale would substitute the court's business judgment for the corporation's. "If what management did was illegal, . . . it should be enjoined. If it wasn't illegal, it should be allowed even if philosophically unpalatable and, if a court cannot tell, it seems . . . that this is what the business judgment rule is all about and the nod should be given to those who are vested with the business decision making responsibility." Edelman v. Fruehauf Corp., 798 F.2d 882, 889 (6th Cir.1986) (Guy, J., dissenting). In short, evaluating the costs and benefits of golden parachutes is quintessentially a job for corporate boards, and not for federal courts.

In Delaware, whose law the parties agreed would govern disputes under this contract, a plaintiff must show that the majority of the board acted in a manner that "rise[s] to the level of gross negligence" before a court may second guess its business judgment. PCS argues that the Arcadian board was misled by incomplete slides and presentations made to it about the golden parachutes, and states that the board did not know the total possible cost of the golden parachutes at the time it approved them. As evidence of neglect of the board's duty of care, PCS points to the statements by Arcadian's chairman about the parachutes that "whatever they cost, they cost," and that it would be PCS's responsibility to pay the severance packages anyway. But even if deemed incriminating, these remarks do not show gross negligence by a majority of the board. Board members had a reasonable amount of accurate information about the severance packages before them when they acted. The lack of a completely accurate total outlay estimate before approval does not rise to the level of gross negligence. According to the deposition of independent board member Chester Vanatta, relied on by the district court, the board understood the nature of the benefits, knew that PCS had approved the severance packages, had a rough idea of the cost and knew what was included, wanted to retain the personnel in case the merger failed to go through, and vetted the severance packages through its compensation committee. Finally, PCS also suggests a measure of self-dealing in the approval of these severance packages, but Mr. Campbell is the only plaintiff who was on the board, and he acknowledged his conflict and abstained from the vote.

The Arcadian board therefore exhibited nothing like the lack of knowledge and the swiftness of deliberation condemned in the Van Gorkom or Hanson cases. See Smith v. Van Gorkom, 488 A.2d 858 (Del.1985); Hanson Trust PLC v. ML SCM Acquisition, Inc., 781 F.2d 264 (2d Cir.1986). Nor does this case feature the kind of insider-dealing on a stacked board decried in Ocilla Indus., Inc. v. Katz, 677 F.Supp. 1291, 1299 (E.D.N.Y.1987). Nor do the severance agreements at issue here approach the possibly wasteful use of corporate assets entailed in the Walt Disney Company's non-fault termination of Michael Ovitz recently adjudicated by the Delaware Supreme Court. See Brehm v.

Eisner, 746 A.2d 244, 253 (Del.2000) (dismissing the action without prejudice on procedural grounds, but observing that "the sheer size of the payout to Ovitz [$140 million for less than 15 months of work] ... pushes the envelope of judicial respect for the business judgment of directors in making compensation decisions.") If the Ovitz severance payment, which included $39 million in cash, only pushes the envelope under Delaware law, then the smaller sum here spread across three executives with longer tenure at their company is well within the confines respected by the business judgment rule.

V

[The court's detailed review of the district court's calculations of the amounts due the plaintiffs is omitted.]

VI

PCS has already received the benefit of the bargain it struck concerning golden parachutes (in having an orderly change in corporate control and in insuring Arcadian's health in the event of a failed effort to merge), and it cannot now refuse payment in return. There was consideration for the assumption agreement insofar as it was bound up in the merger obligations. Golden parachutes are not void as against public policy, nor did the Arcadian board exhibit gross negligence in approving the golden parachutes at issue in this case. Finally, although the district court correctly interpreted the multiplier clause's language based on extrinsic evidence gathered at trial, it committed clear error in counting certain incentive payments that were made in respect of more than two years. For these reasons, the judgment of the district court on partial summary judgment and after trial is AFFIRMED in part, REVERSED in part, and REMANDED back to the district court for further proceedings consistent with this opinion.

———————

ii.   Just Cause as a Limit on the Right to Discharge

CONRAD v. ROFIN–SINAR, INC.

United States District Court, Eastern District of Michigan, 1991.
762 F.Supp. 167.

Cohn, District Judge.

I.

This is an employer-employee wrongful discharge and an unjust enrichment case. Plaintiff Melvin K. Conrad (Conrad) was terminated by his employer, defendant Rofin–Sinar, Inc. (Rofin–Sinar), a manufacturer of laser systems. Conrad says the termination violates a "just cause" employment contract. Alternatively, Conrad, who was a salesperson for Rofin–Sinar, makes a claim in quantum meruit. Now before the Court is

Rofin–Sinar's motion for summary judgment as to all claims. Fed. R.Civ.P. 56(c). Rofin–Sinar says the alleged "just cause" contract is not enforceable because it was made by a representative of Conrad's previous employer, the Industrial Laser Division of Spectra Physics, Inc. [The discussion of Conrad's quantum meruit claims is omitted.—Eds.]

II.

The following facts, as gleaned from deposition testimony, affidavits and documents in the record, are not in dispute.

A.

In early 1985, Conrad applied for a job as laser systems salesman with the Industrial Laser Division (ILD) of Spectra Physics. As a division, ILD has no separate corporate existence. During the application process, Conrad asked about job security. Herbert Dwight (Dwight), the president of Spectra Physics, told Conrad that he would remain employed as long as he did a good job selling laser systems.

Shortly after beginning his employment, Conrad received a personnel manual describing Spectra Physics' policies and practices. It listed specific grounds for discipline and provided for formal yearly performance reviews. Spectra Physics had a separate manual for ILD which: (1) listed the same reasons for discipline as the Spectra Physics manual itself, (2) provided for progressive discipline before termination, and (3) provided for formal performance evaluations.

B.

In March 1988, Spectra Physics sold all of its ILD assets to Siemens Capital Corporation (Siemens) which in turn incorporated Rofin–Sinar, specifically to continue the business of ILD. Rofin–Sinar did not exist before Siemens purchased the assets. After the transaction, Rofin–Sinar informed Spectra Physics customers that ILD "has been sold and is now Rofin–Sinar." All the supervisory personnel who worked at ILD continued to work for Rofin–Sinar in the same or similar capacity.

C.

1.

Before the asset sale, notices were given to Spectra Physics employees stating that their employment with Spectra Physics was terminated, and they would be offered employment by Rofin–Sinar. There is no evidence in the record suggesting Rofin–Sinar issued any policy statement suggesting it would adopt any "just cause" employment contracts which may have been in effect prior to the asset sale. The asset purchase agreement states Rofin–Sinar reserved the right to terminate Spectra Physics employees. It also states that Rofin–Sinar retained Spectra Physics employees under "terms and conditions of employment as [it] may determine in its discretion."

2.

After the asset sale, Conrad continued to work without interruption, at the same salary, under the same commission plan, with the same reporting requirements, with the same vacation plan, hire date, employee number, personnel file, supervisor, office, car and insurance deductions. He was never asked or required to file an employment application or a W–4 income tax form for Rofin–Sinar.

On May 11, 1988, Spectra Physics placed Conrad on probation as a result of a performance review for the period ending March 31, 1988. After the effective date of the purchase of the ILD assets, Conrad's probationary period was continued by Rofin–Sinar.

3.

Rofin–Sinar retained and relied on Spectra Physic's personnel manual. It used the personnel codes, personnel forms and expense reports contained in it.

When Conrad was terminated, Rofin–Sinar followed the termination and exit interview procedures contained in the personnel manual. A Spectra Physics Employee Profile form was generated containing Conrad's original hire date, department number and employee number. The form indicated the termination reason as "42" which is the code in the personnel manual that means "poor performer."

Rofin–Sinar did not develop any additional or different personnel practices before Conrad's termination. It did not notify employees of any changes in personnel policies.

D.

Rofin–Sinar terminated Conrad on January 27, 1989. The precipitating factor in his discharge was that he allegedly withheld information that Ford Motor Company (Ford) was planning to purchase a competitive laser system. Conrad has testified that he did not fail to communicate information to Rofin–Sinar. Conrad's supervisors at Spectra Physics had previously criticized his communication skills. His May 11, 1988 probation was instituted because he had been tardy in submitting certain written reports. Conrad satisfactorily completed his probationary period, and he was not given any written notice of performance problems between May 11, 1988 and his termination. Conrad's sales performance met the goals established by his supervisors.

E.

At the time of his termination, Conrad had been negotiating the sale of two large laser systems. After his termination, Rofin–Sinar received the purchase orders for the two systems. Conrad was not paid commission on the sales. Moreover, after his termination, Rofin–Sinar received other purchase orders on which Conrad had worked.

F.

Conrad's salary structure was embodied in a 1985 letter sent from Tom Liolios (Liolios), a Spectra Physics marketing manager, to Conrad. In the letter, Liolios said Conrad would receive a base salary. In addition, Conrad was eligible to receive incentive payments if he met quarterly sales quotas. The "incentive compensation plan" provided that commissions paid to employees were calculated on the basis of sales order receipts.

III.

A.

The Michigan Supreme Court has held that an employee can enforce an employer's promise not to terminate employment except for just cause. *Toussaint v. Blue Cross & Blue Shield of Michigan,* 408 Mich. 579, 292 N.W.2d 880 (1980). Such an enforceable agreement can result from either: (1) an employer's "express agreement, oral or written" or (2) "an employee's legitimate expectations grounded in an employer's policy statements."

Applying this standard, a reasonable trier of facts may conclude that an implied "just cause" employment contract existed between Spectra Physics and Conrad. The record contains undisputed evidence that Dwight, the president of Spectra Physics, promised Conrad he would remain employed as long as he did a good job. This fact alone is sufficient to support a verdict that Conrad had a "just cause" employment contract with Spectra Physics. Spectra Physics adopted other policies that may have given Conrad a "legitimate expectation" that he had a "just cause" employment contract. In particular, its personnel manual listed grounds for discipline. *Butzer v. Camelot Hall,* 183 Mich. App. 194, 202, 454 N.W.2d 122 (1989) (handbook's listing of acts from which termination would result enhances an employee's legitimate expectation he or she would be terminated only for just cause). The personnel manual also provided for annual performance reviews. *Diggs v. Pepsi–Cola Metropolitan Bottling Co.,* 861 F.2d 914, 918–919 (6th Cir.1988) (employer policy of appraising employees of their performance is evidence of a "just cause" contract). In addition, as Conrad's probation and the personnel manual suggest, Spectra Physics provided for progressive discipline prior to termination. *Langeland v. Bronson Methodist Hospital,* 178 Mich.App. 612, 615–616, 444 N.W.2d 146 (1989) (policy of terminating employees only after a graduated series of disciplinary measures contributes to legitimate expectation that employee would be terminated only for cause).

B.

1.

Ordinarily, a purchaser of assets does not assume the liabilities of the selling corporation. However, under Michigan law, a purchaser of assets assumes the selling corporation's liabilities where: (1) there is an express or implied assumption of liability, (2) the transaction amounts to a consolidation or merger, (3) the transaction was fraudulent, (4) some of the elements of a purchase in good faith were lacking, or where the transfer was without consideration and the creditors of the transferor were not provided for, or (5) the transferee corporation was a mere continuation or reincarnation of the old corporation.[1] The issue of whether the purchasing corporation agrees to assume the predecessor corporation's liabilities is a question of fact for the jury. The presence of such an intention depends on the facts and circumstances of each case. 15 Fletcher, *Cyclopedia of Law of Private Corporations* § 7124 (1990 Rev.Vol.).

2.

Here, there is a dispute of material fact as to whether Rofin–Sinar impliedly agreed to assume liability under the alleged "just cause" employment contract between Conrad and Spectra Physics. Kay Cooper, Rofin–Sinar's vice president of human resources, has submitted an affidavit in which she makes the conclusory statement that Rofin–Sinar did not adopt the policies of Spectra Physics. Nevertheless, a reasonable trier of the fact could conclude from the undisputed facts in Part II that Rofin–Sinar impliedly agreed to assume liability under the contract.

The evidence of record shows that the period of transition after the sale of the ILD assets may best be defined as one of continuity in which Rofin–Sinar availed itself of many of Spectra Physics' practices, policies and work force. Rofin–Sinar failed to promulgate new personnel policies, and it never disclaimed liability under "just cause" employment contracts that may have existed. It used Spectra Physics' personnel manual which, as stated *supra*, indicates the existence of a "just cause" contract. When Rofin–Sinar purchased the ILD assets, Conrad remained on probation. The fact that Rofin–Sinar informed Spectra Physics' customers that it "is now" ILD reflects Rofin–Sinar's intention "to assume all benefits and burdens of its predecessor in the continuation of business." It is also significant that the same persons remained employed in upper management with Rofin–Sinar after the asset purchase sale. *General Foam Fabricators,* 695 F.2d at 287 (continued employment of upper management is evidence of successor company's intent to assume liability under a confidentiality agreement). All of these undisputed facts, when considered *in toto,* allow a finder of the facts to reasonably conclude Rofin–Sinar acceded to most, if not all[2], of Spectra Physics personnel practices,

---

1. Conrad says that it does not need to show that Rofin–Sinar assumed liability under the alleged "just cause" employment contract. Instead, it simply argues that a *Toussaint* claim may be asserted against a successor company like Rofin–Sinar. This contention is meritless and is unsupported by case law. A plaintiff's *Toussaint* claim against a successor company will fail unless it falls within one of the five well-recog-nized exceptions to the general rule that a purchaser of assets is not responsible for the debts and liabilities of the selling corporation.

2. Not all of Spectra Physics' personnel policies remained intact after Rofin–Sinar purchased the ILD assets. For instance, on July 1, 1988, Rofin–Sinar enhanced vacation benefits available to its employees.

including honoring any alleged "just cause" employment contracts.[3]
* * *

b. Does a Collective Bargaining Agreement Make a Difference?

CASE STUDY: FROST AND SUNSHINE II

So far we've been considering the impact of the transfer of ownership on Frost's salaried employees. At Frost's 15 retail stores, however, the sales force is paid on an hourly basis. At 10 of these garden centers, sales clerks are represented by the Retail Clerks Union, which signed a three-year collective bargaining agreement with Frost just five months ago. The wages, hours, and terms and conditions of employment at the five non-unionized stores mimic those negotiated by the RCU.

The union's chief goal in the recently concluded negotiations had been job security. The leaders feel they secured strong language, well worth the cost of a slight reduction in hourly rates. The successors clause says: "Successors. This agreement shall be binding on successors and assigns, and no provisions, terms or obligations herein contained shall be affected, modified, altered, or changed in any respect by the sale, transfer, assignment or change of any kind of the ownership or management of the employer."

Even more important, a complicated provision called "Staffing" commits Frost to retain the existing number of full-time sales clerks at each of the ten unionized garden centers. The union considers this clause important because it goes against the trend in retail of hiring very few full-time employees and lots of part-timers who work no more than 30 hours a week.

Is Sunshine, as the new owner of Frost, obligated to honor the terms of the Frost–RCU bargaining agreement? Need Sunshine bargain with the RCU about wages, hours, and terms and conditions of employment at the unionized retail outlets? If there are outstanding claims by employees against Frost, who remedies them—Susan Frost or Sunshine? Assume the new president of Frost believes it makes good business sense to reduce the number of full-time sales clerks. Can Sunshine, following the transfer of ownership, offer Frost's retail clerks the opportunity to keep working but as part-timers at lower wages and without benefits?

---

3. When denying that it agreed to assume liability under the alleged "just cause" contract, Rofin–Sinar relies most heavily on language in the asset purchase agreement that reserves to Rofin–Sinar the right to terminate Spectra–Physics employees and retain them on its own terms. However, this language is ambiguous and it does not explicitly declare any "just cause" contracts null and void. A reasonable trier of the facts may conclude that: (1) the asset purchase agreement merely gave Rofin–Sinar the discretion to avoid any "just cause" contracts, and (2) Rofin–Sinar subsequently elected not to exercise that discretion. Also, there is no evidence of record that this term of the asset purchase agreement was ever communicated to any Spectra Physics employee.

i. Must Sunshine Honor the Terms of the Frost–RCU Bargaining Agreement?

There are two possible bases for holding Sunshine to the terms of the Frost–RCU bargaining agreement. The first is for the union to claim that the law, in this case the National Labor Relations Act, requires Sunshine, as successor to Frost, to carry forward the terms of its predecessor's bargaining agreement. The second is for the union to try to enforce the terms of the predecessor's bargaining agreement through the vehicle of arbitration. In the Supreme Court cases that follow you will see that the first option, imposition of the terms of the bargaining agreement under the NLRA, is a dead letter; the excerpt from the Supreme Court's opinion in *NLRB v. Burns International Security Services* explains why. The second option, enforcement through arbitration, has some life in it, as the Court explains in the excerpt from *John Wiley & Sons, Inc. v. Livingston*. Our question to you concerns the third Supreme Court opinion in this section, *Howard Johnson Co., Inc. v. Detroit Joint Executive Board:* After *Howard Johnson* just how lively is the option of using arbitration to hold a successor employer to the terms of the collective bargaining agreement signed by its predecessor?

a.) Under the NLRA Sunshine has no obligation to carry forward the terms of the bargaining agreement negotiated by the predecessor

NLRB v. BURNS INTERN. SECURITY SERVICES

Supreme Court of the United States, 1972.
406 U.S. 272, 92 S.Ct. 1571, 32 L.Ed.2d 61.

[Wackenhut Corp. had a contract to provide plant protection service for Lockheed Aircraft. The Wackenhut employees were represented by a union that had negotiated a collective bargaining agreement with Wackenhut. Wackenhut lost its plant protection contract with Lockheed and was replaced by Burns. Burns in turn hired a majority of the plant guards who had formerly worked for Wackenhut. The union brought an action under Section 8(a)(5), claiming Burns was obliged to honor the terms and conditions of employment that had prevailed under the union's collective bargaining agreement with Wackenhut.

The Court in *Burns* concluded that because Burns had hired a majority of the guards who worked for Wackenhut and who continued to perform similar services, it was obligated as a successor to recognize the predecessor's union, an issue we deal with later in this section. However, the Court held that Burns was not bound by the terms of the collective bargaining agreement negotiated and signed by Wackenhut.

The following excerpt sets forth the Court's rationale:]

Mr. Justice White.

It does not follow, however, from Burns' duty to bargain that it was bound to observe the substantive terms of the collective-bargaining contract the union had negotiated with Wackenhut and to which Burns had in no way agreed. Section 8(d) of the Act expressly provides that the existence of such bargaining obligation "does not compel either party to agree to a proposal or require the making of a concession." Congress has consistently declined to interfere with free collective bargaining and has preferred that device, or voluntary arbitration, to the imposition of compulsory terms as a means of avoiding or terminating labor disputes. In its report accompanying the 1935 Act, the Senate Committee on Education and Labor stated:

"The committee wishes to dispel any possible false impression that this bill is designed to compel the making of agreements or to permit governmental supervision of their terms. It must be stressed that the duty to bargain collectively does not carry with it the duty to reach an agreement, because the essence of collective bargaining is that either party shall be free to decide whether proposals made to it are satisfactory."

This Court immediately noted this fundamental theme of the legislation: "[The Act] does not compel any agreement whatever.... The theory of the Act is that free opportunity for negotiation with accredited representatives of employees is likely to promote industrial peace and may bring about the adjustments and agreements which the Act in itself does not attempt to compel." *NLRB v. Jones & Laughlin Steel Corp.,* 301 U.S. 1, 45, 57 S.Ct. 615, 628, 81 L.Ed. 893 (1937).

Section 8(d), 29 U.S.C. § 158(d), made this policy an express statutory mandate, and was enacted in 1947 because Congress feared that "the present Board has gone very far, in the guise of determining whether or not employers had bargained in good faith, in setting itself up as the judge of what concessions an employer must make and of the proposals and counterproposals that he may or may not make.... [U]nless Congress writes into the law guides for the Board to follow, the Board may attempt to carry this process still further and seek to control more and more the terms of collective bargaining agreements."

This history was reviewed in detail and given controlling effect in *H.K. Porter Co. v. NLRB,* 397 U.S. 99, 90 S.Ct. 821, 25 L.Ed.2d 146 (1970). There this Court, while agreeing that the employer violated § 8(a)(5) by adamantly refusing to agree to a dues checkoff, intending thereby to frustrate the consummation of any bargaining agreement, held that the Board had erred in ordering the employer to agree to such a provision:

> "[W]hile the Board does have power ... to require employers and employees to negotiate, it is without power to compel a company or a union to agree to any substantive contractual provision of a collective-bargaining agreement." * * *

"It would be anomalous indeed to hold that while § 8(d) prohibits the Board from relying on a refusal to agree as the sole evidence of bad-faith bargaining, the Act permits the Board to compel agreement in that same dispute. The Board's remedial powers under § 10 of the Act are broad, but they are limited to carrying out the policies of the Act itself. One of these fundamental policies is freedom of contract."

These considerations, evident from the explicit language and legislative history of the labor laws, underlay the Board's prior decisions, which until now have consistently held that, although successor employers may be bound to recognize and bargain with the union, they are not bound by the substantive provisions of a collective-bargaining contract negotiated by their predecessors but not agreed to or assumed by them. * * *

The Board, however, has now departed from this view and argues that the same policies that mandate a continuity of bargaining obligation also require that successor employers be bound to the terms of a predecessor's collective-bargaining contract. It asserts that the stability of labor relations will be jeopardized and that employees will face uncertainty and a gap in the bargained-for terms and conditions of employment, as well as the possible loss of advantages gained by prior negotiations, unless the new employer is held to have assumed, as a matter of federal labor law, the obligations under the contract entered into by the former employer. * * * Here there was no merger or sale of assets, and there were no dealings whatsoever between Wackenhut and Burns. On the contrary, they were competitors for the same work, each bidding for the service contract at Lockheed. Burns purchased nothing from Wackenhut and became liable for none of its financial obligations. Burns merely hired enough of Wackenhut's employees to require it to bargain with the union as commanded by § 8(a)(5) and § 9(a). But this consideration is a wholly insufficient basis for implying either in fact or in law that Burns had agreed or must be held to have agreed to honor Wackenhut's collective-bargaining contract.

We agree with the Court of Appeals that the Board failed to heed the admonitions of the *H.K. Porter* case. Preventing industrial strife is an important aim of federal labor legislation, but Congress has not chosen to make the bargaining freedom of employers and unions totally subordinate to this goal. When a bargaining impasse is reached, strikes and lockouts may occur. This bargaining freedom means both that parties need not make any concessions as a result of Government compulsion and that they are free from having contract provisions imposed upon them against their will. Here, Burns had notice of the existence of the Wackenhut collective-bargaining contract, but it did not consent to be bound by it. The source of its duty to bargain with the union is not the collective-bargaining contract but the fact that it voluntarily took over a bargaining unit that was largely intact and that had been certified within the past year. Nothing in its actions, however, indicated that Burns was assuming the obligations of the contract, and "allowing the Board to compel agreement when the parties themselves are unable to agree would violate the fundamental premise on which the Act is based—private bargaining under governmental supervision of the procedure alone, without any official compulsion over the actual terms of the contract."

We also agree with the Court of Appeals that holding either the union or the new employer bound to the substantive terms of an old collective-bargaining contract may result in serious inequities. A potential employer may be willing to take over a moribund business only if he can make changes in corporate structure, composition of the labor force, work location, task assignment, and nature of supervision. Saddling such an employer with the terms and conditions of employment contained in the old collective-bargaining contract may make these changes impossible and may discourage and inhibit the transfer of capital. On the other hand, a union may have made concessions to a small or failing employer that it would be unwilling to make to a large or economically successful firm. The congressional policy manifest in the Act is to enable the parties to negotiate for any protection either deems appropriate, but to allow the balance of bargaining advantage to be set by economic power realities. Strife is bound to occur if the concessions that must be honored do not correspond to the relative economic strength of the parties.

The Board's position would also raise new problems, for the successor employer would be circumscribed in exactly the same way as the predecessor under the collective-bargaining contract. It would seemingly follow that employees of the predecessor would be deemed employees of the successor, dischargeable only in accordance with provisions of the contract and subject to the grievance and arbitration provisions thereof. Burns would not have been free to replace Wackenhut's guards with its own except as the contract permitted. Given the continuity of employment relationship, the pre-existing contract's provisions with respect to wages, seniority rights, vacation privileges, pension and retirement fund benefits, job security provisions, work assignments and the like would devolve on the successor. Nor would the union commit a § 8(b)(3) unfair labor practice if it refused to bargain for a modification of the agreement effective prior to the expiration date of the agreement. A successor employer might also be deemed to have inherited its predecessor's pre-existing contractual obligations to the union that had accrued under past contracts and that had not been discharged when the business was transferred. "[A] successor may well acquire more liabilities as a result of *Burns* than appear on the face of a contract." Finally, a successor will be bound to observe the contract despite good-faith doubts about the union's majority during the time that the contract is a bar to another representation election. For the above reasons, the Board itself has expressed doubts as to the general applicability of its *Burns* rule.

In many cases, of course, successor employers will find it advantageous not only to recognize and bargain with the union but also to observe the pre-existing contract rather than to face uncertainty and turmoil. Also, in a variety of circumstances involving a merger, stock acquisition, reorganization, or assets purchase, the Board might properly find as a matter of fact that the successor had assumed the obligations under the old contract. Such a duty does not, however, ensue as a matter of law from the mere fact than an employer is doing the same work in the same place with the same employees as his predecessor, as the Board had recognized until its decision in the instant case. We accordingly set aside the Board's finding of a § 8(a)(5) unfair labor practice insofar as it rested on a conclusion that Burns was required to but did not honor the collective-bargaining contract executed by Wackenhut. * * *

---

b.) An arbitrator has authority to order Sunshine to carry forward the terms negotiated by the predecessor

JOHN WILEY & SONS, INC. v. LIVINGSTON

Supreme Court of the United States, 1964.
376 U.S. 543, 84 S.Ct. 909, 11 L.Ed.2d 898.

MR. JUSTICE HARLAN.

I.

District 65, Retail, Wholesale and Department Store Union, AFL–CIO, entered into a collective bargaining agreement with Interscience Publishers, Inc., a publishing firm, for a term expiring on January 31, 1962. The agreement did not contain an express provision making it binding on successors of Interscience. On October 2, 1961, Interscience merged with the petitioner, John Wiley & Sons, Inc., another publishing firm, and ceased to do business as a separate entity. There is no suggestion that the merger was not for genuine business reasons.

At the time of the merger Interscience had about 80 employees, of whom 40 were represented by this Union. It had a single plant in New York City, and did an annual business of somewhat over $1,000,000. Wiley was a much larger concern, having separate office and warehouse facilities and about 300 employees, and doing an annual business of more than $9,000,000. None of Wiley's employees was represented by a union.

In discussions before and after the merger, the Union and Interscience (later Wiley) were unable to agree on the effect of the merger on the collective bargaining agreement and on the rights under it of those covered employees hired by Wiley. The Union's position was that despite the merger it continued to represent the covered Interscience employees taken over by Wiley, and that Wiley was obligated to recognize certain rights of such employees which had "vested" under the Interscience bargaining agreement. Such rights, more fully described below, concerned matters typically covered by collective bargaining agreements, such as seniority status, severance pay, etc. The Union contended also that Wiley was required to make certain pension fund payments called for under the Interscience bargaining agreement.

Wiley, though recognizing for purposes of its own pension plan the Interscience service of the former Interscience employees, asserted that the merger terminated the bargaining agreement for all purposes. It refused to recognize the Union as bargaining agent or to accede to the

Union's claims on behalf of Interscience employees. All such employees, except a few who ended their Wiley employment with severance pay and for whom no rights are asserted here, continued in Wiley's employ.

No satisfactory solution having been reached, the Union, one week before the expiration date of the Interscience bargaining agreement, commenced this action to compel arbitration.

II.

The threshold question in this controversy is who shall decide whether the arbitration provisions of the collective bargaining agreement survived the Wiley–Interscience merger, so as to be operative against Wiley. Both parties urge that this question is for the courts. Past cases leave no doubt that this is correct.

* * * The duty to arbitrate being of contractual origin, a compulsory submission to arbitration cannot precede judicial determination that the collective bargaining agreement does in fact create such a duty.

* * * Wiley, objecting to arbitration, argues that it never was a party to the collective bargaining agreement, and that, in any event, the Union lost its status as representative of the former Interscience employees when they were mingled in a larger Wiley unit of employees. The Union argues that Wiley, as successor to Interscience, is bound by the latter's agreement, at least sufficiently to require it to arbitrate. The Union relies on § 90 of the N.Y. Stock Corporation Law, McKinney's Consol.Laws, c. 59, which provides, among other things, that no "claim or demand for any cause" against a constituent corporation shall be extinguished by a consolidation.[2] Alternatively, the Union argues that, apart from § 90, federal law requires that arbitration go forward, lest the policy favoring arbitration frequently be undermined by changes in corporate organization.

Federal law, fashioned "from the policy of our national labor laws," controls. Textile Workers Union of America v. Lincoln Mills, 353 U.S. 448, 456, 77 S.Ct. 912, 918, 1 L.Ed.2d 972. State law may be utilized so far as it is of aid in the development of correct principles or their application in a particular case, but the law which ultimately results is

2. "The rights of creditors of any constituent corporation shall not in any manner be impaired, nor shall any liability or obligation due or to become due, or any claim or demand for any cause existing against any such corporation or against any stockholder thereof be released or impaired by any such consolidation: but such consolidated corporation shall be deemed to have assumed and shall be liable for all liabilities and obligations of each of the corporations consolidated in the same manner as if such consolidated corporation had itself incurred such liabilities or obligations. The stockholders of the respective constituent corporations shall continue subject to all the liabilities, claims and demands existing against them as such, at or before the consolidation; and no action or proceeding then pending before any court or tribunal in which any constituent corporation is a party, or in which any such stockholder is a party, shall abate or be discontinued by reason of such consolidation, but may be prosecuted to final judgment, as though no consolidation had been entered into; or such consolidated corporation may be substituted as a party in place of any constituent corporation, by order of the court in which such action or proceeding may be pending."

federal. We hold that the disappearance by merger of a corporate employer which has entered into a collective bargaining agreement with a union does not automatically terminate all rights of the employees covered by the agreement, and that, in appropriate circumstances, present here, the successor employer may be required to arbitrate with the union under the agreement.

This Court has in the past recognized the central role of arbitration in effectuating national labor policy. Thus, in Warrior & Gulf Navigation Co., supra, 363 U.S. at 578, 80 S.Ct. 1347, 1351, 4 L.Ed.2d 1409, arbitration was described as "the substitute for industrial strife," and as "part and parcel of the collective bargaining process itself." It would derogate from "[t]he federal policy of settling labor disputes by arbitration," United Steelworkers of America v. Enterprise Wheel & Car Corp., 363 U.S. 593, 596, 80 S.Ct. 1358, 1360, 4 L.Ed.2d 1424, if a change in the corporate structure or ownership of a business enterprise had the automatic consequence of removing a duty to arbitrate previously established; this is so as much in cases like the present, where the contracting employer disappears into another by merger, as in those in which one owner replaces another but the business entity remains the same.

Employees, and the union which represents them, ordinarily do not take part in negotiations leading to a change in corporate ownership. The negotiations will ordinarily not concern the well-being of the employees, whose advantage or disadvantage, potentially great, will inevitably be incidental to the main considerations. The objectives of national labor policy, reflected in established principles of federal law, require that the rightful prerogative of owners independently to rearrange their businesses and even eliminate themselves as employers be balanced by some protection to the employees from a sudden change in the employment relationship. The transition from one corporate organization to another will in most cases be eased and industrial strife avoided if employees' claims continue to be resolved by arbitration rather than by "the relative strength ... of the contending forces," Warrior & Gulf, supra, 363 U.S. at 580, 80 S.Ct. at 1352, 4 L.Ed.2d 1409.

The preference of national labor policy for arbitration as a substitute for tests of strength between contending forces could be overcome only if other considerations compellingly so demanded. We find none. While the principles of law governing ordinary contracts would not bind to a contract an unconsenting successor to a contracting party,[6] a collective bargaining agreement is not an ordinary contract. " ... [I]t is a generalized code to govern a myriad of cases which the draftsmen cannot wholly anticipate.... The collective agreement covers the whole employment relationship. It calls into being a new common law—the common law of a particular industry or of a particular plant." Warrior & Gulf, supra, 363 U.S. at 578–579, 80 S.Ct. at 1351, 4 L.Ed.2d 1409 (footnotes

6. But cf. the general rule that in the case of a merger the corporation which survives is liable for the debts and contracts of the one which disappears. 15 Fletcher, Private Corporations (1961 rev. ed.), § 7121.

omitted). Central to the peculiar status and function of a collective bargaining agreement is the fact, dictated both by circumstance, and by the requirements of the National Labor Relations Act, that it is not in any real sense the simple product of a consensual relationship. Therefore, although the duty to arbitrate, as we have said, must be founded on a contract, the impressive policy considerations favoring arbitration are not wholly overborne by the fact that Wiley did not sign the contract being construed. This case cannot readily be assimilated to the category of those in which there is no contract whatever, or none which is reasonably related to the party sought to be obligated. There was a contract, and Interscience, Wiley's predecessor, was party to it. We thus find Wiley's obligation to arbitrate this dispute in the Interscience contract construed in the context of a national labor policy.

We do not hold that in every case in which the ownership or corporate structure of an enterprise is changed the duty to arbitrate survives. As indicated above, there may be cases in which the lack of any substantial continuity of identity in the business enterprise before and after a change would make a duty to arbitrate something imposed from without, not reasonably to be found in the particular bargaining agreement and the acts of the parties involved. * * * Although Wiley was substantially larger than Interscience, relevant similarity and continuity of operation across the change in ownership is adequately evidenced by the wholesale transfer of Interscience employees to the Wiley plant, apparently without difficulty. * * *

---

c.) An intelligent twelve-year-old can avoid the duty to arbitrate whether predecessor obligations survive a transfer of ownership.

HOWARD JOHNSON CO. INC. v. DETROIT JOINT EXECUTIVE BOARD

Supreme Court of the United States, 1974.
417 U.S. 249, 94 S.Ct. 2236, 41 L.Ed.2d 46.

MR. JUSTICE MARSHALL delivered the opinion of the Court.

Once again we are faced with the problem of defining the labor law obligations of a "successor" employer to the employees of its predecessors. In this case, petitioner Howard Johnson Co. is the bona fide purchaser of the assets of a restaurant and motor lodge. Respondent Union was the bargaining representative of the employees of the previous operators, and had successfully concluded collective-bargaining agreements with them. In commencing its operation of the restaurant, Howard Johnson hired only a small fraction of the predecessors' employees. The question presented in this case is whether the Union may compel Howard Johnson to arbitrate, under the arbitration provisions of the collective-bargaining agreements signed by its predecessors, the extent of its obligations under those agreements to the predecessors' employees.

Prior to the sale at issue here, the Grissoms * * * had operated a Howard Johnson's Motor Lodge and an adjacent Howard Johnson's Restaurant in Belleville, Michigan, under franchise agreements with the petitioner. Employees at both the restaurant and motor lodge were represented by the respondent Hotel & Restaurant Employees & Bartenders International Union. The Grissoms had entered into separate collective-bargaining agreements with the Union covering employees at the two establishments. Both agreements contained dispute settlement procedures leading ultimately to arbitration. Both agreements also provided that they would be binding upon the employer's "successors, assigns, purchasers, lessees or transferees."

On June 16, 1972, the Grissoms entered into an agreement with Howard Johnson to sell it all of the personal property used in connection with operation of the restaurant and motor lodge. The Grissoms retained ownership of the real property, leasing both premises to Howard Johnson. Howard Johnson did not agree to assume any of the Grissoms' obligations, except for four specific contracts relating to operation of the restaurant and motor lodge. On June 28, Howard Johnson mailed the Grissoms a letter, which they later acknowledged and confirmed, clarifying that "[i]t was understood and agreed that the Purchaser ... would not recognize and assume any labor agreements between the Sellers ... and any labor organizations," and that it was further agreed that "the Purchaser does not assume any obligations or liabilities of the Sellers resulting from any labor agreements...."

Transfer of operation of the restaurant and motor lodge was set for midnight, July 23, 1972. On July 9, the Grissoms notified all of their employees that their employment would terminate as of that time. The Union was also notified of the termination of the Grissoms' business. On July 11, Howard Johnson advised the Union that it would not recognize the Union or assume any obligations under the existing collective-bargaining agreements.

After reaching agreement with the Grissoms, Howard Johnson began hiring its own work force. It placed advertisements in local newspapers, and posted notices in various places, including the restaurant and motor lodge. It began interviewing prospective employees on July 10, hired its first employees on July 18, and began training them at a Howard Johnson facility in Ann Arbor on July 20. Prior to the sale, the Grissoms had 53 employees. Howard Johnson commenced operations with 45 employees, 33 engaged in the restaurant and 12 in the motor lodge. Of these, only nine of the restaurant employees and none of the motor lodge employees had previously been employed by the Grissoms. None of the supervisory personnel employed by the Grissoms were hired by Howard Johnson.

* * * At a hearing before the District Court on August 7, the Grissoms admitted that they were required to arbitrate in accordance

with the terms of the collective-bargaining agreements they had signed and that an order compelling arbitration should issue. On August 22, the District Court held that Howard Johnson was also required to arbitrate the extent of its obligations to the former Grissom employees. * * * Howard Johnson appealed the order compelling arbitration, but the Court of Appeals affirmed. * * * We reverse.

Both courts below relied heavily on this Court's decision in *John Wiley & Sons v. Livingston.* * * * As *Wiley* was this Court's first experience with the difficult "successorship" question, its holding was properly cautious and narrow:

> "We hold that the disappearance by merger of a corporate employer which has entered into a collective bargaining agreement with a union does not automatically terminate all rights of the employees covered by the agreement, and that, in appropriate circumstances, present here, the successor employer may be required to arbitrate with the union under the agreement."

Mr. Justice Harlan, writing for the Court, emphasized "the central role of arbitration in effectuating national labor policy" and preventing industrial strife, and the need to afford some protection to the interests of the employees during a change of corporate ownership.

The courts below recognized that the reasoning of *Wiley* was to some extent inconsistent with our more recent decision in *NLRB v. Burns International Security Services.* * * *

We find it unnecessary, however, to decide in the circumstances of this case whether there is any irreconcilable conflict between *Wiley* and *Burns.* We believe that even on its own terms, *Wiley* does not support the decision of the courts below. The Court in *Burns* recognized that its decision "turn[ed] to a great extent on the precise facts involved here." The same observation could have been made in *Wiley,* as indeed it could be made in this case. In our development of the federal common law under § 301, we must necessarily proceed cautiously, in the traditional case-by-case approach of the common law. Particularly in light of the difficulty of the successorship question, the myriad factual circumstances and legal contexts in which it can arise, and the absence of congressional guidance as to its resolution, emphasis on the facts of each case as it arises is especially appropriate. The Court was obviously well aware of this in *Wiley,* as its guarded, almost tentative statement of its holding amply demonstrates.

When the focus is placed on the facts of these cases, it becomes apparent that the decision below is an unwarranted extension of *Wiley* beyond any factual context it may have contemplated. Although it is true that both *Wiley* and this case involve § 301 suits to compel arbitration, the similarity ends there. *Wiley* involved a merger, as a result of which the initial employing entity completely disappeared. In contrast, this case involves only a sale of some assets, and the initial employers remain in existence as viable corporate entities, with substantial revenues from the lease of the motor lodge and restaurant to Howard Johnson. Although we have recognized that ordinarily there is no basis for distinguishing among mergers, consolidations, or purchases of assets in the analysis of successorship problems, see *Golden State Bottling Co. v. NLRB,* 414 U.S. 168, 182–183, n. 5, 94 S.Ct. 414, 424, 38 L.Ed.2d 388 (1973), we think these distinctions are relevant here for two reasons. First, the merger in *Wiley* was conducted "against a background of state law that embodied the general rule that in merger situations the surviving corporation is liable for the obligations of the disappearing corporation," which suggests that holding Wiley bound to arbitrate under its predecessor's collective-bargaining agreement may have been fairly within the reasonable expectations of the parties. Second, the disappearance of the original employing entity in the *Wiley* merger meant that unless the union were afforded some remedy against Wiley, it would have no means to enforce the obligations voluntarily undertaken by the merged corporation, to the extent that those obligations vested prior to the merger or to the extent that its promises were intended to survive a change of ownership. Here, in contrast, because the Grissom corporations continue as viable entities with substantial retained assets, the Union does have a realistic remedy to enforce their contractual obligations. Indeed, the Grissoms have agreed to arbitrate the extent of their liability to the Union and their former employees; presumably this arbitration will explore the question whether the Grissoms breached the successorship provisions of their collective-bargaining agreements, and what the remedy for this breach might be.[3]

Even more important, in *Wiley* the surviving corporation hired *all* of the employees of the disappearing corporation. Although, under *Burns,* the surviving corporation may have been entitled to make substantial changes in its operation of the enterprise, the plain fact is that it did not. As the arbitrator in *Wiley* subsequently stated:

> "Although the Wiley merger was effective on October 2, 1961, the former Interscience employees continued to perform the same work on the same products under the same management at the same work place as before the change in the corporate employer." Interscience Encyclopedia, Inc., 55 Lab.Arb. 210, 218 (1970).

The claims which the union sought to compel Wiley to arbitrate were thus the claims of Wiley's employees as to the benefits they were entitled to receive in connection with their employment. It was on this basis that the Court in *Wiley* found that there was the "substantial continuity of identity in the business enterprise," which it held necessary before the successor employer could be compelled to arbitrate.

---

3. The Union apparently did not explore another remedy which might have been available to it prior to the sale, i.e., moving to enjoin the sale to Howard Johnson on the ground that this was a breach by the Grissoms of the successorship clauses in the collective-bargaining agreements. The mere existence of the successorship clauses in the bargaining agreements between the Union and the Grissoms, however, cannot bind Howard Johnson either to the substantive terms of the agreements or to the arbitration clauses thereof, absent the continuity required by *Wiley,* when it is perfectly clear the Company refused to assume any obligations under the agreements.

Here, however, Howard Johnson decided to select and hire its own independent work force to commence its operation of the restaurant and motor lodge.[5] It therefore hired only nine of the 53 former Grissom employees and none of the Grissom supervisors. The primary purpose of the Union in seeking arbitration here with Howard Johnson is not to protect the rights of Howard Johnson's employees; rather, the Union primarily seeks arbitration on behalf of the former Grissom employees who were *not* hired by Howard Johnson. It is the Union's position that Howard Johnson was bound by the pre-existing collective-bargaining agreement to employ all of these former Grissom employees, except those who could be dismissed in accordance with the "just cause" provision or laid off in accordance with the seniority provision. It is manifest from the Union's efforts to obtain injunctive relief requiring the Company to hire all of these employees that this is the heart of the controversy here. Indeed, at oral argument, the Union conceded that it would be making the same argument here if Howard Johnson had not hired any of the former Grissom employees, and that what was most important to the Union was the prospect that the arbitrator might order the Company to hire all of these employees.

What the Union seeks here is completely at odds with the basic principles this Court elaborated in *Burns.* We found there that nothing in the federal labor laws "requires that an employer ... who purchases the assets of a business be obligated to hire all of the employees of the predecessor though it is possible that such an obligation might be assumed by the employer." *Burns* emphasized that "[a] potential employer may be willing to take over a moribund business only if he can make changes in corporate structure, composition of the labor force, ... and nature of supervision." We rejected the Board's position in part because "[i]t would seemingly follow that employees of the predecessor would be deemed employees of the successor, dischargeable only in accordance with provisions of the contract and subject to the grievance and arbitration provisions thereof. Burns would not have been free to replace Wackenhut's guards with its own except as the contract permitted." Clearly, *Burns* establishes that Howard Johnson had the right not to hire any of the former Grissom employees, if it so desired.[8] The

5. It is important to emphasize that this is not a case where the successor corporation is the "alter ego" of the predecessor, where it is "merely a disguised continuance of the old employer." Such cases involve a mere technical change in the structure or identity of the employing entity, frequently to avoid the effect of the labor laws, without any substantial change in its ownership or management. In these circumstances, the courts have had little difficulty holding that the successor is in reality the same employer and is subject to all the legal and contractual obligations of the predecessor.

There is not the slightest suggestion in this case that the sale of the restaurant and motor lodge by the Grissoms to Howard Johnson was in any sense a paper transaction without meaningful impact on the ownership or operation of the enterprise. * * *

8. Of course, it is an unfair labor practice for an employer to discriminate in hiring or retention of employees on the basis of union membership or activity under § 8(a)(3) of the National Labor Relations Act. Thus, a new owner could not refuse to hire the employees of his predecessor solely because they were union members or to avoid having to recognize the union. There is no suggestion in this case that Howard Johnson in any way discriminated in its

Union's effort to circumvent this holding by asserting its claims in a § 301 suit to compel arbitration rather than in an unfair labor practice context cannot be permitted.

We do not believe that *Wiley* requires a successor employer to arbitrate in the circumstances of this case.[9] The Court there held that arbitration could not be compelled unless there was "substantial continuity of identity in the business enterprise" before and after a change of ownership, for otherwise the duty to arbitrate would be "something imposed from without, not reasonably to be found in the particular bargaining agreement and the acts of the parties involved." This continuity of identity in the business enterprise necessarily includes, we think, a substantial continuity in the identity of the work force across the change in ownership. The *Wiley* Court seemingly recognized this, as it found the requisite continuity present there in reliance on the "wholesale transfer" of Interscience employees to Wiley. This view is reflected in the emphasis most of the lower courts have placed on whether the successor employer hires a majority of the predecessor's employees in determining the legal obligations of the successor in § 301 suits under *Wiley*. This interpretation of *Wiley* is consistent also with the Court's concern with affording protection to those employees who are in fact retained in "[t]he transition from one corporate organization to another" from sudden changes in the terms and conditions of their employment, and with its belief that industrial strife would be avoided if these employees' claims were resolved by arbitration rather than by " 'the relative strength ... of the contending forces.' " At the same time, it recognizes that the employees of the terminating employer have no legal right to continued employment with the new employer, and avoids the difficulties inherent in the Union's position in this case. This holding is compelled, in our view, if the protection afforded employee interests in a change of ownership by *Wiley* is to be reconciled with the new employer's right to operate the enterprise with his own independent labor force.

Since there was plainly no substantial continuity of identity in the work force hired by Howard Johnson with that of the Grissoms, and no express or implied assumption of the agreement to arbitrate, the courts

hiring against the former Grissom employees because of their union membership, activity, or representation.

9. * * * The question whether Howard Johnson is a "successor" is simply not meaningful in the abstract. Howard Johnson is of course a successor employer in the sense that it succeeded to operation of a restaurant and motor lodge formerly operated by the Grissoms. But the real question in each of these "successorship" cases is, on the particular facts, what are the legal obligations of the new employer to the employees of the former owner or their representative? The answer to this inquiry requires analysis of the interests of the new employer and the employees and of the policies of the labor laws in light of the facts of each

case and the particular legal obligation which is at issue, whether it be the duty to recognize and bargain with the union, the duty to remedy unfair labor practices, the duty to arbitrate, etc. There is, and can be, no single definition of "successor" which is applicable in every legal context. A new employer, in other words, may be a successor for some purposes and not for others.

Thus, our holding today is that Howard Johnson was not required to arbitrate with the Union representing the former Grissom employees in the circumstances of this case. We necessarily do not decide whether Howard Johnson is or is not a "successor employer" for any other purpose.

below erred in compelling the Company to arbitrate the extent of its obligations to the former Grissom employees. Accordingly, the judgment of the Court of Appeals must be reversed.

Mr. Justice Douglas, dissented.

Questions

1. Assume that Frost gives notices of termination to all employees, effective midnight of the day before Sunshine takes over. Sunshine intends to operate the Frost businesses with no interruption and takes out an ad in local newspapers that it is hiring. Frost's employees apply for the jobs. Sunshine hires one-fourth of the Frost workforce, telling the remaining three-fourths of Frost's employees that Sunshine has established a cap on the percentage of Frost employees who will be hired. Do the former Frost employees who no longer have jobs have any legal recourse?

2. Sunshine wants to restructure operations by replacing most full-time clerks with a part-time sales force. Will this change in operations sufficiently destroy continuity of operations so that an arbitrator will not order continuation of significant terms of the collective bargaining agreement? If not, what additional measures should Susan Frost or Sunshine take?

ii. Must Sunshine Bargain with the RCU?

Let's assume that Sunshine has no continuing obligation to follow the terms of the Frost–RCU collective bargaining agreement. Can Sunshine unilaterally change most full-time positions to part-time ones? Must the company bargain with the union about the proposed wages, hours, and terms and conditions of employment? If the company wants to retain the Frost workforce, may it nonetheless offer them part-time jobs at reduced hourly wages and with no benefits?

FALL RIVER DYEING & FINISHING CORP. v. NLRB

Supreme Court of the United States, 1987.
482 U.S. 27, 107 S.Ct. 2225, 96 L.Ed.2d 22.

Justice Blackmun delivered the opinion of the Court.*

I

For over 30 years before 1982, Sterlingwale operated a textile dyeing and finishing plant in Fall River, Mass. Its business consisted basically of two types of dyeing, called, respectively, "converting" and "commission." Under the converting process, which in 1981 accounted for 60% to 70% of its business, Sterlingwale bought unfinished fabrics for its own account, dyed and finished them, and then sold them to apparel manufacturers. In commission dyeing, which accounted for the remainder of

* Justice White joins only Parts I and III
of this opinion.

its business, Sterlingwale dyed and finished fabrics owned by customers according to their specifications. The financing and marketing aspects of converting and commission dyeing are different. Converting requires capital to purchase fabrics and a sales force to promote the finished products. The production process, however, is the same for both converting and commission dyeing.

In the late 1970's the textile-dyeing business, including Sterlingwale's, began to suffer from adverse economic conditions and foreign competition. After 1979, business at Sterlingwale took a serious turn for the worse because of the loss of its export market, and the company reduced the number of its employees. Finally, in February 1982, Sterlingwale laid off all its production employees, primarily because it no longer had the capital to continue the converting business. It retained a skeleton crew of workers and supervisors to ship out the goods remaining on order and to maintain the corporation's building and machinery. In the months following the layoff, Leonard Ansin, Sterlingwale's president, liquidated the inventory of the corporation and, at the same time, looked for a business partner with whom he could "resurrect the business." Ansin felt that he owed it to the community and to the employees to keep Sterlingwale in operation.

For almost as long as Sterlingwale had been in existence, its production and maintenance employees had been represented by the United Textile Workers of America, AFL–CIO, Local 292 (Union). The most recent collective-bargaining agreement before Sterlingwale's demise had been negotiated in 1978 and was due to expire in 1981. By an agreement dated October 1980, however, in response to the financial difficulties suffered by Sterlingwale, the Union agreed to amend the 1978 agreement to extend its expiration date by one year, until April 1, 1982, without any wage increase and with an agreement to improve labor productivity. In the months following the final February 1982 layoff, the Union met with company officials over problems involving this job action, and, in particular, Sterlingwale's failure to pay premiums on group-health insurance. In addition, during meetings with Ansin, Union officials told him of their concern with Sterlingwale's future and their interest in helping to keep the company operating or in meeting with prospective buyers.

In late summer 1982, however, Sterlingwale finally went out of business. It made an assignment for the benefit of its creditors, primarily Ansin's mother, who was an officer of the corporation and holder of a first mortgage on most of Sterlingwale's real property, and the Massachusetts Capital Resource Corporation (MCRC), which held a security interest on Sterlingwale's machinery and equipment. Ansin also hired a professional liquidator to dispose of the company's remaining assets, mostly its inventory, at auction.

During this same period, a former Sterlingwale employee and officer, Herbert Chace, and Arthur Friedman, president of one of Sterlingwale's major customers, Marcamy Sales Corporation (Marcamy), formed petitioner Fall River Dyeing & Finishing Corp. Chace, who had resigned from Sterlingwale in February 1982, had worked there for 27 years, had been vice president in charge of sales at the time of his departure, and had participated in collective bargaining with the Union during his tenure at Sterlingwale. Chace and Friedman formed petitioner with the intention of engaging strictly in the commission-dyeing business and of taking advantage of the availability of Sterlingwale's assets and work-force. Accordingly, Friedman had Marcamy acquire from MCRC and Ansin's mother Sterlingwale's plant, real property, and equipment, and convey them to petitioner. Petitioner also obtained some of Sterling-wale's remaining inventory at the liquidator's auction. Chace became petitioner's vice president in charge of operations and Friedman became its president.

In September 1982, petitioner began operating out of Sterlingwale's former facilities and began hiring employees. It advertised for workers and supervisors in a local newspaper, and Chace personally got in touch with several prospective supervisors. Petitioner hired 12 supervisors, of whom 8 had been supervisors with Sterlingwale and 3 had been produc-tion employees there. In its hiring decisions for production employees, petitioner took into consideration recommendations from these supervi-sors and a prospective employee's former employment with Sterlingwale. Petitioner's initial hiring goal was to attain one full shift of workers, which meant from 55 to 60 employees. Petitioner planned to "see how business would be" after this initial goal had been met and, if business permitted, to expand to two shifts. The employees who were hired first spent approximately four to six weeks in start-up operations and an additional month in experimental production.

By letter dated October 19, 1982, the Union requested petitioner to recognize it as the bargaining agent for petitioner's employees and to begin collective bargaining. Petitioner refused the request, stating that, in its view, the request had "no legal basis." At that time, 18 of petitioner's 21 employees were former employees of Sterlingwale. By November of that year, petitioner had employees in a complete range of jobs, had its production process in operation, and was handling customer orders; by mid-January 1983, it had attained its initial goal of one shift of workers. Of the 55 workers in this initial shift, a number that represented over half the workers petitioner would eventually hire, 36 were former Sterlingwale employees. Petitioner continued to expand its workforce, and by mid-April 1983 it had reached two full shifts. For the first time, ex-Sterlingwale employees were in the minority but just barely so (52 or 53 out of 107 employees).

Although petitioner engaged exclusively in commission dyeing, the employees experienced the same conditions they had when they were working for Sterlingwale. The production process was unchanged and the employees worked on the same machines, in the same building, with the same job classifications, under virtually the same supervisors. Over half the volume of petitioner's business came from former Sterlingwale customers, and, in particular, Marcamy.

On November 1, 1982, the Union filed an unfair labor practice charge with the Board, alleging that in its refusal to bargain petitioner had violated §§ 8(a)(1) and (5) of the National Labor Relations Act (NLRA). * * *

II

Fifteen years ago in *NLRB v. Burns International Security Services, Inc.,* 406 U.S. 272, 92 S.Ct. 1571, 32 L.Ed.2d 61 (1972), this Court first dealt with the issue of a successor employer's obligation to bargain with a union that had represented the employees of its predecessor. In *Burns,* about four months before the employer transition, the security-guard employees of Wackenhut Corp. had chosen a particular union as their bargaining representative and that union had negotiated a collective-bargaining agreement with Wackenhut. Wackenhut, however, lost its service contract on certain airport property to Burns. Burns proceeded to hire 27 of the Wackenhut guards for its 42–guard operation at the airport. Burns told its guards that, as a condition of their employment, they must join the union with which Burns already had collective-bargaining agreements at other locations. When the union that had represented the Wackenhut employees brought unfair labor practice charges against Burns, this Court agreed with the Board's determination that Burns had an obligation to bargain with this union. We observed:

> "In an election held but a few months before, the union had been designated bargaining agent for the employees in the unit and a majority of these employees had been hired by Burns for work in the identical unit. It is undisputed that Burns knew all the relevant facts in this regard and was aware of the certification and of the existence of a collective-bargaining contract. In these circumstances, it was not unreasonable for the Board to conclude that the union certified to represent all employees in the unit still represented a majority of the employees and that Burns could not reasonably have entertained a good-faith doubt about that fact. Burns' obligation to bargain with the union over terms and conditions of employment stemmed from its hiring of Wackenhut's employees and from the recent election and Board certification."

Although our reasoning in *Burns* was tied to the facts presented there, we suggested that our analysis would be equally applicable even if a union with which a successor had to bargain had not been certified just before the transition in employers. We cited with approval Board and Court of Appeals decisions where it "ha[d] been consistently held that a mere change of employers or of ownership in the employing industry is not such an unusual circumstance' as to affect the force of the Board's certification within the normal operative period if a majority of employees after the change of ownership or management were employed by the preceding employer." Several of these cases involved successorship situations where the union in question had not been certified only a short time before the transition date.

Moreover, in defining "the force of the Board's certification within the normal operative period," we referred in *Burns* to two presumptions regarding a union's majority status following certification. First, after a union has been certified by the Board as a bargaining-unit representative, it usually is entitled to a conclusive presumption of majority status for one year following the certification. Second, after this period, the union is entitled to a rebuttable presumption of majority support.

These presumptions are based not so much on an absolute certainty that the union's majority status will not erode following certification, as on a particular policy decision. The overriding policy of the NLRA is "industrial peace." The presumptions of majority support further this policy by "promot[ing] stability in collective-bargaining relationships, without impairing the free choice of employees." In essence, they enable a union to concentrate on obtaining and fairly administering a collective-bargaining agreement without worrying that, unless it produces immediate results, it will lose majority support and will be decertified. The presumptions also remove any temptation on the part of the employer to avoid good-faith bargaining in the hope that, by delaying, it will undermine the union's support among the employees. The upshot of the presumptions is to permit unions to develop stable bargaining relationships with employers, which will enable the unions to pursue the goals of their members, and this pursuit, in turn, will further industrial peace.

The rationale behind the presumptions is particularly pertinent in the successorship situation and so it is understandable that the Court in *Burns* referred to them. During a transition between employers, a union is in a peculiarly vulnerable position. It has no formal and established bargaining relationship with the new employer, is uncertain about the new employer's plans, and cannot be sure if or when the new employer must bargain with it. While being concerned with the future of its members with the new employer, the union also must protect whatever rights still exist for its members under the collective-bargaining agreement with the predecessor employer. Accordingly, during this unsettling transition period, the union needs the presumptions of majority status to which it is entitled to safeguard its members' rights and to develop a relationship with the successor.

The position of the employees also supports the application of the presumptions in the successorship situation. If the employees find themselves in a new enterprise that substantially resembles the old, but without their chosen bargaining representative, they may well feel that their choice of a union is subject to the vagaries of an enterprise's transformation. This feeling is not conducive to industrial peace. In addition, after being hired by a new company following a layoff from the old, employees initially will be concerned primarily with maintaining their new jobs. In fact, they might be inclined to shun support for their former union, especially if they believe that such support will jeopardize their jobs with the successor or if they are inclined to blame the union for their layoff and problems associated with it. Without the presumptions of majority support and with the wide variety of corporate transformations possible, an employer could use a successor enterprise as a way of getting rid of a labor contract and of exploiting the employees' hesitant attitude towards the union to eliminate its continuing presence.

In addition to recognizing the traditional presumptions of union majority status, however, the Court in *Burns* was careful to safeguard " 'the rightful prerogative of owners independently to rearrange their businesses.' " We observed in *Burns* that, although the successor has an obligation to bargain with the union, it "is ordinarily free to set initial terms on which it will hire the employees of a predecessor," and it is not bound by the substantive provisions of the predecessor's collective-bargaining agreement. We further explained that the successor is under no obligation to hire the employees of its predecessor, subject, of course, to the restriction that it not discriminate against union employees in its hiring. Thus, to a substantial extent the applicability of *Burns* rests in the hands of the successor. If the new employer makes a conscious decision to maintain generally the same business and to hire a majority of its employees from the predecessor, then the bargaining obligation of § 8(a)(5) is activated. This makes sense when one considers that the employer *intends* to take advantage of the trained workforce of its predecessor.

Accordingly, in *Burns* we acknowledged the interest of the successor in its freedom to structure its business and the interest of the employees in continued representation by the union. We now hold that a successor's obligation to bargain is not limited to a situation where the union in question has been recently certified. Where, as here, the union has a rebuttable presumption of majority status, this status continues despite the change in employers. And the new employer has an obligation to bargain with that union so long as the new employer is in fact a successor of the old employer and the majority of its employees were employed by its predecessor.

III

We turn now to the three rules, as well as to their application to the facts of this case, that the Board has adopted for the successorship situation. The Board, of course, is given considerable authority to interpret the provisions of the NLRA. If the Board adopts a rule that is rational and consistent with the Act, then the rule is entitled to deference from the courts. Moreover, if the Board's application of such a rational rule is supported by substantial evidence on the record, courts should enforce the Board's order. These principles also guide our review of the Board's action in a successorship case.

A

In *Burns* we approved the approach taken by the Board and accepted by courts with respect to determining whether a new company was indeed the successor to the old. This approach, which is primarily factual in nature and is based upon the totality of the circumstances of a given situation, requires that the Board focus on whether the new company has "acquired substantial assets of its predecessor and continued, without interruption or substantial change, the predecessor's business operations." Hence, the focus is on whether there is "substantial continuity" between the enterprises. Under this approach, the Board examines a number of factors: whether the business of both employers is essentially the same; whether the employees of the new company are doing the same jobs in the same working conditions under the same supervisors; and whether the new entity has the same production process, produces the same products, and basically has the same body of customers.

In conducting the analysis, the Board keeps in mind the question whether "those employees who have been retained will understandably view their job situations as essentially unaltered." This emphasis on the employees' perspective furthers the Act's policy of industrial peace. If the employees find themselves in essentially the same jobs after the employer transition and if their legitimate expectations in continued representation by their union are thwarted, their dissatisfaction may lead to labor unrest.

Although petitioner does not challenge the Board's "substantial continuity" approach, it does contest the application of the rule to the facts of this case. * * * [W]e find that the Board's determination that there was "substantial continuity" between Sterlingwale and petitioner and that petitioner was Sterlingwale's successor is supported by substantial evidence in the record. Petitioner acquired most of Sterlingwale's real property, its machinery and equipment, and much of its inventory and materials.[10] It introduced no new product line. Of particular significance is the fact that, from the perspective of the employees, their jobs did not change. Although petitioner abandoned converting dyeing in exclusive favor of commission dyeing, this change did not alter the essential nature of the employees' jobs, because both types of dyeing involved the same production process. The job classifications of petitioner were the same as those of Sterlingwale; petitioners' employees worked on the same machines under the direction of supervisors most of whom were former supervisors of Sterlingwale. The record, in fact, is clear that petitioner acquired Sterlingwale's assets with the express purpose of taking advantage of its predecessor's workforce.

We do not find determinative of the successorship question the fact that there was a 7–month hiatus between Sterlingwale's demise and petitioner's start-up. Petitioner argues that this hiatus, coupled with the fact that its employees were hired through newspaper advertisements— not through Sterlingwale employment records, which were not transferred to it—resolves in its favor the "substantial continuity" question. Yet such a hiatus is only one factor in the "substantial continuity"

---

10. Petitioner makes much of the fact that it purchased the assets of Sterlingwale on the "open market." Petitioner, however, overlooks the fact that it was formed with the express purpose of acquiring Sterlingwale's assets, a purpose it accomplished by having its parent company acquire some of Sterlingwale's major assets and then transferring them to petitioner. So long as there are other indicia of "substantial continuity," the way in which a successor obtains the predecessor's assets is generally not determinative of the "substantial continuity" question.

calculus and thus is relevant only when there are other indicia of discontinuity. Conversely, if other factors indicate a continuity between the enterprises, and the hiatus is a normal start-up period, the "totality of the circumstances" will suggest that these circumstances present a successorship situation.

For the reasons given above, this is a case where the other factors suggest "substantial continuity" between the companies despite the 7–month hiatus. Here, moreover, the extent of the hiatus between the demise of Sterlingwale and the start-up of petitioner is somewhat less than certain. After the February layoff, Sterlingwale retained a skeleton crew of supervisors and employees that continued to ship goods to customers and to maintain the plant. In addition, until the assignment for the benefit of the creditors late in the summer, Ansin was seeking to resurrect the business or to find a buyer for Sterlingwale. The Union was aware of these efforts. Viewed from the employees' perspective, therefore, the hiatus may have been much less than seven months. Although petitioner hired the employees through advertisements, it often relied on recommendations from supervisors, themselves formerly employed by Sterlingwale, and intended the advertisements to reach the former Sterlingwale workforce.[11]

Accordingly, we hold that, under settled law, petitioner was a successor to Sterlingwale. We thus must consider if and when petitioner's duty to bargain arose.

B

In *Burns,* the Court determined that the successor had an obligation to bargain with the union because a majority of its employees had been employed by Wackenhut. The "triggering" fact for the bargaining obligation was this composition of the successor's workforce.[12] The Court, however, did not have to consider the question *when* the successor's obligation to bargain arose: Wackenhut's contract expired on June 30 and Burns began its services with a majority of former Wackenhut

---

11. Similarly, in light of the general continuity between Sterlingwale and petitioner from the perspective of the employees, we do not find determinative the differences between the two enterprises cited by petitioner. Petitioner's change in marketing and sales appears to have had no effect on the employer-employee relationship. That petitioner did not assume Sterlingwale's liabilities or trade name also is not sufficient to outweigh the other factors. Moreover, the mere reduction in petitioner's size, in comparison to that of Sterlingwale does not change the nature of the company so as to defeat the employees' expectations in continued representation by their union.

12. After *Burns,* there was some initial confusion concerning this Court's holding. It was unclear if workforce continuity would turn on whether a majority of the successor's employees were those of the predecessor or on whether the successor had hired a majority of the predecessor's employees. Compare 406 U.S., at 281, 92 S.Ct., at 1579 ("a majority of the employees hired by the new employer are represented by a recently certified bargaining agent"), with id., at 278, 92 S.Ct., at 1577 ("the union had been designated bargaining agent for the employees in the unit and a majority of these employees had been hired by Burns"). See also Howard Johnson Co. v. Hotel Employees, 417 U.S., at 263, 94 S.Ct., at 2244 ("successor employer hires a majority of the predecessor's employees"); Golden State Bottling Co. v. NLRB, 414 U.S., at 184, n. 6, 94 S.Ct., at 425, n. 6 (same). The Board, with the approval of the Courts of Appeals, has adopted the former interpretation. This issue is not presented by the instant case.

guards on July 1. In other situations, as in the present case, there is a start-up period by the new employer while it gradually builds its operations and hires employees. In these situations, the Board, with the approval of the Courts of Appeals, has adopted the "substantial and representative complement" rule for fixing the moment when the determination as to the composition of the successor's workforce is to be made. If, at this particular moment, a majority of the successor's employees had been employed by its predecessor, then the successor has an obligation to bargain with the union that represented these employees. * * *

Petitioner contends that the Board's representative complement rule is unreasonable, given that it injures the representation rights of many of the successor's employees and that it places significant burdens upon the successor, which is unsure whether and when the bargaining obligation will arise. According to petitioner, if majority status is determined at the "full complement" stage, all the employees will have a voice in the selection of their bargaining representative, and this will reveal if the union truly has the support of most of the successor's employees. This approach, however, focuses only on the interest in having a bargaining representative selected by the majority of the employees. It fails to take into account the significant interest of employees in being represented as soon as possible. The latter interest is especially heightened in a situation where many of the successor's employees, who were formerly represented by a union, find themselves after the employer transition in essentially the same enterprise, but without their bargaining representative. Having the new employer refuse to bargain with the chosen representative of these employees "disrupts the employees' morale, deters their organizational activities, and discourages their membership in unions." Accordingly, petitioner's "full complement" proposal must fail.

* * * The Court of Appeals observed that by mid-January petitioner "had hired employees in virtually all job classifications, had hired at least fifty percent of those it would ultimately employ in the majority of those classifications, and it employed a majority of the employees it would eventually employ when it reached full complement." At that time petitioner had begun normal production. Although petitioner intended to expand to two shifts, and, in fact, reached this goal by mid-April, that expansion was contingent expressly upon the growth of the business. Accordingly, as found by the Board and approved by the Court of Appeals, mid-January was the period when petitioner reached its "substantial and representative complement." Because at that time the majority of petitioner's employees were former Sterlingwale employees, petitioner had an obligation to bargain with the Union then.

C

We also hold that the Board's "continuing demand" rule is reasonable in the successorship situation. The successor's duty to bargain at the "substantial and representative complement" date is triggered only when the union has made a bargaining demand. Under the "continuing demand" rule, when a union has made a premature demand that has been rejected by the employer, this demand remains in force until the moment when the employer attains the "substantial and representative complement." * * *

JUSTICE POWELL, with whom THE CHIEF JUSTICE and JUSTICE O'CONNOR join, dissenting.

[A] decision by the NLRB that one company is a successor of another is entitled to deference, and its conclusions will be upheld if they are based on substantial record evidence. The critical question in determining successorship is whether there is "substantial continuity" between the two businesses. Here the Board concluded that there was sufficient continuity between petitioner and Sterlingwale, primarily because the workers did the same finishing work on the same equipment for petitioner as they had for their former employer. In reaching this conclusion, however, the Board, and now the Court, give virtually no weight to the evidence of *dis*continuity, that I think is overwhelming.

In this case the undisputed evidence shows that petitioner is a completely separate entity from Sterlingwale. There was a clear break between the time Sterlingwale ceased normal business operations in February 1982 and when petitioner came into existence at the end of August. In addition, it is apparent that there was no direct contractual or other business relationship between petitioner and Sterlingwale. Although petitioner bought some of Sterlingwale's inventory, it did so by outbidding several other buyers on the open market. Also, the purchases at the public sale involved only tangible assets. Petitioner did not buy Sterlingwale's trade name or good will, nor did it assume any of its liabilities. And while over half of petitioner's business (measured in dollars) came from former Sterlingwale customers, apparently this was due to the new company's skill in marketing its services. There was no sale or transfer of customer lists, and given the 9-month interval between the time that Sterlingwale ended production and petitioner commenced its operations in November, the natural conclusion is that the new business attracted customers through its own efforts. No other explanation was offered. * * *

The Court nevertheless is unpersuaded. It views these distinctions as not directly affecting the employees' expectations about their job status or the status of the union as their representative, even though the CBA with the defunct corporation had long since expired. Yet even from the employees' perspective, there was little objective evidence that the jobs with petitioner were simply a continuation of those at Sterlingwale. When all of the production employees were laid off indefinitely in February 1982, there could have been little hope—and certainly no reasonable expectation—that Sterlingwale would ever reopen. Nor was it reasonable for the employees to expect that Sterlingwale's failed textile operations would be resumed by a corporation not then in existence. The CBA had expired in April with no serious effort to renegotiate it, and with several of the employees' benefits left unpaid. The possibility of further employment with Sterlingwale then disappeared entirely in August 1982 when the company liquidated its remaining assets. Cf. *Textile Workers Union v. Darlington Manufacturing Co.*, 380 U.S. 263, 274, 85 S.Ct. 994, 1002, 13 L.Ed.2d 827 (1965) (the "closing of an entire business . . . ends the employer-employee relationship"). After petitioner was organized, it advertised for workers in the newspaper, a move that hardly could have suggested to the old workers that they would be reinstated to their former positions. The sum of these facts inevitably would have had a negative "effect on the employees' expectations of rehire." The former employees engaged by petitioner found that the new plant was smaller, and that there would be fewer workers, fewer shifts, and more hours per shift than at their prior job. Moreover, as petitioner did not acquire Sterlingwale's personnel records, the benefits of having a favorable work record presumably were lost to these employees.

In deferring to the NLRB's decision, the Court today extends the successorship doctrine in a manner that could not have been anticipated by either the employer or the employees. I would hold that the successorship doctrine has no application when the break in continuity between enterprises is as complete and extensive as it was here.

II

Even if the evidence of genuine continuity were substantial, I could not agree with the Court's decision. As we have noted in the past, if the presumption of majority support for a union is to survive a change in ownership, it must be shown that there is both a continuity of conditions *and* a continuity of work force. *Howard Johnson Co. v. Hotel Employees.* This means that unless a majority of the new company's workers had been employed by the former company, there is no justification for assuming that the new employees wish to be represented by the former union, or by any union at all. Indeed, the rule hardly could be otherwise. It would be contrary to the basic principles of the NLRA simply to presume in these cases that a majority of workers supports a union when more than half of them have never been members, and when there has been no election. * * *

As the Court notes, the substantial complement rule reflects the need to balance "the objective of insuring maximum employee participation in the selection of a bargaining agent against the goal of permitting employees to be represented as quickly as possible." The decision today "balances" these interests by over-protecting the latter and ignoring the former. In an effort to ensure that some employees will not be deprived of representation for even a short time, the Court requires petitioner to recognize a union that has never been elected or accepted by a majority of its workers. For the reasons stated, I think that the Court's decision is unfair both to petitioner, who hardly could have anticipated the date chosen by the Board, and to most of petitioner's employees, who were denied the opportunity to choose their union. I dissent.

---

c. *Perspectives*

JOIN THE DISCUSSION * * *

Eileen's class is talking about the interplay between legal regulation and control through the market when ownership changes. At various points, noted as * * *, you are invited to join the discussion.

> *Eileen:* I wonder if the class thinks the Court reached the right result in the successor cases under the NLRA? There's a pretty heavy emphasis on protecting capital mobility. First, *Burns* assumes capital mobility would be inhibited if successor employers are subject to the terms and conditions negotiated by the predecessors. Then *Howard Johnson* and *Fall River Dyeing* emphasize the concern for capital mobility by making it so easy for an employer to tailor the facts to avoid successor designation and obligations.

> *Vivian:* There's something peculiar about this. In *Campbell v. Potash Corp.* we saw the court enforcing "golden parachutes" which require acquiring companies to take care of executives who lose their jobs, to the tune of two or three years' salary plus stock options, incentive bonuses, benefits, etc. This must have some deterrent effect on capital mobility and transfers of ownership; at the very least, it reduces the purchase price and opens up the possibility of litigation by disgruntled shareholders. How come a device for protecting executives is binding on the acquiring company, while a collective bargaining agreement, which protects the ordinary worker, is not? Is it simply the difference between gold and tin?

> *Eileen:* Good point. Can anyone explain why costly executive parachutes are viewed as a routine cost of doing business while carrying forward the terms of bargaining agreements is considered a drag on the economy?

> *Herb:* Easy. Golden parachutes get rid of unwanted executives. They open up opportunities for innovation and fresh managerial perspectives. They accomplish the same thing as the rule against involuntary assumption of bargaining agreements.

> *Vivian:* But that's not fair to the ordinary worker who gets shunted aside without any compensation.

> *Herb: Howard Johnson* takes care of that. Look at footnote 3 where Justice Marshall observes that the union could have petitioned for an injunction against the Grissoms for breaching the successors clause. We know it's bloody unlikely that a court will

actually enjoin a sale, but the threat of delay gives the union leverage to negotiate serious severance benefits for the discarded employees. How the Grissoms and Howard Johnson allocate the burden of paying for this settlement is between them.

Eileen: Herb has, I guess, restated the question. Why is the workers' interest in job security subordinated to the "rightful prerogatives of employers to rearrange their businesses?"

* * *

Eileen: Is there any other way the Court could have approached the successorship issue so as to accommodate the interests of both capital and labor?

Yvette: I think the Court was so captured by the rhetoric of capital mobility that it mischaracterized the issue. The constraints imposed by the NLRA wouldn't have been anti-competitive. After all, in any capital transfer case under the Act, except where motive may be unlawful under 8(a)(3), the issue isn't whether the move should be banned. Rather, it's whether the union has any say in whether the move is to be made and what the conditions should be at the new location. It's a body of law that would give workers a voice, not a veto power. There are plenty of accounts showing that workers and employers can work these things out jointly. And American companies doing business in Europe are obligated to notify and consult workers and unions when a transfer of ownership is being considered.

Mark: Granting unions even greater participatory rights in successorship situations in America isn't much by itself, is it? What leverage does a union have? The unions can't even use effective secondary economic activity.

Herb: Why do you assume the gains from worker participation will outweigh the burden on the market? I think in the long run we're worse off if we try to inhibit corporate changes. Capital flows to more efficient firms and more viable technologies. Older jobs may disappear, but new ones are created. The theory goes that if a company cannot operate efficiently, it's pointless to try to keep it operating through restrictive legislation. In the last analysis that's how I understand our old friend the *U.S. Steel* case [in Chapter One]. It was good that U.S. Steel was able to pull out of an outmoded structure and invest in other industries. Same reasoning applies to OSHA regulations: if compliance bankrupts a company, as compared to the entire industry, so be it; the company was marginal and wouldn't have stayed in operation for long.

Thaddeus: I agree with Herb, both on his economic grounds and on moral grounds. The choice isn't between market regulation and participatory decision-making. It's between market regulation and the coercive power of the government. Richard MacKenzie said it best: "[M]oving from reliance on the market to reliance on the government does not necessarily uplift the integrity of the unscrupulous among us and does not secure the 'pursuit of happiness.' ... [I]n the final analysis for free markets to exist, people must value freedom for itself. This means that we must allow, within broad limits, each individual to do what he or she wants, that we must assert his or her ethical right to do so. That is the bottom line." [R. MacKenzie, Bound To Be Free 43–44, 72 (1982).]

Vivian: So organized labor would be better off in an entirely unregulated arena, left to make its case without the protections and limitations of law?

Alvin: But aren't there considerations other than efficiency in deciding whether the law should intervene in market choices? Aren't we concerned as a society with meeting social, family and individual needs that aren't necessarily measured by efficiency? We live, among other things, for love, laughs, beauty, status, the surge of adrenalin, mental and sexual stimulation, happiness, and on and on. Why does only efficiency count?

* * *

Eileen: This has been an interesting theoretical discussion, but let's return to the ground. Specifically, let's talk about how a lawyer is supposed to deal with the law as it actually exists. What kind of advice will you give a corporate client like Sunshine after you explain the law of successorship under *Fall River Dyeing* and *Howard Johnson?*

* * *

Sly: I'm bothered when I compare the wrongful discharge case, *Rofin–Sinar,* with *Howard Johnson.* The plaintiff in *Rofin–Sinar* was able to enforce an implied just cause limitation on the right to discharge against a successor employer, while the staff at Grissom's could be let go despite just cause language and a successorship clause in the collective bargaining agreement.

Herb: But the Grissom staff was never hired by HoJos.

Sarah: Assume they had been. HoJos still wouldn't have been bound to the just cause standard in the bargaining agreement. That's *Burns.*

Herb: It's always possible an arbitrator would find sufficient continuity to require successor compliance with the just cause standard. Just like the court in *Rofin–Sinar* found adequate indicia to hold the successor to the just cause standard promised by its predecessor.

Eileen: I'd be interested in seeing such an arbitration decision, if you come across one.

Sly: Well, maybe now that courts enforce just cause promises and covenants not to compete across a transfer of ownership, maybe the labor law successorship rules will change.

* * *

Vivian: What about claims by employees that arose before the transfer of ownership? Let's say that six months before the closing, Susan Frost fires a black woman who is trying to organize at one of the nonunion facilities. In the fullness of time, the EEOC, the NLRB, and the courts determine her firing violated Title VII and the NLRA. Part of the remedy is reinstatement. If Susan Frost is in retirement in Santa Fe, does that mean the organizer gets backpay but no job?

Eileen: In *Golden State Bottling Co., Inc. v. NLRB,* 414 U.S. 168, 94 S.Ct. 414, 38 L.Ed.2d 388 (1973), the Court held that where the acquiring corporation had notice of the violation at the time of the acquisition, it was liable to remedy any existing unfair labor practices. Lower federal courts have applied the *Golden State Bottling* reasoning to cases arising under Title VII, ADEA and the Rehabilitation Act.

Thaddeus: Why does the successor have the obligation to remedy unfair labor practices it knew of at the acquisition, but not the absolute obligation to bargain with the union or honor the terms of the predecessor's collective bargaining agreement, even if the successor knew such an agreement existed?

Vivian: Maybe there's a real tiger lurking in the *Golden State* decision. If an employer was in violation of the duty to bargain at the time of the transfer of ownership and the successor acquired with knowledge, maybe the successor has to bargain in order to remedy the predecessor's unfair labor practice.

[Can Vivian be right? Will a court enforce a bargaining order in the absence of workforce continuity? If a court ordered the successor to remedy the predecessor's refusal to bargain by bargaining, what success at the bargaining table could you expect from a union foisted on employees by court order?—Eds.]

C. INTERNATIONAL BUSINESS TRANSACTIONS AND THE LAW OF WORK*

The increasing globalization of commercial relations means that many companies have employees in more than one country: The Disney Company runs a theme park in France as well as entertainment parks in Florida and California; BMW has factories in the United States and Germany; accounting giants like PricewaterhouseCoopers have offices throughout the world. Nike, headquartered in Oregon, manufactures

* Thanks to Lance Compa for his help in preparing these materials for the second edition and in reviewing them for this edition. Errors are the authors' responsibility.

none of its products in the United States, but has contracts with suppliers in many of the world's poorest countries.

Which country's laws govern these employment relationships? If Disney offers health benefits to its French employees, do those benefits automatically vest per French law or can the plan documents make the benefits presumptively terminable under ERISA? If BMW pays its American employees in South Carolina straight-time wages for 40 hours a week and for a two week vacation, has the company violated German law which requires German employers to pay overtime after a 35-hour work week and to provide five weeks of paid vacation? If Pricewaterhouse-Coopers advertises for "a manager no older than 35 years of age" for its Moscow office, does the ADEA apply or is Russian law, which permits age-based hiring decisions, controlling? Must an electronics employer in Malaysia bargain with the collective representative chosen by its Malaysian employees or can the company simply point out that the Malaysian government denies electronic workers the right to independent representation? If employees in Indiana lose their jobs as a result of General Electric's moving operations to Mexico where labor costs are lower, do the United States employees have any recourse against General Electric in the United States? In Mexico? If the conditions and wages offered by Nike in Vietnam are significantly inferior to the minimum standards found in American workplaces, do the Vietnamese workers have claims under any American state or federal legislation? Should it matter that trade between the United States and Vietnam is greatly enhanced pursuant to bi-or multi-lateral trade agreements that, in effect, subsidize Vietnamese imports into the United States? Should trade rights be tied to labor rights?

1. EXTRATERRITORIALITY: DOMESTIC JURISDICTION DETERMINED BY STATUTE OR TREATY

Legal regulation of the employment relationship has traditionally been a matter of local or domestic law. Thus, benefits offered to French national employees in Paris by Disney would vest under French law; BMW could pay its American employees in South Carolina straight time for 40 hours of work and limit their vacation weeks to two; Pricewater-houseCoopers would not face a lawsuit by its Russian employees in connection with a hiring policy that specified an upper age limit; the Malaysian electronics employer can ignore its workers' trade union; GE could move operations to Mexico or anywhere else in the absence of anti-union motivation; and Nike must comply with the domestic law of Vietnam and the other countries in which it contracts for its products.

One reason for expecting companies doing business abroad to conform their practices to local law is respect for the principle of sovereignty. A closely connected concern is to avoid unintended clashes between countries' laws that might result in international discord. In the United States, the Supreme Court responded to these considerations by adopting a presumption against extraterritorial application of domestic laws, including labor and employment statutes. The presumption can be rebutted only by a clear Congressional expression of a statute's extraterritorial reach.

At the time the Court established the presumption against extraterritorial jurisdiction few American companies employed persons abroad and Congress rarely analyzed whether to extend the reach of American statutes beyond domestic borders. Consider the presumption against extraterritoriality in the following cases, one of which involves a federal statute from the 1890's, the other a 1984 amendment to the ADEA.

VAN BLARICOM v. BURLINGTON NORTHERN R.R. CO.

United States Court of Appeals, Ninth Circuit, 1994.
17 F.3d 1224.

BRUNETTI, CIRCUIT JUDGE.

The issue presented in this case is whether the Interstate Commerce Commission ("ICC") has the authority to enforce labor protective conditions adopted in compliance with the Interstate Commerce Act extraterritorially on behalf of a Canadian citizen, working in Canada for an American rail carrier. We hold that it does not.

I. FACTS AND PROCEEDINGS

Paul Van Blaricom, a Canadian citizen, was an employee of Northern Pacific Railway Co., which merged with several U.S. and Canadian railroads to form Burlington Northern Railroad Co. ("Burlington") in 1970. The ICC approved the merger agreement, which extended the collective bargaining agreement protections the railroads had negotiated for union employees to non-union employees as required by the Interstate Commerce Act, 49 U.S.C. § 11347. These labor protective conditions included guaranteed compensation for the rest of an employee's working life upon any reduction in force.

After the merger, Van Blaricom was employed by Burlington as an "exempt" or non-union clerk in Canada until his position was abolished by Burlington in 1988.

Van Blaricom brought this action in district court for breach of the labor protective conditions of the merger agreement established in Northern Lines and approved by the ICC. The district court stayed the action pending determination by the ICC of several issues including whether the labor protective conditions adopted for non-union employees in the Northern Lines merger agreement applied to Van Blaricom, a Canadian citizen working in Canada.[1] The ICC concluded that it did not

---

1. The questions referred to the ICC included:

   (1) Whether the labor protective conditions adopted for exempt employees in the Northern Lines merger agreement

apply to plaintiff, a Canadian citizen employed by defendant in Canada;

   (2) Whether such conditions have been breached by defendant as to plaintiff; and

   (3) The damages, if any, to which plaintiff is entitled.

have jurisdiction and lacked the authority to enforce the employment protections on Van Blaricom's behalf. Great N. Pac. & Burlington Lines—Merger—*Great N. Ry. In the Matter of Paul E. Van Blaricom*, 6 I.C.C.2d 919 (1990). Van Blaricom appealed the ICC's decision to the district court, where the decision was affirmed on summary judgment.

II. DISCUSSION

A grant of summary judgment is reviewed de novo, applying the same standards used by the district court.

Pursuant to the Administrative Procedure Act, agency decisions must be set aside if they are "arbitrary, capricious, an abuse of discretion, or otherwise not in accordance with law." 5 U.S.C. § 706(2)(A). In reviewing an agency's interpretation of a statute, the court must reject those constructions that are contrary to clear congressional intent or frustrate the policy that Congress sought to implement. If a statute is silent or ambiguous on a particular point, however, the court defers to the agency's interpretation.

Congress has the authority to enforce its laws beyond the territorial boundaries of the United States. Unless Congress has clearly expressed a contrary intent, however, federal statutory law is presumed to apply only within the territorial jurisdiction of the United States. *Foley Bros. v. Filardo,* 336 U.S. 281, 284–85, 69 S.Ct. 575, 93 L.Ed. 680 (1949).

In *Foley Bros.,* the Court held that the Eight Hour Law did not apply extraterritorially, since "nothing in the Act itself ... nor in the legislative history ... [led] to the belief that Congress entertained any intention other than the normal one." The Court explained:

> The canon of construction which teaches that legislation of Congress, unless a contrary intent appears, is meant to apply only within the territorial jurisdiction of the United States, is a valid approach whereby unexpressed congressional intent may be ascertained. It is based on the assumption that Congress is primarily concerned with domestic conditions.

Assuming Congress is primarily concerned with domestic conditions "serves to protect against unintended clashes between our laws and those of other nations which could result in international discord." *EEOC v. Arabian Am. Oil Co.,* 499 U.S. 244, 248, 111 S.Ct. 1227, 113 L.Ed.2d 274 (1991). The presumption against extraterritoriality also reflects the deference of courts to Congress, which "alone has the facilities necessary to make fairly such an important policy decision." *Benz v. Compania Naviera Hidalgo, S.A.,* 353 U.S. 138, 147, 77 S.Ct. 699, 1 L.Ed.2d 709 (1957).

The Supreme Court has required a "clear expression" of Congressional intent to apply legislation extraterritorially, making this presumption difficult to overcome. For example, in *Benz,* the Court considered

After concluding that it did not have jurisdiction to enforce the labor protective conditions, the ICC found it unnecessary to answer questions 2 and 3.

whether the striking crew of a foreign vessel could invoke the protection of the Labor Management Relations Act while in United States waters. The Court denied extraterritorial effect to the Act, holding that "to run interference in such a delicate field of international relations there must be present the affirmative intention of the Congress clearly expressed." Similarly, in *Foley Bros.*, the Court reasoned that Congress would not ordinarily apply domestic wage and hour provisions to aliens working abroad on United States public work projects and that the absence of a distinction in the Act between citizens and aliens was strong evidence of congressional intent not to do so. The Court stated: "An intention so to regulate labor conditions which are the primary concern of a foreign country should not be attributed to Congress in the absence of a clearly expressed purpose."

Van Blaricom argues that labor protective conditions adopted in compliance with 49 U.S.C. § 11347 extend to all "affected employees" regardless of citizenship or situs of work.

49 U.S.C. § 11347 provides in part:

When a rail carrier is involved in a transaction for which approval is sought . . . the Interstate Commerce Commission shall require the carrier to provide a fair arrangement at least as protective to the interest of employees who are affected by the transaction as the terms imposed under this section before February 5, 1976, and the terms established under section 405 of the Rail Passenger Service Act (49 U.S.C. 565).

While section 11347 does not specifically limit its application to United States citizens, it does not contain a "clear expression" of Congressional intent to apply the legislation extraterritorially. Additionally, the jurisdictional reach of the Interstate Commerce Act is governed by 49 U.S.C. § 10501, which provides in pertinent part:

(a) Subject to this chapter and other law, the Interstate Commerce Commission has jurisdiction over transportation

(2) to the extent such jurisdiction is not limited by subsection (b) of this section or the extent the transportation is *in the United States* and is between a place in—

(G) the United States and a place in a foreign Country.

49 U.S.C. § 10501(a)(2)(G) (emphasis added).[2]

The presumption against extraterritoriality, in conjunction with Congress' specific language in § 10501 limiting the jurisdiction of the ICC to transportation "in the United States," compels the conclusion

2. The wording of the predecessor language to this provision was even more clearly limited to domestic transportation. It provided that the Act applied to transportation "from or to any place in the United States to or from a foreign country, but only in so far as such transportation or transmission takes place within the United States." Transportation Act, 1920, § 400(1), ch. 91, 41 Stat. 474 (originally codified at 49 U.S.C. § 1(1)).

that the ICC does not have the authority to enforce the labor protective conditions extraterritorially.

AFFIRMED.

Notes

1. The court in *Van Blaricom* applies the traditional rule against extraterritorial application of United States domestic law, but the worlds of trade and commerce have changed considerably in recent years. Indeed, the parties in *Van Blaricom* seem to have assumed that they had the power to negotiate the terms of a merger that would bind the United States company and benefit Canadian citizens working for the company in Canada. Should the presumption against extraterritoriality be reconsidered in light of the changed world economy? Where a United States corporation controls companies and operations in other nations, should the presumption be that United States employment laws apply to the foreign operations, unless Congress clearly determines otherwise?

2. Older statutes like the NLRA that contain no expressions of extraterritorial force are unlikely to be amended, not because of a judgment that the NLRA should apply only to domestically-based labor-management disputes but because any modest attempt to amend the NLRA carries the likelihood of pitched battles between labor and management over all aspects of the existing law. If amendment of the NLRA to reflect international economic realities is a good idea that is frustrated for political reasons, how will the law ever respond to the actual needs of business and labor in a global economy?

MORELLI v. CEDEL

United States Court of Appeals, Second Circuit, 1998.
141 F.3d 39..

CUDAHY, CIRCUIT JUDGE:

This appeal requires us to decide whether the domestic employees of certain foreign corporations are protected under the Age Discrimination in Employment Act of 1967 (the ADEA), and, if so, whether a foreign corporation's *foreign* employees are counted for the purpose of determining whether the corporation has enough employees to be subject to the ADEA. We answer both questions in the affirmative.

BACKGROUND

* * *

As alleged in the complaint, the facts relevant to this appeal are as follows. The plaintiff, Ida Morelli, was born on April 11, 1939. The defendant is a Luxembourg bank. On or about June 29, 1984, the defendant hired the plaintiff to work in its New York office. On or about February 26, 1993, the plaintiff became an assistant to Dennis Sabourin, a manager in the defendant's New York office. Mr. Sabourin summoned the then 54–year-old plaintiff to his office on January 18, 1994, handed her a separation agreement, and insisted that she sign it.

Under the terms of the separation agreement, a copy of which was attached to the complaint, the plaintiff would resign, effective April 30, 1994. She would continue to receive her salary and benefits until the effective date of her resignation, but she would be relieved of her duties as an employee, effective immediately. Both the defendant and the employee would renounce all claims arising out of "their past working relationship." Mr. Sabourin told the plaintiff that she would receive the three months' severance pay, medical coverage for three months, and her pension only on the condition that she sign the agreement on the spot. The plaintiff had never seen the separation agreement before and had no warning that she was going to be asked to resign. But in the face of Mr. Sabourin's ultimatum, she did sign the agreement immediately and returned it to him. The defendant, however, never provided her with a pension distribution.

DISCUSSION

1. Age Discrimination

    (a) Does the ADEA cover a U.S.-based branch of a foreign employer?

The ADEA was enacted in 1967 to prevent discrimination by employers on the basis of age.

In order to determine whether the defendant is subject to the ADEA, we must first determine whether the ADEA generally protects the employees of a branch of a foreign employer located in the United States.

It is undisputed that Cedel is a foreign employer with fewer than 20 employees in its sole U.S. branch. There being no contested facts on the motion to dismiss under Rule 12(b)(1), we review the district court's dismissal de novo.

Section 4(h)(2) of the ADEA provides that "[t]he prohibitions of [the ADEA] shall not apply where the employer is a foreign person not controlled by an American employer." 29 U.S.C. § 623(h)(2). At a minimum, this provision means that the ADEA does not apply to the *foreign* operations of foreign employers–unless there is an American employer behind the scenes. An absolutely literal reading of § 4(h)(2) might suggest that the ADEA also does not apply to the *domestic* operations of foreign employers. But the plain language of § 4(h)(2) is not necessarily decisive if it is inconsistent with Congress' clearly expressed legislative purpose.

Section 4(h)(2) was not part of the original ADEA. It was added in 1984. The context in which it was added reveals that Congress' purpose was not to exempt the domestic workplaces of foreign employers from the ADEA's prohibition of age discrimination. Instead, the purpose of adding this exclusion was to limit the reach of an extraterritorial amendment adopted as part of the same legislation.* * *

The 1984 amendments amplified the definition of "employee" in § 11(f) of the ADEA, which had previously embraced any "individual employed by any employer," except for certain elected public officials and political appointees. One of the 1984 amendments specified that "[t]he term employee' includes any individual who is a citizen of the United States employed by an employer in a workplace in a foreign country."

Companion amendments dealt with the cases of foreign persons not controlled by an American employer—now § 4(h)(2) of the ADEA—and foreign corporations controlled by American employers—now § 4(h)(1):

> If an employer controls a corporation whose place of incorporation is in a foreign country, any practice by such corporation prohibited under this section shall be presumed to be such practice by such employer.

[codified at 29 U.S.C. § 623(h)(1)] The amendments also included a "foreign law exception"—now ADEA § 4(f)(1)—insulating employers from liability for "practices involv [ing] an employee in a workplace in a foreign country" where compliance with the ADEA "would cause [the] employer, or a corporation controlled by such employer, to violate the laws of the country in which such workplace is located."[codified at 29 U.S.C. § 623(f)(1)]

The 1984 revision to the definition of "employee" in § 11(f) was intended "to assure that the provisions of the ADEA would be applicable to any citizen of the United States who is employed by an American employer in a workplace outside the United States." S.Rep. 98–467, at 27 (1984); see EEOC v. Arabian American Oil Co., 499 U.S. 244, 258–59, 111 S.Ct. 1227, 1235–36, 113 L.Ed.2d 274 (1991). The other 1984 amendments, to § 4 of ADEA, conform the ADEA's reach to "the well-established principle of sovereignty, that no nation has the right to impose its labor standards on another country." S.Rep. at 27. Thus § 4(h)(2) of the ADEA merely limits the scope of the amended definition of employee, so that an employee at a workplace in a foreign country is not protected under the ADEA if the employer is a foreign person not controlled by an American employer. See id. at 27–28 ("[T]he amendment ... does not apply to foreign companies which are not controlled by U.S. firms.") (emphasis added). There is no evidence in the legislative history that these amendments were intended to restrict the application of the ADEA with respect to the *domestic* operations of foreign employers.

Further, the plain language of the corresponding foreign-employer exclusions in Title VII of the Civil Rights Act of 1964, 42 U.S.C. §§ 2000e–2000e–17, and the Americans with Disabilities Act of 1990 (ADA), 42 U.S.C. §§ 12101–12213, indicates that a foreign employer's domestic operations are not excluded from the reach of those statutes. The Title VII and ADA exclusions are expressly limited to the "*foreign operations* of an employer that is a foreign person not controlled by an American employer," 42 U.S.C. §§ 2000e-1(c)(2), 12112(c)(2)(B) (emphasis added), so these employment discrimination statutes would apply to a foreign company's domestic operations. It is not apparent why the domestic operations of foreign companies should be subject to Title VII and the ADA, but not to the ADEA. The legislative history of the comparable foreign-employer exemptions of those laws—both added as part of the Civil Rights Act of 1991—contains no indication that Congress intended any such difference in scope between the ADEA and Title VII or the ADA.

If § 4(h)(2) does not exempt the domestic operations of foreign companies from the ADEA, there is no other basis for such an exemption. Because "[t]he Age Discrimination Act is remedial and humanitarian legislation," it should be "construed liberally to achieve its purpose of protecting older employees from discrimination." Moses v. Falstaff Brewing Corp., 525 F.2d 92, 93 (8th Cir.1975). The exemption of the domestic operations of foreign employers from the ADEA would only undermine the purpose of the ADEA to "promote employment of older persons based on their ability rather than age." 29 U.S.C. § 621(b). International comity does not require such an exemption; the 1984 amendments anticipate that American corporations operating abroad will be subject to foreign labor laws, and Congress presumably contemplated that the operations of foreign corporations here will be subject to U.S. labor laws.

We have previously concluded that even when a foreign employer operating in the United States can invoke a Friendship, Commerce and Navigation treaty to justify employing its own nationals, this "does not give [the employer] license to violate American laws prohibiting discrimination in employment." Avigliano v. Sumitomo Shoji America, Inc., 638 F.2d 552, 558 (2d Cir.1981), *vacated on other grounds*, 457 U.S. 176, 102 S.Ct. 2374, 72 L.Ed.2d 765 (1982); *see also* MacNamara v. Korean Air Lines, 863 F.2d 1135, 1141 (3d Cir.1988) ("'[A] foreign business may not deliberately undertake to reduce the age of its workforce by replacing older Americans with younger foreign nationals.") Although the Supreme Court vacated our judgment in that case on the grounds that the defendant could not invoke the treaty, the Court observed that "the highest level of protection afforded by commercial treaties" to foreign corporations operating in the United States is generally no more than "equal treatment with domestic corporations." Here equal treatment would require that antidiscrimination rules apply to foreign enterprises' U.S. branches, since "defending personnel decisions is a fact of business life in contemporary America and is a burden that the domestic competitors of foreign enterprise have been required to shoulder," MacNamara, 863 F.2d at 1147. Also, U.S. subsidiaries of foreign corporations are generally subject to U.S. antidiscrimination laws, *see, e.g.,* Fortino v. Quasar Co., 950 F.2d 389, 393–94 (7th Cir.1991), and, absent treaty protection—not an issue in this case—a U.S. branch of a foreign corporation is not entitled to an immunity not enjoyed by such subsidiaries.

We therefore agree with the E.E.O.C., the agency charged with the enforcement of the ADEA, that the law generally applies "to foreign firms operating on U.S. soil." E.E.O.C. Policy Guidance, N–915.039, Empl.Prac.Guide (CCH) 5183, 6531 (March 3, 1989). For the reasons we have discussed, we are confident that Congress has never clearly expressed a contrary intent. *See* Regions Hosp. v. Shalala, 522 U.S. 448, 457, 118 S.Ct. 909, 915, 139 L.Ed.2d 895 (1998).

(b) Are employees based abroad counted in determining whether a U.S.-based branch of a foreign employer is subject to the ADEA?

Cedel will still not be subject to the ADEA by virtue of its U.S. operations unless Cedel is an "employer" under the ADEA. A business must have at least twenty "employees" to be an "employer." 29 U.S.C. § 630(b). Cedel maintains that, in the case of foreign employers, only domestic employees should be counted. The district court agreed, and, since Cedel had fewer than 20 employees in its U.S. branch, the court granted Cedel's motion to dismiss for lack of subject matter jurisdiction without considering the number of Cedel's overseas employees.

The initial version of the ADEA, adopted in 1967, did not apply to employers with fewer than 25 employees. (For a brief transitional period, employers with fewer than 50 employees were not subject to the ADEA.) In 1974, the threshold was lowered to its present level. We first consider whether the ADEA's definition of "employee" might somehow support Cedel's position. Prior to the 1984 amendments, the definition of an employee was simply "an individual employed by any employer," with exceptions, noted above, not relevant in the present case. This language provides no basis for counting only domestic employees. (Neither does the reasoning of the cases limiting the reach of the pre–1984 ADEA to domestic workplaces, since the portions of the FLSA incorporated into the ADEA—in particular § 13(f) of the FLSA—do not purport to modify the definition of employee under § 3(e) of the FLSA.)

The 1984 amendments supplemented the definition of employee in § 11(f) of the ADEA to include U.S. citizens employed in a foreign workplace. This revision to § 11(f) does not establish that the employees, wherever located, of a foreign corporation with a U.S. branch are not "employees" under the ADEA, for it makes no distinction between foreign and domestic employers. As discussed above, the function of adding § 4(h)(2) in 1984 was only to limit a foreign-based employer's ADEA liability with respect to employees in a foreign workplace, and so § 4(h)(2) provides no grounds for counting only Cedel's domestic employees. The word "employee" does not even appear in § 4(h); if Congress had wished to restrict the definition of "employee" to exclude a foreign employer's foreign workers, it certainly could have done so directly when it amended § 11(f) in 1984. The 1984 foreign law exception (§ 4(f)(1)) also does not aid Cedel.

The district court reasoned that the overseas employees of foreign employers should not be counted because they are not protected by the ADEA. But there is no requirement that an employee be protected by the

ADEA to be counted; an enumeration, for the purpose of ADEA coverage of an employer, includes employees under age 40, who are also unprotected, *see* 29 U.S.C. § 631(a). The nose count of employees relates to the scale of the employer rather than to the extent of protection.

The legislative history of the ADEA does not address the minimum employee requirement. The ADEA was modeled in large part on Title VII, however, *see* McKennon v. Nashville Banner Publ'g Co., 513 U.S. 352, 357, 115 S.Ct. 879, 884, 130 L.Ed.2d 852 (1995), and we have previously identified several reasons for Title VII's minimum-employee requirement, *see* 42 U.S.C. § 2000e(b) (15 or more employees). These include the burdens of compliance and potential litigation costs, "the protection of intimate and personal relations existing in small businesses, potential effects on competition and the economy, and the constitutionality of Title VII under the Commerce Clause." Tomka, 66 F.3d at 1314.

None of these reasons suggests that whether a foreign employer is subject to the ADEA should turn on the size of its U.S. operations alone. Cedel contends that because it has fewer than 20 employees in the United States, it is the equivalent of a small U.S. employer. This is implausible with respect to compliance and litigation costs; their impact on Cedel is better gauged by its worldwide employment. Cedel would not appear to be any more a boutique operation in the United States than would a business with ten employees each in offices in, say, Alaska and Florida, which would be subject to the ADEA. Further, a U.S. corporation with many foreign employees but fewer than 20 domestic ones would certainly be subject to the ADEA.

Accordingly, in determining whether Cedel satisfies the ADEA's 20–employee threshold, employees cannot be ignored merely because they work overseas. We therefore vacate the judgment on the plaintiff's ADEA count.

2.   ERISA [omitted] * * *

THE EFFECT OF TREATIES

There is an important exception to the proposition that foreign-based employers doing business in the United States must comply with United States laws. Treaties between the United States and other countries may provide a safe harbor for a foreign employer that engages in employment practices that would violate American law if engaged in by a United States employer. For example, the Friendship, Commerce and Navigation Treaty between the United States and Japan (1953 FCN Treaty) provides in Article VIII(1) that "companies of either party shall be permitted to engage, within the territories of the other party, accountants and other technical experts, executive personnel, attorneys, agents and other specialists of their choice." Under Article VIII(1) may a

Japanese company doing business in the United States give a preference to its citizens in filling managerial positions? As Judge Posner explains in the excerpt that follows, this is not national origin discrimination prohibited by Title VII, but discrimination on the ground of citizenship expressly provided for in a treaty between the two countries.

FORTINO v. QUASAR COMPANY

United States Court of Appeals, Seventh Circuit, 1991.
950 F.2d 389.

[Plaintiffs were former American executives of Quasar, the American subsidiary of a Japanese company. Plaintiffs charged Quasar with discrimination on the grounds of national origin and age. Defendant appealed from a finding of liability and award of $2.5 million in damages plus attorneys fees and costs. The finding of age discrimination was reversed and remanded for a new trial. The court's disposition of the national origin claim follows.]

POSNER, CIRCUIT JUDGE * * *

Quasar markets in the United States products made in Japan by Matsushita, which assigns several of its own financial and marketing executives to Quasar on a temporary basis. They are employees of Quasar and are under its day-to-day control but they also retain their status as employees of Matsushita and are designated as "MEI [Matsushita Electric Industrial] personnel" on Quasar's books. Quasar does not evaluate their performance—Matsushita does, and also keeps their personnel records and fixes their salaries and assists with the relocation of their families to the United States during the period of the assignment. These executives enter this country under "E–1." or "E–2." temporary visas, which permit the holder of the visa to work here, provided (so far as applicable to this case, which involves Japanese executives) that the work is executive or supervisory in character, the worker is a Japanese citizen, the company he is working for in the U.S. is at least half owned by Japanese nationals and has substantial trade or investment relations with Japan, and he is doing work authorized by the Treaty of Friendship, Commerce and Navigation between the United States and Japan.

In 1986 there were ten of these Japanese expatriate executives working for Quasar. (The parties call them "expatriates," though in common parlance the word is not applied to a person on merely temporary assignment to another country.) One was named Nishikawa. In 1985 Quasar had lost $20 million, and Nishikawa had been sent by Matsushita to prevent a recurrence of the loss. He was put in charge of Quasar and proceeded to reorganize the company, in the process reducing the work force, including management, by half. The three plaintiffs were among the American executives of non-Japanese origin who were discharged. None of the Japanese expatriate executives was discharged, although it appears that two were rotated back to Japan and replaced by only one new expatriate. Far from being discharged, the expatriates received salary increases; the American executives of Quasar who were not discharged did not. Two out of Quasar's three Japanese–American employees were also discharged, but none of these was an executive.

Article VIII(1) of the treaty authorizes "companies of either Party [i.e., the U.S. and Japan], to engage, within the territories of the other Party ... executive personnel ... of their choice." The propriety of Matsushita's assigning its own executives to Quasar is further confirmed by the issuance of E–1 and E–2 visas to the Japanese expatriate executives. Nevertheless the district judge based his conclusion that Quasar had violated Title VII on the better treatment the company gave the Japanese expatriates compared to its American executives in 1986: it discharged none of the former but many of the latter, and it gave raises to all of the former and none of the latter. This was favoritism all right, but discrimination in favor of foreign executives given a special status by virtue of a treaty and its implementing regulations is not equivalent to discrimination on the basis of national origin.

We may assume that just as Title VII protects whites from discrimination in favor of blacks as well as blacks from discrimination in favor of whites, so it protects Americans of non-Japanese origin from discrimination in favor of persons of Japanese origin. Title VII does not, however, forbid discrimination on grounds of citizenship. *Espinoza v. Farah Mfg. Co.*, 414 U.S. 86, 94 S.Ct. 334, 38 L.Ed.2d 287 (1973). Of course, especially in the case of a homogeneous country like Japan, citizenship and national origin are highly correlated; almost all citizens of Japan were born there. But to use this correlation to infer national-origin discrimination from a treaty-sanctioned preference for Japanese citizens who happen also to be of Japanese national origin would nullify the treaty. This is true whether the correlation is used to prove intentional discrimination, as in this case, or to establish a disparate impact that the employer must justify on nondiscriminatory grounds. The exercise of a treaty right may not be made the basis for inferring a violation of Title VII. By virtue of the treaty, "foreign businesses clearly have the right to choose citizens of their own nation as executives *because they are such citizens*." *MacNamara v. Korean Air Lines*, 863 F.2d 1135, 1144 (3d Cir.1988) (emphasis in original). That right would be empty if the subsidiary could be punished for treating its citizen executives differently from American executives on the ground that, since the former were of Japanese national origin and the latter were not, it was discriminating on the basis of national origin. Title VII would be taking back from the Japanese with one hand what the treaty had given them with the other. This collision is avoided by holding national origin and citizenship separate. That was not done here.

But can Quasar, not being a Japanese company in the technical sense in which this term is used in the treaty, rely on the treaty even to the limited extent suggested? *Sumitomo Shoji America, Inc. v. Avagliano*, 457 U.S. 176, 102 S.Ct. 2374, 72 L.Ed.2d 765 (1982), held that an American subsidiary of a foreign parent was not protected by the treaty. But there was no contention that the parent had dictated the subsidiary's discriminatory conduct, and the Court left open the question whether the subsidiary might in such a case assert any of its parent's treaty rights. We think it must be allowed to in a case such as this, at least to the extent necessary to prevent the treaty from being set at naught. A judgment that forbids Quasar to give preferential treatment to the expatriate executives that its parent sends would have the same effect on the parent as it would have if it ran directly against the parent: it would prevent Matsushita from sending its own executives to manage Quasar in preference to employing American citizens in these posts.

But suppose a Japanese company buys an American company, fires all of its new subsidiary's occidental executives because it is prejudiced against occidentals, and replaces them with Japanese citizens. The question would then arise whether the treaty of friendship in effect confers a blanket immunity from Title VII. On this there are different views. We need not choose sides in this case, because (setting to one side the question of age discrimination, discussed next) there is no evidence of discrimination here save what is implicit in wanting your own citizens to run your foreign subsidiary. There is no evidence that if John Fortino had had three or for that matter four Japanese grandparents he would not have been fired. No favoritism was shown Quasar's Japanese–American employees, which would have been true national-origin discrimination since they are not citizens of Japan; and whatever his ancestry, Fortino would have had the irremediable disability of not being an executive of Matsushita. That was the real source of the "prejudice" against him, and it is not prejudice based on national origin. It may have had a similar effect to national-origin prejudice (though not identical— for look what happened to Quasar's Japanese–American employees) because of the correlation between citizenship and national origin, but the treaty prevents equating the two forms of discrimination or, what as a practical matter would amount to the same thing, allowing the first to be used to prove the second. If this conclusion seems callous toward the Americans who lost their jobs at Quasar, we remind that the rights granted by the treaty are reciprocal. There are Americans employed abroad by foreign subsidiaries of U.S. companies who, but for the treaty, would lose their jobs to foreign nationals. Indeed, the treaty provision was inserted at the insistence of the United States. Japan was opposed to it. * * *

Note

Is Judge Posner correct? Why should a foreign company that chooses to do business in the United States by incorporating a wholly owned subsidiary, rather than by opening a branch office, have the benefit of both the limited liability assured by corporate law *and* the protection of the Treaty?

2. DOMESTIC JURISDICTION DECLINED: FORUM NON CONVENIENS

Even if there is a statutory basis for a court to take jurisdiction of a claimed legal injury that occurred outside the United States, challenges to the conduct of American-based multinationals abroad may founder as United States courts exercise their discretion to decline jurisdiction, pursuant to the doctrine known as forum non conveniens (FNC).

The central inquiry is on the convenience of the plaintiff's chosen jurisdiction, but there is no bright line test for making this determination. The Supreme Court has emphasized both the fact specific nature of the inquiry and the breadth of the trial court's discretion to determine "if the balance of conveniences suggests that trial in the [plaintiff's] chosen forum would be unnecessarily burdensome." Piper Aircraft Co. v. Reyno, 454 U.S. 235, 256, 102 S.Ct. 252, 70 L.Ed.2d 419 (1981)(holding that one factor, the differences between American and foreign substantive law, was not entitled to substantial weight). Initially, the court inquires into the adequacy of the alternative forum to provide an effective remedy. If the foreign jurisdiction does not recognize a cause of action but the United States does, or if the foreign jurisdiction's dispute resolution system is so inadequate that a plaintiff would be unable to litigate, FNC does not apply. But mere differences in procedures (e.g., the unavailability of liberal discovery, the absence of trial by jury) or remedies (e.g., the unavailability of punitive damages) are generally insufficient for a court to choose to exercise jurisdiction. If the foreign jurisdiction does not provide an adequate alternative, the court further investigates the balance of conveniences, looking at factors such as the convenience and expense to the parties of conducting the trial in view of the location of evidence, witnesses, parties and counsel (private factors); and the burdens on the American judicial system, the foreign jurisdiction's interest in the subject matter of the litigation, and the foreign jurisdiction's greater familiarity with applicable foreign substantive law (public factors).

In the context of the workplace, litigation has focused on unsafe working conditions and substandard pay of workers employed in the foreign operations of multinational companies. To date most of these suits have been dismissed pursuant to FNC; but they are important because they educate the judiciary about conditions for which American-based companies have at least some moral responsibility and because the litigation is coupled with media campaigns designed to raise general public awareness. See e.g. Torres v. Southern Peru Copper Corp., 113 F.3d 540 (5th Cir.1997)(dismissing personal injury action by Peruvian citizens against mining company domiciled in Delaware); Delgado v. Shell Oil Co., 890 F.Supp. 1324 (S.D.Tex.1995)(dismissing several products liability actions against American-based manufacturers, marketers, distributors and sellers of nematocide, brought by citizens of 12 foreign counties seeking damages for injuries stemming from alleged exposure to

nematocide while working on farms in 23 foreign countries); and Barrantes Cabalceta v. Standard Fruit Co., 667 F.Supp. 833
(S.D.Fla.1987)(dismissing unspecified claims of defendant's negligence
causing injuries to employees located in Latin America). For an excellent
discussion of the policy issues concerning FNC, see Judge Doggett's
concurring opinion in Dow Chemical and Shell Oil v. Castro Alfaro, 786
S.W.2d 674 (Tex.1990).

3. DOMESTIC SUBSTANTIVE LAW APPLIED

Assuming that a court has jurisdiction to hear a claim that crosses
national boundaries, how does the substantive law developed for domestic transactions apply?

LABOR UNION OF PICO KOREA LTD.
v. PICO PRODUCTS, INC.

United States District Court, Northern District of New York, 1991.
1991 WL 299121, affirmed 968 F.2d 191 (2d Cir.1992), *cert. denied*
506 U.S. 985, 113 S.Ct. 493, 121 L.Ed.2d 431 (1992).

[Pico Products (Pico) is a New York based corporation with its
principal place of business in New York. Pico Macom (Macom), a
Delaware corporation with its principal place of business in California, is
a wholly-owned subsidiary of Pico. Pico Korea (Korea), a South Korean
corporation with its principal place of business in Seoul, is in turn a
wholly owned subsidiary of Macom.

In 1985 Korea was incorporated to manufacture electronic components. Macom purchased most of Korea's products and controlled distribution of the remainder. In April 1988 Korea had cash problems and
Macom advanced the needed capital. In June 1988 Korea workers formed
a union pursuant to the laws of the Republic of Korea. A one-year
bargaining agreement between the union and Korea was signed on
November 15, 1988, by James D. O'Connell, Korea's president. From
1986 to early 1989 O'Connell was also the executive vice-president of
Pico Products, a member of the Board of Directors of Macom, and the
only person serving as a director of the three corporations.

The bargaining agreement provided for, inter alia, (1) timely payment of wages, (2) wage payments in the event of work suspensions
beyond two days, (3) severance pay, and (4) notification to the union in
the event of shut downs and reductions of personnel.

On February 23, 1989 the Pico products' Board of Directors instructed Macom to cease providing capital to Korea. Subsequently Korea
closed operations.—Eds.]

McAVOY, DISTRICT JUDGE. * * *

The employees of Pico Korea were not paid for wages earned for
work performed during the month of February, 1989. In addition, these
employees were not provided with notice of the shutdown or paid

suspension or severance pay. Following the shutdown, the members of the plaintiff labor union took control of the Boochun City plant and attempted to continue production with the remaining available resources. The plaintiff Sun Rye Hong admitted that the seizure of the plant continued for approximately two months. During this time, union members sent fax telegrams to [Pico Products' chairman of the board] Hitchcock demanding negotiations on the back pay and contract terms.

Eventually, the plaintiffs sought to remedy the purported breaches of the CBA under the provisions of American law and * * * two causes of action remain. This first, a breach of contract theory, attempts to hold the parent corporation, Pico Products, liable for its second tier subsidiary's obligations arising under the CBA. The second alleges a cause of action for the tortious interference with the CBA. The parties have stipulated that New York's choice of law rules mandate that New York law controls the remaining causes of action.

II.

DISCUSSION

A. Breach of Contract

Plaintiffs' breach of contract theory attempts to "pierce the corporate veil" and hold the New York defendant liable for breach of the CBA as if it were a party to the agreement. The plaintiffs allege that the parent corporation, Pico Products, so dominated the operations of the Korean subsidiary that the Korean corporation was but a puppet of the New York corporation. The control, the plaintiffs allege, came both in the form of overt decision making at the New York corporation as well as in more disjointed forms. As to the latter, the plaintiffs claim that the defendant controlled the fate of the Korean subsidiary by controlling the flow of essential working capital being advanced from Pico Product's first tier subsidiary, Pico Macom. When it became apparent that the recently entered CBA was infringing upon the parent's otherwise available profits, the plaintiffs claim, the defendant used its control to close the Korean subsidiary and to prevent the subsidiary from honoring the terms of the CBA

In as much as Defendant Pico Products is not a signatory to the CBA, the plaintiffs now attempt to impose liability via a "piercing of the corporate veil/alter ego" theory. In opposition, the defendants' argue that there was not sufficient control to impose liability upon a parent corporation for the acts of a subsidiary.

(i) Corporate Separateness

A corporation is entitled to a presumption that it is an entity which is separate from its sister corporations, subsidiaries, and shareholders. *Sampsell v. Imperial Paper & Color Corp.*, 313 U.S. 215, 61 S.Ct. 904 (1941). Thus, as a general rule a parent corporation is not liable for the acts of a subsidiary. However, a court may disregard the separate legal identity of the parent and subsidiary corporation if it is shown that the parent has ignored the subsidiary's wall of separate corporate identity. If it is shown that a parent corporation used a subsidiary as a "department" rather than treating it as an independent concern, New York law allows the parent corporation to be held accountable for the contracts of its subsidiary.

(ii) Piercing the Corporate Veil

"In order to overcome the presumption of separateness, what must be shown is that the parent is the 'alter ego' of the subsidiary and that the subsidiary is the 'mere instrumentality' of the parent." *Fidenas AG v. Honeywell Inc.,* 501 F.Supp. 1029, 1036 (S.D.N.Y.1980) (applying New York law). Under this "alter ego/mere instrumentality" approach to piercing the corporate veil, New York law requires that the plaintiffs plead and prove:

> 1. Control, not mere majority or complete stock control, but complete domination, not only of finances but of policy and business practices in respect to the transaction attacked so that the corporate entity as to this transaction had *at the time* no separate mind, will or existence of its own; and

> 2. Such control must have been used by the defendant to commit fraud or wrong, to perpetrate the violation of a statutory or other positive legal duty, or a dishonest and unjust act in contravention of plaintiff's legal rights; and

> 3. The aforesaid control and breach of duty must proximately cause the injury or unjust loss complained of. [Emphasis in original.]

The plaintiffs in the instant action claim that the parent corporation, Pico Products, controlled the operations of the Korean subsidiary via interlocking directorates and officers, a majority stockholding, and financial control of the Korean corporation to such a degree as to render the Korean concern nothing more than a "plant" operating at the desire and direction of the New York parent. Further, the plaintiffs claim that the control exerted by the parent was used to close the Korean concern without notice or negotiations, thus breaching the collective bargaining agreement. As such, the plaintiffs allege that they were injured and that their injuries stemmed from Pico Products' actions.

Nevertheless, the term "complete domination and control" is malleable at best and open to differing interpretation. In an attempt to more clearly define its parameters, the New York Court of Appeals has stated:

> [L]iability can never be predicated solely upon the fact of a parent corporation's ownership of a controlling interest in the shares of the subsidiary. At the very least there must be direct intervention by the parent in the management of the subsidiary to such an extent that 'the subsidiary's paraphernalia of incorporation, directors, and officers' are completely ignored.

Other courts have offered lists of factors which may be used to determine "complete domination." These factors include:

a.   Whether the parent corporation owns all or most of the subsidiary;

b.   Whether the parent and subsidiary have common directors or officers;

c.   Whether the parent corporation finances the subsidiary;

d.   Whether the parent corporation subscribes to all the capital stock of the subsidiary or otherwise causes its incorporation;

e.   Whether the subsidiary has grossly inadequate capital;

f.   Whether the parent corporation pays the salaries and other expenses or losses of the subsidiary;

g.   Whether the subsidiary has substantially no business except with the parent corporation or no assets except those conveyed to it by the parent corporation;

h.   Whether in the papers of the parent corporation or in the statements of its officers, the subsidiary is described as a department or division of the parent corporation, or its business or financial responsibility is referred to as the parent corporation's own;

i.   Whether the parent corporation uses the property of the subsidiary as its own;

j.   Whether the directors or executives of the subsidiary do not act independently in the interest of the subsidiary but take their orders from the parent corporation in the latter's interest;

k.   Whether the formal legal requirements of the subsidiary are not observed.

(iii) Proof at Trial

The proof at trial revealed that Pico Korea lacked autonomy over all but the most basic daily operations. On a wide-scale operational level, Pico Korea was clearly controlled by others. However, this court must conclude that there is insufficient proof to conclude that this control was within the hands of the defendant Pico Products.

At trial it was proved that Pico Macom controlled the monthly influx of capital into the Korean corporation. Pico Products was not made aware of this "deficit funding" until well after the practice had been established. Thus, it was Pico Macom who must be said to have "financed" the corporation. Such a decision by Pico Macom to provide the deficit funding was only logical as it was Pico Macom, not Pico Products, that was the sole buyer of the Korean corporation's products. Further, the stock of the Korean corporation was wholly owned by Pico Macom, not Pico Products. Thus, it must be concluded that Pico Products' financial control of the Korean corporation was de minimis at best.

Although there is evidence that the Korean corporation controlled many of its own daily operations, (the corporation was incorporated under the laws of Korea; it had its own bank accounts, tax returns, and auditors; it controlled the hiring and firing of the non-management work force; and it took loans in its own name), the overwhelming impact of the evidence is that on an operational level the corporation was controlled by others. Indeed, the president of Pico Korea, James D. O'Connell, lacked autonomy and took his orders from individuals who sat on the boards of both Pico Macom and Pico Products. Nevertheless, the plaintiffs have not meet [sic] their burden of proving that it was the corporation of Pico Products and not Pico Macom from where these directors gained their authority to control O'Connell.

While it is true that O'Connell and the manager of operations, Young Gu Kim, were hired by Bernard Hitchcock, Mr. Hitchcock sat on the boards of both Pico Products and Pico Macom. Without proof that Hitchcock was acting on behalf of Pico Products when he took this action, the element of control by the defendant is lost. In the same vein, the claim by the plaintiff that there existed interlocking directorates between the parent corporation and its various subsidiaries is of little value. Here, there existed only one interlocking director between the Korean corporation plaintiff and defendant—James O'Connell. This hardly arises to the level of being so intertwined that the paraphernalia of the subsidiary is disregarded.

While it is also true that the parent corporation's annual report and 10–K Statement referred to the Korean corporation as "belonging" to it, the court may view this as only one factor in its determination. That the New York corporation took responsibility for "winding up" the Korean corporation after its closure and retained Korean legal counsel for this purpose indicates nothing more than that the defendant sought to protect its economic interest. These factors "seem to represent fairly common relationships between the parent corporation and subsidiaries rather than the 'alter ego' or 'mere instrumentality' relationship required for piercing the corporate veil."

(iv) Conclusion

Thus, the facts of the case do not reveal that the first element of the *Lowendahl* test is satisfied as to defendant Pico Products. The stark reality of the situation at hand is that the defendant has insulated itself from liability via the very corporate structure the plaintiff now wishes to destroy. However, it is well recognized that the primary purpose of forming a corporation is to enable shareholders to avoid personal liability. The laws of New York condone the use of the corporate entity to avoid personal liability. "With few exceptions, New York courts continue to treat the corporate veil as 'nearly impregnable' and to adhere to the general rule that courts will not 'pierce the corporate veil' or disregard the corporate entity by imposing personal liability on shareholders or on a parent or affiliated corporations."

As the defendant has correctly stated, to prevail on their contract theory, the plaintiffs must pierce two corporate veils, not one. The layering of separate corporate entities, whereby Pico Products is insulated by the corporate walls of both Pico Korea and Pico Macom, serves effectively to protect the parent. Thus, the defendant, as stockholder or as parent corporation, is not liable for the subsidiary's breach of contract. Whether another entity has dominated or controlled Pico Korea is beyond the scope of the plaintiffs' action and is therefore not addressed by this court.

B. Tortious Interference With Contract

The theory underlying the plaintiffs' tortious interference cause of action is that the defendant Pico Products took deliberate action calculated to close Pico Korea thereby preventing Pico Korea from complying with the terms of the collective bargaining agreement. Among the plaintiffs' contentions are allegations that anti-union animus on the part of the directors of Pico Products so fueled their decisions that they took this deliberate [sic] despite knowledge that a CBA existed. The plaintiffs contend that this action, namely, a directive to Pico Macom to cease funding to Pico Korea, was done with the intent of swiftly shutting down the Korean subsidiary and thereby preventing the officers of the Korean corporation from honoring the obligations arising under the CBA. The defendant claims, however, that it acted within the confines of the applicable law and that all actions were justifiable.

(i) Elements

To make out a cause of action for tortious interference under New York law the plaintiff must show that (i) it had a valid and binding agreement with another party; (ii) the alleged interferer knew of the agreement yet acted intentionally to induce its breach; (iii) the agreement was consequently breached; and (iv) damage resulted from the breach.

The court finds that a valid and binding contract existed between the plaintiff and Pico Korea; that the directors of Pico Products were aware of the contract existing between these two parties but took deliberate action, realizing full well the consequences and impact of such action, and ordered the cessation of funding to Pico Korea thereby inducing (or, more appropriately, causing) the contract to be breached; that the contract was breached by the failure of Pico Korea to abide by [specified] terms and conditions; and that the plaintiffs have suffered damages as a result of the breach.

(ii) Felsen Privilege

Nevertheless, the legal inquiry may not end here. Throughout this case the defendant has argued a corporate privilege arising under New York law. *See Felsen v. Sol Café Mfg. Corp.,* 24 N.Y.2d 682, 686, 301 N.Y.S.2d 610, 613 (1969). This privilege, referred to by this court as the "Felsen Privilege," insulates parent corporations' actions which cause their subsidiaries to breach contracts. However, the New York courts have held that this privilege is not without limitations and applies only when the parent's actions are motivated by a justifiable business purpose (such as the protection of its economic interests). This privilege does not apply if it is shown that the parent's action is motivated primarily by malice or some other unjustifiable purpose. * * *

(iii) Proof at Trial

At trial, various directors of the defendant corporation were called to the stand. All testified that they were aware of the collective bargaining agreement between the plaintiffs and Pico Korea, yet each claimed a justifiable business reason for the decision that eventually closed the Korean concern. One director summed up the testimony of the others when he claimed that, from a financial perspective, the Korean corporation was "hemorrhaging." To have allowed the losses to continue, the directors claimed, would have jeopardized the entire Pico conglomerate.

The business and economic reports produced by the defendant supported their allegations. These clearly showed that Pico Korea ceased being profitable in April, 1988. After this time, its lifeline consisted solely of capital advances, referred to as "deficit funding," from Pico Macom. The purpose was to keep the Korean corporation solvent in the hope that it could regain its self-sufficiency in the future. Nevertheless, the directors of Pico Products claimed that in the face of raising labor costs, increasing labor unrest, and a drastic decrease in levels of both production and quality, Pico Korea labored simply to remain afloat. * * *

(iv) Malicious Intent

The plaintiffs contend that the very admission by the various directors that "labor costs and unrest" entered into the calculus leading to the decision to stop funding evidences a malicious intent. * * *

Focusing once again on the Felsen Privilege, the court is faced with a difficult decision. It must determine whether the defendant's intentional interference with the collective bargaining agreement was primarily motivated by malice, or whether justifiable business reasons formed the primary impetus for such action. Black's Law Dictionary, Fifth Edition, defines malice as "[t]he intentional doing of a wrongful act without just cause or excuse, with an intent to inflict an injury or under circumstances that the law will imply an evil intent." The definition does little to advance the inquiry. The definition of malice and the Felsen Privilege are redundant. Both prohibit the doing of an otherwise wrongful act *unless* there is justifiable cause. The question then becomes, what is a justifiable cause?

In 1980 the New York State Court of Appeals, in the case of *Guard–Life Corp. v. S. Parker Hardware Mfg.*, 50 N.Y.2d 183, 428 N.Y.S.2d 628 (1980), had the opportunity to examine the tort of intentional interference with a contract. While the central focus of the *Guard–Life* case involved the question of liability arising when the questioned contract was void or voidable, the Court's discussion of the state-of-mind element of the tort is applicable here. There, the New York court recognized that the tort of interference with contractual relations, as defined by the Restatement of Torts 2d, applied to one who *improperly* interferes with the performance of a contract. In recognizing the distinction in the use of the term "improper" as opposed to the phrase "without justification," the Court stated:

> The keystone of the statement is the adverb "improperly"—a term selected in preference to the phrase "without justification" appearing frequently in judicial decisions and giving rise to questions of burden of proof—the definition of which is inconstant and mutable, drawing its substance from the circumstances of the particular situation at hand.

(v) Relevant Circumstances

Further drawing from the Restatement of Torts 2d, the *Guard–Life* court elaborated on which circumstances should be considered when determining whether, as must be done under *Felsen*, the interference was proper or improper. Included among the factors to be considered "are the nature of the conduct of the person who interferes (a chief factor in determining whether conduct is improper), the interest of the party being interfered with, the relationship between the parties," the motives and interests sought to be advanced by the one who interferes, and the social interests involved.

Here, the nature of the conduct of the interferer, Pico Products, was not in itself wrongful. Pico Products did not interfere by way of fraud, violence, misrepresentation, or unjustifiable civil or criminal legal actions—the more common forms of "wrongful" interference. In the same vein, the professed motives and interests sought to be advanced by Pico Products were of the type historically recognized as proper. The protection of the economic interests of shareholders has, from the date of *Felsen,* been recognized as a proper motive within the State of New York. Further, the legal relationship of the parties here is of little consequence. Plaintiff and defendant had no legal relationship and thus Pico Products owed no affirmative duty to the plaintiff union.

And finally, the societal interests involved, while always favorable to the sanctity of contracts, weigh in favor of the defendant's actions. Indeed, this is the law as established by the New York Court of Appeals in *Felsen*. In explaining the superiority of societal interests in the economic rights of shareholders, the *Felsen* court stated:

> "Procuring the breach of a contract in the exercise of an equal of [sic] superior right is acting with just cause or excuse, and it is justification for what would otherwise be an actionable wrong." Thus, Chock Full O'Nuts, as the sole stockholder of Sol Café, had an existing economic interest in the affairs of Sol Café which it was privileged to attempt to protect when it "interfered" with plaintiff's contract of employment with Sol Café.

(vi) Anti–Union Animus

The plaintiffs' allegations of anti-union animus on the part of the defendant is of little moment to this court's ultimate conclusion. While the defendant's directors have openly admitted that a primary factor in their decision was the rising labor costs at Pico Korea, such concerns, in this context, do not evidence a malicious character. Workers in the international market, those beyond the reaches of our Constitution and the Commerce Clause which provides the basis for our national labor laws, are not afforded protection from actions which may be detrimental to collective bargaining. * * * Pico Products' action must be viewed as a purely economic based decision, the type of action expressly sanctioned by New York law. Pico Products' action was motivated by its desire to protect its economic interests, not out of disdain for unionism. As the New York courts have held, such a motivation is justifiable.

(vii) Conclusion

Consequently, this court finds that Pico Products' action in inducing the breach of the contract was not malicious, but rather was motivated by justifiable concerns. Thus, under the holding of *Felsen* and its progeny, no liability adheres to the defendant's action.

III.

CONCLUSION

For the reasons set out in this Memorandum Decision, this court finds that the plaintiffs have failed to present evidence sufficient to impose liability upon the defendant for either of the two remaining claims. Consequently, this court instructs the Clerk of the Court to enter judgment for the defendant on both the contract and tortious interference causes of action.

Note

On appeal the Korean union argued that Pico Products' liability for Pico Korea's unmet obligations under the collective bargaining agreement should have been addressed as a breach of a bargaining agreement under section 301 of the NLRA. The court of appeals held that the dispute did not fall within the territorial scope of section 301. *See Labor Union of Pico Korea v. Pico Products,* 968 F.2d 191 (2d Cir.1992), *cert. denied* 506 U.S. 985, 113 S.Ct. 493, 121 L.Ed.2d 431 (1992).

NOTE ON DOE v. UNOCAL

Local Union v. Pico is but one example of workers' attempts to hold United States-based multinational companies liable for harms occurring in foreign countries. Most claims founder, as did Local Union v. Pico, on doctrines of state law originally designed to promote business by shielding investors from personal liability which are now used to avoid entity liability altogether. See generally, Lynn M. LoPucki, The End of Liability, 106 Yale L.J. 1 (1996).

Another example is Doe v. Unocal Corp., 110 F.Supp.2d 1294, 1308–1310 (C.D.Cal.2000), in which plaintiffs claimed that Unocal Corp., along with the Burmese military, used forced labor in the construction of a pipeline, jointly owned by Unocal, Total (a French corporation), and the Burmese (aka Myanmar) government. Having decided that forced labor qualifies as a human rights violation within the meaning of the Alien Torts Claims Act, 28 U.S.C. § 1350,[1] and that the Burmese military utilized forced labor in the building of the pipeline, the district court then analyzed whether Unocal could be held liable:

> To prevail on their ATCA claim against Unocal, Plaintiffs must establish that Unocal is legally responsible for the Myanmar military's forced labor practices. Plaintiffs contend that under international law principles of direct and vicarious liability, Unocal is legally responsible for the Myanmar military's forced labor practices. Specifically, Plaintiffs cite three decisions issued by United States Military Tribunals after World War II involving the prosecution of German industrialists for their participation in the Third Reich's slave labor policies. Plaintiffs argue that under these holdings, knowledge and approval of acts is sufficient for a finding of liability.

> During World War II, German industrial firms found themselves caught between the Nazi government's fixed production quotas and a severe wartime labor shortage. In 1942, the Reich Labor Office implemented a massive slave-labor program utilizing foreign civilians, prisoners of war, and concentration camp inmates. The German government compelled German factories to employ the slave-laborers and severely punished industrialists for failing to meet the production quotas.

> [After Germany's defeat, the four victorious Powers, the United States, Great Britain, France, and Russia, formed a "Control Council" to establish a uniform legal basis in Germany for the prosecution of war criminals and other offenders of international law. Control Council Law No. 10 recognized many international crimes; six U.S. Military Tribunals conducted twelve trials before American civilian judges.] The defendants in these proceedings were prominent figures in Hitler's Germany and included diplomats and politicians, military leaders, SS leaders, professionals, and jurists. Three of these twelve cases involved the prosecution of German industrialists charged with war crimes and crimes against humanity relating to slave labor and to the plunder and expropriation of property in occupied countries.

---

1. The Alien Tort Claims Act ("ATCA") states:

The district courts shall have original jurisdiction of any civil action by an alien for a tort only, committed in violation of the law of nations or a treaty of the United States.

28 U.S.C. § 1350. According to the district court, "[t]he ATCA provides both subject matter jurisdiction and a cause of action. To state a claim under the ATCA, a plaintiff must allege (1) a claim by an alien, (2) alleging a tort, and (3) a violation of the law of nations (international law). The parties do not dispute that the first two elements are satisfied. The issue is whether the conduct of the Myanmar military violated international law, and if so, whether Unocal is liable for these violations."

In the first of the three industrialist cases, *United States of America v. Friedrich Flick*, "The Flick Case," 6 Trials of War Criminals Before the Nuremberg Military Tribunals Under Control Council Law No. 10 (1952), Frederick Flick, a dominant figure in the German steel industry, and five of his business associates, were charged with participating in the Third Reich's slave labor program. The Tribunal concluded that four of the six defendants were entitled to the affirmative defense of necessity and were therefore not guilty. In reaching its decision, the Tribunal acknowledged that the German slave labor program was created and supervised by the Nazi government and that it would have been futile and dangerous for these defendants to have objected. Two of the defendants were convicted. The Tribunal found that Bernhard Weiss, with the knowledge and approval of his superior Frederick Flick, sought an increase in the factory's production quota of freight cars and attempted to procure a corresponding increase in his firm's allotment of forced laborers. These active steps to participate in the Reich's slave labor program, reasoned the Tribunal, deprived these two defendants of the necessity defense.

In the second industrialist case, *United States of America v. Carl Krauch*, "The Farben Case," twenty-three members of I.G. Farben, a German chemical and pharmaceutical company, were tried for utilizing slave labor. Like the Flick defendants, the Farben defendants invoked the necessity defense and testified that they were under such oppressive coercion and compulsion that they cannot be said to have acted with criminal intent. The Tribunal found five of the defendants guilty on grounds that they, "like Weiss and Flick, were not moved by a lack of moral choice, but, on the contrary, embraced the opportunity to take full advantage of the slave-labor program. Indeed, it might be said that they were, to a very substantial degree, responsible for broadening the scope of that reprehensible system." The Tribunal further found that defendant Krauch was "a willing participant in the crime of enslavement." As for the balance of the defendants, the Tribunal found that they all knew that forced labor was being utilized and that they acquiesced in this practice under the Reich's pressure. However, because these defendants did not exercise initiative in obtaining forced labor, they were acquitted.

Finally, in *United States of America v. Alfried Felix Alwyn Krupp von Bohlen und Halbach*, "The Krupp Case," the defendants were twelve members of the Krupp organization, a German company in the business of producing steel and iron products. The Tribunal found the defendants guilty of employing slave labor because their will was not overpowered by the Third Reich "but instead coincide[d] with the will of those from whom the alleged compulsion emanate[d]." Moreover, the "Krupp firm had manifested not only its willingness but its ardent desire to employ forced labor."

The Court disagrees with Plaintiffs that these cases hold that an industrialist is liable where he or she has knowledge that someone else would commit abuses. Rather, liability requires participation or cooperation in the forced labor practices. In the Flick Case, Weiss took "active steps" with the "knowledge and approval" of his superior to procure forced laborers so that the company could increase its production quota. The Tribunal's guilty verdict rested not on the defendants' knowledge and acceptance of benefits of the forced labor, but on their active participation in the unlawful conduct.

Plaintiffs also argue that *Iwanowa v. Ford Motor Co.,* 67 F.Supp.2d 424 (D.N.J.1999), supports their argument that Unocal is liable for the Myanmar military's forced labor practices. In Iwanowa, the plaintiff alleged that after being abducted by Nazi troops and transported from Rostov, Russia to Germany, Ford Werke, a German subsidiary of Ford Motor Co., purchased her and forced her to perform heavy labor from 1942 until Germany surrendered in 1945. The district court denied Ford's motion to dismiss for lack of jurisdiction, finding there to be jurisdiction for the plaintiff's claims of slave labor under the ATCA. The court held that Ford Werke's "use of unpaid, forced labor during World War II violated clearly established norms of customary international law."

In this case, there are no facts suggesting that Unocal sought to employ forced or slave labor. In fact, the Joint Venturers expressed concern that the Myanmar government was utilizing forced labor in connection with the Project. In turn, the military made efforts to conceal its use of forced labor. The evidence does suggest that Unocal knew that forced labor was being utilized and that the Joint Venturers benefitted from the practice. However, because such a showing is insufficient to establish liability under international law, Plaintiffs' claim against Unocal for forced labor under the Alien Tort Claims Act fails as a matter of law.

In Sept. 2001, a court refused to dismiss similar claims, framed as violation of the California constitution and statutes. See Roe III v. Unocal (Cal. Sup. Ct.) reported at 170 DLR A–10 (2001).

D. TRANSNATIONAL LABOR STANDARDS AND THE GLOBAL ECONOMY

As we have seen, American labor and employment laws do not automatically apply to domestic workers plying their trades outside the United States or to foreign workers laboring in the United States. Are there, however, labor standards which apply transnationally? And if so, how are they set?

Section I introduces the concept of transnational labor rights and sketches the range of labor rights that have been proposed. Section 2 explores the connection between international trade and labor standards.

Finally, section 3 offers examples of institutional means to establish labor standards transnationally.

1. TRANSNATIONAL LABOR RIGHTS

JANET DINE,
HUMAN RIGHTS AND COMPANY LAW

in Human Rights Standards and the Responsibility
of Transnational Corporations,
ed. Michael K. Addo.
209, 209–212 (1999).

Valticos puts forward three purposes for international labour law: as an aid to fair competition, as furthering the cause of peace, but, overwhelmingly as "the concept of social justice" for its own sake. Drzewicki agrees that "whatever the historical motives at the outset were, the philosophy of social justice has remained the prime objective of the International Labour Organization [ILO]." The Constitution of the ILO (revised 1946) states that "labor is not a commodity" and that "all human beings, irrespective of race, creed or sex, have the right to pursue both their material well-being and their spiritual development in conditions of freedom and dignity, of economic security and equal opportunity." The reasons for concluding international treaties on labour rights may thus be seen as primarily protective of employees, redressing the imbalance of their otherwise enfeebled status. However, the treaties themselves are embedded in the "junior branch" of human rights laws. * * *

[The perceived distinction between public rights, i.e., civil and political rights, and private rights, i.e., social, economic and cultural rights, has had significant impact.] The original division between civil and political rights on the one hand and economic social and cultural rights on the other stemmed from "a controversial and contested" decision of the UN General Assembly in 1951 which was based on the underlying assumption that civil and political rights were absolute, immediate and justiciable whereas economic, social and cultural rights were programmatic and would be costly to implement. Even where the rights are formulated as creating legally binding obligations on contracting states, individuals have no right of enforcement[.] * * * [T]his "neat distinction" is now too simplistic[;] it is nevertheless true that the rights built into economic, social and cultural treaties are less well known generally and less easy to enforce. Labour rights are "quite far from reaching a reasonable degree of their juridization." From the perspective of the detractors of economic, social and political rights their nature has provided two apparently contradictory arguments: on the one hand the rights would be too costly and burdensome to implement; on the other their vague nature and lack of standards means they are not rights at all, mere ephemera. * * *

LANCE COMPA, THE MULTILATERAL AGREEMENT ON INVESTMENT AND INTERNATIONAL LABOR RIGHTS: A FAILED CONNECTION

31 Cornell International Law Journal 683, 697–700.
1998.

The first element in an international labor rights regime is a set of norms with extraterritorial reach. Among current labor rights regimes, there are two poles of normative formulations. One is devoted to a relatively narrow "core." The other is more expansive. At extremes, the number of norms can actually vary from one, such as with some corporate codes or social labeling schemes which are limited to the issue of child labor, to the 176 Conventions of the ILO (although the ILO cites only seven as "human rights" Conventions).

Inside these extremes, the elaboration of labor rights norms generally follows "core" and "core-plus" tracks. The core track contains a limited number of standards usually addressing freedom of association (and related rights of organization and collective bargaining), forced labor, child labor, and non-discrimination. The standards reflect fundamental human rights that cannot vary based on a country's level of development.

Advocates of core standards argue that limiting a labor rights regime to universal human rights standards sustains a consensus in favor of labor rights. Sticking to a narrow, non-economic core disarms critics who see a labor standards-trade link as a form of protectionism in disguise, meant to deprive developing countries of their comparative advantage in low labor costs.

The other current model goes beyond the so-called "core" to embrace social and economic standards related to wages, hours, and working conditions, usually bringing the number of specific standards closer to a dozen. A wider set of norms is more responsive to workers' concrete concerns and needs, and addresses some governments' attempts to gain trade advantages through economic and social repression. For example, the NAFTA [North America Free Trade Agreement between Canada, Mexico and the United States] and the EU [European Union, an alliancee between European countries] set out eleven and twelve basic labor standards, respectively, that mix human rights with social and economic concerns. Taken as a whole, the UN's International Bill of Rights covers more than a dozen labor-related concerns. Most corporate codes of conduct contain more than core-norm construction, but do not usually reach as many concerns as the NAALC [North American Agreement on Labor Cooperation, the side agreement to NAFTA dealing with labor rights], EU, and UN formulations. Generally, they cover working hours and occupational safety and health; rarely do they address cost factors like wages and benefits beyond compliance with relevant domestic laws.

Scope of Norms in Selected International Labor Rights Instruments:

1) "Core" Norm Construction

Frameworks based on core labor standards include the following:

[European Union General System of Preferences] EU GSP system:

—freedom of association;

—the right to bargain collectively;

—limits on child labor.

World Bank:

—freedom of association;

—the right to collective bargaining;

—elimination of forced labor;

—elimination of exploitative forms of child labor;

—non-discrimination in employment.

[] OECD:

—freedom of association;

—collective bargaining;

—elimination of exploitative forms of child labor;

—prohibition of forced labor;

—non-discrimination in employment.

ILO Human Rights Conventions:

—freedom of association and protection of the right to organize;

—the right to organize and bargain collectively;

—minimum age for admission to employment;

—abolition of forced labor (2 conventions);

—non-discrimination in employment;

—equal pay for men and women.

World Trade Organization [WTO]:

The WTO has affirmed a "commitment to the observance of internationally recognized core [labour] standards" and declared that the ILO "is the competent body to set and deal with these standards."

2) "Core–Plus" Formulations:

U.S. GSP and other domestic U.S.trade laws:

—the right of association;

—the right to organize and bargain collectively;

—prohibition of forced labor;

—limits on child labor;

—"acceptable conditions" on minimum wages, hours of work, and occupational safety and health;

EU Community Charter of Fundamental Social Rights for Workers:

—the right to freedom of movement;

—free employment and fair remuneration;

—the improvement of living and working conditions;

—the right to social protection;

—the right to freedom of association and collective bargaining;

—the right to vocational training;

—the right of men and women to equal treatment;

—the right to information, consultation, and participation;

—the right to health and safety in the workplace;

—the protection of children and adolescents in employment;

—the protection of elderly persons in employment;

—protection of persons with disabilities in employment.

Labor Principles of the North American Agreement on Labor Cooperation (NAALC):

—freedom of association and protection of the right to organize;

—the right to bargain collectively;

—the right to strike;

—prohibition of forced labor;

—labor protections for children and young persons;

—minimum employment standards, such as minimum wages and overtime pay, covering wage earners, including those not covered by collective agreements;

—elimination of employment discrimination on the basis of such grounds as race, religion, age, sex, or other grounds as determined by each Party's domestic laws;

—equal pay for men and women;

—prevention of occupational injuries and illnesses;

—compensation in cases of occupational injuries and illnesses;

—protection of migrant workers.

Apparel Industry Partnership Code of Conduct:

—forced labor;

—child labor;

—harassment or abuse;

—non-discrimination;

—health and safety;

—freedom of association and collective bargaining;

—wages and benefits;

—hours of work;

—overtime compensation;

Levi Strauss Code of Conduct:

—wages and benefits;

—working hours;

—child labor;

—prison labor/forced labor;

—non-discrimination;

—disciplinary practices (i.e., "corporal punishment or other forms of mental or physical coercion.")

Reebok Code of Conduct:

—non-discrimination;

—working hours/overtime;

—forced or compulsory labor;

—fair wages;

—child labor;

—freedom of association;

—safe and healthy work environment.

Like the Cheshire Cat's grin, an elaboration of international labor norms is just floating in air without attaching some level of obligation to respect the norms. Like norms, obligations vary in their number and level of detail. In some instruments, a single phrase announces the obligation, while in others, a detailed statement lays out myriad obligations.

CLYDE SUMMERS
THE BATTLE IN SEATTLE: FREE TRADE,
LABOR RIGHTS AND SOCIETAL VALUES

22 U. Pa. J. Int'l Economic L. 61, 66–68.
Spring 2001.

"[C]ore" labor standards * * * are defined in the ILO Declaration of Fundamental Principles and Rights of Work as: (1) freedom of association and effective recognition of the right to bargain collectively; (2) elimination of all forms of forced labor; (3) effective abolition of child labor; and (4) elimination of discrimination in employment and occupation. These "core" labor rights have been designated by the ILO as the four fundamental rights that all [180] members of the ILO [including the United States] are obligated "to respect, promote and realize in good faith,'' regardless of whether the member has ratified relevant ILO conventions. * * *

It is crucial to recognize three characteristics of these core labor rights. First, these rights do not focus on low wages. Forced labor is prohibited not because goods produced under such conditions compete unfairly, but because it denies workers their freedom. Child labor is prohibited not because it is cheap but because children's growth and development should not be stunted by wage work. Even if a child were paid the same wage as her father, allowing her to enter the labor market would violate this standard. The operative principle is that children should be shielded from the burdens of wage labor. Prohibition of discrimination reaches beyond wage costs to protect workers' equal right to work and the right to equal treatment on the job, as a part of their basic human right to be treated equally. The right to free association and collective bargaining is protected as a human right regardless of whether the union is able to bargain for a living wage.

There is no suggestion that there should be a global minimum wage or that a right to a ''fair wage'' or even a ''living wage'' is a core labor right. There is general acceptance that the differential in wages due to the availability of cheap labor serves as a legitimate comparative advantage in international trade and that low wage countries should not be deprived of this advantage. It should be noted that the European Union over a period of forty years has established uniform standards on a multitude of labor rights, but it has not even considered establishing a community-wide minimum wage. The comparative advantage of the differential in wage rates is preserved.

Second, these core labor rights are, at most, minimal. They encompass only seven of the ILO Conventions, all seven of which are almost universally accepted. One hundred twenty-seven countries have ratified ILO Convention No. 87 on Freedom of Association and the Right to Organize; 145 have ratified Convention No. 98 on the Right to Bargain collectively; 141 countries have ratified Convention No. 111 on Discrimination; 151 countries have ratified Convention No. 29 on Forced Labor; and 84 countries have ratified Convention No. 138 on Child Labor. * * *

Observance of these core labor rights would have minimal impact on labor costs. To be sure, prohibiting forced labor or child labor may reduce the supply of labor and thereby increase the wage level, reducing a country's competitive advantage. The effect on wages, however, would not measurably reduce an underdeveloped country's comparative advantage in labor costs over developed countries. In any case, the competitive advantage gained by slavery or child labor is not an advantage to be shielded by free trade. The same is true of any advantage gained by discrimination. Observance of the right to organize and bargain collectively may ultimately have more impact on wage rates, but none of the countries objecting to enforcing core labor rights claimed that they were entitled to a comparative advantage gained by prohibiting workers from joining unions.

There are a number of other important and widely recognized labor rights that are not protected by the "core" labor rights: the right to a safe and healthful place of work, limits on the hours of work, rights to periods of rest, and protection against abusive treatment. None of these involve wage rates, and though some of them might entail labor costs, they would not deny any developing country the comparative advantage they obtain by offering cheap labor.

Third, the four core labor rights are more than labor rights; they are recognized internationally as human rights. The core rights go beyond those belonging to individuals as workers; they belong to individuals as human beings. Accordingly, the core rights have become recognized as human rights. They are articulated in the Universal Declaration of Human Rights, the International Covenant on Civil and Political Rights, the International Covenant on Economic, Social and Cultural Rights, and a number of other human rights conventions. To bar imports because they have been produced in violation of these rights is not an economic regulation but a social regulation. The enforcement mechanism is economic, but the interests protected are human rights. This significantly shifts the focus of the free trade debate. The issue is not simply one of economic efficiency—whether free trade will promote economic growth—but one of humanitarian concern, whether free trade serves to promote or deny basic human values. * * *

Questions

1. Does linking labor rights with trade rights mean penalizing the imports of countries whose labor standards fall below a minimum agreed on by other countries?

2. What arguments could you put forward on behalf of linking trade and labor rights?

3. How would you make the case against establishing a link between trade and labor rights?

2. INTERNATIONAL TRADE AND LABOR STANDARDS

To illustrate how establishment of labor standards necessarily implicates the regulation of international business and international investment, Bennett Harrison, an economist, and Donald Dowling, a management consultant, evaluate business operations in the global economy. Although the excerpts focus on the manufacturing process of the Nike company, the issues raised by Harrison and Dowling appear in most discussions of labor rights in the global economy. And Frances Olsen reminds us that ideas, like financial capital, may be hypermobile.

BENNETT HARRISON, LEAN AND MEAN: THE CHANGING LANDSCAPE OF CORPORATE POWER IN THE AGE OF FLEXIBILITY

206–213 (1994).

No product sold in America (or Europe, or the Far East) today is more well known than Nike's running shoes. Like cars, hamburgers, and furniture, Nike shoes (the name *Nike* stands for the goddess of victory in Greek mythology) come in literally dozens of models, from the relatively cheap to the very expensive, from the (literally) pedestrian to the stylish. Although Nike is legally registered as an American corporation, not one of the 40 million pairs of running shoes that Nike produces annually is manufactured within the United States: *everything* is subcontracted from elsewhere.

As reconstructed by Michael T. Donaghu and Richard Barff, two Dartmouth College geographers (one of whom worked for the company for a time), Nike's global division of labor is an exemplar of the principle of * * * concentration without centralization. That principle is intended to capture the continuing dispersal of production, but ultimately under the technical and financial control of managers in a relatively small number of big multiregional, multisectoral, multinational corporations and their strategic allies. Nike is such a network firm, whose management has found ways to connect the lowest-paying unskilled jobs with the highest-paying skilled R & D jobs, classic mass production with flexibly automated technology, and the First World with the Third.* * *

The Nike production system is organized into two broad tiers. In the first of these tiers, "developed partners" located mainly in Taiwan and South Korea work closely with the R & D personnel in Oregon to make the firm's most expensive, high-end footwear (by *partners*, Nike managers mean contractors and suppliers who share some joint responsibility with the core firm, for design or for evaluation of production methods). The Asian partners contract out most of the work to local low-wage subcontractors.

"Volume producers" are considerably larger, more vertically integrated companies with their own leather tanneries and rubber factories that manufacture more standardized products and sell to several buyers, of whom Nike is only one. Production and sales are highly variable from one month to the next.

Finally within this tier, Nike has created what it calls "developing sources"—producers located in Thailand, Indonesia, Malaysia, and China. These are the lowest-wage, low-and semiskilled operations that Nike is gradually upgrading ("bringing along"). Technicians from the United States, Taiwan, and South Korea are assigned to work in these "developing" facilities, often on a rotating basis (Nike calls this its "expatriate program"). Such sources often take the form of joint ventures between

the Taiwanese or South Korean "big brothers" and the less industrialized Southeast Asian "little brothers."

Nike managers explicitly acknowledge the advantages of this spatial
division of labor within the first tier. Apart from "hedg[ing] against
currency fluctuations, tariffs and duties [and] political climate change
. . . in the long run [this arrangement] keeps pressure on the first tier
producers to keep production costs low as developing sources mature
into full-blown developed partners."

The second tier of the Nike production network consists of the many
material, component, and subassembly sources. Predictably, the least
complicated elements may be produced at any of the network's locations
in the United States, Europe, or Southeast Asia. But some elements,
such as the air cushions that pad all modern athletic shoes, either
require skilled labor to turn them out, or make use of proprietary
technology or designs. These tend to be located in the vicinity of the
Oregon headquarters, where engineers and others can be exchanged
easily and frequently—an example of * * * "specialization subcontracting" * * *. As the physical infrastructure and human capital of the
"little brothers" is upgraded over time, Nike anticipates that a growing
fraction of its second-tier suppliers will be located in Asia.

Clearly, the Nike production system has undergone a substantial
evolution since the 1970s. Yet it remains a dualistic system, combining
high-wage and low-wage, specialized and standardized production, core
and periphery. As Donaghu and Barff put it:

> When NIKE's shoes were first produced in Asia, Japan represented
> the core and other nations constituted the periphery. Today, NIKE's
> intraregional division of labor in South East Asia simply based on
> labor costs has S. Korea and Taiwan as the core and China,
> Thailand, Malaysia, and Indonesia as the periphery. Japan, with
> average manufacturing hourly wages very close to those of the
> United States, is still a supplier of materials, but is no longer a site
> of production for NIKE athletic shoes. . . . [However,] there is no
> evidence to suggest that production has shifted as markets have
> developed. In fact, there is evidence to the contrary. The English,
> Irish and American plants all ended production of NIKE athletic
> shoes in the mid 1980s, even as demand for Nike running shoes was
> accelerating in all three countries.

Interviews with the American managers revealed that they clearly
perceived the flexibility of this production system as residing in a
combination of low cost, spread risk, and—most of all—"the speed by
which a design for a new model of shoe is transformed into a product at
the market." This turnaround time is partly a function of using highly
disciplined labor and partly of deploying "mass production techniques by
simplifying work stations and updating existing machinery." For example:

> a new machine was introduced that could automatically position the
> needle and trim excess thread for the operator. This kind of labor

saving change is hardly revolutionary and can be specifically associated with the continuation of Fordist means of production. The only elements of NIKE's system that could be classified as flexible machinery [are] the computer-aided design and computer-aided engineering used in the Beaverton [U.S.] R & D facility, and some numerically-controlled molding machines used by one or two South Korean subcontractors.

The other aspect of flexibility in this system is the core firm's adeptness at shifting productive capital from one place to another. Nike "has opened plants and begun contracts only to end them within only a matter of a year or two. It also utilizes capacity subcontracting methods to meet variable market demand."

Throughout the first tier, as much as 80 percent of sales to the final assemblers of the footwear are "prepurchased," meaning that Nike effectively advances capital to the members of what, after all, clearly has features that resemble a far-flung putting-out system. And while Nike's subcontractors themselves tend to be vertically disintegrated and may in some cases be locally agglomerated, and while customer-supplier relations may sometimes be described as reciprocal, or at least not confrontational, "by any definition, [Nike's] method of physically producing athletic shoes is mass production." At the level of the global network, "the company still relies on large volume production by [mostly] semi- and unskilled labor," linked to high-tech R & D and sophisticated financial management situated in the United States.

* * * Nike is a neo-Fordist firm, whose flexibility derives mainly from its managers' ability to construct and govern a dualistic system characterized by concentration without centralization. Its profitability derives directly from its managers being so cleverly able to manage the dark side. * * *

What does Harrison mean by "the dark side?" If he is referring to the conditions under which Nike's low paid workforce operates, how does he know that side is "dark?" Consider the observations of Donald Dowling:

DONALD C. DOWLING, JR.
THE MULTINATIONAL'S MANIFESTO ON SWEATSHOPS, TRADE/LABOR LINKAGE, AND CODE OF CONDUCT

8 Tulsa J. Comp. & Int'l L. 27, 39–40, 43–46 (Fall 2000).

[Dowling begins by comparing workplace regulation in the United States at the federal level with the laws in various developing countries; he emphasizes that the more stringent standards appear in the laws of the developing countries. What he neglects to mention is that in the

United States, standards legislation is usually enacted by the state legislatures not by the federal government (although federal laws on taxes and spending may act as incentives for the states to legislate standards). Having established the rigorous rules in developing countries regarding minimum workplace protections, child labor, forced labor, labor union rights and mandatory benefits, Dowling then moves to the question of enforcement.]

Activists' charges of weak employment law enforcement are undoubtedly true in some workplaces. But most of the bad enforcement is at the level of purely local employers—that is, the mom-and-pops in poor countries that make stuff purely for the domestic market (and, therefore, lie beyond the reach of multinationals and those who work in world trade, like the WTO, the IMF, the World Bank, and U.S. Congress). Small, local employers are the most likely to cruise along under local regulators' radar.

But everything changes when we look at poor-country labor law enforcement against multinationals and local companies who sell goods in international trade. Poor countries do a good job enforcing worker protection and anti-sweatshop laws against players in global commerce. Indeed, a third-world bureaucrat whose job is to enforce local labor laws has a political incentive to crack down on the big, foreign-based companies and their suppliers. (Overseas, American multinationals make popular targets; they are symbols of American economic and cultural imperialism. Think of Jose Bove, the French protester who rode to fame by dismantling a McDonald's; think of all the hullabaloo about Nike's factories abroad; think of the regulators in India who made a splash a few years ago by denying Kentucky Fried Chicken a license to do business.) Busting a big multinational—particularly an American one—can be a career-making move for a third-world labor law enforcer. And, politics aside, larger workforces have higher visibility on enforcers' radar screens; it is tough for a giant to hide. (Most multinationals and local companies making goods for world trade are bigger than most poor-country companies involved only in domestic commerce.)

Anecdotal evidence bears out the logic. Contrary to what activists tell you, in poor countries multinationals and employers engaged in world trade boast good compliance records. The Mexican maquiladora factories I have toured were well maintained, nice-looking places even by U.S. standards. One I saw even gives employees spotless tennis and jai alai courts. In my experience, U.S.-run maquiladoras in Mexico abide by the law. Go to Monterrey, Mexico, where hundreds of U.S.-based companies make stuff for the U.S. market. At quitting time, ask the thousands of Monterrey factory workers you see whether they get their premium-pay vacation, their thirteenth-month salary, their annual profit-sharing check, their free or subsidized lunches, and their severance pay when they are fired. The answer will be "sí."

According to the Wall Street Journal, "in El Salvador, women workers at [Nike supplier] Hilasal's textile plant in San Salvador have company doctors, a pediatric clinic, maternity leave and a company-subsidized store." One big Brazilian company I once worked with offers its factory workers an on-site medical clinic—that actually does surgery. While Nike gets criticized because its supplier factories in Vietnam pay workers $55 per month, that is over double the average—not minimum—Vietnamese per capita income ($26 per month). Supporting all this, documents I see in merger and acquisition deals (as part of "due diligence") show that poor country workers in multinationals' factories do get their agüinaldo Christmas bonuses, their premium-pay vacations, their profit-sharing, their free child-care, and most everything else in which they have a legal right. And my experience in deals shows poor-country workers, far more often than their U.S. counterparts, actually belong to labor unions and come under collective agreements.

* * *

C. If Third–World Anti–Sweatshop Laws Are So Strong and Enforcement Is So Good, Then How to Account for All the Horror Stories?

If what we said up to now is true (and it is), that means the poor countries of the world have, on their books, better laws protecting workers and banning sweatshops than the U.S. has. And it also means that third-world nations do enforce their laws against multinationals and local companies making goods for world trade. But surely you are skeptical. Surely you are asking, if poor countries' laws do adequately protect workers from sweatshop conditions, and if poor countries do adequately enforce worker protection laws against multinationals and companies involved in world trade, then why on earth do we in rich countries hear so much about horrid third-world employment conditions? This is a good question, and it has three good answers: low but livable wages, local employment, and comparing "apples" with "oranges."

1. LOW BUT LIVABLE WAGES

In poor countries people are, by definition, poor. Although we have noted that poor countries often require employers to give cash benefits in addition to wages (paid Sundays, profit sharing, Christmas bonuses), no one denies that by rich-country standards, even total compensation packages for manual labor in poor countries are very low and always will be. (Jesus Christ said "the poor will always be with us.") Yet while by rich-country standards base wage rates in the developing world can be incredibly low, they are still livable; no one claims poor-country workers with full-time jobs (or their families) are starving, naked, or homeless. Nevertheless, field hands in India can earn less than 50 cents a day; doctors in Cuba earn under $10 per month; per capita annual income in places like Chad can run under $100. (But this is not always the case: blue-collar workers in more advanced parts of the developing world, such as Argentina, Mexico, and South Korea, earn thousands or tens of thousands of dollars per year.)

While we in rich countries can be shocked to hear about the incredibly low wages that poor-country laborers earn, always remember: low wages are better than no wages. This point came home to me in September 2000, when Pulitzer Prize-winning journalists Nicholas Kristof and Sheryl WuDunn (who specialize in Asia reporting) wrote an article in the New York Times Sunday Magazine called Two Cheers for Sweatshops. According to Kristof and WuDunn:

> We moved to Asia outraged by sweatshops. In time, though, we came to accept that the simplest way to help the poorest Asians would be to buy more from sweatshops, not less. It may sound silly to say that sweatshops offer a route to prosperity, when wages in the poorest countries are sometimes less than $1 a day. Still, for an impoverished Indonesian or Bangladeshi woman with a handful of kids who would otherwise drop out of school and risk dying of mundane diseases like diarrhea, $1 or $2 a day can be a life-transforming wage.

"For all the misery they engender," Kristof and WuDunn concluded, "sweatshops at least offer a precarious escape from the poverty that is the developing world's greatest problem." But why not force multinational employers and companies involved in world trade in these countries to pay more? Kristof and WuDunn explain that "if companies are scolded for paying those wages," then "labor costs" will rise "across the board." This, in turn, "encourages less well established companies to mechanize and to reduce the number of employees needed," or else it "shifts manufacturing to marginally richer areas."

Still skeptical? Talk to University of Puget Sound student Elie Wasser, an activist crusader who traveled to Managua, Nicaragua to investigate and blow the whistle on exploitive multinationals. In October 2000, Rolling Stone ran an article with the news that when crusaders like Wasser investigate poor-country factories, even they end up conceding that multinationals offer decent jobs with tolerable conditions and livable, above-minimum wages. Rolling Stone quotes Wasser: "Before I came here [to Managua], I knew sweatshops were bad. But now I realize it would be disastrous if the factories in the Free Trade Zone and the jobs they provide were taken away." (And Rolling Stone reports that Wasser's Managua trip left a companion activist, Duke sophomore Jonelle Grant, filled with "self-doubt" and "equivocation" because she could not in good conscience label the Nicaraguan garment factory she had investigated a "sweatshop!")

2. LOCAL EMPLOYERS

Apart from low but livable wages, a second reason we hear so much about sweatshops in poor countries has to do with abuses by local employers not involved in world trade and outside the reach of the WTO, the IMF, the World Bank, and the U.S. Congress. We already discussed this issue in the context of child labor enforcement; as with child labor, the more gruesome third-world sweatshop horror stories we hear involve purely-local jobs tucked well away from big multinationals and the world trade community.

A great example: the New York Times recently did a splashy expose of horrid work conditions in China's "shoe town," Bishan. Bishan shoemakers toil long hours for a pittance in dank factories using glues that emit benzene fumes causing severe anemia and leukemia. But Bishan shoes are not Prada, they are not Nike, and they are not even Payless. Bishan shoes retail for $4 a pair and get sold domestically to Chinese peasants who cannot afford better. No one—not even the most strident defender of human rights—blames Bishan's horrors on any Western multinational, because Bishan factories are locally-owned mom-and-pop outfits. Yet you cannot even accuse the moms-or-pops of exploiting workers; Bishan factory owners toil as hard as their workers, and their factories are inside their own houses—meaning factory owners and their families inhale more benzene than anyone!

No one denies local employment stories like this are awful. And no one has figured out how to solve these local employment problems. Our point is simply that the way to solve local employment problems is not to tie the hands of the very Western multinationals offering the highest paying, safest, and most comfortable jobs. Nor is the way to solve local employment problems to pretend that local domestic tragedies are world trade issues implicating the giant multinationals and companies involved in world trade.

3. Comparing "Apples" with "Oranges"

Low but livable wages and the "local employers" issue aside, the third reason that the poor-country sweatshop horror stories we hear sound so grim has to do with our tendency to compare "apples" with "oranges," between rich and poor-country workplaces. When you hear about bad work standards in poor countries, be sure you compare low-wage factory jobs in the third world to the harsh realities of low-wage gritty work in the first world.

Macroeconomic trends have shifted so much heavy production out of rich countries that most Americans do not know any manual laborers in bad jobs. Therefore, we forget how harsh low-wage factory life still is in the U.S. We end up comparing the media's descriptions of, for example, Nike factories in Vietnam to, say, our air-conditioned office cubicles, or, at worst, to deep-fryer duty at a local Burger King. That comparison is unfair. The next time you hear a description of a third-world sweatshop, compare it to a comparable American job, like a laborer in a West Virginia coal mine or a harvester on a Florida sugarcane farm. Or take the example of a law-abiding non-union metal castings factory in Ohio, where American laborers toil, for little over minimum wage, in Dickensian conditions, pouring molten steel in dirty buildings that, in summer, get hot enough to bake food. These are real "sweatshops." I toured one once, wearing a suit, and had a hard time looking workers in the eye.

Only if you understand how tough low-wage manual factory labor is right here in our country can you appreciate the sincerity of C.T. Park, a South Korean who owns a 10,000–employee factory in Vietnam making Nike shoes. Park, whose facility was recently the target of rich-country human rights activists' complaints, laments, "I had pride in my factory. And then suddenly it was the worst factory in the world." * * *

Perhaps Harrison's reference to the "dark side" was prompted by the concern that companies are abandoning workforces in what Dowling calls the "rich countries" for the less costly employees in developing countries. Indeed, many commentators combine their concerns that the global economy is based on low wage, exploited labor *and* that workers in the countries with higher labor standards are losing jobs to workers who have been unable to raise theirs. Leaders of developed countries argue, as does Dowling, that imposition of labor rights is a disguised form of protectionism sought by United States unions that want to keep middle class wages in the pockets of their constituents. How would Clyde Summers respond?

FRANCES E. OLSEN, SYMPOSIUM: GLOBAL DYNAMICS OF UNFAIR EMPLOYMENT

4 Employee Rights and Employment Policy Journal 171, 171–74.
2000.

* * * Much of what people write on the topic in law reviews focuses on the issue of whether competition in the global market does or does not damage labor standards around the world. That is one face of globalization, and I wouldn't want to underestimate its importance. * * *

But my talk this morning will focus on a second face of globalization and what effects it may have on labor conditions. The example I want to use to illustrate this second face of globalization is sexual harassment.

The experience of sexual harassment is very old. It seems to date back as far as man's oppression of women. The concept that sexual imposition is sexual harassment is of much more recent vintage. At least by the early 1970s, women workers began coming to lawyers throughout the U.S. with stories of co-workers or bosses sexually molesting them and firing them when they refused sexual overtures. The Civil Rights Act of 1964, which said that there should be no discrimination in employment on the basis of race or sex, empowered these women to come to lawyers to see whether there might be a legal remedy.

[The discussion of the hesitancy of federal courts to recognize claims of sexual harassment as sex discrimination is omitted. Eds.]

By 1980, the EEOC had issued its guidelines on sexual harassment and the cause of action began to feel established. Of course, women in the United States continued to try to handle 99 percent of sexual harassment situations as best they could informally as they had always tried in the past. But, the public silence was broken and the balance of power gradually shifted. Women had a label for our experience that gave us a greater sense of entitlement. The greater sense of entitlement gave us more options for making men stop the behavior, gave us more room to maneuver, and allowed us to work out better solutions informally. Sexual harassment was wrong, it was illegal, it was not just a workplace misfortune, and not just bad workplace conditions. This redefinition of the workplace experience was more important than any money that actually changed hands in damage awards. The idea that men sexually hassling women at work is not natural, not inevitable, not good-natured fun, was cemented by the few cases that were brought and it had an effect on virtually everyone. It empowered the men who opposed hassling women; it undermined the sense of entitlement assumed by the harassers; and, most of all, it reinforced the notion that sexual harassment was wrong and that all women had a right to have it stopped. It was this sense that women shouldn't have to put up with sexual harassment that has begun to spread around the globe.

In 1986, the Commission of the European Community initiated a country-by-country survey to see what laws existed in the European Union countries to deal with sex in the workplace—sexual demands, coercion, hassling. The study was published in 1988, and by 1990 the Council issued a Resolution on the Protection of the Dignity of Women and Men at Work. It is this notion of worker dignity that ties sexual harassment so closely to other labor law issues.

David Gregory, in his recent article on Dorothy Day, offers a good reminder of the central role that the notion of workers' dignity has played in strikes and other labor actions. This linkage is particularly important in European countries with strong labor movements. In some of these countries, the unions play a central role in preventing harassment.

In 1987, the Canadian Supreme Court decided Robichaud v. Canada, condemning sexual harassment as a form of sex discrimination in violation of the Canadian Human Rights Act. New Zealand enacted the Employment Contracts Act of 1991 which specifies that all employment contracts shall include effective procedures to be followed when an employee complains of sexual harassment, including peer harassment from a co-worker or third party harassment from a client or customer of the employer. The employee is deemed to have a personal grievance against the employer if it fails to take all practicable steps to prevent a repetition of the harassment. The New Zealand law also specifies that neither the employer nor the employment tribunal may take account of the employee's previous sexual experience or reputation. In this sense, the New Zealand law goes further and is more progressive than the law in the U.S.

The notion that sexual harassment is a legal wrong and that women are entitled to work without having to fend off sexual overtures has spread to Japan also. In April 1992, a woman in Fukuoka, Japan won that country's first sexual harassment case—a case of hostile environment harassment. The case drew enormous publicity and during the past eight years the concept of sexual harassment, or sekushuara harasumento, has had a tremendous effect throughout Japan. Only a handful of cases have been brought—Japan is much less litigious than the U.S. or Europe—and in the end these cases that have been brought have focused on a tort theory more than a civil rights or an employment discrimination theory. Companies and universities have been drafting sexual harassment guidelines and women in Japan have begun seeing freedom from sexual harassment as a part of their entitlement to dignity.

One could look at these developments from a comparative law perspective as an interesting case of lateral transplants, and there are some insights to be gained from such a perspective. But, I think that would miss what I see as the more important issue. Globalization means that ideas can spread like wildfire. The idea that women don't have to put up with sexual aggression at work or at school has infected the world. The laws against sexual harassment in their various diverse forms arise from the pressure exerted upon the law by the idea that sexual harassment is a wrong against women.

The second face of globalization is the organizing power of ideas. This second face of globalization is just as important in other fields also, fields where discussions sometimes focus more narrowly on just the first, market-competition face of globalization. The idea that children shouldn't have to work and especially that they shouldn't have to work while their parents suffer unemployment is an idea that spreads globally and an idea around which we can organize international solidarity. * * *

3. INSTITUTIONAL APPROACHES

We now turn to what Sol Picciotto calls "the spaghetti bowl or spider's web" of global regulation. Katherine Stone describes and evaluates the approach taken by the European Union. Katherine Hagen and Clyde Summers discuss the genesis and early history of NAFTA. Bob Hepple examines private corporate codes of conduct which "exist because of the absence of an enforceable internationally agreed labor regime."

KATHERINE VAN WEZEL STONE,
LABOR AND THE GLOBAL ECONOMY: FOUR APPROACHES
TO TRANSNATIONAL LABOR REGULATION

16 Michigan Journal of International Law 987, 998–1006.
1995.

TWO EUROPEAN APPROACHES TO TRANSNATIONAL LABOR REGULATION

Each of the member states of the European Union has its own legal history, customs, norms, and cultures that have shaped its system of labor rights. Each state has developed a large body of legal rules, statutes, regulations and procedures which establish employment standards for individual workers, including statutory minimum wages, unemployment and job training provisions, and so forth. In addition, each EU country has its own distinct legal and institutional structure of collective bargaining which differs markedly from each of the others.

For example, German labor laws provide for industry-wide unions which engage in industry-wide collective bargaining at the national-level. At the same time, German unions have the legal right to participate both on corporate boards of directors and in work councils at the workplace. In France, there are several competing national unions in each industry, each of which engages in bargaining at both the national and local level, resulting in fragmented bargaining. There are no legally established co-determination rights but there are extensive protections for individual employment and for collective action. In Great Britain, unions engage in collective bargaining but have no co-determination rights and relatively few legally enforceable rights of any sort. Other countries have other union structures and legal regimes of collective bargaining, all of which give protection to some form of collective bargaining, but no two of which are identical. In addition, EU countries differ on the forum used to enforce collective labor rights: some have a system of labor courts to enforce collective labor rights, some rely on specialized administrative tribunals, and some on courts of general jurisdiction.

The EU addresses this plurality of regulation in two ways. One approach, known as preemptive legislation, includes treaty provisions and EU r'eglements [regulations] that are directly applicable to citizens of the member states. These regulations set uniform rules for certain labor rights and have priority over conflicting national legislation. Thus, they are a form of unified transnational labor legislation.

The other approach is known as harmonization. Harmonization involves structured incentives and pressures created by the EU legal rules which induce the member states to bring their separate labor laws into conformity. Harmonization occurs directly, through EU Directives, and indirectly through collateral regulations. It is a strategy of regulation that is based both upon the short-term acceptance of differences in regulatory regimes and the assumption that, over time, these differences will fade and there will emerge one set of norms, rules and procedures.

1. Preemptive Legislation

The European Economic Community Treaty (EEC Treaty) sets out specific provisions of supranational law in certain areas, and sets up structures for EU-wide regulation in other areas. There are very few specific provisions in the EEC Treaty that bear directly on labor law. The few labor provisions that do exist can be found in Title III, The Free Movement of Persons, Services, and Capital. Under Title III, there are provisions concerning the freedom of movement of employees, and provisions concerning the treatment of and social benefits for migrant workers. There are also provisions concerning professional workers. Elsewhere in the EEC Treaty there are provisions that mandate equal treatment between male and female workers. However, these provisions state general principles, and have not, in themselves, given rise to enforceable rights. * * *

In 1989, European lawmakers attempted to enact a Community Charter of Fundamental Social Rights of Workers (known as the "Social Charter"). The Social Charter contained a list of "Fundamental Social Rights of Workers," which included occupational health and safety protections, guarantees for the right to organize and bargain collectively, rights to adequate social welfare benefits, workplace consultation and participation rights, and protection for children, older workers, and the disabled. Eleven of the twelve member states approved the Social Charter—all but the United Kingdom. As a result, the eleven states that ratified the Social Charter have treated it as a mandate for the European Commission to formulate directives for the protection of labor and the promotion of collective bargaining.

2. Harmonization

As discussed, the EEC Treaty makes it possible to unify some employment rights by means of multilateral r'eglements, but the Council of Ministers has not yet pursued this course of action. Rather, in most instances, the Council has attempted to encourage its member nations to "harmonize" their labor and employment laws. The goal of harmonization is to provide incentives for convergence, or what the EU scholars call "approximation," between collective bargaining systems. Harmonization occurs in two ways: through EU Directive, and through indirect pressures imposed by regulation in other areas that have a collateral impact on labor matters.

(a) Direct Harmonization

An EU directive is a regulation enacted by the EU Council which the member states must then enact into their domestic legislation. There is a time period within which the member states are required to "transpose" the directive into their own domestic law. Usually the directive sets minimum standards in a particular area which the member states must then "transpose" in ways that are consistent with their own distinct labor law system.

There are presently EU Directives in effect in several areas of labor regulation. In 1975, the EU lawmakers adopted a directive on collective redundancies, also known as dismissals for economic reasons. This directive provided that firms who intend to implement a mass layoff must notify workers affected and confer with the worker representatives. In 1977 a directive designed to protect workers faced with takeovers and other changes in the ownership of their firms was adopted. The 1977 directive provides that employees of companies that were involved in a transfer of ownership of the entire company or a part thereof must have their preexisting contractual rights, including collective bargaining rights, honored by the new entity. A 1980 directive on insolvencies provided that firms must guarantee payment of workers' outstanding wage claims and benefits prior to the commencement of insolvency proceedings.

There have also been directives addressing workplace safety and health and equal treatment for women and men. In addition, the EU is considering several directives concerning part-time workers, service workers and temporary workers.

In 1992 at Maastricht, eleven of the twelve EU member states agreed to a Protocol on Social Policy. In the negotiations leading up to the Maastricht Agreement, there were considerable pressures to enlarge the EEC Treaty's social policy provisions. Due to the United Kingdom's continued opposition, however, there was no unanimous agreement. Instead, provisions based on the previous Social Charter were annexed as a Social Agreement accepted by all except the UK, and these eleven member states were authorized by the Protocol on Social Policy to utilize the mechanisms of the EEC for the purposes of implementing that Agreement. This UK 'opt-out' means that the Social Policy proposals which the UK government is unwilling to accept may be agreed upon among the other member states and become binding on all except the UK.

The Maastrict Protocol, also known as the Social Agreement, made a number of changes in the manner in which labor directives are implemented. Most significantly, it provided that labor directives can be implemented through collective bargaining agreements as well as through legislation and administrative regulation. In addition, the 1992 Maastricht Protocol on Social Policy expanded the legislative capacity of the EU. It set out a series of issues on which the EU could legislate on the basis of majority voting, rather than unanimity which had previously been required. These areas include health and safety protection, working conditions, workers' information and consultation rights, and equality between men and women.

Article 2(6) of the Social Agreement makes it clear that most collective labor rights are excluded from majority voting. It states that "the provisions of this Article shall not apply to pay, the right of association, the right to strike or the right to impose lock-outs." Thus, unanimous voting was retained for directives in the areas of job security, representation, and collective defense of workers' interests.

To date, the EU has not attempted to legislate or harmonize in the field of collective bargaining law. It has, however, attempted to legislate works councils. In September 1994, the first Directive was issued under the Social Agreement, providing for the establishment of European Works Councils or other consultative procedures by all European multi-national enterprises. These are workplace-based organizations established for the purpose of consultation and sharing information, not for purposes of providing worker representation. A number of multinationals have moved to set up such Works Councils, and although it is not legally binding on the UK, some have included their UK workers in the arrangements.

EU directives have force only to the extent that they are implemented by the member states. As a consequence, the actual meaning of the directives can vary greatly between states. However, in Francovich v. Italy, a landmark decision in 1991, the European Court of Justice ruled that a member country could be held liable to an individual worker for restitution if it failed to enact a labor protection directive. In that case, two Italian workers sued the Italian government for failing to implement the 1980 Directive concerning worker protection in the event of an employer's insolvency. The Court ruled that it is "inherent in the Treaty system" that the member states are liable to individuals who are damaged by the state's failure to implement directives. This decision will give added enforcement power to the directives, and may lead to a uniform interpretation of the precise rights and protections contained in them. If that happens, the directives will come to resemble the preemptive legislation of the r'eglements discussed above.

(b) Indirect Harmonization

In addition to harmonization by means of EU labor directives, the EU can harmonize labor regulation indirectly by means of regulations and directives in other areas of law. For example, labor policy is implicated by regulations and directives in the area of corporate law. The EU has a long-standing draft directive on the structure of stock corporations and a proposal for a European-wide stock corporation. However, the proposals have not yet been enacted, due largely to disagreement about the proper role of labor in the structure of the corporation. Some member states have extensive codetermination rights for workers built into their current laws on corporate structures, while some states do not. The EU states have not been able to agree whether or not to include codetermination rights in the EU directive on corporate structure, so the directive has not yet been adopted. However, if any directive on corporate structure were adopted, it would have a profound effect on labor's participation rights in all EU nations.

Similarly, any EU directive on insolvency could have a significant impact on labor. For example, French insolvency law has, as one of its primary objectives, the preservation of workers' jobs. Under French bankruptcy law, this objective has a higher priority than the protection of stockholders. If this principle is carried over into a European-wide bankruptcy code, it could give labor unions substantial participation rights in bankruptcy proceedings and a greater role in the structure of their firms.

3. *Observations about the European Approaches*

As we have seen, the EU has utilized r'eglements and directives to set minimum standards in some areas of employment regulation, but it has not attempted to harmonize collective labor regulations. The different approaches toward individual employment regulation and collective labor regulation is understandable in the context of European labor relations systems. Prior to European integration, each EU country had its own legislation establishing a bundle of minimal terms for employment contracts—terms such as minimum wage rates, old age assistance, maximum hours, occupational health and safety protection, health insurance, disability provisions, or job security protection. Frequently these employment standards were similar in structure but differed in their quantitative dimension, such as the precise amount of the minimum wage or the total sum paid for a particular disability. Because the differences between countries' labor standards were quantitative rather than qualitative, it has been possible to devise a single set of minimal terms which all member countries are required to adopt. Once a unified set of minimal terms is mandated, each country can adjust its own terms upward or downward to comply with the mandate. No vested interests are disrupted, no labor leaders lose their constituencies, no labor lawyers lose the value of their expertise, and no individual workers lose their jobs. Thus it has been feasible to develop transnational labor standards for individual labor rights within the EU, and to make them mandatory by means of EU-level legislation.

However, when it comes to transnational regulation of collective labor relations, neither harmonization nor preemptive legislation is likely to be a simple expedient. In the area of collective bargaining, each country's own institutions, customs, and labor relations practices have given rise to labor organizations, employer organizations, and labor relations professionals who have a vested stake in the continuation of their own national system. Each country's incumbent labor relations personae, whether they represent a management, labor or neutral perspective, can be expected to resist efforts at transformations that threaten their own particular niche, role, or expertise. They will resist any transnational regulation that attempts to supersede those local regulations, even one that would benefit their own country's labor movement generally. Hence, for collective labor rights, both harmonization and preemption may be slow to develop.

A. Preemptive Legislation

The model of regulation that is most likely to limit runaway shops, prevent labor standards races-to-the-bottom and discourage regulatory competition is the one that is most effective at setting uniform labor standards across national boundaries. Uniformity in labor standards would prevent the phenomenon of regulation-shopping, in which corporations move to the least restrictive regulatory environment. Uniformity would also eliminate union fears that by advocating protective legislation, they are contributing to capital flight and costing union members their jobs. Where uniformity in labor regulation cannot be achieved for either political or pragmatic reasons, an alternative is to adopt regulations that set a floor of rights, such as a minimum wage or minimum safety standards, above which parties can further negotiate. If the floor of labor rights is high enough, it will also have a deterrent effect on runaway shops and races-to-the-bottom, although not as powerful a deterrent as uniform labor standards.

In theory, uniformity can be achieved most effectively through the EU model of preemptive legislation since the very purpose of this model is to set uniform employment standards. To the extent that the EU Commission has the power to set rules and enforce regulations for labor standards in its member countries, it minimizes the possibility of a labor standards race-to-the-bottom.

In addition to setting uniform standards directly, the EU could legislate rules that would encourage the development of transnational unions which could then bargain for uniform transnational labor standards. That is, preemptive legislation has the potential of creating a uniform set of legal regulations to facilitate cross-border collective bargaining. This would make it more feasible for unions to organize and coordinate bargaining strategies on a transnational basis. Accordingly, preemptive legislation is a strategy that could prevent organizational fragmentation and counteract the weakening of labor's bargaining power that globalization initially creates.

A further strength of the preemptive legislation model is that it furthers the goal of encouraging international cooperation. Indeed, both of the European integrative approaches have as their goal not merely integration, but actual unification of regulatory regimes. These approaches carry the prospect of developing, over time, shared norms and collaborative means by which to implement those norms. Furthermore, the integrative models are part of an economic strategy that has a political goal—to achieve the unification of Europe into a single political, juridical and economic unit. Thus, the preemptive legislation model, as well as the harmonization model, is likely to foster international cooperation and interdependency that will make overt international aggression between EU members less likely.

The limitations on the preemptive legislation model are primarily practical ones. The model requires multilateral action for its implementation, and it is extremely difficult to gain the necessary consensus to actually set labor standards. To date, the European Commission has only utilized its legislative power to set labor standards on a few issues, and it has not attempted to set any uniform rules governing collective bargaining, strikes, and other forms of collective action. Indeed, most observers predict that the EU is unlikely to attempt any preemptive legislative, or even harmonization, in the area of unionism or collective bargaining in the foreseeable future. Therefore, while the preemptive legislation model could theoretically eliminate barriers to trade by equalizing labor standards and labor rights, in practice it is not likely to do so in the near future. And, without a uniform framework of legal rules to govern collective bargaining, the preemptive legislation model cannot prevent organizational fragmentation or the weakening of labor's bargaining power that globalization entails.

There is a further drawback to the preemptive legislation model. Both integrative models are well suited to further the goals of international cooperation, world peace, and the establishment of a floor of labor standards, but they are not necessarily the models that will provide the highest labor standards or the best legal protection for workers. The integrative models rely on consensus between nations, so that there is a tendency for least common denominator regulations to emerge. This is the phenomenon of "harmonization downward" that has been widely discussed amongst scholars in the European Community. The dynamic of harmonization downward was apparent in 1989 when the EU nations could not enact the Social Charter due to the objections of Great Britain. It is a dynamic that could, under an integrative model of labor regulation, lead to the triumph of the weakest regulatory regime.

There is yet another problem with the model of preemptive legislation. One of the most important goals of transnational labor regulation is to preserve a role for labor in political life and to preserve labor's political clout. The preemptive legislation model diminishes the role of labor unions in politics by taking issues of labor relations out of the reach of the national political processes and placing them in multilateral agencies. Preemptive legislation by definition moves labor legislation from the national political arena into a multilateral arena. At present, unions exist in nation-specific environments; they are not major players in transnational decision-making bodies. In the EU Commission, votes are cast by country, not by political party or constituency-based group. Yet national unions are rarely powerful enough in their home countries to be empowered to speak for the country's national interest in an international policy-making setting. As a result, under preemptive legislation, the influence of national unions becomes diluted and mediated.

B. Harmonization

The harmonization model of transnational labor regulation is similar to preemptive legislation in most respects. That is, it fosters uniformity in labor standards, thus counteracting labor standards races-to-the-bottom. It also establishes a floor of labor standards and fosters international labor cooperation.

There are, however, some differences in the ability of the two integrative models to achieve the policy goals discussed above. First, harmonization, unlike preemptive legislation, relies on unilateral action by each member country. This feature makes it highly unlikely that directives on labor standards will be implemented in the same way in all the EU countries. To the contrary, harmonization permits a wide range of variation as to the appropriate way to implement directives. Thus, harmonization is less likely to create uniformity in labor regulations than will preemptive legislation. To the extent that uniformity in regulation is desirable as an antidote to labor standards races-to-the-bottom, harmonization is less effective than preemptive legislation.

Harmonization can, however, establish a floor of rights. But in doing so, it shares with preemptive legislation the potential problem of setting a least common denominator floor, and thus of levelling downward.

Harmonization has several advantages over the other models as well. First, harmonization relies on unilateral action for implementation after shared norms are articulated in the form of directives. From a practical vantage point, this suggests that as difficult as it may be to enact labor directives at the transnational level due to the difficulties of reaching international consensus, it might be easier to reach consensus when countries know they will retain autonomy at the implementation stage. Indeed, the fact that the EU has many more directives than r'eglements on labor issues bears out this insight.

Second, harmonization is a model of labor regulation that secures a larger role for labor in national politics than does preemptive legislation. As with preemptive legislation, harmonization directives require that legal norms be set multilaterally, so the role of domestic labor unions in the norm-setting process is diminished. However, unlike preemptive legislation, harmonization requires legislation to be enacted at the domestic level to implement the directives. It thus presumes that labor regulations will be debated, adopted, and interpreted at the level of the nation-state. Consequently, harmonization will enable, indeed require, unions to continue their efforts to influence lawmakers and other decision-makers at the national level.

Another possible advantage of harmonization over preemptive legislation is that it is possibly more conducive to international peace and cooperation. Harmonization sets in motion a process by which countries bring their regulatory frameworks into consistency with one another. It does not involve the external imposition of regulations, but it does provide structured incentives for nations to alter their regulations in a consistent way. Given the emphasis on internal change of a country's regulations, harmonization may be a process that engenders less conflict, opposition, and backlash than preemptive legislation. * * *

In North America, reduction of trade barriers also included consideration of national labor standards. But in contrast to the European Union, the signatories to the North American Free Trade Agreement

(Canada, Mexico and the United States) rejected transnational norms. Instead, as Katherine Hagen emphasizes, each country will continue to make and enforce its own labor and employment laws. According to the side agreement on labor each country will set up a National Administration Office (NAO) empowered to investigate claims of failure by the other countries to enforce their own labor and employment laws. Through reports and conciliation it is hoped that the NAOs can insure that countries honor their own laws. With regard to persistent claims of noncompliance with child labor, minimum wage and occupational health and safety laws, arbitration is available. Clyde Summer reviews the early impact of cross-border monitoring.

KATHERINE A. HAGEN
FUNDAMENTALS OF LABOR ISSUES AND NAFTA

27 U.C. Davis L.Rev. 917, 924–930.
(1994).

One of the key objectives of the labor agreement is "to promote, to the maximum extent possible," certain labor principles. These principles are not embodied in the labor agreement itself but are identified in an annex to the labor agreement. These principles, furthermore, are only "guiding principles" which, the annex states, "the Parties are committed to promote, subject to each Party's domestic law, but do not establish common minimum standards for their domestic law." These are important qualifiers. The principles are not only subject to being promoted in the context of domestic law, they are also not intended to serve as a minimum standard. The annex goes on to state that the principles "indicate broad areas of concern where the Parties have developed, each in its own way, laws, regulations, procedures and practices that protect the rights and interests of their respective workforces." Again, the emphasis has been placed on domestic interpretation, rather than trilateral standards.

The principles, then, are not even intended to create an acknowledgment of common minimum standards. There is recognition elsewhere in the Agreement that each Party "shall ensure that its labor laws and regulations provide for high labor standards ... and shall continue to strive to improve those standards...." Nonetheless, it appears to be very carefully stated that the principles themselves are not deemed to be these standards. Therefore, domestic labor law was retained for the definition of common standards, and the enunciation of "guiding principles" was deliberately kept separate from the identification of standards for implementation in the agreement.

* * * [T]he discussions among the three governments led gradually but steadily to a modest, multi-tiered approach. This multi-tiered approach encompassed both cooperative activity and limited investigative and enforcement authority regarding these guiding principles. The labor agreement establishes a Commission for Labor Cooperation which shall

consist of a ministerial Council and a small Secretariat, headquartered in Dallas, Texas. A National Administrative Office (N.A.O.) in each of the three countries will also assist the Commission. The Council, the Secretariat, and the N.A.O.'s constitute the new structure for trilateral activities.

Each government has the obligation to promote compliance and effectively enforce its respective labor laws. Each government must also ensure appropriate access to enforcement mechanisms to "persons with a legally recognized interest under its law in a particular matter . . . ." Finally, each must ensure certain procedural guarantees that are "fair, equitable and transparent" before tribunals that are "impartial and independent and do not have any substantial interest in the outcome of the matter" and with available remedies to "ensure enforcement of [each country's] labor rights." These domestic remedies must be addressed before any enforcement can be considered at the trilateral level, but the agreement does not appear to require that these remedies be exhausted.* * *

With regard to the concerns that critics of NAFTA raise, very little was actually resolved—or could have been resolved—in the supplemental labor agreement. The key areas for trilateral enforcement ultimately were limited to labor laws affecting occupational safety and health, child labor, and minimum wages, where such laws are mutually recognized and trade-related, and where there is a persistent pattern of failure by the government to enforce its laws in these areas. Wage differentials, the interaction between unions and governments, and the applicability of labor laws generally to the informal sector were not included in this framework, although there was accommodation to the issue of inadequate enforcement of basic worker rights in the threshold areas. The narrow scope of the enforcement mechanisms reflects the difficulties of truly establishing transnational labor standards as a criterion of domestic labor policy, but the fact that some consensus does exist is encouraging. * * *

CLYDE SUMMERS,
NAFTA'S LABOR SIDE AGREEMENT
AND INTERNATIONAL LABOR STANDARDS

3 Journal of Small and Emerging Business Law173, 175–187.
(1999).

Describing how a specific submission is processed is the best way to provide the necessary background for examining how and to what extent the Agreement promotes the standards articulated in the Labor Principles.

Submission 940003, filed with the U.S. NAO by organizations in the United States and Mexico, alleged that Sony Corporation at its Maquiladora plant in Nuevo Laredo had violated the law by denying employees freedom of association and the right to organize and had violated minimum employment standards relating to hours of work and holiday work. More specifically, the submission alleged that Sony, by discharging many of the dissidents, had interfered with an attempt by dissatisfied workers to challenge the leadership of their union in order to obtain more democratic representation within the union. The union was affiliated with the Confederation of Mexican Workers (CTM), the official Mexican labor federation.

The submission alleged a variety of actions by Sony against the dissidents. For example, it alleged that Sony suspended an elected union delegate on a charge of complaining about a work rule change after she was removed from her union position because of criticizing the union leadership. A production chief was demoted for speaking out against the CTM leadership, and there was a general campaign of intimidation by Sony directed at workers organizing an alternate dissident slate of union delegates. The delegate election was held after a twelve hour notice, not all employees received notice, and the election was by a show of hands, with company officials observing who voted for the dissident slate. The submission alleged that the company collaborated with the police in violently suppressing a work stoppage triggered by the election and that additional reprisals were taken against workers who supported the opposition slate.

The submission also charged that the Mexican government had thwarted the attempts by the workers to register an independent union to represent the workers at Sony. The Conciliation and Arbitration Board (CAB) refused to accept their petition to register on the grounds that the workers were already represented by an existing collective bargaining agreement with the CTM union and because the petition was not submitted in triplicate.

The NAO, in accepting the submission, stated that its review would focus on " 'compliance with, and effective enforcement of, labor laws that guarantee the right of association and the right to organize freely and prohibit the dismissal of workers because of efforts to exercise those rights.' " After receiving information from the submitters, the company, the Mexican NAO, and an expert legal consultant, the NAO held a public hearing at which a number of workers and legal experts testified. The NAO issued its Public Report of Review, which made the following findings:

> 1) On the face of the evidence "it appears plausible" that the employees were discharged for union activities. "[E]conomic realities facing these Mexican workers make it very difficult to seek redress from the proper Mexican authorities. . . ." Discharged employees do not have the financial resources to pursue reinstatement before the CABs, which they do not consider impartial. As a result, they accept the employer's offer to let them resign in order to receive severance pay, thereby surrendering their ability to pursue charges of illegal

discrimination. They accept immediate severance pay rather than wait and risk receiving nothing through the CAB.

2) Evidence supports the complaints about the election and that workers do not have access to their union by law or collective agreements. "The [Federal Labor Law] appears to leave the conduct of internal union affairs largely in the hands of the unions themselves.... [I]t remains unclear whether there are applicable laws dealing with these issues and whether the workers have any viable recourse against improper union actions."

3) In the work stoppage that followed the election, "the allegations of police violence are disturbing," but the evidence is conflicting. The company stated that its investigation found that no violence was used.

4) Expert testimony indicated that the CAB was specifically empowered to remedy the technical defects in the application or registration. Although the application may be resubmitted, the delay involved in resubmitting "arguably caused the interested workers irreparable harm" because several of those who signed the original petition, including the leaders, had been dismissed. Further, the CAB acknowledged that the leader of the CTM union had filed a letter opposing registration. This "tends to support the allegations" that the CAB permitted the CTM union to be involved in the registration process of an independent union.

On the basis of these findings, the Report stated that it would take the following action:

1) "[T]he NAO will continue to pursue trinational programs under the NAALC which emphasize exchanges on laws and procedures to protect workers from dismissal for exercising their rights to organize and to freedom of association...." It will also add to the agenda the question of availability of private action and procedural guarantees when the union violates its own governing instruments.

2) "[T]he U.S. NAO will conduct a study to explore the practices and findings of the local CABs with respect to workers' complaints of unjustified dismissals...."

3) Because "compliance with and effective enforcement of the laws pertaining to union recognition are fundamental to ensuring the right to organize and freedom of association, the NAO recommends that ministerial consultations are appropriate to further address the operation of the union registration process."

In accordance with the Agreement, ministerial consultations were held between the two secretaries of labor. They negotiated an "Agreement on Implementation," which provided for three activities: (1) a joint work program, which consisted of three trinational public seminars on union registration and certification; (2) a study by independent experts on Mexican labor law dealing with union registration; and (3) a series of meetings between officials of the Mexican Department of Labor and Social Welfare and parties to union registration at Sony.

Twenty months after its Report and six months after the Report on Ministerial Consultation, the NAO issued a follow-up report that found the following:

(1) All of the workers dismissed by Sony remained unemployed and believed they had been blacklisted, so they were unable to obtain work in Nuevo Laredo.

(2) The opposition political party, the National Action Party (PAN), proposed legislation that would make registration a procedural formality with no discretionary authority in local tribunals. It also would transfer jurisdiction over CABs from the executive branch to the judicial branch and end the current tripartite structure, which gave dominant voice to those allied with the CTM, the official labor confederation. There is no indication that this legislation has any chance of being adopted.

(3) The Mexican government promoted tripartite negotiations leading to the signing of a document, "Principles of the New Labor Culture," which addresses the issues of union democracy and union registration, including the impartiality of labor tribunals in very general terms. The legal and practical effects of this document are not discussed.

(4) The Supreme Court of Mexico, in two unanimous decisions unrelated to NAALC submissions, found unconstitutional provisions of two state statutes that prohibited employees from forming more than one union in a workplace.

The story is long, but the moral is simple. The submission involved charges of violations of the first three Labor Principles that the Agreement was intended to "promote to the maximum extent possible"— freedom of association, the right to bargain collectively, and the right to strike. These are considered the most basic internationally recognized labor standards. After extensive investigation and hearings that produced substantial evidence that these standards had been violated, the NAO made no definite findings of violation and provided no remedy. The mouse brought forth by the mountain's labors was an agreement by the secretaries of labor to hold three seminars, study Mexican labor law, and schedule meetings between Mexican labor officials and parties to the union registration.

This case is not unique; it is a paradigm of all the submissions— allegations of employer conduct that violated the declared labor principles; allegations of the failure of government institutions to enforce those principles; extensive inquiry or hearings producing substantial evidence supporting the allegations; no remedy for the victims; and, at most, an agreement by the ministers to exchange information, hold seminars, organize a conference, or make a study.

This raises the question of why the Agreement so totally fails to enforce the standards set forth in the Labor Principles. First, the Agreement creates no private rights or duties; it is an agreement solely between the two countries binding only on the governments. It explicitly excludes any private right of action. Although the submission alleges specific violations as to individuals or unions, and the procedure is shaped as an inquiry into those violations, the purpose is not to provide remedies for victimized workers. Rather, it is to determine whether the government is failing to fulfill its obligations under the Agreement. The response is to be negotiated by the ministers on behalf of their governments. If they are unable to agree (which has not yet happened), there may be successive procedural steps that may possibly lead to a sanction; however, these additional procedures and potential sanctions are not available for cases involving the first three labor principles involved in this submission.

Second, and most crucial, the objectives set forth in Part One of the Agreement, which incorporate by reference the Labor Principles, are only declared goals and do not create binding obligations. The obligations are set out in Part Two, which states that "[e]ach Party shall promote compliance with and effectively enforce its labor law through appropriate government action...." In short, the binding obligation of each government is to observe and enforce its own laws. The Labor Principles are only "guiding principles," not binding obligations. They establish no "common minimum standards," but only indicate "broad areas of concern" that the parties are to promote, "each in its own way."
* * *

The declaration of the Labor Principles can make little concrete contribution toward those ends because the obligation to promote those Principles is limited to each country's complying with and enforcing its own laws. The operative content of the Labor Principles is what the laws of each country say it is, nothing more and nothing less.* * *

In summary, the NAALC declares the Labor Principles only as goals, not as binding labor standards. Each country remains free to define and observe its own standards. The internalization of international conventions has potential for establishing binding labor standards, but this process depends on the conventions each country has ratified. The procedural requirements do not articulate or develop labor standards, but they can reinforce the implementation of the standards that the laws and conventions of each country establish. * * *

After five years there has been measurable, or even visible, progress on only two of the objectives set forth in Part One of the Agreement: encouraging cooperation to promote innovation and encouraging publication and exchange of information. On the stated objectives to "improve working conditions and living standards, ... promote ... the labor principles, ... promote compliance with, and effective enforcement by each Party of, its labor law, [and] foster transparency in the administration of labor law," there has been little, if any, visible progress.

This bleak picture of enforcement of treaty obligations through the submission process leaves out of account the intangible, but perhaps more important, contributions of the Agreement. First, there has been significant development of cross-border relations and informal institutions, which provide a base for improved labor conditions. Second, the very articulation of the Labor Principles in a formal Agreement gives these labor standards a definiteness and salience with a moral claim to be observed. The submission process raises to public view and places in sharp focus the too easily ignored failures to live up to those standards. There is some evidence that the process has led to some changes in attitudes and practices. Third, the Agreement is only five years old, starting with a protective jealousy of sovereignty and a hesitancy to press for changes. As the cross-boundary institutions grow and the public forum makes each party confront its own failures to comply with the standards, there may develop a greater readiness to treat the Objectives as obligations.

However, it still must be said that, from the viewpoint of workers who placed hope in the realization of the stated Objectives and the declared Labor Principles, the submission process has held the promise to the ear, but broken it to the heart.

How would NAFTA's cross-border monitoring fare if analyzed by the criteria Prof. Stone used to analyze preemptive legislation and harmonization?

BOB HEPPLE,
A RACE TO THE TOP:
INTERNATIONAL INVESTMENT GUIDELINES
AND CORPORATE CODES OF CONDUCT

20 Comparative Labor Law & Policy Journal. 347, 357–363.
1999.

Private corporate codes exist because of the absence of an enforceable internationally agreed labor regime * * *

Most private codes are issued by individual companies, but some emanate from private business organizations and others involve NGOs and trade unions. What they have in common is that they are voluntary written commitments to observe certain standards in the conduct of business. They may cover a number of broad areas of ethical conduct, namely fair business practices, observance of the rule of law, environmental stewardship, corporate citizenship and fair employment and labor rights. Fair business practices and fair employment and labor rights are the most frequently mentioned subjects. But the choice of particular labor issues is highly selective and seems to depend on the size of the company, the industry sector and the importance of the issue to the company's operations. So of the codes surveyed by the ILO, those in the textile, clothing and footwear sector, where abuses of child and forced labor have been well-publicized, tended to concentrate on these issues, while health and safety got special attention in the chemical and transport sectors. In the UK survey, not all supplier codes included a provision on equality. While some UK codes included a reference to freedom of association, none of the UK company codes made explicit reference to collective bargaining. Even internationally, only fifteen percent of codes in the ILO survey addressed freedom of association and only some of these referred to collective bargaining. The same survey found examples of codes aimed at the elimination of trade unions, or expressing a preference for individualized non-union representation.* * *

The credibility of a private company code depends first on how it is made and interpreted, and secondly on how it is monitored and implemented. Is the code a genuine attempt to change corporate behavior or is it simply a public relations exercise? One indicator of this is whether the code was unilaterally adopted by the company or was negotiated with trade unions or NGOs. The ICFTU Working Party on Multinational Companies []alleged that some early codes were a form of avoidance of unions, and that very few codes respected trade union rights. Moreover, it was said that some companies sought to engage in a dialogue with NGOs as a substitute for dealing with trade unions. The picture seems to be changing as international unions adopt a more strategic role toward their involvement in the making and implementation of codes. However, the fundamental problem is that international trade union structure cannot match the globalized activities of TNCs and negotiate framework agreements covering all the countries in which a TNC operates. Although there are some agreements between TNCs and international trade secretariats, and also some between national unions and TNCs covering the labor practices of suppliers or sub-contractors of the TNC, these are, in the ICFTU's words, only "the first building blocks in an international system of industrial relations."

The main criticism of corporate codes is that of ineffective implementation. Codes launched in the glare of publicity in the TNC's host country are not infrequently unknown, unavailable nor unimplemented in the producing country, and workers in that country have no means of reporting non-compliance. There is an absence of monitoring (i.e., checking that the code is followed), a lack of training and incentives encouraging managers to comply (e.g., performance bonuses), and of sanctions on those who do not comply. So far as monitoring is concerned, the [United States Council for Business] USCIB SA 8000 standard draws a distinction between (1) internal or first-party assessment within the company itself; (2) second-party assessment by a purchaser of company products against a standard selected by the purchaser (e.g., a brand-name retailer assesses its manufacturing supplier); and (3) third-party assessment, in which an external audit body—neither a purchaser nor consultant employed by the company—imposes a uniform standard (e.g., an industry association, NGO or certification agency), leading to certification of the company as meeting the required standard. The OECD survey found that a significant number of companies did not deal with the issue of monitoring at all, and of those that did so, almost all stated that in-house staff would monitor compliance. Although several of the codes in the UK survey referred to the use of their regular monitoring systems, none of them made reference to the use of unions or other civil society organizations as intermediaries in consultations with the workers involved. The ICFTU Working Party argued that without effective trade union and worker participation, there could be no effective monitoring. By "effective monitoring" is meant (1) auditable standards, with fairly precise requirements as to performance, and (2) verification, which may be limited to ensuring that there is an adequate system of internal monitoring, or may itself verify the achievement of the standards. A satisfactory outcome might lead to certification or accreditation, indicating that the product was made under conditions required by the code. Such procedures are, however, still largely an aspiration and not a reality.

So far as sanctions are concerned, corporate codes are generally toothless. In the OECD survey, codes made little reference to the consequences of non-compliance. A few mentioned some form of corrective action, including working with suppliers or business partners to make improvements. Even fewer stated that non-compliance could lead to termination of a contract or business relationship, and it is not clear whether this sanction has ever been invoked. None of the codes in the OECD survey provided for government involvement.

In summary, what is clear from all the reviews of corporate codes is that these private sector initiatives generally impose lower standards and are more selective in their choice of human and labor rights than the public regulatory frameworks, and that they are inadequately monitored and enforced. * * *

The struggle to restrain the unbridled power of TNCs is the greatest task of contemporary labor law on an international scale. Can public international labor law—by which is meant broadly, the obligations binding on nation states—and national labor laws play any significant part in this process? Harry Arthurs has persuasively argued that,

> [T]he enfeeblement of the nation state and the failure to produce an effective substitute for the state at transnational level may refocus attention on local struggles, on indigenous, implicit and informal lawmaking, on movements which have not become juridified but which actually draw their sustenance and strength from grass-roots involvement.

Political campaigns have, indeed, been built around codes and social labels, particularly on issues such as child labor, forcing TNCs to adhere to their voluntary commitments. But single issue campaigns can have unforeseen consequences—such as increased family poverty in developing countries—if they are directed from the TNC's home state without the involvement of local communities and (where they exist) trade unions in the producing country, and without positive measures to strengthen the local economy and educational system of that country. Other core rights, such as freedom of association and the right to effective collective bargaining, rarely evoke the same sympathy as child or forced labor. "Core-plus" rights—such as those to information and consultation for workers' representatives mentioned in the OECD Guidelines—are toughest of all targets.

If global commodity chains dominated by TNCs are to be used to disseminate "best practices," then both the international instruments and national legislation need to be strengthened so as to ensure that: (1) corporate codes specify at least the ILO's core standards, suitably expanded in the light of local conditions; (2) TNCs are placed under legal obligations requiring them to take reasonable steps to ensure compliance with those standards, not only with respect to their direct employees, but also their contractors and sub-contractors; (3) there is independent monitoring of compliance with those standards by local workers' representatives and independent experts; and, (4) there is an effective complaints mechanism at the national and international level. The challenge for labor lawyers is to help build institutions such as these that will empower local communities in their struggles for decent labor standards.

Index

References are to Pages

AFFIRMATIVE ACTION
Equal employment opportunity law, 107-127

AGE
Equal employment opportunity law, 147-152

AIDS
Health and safety, workplace, 665-667

AMERICANS WITH DISABILITIES ACT
Arbitration award, 673
Pregnancy, 596 et seq.

ARBITRATION
Americans with Disabilities Act, 673
Arbitrators, establishment of body to license, select, and monitor, 189
Cause and arbitration, 39
Conflict of statute and contract, 171-189
Domestic partner benefits, 460
Enforcing collective bargaining agreement, 466-487
Refusals to work over health and safety issues, 611-616

ATTORNEY'S FEES
Wrongful dismissal, 69, 70

AT-WILL EMPLOYMENT
Generally, 11-72
Implied-in-fact promises of job security, 62-72
Implied-in-law good faith and fair dealing, 54-62
Judicial and legislative rejection of absolute at-will employment, 39
Statutory law, 70-72

BANKRUPTCY
Reorganization under Chapter 11 of Bankruptcy Code, job security, 708 et seq.

BARGAINING ORDERS
Collective bargaining, 318 et seq.

BARGAINING UNITS
Collective bargaining, 289-309

BONA FIDE OCCUPATIONAL QUALIFICATION (BFOQ)
Equal employment opportunity law, 101-107
Fetal-protection, sex-specific policies, 580 et seq.

CAPITAL MOBILITY
Economic Security and Capital Mobility, this index

CIVIL RIGHTS ACT OF 1964, TITLE VII
Pregnancy, 580 et seq.

COERCION
Collective bargaining, 499 et seq.

COLLECTIVE BARGAINING
Unions, this index

COMMON LAW
Health and safety, common law and employee injuries, 528-531

COMPENSATION
Statistics, 9

COMPETITION
Covenants Not To Compete, this index

CONCERTED ACTIVITIES
Health and safety, protected concerted activities, 616-625
Unions, this index

CONTINGENT WORKERS
Generally, 9

CONTRACTS
At-Will Employment, this index
Collective bargaining agreement, applying and enforcing, 466-487
Conflict of statute and contract, 171-189
Covenants not to compete, 165-171

COVENANTS NOT TO COMPETE
Generally, 165-171

DAMAGES
Wrongful dismissal, 69, 70

DISABILITY
Equal employment opportunity law, 152-164

DISCLOSURES
Right-to-know Legislation, this index

DISCRIMINATION
Equal employment opportunity law, 89-101

DISPARATE IMPACT
Equal employment opportunity law, 82-89

DISPARATE TREATMENT
Equal employment opportunity law, 89-101

DISPROPORTIONALITY
Equal employment opportunity law, 82-89

DISSENTING UNION MEMBERS
Unions, 270-273

DOMESTIC PARTNER BENEFITS
Public sector arbitration, 460 et seq.

DOMESTIC SUBSTANTIVE LAW
International business transactions and law of work, application of domestic substantive law to international claim, 834-845

ECONOMIC SECURITY AND CAPITAL MOBILITY
Generally, 682-846
Bankruptcy, reorganization under Chapter 11 of Bankruptcy Code, 708 et seq.
Changes, economic, 683-698
Domestic substantive law, application to international claim, 834-845
Elimination of jobs to cut costs
    Early retirement incentives to eligible employees, 733
    Firing people, 728, 729
    Voluntary separations combined with generous severance benefits, 729
Extraterritoriality, jurisdiction over international business transactions and law of work, 820-832
Forum non convenience, international business transactions and law of work, 833, 834
Free enterprise capitalism, 683-698
Globalization. International business transactions and law of work, below
Going out of business, 698-708
International business transactions and law of work
    Generally, 819-846
    Domestic substantive law, application to international claim, 834-845
    Extraterritoriality, 820-832
    Forum non convenience, 833, 834
    Jurisdiction, domestic jurisdiction as determined by statute or treaty, 820-832

ECONOMIC SECURITY AND CAPITAL MOBILITY—Cont'd
International business transactions and law of work—Cont'd
    Labor standards. Transnational labor standards and global economy, below
    Treaties, effect of, 829-833
International trade and labor standards, 852 et seq.
Jurisdiction, domestic jurisdiction over international claim as determined by statute or treaty, 820-832
Labor market changes and effects, 691 et seq.
Labor standards. Transnational labor standards and global economy, below
Law of work. International business transactions and law of work, above
Layoffs. Elimination of jobs to cut costs, above
Ownership transfer, 774 et seq.
Reorganization under Chapter 11 of Bankruptcy Code, 708 et seq.
Responses to accelerated capital mobility
    Elimination of jobs, above
    Going out of business, 698-708
    Ownership transfer, 774 et seq.
    Reorganization under Chapter 11 of Bankruptcy Code, 708 et seq.
    Restructuring to cut costs, 727-774
    Sale of business, 774 et seq.
    Worker Adjustment and Retraining Notification Act (WARN), 699 et seq.
Sale of business, 774 et seq.
Transnational labor standards and global economy
    Generally, 845, 846
    Institutional approaches, 862 et seq.
    International trade and labor standards, 852 et seq.
    Labor rights, transnational, 846 et seq.
Treaties, effect of treaties on international business transactions and law of work, 829-833
Worker Adjustment and Retraining Notification Act (WARN), 699 et seq.

ELECTRONIC WORKPLACES
Unions, organizing issues, 337-348

ELIMINATION OF JOBS TO CUT COSTS
Economic Security and Capital Mobility, this index

EQUAL EMPLOYMENT OPPORTUNITY LAW
Generally, 72 et seq.
Affirmative action, 107-127
Age, 147-152
Bona fide occupational qualification (BFOQ), 101-107
Claims, filing, 188, 189
Disability, 152-164
Discrimination, intentional, 89-101

EQUAL EMPLOYMENT OPPORTUNITY LAW—Cont'd
Disparate impact, 82-89
Disparate treatment, 89-101
Disproportionality, 82-89
Filing claims, 188, 189
Harassing behavior, 135-143
Intentional discrimination, 89-101
Models of proof, 82-89
Overview, 72 et seq.
Pregnancy, 143-147
Reasonable accommodation, 127-134

ERGONOMIC ISSUES
Generally, 605-607

EXCLUSIVITY
Unions, 254-289

EXTRATERRITORIALITY
Jurisdiction over international business transactions and law of work, 820-832

FAIR REPRESENTATION
Health and safety, 649
Unions, exclusivity and duty of fair representation, 274-285

FAIR TREATMENT OF WORKERS
Generally, 1-199
Arbitration, this index
Attorney's fees, wrongful dismissal, 69, 70
At-Will Employment, this index
Cause and arbitration, 39
Compensation statistics, 9
Concerted activities. Unions, this index
Conflict of statute and contract, 171-189
Contingent workers, 9
Covenants not to compete, 165-171
Damages, wrongful dismissal, 69, 70
Education level and income, 10
Efficiency, reconciliation of fairness with, 23 et seq.
Enforcement of workplace rights, models for, 6
Equal Employment Opportunity Law, this index
Good faith and fair dealing, implied-in-law, 54-62
Implied-in-fact promises of job security, 62-72
Implied-in-law good faith and fair dealing, 54-62
Job security
    Implied-in-fact promises of job security, 62-72
    Statutory efforts to enhance job security, 37
Models for enforcement of workplace rights, 6
Sectors, employment by industry, 8
Security, job. Job security, above
Statistics about employment, 7
Toolbox of sources of potential relief, 4

FAIR TREATMENT OF WORKERS—Cont'd
Types of work, employment by occupation, 8
Unions, this index

FORUM NON CONVENIENCE
International business transactions and law of work, 833, 834

FREE ENTERPRISE CAPITALISM
Economic security and capital mobility, 683-698

GLOBAL ECONOMIC WEAPONS
Unions, 487-519

GLOBALIZATION
Economic Security and Capital Mobility, this index

GOING OUT OF BUSINESS
Economic security and capital mobility, 698-708

GOOD FAITH AND FAIR DEALING
At-will employment, implied-in-law good faith and fair dealing, 54-62

GOVERNANCE
Participation in Workplace Governance, this index

GRADUATE STUDENTS
Unions, 307-309

HARASSING BEHAVIOR
Equal employment opportunity law, 135-143

HEALTH AND SAFETY
Generally, 520-681
Activism by workers
    Generally, 607 et seq.
    Arbitration and refusals to work, 611-616
    Collective action without representation, 625
    Concerted activities protected, 616-625
    Protected concerted activities, 616-625
    Refusals to work, 611-616
    Union's obligation to provide safe work place, 633-662
AIDS, 665-667
Americans with Disabilities Act, 673
Arbitration and refusals to work, 611-616
Collective action without representation, 625
Common law and employee injuries, 528-531
Concerted activities protected, 616-625
Ergonomic issues, 605-607
Occupational Safety and Health Act of 1970, this index
Refusals to work, 611-616
Rehabilitation Act of 1973, 667-673
Union's obligation to provide safe work place, 633-662

HEALTH AND SAFETY—Cont'd
Workers' compensation laws, 531-537

IMPASSES
Collective bargaining, 390-394

INJUNCTIONS
Collective bargaining, injunction under NLRA, 366-368

INTERNATIONAL BUSINESS TRANSACTIONS AND LAW OF WORK
Economic Security and Capital Mobility, this index

JOB SECURITY
Economic Security and Capital Mobility, this index
Fair Treatment of Workers, this index

JURISDICTION
International business transactions and law of work, domestic jurisdiction over international claim as determined by statute or treaty, 820-832

LABOR STANDARDS
Economic Security and Capital Mobility, this index

LAYOFFS
Economic Security and Capital Mobility, this index

MEDICAL STUDENTS
Unions, 307-309

NON-UNION WORKPLACES
Economic weapons of non-union workers, 450-459
Health and safety, collective action without representation, 625
Protections during representation process, 350-352
Rights of workers, judicial and statutory, 220 et seq.

OCCUPATIONAL SAFETY AND HEALTH ACT OF 1970
Generally, 538-577
Assessing risks, 540-565
Balancing values, 540-565
Cost-benefit analysis under OSHA, 550-565
Disclosure obligations, 565-577
Executive Order 12866, 557, 558
Feasibility, 551 et seq.
Fetal-protection, sex-specific policies, 580 et seq.
Information, learning about risks, 565-577
Life, value of, 550-565
Pregnancy, 576 et seq.
Refusals to work, 626
Right-to-know Legislation, this index
Sex-specific fetal-protection policies, 580 et seq.

OCCUPATIONAL SAFETY AND HEALTH ACT OF 1970—Cont'd
Steel-erection standards, 558 et seq.

OCCUPATIONS
Types of work, statistics, 8

ORGANIZATION
Unions, this index

OSHA
Occupational Safety and Health Act of 1970, this index

PARTICIPATION IN WORKPLACE GOVERNANCE
Generally, 200 et seq.
Bargaining units. Unions, this index
Bridge between union and non-union models, potential, 220 et seq.
Collective bargaining. Unions, this index
Exclusivity, 254-289
Informal worker representation, 227-252
Minority workers, exclusivity and concerted action by, 259 et seq.
Modes of worker participation, 205 et seq.
Non-Union Workplaces, this index
Premature union recognition, 240 et seq.
Representation, boundaries, perks and obligations of, 252-309
TEAM Act, 239
Unions, this index

PREGNANCY
Americans with Disabilities Act, 596 et seq.
Civil Rights Act of 1964, Title VII, 580 et seq.
Collective bargaining agreement, 597 et seq.
Equal employment opportunity law, 143-147
Occupational Safety and Health Act of 1970, 576 et seq., 591 et seq.

PUBLIC SECTOR
Unions, public sector model of collective bargaining, 459-466

REASONABLE ACCOMMODATION
Equal employment opportunity law, 127-134

REFUSALS TO WORK
Health and safety, 611-616

REHABILITATION ACT OF 1973
Health and safety, 667-673

REPLACEMENT WORKERS
Generally, 408-423

REPRESENTATION
Unions, this index

RIGHT-TO-KNOW LEGISLATION
Generally, 566-577
Development, 566-577
NLRA, legislation under, 567-577

RIGHT-TO-KNOW LEGISLATION—Cont'd
Right to Know statutes, 571-577

SAFETY
Health and Safety, this index

SALE OF BUSINESS
Economic security and capital mobility, 774
    et seq.

SECURITY
Economic Security and Capital Mobility,
    this index
Fair Treatment of Workers, this index

STATISTICS
Employment, 7

STUDENTS
Unions, medical students and graduate stu-
    dents, 307-309

SURFACE BARGAINING
Unions, 355-360

TREATIES
International business transactions and law
    of work, effect of treaties on, 829-833

UNIONS
Agreement, applying and enforcing, 466-487
Arbitration, enforcing collective bargaining
    agreement, 467 et seq.
Bargaining orders, 318 et seq.
Bargaining units, 289-309
Benefits to workers, 210 et seq.
Cartel, assumption of labor cartel as source
    of union wage increases, 218-226
Coercion, collective bargaining, 499 et seq.
Collective bargaining
    Generally, 207 et seq.
    Agreement, applying and enforcing,
        466-487
    Applying and enforcing collective bar-
        gaining agreement, 466-487
    Arbitration, enforcing collective bargain-
        ing agreement, 467 et seq.
    Bargaining orders, 318 et seq.
    Bargaining units, 289-309
    Benefits to workers, 210 et seq.
    Cartel, assumption of labor cartel as
        source of union wage increases,
        218-226
    Contract, applying and enforcing collec-
        tive bargaining agreement,
        466-487
    Costs of collective bargaining as posi-
        tional externalities, 358-360
    Dissenting union members, employers
        and unions, 270-273
    Domestic partner benefits, 460 et seq.
    Duty to bargain, 386-390
    Economic activities, union control over
        and persuasion of those who do
        not honor union's, 441-450
    Effects bargaining, 394 et seq.

UNIONS—Cont'd
Collective bargaining—Cont'd
    Electronic workplaces, organizing issues,
        337-348
    Enforcing collective bargaining agree-
        ment, 466-487
    Exclusivity, 254-289
    Fair representation, exclusivity and duty
        of, 274-285
    Impasse in bargaining, 390-394
    Information, right to information in bar-
        gaining, 396-398
    Injunction under NLRA, 366-368
    Judicial intervention, 400-413
    Mandatory subjects of collective bargain-
        ing, 372-386
    Neutrality, 511 et seq.
    Public sector model, 459-466
    Regulation of collective bargaining, 352
    Replacement workers, 408-423
    Scope of duty to bargain, 386-390
    Striker replacement bill, consideration
        of, 408-423
    Students, medical students and graduate
        students, 307-309
    Surface bargaining, 355-360
Concerted activities
    Generally, 190-197
    Concertedness, requirement of, 191, 192
    Minority workers, exclusivity and con-
        certed action by, 259 et seq.
    Motive in anti-union setting, 197-199
    Protected and nonprotected concerted
        activity, 192-197
Contract, applying and enforcing collective
    bargaining agreement, 466-487
Costs of collective bargaining as positional
    externalities, 358-36-
Dissenting union members, employers and
    unions, 270-273
Domestic partner benefits, 460 et seq.
Dues, dissenting employees and fair share
    charges, 280 et seq.
Duty to bargain, 386-390
Economic activities, union control over and
    persuasion of those who do not honor
    union's, 441-450
Economic weapons, 398 et seq., 487 et seq.
Effects bargaining, 394 et seq.
Electronic workplaces, organizing issues,
    337-348
Exclusivity, 254-289
Fair representation, exclusivity and duty of,
    274-285
Fair share charges, 280 et seq.
Future directions in union representation,
    300-307
Global economic weapons, 487-519
Health and safety, union's obligation to
    provide safe work place, 633-662
Impasse in bargaining, 390-394
Information, right to information in bar-
    gaining, 396-398
Injunction under NLRA, 366-368

UNIONS—Cont'd
Judicial intervention in collective bargaining, 400-413
Mandatory subjects of collective bargaining, 372-386
Market, unions and the, 215 et seq.
Membership, duty to join union and meaning, 286-289
Minority workers, exclusivity and concerted action by, 259 et seq.
Neutrality, 511 et seq.
Organization
    Process of representation, 309
    Unionization of workers, 10
Premature union recognition, 240 et seq.
Public sector model of collective bargaining, 459-466
Regulation of collective bargaining, 352 et seq.
Replacement workers, 408-423
Representation

UNIONS—Cont'd
Representation—Cont'd
    Boundaries, perks and obligations of, 252-309
    Process of representation, 309 et seq.
Safe work place, union's obligation to provide, 633-662
Scope of duty to bargain, 386-390
Students, medical students and graduate students, 307-309
Surface bargaining, 355-360

WORKER ADJUSTMENT AND RETRAINING NOTIFICATION ACT (WARN)
Economic security and capital mobility, 699 et seq.

WORKERS' COMPENSATION LAWS
Generally, 531-537

WORKPLACE GOVERNANCE
Participation in Workplace Governance, this index

†